Microsoft Office 2016

Grand Valley State University

Patrick Carey I Carol DesJardins I Ann Shaffer I Mark Shellman
Sasha Vodnik

CENGAGE
Learning·

Australia • Brazil • Japan • Korea • Mexico • Singapore • Spain • United Kingdom • United States

Microsoft Office 2016: Grand Valley State University

New Perspectives Microsoft® Office 365 & Office 2016: Introductory, 1st Edition
Patrick Carey I Carol DesJardins I Ann Shaffer I Mark Shellman Sasha Vodnik

© 2017 Cengage Learning. All rights reserved.

New Perspectives Microsoft® Office 365 & Office 2016: Intermediate, 1st Edition
Patrick Carey I Carol DesJardins I Ann Shaffer I Mark Shellman Sasha Vodnik

© 2017 Cengage Learning. All rights reserved.

For product information and technology assistance, contact us at
Cengage Learning Customer & Sales Support, 1-800-354-9706

For permission to use material from this text or product,
submit all requests online at **cengage.com/permissions**
Further permissions questions can be emailed to
permissionrequest@cengage.com

This book contains select works from existing Cengage Learning resources and was produced by Cengage Learning Custom Solutions for collegiate use. As such, those adopting and/or contributing to this work are responsible for editorial content accuracy, continuity and completeness.

Compilation © 2016 Cengage Learning

ISBN: 978-1-337-05682-3

Cengage Learning
20 Channel Center Street
Boston, MA 02210
USA

Cengage Learning is a leading provider of customized learning solutions with office locations around the globe, including Singapore, the United Kingdom, Australia, Mexico, Brazil, and Japan. Locate your local office at: **www.international.cengage.com/region**.

Cengage Learning products are represented in Canada by Nelson Education, Ltd.

For your lifelong learning solutions, visit **www.cengage.com/custom**.

Visit our corporate website at **www.cengage.com**.

Brief Contents

Productivity Apps for School and Work

Corinne Hoisington

Lochlan keeps track of his class notes, football plays, and internship meetings with OneNote.

Zoe is using the annotation features of Microsoft Edge to take and save web notes for her research paper.

Nori is creating a Sway site to highlight this year's activities for the Student Government Association.

Hunter is adding interactive videos and screen recordings to his PowerPoint resume.

© Rawpixel/Shutterstock.com

Being computer literate no longer means mastery of only Word, Excel, PowerPoint, Outlook, and Access. To become technology power users, Hunter, Nori, Zoe, and Lochlan are exploring Microsoft OneNote, Sway, Mix, and Edge in Office 2016 and Windows 10.

In this Module

Learn to use productivity apps!
Links to companion **Sways**, featuring **videos** with hands-on instructions, are located on www.cengagebrain.com.

Introduction to OneNote 2016

notebook | section tab | To Do tag | screen clipping | note | template | Microsoft OneNote Mobile app | sync | drawing canvas | inked handwriting | Ink to Text

As you glance around any classroom, you invariably see paper notebooks and notepads on each desk. Because deciphering and sharing handwritten notes can be a challenge, Microsoft OneNote 2016 replaces physical notebooks, binders, and paper notes with a searchable, digital notebook. OneNote captures your ideas and schoolwork on any device so you can stay organized, share notes, and work with others on projects. Whether you are a student taking class notes as shown in Figure 1 or an employee taking notes in company meetings, OneNote is the one place to keep notes for all of your projects.

Figure 1: OneNote 2016 notebook

Each **notebook** is divided into sections, also called **section tabs**, by subject or topic.

Use **To Do tags**, icons that help you keep track of your assignments and other tasks.

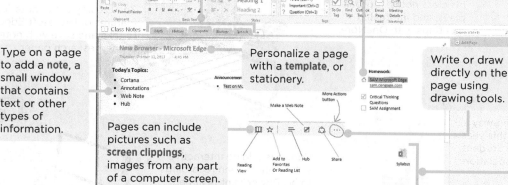

Type on a page to add a **note**, a small window that contains text or other types of information.

Personalize a page with a **template**, or stationery.

Write or draw directly on the page using drawing tools.

Pages can include pictures such as **screen clippings**, images from any part of a computer screen.

Attach files and enter equations so you have everything you need in one place.

Creating a OneNote Notebook

OneNote is divided into sections similar to those in a spiral-bound notebook. Each OneNote notebook contains sections, pages, and other notebooks. You can use OneNote for school, business, and personal projects. Store information for each type of project in different notebooks to keep your tasks separate, or use any other organization that suits you. OneNote is flexible enough to adapt to the way you want to work.

When you create a notebook, it contains a blank page with a plain white background by default, though you can use templates, or stationery, to apply designs in categories such as Academic, Business, Decorative, and Planners. Start typing or use the buttons on the Insert tab to insert notes, which are small resizable windows that can contain text, equations, tables, on-screen writing, images, audio and video recordings, to-do lists, file attachments, and file printouts. Add as many notes as you need to each page.

Syncing a Notebook to the Cloud

OneNote saves your notes every time you make a change in a notebook. To make sure you can access your notebooks with a laptop, tablet, or smartphone wherever you are, OneNote uses cloud-based storage, such as OneDrive or SharePoint. **Microsoft OneNote Mobile app**, a lightweight version of OneNote 2016 shown in Figure 2, is available for free in the Windows Store, Google Play for Android devices, and the AppStore for iOS devices.

If you have a Microsoft account, OneNote saves your notes on OneDrive automatically for all your mobile devices and computers, which is called **syncing**. For example, you can use OneNote to take notes on your laptop during class, and then open OneNote on your phone to study later. To use a notebook stored on your computer with your OneNote Mobile app, move the notebook to OneDrive. You can quickly share notebook content with other people using OneDrive.

Figure 2: Microsoft OneNote Mobile app

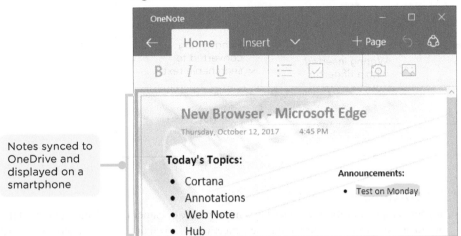

Notes synced to OneDrive and displayed on a smartphone

Taking Notes

Use OneNote pages to organize your notes by class and topic or lecture. Beyond simple typed notes, OneNote stores drawings, converts handwriting to searchable text and mathematical sketches to equations, and records audio and video.

OneNote includes drawing tools that let you sketch freehand drawings such as biological cell diagrams and financial supply-and-demand charts. As shown in Figure 3, the Draw tab on the ribbon provides these drawing tools along with shapes so you can insert diagrams and other illustrations to represent your ideas. When you draw on a page, OneNote creates a **drawing canvas**, which is a container for shapes and lines.

On the Job Now

OneNote is ideal for taking notes during meetings, whether you are recording minutes, documenting a discussion, sketching product diagrams, or listing follow-up items. Use a meeting template to add pages with content appropriate for meetings.

Figure 3: Tools on the Draw tab

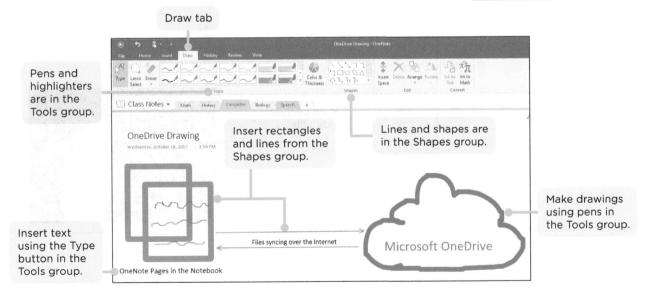

Draw tab

Pens and highlighters are in the Tools group.

Insert rectangles and lines from the Shapes group.

Lines and shapes are in the Shapes group.

Make drawings using pens in the Tools group.

Insert text using the Type button in the Tools group.

Files syncing over the Internet

Microsoft OneDrive

Converting Handwriting to Text

When you use a pen tool to write on a notebook page, the text you enter is called **inked handwriting**. OneNote can convert inked handwriting to typed text when you use the **Ink to Text** button in the Convert group on the Draw tab, as shown in Figure 4. After OneNote converts the handwriting to text, you can use the Search box to find terms in the converted text or any other note in your notebooks.

Figure 4: Converting handwriting to text

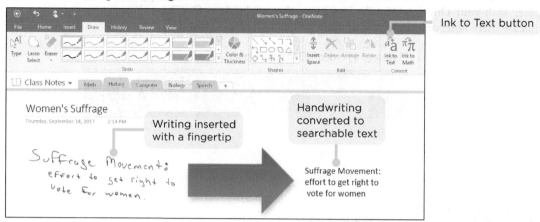

Ink to Text button

Women's Suffrage
Thursday, September 14, 2017   2:14 PM

Suffrage Movement: effort to get right to vote for women.

Writing inserted with a fingertip

Handwriting converted to searchable text

Suffrage Movement: effort to get right to vote for women

Recording a Lecture

If your computer or mobile device has a microphone or camera, OneNote can record the audio or video from a lecture or business meeting as shown in **Figure 5**. When you record a lecture (with your instructor's permission), you can follow along, take regular notes at your own pace, and review the video recording later. You can control the start, pause, and stop motions of the recording when you play back the recording of your notes.

Figure 5: Video inserted in a notebook

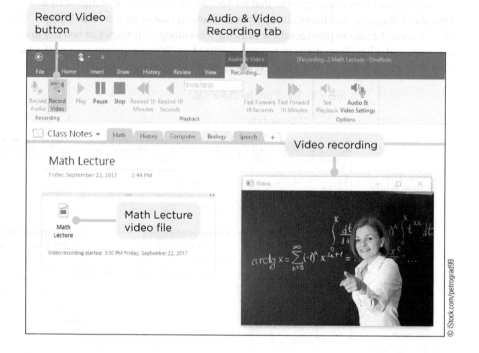

Record Video button

Audio & Video Recording tab

Video recording

Math Lecture
Friday, September 22, 2017   2:44 PM

Math Lecture

Math Lecture video file

Video recording started: 3:00 PM Friday, September 22, 2017

© iStock.com/petrograd99

Try This Now

1: Taking Notes for a Week

As a student, you can get organized by using OneNote to take detailed notes in your classes. Perform the following tasks:

    a. Create a new OneNote notebook on your Microsoft OneDrive account (the default location for new notebooks). Name the notebook with your first name followed by "Notes," as in **Caleb Notes**.

    b. Create four section tabs, each with a different class name.

    c. Take detailed notes in those classes for one week. Be sure to include notes, drawings, and other types of content.

    d. Sync your notes with your OneDrive. Submit your assignment in the format specified by your instructor.

2: Using OneNote to Organize a Research Paper

You have a research paper due on the topic of three habits of successful students. Use OneNote to organize your research. Perform the following tasks:

    a. Create a new OneNote notebook on your Microsoft OneDrive account. Name the notebook **Success Research**.

    b. Create three section tabs with the following names:

- **Take Detailed Notes**
- **Be Respectful in Class**
- **Come to Class Prepared**

    c. On the web, research the topics and find three sources for each section. Copy a sentence from each source and paste the sentence into the appropriate section. When you paste the sentence, OneNote inserts it in a note with a link to the source.

    d. Sync your notes with your OneDrive. Submit your assignment in the format specified by your instructor.

3: Planning Your Career

Note: This activity requires a webcam or built-in video camera on any type of device.

Consider an occupation that interests you. Using OneNote, examine the responsibilities, education requirements, potential salary, and employment outlook of a specific career. Perform the following tasks:

    a. Create a new OneNote notebook on your Microsoft OneDrive account. Name the notebook with your first name followed by a career title, such as **Kara - App Developer**.

    b. Create four section tabs with the names **Responsibilities, Education Requirements, Median Salary**, and **Employment Outlook**.

    c. Research the responsibilities of your career path. Using OneNote, record a short video (approximately 30 seconds) of yourself explaining the responsibilities of your career path. Place the video in the Responsibilities section.

    d. On the web, research the educational requirements for your career path and find two appropriate sources. Copy a paragraph from each source and paste them into the appropriate section. When you paste a paragraph, OneNote inserts it in a note with a link to the source.

    e. Research the median salary for a single year for this career. Create a mathematical equation in the Median Salary section that multiplies the amount of the median salary times 20 years to calculate how much you will possibly earn.

    f. For the Employment Outlook section, research the outlook for your career path. Take at least four notes about what you find when researching the topic.

    g. Sync your notes with your OneDrive. Submit your assignment in the format specified by your instructor.

Learn to use OneNote!
Links to companion **Sways**, featuring **videos** with hands-on instructions, are located on www.cengagebrain.com.

Introduction to Sway

Sway site | responsive design | Storyline | card | Creative Commons license | animation emphasis effects | Docs.com

Expressing your ideas in a presentation typically means creating PowerPoint slides or a Word document. Microsoft Sway gives you another way to engage an audience. Sway is a free Microsoft tool available at Sway.com or as an app in Office 365. Using Sway, you can combine text, images, videos, and social media in a website called a **Sway site** that you can share and display on any device. To get started, you create a digital story on a web-based canvas without borders, slides, cells, or page breaks. A Sway site organizes the text, images, and video into a **responsive design**, which means your content adapts perfectly to any screen size as shown in **Figure 6**. You store a Sway site in the cloud on OneDrive using a free Microsoft account.

Figure 6: Sway site with responsive design

You can display a Sway presentation in a web browser.

Sway uses responsive design to make sure pages fit perfectly on any device.

Creating a Sway Presentation

You can use Sway to build a digital flyer, a club newsletter, a vacation blog, an informational site, a digital art portfolio, or a new product rollout. After you select your topic and sign into Sway with your Microsoft account, a **Storyline** opens, providing tools and a work area for composing your digital story. See **Figure 7**. Each story can include text, images, and videos. You create a Sway by adding text and media content into a Storyline section, or **card**. To add pictures, videos, or documents, select a card in the left pane and then select the Insert Content button. The first card in a Sway presentation contains a title and background image.

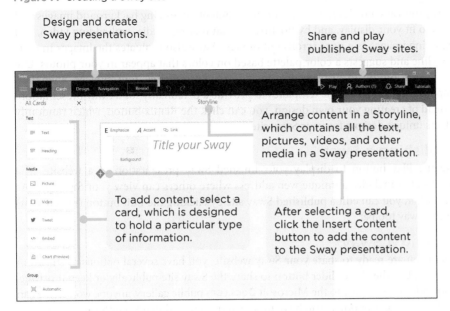

Design and create Sway presentations.

Share and play published Sway sites.

Arrange content in a Storyline, which contains all the text, pictures, videos, and other media in a Sway presentation.

To add content, select a card, which is designed to hold a particular type of information.

After selecting a card, click the Insert Content button to add the content to the Sway presentation.

Adding Content to Build a Story

As you work, Sway searches the Internet to help you find relevant images, videos, tweets, and other content from online sources such as Bing, YouTube, Twitter, and Facebook. You can drag content from the search results right into the Storyline. In addition, you can upload your own images and videos directly in the presentation. For example, if you are creating a Sway presentation about the market for commercial drones, Sway suggests content to incorporate into the presentation by displaying it in the left pane as search results. The search results include drone images tagged with a **Creative Commons license** at online sources as shown in **Figure 8**. A Creative Commons license is a public copyright license that allows the free distribution of an otherwise copyrighted work. In addition, you can specify the source of the media. For example, you can add your own Facebook or OneNote pictures and videos in Sway without leaving the app.

On the Job Now

If you have a Microsoft Word document containing an outline of your business content, drag the outline into Sway to create a card for each topic.

Figure 8: Images in Sway search results

Select the source of media objects

Information about Creative Commons licenses

Storyline title

The Market for Commercial Drones

Drag an image to the picture placeholder box

Suggested images in the search results

On the Job Now

If your project team wants to collaborate on a Sway presentation, click the Authors button on the navigation bar to invite others to edit the presentation.

Designing a Sway

Sway professionally designs your Storyline content by resizing background images and fonts to fit your display, and by floating text, animating media, embedding video, and removing images as a page scrolls out of view. Sway also evaluates the images in your Storyline and suggests a color palette based on colors that appear in your photos. Use the Design button to display tools including color palettes, font choices, **animation emphasis effects**, and style templates to provide a personality for a Sway presentation. Instead of creating your own design, you can click the Remix button, which randomly selects unique designs for your Sway site.

Publishing a Sway

Use the Play button to display your finished Sway presentation as a website. The Address bar includes a unique web address where others can view your Sway site. As the author, you can edit a published Sway site by clicking the Edit button (pencil icon) on the Sway toolbar.

Sharing a Sway

When you are ready to share your Sway website, you have several options as shown in Figure 9. Use the Share slider button to share the Sway site publically or keep it private. If you add the Sway site to the Microsoft **Docs.com** public gallery, anyone worldwide can use Bing, Google, or other search engines to find, view, and share your Sway site. You can also share your Sway site using Facebook, Twitter, Google+, Yammer, and other social media sites. Link your presentation to any webpage or email the link to your audience. Sway can also generate a code for embedding the link within another webpage.

Figure 9: Sharing a Sway site

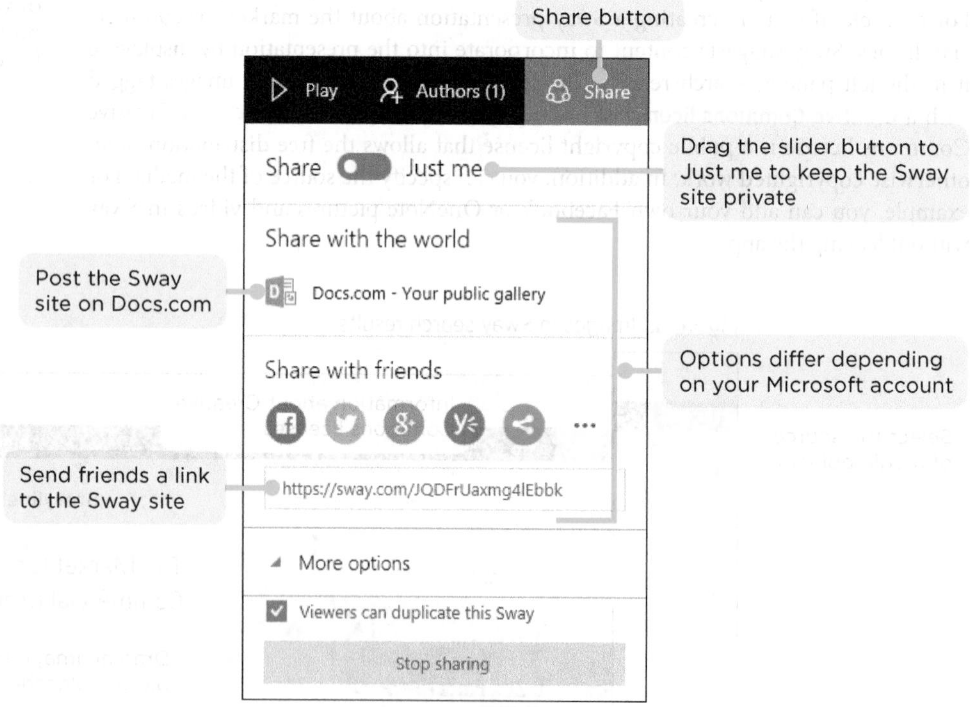

Try This Now

Learn to use Sway!
Links to companion **Sways**, featuring **videos** with hands-on instructions, are located on www.cengagebrain.com.

1: Creating a Sway Resume

Sway is a digital storytelling app. Create a Sway resume to share the skills, job experiences, and achievements you have that match the requirements of a future job interest. Perform the following tasks:

    a. Create a new presentation in Sway to use as a digital resume. Title the Sway Storyline with your full name and then select a background image.

    b. Create three separate sections titled **Academic Background, Work Experience**, and **Skills**, and insert text, a picture, and a paragraph or bulleted points in each section. Be sure to include your own picture.

    c. Add a fourth section that includes a video about your school that you find online.

    d. Customize the design of your presentation.

    e. Submit your assignment link in the format specified by your instructor.

2: Creating an Online Sway Newsletter

Newsletters are designed to capture the attention of their target audience. Using Sway, create a newsletter for a club, organization, or your favorite music group. Perform the following tasks:

    a. Create a new presentation in Sway to use as a digital newsletter for a club, organization, or your favorite music group. Provide a title for the Sway Storyline and select an appropriate background image.

    b. Select three separate sections with appropriate titles, such as Upcoming Events. In each section, insert text, a picture, and a paragraph or bulleted points.

    c. Add a fourth section that includes a video about your selected topic.

    d. Customize the design of your presentation.

    e. Submit your assignment link in the format specified by your instructor.

3: Creating and Sharing a Technology Presentation

To place a Sway presentation in the hands of your entire audience, you can share a link to the Sway presentation. Create a Sway presentation on a new technology and share it with your class. Perform the following tasks:

    a. Create a new presentation in Sway about a cutting-edge technology topic. Provide a title for the Sway Storyline and select a background image.

    b. Create four separate sections about your topic, and include text, a picture, and a paragraph in each section.

    c. Add a fifth section that includes a video about your topic.

    d. Customize the design of your presentation.

    e. Share the link to your Sway with your classmates and submit your assignment link in the format specified by your instructor.

Introduction to Office Mix

add-in | clip | slide recording | Slide Notes | screen recording | free-response quiz

To enliven business meetings and lectures, Microsoft adds a new dimension to presentations with a powerful toolset called Office Mix, a free add-in for PowerPoint. (An **add-in** is software that works with an installed app to extend its features.) Using Office Mix, you can record yourself on video, capture still and moving images on your desktop, and insert interactive elements such as quizzes and live webpages directly into PowerPoint slides. When you post the finished presentation to OneDrive, Office Mix provides a link you can share with friends and colleagues. Anyone with an Internet connection and a web browser can watch a published Office Mix presentation, such as the one in Figure 10, on a computer or mobile device.

Figure 10: Office Mix presentation

Adding Office Mix to PowerPoint

To get started, you create an Office Mix account at the website mix.office.com using an email address or a Facebook or Google account. Next, you download and install the Office Mix add-in (see Figure 11). Office Mix appears as a new tab named Mix on the PowerPoint ribbon in versions of Office 2013 and Office 2016 running on personal computers (PCs).

Figure 11: Getting started with Office Mix

Capturing Video Clips

A **clip** is a short segment of audio, such as music, or video. After finishing the content on a PowerPoint slide, you can use Office Mix to add a video clip to animate or illustrate the content. Office Mix creates video clips in two ways: by recording live action on a webcam and by capturing screen images and movements. If your computer has a webcam, you can record yourself and annotate the slide to create a **slide recording** as shown in **Figure 12**.

On the Job Now

Companies are using Office Mix to train employees about new products, to explain benefit packages to new workers, and to educate interns about office procedures.

Figure 12: Making a slide recording

When you are making a slide recording, you can record your spoken narration at the same time. The **Slide Notes** feature works like a teleprompter to help you focus on your presentation content instead of memorizing your narration. Use the Inking tools to make annotations or add highlighting using different pen types and colors. After finishing a recording, edit the video in PowerPoint to trim the length or set playback options.

The second way to create a video is to capture on-screen images and actions with or without a voiceover. This method is ideal if you want to show how to use your favorite website or demonstrate an app such as OneNote. To share your screen with an audience, select the part of the screen you want to show in the video. Office Mix captures everything that happens in that area to create a **screen recording**, as shown in **Figure 13**. Office Mix inserts the screen recording as a video in the slide.

On the Job Now

To make your video recordings accessible to people with hearing impairments, use the Office Mix closed-captioning tools. You can also use closed captions to supplement audio that is difficult to understand and to provide an aid for those learning to read.

Figure 13: Making a screen recording

Inserting Quizzes, Live Webpages, and Apps

To enhance and assess audience understanding, make your slides interactive by adding quizzes, live webpages, and apps. Quizzes give immediate feedback to the user as shown in Figure 14. Office Mix supports several quiz formats, including a **free-response quiz** similar to a short answer quiz, and true/false, multiple-choice, and multiple-response formats.

Figure 14: Creating an interactive quiz

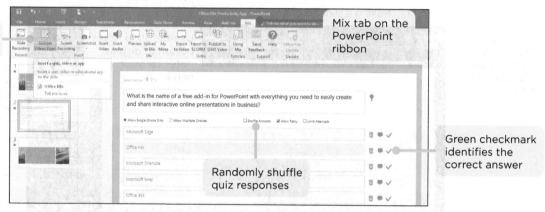

Quizzes Videos Apps button

Mix tab on the PowerPoint ribbon

Randomly shuffle quiz responses

Green checkmark identifies the correct answer

Sharing an Office Mix Presentation

When you complete your work with Office Mix, upload the presentation to your personal Office Mix dashboard as shown in Figure 15. Users of PCs, Macs, iOS devices, and Android devices can access and play Office Mix presentations. The Office Mix dashboard displays built-in analytics that include the quiz results and how much time viewers spent on each slide. You can play completed Office Mix presentations online or download them as movies.

Figure 15: Sharing an Office Mix presentation

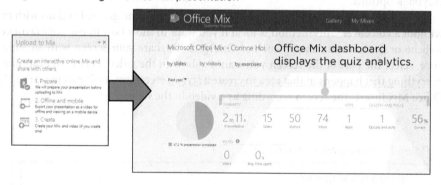

Office Mix dashboard displays the quiz analytics.

Try This Now

Learn to use Office Mix!
Links to companion **Sways**, featuring **videos** with hands-on instructions, are located on www.cengagebrain.com.

1: Creating an Office Mix Tutorial for OneNote

Note: This activity requires a microphone on your computer.

Office Mix makes it easy to record screens and their contents. Create PowerPoint slides with an Office Mix screen recording to show OneNote 2016 features. Perform the following tasks:

a. Create a PowerPoint presentation with the Ion Boardroom template. Create an opening slide with the title **My Favorite OneNote Features** and enter your name in the subtitle.

b. Create three additional slides, each titled with a new feature of OneNote. Open OneNote and use the Mix tab in PowerPoint to capture three separate screen recordings that teach your favorite features.

c. Add a fifth slide that quizzes the user with a multiple-choice question about OneNote and includes four responses. Be sure to insert a checkmark indicating the correct response.

d. Upload the completed presentation to your Office Mix dashboard and share the link with your instructor.

e. Submit your assignment link in the format specified by your instructor.

2: Teaching Augmented Reality with Office Mix

Note: This activity requires a webcam or built-in video camera on your computer.

A local elementary school has asked you to teach augmented reality to its students using Office Mix. Perform the following tasks:

a. Research augmented reality using your favorite online search tools.

b. Create a PowerPoint presentation with the Frame template. Create an opening slide with the title **Augmented Reality** and enter your name in the subtitle.

c. Create a slide with four bullets summarizing your research of augmented reality. Create a 20-second slide recording of yourself providing a quick overview of augmented reality.

d. Create another slide with a 30-second screen recording of a video about augmented reality from a site such as YouTube or another video-sharing site.

e. Add a final slide that quizzes the user with a true/false question about augmented reality. Be sure to insert a checkmark indicating the correct response.

f. Upload the completed presentation to your Office Mix dashboard and share the link with your instructor.

g. Submit your assignment link in the format specified by your instructor.

3: Marketing a Travel Destination with Office Mix

Note: This activity requires a webcam or built-in video camera on your computer.

To convince your audience to travel to a particular city, create a slide presentation marketing any city in the world using a slide recording, screen recording, and a quiz. Perform the following tasks:

a. Create a PowerPoint presentation with any template. Create an opening slide with the title of the city you are marketing as a travel destination and your name in the subtitle.

b. Create a slide with four bullets about the featured city. Create a 30-second slide recording of yourself explaining why this city is the perfect vacation destination.

c. Create another slide with a 20-second screen recording of a travel video about the city from a site such as YouTube or another video-sharing site.

d. Add a final slide that quizzes the user with a multiple-choice question about the featured city with five responses. Be sure to include a checkmark indicating the correct response.

e. Upload the completed presentation to your Office Mix dashboard and share your link with your instructor.

f. Submit your assignment link in the format specified by your instructor.

Introduction to Microsoft Edge

Reading view | Hub | Cortana | Web Note | Inking | sandbox

Bottom Line

- Microsoft Edge is the name of the new web browser built into Windows 10.
- Microsoft Edge allows you to search the web faster, take web notes, read webpages without distractions, and get instant assistance from Cortana.

Microsoft Edge is the default web browser developed for the Windows 10 operating system as a replacement for Internet Explorer. Unlike its predecessor, Edge lets you write on webpages, read webpages without advertisements and other distractions, and search for information using a virtual personal assistant. The Edge interface is clean and basic, as shown in Figure 16, meaning you can pay more attention to the webpage content.

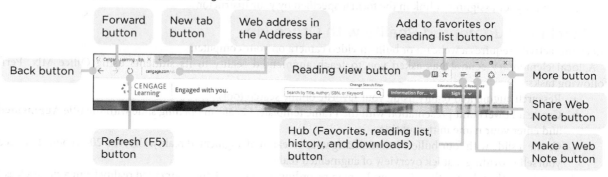

Figure 16: Microsoft Edge tools

- Forward button
- New tab button
- Web address in the Address bar
- Add to favorites or reading list button
- Back button
- Reading view button
- More button
- Refresh (F5) button
- Hub (Favorites, reading list, history, and downloads) button
- Share Web Note button
- Make a Web Note button

Learn to use Edge!

Links to companion **Sways**, featuring **videos** with hands-on instructions, are located on www.cengagebrain.com.

On the Job Now

Businesses started adopting Internet Explorer more than 20 years ago simply to view webpages. Today, Microsoft Edge has a different purpose: to promote interaction with the web and share its contents with colleagues.

Browsing the Web with Microsoft Edge

One of the fastest browsers available, Edge allows you to type search text directly in the Address bar. As you view the resulting webpage, you can switch to **Reading view**, which is available for most news and research sites, to eliminate distracting advertisements. For example, if you are catching up on technology news online, the webpage might be difficult to read due to a busy layout cluttered with ads. Switch to Reading view to refresh the page and remove the original page formatting, ads, and menu sidebars to read the article distraction-free.

Consider the **Hub** in Microsoft Edge as providing one-stop access to all the things you collect on the web, such as your favorite websites, reading list, surfing history, and downloaded files.

Locating Information with Cortana

Cortana, the Windows 10 virtual assistant, plays an important role in Microsoft Edge. After you turn on Cortana, it appears as an animated circle in the Address bar when you might need assistance, as shown in the restaurant website in Figure 17. When you click the Cortana icon, a pane slides in from the right of the browser window to display detailed information about the restaurant, including maps and reviews. Cortana can also assist you in defining words, finding the weather, suggesting coupons for shopping, updating stock market information, and calculating math.

Figure 17: Cortana providing restaurant information

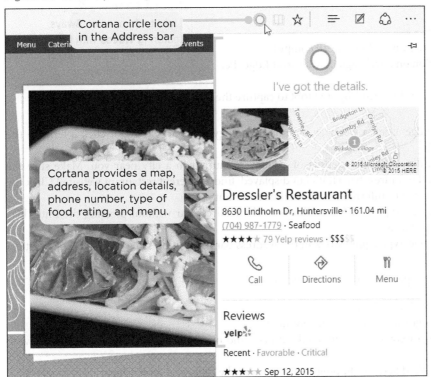

Cortana circle icon in the Address bar

Cortana provides a map, address, location details, phone number, type of food, rating, and menu.

Annotating Webpages

One of the most impressive Microsoft Edge features are the **Web Note** tools, which you use to write on a webpage or to highlight text. When you click the Make a Web Note button, an **Inking** toolbar appears, as shown in **Figure 18**, that provides writing and drawing tools. These tools include an eraser, a pen, and a highlighter with different colors. You can also insert a typed note and copy a screen image (called a screen clipping). You can draw with a pointing device, fingertip, or stylus using different pen colors. Whether you add notes to a recipe, annotate sources for a research paper, or select a product while shopping online, the Web Note tools can enhance your productivity. After you complete your notes, click the Save button to save the annotations to OneNote, your Favorites list, or your Reading list. You can share the inked page with others using the Share Web Note button.

On the Job Now

To enhance security, Microsoft Edge runs in a partial sandbox, an arrangement that prevents attackers from gaining control of your computer. Browsing within the **sandbox** protects computer resources and information from hackers.

Figure 18: Web Note tools in Microsoft Edge

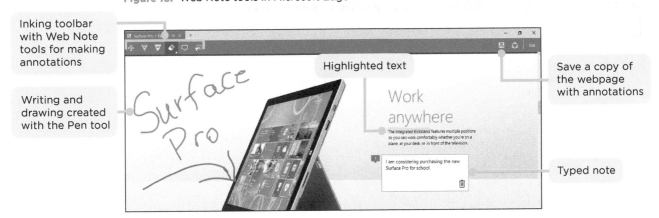

Inking toolbar with Web Note tools for making annotations

Highlighted text

Save a copy of the webpage with annotations

Writing and drawing created with the Pen tool

Typed note

Try This Now

Learn to use Edge!

Links to companion **Sways**, featuring **videos** with hands-on instructions, are located on www.cengagebrain.com.

1: Using Cortana in Microsoft Edge

Note: This activity requires using Microsoft Edge on a Windows 10 computer.

Cortana can assist you in finding information on a webpage in Microsoft Edge. Perform the following tasks:

a. Create a Word document using the Word Screen Clipping tool to capture the following screenshots.

- Screenshot A—Using Microsoft Edge, open a webpage with a technology news article. Right-click a term in the article and ask Cortana to define it.
- Screenshot B—Using Microsoft Edge, open the website of a fancy restaurant in a city near you. Make sure the Cortana circle icon is displayed in the Address bar. (If it's not displayed, find a different restaurant website.) Click the Cortana circle icon to display a pane with information about the restaurant.
- Screenshot C—Using Microsoft Edge, type **10 USD to Euros** in the Address bar without pressing the Enter key. Cortana converts the U.S. dollars to Euros.
- Screenshot D—Using Microsoft Edge, type **Apple stock** in the Address bar without pressing the Enter key. Cortana displays the current stock quote.

b. Submit your assignment in the format specified by your instructor.

2: Viewing Online News with Reading View

Note: This activity requires using Microsoft Edge on a Windows 10 computer.

Reading view in Microsoft Edge can make a webpage less cluttered with ads and other distractions. Perform the following tasks:

a. Create a Word document using the Word Screen Clipping tool to capture the following screenshots.

- Screenshot A—Using Microsoft Edge, open the website **mashable.com**. Open a technology article. Click the Reading view button to display an ad-free page that uses only basic text formatting.
- Screenshot B—Using Microsoft Edge, open the website **bbc.com**. Open any news article. Click the Reading view button to display an ad-free page that uses only basic text formatting.
- Screenshot C—Make three types of annotations (Pen, Highlighter, and Add a typed note) on the BBC article page displayed in Reading view.

b. Submit your assignment in the format specified by your instructor.

3: Inking with Microsoft Edge

Note: This activity requires using Microsoft Edge on a Windows 10 computer.

Microsoft Edge provides many annotation options to record your ideas. Perform the following tasks:

a. Open the website **wolframalpha.com** in the Microsoft Edge browser. Wolfram Alpha is a well-respected academic search engine. Type **US$100 1965 dollars in 2015** in the Wolfram Alpha search text box and press the Enter key.

b. Click the Make a Web Note button to display the Web Note tools. Using the Pen tool, draw a circle around the result on the webpage. Save the page to OneNote.

c. In the Wolfram Alpha search text box, type the name of the city closest to where you live and press the Enter key. Using the Highlighter tool, highlight at least three interesting results. Add a note and then type a sentence about what you learned about this city. Save the page to OneNote. Share your OneNote notebook with your instructor.

d. Submit your assignment link in the format specified by your instructor.

Essential Computer Concepts

Learning About the Components of Computer Systems

OBJECTIVES

- Compare the types of computers
- Describe the components of a computer system
- Learn how data is represented to a computer
- Learn how data is transmitted
- Learn about processing hardware
- Understand memory and storage
- Describe peripheral devices and understand how to connect them
- Learn about the hardware and software used to establish a network connection
- Explain how Internet access, email, and the World Wide Web affect the use of computers
- Describe potential security threats to computers and protection methods
- Discuss the types of system software and their functions
- Identify popular application software
- Learn about cloud computing

Case | *Oceanside Fish Market*

Two years ago, Jen and Sean Fuller started selling fresh fish at their new store Oceanside Fish Market in Newport, Rhode Island. Their business grew rapidly by word of mouth as people discovered their fresh fish and excellent customer service. Jen and Sean have spent so much time building their business that they haven't had time to research and purchase an updated computer system. They need to buy a computer soon because several of their suppliers are switching to all-electronic ordering systems. Also, customers have begun asking if the market has a website from which they could order. Jen and Sean ask you to research and recommend a computer system that fits their needs. They want a system that will grow with their business, but they have a limited budget to start (approximately $2000). They ask you to help them decide what to buy.

In this module, you will learn about computers and their components. You will learn how data is represented, processed, and stored. You will examine input and output devices, how information is transmitted between computers, and ways to secure that information. Finally, you will learn about system and application software, and cloud computing.

STARTING DATA FILES

There are no starting Data Files needed for this module.

Visual Overview:

The monitor, keyboard, and mouse are **peripheral devices**, which are hardware components that are not part of the internal components of the computer.

The **motherboard**, **CPU**, **hard disk**, and **cards** that expand the capabilities of the motherboard are inside the tower in a desktop computer or in the monitor in an all-in-one computer.

Output is the results of the computer processing input. The **monitor** is the device that displays the output from a computer.

Input is data or instructions you type into the computer. The **keyboard** is the most frequently used input device.

Pointing devices control the **pointer**, which is a small arrow or other symbol displayed on the monitor that you use to select commands and manipulate text or graphics. The most popular pointing device for a desktop computer is a **mouse**.

Our award-winning computers offer strong performance at a reasonable price. MicroPlus computers feature superior engineering, starting with a processor and a motherboard designed specifically to take advantage of the latest technological advancements. Of course, you are covered by our one-year parts and labor warranty.*

2017
BEST
TECH
!

COMPUTER
CHOICE
TOP
AWARD

QUALITY
PICK
2017

All credit cards welcome. Call 1-800-555-0000 today!

*ON-SITE SERVICE AVAILABLE FOR HARDWARE ONLY AND MAY NOT BE AVAILABLE IN CERTAIN REMOTE AREAS. SHIPPING AND HANDLING EXTRA. RETURNS ACCEPTED; CALL FOR AN RMA NUMBER (SEE YOUR INVOICE FOR DETAILS). ALL RETURNS MUST BE IN ORIGINAL BOX WITH ALL MATERIALS. DEFECTIVE PRODUCTS REPAIRED AT THE DISCRETION OF MICROPLUS. PRICES AND AVAILABILITY SUBJECT TO CHANGE WITHOUT NOTICE.

Photo source: ©iStock.com/sweetym

Computer Advertisement

This desktop PC is powerful enough to meet your most demanding computing needs.

> Specifications are the technical details about each component.

SPECIFICATIONS

Processor: Quad-core 4th generation Intel© Core™ i7-4790 processor (8MB cache, 4.00 GHz)

Memory: 8GB DDR3 SDRAM (expandable to 32 GB)

Graphics: Integrated graphics processor

Hard drive: 1TB SATA

Monitor: MicroPlus 22-inch LED monitor with built-in speakers

Keyboard: MicroPlus ergonomic keyboard

Mouse: MicroPlus wireless optical mouse

Optical drive: Blu-ray Reader and DVD Recordable (reads and writes to DVD/CD)

Networking and wireless: MicroPlus Wireless Zoom and Bluetooth 4.0

Operating system: Microsoft Windows 10, 64-bit

USB ports: 6 USB ports (3 high-speed)

Speakers: Built into monitor

Digital media card reader: 7-in-1 (Secure Media (SM), Secure Digital (SD), Secure Digital High Capacity (SDHC), SDXC, Memory Stick (MS), Memory Stick Pro (MS Pro), and MultiMediaCard (MMC))

Printer (not shown): Wireless MicroPlus PhotoPlus color inket printer and scanner

Installed software: 60-day trial of Microsoft Office 365 and 30-day trial of Norton AntiVirus

> **Special!**
> *Add a Windows or Android tablet for only $109!.*
> **Ask for details.**

> The **central processing unit (CPU)** or **processor** is mounted on the motherboard and is responsible for executing instructions to process data.

> **Memory** is a set of storage locations on the motherboard.

> A **hard disk drive** (also called a **hard drive** or a **hard disk**) is the most common magnetic storage device.

> A **DVD** is an optical storage device that stores 4.7 GB of data in a single layer on one side and up to 17.1 GB of data in dual layers on both sides. A **CD** is an optical storage device that stores up to 700 MB in a single layer on one side. A **Blu-ray disc** is an optical storage device that stores up to 500 GB of high-definition video on up to 20 layers.

> A **port** is an opening on a computer connected to a card or to an appropriate place on the motherboard into which you can plug a connector. A **USB (Universal Serial Bus) port** is a high-speed port used to connect many types of peripheral devices to the computer.

What Is a Computer?

Computers are essential tools in almost all kinds of activity in virtually every type of business. A **computer** is an electronic device that accepts information and instructions from a user, manipulates the information according to the instructions, displays the information in some way, and stores the information for retrieval later. It is a versatile tool with the potential to perform many different tasks. Computers and prices are constantly changing, but most of today's computers are well suited to running a small business.

PROSKILLS

Decision Making: Why Learn Basic Computer Concepts?

Although it's not necessary to become an expert in computers before purchasing one, it is a good idea to familiarize yourself with terminology and gain a basic understanding of how computers work before you spend your hard-earned money. Understanding the functions and capabilities of each system component helps you to make informed decisions so that you can purchase a system that will fulfill your needs within your budget.

TIP

In common usage, the term "PC" refers to personal computers that use Microsoft Windows. Personal computers that are sold only by Apple, Inc. are referred to as Macs (short for Macintosh).

Personal computers (**PCs**) are computers typically used by one person in a home or an office. A PC is used for general computing tasks such as word processing, manipulating numbers, working with photographs or graphics, exchanging email, and accessing the Internet.

There are several types of PCs. **Desktop computers** are designed to sit on a desk and run on power from an electrical outlet. The computer in the advertisement shown in the Visual Overview is a desktop computer, and the computer shown in Figure 1 is also a desktop computer. **All-in-one computers** are desktop computers, but the motherboard and CPU are part of the monitor instead of in a separate tower.

Figure 1	Desktop computer

Source: ©iStock.com/Alex Slobodkin

Laptop computers (also referred to as **notebook computers**) are small, lightweight, and designed for portability. They can run on power supplied by an electrical outlet or on battery power. The computer shown in Figure 2 is a laptop.

Figure 2   Laptop computer

Source: Yulia Nikulyasha Nikitina/Shutterstock.com

Tablet computers are personal computers also designed for portability, but they are usually thinner than laptops or netbooks because they do not have a keyboard, and they have a **touchscreen**—a display that, while showing you information, allows you to touch it with your finger or a stylus, a pen-like device used to interact with touchscreens, to input commands. Tablets vary widely in the tasks they can do. Figure 3 shows two brands of tablets.

Figure 3   Tablets

Apple iPad   Samsung Galaxy Note

Source: ©iStock.com/Bajak; olegganko/Shutterstock.com

The prices for desktop computers, laptops, netbooks, and tablets range widely from as low as $150 to as much as several thousands of dollars for high-end machines.

Mobile devices are small computers that are designed to fit in the palm of your hand, run on batteries, and usually have more limited capabilities than PCs. A **smartphone** is a mobile device that is used to make and receive phone calls; send and receive text messages; video chat; maintain a contact list and calendar for scheduling appointments; send email; connect to the Internet; play music; take photos or video; and even perform some of the same functions as a PC, such as word processing. To use all the capabilities of a smartphone, you need a contract with a cell phone company and must pay a fee, either monthly or pay as you go, for access to its phone network and to the Internet. A **wearable device** is a type of mobile device that attaches to a person and is worn like a piece of jewelry or clothing. Two examples of wearable devices are fitness trackers and smartwatches. Figure 4 shows a smartphone and a smartwatch.

Figure 4   Mobile devices

Samsung Galaxy smartphone   Apple Watch smartwatch

Source: ©iStock.com/guvendemir; ©iStock.com/killerbayer

Small and large businesses use PCs extensively. Some businesses, government agencies, and other institutions also use larger and faster types of computers, such as servers, mainframes, and supercomputers. A **server** is a computer that stores programs and data for multiple users. Authorized users connect to the server to run programs or access files. **Mainframe computers** are used by larger businesses and government agencies to centrally store, process, and manage large amounts of data.

The largest and fastest computers, called **supercomputers**, were first developed for high-volume computing tasks such as weather prediction. Supercomputers, like the one owned by NASA shown in Figure 5, are also used by large corporations and government agencies when the tremendous volume of data would seriously delay processing on a mainframe computer. Supercomputers can cost millions of dollars. However, a supercomputer's processing speed is so much faster than that of PCs and mainframes that the investment is worthwhile for agencies that need it.

Figure 5   Supercomputer

Courtesy of NASA

Your initial recommendation to Jen and Sean will be for them to purchase a desktop PC similar to the one shown in the advertisement in the Visual Overview because most daily tasks can be performed very efficiently using one, and it will not require a large initial investment. They also might want to consider a getting a laptop or tablet so that they can work in locations other than the store.

Converging Technologies

Every year, the lines between the types of computers are getting more blurry. Mobile devices such as smartphones are more powerful than the first laptops were, and today's desktop PCs are more powerful than the mainframe computers of a few decades ago. Tablets, which are available in several sizes and with varying capabilities, can be considered mobile devices rather than PCs. As new technologies are developed, consumers will need fewer and fewer devices to accomplish their tasks.

A computer has both hardware and software. **Hardware** is the physical components of a computer. **Software** is the intangible components of a computer system, particularly **programs**, which are the lists of instructions the computer needs to perform a specific task. For example, you can use word-processing software to type memos, letters, and reports, and you can use accounting software to maintain information about what customers owe you, display a graph showing the timing of customer payments, or keep track of your personal finances.

The advertisement in the Visual Overview includes several specifications describing the hardware and software included in the computer system shown.

Processing Hardware

The hardware and software of a computer work together to process data and commands. **Processing** is modifying data and executing commands. **Commands** are instructions to the computer on how to process the data. For example, you issue a command in the word-processing program to instruct the computer to center the title in a report.

Processing tasks occur on the **motherboard**, which contains the processing hardware— the computer's major electronic components—and is located inside the computer. The motherboard is a **circuit board**, which is a rigid piece of insulating material with **circuits**, or electrical paths, on it that control specific functions. See Figure 6.

Figure 6	Motherboard

Courtesy of Intel Corporation

The CPU consists of transistors and electronic circuits on a silicon **chip**, which is an integrated circuit embedded in semiconductor material that is mounted on the motherboard and is responsible for executing instructions to process data. Figure 7 shows a CPU for a PC.

Figure 7	CPU for a PC

Source: ©iStock.com/4kodiak

Most PCs have a 64-bit processor, which means they can process 64 bits at a time. Some older PCs have 32-bit processors. A **dual-core processor**, which has two processors on a single chip, can process information up to twice as fast as a **single-core processor**, which has one processor on the chip. Likewise, a **quad-core processor**, with four processors on a chip, processes information up to four times faster than a single-core processor.

Cards (sometimes called **expansion cards**) are circuit boards that are inserted into electrical connectors on the motherboard called **slots** (sometimes called **expansion slots**) to expand the capabilities of the motherboard. A sound card, for example, translates the digital audio information from the computer into analog sounds that the human ear can hear. To display graphics and video, a computer must have a graphics card. The graphics card controls the signals the computer sends to the monitor. Some motherboards have a built-in graphics processor instead.

Input Devices

You use an **input device**, such as a keyboard or a mouse, to input data and issue commands. In Figure 8, the top keyboard is a standard keyboard. The bottom keyboard in Figure 8 is **ergonomic**, which means that it has been designed to fit the natural placement of your hands and should reduce the risk of repetitive motion injuries. Many keyboards, like the ones shown, have additional keys programmed as shortcut keys to commonly used functions.

Figure 8 ▶ **Keyboards**

Source: Petr Malyshev/Shutterstock.com; Creativa Images/Shutterstock.com

When you use a pointing device to move the pointer on the screen and then click, you are providing input by issuing an instruction. The most common pointing device is a mouse, shown on the left in Figure 9. To move the pointer using a mouse, you slide the entire mouse around on your desk. To select items on the screen or execute an instruction, you point to something and then click a button on the mouse. A mouse usually has a **scroll wheel** that you roll to scroll the page on the screen and that also might function as a button. A **trackball**, such as the one shown in the middle in Figure 9, is similar to a mouse except that you control the movement of the pointer by moving only the ball. Notebook computers are usually equipped with a touchpad, as shown on the right in Figure 9. A **touchpad** is a touch-sensitive device on which you drag your finger to control the pointer. The buttons are located below the touchpad. When you use a touchscreen, there is no pointer. Instead, you tap or swipe your finger across the screen to input commands or scroll. If you do not have a touchscreen, you can use an external touchpad to use the same commands as with a touchscreen.

Figure 9 ▶ **Personal computer pointing devices**

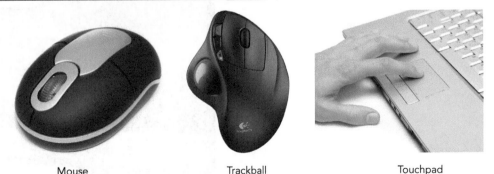

Mouse   Trackball   Touchpad

Source: NIKSPHOTO dot COM/Shutterstock.com; Courtesy of Logitech; Source: INSAGO/Shutterstock.com

A **scanner** transfers the content on a piece of paper into memory. When you place a piece of paper on the glass, a beam of light moves across the glass, similar to a photocopier, and the images or words on the paper are stored as digital information.

You can scan a document or a photo and save it as an image file, or you can scan a document and have the text "read" by the scanner and saved in a document file for editing later.

Microphones are another type of input device. You can use them to record sound for certain types of files, or, if you have voice-recognition software, you can use them to input data and commands.

Web cams are included with many computers. With a **web cam**, you can send pictures and video of yourself to others. You can also use a web cam to talk to others using a video phone service, such as Skype, that connects over the Internet.

The input devices that come with the system advertised in the Visual Overview are a mouse, an ergonomic keyboard, and a scanner that is built into the printer.

Understanding Assistive Technology

People with physical impairments or disabilities can use computers because of technology that makes computers accessible. This technology is called **assistive technology**, and the individual devices are called **assistive devices**. For example, people who cannot use their arms or hands instead can use foot, head, or eye movements to control the pointer. People with poor vision can use keyboards with large keys for input, screen enlargers to enlarge the type and images on the monitor, or screen readers to read the content on the screen aloud. Computers have even been developed that can be controlled by a person's thoughts—that is, the brain's electromagnetic waves.

Output Devices

Output devices store or show you output. The most common devices for displaying output are monitors and printers. The monitor shown in Figure 10 is a **flat screen monitor** or a **flat panel monitor**. Some flat screen monitors use **LCD** (**liquid crystal display**) technology, which creates the image you see on the screen by manipulating light within a layer of liquid crystal. This is the same technology used in digital watches or the time display on a microwave oven. LCD monitors require a backlight. Flat screen monitors labeled as **LED** (**light emitting diode**) monitors use LEDs to provide the backlight. LED backlighting is more energy efficient than ordinary backlighting.

Figure 10   **Flat screen monitor**

Source: ©iStock.com/Alex Slobodkin

Screen size is the diagonal measurement from one corner of the screen to the other (not including the plastic housing). Desktop monitors range from 18 to 32 inches. Most monitors on laptops are approximately 15 or 17 inches.

Monitor screens are divided into a matrix of small dots called **pixels**. The number of pixels the monitor displays is the **screen resolution**, which is expressed as horizontal and vertical measurements, such as 1366x768, 1600x900, or 1920x1200. The higher these numbers are, the smaller the objects appear because more objects can fit on the screen at once.

TIP

The viewing angle is not always listed in computer ads.

The horizontal **viewing angle** indicates how far to the side you can be and still see the images on the screen clearly, and the vertical viewing angle indicates how far above or below the monitor you can be. It is measured in degrees up to 180. The higher the number, the wider the viewing angle. If the measurement is written as a fraction in the manufacturer's description of a monitor, the top number is the horizontal viewing angle and the bottom is the vertical viewing angle.

The monitor included with the computer advertised in the Visual Overview is a 22-inch flat screen LED monitor.

A **printer** produces a paper copy of the text or graphics processed by the computer. Printed computer output is called **hard copy** because it is more tangible than the electronic version found in the computer or on the monitor.

Laser printers, such as the one shown on the left in Figure 11, use the same technology as a photocopier to create a temporary image on paper and then spray it with a powdery substance called **toner**. The speed of laser printers is measured in **pages per minute** (**ppm**). Laser printers are a popular choice for businesses because they produce high-quality output quickly and efficiently.

Figure 11	Printers

Laser printer

Inkjet printer

Source: Ihor Pasternak/Shutterstock.com; Courtesy of Epson America Inc.

TIP

Although the ppm speed is useful for comparing a printer's speed to other printers, it is not necessarily an indication of how fast the printer will print when you use it; that is dependent on how much text and graphics appear on the pages being printed.

Inkjet printers, such as the one shown on the right in Figure 11, spray ink onto paper. The quality of the inkjet output is comparable to a laser printer's output. The speed of inkjet printers is also measured in pages per minute. Although inkjet printers and ink cartridges are less expensive than laser printers and toner cartridges, the ink for inkjet printers needs to be replaced far more often than the toner for laser printers. Inkjet printers are popular for home use. Most inkjet printers are called "all-in-one" because they include a scanner, a photocopier, and fax capabilities.

Another type of printer is the dot matrix printer. **Dot matrix printers** transfer ink to the paper by striking a ribbon with pins. Dot matrix printers are most often used to print a large number of pages fairly quickly, or multipage, continuous forms such as payroll checks. The speed of dot matrix printers is measured in **characters per second** (**cps**).

Speakers allow you to hear sounds from the computer. Speakers can be separate peripheral devices attached to the computer, or they can be built into the computer or monitor.

In the computer advertised in the Visual Overview, speakers are built into the monitor. It also includes a color inkjet printer, although it is not shown. Jen and Sean might want to consider upgrading to a color laser printer that will enable them to print high-quality correspondence, advertisements, and brochures.

Connecting Peripheral Devices

An external peripheral device connects to the computer either via a cable from the device to the computer or wirelessly. If you are using a cable, the cable connects to the computer in a port. Some types of wireless connections require a wireless transmitter to be inserted into a port. Personal computers can have several types of ports. See Figure 12. Ports are connected to cards or to appropriate places on the motherboard.

Figure 12   **Ports on a typical desktop PC**

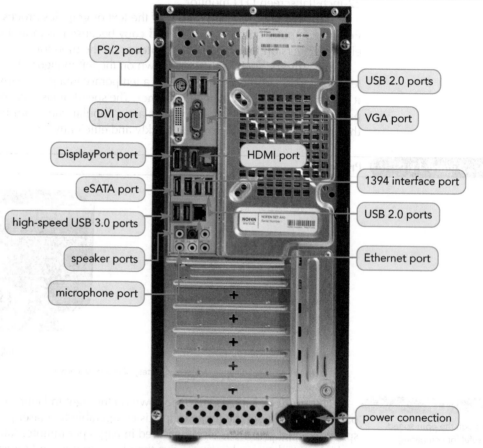

PS/2 port

USB 2.0 ports

DVI port

VGA port

DisplayPort port

HDMI port

eSATA port

1394 interface port

high-speed USB 3.0 ports

USB 2.0 ports

speaker ports

Ethernet port

microphone port

power connection

Source: Quiet PC LLP

Monitors are connected to computers through display ports. **HDMI (high-definition multimedia interface)** and **DisplayPort ports** transmit video and audio digitally. **DVI (digital video interface) ports** transmit video digitally. **VGA (video graphics array) ports** transmit analog video. Speakers and a microphone connect to a computer via ports on the sound card. Older style wired keyboards and mice connect via **PS/2 ports**; most wired keyboard and mice that you buy now connect via USB ports. A wireless keyboard or mouse often connects via a small connector that plugs into a USB port. Printers also connect via a USB port.

Ethernet ports allow data to be transmitted at high speeds so they are used to connect computers to one another or to the Internet. You can connect to another computer, a **modem** (a device that connects your computer to a standard telephone jack or to a cable connection), or sometimes directly to the Internet using an Ethernet port. 1394 interface and eSATA are also high-speed ports. These two types of ports are not typically found on personal PCs.

USB ports are either version 1, 2, or 3, with version 3 able to transmit data the fastest. The latest version, 3.1. USB ports, are high-speed ports that are not dedicated to any particular peripheral device.

To connect a device to a USB port, you need a USB connector, which is a metal tab attached to a cable, wireless transmitter, or flash drive that inserts into the USB port. There are three types of USB ports and connectors: type A, type B, and type C. Type A ports are found on PCs (refer back to Figure 12). Type A and two different type B connectors are shown in Figure 13. Another type B port and connector is larger and square; that shape type B port is often found on printers. USB cables usually have a type A connector on one end and a type B connector on the other end—the type A connector plugs into the type A port on a PC, and the type B connector plugs into the type B port on another device, such as a printer, smartphone, or a tablet. USB type C is a new connector that fits into type C ports. USB type C ports are version 3.1, and because of their design, they can transmit data much faster than other types. They are currently available on only a few devices, such as the newest Google Chromebook and the newest Apple Macbook. The computer shown in the advertisement in the Visual Overview has six USB ports, three of which are high-speed ports.

Figure 13	USB connectors

micro-USB connector   mini-USB connector   USB type A connector
(USB type B)   (USB type B)

Source: Tuomas Lehtinen/Shutterstock.com

Data Representation

Data refers to the words, numbers, figures, sounds, and graphics that describe people, events, things, and ideas. Like a light bulb, the computer interprets every signal as either "on" or "off" by using the number 1 to represent "on" and the number 0 to represent "off." Each of these numbers, called **binary digits**, or **bits**, is the smallest piece of data a computer can process.

Each character you type is represented by 8 bits. For example, as Figure 14 shows, the 8 bits that represent the number 0 are 00000000, with all eight bits "off" or set to 0; the eight bits that represent the integer value 1 are 00000001; and the eight bits that represent 255 are 11111111.

| Figure 14 | Binary representation of numbers |

Number	Binary Representation
0	00000000
1	00000001
2	00000010
3	00000011
4	00000100
5	00000101
6	00000110
7	00000111
8	00001000
.	.
.	.
.	.
253	11111101
254	11111110
255	11111111

A series of eight bits is called a **byte**. Processing capacity, storage capacity, and file sizes are all measured in bytes. A **kilobyte** (**KB** or simply **K**) is 1024 bytes, or approximately one thousand bytes; a **megabyte** (**MB**) is 1,048,576 bytes, or about one million bytes; a **gigabyte** (**GB**) is 1,073,741,824 bytes, or about one billion bytes; a **terabyte** (**TB**) is 1024 GB, or approximately one trillion bytes; and a **petabyte** (**PB**) is approximately 1000 terabytes.

Memory

A computer has several types of memory. **Random access memory** (**RAM**), which consists of chips on cards that plug into the motherboard, temporarily holds programs and data while the computer is on and allows the computer to access that information randomly; in other words, RAM doesn't need to access data in the same sequence in which it was stored. For example, when you write a report, the CPU temporarily copies the word-processing program into RAM so that the CPU can quickly access the instructions you need as you type and format the report. The characters you type are also stored in RAM. RAM is **volatile memory** or **temporary memory** because it constantly changes while the computer is on and clears when the computer is turned off. Most PCs use DDR SDRAM, which stands for "double data rate synchronous dynamic random access memory." RAM is measured in gigabytes (GB).

Cache memory, sometimes called RAM cache or CPU cache, is a special, high-speed memory chip on the motherboard or CPU. Because the computer can access cache memory more quickly than RAM, frequently and recently accessed data and commands are stored there instead of in RAM.

The computer advertised in the Visual Overview has 8 GB of SDRAM and 8 MB of cache memory. Next to the RAM specification, the note "expandable to 32 GB" indicates that you can add more RAM to this computer.

Read-only memory (ROM) is a chip on the motherboard prerecorded with instructions the computer uses to check its components to ensure they are working, and to activate the software that provides the computer's basic functionality when you turn it on. This set of instructions, called the BIOS (basic input/output system), tells the computer to initialize the motherboard, how to recognize devices connected to the computer, and to start the boot process. The boot process is the set of events that occurs between the moment you turn on the computer and the moment you can begin to use the computer. This is why turning on the computer is sometimes called booting up. ROM never changes and remains intact when the computer is turned off; therefore, it is called nonvolatile memory or permanent memory.

Complementary metal oxide semiconductor (CMOS, pronounced "SEE-moss") memory is a chip installed on the motherboard that is activated during the boot process and identifies where essential software is stored. A small rechargeable battery powers CMOS so its contents are saved when the computer is turned off. Unlike ROM, which cannot be changed, CMOS changes every time you add or remove hardware; therefore, CMOS is often referred to as semipermanent memory. CMOS stores the date and time because it retains its contents when the computer is turned off.

INSIGHT

Upgrading RAM

One of the easiest ways to make your computer run faster is to add more RAM. The more RAM a computer has, the more instructions and data it can store. You can often add more RAM to a computer by installing additional memory cards on the motherboard. Currently, you can buy cards that contain as little as 512 MB RAM or as much as 128 GB of RAM, and usually you can add more than one card. Check your computer's specifications to see what size RAM cards fit the slots on your motherboard.

Storage Media

Because RAM retains data only while the computer is powered on, your computer must have a more permanent storage option. Storage is where the data you create and the instructions you use remain when you are not using them. All data and instructions are stored as files. A file is a named collection of stored data. An executable file contains the instructions that tell a computer how to perform a specific task; for instance, the files used when the computer starts are executable. A data file is created by a user; for instance, a report you write with a word-processing program can be saved as a data file. A storage device receives data from RAM and stores it on a storage medium, such as a hard disk drive or a USB drive, CD, or DVD. Later, the data can be read and sent back to RAM to use again. The information stored in RAM can be retrieved more quickly than information that is stored permanently.

Magnetic storage media store data as magnetized particles on a surface. Before data is stored on magnetic media, the particles in the magnetic surface of the disk are scattered in random patterns. The read-write heads above the disk magnetize the particles to represent data.

Figure 15 shows a hard disk, a common magnetic storage device. It contains several magnetic oxide-covered metal platters that are usually sealed in a case inside the computer. The hard disk described in the ad in the Visual Overview has a capacity of 1 TB. Although this might seem like a high number, a computer fully loaded with typical software can easily use 18 to 20 GB of space, and disks fill up surprisingly quickly as you add data and multimedia files (pictures, music, and video).

| Figure 15 | Inside a hard disk drive |

Source: ©iStock.com/Tyler Boyes

Solid state media stores data as 1s and 0s that are turned on and off with electrical signals. Solid state drives (SSDs) are hard drives that are faster and tend to be more reliable than magnetic hard drives. However, they are also significantly more expensive than magnetic hard drives, almost twice as much per gigabyte of storage space.

Flash memory cards, like the one shown in Figure 16, are small, portable cards encased in hard plastic to which data can be written and rewritten using electrical signals. They are used in digital cameras, mobile devices, video game controllers, and other devices. Because they are fairly inexpensive, some people use them as permanent storage for things like pictures or videos, and just purchase a new card when one fills up. Flash memory cards are inserted into computers using a card reader, which, on a desktop, is usually a slot on the front of the tower. The computer shown in the Visual Overview comes with a card reader so that you can insert flash memory cards and copy their contents to the hard drive.

| Figure 16 | Flash memory card |

Courtesy of Kingston Technology Company, Inc.

A popular type of flash memory is a USB flash storage device, also called a USB drive or a flash drive. See Figure 17. USB drives for PCs are available in a wide range of sizes from 1 to 1000 GB of data. Most users don't need USB drives larger than 128 GB. They are popular for use as a secondary or backup storage device for data typically stored on a hard disk drive. USB drives plug directly into the PC; the computer recognizes the device as another disk drive.

| Figure 17 | USB flash storage device |

Courtesy of Kingston Technology Company, Inc.

Optical storage devices, such as CDs and DVDs, are polycarbonate discs coated with a reflective metal on which data is recorded as a trail of tiny pits or dark spots on the surface of the disc. The data that these pits or spots represent can then be "read" with a beam of laser light. Optical storage media are very durable but not indestructible. Take care not to scratch the disc surface or expose it to high temperatures.

To store data on a CD, you need to record it on a **CD-R** (**compact disc recordable**) or **CD-RW** (**compact disc rewritable**) disc. CDs that you buy with software or music already on them are **CD-ROMs** (**compact disc read-only memory**)—you can read from them, but you cannot record additional data onto them.

On a CD-R, after the data is recorded and finalized, you cannot erase or modify it. In contrast, you can re-record a CD-RW. Recordable DVD drives are also available. As with CDs, you can buy a DVD to which you can record only once, or a rewritable DVD to which you can record and then re-record data. Recordable DVDs come in two formats—**DVD-R** and **DVD+R**. Likewise, re-recordable DVDs come in two formats— **DVD-RW** and **DVD+RW**. DVD drives on most computers are capable of reading from and writing to both -RW and +RW DVDs and CDs, as well as DVDs with two layers. **BD-R** are Blu-ray discs that you can record to once, and **BD-RE** are Blu-ray discs that you can record to multiple times. You need a Blu-ray drive to use Blu-ray discs.

Although CDs, DVDs, and Blu-ray discs are the same physical size, the amount of data they can store is very different. Refer to the Visual Overview for more information about the storage capacities of optical storage devices.

The computer shown in the ad in the Visual Overview includes an optical drive that can play Blu-ray discs and play and record DVDs and CDs. You'll recommend that Jen and Sean purchase a computer with a DVD drive that can record DVDs. You'll also recommend at least a 1 TB hard drive and at least 8 GB of RAM.

Networks

A **network** connects one computer to other computers and peripheral devices, enabling you to share data and resources with others. Each computer that is part of the network must have a **network adapter** to create a communications connection between the computer and the network. In wired connections, a cable is used to connect the network adapter port to the network. **Network software** establishes the communications protocols that will be observed on the network and controls the "traffic flow" as data travels throughout the network.

Some networks have one or more servers that act as the central storage location for programs and provide mass storage for most of the data used on the network. A network consisting of computers dependent on a server is called a **client/server network**. The dependent computers are the **clients**. These computers are dependent on the server because it contains most of the data and software. When a network does not have a server, all the computers are essentially equal, and programs and data are distributed among them. This is called a **peer-to-peer network**. A **router** connects devices on a network and controls traffice between the devices so all the devices can access the network. Figure 18 illustrates a typical network configuration.

Figure 18 ● **Typical network configuration**

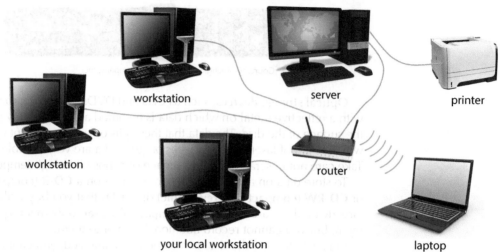

workstation   server   printer

workstation

router

your local workstation   laptop

Source: Eugene Shapovalov/Shutterstock.com; Dmitry Melnikov/Shutterstock.com; Oleksiy Mark/Shutterstock.com; Maxx-Studio/Shutterstock.com; Ihor Pasternak/Shutterstock.com

In a **local area network** (**LAN**), computers and peripheral devices are located relatively close to each other, generally in the same building. A **wide area network** (**WAN**) consists of multiple LANs connected together. The Internet is the largest example of a WAN. In a **wireless local area network** (**WLAN**), computers and peripherals use high-frequency radio waves instead of wires to connect in a network. A **personal area network** (**PAN**) is a network that allows two or more devices located close to each other to communicate or to connect a device to the Internet.

Data Communications

The transmission of data from a computer to a peripheral device or from one computer to another is called **data communications**. The four essential components of data communications are a sender, a receiver, a channel, and a protocol. The computer that originates the message is the **sender**. The message is sent over some type of **channel**, such as telephone or coaxial cable, a microwave or radio signal, or optical fibers. The computer or device at the message's destination is called the **receiver**. The rules that establish an orderly transfer of data between the sender and the receiver are **protocols**.

Data can be transmitted via a wired or wireless connection. To transmit data via a wired connection, you need to connect a cable to a port on the computer and connect the other end to another computer or peripheral device. To transmit data wirelessly, the appropriate hardware must be built into or attached to a computer.

Two common ways to transmit data wirelessly over short distances are **Bluetooth** and **Certified Wireless USB**, which both use short-range radio waves to connect one device to another. The devices must each have a Bluetooth or Wireless USB transmitter. The two devices must be near each other, although the newest versions of Bluetooth allow the devices to be up to 300 feet from each other.

Wi-Fi (short for wireless fidelity) is a standard radio frequency established by the Institute of Electrical and Electronics Engineers (IEEE) that allows you to transmit data wirelessly over medium-range distances. The distance and speed at which data transfers varies depending on the hardware and the Wi-Fi version. The distance can range from 100 to 900 feet. Wi-Fi is the standard used to connect to the Internet at Wi-Fi hotspots, such as a public library, an airport, a college campus, or another public spot such as Starbucks or McDonald's.

WiMAX (short for **Worldwide Interoperability for Microwave Access**), another standard defined by the IEEE, allows computer users to connect over many miles. A WiMAX tower sends signals to a WiMAX receiver built or plugged into a computer. WiMAX towers can communicate with each other or with a company that provides connections to the Internet.

3G and **4G** are the standards used by cell phone companies to transmit data. Exactly what is used to transmit data depends on the type of network and the phone in use. Some cell phones use mobile WiMAX to provide access to their 4G networks. A newer wireless standard used by some cell phone companies to deliver access to their 4G networks is **LTE** (**long-term evolution**). To access 3G and 4G networks, you need to have a contract with a cell phone provider, such as AT&T, Verizon, or Sprint, and a smartphone, tablet, or other device that can access the network.

The Internet

The **Internet** is the largest network in the world. People use the Internet to send **email**, messages sent from one user's computer to another user's computer. The **World Wide Web**, or simply the **web**, is a huge collection of information stored on network servers around the world. The information is stored as a type of file called a **webpage**, which can include text, graphics, sound, animation, and video. A collection of webpages is a **website**. A **hyperlink**, or **link**, is text, a graphic, or another object on a webpage programmed to connect to another webpage or file on any web server in the world. A **web browser** is software that you use to navigate the web. Figure 19 shows a webpage on the Library of Congress website.

Figure 19   **Webpage on the World Wide Web**

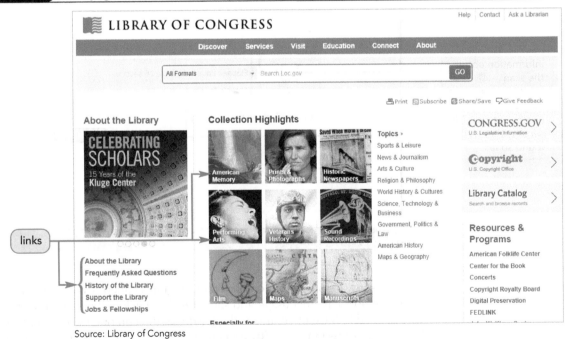

Source: Library of Congress

To connect to the Internet, you need a wireless connection or a modem. Most computers come with a built-in network and wireless adapters, and a modem to connect to phone lines. To use a high-speed connection over phone lines, such as **DSL** (**digital subscriber line**), or over a cable connection, you need to purchase an external DSL or cable modem. High-speed connections are often called **broadband connections**.

A broadband connection will enable Jen and Sean to connect to suppliers at other locations without waiting an undue amount of time to send and receive data. You decide to include the benefits of Internet and web access in your recommendation to Jen and Sean. Specifically, you plan to convince them that they could sell their products over the Internet.

Security Threats on Your Computer

After a computer is connected to a network, it is essential to protect the computer against possible threats from people intent on stealing information or causing malicious damage. **Malware** is a broad term that describes any program that is intended to cause harm or convey information to others without the owner's permission. One type of malware is a **virus**, which instructs your computer to perform annoying or destructive activities, such as erasing or damaging data and programs on your hard disk. Worms and Trojan horses are specific types of viruses. **Antivirus software** searches executable files for the sequences of characters that might cause harm, and disinfects the files by erasing or disabling those commands. Figure 20 shows the dialog box that appears when you use Trend Micro's free antivirus program on its website to scan your computer for potential threats. The computer advertised in the Visual Overview comes with a 30-day trial version of antivirus software.

Figure 20	Antivirus scan in progress

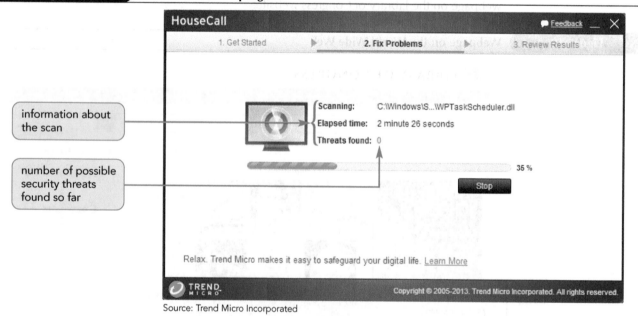

information about the scan

number of possible security threats found so far

Source: Trend Micro Incorporated

Some software programs contain other programs called **spyware** that track a computer user's Internet usage and send this data back to the company or person who created it. Most often, this is done without the computer user's permission or knowledge. **Anti-spyware software** can detect these programs and delete them. **Adware** is software installed along with another program, usually with the user's permission, that generates advertising revenue for the program's creator by displaying targeted ads to the program's user.

Malware on one computer sometimes tries to access another computer without the owner's permission. A **firewall**, which can be either hardware (usually built into a router) or software, prevents this from happening.

Another way criminals try to gain access to personal information stored on computers connected to the Internet is to trick people into visiting a spoofed website. A **spoofed site** is a website set up to look exactly like another website, such as a bank's website. The spoofed site attempts to convince customers of the real site to enter personal information, such as credit card numbers, Social Security numbers, and passwords, so that the thief collecting the information can use it to steal the customer's money or identity.

One way criminals get people to visit spoofed sites is by **phishing**, which is the practice of sending email messages to customers or potential customers of a legitimate website asking them to click a link in the email message. The link leads to a spoofed site where the user is asked to "verify" personal information. If you receive a message like this, never click the link in the message. Instead, use a web browser to visit the organization's website.

INSIGHT

Protecting Information with Passwords

You can protect data on your computer by using passwords. When you set up accounts on your computer for multiple users, consider requiring that users sign in with a username and password before they can use the computer. This is known as **logging in** or **logging on**. You can also protect individual files on your computer so that people who try to open or alter a file need to type the password before they are allowed access to the file. Many websites require a username and password to access the information stored on it. To prevent anyone from guessing your passwords, you should always create and use strong passwords. A **strong password** consists of at least eight characters of upper- and lowercase letters and numbers. Avoid using common personal information, such as birthdays and addresses, in your password.

Computer Software

Software can be divided into two major categories—system software and application software. **System software** helps the computer carry out its basic operating tasks. **Application software** helps the user carry out a variety of specific tasks.

System Software

System software manages the fundamental operations of your computer, such as loading programs and data into memory, executing programs, saving data to disks, displaying information on the monitor, and transmitting data through a port to a peripheral device. There are four types of system software—operating systems, utilities, device drivers, and programming languages. An **operating system** performs the following tasks:

- Controls the flow of input and output
- Allocates hardware resources, such as memory and processing time, so programs run properly; this allows computers to **multitask**—start and run more than one program at a time, such as producing a document in your word-processing program while you check your email
- Manages files on your storage devices so that you can open and save them
- Maintains security, such as requiring a username and password to use the computer
- Guards against and detects equipment failure by checking electronic circuits periodically, and then notifying the user if there is a problem by displaying a warning message on the screen

Utilities augment the operating system by taking over some of its responsibility for allocating hardware resources. Many utilities come with the operating system, but some independent software developers offer utilities for sale separately. **Device drivers** are computer programs that handle the transmission protocol between a computer and its peripherals by establishing communication between a computer and a device. When you add a device to an existing computer, part of its installation includes adding its device driver to the computer's configuration. **Programming languages** are software that a programmer uses to write computer instructions. Some examples of popular programming languages are BASIC, Visual Basic, C, C++, C#, Java, and Delphi.

Microsoft Windows, used on many PCs, and the Mac OS, used exclusively on Apple computers, provide a **graphical user interface** (**GUI**, pronounced "goo-ey"), which allows the user to manipulate graphics, icons, and dialog boxes to execute commands. In addition to the operating system, Windows and the Mac OS also include utilities, device drivers, and some application programs that perform common tasks. Figure 21 shows the Start menu open on the Microsoft Windows 10 desktop.

| Figure 21 | Windows 10 Start button |

Windows 10, the newest version of the Windows operating system, requires a computer with at least a 1 GHz processor, 1 GB of RAM for the 32-bit version or 2 GB of RAM for the 64-bit version, a DirectX 9 graphics processor, and 16 GB of available space on the hard disk for the 32-bit version or 20 GB for the 64-bit version. Keep in mind that these are the minimum recommendations.

Application Software

The primary factor in choosing specifications for a computer you purchase is the software you will be using. Application software enables you to perform specific computer tasks, such as document production, spreadsheet calculations, and database management.

Document production software includes word-processing software, desktop publishing software, email editors, and web authoring software. All of these production tools have a variety of features that assist you in writing and formatting documents, including changing the style of type or adding color and design elements. Most offer tools to help you avoid typographical and spelling errors, as shown in the document in Figure 22. The document in the figure was created in Microsoft Word 2016, the word-processing program included with Microsoft Office 2016. Many programs also provide grammar-checking and thesaurus tools to improve your writing by offering suggestions and alternatives.

Figure 22	Document with a misspelled word

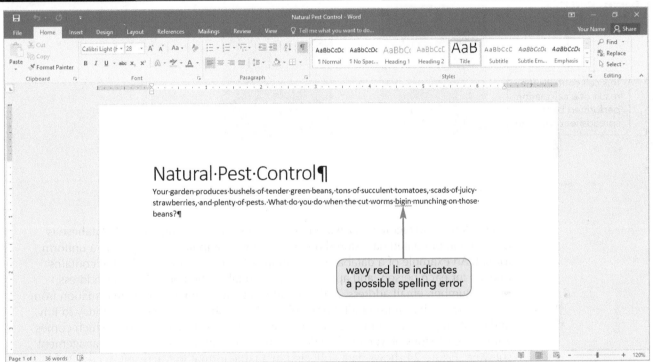

Spreadsheet software is a numerical analysis tool that both businesses and individuals use extensively. Spreadsheet software creates a **worksheet** composed of a grid of columns and rows. Each column is lettered, and each row is numbered. The intersection of a column and a row is a **cell**. You type numbers into the cells, and then create mathematical formulas in other cells that perform calculations using these numbers. With the appropriate data and formulas, you can use an electronic spreadsheet to prepare financial reports, analyze investment portfolios, calculate amortization tables, examine alternative bid proposals, and project income, as well as perform many other tasks involved in making informed business decisions. You can also use spreadsheet software to produce graphs and reports based upon the data. A worksheet created in Microsoft Excel 2016, which is included with Microsoft Office 2016, is shown in Figure 23 and includes a simple calculation and a chart that represents the data in the spreadsheet.

Figure 23   Worksheet with numerical data and a graph

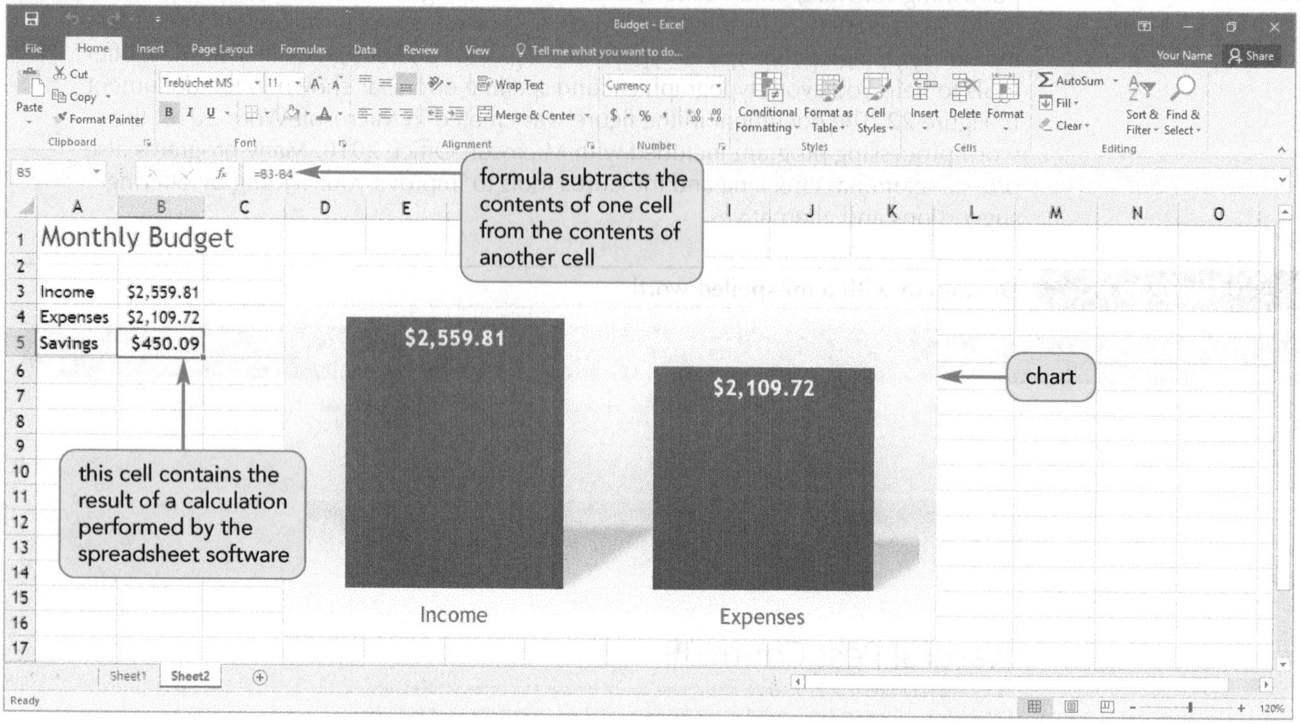

Database management software lets you collect and manage data. A **database** is a collection of related data stored on one or more computers organized in a uniform format. An example of a database is an address book or a contacts list that contains one tab for each person, and appearing on each tab is the person's name, address, phone number, email address, and birthdate. You can extract specific information from a database, such as a list of all the people in the database who have a birthday in July, and create reports to list the data in many ways. Microsoft Access 2016, which comes with some versions of Microsoft Office 2016, is an example of database management software. Figure 24 shows data collected in a table format in Microsoft Access 2016.

Figure 24   **Data in Microsoft Access 2016**

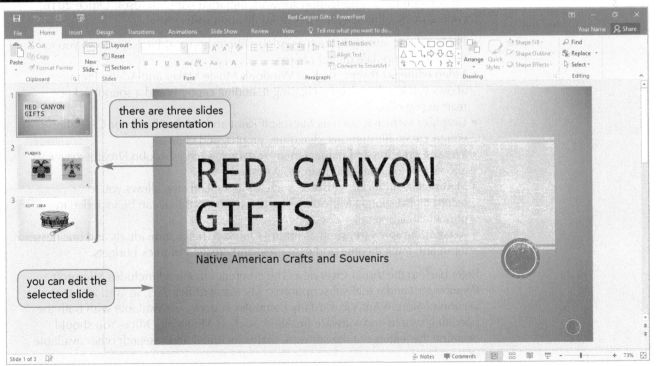

Presentation software allows you to display or project text, graphics, video, and other information to a group; print them for quick reference; or transmit them to remote computers. Figure 25 shows a slide from a presentation created in Microsoft PowerPoint 2016, which is part of the suite of programs included with Microsoft Office 2016.

Figure 25   **Slide in Microsoft PowerPoint 2016**

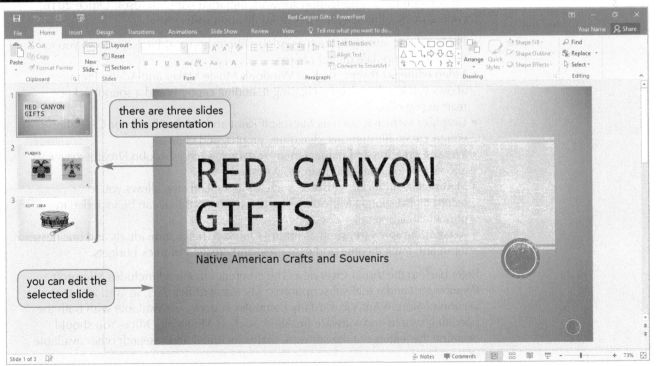

Information management software allows people to keep track of their schedules, appointments, contacts, and to-do lists. Some information software allows you to synchronize information between a handheld device such as a smartphone and a desktop or notebook computer. Microsoft Outlook 2016, the information manager and email software that comes with Microsoft Office 2016, is shown in Figure 26.

Figure 26   Microsoft Outlook 2016 program window

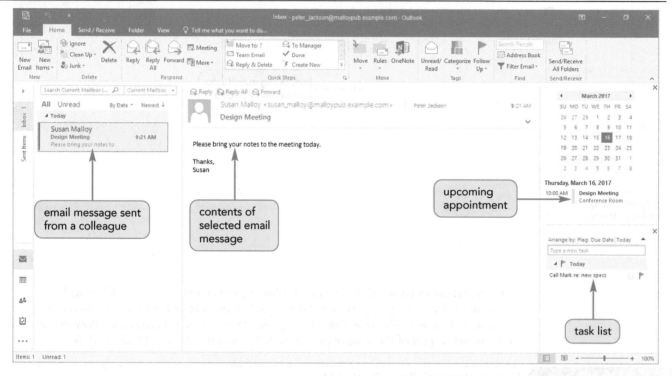

In addition to the application software included with Microsoft Office 2016, there are many other useful types of application software:

- **Photo editing software**, such as Adobe Photoshop and Picasa, allows you to edit and manipulate digital photos.
- **Video editing software**, such as Windows Movie Maker and Adobe Premiere, allows you to edit video by clipping it, adding captions and a soundtrack, or rearranging clips.
- **Graphics software**, such as Microsoft Paint and Adobe Illustrator CS6, allows you to create illustrations, diagrams, graphs, and charts.
- **Website creation and management software**, such as Adobe Dreamweaver, allows you to create and manage websites.
- **Multimedia authoring software**, such as Adobe Director, allows you to record digital sound files, video files, and animations that can be included in presentations and other documents.
- **Accounting software**, such as Intuit's Quicken, helps individuals and businesses input and track income and expenses, and create and track budgets.

Refer back to the Visual Overview. The computer in the ad includes Microsoft Windows 10 and a trial subscription to Microsoft Office 365, as well as a trial version of Norton AntiVirus. Many computer systems are available with both the operating system and software installed, such as Microsoft Office. You should examine the features of the software that is included and research other available options.

Computing in the Cloud

Cloud computing means that data, applications, and even resources are stored on servers accessed over the Internet rather than on users' computers, and you access only what you need when you need it. Many individuals and companies are moving toward the **cloud**—servers that are connected to the Internet and are used to provide access to and storage for data, resources, and programs—for at least some of their needs. For example, some companies provide space and computing power to developers for a fee. Individuals might subscribe to a backup service such as Carbonite or Mozy so that their data is automatically backed up on a computer at the physical location of those companies.

Microsoft Office Online and Google Docs editors provide both free and paid versions of various applications that you access by logging in to their websites. Office 365 is a subscription to Microsoft cloud services. There are different plans available for home and business users, but most of the plans include access to Microsoft Office programs, such as Word, Excel, PowerPoint, and so on. With Office 365, you can sign in to your account from any computer running Windows 7, Windows 8, Windows 8.1, or Windows 10 and use the services you are subscribed to.

In addition to using services over the Internet, many people store files on servers accessed over the Internet. For example, OneDrive is space on Microsoft servers where you can store files in public or private folders, or in folders that you make available to only people you specify. To access OneDrive, you need a free Microsoft account. Figure 27 shows a user's OneDrive. Many other companies offer storage space for files on their servers as well, such as Google Drive, Dropbox, and Box.

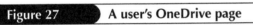

Figure 27   **A user's OneDrive page**

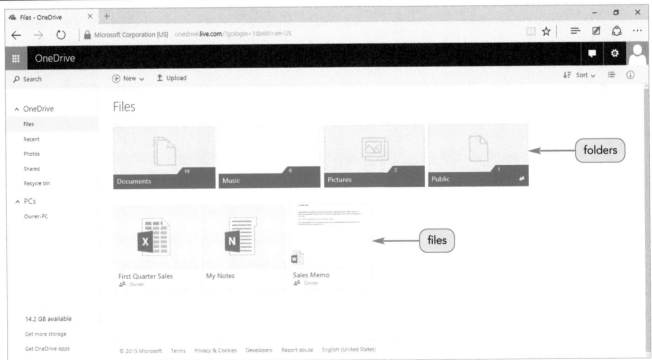

Putting It All Together

Your recommendation for Jen and Sean will include a PC with 8 GB of RAM, a 1 TB hard drive, and at least a 2.90 GHz processor, as well as document production, spreadsheet, and database management software, such as Microsoft Word, Excel, and Access. You want them to also add photo editing software; but because several free programs, such as Windows Photo Gallery, will probably suit their needs, they don't need to purchase that now. In addition, you will recommend that they purchase accounting software specifically designed for small businesses, such as Sage 50 Pro Accounting or QuickBooks. You will also recommend that they consider buying a high-speed modem and a router. The router will provide firewall protection now and will enable them to easily set up a network when they expand their computer system. To complete their system, you will recommend that they purchase a 24-inch LED monitor and a color laser printer. Finally, you will suggest that they sign up for a free Microsoft account and use the free space available on OneDrive to share and back up their files.

Review Questions

PRACTICE

1. Which of the following would not be considered a PC?
   - a. mainframe
   - b. desktop
   - c. tablet PC
   - d. laptop

2. The intangible components of a computer system, including the programs, are called:
   - a. peripherals
   - b. hardware
   - c. price
   - d. software

3. To display graphics, a computer needs a monitor and a(n):
   - a. expansion port
   - b. graphics port
   - c. sound card
   - d. graphics card or processor

4. What part of the computer is responsible for executing instructions to process information?
   - a. peripheral device
   - b. motherboard
   - c. CPU
   - d. card

5. Keyboards, monitors, and printers are all examples of which of the following?
   - a. peripheral devices
   - b. output devices
   - c. software
   - d. input devices

6. Which of the following is a pointing device that allows you to control the pointer by moving the entire device around on a surface?
   - a. mouse
   - b. trackball
   - c. touchpad
   - d. touchscreen

7. What do you call each 1 or 0 used in the representation of computer data?
   - a. a pixel
   - b. a point
   - c. a bit
   - d. a byte

8. What is a gigabyte?
   - a. about a billion bits
   - b. about a billion bytes
   - c. 10,000 kilobytes
   - d. one-half of a petabyte

9. The transmission protocol between a computer and a peripheral device is handled by a:
   - a. sender
   - b. device driver
   - c. card
   - d. channel

10. What are high-speed connections to the Internet often called?
    - a. broadband connections
    - b. Wi-Fi
    - c. cables
    - d. wireless connections

11. Which of the following temporarily stores data and programs while you are using them?
    - a. RAM
    - b. ROM
    - c. peripherals
    - d. the hard disk

12. When you turn the computer on, which of the following permanently stores the set of instructions that the computer uses to activate the software that controls the processing function?
    - a. RAM
    - b. ROM
    - c. cache
    - d. the hard disk

13. What do you call a named collection of data stored on a disk?
    - a. a file
    - b. a pixel
    - c. a protocol
    - d. the operating system

14. Which of the following is not a permanent storage medium?
    - a. hard disk
    - b. DVD
    - c. cache
    - d. optical disk

15. Which of the following prevents unauthorized access to a computer by another computer?
    a. spyware
    c. firewall
    b. antivirus software
    d. DNS server

16. Which of the following is not a function of an operating system?
    a. allocates hardware resources
    c. carries out a specific task for the user
    b. controls the flow of input and output
    d. manages storage space

17. Which of the following is system software?
    a. Microsoft Windows
    c. Microsoft Excel
    b. Microsoft Word
    d. Microsoft Paint

18. What are the technical details about each hardware component called?

19. What is processing?

20. What is an opening on a computer connected to a card or to a place on the motherboard into which you can plug a connector?

21. What is the set of events that occurs between the moment you turn on the computer and the moment you can begin to use the computer?

22. What is a printed copy of computer output called?

23. What is the chip installed on the motherboard that is activated during the boot process and identifies where essential software is stored?

24. What type of storage uses flash memory technology and is approximately twice as expensive as a magnetic hard drive?

25. What must each computer that is part of the network have installed in order to connect it to the network?

26. What connects devices on a network so all the devices can access network components?

27. What is a program that instructs a computer to perform annoying or destructive activities?

28. What is software that a programmer uses to write computer instructions?

29. What is the term that describes starting and running more than one program at a time?

30. What is the term that describes data, applications, and resources being stored on servers accessed over the Internet rather than on users' computers?

APPLY

Case Problem

There are no Data Files needed for this Case Problem.

You are buying a new computer. You want the computer to run Microsoft Office 2016 or Office 365, and you want to make sure you are protected against security threats. You need to decide if you want a desktop, a laptop, or a tablet. You also need a printer. However, you have a limited budget and can spend no more than $900 for everything (all hardware and software).

To help you organize your information, use the table shown in Figure 28.

Figure 28   **System requirements table**

	Your Requirements	Computer Retailer #1	Computer Retailer #2	Computer Retailer #3
Windows 10				
Microsoft Office (version of Office 2016 or Office 365)				
Brand of computer, if any				
Processor (brand and speed)				
RAM (amount)				
Hard disk (size)				
Flash memory card reader				
Number of high-speed USB ports				
Total number of USB ports				
Monitor (type and size)				
Keyboard				
Mouse				
Printer (type and speed)				
Speakers				
Antivirus software				
Firewall (software or router with built-in firewall)				
System price				
Additional costs				
Total price				

1. Decide whether you want a desktop, a laptop, or a tablet, and then enter that in the table.
2. If you decide to get a laptop or a tablet, consider whether you will need an external keyboard and mouse, and whether you want to purchase a large monitor so that you can use the smaller computer more comfortably.
3. Decide which edition of Office you want—a version of Office 2016 or Office 365—and enter it in the first column of the table. Search the Microsoft website to find a description of the software included with each edition of Office, and then search for the hardware requirements for running the edition that you chose. If necessary, change the hardware requirements in the table.

4. Research the cost of your new computer system. To begin, visit local stores, look at advertisements, or search the web for computer system retailers. Most computer retailers sell complete systems that come with all the necessary hardware, an operating system, and additional software already installed. Consider visiting a small, local computer store that has the capability to custom-build a desktop system for you or sell you a refurbished laptop with a guarantee. In the Computer Retailer #1 column of the table, fill in the specifications for the system you chose. If any item listed as a minimum requirement is not included with the system you chose, find the cost of adding that item and enter the price in the table. Repeat this process with systems from two other retailers, entering the specifications in the Computer Retailer #2 and Computer Retailer #3 columns.

5. If the system you chose does not come with a printer, add a color inkjet printer priced within your budget.

6. If the system you chose does not come with antivirus software, search the web for the cost, if any, of an antivirus software package. Make sure you look up reviews of the package you choose. Decide whether to purchase this software or download free software, and enter this cost in the table.

7. If you decide you need a router with a built-in firewall, search the web for the price of one. Enter this information in the table.

8. Total the costs you entered in the table for the various items. Is the total cost $900 or less? If not, revisit some of the items. Can you get a less expensive printer? Do you need to downgrade to a less expensive monitor? Likewise, if you are under budget, upgrade a part of your system. For example, if the system you chose meets only the minimum requirements for running Windows and Office, consider upgrading the processor or adding more RAM. Or perhaps you can afford to upgrade the monitor to a larger one. Reevaluate your choices if necessary and try to get your total cost close to $900.

Managing Your Files

Organizing Files and Folders with Windows 10

OBJECTIVES

- Plan the organization of files and folders
- Use File Explorer to view and manage folders and files
- Open and save files
- Create folders
- Copy and move files and folders
- Find files and information with Cortana
- Compress and extract files

Case | *Miami Trolleys*

After college, Diego and Anita Marino moved to Miami, Florida, and started Miami Trolleys, a sightseeing company that provides guided tours of Miami on a hop-on, hop-off trolley. As marketing manager, Diego is in charge of creating resources that describe the tours and sights in Miami. He hired you to help him develop marketing materials and use computer tools to organize photos, illustrations, and text documents to promote the business. For your first task, Diego asks you to organize the files on his new computer. Although he has only a few files, he wants to use a logical organization to help him find his work as he stores more files and folders on the computer.

In this module, you'll work with Diego to devise a strategy for managing files. You'll learn how Windows 10 organizes files and folders, and you'll examine Windows 10 file management tools. You'll create folders and organize files within them. You'll also use techniques to display the information you need in folder windows and explore options for working with compressed files.

Note: With the release of Windows 10, Microsoft is taking a new approach to software publication called "Windows as a Service." With this approach, Microsoft is constantly providing updates to Windows instead of releasing new versions periodically. This means that Windows features might change over time, including how they look and how you interact with them. The information provided in this text was accurate at the time this book was published.

STARTING DATA FILES

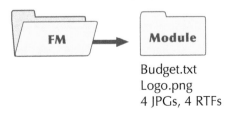

FM → **Module**
Budget.txt
Logo.png
4 JPGs, 4 RTFs

Review
Background.png
Events.xlsx
2 JPGs, 3 RTFs

Case1
Designers.txt
4 JPGs, 5 RTFs

Case2
Estimate Tips.txt
Plan Projects.txt
4 RTFs, 6 XLSXs

Visual Overview:

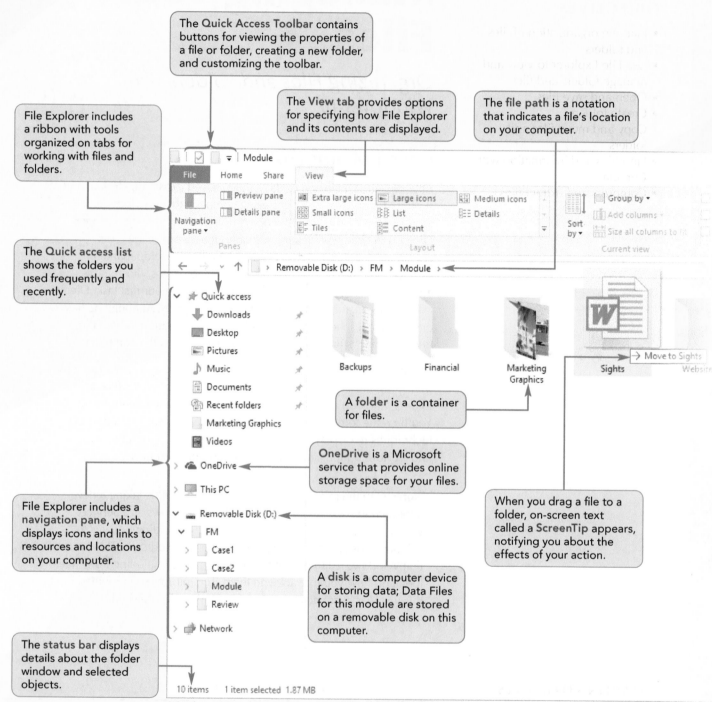

The Quick Access Toolbar contains buttons for viewing the properties of a file or folder, creating a new folder, and customizing the toolbar.

The View tab provides options for specifying how File Explorer and its contents are displayed.

The file path is a notation that indicates a file's location on your computer.

File Explorer includes a ribbon with tools organized on tabs for working with files and folders.

The Quick access list shows the folders you used frequently and recently.

A folder is a container for files.

OneDrive is a Microsoft service that provides online storage space for your files.

File Explorer includes a navigation pane, which displays icons and links to resources and locations on your computer.

When you drag a file to a folder, on-screen text called a ScreenTip appears, notifying you about the effects of your action.

A disk is a computer device for storing data; Data Files for this module are stored on a removable disk on this computer.

The status bar displays details about the folder window and selected objects.

©iStock.com/Meinzahn, ©iStock.com/Betelgejze, ©iStock.com/Vladone, ©iStock.com/Ivan Cholakov

Files in a Folder Window

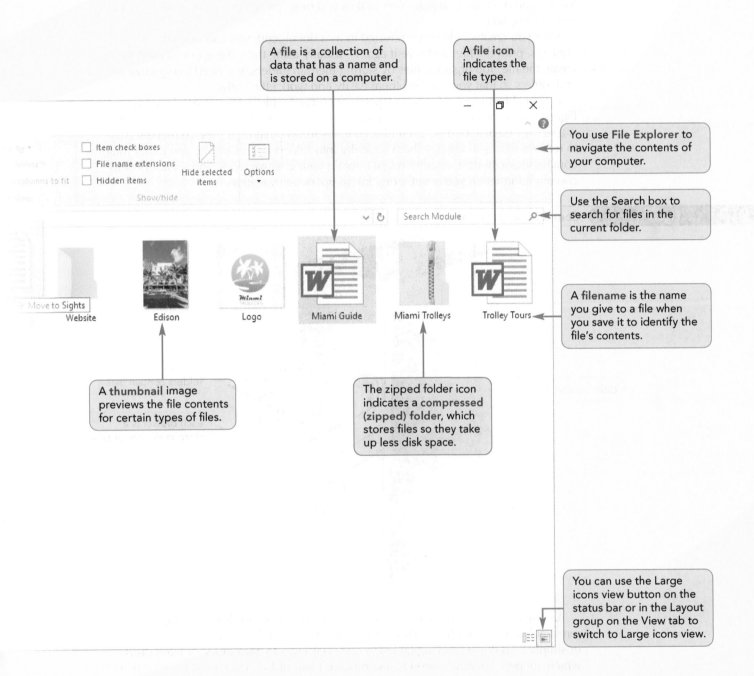

A file is a collection of data that has a name and is stored on a computer.

A file icon indicates the file type.

You use **File Explorer** to navigate the contents of your computer.

Use the Search box to search for files in the current folder.

A filename is the name you give to a file when you save it to identify the file's contents.

A thumbnail image previews the file contents for certain types of files.

The zipped folder icon indicates a **compressed (zipped) folder**, which stores files so they take up less disk space.

You can use the Large icons view button on the status bar or in the Layout group on the View tab to switch to Large icons view.

Item check boxes
File name extensions
Hidden items
Hide selected items
Options
Show/hide

Search Module

Move to Sights
Website
Edison
Logo
Miami Guide
Miami Trolleys
Trolley Tours

Organizing Files and Folders

Your typical computer session usually begins with starting an app and opening a file. You view, add, or change the file contents, and then save and close the file. Because most of your work involves files, you need to understand how to save and organize files, so you can easily find and open them when necessary. Knowing how to save, locate, and organize computer files makes you more productive when you are working with a computer.

After you create a file (often referred to as a document), you can open it, edit its contents, print the file, and save it again—usually using the same app you used to create the file. You organize files by storing them in folders. You need to organize files and folders so that you can find them easily and work efficiently.

A file cabinet is a common metaphor for computer file organization. As shown in Figure 1, a computer is like a file cabinet that has two or more drawers—each drawer is a storage device, or disk. Each disk contains folders that hold files. To make it easy to retrieve files, you arrange them logically into folders. For example, one folder might contain financial data, another might contain your creative work, and another could contain information you're gathering for an upcoming vacation.

| Figure 1 | Computer as a file cabinet |

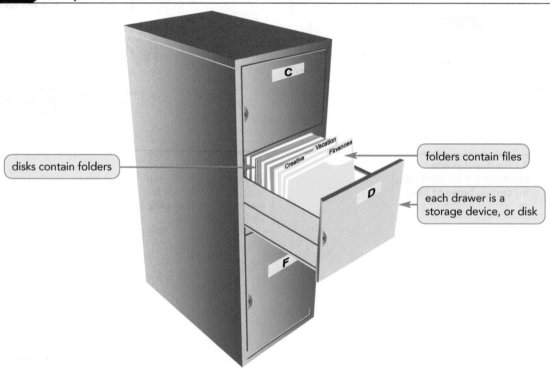

disks contain folders

folders contain files

each drawer is a storage device, or disk

A computer can store folders and files on different types of disks, ranging from removable media—such as **USB flash drives** (also called thumb drives, flash drives, or simply USB drives) and digital video discs (DVDs)—to **hard disks**, or fixed disks, which are permanently housed in a computer. Hard disks are the most popular type of computer storage because they provide an economical way to store many gigabytes of data. (A **gigabyte**, or **GB**, is about 1 billion bytes, with each byte roughly equivalent to a character of data.)

To have your computer access a removable disk, you must insert the disk into a **drive**, which is a device that can retrieve and sometimes record data on a disk. A computer's hard disk is already contained in a drive inside the computer, so you don't need to insert it each time you use the computer.

A computer distinguishes one drive from another by assigning each a drive letter. The hard disk is assigned to drive C. The remaining drives can have any other letters but are usually assigned in the order that the drives were installed on the computer—so your USB drive might be drive D, drive E, or drive F.

If you are using a tablet or a recent-model laptop, it might not have drives for removable disks. Instead, you store files on the hard disk or in the **cloud**, a location on a large computer called a **server**, which you access through the Internet or other network. (A **network** is two or more computers connected together to share resources.) As a Windows 10 user, you probably have OneDrive, a Microsoft service that provides access to a server where you can store your files instead of using a hard disk or removable disk. Your school might also provide a cloud location for storing your files.

Understanding How to Organize Files and Folders

Windows 10 stores thousands of files in many folders on the hard disk of your computer. Windows 10 needs these system files to display the desktop, use drives, and perform other operating system tasks. To keep the system stable and to find files quickly, Windows organizes the folders and files in a hierarchy, or **file system**. At the top of the hierarchy, Windows stores folders and important files that it needs when you turn on the computer. This location, called the **root directory**, is usually drive C (the hard disk). As Figure 2 shows, the root directory contains all the other folders and files on the computer. The figure also shows that folders can contain other folders. An effectively organized computer contains a few folders in the root directory, and those folders contain other folders, also called **subfolders**.

Figure 2	Organizing folders and files on a hard disk

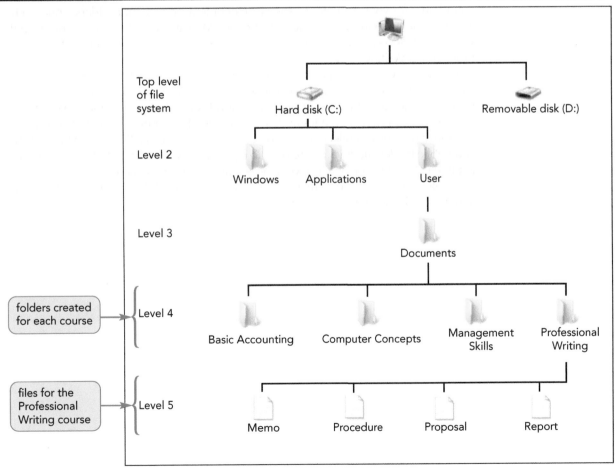

INSIGHT

Root Directory in a File System

The root directory in the Windows file system is for system files and folders only. You should not store your own work in the root directory because your files could interfere with Windows or an app. (If you are working in a computer lab, you might not be allowed to access the root directory.)

Do not delete or move any files or folders from the root directory of the hard disk; doing so could disrupt the system so that you can't start or run the computer. In fact, you should not reorganize or change any folder that contains installed software because Windows 10 expects to find the files for specific apps within certain folders.

In Figure 2, folders containing software are stored at level 2 of the file system. If you reorganize or change these folders, Windows 10 can't locate and start the apps stored in those folders. Likewise, you should not make changes to the folder (usually named Windows) that contains the Windows 10 operating system.

Level 2 of the file system also includes a folder for your user account, such as the User folder. This folder contains all of your system settings, preferences, and other user account information. It also contains subfolders, such as the Documents folder, for your personal files.

The folders in level 3 of the file system are designed to contain subfolders for your personal files. You can create as many subfolders at level 4 of the file system as you need to store other folders and files and keep them organized.

Figure 2 shows how you could organize your files on a hard disk if you were taking a full semester of business classes. To duplicate this organization, you would open the main folder for your documents, such as Documents, create four folders—one each for the Basic Accounting, Computer Concepts, Management Skills, and Professional Writing courses—and then store the writing assignments you complete in the Professional Writing folder.

If you store your files on OneDrive or removable media, such as a USB drive, you can use a simpler organization because you do not have to account for system files. In general, the larger the medium, the more levels of folders you should use because large media can store more files and, therefore, need better organization. For example, OneDrive provides a collection of folders such as Documents, Favorites, Music, Pictures, and Public by default. If you were organizing your files on your 15 GB OneDrive, you could create folders in the top-level Documents folder for each course (Basic Accounting, Computer Concepts, Management Skills, and Professional Writing), and each of those folders could contain the appropriate files.

PROSKILLS

Decision Making: Determining Where to Store Files

When you create and save files on your computer's hard disk, you should store them in subfolders. The top level of the hard disk is off-limits for your files because they could interfere with system files. If you are working on your own computer, store your files within the Documents folder, which is where many apps save your files by default. When you use a computer on the job, your employer might assign a main folder to you for storing your work. In either case, if you simply store all your files in one folder, you will soon have trouble finding the files you want. Instead, you should create subfolders within a main folder to separate files in a way that makes sense for you.

Even if you store most of your files in the cloud, such as on OneDrive, or on removable media, such as USB drives, you still need to organize those files into folders and subfolders. Before you start creating folders in any location, you need to plan the organization you will use. Following your plan increases your efficiency because you don't have to pause and decide which folder to use when you save your files. A file organization plan also makes you more productive in your computer work—the next time you need a particular file, you'll know where to find it.

Exploring Files and Folders

As shown in the Visual Overview, you use File Explorer to explore the files and folders on your computer. File Explorer displays the contents of your computer by using icons to represent drives, folders, and files. When you start File Explorer, it opens to show the contents of the Quick access list, which are the folders and files you used frequently and recently, making it easy to find the files you work with often.

The File Explorer window is divided into two sections, called panes. The left pane is the navigation pane, which contains icons and links to locations on your computer. The right pane displays the contents of the location selected in the navigation pane. If the navigation pane showed all the contents on your computer at once, it could be a very long list. Instead, you open drives and folders only when you want to see what they contain. For example, to display the hierarchy of the folders and other locations on your computer, you select the This PC icon in the navigation pane, and then select the icon for a drive, such as OS (C:) or Removable Disk (D:). (The OS stands for operating system.) You can then open and explore folders on that drive.

If a folder contains undisplayed subfolders, an expand icon appears to the left of the folder icon. (The same is true for drives.) To view the folders contained in an object, you click the expand icon. A collapse icon then appears next to the folder icon; click the collapse icon to hide the folder's subfolders. To view the files contained in a folder, you click the folder icon, and the files appear in the right pane. See Figure 3.

| Figure 3 | Viewing files in File Explorer |

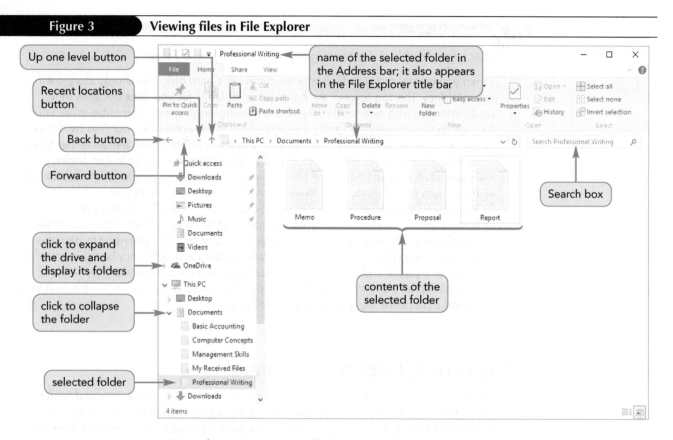

Using the navigation pane helps you explore your computer and orients you to your current location. As you move, copy, delete, and perform other tasks with the files and folders in the right pane of File Explorer, you can refer to the navigation pane to see how your changes affect the overall organization.

In addition to using the navigation pane, you can explore your computer in File Explorer using the following navigation techniques:

- Opening drives and folders in the right pane—To view the contents of a drive or folder, double-click the drive or folder icon in the right pane of File Explorer.
- Using the Address bar—You can use the Address bar to navigate to a different folder. The Address bar displays the file path for your current folder. (Recall that a file path shows the location of a folder or file.) Click a folder name such as Documents in the Address bar to navigate to that folder, or click an arrow button to navigate to a different location in the folder's hierarchy.
- Clicking the Back, Forward, Recent locations, and Up to buttons—Use the Back, Forward, and Recent locations buttons to navigate to other folders you have already opened. Use the Up to button to navigate up to the folder containing the current folder.
- Using the Search box—To find a file or folder stored in the current folder or its subfolders, type a word or phrase in the Search box. The search begins as soon as you start typing. Windows finds files based on text in the filename, text within the file, and other properties of the file.

You'll practice using some of these navigation techniques later in the module. Right now, you'll show Diego how to open File Explorer and then navigate to the Documents folder using the Quick access list and the This PC icon. Your computer should be turned on and displaying the desktop.

To open File Explorer:

▶ **1.** Click the **File Explorer** button 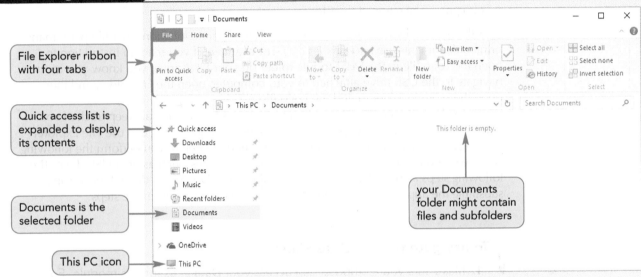 on the taskbar. The File Explorer window opens, displaying the contents of the Quick access list.

▶ **2.** Click the **Documents** icon in the navigation pane to display its contents in the right pane. See Figure 4. The contents of your computer will differ.

Trouble? If your window displays icons in a view different from the one shown in the figure, you can still explore files and folders. The same is true for all figures in this session.

Figure 4	Contents of the Documents folder

File Explorer ribbon with four tabs

Quick access list is expanded to display its contents

Documents is the selected folder

This PC icon

your Documents folder might contain files and subfolders

▶ **3.** In the navigation pane of the open folder window, click the **This PC** icon. The right pane displays the devices and drives on the computer and the locations for storing your work files, including the Documents folder.

▶ **4.** In the right pane, double-click the **Documents** folder to display its contents.

The Documents folder is designed to store your files—the notes, reports, spreadsheets, presentations, and other files that you create, edit, and manipulate in an app. The Quick access list provides access to folders that most users open frequently. In addition to the Documents folder, This PC displays other default folders, such as the Pictures folder and the Music folder. Although the Pictures folder is designed to store graphics and the Music folder is designed to store music files, you can store graphics, music, or any other type of file in the Documents folder, especially if doing so makes it easier to find these files when you need them. As you create more folders, they are listed in the navigation pane.

Navigating to Your Data Files

To navigate to the files you want, it helps to know the file path because it tells you exactly where the file is stored in the hierarchy of drives and folders on your computer. For example, the Logo file is stored in the Module subfolder of the FM folder. If you are working on a USB drive, for example, the Address bar would show the following file path for the Logo file:

Removable Disk (D:) > FM > Module > Logo.png

This path has four parts, with each part separated by an arrow button:

- Removable Disk (D:)—The drive name, including the drive letter followed by a colon, which indicates a drive rather than a folder
- FM—The top-level folder on drive D
- Module—A subfolder in the FM folder
- Logo.png—The name of the file

Although File Explorer uses arrow buttons to separate locations in a file path, many printed documents use backslashes (\ ). For example, if you read an instruction to open the Logo file in the FM\Module folder on your USB drive, you know you must navigate to the USB drive attached to your computer, open the FM folder, and then open the Module folder to find the Logo file.

File Explorer displays the file path in the Address bar so you can keep track of your current location as you navigate between drives and folders. You can use File Explorer to navigate to the Data Files you need for this module. Before you perform the following steps, you should know where you stored your Data Files, such as on a USB drive. The following steps assume that drive is Removable Disk (D:), a USB drive. If necessary, substitute the appropriate drive on your system when you perform the steps.

To navigate to your Data Files:

1. Make sure your computer can access your Data Files for this module. For example, if you are using a USB drive, insert the drive into the USB port.

   Trouble? If you don't have the starting Data Files, you need to get them before you can proceed. Your instructor will either give you the Data Files or ask you to obtain them from a specified location (such as a network drive). If you have any questions about the Data Files, see your instructor or technical support person for assistance.

2. In the navigation pane of File Explorer, click the **expand** icon ⟩ next to the drive containing your Data Files, such as Removable Disk (D:). A list of the folders on that drive appears below the drive name.

3. If the list of folders does not include the FM folder, continue clicking the **expand** icon ⟩ to navigate to the folder that contains the FM folder.

4. Click the **expand** icon ⟩ next to the FM folder to expand the folder, and then click the **FM** folder so that its contents appear in the navigation pane and in the right pane of the folder window. The FM folder contains the Case1, Case2, Module, and Review folders, as shown in Figure 5. The other folders on your computer might vary.

| Figure 5 | Navigating to the FM folder |

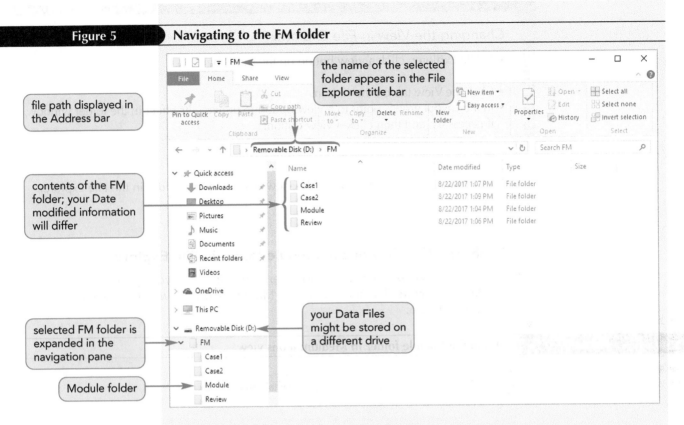

file path displayed in the Address bar

the name of the selected folder appears in the File Explorer title bar

contents of the FM folder; your Date modified information will differ

your Data Files might be stored on a different drive

selected FM folder is expanded in the navigation pane

Module folder

▶ **5.** In the navigation pane, click the **Module** folder. The files it contains appear in the right pane.

Trouble? If the Module folder does not appear in the navigation pane, you did not click the expand icon next to the FM folder to expand the folder. Click the expand icon ⟩ next to the FM folder, and then repeat Step 5.

Before you begin working with individual files and folders, you might want to change the appearance of the File Explorer window to suit your preferences. You'll do so next so you can see more details about folders and files.

Changing the View

TIP

The default view for the Pictures folder is Large icons view, which provides a thumbnail image of the file contents.

File Explorer provides eight ways to view the contents of a folder: Extra large icons, Large icons, Medium icons, Small icons, List, Details, Tiles, and Content. For example, the files in the Module folder are currently displayed in Details view, which is the default view for all folders except those stored in the Pictures folder and its subfolders. Details view displays a small icon to identify each file's type and lists file details in columns, such as the date the file was last modified, the file type, and the size of the file. Although only Details view lists the file details, you can also see these details in any other view by pointing to a file to display a ScreenTip.

To change the view of File Explorer to any of the eight views, you use the View tab on the ribbon. To switch quickly between Details view and Large icons view, you can use the view buttons on the status bar.

REFERENCE

Changing the View in File Explorer

- In File Explorer, click a view button on the status bar.

or

- Click the View tab on the ribbon.
- In the Layout group, point to a view option to preview its effect in the folder window, if necessary, and then click a view option.

You'll show Diego how to change the view of the Module folder in the File Explorer window.

To change the view of the Module folder in File Explorer:

1. Click the **View** tab on the ribbon, and then in the Layout group, click **Medium icons**. The files appear in Medium icons view in File Explorer. See Figure 6.

Figure 6   **Files in the Module folder in Medium icons view**

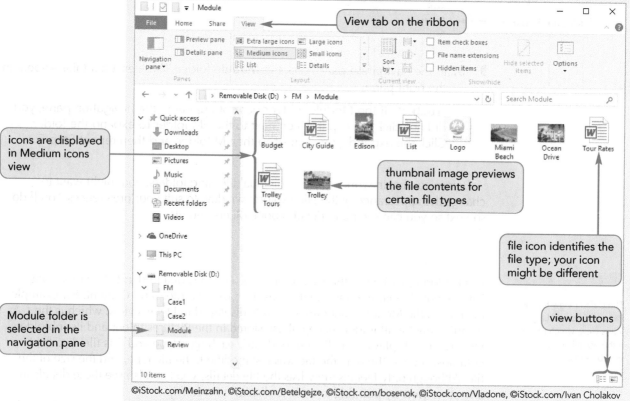

©iStock.com/Meinzahn, ©iStock.com/Betelgejze, ©iStock.com/bosenok, ©iStock.com/Vladone, ©iStock.com/Ivan Cholakov

Trouble? Because the icons used to identify types of files depend on the apps installed on your computer, the file icons that appear in your window might be different.

TIP

When you change the
view, it applies only to the
current folder.

2. On the status bar, click the **Large icons view** button 🖼. The window shows the files with large icons and no file details.

3. On the status bar, click the **Details view** button ▦. The window shows the files with small icons and lists the file details.

No matter which view you use, you can sort the file list by the name of the files (the default sort order) or another detail, such as size, type, or date. When you **sort** files, you list them in ascending order (A to Z, 0 to 9, or earliest to latest date) or descending order (Z to A, 9 to 0, or latest to earliest date) by a file detail. If you're viewing music files, you can sort by details such as contributing artists or album title; if you're viewing picture files, you can sort by details such as date taken or size. Sorting can help you find a particular file in a long file listing. For example, suppose you want to work on a document that you know you edited on June 18, 2017, but you can't remember the name of the file. You can sort the file list by date modified to find the file you want.

When you are working in Details view in File Explorer, you sort a list of folders and files by clicking a column heading that appears at the top of the list. In other views, you use the View tab on the ribbon to sort. In the Current view group, click the Sort by button, and then click a file detail.

TIP

To sort by a file detail that
does not appear
as a column heading,
right-click any column
heading and then select
a file detail on the
shortcut menu.

To sort the file list by date modified:

1. At the top of the file list, click the **Date modified** column heading. The down arrow that appears above the label of the column heading indicates that the files are sorted in descending (newest to oldest) order by the date the file was modified. At the top of the list is the List file, which was modified on August 18, 2017.

Trouble? If your folder window does not contain a Date modified column, right-click any column heading, click Date modified on the shortcut menu, and then repeat Step 1.

2. Click the **Date modified** column heading again. The up arrow above the Date modified label indicates that the sort order is reversed, with the files listed in ascending (oldest to newest) order.

3. Click the **Name** column heading to sort the files in alphabetical order by name. The Budget file is now listed first.

Now that Diego is comfortable working in File Explorer, you're ready to show him how to manage his files and folders.

Managing Files and Folders

As discussed earlier, you manage your personal files and folders by storing them according to a logical organization so that they are easy to find later. You can organize files as you create, edit, and save them, or you can do so later by creating folders, if necessary, and then moving and copying files into the folders.

To create a file-organization plan for Diego's files, you can begin by reviewing Figure 6 to look for files that logically belong together. In the Module folder, Edison, Logo, Miami Beach, Ocean Drive, and Trolley are all graphics files that Diego uses for marketing Miami Trolleys. The City Guide and Trolley Tours files contain descriptions of sights in Miami for customers. The Budget and Tour Rates files relate to business finances. Diego thinks the List file contains a task list for creating a website, but he isn't sure of its contents. He does recall creating the file using WordPad, a text-editing tool provided with Windows 10.

If the List file does contain a website task list, you can organize the files by creating four folders—one for graphics, one for tours, another for the financial files, and a fourth folder for files about the website. When you create a folder, you give it a name, preferably one that describes its contents. A folder name can have up to 255 characters, and any character is allowed, except / \ : * ? " < > and |. Considering these conventions, you could create four folders to contain Diego's files, as follows:

- Marketing Graphics folder—Edison, Logo, Miami Beach, Ocean Drive, and Trolley files
- Sights folder—City Guide and Trolley Tours files
- Financial folder—Budget and Tour Rates files
- Website folder—List file

Before you start creating folders according to this plan, you need to verify the contents of the List file. You can do so by opening the file.

Opening a File

You can open a file from a running app or from File Explorer. To open a file in a running app, you select the app's Open command to access the Open dialog box, which you use to navigate to the file you want, select the file, and then open it. In the Open dialog box, you use the same tools that are available in File Explorer to navigate to the file you want to open. If the app you want to use is not running, you can open a file by double-clicking it in the right pane of File Explorer. The file usually opens in the app that you used to create or edit it.

Diego says that he might want to edit the List file to add another task. You'll show him how to use File Explorer to open and edit the file in WordPad, which he used to create the file.

TIP

In File Explorer, you can also double-click a file to open it in the default app for that file type.

To open and edit the List file:

1. In the right pane of File Explorer, right-click the **List** file, and then click **Open with** on the shortcut menu to display the How do you want to open this file? dialog box, which lists apps that can open the file.

   Trouble? If a shortcut menu appears when you click Open with, click WordPad and skip Step 2. If WordPad is not an option on the shortcut menu, click Choose another app, click More apps, scroll down the list if necessary to display WordPad, and then continue with Step 2.

2. Click **WordPad** and then click the **OK** button to open the List file in WordPad. The file contains a task list for the Miami Trolleys website, which includes three items.

   Trouble? If the dialog box does not include WordPad, click More apps, scroll down the list, click WordPad, and then click the OK button.

3. Press the **Ctrl+End** keys to move the insertion point to the end of the document, press the **Enter** key if necessary to start a new line, and then type **4. Include tool for customer comments.**

Now that you've added text to the List file, you need to save it to preserve the changes you made.

Saving a File

As you are creating or editing a file, you should save it frequently so you don't lose your work. When you save a file, you need to decide what name to use for the file and where to store it. Most apps provide a default location for saving a file, which makes it easy to find the file again later. However, you can select a different location depending on where you want to store the file.

Besides a storage location, every file must have a filename, which provides important information about the file, including its contents and purpose. A filename such as Miami Tours.docx has the following three parts:

- Main part of the filename—When you save a file, you need to provide only the main part of the filename, such as "Miami Tours."
- Dot—The dot (.) separates the main part of the filename from the filename extension.
- Filename extension—The **filename extension** includes the three or four characters that follow the dot in the filename and identify the file's type, such as .docx.

The main part of a filename can have up to 255 characters. This gives you plenty of room to name your file accurately enough so that you'll recognize the contents of the file just by looking at the filename. You can use spaces and certain punctuation symbols in your filenames. However, filenames cannot contain the symbols / \ : * ? " < > or | because these characters have special meanings in Windows 10.

Windows and other software add the dot and the extension to a filename, although File Explorer does not display them by default. Instead, File Explorer shows the file icon associated with the filename extension or a thumbnail for some types of files, such as graphics.

When you save a newly created file, you use the Save As dialog box to provide a filename and select a location in which to store the file. You can create a folder for the new file at the same time as you save the file. When you edit a file you saved previously, you can use the app's Save command to save the changes you made to the file, keeping the same name and location. If you want to save the edited file with a different name or in a different location, however, you need to use the Save As dialog box to specify the new name or location.

As with the Open dialog box, you specify the file location in the Save As dialog box using the same navigation techniques and tools that are available in File Explorer. To make sure that the Save As dialog box displays these tools, you might need to click the Browse Folders button to expand the dialog box. In addition, the Save As dialog box always includes a File name box where you specify a filename.

INSIGHT

Saving Files on OneDrive

OneDrive is a Microsoft service that provides up to 15 GB of online storage space for your files by default. You can purchase additional storage space if you need it. Some Windows 10 applications, such as Microsoft Office, include OneDrive as a location for saving and opening files. If you have a Microsoft account, you can select a folder on your OneDrive to save the document online. (If you don't have a Microsoft account, you can sign up for one by visiting the OneDrive website.) Because the file is stored online, it takes up no storage space on your computer and is available from any computer with an Internet connection. You access the document by opening it in an Office application or by visiting the OneDrive website (https://onedrive.live.com/about/en-us/) and then signing in to your Microsoft account. Look for a link or button that lets you display your OneDrive. To share the document with other people, you can send them a link to the document via email. They can use the link to access the document even if they do not have a Microsoft account.

One reason that Diego had trouble remembering the contents of the List file is that "List" is not a descriptive name. A better name for this file is Task List. You will save this document in the Module subfolder of the FM folder provided with your Data Files. You will also use the Save As dialog box to specify a new name for the file as you save it.

To save the List file with a new name:

▶ **1.** In the WordPad window, click the **File** tab on the ribbon to display commands for working with files.

▶ **2.** Click **Save as** to open the Save As dialog box, as shown in Figure 7. The Module folder is selected as the storage location for this file because you opened the file from this folder.

    Trouble? If the navigation pane does not appear in the Save As dialog box, click the Browse Folders button. The Browse Folders button toggles to become the Hide Folders button.

Figure 7	Saving a file using the Save As dialog box

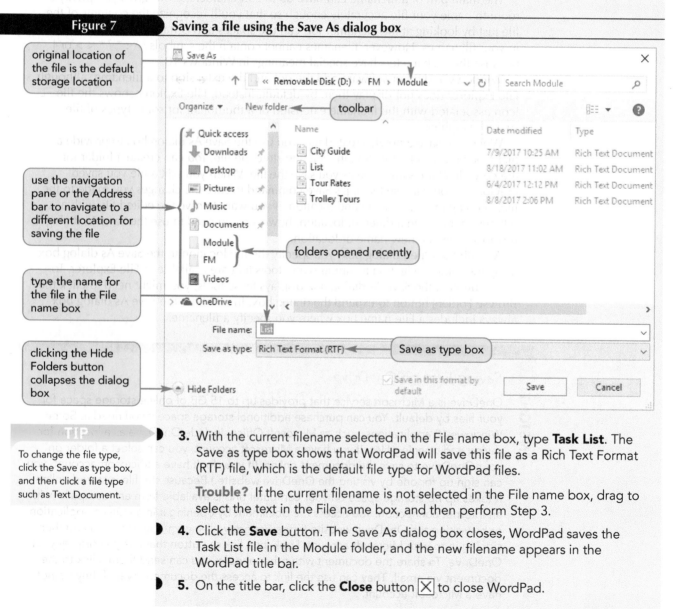

original location of the file is the default storage location

toolbar

use the navigation pane or the Address bar to navigate to a different location for saving the file

folders opened recently

type the name for the file in the File name box

clicking the Hide Folders button collapses the dialog box

Save as type box

TIP

To change the file type, click the Save as type box, and then click a file type such as Text Document.

▶ **3.** With the current filename selected in the File name box, type **Task List**. The Save as type box shows that WordPad will save this file as a Rich Text Format (RTF) file, which is the default file type for WordPad files.

    Trouble? If the current filename is not selected in the File name box, drag to select the text in the File name box, and then perform Step 3.

▶ **4.** Click the **Save** button. The Save As dialog box closes, WordPad saves the Task List file in the Module folder, and the new filename appears in the WordPad title bar.

▶ **5.** On the title bar, click the **Close** button ⊠ to close WordPad.

Now you're ready to start creating the folders you need to organize Diego's files.

Creating Folders

You originally proposed creating four new folders for Diego's files: the Marketing Graphics, Sights, Financial, and Website folders. Diego asks you to create these folders now. After that, you'll move his files to the appropriate folders. You create folders in File Explorer using one of three methods: using the New folder button in the New group on the Home tab, using the New folder button on the Quick Access Toolbar, or right-clicking to display a shortcut menu that includes the New command.

Guidelines for Creating Folders

Keep the following guidelines in mind as you create folders:

- Keep folder names short yet descriptive of the folder's contents. Long folder names can be more difficult to display in their entirety in folder windows, so use names that are short but clear. Choose names that will be meaningful later, such as project names or course numbers.
- Create subfolders to organize files. If a file list in File Explorer is so long that you must scroll the window, you should probably organize those files into subfolders.
- Develop standards for naming folders. Use a consistent naming scheme that is clear to you, such as one that uses a project name as the name of the main folder and includes step numbers in each subfolder name (for example, 1-Outline, 2-First Draft, 3-Final Draft, and so on).

In the following steps, you will create the four folders for Diego in your Module folder. Because it is easier to work with files using large file icons, you'll switch to Large icons view first.

To create folders:

▶ 1. On the status bar in the File Explorer window, click the **Large icons view** button ▦ to switch to Large icons view.

▶ 2. Click the **Home** tab on the ribbon.

▶ 3. In the New group, click the **New folder** button. A folder icon with the label "New folder" appears in the right pane of the File Explorer window. See Figure 8.

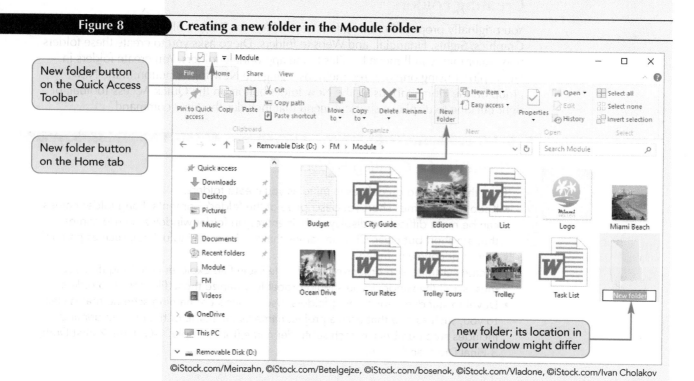

Figure 8 · **Creating a new folder in the Module folder**

New folder button on the Quick Access Toolbar

New folder button on the Home tab

new folder; its location in your window might differ

©iStock.com/Meinzahn, ©iStock.com/Betelgejze, ©iStock.com/bosenok, ©iStock.com/Vladone, ©iStock.com/Ivan Cholakov

Trouble? If the "New folder" name is not selected, right-click the new folder, click Rename on the shortcut menu, and then continue with Step 4.

Windows uses "New folder" as a placeholder and selects the text so that you can replace it immediately by typing a new name. You do not need to press the Backspace or Delete key to delete the text.

4. Type **Marketing Graphics** as the folder name, and then press the **Enter** key. The new folder is named Marketing Graphics and is the selected item in the right pane. To create a second folder, you can use a shortcut menu.

5. Right-click a blank area in the right pane, point to **New** on the shortcut menu, and then click **Folder**. A folder icon appears in the right pane with the "New folder" text selected.

6. Type **Sights** as the name of the new folder, and then press the **Enter** key. To create the third folder, you can use the Quick Access Toolbar.

7. On the Quick Access Toolbar, click the **New folder** button ▢, type **Financial**, and then press the **Enter** key to create and name the folder.

8. Using the method you prefer, create the last new subfolder in the Module folder, and name it **Website**.

After creating four folders, you're ready to organize Diego's files by moving them into the appropriate folders.

Moving and Copying Files and Folders

You can either move or copy a file from its current location to a new location. **Moving** a file removes it from its current location and places it in a new location that you specify. **Copying** a file places a duplicate version of the file in a new location that you specify, while leaving the original file intact in its current location. You can also move and copy folders. When you do, you move or copy all the files contained in the folder. (You'll practice moving and copying folders in the Case Problems at the end of this module.)

In File Explorer, you can move and copy files by using the Move to or Copy to buttons in the Organize group on the Home tab, the Copy and Cut commands on a file's shortcut menu, or keyboard shortcuts. When you copy or move files using these methods, you are using the **Clipboard**, a temporary storage area for files and information that you copy or move from one location to place in another.

You can also move files by dragging them in the File Explorer window. You will now organize Diego's files by moving them to the appropriate folders you have created. You'll start by moving the Budget file to the Financial folder by dragging the file.

To move a file by dragging it:

1. In File Explorer, point to the **Budget** file in the right pane, and then press and hold the left mouse button.

2. While still pressing the mouse button, drag the **Budget** file to the **Financial** folder. See Figure 9.

Figure 9	Dragging a file to move it to a folder

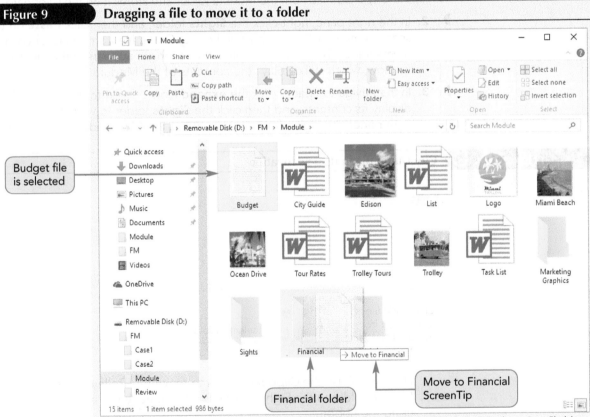

©iStock.com/Meinzahn, ©iStock.com/Betelgejze, ©iStock.com/bosenok, ©iStock.com/Vladone, ©iStock.com/Ivan Cholakov

3. When the Move to Financial ScreenTip appears, release the mouse button. The Budget file is removed from the main Module folder and stored in the Financial subfolder.

   Trouble? If you released the mouse button before the Move to Financial ScreenTip appeared, press the Ctrl+Z keys to undo the move, and then repeat Steps 1–3.

TIP

If you drag a file or folder to a location on a different drive, the file is copied, not moved, to preserve the file in its original location.

Trouble? If you moved a file other than the Budget file, press the Ctrl+Z keys to undo the move, and then repeat Steps 1–3.

▶ **4.** In the right pane, double-click the **Financial** folder to verify that it contains the Budget file.

Trouble? If the Budget file does not appear in the Financial folder, you probably moved it to a different folder. Press the Ctrl+Z keys to undo the move, and then repeat Steps 1–4.

▶ **5.** Click the **Back** button ← in the Address bar to return to the Module folder. Windows sorts the Module folder to list the subfolders first followed by the files.

You'll move the remaining files into the folders using the Clipboard.

To move files using the Clipboard:

▶ **1.** Right-click the **City Guide** file, and then click **Cut** on the shortcut menu. Although the file icon still appears selected, though dimmed, Windows removes the City Guide file from the Module folder and stores it on the Clipboard.

▶ **2.** In the right pane, right-click the **Sights** folder, and then click **Paste** on the shortcut menu. Windows pastes the City Guide file from the Clipboard to the Sights folder. The City Guide file icon no longer appears in the File Explorer window, which still displays the contents of the Module folder.

▶ **3.** In the navigation pane, click the **expand** icon ⟩ next to the Module folder to display its contents, and then click the **Sights** folder to view its contents in the right pane. The Sights folder now contains the City Guide file. See Figure 10.

Figure 10	City Guide file in its new location

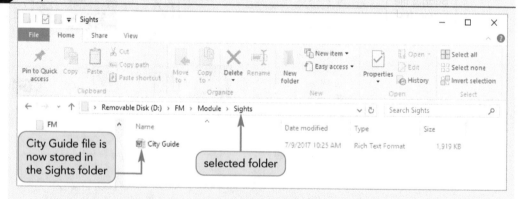

Next, you'll use the Clipboard again to move the Trolley Tours file from the Module folder to the Sights folder. But this time, you'll access the Clipboard using the ribbon.

▶ **4.** In the Address bar, point to the **Up to** button ↑ to display its ScreenTip (Up to "Module"), click the **Up to** button ↑ to return to the Module folder, and then click the **Trolley Tours** file to select it.

Trouble? If you clicked the Up to button ↑ twice, click the Module folder in the navigation pane and then click the Trolley Tours file.

▶ **5.** On the Home tab, in the Clipboard group, click the **Cut** button to remove the Trolley Tours file from the Module folder and temporarily store it on the Clipboard.

6. In the navigation pane, click the **Sights** folder to display its contents in the right pane.

7. In the Clipboard group, click the **Paste** button to paste the Trolley Tours file in the Sights folder. The Sights folder now contains the City Guide and Trolley Tours files.

Finally, you'll move the Task List file from the Module folder to the Website folder using the Move to button in the Organize group on the Home tab. This button and the Copy to button are ideal when you want to move or copy files without leaving the current folder. When you select a file and then click the Move to or Copy to button, a list of locations appears, including the Windows standard folders (Documents, Pictures, Music, and Videos) and one or more folders you open frequently. You can click a location in the list to move the selected file to that folder. You can also select the Choose location option to open the Move Items or Copy Items dialog box, and then select a location for the file, which you'll do in the following steps.

To move a file using the Move to button:

1. In the Address bar, click **Module** to return to the Module folder, and then click the **Task List** file to select it.

2. On the Home tab, in the Organize group, click the **Move to** button to display a list of locations to which you can move the selected file. The Website folder is not included on this list because you haven't opened it yet.

3. Click **Choose location** to open the Move Items dialog box. See Figure 11. The locations in your Move Items dialog box will differ.

| Figure 11 | Move Items dialog box |

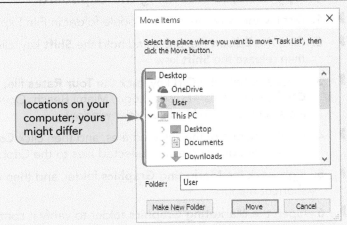

locations on your computer; yours might differ

4. If necessary, scroll the list of locations, and then click the **expand** icon ▷ next to the drive containing your Data Files, such as Removable Disk (D:).

5. Navigate to the **FM > Module** folder, and then click the **Website** folder to select it.

6. Click the **Move** button to close the dialog box and move the Task List file to the Website folder.

7. Open the Website folder to confirm that it contains the Task List file.

One way to save steps when moving or copying multiple files or folders is to select all the files and folders you want to move or copy, and then work with them as a group. You can use several techniques to select multiple files or folders at the same time, which are described in Figure 12.

Figure 12   **Selecting multiple files or folders**

Items to Select in the Right Pane of File Explorer	Method
Files or folders listed together	Click the first item, press and hold the Shift key, click the last item, and then release the Shift key.
	or
	Drag the pointer to create a selection box around all the items you want to include.
Files or folders not listed together	Press and hold the Ctrl key, click each item you want to select, and then release the Ctrl key.
All files and folders	Click the Select all button in the Select group on the Home tab.

Items to Deselect in the Right Pane of File Explorer	Method
Single file or folder in a selected group	Press and hold the Ctrl key, click each item you want to remove from the selection, and then release the Ctrl key.
All selected files and folders	Click a blank area of the File Explorer window.

Next, you'll copy the five graphics files from the Module folder to the Marketing Graphics folder using the Clipboard. To do this efficiently, you will select multiple files at the same time.

To copy multiple files using the Clipboard:

1. Display the contents of the Module folder in File Explorer.

2. Click the **Edison** file, press and hold the **Shift** key, click the **Trolley** file, and then release the **Shift** key.

3. Press and hold the **Ctrl** key, click the **Tour Rates** file, and then release the **Ctrl** key. Five files—Edison, Logo, Miami Beach, Ocean Drive, and Trolley—are selected in the Module folder window.

4. Right-click one of the selected files, and then click **Copy** on the shortcut menu. Windows copies the selected files to the Clipboard.

5. Right-click the **Marketing Graphics** folder, and then click **Paste** on the shortcut menu.

6. Open the **Marketing Graphics** folder to verify it contains the five files you copied, and then return to the Module folder. The Tour Rates file contains financial information, so you can move it to the Financial folder.

7. Right-click the **Tour Rates** file, and then click **Cut** on the shortcut menu.

8. Double-click the **Financial** folder to open it, right-click a blank area of the right pane, and then click **Paste** on the shortcut menu.

INSIGHT

Duplicating Your Folder Organization

If you work on two computers, such as one computer at an office or school and another computer at home, you can duplicate the folders you use on both computers to simplify the process of transferring files from one computer to another. For example, if you have four folders in your Documents folder on your work computer, copy these four folders to the Documents folder on your OneDrive or USB drive. If you change a file on the hard disk of your home computer, you can copy the most recent version of the file to the corresponding folder on your OneDrive or USB drive so the file is available when you are at work. You also then have a **backup**, or duplicate copy, of important files. Having a backup of your files is invaluable if your computer has a fatal error.

All the files that originally appeared in the Module folder are now stored in appropriate subfolders. You can streamline the organization of the Module folder by deleting the duplicate files you no longer need.

Deleting Files and Folders

TIP

In most cases, a file deleted from a USB drive does not go into the Recycle Bin. Instead, it is deleted when Windows 10 removes its icon, and the file cannot be recovered.

You should periodically delete files and folders you no longer need so that your main folders and disks don't get cluttered. In a folder window, you delete a file or folder by deleting its icon. When you use File Explorer to delete a file from a hard disk, including a OneDrive file, Windows 10 removes the file from the folder but stores the file contents in the Recycle Bin. The Recycle Bin is an area on your hard disk that holds deleted files until you remove them permanently. When you delete a folder from the hard disk, the folder and all of its files are stored in the Recycle Bin. If you change your mind and want to retrieve a deleted file or folder, you can double-click the Recycle Bin, right-click the file or folder you want to retrieve, and then click Restore. However, after you empty the Recycle Bin, you can no longer recover the files it contained.

Because you copied the Edison, Logo, Miami Beach, Ocean Drive, and Trolley files to the subfolders in the Module folder, you can safely delete the original files. As is true for moving, copying, and renaming files and folders, you can delete a file or folder in many ways, including using a shortcut menu or selecting one or more files and then pressing the Delete key.

To delete files in the Module folder:

1. Use any technique you've learned to navigate to and display the **FM > Module** folder.

2. In the right pane, click **Edison**, press and hold the **Shift** key, click **Trolley**, and then release the **Shift** key. All files in the Module folder are now selected. None of the subfolders should be selected.

3. Right-click the selected files, and then click **Delete** on the shortcut menu. A message box appears, asking if you're sure you want to move these files to the Recycle Bin.

Make sure you have copied the selected files to the Marketing Graphics folder before completing this step.

4. Click the **Yes** button to confirm that you want to delete the files.

   Trouble? If you are working with files on a hard disk, Windows does not ask if you want to permanently delete the files. Skip Step 4.

Renaming Files

After creating and naming a file or folder, you might realize that a different name would be more meaningful or descriptive. You can easily rename a file or folder by using the Rename command on the file's shortcut menu.

Now that you've organized Diego's files into folders, he reviews your work and notes that the City Guide file in the Sights folder could contain information about any city. He recommends that you rename that file to give it a more descriptive filename. The City Guide file was originally created to store text specifically about sights on Miami, so you'll rename the file Miami Guide.

To rename the City Guide file:

▶ **1.** In the right pane of the File Explorer window, double-click the **Sights** folder to display its contents.

▶ **2.** Right-click the **City Guide** file, and then click **Rename** on the shortcut menu. The filename is highlighted, and a box appears around it.

▶ **3.** Type **Miami Guide** and then press the **Enter** key. The file now appears with the new name.

Trouble? If you make a mistake while typing and you haven't pressed the Enter key yet, press the Backspace key until you delete the mistake and then complete Step 3. If you've already pressed the Enter key, repeat Steps 2 and 3 to rename the file again.

Trouble? If your computer is set to display filename extensions, a message might appear asking if you are sure you want to change the filename extension. Click the No button and then repeat Steps 2 and 3.

TIP

To rename a file, you can also click the file, pause, click it again to select the filename, and then type to enter a new filename.

Now that the Miami Guide file has a more descriptive name, Diego asks you to copy the Sights folder containing the Miami Guide file to the Documents folder. Anita will need this file the next time she uses Diego's computer. To copy the folder, you'll use the key combinations for copying and pasting. (When you use a **key combination**, you press two or more keys to access a feature or perform a command efficiently.)

To copy the Sights folder using key combinations:

▶ **1.** Return to the Module folder.

▶ **2.** If necessary, click the **Sights** folder to select it, and then press the **Ctrl+C** keys to copy the folder.

▶ **3.** In the navigation pane, click the **Documents** folder, and then press the **Ctrl+V** keys to paste the folder.

▶ **4.** Open each file in the Documents > Sights folder, add your name at the beginning of the file, save the file, and then close it.

TIP

To cut a file or folder and store it on the Clipboard, press the Ctrl+X keys.

Finding Files and Information with Cortana

Cortana is an electronic personal assistant that Windows 10 provides to help you find files, search the web, keep track of information, and answer your questions. For example, you can ask Cortana to tell a joke, remind you about an appointment, or find a document you were working on before you took a break.

Cortana is turned off by default. If you have a Microsoft account, you can turn on Cortana and use it. Turning on Cortana involves agreeing to let it collect information about you. If you use more than one Windows device, Cortana uses the information you provide to keep the devices in sync.

After you turn on Cortana, it responds to text you enter in the Ask me anything box. For example, you can enter the first few characters of a filename to have Cortana display the file in a search results list. Click the file to open it in its default app. If your computer has a microphone, you can also set up Cortana to respond to your voice. You can then say "Hey, Cortana" to let Cortana know you want to find something. Cortana uses the next words you speak as search text. For example, you can say "Find files I edited today" to have Cortana respond appropriately.

If you ask questions, Cortana responds to them based on information stored in its **Notebook**, which is where Cortana keeps track of what you like, such as your interests and favorite places, and what you want it to do, such as display reminders or information that might interest you. Settings in the People and Maps Windows apps also affect Cortana. For example, if you identify a contact as a friend, Cortana can remind you to call that person. As you work in Windows and apps, Cortana can take note of your preferences and what you're doing when you ask for information to give personalized answers and recommendations.

In the following steps, you set up and turn on Cortana for the first time. If your taskbar includes the Ask me anything box, Cortana is already turned on. Skip the following steps and continue with the next set of steps.

To set up and turn on Cortana for the first time:

▶ **1.** Click the **Search the web and Windows** box on the taskbar. Cortana opens and displays some of the tasks it can do for you. See Figure 13.

Figure 13   **Turning on Cortana**

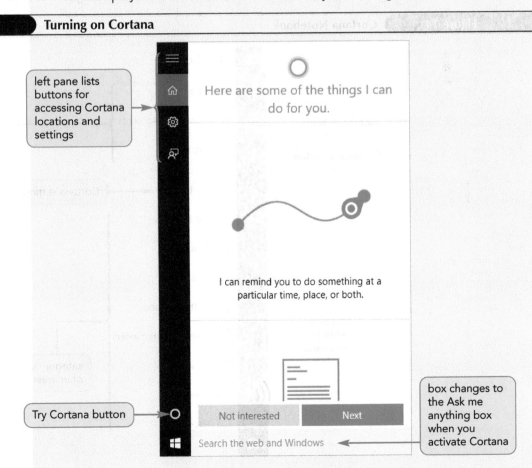

left pane lists buttons for accessing Cortana locations and settings

Here are some of the things I can do for you.

I can remind you to do something at a particular time, place, or both.

Try Cortana button

Not interested   Next

Search the web and Windows

box changes to the Ask me anything box when you activate Cortana

Trouble? If Cortana does not look like Figure 13, click the Try Cortana button ◉ in the left pane.

▶ **2.** Click the **Next** button. A notice appears explaining that Cortana will collect and use information and store it in its Notebook.

▶ **3.** Click the **I agree** button. Cortana asks for a name to use when addressing you.

▶ **4.** Type your first name, and then click the **Next** button. Cortana displays a few starter interests, webpages, and search text that might suit you based on information in your Microsoft account.

▶ **5.** Click the **Got it** button. Cortana stores the webpage information and search text in your Notebook.

You can access the Notebook and configure information about yourself, such as favorite locations, upcoming events, and entertainment preferences. Diego wants to explore his Notebook and learn how to add a reminder for meetings and other events. Before entering a reminder, check to make sure Cortana is set up to store meeting and reminder information.

To access the Cortana Notebook and view reminders:

▶ **1.** In the left pane, click the **Notebook** button ⬚. Cortana displays the Notebook menu. See Figure 14. The top part of the Notebook menu lists categories of general information about you, your accounts, and your settings. The bottom part lists a Cortana setting and categories of interests.

Figure 14	Cortana Notebook

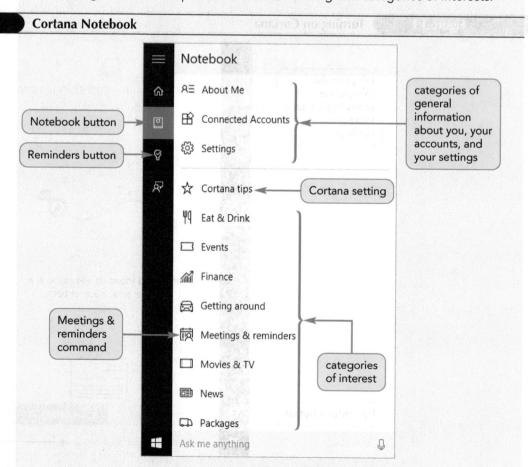

2. Click **Meetings & reminders** on the Notebook menu to display the settings for meetings and reminders. All of the settings in this category are activated by default.

3. In the left pane, click the **Reminders** button. The right pane displays tools for entering a reminder.

4. Click the **Add** button ➕ to display boxes for entering reminder information. Diego doesn't have all the details for a reminder now, so you can cancel the reminder.

5. Click the **Cancel** button.

Finally, you can use Cortana to find files on your computer and information on webpages. By default, Cortana searches the hard drive and OneDrive, but not removable disks, to find files. When you enter text or speak to Cortana, you can use natural language instead of computer commands. For example, you'll show Diego how to find files he added to the Documents folder today.

To use Cortana to find files:

1. Click in the **Ask me anything** box.

2. Type **find files I added today** and then press the **Enter** key. Cortana displays a list of files added to the hard drive or OneDrive today, including the Miami Guide and Trolley Tours files in the Sights folder on the hard drive. See Figure 15. The files you find and their details might differ.

Figure 15	Search results

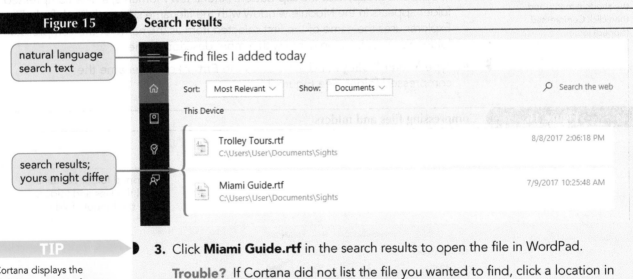

natural language search text → find files I added today

search results; yours might differ

Sort: Most Relevant ⌄   Show: Documents ⌄   🔍 Search the web

This Device

Trolley Tours.rtf   8/8/2017 2:06:18 PM
C:\Users\User\Documents\Sights

Miami Guide.rtf   7/9/2017 10:25:48 AM
C:\Users\User\Documents\Sights

TIP

Cortana displays the filename extension for each file it finds, even if you set File Explorer to hide filename extensions.

3. Click **Miami Guide.rtf** in the search results to open the file in WordPad.

   Trouble? If Cortana did not list the file you wanted to find, click a location in the Other places to look list to continue searching.

4. Click the **Close** button ☒ to close WordPad.

Searching for Files without Cortana

If you are not using Cortana, you can still search for files. Suppose you forgot where you stored a file, what filename you used, or when you last modified the file. You can find the file by clicking in the Search box in File Explorer, typing text that appears at the beginning of the filename, and then using the options on the Search Tools Search tab.

INSIGHT

Working with Compressed Files

You compress a file or a folder of files so it occupies less space on the disk. It can be useful to compress files before transferring them from one location to another, such as from your hard disk to a removable disk or vice versa, or from one computer to another via email. You can then transfer the files more quickly. Also, if you or your email contacts can send and receive files only up to a certain size, compressing large files might make them small enough to send and receive.

You can compress one or more files in File Explorer using the Zip button, which is located in the Send group on the Share tab of the ribbon. Windows stores the compressed files in a special type of folder called an **archive**, or a compressed (zipped) folder. File Explorer uses an icon of a folder with a zipper to represent a compressed folder. To compress additional files or folders, you drag them into the compressed folder. You can open a file directly from a compressed folder, although you cannot modify the file. To edit and save a compressed file, you must extract it first. When you **extract** a file, you create an uncompressed copy of the file in a folder you specify. The original file remains in the compressed folder.

You suggest that you compress the files and folders in the Module folder so that Diego can more quickly transfer them to another location.

To compress the folders and files in the Module folder:

TIP

Another way to compress files is to select the files, right-click the selection, point to Send to on the shortcut menu, and then click Compressed (zipped) folder.

1. In File Explorer, navigate to the **FM > Module** folder, and then select all the folders in the Module folder.

2. Click the **Share** tab on the ribbon.

3. In the Send group, click the **Zip** button. After a few moments, a new compressed folder appears in the Module window with the filename selected. By default, File Explorer uses the name of the first selected item as the name of the compressed folder. You'll replace the name with a more descriptive one.

4. Type **Miami Trolleys** and then press the **Enter** key to rename the compressed folder. See Figure 16.

Figure 16 Compressing files and folders

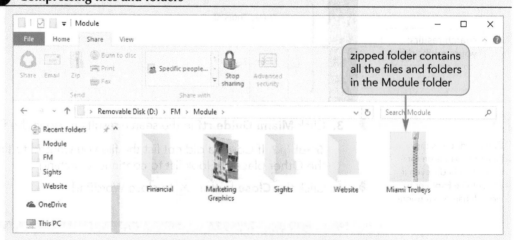

5. Double-click the **Miami Trolleys** compressed folder to open it, open the **Sights** folder, and then note the size of the compressed Miami Guide file, which is 532 KB.

6. Navigate back to the Module folder.

You can move and copy the files and folders from an opened compressed folder to other locations, although you cannot rename the files. More often, you extract all of the files from the compressed folder to a new location that you specify, preserving the files in their original folders as appropriate.

To extract the compressed files:

▶ 1. If necessary, click the **Miami Trolleys** compressed folder to select it, and then click the **Compressed Folder Tools Extract** tab on the ribbon.

▶ 2. Click the **Extract all** button. The Extract Compressed (Zipped) Folders Wizard starts and opens the Select a Destination and Extract Files dialog box.

▶ 3. Press the **End** key to deselect the path in the box and move the insertion point to the end of the path, press the **Backspace** key as many times as necessary to delete the Miami Trolleys text, and then type **Backups**. The final three parts of the path in the box should be FM > Module > Backups. See Figure 17.

| Figure 17 | Extracting files from a compressed folder |

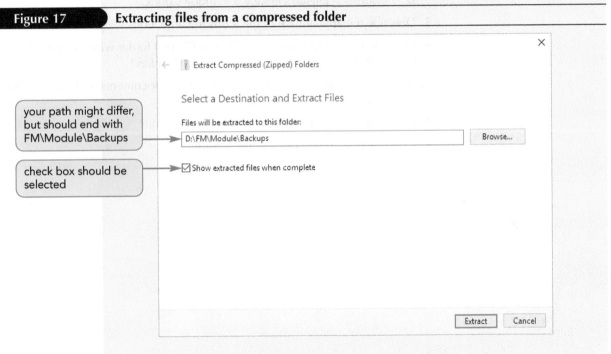

▶ 4. Make sure the Show extracted files when complete check box is checked, and then click the **Extract** button. Windows extracts the files and then opens the Backups folder, showing the Financial, Marketing Graphics, Sights, and Website folders.

▶ 5. Open each folder to make sure it contains the files you worked with in this module. When you open the Sights folder, note the uncompressed size of the Miami Guide file, which is 1,932 KB, nearly four times as large as its compressed version.

▶ 6. Close all open windows.

In this module, you examined the purpose of organizing files and folders, and you planned and created an organization for a set of related files and folders. You also explored your computer using File Explorer and learned how to navigate to your Data Files using the navigation pane. You used File Explorer to manage files and folders by opening and saving files; creating folders; and selecting, moving, and copying files. You also renamed and deleted files according to your organization plan. Finally, you used Cortana to find files and then compressed and extracted files.

Quick Check

REVIEW

1. Why should you take the time to organize files and folders?

2. Windows organizes the folders and files in a hierarchy, or _____.

3. In File Explorer, what does the navigation pane contain?

4. Explain how to use File Explorer to navigate to a file in the following location: D: > Courses > Digital Literacy > Windows.docx.

5. Describe the appearance of file icons in Large icons view.

6. What do you select if you click the first file in a folder window, press the Ctrl key, click the last file, and then release the Ctrl key?

7. What happens when you drag a file from the Documents folder on the hard drive to the Pictures folder on the hard drive?

8. Where does Cortana store information about you?

9. Describe how to compress a file or folder.

Review Assignments

PRACTICE

Data Files needed for the Review Assignments: Background.png, Calendar.rtf, Events.xlsx, Skyline.jpg, Visit.rtf, Walking.rtf, Welcome.jpg

Diego has saved a few files from his old computer to a removable disk. He gives you these files in a single, unorganized folder and asks you to organize them logically into subfolders. He needs at least one subfolder for files related to a newsletter he is planning. Devise a plan for managing the files, and then create the subfolders you need. Rename, copy, and move files, and then delete unnecessary or duplicate files. Perform other management tasks to make it easy for Diego to work with these files and folders. Complete the following steps:

1. Use File Explorer to navigate to and open the FM > Review folder provided with your Data Files. Examine the seven files in this folder, and consider the best way to organize the files.
2. Open the **Visit** text file in WordPad, and then add the following line to the end of the document: **Oct - Pleasant**
3. Save the document as **When to Visit** in the Review folder. Close the WordPad window.
4. In the Review folder, create three folders: **Business**, **Newsletter**, and **Tours**.
5. To organize the files into the correct folders:
   - Move the Background and Calendar files from the Review folder to the Business folder.
   - Move the Events and When to Visit files to the Newsletter folder.
   - Move the Skyline, Walking, and Welcome files to the Tours folder.
6. Rename the Walking file in the Tours folder as **Walking Tours**, and then copy the Walking Tours file to the Newsletter folder.
7. Rename the Calendar file in the Business folder as **2017 Calendar**.
8. Delete the **Visit** file from the Review folder.
9. Create a compressed (zipped) folder in the Review folder named **Miami** that contains all the files and folders in the Review folder.
10. Extract the contents of the Miami compressed folder to a new folder named **Miami Backups** in the Review folder. (*Hint*: The file path will end with \FM\Review\Miami Backups.)
11. Close all open windows.

Case Problem 1

APPLY

Data Files needed for this Case Problem: Advanced Classes.rtf, Beginner Classes.rtf, Designers.txt, Detail.jpg, Intermediate Classes.rtf, Kids Classes.rtf, Lampshade.jpg, Modern.jpg, Round.jpg, Studio.rtf

Art Glass Studio   Shannon Beecher started the Art Glass Studio in Lake George, New York, to provide custom stained-glass works for residential and commercial buildings. The business also holds classes on stained-glass techniques for children and adults. Knowing you are multitalented, Shannon hired you to help her manage the front end of the studio and other parts of her growing business, including electronic business files. Your first task is to organize the files on her new Windows 10 computer. Complete the following steps:

1. Open File Explorer. In the FM > Case1 folder provided with your Data Files, create three folders: **Classes**, **Designs**, and **Marketing**.
2. Move the Advanced Classes, Beginner Classes, Intermediate Classes, and Kids Classes files from the Case1 folder to the Classes folder.
3. Rename the four files in the Classes folder by deleting the word Classes from each name.
4. Move the four JPG files from the Case1 folder to the Designs folder.
5. Copy the remaining two files to the Marketing folder.

6. Copy the Designers file to the Designs folder.

7. Delete the Designers and Studio files from the Case1 folder.

⊕ **Explore** 8. Make a copy of the Designs folder in the Case1 folder. The name of the duplicate folder appears as Designs - Copy. Rename the Designs - Copy folder as **Beecher Designs**.

9. Copy the Advanced file from the Classes folder to the Beecher Designs folder. Rename this file **Classes**.

10. Compress the four photo files in the Beecher Designs folder in a new compressed folder named **Photos**.

11. Move the compressed Photos folder to the Case1 folder.

12. Close File Explorer.

TROUBLESHOOT

Case Problem 2

Data Files needed for this Case Problem: Estimate Tips.txt, Estimate01.xls, Estimate02.xlsx, Estimate03.xlsx, Planner01.xlsx, Planner02.xlsx, Planner03.xlsx, Project Plans.txt, Steps1.rtf, Steps1 – Copy.rtf, Steps2.rtf, Steps2 – Copy.rtf

Avant Web Design Dante Havens is the owner of Avant Web Design, a new website design company in Austin, Texas. You work as a part-time technology assistant at the company and spend some of your time organizing business files. Dante recently upgraded to Windows 10 and asks you to examine the folder structure and file system on his computer and then begin organizing the files logically. Complete the following steps:

1. Navigate to the FM > Case2 folder provided with your Data Files, and then examine the files in this folder. Based on the filenames and file types, begin to create an organization plan for the files.

⚙ **Troubleshoot** 2. Open the Steps1 and the Steps1 - Copy files, and consider the problem these files could cause. Close the files and then fix the problem.

⚙ **Troubleshoot** 3. Open the Steps2 and the Steps2 - Copy files, and compare their contents. Change the filenames to clarify the purpose and contents of the files.

4. Complete the organization plan for Dante's files. In the FM > Case2 folder, create the subfolders you need according to your plan.

5. Move the files in the Case2 folder to the subfolders you created. When you finish, the Case2 folder should contain at least two subfolders containing files.

6. Rename the spreadsheet files in each subfolder according to the following descriptions.
   - Estimate01: **Website estimate**
   - Estimate02: **Cost estimates**
   - Estimate03: **Event estimate**
   - Planner01: **Travel expense planner**
   - Planner02: **Project planner**
   - Planner03: **Balance sheet**

⚙ **Troubleshoot** 7. Make sure all files have descriptive names that accurately reflect their contents.

⚙ **Troubleshoot** 8. Based on the work you did in Steps 6 and 7, move files as necessary to improve the file organization.

9. Close File Explorer.

OBJECTIVES

- Learn about the Internet and the web
- Start Microsoft Edge
- Develop search techniques for locating information on the web
- Use a search engine to conduct a search
- Evaluate your search results
- Use the information you find legally and accurately
- Document web resources

Internet Basics and Information Literacy

Using Microsoft Edge to Conduct Research

Case | *Tabor University*

Irene Jacobson is a graduate student studying environmental engineering at Tabor University. She is writing a report on residential energy usage. Irene wants to research information about innovative technologies that save energy and money for homeowners. She has already researched alternative and renewable energy resources such as wind, solar, and hydropower. Now she wants to find out more about the changing lightbulb technology. She has asked for your help in finding the most current information about this technology. Having recently bought a new computer running Windows 10 and Microsoft Edge, she suggests that you use her computer to conduct the research.

STARTING DATA FILES

There are no starting Data Files needed for this module.

Visual Overview:

Tabs are used to open multiple webpages simultaneously in one browser window.

The New tab button opens a tab for displaying another webpage.

The Address bar is where you enter the URL (uniform resource locator), the address of the webpage you want to view.

 Department of Energy × +

← → ↻ | energy.gov

The Back button redisplays a previously viewed webpage. The Forward button returns you to the more recently viewed webpage.

Webpages often provide navigation tools for access to other webpages.

 **ENERGY.GOV**

PUBLIC SERVICES   SCIENCE & INNOVATION   ⚡ ENERGY SAVER

A webpage is a document created with a special programming language that displays in a web browser. A home page is the webpage that appears when the browser starts or the main page of a website.

MAP: Climate Change and the U.S. Energy Sector

Check out our map to find out how climate change impacts the energy sector, and doing to help.

A hyperlink (or link) is text or a graphic that, when clicked, connects and displays another part of the webpage or a different webpage.

READ MORE ❯

The Microsoft Edge button on the taskbar opens the web browser on the desktop.

⊞ Search the web and Windows

Source: U.S. Department of Energy

Microsoft Edge

Click to display the Hub, the pane where you can access favorite webpages, open webpages saved to your Reading list, and view the history of previously visited webpages.

The Microsoft Edge navigation bar includes tools for navigating and managing websites you visit.

Most webpages have a search box in which you can enter keywords, which are specific words and phrases that describe a topic of interest.

Microsoft Edge is a web browser, or browser, an app that locates, retrieves, and displays webpages.

Search Energy.gov

ENERGY SAVER   ABOUT ENERGY.GOV   OFFICES >

ENERGY SAVER
SAVINGS AND REBATES

Select your state to find tax credits, rebates and savings.

All   GO

RENEWABLE ENERGY

...ergy Sector
...energy sector, and what the Department is

THE NATIONAL LABS

11:59 AM
10/27/2017

Understanding the Internet and the World Wide Web

The **web**, (short for **World Wide Web**), is a collection of electronic documents or files—called webpages—that are available through the Internet. The **Internet** is a worldwide collection of computer networks that allows people to communicate and exchange information. Webpages are stored on **web servers**, which are computers connected to the Internet that manage the display of the webpages. A collection of related webpages is called a **website**. Webpages are connected by hyperlinks, or links, which you click to move from one webpage to another.

Starting Microsoft Edge

You use a web browser to access, retrieve, and display webpages from a computer that is connected to the Internet. Common browsers include Microsoft Edge, Mozilla Firefox, Google Chrome, Apple Safari, and Opera. Microsoft Edge (or simply Edge) is the default web browser in Windows 10. Edge provides all of the tools you need to communicate, access, and share information on the web.

To conduct Irene's research about lightbulbs, you will begin by starting Edge and visiting a website.

INSIGHT

Connecting to the Internet

To access information on the web, you must use a computer that is connected to the Internet. Common Internet connections include cable, DSL (digital subscriber line), dial-up, and wireless networks. A **wireless** network uses radio frequency signals to transmit data between computers and devices, such as routers, that are physically connected to a network. Home connections require an account with an **Internet service provider (ISP)**, a company that provides Internet access by connecting your computer to one of its servers via a telephone or cable modem. When you are logged on to your ISP account, you use a web browser to access, retrieve, and display webpages.

When you start Edge, the home page set for your browser appears in the browser window.

TIP

To start the browser quickly, click the Microsoft Edge button on the Windows taskbar.

To start Edge:

1. On the Windows taskbar, click the **Start** button ⊞. The Start menu opens.

2. Click **All apps** on the Start menu, scroll the list, and then click **Microsoft Edge**. Edge starts, displaying its home page, which appears in the Start tab.

3. If the browser window does not fill the screen, click the **Maximize** button ☐ on the title bar.

Entering a URL in the Address Bar

A URL identifies where a webpage is located on the Internet. For example, a URL for a webpage on the U.S. Department of Energy website is http://www.energy.gov/energygov/index.php. A URL consists of the following parts:

- The first part of the URL, http://, is the **protocol**, which is a set of rules that computers use to exchange files. Hypertext Transfer Protocol (HTTP) and File Transfer Protocol (FTP) are two of the most common protocols used on the Internet. In this example, http:// is the protocol.

TIP
Generally, organizations use URLs that include their name, making it easier to find their site.

- The second part of the URL, www.energy.gov, specifies the location of the web server. The prefix is often www, but it can be something else or omitted entirely. The next part provides a unique name for the website, and the last part identifies the type of website. In this example, energy is the unique name, and .gov indicates that it is a government agency. Other categories include .com (commercial enterprise), .edu (educational institutions), .mil (U.S. military units or agencies), .net (network service providers or resources), .org (organizations, usually not-for-profit), and .biz (businesses).
- The third portion of the URL, /energygov/ in this example, provides the path for the folder in which the webpage file is located. The path can include more than one folder.
- A URL might also include the filename of the webpage as the last part of the URL, such as index.php. However, because many pages are now dynamic, displaying content stored in a database or in different folders, you might not see a filename.

INSIGHT

IP Addresses and Domain Names

The web server address corresponds to an Internet Protocol (IP) address. An **IP address** is a unique number consisting of four sets of numbers from 0 to 255, separated by periods (such as 216.35.148.4), that identifies the server or computer connected to the Internet. Because IP addresses can be difficult to remember, web addresses use a **domain name**, which is a unique string of letters and/or numbers that are easy to remember, such as energy.gov in the previous example. Some URLs include a filename after the domain name. If a URL does not include a filename, many web browsers will download the file that contains the website's home page—for example, index.htm or index.php.

To display a specific webpage, you can enter its URL in the Address bar. As you type, the names or URLs of other webpages you have visited that start with the same characters appear in a list below the Address bar. URLs are not case sensitive, so you can type them in all lowercase letters, even though some longer URLs use a mix of uppercase and lowercase letters to distinguish the different words in the address.

You will begin your research into light bulbs by visiting the U.S Department of Energy website. You can type the URL for the website into the Address bar in the Edge browser window.

TIP
You can omit the http:// and www when you enter the URL because Edge recognizes the entry in the Address bar as a URL.

To go to the Department of Energy website by entering its URL:

1. Click in the **Address bar**, and then type **energy.gov**. As you type, Edge displays a list of websites that begin with the same letters you enter.

2. Press the **Enter** key. The Department of Energy home page, shown in the Visual Overview, appears in the browser window. The content you see might differ because webpages are dynamic and their content is updated frequently.

Although there are millions of websites designed for a multitude of purposes and audiences, most websites are organized similarly. The home page provides basic information about the individual or organization and includes a navigation bar with links to other pages of information. The number of additional pages depends on how much information there is to share. Common pages include a Contact page that contains information about how to get in touch with the organization; an About page that contains information about the organization such as its history, mission, and staff; and a Products or Services or Topics page that contains information about the items the organization sells, the services it provides, or topics it has information about. Depending on the amount of information included, each top-level page could be linked to additional pages with more details or related information. In addition, each page usually includes a link to return to the site's home page.

INSIGHT

Opening Web Pages in Internet Explorer

Since the start of the World Wide Web, standards have continually evolved and changed. Edge is intended to work with the most current versions of webpages. Webpages that were created using earlier standards might not display correctly in Edge. In those instances, you can open the webpage in Internet Explorer, an earlier version of the Microsoft web browser. To open a webpage in Internet Explorer, click the More button in the navigation bar in the Edge browser window, and then click Open with Internet Explorer. Internet Explorer starts and displays that webpage in a new tab.

Using Links to Explore Websites

Clicking a link displays a new webpage in the browser window, replacing the previous page. Likewise, the URL in the Address box changes to correspond to the new webpage.

You can use links to navigate a website and locate information. The Department of Energy home page has links to a variety of resources. Its navigation bar includes the following categories: PUBLIC SERVICES, SCIENCE & INNOVATION, ENERGY SAVER, ABOUT ENERGY.GOV, and OFFICES. When you click a category, a menu with links to additional webpages appears.

Irene is interested in learning more about LED lights and might want to include the information in her paper. You will begin to navigate the site to find out more information about LED lights.

Note: The web is a dynamic medium, and websites and webpages are updated frequently. As you work through this module, if you cannot find a specific link mentioned in a step, the page content has been updated. In those instances, choose a different link to click.

To use links to navigate webpages on the Department of Energy website:

▶ **1.** In the Department of Energy navigation bar, point to **ENERGY SAVER**. A menu of links appears.

▶ **2.** On the ENERGY SAVER menu, point to the **Lighting** link. The pointer changes to ⏍, and a ScreenTip lists the URL of the page that the link will open. See Figure 1.

Figure 1   **Links on a webpage**

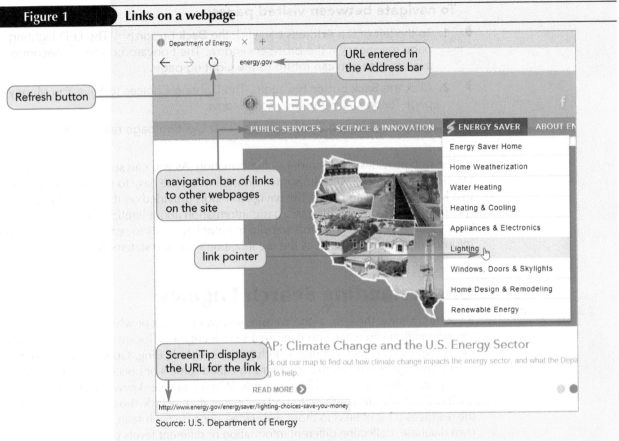

Source: U.S. Department of Energy

3. Click the **Lighting** link. The Lighting Choices to Save You Money page loads. It includes information about different lighting options.

4. In the navigation pane on the left, click the **LEDs** link to load the LED Lighting page, and then read the information about LED lighting.

5. In the Energy Savings section, click the **how energy-efficient lightbulbs compare with traditional incandescents** link to load the corresponding page, and then read how energy efficient lightbulbs compare with traditional incandescent lightbulbs.

Moving Between Viewed Pages

TIP

If a webpage doesn't load quickly or correctly, click the Refresh button located to the right of the Forward button to try again.

You can move back and forth between the different webpages you have viewed during a browsing session. As shown in the Visual Overview, the Back button and the Forward button appear to the left of the Address bar. Clicking the Back button redisplays the previous webpage you visited. You can continue backward through the visited pages until you reach the first page that opened when you started Edge. Once you navigate back a page, the Forward button becomes available so you can return to the more recent pages you visited.

You will move between the pages you have viewed.

To navigate between visited pages:

▶ **1.** To the left of the Address bar, click the **Back** button ⬅. The LED Lighting page reappears in the browser window. The Forward button ➡ becomes available, so you can return to the Lighting page.

▶ **2.** Click the **Back** button ⬅ again. The Lighting Choices to Save You Money page reappears in the browser window.

▶ **3.** Click the **Forward** button ➡. The LED Lighting page reappears.

The web provides a vast amount of information. As you can see from visiting the Department of Energy website, some information can be easy to find by going directly to a known website and using the navigation tools provided on the site to locate specific information—in this case, basic information about lighting. You also could have used the search box on the website to enter keywords to search for more specific information on the site, such as the organization's mission statement.

Understanding Search Engines

If you don't know the URL of the website you want to visit or which website contains the information you want, you can use a **search engine** to locate webpages related to the keywords you enter. Popular search engines include Bing, Google, and Yahoo!

Search engines use automated programs called spiders or bots to compile databases of webpages that are indexed by keywords. When you enter keywords in a search engine, it searches its database to find webpages that include those keywords and shows the results as a list of links to those webpages. Because each search engine creates its own database, collecting different information or different levels of detail, the results delivered by each search engine can be different.

Each search engine has its own website. From the search engine's home page, you can enter keywords for your topic in a search box, and then click the search button or press the Enter key to conduct the search. The search results page that appears includes a list of links to pages that contain your search words. The links are arranged in descending order by relevancy—the pages that seem more related to your search term appear at the top of the list. Other webpages at the search engine site let you search for images, videos, news, and so forth.

TIP

Edge can differentiate between a URL and keywords for a search engine because a URL includes a domain name and keywords do not.

Because search engines are the most effective way to locate information on the web, the Address bar in Edge also provides access to its default search engine, Bing. Instead of entering a URL, you can enter keywords that relate to your search topic in the Address bar and then press the Enter key. The search engine's results page, which contains links to other webpages, appears—the same as if you entered the keywords in the search box on the search engine site's home page.

While visiting the Department of Energy website, you found some information on cost savings from using LED lightbulbs. To help Irene verify this information, you can broaden your search by using a search engine to locate more resources on this topic.

Finding Information on the Web

Organizations and individuals use the web for a variety of reasons. Businesses use websites to sell or advertise their products and to communicate information to customers or employees. Individuals use the web to find a wide variety of information, to communicate and share information with others, and to purchase products and services. Because so much information is available, you need a way to sift through and find the information that is relevant to your needs. To do this, you first must develop a search strategy.

Formulating a Search Strategy

When you are looking for information on the web, it is important to figure out exactly what you want to find and how to find it before you start. This means developing a search strategy so you can find the information you need efficiently and effectively. Otherwise, you will find a lot of information, but not necessarily the information you need or want. Before beginning your search, develop a search strategy by doing the following:

- **Identify your topic.** You want to pinpoint the main concept, subject, or issue that you want to research. You can do this by formulating a question. For example, Irene might formulate the question "What is the cost savings of an LED lightbulb?" or "How much will I save using LED lightbulbs?" or "How efficient are LED lights?"
- **List keywords associated with your topic.** Keywords should be specific words and phrases that are connected to your main topic, such as unique words, names, abbreviations, or organizations. At this point, you should jot down any keywords you think might be relevant. For Irene's research, keywords might include "LED lightbulbs," "lightbulb comparison," "cost savings," and "efficiency."
- **Refine your keywords list.** Once you have a list of potential keywords, you need to review them to determine which are most relevant, identify synonyms that might provide better results, and consider if the keywords provide a complete representation of your topic. Add, remove, and modify the list as needed. You want to use keywords that are most likely to be on the webpages you want to find. For example, Irene might refine her list to the keywords "LED lights" and "cost savings."
- **Develop your search query.** A **search query** is a question that includes the keywords you identified as most closely related to your topic. Be descriptive and specific, and combine keywords to pare the search results to the most relevant. The more descriptive and complete your search query is, the better and more accurate the results. For example, Irene might find that "LED lights" and "cost savings" will return many hits, but "cost savings of LED lights" will return fewer, more specific results.
- **Refine your search query.** As you review the initial results from your search query, you might not find the exact information you were looking for. However, you might discover related information that will help you refine your search query. For example, you might find additional keywords you could add to your query to locate more specific information related to your topic. Conversely, you might need to remove a keyword because it's leading to incorrect or misleading results. Likewise, you might need to change some of the keywords to synonyms to obtain better results. In fact, you might need to adjust your search query several times to refine the results to locate the specific information you wanted to find.

You will use a search engine to implement Irene's search strategy for finding the cost savings of using LED lights. Because you are working with Edge on the desktop, you can use other desktop apps (short for applications) to compile your research as you go. For example, you might want to use WordPad, a basic word-processing program, or Paint, a simple computer graphics program, that come with Windows, to record some of the information you gathered and to begin outlining a report.

Using a Search Engine

You can use the Address bar to access a search engine, or you can go directly to a search engine's home page to access all of its features and functionality. Either way, the search results appear in the browser window. At the top of the results page, the search box shows the current search words. You can enter new keywords to start a new search at any time. The number of results indicates the number of **hits**, which are pages containing content that matches your search words. Hits are generally organized in order of relevancy. The first line contains a link with a headline of the page, the second line shows the URL, and the next lines display a more detailed summary or description of what you will find on the page. Also, website owners can purchase a paid placement or ad to get a hit to appear in the first page of search results that include a specific keyword—even if it is not the most relevant. Ads are labeled as ads and appear in the right column of the page or sometimes at the top of the page.

You will use Bing to implement Irene's search strategy for finding the cost savings with LED lights.

To use the Bing search engine:

TIP

Keywords are not case sensitive. Typing "led" is the same as typing "LED."

1. Click in the **Address bar** to select the URL of the current page, type **cost savings with led lights** as the search query, and then press the **Enter** key. The search query is sent to Bing. After a moment, the search results appear on the screen. See Figure 2.

Figure 2   **Search results returned by Bing**

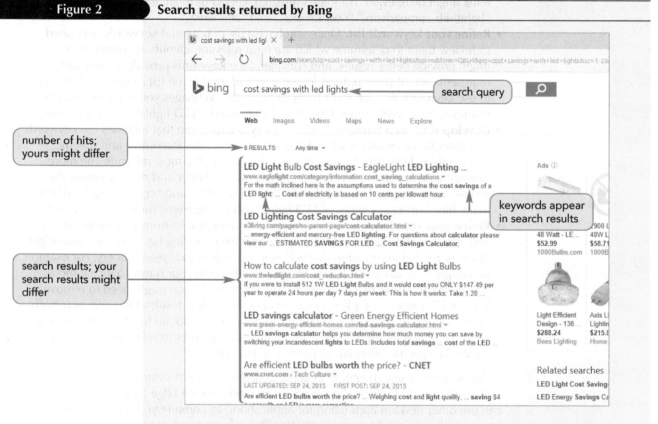

number of hits; yours might differ

search query

keywords appear in search results

search results; your search results might differ

2. Click one of the links in the search results that is not an ad. The webpage replaces the search results.

3. Review the content of the web page, and then click the **Back** button ⬅ to return to the search results page.

You should review the links that appear in the search results, looking for ones that seem to have the information most related to the topic you are researching. The description following each search result highlights the keywords from your search, giving you some indication of how relevant that search result might be to your topic.

It is also a good idea to conduct your search using multiple search engines. Different search engines return different results depending on which part of the web the search engine accesses. Also, each search engine uses a unique ranking system when listing search results. Tabbed browsing can make it convenient to compare search results from multiple search engines.

Using Tabbed Browsing

Tabbed browsing allows multiple webpages to display in the same browser window. With tabbed browsing, you can open a tab for each webpage you visit and to which you might want to return to quickly. Opening multiple pages in tabs lets you easily compare the content of different pages or follow a pathway of information without losing your starting point.

REFERENCE

Opening Tabs for Browsing

- Click the New tab button.
- In the Address box, enter the URL for the webpage you want to visit, and then press the Enter key.

or

- Press and hold the Ctrl key as you click a link on a webpage to open a new webpage in a new tab.

or

- Right-click a link on a webpage, and then on the shortcut menu, click Open in new tab.

You will open a new tab so that you can visit the Google search engine site and perform the same search with a different search engine.

To open, switch between, and close tabs in Edge:

▶ **1.** To the right of the first tab, click the **New tab** button ⊞. A new tab opens with the insertion point blinking in the Search or enter web address box. Depending on your settings, you might also see a Top sites section with links to popular websites or those you have recently visited or saved as a favorite; you can click a tile to open that webpage in the tab. See Figure 3.

| Figure 3 | Tabbed browsing |

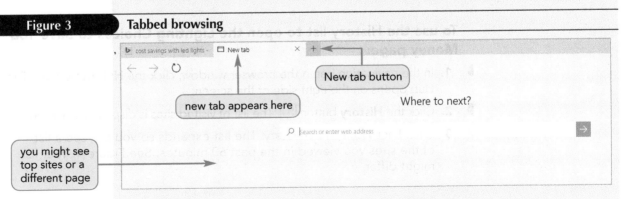

▶ **2.** In the Search or enter web address box, type **google.com** and then press the **Enter** key. The Google home page opens with a search box.

Trouble? If a message appears about making Google the default search engine or getting Google Chrome, click the Close button ☒.

3. Click in the search box, type **cost savings with led lights**, and then press the **Enter** key. The search query is sent to Google. After a moment, the search results appear on the screen.

4. Review the search results. Notice the number of hits and the first three websites listed in the results. You will return to the Bing search results, so you can compare them with the Google search results.

5. Click the **Bing** tab to redisplay the Bing search results, and then look for differences in the search results. For example, the number of hits on Bing will differ from the number of hits on Google, and the list of results might have different hits at the top or the same hits but in a different order.

   You will open pages from the search results in different tabs so you can leave the search results open in the original tab.

6. Press and hold the **Ctrl** key as you click a promising link in the Bing search results, and then release the **Ctrl** key. The linked webpage opens in a new tab, but the Bing search results tab remains active.

7. In the Bing search results, right-click the link for another page with promising information, and then click **Open in new tab** on the shortcut menu. The page opens in another tab.

8. Point to the **Google** tab to display its thumbnail, and then click the **Close tab** button ☒. The page with the Google search results closes, leaving the other tabs available.

To open a link on a new tab, be sure to press and hold the Ctrl key. If you don't, the link will open on the current tab, replacing the page displayed.

Using the History List

TIP

Some suggestions that appear when you start typing a URL in the Address bar are based on your History list.

The **History list** tracks the webpages you visit over a certain time period, not just during one browsing session. The History list contains the URLs for the websites and webpages that you have visited using Edge. By default, the entries in the History list are organized into time and date folders (Last hour, Today, Yesterday, Last week, and sometimes specific days). Each folder contains the webpages you visited appear in chronological order.

   You will use the History list to open the Lighting Choices to Save You Money page you viewed earlier.

To use the History list to open the Lighting Choices to Save You Money page:

1. In the navigation bar in the browser window, click the **Hub** button ☰. The Hub opens on the right side of the screen.

2. Click the **History** button 🕔. The list of visited sites is displayed chronologically.

3. Click **Last Hour**, if necessary. The list expands so you can see a list of the sites you viewed in the past 60 minutes. See Figure 4. Your list might differ.

Figure 4	History list in the Hub pane

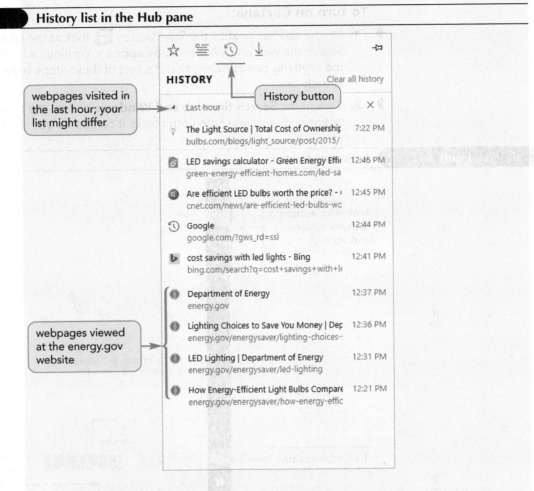

webpages visited in the last hour; your list might differ

History button

webpages viewed at the energy.gov website

HISTORY　　　　Clear all history

◢ Last hour　　　　　　　　　×

The Light Source | Total Cost of Ownership　7:22 PM
bulbs.com/blogs/light_source/post/2015/

LED savings calculator - Green Energy Effi　12:46 PM
green-energy-efficient-homes.com/led-sa

Are efficient LED bulbs worth the price? -　12:45 PM
cnet.com/news/are-efficient-led-bulbs-wo

Google　　　　　　　　　　12:44 PM
google.com/?gws_rd=ssl

cost savings with led lights - Bing　　　12:41 PM
bing.com/search?q=cost+savings+with+l

Department of Energy　　　　12:37 PM
energy.gov

Lighting Choices to Save You Money | Dep　12:36 PM
energy.gov/energysaver/lighting-choices-

LED Lighting | Department of Energy　　12:31 PM
energy.gov/energysaver/led-lighting

How Energy-Efficient Light Bulbs Compare　12:21 PM
energy.gov/energysaver/how-energy-effic

▶ **4.** Click **Lighting Choices to Save You Money** to open the same page you viewed earlier. This webpage replaces the Bing search results in the active tab.

Finding Information with Cortana

Another way to search for information is with Cortana. **Cortana** is an electronic personal assistant that Windows 10 provides to help you find files, search the web, keep track of information, and answer your questions. You control what Cortana knows about you. Cortana stores details you provide about yourself, your accounts, and your preferences in categories such as Eat & Drink, Events, Finance, and News in its Notebook. Cortana uses this information to provide personalized answers to your questions and display content that you might find interesting. You can also have Cortana reference information in the Window apps, such as People and Maps, so it can remind you about times, places, and people you add.

If you want to use Cortana, you must turn it on, or activate it, which requires a Microsoft account, and you must agree to let it collect information about you. You can tell whether Cortana is on by the text that appears in the box on the taskbar next to the Start button. If the box is labeled, "Ask me anything," then Cortana is on. If the box is labeled, "Search the web and Windows," Cortana is off. You can use the Try Cortana button that appears in the left pane when you click in the Search the web and Windows box on the taskbar to turn on Cortana.

To look up information using Cortana, you'll begin by checking whether Cortana is on.

To turn on Cortana:

▶ **1.** On the taskbar, next to the Start button ⊞, look at the label in the box. If the Search the web and Windows box appears, continue with Step 2. If the Ask me anything box appears, skip the rest of these steps because Cortana is already on.

▶ **2.** Click in the **Search the web and Windows** box on the taskbar. The menu opens and displays some of the tasks it can do for you. See Figure 5.

Figure 5	Activating Cortana

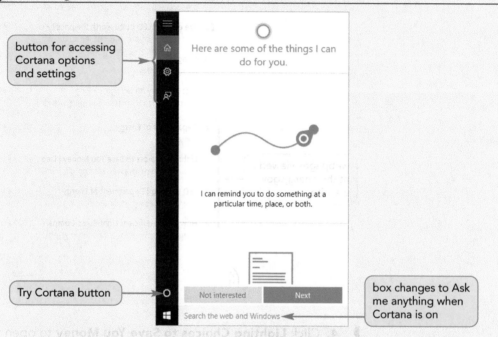

button for accessing Cortana options and settings

Here are some of the things I can do for you.

I can remind you to do something at a particular time, place, or both.

Try Cortana button

Not interested   Next

box changes to Ask me anything when Cortana is on

Search the web and Windows

Trouble? If your screen does not look like Figure 5, click the Try Cortana button ◉ in the left pane, and then continue with Step 3 if you see a list of tasks and continue with Step 4 if you see a notice about information that Cortana will collect and use.

▶ **3.** Click the **Next** button. A notice appears explaining that Cortana will collect your information and store it in its Notebook.

TIP
If the button labels on your screen differ, click the ones that turn on Cortana.

▶ **4.** Click the **Use Cortana** button. Cortana asks for a name to use when addressing you.

▶ **5.** Type your first name, click the **Settings** button, click the **Settings** button, and then sign in. Cortana displays a few starter interests, webpages, and search text that might suit you based on information in your Microsoft account.

▶ **6.** Click the **Got it** button. Cortana stores the webpage information and search text in your Notebook.

Once Cortana is on, you can use the Ask me anything box on the taskbar to have Cortana find the answer to any question.

Cortana uses your browsing history from Edge to help you locate information. For example, you can type the URL for a webpage you want to open in Edge, or you can enter your search query and view the results in the pane. If your computer has a microphone, you can also set up Cortana to respond to your voice. You can say, "Hey, Cortana" followed by what you want to find. For example, you can say "Open the Energy.gov webpage" or "Find the cost savings for LED lights" to have Cortana open the webpage or display the search results.

Cortana can also provide information about text you select on a webpage that is open in Edge. Information from other webpages about the selected text or search results using the selected text as your search query appear in the pane that opens along the right side of the web browser window. You'll use Cortana to find information.

To ask Cortana for information about selected text in a webpage:

▶ 1. Click in the **Ask me anything** box on the taskbar, and then type **cost savings for LED lights**. Cortana lists the search results for your query.

   Trouble? If Edge opens, you pressed the Enter key after typing the search query. Continue with Step 3.

▶ 2. Click a promising link in the search results. The page opens in a new tab.

▶ 3. On the new tab or any other tab, select **LEDs** or **LED lightbulbs** or a similar phrase somewhere on the webpage in order to find information about the selected text.

▶ 4. Right-click the selected text, and then click **Ask Cortana** on the shortcut menu. For example, if you select LEDs in a webpage, an explanation of light-emitting diode from Wikipedia appears in the pane followed by links to related people, related search queries that you might want to try, and a link to search for LED light on Bing. See Figure 6.

Figure 6   **Ask Cortana results in the browser window**

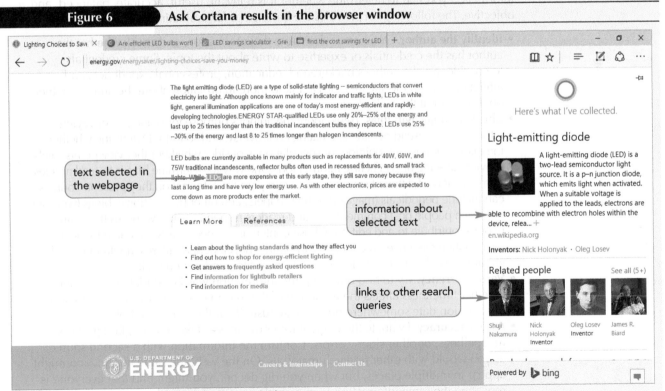

Source: U.S. Department of Energy

▶ 5. Click in a blank area of the webpage to close the Cortana pane, and then close the tab.

If you no longer want to use Cortana, you can turn it off. If, at any point, you decide to use Cortana again, you can switch it back on.

To turn off Cortana:

▶ **1.** On the taskbar, click in the **Ask me anything** box, and then click the **Notebook** button 🔲 on the left side of the Cortana pane.

▶ **2.** In the Notebook pane, click **Settings**. The Settings pane opens.

▶ **3.** At the top of the Settings pane, click the **slider button** to change On to Off. Cortana is now off, and the Ask me anything box returns to the Search the web and Windows box.

▶ **4.** Press the **Esc** key to close the pane and return to the desktop.

Now that you have implemented Irene's search strategy, she needs to determine if the results meet her needs.

Evaluating the Search Results

You should always review and evaluate all of the information you find on the web to identify its author, source, and accuracy and to evaluate the usefulness of the information. The cost of publishing on the web is low, and anyone who has access to a computer connected to the Internet can publish content. The content of webpages is not regulated or verified. Although information can be and is updated regularly, there is plenty of outdated information on the web. As you gather facts, be sure to read the information you find to determine whether it is relevant, useful, accurate, balanced, and objective. The following list provides the basic steps for evaluating your search results:

- **Identify the author.** Determine who wrote the information, and check whether the author has the credentials or expertise to write about the topic. Some credentials to consider are the author's background, education, professional experience, and affiliations. Often the site includes a link to more information about the author—either on the site or at the author's site.
- **Check for objectivity/bias.** Think about the author's purpose for writing—conveying information, persuading others, creating controversy, and so forth. Determine whether the information is fact, opinion, or speculation. Consider whether other viewpoints might provide differing or conflicting information. One way to determine bias is to read articles from a variety of different sources and to compare the information they present. Sources can include periodicals (magazines, newspapers, and other publications), blogs (websites on which people post commentaries and readers respond), wikis (websites that many people contribute to and edit but whose content is not necessarily validated for accuracy), online references (dictionaries, thesauri, encyclopedias, atlases, quotations, and grammar checkers), government sites, business sites, and personal sites.
- **Verify currency.** Try to find out when the information was last updated. Consider whether timeliness affects the reliability of the information. Most webpages include a last revision date somewhere on the page (usually at the top or the bottom).
- **Assess accuracy.** Evaluate the content for correctness—take note of glaring errors, misspellings, or other sloppy errors. Confirm the information with a second source, as you would with other research materials. On the web, the same information might appear in multiple places, but when you dig deeper, you might find that everyone is repeating the same information from a single source.
- **Determine validity.** Look at the source of the site to determine whether this is a trustworthy information resource. Consider who owns the website on which you found the information—a recognized, legitimate publication or an individual. Check whether the website has a stated goal that might influence how it presents

information or what information it presents. From the About and Contact pages, you can check out the site's history, read mission or vision statements, and find the address and details about key staff. You can also search the web to find reviews of the source.

- **Consider relevancy.** As a final step, you need to consider whether the information you find is relevant to your topic. You will encounter a lot of interesting information as you go, and it's easy to get lost in tangential information.

Based on her evaluation, Irene can determine whether the information you found is useful. For example, Figure 7 shows Irene's evaluation of one of the webpages from the search results. Although this webpage provides information on her topic, given her evaluation, she might want to continue looking for more information.

Figure 7 | **Webpage evaluated for usefulness to search topic**

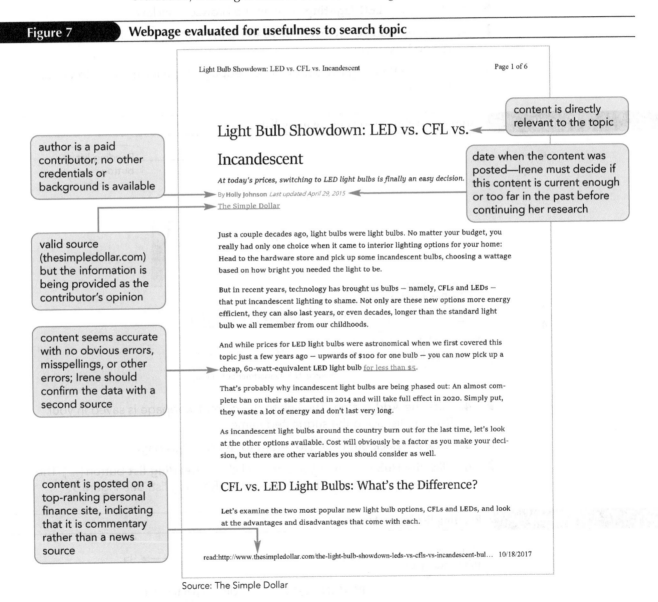

Source: The Simple Dollar

If the information meets your needs, Edge provides several ways to save the information, so you can access it later as you continue the research.

Saving Webpages to Your Reading List

You can create a **Reading list** by saving links to webpages that you want to read later. This is helpful during research as you find pages you want to read more closely or refer back to later. The webpages in your Reading list are available in the Hub pane.

Irene may want to read the information on the LED Lighting page more completely as she works on her report. You will save the LED Lighting page in your Reading list to review more thoroughly later.

To save the LED Lighting page in your Reading list:

▸ **1.** Display the **LED Lighting** page in the browser window.

▸ **2.** Click the **Add to favorites or reading list** button ☆ in the Address bar. A dialog box opens.

▸ **3.** Click the **Reading list** button. The webpage appears in the dialog box. See Figure 8.

Figure 8　Adding a webpage to your Reading list

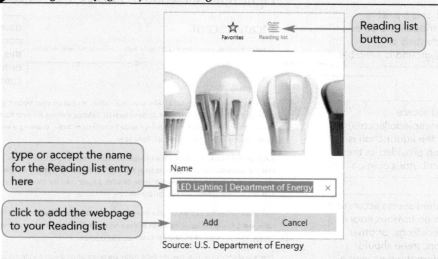

type or accept the name for the Reading list entry here

click to add the webpage to your Reading list

Reading list button

Name

LED Lighting | Department of Energy ✕

Add　　　Cancel

Source: U.S. Department of Energy

▸ **4.** Click the **Add** button. The link to the current webpage is saved in your Reading list using the suggested name.

▸ **5.** Click the **Back** button ← to return to the previous page.

▸ **6.** Click the **Hub** button ≡, and then click the **Reading list** button ☰. The webpage you just saved appears in your Reading list. See Figure 9.

Figure 9　Reading list in the Hub

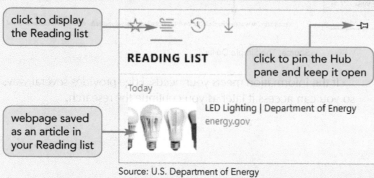

click to display the Reading list

click to pin the Hub pane and keep it open

webpage saved as an article in your Reading list

READING LIST

Today

LED Lighting | Department of Energy
energy.gov

Source: U.S. Department of Energy

You'll be working with the Hub, so you'll pin the Hub to keep the pane open along the right side of the browser window.

▶ **7.** In the upper-right corner of the Hub pane, click the **Pin this pane** button ⊞. The Hub pane will remain open until you close it.

▶ **8.** Click **LED Lighting | Department of Energy** in the Reading list. The page is displayed again in the browser window.

Using Reading View

As you focus on reviewing a webpage, you might want to maximize the amount of space available on the screen for viewing the actual content. Reading view hides page banners, navigation bars and links for navigating the site, links to related content, advertisements, and anything else that is not part of the main article on the page. Reading view lets you see more of the main page content so that you have to scroll less and see fewer distractions.

You will look at the LED Lighting page in Reading view to focus on the main content of the webpage.

To read the LED Lighting page in Reading view:

▶ **1.** In the Address bar, click the **Reading view** button 🕮. The page switches to Reading view, leaving only the main page content visible on the screen. See Figure 10. In some instances, the page content might include a photo, but usually it is only text.

Figure 10   **Webpage in Reading view**

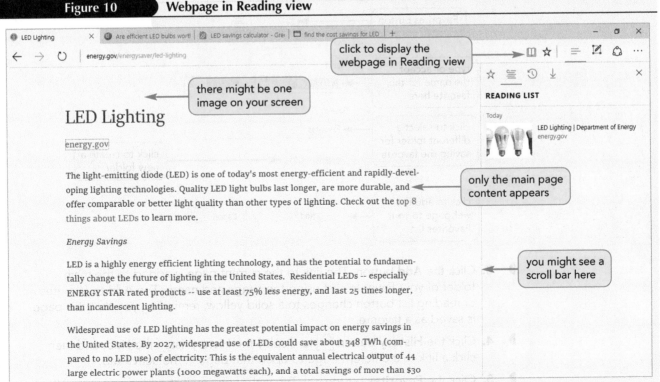

Source: U.S. Department of Energy

▶ **2.** Scroll through the webpage, noticing that no other page content is visible.

▶ **3.** In the Address bar, click the **Reading view** button 🕮 again. The page returns to Normal view, showing all the banners and links and related content again.

Adding Webpages to Your Favorites List

Web addresses can be very long and, as a result, difficult to remember. In Edge, you can add the URL of a website to the **Favorites list**, a feature that you can use to store and organize a list of webpages you want to revisit. When you add a webpage to your Favorites list, you can specify a name for that favorite and select a folder in which to save that favorite. Using folders to organize your Favorites list makes it easier to find a favorite when you need it. Your favorites are available in the Favorites list in the Hub pane.

Irene will want you to refer back to the LED Lighting page as she completes her report, so you will add that page to your Favorites list.

To add the LED Lighting page to your Favorites list:

▶ **1.** With the LED Lighting page displayed in the browser window, click the **Add to favorites or reading list** button ☆ in the Address bar. A dialog box opens.

▶ **2.** Click the **Favorites** button ☆ at the top of the dialog box. You can accept the suggested name or change it. Favorites is the default folder, but you can create or select a different folder, including the Favorites bar. See Figure 11.

| Figure 11 | Add a Favorite dialog box |

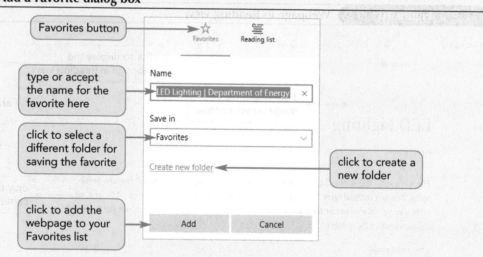

3. Click the **Add** button. The link to the current page is added to the main folder of your Favorites list using the suggested name. The Add to favorites or reading list button changes to a solid yellow, reminding you that this page is saved as a favorite.

▶ **4.** Click the **History** button 🕓 to display the History list in the Hub, and then click a link to a different page to open that page in the active tab.

▶ **5.** Click the **Favorites** button ☆. The webpage you just added appears in the Favorites list. See Figure 12.

Figure 12   Favorites list in the Hub

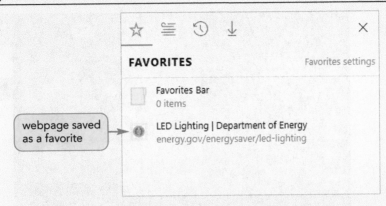

webpage saved as a favorite

6. Click the **LED Lighting** favorite. The page is displayed again in the browser window.

Pinning Webpages to the Start Menu

You can pin a page to the Start menu so you can open the webpage directly from the Start menu without first starting Edge. Display the webpage you want to pin, click the More actions button in the Edge navigation bar, and then click Pin this page to Start. A tile for that webpage appears on the Start menu. When you click the tile for the pinned page, the webpage opens in a new browser window.

You will pin the LED Lighting page to the Start menu for Irene.

To pin the LED Lighting page to the Start menu:

1. With the LED Lighting page displayed in the browser window, click the **More** button ⋯ to open the menu of actions you can perform in Edge.

2. On the menu, click **Pin this page to Start**. A dialog box opens, asking if you want to pin this tile to Start.

3. Click the **Yes** button. A tile for the LED Lighting page is added to the Start menu.

4. Click the **Close tab** button ☒ to close the tab displaying the LED Lighting home page.

5. Click the **Start** button ⊞, and then scroll the right pane to the bottom until you see the LED Lighting tile you added to the Start menu. See Figure 13.

Figure 13   **Tile for pinned site on the Start menu**

6. Click the **LED Lighting** tile. The LED Lighting page opens in a new tab in the Edge browser window.

You should delete the tiles for pinned pages that you no longer need to avoid unwanted clutter on your Start menu. You will unpin the tile for the LED Lighting page directly from the Start menu.

To unpin the tile for the LED Lighting page:

1. Click the **Start** button ▦, and then scroll the right pane to the bottom until you see the LED Lighting tile you added to the Start menu.

2. Right-click the **LED Lighting** tile. A shortcut menu opens with options to unpin the page from Start, resize the tile, or turn off the live tile.

3. Click **Unpin from Start**. The LED Lighting tile is removed from the Start menu.

4. Press the **Esc** key to close the Start menu.

TIP

A live tile on the Start menu frequently changes the content it's displaying.

Before Irene compiles and uses information on the latest lighting technology in her report, she needs to understand the rules of copyright and fair use. This knowledge will help her determine what information she can use for her own purposes and how to properly cite its source.

Using the Information You Find

The content you find on the web is a form of **intellectual property**, which includes all creations of the human mind, such as original ideas and creative works presented in a form that can be shared or that others can recreate, emulate, or manufacture. On a webpage, intellectual property includes the text, images, and videos on the page, as well as the design of the page itself. Intellectual property as a tangible expression of an idea is protected just like other tangible forms of property, such as houses and cars. Each country has its own rules and laws governing intellectual property rights and protection. In the United States, intellectual property is protected through patents, trademarks, trade secrets, and copyrights.

A **copyright** is a protection granted by law to the author or creator of an original work who creates a tangible expression of that work or creation. Creations that can be copyrighted include virtually all forms of artistic or intellectual expression, such as books, music, artwork, audio and video recordings, architectural drawings, choreographic works, product packaging, and computer software. The tangible form of the work can be words, numbers, notes, sounds, pictures, and so forth. A collection of facts can be copyrighted but only if the collection is arranged, coordinated, or selected in a way that causes the resulting work to rise to the level of an original work. Copyright protection exists whether the work is published or unpublished.

The copyright is in effect for the length of time specified in the copyright law and gives the author or creator the exclusive right to reproduce, adapt, distribute, publicly perform, publicly display, or sell the work. In the United States, under the 1976 Copyright Act, works created after 1977 are protected for the life of the author (or the last surviving author in the case of a "joint work" with multiple authors) plus another 70 years. Works made for hire and anonymous or pseudonymous works are protected for 95 years from the date of publication or 120 years from the date of creation, whichever is earlier. The copyright holder can transfer, license, sell, donate, or leave the copyright to his or her heirs. Works created before 1978 are protected under the 1909 Copyright Act and have more complex and variable terms of copyright.

Determining Fair Use

U.S. copyright law allows people to use portions of copyrighted works without obtaining permission from the copyright holder if that use is a fair use. Section 107 of the 1976 Copyright Act lists criticism, comment, news reporting, teaching, scholarship, and research as examples of uses that may be eligible for fair use. However, the circumstances surrounding a particular use determine whether that use is considered fair. Keep in mind that the legal definition of fair use is intentionally broad and can be difficult to interpret. As a result, many disputes about whether a use is fair have landed in court. Courts generally consider the following four factors when determining fair use:

- **The purpose and character of the new work**—This factor considers such issues as whether the use adds something new to the body of knowledge and arts or just reproduces the work, and whether the use is commercial or for nonprofit educational purposes.
- **The nature of the copyrighted work**—In general, more creative works have stronger protection than factual works. Keep in mind that an unpublished work has the same copyright protections for fair use as a published work.
- **The amount and substantiality of the portion used in relation to the copyrighted work as a whole** (in other words, how much of the copyrighted work was used)—The less work that is used, the more likely it falls under fair use. However, using even a small amount of the work can be copyright infringement if it is the heart of the work.
- **The effect of the use on the potential market, or value, of the copyrighted work**—For example, does the use of the copyrighted material hurt the market for the original work, and does it impair or limit the ability of the copyright owner to earn income or otherwise benefit from the work?

Again, no hard-and-fast rule determines fair use. If you are unsure whether your use is indeed fair use, the safest course of action is to contact the copyright owner and ask for permission to use the work.

Identifying Works in the Public Domain

Once the term of the copyright has expired, the work moves into the **public domain**, which means that anyone is free to copy the work without requesting permission from the last copyright holder. Older literary works, such as *A Tale of Two Cities* by Charles Dickens published in 1859, are in the public domain and can be reproduced freely. Songs or musical works published earlier than 1922, such as "The Star-Spangled Banner" written by Francis Scott Key in 1814, are also in the public domain in the United States. However, if a publisher creates a new print edition of the public domain literary work or an orchestra makes an audio recording of the public domain musical work, the book or performance is a separate work that can be copyrighted and protected under current copyright laws.

Authors or creators can place their work into the public domain voluntarily at any time. For example, some websites provide graphics files that visitors can use free of charge. You can include public domain content on a webpage, in a paper, or in any other form of creative expression. However, you should still acknowledge the source of the public domain material and not represent the work as your own, which is plagiarism.

Avoiding Plagiarism

The web makes it very easy to copy someone else's work. If you use someone else's work, whether the work is in the public domain or protected by copyright, you must cite the source of the material. Failure to cite the source of material that you use is called **plagiarism**. Claiming someone else's work as your own is a serious legal violation that can lead to a failing grade, being expelled from school, being fired from a job, or being subjected to a hefty fine or prosecution.

Plagiarism can be as simple as including a sentence or two from someone else's work without using quotation marks or attribution. It can be as blatant as duplicating substantial parts of someone else's work and claiming them as your own. It can be more subtle, such as paraphrasing someone else's content without a proper citation of the source. Another form of plagiarism is when students purchase essays, term papers, and even theses or dissertations from commercial services and then pass them off as their own.

To ensure that you don't unintentionally plagiarize someone else's work, be sure to properly reference the sources of works that you use. Keep in mind that just including a source citation is not enough if you plan to use the finished product commercially. You must also obtain the copyright holder's permission if you want to use the work in a way that falls outside of fair use.

TIP

For more information about current U.S. copyright law, you can visit the United States Copyright Office website at copyright.gov.

Documenting Web Resources

To avoid charges of plagiarism, all works you reference—whether they are protected by copyright, in the public domain, or considered fair use—need to be documented. This gives proper credit to the original authors as well as provides readers with the information they need to find and review the works you used.

However, documentation can become a challenge when you are referencing a webpage. Because the web is a dynamic medium, the content of any given page can change in an instant. Also, its URL can change or disappear from day to day. Unlike published books and journals, which have a physical existence, a webpage exists only in an HTML document on a web server computer. If the file's name or location changes, or if the web server is disconnected from the Internet, the page is no longer accessible.

For academic research, the two most widely followed standards for citations are those of the American Psychological Association (APA) and the Modern Language Association (MLA). The APA and MLA formats for webpage citations are similar. Figure 14 shows both APA and MLA citations for a specific webpage and how the citation information is obtained from the webpage.

Figure 14	Webpage citations

APA Citation

Johnson, H. (2015). Light Bulb Showdown. In *The Simple Dollar*. Retrieved October 18, 2017, from http://www.thesimpledollar.com

MLA Citation

Johnson, Holly. "Light Bulb Showdown." *The Simple Dollar*. Soda, 29 April 2015. Web. 18 October 2017. <http://www.thesimpledollar.com/the-light-bulb-showdown-leds-vs-cfls-vs-incandescent-bulbs-whats-the-best-deal-now-and-in-the-future>.

Be aware, however, that both the APA and MLA standards change from time to time. Consult these organizations' websites as well as the APA and MLA style guides for the latest rules and updates to these styles before using them. Also, always check to see if your instructor or editor (for work you are submitting for publication) has established other guidelines.

Saving Webpages with Web Notes

Rather than using the resources to print and the space to store, many people prefer to document their work by saving a static version of webpages in a file. As a reminder of why you wanted to save those webpages, you might want to add notes and highlights to particular sections, phrases, or images. With a **Web Note**, you can save a webpage with your handwritten or typed notes and highlights and even clip a section of the webpage to save. You can save the Web Note to OneNote, as a favorite, or to your Reading list.

You will annotate the LED Lighting page using the Make a Web Note tools so you can share this information with Irene.

To annotate the LED Lighting page with Web Notes:

1. With the LED Lighting page displayed in the browser window, click the **Make a Web Note** button in the navigation bar. A toolbar appears above a static copy of the page with buttons for adding and erasing notes and highlights, clipping a section of the page, and saving or sharing the Web Note page.

2. Click the **Pen** button on the toolbar, and then drag the pointer to circle a section heading on the webpage.

   Trouble? If you don't like how you drew the circle, click the Eraser button, and then drag the pointer over the ink to remove it.

3. Click the **Highlighter** button on the toolbar, and drag the pointer across an important point on the webpage to highlight it.

4. Click the **Add a typed note** button on the toolbar, click on the webpage to insert a numbered note, and then type **You might want to include this in your report.** as the note. See Figure 15.

TIP

You can click the Pen or Highlighter button a second time to choose an ink color and size.

Figure 15 — Making Web Notes

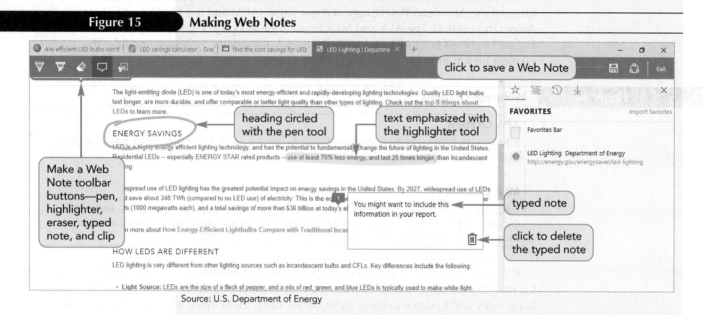

Source: U.S. Department of Energy

You can use the Clip button 📷 to save only part of the webpage in the web note.

▶ **5.** Click the **Save Web Note** button 💾 on the toolbar. A dialog box opens so you can choose where to save the Web Notes and with what name.

▶ **6.** Click the **Reading list** button at the top of the dialog box. See Figure 16.

Figure 16 — Saving a Web Note

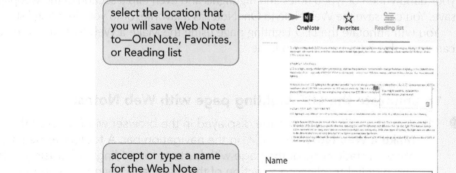

Source: U.S. Department of Energy

▶ **7.** Click the **Save** button. The Web Notes – LED Lighting page is saved to the Reading list with the suggested name.

▶ **8.** Click the **Exit** button on the toolbar. Edge returns to the dynamic webpage.

You access Web Notes you saved as favorites or added to your Reading list from the Hub just like any other favorite or Reading list entry. You will open the Web Notes – LED Lighting page you plan to share with Irene.

To open the Web Notes – LED Lighting page from your Reading list:

▶ **1.** Click the **Reading list** button ▤ at the top of the Hub pane. The Web Notes – LED Lighting page is at the top of your Reading list.

▶ **2.** Click the **Web Notes – LED Lighting**. The static webpage with your notes and highlights opens in the current tab.

▶ **3.** If necessary, click the **Expand typed note 1** icon ⬇ on the Web Notes page to expand the note box, and then read the note.

Deleting Items from the Hub

When you no longer need webpages and Web Notes you saved as favorites or saved to your Reading list, you can delete them from the Hub. This keeps the entries current and streamlined. You can also clear your History list so that Edge no longer remembers webpages that you have viewed.

You will delete the webpages and Web Notes from your Favorites and Reading lists and clear the History list.

To remove Reading list entries and favorites from the Hub:

▶ **1.** In the Reading list, right-click the **LED Lighting** link. A shortcut menu opens.

▶ **2.** On the shortcut menu, click **Delete**. The LED Lighting webpage is deleted from your Reading list.

▶ **3.** Right-click the **Web Notes – LED Lighting**, and then click **Delete** on the shortcut menu. The Web Note is deleted from your Reading list.

▶ **4.** In the Hub, click the **Favorites** button ☆.

▶ **5.** In the Favorites list, right-click the **LED Lighting** favorite. A shortcut menu opens with options for working with favorites, including opening the favorite in new tab, creating a new folder to store the favorite in, renaming the favorite, and removing the favorite from the list.

> **TIP**
>
> You can also click the solid yellow Add to favorites or reading list button to reopen the dialog box and then click the Delete button.

▶ **6.** On the shortcut menu, click **Delete**. The LED Lighting favorite is deleted from the Hub.

▶ **7.** At the top of the Hub pane, click the **History** button 🕔, and then click the **Clear all history** link. The Clear browsing data options appear in the pane.

▶ **8.** Click check boxes as needed until only the **Browsing history** check box has a checkmark, and then click the **Clear** button.

▶ **9.** After the All clear! message appears, click in any blank area of the current webpage to redisplay the Hub pane.

▶ **10.** Click the **Close** button ☒ in the upper-left corner to close the Hub pane.

Printing a Webpage

The web is a dynamic medium, so pages can be removed or changed without warning. When doing research, you might want to print copies of pages that you have used during your research to document the information.

Webpages are not necessarily designed with printing in mind. Before you print a webpage, it is a good idea to preview it to ensure that the text and graphics fit well on the page. If necessary, you can change the settings to adjust the webpage to fit better on the page. The Print dialog box shows a preview of the printed page based on the current print settings. You can change any of these settings, which include selecting a different printer or printing to PDF, selecting the pages to print, changing the page orientation between portrait (where the page is taller than it is wide) and landscape (where the page is wider than it is tall), changing the scale to force the content to fit on a specific number of pages adjust the margins, turning the display of headers and footers on or off, and changing the paper size. Also, many webpages provide a link to a separate printer-friendly version of the page. This option controls what is printed, including only essential information and ensuring that it will print in an appropriate format.

You will preview and print one of the pages with promising information that you found.

To preview and print the LED Lighting webpage:

TIP

If the preview has two or more pages, click the Next Page button to view the subsequent pages.

1. Display the **LED Lighting** webpage or another webpage in the browser window.

2. Click the **More** button ⋯, and then click **Print** on the menu. The Print dialog box opens. See Figure 18. The options will differ, depending on the printer available to you.

Figure 17   **Print dialog box**

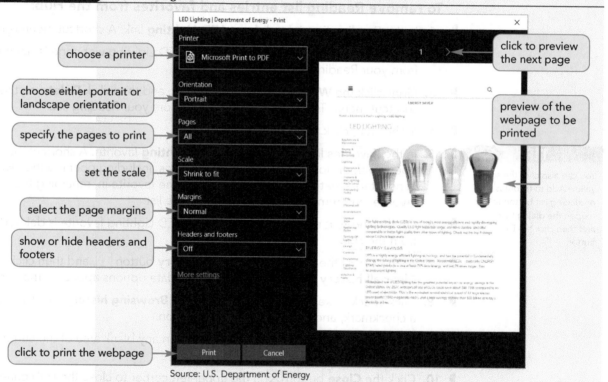

choose a printer

choose either portrait or landscape orientation

specify the pages to print

set the scale

select the page margins

show or hide headers and footers

click to print the webpage

click to preview the next page

preview of the webpage to be printed

Source: U.S. Department of Energy

3. In the Printer section, click the printer you want to use, if necessary, and then review the orientation, scale, and other settings.

Check with your instructor about whether to print the webpage.

4. If you are instructed to print, click the **Print** button. Otherwise, click the **Cancel** button.

Sharing Webpages, Web Notes, or Screenshots

You can share the current webpage, a Web Note, or a screenshot of the current webpage or Web Note with other people or apps. The Share pane lists all of the ways you can share the current webpage. For example, you can send the current webpage to Flipboard, Mail, OneNote, the Reading List app, or Twitter. These options change when you choose to share a screenshot of the current webpage or a Web Note.

To share the LED Lighting page:

▶ **1.** To the right of the Address bar, click the **Share Web Note** button 🔲. The Share pane opens with a list of different ways you can share the webpage.

▶ **2.** Click the **LED Lighting** link at the top of the Share pane. A menu opens with options to share the current webpage or a screenshot of the current webpage.

▶ **3.** Click **Screenshot**. The list of apps changes to reflect those that you can use to share a screenshot.

   Irene doesn't want you to share the webpage at this time.

▶ **4.** Press the **Esc** key to close the Share pane.

You have completed all of the research that Irene wants for now, so you will close the browser.

To close Edge:

▶ **1.** On the Edge title bar, click the **Close** button ⊠. A dialog box opens, asking whether you want to close all tabs.

   Trouble? If the dialog box asking if you want to close all tabs does not open, someone has already select the Always close all tabs check box. All tabs close when you close Microsoft Edge. Skip Step 2.

▶ **2.** Click the **Close all** button to close any open tabs close and exit Edge.

Irene will include the information you researched in her report.

PROSKILLS

Written Communication: Organizing Your Research

Research is the first step toward conveying information and facts in a written report. When you summarize your research results, how you organize the information and write the report is just as important as the quality of the research that you have done. If you do an excellent job gathering the facts, be sure to deliver a report that is clear and easy to understand. This ensures that your audience benefits from your hard work and gets the information it needs. A lack of clarity can introduce noise into the communication and prevent readers from getting the message you intend to convey.

As you research a topic, be sure to take accurate notes about what you learn. Remember to include complete information about your sources, so you can cite them as needed in your report. After you finish your research, organize your notes into a logical order so that you can present the information clearly and succinctly. This is also a good way to check whether you need to locate additional information.

As you begin writing, make sure it is apparent why you are writing in the first place. Are you writing to inform, to entertain, or to express your opinion? When writing a factual report, your opinions are not relevant and should not be included. Next, determine the appropriate writing style—formal or informal. If you are writing for a professor or supervisor, use a more formal tone than you would in a casual email to a colleague, friend, or family member.

When you have finished your report, be sure to read it carefully, keeping the recipient's viewpoint in mind. Make sure your points are clear and are presented in a logical order. Also, check your spelling and grammar, and correct any errors that you find. However, do not rely only on spelling and grammar checkers because they do not always find all errors. You might find it helpful to read what you have written out loud to determine whether your intended message and tone are coming through clearly. As a final step, you could ask a friend or colleague to read your final report and provide feedback.

Irene thanks you for the information about LED lighting that you found using Edge. She is confident that she can find additional relevant information and that she can compile and document her sources appropriately.

REVIEW

Quick Check

1. What are the two functions of the Address bar?
2. What are the basic steps for developing a search strategy?
3. Why should you conduct a search using multiple search engines?
4. Why would you want to use tabbed browsing?
5. What is the difference between the History list and the Favorites list?
6. Why should you review and evaluate information you find on the web?
7. What is the difference between the Reading list and the Reading view?
8. What is plagiarism, and how can you avoid it?

Review Assignments

There are no Data Files needed for the Review Assignments.

Irene wants to gather information about another way technology is saving energy and money. She has been researching hybrid and electric cars. Now Irene wants to research fuel cell vehicles. She wants to know what fuel cells vehicles are, the how they work, and the benefits and challenges of fuel cells. Complete the following:

1. Start Edge, and then visit the Fuel Economy website by entering its URL **fueleconomy.gov** in the Address bar.
2. Click links on the page to navigate the site, looking for basic information about fuel cell vehicles.
3. Formulate a search strategy for finding the information Irene wants to gather for her report.
4. Use the Address bar or the Search the web and Windows box or the Ask me anything box to implement the search strategy you developed.
5. Open a new tab, visit the website for a different search engine (such as Google, Bing, or Yahoo!), and then implement the same search strategy using that search engine.
6. Compare the results of the two search engines, and then open three promising pages on new tabs.
7. Evaluate one of the pages you opened to determine whether it is relevant, useful, accurate, balanced, and objective.
8. Make a Web Note from the page you evaluated, and use the Web Note tools to record your evaluation summaries and a complete citation for the webpage.
9. Save the Web Note in your Reading list using the suggested name.
10. Open the Web Note you saved in your Reading list, and then print the note or share it as instructed.
11. Delete the Web Note from your Reading list.

Case Problem 1

There are no Data Files needed for this Case Problem.

Home Composting   Ruth Simmons wants to start composting at home. She already knows that composting turns organic matter, such as plants, into fertilizer through decomposition. Now she wants to know how to make a compost bin in her backyard. She asks you to research a simple compost bin to build and find out what she should put in the bin to create the compost. Complete the following steps:

1. Formulate a search strategy for finding the information Ruth wants to gather about composting.
2. Start Edge, and then implement the search strategy you developed using the default search engine.
3. On a new tab, repeat the search strategy using a different search engine.
4. Compare the results of the two search engines, and then open three promising pages on new tabs.
5. Evaluate the pages you opened to find one that is relevant, useful, accurate, balanced, and objective.
6. Make a Web Note from at least one page you evaluated. Use the Web Note tools to record your evaluation notes.
7. Include a complete citation for the webpage in the Web Note.
8. Save the Web Note webpage using its default name in your Reading list.
9. Open the Web Note you saved in your Reading list, and then print the note or share it as specified by your instructor.
10. Delete the Web Note from your Reading list.

RESEARCH

Case Problem 2

There are no Data Files needed for this Case Problem.

House Painting   Milo Peterson is planning to paint his home this summer. Before he chooses a color and brand, he needs to decide whether the exterior paint should be oil or latex. He asks you to research the two types of exterior paints, including the differences between them as well as the advantages and disadvantages of using each type of paint. He also asks you to recommend which type of paint he should use based on your research. Complete the following steps:

1. Formulate a search strategy for finding the information Milo wants to gather about exterior paints.
2. Start Edge and then implement the search strategy you developed. Repeat your strategy on a different search engine.
3. Open as many pages as needed to find information about the differences between the two types of exterior paints and the advantages of one versus the other.
4. Evaluate the pages you opened to find at least one that is relevant, useful, accurate, balanced, and objective.
5. Make a Web Note on the page or pages you evaluated using the Web Note tools to record your evaluation notes. Include a complete citation for the webpage or webpages.
6. Print or share the Web Notes webpage using its default name as specified by your instructor.
7. Start WordPad and then record the information you found as well as your recommendation. Be sure to document your sources.

OBJECTIVES

Session 1.1
- Create and save a document
- Enter text and correct errors as you type
- Use AutoComplete and AutoCorrect
- Select text and move the insertion point
- Undo and redo actions
- Adjust paragraph spacing, line spacing, and margins
- Preview and print a document
- Create an envelope

Session 1.2
- Open an existing document
- Use the Spelling and Grammar task panes
- Change page orientation, font, font color, and font size
- Apply text effects and align text
- Copy formatting with the Format Painter
- Insert a paragraph border and shading
- Delete, insert, and edit a photo
- Use Word Help

Creating and Editing a Document

Writing a Business Letter and Formatting a Flyer

Case | *Villa Rio Records*

Villa Rio Records, in Wilmington, Delaware, specializes in vinyl records, which have been making a comeback in the past few years. To replenish the store's stock, the purchasing manager, Leo Barinov, frequently appraises and bids on record collections from around the state. Leo has asked you to create a cover letter to accompany an appraisal that he needs to send to a potential seller and an envelope for sending an appraisal to another potential seller. He also wants your help creating a flyer reminding store customers that Villa Rio Records buys old vinyl records.

You will create the letter and flyer using **Microsoft Office Word 2016** (or simply **Word**), a word-processing program. You'll start by opening Word and saving a new document. Then you'll type the text of the cover letter and print it. In the process of entering the text, you'll learn several ways to correct typing errors and how to adjust paragraph and line spacing. When you create the envelope, you'll learn how to save it as part of a document for later use. As you work on the flyer, you will learn how to open an existing document, change the way text is laid out on the page, format text, and insert and resize a photo. Finally, you'll learn how to use Word's Help system.

STARTING DATA FILES

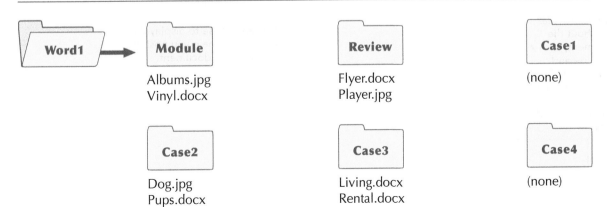

Word1 →	Module	Review	Case1
	Albums.jpg Vinyl.docx	Flyer.docx Player.jpg	(none)
	Case2	Case3	Case4
	Dog.jpg Pups.docx	Living.docx Rental.docx	(none)

Session 1.1 Visual Overview:

The **Quick Access Toolbar** is a collection of buttons that provides one-click access to commonly used commands, such as Save, Undo, and Repeat; you might see additional buttons here.

Each **tab** includes commands related to particular activities or tasks. The Home tab includes options for formatting and editing text.

The **title bar** displays the name of the open file and the program.

The **ribbon** is the main set of buttons and other tools you can use to complete tasks. It is organized into tabs and groups.

The dark gray areas on the ruler represent the document's margins. **Margins** are the blank spaces around the edges of a document's content.

The **insertion point** shows where characters will appear when you start typing.

The **paragraph mark** indicates the end of a paragraph. It is visible only if nonprinting characters are turned on. **Nonprinting characters** appear on the screen but not on the printed page.

Buttons for related commands are organized on a tab in **groups**. The buttons in this group can be used to change the appearance of a paragraph.

The **status bar** provides information about the current document, such as the current page and number of words in the document; it also contains buttons and other controls for working with the document.

You can choose to display the rulers, which help you position elements in a document.

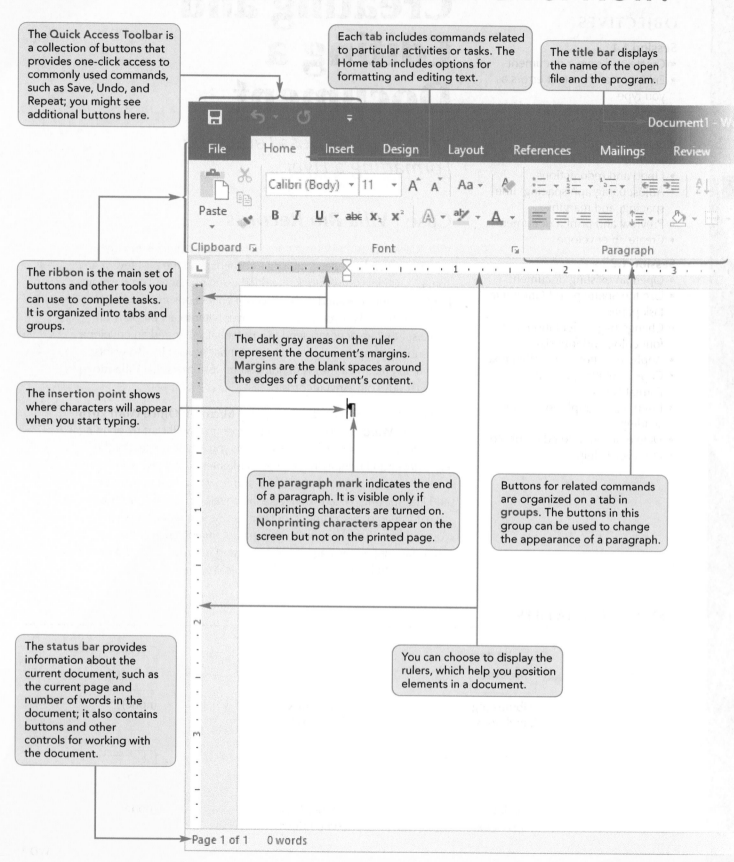

The Word Window

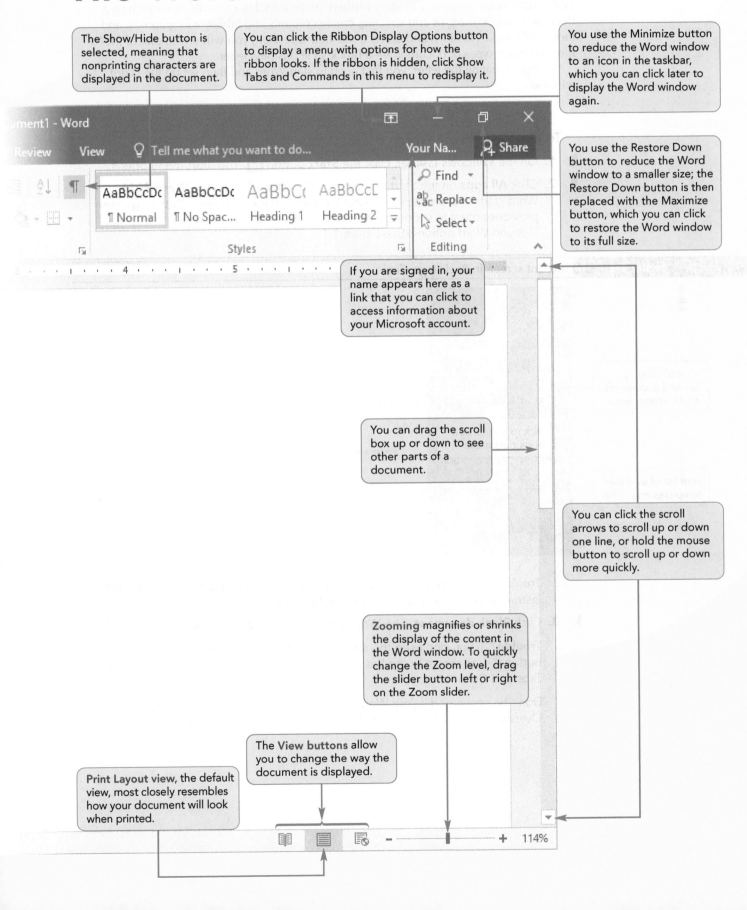

The Show/Hide button is selected, meaning that nonprinting characters are displayed in the document.

You can click the Ribbon Display Options button to display a menu with options for how the ribbon looks. If the ribbon is hidden, click Show Tabs and Commands in this menu to redisplay it.

You use the Minimize button to reduce the Word window to an icon in the taskbar, which you can click later to display the Word window again.

You use the Restore Down button to reduce the Word window to a smaller size; the Restore Down button is then replaced with the Maximize button, which you can click to restore the Word window to its full size.

If you are signed in, your name appears here as a link that you can click to access information about your Microsoft account.

You can drag the scroll box up or down to see other parts of a document.

You can click the scroll arrows to scroll up or down one line, or hold the mouse button to scroll up or down more quickly.

Zooming magnifies or shrinks the display of the content in the Word window. To quickly change the Zoom level, drag the slider button left or right on the Zoom slider.

The View buttons allow you to change the way the document is displayed.

Print Layout view, the default view, most closely resembles how your document will look when printed.

Starting Word

With Word, you can quickly create polished, professional documents. You can type a document, adjust margins and spacing, create columns and tables, add graphics, and then easily make revisions and corrections. In this session, you will create one of the most common types of documents—a block-style business letter.

To begin creating the letter, you first need to start Word and then set up the Word window.

To start Microsoft Word:

▶ **1.** On the Windows taskbar, click the **Start** button ⊞. The Start menu opens.

▶ **2.** Click **All apps** on the Start menu, scroll the list, and then click **Word 2016**. Word starts and displays the Recent screen in Backstage view. **Backstage view** provides access to various screens with commands that allow you to manage files and Word options. See Figure 1-1.

| Figure 1-1 | Recent screen in Backstage view |

a list of recently opened documents might appear here

click to open a new, blank document

your list of available templates may differ

Trouble? If you don't see Word 2016 on the Windows Start menu, ask your instructor or technical support person for help.

▶ **3.** Click **Blank document**. The Word window opens, with the ribbon displayed.

Trouble? If you don't see the ribbon, click the Ribbon Display Options button 🖽, as shown in the Session 1.1 Visual Overview, and then click Show Tabs and Commands.

Don't be concerned if your Word window doesn't match the Session 1.1 Visual Overview exactly. You'll have a chance to adjust its appearance shortly.

Working in Touch Mode

You can interact with the Word screen using a mouse, or, if you have a touchscreen, you can work in Touch Mode, using a finger instead of the mouse pointer. In **Touch Mode**, extra space around the buttons on the ribbon makes it easier to tap the specific button you need. The figures in this text show the screen with Mouse Mode on, but it's helpful to learn how to switch back and forth between Touch Mode and Mouse Mode.

Note: The following steps assume that you are using a mouse. If you are instead using a touch device, please read these steps but don't complete them so that you remain working in Touch Mode.

To switch between Touch and Mouse Mode:

▶ **1.** On the Quick Access Toolbar, click the **Customize Quick Access Toolbar** button ⯆ to open the menu. The Touch/Mouse Mode command near the bottom of the menu does not have a checkmark next to it, indicating that it is currently not selected.

> **Trouble?** If the Touch/Mouse Mode command has a checkmark next to it, press the Esc key to close the menu, and then skip to Step 3.

▶ **2.** On the menu, click **Touch/Mouse Mode**. The menu closes, and the Touch/Mouse Mode button 👆 ⯆ appears on the Quick Access Toolbar.

▶ **3.** On the Quick Access Toolbar, click the **Touch/Mouse Mode** button 👆 ⯆. A menu opens with two options—Mouse and Touch. The icon next to Mouse is shaded blue to indicate it is selected.

> **Trouble?** If the icon next to Touch is shaded blue, press the Esc key to close the menu and skip to Step 5.

▶ **4.** On the menu, click **Touch**. The menu closes, and the ribbon increases in height so that there is more space around each button on the ribbon. See Figure 1-2.

Figure 1-2	Word window in Touch Mode

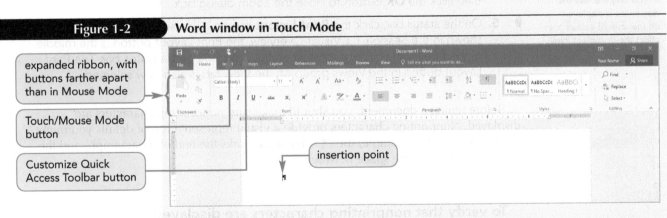

expanded ribbon, with buttons farther apart than in Mouse Mode

Touch/Mouse Mode button

Customize Quick Access Toolbar button

insertion point

> **Trouble?** If you are working with a touchscreen and want to use Touch Mode, skip Steps 5 and 6.

▶ **5.** On the Quick Access Toolbar, click the **Touch/Mouse Mode** button 👆 ⯆, and then click **Mouse**. The ribbon changes back to its Mouse Mode appearance, as shown in the Session 1.1 Visual Overview.

▶ **6.** On the Quick Access Toolbar, click the **Customize Quick Access Toolbar** button ⯆, and then click **Touch/Mouse Mode** to deselect it. The Touch/Mouse Mode button is removed from the Quick Access Toolbar.

Setting Up the Word Window

Before you start using Word, you should make sure you can locate and identify the different elements of the Word window, as shown in the Session 1.1 Visual Overview. In the following steps, you'll make sure your screen matches the Visual Overview.

To set up your Word window to match the figures in this book:

1. If the Word window does not fill the entire screen, click the **Maximize** button ☐ in the upper-right corner of the Word window.

   The insertion point on your computer should be positioned about an inch from the top of the document, as shown in Figure 1-2, with the top margin visible.

   Trouble? If the insertion point appears at the top of the document, with no white space above it, position the mouse pointer between the top of the document and the horizontal ruler, until it changes to ⬍, double-click, and then scroll up to top of the document.

2. On the ribbon, click the **View** tab. The ribbon changes to show options for changing the appearance of the Word window.

3. In the Show group, click the **Ruler** check box to insert a checkmark, if necessary. If the rulers were not displayed, they are displayed now.

   Next, you'll change the Zoom level to a setting that ensures that your Word window will match the figures in this book. To increase or decrease the screen's magnification, you could drag the slider button on the Zoom slider in the lower-right corner of the Word window. But to choose a specific Zoom level, it's easier to use the Zoom dialog box.

4. In the Zoom group, click the **Zoom** button to open the Zoom dialog box. Double-click the current value in the **Percent** box to select it, type **120**, and then click the **OK** button to close the Zoom dialog box.

5. On the status bar, click the **Print Layout** button 🖺 to select it, if necessary. As shown in the Session 1.1 Visual Overview, the Print Layout button is the middle of the three View buttons located on the right side of the status bar. The Print Layout button in the Views group on the View tab is also now selected.

Before typing a document, you should make sure nonprinting characters are displayed. Nonprinting characters provide a visual representation of details you might otherwise miss. For example, the (¶) character marks the end of a paragraph, and the (•) character marks the space between words.

To verify that nonprinting characters are displayed:

1. On the ribbon, click the **Home** tab.

2. In the blank Word document, look for the paragraph mark (¶) in the first line of the document, just to the right of the blinking insertion point.

   Trouble? If you don't see the paragraph mark, click the Show/Hide ¶ button ¶ in the Paragraph group.

   In the Paragraph group, the Show/Hide ¶ button should be highlighted in gray, indicating that it is selected, and the paragraph mark (¶) should appear in the first line of the document, just to the right of the insertion point.

Saving a Document

Before you begin working on a document, you should save it with a new name. When you use the Save button on the Quick Access Toolbar to save a document for the first time, Word displays the Save As screen in Backstage view. In the Save As screen, you can select the location where you want to store your document. After that, when you click the Save button, Word saves your document to the same location you specified earlier and with the same name.

To save the document:

▶ **1.** On the Quick Access Toolbar, click the **Save** button 🔲. Word switches to the Save As screen in Backstage view, as shown in Figure 1-3.

Figure 1-3	Save As screen in Backstage view

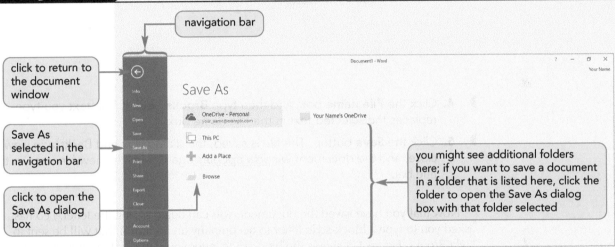

navigation bar

click to return to the document window

Save As selected in the navigation bar

click to open the Save As dialog box

you might see additional folders here; if you want to save a document in a folder that is listed here, click the folder to open the Save As dialog box with that folder selected

Because a document is now open, more commands are available in Backstage view than when you started Word. The **navigation bar** on the left contains commands for working with the open document and for changing settings that control how Word works.

▶ **2.** Click the **Browse** button. The Save As dialog box opens.

Trouble? If your instructor wants you to save your files to your OneDrive account, click OneDrive - Personal, and then log in to your account.

▶ **3.** Navigate to the location specified by your instructor. The default filename, "Doc1," appears in the File name box. You will change that to something more descriptive. See Figure 1-4.

Figure 1-4 **Save As dialog box**

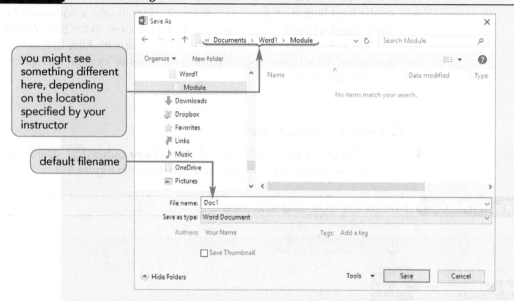

you might see something different here, depending on the location specified by your instructor

default filename

▶ **4.** Click the **File name** box, and then type **Brooks Letter**. The text you type replaces the selected text in the File name box.

▶ **5.** Click the **Save** button. The file is saved, the dialog box and Backstage view close, and the document window appears again, with the new filename in the title bar.

Now that you have saved the document, you can begin typing the letter. Leo has asked you to type a block-style letter to accompany an appraisal that will be sent to Jayla Brooks. Figure 1-5 shows the block-style letter you will create in this module.

Figure 1-5   **Completed block-style letter**

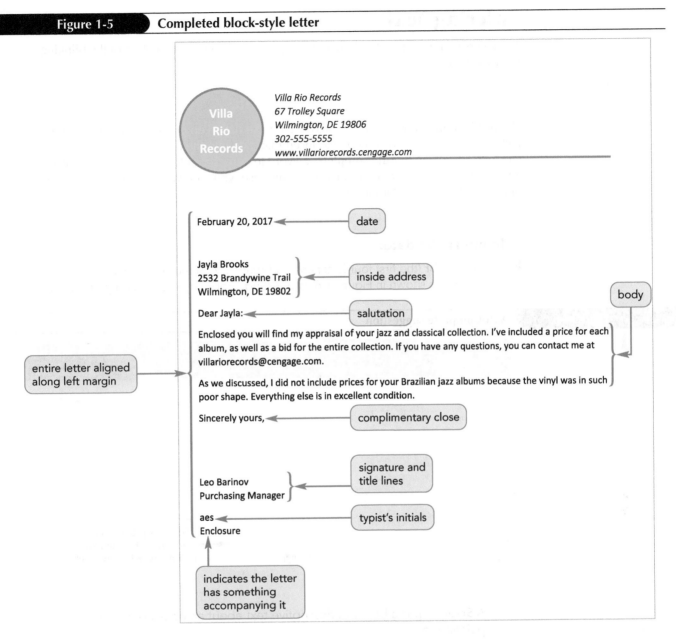

Written Communication: Creating a Business Letter

Several styles are considered acceptable for business letters. The main differences among the styles have to do with how parts of the letter are indented from the left margin. In the block style, which you will use in this module, each line of text starts at the left margin. In other words, nothing is indented. Another style is to indent the first line of each paragraph. The choice of style is largely a matter of personal preference, or it can be determined by the standards used in a particular business or organization. To further enhance your skills in writing business correspondence, you should consult an authoritative book on business writing that provides guidelines for creating a variety of business documents, such as *Business Communication: Process & Product*, by Mary Ellen Guffey.

Entering Text

The letters you type in a Word document appear at the current location of the blinking insertion point.

Inserting a Date with AutoComplete

The first item in a block-style business letter is the date. Leo plans to send the letter to Jayla on February 20, so you need to insert that date into the document. To do so, you can take advantage of **AutoComplete**, a Word feature that automatically inserts dates and other regularly used items for you. In this case, you can type the first few characters of the month and let Word insert the rest.

To insert the date:

▶ **1.** Type **Febr** (the first four letters of "February"). A ScreenTip appears above the letters, as shown in Figure 1-6, suggesting "February" as the complete word.

Figure 1-6	AutoComplete suggestion

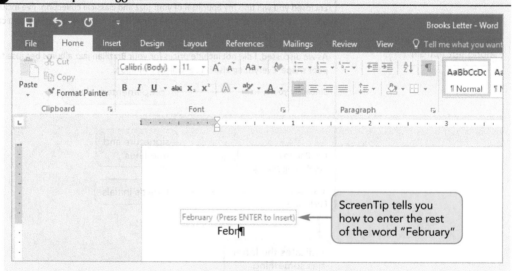

A **ScreenTip** is a box with descriptive text about an object or button you are pointing to.

If you wanted to type something other than "February," you could continue typing to complete the word. In this case, you want to accept the AutoComplete suggestion.

▶ **2.** Press the **Enter** key. The rest of the word "February" is inserted in the document. Note that AutoComplete works for long month names like February but not shorter ones like May, because "Ma" could be the beginning of many words besides "May."

▶ **3.** Press the **spacebar**, type **20, 2017** and then press the **Enter** key twice, leaving a blank paragraph between the date and the line where you will begin typing the inside address, which contains the recipient's name and address. Notice the nonprinting character (•) after the word "February" and before the number "20," which indicates a space. Word inserts this nonprinting character every time you press the spacebar.

Trouble? If February happens to be the current month, you will see a second AutoComplete suggestion displaying the current date after you press the spacebar. To ignore that AutoComplete suggestion, continue typing the rest of the date, as instructed in Step 3.

Continuing to Type the Block-Style Letter

In a block-style business letter, the inside address appears below the date, with one blank paragraph in between. Some style guides recommend including even more space between the date and the inside address. But in the short letter you are typing, more space would make the document look out of balance.

To insert the inside address:

1. Type the following information, pressing the **Enter** key after each item:

   Jayla Brooks

   2532 Brandywine Trail

   Wilmington, DE 19802

   Remember to press the Enter key after you type the ZIP code. Your screen should look like Figure 1-7. Don't be concerned if the lines of the inside address seem too far apart. You'll use the default spacing for now, and then adjust it after you finish typing the letter.

Figure 1-7	Letter with inside address

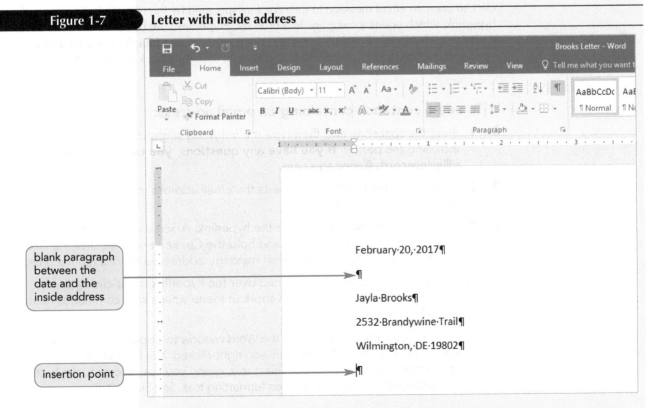

blank paragraph between the date and the inside address

insertion point

Trouble? If you make a mistake while typing, press the Backspace key to delete the incorrect character, and then type the correct character.

Now you can move on to the salutation and the body of the letter. As you type the body of the letter, notice that Word automatically moves the insertion point to a new line when the current line is full.

To type the salutation and the body of the letter:

1. Type **Dear Jayla:** and then press the **Enter** key to start a new paragraph for the body of the letter.

2. Type the following sentence, including the period: **Enclosed you will find my appraisal of your jazz and classical collection.**

3. Press the **spacebar**. Note that you should only include one space between sentences.

4. Type the following sentence, including the period: **I've included a price for each album, as well as a bid for the complete collection.**

5. On the Quick Access Toolbar, click the **Save** button 🔲. Word saves the document as Brooks Letter to the same location you specified earlier.

The next sentence you need to type includes Leo's email address.

Typing a Hyperlink

When you type an email address and then press the spacebar or the Enter key, Word converts it to a hyperlink, with blue font and an underline. A **hyperlink** is text or a graphic you can click to jump to another file or to somewhere else in the same file. The two most common types of hyperlinks are: 1) an email hyperlink, which you can click to open an email message to the recipient specified by the hyperlink; and 2) a web hyperlink, which opens a webpage in a browser. Hyperlinks are useful in documents that you plan to distribute via email. In printed documents, where blue font and underlines can be distracting, you'll usually want to convert a hyperlink back to regular text.

To add a sentence containing an email address:

1. Press the spacebar, and then type the following sentence, including the period: **If you have any questions, you can contact me at villariorecords@cengage.com.**

2. Press the **Enter** key. Word converts the email address to a hyperlink, with blue font and an underline.

3. Position the mouse pointer over the hyperlink. A ScreenTip appears, indicating that you could press and hold the Ctrl key and then click the link to follow it—that is, to open an email message addressed to Villa Rio Records.

4. With the mouse pointer positioned over the hyperlink, right-click—that is, press the right mouse button. A shortcut menu opens with commands related to working with hyperlinks.

   You can right-click many items in the Word window to display a **shortcut menu** with commands related to the item you right-clicked. The **Mini toolbar** also appears when you right-click or select text, giving you easy access to the buttons and settings most often used when formatting text. See Figure 1-8.

Figure 1-8   **Shortcut menu**

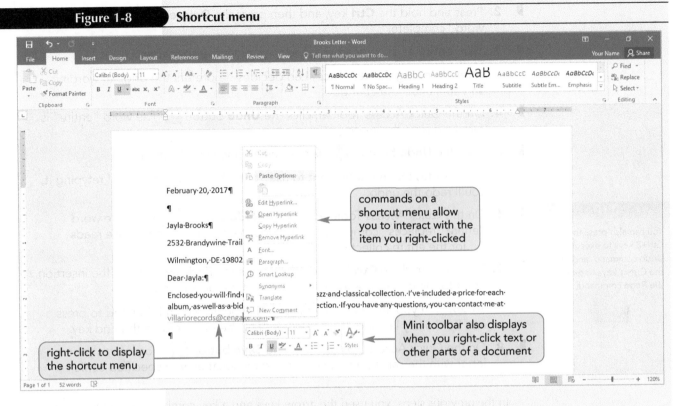

commands on a shortcut menu allow you to interact with the item you right-clicked

right-click to display the shortcut menu

Mini toolbar also displays when you right-click text or other parts of a document

5. Click **Remove Hyperlink** in the shortcut menu. The shortcut menu and the Mini toolbar are no longer visible. The email address is now formatted in black, like the rest of the document text.

6. On the Quick Access Toolbar, click the **Save** button 🖫.

Using the Undo and Redo Buttons

To undo (or reverse) the last thing you did in a document, click the Undo button on the Quick Access Toolbar. To restore your original change, click the Redo button, which reverses the action of the Undo button (or redoes the undo). To undo more than your last action, you can continue to click the Undo button, or you can click the Undo button arrow on the Quick Access Toolbar to open a list of your most recent actions. When you click an action in the list, Word undoes every action in the list up to and including the action you clicked.

Leo asks you to change the word "complete" to "entire" in the second-to-last sentence you typed. You'll make the change now. If Leo decides he doesn't like it after all, you can always undo it. To delete a character, space, or blank paragraph to the right of the insertion point, you use the Delete key; or to delete an entire word, you can press the Ctrl+Delete keys. To delete a character, space, or blank paragraph to the left of the insertion point, you use the Backspace key; or to delete an entire word, you can press the Ctrl+Backspace keys.

To change the word "complete":

1. Press the ↑ key once and then press the → key as necessary to move the insertion point to the left of the "c" in the word "complete."

▶ **2.** Press and hold the **Ctrl** key, and then press the **Delete** key to delete the word "complete."

▶ **3.** Type **entire** as a replacement, and then press the **spacebar**.

After reviewing the sentence, Leo decides he prefers the original wording, so you'll undo the change.

▶ **4.** On the Quick Access Toolbar, click the **Undo** button ↩. The word "entire" is removed from the sentence.

▶ **5.** Click the **Undo** button ↩ again to restore the word "complete."

Leo decides that he does want to use "entire" after all. Instead of retyping it, you'll redo the undo.

TIP

You can also press the Ctrl+Z keys to execute the Undo command, and press the Ctrl+Y keys to execute the Redo command.

▶ **6.** On the Quick Access Toolbar, click the **Redo** button ↪ twice. The word "entire" replaces "complete" in the document, so that the phrase reads "...for the entire collection."

▶ **7.** Press and hold the **Ctrl** key, and then press the **End** key to move the insertion point to the blank paragraph at the end of the document.

Trouble? If you are working on a small keyboard, you might need to press and hold a key labeled "Function" or "FN" before pressing the End key.

▶ **8.** On the Quick Access Toolbar, click the **Save** button 🖫. Word saves your letter with the same name and to the same location you specified earlier.

In the previous steps, you used the arrow keys and a key combination to move the insertion point to specific locations in the document. For your reference, Figure 1-9 summarizes the most common keystrokes for moving the insertion point in a document.

Figure 1-9 **Keystrokes for moving the insertion point**

To Move the Insertion Point	Press
Left or right one character at a time	← or →
Up or down one line at a time	↑ or ↓
Left or right one word at a time	Ctrl+← or Ctrl+→
Up or down one paragraph at a time	Ctrl+↑ or Ctrl+↓
To the beginning or to the end of the current line	Home or End
To the beginning or to the end of the document	Ctrl+Home or Ctrl+End
To the previous screen or to the next screen	Page Up or Page Down
To the top or to the bottom of the document window	Alt+Ctrl+Page Up or Alt+Ctrl+Page Down

Correcting Errors as You Type

As you have seen, you can use the Backspace or Delete keys to remove an error, and then type a correction. In many cases, however, Word's AutoCorrect feature will do the work for you. Among other things, **AutoCorrect** automatically corrects common typing errors, such as typing "adn" instead of "and." For example, you might have noticed AutoCorrect at work if you forgot to capitalize the first letter in a sentence as you typed the letter. After you type this kind of error, AutoCorrect automatically corrects it when you press the spacebar, the Tab key, or the Enter key.

Word draws your attention to other potential errors by marking them with wavy underlines. If you type a word that doesn't match the correct spelling in Word's dictionary, or if a word is not in the dictionary at all, a wavy red line appears beneath it. A wavy red underline also appears if you mistakenly type the same word twice in a row. Misused words (for example, "you're" instead of "your") are underlined with a wavy blue line, as are problems with possessives, punctuation, and plurals.

You'll see how this works as you continue typing the letter and make some intentional typing errors.

To learn more about correcting errors as you type:

1. Type the following sentence, including the errors shown here: **as we discussed, I did not include priices for you're Brazilian jazz albums because teh vynil was in such poor shape. Everything else else is in excellent condition.**

   As you type, AutoCorrect changes the lowercase "a" at the beginning of the sentence to uppercase. It also changes "priices" to "prices and "teh" to "the." Also, the incorrectly used word "you're" is marked with a wavy blue underline. The spelling error "vynil" and the second "else" are marked with wavy red underlines. See Figure 1-10.

Figure 1-10	Errors marked in the document

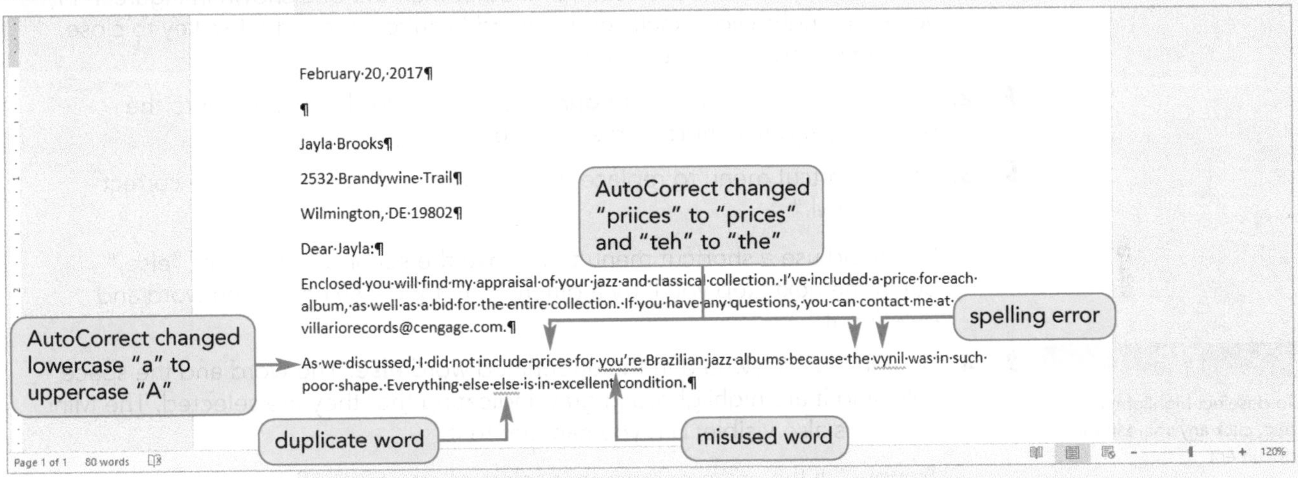

February·20,·2017¶

¶

Jayla·Brooks¶

2532·Brandywine·Trail¶

Wilmington,·DE·19802¶

Dear·Jayla:¶

Enclosed·you·will·find·my·appraisal·of·your·jazz·and·classical·collection.·I've·included·a·price·for·each· album,·as·well·as·a·bid·for·the·entire·collection.·If·you·have·any·questions,·you·can·contact·me·at· villariorecords@cengage.com.¶

As·we·discussed,·I·did·not·include·prices·for·you're·Brazilian·jazz·albums·because·the·vynil·was·in·such· poor·shape.·Everything·else·else·is·in·excellent·condition.¶

AutoCorrect changed "priices" to "prices" and "teh" to "the"

spelling error

AutoCorrect changed lowercase "a" to uppercase "A"

duplicate word

misused word

Page 1 of 1   80 words   120%

To correct an error marked with a wavy underline, you can right-click the error and then click a replacement in the shortcut menu. If you don't see the correct word in the shortcut menu, click anywhere in the document to close the menu, and then type the correction yourself. You can also bypass the shortcut menu entirely and simply delete the error and type a correction.

To correct the spelling and grammar errors:

▶ **1.** Right-click **you're** to display the shortcut menu shown in Figure 1-11.

Figure 1-11	Shortcut menu with suggested spelling

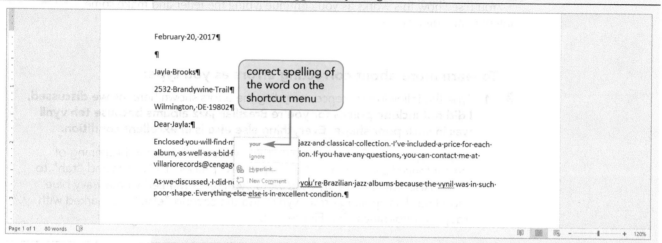

February·20,·2017¶

¶

Jayla·Brooks¶

2532·Brandywine·Trail¶

correct spelling of
the word on the
shortcut menu

Wilmington,·DE·19802¶

Dear·Jayla:¶

Enclosed·you·will·find·m... jazz·and·classical·collection.·I've·included·a·price·for·each·
album,·as·well·as·a·bid·f... your ...ion.·If·you·have·any·questions,·you·can·contact·me·at·
villariorecords@cengag... Ignore

As·we·discussed,·I·did·n... Hyperlink... you're·Brazilian·jazz·albums·because·the·vynil·was·in·such·
poor·shape.·Everything·else·else·is·in·excellent·condition.¶
New Comment

Page 1 of 1   80 words   120%

Trouble? If you see a shortcut menu other than the one shown in Figure 1-11, you didn't right-click exactly on the word "you're." Press the Esc key to close the menu, and then repeat Step 1.

▶ **2.** On the shortcut menu, click **your**. The correct word is inserted into the sentence, and the shortcut menu closes.

▶ **3.** Use a shortcut menu to replace the spelling error "vynil" with the correct word "vinyl."

You could use a shortcut menu to remove the second instance of "else," but in the next step you'll try a different method—selecting the word and deleting it.

▶ **4.** Double-click anywhere in the underlined word **else**. The word and the space following it are highlighted in gray, indicating that they are selected. The Mini toolbar is also visible, but you can ignore it.

Trouble? If the entire paragraph is selected, you triple-clicked the word by mistake. Click anywhere in the document to deselect it, and then repeat Step 4.

▶ **5.** Press the **Delete** key. The second instance of "else" and the space following it are deleted from the sentence.

▶ **6.** On the Quick Access Toolbar, click the **Save** button 🔲.

You can see how quick and easy it is to correct common typing errors with AutoCorrect and the wavy underlines, especially in a short document that you are typing yourself. If you are working on a longer document or a document typed by someone else, you'll also want to have Word check the entire document for errors. You'll learn how to do this in Session 1.2.

Next, you'll finish typing the letter.

To finish typing the letter:

▶ **1.** Press the **Ctrl+End** keys. The insertion point moves to the end of the document.

▶ **2.** Press the **Enter** key, and then type **Sincerely yours,** (including the comma).

▶ **3.** Press the **Enter** key three times to leave space for the signature.

▶ **4.** Type **Leo Barinov** and then press the **Enter** key. Because Leo's last name is not in Word's dictionary, a wavy red line appears below it. You can ignore this for now.

TIP

You need to include your initials in a letter only if you are typing it for someone else.

▶ **5.** Type your first, middle, and last initials in lowercase, and then press the **Enter** key. AutoCorrect wrongly assumes your first initial is the first letter of a new sentence and changes it to uppercase. If your initials do not form a word, a red wavy underline appears beneath them. You can ignore this for now.

▶ **6.** On the Quick Access Toolbar, click the **Undo** button 🔄. Word reverses the change, replacing the uppercase initial with a lowercase one.

▶ **7.** Type **Enclosure**. At this point, your screen should look similar to Figure 1-12.

Figure 1-12	Letter to Jayla Brooks

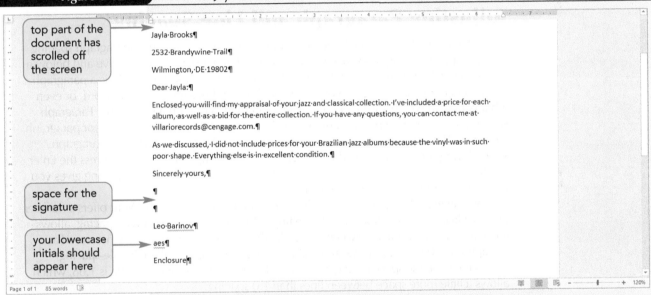

- top part of the document has scrolled off the screen

Jayla·Brooks¶

2532·Brandywine·Trail¶

Wilmington,·DE·19802¶

Dear·Jayla:¶

Enclosed·you·will·find·my·appraisal·of·your·jazz·and·classical·collection.·I've·included·a·price·for·each·album,·as·well·as·a·bid·for·the·entire·collection.·If·you·have·any·questions,·you·can·contact·me·at·villariorecords@cengage.com.¶

As·we·discussed,·I·did·not·include·prices·for·your·Brazilian·jazz·albums·because·the·vinyl·was·in·such·poor·shape.·Everything·else·is·in·excellent·condition.¶

Sincerely·yours,¶

- space for the signature

¶

¶

Leo·Barinov¶

- your lowercase initials should appear here

aes¶

Enclosure¶

Page 1 of 1   85 words

Notice that as you continue to add lines to the letter, the top part of the letter scrolls off the screen. For example, in Figure 1-12, you can no longer see the date.

▶ **8.** Save the document.

Now that you have finished typing the letter, you need to proofread it.

Proofreading a Document

After you finish typing a document, you need to proofread it carefully from start to finish. Part of proofreading a document in Word is removing all wavy underlines, either by correcting the text or by telling Word to ignore the underlined text because it isn't really an error. For example, Leo's last name is marked as an error, when in fact it is spelled correctly. You need to tell Word to ignore "Barinov" wherever it occurs in the letter. You need to do the same for your initials.

To proofread and correct the remaining marked errors in the letter:

▶ **1.** Right-click **Barinov**. A shortcut menu opens.

▶ **2.** On the shortcut menu, click **Ignore All** to indicate that Word should ignore the word "Barinov" each time it occurs in this document. (The Ignore All option can be particularly helpful in a longer document.) The wavy red underline disappears from below Leo's last name.

▶ **3.** If you see a wavy red underline below your initials, right-click your initials. On the shortcut menu, click **Ignore All** to remove the red wavy underline.

▶ **4.** Read the entire letter to proofread it for typing errors. Correct any errors using the techniques you have just learned.

▶ **5.** Save the document.

The text of the letter is finished. Now you need to think about its appearance—that is, you need to think about the document's **formatting**. First, you need to adjust the spacing in the inside address.

Adjusting Paragraph and Line Spacing

When typing a letter, you might need to adjust two types of spacing—paragraph spacing and line spacing. **Paragraph spacing** is the space that appears directly above and below a paragraph. In Word, any text that ends with a paragraph mark symbol (¶) is a paragraph. So, a **paragraph** can be a group of words that is many lines long, a single word, or even a blank line, in which case you see a paragraph mark alone on a single line. Paragraph spacing is measured in points; a **point** is 1/72 of an inch. The default setting for paragraph spacing in Word is 0 points before each paragraph and 8 points after each paragraph. When laying out a complicated document, resist the temptation to simply press the Enter key to insert extra space between paragraphs. Changing the paragraph spacing gives you much more control over the final result.

Line spacing is the space between lines of text within a paragraph. Word offers a number of preset line spacing options. The 1.0 setting, which is often called **single-spacing**, allows the least amount of space between lines. All other line spacing options are measured as multiples of 1.0 spacing. For example, 2.0 spacing (sometimes called **double-spacing**) allows for twice the space of single-spacing. The default line spacing setting is 1.08, which allows a little more space between lines than 1.0 spacing.

Now consider the line and paragraph spacing in the Brooks letter. The three lines of the inside address are too far apart. That's because each line of the inside address is actually a separate paragraph. Word inserted the default 8 points of paragraph spacing after each of these separate paragraphs. See Figure 1-13.

Figure 1-13   Line and paragraph spacing in the letter to Jayla Brooks

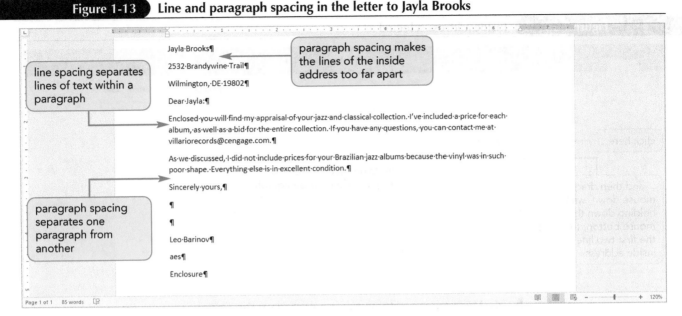

To follow the conventions of a block-style business letter, the three paragraphs that make up the inside address should have the same spacing as the lines of text within a single paragraph—that is, they need to be closer together. You can accomplish this by removing the 8 points of paragraph spacing after the first two paragraphs in the inside address. To conform to the block-style business letter format, you also need to close up the spacing between your initials and the word "Enclosure" at the end of the letter.

To adjust paragraph and line spacing in Word, you use the Line and Paragraph Spacing button in the Paragraph group on the Home tab. Clicking this button displays a menu of preset line spacing options (1.0, 1.15, 2.0, and so on). The menu also includes two paragraph spacing options that allow you to add 12 points before a paragraph or remove the default 8 points of space after a paragraph.

Next you'll adjust the paragraph spacing in the inside address and after your initials. In the process, you'll also learn some techniques for selecting text in a document.

To adjust the paragraph spacing in the inside address and after your initials:

1. Move the pointer to the white space just to the left of "Jayla Brooks" until it changes to a right-facing arrow ⌐.

2. Click the mouse button. The entire name, including the paragraph symbol after it, is selected.

   Trouble? If the Mini toolbar obscures your view of Jayla's name, move the mouse pointer away from the address to close the Mini toolbar.

3. Press and hold the mouse button, drag the pointer ⌐ down to select the next paragraph of the inside address as well, and then release the mouse button.

   The name and street address are selected as well as the paragraph marks at the end of each paragraph. You did not select the paragraph containing the city, state, and ZIP code because you do not need to change its paragraph spacing. See Figure 1-14.

TIP

The white space in the left margin is sometimes referred to as the selection bar because you click it to select text.

Figure 1-14   Inside address selected

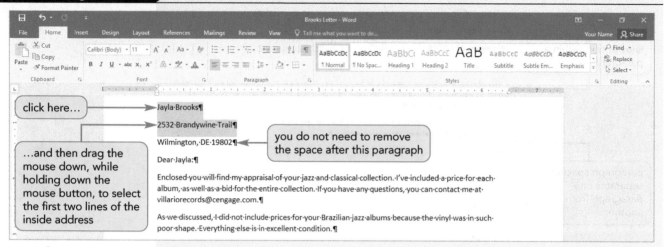

4. Make sure the Home tab is selected on the ribbon.

5. In the Paragraph group on the Home tab, click the **Line and Paragraph Spacing** button. A menu of line spacing options appears, with two paragraph spacing options at the bottom. See Figure 1-15.

Figure 1-15   Line and paragraph spacing options

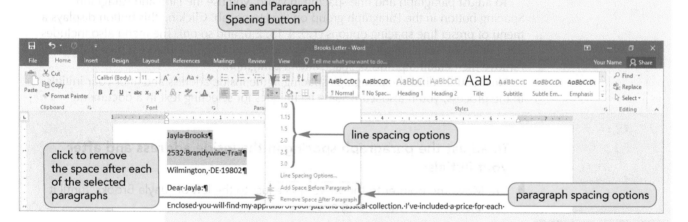

At the moment, you are interested only in the paragraph spacing options. Your goal is to remove the default 8 points of space after the first two paragraphs in the inside address.

6. Click **Remove Space After Paragraph**. The menu closes, and the paragraphs are now closer together.

7. Double-click your initials to select them and the paragraph symbol after them.

8. In the Paragraph group, click the **Line and Paragraph Spacing** button, click **Remove Space After Paragraph**, and then click anywhere in the document to deselect your initials.

Another way to compress lines of text is to press the Shift+Enter keys at the end of a line. This inserts a **manual line break**, also called a **soft return**, which moves the insertion point to a new line without starting a new paragraph. You will use this technique now as you add Leo's title below his name in the signature line.

To use a manual line break to move the insertion point to a new line without starting a new paragraph:

▶ **1.** Click to the right of the "v" in "Barinov."

▶ **2.** Press the **Shift+Enter** keys. Word inserts a small arrow symbol ⏎, indicating a manual line break, and the insertion point moves to the line below Leo's name.

▶ **3.** Type **Purchasing Manager**. Leo's title now appears directly below his name with no intervening paragraph spacing, just like the lines of the inside address.

▶ **4.** Save the document.

INSIGHT

Understanding Spacing Between Paragraphs

When discussing the correct format for letters, many business style guides talk about single-spacing and double-spacing between paragraphs. In these style guides, to single-space between paragraphs means to press the Enter key once after each paragraph. Likewise, to double-space between paragraphs means to press the Enter key twice after each paragraph. With the default paragraph spacing in Word 2016, however, you need to press the Enter key only once after a paragraph. The space Word adds after a paragraph is not quite the equivalent of double-spacing, but it is enough to make it easy to see where one paragraph ends and another begins. Keep this in mind if you're accustomed to pressing the Enter key twice; otherwise, you could end up with more space than you want between paragraphs.

As you corrected line and paragraph spacing in the previous set of steps, you used the mouse to select text. Word provides multiple ways to select, or highlight, text as you work. Figure 1-16 summarizes these methods and explains when to use them most effectively.

Figure 1-16   **Methods for selecting text**

To Select	Mouse	Keyboard	Mouse and Keyboard
A word	Double-click the word	Move the insertion point to the beginning of the word, press and hold Ctrl+Shift, and then press →	
A line	Click in the white space to the left of the line	Move the insertion point to the beginning of the line, press and hold Shift, and then press ↓	
A sentence	Click at the beginning of the sentence, then drag the pointer until the sentence is selected		Press and hold Ctrl, then click any location within the sentence
Multiple lines	Click and drag in the white space to the left of the lines	Move the insertion point to the beginning of the first line, press and hold Shift, and then press ↓ until all the lines are selected	
A paragraph	Double-click in the white space to the left of the paragraph, or triple-click at any location within the paragraph	Move the insertion point to the beginning of the paragraph, press and hold Ctrl+Shift, and then press ↓	
Multiple paragraphs	Click in the white space to the left of the first paragraph you want to select, and then drag to select the remaining paragraphs	Move the insertion point to the beginning of the first paragraph, press and hold Ctrl+Shift, and then press ↓ until all the paragraphs are selected	
An entire document	Triple-click in the white space to the left of the document text	Press Ctrl+A	Press and hold Ctrl, and click in the white space to the left of the document text
A block of text	Click at the beginning of the block, then drag the pointer until the entire block is selected		Click at the beginning of the block, press and hold Shift, and then click at the end of the block
Nonadjacent blocks of text			Press and hold Ctrl, then drag the mouse pointer to select multiple blocks of nonadjacent text

Adjusting the Margins

Another important aspect of document formatting is the amount of margin space between the document text and the edge of the page. You can check the document's margins by changing the Zoom level to display the entire page.

To change the Zoom level to display the entire page:

1. On the ribbon, click the **View** tab.

2. In the Zoom group, click the **One Page** button. The entire document is now visible in the Word window. See Figure 1-17.

| Figure 1-17 | Document zoomed to show entire page |

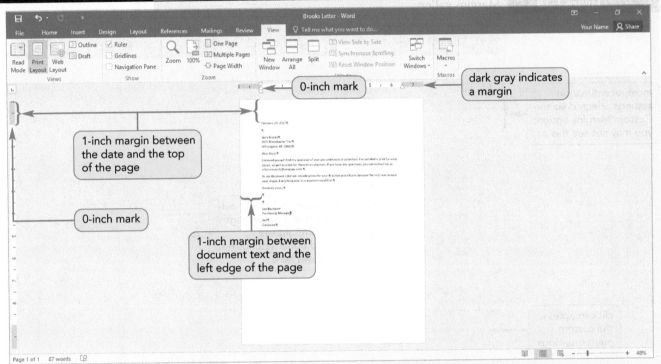

On the rulers, the margins appear dark gray. By default, Word documents include 1-inch margins on all sides of the document. By looking at the vertical ruler, you can see that the date in the letter, the first line in the document, is located 1 inch from the top of the page. Likewise, the horizontal ruler indicates the document text begins 1 inch from the left edge of the page.

Reading the measurements on the rulers can be tricky at first. On the horizontal ruler, the 0-inch mark is like the origin on a number line. You measure from the 0-inch mark to the left or to the right. On the vertical ruler, you measure up or down from the 0-inch mark.

Leo plans to print the letter on Villa Rio Records letterhead, which includes a graphic and the company's address. To allow more blank space for the letterhead, and to move the text down so that it doesn't look so crowded at the top of the page, you need to increase the top margin. The settings for changing the page margins are located on the Layout tab on the ribbon.

To change the page margins:

▶ 1. On the ribbon, click the **Layout** tab. The Layout tab displays options for adjusting the layout of your document.

▶ 2. In the Page Setup group, click the **Margins** button. The Margins gallery opens, as shown in Figure 1-18.

Figure 1-18   **Margins gallery**

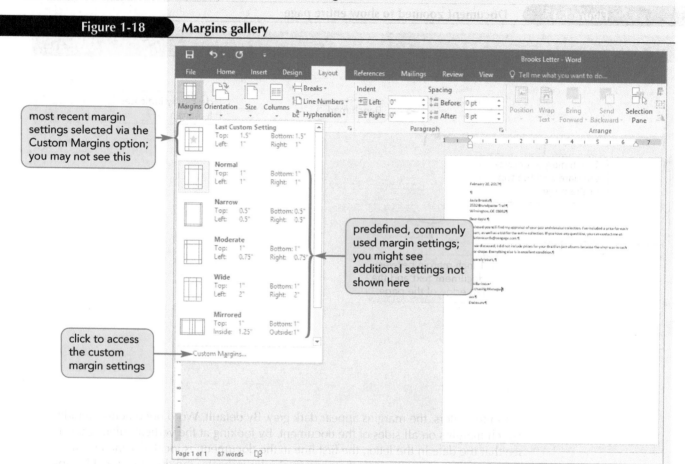

most recent margin settings selected via the Custom Margins option; you may not see this

predefined, commonly used margin settings; you might see additional settings not shown here

click to access the custom margin settings

In the Margins gallery, you can choose from a number of predefined margin options, or you can click the Custom Margins command to select your own settings. After you create custom margin settings, the most recent set appears as an option at the top of the menu. For the Brooks Letter document, you will create custom margins.

▶ 3. Click **Custom Margins**. The Page Setup dialog box opens with the Margins tab displayed. The default margin settings are displayed in the boxes at the top of the Margins tab. The top margin of 1" is already selected, ready for you to type a new margin setting.

▶ 4. In the Top box in the Margins section, type **2.5**. You do not need to type an inch mark ("). See Figure 1-19.

Figure 1-19   Creating custom margins in the Page Setup dialog box

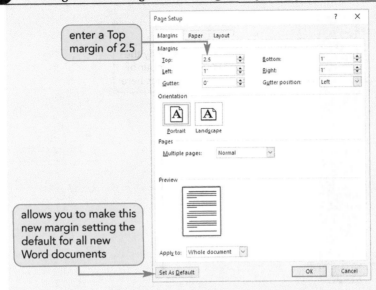

enter a Top margin of 2.5

allows you to make this new margin setting the default for all new Word documents

5. Click the **OK** button. The text of the letter is now lower on the page. The page looks less crowded, with room for the company's letterhead.

6. Change the Zoom level back to **120%**, and then save the document.

For most documents, the Word default of 1-inch margins is fine. In some professional settings, however, you might need to use a particular custom margin setting for all your documents. In that case, define the custom margins using the Margins tab in the Page Setup dialog box, and then click the Set As Default button to make your settings the default for all new documents. Keep in mind that most printers can't print to the edge of the page; if you select custom margins that are too narrow for your printer's specifications, Word alerts you to change your margin settings.

Previewing and Printing a Document

To make sure the document is ready to print, and to avoid wasting paper and time, you should first review it in Backstage view to make sure it will look right when printed. Like the One Page zoom setting you used earlier, the Print option in Backstage view displays a full-page preview of the document, allowing you to see how it will fit on the printed page. However, you cannot actually edit this preview. It simply provides one last opportunity to look at the document before printing.

To preview the document:

1. Proofread the document one last time, and correct any remaining errors.

2. Click the **File** tab to display Backstage view.

3. In the navigation bar, click **Print**.

The Print screen displays a full-page version of your document, showing how the letter will fit on the printed page. The Print settings to the left of the preview allow you to control a variety of print options. For example, you can change the number of copies from the default setting of "1." The 1 Page Per Sheet button opens a menu where you can choose to print multiple pages on a single sheet of paper or to scale the printed page to a particular paper size. You can also use the navigation controls at the bottom of the screen to display other pages in a document. See Figure 1-20.

Figure 1-20   **Print settings in Backstage view**

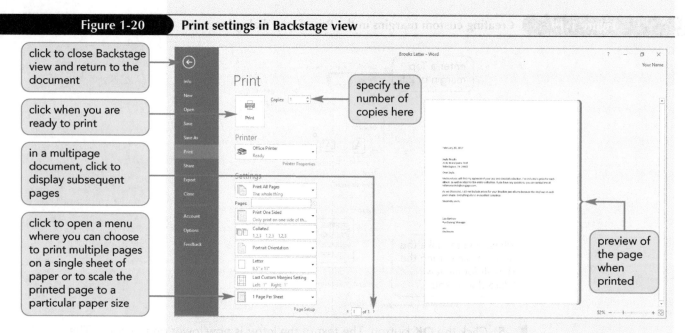

click to close Backstage view and return to the document

click when you are ready to print

in a multipage document, click to display subsequent pages

click to open a menu where you can choose to print multiple pages on a single sheet of paper or to scale the printed page to a particular paper size

specify the number of copies here

preview of the page when printed

4. Review your document and make sure its overall layout matches that of the document in Figure 1-20. If you notice a problem with paragraph breaks or spacing, click the **Back** button ⬅ at the top of the navigation bar to return to the document, make any necessary changes, and then start again at Step 2.

At this point, you can print the document or you can leave Backstage view and return to the document in Print Layout view. In the following steps, you should print the document only if your instructor asks you to. If you will be printing the document, make sure your printer is turned on and contains paper.

To leave Backstage view or to print the document:

1. Click the **Back** button at the top of the navigation bar ⬅ to leave Backstage view and return to the document in Print Layout view, or click the **Print** button. Backstage view closes, and the letter prints if you clicked the Print button.

2. Click the **File** tab, and then click **Close** in the navigation bar to close the document without closing Word.

Next, Leo asks you to create an envelope he can use to send an appraisal to another potential record seller.

Creating an Envelope

Before you can create the envelope, you need to open a new, blank document. To create a new document, you can start with a blank document—as you did with the letter to Jayla Brooks—or you can start with one that already contains formatting and generic text commonly used in a variety of professional documents, such as a fax cover sheet or a memo. These preformatted files are called **templates**. You could use a template to create a formatted envelope, but first you'll learn how to create one on your own in a new, blank document. You'll have a chance to try out a template in the Case Problems at the end of this module.

To create a new document for the envelope:

▶ **1.** Click the **File** tab, and then click **New** in the navigation bar. The New screen is similar to the one you saw when you first started Word, with a blank document in the upper-left corner, along with a variety of templates. See Figure 1-21.

| Figure 1-21 | New options in Backstage view |

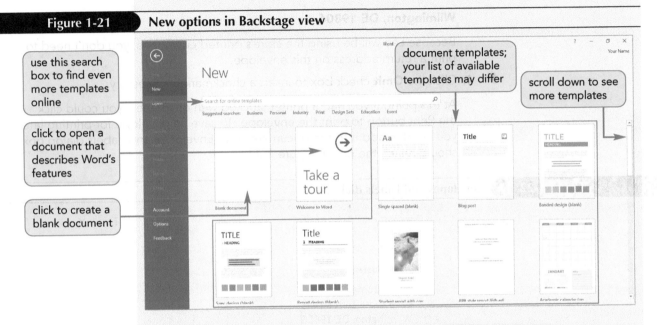

- use this search box to find even more templates online
- document templates; your list of available templates may differ
- scroll down to see more templates
- click to open a document that describes Word's features
- click to create a blank document

▶ **2.** Click **Blank document**. A new document named Document2 opens in the document window, with the Home tab selected on the ribbon.

▶ **3.** If necessary, change the Zoom level to **120%**, and display nonprinting characters and the rulers.

▶ **4.** Save the new document as **Gomez Envelope** in the location specified by your instructor.

To create the envelope:

▶ **1.** On the ribbon, click the **Mailings** tab. The ribbon changes to display the various Mailings options.

▶ **2.** In the Create group, click the **Envelopes** button. The Envelopes and Labels dialog box opens, with the Envelopes tab displayed. The insertion point appears in the Delivery address box, ready for you to type the recipient's address. Depending on how your computer is set up, and whether you are working on your own computer or a school computer, you might see an address in the Return address box.

▶ **3.** In the Delivery address box, type the following address, pressing the Enter key to start each new line:

Alexis Gomez

6549 West 16th Street

Wilmington, DE 19806

Because Leo will be using the store's printed envelopes, you don't need to print a return address on this envelope.

▶ **4.** Click the **Omit** check box to insert a checkmark, if necessary.

At this point, if you had a printer stocked with envelopes, you could click the Print button to print the envelope. To save an envelope for printing later, you need to add it to the document. Your Envelopes and Labels dialog box should match the one in Figure 1-22.

Figure 1-22   **Envelopes and Labels dialog box**

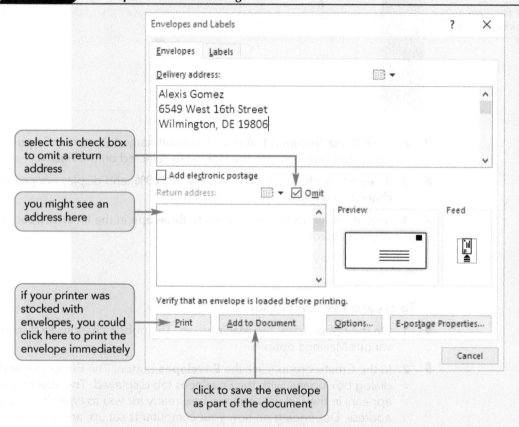

select this check box to omit a return address

you might see an address here

if your printer was stocked with envelopes, you could click here to print the envelope immediately

click to save the envelope as part of the document

▶ **5.** Click the **Add to Document** button. The dialog box closes, and you return to the document window. The envelope is inserted at the top of your document, with 1.0 line spacing. The double line with the words "Section Break (Next Page)" is related to how the envelope is formatted and will not be visible when you print the envelope. The envelope will print in the standard business envelope format. In this case, you added the envelope to a blank document, but you could also add an envelope to a completed letter, in which case Word adds the envelope as a new page before the letter.

▶ **6.** Save the document. Leo will print the envelope later, so you can close the document now.

▶ **7.** Click the **File** tab, and then click **Close** in the navigation bar. The document closes, but Word remains open.

You're finished creating the cover letter and the envelope. In the next session, you will modify a flyer by formatting the text and adding a photo.

INSIGHT

Creating Documents with Templates

Microsoft offers predesigned templates for all kinds of documents, including calendars, reports, and thank-you cards. You can use the scroll bar on the right of the New screen (shown earlier in Figure 1-21) to scroll down to see more templates, or you can use the Search for online templates box in the New screen to search among thousands of other options available at Office.com. When you open a template, you actually open a new document containing the formatting and text stored in the template, leaving the original template untouched. A typical template includes placeholder text that you replace with your own information.

Templates allow you to create stylish, professional-looking documents quickly and easily. To use them effectively, however, you need to be knowledgeable about Word and its many options for manipulating text, graphics, and page layouts. Otherwise, the complicated formatting of some Word templates can be more frustrating than helpful. As you become a more experienced Word user, you'll learn how to create your own templates.

REVIEW

Session 1.1 Quick Check

1. What Word feature automatically inserts dates and other regularly used items for you?

2. In a block-style letter, does the inside address appear above or below the date?

3. Explain how to display nonprinting characters.

4. Explain how to use a hyperlink in a Word document to open a new email message.

5. Define the term "line spacing."

6. Explain how to display a shortcut menu with options for correcting a word with a wavy red underline.

Session 1.2 Visual Overview:

Alignment buttons control the text's alignment—that is, the way it lines up horizontally between the left and right margins. Here, the Center button is selected because the text containing the insertion point is center-aligned.

You can click the Clear All Formatting button to restore selected text to the default font, font size, and color.

Clicking the Format Painter button displays the Format Painter pointer, which you can use to copy formatting from the selected text to other text in the document.

The Font group on the Home tab includes the Font box and the Font size box for setting the text's font and the font size, respectively. A font is a set of characters that uses the same typeface.

This document has a landscape orientation, meaning it is wider than it is tall.

You can insert a photo or another type of picture in a document by using the Pictures button located on the Insert tab of the ribbon. After you insert a photo or another picture, you can format it with a style that adds a border or a shadow or changes its shape.

You click the Shading button arrow to apply a colored background to a selected paragraph.

The boldface and blue font color applied to this text are examples of formatting that you should use sparingly to draw attention to a specific part of a document.

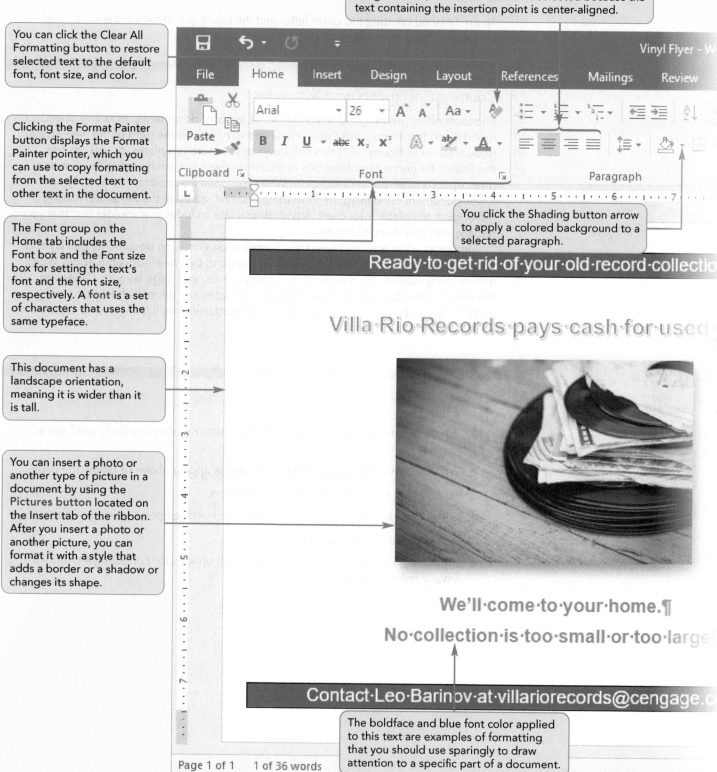

iravgustin/Shutterstock.com

Formatting a Document

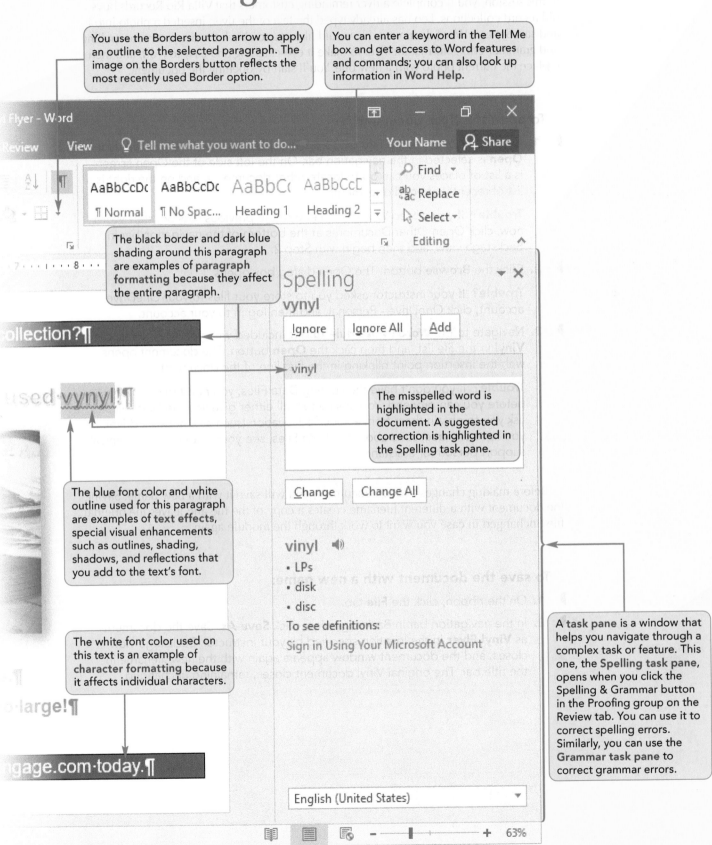

You use the Borders button arrow to apply an outline to the selected paragraph. The image on the Borders button reflects the most recently used Border option.

You can enter a keyword in the Tell Me box and get access to Word features and commands; you can also look up information in **Word Help**.

The black border and dark blue shading around this paragraph are examples of **paragraph formatting** because they affect the entire paragraph.

The misspelled word is highlighted in the document. A suggested correction is highlighted in the Spelling task pane.

The blue font color and white outline used for this paragraph are examples of **text effects**, special visual enhancements such as outlines, shading, shadows, and reflections that you add to the text's font.

The white font color used on this text is an example of **character formatting** because it affects individual characters.

A task pane is a window that helps you navigate through a complex task or feature. This one, the Spelling task pane, opens when you click the Spelling & Grammar button in the Proofing group on the Review tab. You can use it to correct spelling errors. Similarly, you can use the **Grammar task pane** to correct grammar errors.

Opening an Existing Document

In this session, you'll complete a flyer reminding customers that Villa Rio Records buys old record collections. Leo has already typed the text of the flyer, inserted a photo into it, and saved it as a Word document. He would like you to check the document for spelling and grammar errors, format the flyer to make it eye-catching and easy to read, and then replace the current photo with a new one. You'll start by opening the document.

To open the flyer document:

1. On the ribbon, click the **File** tab to open Backstage view, and then verify that **Open** is selected in the navigation bar. On the left side of the Open screen is a list of places you can go to locate other documents, and on the right is a list of recently opened documents.

   Trouble? If you closed Word at the end of the previous session, start Word now, click Open Other Documents at the bottom of the navigation bar in Backstage view, and then begin with Step 2.

2. Click the **Browse** button. The Open dialog box opens.

   Trouble? If your instructor asked you to store your files to your OneDrive account, click OneDrive - Personal, and then log in to your account.

3. Navigate to the **Word1 > Module folder** included with your Data Files, click **Vinyl** in the file list, and then click the **Open** button. The document opens with the insertion point blinking in the first line of the document.

   Trouble? If you don't have the starting Data Files, you need to get them before you can proceed. Your instructor will either give you the Data Files or ask you to obtain them from a specified location (such as a network drive). If you have any questions about the Data Files, see your instructor or technical support person for assistance.

Before making changes to Leo's document, you will save it with a new name. Saving the document with a different filename creates a copy of the file and leaves the original file unchanged in case you want to work through the module again.

To save the document with a new name:

1. On the ribbon, click the **File** tab.

2. In the navigation bar in Backstage view, click **Save As**. Save the document as **Vinyl Flyer** in the location specified by your instructor. Backstage view closes, and the document window appears again with the new filename in the title bar. The original Vinyl document closes, remaining unchanged.

PROSKILLS

Decision Making: Creating Effective Documents

Before you create a new document or revise an existing document, take a moment to think about your audience. Ask yourself these questions:

- Who is your audience?
- What do they know?
- What do they need to know?
- How can the document you are creating change your audience's behavior or opinions?

Every decision you make about your document should be based on your answers to these questions. To take a simple example, if you are creating a flyer to announce an upcoming seminar on college financial aid, your audience would be students and their parents. They probably all know what the term "financial aid" means, so you don't need to explain that in your flyer. Instead, you can focus on telling them what they need to know—the date, time, and location of the seminar. The behavior you want to affect, in this case, is whether or not your audience will show up for the seminar. By making the flyer professional looking and easy to read, you increase the chance that they will.

You might find it more challenging to answer these questions about your audience when creating more complicated documents, such as corporate reports. But the focus remains the same—connecting with the audience. As you are deciding what information to include in your document, remember that the goal of a professional document is to convey the information as effectively as possible to your target audience.

Before revising a document for someone else, it's a good idea to familiarize yourself with its overall structure.

To review the document:

1. Verify that the document is displayed in Print Layout view and that nonprinting characters and the rulers are displayed. For now, you can ignore the wavy underlines that appear in the document.

2. Change the Zoom level to **120%**, if necessary, and then scroll down, if necessary, so that you can read the last line of the document.

At this point, the document is very simple. By the time you are finished, it will look like the document shown in the Session 1.2 Visual Overview, with the spelling and grammar errors corrected. Figure 1-23 summarizes the tasks you will perform.

Figure 1-23 | **Formatting changes requested by Leo**

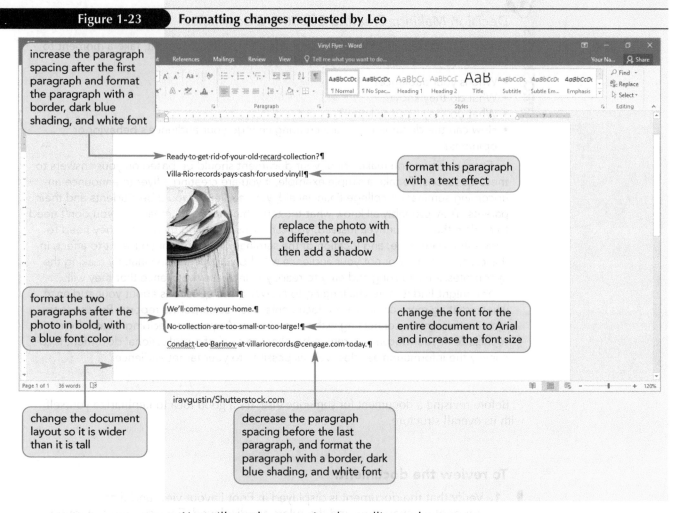

iravgustin/Shutterstock.com

You will start by correcting the spelling and grammar errors.

Using the Spelling and Grammar Task Panes

Word marks possible spelling and grammatical errors with wavy underlines as you type so that you can quickly go back and correct those errors. A more thorough way of checking the spelling in a document is to use the Spelling and Grammar task panes to check a document word by word for a variety of errors. You can customize the spelling and grammar settings to add or ignore certain types of errors.

Leo asks you to use the Spelling and Grammar task panes to check the flyer for mistakes. Before you do, you'll review the various Spelling and Grammar settings.

To review the Spelling and Grammar settings:

▶ **1.** On the ribbon, click the **File** tab, and then click **Options** in the navigation bar. The Word Options dialog box opens. You can use this dialog box to change a variety of settings related to how Word looks and works.

2. In the left pane, click **Proofing**.

Note the four selected options in the "When correcting spelling and grammar in Word" section. The first three options tell you that Word will check for misspellings, grammatical errors, and frequently confused words as you type, marking them with wavy underlines as necessary. The fourth option, "Check grammar with spelling," tells you that Word will check both grammar and spelling when you use the Spelling and Grammar task pane. If you want to check only spelling, you could deselect this check box.

3. In the "When correcting spelling and grammar in Word" section, click the **Settings** button. The Grammar Settings dialog box opens. Here you can control the types of grammar errors Word checks for. All of the boxes are selected by default, which is what you want. See Figure 1-24.

Figure 1-24	Grammar Settings dialog box

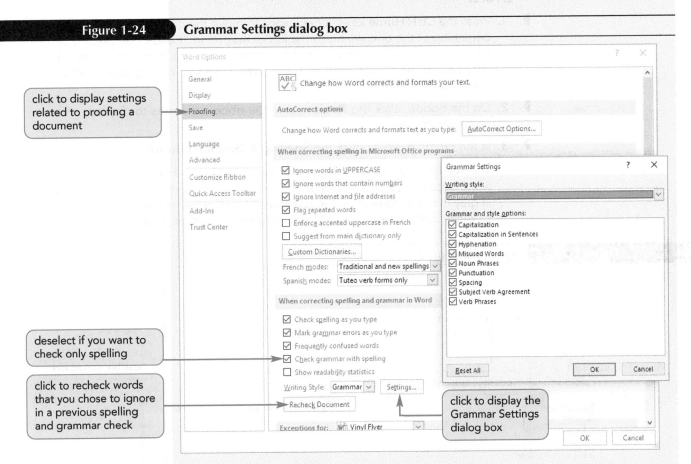

click to display settings related to proofing a document

deselect if you want to check only spelling

click to recheck words that you chose to ignore in a previous spelling and grammar check

click to display the Grammar Settings dialog box

4. Click the **Cancel** button to close the Grammar Settings dialog box and return to the Word Options dialog box.

Note that the results of the Spelling and Grammar checker are sometimes hard to predict. For example, in some documents Word will mark a misused word or duplicate punctuation as errors and then fail to mark the same items as errors in another document. Also, if you choose to ignore a misspelling in a document, and then, without closing Word, type the same misspelled word in another document, Word will probably not mark it as an error. These issues can be especially problematic when working on a document typed by someone else. So to ensure that you get the best possible results, it's a good idea to click the Recheck Document button before you use the Spelling and Grammar checker.

5. Click the **Recheck Document** button, and then click **Yes** in the warning dialog box.

6. In the Word Options dialog box, click the **OK** button to close the dialog box. You return to the Vinyl Flyer document.

Now you are ready to check the document's spelling and grammar. All errors marked with red underlines are considered spelling errors, while all errors marked with blue underlines are considered grammatical errors.

To check the Vinyl Flyer document for spelling and grammatical errors:

1. Press the **Ctrl+Home** keys, if necessary, to move the insertion point to the beginning of the document, to the left of the "R" in "Ready." By placing the insertion point at the beginning of the document, you ensure that Word will check the entire document from start to finish, without having to go back and check an earlier part.

2. On the ribbon, click the **Review** tab. The ribbon changes to display reviewing options.

3. In the Proofing group, click the **Spelling & Grammar** button.

The Spelling task pane opens on the right side of the Word window, with the word "recard" listed as a possible spelling error. The same word is highlighted in gray in the document. In the task pane's list of possible corrections, the correctly spelled word "record" is highlighted in light blue. See Figure 1-25.

Figure 1-25	Spelling task pane

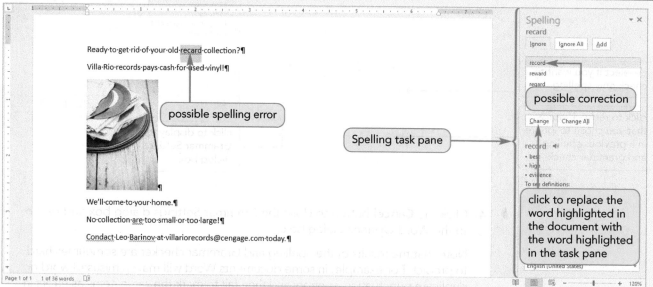

iravgustin/Shutterstock.com

4. In the task pane, click the **Change** button. The misspelled word "recard" is replaced with "record."

Next, Word highlights the second to last sentence, indicating another possible error. The Spelling task pane changes to the Grammar task pane, and the information at the bottom of the task pane explains that the error is related to subject-verb agreement.

5. Verify that "is" is selected in the Grammar task pane, and then click the **Change** button. The first word of the last sentence is now highlighted in the document, and the Grammar task pane changes to the Spelling task pane. You could correct this misspelling by using the options in the Spelling task pane, but this time you'll try typing directly in the document.

6. In the document, click to the right of the "d" in "Condact," press the **Backspace** key, type **t**, and then click the **Resume** button in the Spelling task pane. Leo's last name is now highlighted in the document. Although the Spelling task pane doesn't recognize "Barinov" as a word, it is spelled correctly, so you can ignore it.

7. Click the **Ignore** button in the Spelling task pane. The task pane closes, and a dialog box opens, indicating that the spelling and grammar check is complete.

8. Click the **OK** button to close the dialog box.

PROSKILLS

Written Communication: Proofreading Your Document

Although the Spelling and Grammar task panes are useful tools, they won't always catch every error in a document, and they sometimes flag "errors" that are actually correct. This means there is no substitute for careful proofreading. Always take the time to read through your document to check for errors the Spelling and Grammar task panes might have missed. Keep in mind that the Spelling and Grammar task panes cannot pinpoint inaccurate phrases or poorly chosen words. You'll have to find those yourself. To produce a professional document, you must read it carefully several times. It's a good idea to ask one or two other people to read your documents as well; they might catch something you missed.

You still need to proofread the Vinyl Flyer document. You'll do that next.

To proofread the Vinyl Flyer document:

1. Review the document text for any remaining errors. In the second paragraph, change the lowercase "r" in "records" to an uppercase "R."

2. In the last line of text, replace "Leo Barinov" with your first and last names, and then save the document. Including your name in the document will make it easier for you to find your copy later if you print it on a shared printer.

Now you're ready to begin formatting the document. You will start by turning the page so it is wider than it is tall. In other words, you will change the document's **orientation**.

Changing Page Orientation

Portrait orientation, with the page taller than it is wide, is the default page orientation for Word documents because it is the orientation most commonly used for letters, reports, and other formal documents. However, Leo wants you to format the flyer in **landscape orientation**—that is, with the page turned so it is wider than it is tall—to better accommodate the photo. You can accomplish this task by using the Orientation button located on the Layout tab on the ribbon. After you change the page orientation, you will select narrower margins so you can maximize the amount of color on the page.

To change the page orientation:

▶ **1.** Change the document Zoom level to **One Page** so that you can see the entire document.

▶ **2.** On the ribbon, click the **Layout** tab. The ribbon changes to display options for formatting the overall layout of text and images in the document.

▶ **3.** In the Page Setup group, click the **Orientation** button, and then click **Landscape** on the menu. The document changes to landscape orientation.

▶ **4.** In the Page Setup group, click the **Margins** button, and then click the **Narrow** option on the menu. The margins shrink from 1 inch to .5 inch on all four sides. See Figure 1-26.

Figure 1-26	Document in landscape orientation with narrow margins

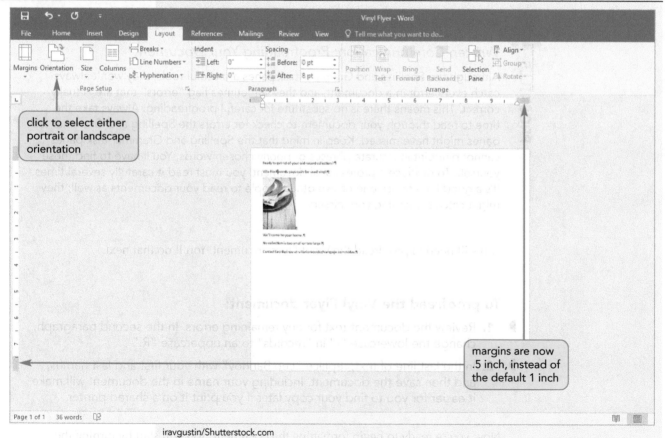

click to select either portrait or landscape orientation

margins are now .5 inch, instead of the default 1 inch

iravgustin/Shutterstock.com

Changing the Font and Font Size

Leo typed the document in the default font size, 11 point, and the default font, Calibri, but he would like to switch to the Arial font instead. Also, he wants to increase the size of all five paragraphs of text. To apply these changes, you start by selecting the text you want to format. Then you select the options you want in the Font group on the Home tab.

To change the font and font size:

▶ **1.** On the ribbon, click the **Home** tab.

▶ **2.** Change the document Zoom level to **120%**.

▶ **3.** To verify that the insertion point is located at the beginning of the document, press the **Ctrl+Home** keys.

▶ **4.** Press and hold the **Shift** key, and then click to the right of the second paragraph marker, at the end of the second paragraph of text. The first two paragraphs of text are selected, as shown in Figure 1-27.

Figure 1-27 ▶ **Selected text, with default font displayed in Font box**

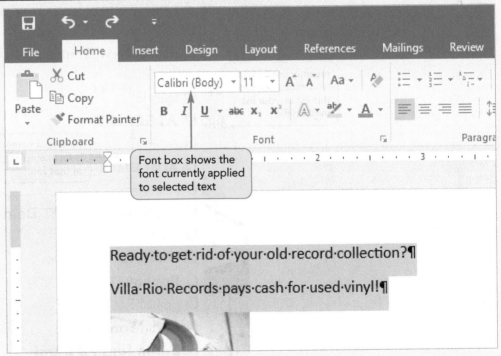

Font box shows the font currently applied to selected text

Ready·to·get·rid·of·your·old·record·collection?¶

Villa·Rio·Records·pays·cash·for·used·vinyl!¶

iravgustin/Shutterstock.com

The Font box in the Font group displays the name of the font applied to the selected text, which in this case is Calibri. The word "Body" next to the font name indicates that the Calibri font is intended for formatting body text. **Body text** is ordinary text, as opposed to titles or headings.

▶ **5.** In the Font group on the Home tab, click the **Font** arrow. A list of available fonts appears, with Calibri Light and Calibri at the top of the list. Calibri is highlighted in gray, indicating that this font is currently applied to the selected text. The word "Headings" next to the font name "Calibri Light" indicates that Calibri Light is intended for formatting headings.

Below Calibri Light and Calibri, you might see a list of fonts that have been used recently on your computer, followed by a complete alphabetical list of all available fonts. (You won't see the list of recently used fonts if you just installed Word.) You need to scroll the list to see all the available fonts. Each name in the list is formatted with the relevant font. For example, the name "Arial" appears in the Arial font. See Figure 1-28.

Figure 1-28 Font list

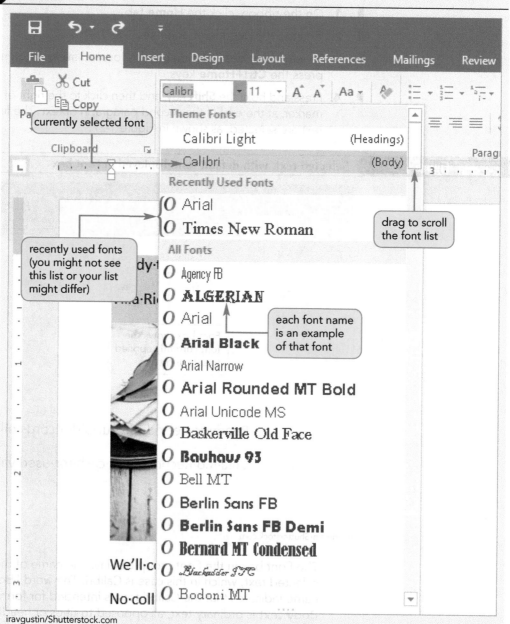

iravgustin/Shutterstock.com

6. Without clicking, move the pointer over a dramatic-looking font in the font list, such as Algerian or Arial Black, and then move the pointer over another font.

The selected text in the document changes to show a Live Preview of the font the pointer is resting on. **Live Preview** shows the results that would occur in your document if you clicked the option you are pointing to.

7. When you are finished reviewing the Font list, click **Arial**. The Font menu closes, and the selected text is formatted in Arial.

Next, you will make the text more eye-catching by increasing the font size. The Font Size box currently displays the number "11," indicating that the selected text is formatted in 11-point font.

8. Verify that the first two paragraphs are still selected, and then click the **Font Size** arrow in the Font group to display a menu of font sizes. As with the Font menu, you can move the pointer over options in the Font Size menu to see a Live Preview of that option.

TIP

To restore selected text to its default appearance, click the Clear All Formatting button in the Font group on the Home tab.

9. On the Font Size menu, click **22**. The selected text increases significantly in size, and the Font Size menu closes.

10. Select the three paragraphs of text below the photo, format them in the Arial font, and then increase the paragraph's font size to 22 points.

11. Click a blank area of the document to deselect the text, and then save the document.

Leo examines the flyer and decides he would like to apply more character formatting, which affects the appearance of individual characters, in the middle three paragraphs. After that, you can turn your attention to paragraph formatting, which affects the appearance of the entire paragraph.

Applying Text Effects, Font Colors, and Font Styles

To really make text stand out, you can use text effects. You access these options by clicking the Text Effects and Typography button in the Font group on the Home tab. Keep in mind that text effects can be very dramatic. For formal, professional documents, you probably need to use only **bold** or *italic* to make a word or paragraph stand out.

Leo suggests applying text effects to the second paragraph.

To apply text effects to the second paragraph:

1. Scroll up, if necessary, to display the beginning of the document, and then click in the selection bar to the left of the second paragraph. The entire second paragraph is selected.

2. In the Font group on the Home tab, click the **Text Effects and Typography** button A ·.

A gallery of text effects appears. Options that allow you to fine-tune a particular text effect, perhaps by changing the color or adding an even more pronounced shadow, are listed below the gallery. A **gallery** is a menu or grid that shows a visual representation of the options available when you click a button.

3. In the middle of the bottom row of the gallery, place the pointer over the blue letter "A." This displays a ScreenTip with the text effect's full name: Fill - Blue, Accent 1, Outline - Background 1, Hard Shadow - Accent 1. A Live Preview of the effect appears in the document. See Figure 1-29.

Figure 1-29   **Live Preview of a text effect**

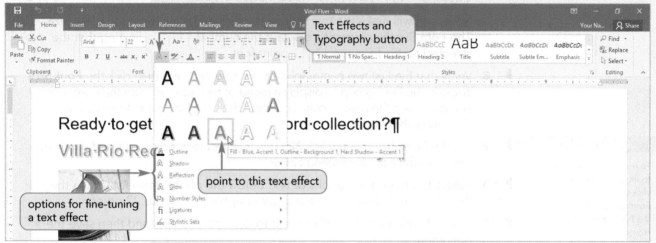

iravgustin/Shutterstock.com

4. In the bottom row of the gallery, click the blue letter "A." The text effect is applied to the selected paragraph and the Text Effects gallery closes. The second paragraph is formatted in blue, as shown in the Session 1.2 Visual Overview. On the ribbon, the Bold button in the Font group is now highlighted because bold formatting is part of this text effect.

Next, to make the text stand out a bit more, you'll increase the font size. This time, instead of using the Font Size button, you'll use a different method.

5. In the Font group, click the **Increase Font Size button** A˘. The font size increases from 22 points to 24 points.

6. Click the **Increase Font Size button** A˘ again. The font size increases to 26 points. If you need to decrease the font size of selected text, you can use the Decrease Font Size button.

Leo asks you to emphasize the third and fourth paragraphs by adding bold and a blue font color.

To apply a font color and bold:

1. Select the third and fourth paragraphs of text, which contain the text "We'll come to your home. No collection is too small or too large!"

2. In the Font group on the Home tab, click the **Font Color button arrow** A˘. A gallery of font colors appears. Black is the default font color and appears at the top of the Font Color gallery, with the word "Automatic" next to it.

The options in the Theme Colors section of the menu are complementary colors that work well when used together in a document. The options in the Standard Colors section are more limited. For more advanced color options, you could use the More Colors or Gradient options. Leo prefers a simple blue.

Trouble? If the third and fourth paragraphs turned red, you clicked the Font Color button A instead of the arrow next to it. On the Quick Access Toolbar, click the Undo button ↩, and then repeat Step 2.

3. In the Theme Colors section, place the mouse pointer over the square that's second from the right in the top row. A ScreenTip with the color's name, "Blue, Accent 5," appears. A Live Preview of the color appears in the document, where the text you selected in Step 1 now appears formatted in blue. See Figure 1-30.

| Figure 1-30 | Font Color gallery showing a Live Preview |

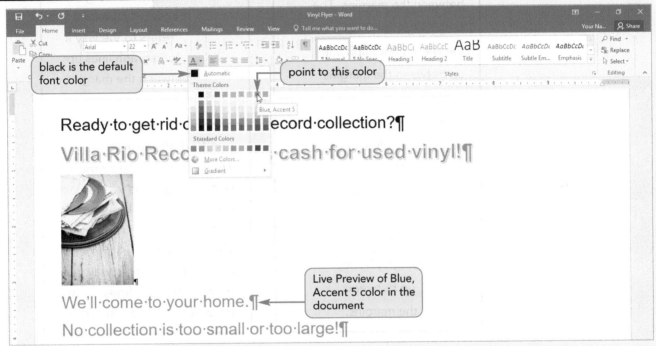

iravgustin/Shutterstock.com

4. Click the **Blue, Accent 5** square. The Font color gallery closes, and the selected text is formatted in blue. On the Font Color button, the bar below the letter "A" is now blue, indicating that if you select text and click the Font Color button, the text will automatically change to blue.

5. In the Font group, click the **Bold** button **B**. The selected text is now formatted in bold, with thicker, darker lettering.

TIP

You can use other buttons in the Font group on the Home tab to apply other character attributes, such as underline, italic, or superscript.

Next, you will complete some paragraph formatting, starting with paragraph alignment.

Aligning Text

Alignment refers to how text and graphics line up between the page margins. By default, Word aligns text along the left margin, with the text along the right margin **ragged**, or uneven. This is called **left alignment**. With **right alignment**, the text is aligned along the right margin and is ragged along the left margin. With **center alignment**, text is centered between the left and right margins and is ragged along both the left and right margins. With **justified alignment**, full lines of text are spaced between both the left and the right margins, and no text is ragged. Text in newspaper columns is often justified. See Figure 1-31.

Figure 1-31   **Varieties of text alignment**

left alignment

The term "alignment" refers to the way a paragraph lines up between the margins. The term "alignment" refers to the way a paragraph lines up between the margins.

right alignment

The term "alignment" refers to the way a paragraph lines up between the margins. The term "alignment" refers to the way a paragraph lines up between the margins.

center alignment

The term "alignment" refers to the way a paragraph lines up between the margins.

justified alignment

The term "alignment" refers to the way a paragraph lines up between the margins. The term "alignment" refers to the way a paragraph lines up between the margins.

The Paragraph group on the Home tab includes a button for each of the four major types of alignment described in Figure 1-31: the Align Left button, the Center button, the Align Right button, and the Justify button. To align a single paragraph, click anywhere in that paragraph, and then click the appropriate alignment button. To align multiple paragraphs, select the paragraphs first, and then click an alignment button.

You need to center all the text in the flyer now. You can center the photo at the same time.

To center-align the text:

> Use the Ctrl+A keys to select the entire document, instead of dragging the mouse pointer. It's easy to miss part of the document when you drag the mouse pointer.

▸ **1.** Make sure the Home tab is still selected, and press the **Ctrl+A** keys to select the entire document.

▸ **2.** In the Paragraph group, click the **Center** button ≡, and then click a blank area of the document to deselect the selected paragraphs. The text and photo are now centered on the page, similar to the centered text shown earlier in the Session 1.2 Visual Overview.

▸ **3.** Save the document.

Adding a Paragraph Border and Shading

A **paragraph border** is an outline that appears around one or more paragraphs in a document. You can choose to apply only a partial border—for example, a bottom border that appears as an underline under the last line of text in the paragraph—or an entire box around a paragraph. You can select different colors and line weights for the border as well, making it more or less prominent as needed. You apply paragraph borders using the Borders button in the Paragraph group on the Home tab. **Shading** is background color that you can apply to one or more paragraphs and can be used in conjunction with a border for a more defined effect. You apply shading using the Shading button in the Paragraph group on the Home tab.

Now you will apply a border and shading to the first paragraph, as shown earlier in the Session 1.2 Visual Overview. Then you will use the Format Painter to copy this formatting to the last paragraph in the document.

To add shading and a paragraph border:

▶ **1.** Select the first paragraph. Be sure to select the paragraph mark at the end of the paragraph.

▶ **2.** On the Home tab, in the Paragraph group, click the **Borders button arrow** ⊞ ▾. A gallery of border options appears, as shown in Figure 1-32. To apply a complete outline around the selected text, you use the Outside Borders option.

| Figure 1-32 | Border gallery |

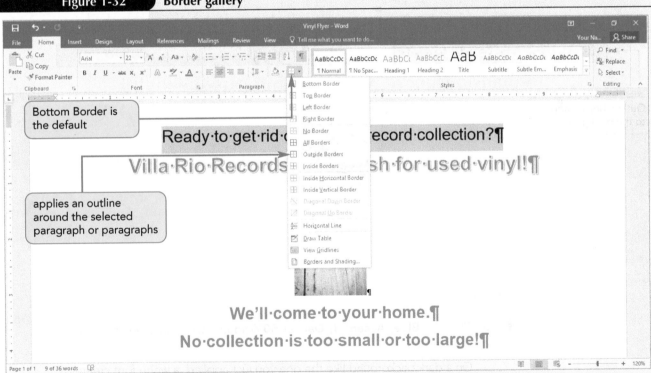

iravgustin/Shutterstock.com

Trouble? If the gallery does not open and instead the paragraph becomes underlined with a single underline, you clicked the Borders button ⊞ instead of the arrow next to it. On the Quick Access Toolbar, click the Undo button ↺, and then repeat Step 2.

3. In the Border gallery, click **Outside Borders**. The menu closes and a black border appears around the selected paragraph, spanning the width of the page. In the Paragraph group, the Borders button ⊞ changes to show the Outside Borders option.

   Trouble? If the border around the first paragraph doesn't extend all the way to the left and right margins and instead encloses only the text, you didn't select the paragraph mark as directed in Step 1. Click the Undo button ↶ repeatedly to remove the border, and begin again with Step 1.

4. In the Paragraph group, click the **Shading button arrow** 🖌▾. A gallery of shading options opens, divided into Theme Colors and Standard Colors. You will use a shade of dark blue in the fifth column from the left.

5. In the bottom row in the Theme Colors section, move the pointer over the square in the fifth column from the left to display a ScreenTip that reads "Blue, Accent 1, Darker 50%." A Live Preview of the color appears in the document. See Figure 1-33.

Figure 1-33   **Shading gallery with a Live Preview displayed**

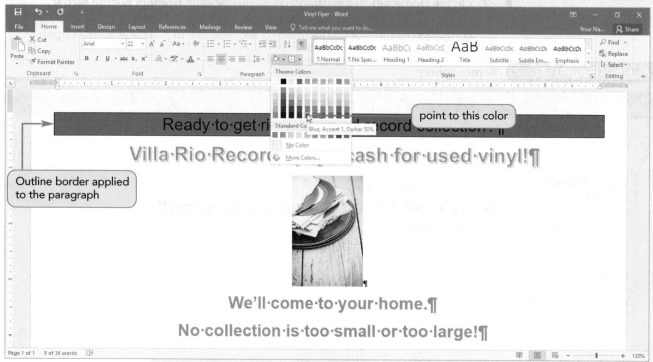

iravgustin/Shutterstock.com

---

6. Click the **Blue, Accent 1, Darker 50%** square to apply the shading to the selected text.

   On a dark background like the one you just applied, a white font creates a striking effect. Leo asks you to change the font color for this paragraph to white.

7. Make sure the Home tab is still selected.

8. In the Font group, click the **Font Color button arrow** 🅰▾ to open the Font Color gallery, and then click the **white** square in the top row of the Theme Colors. The Font Color gallery closes, and the paragraph is now formatted with white font.

9. Click a blank area of the document to deselect the text, review the change, and then save the document. See Figure 1-34.

| Figure 1-34 | Paragraph formatted with dark blue shading, a black border, and white font |

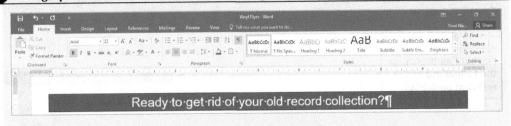

To add balance to the flyer, Leo suggests formatting the last paragraph in the document with the same shading, border, and font color as the first paragraph. You'll do that next.

Copying Formatting with the Format Painter

You could select the last paragraph and then apply the border, shading, and font color one step at a time. But it's easier to copy all the formatting from the first paragraph to the last paragraph using the Format Painter button in the Clipboard group on the Home tab.

Using the Format Painter

- Select the text whose formatting you want to copy.
- On the Home tab, in the Clipboard group, click the Format Painter button; or to copy formatting to multiple sections of nonadjacent text, double-click the Format Painter button.
- The mouse pointer changes to the Format Painter pointer, the I-beam pointer with a paintbrush.
- Click the words you want to format, or drag to select and format entire paragraphs.
- When you are finished formatting the text, click the Format Painter button again to turn off the Format Painter.

You'll use the Format Painter now.

To use the Format Painter:

1. Change the document Zoom level to One Page so you can easily see both the first and last paragraphs.

2. Select the first paragraph, which is formatted with the dark blue shading, the border, and the white font color.

3. On the ribbon, click the **Home** tab.

4. In the Clipboard group, click the **Format Painter** button to activate, or turn on, the Format Painter.

5. Move the pointer over the document. The pointer changes to the Format Painter pointer ⌖ when you move the mouse pointer near an item that can be formatted. See Figure 1-35.

Figure 1-35   **Format Painter**

Format Painter is turned on

Format Painter copies the formatting of the selected paragraph

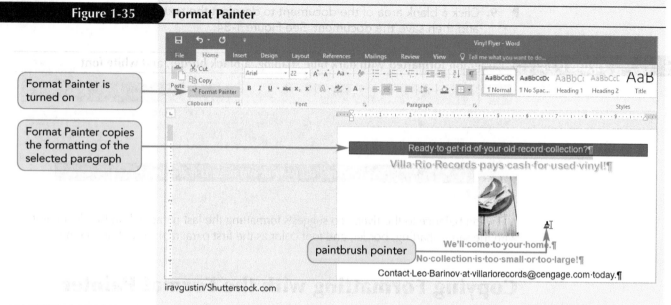

paintbrush pointer

iravgustin/Shutterstock.com

TIP

To turn off the Format Painter without using it, press the Esc key.

6. Click and drag the Format Painter pointer ▲🖌 to select the last paragraph in the document. The paragraph is now formatted with dark blue shading, a black border, and white font. The mouse pointer returns to its original I-beam shape.

Trouble? If the text in the newly formatted paragraph wrapped to a second line, replace your full name with your first name, or, if necessary, use only your initials so the paragraph is only one line long.

7. Click anywhere in the document to deselect the text, review the change, and then save the document.

You're almost finished working on the document's paragraph formatting. Your last step is to increase the paragraph spacing below the first paragraph and above the last paragraph. This will give the shaded text even more weight on the page. To complete this task, you will use the settings on the Layout tab, which offer more options than the Line and Paragraph Spacing button on the Home tab.

To increase the paragraph spacing below the first paragraph and above the last paragraph:

1. Click anywhere in the first paragraph, and then click the **Layout** tab. On this tab, the Paragraph group contains settings that control paragraph spacing. Currently, the paragraph spacing for the first paragraph is set to the default 0 points before the paragraph and 8 points after.

2. In the Paragraph group, click the **After** box to select the current setting, type **42**, and then press the **Enter** key. The added space causes the second paragraph to move down 42 points.

3. Click anywhere in the last paragraph.

4. On the Layout tab, in the Paragraph group, click the **Before** box to select the current setting, type **42**, and then press the **Enter** key. The added space causes the last paragraph to move down 42 points.

INSIGHT

Formatting Professional Documents

In more formal documents, use color and special effects sparingly. The goal of letters, reports, and many other types of documents is to convey important information, not to dazzle the reader with fancy fonts and colors. Such elements only serve to distract the reader from your main point. In formal documents, it's a good idea to limit the number of colors to two and to stick with left alignment for text. In a document like the flyer you're currently working on, you have a little more leeway because the goal of the document is to attract attention. However, you still want it to look professional.

Finally, Leo wants you to replace the photo with one that will look better in the document's new landscape orientation. You'll replace the photo, and then you'll resize it so that the flyer fills the entire page.

Working with Pictures

A **picture** is a photo or another type of image that you insert into a document. To work with a picture, you first need to select it. Once a picture is selected, a contextual tab—the Picture Tools Format tab—appears on the ribbon, with options for editing the picture and adding effects such as a border, a shadow, a reflection, or a new shape. A **contextual tab** appears on the ribbon only when an object is selected. It contains commands related to the selected object so that you can manipulate, edit, and format the selected object. You can also use the mouse to resize or move a selected picture. To insert a new picture, you use the Pictures button in the Illustrations group on the Insert tab.

To delete the current photo and insert a new one:

▶ **1.** Click the photo to select it.

The circles, called **handles**, around the edge of the photo indicate the photo is selected. The Layout Options button, to the right of the photo, gives you access to options that control how the document text flows around the photo. You don't need to worry about these options now. Finally, note that the Picture Tools Format tab appeared on the ribbon when you selected the photo. See Figure 1-36.

Figure 1-36   **Selected photo**

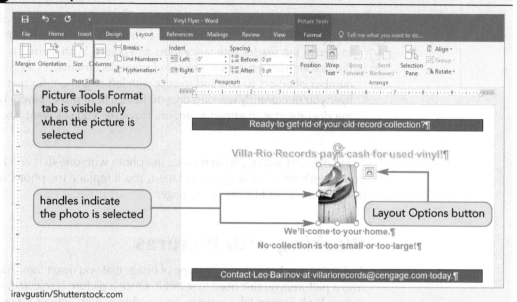

iravgustin/Shutterstock.com

▶ **2.** Press the **Delete** key. The photo is deleted from the document. The insertion point blinks next to the paragraph symbol. You will insert the new photo in that paragraph.

▶ **3.** On the ribbon, click the **Insert** tab. The ribbon changes to display the Insert options.

▶ **4.** In the Illustrations group, click the **Pictures** button. The Insert Picture dialog box opens.

▶ **5.** Navigate to the **Word1 > Module folder** included with your Data Files, and then click **Albums** to select the file. The name of the selected file appears in the File name box.

▶ **6.** Click the **Insert** button to close the Insert Picture dialog box and insert the photo. A different album image, with the albums in the upper-right corner, appears in the document, below the second paragraph. The photo is selected, as indicated by the handles on its border. The newly inserted photo is so large that it appears on a second page.

Now you need to shrink the photo to fit the available space on the first page. You could do so by clicking one of the picture's corner handles, holding down the mouse button, and then dragging the handle to resize the picture. But using the Shape Height and Shape Width boxes on the Picture Tools Format tab gives you more precise results.

To resize the photo:

▶ **1.** Make sure the Picture Tools Format tab is still selected on the ribbon.

▶ **2.** In the Size group on the far right edge of the ribbon, locate the Shape Height box, which tells you that the height of the selected picture is currently 6.67". The Shape Width box tells you that the width of the picture is 10". As you'll see in the next step, when you change one of these measurements, the other changes accordingly, keeping the overall shape of the picture the same. See Figure 1-37.

Figure 1-37   **Shape Height and Shape Width boxes**

Shape Height box shows the current height

Shape Width box shows the current width

click the up arrow to increase the picture's height

you could also drag a corner handle to resize the picture

iravgustin/Shutterstock.com

> **3.** Click the **down arrow** in the Shape Height box in the Size group. The photo decreases in size slightly. The measurement in the Shape Height box decreases to 6.6", and the measurement in the Shape Width box decreases to 9.9".

> **4.** Click the **down arrow** in the Shape Height box repeatedly until the picture is 3.3" tall and 4.95" wide. As the photo shrinks, it moves back to page 1, along with the text below it. The entire flyer should again appear on one page.

Finally, to make the photo more noticeable, you can add a **picture style**, which is a collection of formatting options, such as a frame, a rounded shape, and a shadow. You can apply a picture style to a selected picture by clicking the style you want in the Picture Styles gallery on the Picture Tools Format tab. In the following steps, you'll start by displaying the gallery.

To add a style to the photo:

> **1.** Make sure the Picture Tools Format tab is still selected on the ribbon.

> **2.** In the Picture Styles group, click the **More** button to the right of the Picture Styles gallery to open the gallery and display more picture styles. Some of the picture styles simply add a border, while others change the picture's shape. Other styles combine these options with effects such as a shadow or a reflection.

> **3.** Place the mouse pointer over various styles to observe the Live Previews in the document, and then place the mouse pointer over the Drop Shadow Rectangle style, which is the middle style in the top row. See Figure 1-38.

Figure 1-38 **Previewing a picture style**

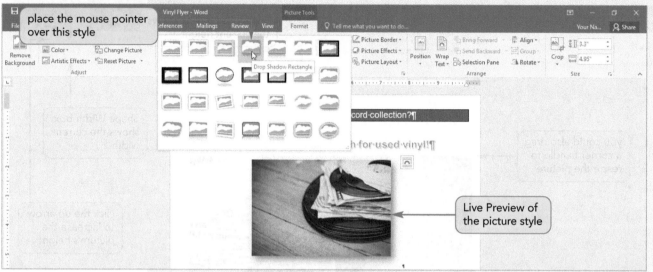

iravgustin/Shutterstock.com

TIP

To return a picture to its original appearance, click the Reset Picture button in the Adjust group on the Picture Tools Format tab.

4. In the gallery, click the **Drop Shadow Rectangle** style to apply it to the photo and close the gallery. The photo is formatted with a shadow on the bottom and right sides, as shown earlier in the Session 1.2 Visual Overview.

5. Click anywhere outside the photo to deselect it, and then save the document.

Working with Inline Pictures

By default, when you insert a picture in a document, it is treated as an inline object, which means its position changes in the document as you add or delete text. Also, because it is an inline object, you can align the picture just as you would align text, using the alignment buttons in the Paragraph group on the Home tab. Essentially, you can treat an inline picture as just another paragraph.

When you become a more advanced Word user, you'll learn how to wrap text around a picture so that the text flows around the picture—with the picture maintaining its position on the page no matter how much text you add to or delete from the document. The alignment buttons don't work on pictures that have text wrapped around them. Instead, you can drag the picture to the desired position on the page.

The flyer is complete and ready for Leo to print later. Because Leo is considering creating a promotional brochure that would include numerous photographs, he asks you to look up more information about inserting pictures. You can do that using Word's Help system.

Getting Help

To get the most out of Help, your computer must be connected to the Internet so it can access the reference information stored at Office.com. The quickest way to look up information is to use the Tell Me box—which appears with the text "Tell me what you want to do…" within it—on the ribbon. You can also use the Tell Me box to quickly access Word features.

To look up information in Help:

TIP

To search the web for information on a word or phrase in a document, select the text, click the Review tab, and then click the Smart Lookup button in the Insights group.

▶ **1.** Verify that your computer is connected to the Internet, and then, on the ribbon, click the **Tell Me** box, and type **insert pictures**. A menu of Help topics related to inserting pictures opens. You could click one of the topics in the menu, or you could click the Get Help on "insert pictures" command at the bottom of the menu to open a Word 2016 Help window, where you could continue to search Office.com for more information on inserting pictures. If you prefer to expand your search to the entire web, you could click the Smart Lookup command at the bottom of the menu to open an Insights task pane with links to articles from Wikipedia and other sources. You could also press Enter at this point to open the Insert Pictures dialog box.

▶ **2.** Click **Get Help on "insert pictures."** After a slight pause, the Word 2016 Help window opens with links to information about inserting pictures. You might see the links shown in Figure 1-39, or you might see other links.

Figure 1-39   **Word Help window**

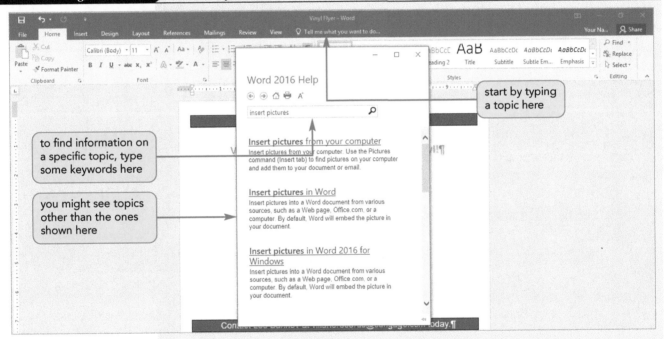

▶ **3.** Click the first link, and then read the article to see if it contains any information about inserting pictures that might be useful to Leo. Note that to print information about a topic, you can click the Print button near the top of the Word Help window.

▶ **4.** When you are finished reading the article, click the **Back** button ⊖ near the top of the Word 2016 Help window to return to the previous list of links.

▶ **5.** Click the **Home** button ⌂ to go to the home page.

▶ **6.** Click the **Close** button ⊠ in the upper-right corner to close the Word 2016 Help window.

▶ **7.** Click the **File** tab, and then click **Close** in the navigation bar to close the document without closing Word.

Word Help is a great way to learn about and access Word's many features. Articles and videos on basic skills provide step-by-step guides for completing tasks, while more elaborate, online tutorials walk you through more complicated tasks. Be sure to take some time on your own to explore Word Help so you can find the information and features you want when you need it.

REVIEW

Session 1.2 Quick Check

1. Explain how to accept a spelling correction suggested by the Spelling task pane.
2. What orientation should you choose if you want your document to be wider than it is tall?
3. What is the default font size?
4. What is a gallery?
5. What is the default text alignment?
6. Explain two important facts about a picture inserted as an inline object.

Review Assignments

Data Files needed for the Review Assignments: Flyer.docx, Player.jpg

Leo asks you to write a cover letter to accompany a bid for a collection of reggae albums. After that, he wants you to create an envelope for the letter and to format a flyer reminding customers that Villa Rio Records buys vintage record players in addition to vintage vinyl. Change the Zoom level as necessary while you are working. Complete the following steps:

1. Open a new, blank document and then save the document as **Huang Letter** in the location specified by your instructor.

2. Type the date **February 19, 2017** using AutoComplete for "February."

3. Press the Enter key twice, and then type the following inside address, using the default paragraph spacing and pressing the Enter key once after each line:

    Sabrina Huang

    52 East Dana Parkway

    Wilmington, DE 19802

4. Type **Dear Ms. Huang:** as the salutation, press the Enter key, and then type the following as the body of the letter:

    Enclosed you will find my appraisal of your reggae collection. Please note that you also included some classic rock albums. I've included a separate bid for those titles, as well as a bid for the combined collections.

    I enjoyed our conversation about gospel music of the 1950s. Please let me know if you are looking for more albums from that era. You can see our complete gospel collection online at www.villariorecords.cengage.com.

5. Press the Enter key, type **Sincerely yours,** as the complimentary closing, press the Enter key three times, type **Leo Barinov** as the signature line, insert a manual line break, and type **Purchasing Manager** as his title.

6. Press the Enter key, type your initials, insert a manual line break, and then use the Undo button to make your initials all lowercase, if necessary.

7. Type **Enclosure** and save the document.

8. Scroll to the beginning of the document and proofread your work. Remove any wavy underlines by using a shortcut menu or by typing a correction yourself. Remove the hyperlink formatting from the web address.

9. Remove the paragraph spacing from the first two lines of the inside address.

10. Change the top margin to 2.75 inches. Leave the other margins at their default settings.

11. Save your changes to the letter, preview it, print it if your instructor asks you to, and then close it.

12. Create a new, blank document, and then create an envelope. Use Sabrina Huang's address (from Step 3) as the delivery address. Use your school's name and address for the return address. Add the envelope to the document. If you are asked if you want to save the return address as the new return address, click No.

13. Save the document as **Huang Envelope** in the location specified by your instructor, and then close the document.

14. Open the document **Flyer**, located in the Word1 > Review folder included with your Data Files, and then check your screen to make sure your settings match those in the module.

15. Save the document as **Record Player Flyer** in the location specified by your instructor.

16. Use the Recheck Document button in the Word Options dialog box to reset the Spelling and Grammar checker, and then use the Spelling and Grammar task panes to correct any errors marked with wavy underlines.

17. Proofread the document and correct any other errors. Be sure to change "Today" to **today** in the last paragraph.

18. Change the page orientation to Landscape and the margins to Narrow.

19. Format the document text in 22-point Times New Roman font.

20. Center the text and the photo.

21. Format the first paragraph with an outside border, and then add orange shading, using the Orange, Accent 2, Darker 25% color in the Theme Colors section of the Shading gallery. Format the paragraph text in white.

22. Format the last paragraph in the document using the same formatting you applied to the first paragraph.

23. Increase the paragraph spacing after the first paragraph to 42 points. Increase the paragraph spacing before the last paragraph in the document to 42 points.

24. Format the second paragraph with the Fill - Orange, Accent 2, Outline - Accent 2 text effect. Increase the paragraph's font size to 26 points.

25. Format the text in the third and fourth paragraphs (the first two paragraphs below the photo) in orange, using the Orange, Accent 2, Darker 50% font color, and then add bold and italic.

26. Delete the photo and replace it with the **Player.jpg** photo, located in the Word1 > Review folder included with your Data Files.

27. Resize the new photo so that it is 3.8" tall, and then add the Soft Edge Rectangle style in the Pictures Styles gallery.

28. Save your changes to the flyer, preview it, and then close it.

29. Use Word Help to look up the topic **work with pictures**. Read the first article, return to the Help home page, and then close Help.

Case Problem 1

APPLY

There are no Data Files needed for this Case Problem.

Brightly Water Quality Consultants   You are a program administrator at Brightly Water Quality Consultants, in Springfield, Missouri. Over the past few months, you have collected handwritten journals from local residents documenting their daily water use. Now you need to send the journals to the researcher in charge of compiling the information. Create a cover letter to accompany the journals by completing the following steps. Because your office is currently out of letterhead, you'll start the letter by typing a return address. As you type the letter, remember to include the appropriate number of blank paragraphs between the various parts of the letter. Complete the following steps:

1. Open a new, blank document, and then save the document as **Brightly Letter** in the location specified by your instructor. If necessary, change the Zoom level to 120%.

2. Type the following return address, using the default paragraph spacing and replacing [Your Name] with your first and last names:
   [Your Name]
   Brightly Water Quality Consultants
   39985 Pepperdine Avenue, Suite 52
   Springfield, MO 65806

3. Type **November 6, 2017** as the date, leaving a blank paragraph between the last line of the return address and the date.

4. Type the following inside address, using the default paragraph spacing and leaving the appropriate number of blank paragraphs after the date:
   Dr. Albert Strome
   4643 College Drive
   Columbia, MO 65211

5. Type **Dear Dr. Strome:** as the salutation.

6. To begin the body of the letter, type the following paragraph:
Enclosed please find the journals our participants have completed. I should have thirty more by the end of next month, but I thought you would like to get started on these now. Please review the enclosed journals, and then call or email me with your answers to these questions:

7. Add the following questions as separate paragraphs, using the default paragraph spacing:
Did the participants include enough helpful information?
Should we consider expanding the program to additional communities?
Can you complete your analysis by early March?

8. Insert a new paragraph before the second question, and then add the following as the new second question in the list: **Is the journal format useful, or would you prefer a simple questionnaire?**

9. Insert a new paragraph after the last question, and then type the complimentary closing **Sincerely,** (including the comma).

10. Leave the appropriate amount of space for your signature, type your full name, insert a manual line break, and then type **Program Administrator**.

11. Type **Enclosure** in the appropriate place.

12. Use the Recheck Document button in the Word Options dialog box to reset the Spelling and Grammar checker, and then use the Spelling and Grammar task panes to correct any errors. Instruct the Spelling task pane to ignore the recipient's name.

13. Italicize the four paragraphs containing the questions.

14. Remove the paragraph spacing from the first three lines of the return address. Do the same for the first two paragraphs of the inside address.

15. Center the four paragraphs containing the return address, format them in 16-point font, and then add the Fill – Gray – 50%, Accent 3, Sharp Bevel text effect.

16. Save the document, preview it, and then close it.

17. Create a new, blank document, and create an envelope. Use Dr. Strome's address (from Step 4) as the delivery address. Use the return address shown in Step 2. Add the envelope to the document. If you are asked if you want to save the return address as the new return address, click No.

18. Save the document as **Strome Envelope** in the location specified by your instructor, and then close the document.

Case Problem 2

CREATE

Data Files needed for this Case Problem: Dog.jpg, Pups.docx

Pups & Pals Pet Care   You work as the sales and scheduling coordinator at Pups & Pals Pet Care, a dog-walking service in San Antonio, Texas. You need to create a flyer promoting the company's services. Complete the following steps:

1. Open the document **Pups** located in the Word1 > Case2 folder included with your Data Files, and then save the document as **Pups & Pals Flyer** in the location specified by your instructor.

2. In the document, replace "Student Name" with your first and last names.

3. Use the Recheck Document button in the Word Options dialog box to reset the Spelling and Grammar checker, and then use the Spelling and Grammar task panes to correct any errors. Instruct the Spelling task pane to ignore your name if Word marks it with a wavy underline.

4. Change the page margins to Narrow.

5. Complete the flyer as shown in Figure 1-40. Use the photo **Dog.jpg** located in the Word1 > Case2 folder included with your Data Files. Use the default line spacing and paragraph spacing unless otherwise specified in Figure 1-40.

Figure 1-40   **Formatted Pups & Pals flyer**

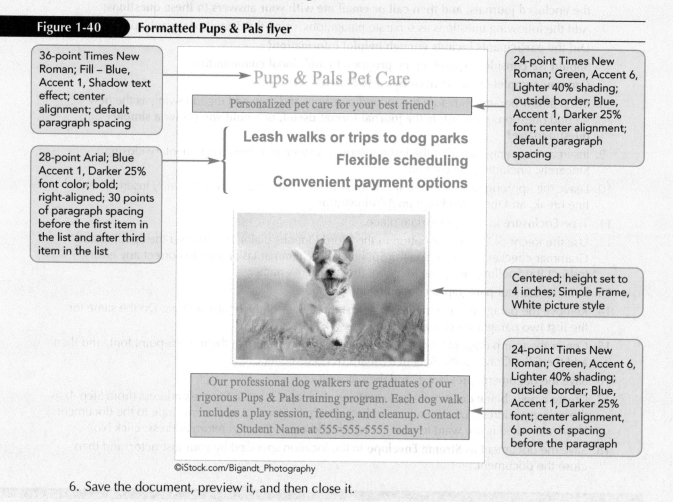

36-point Times New Roman; Fill – Blue, Accent 1, Shadow text effect; center alignment; default paragraph spacing

28-point Arial; Blue Accent 1, Darker 25% font color; bold; right-aligned; 30 points of paragraph spacing before the first item in the list and after third item in the list

24-point Times New Roman; Green, Accent 6, Lighter 40% shading; outside border; Blue, Accent 1, Darker 25% font; center alignment; default paragraph spacing

Centered; height set to 4 inches; Simple Frame, White picture style

24-point Times New Roman; Green, Accent 6, Lighter 40% shading; outside border; Blue, Accent 1, Darker 25% font; center alignment; 6 points of spacing before the paragraph

©iStock.com/Bigandt_Photography

6. Save the document, preview it, and then close it.

Case Problem 3

Data Files needed for this Case Problem: Living.docx, Rental.docx

Salt Lake Synergy Vacation Rentals   You work as the office manager for Salt Lake Synergy Vacation Rentals, a service that rents apartments and houses in Salt Lake City, Utah, to out-of-town visitors. One of the company's rental agents needs to complete a letter to accompany a photo of a rental property. The letter is almost finished, but the agent needs help correcting errors and formatting the text to match the block style. The photo itself is stored in a separate document. The agent mistakenly applied a picture style to the photo that is inappropriate for professional correspondence. She asks you to remove the picture style and then format the page. Complete the following steps:

1. Open the document **Rental** located in the Word1 > Case3 folder included with your Data Files, and then save the document as **Rental Letter** in the location specified by your instructor.

2. Use the Recheck Document button in the Word Options dialog box to reset the Spelling and Grammar checker, and then use the Spelling and Grammar task panes to correct any errors, typing directly in the document as necessary.

⚙ **Troubleshoot** 3. Make any necessary changes to ensure that the letter matches the formatting of a block-style business letter, including the appropriate paragraph spacing. Keep in mind that the letter will include an enclosure. Include your initials where appropriate.

☼ **Troubleshoot** 4. The letterhead for Salt Lake Synergy Vacation Rentals requires a top margin of 2.5 inches. Determine if the layout of the letter will work with the letterhead, make any necessary changes, and then save the letter.

5. Save the document and preview it.

6. Move the cursor to the beginning of the letter, and then create an envelope. Use the delivery address taken from the letter, but edit the delivery address to remove the salutation, if necessary. Click the Omit check box to deselect it (if necessary), and then, for the return address, type your school's name and address. Add the envelope to the Rental Letter document. If you are asked if you want to save the return address as the new default return address, answer No.

7. Save the document, preview both pages, and then close it.

8. Open the document **Living** located in the Word1 > Case3 folder included with your Data Files, and then save the document as **Living Area Photo** in the location specified by your instructor.

☼ **Troubleshoot** 9. Reset the picture to its original appearance, before the agent mistakenly added the style with the reflection.

☼ **Troubleshoot** 10. Modify the page layout and margins and adjust the size of the photo so the photo fills as much of the page as possible without overlapping the page margins.

11. Save the document, preview it, and then close it.

Case Problem 4

There are no Data Files needed for this Case Problem.

Palomino Lighting Manufacturers   As an assistant facilities manager at Palomino Lighting Manufacturers, you are responsible for alerting the staff when clients plan to visit the factory. In addition to sending out a company-wide email, you also need to post a memo in the break room. Complete the following steps:

⊕ **Explore** 1. Open a new document—but instead of selecting the Blank document option, search for a memo template online. In the list of search results, click the Memo (Simple design) template, and then click the Create button. (Note: If you don't see that template, pick another with a simple style and the word "Memo" at the top. You will need to adapt the steps in this Case Problem to match the design of the template you use.) A memo template opens in the Word window.

2. Save the document as **Visit Memo** in the location specified by your instructor. If you see a dialog box indicating that the document will be upgraded to the newest file format, click the OK button. Note that of the hundreds of templates available online, only a small portion have been created in the most recent version of Word, so you will often see this dialog box when working with templates.

⊕ **Explore** 3. In the document, click the text "[Company name]." The placeholder text appears in a box with gray highlighting. The box containing the highlighted text (with the small rectangle attached) is called a document control. You can enter text in a document control just as you enter text in a dialog box. Type **Palomino Lighting Manufacturers**, and then press the Tab key. The "[Recipient names]" placeholder text now appears in a document control next to the word "To." (*Hint*: As you work on the memo in the following steps, keep in mind that if you accidentally double-click the word "memo" at the top of the document, you will access the header portion of the document, which is normally closed to editing. In that case, press the Esc key to return to the main document.)

4. Type **All Personnel** and then press the Tab key twice. A document control is now visible to the right of the word "From." Depending on how your computer is set up, you might see your name or another name here, or the document control might be empty. Delete the name, if necessary, and then type your first and last names.

Explore 5. Continue using the Tab key to edit the remaining document controls as indicated below. If you press the Tab key too many times and accidentally skip a document control, you can click the document control to select it.

- In the CC: document control, delete the placeholder text.
- In the Date document control, click the down arrow, and then click the current date in the calendar.
- In the Re: document control, type **Client Visit**.
- In the Comments document control, type **Representatives from Houghton Contractors are scheduled to tour the factory this Tuesday morning. Please greet them warmly, and be prepared to answer any questions they might have.**

6. Use the Recheck Document button in the Word Options dialog box to reset the Spelling and Grammar checker, and then use the Spelling and Grammar task panes to correct any underlined errors. Proofread the document to look for any additional errors.

7. Save the document, preview it, and then close it.

MODULE **2**

Navigating and Formatting a Document

Editing an Academic Document According to MLA Style

OBJECTIVES

Session 2.1
- Read, reply to, delete, and add comments
- Create bulleted and numbered lists
- Move text using drag and drop
- Cut and paste text
- Copy and paste text
- Navigate through a document using the Navigation pane
- Find and replace text
- Format text with styles
- Apply a theme to a document

Session 2.2
- Review the MLA style for research papers
- Indent paragraphs
- Insert and modify page numbers
- Create citations
- Create and update a bibliography
- Modify a source

Case | *Quincy Rivers College*

Carolina Frey, an architecture student at Quincy Rivers College, is doing a student internship at Wilson and Page Design, an architecture firm in Minneapolis, Minnesota. She has written a handout describing the process of acquiring LEED certification, which serves as proof that a home has been constructed according to strict environmental guidelines specified by the U.S. Green Building Council. She asks you to help her finish the handout. The text needs some reorganization and other editing. The handout also needs formatting so the finished document looks professional and is easy to read.

Carolina is also taking an architecture history class and is writing a research paper on the history of architecture. To complete the paper, she needs to follow a set of very specific formatting and style guidelines for academic documents.

Carolina has asked you to help her edit these two very different documents. In Session 2.1, you will review and respond to some comments in the handout and then revise and format that document. In Session 2.2, you will review the MLA style for research papers and then format Carolina's research paper to match the MLA specifications.

STARTING DATA FILES

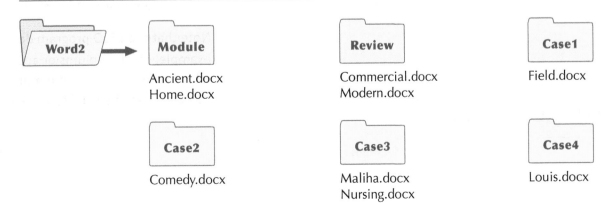

Word2 → **Module**
Ancient.docx
Home.docx

Review
Commercial.docx
Modern.docx

Case1
Field.docx

Case2
Comedy.docx

Case3
Maliha.docx
Nursing.docx

Case4
Louis.docx

Session 2.1 Visual Overview:

Use the Bullets button to create a bulleted list from selected paragraphs.

Use the Numbering button to create a numbered list from selected paragraphs.

The Navigation pane allows you to search for text in the document, with the results highlighted in yellow in the document.

Click the **Search for more things button** to access advanced search tools, or to select something to search for besides text.

You can type the text you want to search for here.

The search text you enter in the Navigation pane is highlighted wherever it appears in the document.

This text is formatted with the Heading 1 style for the Office theme.

The bullet before each of these paragraphs identifies the four paragraphs as items in a list.

This document has two pages.

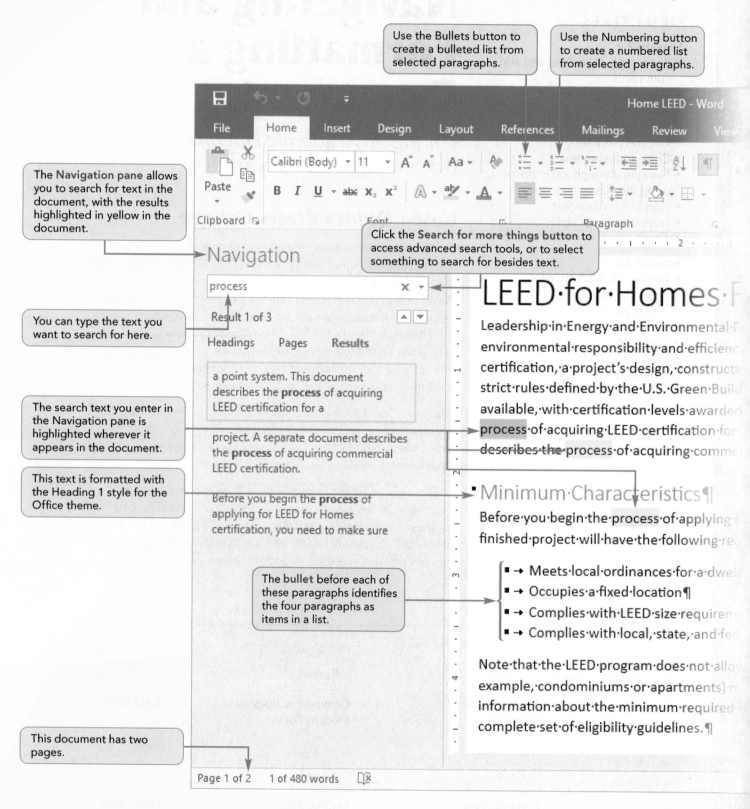

Working with Lists and Styles

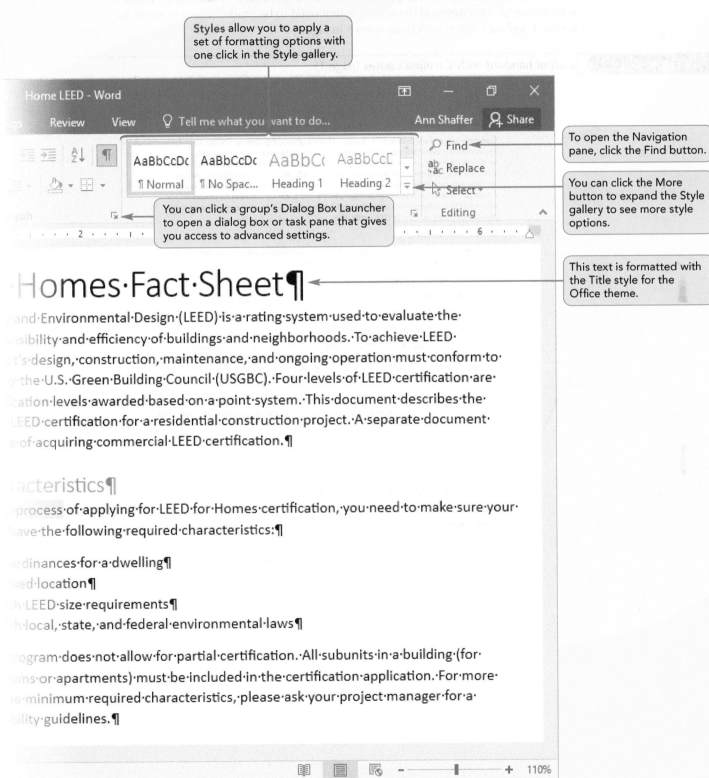

Styles allow you to apply a set of formatting options with one click in the Style gallery.

To open the Navigation pane, click the Find button.

You can click the More button to expand the Style gallery to see more style options.

You can click a group's Dialog Box Launcher to open a dialog box or task pane that gives you access to advanced settings.

This text is formatted with the Title style for the Office theme.

Homes·Fact·Sheet¶

and·Environmental·Design·(LEED)·is·a·rating·system·used·to·evaluate·the·
sibility·and·efficiency·of·buildings·and·neighborhoods.·To·achieve·LEED·
t's·design,·construction,·maintenance,·and·ongoing·operation·must·conform·to·
y·the·U.S.·Green·Building·Council·(USGBC).·Four·levels·of·LEED·certification·are·
cation·levels·awarded·based·on·a·point·system.·This·document·describes·the·
LEED·certification·for·a·residential·construction·project.·A·separate·document·
s·of·acquiring·commercial·LEED·certification.¶

acteristics¶

process·of·applying·for·LEED·for·Homes·certification,·you·need·to·make·sure·your·
ave·the·following·required·characteristics:¶

rdinances·for·a·dwelling¶
ed·location¶
h·LEED·size·requirements¶
h·local,·state,·and·federal·environmental·laws¶

rogram·does·not·allow·for·partial·certification.·All·subunits·in·a·building·(for·
ms·or·apartments)·must·be·included·in·the·certification·application.·For·more·
e·minimum·required·characteristics,·please·ask·your·project·manager·for·a·
ility·guidelines.¶

Reviewing the Document

Before revising a document for someone else, it's a good idea to familiarize yourself with its overall structure and the revisions that need to be made. Take a moment to review Carolina's notes, which are shown in Figure 2-1.

Figure 2-1 **Draft of handout with Carolina's notes (page 1)**

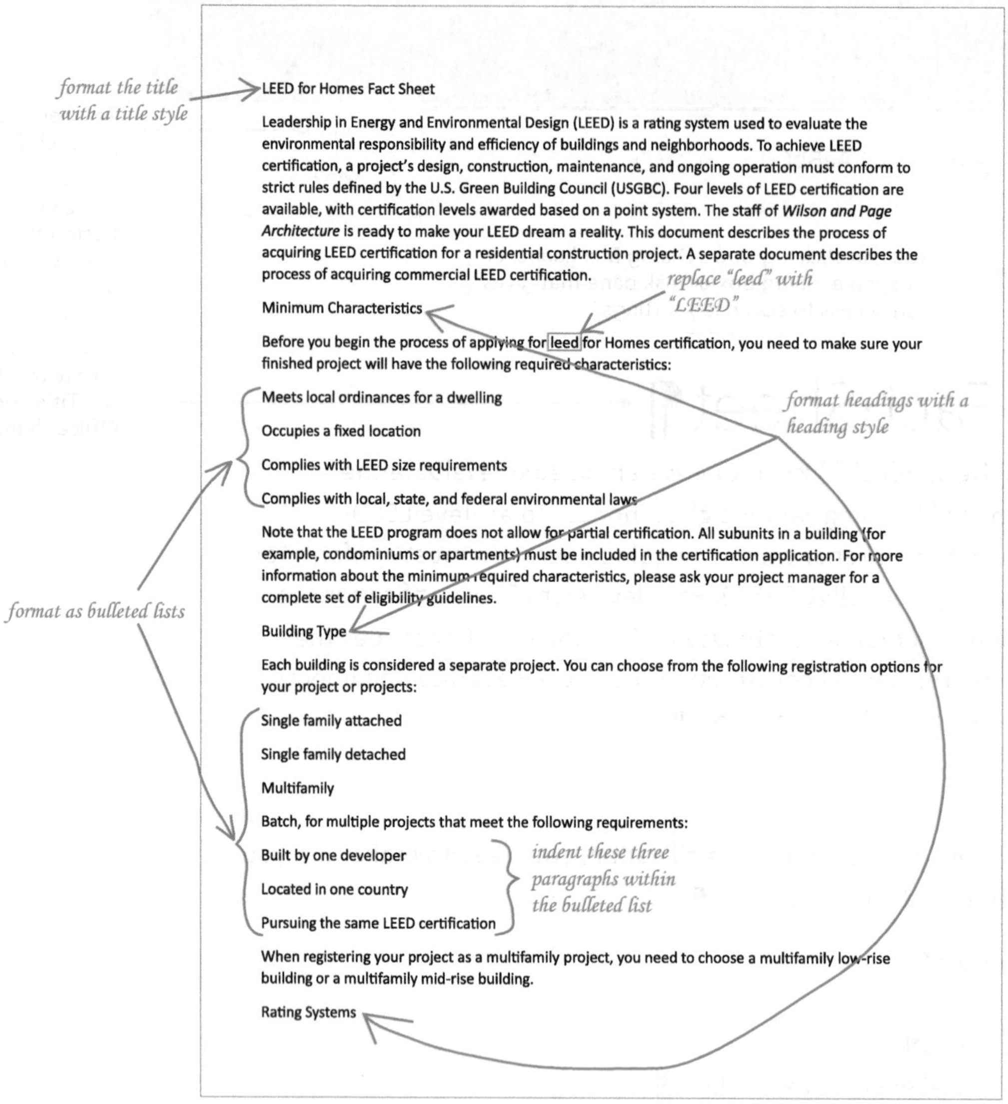

format the title with a title style

LEED for Homes Fact Sheet

Leadership in Energy and Environmental Design (LEED) is a rating system used to evaluate the environmental responsibility and efficiency of buildings and neighborhoods. To achieve LEED certification, a project's design, construction, maintenance, and ongoing operation must conform to strict rules defined by the U.S. Green Building Council (USGBC). Four levels of LEED certification are available, with certification levels awarded based on a point system. The staff of *Wilson and Page Architecture* is ready to make your LEED dream a reality. This document describes the process of acquiring LEED certification for a residential construction project. A separate document describes the process of acquiring commercial LEED certification.

replace "leed" with "LEED"

Minimum Characteristics

Before you begin the process of applying for leed for Homes certification, you need to make sure your finished project will have the following required characteristics:

format headings with a heading style

Meets local ordinances for a dwelling

Occupies a fixed location

Complies with LEED size requirements

Complies with local, state, and federal environmental laws

Note that the LEED program does not allow for partial certification. All subunits in a building (for example, condominiums or apartments) must be included in the certification application. For more information about the minimum required characteristics, please ask your project manager for a complete set of eligibility guidelines.

format as bulleted lists

Building Type

Each building is considered a separate project. You can choose from the following registration options for your project or projects:

Single family attached

Single family detached

Multifamily

Batch, for multiple projects that meet the following requirements:

Built by one developer

Located in one country

Pursuing the same LEED certification

indent these three paragraphs within the bulleted list

When registering your project as a multifamily project, you need to choose a multifamily low-rise building or a multifamily mid-rise building.

Rating Systems

| Figure 2-1 | Draft of handout with Carolina's notes (page 2) |

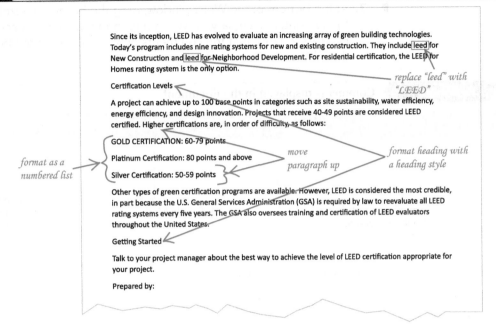

Carolina also included additional guidance in some comments she added to the document file. A **comment** is like an electronic sticky note attached to a word, phrase, or paragraph in a document. Comments appear in the margin, along with the name of the person who added them. Within a single document, you can add new comments, reply to existing comments, and delete comments.

You will open the document now, save it with a new name, and then review Carolina's comments in Word.

To open and rename the document:

1. Open the document **Home** located in the Word2 > Module folder included with your Data Files.

2. Save the document as **Home LEED** in the location specified by your instructor.

3. Verify that the document is displayed in Print Layout view, that the Zoom level is set to **120%**, and that the rulers and nonprinting characters are displayed.

4. On the ribbon, click the **Review** tab to display the tools used for working with comments. Comments can be displayed in several different ways, so your first step is to make sure the comments in the Home LEED document are displayed to match the figures in this book—using Simple Markup view.

5. In the Tracking group, click the **Display for Review** arrow, and then click **Simple Markup** to select it, if necessary. At this point, you might see comment icons to the right of the document text, or you might see the full text of each comment.

6. In the Comments group, click the **Show Comments** button several times to practice displaying and hiding the comments, and then, when you are finished, make sure the Show Comments button is selected so the full text of each comment is displayed.

7. At the bottom of the Word window, drag the horizontal scroll bar all the way to the right, if necessary, so you can read the full text of each comment. See Figure 2-2. Note that the comments on your screen might be a different color than the ones shown in the figure.

Figure 2-2 **Comments displayed in the document**

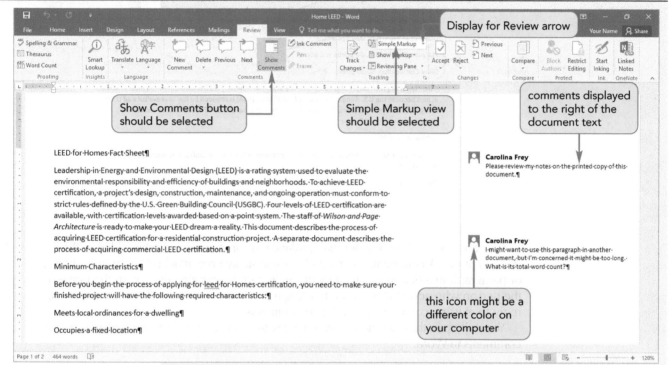

Keep in mind that when working on a small monitor, it can be helpful to switch the document Zoom level to Page Width, in which case Word automatically reduces the width of the document to accommodate the comments on the right.

8. Read the document, including the comments. The handout includes the title "LEED for Homes Fact Sheet" at the top, as well as headings (such as "Minimum Characteristics" and "Building Type") that divide the document into parts. Right now the headings are hard to spot because they don't look different from the surrounding text. Carolina used the default font size, 11-point, and the default font, Calibri (Body), for all the text in the document. Note, too, that the document includes some short paragraphs that would work better as bulleted or numbered lists.

9. Scroll down until you can see the first line on page 2 (which begins "Since its inception…"), and then click anywhere in that sentence. The message "Page 2 of 2" in the status bar, in the lower-left corner of the Word window, tells you that the insertion point is currently located on page 2 of the two-page document. The shaded space between the first and second pages of the document indicates a page break. To hide the top and bottom margins in a document, as well as the space between pages, you can double-click the shaded space between any two pages.

10. Position the mouse pointer over the shaded space between page 1 and page 2 until the pointer changes to ⊞, and then double-click. The shaded space disappears. Instead, the two pages are now separated by a gray, horizontal line.

Trouble? If the Header & Footer Tools Design contextual tab appears on the ribbon, you double-clicked the top or bottom of one of the pages, instead of in the space between them. Click the Close Header and Footer button on the Header & Footer Tools Design tab, and then repeat Step 10.

▶ **11.** Use the ⇕ pointer to double-click the gray horizontal line between pages 1 and 2. The shaded space between the two pages is redisplayed.

Working with Comments

Now that you are familiar with the Home LEED document, you can review and respond to Carolina's comments. The Comment group on the Review tab includes helpful tools for working with comments.

Working with Comments

- On the ribbon, click the Review tab.
- To display comments in an easy-to-read view, in the Tracking group, click the Display for Review button, and then click Simple Markup.
- To see the text of each comment in Simple Markup view, click the Show Comments button in the Comments group.
- To move the insertion point to the next or previous comment in the document, click the Next button or the Previous button in the Comments group.
- To delete a comment, click anywhere in the comment, and then click the Delete button in the Comments group.
- To delete all the comments in a document, click the Delete button arrow in the Comments group, and then click Delete All Comments in Document.
- To add a new comment, select the document text you want to comment on, click the New Comment button in the Comments group, and then type the comment text.
- To reply to a comment, click the Reply button to the right of the comment, and then type your reply.
- To indicate that a comment or an individual reply to a comment is no longer a concern, right-click the comment or reply, and then click Mark Comment Done in the shortcut menu. To mark a comment and all of the replies attached to it as done, right-click the original comment, and then click Mark Comment Done.

To review and respond to the comments in the document:

▶ **1.** Press the **Ctrl+Home** keys to move the insertion point to the beginning of the document.

▶ **2.** On the Review tab, in the Comments group, click the **Next** button. The first comment now has an outline, indicating that it is selected. See Figure 2-3.

Figure 2-3   **Comment attached to document text**

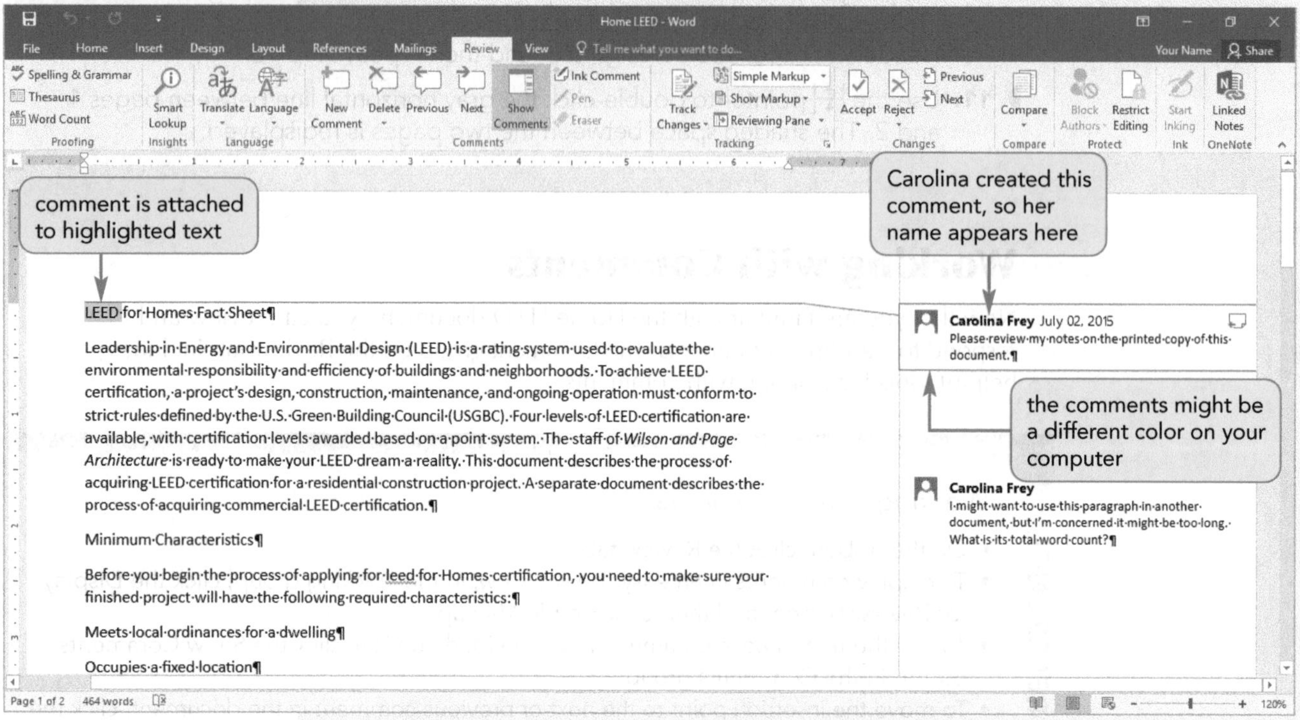

comment is attached to highlighted text

Carolina created this comment, so her name appears here

the comments might be a different color on your computer

LEED for Homes Fact Sheet¶

Leadership in Energy and Environmental Design (LEED) is a rating system used to evaluate the environmental responsibility and efficiency of buildings and neighborhoods. To achieve LEED certification, a project's design, construction, maintenance, and ongoing operation must conform to strict rules defined by the U.S. Green Building Council (USGBC). Four levels of LEED certification are available, with certification levels awarded based on a point system. The staff of *Wilson and Page Architecture* is ready to make your LEED dream a reality. This document describes the process of acquiring LEED certification for a residential construction project. A separate document describes the process of acquiring commercial LEED certification.¶

Minimum Characteristics¶

Before you begin the process of applying for leed for Homes certification, you need to make sure your finished project will have the following required characteristics:¶

Meets local ordinances for a dwelling¶

Occupies a fixed location¶

Carolina Frey July 02, 2015
Please review my notes on the printed copy of this document.¶

Carolina Frey
I might want to use this paragraph in another document, but I'm concerned it might be too long. What is its total word count?¶

In the document, the text "LEED" is highlighted. A line connects the comment to "LEED," indicating that the comment is attached to that text. Because Carolina created the comment, her name appears at the beginning of the comment, followed by the date on which she created it. The insertion point blinks at the beginning of the comment and is ready for you to edit the comment if you want.

3. Read the comment, and then in the Comments group, click the **Next** button to select the next comment. According to this comment, Carolina wants to know the total word count of the paragraph the comment is attached to. You can get this information by selecting the entire paragraph and locating the word count in the status bar.

4. Triple-click anywhere in the second paragraph of the document (which begins "Leadership in Energy and Environmental Design…") to select the paragraph. In the status bar, the message "105 of 464 words" tells you that 105 of the document's 464 words are currently selected. So the answer to Carolina's question is 105.

5. Point to the second comment to select it again, click the **Reply** button 🔲, and then type **105**. Your reply appears below Carolina's original comment.

Trouble? If you do not see the Reply button in the comment box, drag the horizontal scroll bar at the bottom of the Word window to the right until you can see it.

If you are logged in, the name that appears in your reply comment is the name associated with your Microsoft account. If you are not logged in, the name in the Reply comment is taken from the User name box on the General tab of the Word Options dialog box. You can quickly open the General tab of the Word Options dialog box by clicking the Dialog Box Launcher in the

Tracking group on the Review tab, and then clicking Change User Name. From there, you can change the username and the initials associated with your copy of Word. To override the name associated with your Microsoft account and use the name that appears in the User name box in the Word Options dialog box instead, select the "Always use these values regardless of sign in to Office" check box. However, there is no need to change these settings for this module, and you should never change them on a shared computer at school unless specifically instructed to do so by your instructor.

6. In the Comments group, click the **Next** button to move the insertion point to the next comment, which asks you to insert your name after "Prepared by:" at the end of the document.

7. Click after the colon in "Prepared by:", press the **spacebar**, and then type your first and last names. To indicate that you have complied with Carolina's request by adding your name, you could right-click the comment, and then click Mark Comment Done. However, in this case, you'll simply delete the comment. Carolina also asks you to delete the first comment in the document.

8. Click anywhere in the final comment, and then in the Comments group, click the **Delete** button.

9. In the Comments group, click the **Previous** button three times to select the comment at the beginning of the document, and then click the **Delete** button to delete the comment.

As you reviewed the document, you might have noticed that, on page 2, one of the certification levels appears in all uppercase letters. This is probably just a typing mistake. You can correct it and then add a comment that points out the change to Carolina.

To correct the mistake and add a comment:

1. Scroll down to page 2, and then, in the fourth paragraph on the page, select the text **GOLD CERTIFICATION**.

2. On the ribbon, click the **Home** tab.

3. In the Font group, click the **Change Case** button Aa , and then click **Capitalize Each Word**. The text changes to read "Gold Certification."

4. Verify that the text is still selected, and then click the **Review** tab on the ribbon.

5. In the Comments group, click the **New Comment** button. A new comment appears, with the insertion point ready for you to begin typing.

6. In the new comment, type **I assumed you didn't want this all uppercase, so I changed it.** and then save the document.

   You can now hide the text of the comments because you are finished working with them.

7. In the Comments group, click the **Show Comments** button. A "See comments" icon now appears in the document margin rather than on the right side of the Word screen. The "See comments" icon alerts you to the presence of a comment without taking up all the space required to display the comment text. You can click a comment icon to read a particular comment without displaying the text of all the comments.

8. Click the **See comments** icon . The comment icon is highlighted, and the full comment is displayed, as shown in Figure 2-4.

Figure 2-4   Document with the See comments icon

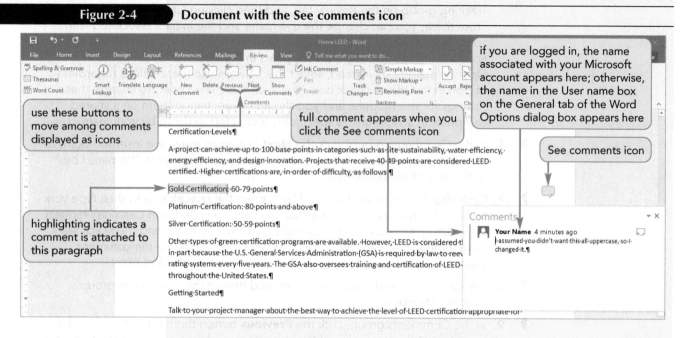

9. Click anywhere outside the comment to close it.

Creating Bulleted and Numbered Lists

A **bulleted list** is a group of related paragraphs with a black circle or other character to the left of each paragraph. For a group of related paragraphs that have a particular order (such as steps in a procedure), you can use consecutive numbers instead of bullets to create a **numbered list**. If you insert a new paragraph, delete a paragraph, or reorder the paragraphs in a numbered list, Word adjusts the numbers to make sure they remain consecutive.

PROSKILLS

Written Communication: Organizing Information in Lists

Bulleted and numbered lists are both great ways to draw the reader's attention to information. But it's important to know how to use them. Use numbers when your list contains items that are arranged by priority in a specific order. For example, in a document reviewing the procedure for performing CPR, it makes sense to use numbers for the sequential steps. Use bullets when the items in the list are of equal importance or when they can be accomplished in any order. For example, in a resume, you could use bullets for a list of professional certifications.

To add bullets to a series of paragraphs, you use the Bullets button in the Paragraph group on the Home tab. To create a numbered list, you use the Numbering button in the Paragraph group instead. Both the Bullets button and the Numbering button have arrows you can click to open a gallery of bullet or numbering styles.

Carolina asks you to format the list of minimum characteristics on page 1 as a bulleted list. She also asks you to format the list of building types on page 1 as a separate bulleted list. Finally, you need to format the list of certification levels on page 2 as a numbered list, in order of difficulty.

To apply bullets to paragraphs:

1. Scroll up until you see the paragraphs containing the list of minimum characteristics (which begins with "Meets local ordinances for a dwelling…"), and then select this paragraph and the three that follow it.

2. On the ribbon, click the **Home** tab.

TIP

The Bullets button is a toggle button, which means you can click it to add or remove bullets from selected text.

3. In the Paragraph group, click the **Bullets** button. Black circles appear as bullets before each item in the list. Also, the bulleted list is indented and the paragraph spacing between the items is reduced.

   After reviewing the default, round bullet in the document, Carolina decides she would prefer square bullets.

4. In the Paragraph group, click the **Bullets button arrow**. A gallery of bullet styles opens. See Figure 2-5.

Figure 2-5 **Bullets gallery**

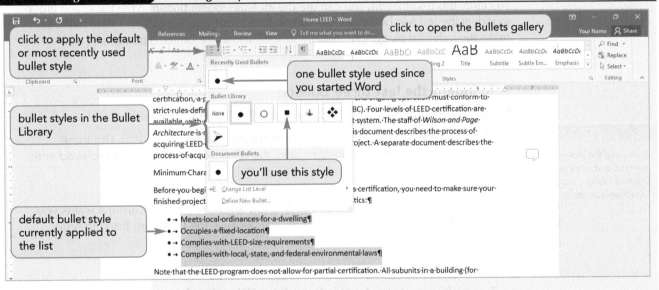

The Recently Used Bullets section appears at the top of the gallery of bullet styles; it displays the bullet styles that have been used since you started Word, which, in this case, is just the round black bullet style that was applied by default when you clicked the Bullets button. The **Bullet Library**, which offers a variety of bullet styles, is shown below the Recently Used Bullets. To create your own bullets from a picture file or from a set of predesigned symbols including diamonds, hearts, or Greek letters, click Define New Bullet, and then click the Symbol button or the Picture button in the Define New Bullet dialog box.

5. Move the mouse pointer over the bullet styles in the Bullet Library to see a Live Preview of the bullet styles in the document. Carolina prefers the black square style.

6. In the Bullet Library, click the **black square**. The round bullets are replaced with square bullets.

Next, you need to format the list of building types on page 1 with square bullets. When you first start Word, the Bullets button applies the default, round bullets you saw earlier. But after you select a new bullet style, the Bullets button applies the last bullet style you used. So, to add square bullets to the decorating styles list, you just have to select the list and click the Bullets button.

To add bullets to the list of building types:

▶ **1.** Scroll down in the document, and select the paragraphs listing the building types, starting with "Single family attached" and ending with "Pursuing the same LEED certification."

▶ **2.** In the Paragraph group, click the **Bullets** button. The list is now formatted with square black bullets.

The list is finished except for one issue. The "Batch" building type has three subrequirements, but that's not clear because of the way the list is currently formatted. To clarify this information, you can use the Increase Indent button in the Paragraph group to indent the last two bullets. When you do this, Word inserts a different style bullet to make the indented paragraphs visually subordinate to the bulleted paragraphs above.

To indent the last three bullets:

▶ **1.** In the list of building types, select the last three paragraphs.

▶ **2.** In the Paragraph group, click the **Increase Indent** button. The three paragraphs move to the right, and the black square bullets are replaced with open circle bullets.

TIP

To remove the indent from selected text, click the Decrease Indent button in the Paragraph group.

Next, you will format the list of certification levels on page 2. Carolina wants you to format this information as a numbered list because the levels are listed in order of difficulty.

To apply numbers to the list of certification levels:

▶ **1.** Scroll down to page 2 until you see the "Gold Certification: 60-79 points" paragraph. You added a comment to this paragraph earlier, but that will have no effect on the process of creating the numbered list.

▶ **2.** Select the three paragraphs containing the list of certification levels, starting with "Gold Certification: 60-79 points" and ending with "Silver Certification: 50-59 points."

▶ **3.** In the Paragraph group, click the **Numbering** button. Consecutive numbers appear in front of each item in the list. See Figure 2-6.

Figure 2-6   **Numbered list**

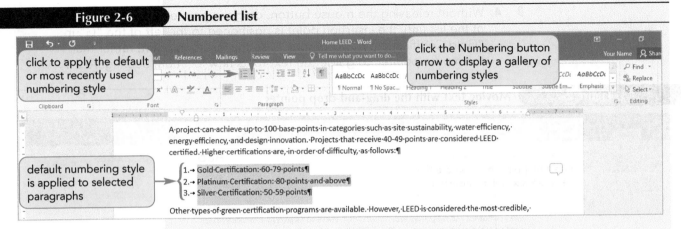

click to apply the default or most recently used numbering style

click the Numbering button arrow to display a gallery of numbering styles

default numbering style is applied to selected paragraphs

A·project·can·achieve·up·to·100·base·points·in·categories·such·as·site·sustainability,·water·efficiency,·energy·efficiency,·and·design·innovation.·Projects·that·receive·40-49·points·are·considered·LEED·certified.·Higher·certifications·are,·in·order·of·difficulty,·as·follows:¶

1.→ Gold·Certification:·60-79·points¶
2.→ Platinum·Certification:·80·points·and·above¶
3.→ Silver·Certification:·50-59·points¶

Other·types·of·green·certification·programs·are·available.·However,·LEED·is·considered·the·most·credible,·

▶ **4.** Click anywhere in the document to deselect the numbered list, and then save the document.

As with the Bullets button arrow, you can click the Numbering button arrow, and then select from a library of numbering styles. You can also indent paragraphs in a numbered list to create an outline, in which case the indented paragraphs will be preceded by lowercase letters instead of numbers. To apply a different list style to the outline (for example, with Roman numerals and uppercase letters), select the list, click the Multilevel List button in the Paragraph group, and then click a multilevel list style.

Moving Text in a Document

One of the most useful features of a word-processing program is the ability to move text easily. For example, Carolina wants to reorder the information in the numbered list. You could do this by deleting a paragraph and then retyping it at a new location. However, it's easier to select and then move the text. Word provides several ways to move text—drag and drop, cut and paste, and copy and paste.

Dragging and Dropping Text

To move text with **drag and drop**, you select the text you want to move, press and hold the mouse button while you drag the selected text to a new location, and then release the mouse button.

In the numbered list you just created, Carolina wants you to move the paragraph that reads "Silver Certification: 50-59 points" up so it is the first item in the list.

To move text using drag and drop:

▶ **1.** Select the third paragraph in the numbered list, "Silver Certification: 50-59 points," being sure to include the paragraph marker at the end. The number 3 remains unselected because it's not actually part of the paragraph text.

▶ **2.** Position the pointer over the selected text. The pointer changes to a left-facing arrow.

▶ **3.** Press and hold the mouse button, and move the pointer slightly until the drag-and-drop pointer appears. A dark black insertion point appears within the selected text.

4. Without releasing the mouse button, drag the pointer to the beginning of the list until the insertion point is positioned to the left of the "G" in "Gold Certification: 60-79 points." Use the insertion point, rather than the mouse pointer, to guide the text to its new location. See Figure 2-7.

Figure 2-7   Moving text with the drag-and-drop pointer

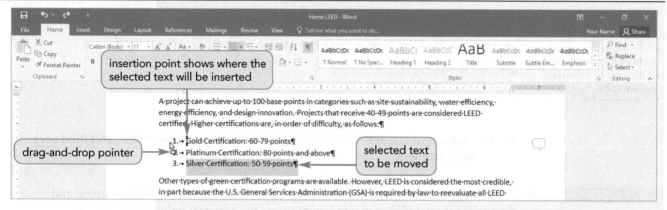

5. Release the mouse button, and then click a blank area of the document to deselect the text. The text "Silver Certification: 50-59 points" is now the first item in the list, and the remaining paragraphs have been renumbered as paragraphs 2 and 3. See Figure 2-8.

Figure 2-8   Text in new location

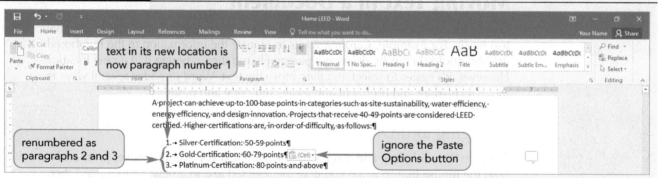

The Paste Options button appears near the newly inserted text, providing access to more advanced options related to pasting text. You don't need to use the Paste Options button right now; it will disappear when you start performing another task.

Trouble? If the selected text moves to the wrong location, click the Undo button ↩ on the Quick Access Toolbar, and then repeat Steps 2 through 5.

6. Save the document.

Dragging and dropping works well when you are moving text a short distance. When you are moving text from one page to another, it's easier to cut, copy, and paste text using the Clipboard.

Cutting or Copying and Pasting Text Using the Clipboard

The **Office Clipboard** is a temporary storage area on your computer that holds objects such as text or graphics until you need them. To **cut** means to remove text or another item from a document and place it on the Clipboard. Once you've cut something, you can paste it somewhere else. To **copy** means to copy a selected item to the Clipboard, leaving the item in its original location. To **paste** means to insert a copy of whatever is on the Clipboard into the document, at the insertion point. When you paste an item from the Clipboard into a document, the item remains on the Clipboard so you can paste it again somewhere else if you want. The buttons for cutting, copying, and pasting are located in the Clipboard group on the Home tab.

By default, Word pastes text in a new location in a document with the same formatting it had in its old location. To select other ways to paste text, you can use the Paste Options button, which appears next to newly pasted text, or the Paste button arrow in the Clipboard group. Both buttons display a menu of paste options. Two particularly useful paste options are Merge Formatting, which combines the formatting of the copied text with the formatting of the text in the new location, and Keep Text Only, which inserts the text using the formatting of the surrounding text in the new location.

When you need to keep track of multiple pieces of cut or copied text, it's helpful to open the **Clipboard task pane**, which displays the contents of the Clipboard. You open the Clipboard task pane by clicking the Dialog Box Launcher in the Clipboard group on the Home tab. When the Clipboard task pane is displayed, the Clipboard can store up to 24 text items. When the Clipboard task pane is not displayed, the Clipboard can hold only the most recently copied item.

Carolina would like to move the third-to-last sentence under the "LEED for Homes Fact Sheet" heading on page 1. You'll use cut and paste to move this sentence to a new location.

To move text using cut and paste:

1. Make sure the Home tab is selected on the ribbon.

2. Scroll up until you can see the second paragraph in the document, just below the "LEED for Homes Fact Sheet" heading.

3. Press and hold the **Ctrl** key, and then click anywhere in the third-to-last sentence of the second paragraph, which reads "The staff of *Wilson and Page Architecture* is ready to make your LEED dream a reality." The entire sentence and the space following it are selected.

4. In the Clipboard group, click the **Cut** button. The selected text is removed from the document and copied to the Clipboard.

5. Scroll down to page 2, and then click at the beginning of the second-to-last paragraph in the document, just to the left of the "T" in "Talk to your project manager...."

6. In the Clipboard group, click the **Paste** button. The sentence and the space following it are displayed in the new location. The Paste Options button appears near the newly inserted sentence.

   Trouble? If a menu opens below the Paste button, you clicked the Paste button arrow instead of the Paste button. Press the Esc key to close the menu, and then repeat Step 6, taking care not to click the arrow below the Paste button.

7. Save the document.

TIP

You can also press the Ctrl+X keys to cut selected text. Press the Ctrl+V keys to paste the most recently copied item.

Carolina explains that she'll be using some text from the Home LEED document as the basis for another department handout. She asks you to copy that information and paste it into a new document. You can do this using the Clipboard task pane.

To copy text to paste into a new document:

▶ **1.** In the Clipboard group, click the **Dialog Box Launcher**. The Clipboard task pane opens on the left side of the document window, as shown in Figure 2-9.

| Figure 2-9 | Clipboard task pane |

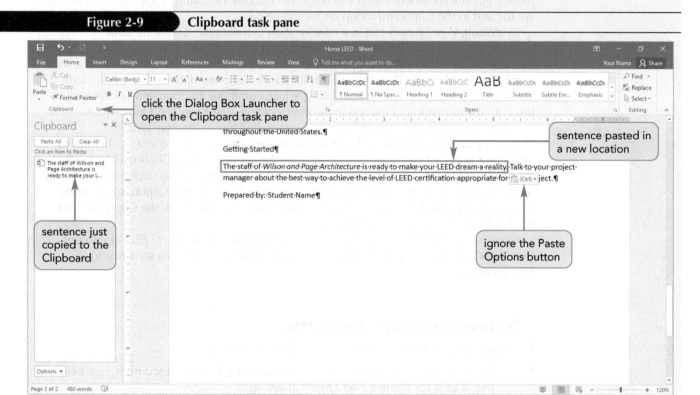

Notice the Clipboard contains the sentence you copied in the last set of steps, although you can see only the first part of the sentence.

▶ **2.** Scroll up, if necessary, and then locate the first sentence on page 2.

▶ **3.** Press and hold the **Ctrl** key, and then click anywhere in the first sentence on page 2, which begins "A project can achieve up to 100...." The sentence and the space following it are selected.

▶ **4.** In the Clipboard group, click the **Copy** button. The first part of the sentence appears at the top of the Clipboard task pane, as shown in Figure 2-10. You can also copy selected text by pressing the Ctrl+C keys.

Figure 2-10   Items in the Clipboard task pane

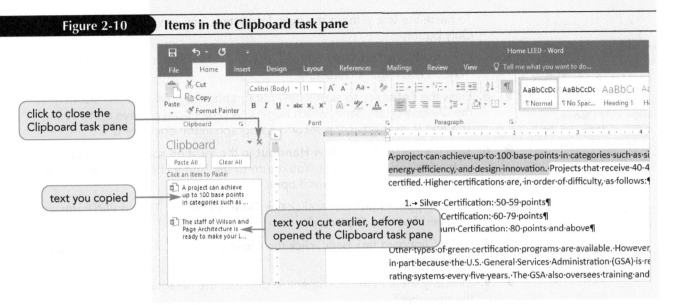

Now you can use the Clipboard task pane to insert the copied text into a new document.

To insert the copied text into a new document:

1. Open a new, blank document. If necessary, open the Clipboard task pane.

2. In the Clipboard task pane, click the second item in the list of copied items, which begins "The staff of *Wilson and Page Architecture* is ready...." The text is inserted in the document and the company name, "Wilson and Page Architecture," retains its italic formatting.

   Carolina doesn't want to keep the italic formatting in the newly pasted text. You can remove this formatting by using the Paste Options button, which is visible just below the pasted text.

3. Click the **Paste Options** button 📋 (Ctrl) ▾ in the document. The Paste Options menu opens, as shown in Figure 2-11.

Figure 2-11   Paste Options menu

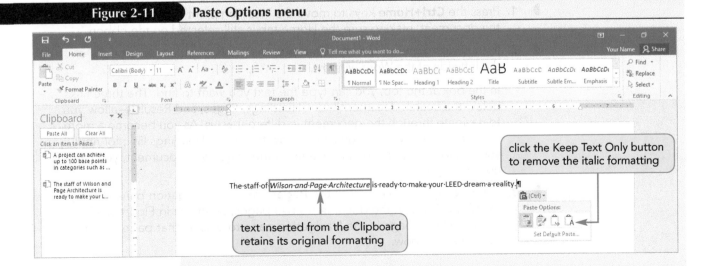

To paste the text without the italic formatting, you can click the Keep Text Only button.

TIP

To select a paste option before pasting an item, click the Paste button arrow in the Clipboard group, and then click the paste option you want.

▶ **4.** Click the **Keep Text Only** button 🄰. Word removes the italic formatting from "Wilson and Page Architecture."

▶ **5.** Press the **Enter** key to start a new paragraph, and then click the first item in the Clipboard task pane, which begins "A project can achieve up to 100...." The text is inserted as the second paragraph in the document.

▶ **6.** Save the document as **New Handout** in the location specified by your instructor, and then close it. You return to the Home LEED document, where the Clipboard task pane is still open.

▶ **7.** In the Clipboard task pane, click the **Clear All** button. The copied items are removed from the Clipboard.

▶ **8.** In the Clipboard task pane, click the **Close** button ☒. The Clipboard task pane closes.

▶ **9.** Click anywhere in the document to deselect the paragraph, and then save the document.

Using the Navigation Pane

The Navigation pane simplifies the process of moving through a document page by page. You can also use the Navigation pane to locate a particular word or phrase. You start by typing the text you're searching for—the **search text**—in the Search box at the top of the Navigation pane. As shown in the Session 2.1 Visual Overview, Word highlights every instance of the search text in the document. At the same time, a list of the **search results** appears in the Navigation pane. You can click a search result to go immediately to that location in the document.

To become familiar with the Navigation pane, you'll use it to navigate through the Home LEED document page by page. You'll start by moving the insertion point to the beginning of the document.

To navigate through the document page by page:

▶ **1.** Press the **Ctrl+Home** keys to move the insertion point to the beginning of the document, making sure the Home tab is still selected on the ribbon.

▶ **2.** In the Editing group, click the **Find** button. The Navigation pane opens on the left side of the Word window.

In the box at the top, you can type the text you want to find. The three links below the Search document box—Headings, Pages, and Results—allow you to navigate through the document in different ways. As you become a more experienced Word user, you'll learn how to use the Headings link; for now, you'll ignore it. To move quickly among the pages of a document, you can use the Pages link.

▶ **3.** In the Navigation pane, click the **Pages** link. The Navigation pane displays thumbnail icons of the document's two pages, as shown in Figure 2-12. You can click a page in the Navigation pane to display that page in the document window.

Figure 2-12   Document pages displayed in the Navigation pane

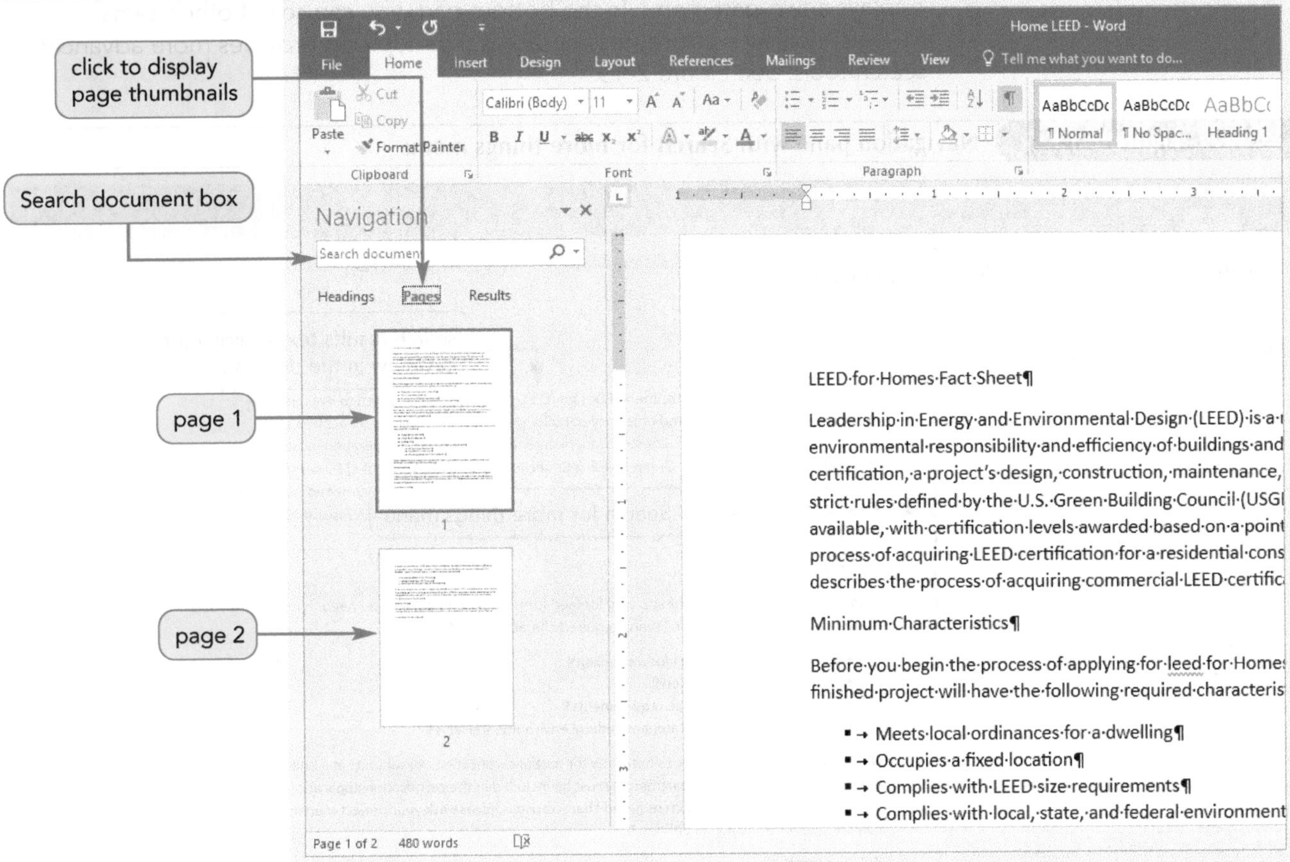

4. In the Navigation pane, click the **page 2** thumbnail. Page 2 is displayed in the document window, with the insertion point blinking at the beginning of the page.

5. In the Navigation pane, click the **page 1** thumbnail to move the insertion point back to the beginning of the document.

Carolina thinks she might have mistakenly used "leed" when she actually meant to use "LEED" in certain parts of the document. She asks you to use the Navigation pane to find all instances of "leed."

To search for "leed" in the document:

1. In the Navigation pane, click the **Results** link, click the **Search document** box, and then type **leed**. You do not have to press the Enter key.

Every instance of the word "leed" is highlighted in yellow in the document. The yellow highlight is only temporary; it will disappear as soon as you begin to perform any other task in the document. A full list of the 20 search results is displayed in the Navigation pane. Some of the search results contain "LEED" (with all uppercase letters), while others contain "leed" (with all lowercase letters). To narrow the search results, you need to tell Word to match the case of the search text.

2. In the Navigation pane, click the **Search for more things** button ▼. This displays a two-part menu. In the bottom part, you can select other items to search for, such as graphics or tables. The top part provides more advanced search tools. See Figure 2-13.

Figure 2-13 Navigation pane with Search for more things menu

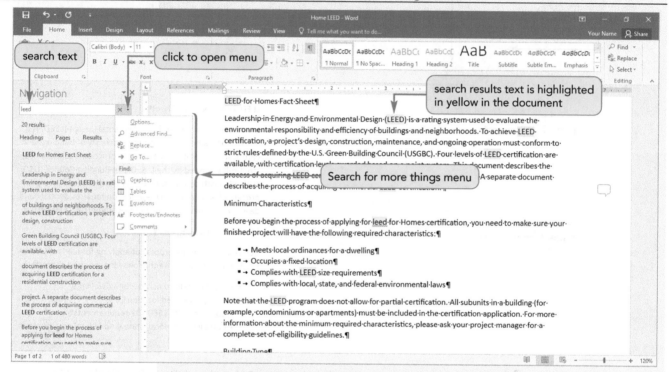

3. At the top of the Search for more things menu, click **Options** to open the Find Options dialog box.

The check boxes in this dialog box allow you to fine-tune your search. For example, to ensure that Word finds the search text only when it appears as a separate word and not when it appears as part of another word, you could select the Find whole words only check box. Right now, you are concerned only with making sure the search results have the same case as the search text.

4. Click the **Match case** check box to select it, and then click the **OK** button to close the Find Options dialog box. Now you can search the document again.

5. Press the **Ctrl+Home** keys to move the insertion point to the beginning of the document, click the **Search document** box in the Navigation pane, and then type **leed**. This time, there are only three search results in the Navigation pane, and they contain the lowercase text "leed."

To move among the search results, you can use the up and down arrows in the Navigation pane.

6. In the Navigation pane, click the **down arrow** button ▼. Word selects the first instance of "leed" in the Navigation pane, as indicated by a blue outline. Also, in the document, the first instance has a gray selection highlight over the yellow highlight. See Figure 2-14.

Figure 2-14   Navigation pane with the first search result selected

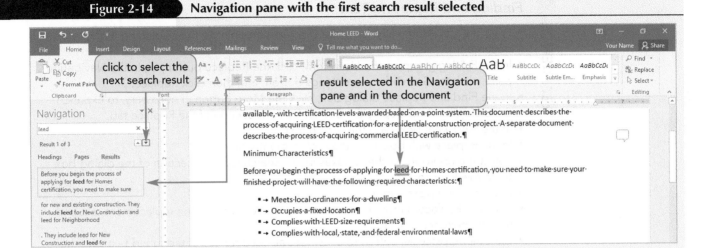

Trouble? If the second instance of "leed" is selected in the Navigation pane, then you pressed the Enter key after typing "leed" in Step 5. Click the up arrow button ▲ to select the first instance.

7. In the Navigation pane, click the **down arrow** button ▼. Word selects the second instance of "leed" in the document and in the Navigation pane.

8. Click the **down arrow** button ▼ again to select the third search result, and then click the **up arrow** button ▲ to select the second search result again.

   You can also select a search result in the document by clicking a search result in the Navigation pane.

9. In the Navigation pane, click the third search result (which begins ". They include leed for New Construction..."). The third search result is selected in the document and in the Navigation pane.

After reviewing the search results, Carolina decides she would like to replace the three instances of "leed" with "LEED." You can do that by using the Find and Replace dialog box.

Finding and Replacing Text

To open the Find and Replace dialog box from the Navigation pane, click the Search for more things button, and then click Replace. This opens the **Find and Replace dialog box**, with the Replace tab displayed by default. The Replace tab provides options for finding a specific word or phrase in the document and replacing it with another word or phrase. To use the Replace tab, type the search text in the Find what box, and then type the text you want to substitute in the Replace with box. You can also click the More button on the Replace tab to display the Search Options section, which includes the same options you saw earlier in the Find Options dialog box, including the Find whole words only check box and the Match case check box.

After you have typed the search text and selected any search options, you can click the Find Next button to select the first occurrence of the search text; you can then decide whether to substitute the search text with the replacement text.

REFERENCE

Finding and Replacing Text

- Press the Ctrl+Home keys to move the insertion point to the beginning of the document.
- In the Editing group on the Home tab, click the Replace button; or, in the Navigation pane, click the Search for more things button, and then click Replace.
- In the Find and Replace dialog box, click the More button, if necessary, to expand the dialog box and display the Search Options section of the Replace tab.
- In the Find what box, type the search text.
- In the Replace with box, type the replacement text.
- Select the appropriate check boxes in the Search Options section of the dialog box to narrow your search.
- Click the Find Next button.
- Click the Replace button to substitute the found text with the replacement text and find the next occurrence.
- Click the Replace All button to substitute all occurrences of the found text with the replacement text without reviewing each occurrence. Use this option only if you are absolutely certain that the results will be what you expect.

You'll use the Find and Replace dialog box now to replace three instances of "leed" with "LEED."

To replace three instances of "leed" with "LEED":

1. Press the **Ctrl+Home** keys to move the insertion point to the beginning of the document.

2. In the Navigation pane, click the **Search for more things** button ▼ to open the menu, and then click **Replace**. The Find and Replace dialog box opens with the Replace tab on top.

   The search text you entered earlier in the Navigation pane, "leed," appears in the Find what box. If you hadn't already conducted a search, you would need to type your search text now. Because you selected the Match case check box earlier in the Find Options dialog box, "Match Case" appears below the Find what box.

3. In the lower-left corner of the dialog box, click the **More** button to display the search options. Because you selected the Match case check box earlier in the Find Options dialog box, it is selected here.

   Trouble? If you see the Less button instead of the More button, the search options are already displayed.

4. Click the **Replace with** box, and then type **LEED**.

5. Click the **Find Next** button. Word highlights the first instance of "leed" in the document. See Figure 2-15.

Figure 2-15   **Find and Replace dialog box**

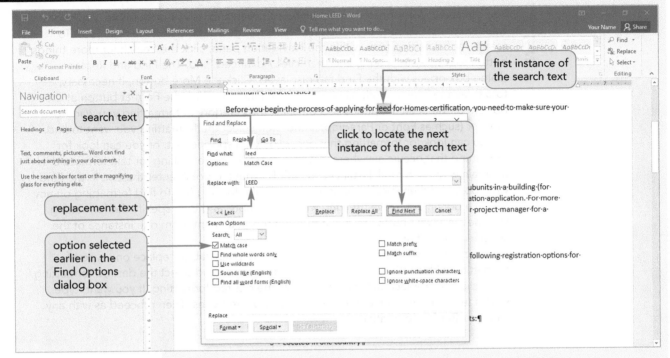

6. Click the **Replace** button. Word replaces "leed" with "LEED," so the text reads "applying for LEED for Homes certification." Then, Word selects the next instance of "leed." If you do not want to make a replacement, you can click the Find Next button to skip the current instance of the search text and move onto the next. In this case, however, you do want to make the replacement.

7. Click the **Replace** button. Word selects the last instance of "leed," which happens to be located in the same sentence.

8. Click the **Replace** button. Word makes the substitution, so the text reads "LEED for Neighborhood Development," and then displays a message box telling you that Word has finished searching the document.

9. Click the **OK** button to close the message box, and then in the Find and Replace dialog box, click the **Close** button.

You are finished with the Navigation pane, so you can close it. But first you need to restore the search options to their original settings. It's a good practice to restore the original search settings so that future searches are not affected by any settings you used for an earlier search.

To restore the search options to their original settings:

1. In the Navigation pane, open the **Find Options** dialog box, deselect the **Match case** check box, and then click the **OK** button to close the Find Options dialog box.

2. Click the **Close** button ☒ in the upper-right corner of the Navigation pane.

3. Save the document.

INSIGHT

Searching for Formatting

You can search for formatting just as you can search for text. For example, you might want to check a document to look for text formatted in bold and the Arial font. To search for formatting from within the Navigation pane, click the Search for more things button to display the menu, and then click Advanced Find. The Find and Replace dialog box opens with the Find tab displayed. Click the More button, if necessary, to display the Search Options section of the Find tab. Click the Format button at the bottom of the Search Options section, click the category of formatting you want to look for (such as Font or Paragraph), and then select the formatting you want to find.

You can look for formatting that occurs only on specific text, or you can look for formatting that occurs anywhere in a document. If you're looking for text formatted in a certain way (such as all instances of "LEED" that are bold), enter the text in the Find what box, and then specify the formatting you're looking for. To find formatting on any text in a document, leave the Find what box empty, and then specify the formatting. Use the Find Next button to move through the document, from one instance of the specified formatting to another.

You can follow the same basic steps on the Replace tab to replace one type of formatting with another. First, click the Find what box and select the desired formatting. Then click the Replace with box and select the desired formatting. If you want, type search text and replacement text in the appropriate boxes. Then proceed as with any Find and Replace operation.

Now that the text in the Home LEED document is final, you will turn your attention to styles and themes, which affect the look of the entire document.

Working with Styles

A style is a set of formatting options that you can apply by clicking an icon in the Style gallery on the Home tab. Each style is designed for a particular use. For example, the Title style is intended for formatting the title at the beginning of a document.

All the text you type into a document has a style applied to it. By default, text is formatted in the Normal style, which applies 11-point Calibri font, left alignment, 1.08 line spacing, and a small amount of extra space between paragraphs. In other words, the Normal style applies the default formatting you learned about when you first began typing a Word document.

Note that some styles apply **paragraph-level formatting**—that is, they are set up to format an entire paragraph, including the paragraph and line spacing. The Normal, Heading, and Title styles all apply paragraph-level formatting. Other styles apply **character-level formatting**—that is, they are set up to format only individual characters or words (for example, emphasizing a phrase by adding italic formatting and changing the font color).

One row of the Style gallery is always visible on the Home tab. To display the entire Style gallery, click the More button in the Styles group. After you begin applying styles in a document, the visible row of the Style gallery changes to show the most recently used styles.

You are ready to use the Style gallery to format the document title.

To display the entire Style gallery and then format the document title with a style:

1. Make sure the Home tab is still selected and locate the More button in the Styles group, as shown earlier in the Session 2.1 Visual Overview.

2. In the Styles group, click the **More** button. The Style gallery opens, displaying a total of 16 styles arranged in two rows, as shown in Figure 2-16. If your screen is set at a lower resolution than the screenshots in this book, the Style gallery on your screen might contain more than two rows.

Figure 2-16	Displaying the Style gallery

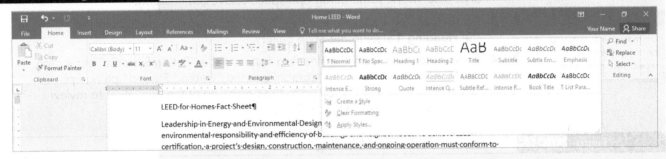

You don't actually need any of the styles in the bottom row now, so you can close the Style gallery.

3. Press the **Esc** key to close the Style gallery.

4. Click anywhere in the first paragraph, "LEED for Homes Fact Sheet," if necessary, and then point to (but don't click) the **Title** style, which is the fifth style from the left in the top row of the gallery. The ScreenTip "Title" is displayed, and a Live Preview of the style appears in the paragraph containing the insertion point, as shown in Figure 2-17. The Title style changes the font to 28-point Calibri Light.

Figure 2-17	Title style in the Style gallery

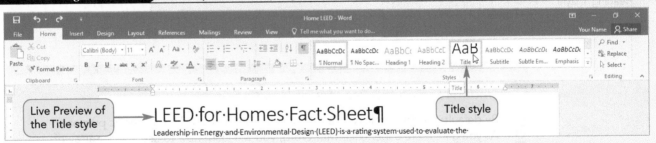

5. Click the **Title** style. The style is applied to the paragraph. To finish the title, you need to center it.

6. In the Paragraph group, click the **Center** button ▤. The title is centered in the document.

Next, you will format the document headings using the heading styles, which have different levels. The highest level, Heading 1, is used for the major headings in a document, and it applies the most noticeable formatting with a larger font than the other heading styles. (In heading styles, the highest, or most important, level has the lowest number.) The Heading 2 style is used for headings that are subordinate to the highest level headings; it applies slightly less dramatic formatting than the Heading 1 style.

The Home LEED handout only has one level of headings, so you will apply only the Heading 1 style.

To format text with the Heading 1 style:

1. Click anywhere in the "Minimum Characteristics" paragraph.

2. On the Home tab, in the Style gallery, click the **Heading 1** style. The paragraph is now formatted in blue, 16-point Calibri Light. The Heading 1 style also inserts some paragraph space above the heading.

TIP

On most computers, you can press the F4 key to repeat your most recent action.

3. Scroll down, click anywhere in the "Building Type" paragraph, and then click the **Heading 1** style in the Style gallery.

4. Repeat Step 3 to apply the Heading 1 style to the "Rating Systems" paragraph, the "Certification Levels" paragraph, and the "Getting Started" paragraph. When you are finished, scroll up to the beginning of the document to review the new formatting. See Figure 2-18.

| Figure 2-18 | **Document with Title and Heading 1 styles** |

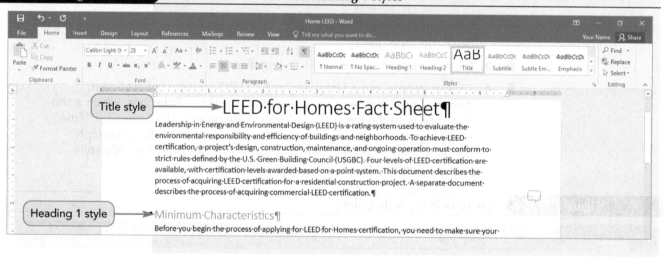

Understanding the Benefits of Heading Styles

INSIGHT

By default, the Style gallery offers 16 styles, each designed for a specific purpose. As you gain more experience with Word, you will learn how to use a wider array of styles. You'll also learn how to create your own styles. Styles allow you to change a document's formatting in an instant. But the benefits of heading styles go far beyond attractive formatting. Heading styles allow you to reorganize a document or generate a table of contents with a click of the mouse. Also, heading styles are set up to keep a heading and the body text that follows it together, so a heading is never separated from its body text by a page break. Each Word document includes nine levels of heading styles, although only the Heading 1 and Heading 2 styles are available by default in the Style gallery. Whenever you use the lowest heading style in the Style gallery, the next-lowest level is added to the Style gallery. For example, after you use the Heading 2 style, the Heading 3 style appears in the Styles group in the Style gallery.

After you format a document with a variety of styles, you can alter the look of the document by changing the document's theme.

Working with Themes

A **theme** is a coordinated collection of fonts, colors, and other visual effects designed to give a document a cohesive, polished look. A variety of themes are installed with Word, with more available online at Templates.office.com. When you open a new, blank document in Word, the Office theme is applied by default. To change a document's theme, you click the Themes button, which is located in the Document Formatting group on the Design tab, and then click the theme you want. Pointing to the Themes button displays a ScreenTip that tells you what theme is currently applied to the document.

When applying color to a document, you usually have the option of selecting a color from a palette of colors designed to match the current theme or from a palette of standard colors. For instance, recall that the colors in the Font Color gallery are divided into Theme Colors and Standard Colors. When you select a Standard Color, such as Dark Red, that color remains the same no matter which theme you apply to the document. But when you click one of the Theme Colors, you are essentially telling Word to use the color located in that particular spot on the Theme Colors palette. Then, if you change the document's theme later, Word substitutes a color from the same location on the Theme Colors palette. This ensures that all the colors in a document are drawn from a group of colors coordinated to look good together. So as a rule, if you are going to use multiple colors in a document (perhaps for paragraph shading and font color), it's a good idea to stick with the Theme Colors.

A similar substitution takes place with fonts when you change the theme. However, to understand how this works, you need to understand the difference between headings and body text. Carolina's document includes the headings "Minimum Characteristics," "Building Type," "Rating Systems," "Certification Levels," and "Getting Started"—all of which you have formatted with the Heading1 style. The title of the document, "LEED for Homes Fact Sheet," is now formatted with the Title style, which is also a type of heading style. Everything else in the Home LEED document is body text.

To ensure that your documents have a harmonious look, each theme assigns a font for headings and a font for body text. Typically, in a given theme, the same font is used for both headings and body text, but not always. In the Office theme, for instance, they are slightly different; the heading font is Calibri Light, and the body font is Calibri. These two fonts appear at the top of the Font list as "Calibri Light (Headings)" and "Calibri (Body)" when you click the Font box arrow in the Font group on the Home tab. When you begin typing text in a new document with the Office theme, the text is formatted as body text with the Calibri font by default.

When applying a font to selected text, you can choose one of the two theme fonts at the top of the Font list, or you can choose one of the other fonts in the Font list. If you choose one of the other fonts and then change the document theme, that font remains the same. But if you use one of the theme fonts and then change the document theme, Word substitutes the appropriate font from the new theme. When you paste text into a document that has a different theme, Word applies the theme fonts and colors of the new document. To retain the original formatting, use the Keep Source Formatting option in the Paste Options menu.

Figure 2-19 compares elements of the default Office theme with the Integral theme. The Integral theme was chosen for this example because, like the Office theme, it has different heading and body fonts.

TIP

Each document theme is designed to convey a specific look and feel. The Office theme is designed to be appropriate for standard business documents. Other themes are designed to give documents a flashier look.

Figure 2-19   **Comparing the Office theme to the Integral theme**

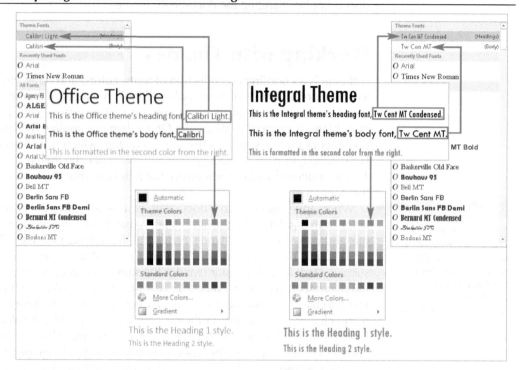

Because Carolina has not yet selected a new theme, the Office theme is currently applied to the Home LEED document. However, she thinks the Berlin theme might be more appropriate for the Home LEED document. She asks you to apply it now.

To change the document's theme:

1. If necessary, press the **Ctrl+Home** keys to move the insertion point to the beginning of the document. With the title and first heading visible, you will more easily see what happens when you change the document's theme.

2. On the ribbon, click the **Design** tab.

3. In the Document Formatting group, point to the **Themes** button. A ScreenTip appears containing the text "Current: Office Theme" as well as general information about themes.

4. In the Document Formatting group, click the **Themes** button. The Themes gallery opens. Because Microsoft occasionally updates the available themes, you might see a different list than the one shown in Figure 2-20.

Figure 2-20   Themes gallery

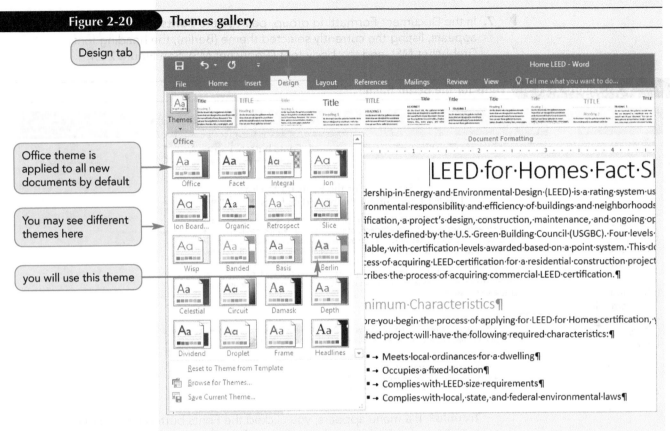

Design tab

Office theme is applied to all new documents by default

You may see different themes here

you will use this theme

▶ **5.** Move the mouse pointer (without clicking it) over the various themes in the gallery to see a Live Preview of each theme in the document. The heading and body fonts as well as the heading colors change to reflect the fonts associated with the various themes.

▶ **6.** In the Themes gallery, click the **Berlin** theme. The text in the Home LEED document changes to the body and heading fonts of the Berlin theme, with the headings formatted in dark orange. To see exactly what the Berlin theme fonts are, you can point to the Fonts button in the Document Formatting group.

   Trouble? If you do not see the Berlin theme in your Themes gallery, click a different theme.

7. In the Document Formatting group, point to the **Fonts** button. A ScreenTip appears, listing the currently selected theme (Berlin), the heading font (Trebuchet MS), and the body font (Trebuchet MS). See Figure 2-21.

Figure 2-21   **Fonts for the Berlin theme**

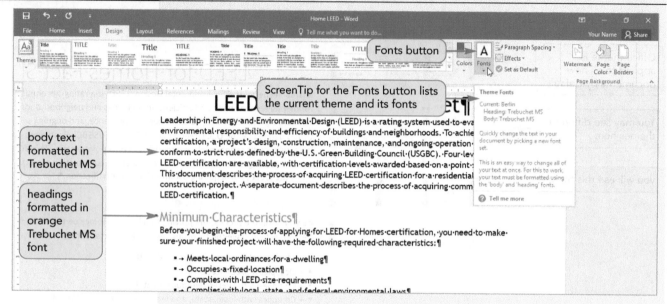

Trouble? If a menu appears, you clicked the Fonts button instead of pointing to it. Press the Esc key, and then repeat Step 7.

8. Save your changes and then close the document.

Carolina's Home LEED document is ready to be handed in to her supervisor. The use of styles, bulleted and numbered lists, and a new theme gives the document a professional look appropriate for use in a business handout.

INSIGHT

Personalizing the Word Interface

The Word Options dialog box allows you to change the look of the Word interface. For starters, you can change the Office Theme from the default setting (Colorful) to Dark Gray or White. Note that in this context, "Office Theme" refers to the colors of the Word interface, and not the colors and fonts used in a Word document. You can also use the Office Background setting to add graphic designs, such as clouds or stars, to the Word interface. To get started, click the File tab, click Options in the navigation bar, and then select the options you want in the Personalize your copy of Microsoft Office section of the Word Options dialog box.

REVIEW

Session 2.1 Quick Check

1. When you reply to a comment, what name appears in the reply?
2. When should you use a numbered list instead of a bulleted list?
3. How can you ensure that the Navigation pane will find instances of "LEED" instead of "leed"?
4. What style is applied to all text in a new document by default?
5. What theme is applied to a new document by default?

Session 2.2 Visual Overview:

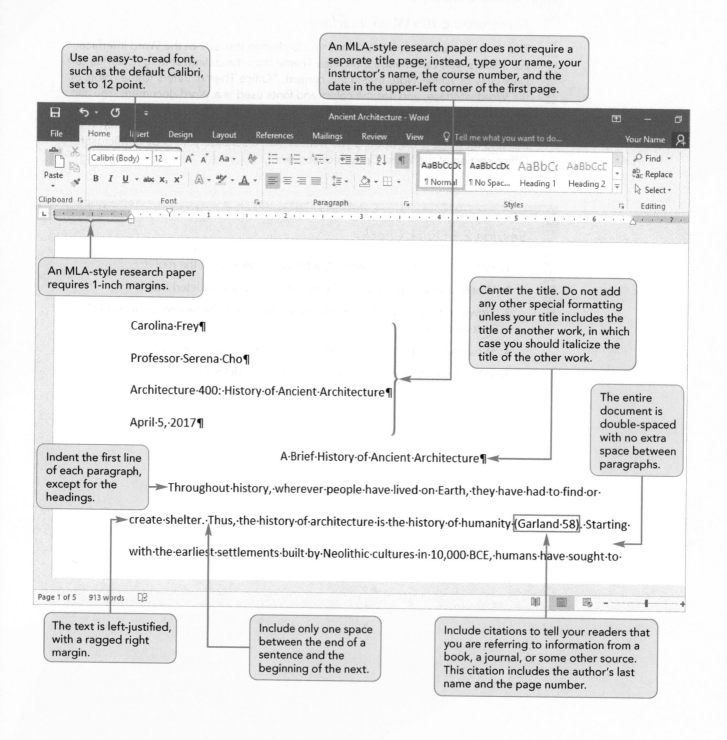

Use an easy-to-read font, such as the default Calibri, set to 12 point.

An MLA-style research paper does not require a separate title page; instead, type your name, your instructor's name, the course number, and the date in the upper-left corner of the first page.

An MLA-style research paper requires 1-inch margins.

Center the title. Do not add any other special formatting unless your title includes the title of another work, in which case you should italicize the title of the other work.

The entire document is double-spaced with no extra space between paragraphs.

Indent the first line of each paragraph, except for the headings.

The text is left-justified, with a ragged right margin.

Include only one space between the end of a sentence and the beginning of the next.

Include citations to tell your readers that you are referring to information from a book, a journal, or some other source. This citation includes the author's last name and the page number.

Carolina·Frey¶

Professor·Serena·Cho¶

Architecture·400:·History·of·Ancient·Architecture¶

April·5,·2017¶

A·Brief·History·of·Ancient·Architecture¶

Throughout·history,·wherever·people·have·lived·on·Earth,·they·have·had·to·find·or·

create·shelter.·Thus,·the·history·of·architecture·is·the·history·of·humanity·(Garland·58)·.·Starting·

with·the·earliest·settlements·built·by·Neolithic·cultures·in·10,000·BCE,·humans·have·sought·to·

MLA Formatting Guidelines

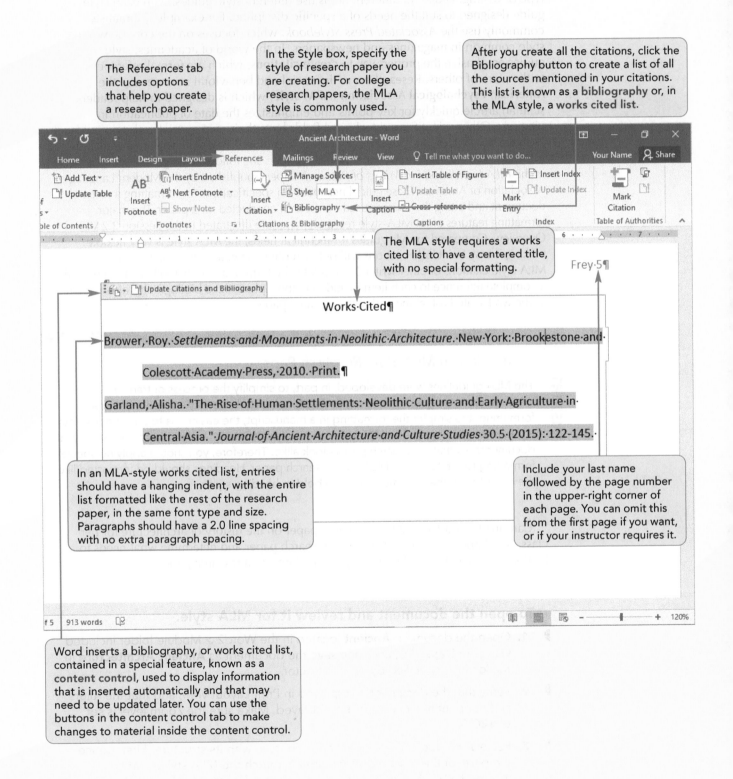

The References tab includes options that help you create a research paper.

In the Style box, specify the style of research paper you are creating. For college research papers, the MLA style is commonly used.

After you create all the citations, click the Bibliography button to create a list of all the sources mentioned in your citations. This list is known as a **bibliography** or, in the MLA style, a **works cited list**.

The MLA style requires a works cited list to have a centered title, with no special formatting.

Frey 5¶

Works Cited¶

Brower, Roy. *Settlements and Monuments in Neolithic Architecture.* New York: Brookestone and Colescott Academy Press, 2010. Print.¶

Garland, Alisha. "The Rise of Human Settlements: Neolithic Culture and Early Agriculture in Central Asia." *Journal of Ancient Architecture and Culture Studies* 30.5 (2015): 122-145.

In an MLA-style works cited list, entries should have a hanging indent, with the entire list formatted like the rest of the research paper, in the same font type and size. Paragraphs should have a 2.0 line spacing with no extra paragraph spacing.

Include your last name followed by the page number in the upper-right corner of each page. You can omit this from the first page if you want, or if your instructor requires it.

Word inserts a bibliography, or works cited list, contained in a special feature, known as a **content control**, used to display information that is inserted automatically and that may need to be updated later. You can use the buttons in the content control tab to make changes to material inside the content control.

Reviewing the MLA Style

A **style guide** is a set of rules that describe the preferred format and style for a certain type of writing. People in different fields use different style guides, with each style guide designed to suit the needs of a specific discipline. For example, journalists commonly use the *Associated Press Stylebook*, which focuses on the concise writing style common in magazines and newspapers. In the world of academics, style guides emphasize the proper way to create **citations**, which are formal references to the work of others. Researchers in the social and behavioral sciences use the **American Psychological Association (APA) style**, which is designed to help readers scan an article quickly for key points and emphasizes the date of publication in citations. Other scientific and technical fields have their own specialized style guides.

In the humanities, the **Modern Language Association (MLA) style** is widely used. This is the style Carolina has used for her research paper. She followed the guidelines specified in the *MLA Handbook for Writers of Research Papers*, published by the Modern Language Association of America. These guidelines focus on specifications for formatting a research document and citing the sources used in research conducted for a paper. The major formatting features of an MLA-style research paper are illustrated in the Session 2.2 Visual Overview. Compared to style guides for technical fields, the MLA style is very flexible, making it easy to include citations without disrupting the natural flow of the writing. MLA-style citations of other writers' works take the form of a brief parenthetical entry, with a complete reference to each item included in the alphabetized bibliography, also known as the works cited list, at the end of the research paper.

INSIGHT

Formatting an MLA-Style Research Paper

The MLA guidelines were developed, in part, to simplify the process of transforming a manuscript into a journal article or a chapter of a book. The style calls for minimal formatting; the simpler the formatting in a manuscript, the easier it is to turn the text into a published document. The MLA guidelines were also designed to ensure consistency in documents, so that all research papers look alike. Therefore, you should apply no special formatting to the text in an MLA-style research paper. Headings should be formatted like the other text in the document, with no bold or heading styles.

Carolina has started writing a research paper on the history of architecture for her class. You'll open the draft of Carolina's research paper and determine what needs to be done to make it meet the MLA style guidelines for a research paper.

To open the document and review it for MLA style:

▸ **1.** Open the document **Ancient** located in the Word2 > Module folder included with your Data Files, and then save the document as **Ancient Architecture** in the location specified by your instructor.

▸ **2.** Verify that the document is displayed in Print Layout view, and that the rulers and nonprinting characters are displayed. Make sure the Zoom level is set to **120%**.

▸ **3.** Review the document to familiarize yourself with its structure. First, notice the parts of the document that already match the MLA style. Carolina included a block of information in the upper-left corner of the first page, giving her name, her instructor's name, the course name, and the date. The title at the top of the first page also meets the MLA guidelines in that it is centered and does not have any special formatting. The headings

("Neolithic Settlements," "Egyptian Construction," "The Civic-Minded Greeks," and "Roman Achievement") have no special formatting; but unlike the title, they are left-aligned. Finally, the body text is left-aligned with a ragged right margin, and the entire document is formatted in the same font, Calibri, which is easy to read.

What needs to be changed in order to make Carolina's paper consistent with the MLA style? Currently, the entire document is formatted using the default settings, which are the Normal style for the Office theme. To transform the document into an MLA-style research paper, you need to complete the checklist shown in Figure 2-22.

| Figure 2-22 | Checklist for formatting a default Word document to match the MLA style |

✓ Double-space the entire document.

✓ Remove paragraph spacing from the entire document.

✓ Increase the font size for the entire document to 12 points.

✓ Indent the first line of each body paragraph .5 inch from the left margin.

✓ Add the page number (preceded by your last name) in the upper-right corner of each page. If you prefer, you can omit this from the first page.

You'll take care of the first three items in the checklist now.

To begin applying MLA formatting to the document:

1. Press the **Ctrl+A** keys to select the entire document.

2. Make sure the Home tab is selected on the ribbon.

3. In the Paragraph group, click the **Line and Paragraph Spacing** button, and then click **2.0**.

4. Click the **Line and Spacing** button again, and then click **Remove Space After Paragraph**. The entire document is now double-spaced, with no paragraph spacing, and the entire document is still selected.

5. In the Font group, click the **Font Size** arrow, and then click **12**. The entire document is formatted in 12-point font.

6. Click anywhere in the document to deselect the text.

7. In the first paragraph of the document, replace Carolina's name with your first and last names, and then save the document.

Now you need to indent the first line of each body paragraph.

Indenting a Paragraph

Word offers a number of options for indenting a paragraph. You can move an entire paragraph to the right, or you can create specialized indents, such as a **hanging indent**, where all lines except the first line of the paragraph are indented from the left margin. As you saw in the Session 2.2 Visual Overview, all the body paragraphs (that is, all the paragraphs except the information in the upper-left corner of the first page, the title, and the headings) have a first-line indent in MLA research papers. Figure 2-23 shows some examples of other common paragraph indents.

Figure 2-23 **Common paragraph indents**

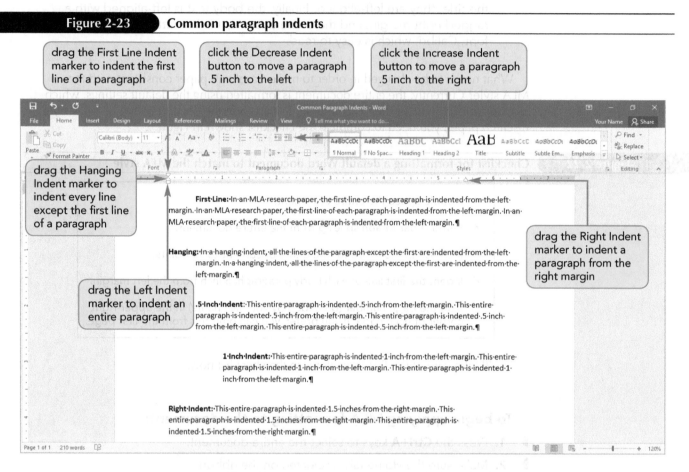

To quickly indent an entire paragraph .5 inch from the left, position the insertion point in the paragraph you want to indent, and then click the Increase Indent button in the Paragraph group on the Home tab. You can continue to indent the paragraph in increments of .5 inch by repeatedly clicking the Increase Indent button. To move an indented paragraph back to the left .5 inch, click the Decrease Indent button.

To create first-line, hanging, or right indents, you can use the indent markers on the ruler. First, click in the paragraph you want to indent or select multiple paragraphs. Then drag the appropriate indent marker to the left or right on the horizontal ruler. The indent markers are small and can be hard to see. As shown in Figure 2-23, the **First Line Indent marker** looks like the top half of an hourglass; the **Hanging Indent marker** looks like the bottom half. The rectangle below the Hanging Indent marker is the **Left Indent marker**. The **Right Indent marker** looks just like the Hanging Indent marker except that it is located on the far-right side of the horizontal ruler.

Note that when you indent an entire paragraph using the Increase Indent button, the three indent markers, shown stacked on top of one another in Figure 2-23, move as a unit along with the paragraphs you are indenting.

In Carolina's paper, you will indent the first lines of the body paragraphs .5 inch from the left margin, as specified by the MLA style.

To indent the first line of each paragraph:

1. On the first page of the document, just below the title, click anywhere in the first main paragraph, which begins "Throughout history...."

2. On the horizontal ruler, position the mouse pointer over the First Line Indent marker 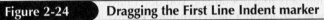. When you see the ScreenTip that reads "First Line Indent," you know the mouse is positioned correctly.

3. Press and hold the mouse button as you drag the **First Line Indent** marker ▽ to the right, to the .5-inch mark on the horizontal ruler. As you drag, a vertical guideline appears over the document, and the first line of the paragraph moves right. See Figure 2-24.

Figure 2-24 ▶ **Dragging the First Line Indent marker**

First Line Indent marker

.5-inch mark

guideline appears as you drag the indent marker and the first line of the paragraph moves right

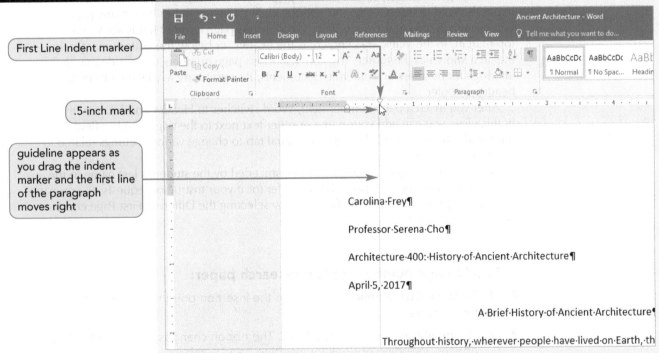

Carolina·Frey¶

Professor·Serena·Cho¶

Architecture·400:·History·of·Ancient·Architecture¶

April·5,·2017¶

A·Brief·History·of·Ancient·Architecture¶

Throughout·history,·wherever·people·have·lived·on·Earth,·th

TIP

You can also click the Dialog Box Launcher in the Paragraph group and then adjust the Indentation settings for one or more selected paragraphs.

4. When the First Line Indent marker ▽ is positioned at the .5-inch mark on the ruler, release the mouse button. The first line of the paragraph containing the insertion point indents .5 inch, and the vertical guideline disappears.

5. Scroll down, if necessary, click anywhere in the next paragraph in the document (which begins "In this paper, I will present..."), and then drag the **First Line Indent** marker ▽ to the right, to the .5-inch mark on the horizontal ruler. As you move the indent marker, you can use the vertical guideline to ensure that you match the first-line indent of the preceding paragraph.

   You could continue to drag the indent marker to indent the first line of the remaining body paragraphs, but it's faster to use the Repeat button on the Quick Access Toolbar.

6. Scroll down and click in the paragraph below the "Neolithic Settlements" heading, and then on the Quick Access Toolbar, click the **Repeat** button ↻.

7. Click in the next paragraph, at the top of page 2 (which begins "The rise of agriculture introduced..."), and then click the **Repeat** button ↻.

▶ 8. Continue using the **Repeat** button ⟳ to indent the first line of all of the remaining body paragraphs. Take care not to indent the headings, which in this document are formatted just like the body text.

▶ 9. Scroll to the top of the document, verify that you have correctly indented the first line of each body paragraph, and then save the document.

Next, you need to insert page numbers.

Inserting and Modifying Page Numbers

When you insert page numbers in a document, you don't have to type a page number on each page. Instead, you can insert a **page number field**, which is an instruction that tells Word to insert a page number on each page, no matter how many pages you eventually add to the document. Word inserts page number fields above the top margin, in the blank area known as the **header**, or below the bottom margin, in the area known as the **footer**. You can also insert page numbers in the side margins, although for business or academic documents, it's customary to place them in the header or footer.

After you insert a page number field, Word switches to Header and Footer view. In this view, you can add your name or other text next to the page number field or use the Header & Footer Tools Design contextual tab to change various settings related to headers and footers.

The MLA style requires a page number preceded by the student's last name in the upper-right corner of each page. If you prefer (or if your instructor requests it), you can omit the page number from the first page by selecting the Different First Page check box on the Design tab.

To add page numbers to the research paper:

▶ 1. Press the **Ctrl+Home** keys to move the insertion point to the beginning of the document.

▶ 2. On the ribbon, click the **Insert** tab. The ribbon changes to display the Insert options, including options for inserting page numbers.

TIP

To remove page numbers from a document, click the Remove Page Numbers command on the Page Number menu.

▶ 3. In the Header & Footer group, click the **Page Number** button to open the Page Number menu. Here you can choose where you want to position the page numbers in your document—at the top of the page, at the bottom of the page, in the side margins, or at the current location of the insertion point.

▶ 4. Point to **Top of Page**. A gallery of page number styles opens. You can scroll the list to review the many styles of page numbers. Because the MLA style calls for a simple page number in the upper-right corner, you will use the Plain Number 3 style. See Figure 2-25.

Figure 2-25 **Gallery of page number styles**

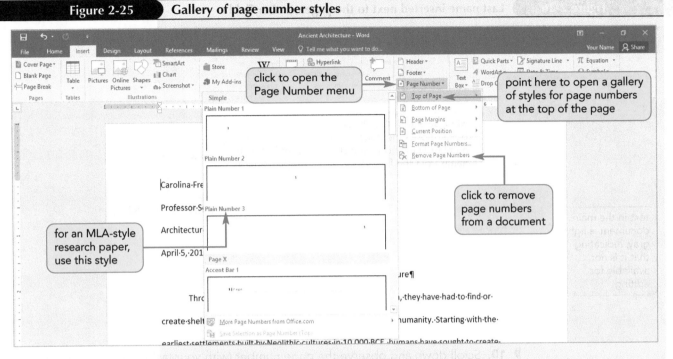

5. In the gallery, click the **Plain Number 3** style. The Word window switches to Header and Footer view, with the page number for the first page in the upper-right corner. The page number has a gray background, indicating that it is actually a page number field and not simply a number that you typed.

The Header & Footer Tools Design tab is displayed on the ribbon, giving you access to a variety of formatting options. The insertion point blinks to the left of the page number field, ready for you to add text to the header if you wish. Note that in Header and Footer view, you can type only in the header or footer areas. The text in the main document area is a lighter shade of gray, indicating that it cannot be edited in this view.

6. Type your last name, and then press the **spacebar**. If you see a wavy red line below your last name, right-click your name, and then click **Ignore All** on the Shortcut menu.

7. Select your last name and the page number field.

8. In the Mini toolbar, click the **Font Size** button arrow, click **12**, and then click anywhere in the header to deselect it. Now the header's font size matches the font size of the rest of the document. This isn't strictly necessary in an MLA research paper, but some instructors prefer it. The page number no longer has a gray background, but it is still a field, which you can verify by clicking it.

9. Click the **page number field** to display its gray background. See Figure 2-26.

Figure 2-26 **Last name inserted next to the page number field**

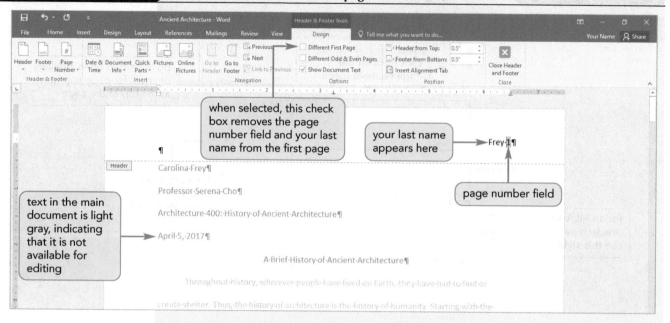

> **10.** Scroll down and observe the page number (with your last name) at the top of pages 2, 3, and 4. As you can see, whatever you insert in the header on one page appears on every page of the document by default.

> **11.** Press the **Ctrl+Home** keys to return to the header on the first page.

> **12.** On the Header & Footer Tools Design tab, in the Options group, click the **Different First Page** check box to insert a check. The page number field and your last name are removed from the first page header. The insertion point blinks at the header's left margin in case you want to insert something else for the first page header. In this case, you don't.

TIP

After you insert page numbers, you can reopen Header and Footer view by double-clicking a page number in Print Layout view.

> **13.** In the Close group, click the **Close Header and Footer** button. You return to Print Layout view, and the Header & Footer Tools Design tab is no longer displayed on the ribbon.

> **14.** Scroll down to review your last name and the page number in the headers for pages 2, 3, and 4. In Print Layout view, the text in the header is light gray, indicating that it is not currently available for editing.

You have finished all the tasks related to formatting the MLA-style research paper. Now Carolina wants your help with creating the essential parts of any research paper—the citations and the bibliography.

Creating Citations and a Bibliography

A bibliography (or, as it is called in the MLA style, the works cited list) is an alphabetical list of all the books, magazine articles, websites, movies, and other works referred to in a research paper. The items listed in a bibliography are known as **sources**. The entry for each source includes information such as the author, the title of the work, the publication date, and the publisher.

Within the research paper itself, you include a parenthetical reference, or citation, every time you quote or refer to a source. Every source included in your citations then has a corresponding entry in the works cited list. A citation should include enough information to identify the quote or referenced material so the reader can easily locate the source in the accompanying works cited list. The exact form for a citation varies depending on the style guide you are using and the type of material you are referencing.

Some style guides are very rigid about the form and location of citations, but the MLA style offers quite a bit of flexibility. Typically, though, you insert an MLA citation at the end of a sentence in which you quote or refer to material from a source. For books or journals, the citation itself usually includes the author's last name and a page number. However, if the sentence containing the citation already includes the author's name, you need to include only the page number in the citation. Figure 2-27 provides some sample MLA citations; the format shown could be used for books or journals. For detailed guidelines, you can consult the *MLA Handbook for Writers of Research Papers, Seventh Edition*, which includes many examples.

Figure 2-27   **MLA guidelines for citing a book or journal**

Citation Rule	Example
If the sentence includes the author's name, the citation should only include the page number.	Peterson compares the opening scene of the movie to a scene from Shakespeare (188).
If the sentence does not include the author's name, the citation should include the author's name and the page number.	The opening scene of the movie has been compared to a scene from Shakespeare (Peterson 188).

Word greatly simplifies the process of creating citations and a bibliography. You specify the style you want to use, and then Word takes care of setting up the citation and the works cited list appropriately. Every time you create a citation for a new source, Word prompts you to enter the information needed to create the corresponding entry in the works cited list. If you don't have all of your source information available, Word also allows you to insert a temporary, placeholder citation, which you can replace later with a complete citation. When you are finished creating your citations, Word generates the bibliography automatically. Note that placeholder citations are not included in the bibliography.

Written Communication: Acknowledging Your Sources

A research paper is a means for you to explore the available information about a subject and then present this information, along with your own understanding of the subject, in an organized and interesting way. Acknowledging all the sources of the information presented in your research paper is essential. If you fail to do this, you might be subject to charges of plagiarism, or trying to pass off someone else's thoughts as your own. Plagiarism is an extremely serious accusation for which you could suffer academic consequences ranging from failing an assignment to being expelled from school.

To ensure that you don't forget to cite a source, you should be careful about creating citations in your document as you type. It's very easy to forget to go back and cite all your sources correctly after you've finished typing a research paper. Failing to cite a source could lead to accusations of plagiarism and all the consequences that entails. If you don't have the complete information about a source available when you are typing your paper, you should at least insert a placeholder citation. But take care to go back later and substitute complete citations for any placeholders.

Creating Citations

Before you create citations, you need to select the style you want to use, which in the case of Carolina's paper is the MLA style. Then, to insert a citation, you click the Insert Citation button in the Citations & Bibliography group on the References tab. If you are citing a source for the first time, Word prompts you to enter all the information required for the source's entry in the bibliography or works cited list. If you are citing an existing source, you simply select the source from the Insert Citation menu.

By default, an MLA citation includes only the author's name in parentheses. However, you can use the Edit Citation dialog box to add a page number. You can also use the Edit Citation dialog box to remove, or suppress, the author's name, so only the page number appears in the citation. However, in an MLA citation, Word will replace the suppressed author name with the title of the source, so you need to suppress the title as well, by selecting the Title check box in the Edit Citation dialog box.

REFERENCE

Creating Citations

- On the ribbon, click the References tab. In the Citations & Bibliography group, click the Style button arrow, and then select the style you want.
- Click in the document where you want to insert the citation. Typically, a citation goes at the end of a sentence, before the ending punctuation.
- To add a citation for a new source, click the Insert Citation button in the Citations & Bibliography group, click Add New Source, enter information in the Create Source dialog box, and then click the OK button.
- To add a citation for an existing source, click the Insert Citation button, and then click the source.
- To add a placeholder citation, click the Insert Citation button, click Add New Placeholder, and then, in the Placeholder Name dialog box, type placeholder text, such as the author's last name, that will serve as a reminder about which source you need to cite. Note that a placeholder citation cannot contain any spaces.
- To add a page number to a citation, click the citation in the document, click the Citation Options button, click Edit Citation, type the page number, and then click the OK button.
- To display only the page number in a citation, click the citation in the document, click the Citation Options button, and then click Edit Citation. In the Edit Citation dialog box, select the Author and Title check boxes to suppress this information, and then click the OK button.

So far, Carolina has referenced information from two different sources in her research paper. You'll select a style and then begin adding the appropriate citations.

To select a style for the citation and bibliography:

1. On the ribbon, click the **References** tab. The ribbon changes to display references options.

2. In the Citations & Bibliography group, click the **Style button** arrow, and then click **MLA Seventh Edition** if it is not already selected.

3. Press the **Ctrl+F** keys to open the Navigation pane.

4. Use the Navigation pane to find the phrase "As at least one historian," which appears on page 2, and then click in the document at the end of that sentence (between the end of the word "standing" and the closing period).

5. Close the **Navigation** pane, and then click the **References** tab on the ribbon, if necessary. You need to add a citation that informs the reader that historian Roy Brauer made the observation described in the sentence. See Figure 2-28.

> Be sure to select the correct citation and bibliography style before you begin.

| Figure 2-28 | MLA style selected and insertion point positioned for new citation |

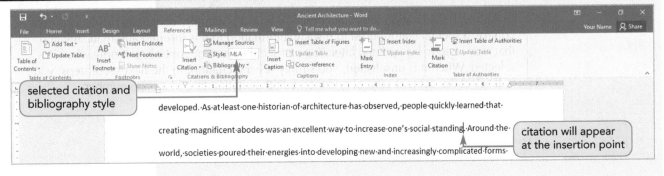

6. In the Citations & Bibliography group, click the **Insert Citation** button to open the menu. At this point, you could click Add New Placeholder on the menu to insert a temporary, placeholder citation. However, because you have all the necessary source information, you can go ahead and create a complete citation.

7. On the menu, click **Add New Source**. The Create Source dialog box opens, ready for you to add the information required to create a bibliography entry for Roy Brauer's book.

8. If necessary, click the **Type of Source** arrow, scroll up or down in the list, and then click **Book**.

9. In the Author box, type **Roy Brauer**.

10. Click in the **Title** box, and then type **Settlements and Monuments in Neolithic Architecture**.

11. Click in the **Year** box, and then type **2010**. This is the year the book was published. Next, you need to enter the name and location of the publisher.

12. Click the **City** box, type **New York**, click the **Publisher** box, and then type **Brookstone and Colescott Academy Press**.

Finally, you need to indicate the medium used to publish the book. In this case, Carolina used a printed copy, so the medium is "Print." For books or journals published online, the correct medium would be "Web."

13. Click the **Medium** box, and then type **Print**. See Figure 2-29.

TIP

When entering information in a dialog box, you can press the Tab key to move the insertion point from one box to another.

Figure 2-29	Create Source dialog box with information for the first source

14. Click the **OK** button. Word inserts the parenthetical "(Brauer)" at the end of the sentence in the document.

Although the citation looks like ordinary text, it is actually contained inside a content control, a special feature used to display information that is inserted automatically and that may need to be updated later. You can see the content control itself only when it is selected. When it is unselected, you simply see the citation. In the next set of steps, you will select the content control and then edit the citation to add a page number.

To edit the citation:

1. In the document, click the citation **(Brauer)**. The citation appears in a content control, which is a box with a tab on the left and an arrow button on the right. The arrow button is called the Citation Options button.

2. Click the **Citation Options** button ⬛. A menu of options related to editing a citation opens, as shown in Figure 2-30.

Figure 2-30 ▶ **Citation Options menu**

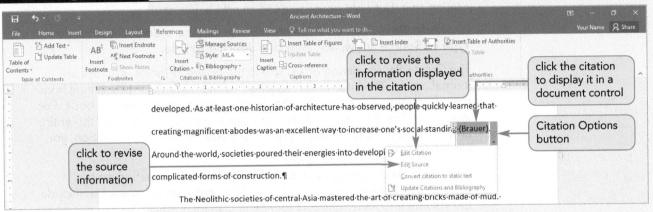

To edit the information about the source, you click Edit Source. To change the information that is displayed in the citation itself, you use the Edit Citation option.

3. On the Citation Options menu, click **Edit Citation**. The Edit Citation dialog box opens, as shown in Figure 2-31.

Figure 2-31 ▶ **Edit Citation dialog box**

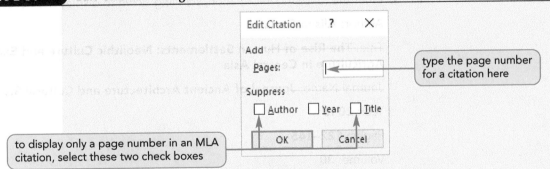

To add a page number for the citation, you type the page number in the Pages box. If you want to display only the page number in the citation (which would be necessary if you already mentioned the author's name in the same sentence in the text), then you would also select the Author and Title check boxes in this dialog box to suppress this information.

4. Type **37** to insert the page number in the Pages box, click the **OK** button to close the dialog box, and then click anywhere in the document outside the citation content control. The revised citation now reads "(Brauer 37)."

Next, you will add two more citations, both for the same journal article.

To insert two more citations:

▶ 1. Scroll up to display the last paragraph on page 1, and then click at the end of the first sentence in that paragraph (which begins "According to Alisha Garland..."), between the word "animals" and the period. This sentence mentions historian Alisha Garland; you need to add a citation to one of her journal articles.

▶ 2. In the Citations & Bibliography group, click the **Insert Citation** button to open the Insert Citation menu. Notice that Roy Brauer's book is now listed as a source on this menu. You could click Brauer's book on the menu to add a citation to it, but right now you need to add a new source.

▶ 3. Click **Add New Source** to open the Create Source dialog box, click the **Type of Source** arrow, and then click **Journal Article**.

The Create Source dialog box displays the boxes, or fields, appropriate for a journal article. The information required to cite a journal article differs from the information you entered earlier for the citation for the Brauer book. For journal articles, you are prompted to enter the page numbers for the entire article. If you want to display a particular page number in the citation, you can add it later.

By default, Word displays boxes, or fields, for the information most commonly included in a bibliography. In this case, you also want to include the volume and issue numbers for Alisha Garland's article, so you need to display more fields.

▶ 4. In the Create Source dialog box, click the **Show All Bibliography Fields** check box to select this option. The Create Source dialog box expands to allow you to enter more detailed information. Red asterisks highlight the fields that are recommended, but these recommended fields don't necessarily apply to every source.

▶ 5. Enter the following information, scrolling down to display the necessary boxes:

Author: **Alisha Garland**

Title: **The Rise of Human Settlements: Neolithic Culture and Early Agriculture in Central Asia**

Journal Name: **Journal of Ancient Architecture and Cultural Studies**

Year: **2015**

Pages: **122–145**

Volume: **30**

Issue: **5**

Medium: **Web**

When you are finished, your Create Source dialog box should look like the one shown in Figure 2-32.

Figure 2-32   Create Source dialog box with information for the journal article

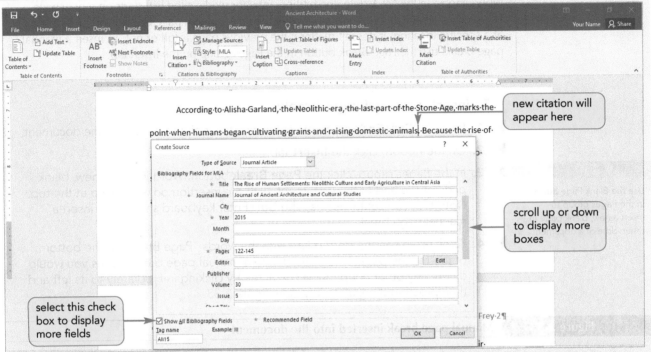

According to Alisha Garland, the Neolithic era, the last part of the Stone Age, marks the point when humans began cultivating grains and raising domestic animals. Because the rise of

> *new citation will appear here*

> *scroll up or down to display more boxes*

> *select this check box to display more fields*

Create Source

Type of Source: Journal Article

Bibliography Fields for MLA

* Title: The Rise of Human Settlements: Neolithic Culture and Early Agriculture in Central Asia
* Journal Name: Journal of Ancient Architecture and Cultural Studies
City:
* Year: 2015
Month:
Day:
* Pages: 122-145
Editor: [Edit]
Publisher:
Volume: 30
Issue: 5

☑ Show All Bibliography Fields   * Recommended Field

Tag name: AlI15   Example: III   [OK] [Cancel]

6. Click the **OK** button. The Create Source dialog box closes, and the citation "(Garland)" is inserted in the text. Because the sentence containing the citation already includes the author's name, you will edit the citation to include the page number and suppress the author's name.

7. Click the **(Garland)** citation to display the content control, click the **Citation Options** button, and then click **Edit Citation** to open the Edit Citation dialog box.

8. In the Pages box, type **142**, and then click the **Author** and **Title** check boxes to select them. You need to suppress both the author's name and the title because otherwise Word will replace the suppressed author name with the title. When using the MLA style, you don't ever have to suppress the year because the year is never included as part of an MLA citation. When working in other styles, however, you might need to suppress the year.

9. Click the **OK** button to close the Edit Citation dialog box, and then click anywhere outside the content control to deselect it. The end of the sentence now reads "…raising domestic animals (142)."

10. Use the Navigation pane to find the sentence that begins "The Neolithic societies of central Asia…" on the second page. Click at the end of the sentence, to the left of the period after "mud," and then close the Navigation pane.

11. On the References tab, in the Citations & Bibliography group, click the **Insert Citation** button, and then click the **Garland, Alisha** source at the top of the menu. You want the citation to refer to the entire article instead of just one page, so you will not edit the citation to add a specific page number.

12. Save the document.

You have entered the source information for two sources.

Inserting a Page Break

Once you have created a citation for a source in a document, you can generate a bibliography. In the MLA style, the bibliography (or works cited list) starts on a new page. So your first step is to insert a manual page break. A **manual page break** is one you insert at a specific location; it doesn't matter if the previous page is full or not. To insert a manual page break, use the Page Break button in the Pages group on the Insert tab.

To insert a manual page break:

▶ **1.** Press the **Ctrl+End** keys to move the insertion point to the end of the document.

▶ **2.** On the ribbon, click the **Insert** tab.

TIP

Use the Blank Page button in the Pages group to insert a new, blank page in the middle of a document.

▶ **3.** In the Pages group, click the **Page Break** button. Word inserts a new, blank page at the end of the document, with the insertion point blinking at the top. Note that you could also use the Ctrl+Enter keyboard shortcut to insert a manual page break.

▶ **4.** Scroll up to see the dotted line with the words "Page Break" at the bottom of the text on page 4. You can delete a manual page break just as you would delete any other nonprinting character, by clicking immediately to its left and then pressing the Delete key. See Figure 2-33.

Figure 2-33 **Manual page break inserted into the document**

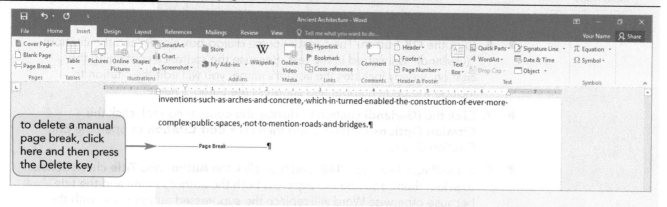

Now you can insert the bibliography on the new page 5.

Generating a Bibliography

When you generate a bibliography, Word scans all the citations in the document, collecting the source information for each citation, and then it creates a list of information for each unique source. The format of the entries in the bibliography will reflect the style you specified when you created your first citation, which in this case is the MLA style. The bibliography itself is a **field**, similar to the page number field you inserted earlier in this session. In other words, it is really an instruction that tells Word to display the source information for all the citations in the document. Because it is a field and not actual text, you can easily update the bibliography later to reflect any new citations you might add.

You can choose to insert a bibliography as a field directly in the document, or you can insert a bibliography enclosed within a content control that also includes the heading "Bibliography" or "Works Cited." Inserting a bibliography enclosed in a content control is best because the content control includes a useful button that you can use to update your bibliography if you make changes to the sources.

To insert the bibliography:

1. Scroll down so you can see the insertion point at the top of page 5.

2. On the ribbon, click the **References** tab.

3. In the Citations & Bibliography group, click the **Bibliography** button. The Bibliography menu opens, displaying three styles with preformatted headings—"Bibliography," "References," and "Works Cited." The Insert Bibliography command at the bottom inserts a bibliography directly in the document as a field, without a content control and without a preformatted heading. See Figure 2-34.

Figure 2-34   **Bibliography menu**

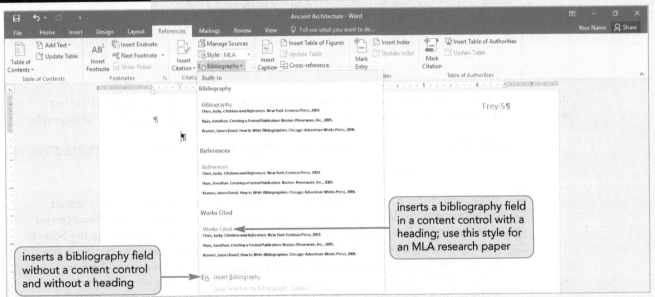

inserts a bibliography field in a content control with a heading; use this style for an MLA research paper

inserts a bibliography field without a content control and without a heading

---

4. Click **Works Cited**. Word inserts the bibliography, with two entries, below the "Works Cited" heading. The bibliography text is formatted in Calibri, the default font for the Office theme. The "Works Cited" heading is formatted with the Heading 1 style.

   To see the content control that contains the bibliography, you need to select it.

5. Click anywhere in the bibliography. Inside the content control, the bibliography is highlighted in gray, indicating that it is a field and not regular text. The content control containing the bibliography is also now visible in the form of a rectangular border and a tab with two buttons. See Figure 2-35.

| Figure 2-35 | Bibliography displayed in a content control |

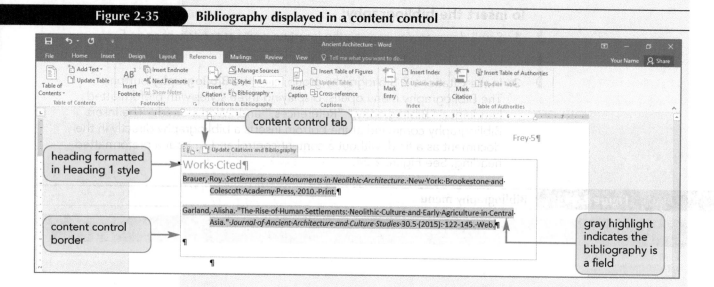

As Carolina looks over the works cited list, she realizes that she misspelled the last name of one of the authors. You'll correct the error now and then update the bibliography.

INSIGHT

Managing Sources

When you create a source, Word adds it to a Master List of all the sources created on your computer. Word also adds each new source to the Current List of sources for that document. Both the Master List and the Current List are accessible via the Source Manager dialog box, which you open by clicking the Manage Sources button in the Citations & Bibliography group on the References tab. Using this dialog box, you can copy sources from the Master List into the Current List and vice versa. As you begin to focus on a particular academic field and turn repeatedly to important works in your chosen field, you'll find this ability to reuse sources very helpful.

Modifying an Existing Source

To modify information about a source, you click a citation to that source in the document, click the Citation Options button on the content control, and then click Edit Source. Depending on how your computer is set up, after you are finished editing the source, Word may prompt you to update the Master List and the source information in the current document. In almost all cases, you should click Yes to ensure that the source information is correct in all the places it is stored on your computer.

To edit a source in the research paper:

1. Click in the blank paragraph below the bibliography content control to deselect the bibliography.

2. Scroll up to display the first paragraph on page 2, and then click the **(Brauer 37)** citation you entered earlier in the second-to-last sentence in the paragraph. The content control appears around the citation.

3. Click the **Citation Options** button ⬚, and then click **Edit Source**. The Edit Source dialog box opens. Note that Word displays the author's last name first in the Author box, just as it would appear in a bibliography.

4. In the **Author** box, double-click **Brauer** to select the author's last name, and then type **Brower**. The author's name now reads "Brower, Roy."

5. Click the **OK** button. The revised author name in the citation now reads "(Brower 37)."

   Trouble? If you see a message dialog box asking if you want to update the master source list and the current document, click the Yes button.

6. Click anywhere on the second page to deselect the citation content control. The revised author name in the citation now reads "(Brower 37)."

7. Save the document.

You've edited the document text and the citation to include the correct spelling of "Brower," but now you need to update the bibliography to correct the spelling.

Updating and Finalizing a Bibliography

The bibliography does not automatically change to reflect edits you make to existing citations or to show new citations. To incorporate the latest information stored in the citations, you need to update the bibliography. To update a bibliography in a content control, click the bibliography, and then, in the content control tab, click Update Citations and Bibliography. To update a bibliography field that is not contained in a content control, right-click the bibliography, and then click Update Field on the shortcut menu.

To update the bibliography:

1. Scroll down to page 5 and click anywhere in the works cited list to display the content control.

2. In the content control tab, click **Update Citations and Bibliography**. The works cited list is updated, with "Brauer" changed to "Brower" in the first entry.

Carolina still has a fair amount of work to do on her research paper. After she finishes writing it and adding all the citations, she will update the bibliography again to include all her cited sources. At that point, you might think the bibliography would be finished. However, a few steps remain to ensure that the works cited list matches the MLA style. To finalize Carolina's works cited list to match the MLA style, you need to make the changes shown in Figure 2-36.

Figure 2-36   **Steps for finalizing a Word bibliography to match MLA guidelines for the works cited list**

1. Format the "Works Cited" heading to match the formatting of the rest of the text in the document.

2. Center the "Works Cited" heading.

3. Double-space the entire works cited list, including the heading, and remove extra space after the paragraphs.

4. Change the font size for the entire works cited list to 12 points.

To format the bibliography as an MLA-style works cited list:

▶ 1. Click in the **Works Cited** heading, and then click the **Home** tab on the ribbon.

▶ 2. In the Styles group, click the **Normal** style. The "Works Cited" heading is now formatted in Calibri body font like the rest of the document. The MLA style for a works cited list requires this heading to be centered.

▶ 3. In the Paragraph group, click the **Center** button.

▶ 4. Select the entire works cited list, including the heading. Change the font size to **12** points, change the line spacing to **2.0**, and then remove the paragraph spacing after each paragraph.

▶ 5. Click below the content control to deselect the works cited list, and then review your work. See Figure 2-37.

Figure 2-37 **MLA-style Works Cited list**

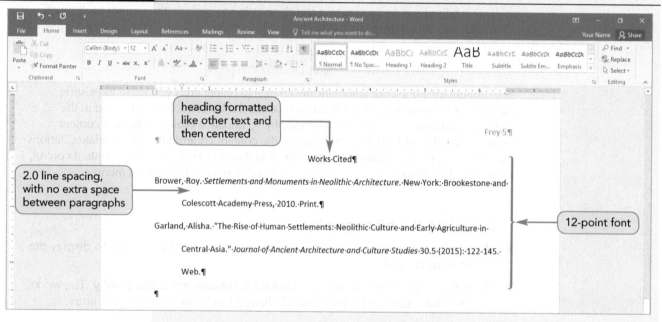

▶ 6. Save the document and close it.

Carolina's research paper now meets the MLA style guidelines.

Session 2.2 Quick Check

REVIEW

1. List the five tasks you need to perform to make a default Word document match the MLA style.

2. How can you quickly repeat the action you just performed?

3. Explain how to remove a page number from the first page of a document.

4. What is the default form of an MLA citation in Word?

5. Explain how to edit a citation to display only the page number.

6. Explain how to generate a works cited list.

Review Assignments

Data Files needed for the Review Assignments: Commercial.docx, Modern.docx

Because the Home LEED document turned out so well, Carolina has been asked to create a handout describing LEED certification for commercial buildings. Carolina asks you to help her revise and format the document. She also asks you to create a document listing projects that are suitable for this type of LEED certification. Finally, as part of her architecture history class, Carolina is working on a research paper on the history of modern architecture. She asks you to help her format the paper according to the MLA style and to create some citations and a bibliography. She has inserted the uppercase word "CITATION" wherever she needs to insert a citation. Complete the following steps:

1. Open the document **Commercial** located in the Word2 > Review folder included with your Data Files, and then save the document as **Commercial LEED** in the location specified by your instructor.

2. Read the first comment, which provides an overview of the changes you will be making to the document in the following steps. Perform the task described in the second comment, and then delete both comments.

3. In the middle of page 1, revise the text "SPECIAL PROJECTS" so that only the first letter of each word is capitalized. Attach a comment to this paragraph that explains the change.

4. Near the end of page 2, move the "Getting Started" heading up to position it before the paragraph that begins "Talk to your project manager...."

5. Replace the second instance of "Design" with "design," being sure to match the case.

6. On page 1, format the list of suitable projects as a bulleted list with square bullets, starting with "Schools, including..." and ending with "Clinics, hospitals, and other healthcare facilities." Do the same for the list of special projects, starting with "Mixed-use projects..." and ending with "No larger than 25,000 square feet.") Then indent the three requirements for multiple structures so they are formatted with an open circle bullet.

7. At the top of page 2, format the three steps for developing a certification plan as a numbered list, using the "1), 2), 3)" numbering style.

8. In the numbered list, move paragraph 3 ("Establish target certification level...") up to make it paragraph 2.

9. Format the title "Commercial LEED Fact Sheet" using the Title style. Format the following headings with the Heading 1 style: "Suitable Projects," "Special Projects," "Location," "Developing a Certification Plan," and "Getting Started."

10. Change the document theme to the Ion theme. If the Ion theme isn't included in your Themes gallery, choose a different theme.

11. Display the Clipboard task pane. On page 1, copy the bulleted list of suitable projects (which begins "Schools, including entire college campuses...") to the Clipboard, and then copy the "Suitable Projects" heading to the Clipboard. To ensure that you copy the heading formatting, be sure to select the paragraph mark after "Suitable Projects" before you click the Copy button.

12. Open a new, blank document, and then save the document as **Suitable Projects** in the location specified by your instructor.

13. At the beginning of the document, paste the heading "Suitable Projects," and then, from the Paste Options menu, apply the Keep Source Formatting option. Below the heading, paste the list of suitable projects.

14. At the end of the document, insert a new paragraph, and then type **Prepared by:** followed by your first and last names.

15. Save the Suitable Projects document and close it.

16. In the Commercial LEED document, clear the contents of the Clipboard task pane, close the Clipboard task pane, save the document, and then close it.

17. Open the document **Modern** located in the Word2 > Review folder included with your Data Files.

18. Save the document as **Modern Architecture** in the location specified by your instructor.

19. In the first paragraph, replace Carolina's name with your own.

20. Adjust the font size, line spacing, paragraph spacing, and paragraph indents to match the MLA style.

21. Insert your last name and a page number on every page except the first. Use the same font size as in the rest of the document.

22. If necessary, select MLA Seventh Edition as the citations and bibliography style.

23. Use the Navigation pane to highlight all instances of the uppercase word "CITATION." Keep the Navigation pane open so you can continue to use it to find the locations where you need to insert citations in Steps 24–28.

24. Delete the first instance of "CITATION" and the space before it, and then create a new source with the following information:

    Type of Source: **Book**

    Author: **Lincoln Mayfield**

    Title: **Very Modern Architecture: A History in Words and Photos**

    Year: **2014**

    City: **Cambridge**

    Publisher: **Boston Pines Press**

    Medium: **Print**

25. Edit the citation to add **105** as the page number. Display only the page number in the citation.

26. Delete the second instance of "CITATION" and the space before it, and then create a new source with the following information:

    Type of Source: **Journal Article**

    Author: **Odessa Robinson**

    Title: **Modern Architecture in the Modern World**

    Journal Name: **Atlantis Architecture Quarterly: Criticism and Comment**

    Year: **2015**

    Pages: **68–91**

    Volume: **11**

    Issue: **2**

    Medium: **Web**

27. Edit the citation to add **80** as the page number.

28. Delete the third instance of "CITATION" and the space before it, and then insert a citation for the book by Lincoln Mayfield.

29. At the end of the document, start a new page and insert a bibliography in a content control with the heading "Works Cited."

30. In the second source you created, change "**Robinson**" to "**Robbins**" and then update the bibliography.

31. Finalize the bibliography to create an MLA-style works cited list.

32. Save the Modern Architecture document, and close it.

33. Close any other open documents.

Case Problem 1

Data File needed for this Case Problem: Field.docx

Hilltop Elementary School   Crystal Martinez, a fourth-grade teacher at Hilltop Elementary School, created a flyer to inform parents and guardians about an upcoming field trip. It's your job to format the flyer to make it look professional and easy to read. Crystal included comments in the document explaining what she wants you to do. Complete the following steps:

1. Open the document **Field** located in the Word2 > Case1 folder included with your Data Files, and then save the file as **Field Trip Flyer** in the location specified by your instructor.

2. Format the document as directed in the comments. After you complete a task, delete the relevant comment. Respond "Yes" to the comment asking if October 20 is the correct date. When you are finished with the formatting, the comment with the question and the comment with your reply should be the only remaining comments.

3. Move up the second bulleted item (which begins "Email me at...") to make it the first bulleted item in the list.

4. Change the theme to the Slice theme, and then attach a comment to the title listing the heading and body fonts applied by the Slice theme.

5. Save the document, and then close it.

Case Problem 2

Data File needed for this Case Problem: Comedy.docx

Frederick Douglass College   Liam Shelton is a student at Frederick Douglass College. He's working on a research paper, which is only partly finished, about the types of comedy used in plays and films. He inserted the uppercase word "CITATION" wherever he needs to insert a citation. Liam asks you to help him format this early draft to match the MLA style. He also asks you to help him create some citations and a first attempt at a bibliography. He will update the bibliography later, after he finishes writing the research paper. Complete the following steps:

1. Open the document **Comedy** located in the Word2 > Case2 folder included with your Data Files, and then save the document as **Comedy Paper** in the location specified by your instructor.

2. In the first paragraph, replace "Liam Shelton" with your name, and then adjust the font size, line spacing, paragraph spacing, and paragraph indents to match the MLA style.

3. Insert your last name and a page number in the upper-right corner of every page except the first page in the document. Use the same font size as in the rest of the document.

4. If necessary, select MLA Seventh Edition as the citations and bibliography style.

5. Use the Navigation pane to find three instances of the uppercase word "CITATION."

6. Delete the first instance of "CITATION" and the space before it, and then create a new source with the following information:

   Type of Source: **Book**
   Author: **Danyl Taylor**
   Title: **Comedy: The Happy Art**
   Year: **2013**
   City: **Chicago**
   Publisher: **Singleton University Press**
   Medium: **Print**

7. Edit the citation to add **135** as the page number. Suppress the author's name and the title.

8. Delete the second instance of "CITATION" and the space before it, and then create a new source with the following information:

   Type of Source: **Sound Recording**

   Performer: **Anne Golden**

   Title: **Slapstick Sample**

   Album Title: **Sounds of the Renaissance**

   Production Company: **Foley Studio Productions**

   Year: **1995**

   Medium: **CD**

   City: **Los Angeles**

9. Edit the citation to suppress the Author and the Year, so that it displays only the title.

10. Delete the third instance of "CITATION" and the space before it, and then insert a second reference to the book by Danyl Taylor.

11. Edit the citation to add **65** as the page number.

12. At the end of the document, start a new page, and then insert a bibliography with the preformatted heading "Works Cited."

13. Edit the last source you created, changing the date to **2000**.

14. Update the bibliography so it shows the revised date.

15. Finalize the bibliography so that it matches the MLA style.

16. Save the Comedy Paper document, and close it.

Case Problem 3

CREATE

Data Files needed for this Case Problem: Maliha.docx, Nursing.docx

Emergency Room Nurse   Maliha Shadid has more than a decade of experience as a nurse in several different settings. After moving to a new city, she is looking for a job as an emergency room nurse. She has asked you to edit and format her resume. As part of the application process, she will have to upload her resume to employee recruitment websites at a variety of hospitals. Because these sites typically request a simple page design, Maliha plans to rely primarily on heading styles and bullets to organize her information. When the resume is complete, she wants you to remove any color applied by the heading styles. She also needs help formatting a document she created for a nursing organization for which she volunteers. Complete the following steps:

1. Open the document **Maliha** located in the Word2 > Case3 folder included with your Data Files, and then save the file as **Maliha Resume** in the location specified by your instructor.

2. Read the comment included in the document, and then perform the task it specifies.

3. Respond to the comment with the response **I think that's a good choice for the theme.**, and then mark Maliha's comment as done.

4. Replace all occurrences of "Lawrencekansas" with **Lawrence, Kansas**.

5. Format the resume as shown in Figure 2-38. To ensure that the resume fits on one page, pay special attention to the paragraph spacing settings specified in Figure 2-38.

6. In the email address, replace "Maliha Shadid" with your first and last names, separated by an underscore, and then save the document and close it.

Figure 2-38   **Formatting for Maliha Shadid's resume**

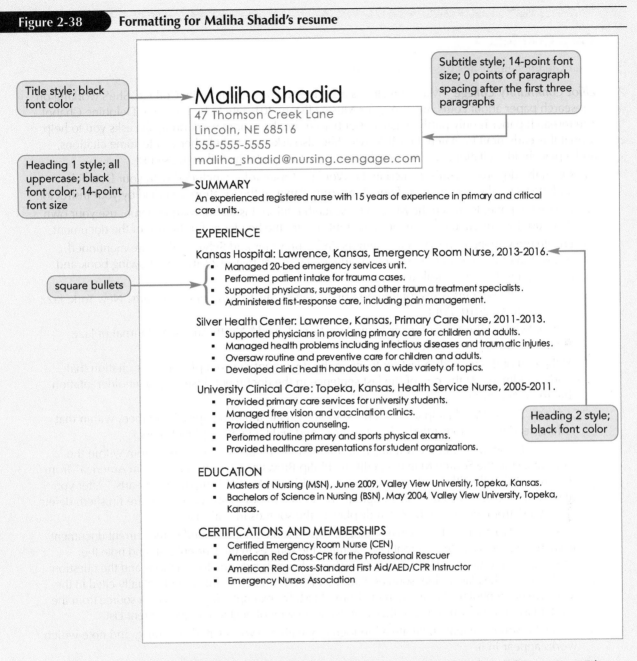

Title style; black font color

Heading 1 style; all uppercase; black font color; 14-point font size

square bullets

Subtitle style; 14-point font size; 0 points of paragraph spacing after the first three paragraphs

Heading 2 style; black font color

Maliha Shadid

47 Thomson Creek Lane
Lincoln, NE 68516
555-555-5555
maliha_shadid@nursing.cengage.com

SUMMARY

An experienced registered nurse with 15 years of experience in primary and critical care units.

EXPERIENCE

Kansas Hospital: Lawrence, Kansas, Emergency Room Nurse, 2013-2016.
- Managed 20-bed emergency services unit.
- Performed patient intake for trauma cases.
- Supported physicians, surgeons and other trauma treatment specialists.
- Administered first-response care, including pain management.

Silver Health Center: Lawrence, Kansas, Primary Care Nurse, 2011-2013.
- Supported physicians in providing primary care for children and adults.
- Managed health problems including infectious diseases and traumatic injuries.
- Oversaw routine and preventive care for children and adults.
- Developed clinic health handouts on a wide variety of topics.

University Clinical Care: Topeka, Kansas, Health Service Nurse, 2005-2011.
- Provided primary care services for university students.
- Managed free vision and vaccination clinics.
- Provided nutrition counseling.
- Performed routine primary and sports physical exams.
- Provided healthcare presentations for student organizations.

EDUCATION
- Masters of Nursing (MSN), June 2009, Valley View University, Topeka, Kansas.
- Bachelors of Science in Nursing (BSN), May 2004, Valley View University, Topeka, Kansas.

CERTIFICATIONS AND MEMBERSHIPS
- Certified Emergency Room Nurse (CEN)
- American Red Cross-CPR for the Professional Rescuer
- American Red Cross-Standard First Aid/AED/CPR Instructor
- Emergency Nurses Association

7. Open the document **Nursing** located in the Word2 > Case3 folder included with your Data Files, and then save the file as **Nursing Foundation** in the location specified by your instructor. Search for the text "Your Name", and then replace it with your first and last names.

8. Select the three paragraphs below your name, and then decrease the indent for the selected paragraphs so that they align at the left margin. Create a .5-inch hanging indent for the selected paragraphs.

9. Change the document theme to Facet, and then add a comment to the first word in the document that reads "**I changed the theme to Facet.**" (If Facet is not an option in your Themes gallery, choose a different theme, and then include that theme name in the comment.)

10. Use the Advanced Find dialog box to search for bold formatting. Remove the bold formatting from the fourth bold element in the document, and then add a comment to that element that reads "**I assumed bold here was a mistake, so I removed it.**"

11. Save and close the document.

CHALLENGE

Case Problem 4

Data File needed for this Case Problem: Louis.docx

Elliot Community College   Maria Taketou is a student at Elliot Community College. She's working on a research paper about Louis Armstrong for Music History 201, taught by Professor Delphine Chabot. The research paper is only partly finished, but before she does more work on it, she asks you to help format this early draft to match the MLA style. She also asks you to help her create some citations, add a placeholder citation, and manage her sources. Complete the following steps:

1. Open the document **Louis** located in the Word2 > Case4 folder included with your Data Files, and then save the document as **Louis Armstrong Paper** in the location specified by your instructor.

2. Revise the paper to match the MLA style, seventh edition. Instead of Maria's name, use your own. Also, use the current date. Use the same font size for the header as for the rest of the document.

3. Locate the sentences in which the authors Philip Brewster and Sylvia Cohen are mentioned. At the end of the appropriate sentence, add a citation for page 123 in the following book and one for page 140 in the following journal article:

   Brewster, Philip. Louis Armstrong in America: King of Music, King of Our Hearts. New York: Jazz Notes Press, 2010. Print.

   Cohen, Sylvia. "The New Orleans Louis Armstrong Loved." North American Journal of Jazz Studies (2015): 133–155. Web.

4. At the end of the second-to-last sentence in the document, insert a placeholder citation that reads "Feldman." At the end of the last sentence in the document, insert a placeholder citation that reads "Harrison."

⊕ **Explore** 5. Use Word Help to look up the topic "Create a bibliography," and then, within that article, read the sections titled "Find a source" and "Edit a citation placeholder."

⊕ **Explore** 6. Open the Source Manager, and search for the name "Brewster." From within the Current List in the Source Manager, edit the Philip Brewster citation to delete "in America" from the title, so that the title reads "Louis Armstrong: King of Music, King of Our Hearts." After you make the change, if you are asked, update the source in both lists. When you are finished, delete "Brewster" from the Search box to redisplay all the sources in both lists.

⊕ **Explore** 7. From within the Source Manager, copy a source not included in the current document from the Master List to the Current List. Examine the sources in the Current List, and note the checkmarks next to the two sources for which you have already created citations and the question marks next to the placeholder sources. Sources in the Current list that are not actually cited in the text have no symbol next to them in the Current List. For example, if you copied a source from the Master List into your Current List, that source has no symbol next to it in the Current List.

8. Close the Source Manager, create a bibliography with a "Works Cited" heading, and note which works appear in it.

⊕ **Explore** 9. Open the Source Manager, and then edit the Feldman placeholder source to include the following information about a journal article:

   Feldman, Jamal. "King Joe Oliver, Music Master." Jazz International Journal (2015): 72–89. Web.

10. Update the bibliography.

⊕ **Explore** 11. Open Microsoft Edge, and use the web to research the difference between a works cited list and a works consulted list. If necessary, open the Source Manager, and then delete any uncited sources from the Current List to ensure that your document contains a true works cited list, as specified by the MLA style, and not a works consulted list. (Maria will create a full citation for the "Harrison" placeholder later.)

12. Update the bibliography, finalize it so it matches the MLA style, save the document, and close it.

WORD

Creating Tables and a Multipage Report

Writing a Recommendation

OBJECTIVES

Session 3.1
- Review document headings in the Navigation pane
- Reorganize document text using the Navigation pane
- Collapse and expand body text in a document
- Create and edit a table
- Sort rows in a table
- Modify a table's structure
- Format a table

Session 3.2
- Set tab stops
- Turn on automatic hyphenation
- Create footnotes and endnotes
- Divide a document into sections
- Create a SmartArt graphic
- Create headers and footers
- Insert a cover page
- Change the document's theme
- Review a document in Read Mode

Case | *Vista Grande Neighborhood Center*

Hillary Sanchez is the managing director of the Vista Grande Neighborhood Center, a nonprofit organization that provides social services and community programming for the Vista Grande neighborhood in Tucson, Arizona. Hillary hopes to begin offering exercise and nutrition classes at the center. She has written a multiple-page report for the center's board of directors summarizing basic information about the proposed classes. She has asked you to finish formatting the report. Hillary also needs your help adding a table and a diagram to the end of the report.

In this module, you'll use the Navigation pane to review the document headings and reorganize the document. You will also insert a table, modify it by changing the structure and formatting, set tab stops, create footnotes and endnotes, hyphenate the document, and insert a section break. In addition, you'll create a SmartArt graphic and add headers and footers. Finally, you will insert a cover page and review the document in Read Mode.

STARTING DATA FILES

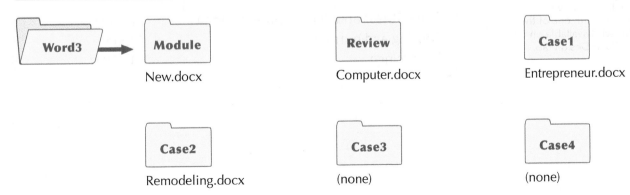

Word3 → Module
New.docx

Review
Computer.docx

Case1
Entrepreneur.docx

Case2
Remodeling.docx

Case3
(none)

Case4
(none)

Session 3.1 Visual Overview:

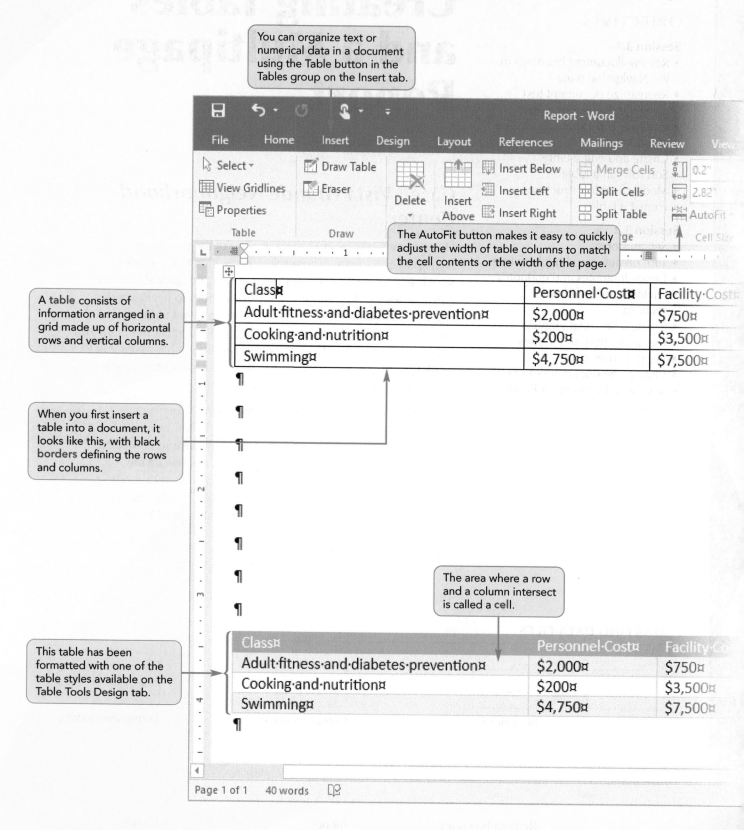

You can organize text or numerical data in a document using the Table button in the Tables group on the Insert tab.

The AutoFit button makes it easy to quickly adjust the width of table columns to match the cell contents or the width of the page.

A table consists of information arranged in a grid made up of horizontal rows and vertical columns.

When you first insert a table into a document, it looks like this, with black borders defining the rows and columns.

The area where a row and a column intersect is called a cell.

This table has been formatted with one of the table styles available on the Table Tools Design tab.

Class¤	Personnel·Cost¤	Facility·Cost¤
Adult·fitness·and·diabetes·prevention¤	$2,000¤	$750¤
Cooking·and·nutrition¤	$200¤	$3,500¤
Swimming¤	$4,750¤	$7,500¤

Class¤	Personnel·Cost¤	Facility·Co...
Adult·fitness·and·diabetes·prevention¤	$2,000¤	$750¤
Cooking·and·nutrition¤	$200¤	$3,500¤
Swimming¤	$4,750¤	$7,500¤

Organizing Information in Tables

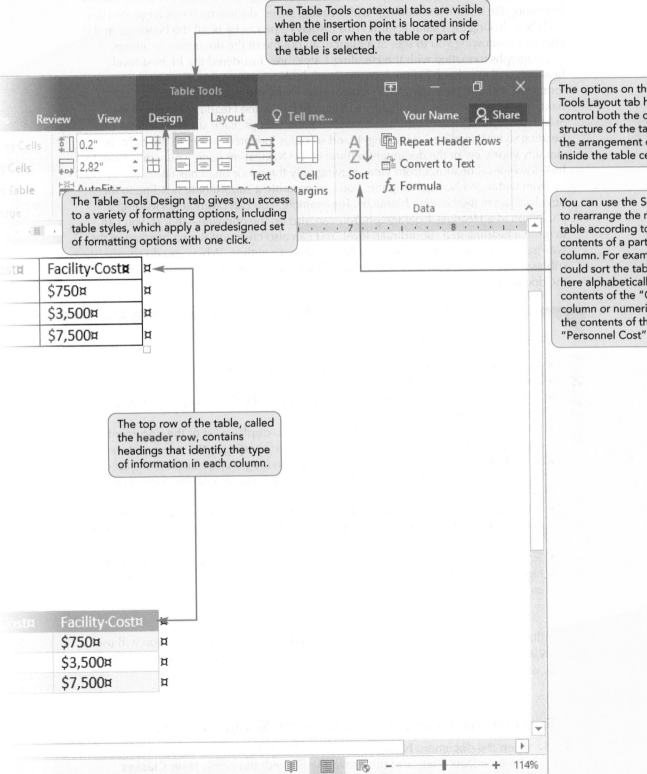

The Table Tools contextual tabs are visible when the insertion point is located inside a table cell or when the table or part of the table is selected.

The options on the Table Tools Layout tab help you control both the overall structure of the table and the arrangement of data inside the table cells.

The Table Tools Design tab gives you access to a variety of formatting options, including table styles, which apply a predesigned set of formatting options with one click.

You can use the Sort button to rearrange the rows of a table according to the contents of a particular column. For example, you could sort the table shown here alphabetically by the contents of the "Class" column or numerically by the contents of the "Personnel Cost" column.

The top row of the table, called the header row, contains headings that identify the type of information in each column.

Working with Headings in the Navigation Pane

When used in combination with the Navigation pane, Word's heading styles make it easier to navigate through a long document and to reorganize a document. You start by formatting the document headings with heading styles, displaying the Navigation pane, and then clicking the Headings link. This displays a hierarchy of all the headings in the document, allowing you to see, at a glance, an outline of the document headings.

Paragraphs formatted with the Heading 1 style are considered the highest-level headings and are aligned at the left margin of the Navigation pane. Paragraphs formatted with the Heading 2 style are considered **subordinate** to Heading 1 paragraphs and are indented slightly to the right below the Heading 1 paragraphs. Subordinate headings are often referred to as **subheadings**. Each successive level of heading styles (Heading 3, Heading 4, and so on) is indented farther to the right. To simplify your view of the document outline in the Navigation pane, you can choose to hide lower-level headings from view, leaving only the major headings visible.

From within the Navigation pane, you can **promote** a subordinate heading to the next level up in the heading hierarchy. For example, you can promote a Heading 2 paragraph to a Heading 1 paragraph. You can also do the opposite—that is, you can **demote** a heading to a subordinate level. You can also click and drag a heading in the Navigation pane to a new location in the document's outline. When you do so, any subheadings—along with their subordinate body text—move to the new location in the document.

REFERENCE

Working with Headings in the Navigation Pane

- Format the document headings using Word's heading styles.
- On the ribbon, click the Home tab.
- In the Editing group, click the Find button, or press the Ctrl+F keys, to display the Navigation pane.
- In the Navigation pane, click the Headings link to display a list of the document headings, and then click a heading to display that heading in the document window.
- In the Navigation pane, click a heading, and then drag it up or down in the list of headings to move that heading and the body text below it to a new location in the document.
- In the Navigation pane, right-click a heading, and then click Promote to promote the heading to the next-highest level. To demote a heading, right-click it, and then click Demote.
- To hide subheadings in the Navigation pane, click the Collapse arrow next to the higher level heading above them. To redisplay the subheadings, click the Expand arrow next to the higher-level heading.

Hillary saved the draft of her report as a Word document named New. You will use the Navigation pane to review the outline of Hillary's report and make some changes to its organization.

To review the document headings in the Navigation pane:

1. Open the document **New** located in the Word3 > Module folder included with your Data Files, and then save the file with the name **New Classes Report** in the location specified by your instructor.

2. Verify that the document is displayed in Print Layout view and that the rulers and nonprinting characters are displayed.

3. Make sure the Zoom level is set to **120%**, and that the Home tab is selected on the ribbon.

4. Press the **Ctrl+F** keys. The Navigation pane opens to the left of the document.

5. In the Navigation pane, click the **Headings** link. The document headings are displayed in the Navigation pane, as shown in Figure 3-1. The blue highlighted heading ("Summary") indicates that part of the document currently contains the insertion point.

Figure 3-1	Headings displayed in the Navigation pane

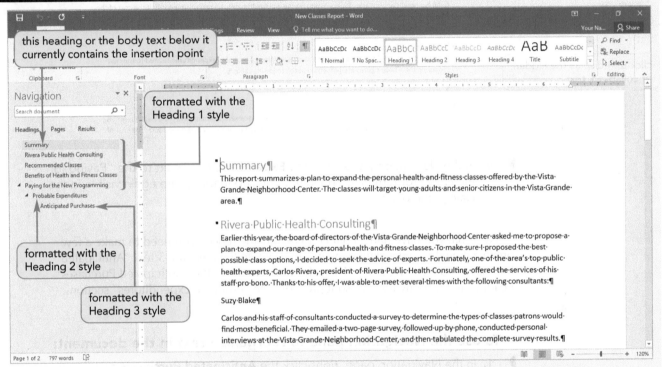

6. In the Navigation pane, click the **Recommended Classes** heading. Word displays the heading in the document window, with the insertion point at the beginning of the heading. The "Recommended Classes" heading is highlighted in blue in the Navigation pane.

7. In the Navigation pane, click the **Paying for the New Programming** heading. Word displays the heading in the document window. In the Navigation pane, you can see that there are subheadings below this heading.

8. In the Navigation pane, click the **Collapse** arrow ◢ next to the "Paying for the New Programming" heading. The subheadings below this heading are no longer visible in the Navigation pane. This has no effect on the text in the actual document. See Figure 3-2.

Figure 3-2   **Heading 2 and Heading 3 text hidden in Navigation pane**

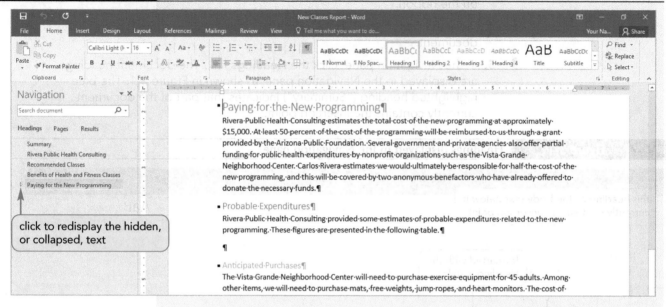

click to redisplay the hidden, or collapsed, text

▶ **9.** In the Navigation pane, click the **Expand** arrow ▷ next to the "Paying for the New Programming" heading. The subheadings are again visible in the Navigation pane.

Now that you have had a chance to review the report, you need to make a few organizational changes. Hillary wants to promote the Heading 3 text "Anticipated Purchases" to Heading 2 text. Then she wants to move the "Anticipated Purchases" heading and its body text up, so it precedes the "Probable Expenditures" section.

To use the Navigation pane to reorganize text in the document:

▶ **1.** In the Navigation pane, right-click the **Anticipated Purchases** heading to display the shortcut menu.

▶ **2.** Click **Promote**. The heading moves to the left in the Navigation pane, aligning below the "Probable Expenditures" heading. In the document window, the text is now formatted with the Heading 2 style, with its slightly larger font.

▶ **3.** In the Navigation pane, click and drag the **Anticipated Purchases** heading up. As you drag the heading, the pointer changes to ⬚, and a blue guideline is displayed. You can use the guideline to position the heading in its new location.

▶ **4.** Position the guideline directly below the "Paying for the New Programming" heading, as shown in Figure 3-3.

Figure 3-3   Moving a heading in the Navigation pane

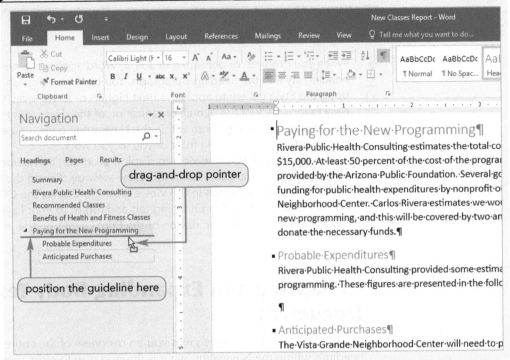

5. Release the mouse button. The "Anticipated Purchases" heading is displayed in its new position in the Navigation pane, as the second-to-last heading in the outline. The heading and its body text are displayed in their new location in the document, before the "Probable Expenditures" heading. See Figure 3-4.

Figure 3-4   Heading and body text in new location

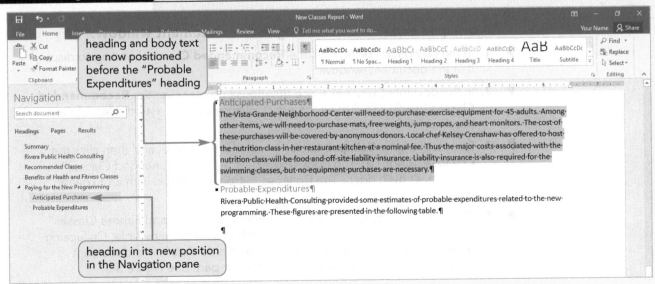

6. Click anywhere in the document to deselect the text, and then save the document.

Hillary also wants you to move the "Recommended Classes" heading and its accompanying body text. You'll do that in the next section, using a different method.

INSIGHT

Promoting and Demoting Headings

When you promote or demote a heading, Word applies the next higher- or lower-level heading style to the heading paragraph. You could accomplish the same thing by using the Style gallery to apply the next higher- or lower-level heading style, but it's easy to lose track of the overall organization of the document that way. By promoting and demoting headings from within the Navigation pane, you ensure that the overall document outline is right in front of you as you work.

You can also use Outline view to display, promote, and demote headings and to reorganize a document. Turn on Outline view by clicking the View tab, and then clicking the Outline button in the Views group to display the Outlining contextual tab on the ribbon. To hide the Outlining tab and return to Print Layout view, click the Close Outline View button on the ribbon or the Print Layout button in the status bar.

Collapsing and Expanding Body Text in the Document

Because the Navigation pane gives you an overview of the entire document, dragging headings within the Navigation pane is the best way to reorganize a document. However, you can also reorganize a document from within the document window, without using the Navigation pane, by first hiding, or collapsing, the body text below a heading in a document. After you collapse the body text below a heading, you can drag the heading to a new location in the document. When you do, the body text moves along with the heading, just as if you had dragged the heading in the Navigation pane. You'll use this technique now to move the "Recommended Classes" heading and its body text.

To collapse and move a heading in the document window:

1. In the Navigation pane, click the **Recommended Classes** heading to display it in the document window.

2. In the document window, place the mouse pointer over the **Recommended Classes** heading to display the gray Collapse button ◢ to the left of the heading.

3. Point to the gray **Collapse** button ◢ until it turns blue, and then click the **Collapse** button ◢. The body text below the "Recommended Classes" heading is now hidden. The Collapse button is replaced with an Expand button.

4. Collapse the body text below the "Benefits of Health and Fitness Classes" heading. The body text below that heading is no longer visible. Collapsing body text can be helpful when you want to hide details in a document temporarily, so you can focus on a particular part. See Figure 3-5.

| Figure 3-5 | Body text collapsed in the document |

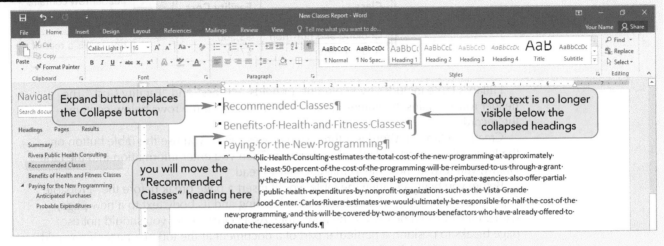

5. In the document, select the **Recommended Classes** heading, including the paragraph mark at the end of the paragraph.

6. Click and drag the heading down. As you drag, a dark black insertion point moves along with the mouse pointer.

7. Position the dark black insertion point to the left of the "P" in the "Paying for the New Programming" heading, and then release the mouse button. The "Recommended Classes" heading and its body text move to the new location, before the "Paying for the New Programming" heading.

   Finally, you need to expand the body text below the two collapsed headings.

8. Click anywhere in the document to deselect the text.

9. Point to the **Expand** button ▷ to the left of the "Recommended Classes" heading until it turns blue, and then click the **Expand** button ▶ to redisplay the body text below the heading.

10. Point to the **Expand** button ▷ to the left of the "Benefits of Health and Fitness Classes" heading until it turns blue, and then click the **Expand** button ▶ to redisplay the body text below the heading.

11. Save the document.

The document is now organized the way Hillary wants it. Next, you need to create a table summarizing her data on probable expenditures.

Inserting a Blank Table

TIP

The terms "table," "field," and "record" are also used to discuss information stored in database programs, such as Microsoft Access.

A table is a useful way to present information that is organized into categories, or **fields**. For example, you could use a table to organize contact information for a list of clients. For each client, you could include information in the following fields: first name, last name, street address, city, state, and ZIP code. The complete set of information about a particular client is called a **record**. In a typical table, each column is a separate field, and each row is a record. A header row at the top contains the names of each field.

The sketch in Figure 3-6 shows what Hillary wants the table in her report to look like.

Figure 3-6   Table sketch

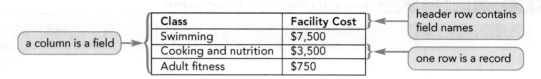

Hillary's table includes two columns, or fields—"Class" and "Facility Cost." The header row contains the names of these two fields. The three rows below contain the records.

Creating a table in Word is a three-step process. First, you use the Table button on the Insert tab to insert a blank table structure. Then you enter information into the table. Finally, you format the table to make it easy to read.

Before you begin creating the table, you'll insert a page break before the "Probable Expenditures" heading. This will move the heading and its body text to a new page, with plenty of room below for the new table. As a general rule, you should not use page breaks to position a particular part of a document at the top of a page. If you add or remove text from the document later, you might forget that you inserted a manual page break, and you might end up with a document layout you didn't expect. By default, Word heading styles are set up to ensure that a heading always appears on the same page as the body text paragraph below it, so you'll never need to insert a page break just to move a heading to the same page as its body text. However, in this case, a page break is appropriate because you need the "Probable Expenditures" heading to be displayed at the top of a page with room for the table below.

To insert a page break and insert a blank table:

▶ **1.** In the Navigation pane, click **Probable Expenditures** to display the heading in the document, with the insertion point to the left of the "P" in "Probable."

▶ **2.** Close the Navigation pane, and then press the **Ctrl+Enter** keys to insert a page break. The "Probable Expenditures" heading and the body text following it move to a new, third page.

▶ **3.** Scroll to position the "Probable Expenditures" heading at the top of the Word window, and then press the **Ctrl+End** keys to move the insertion point to the blank paragraph at the end of the document.

▶ **4.** On the ribbon, click the **Insert** tab.

▶ **5.** In the Tables group, click the **Table** button. A table grid opens, with a menu at the bottom.

▶ **6.** Use the mouse pointer to point to the **upper-left cell** of the grid, and then move the mouse pointer down and across the grid to highlight two columns and four rows. (The outline of a cell turns orange when it is highlighted.) As you move the pointer across the grid, Word indicates the size of the table (columns by rows) at the top of the grid. A Live Preview of the table structure is displayed in the document. See Figure 3-7.

Figure 3-7   Inserting a blank table

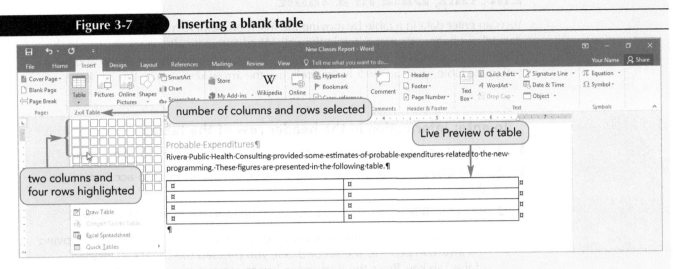

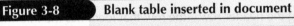

▶ **7.** When the table size is 2×4, click the lower-right cell in the block of selected cells. An empty table consisting of two columns and four rows is inserted in the document, with the insertion point in the upper-left cell. See Figure 3-8.

Figure 3-8   Blank table inserted in document

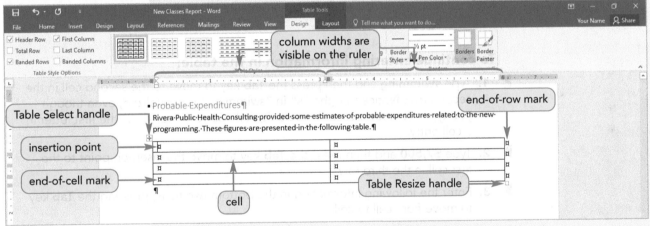

The two columns are of equal width. Because nonprinting characters are displayed in the document, each cell contains an end-of-cell mark, and each row contains an end-of-row mark, which are important for selecting parts of a table. The Table Select handle ⊞ is displayed at the table's upper-left corner. You can click the Table Select handle ⊞ to select the entire table, or you can drag it to move the table. You can drag the Table Resize handle ▢, which is displayed at the lower-right corner, to change the size of the table. The Table Tools Design and Layout contextual tabs are displayed on the ribbon.

Trouble? If you inserted a table with the wrong number of rows or columns, click the Undo button ↺ on the Quick Access Toolbar to remove the table, and then repeat Steps 4 through 7.

The blank table is ready for you to begin entering information.

Entering Data in a Table

You can enter data in a table by moving the insertion point to a cell and typing. If the data takes up more than one line in the cell, Word automatically wraps the text to the next line and increases the height of that row. To move the insertion point to another cell in the table, you can click in that cell, use the arrow keys, or use the Tab key.

To enter information in the header row of the table:

▶ **1.** Verify that the insertion point is located in the upper-left cell of the table.

▶ **2.** Type **Class**. As you type, the end-of-cell mark moves right to accommodate the text.

▶ **3.** Press the **Tab** key to move the insertion point to the next cell to the right.

   Trouble? If Word created a new paragraph in the first cell rather than moving the insertion point to the second cell, you pressed the Enter key instead of the Tab key. Press the Backspace key to remove the paragraph mark, and then press the Tab key to move to the second cell in the first row.

▶ **4.** Type **Facility Cost** and then press the **Tab** key to move to the first cell in the second row.

You have finished entering the header row—the row that identifies the information in each column. Now you can enter the information about the various expenditures.

To continue entering information in the table:

▶ **1.** Type **swimming** and then press the **Tab** key to move to the second cell in the second row. Notice that the "s" in "swimming" is capitalized, even though you typed it in lowercase. By default, AutoCorrect capitalizes the first letter in a cell entry.

▶ **2.** Type **$7,500** and then press the **Tab** key to move the insertion point to the first cell in the third row.

▶ **3.** Enter the following information in the bottom two rows, pressing the **Tab** key to move from cell to cell:

   Cooking and nutrition; $3,500

   Adult fitness; $750

At this point, the table consists of a header row and three records. Hillary realizes that she needs to add one more row to the table. You can add a new row to the bottom of a table by pressing the Tab key when the insertion point is in the rightmost cell in the bottom row.

To add a row to the table:

▶ **1.** Verify that the insertion point is in the lower-right cell (which contains the value "$750"), and then press the **Tab** key. A new, blank row is added to the bottom of the table.

> **2.** Type **Diabetes prevention**, press the **Tab** key, type **$400**, and then save the document. When you are finished, your table should look like the one shown in Figure 3-9.

Figure 3-9 **Table with all data entered**

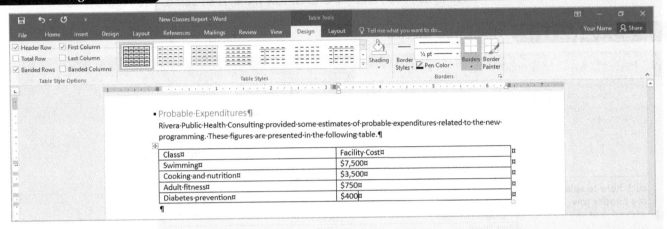

Trouble? If a new row is added to the bottom of your table, you pressed the Tab key after entering "$400". Click the Undo button on the Quick Access Toolbar to remove the extra row from the table.

The table you've just created presents information about expenditures in an easy-to-read format. To make it even easier to read, you can format the header row in bold so it stands out from the rest of the table. To do that, you need to first select the header row.

Selecting Part of a Table

TIP

To merge multiple cells into one cell, select the cells you want to merge, and then click the Merge Cells button in the Merge group on the Table Tools Layout tab.

When selecting part of a table, you need to make sure you select the end-of-cell mark in a cell or the end-of-row mark at the end of a row. If you don't, the formatting changes you make next might not have the effect you expect. The foolproof way to select part of a table is to click in the cell, row, or column you want to select; click the Select button on the Table Tools Layout contextual tab; and then click the appropriate command—Select Cell, Select Column, or Select Row. (You can also click Select Table to select the entire table.) To select a row, you can also click in the left margin next to the row. Similarly, you can click just above a column to select it. After you've selected an entire row, column, or cell, you can drag the mouse to select adjacent rows, columns, or cells.

Note that in the following steps, you'll position the mouse pointer until it takes on a particular shape so that you can then perform the task associated with that type of pointer. Pointer shapes are especially important when working with tables and graphics; in many cases, you can't perform a task until the pointer is the right shape. It takes some patience to get accustomed to positioning the pointer until it takes on the correct shape, but with practice you'll grow to rely on the pointer shapes as a quick visual cue to the options currently available to you.

To select and format the header row:

▶ **1.** Position the mouse pointer in the selection bar, to the left of the header row. The pointer changes to a right-facing arrow ⤒.

▶ **2.** Click the mouse button. The entire header row, including the end-of-cell mark in each cell and the end-of-row mark, is selected. See Figure 3-10.

Figure 3-10   **Header row selected**

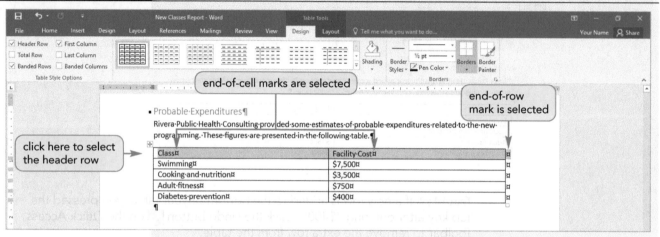

▶ **3.** Press the **Ctrl+B** keys to apply bold to the text in the header row. You can also use the formatting options on the Home tab to format selected text in a table, including adding italic formatting, changing the font, aligning text within cells, or applying a style.

▶ **4.** Click anywhere in the table to deselect the header row, and then save the document.

INSIGHT

Formatting a Multipage Table

In some documents, you might have a long table that extends across multiple pages. To make a multipage table easier to read, you can format the table header row to appear at the top of every page. To do so, click in the header row, click the Table Tools Layout tab, and then click the Properties button in the Table group. In the Table Properties dialog box, click the Row tab, and then select the "Repeat as header row at the top of each page" check box.

Now that you have created a very basic table, you can sort the information in it and improve its appearance.

Sorting Rows in a Table

The term **sort** refers to the process of rearranging information in alphabetical, numerical, or chronological order. You can sort a series of paragraphs, including the contents of a bulleted list, or you can sort the rows of a table.

When you sort a table, you arrange the rows based on the contents of one of the columns. For example, you could sort the table you just created based on the contents of the "Class" column—either in ascending alphabetical order (from A to Z) or in descending alphabetical order (from Z to A). Alternatively, you could sort the table based on the contents of the "Facility Cost" column—either in ascending numerical order (lowest to highest) or in descending numerical order (highest to lowest).

Clicking the Sort button in the Data group on the Table Tools Layout tab opens the Sort dialog box, which provides a number of options for fine-tuning the sort, including options for sorting a table by the contents of more than one column. This is useful if, for example, you want to organize the table rows by last name and then by first name within each last name. By default, Word assumes your table includes a header row that should remain at the top of the table—excluded from the sort.

REFERENCE

Sorting the Rows of a Table

- Click anywhere within the table.
- On the ribbon, click the Table Tools Layout tab.
- In the Data group, click the Sort button.
- In the Sort dialog box, click the Sort by arrow, and then select the header for the column you want to sort by.
- In the Type box located to the right of the Sort by box, select the type of information stored in the column you want to sort by; you can choose Text, Number, or Date.
- To sort in alphabetical, chronological, or numerical order, verify that the Ascending option button is selected. To sort in reverse order, click the Descending option button.
- To sort by a second column, click the Then by arrow, and then select a column header. If necessary, specify the type of information stored in the Then by column, and then confirm the sort order.
- At the bottom of the Sort dialog box, make sure the Header row option button is selected. This indicates that the table includes a header row that should not be included in the sort.
- Click the OK button.

Hillary would like you to sort the contents of the table in ascending numerical order based on the contents of the "Facility Cost" column.

To sort the information in the table:

▶ **1.** Make sure the insertion point is located somewhere in the table.

▶ **2.** On the ribbon, click the **Table Tools Layout** tab.

▶ **3.** In the Data group, click the **Sort** button. The Sort dialog box opens. Take a moment to review its default settings. The leftmost column in the table, the "Class" column, is selected in the Sort by box, indicating the sort will be based on the contents in this column. Because the "Class" column contains text, "Text" is selected in the Type box. The Ascending option button is selected by default, indicating that Word will sort the contents of the "Class" column from A to Z. The Header row option button is selected in the lower-left corner of the dialog box, ensuring the header row will not be included in the sort.

You want to sort the column by the contents of the "Facility Cost" column, so you need to change the Sort by setting.

▶ **4.** Click the **Sort by** button arrow, and then click **Facility Cost**. Because the "Facility Cost" column contains numbers, the Type box now displays "Number". The Ascending button is still selected, indicating that Word will sort the numbers in the "Facility Cost" column from lowest to highest. See Figure 3-11.

Figure 3-11   **Sort dialog box**

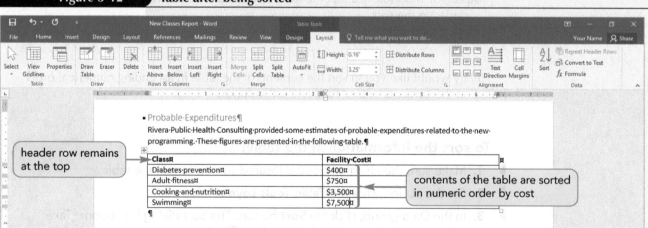

type of data in the "Facility Cost" column

sort based on the contents of the "Facility Cost" column

sort order

header row will be excluded from the sort

▶ **5.** Click the **OK** button to close the Sort dialog box, and then click anywhere in the table to deselect it. Rows 2 through 5 are now arranged numerically, according to the numbers in the "Facility Cost" column, with the "Swimming" row at the bottom. See Figure 3-12.

Figure 3-12   **Table after being sorted**

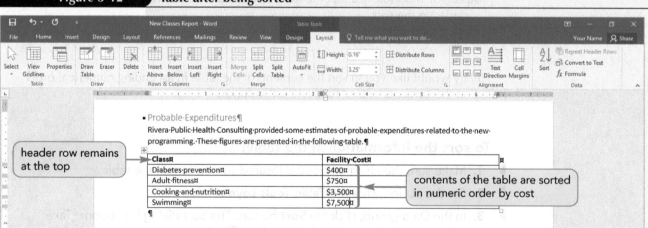

header row remains at the top

contents of the table are sorted in numeric order by cost

▶ **6.** Save the document.

Hillary decides that the table should also include the personnel cost for each item. She asks you to insert a "Personnel Cost" column.

Inserting Rows and Columns in a Table

To add a column to a table, you can use the tools in the Rows & Columns group on the Table Tools Layout tab, or you can use the Add Column button in the document window. To use the Add Column button, make sure the insertion point is located somewhere within the table. When you position the mouse pointer at the top of the table, pointing to the border between two columns, the Add Column button is displayed. When you click that button, a new column is inserted between the two existing columns.

To insert a column in the table:

1. Verify that the insertion point is located anywhere in the table.

2. Position the mouse pointer at the top of the table, so that it points to the border between the two columns. The Add Column button ⊕ appears at the top of the border. A blue guideline shows where the new column will be inserted. See Figure 3-13.

| Figure 3-13 | Inserting a column |

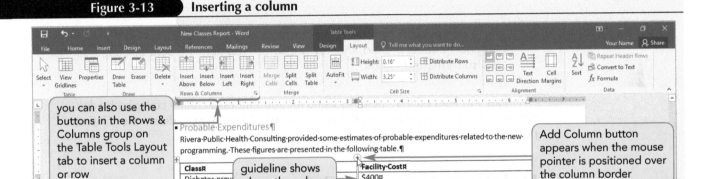

3. Click the **Add Column** button ⊕. A new, blank column is inserted between the "Class" and "Facility Cost" columns. The three columns in the table are narrower than the original two columns, but the overall width of the table remains the same.

4. Click in the top cell of the new column, and then enter the following header and data. Use the ↓ key to move the insertion point down through the column.

Personnel Cost

$500

$2,000

$200

$4,750

Your table should now look like the one in Figure 3-14.

Figure 3-14   New "Personnel Cost" column

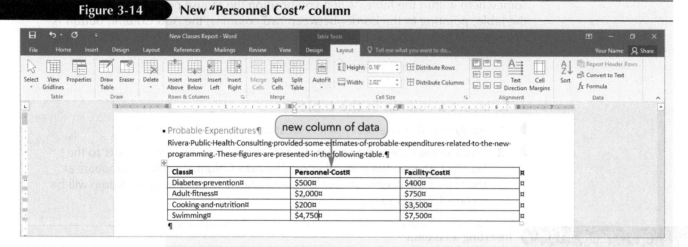

Because you selected the entire header row when you formatted the original headers in bold, the newly inserted header, "Personnel Cost," is also formatted in bold.

Hillary just learned that the costs listed for adult fitness actually cover both adult fitness and diabetes prevention. Therefore, she would like you to delete the "Diabetes prevention" row from the table.

Deleting Rows and Columns

When you consider deleting a row, you need to be clear about whether you want to delete just the contents of the row, or both the contents and the structure of the row. You can delete the contents of a row by selecting the row and pressing the Delete key. This removes the information from the row but leaves the row structure intact. The same is true for deleting the contents of an individual cell, a column, or the entire table. To delete the structure of a row, a column, or the entire table—including its contents—you select the row (or column or the entire table), and then use the Delete button on the Mini toolbar or in the Rows & Columns group on the Table Tools Layout tab. To delete multiple rows or columns, start by selecting all the rows or columns you want to delete.

Before you delete the "Diabetes prevention" row, you need to edit the contents in the third cell in the first column to indicate that the items in that row are for adult fitness and diabetes prevention.

To delete the "Diabetes prevention" row:

▶ **1.** In the cell containing the text "Adult fitness," click to the right of the final "s," press the **spacebar**, and then type **and diabetes prevention**. The cell now reads "Adult fitness and diabetes prevention." Part of the text wraps to a second line within the cell.

   Next, you can delete the "Diabetes prevention" row, which is no longer necessary.

▶ **2.** Click in the selection bar to the left of the **Diabetes prevention** row. The row is selected, with the Mini toolbar displayed on top of the selected row.

3. On the Mini toolbar, click the **Delete** button. The Delete menu opens, displaying options for deleting cells, columns, rows, or the entire table. See Figure 3-15.

Figure 3-15   Deleting a row

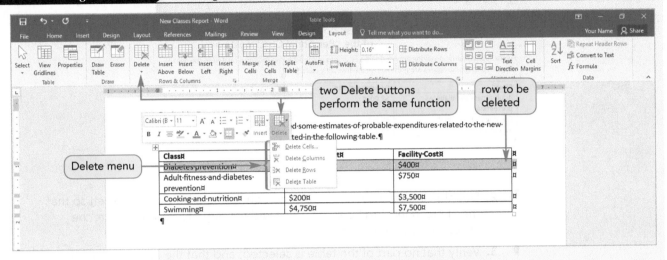

4. Click **Delete Rows**. The "Diabetes prevention" row is removed from the table, and the Mini toolbar disappears.

5. Save your work.

The table now contains all the information Hillary wants to include. Next, you'll adjust the widths of the three columns.

Changing Column Widths

TIP

To change the height of a row, position the mouse pointer over the bottom row border and drag the border up or down.

Columns that are too wide for the material they contain can make a table hard to read. You can change a column's width by dragging the column's right border to a new position. Or, if you prefer, you can double-click a column border to make the column width adjust automatically to accommodate the widest entry in the column. To adjust the width of all the columns to match their widest entries, click anywhere in the table, click the AutoFit button in the Cell Size group on the Table Tools Layout tab, and then click AutoFit Contents. To adjust the width of the entire table to span the width of the page, click the AutoFit button and then click AutoFit Window.

You'll adjust the columns in Hillary's table by double-clicking the right column border. You need to start by making sure that no part of the table is selected. Otherwise, when you double-click the border, only the width of the selected part of the table will change.

To change the width of the columns in the table:

When resizing a column, be sure that no part of the table is selected. Otherwise, you'll resize just the selected part.

1. Verify that no part of the table is selected, and then position the mouse pointer over the right border of the "Personnel Cost" column until the pointer changes to ◄‖►. See Figure 3-16.

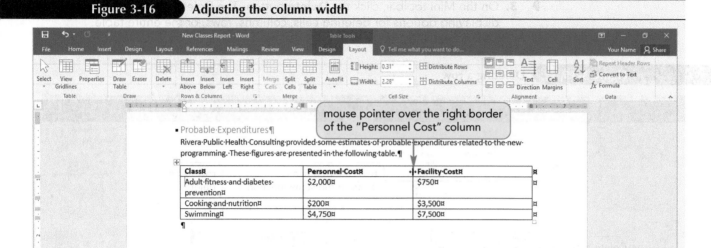

Figure 3-16　**Adjusting the column width**

> ▶ **2.** Double-click the mouse button. The right column border moves left so that the "Personnel Cost" column is just wide enough to accommodate the widest entry in the column.

> ▶ **3.** Verify that no part of the table is selected, and that the insertion point is located in any cell in the table.

> ▶ **4.** Make sure the Table Tools Layout tab is selected on the ribbon.

> ▶ **5.** In the Cell Size group, click the **AutoFit** button, and then click **AutoFit Contents**. All of the table columns adjust so that each is just wide enough to accommodate its widest entry. The text "Adult fitness and diabetes prevention" in row 2 no longer wraps to a second line.

To finish the table, you will add some formatting to improve the table's appearance.

Formatting Tables with Styles

To adjust a table's appearance, you can use any of the formatting options available on the Home tab. To change a table's appearance more dramatically, you can use table styles, which allow you to apply a collection of formatting options, including shading, color, borders, and other design elements, with a single click.

By default, a table is formatted with the Table Grid style, which includes only black borders between the rows and columns, no paragraph spacing, no shading, and the default black font color. You can select a more colorful table style from the Table Styles group on the Table Tools Design tab. Whatever table style you choose, you'll give your document a more polished look if you use the same style consistently in all the tables in a single document.

Some table styles format rows in alternating colors, called **banded rows**, while others format the columns in alternating colors, called **banded columns**. You can choose a style that includes different formatting for the header row than for the rest of the table. Or, if the first column in your table is a header column—that is, if it contains headers identifying the type of information in each row—you can choose a style that instead applies different formatting to the first column.

REFERENCE

Formatting a Table with a Table Style

- Click in the table you want to format.
- On the ribbon, click the Table Tools Design tab.
- In the Table Styles group, click the More button to display the Table Styles gallery.
- Position the mouse pointer over a style in the Table Styles gallery to see a Live Preview of the table style in the document.
- In the Table Styles gallery, click the style you want.
- To apply or remove style elements (such as special formatting for the header row, banded rows, or banded columns), select or deselect check boxes as necessary in the Table Style Options group.

Hillary wants to use a table style that emphasizes the header row with special formatting, does not include column borders, and uses color to separate the rows.

To apply a table style to the Probable Expenditures table:

1. Click anywhere in the table, and then scroll to position the table at the very bottom of the Word window. This will make it easier to see the Live Preview in the next few steps.

2. On the ribbon, click the **Table Tools Design** tab. In the Table Styles group, the plain Table Grid style is highlighted, indicating that it is the table's current style.

3. In the Table Styles group, click the **More** button. The Table Styles gallery opens. The default Table Grid style now appears under the heading "Plain Tables." The more elaborate styles appear below, in the "Grid Tables" section of the gallery.

4. Use the gallery's vertical scroll bar to view the complete collection of table styles. When you are finished, scroll up until you can see the "Grid Tables" heading again.

5. Move the mouse pointer over the style located in the fourth row of the Grid Tables section, first column on the right. See Figure 3-17.

Figure 3-17   **Table Styles gallery**

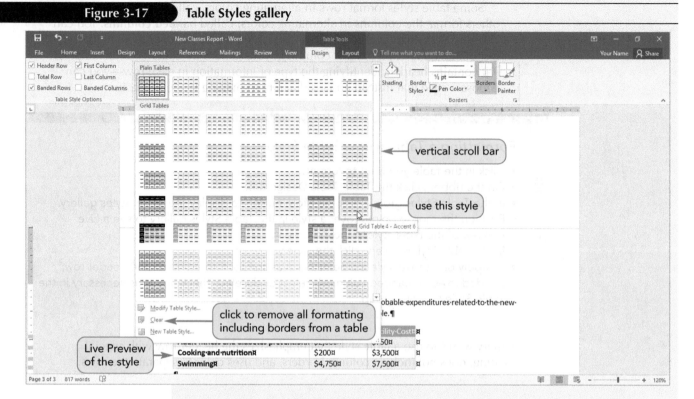

A ScreenTip displays the style's name, "Grid Table 4 - Accent 6." The style consists of a dark green heading row, with alternating rows of light green and white below. A Live Preview of the style is visible in the document.

▶ **6.** Click the **Grid Table 4 - Accent 6** style. The Table Styles gallery closes.

▶ **7.** Scroll to position the table at the top of the Word window, so you can review it more easily. The table's header row is formatted with dark green shading and white text. The rows below appear in alternating colors of light green and white.

The only problem with the newly formatted table is that the text in the first column is formatted in bold. In tables where the first column contains headers, bold would be appropriate—but this isn't the case with Hillary's table. You'll fix this by deselecting the First Column check box in the Table Style Options group on the Table Tools Design tab.

To remove the bold formatting from the first column:

▶ **1.** In the Table Style Options group, click the **First Column** check box to deselect this option. The bold formatting is removed from the entries in the "Class" column. Note that the Header Row check box is selected. This indicates that the table's header row is emphasized with special formatting (dark green shading with white text). The Banded Rows check box is also selected because the table is formatted with banded rows of green and white. Figure 3-18 shows the finished table.

Figure 3-18 **Completed table**

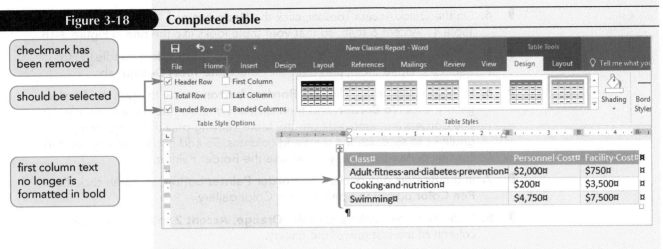

checkmark has been removed

should be selected

first column text no longer is formatted in bold

2. Save the document.

After you apply a table style, it's helpful to know how to remove it in case you want to start over from scratch. The Clear option on the menu below the Table Styles gallery removes the current style from a table, including the borders between cells. When a table has no borders, the rows and columns are defined by **gridlines**, which are useful as guidelines but do not appear when you print the table.

In the following steps, you'll experiment with clearing the table's style, displaying and hiding the gridlines, and removing the table's borders.

To experiment with table styles, gridlines, and borders:

1. In the Table Styles group, click the **More** button, and then click **Clear** in the menu below the gallery. Next, you need to make sure the table gridlines are displayed.

2. On the ribbon, click the **Table Tools Layout** tab.

3. In the Table group, click the **View Gridlines** button, if necessary, to select it. The table now looks much simpler, with no shading or font colors. Instead of the table borders, dotted gridlines separate the rows and columns. The text in the table is spaced farther apart because removing the table style restored the default paragraph and line spacing of the Normal style. The bold formatting that you applied earlier, which is not part of a table style, is visible again.

   It is helpful to clear a table's style and view only the gridlines if you want to use a table to lay out text and graphics on a page, but you want no visible indication of the table itself. You'll have a chance to try this technique in the Case Problems at the end of this module.

   Another option is to remove only the table borders, leaving the rest of the table style applied to the table. To do this, you have to select the entire table. But first you need to undo the style change.

▶ **4.** On the Quick Access Toolbar, click the **Undo** button to restore the Grid Table 4 - Accent 6 style, so that your table looks like the one in Figure 3-18.

▶ **5.** In the upper-left corner of the table, click the **Table Select** handle ⊕ to select the entire table, and then click the **Table Tools Design** tab.

▶ **6.** In the Borders group, click the **Borders button arrow** to open the Borders gallery, click **No Border**, and then click anywhere in the table to deselect it. The borders are removed from the table, leaving only the nonprinting gridlines to separate the rows and columns. To add borders of any color to specific parts of a table, you can use the Border Painter.

▶ **7.** In the Borders group, click the **Border Painter** button, and then click the **Pen Color** button to open the Pen Color gallery.

▶ **8.** In the Pen Color gallery, click the **Orange, Accent 2** square in the sixth column of the first row of the gallery.

▶ **9.** Use the Border Painter pointer to click any gridline in the table. An orange border is added to the cell where you clicked.

▶ **10.** Continue experimenting with the Border Painter pointer, and then press the **Esc** key to turn off the Border Painter pointer when you are finished.

▶ **11.** Reapply the Grid Table 4 - Accent 6 table style to make your table match the one shown earlier in Figure 3-18.

▶ **12.** Save the document and then close it.

PROSKILLS

Problem Solving: Fine-Tuning Table Styles

After you apply a table style to a table, you might like the look of the table but find that it no longer effectively conveys your information or is not quite as easy to read. To solve this problem, you might be inclined to go back to the Table Styles gallery to find another style that might work better. Another method to correct problems with a table style is to identify the table elements with problematic formatting, and then manually make formatting adjustments to only those elements using the options on the Table Tools Design tab. For example, you can change the thickness and color of the table borders using the options in the Borders group, and you can add shading using the Shading button in the Table Styles group. Also, if you don't like the appearance of table styles in your document, consider changing the document's theme and previewing the table styles again. The table styles have a different appearance in each theme. When applying table styles, remember there are many options for attractively formatting the table without compromising the information being conveyed.

In the next session, you'll complete the rest of the report by organizing information using tab stops, creating footnotes and endnotes, dividing the document into sections, inserting headers and footers, and, finally, inserting a cover page.

REVIEW

Session 3.1 Quick Check

1. What kind of style must you apply to a paragraph to make the paragraph appear as a heading in the Navigation pane?

2. What are the three steps involved in creating a table in Word?

3. Explain how to insert a new column in a table.

4. After you enter data in the last cell in the last row in a table, how can you insert a new row?

5. When sorting a table, is the header row included by default?

6. To adjust the width of a table's column to span the width of the page, would you use the AutoFit Contents option or the AutoFit Window option?

Session 3.2 Visual Overview:

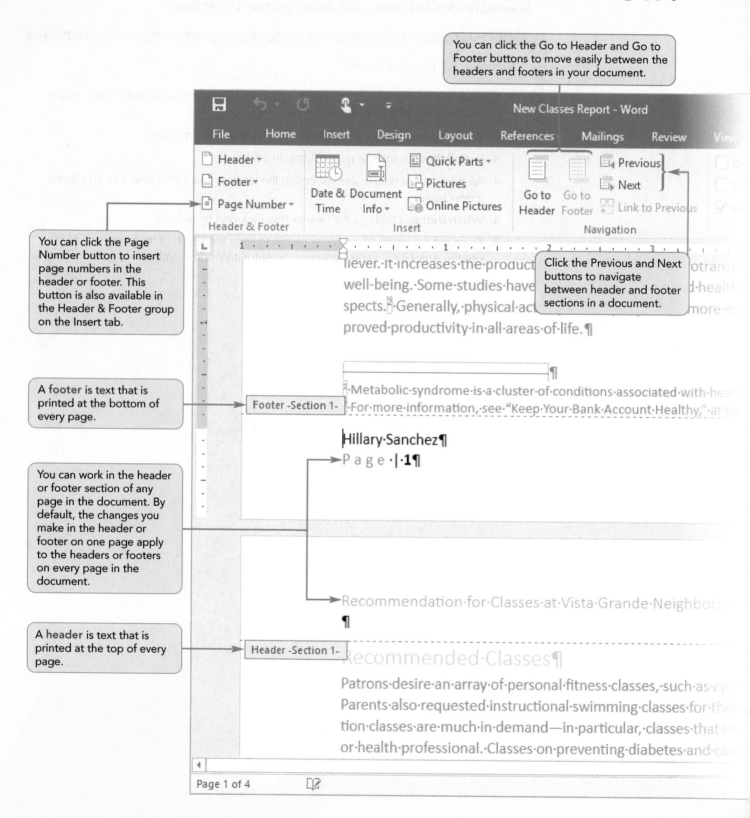

You can click the Go to Header and Go to Footer buttons to move easily between the headers and footers in your document.

You can click the Page Number button to insert page numbers in the header or footer. This button is also available in the Header & Footer group on the Insert tab.

Click the Previous and Next buttons to navigate between header and footer sections in a document.

A footer is text that is printed at the bottom of every page.

You can work in the header or footer section of any page in the document. By default, the changes you make in the header or footer on one page apply to the headers or footers on every page in the document.

A header is text that is printed at the top of every page.

Working with Headers and Footers

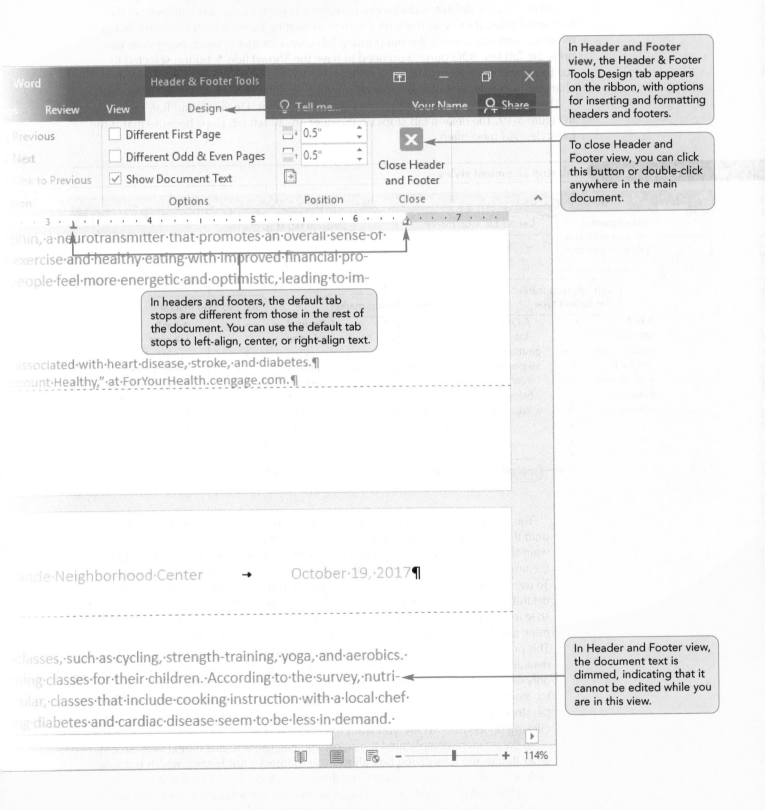

In **Header and Footer** view, the Header & Footer Tools Design tab appears on the ribbon, with options for inserting and formatting headers and footers.

To close Header and Footer view, you can click this button or double-click anywhere in the main document.

In headers and footers, the default tab stops are different from those in the rest of the document. You can use the default tab stops to left-align, center, or right-align text.

In Header and Footer view, the document text is dimmed, indicating that it cannot be edited while you are in this view.

Setting Tab Stops

A **tab stop** (often called a **tab**) is a location on the horizontal ruler where the insertion point moves when you press the Tab key. You can use tab stops to align small amounts of text or data. By default, a document contains tab stops every one-half inch on the horizontal ruler. There's no mark on the ruler indicating these default tab stops, but in the document you can see the nonprinting Tab character that appears every time you press the Tab key. (Of course, you need to have the Show/Hide ¶ button selected to see these nonprinting characters.) A nonprinting tab character is just like any other character you type; you can delete it by pressing the Backspace key or the Delete key.

The five major types of tab stops are Left, Center, Right, Decimal, and Bar, as shown in Figure 3-19. The default tab stops on the ruler are all left tab stops because that is the tab style used most often.

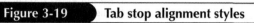
Figure 3-19   Tab stop alignment styles

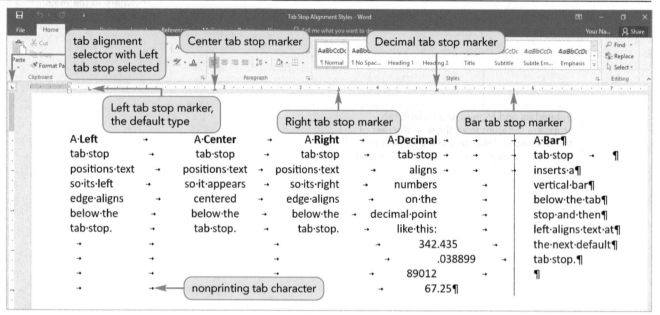

You can use tab stops a few different ways. The simplest is to press the Tab key until the insertion point is aligned where you want it, and then type the text you want to align. Each time you press the Tab key, the insertion point moves right to the next default tab stop, with the left edge of the text aligning below the tab stop. To use a different type of tab stop, or to use a tab stop at a location other than the default tab stop locations (every half-inch on the ruler), first select an alignment style from the tab alignment selector, located at the left end of the horizontal ruler, and then click the horizontal ruler where you want to insert the tab stop. This process is called setting a tab stop. When you set a new tab stop, all of the default tab stops to its left are removed. This means you have to press the Tab key only once to move the insertion point to the newly created tab stop. To set a new tab stop in text you have already typed, select the text, including the nonprinting tab stop characters, and then set the tab stop by selecting an alignment style and clicking on the ruler where you want to set the tab stop.

To create more complicated tab stops, you can use the Tabs dialog box. Among other things, the Tabs dialog box allows you to insert a **dot leader**, which is a row of dots (or other characters) between tabbed text. A dot leader makes it easier to read a long list of tabbed material because the eye can follow the dots from one item to the next. You've probably seen dot leaders used in the table of contents in a book, where the dots separate the chapter titles from the page numbers.

To create a left tab stop with a dot leader, click the Dialog Box Launcher in the Paragraph group on the Home tab, click the Indents and Spacing tab, if necessary, and then click the Tabs button at the bottom of the dialog box. In the Tab stop position box in the Tabs dialog box, type the location on the ruler where you want to insert the tab. For example, to insert a tab stop at the 4-inch mark, type 4. Verify that the Left option button is selected in the Alignment section, and then, in the Leader section, click the option button for the type of leader you want. Click the Set button, and then click the OK button.

REFERENCE

Setting, Moving, and Clearing Tab Stops

- To set a tab stop, click the tab alignment selector on the horizontal ruler until the appropriate tab stop alignment style is displayed, and then click the horizontal ruler where you want to position the tab stop.
- To move a tab stop, drag it to a new location on the ruler. If you have already typed text that is aligned by the tab stop, select the text before dragging the tab stop to a new location.
- To clear a tab stop, drag it off the ruler.

In the New Classes Report document you have been working on, you need to type the list of consultants and their titles. You can use tab stops to quickly format this small amount of information in two columns. As you type, you'll discover whether Word's default tab stops are appropriate for this document or whether you need to set a new tab stop. Before you get started working with tabs, you'll take a moment to explore Word's Resume Reading feature.

To enter the list of consultants using tabs:

1. Open the **New Classes Report** document. The document opens with the "Summary" heading at the top of the Word window. In the lower-right corner, a "Welcome back!" message is displayed briefly and is then replaced with the Resume Reading button 🔲.

2. Point to the **Resume Reading** button 🔲 to expand its "Welcome back!" message. See Figure 3-20.

| Figure 3-20 | "Welcome back!" message displayed in re-opened document |

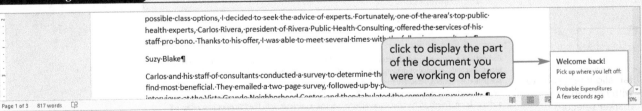

4. Scroll up to display the "Rivera Public Health Consulting" heading on page 1.

5. Confirm that the ruler and nonprinting characters are displayed, and that the document is displayed in **Print Layout** view, zoomed to **120%**.

3. Click the **Welcome back!** message. The document window scrolls down to display the table, which you were working on just before you closed the document.

    6. Click to the right of the last "e" in "Suzy Blake."

    7. Press the **Tab** key. An arrow-shaped tab character appears, and the insertion point moves to the first tab stop after the last "e" in "Blake." This tab stop is the default tab located at the 1-inch mark on the horizontal ruler. See Figure 3-21.

Figure 3-21	Tab character

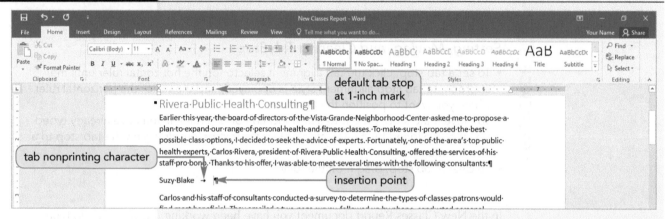

    8. Type **Senior Consultant**, and then press the **Enter** key to move the insertion point to the next line.

    9. Type **Emmanuel Iglesias**, and then press the **Tab** key. The insertion point moves to the next available tab stop, this time located at the 1.5-inch mark on the ruler.

    10. Type **Senior Consultant**, and then press the **Enter** key to move to the next line. Notice that Emmanuel Iglesias's title does not align with Suzy Blake's title on the line above it. You'll fix this after you type the last name in the list.

    11. Type **Carolina Sheffield-Bassinger**, press the **Tab** key, and then type **Project Manager**. See Figure 3-22.

Figure 3-22	List of consultants

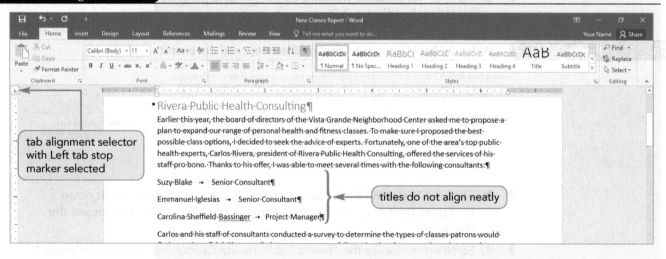

The list of names and titles is not aligned properly. You can fix this by inserting a new tab stop.

To add a new tab stop to the horizontal ruler:

▶ **1.** Make sure the Home tab is displayed on the ribbon, and then select the list of consultants and their titles.

▶ **2.** On the horizontal ruler, click at the 2.5-inch mark. Because the current tab stop alignment style is Left tab, Word inserts a left tab stop at that location. Remember that when you set a new tab stop, all the default tab stops to its left are removed. The column of titles shifts to the new tab stop. See Figure 3-23.

Figure 3-23	Titles aligned at new tab stop

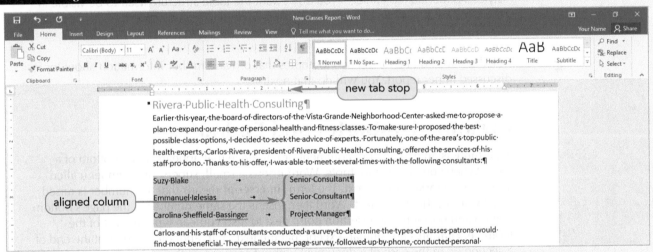

To complete the list, you need to remove the paragraph spacing after the first two paragraphs in the list, so the list looks like it's all one paragraph. You can quickly reduce paragraph and line spacing to 0 points by clicking the No Spacing style in the Styles group. In this case, you want to reduce only the paragraph spacing to 0 points, so you'll use the Line and Paragraph Spacing button instead.

▶ **3.** Select the first two paragraphs in the list, which contain the names and titles for Suzy and Emmanuel.

▶ **4.** In the Paragraph group, click the **Line and Paragraph Spacing** button ▤▾, and then click **Remove Space After Paragraph**.

▶ **5.** Click anywhere in the document to deselect the list, and then save your work.

PROSKILLS

Decision Making: Choosing Between Tabs and Tables

When you have information that you want to align in columns in your document, you need to decide whether to use tabs or tables. Whatever you do, don't try to align columns of data by adding extra spaces with the spacebar. Although the text might seem precisely aligned on the screen, it probably won't be aligned when you print the document. Furthermore, if you edit the text, the spaces you inserted to align your columns will be affected by your edits; they get moved just like regular text, ruining your alignment.

So what is the most efficient way to align text in columns? It depends. Inserting tabs works well for aligning small amounts of information in just a few columns and rows, such as two columns with three rows, but tabs become cumbersome when you need to organize a lot of data over multiple columns and rows. In that case, using a table to organize columns of information is better. Unlike with tabbed columns of data, it's easy to add data to tables by inserting columns. You might also choose tables over tab stops when you want to take advantage of the formatting options available with table styles. As mentioned earlier, if you don't want the table structure itself to be visible in the document, you can clear its table style and then hide its gridlines.

Hillary would like to add two footnotes that provide further information about topics discussed in her report. You will do that next.

Creating Footnotes and Endnotes

A **footnote** is an explanatory comment or reference that appears at the bottom of a page. When you create a footnote, Word inserts a small, superscript number (called a **reference marker**) in the text. The term **superscript** means that the number is raised slightly above the line of text. Word then inserts the same number in the page's bottom margin and positions the insertion point next to it so you can type the text of the footnote. **Endnotes** are similar, except that the text of an endnote appears at the end of a section or, in the case of a document without sections, at the end of the document. (You'll learn about dividing a document into sections later in this module.) By default, the reference marker for an endnote is a lowercase Roman numeral, and the reference marker for a footnote is an ordinary, Arabic numeral.

Word automatically manages the reference markers for you, keeping them sequential from the beginning of the document to the end, no matter how many times you add, delete, or move footnotes or endnotes. For example, if you move a paragraph containing footnote 4 so that it falls before the paragraph containing footnote 1, Word renumbers all the footnotes in the document to keep them sequential.

REFERENCE

Inserting a Footnote or an Endnote

- Click the location in the document where you want to insert a footnote or an endnote.
- On the ribbon, click the References tab.
- In the Footnotes group, click the Insert Footnote button or the Insert Endnote button.
- Type the text of the footnote in the bottom margin of the page, or type the text of the endnote at the end of the document.
- When you are finished typing the text of a footnote or an endnote, click in the body of the document to continue working on the document.

Hillary asks you to insert a footnote that provides more information about some studies mentioned in the report.

To add a footnote to the report:

▶ **1.** Use the Navigation pane to find the phrase "improved financial prospects" on page 1, and then click to the right of the period after "prospects."

▶ **2.** Close the Navigation pane.

▶ **3.** On the ribbon, click the **References** tab.

▶ **4.** In the Footnotes group, click the **Insert Footnote** button. A superscript "1" is inserted to the right of the period after "prospects." Word also inserts the number "1" in the bottom margin below a separator line. The insertion point is now located next to the number in the bottom margin, ready for you to type the text of the footnote.

▶ **5.** Type **For more information, see "Keep Your Bank Account Healthy," at ForYourHealth.cengage.com.** See Figure 3-24.

Figure 3-24   **Inserting a footnote**

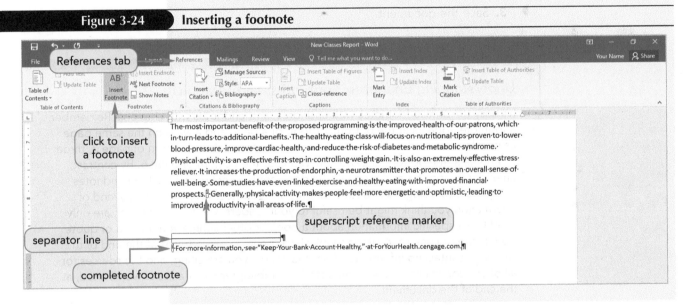

Now, Hillary would like you to insert a second footnote.

To insert a second footnote:

▶ **1.** At the end of the third line of the same paragraph, click at the end of the second sentence to position the insertion point to the right of the period after "syndrome."

▶ **2.** In the Footnotes group, click the **Insert Footnote** button, and then type **Metabolic syndrome is a cluster of conditions associated with heart disease, stroke, and diabetes.** Because this footnote is placed earlier in the document than the one you just created, Word inserts a superscript "1" for this footnote and then renumbers the other footnote as "2." See Figure 3-25.

Figure 3-25   **Inserting a second footnote**

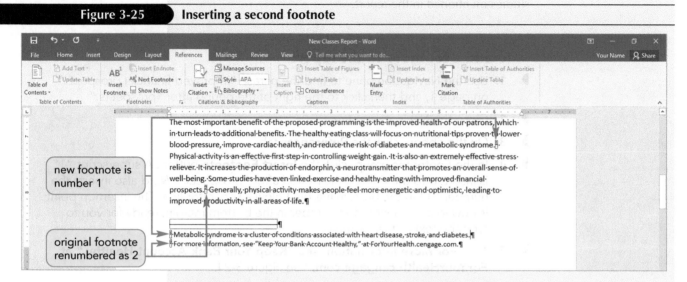

▶   **3.** Save the document.

Understanding Endnotes, Footnotes, and Citations

It's easy to confuse footnotes with endnotes, and endnotes with citations. Remember, a footnote appears at the bottom, or foot, of a page and always on the same page as its reference marker. You might have one footnote at the bottom of page 3, three footnotes at the bottom of page 5, and one at the bottom of page 6. By contrast, an endnote appears at the end of the document or section, with all the endnotes compiled into a single list. Both endnotes and footnotes can contain any kind of information you think might be useful to your readers. Citations, however, are only used to list specific information about a book or other source you refer to or quote from in the document. A citation typically appears in parentheses at the end of the sentence containing information from the source you are citing, and the sources for all of the document's citations are listed in a bibliography, or a list of works cited, at the end of the document.

Now you're ready to address some other issues with the document. First, Hillary has noticed that the right edges of most of the paragraphs in the document are uneven, and she'd like you to try to smooth them out. You'll correct this problem in the next section.

Hyphenating a Document

By default, hyphenation is turned off in Word documents. That means if you are in the middle of typing a word and you reach the end of a line, Word moves the entire word to the next line instead of inserting a hyphen and breaking the word into two parts. This can result in ragged text on the right margin. To ensure a smoother right margin, you can turn on automatic hyphenation—in which case, any word that ends within the last .25 inch of a line will be hyphenated.

To turn on automatic hyphenation in the document:

▶ **1.** Review the paragraph above the footnotes on page 1. The text on the right side of this paragraph is uneven. Keeping an eye on this paragraph will help you see the benefits of hyphenation.

▶ **2.** On the ribbon, click the **Layout** tab.

▶ **3.** In the Page Setup group, click the **Hyphenation** button to open the Hyphenation menu, and then click **Automatic**. The Hyphenation menu closes. Throughout the document, the text layout shifts to account for the insertion of hyphens in words that break near the end of a line. For example, in the last paragraph on page 1, the word "Physical" is now hyphenated. See Figure 3-26.

Figure 3-26	Hyphenated document

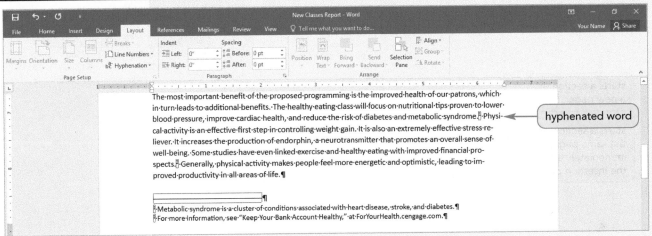

▶ **4.** Save the document.

Hillary plans to post a handout on the bulletin board at the neighborhood center to illustrate the benefits of the new classes, and she wants to include a sample handout in the report. Before you can add the sample of the handout, you need to divide the document into sections.

Formatting a Document into Sections

A **section** is a part of a document that can have its own page orientation, margins, headers, footers, and so on. In other words, each section is like a document within a document. To divide a document into sections, you insert a **section break**. You can select from a few different types of section breaks. One of the most useful is a Next page section break, which inserts a page break and starts the new section on the next page. Another commonly used kind of section break, a Continuous section break, starts the section at the location of the insertion point without changing the page flow. To insert a section break, you click the Breaks button in the Page Setup group on the Layout tab and then select the type of section break you want to insert.

Hillary wants to format the handout in landscape orientation, but the report is currently formatted in portrait orientation. To format part of a document in an orientation different from the rest of the document, you need to divide the document into sections.

To insert a section break below the table:

▶ **1.** Press the **Ctrl+End** keys to move the insertion point to the end of the document, just below the table.

▶ **2.** In the Page Setup group, click the **Breaks** button. The Breaks gallery opens, as shown in Figure 3-27.

Figure 3-27	Breaks gallery

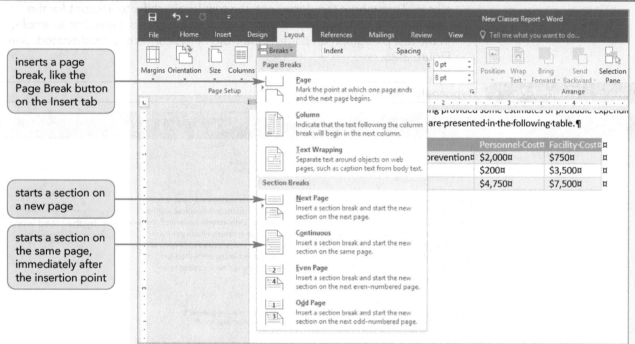

inserts a page break, like the Page Break button on the Insert tab

starts a section on a new page

starts a section on the same page, immediately after the insertion point

The Page Breaks section of the gallery includes options for controlling how the text flows from page to page. The first option, Page, inserts a page break. It has the same effect as pressing the Page Break button on the Insert tab or pressing the Ctrl+Enter keys. The Section Breaks section of the gallery includes four types of section breaks. The two you'll use most often are Next Page and Continuous.

▶ **3.** Under "Section Breaks," click **Next Page**. A section break is inserted in the document, and the insertion point moves to the top of the new page 4.

▶ **4.** Scroll up, if necessary, until you can see the double dotted line and the words "Section Break (Next Page)" below the table on page 3. This line indicates that a new section begins on the next page.

▶ **5.** Save the document.

You've created a new page that is a separate section from the rest of the report. The sections are numbered consecutively. The first part of the document is section 1, and the new page is section 2. Now you can format section 2 in landscape orientation without affecting the rest of the document.

To format section 2 in landscape orientation:

▶ **1.** Scroll down and verify that the insertion point is positioned at the top of the new page 4.

▶ **2.** On the ribbon, click the **View** tab.

▶ **3.** In the Zoom group, click the **Multiple Pages** button, and then change the Zoom level to **30%** so you can see all four pages of the document displayed side by side.

▶ **4.** On the ribbon, click the **Layout** tab.

▶ **5.** In the Page Setup group, click the **Orientation** button, and then click **Landscape**. Section 2, which consists solely of page 4, changes to landscape orientation, as shown in Figure 3-28. Section 1, which consists of pages 1 through 3, remains in portrait orientation.

| Figure 3-28 | Page 4 formatted in landscape orientation |

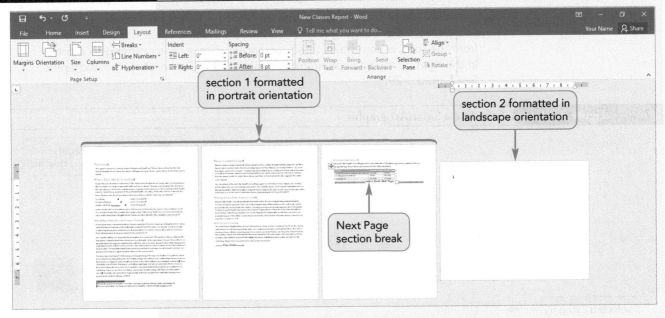

▶ **6.** Change the Zoom level back to **120%**, and then save the document.

Page 4 is now formatted in landscape orientation, ready for you to create Hillary's handout, which will consist of a graphic that shows the benefits of exercise. You'll use Word's SmartArt feature to create the graphic.

Creating SmartArt

A **SmartArt** graphic is a diagram of shapes, such as circles, squares, or arrows. A well-designed SmartArt graphic can illustrate concepts that might otherwise require several paragraphs of explanation. To create a SmartArt graphic, you switch to the Insert tab and then, in the Illustrations group, click the SmartArt button. This opens the Choose a SmartArt Graphic dialog box, where you can select from eight categories of graphics, including graphics designed to illustrate relationships, processes, and hierarchies. Within each category, you can choose from numerous designs. Once inserted into your document, a SmartArt graphic contains placeholder text that you replace with your own text. When a SmartArt graphic is selected, the SmartArt Tools Design and Format tabs appear on the ribbon.

To create a SmartArt graphic:

1. Verify that the insertion point is located at the top of page 4, which is blank.

2. On the ribbon, click the **Insert** tab.

3. In the Illustrations group, click the **SmartArt** button. The Choose a SmartArt Graphic dialog box opens, with categories of SmartArt graphics in the left panel. The middle panel displays the graphics associated with the category currently selected in the left panel. The right panel displays a larger image of the graphic that is currently selected in the middle panel, along with an explanation of the graphic's purpose. By default, All is selected in the left panel.

4. Explore the Choose a SmartArt Graphic dialog box by selecting categories in the left panel and viewing the graphics displayed in the middle panel.

5. In the left panel, click **Relationship**, and then scroll down in the middle panel and click the **Converging Radial** graphic (in the first column, seventh row from the top), which shows three rectangles with arrows pointing to a circle. In the right panel, you see an explanation of the Converging Radial graphic. See Figure 3-29.

Figure 3-29   Selecting a SmartArt graphic

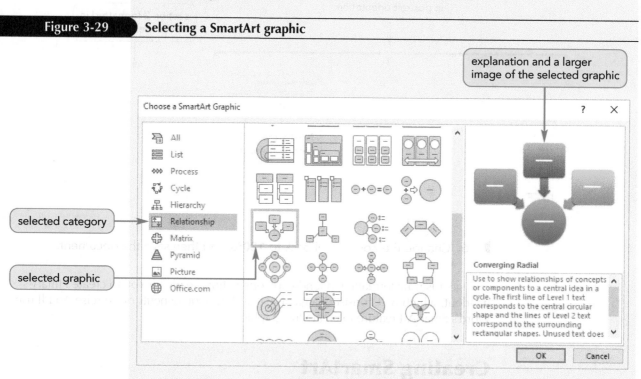

6. Click the **OK** button. The Converging Radial graphic, with placeholder text, is inserted at the top of page 4. The graphic is surrounded by a rectangular border, indicating that it is selected. The SmartArt Tools contextual tabs appear on the ribbon. To the right of the graphic, you also see the Text pane, a small window with a title bar that contains the text "Type your text here." See Figure 3-30.

| Figure 3-30 | SmartArt graphic with Text pane displayed |

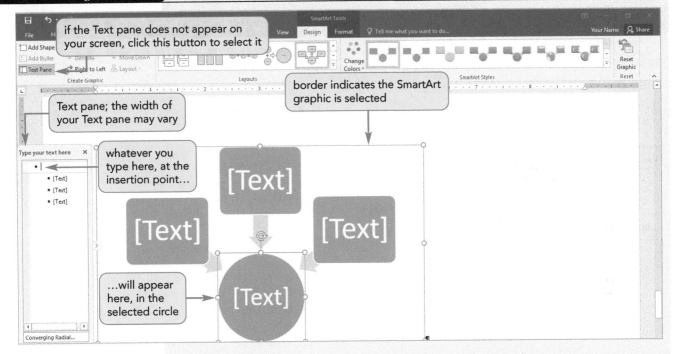

Trouble? If you do not see the Text pane, click the Text Pane button in the Create Graphic group on the SmartArt Tools Design tab to select it.

The insertion point is blinking next to the first bullet in the Text pane, which is selected with an orange rectangle. The circle at the bottom of the SmartArt graphic is also selected, as indicated by the border with handles. At this point, anything you type next to the selected bullet in the Text pane will also appear in the selected circle in the SmartArt graphic.

Trouble? If you see the Text pane but the first bullet is not selected as shown in Figure 3-30, click next to the first bullet in the Text pane to select it.

Now you are ready to add text to the graphic.

To add text to the SmartArt graphic:

1. Type **Better Physical and Mental Health**. The new text is displayed in the Text pane and in the circle in the SmartArt graphic. Now you need to insert text in the three rectangles.

2. Press the ↓ key to move the insertion point down to the next placeholder bullet in the Text pane, and then type **Exercise**. The new text is displayed in the Text pane and in the blue rectangle on the left. See Figure 3-31.

Figure 3-31   New text in Text pane and in SmartArt graphic

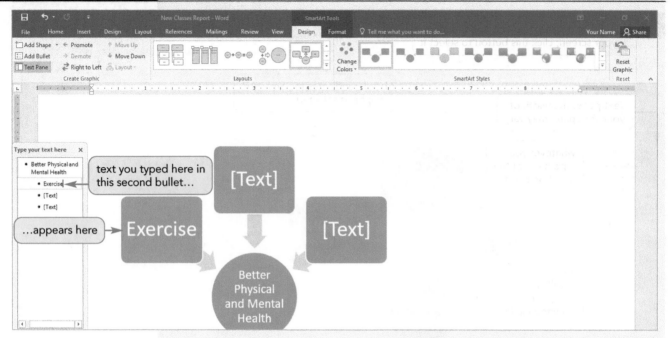

3. Press the ↓ key to move the insertion point down to the next placeholder bullet in the Text pane, and then type **Good Nutrition**. The new text appears in the middle rectangle and in the Text pane. You don't need the third rectangle, so you'll delete it.

4. Press the ↓ key to move the insertion point down to the next placeholder bullet in the Text pane, and then press the **Backspace** key. The rectangle on the right is deleted from the SmartArt graphic. The two remaining rectangles and the circle enlarge and shift position.

5. Make sure the SmartArt Tools Design tab is still selected on the ribbon.

6. In the Create Graphic group, click the **Text Pane** button to deselect it. The Text pane closes.

7. Click in the white area inside the SmartArt border.

Next, you need to resize the SmartArt graphic so it fills the page.

To adjust the size of the SmartArt graphic:

1. Zoom out so you can see the entire page. As you can see on the ruler, the SmartArt is currently 6 inches wide. You could drag the SmartArt border to resize it, just as you can with any graphic, but you will get more precise results using the Size button on the SmartArt Tools Format tab.

2. On the ribbon, click the **SmartArt Tools Format** tab.

3. On the right side of the SmartArt Tools Format tab, click the **Size** button to display the Height and Width boxes.

4. Click the **Height** box, type **6.5**, click the **Width** box, type **9**, and then press the **Enter** key. The SmartArt graphic resizes, so that it is now 9 inches wide and 6.5 inches high, taking up most of the page. See Figure 3-32.

TIP

To add a shape to a SmartArt graphic, click a shape in the SmartArt graphic, click the Add Shape arrow in the Create Graphic group on the SmartArt Tools Design tab, and then click a placement option.

Figure 3-32 **Resized SmartArt**

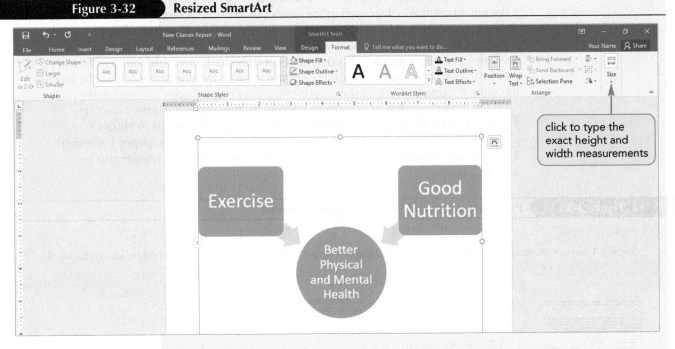

click to type the exact height and width measurements

Trouble? If one of the shapes in the SmartArt graphic was resized, rather than the entire SmartArt graphic, the insertion point was located within the shape rather than in the white space. On the Quick Access Toolbar, click the Undo button 🔄, click in the white area inside the SmartArt border, and then repeat Steps 3 and 4.

5. Click outside the SmartArt border to deselect it, and then review the graphic centered on the page.

Next, you need to insert a header at the top of each page in the report and a footer at the bottom of each page in the report.

Adding Headers and Footers

The first step to working with headers and footers is to open Header and Footer view. You can do that in three ways: (1) insert a page number using the Page Number button in the Header & Footer group on the Insert tab; (2) double-click in the header area (in a page's top margin) or in the footer area (in a page's bottom margin); or (3) click the Header button or the Footer button on the Insert tab.

By default, Word assumes that when you add something to the header or footer on any page of a document, you want the same text to appear on every page of the document. To create a different header or footer for the first page, you select the Different First Page check box in the Options group on the Header & Footer Tools Design tab. When a document is divided into sections, like the New Classes Report document, you can create a different header or footer for each section.

For a simple header or footer, double-click the header or footer area, and then type the text you want directly in the header or footer area, formatting the text as you would any other text in a document. To choose from a selection of predesigned header or footer styles, use the Header and Footer buttons on the Header & Footer Tools Design tab (or on the Insert tab). These buttons open galleries that you can use to select from a number of header and footer styles, some of which include page numbers and graphic elements such as horizontal lines or shaded boxes.

Some styles also include document controls that are similar to the kinds of controls that you might encounter in a dialog box. Any information that you enter in a document control is displayed in the header or footer as ordinary text, but it is also stored in the Word file so that Word can easily reuse it in other parts of the document. For example, later in this module you will create a cover page for the report. Word's predefined cover pages include document controls similar to those found in headers and footers. So if you use a document control to enter the document title in the header, the same document title will show up on the cover page; there's no need to retype it.

In the following steps, you'll create a footer for the whole document (sections 1 and 2) that includes the page number and your name. As shown in Hillary's plan in Figure 3-33, you'll also create a header for section 1 only (pages 1 through 3) that includes the document title and the date. You'll leave the header area for section 2 blank.

Figure 3-33   Plan for headers and footers in Hillary's report

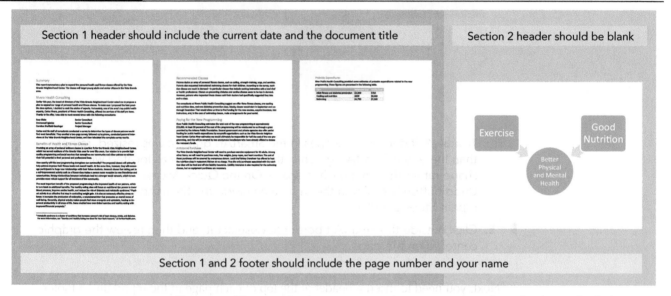

First you will create the footer on page 1, so you can see how the footer fits below the footnotes at the bottom of the page.

To create a footer for the entire document:

▶ 1. Change the Zoom level to **120%**, and then scroll up until you can see the bottom of page 1 and the top of page 2.

▶ 2. Double-click in the white space at the bottom of page 1. The document switches to Header and Footer view. The Header & Footer Tools Design tab is displayed on the ribbon. The insertion point is positioned on the left side of the footer area, ready for you to begin typing. The label "Footer -Section 1-" tells you that the insertion point is located in the footer for section 1. The document text is gray, indicating that you cannot edit it in Header and Footer view. The header area for section 1 is also visible on top of page 2. The default footer tab stops (which are different from the default tab stops in the main document) are visible on the ruler. See Figure 3-34.

| Figure 3-34 | Creating a footer |

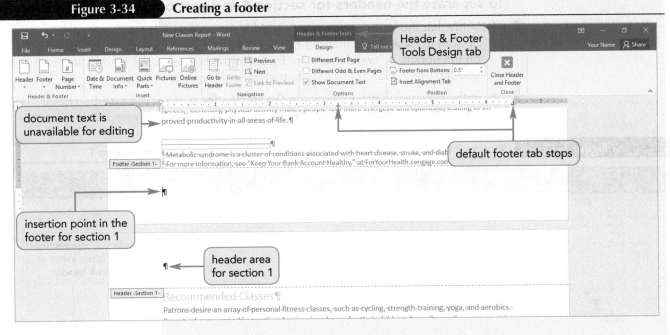

3. Type your first and last names, and then press the **Enter** key. The insertion point moves to the second line in the footer, aligned along the left margin. This is where you will insert the page number.

4. In the Header & Footer group, click the **Page Number** button. The Page Number menu opens. Because the insertion point is already located where you want to insert the page number, you'll use the Current Position option.

5. Point to **Current Position**. A gallery of page number styles opens. Hillary wants to use the Accent Bar 2 style.

6. Click the **Accent Bar 2** style (the third style from the top). The word "Page," a vertical bar, and the page number are inserted in the footer.

Next, you'll check to make sure that the footer you just created for section 1 also appears in section 2. To move between headers or footers in separate sections, you can use the buttons in the Navigation group on the Header & Footer Tools Design tab.

7. In the Navigation group, click the **Next** button. Word displays the footer for the next section in the document—that is, the footer for section 2, which appears at the bottom of page 4. The label at the top of the footer area reads "Footer -Section 2-" and it contains the same text (your name and the page number) as in the section 1 footer. Word assumes, by default, that when you type text in one footer, you want it to appear in all the footers in the document.

TIP

To change the numbering style or to specify a number to use as the first page number, click the Page Number button in the Header & Footer group, and then click Format Page Numbers.

Now you need to create a header for section 1. Hillary does not want to include a header in section 2 because it would distract attention from the SmartArt graphic. So you will first separate the header for section 1 from the header for section 2.

To separate the headers for section 1 and section 2:

1. Verify that the insertion point is located in the section 2 footer area at the bottom of page 4 and that the Header & Footer Tools Design tab is selected on the ribbon. To switch from the footer to the header in the current section, you can use the Go to Header button in the Navigation group.

2. In the Navigation group, click the **Go to Header** button. The insertion point moves to the section 2 header at the top of page 4. See Figure 3-35.

Figure 3-35   **Section 2 header is currently the same as the previous header, in section 1**

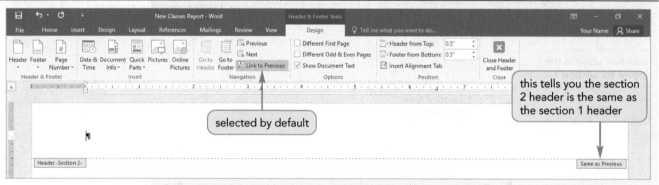

selected by default

this tells you the section 2 header is the same as the section 1 header

Header -Section 2-

Same as Previous

Notice that in the Navigation group, the Link to Previous button is selected. In the header area in the document window, the gray tab on the right side of the header border contains the message "Same as Previous," indicating that the section 2 header is set up to display the same text as the header in the previous section, which is section 1. To make the section 2 header a separate entity, you need to break the link between the section 1 and section 2 headers.

3. In the Navigation group, click the **Link to Previous** button to deselect it. The Same as Previous tab is removed from the right side of the section 2 header border.

4. In the Navigation group, click the **Previous** button. The insertion point moves up to the nearest header in the previous section, which is the section 1 header at the top of page 3. The label "Header -Section 1-" identifies this as a section 1 header.

5. In the Header & Footer group, click the **Header** button. A gallery of header styles opens.

6. Scroll down and review the various header styles, and then click the **Grid** style (eighth style from the top). The placeholder text "[Document title]" is aligned at the left margin. The placeholder text "[Date]" is aligned at the right margin.

7. Click the **[Document title]** placeholder text. The placeholder text is now selected within a document control. See Figure 3-36.

TIP

When you create a header for a section, it doesn't matter what page you're working on as long as the insertion point is located in a header in that section.

Figure 3-36   Adding a header to section 1

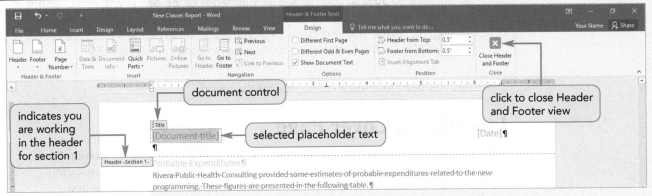

8. Type **Recommendation for Classes at Vista Grande Neighborhood Center**. The text you just typed is displayed in the document control instead of the placeholder text. Next, you need to add the date. The header style you selected includes a date picker document control, which allows you to select the date from a calendar.

9. Click the **[Date]** placeholder text to display an arrow in the document control, and then click the arrow. A calendar for the current month appears, as shown in Figure 3-37. In the calendar, the current date is outlined in dark blue.

Figure 3-37   Adding a date to the section 1 header

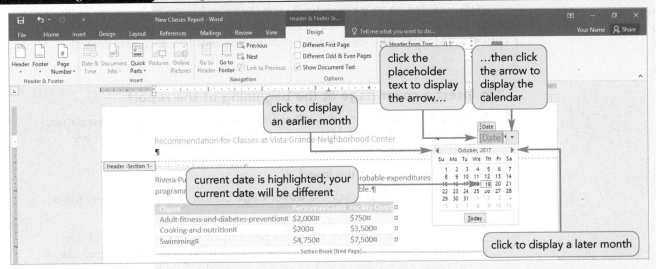

10. Click the current date. The current date, including the year, is inserted in the document control.

11. Scroll up slightly and click anywhere in the Section 1 footer (on the preceding page) to deselect the date document control. You are finished creating the header and footer for Hillary's report, so you can close Header and Footer view and return to Print Layout view.

12. In the Close group, click the **Close Header and Footer** button, or double-click anywhere in the main document, and then save your work.

13. On the ribbon, click the **View** tab.

> **14.** In the Zoom group, click the **Multiple Pages** button, and then change the Zoom level to **30%** so you can see all four pages of the document, including the header at the top of pages 1 through 3 and the footer at the bottom of pages 1 through 4. Take a moment to compare your completed headers and footers with Hillary's plan for the headers and footers shown earlier in Figure 3-33.

Finally, you need to insert a cover page for the report.

Inserting a Cover Page

A document's cover page typically includes the title and the name of the author. Some people also include a summary of the report on the cover page, which is commonly referred to as an abstract. In addition, you might include the date, the name and possibly the logo of your company or organization, and a subtitle. A cover page should not include the document header or footer.

To insert a preformatted cover page at the beginning of the document, you use the Cover Page button on the Insert tab. You can choose from a variety of cover page styles, all of which include document controls in which you can enter the document title, the document's author, the date, and so on. These document controls are linked to any other document controls in the document. For example, you already entered "Recommendation for Classes at Vista Grande Neighborhood Center" into a document control in the header of Hillary's report. So if you use a cover page that contains a similar document control, "Recommendation for Classes at Vista Grande Neighborhood Center" will be displayed on the cover page automatically. Note that document controls sometimes display information entered when either Word or Windows was originally installed on your computer. If your computer has multiple user accounts, the information displayed in some document controls might reflect the information for the current user. In any case, you can easily edit the contents of a document control.

To insert a cover page at the beginning of the report:

> **1.** Verify that the document is still zoomed so that you can see all four pages, and then press the **Ctrl+Home** keys. The insertion point moves to the beginning of the document.

> **2.** On the ribbon, click the **Insert** tab.

> **3.** In the Pages group, click the **Cover Page** button. A gallery of cover page styles opens.

> Notice that the names of the cover page styles match the names of the preformatted header styles you saw earlier. For example, the list includes a Grid cover page, which is designed to match the Grid header used in this document. To give a document a uniform look, it's helpful to use elements with the same style throughout.

> **4.** Scroll down the gallery to see the cover page styles, and then locate the Grid cover page style.

> **5.** Click the **Grid** cover page style. The new cover page is inserted at the beginning of the document.

> **6.** Change the Zoom level to **120%**, and then scroll down to display the report title in the middle of the cover page. The only difference between the title "Recommendation for Classes at Vista Grande Neighborhood Center" here and the title you entered in the document header is that here the title is

TIP

To delete a cover page that you inserted from the Cover Page gallery, click the Cover Page button in the Pages group, and then click Remove Current Cover Page.

displayed in all uppercase. The cover page also includes document controls for a subtitle and an abstract. See Figure 3-38.

Figure 3-38   **Newly inserted cover page**

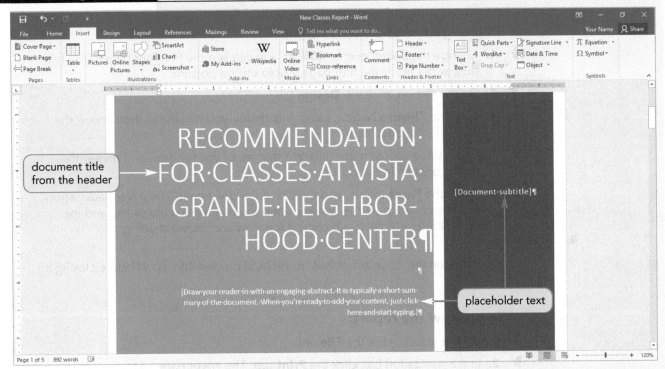

The word "NEIGHBORHOOD" is hyphenated, which looks awkward in a title. You can fix that by changing the document's hyphenation settings.

7. On the ribbon, click the **Layout** tab.

8. In the Page Setup group, click the **Hyphenation** button, and then click **Hyphenation Options**.

9. In the Hyphenation dialog box, click the **Hyphenate words in CAPS** check box to remove the checkmark, and then click the **OK** button. The word "NEIGHBORHOOD" moves to its own line, so the hyphen is no longer necessary.

Next, you need to type a subtitle in the subtitle document control on the right side of the page.

10. Click the **[Document subtitle]** placeholder text, and then type **Rivera Public Health Consulting**. Next, you will remove the abstract document control because you do not need an abstract for this report.

11. Below the document title, right-click the placeholder text that begins **[Draw your reader in...** to display the shortcut menu, and then click **Remove Content Control**. The content control is removed from the cover page.

12. Save the document.

Changing the Theme

The report now contains several formatting elements that are controlled by the document's theme, so changing the theme will affect the document's overall appearance. Hillary suggests that you apply a different theme to the document.

To change the document's theme:

▶ **1.** Change the Zoom level to **40%** so you can see the first four pages side by side, with part of the fifth page visible on the bottom.

▶ **2.** On the ribbon, click the **Design** tab.

▶ **3.** Click the **Themes** button, select any theme you want, and then review the results in the document.

▶ **4.** Apply three or four more different themes of your choice, and review the results of each in the document.

▶ **5.** Apply the **Facet** theme, and then save the document. The cover page is now green and dark gray, the headings and the header text are green, and the table is formatted with a brown header row and brown shading.

Your work on the report is finished. You should preview the report before closing it.

To preview the report:

▶ **1.** On the ribbon, click the **File** tab.

▶ **2.** In the navigation bar, click the **Print** tab. The cover page of the report is displayed in the document preview in the right pane.

▶ **3.** Examine the document preview, using the arrow buttons at the bottom of the pane to display each page.

▶ **4.** If you need to make any changes to the report, return to Print Layout view, edit the document, preview the document again, and then save the document.

▶ **5.** Display the document in Print Layout view.

▶ **6.** Change the Zoom level back to **120%**, and then press the **Ctrl+Home** keys to make sure the insertion point is located on the first page.

Reviewing a Document in Read Mode

The members of the board of directors might choose to print the report, but some might prefer to read it on their computers instead. In that case, they can take advantage of **Read Mode**, a document view designed to make reading on a screen as easy as possible. Unlike Print Layout view, which mimics the look of the printed page with its margins and page breaks, Read Mode focuses on the document's content. Read Mode displays as much content as possible on the screen at a time, with buttons that allow you to display more. Note that you can't edit text in Read Mode. To do that, you need to switch back to Page Layout view.

To display the document in Read Mode:

1. In the status bar, click the **Read Mode** button 📖. The document switches to Read Mode, with a reduced version of the cover page on the left and the first part of the document text on the right. On the left edge of the status bar, the message "Screens 1-2 of 6" explains that you are currently viewing the first two screens out of a total of 6.

Trouble? If your status bar indicates that you have a different number of screens, change the Zoom level as needed so that the document is split into 6 screens.

The title page on the left is screen 1. The text on the right is screen 2. To display more of the document, you can click the arrow button on the right. See Figure 3-39.

Figure 3-39   Document displayed in Read Mode

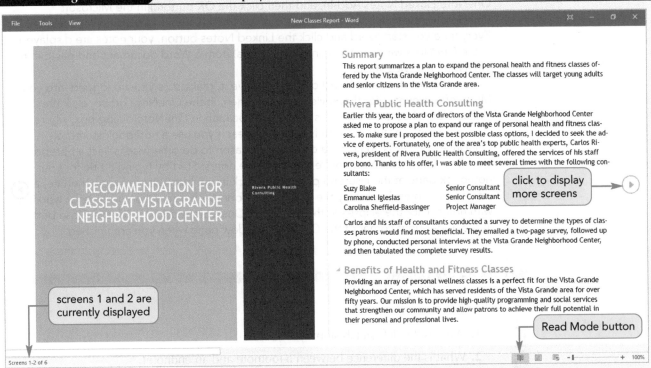

Trouble? If the pages on your screen are not laid out as shown in Figure 3-39, click View on the menu bar, point to Layout, and then click Column Layout.

2. Click the **right arrow** button ⊙ on the right to display screens 3 and 4. A left arrow button is now displayed on the left side of the screen. You could click it to move back to the previous screens.

3. Click the **right arrow** button ⊙ to display screens 5 and 6.

4. Click the **left arrow** button ⊙ on the left as necessary to return to screens 1 and 2, and then click the **Print Layout** button 📄 in the status bar to return to Page Layout view.

5. Close the document.

TIP

To zoom in on a SmartArt graphic, you can double-click it. Click anywhere outside the object zoom window to return to the Read Mode screens.

You now have a draft of the New Classes Report document, including a cover page, the report text, a nicely formatted table, and the SmartArt graphic (in landscape orientation).

Written Communication: Taking Notes

The process of writing a report or other long document usually involves taking notes. It's essential to organize your notes in a way that allows you to write about your topic logically and coherently. It's also important to retain your notes after you finish a first draft, so that you can incorporate additional material from your notes in subsequent drafts.

Clicking the Linked Notes button on the Review tab opens Microsoft OneNote in a window on the right side of the screen. (If you don't see the Linked Notes button, click the File tab to display Backstage view. Click Options in the navigation bar, and then click Add-ins. Click the arrow button in the Manage box, select Com Add-ins, if necessary, and then click the Go button. In the Com Add-ins dialog box, select OneNote Linked Notes Add-In, and then click the OK button.) In the Microsoft OneNote window, you can take notes that are linked to your Microsoft Word account. Every time you start Word and click the Linked Notes button, your notes are displayed in the OneNote window. You can copy material from a Word document and paste it in OneNote, and vice versa.

To get started, open a Word document, save it, make sure you are logged into your Microsoft account, click the Review tab, and then, in the OneNote group, click the Linked Notes button. This opens the Select Location in OneNote dialog box, where you can select a notebook. OneNote works best if you use a notebook stored on OneDrive, so unless you have a compelling reason to do otherwise, select a notebook stored on OneDrive. Now you're ready to take notes. Start by typing a title for your notebook page at the insertion point, then click in the blank space below the title, and start taking notes. To display the OneNote ribbon, with a selection of tools for working with notes, click the ellipses at the top of the OneNote window. Click the Close button in the upper-right corner of the OneNote window pane when you are finished.

Session 3.2 Quick Check

1. What is the default tab stop style?

2. What is the difference between a footnote and an endnote?

3. Explain how to configure Word to hyphenate a document automatically.

4. What is the first thing you need to do if you want to format part of a document in an orientation different from the rest of the document?

5. Explain how to create separate headers for a document with two sections.

6. Explain how to insert a preformatted cover page.

PRACTICE

Review Assignments

Data File needed for the Review Assignments: Computer.docx

The new exercise and nutrition classes at the Vista Grande Neighborhood Center were a success. Now, Hillary Sanchez is organizing a series of computer literacy classes for the neighborhood center staff. She has begun working on a report for the board that outlines basic information about the classes. You need to format the report, add a table containing a preliminary schedule, and create a sample graphic that Hillary could use in a handout announcing the classes. Complete the following steps:

1. Open the document **Computer** located in the Word3 > Review folder included with your Data Files, and then save it as **Computer Classes Report** in the location specified by your instructor.

2. Promote the "Schedule" and "Facility Requirements" headings from Heading 2 text to Heading 1 text, and then move the "Facility Requirements" heading and its body text up above the "Schedule" heading.

3. Insert a page break before the "Schedule" heading. Insert a blank paragraph at the end of the new page 2, and then insert a table using the information shown in Figure 3-40. Format the header row in bold.

Figure 3-40   **Information for training schedule table**

Date	Topic
April 21	Spreadsheets
January 16	The Internet
April 28	Database concepts
April 6	Social media
March 3	Computer maintenance

4. Sort the table by the contents of the "Date" column in ascending order.

5. In the appropriate location in the table, insert a new row for a **Word processing** class on **February 23**.

6. Delete the "Social media" row from the table.

7. Modify the widths of both columns to accommodate the widest entry in each.

8. Apply the Grid Table 4 - Accent 1 style to the table, and then remove the special formatting for the first column.

9. On page 1, replace the text "[instructor names]" with a tabbed list of instructors and their specialties, using the following information: **Casey Sharpless-Dunaway**, **Word processing**; **Marcolo Jimenez**, **Computer maintenance**; **Jin-Hua Lee**, **Database concepts**; **Tommy Halverson**, **Spreadsheets**; **Katrina Yackel**, **The Internet**. Insert a tab after each name, and don't include any punctuation in the list.

10. Use a left tab stop to align the instructors' specialties 2.5 inches from the left margin, and then adjust the list's paragraph spacing so it appears to be a single paragraph.

11. Locate the first sentence below the "Facility Requirements" heading. At the end of that sentence, insert a footnote that reads **Some board members mentioned the possibility of holding classes in the gym, but the instructors prefer the multipurpose room, where microphones are unnecessary.**

12. Turn on automatic hyphenation.

13. After the schedule table on page 2, insert a section break that starts a new, third page, and then format the new page in landscape orientation.

14. Insert a SmartArt graphic that illustrates the requirements of computer literacy. Use the Circle Process graphic from the Process category, and, from left to right, include the following text in the SmartArt diagram: **Hardware Knowledge**, **Software Knowledge**, and **Computer Literacy**. Do not include any punctuation in the SmartArt. Size the SmartArt graphic to fill the page.

15. Create a footer for sections 1 and 2 that aligns your first and last names at the left margin. Insert the page number, without any design elements and without the word "Page," below your name.

16. Separate the section 1 header from the section 2 header, and then create a header for section 1 using the Retrospect header style. Enter **NEW COMPUTER LITERACY CLASSES** as the document title, and select the current date. Note that the document title will be displayed in all uppercase no matter how you type it.

17. Insert a cover page using the Retrospect style. If you typed the document title in all uppercase in the header, it will be displayed in all uppercase here. If you used a mix of uppercase and lowercase in the header, you'll see a mix here. Revise the document title as necessary to make it all uppercase, and then add the following subtitle: **A REPORT FOR THE VISTA GRANDE NEIGHBORHOOD CENTER BOARD OF DIRECTORS**. In the Author document control, replace Hillary Sanchez's name with yours, and then delete the Company Name and Company Address document controls, as well as the vertical bar character between them.

18. Change the document theme to Integral, save and preview the report, and then close it.

Case Problem 1

Data File needed for this Case Problem: Entrepreneur.docx

Boise Entrepreneurs Consortium   You are the assistant business manager of the Boise Entrepreneurs Consortium, a professional organization for technology entrepreneurs and investors in Boise, Idaho. You have been asked to help prepare an annual report for the board of directors. The current draft is not complete, but it contains enough for you to get started. Complete the following steps:

1. Open the document **Entrepreneur** located in the Word3 > Case1 folder included with your Data Files, and then save it as **Entrepreneur Report** in the location specified by your instructor.

2. Adjust the heading levels so that the "Investment Fair" and "Tech Fest" headings are formatted with the Heading 2 style.

3. Move the "Membership Forecast" heading and its body text down to the end of the report.

4. Format the Board of Directors list using a left tab stop with a dot leader at the 2.2-inch mark. (*Hint:* Use the Dialog Box Launcher in the Paragraph group on the Layout tab to open the Paragraph dialog box, and then click the Tabs button at the bottom of the Indents and Spacing tab to open the Tabs dialog box.)

5. At the end of the first paragraph below the "Monthly Technology Lunches" heading, insert the following footnote: **The monthly technology lunches are open to the public.**

6. Locate the "Purpose" heading on page 1. At the end of the body text below that heading, insert the following footnote: **We recently signed a five-year contract renewal with our website host, Boise Web and Media.**

7. Insert a page break that moves the "Membership Forecast" heading to the top of a new page, and then, below the body text on the new page, insert a table consisting of three columns and four rows.

8. In the table, enter the information shown in Figure 3-41. Format the column headings in bold.

Figure 3-41   **Information for membership forecast table**

Membership Type	2017	Projected 2018
Vendor	340	400
Entrepreneur	205	255
Investor	175	200

9. Sort the table in ascending order by membership type.

10. In the appropriate location in the table, insert a row for a **Student** membership type, with **150** members in 2017, and **170** projected members in 2018.

11. Adjust the column widths so each column accommodates the widest entry.

12. Format the table using the Grid Table 4 - Accent 6 table style without banded rows or bold formatting in the first column.

13. Turn on automatic hyphenation.

14. Insert a Blank footer, and then type your name to replace the selected placeholder text in the footer's left margin. In the right margin, insert a page number using the Large Color style. (*Hint*: Press the Tab key twice to move the insertion point to the right margin before inserting the page number, and then insert the page number at the current location.)

15. Insert a cover page using the Sideline style. Enter the company name, **Boise Entrepreneurs Consortium**, and the title, **Annual Report**, in the appropriate document controls. In the subtitle document control, enter **Prepared by [Your Name]** (but replace "[Your Name]" with your first and last names). Delete the Author document control, which might contain a default name inserted by Word, and then insert the current date in the Date document control.

16. Change the document theme to Facet.

17. Save, preview, and then close the document.

Case Problem 2

Data File needed for this Case Problem: **Remodeling.docx**

Customer Evaluation Report   Kitchen Design Magic is a construction and design firm that specializes in high-end, energy-efficient kitchens. Hope Richardson has begun writing a report summarizing the most recent crop of customer evaluation forms. She asks you to review her incomplete draft and fix some problems. Complete the following steps:

1. Open the document **Remodeling** located in the Word3 > Case2 folder included with your Data Files, and then save it as **Remodeling Evaluation Report** in the location specified by your instructor.

⚙ **Troubleshoot** 2. Adjust the document so that the following are true:

   • The "Problems Acquiring Building Permits" heading, its body text, and the SmartArt graphic appear on the last page in landscape orientation, with the rest of the report in portrait orientation.

   • In section 1, the "Summary" heading is displayed at the top of page 2.

   • The document header contains your first and last names but not a content control for the document title.

   • Neither the header nor the footer is displayed on page 1.

   • The footer is not displayed on the last page of the document. (*Hint*: After you break the link between sections, you'll need to delete the contents of the footer in one section.)

⚙ **Troubleshoot** 3. On pages 2 and 3, promote headings as necessary so all the headings are on the same level.

4. Increase the paragraph spacing before the first paragraph, "Kitchen Design Magic," on page 1 as much as necessary so that the paragraph is located at about the 3-inch mark on the vertical ruler. When you're finished, the text should be centered vertically on the page, so it looks like a cover page.

⚙ **Troubleshoot** 5. On page 2, remove any extra rows and columns in the table, and sort the information in a logical way. When you are finished, format it with a style that applies blue (Accent 5) shading to the header row, with banded rows below, and remove any unnecessary bold formatting.

6. Add a fourth shape to the SmartArt Graphic with the text **Submit completed forms, designs, and fee to permit office.** Resize the graphic to fill the white space below the document text.

7. Save the document, review it in Read Mode, preview it, and then close it.

Case Problem 3

CREATE

There are no Data Files needed for this Case Problem.

Tim's Total T's Online Retailer   Tim Washburn recently started a new business, Tim's Total T's, which sells athletic team t-shirts online. A friend has just emailed him a list of potential customers. Tim asks you to create and format a table containing the list of customers. When you're finished with that project, you'll create a table detailing some of his recent repair expenses in his new production facility. Complete the following steps:

1. Open a new, blank document, and then save it as **Customer Table** in the location specified by your instructor.

2. Create the table shown in Figure 3-42.

Figure 3-42   **Advertiser table**

Organization	Contact	Phone
Franklin Metropolitan School District	Sasha Malee	555-555-5555
Haverford Swim Club	Crystal Grenier	555-555-5555
Kingford Bowling	Joyce Garcia	555-555-5555
Tri County Rec League	Terrence O'Hern	555-555-5555

For the table style, start with the Grid Table 4 - Accent 6 table style, and then make any necessary changes. Use the Green, Accent 6, Darker 50% pen color to create a darker border around the outside of the table. The final table should be about 6.5 inches wide and 2 inches tall, as measured on the horizontal and vertical rulers. (*Hint:* Remember that you can drag the Table Resize handle to increase the table's overall size.)

3. Replace "Sasha Malee" with your first and last names.

4. Save, preview, and then close the Customer Table document.

5. Open a new, blank document, and then save it as **Repair Table** in the location specified by your instructor.

6. Create the table shown in Figure 3-43.

Figure 3-43   Expense table

Repair	Completion Date	Expense
Replace bathroom fan	3/5/17	$350.00
Install deadbolt lock	3/16/17	$85.00
Replace broken window pane	3/26/17	$25.50
	Total	$460.50

For the table style, start with the Grid Table 4 - Accent 6 table style, and then make any necessary changes. Use the Green, Accent 6, Darker 50% pen color to create a darker border around the outside of the table. Note that in the bottom row, you'll need to merge two cells and right-align text within the new, merged cell.

7. For the total, use a formula instead of simply typing the amount. (*Hint*: Click in the cell where you want to insert a formula to sum the values, go to the Table Tools Layout tab, click the Formula button in the Data group to open the Formula dialog box, and then click the OK button.)

8. Save, preview, and then close the Repair Table document.

CHALLENGE

Case Problem 4

There are no Data Files needed for this Case Problem.

Sun Star Fund-Raisers   Janita Roush coordinates fund-raising events for the Sun Star Bike and Pedestrian Path in Bloomington, Illinois. She needs a flyer to hand out at an upcoming neighborhood festival, where she hopes to recruit more volunteers. You can use Word's table features to lay out the flyer as shown in Janita's sketch in Figure 3-44. At the very end, you'll remove the table borders.

Figure 3-44   Sketch for Sun Star flyer

Sun Star Fund-Raisers

Bike for Fun!

Sun Star Path Ride
- First Saturday in May
- 50-mile ride
- $20 entrance fee
- Free t-shirt

Sun Star Bike Swap
- First Saturday in April
- $15 swap fee
- Midwest's largest event
- All types of bike gear

Mission
Friends of the Sun Star Path is a nonprofit volunteer organization devoted to supporting the Sun Star Bike and Pedestrian Path through fund-raising and volunteer efforts.

Contact
Janita Roush, **janita@sunstar.cengage.com**, 555-555-5555.

Complete the following steps:

1. Open a new, blank document, and then save it as **Sun Star Flyer** in the location specified by your instructor.

2. Change the document's orientation to landscape.

⊕ **Explore** 3. Use the Table button on the Insert tab to access the Insert Table menu, and then click Draw Table at the bottom of the menu to activate the Draw Table pointer (which looks like a pencil). Click in the upper-left corner of the document (near the paragraph mark), and, using the rulers as guides, drag down and to the right to draw a rectangle that is 9 inches wide and 6 inches high. After you draw the rectangle, you can adjust its height and width using the Height and Width boxes in the Cell Size group on the Table Tools Layout tab, if necessary. (*Hint*: If the Draw Table pointer disappears after you change the table's height and width, you can turn it back on by clicking the Draw Table button in the Draw group on the Table Tools Layout tab.)

⊕ **Explore** 4. Use the Draw Table pointer to draw the columns and rows shown in Figure 3-44. For example, to draw the column border for the "Sun Star Fund-Raisers" column, click the top of the rectangle at the point where you want the right column border to be located, and then drag down to the bottom of the rectangle. Use the same technique to draw rows. (*Hint*: To delete a border, click the Eraser button in the Draw group on the Table Tools Layout tab, click anywhere on the border you want to erase, and then click the Eraser button again to turn it off.)

5. When you are finished drawing the table, turn off the Draw Table pointer by pressing the Esc key.

⊕ **Explore** 6. In the left column, type the text **Sun Star Fund-Raisers**. With the pointer still in that cell, click the Table Tools Layout tab, and then in the Alignment group, click the Text Direction button twice to position the text vertically so that it reads from bottom to top. Using the formatting options on the Home tab, format the text in 36-point font. Use the Align Center button in the Alignment group on the Table Tools Layout tab to center the text in the cell. (*Hint*: You will probably have to adjust and readjust the row and column borders throughout these steps until all the elements of the table are positioned properly.)

7. Type the remaining text as shown in Figure 3-44. To prevent problems with formatting the bulleted lists, press Enter after the text "Free-t-shirt" and after "All types of bike gear," and then remove the bulleted list formatting from the new paragraph, so that an end-of-cell mark appears on a separate line below each bulleted list. Replace "Janita Roush" with your own name, remove the hyperlink formatting from the email address, and format it in bold. Change the font size for "Bike for Fun!" to 36 points, and center-align the text in that cell. Use the Heading 1 style for the following text—"Sun Star Path Ride," "Sun Star Bike Swap," "Mission," and "Contact." Change the font size for this text to 20 points. Center-align the "Sun Star Path Ride" and "Sun Star Bike Swap" headings in their cells. Change the font size for the bulleted lists and the paragraphs below the "Mission" and "Contact" headings to 16 points. If the table expands to two pages, drag a row border up slightly to reduce the row's height. Repeat as necessary until the table fits on one page.

⊕ **Explore** 8. On the Insert tab, use the Shapes button in the Illustrations group to draw the Sun shape (from the Basic Shapes section of the Shapes gallery), similar to the way you drew the table rectangle, by dragging the pointer. Draw the sun in the blank cell in the top row. If the sun isn't centered neatly in the cell, click the Undo button, and try again until you draw a sun that has the same proportions as the one in Figure 3-44. Until you change the theme in the next step, the sun will be blue.

9. Change the document theme to Retrospect.

10. Remove the table borders. When you are finished, your flyer should match the table shown in Figure 3-44, but without the table borders.

11. Save your work, preview the document, and then close it.

MODULE **4**

Enhancing Page Layout and Design

Creating a Newsletter

Case | *Aria Occupational Therapy*

Avanti Saro is a public relations consultant who has been hired to create a newsletter for Aria Occupational Therapy, a clinic that provides rehabilitation services in Portland, Oregon. He has written the text of a newsletter describing the services provided by the clinic's therapists. Now he needs you to transform the text into an eye-catching publication with a headline, photos, drop caps, and other desktop-publishing elements. Avanti's budget doesn't allow him to hire a professional graphic designer to create the document using desktop-publishing software. But there's no need for that because you can do the work for him using Word's formatting, graphics, and page layout tools. After you finish the newsletter, Avanti wants you to save the newsletter as a PDF so he can email it to the printing company. You also need to make some edits to a document that is currently available only as a PDF.

OBJECTIVES

Session 4.1
- Use continuous section breaks for page layout
- Format text in columns
- Insert symbols and special characters
- Distinguish between inline and floating objects
- Wrap text around an object
- Insert and format text boxes
- Insert drop caps

Session 4.2
- Create and modify WordArt
- Insert and crop a picture
- Search for Online Pictures
- Rotate and adjust a picture
- Remove a photo's background
- Balance columns
- Add a page border
- Save a document as a PDF
- Open a PDF in Word

STARTING DATA FILES

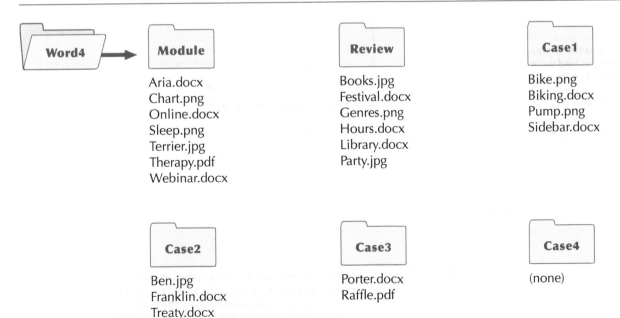

Word4 → **Module**

Aria.docx
Chart.png
Online.docx
Sleep.png
Terrier.jpg
Therapy.pdf
Webinar.docx

Review

Books.jpg
Festival.docx
Genres.png
Hours.docx
Library.docx
Party.jpg

Case1

Bike.png
Biking.docx
Pump.png
Sidebar.docx

Case2

Ben.jpg
Franklin.docx
Treaty.docx

Case3

Porter.docx
Raffle.pdf

Case4

(none)

Session 4.1 Visual Overview:

Desktop publishing is the process of preparing commercial-quality printed material, such as the newsletter shown here, using a desktop or laptop computer. Using Word, you can create documents that have elements of desktop publishing, such as special font treatments, graphics, and page layout options, as well as design elements such as page borders.

This specially formatted text is an example of WordArt, which is created using the WordArt button in the Text group on the Insert tab.

These are examples of text boxes, which are like mini documents within a document.

This photo and the drawing of the person in bed were inserted from files, but you can also use the Online Pictures button in the Illustrations group on the Insert tab to search for photos and drawings on the web.

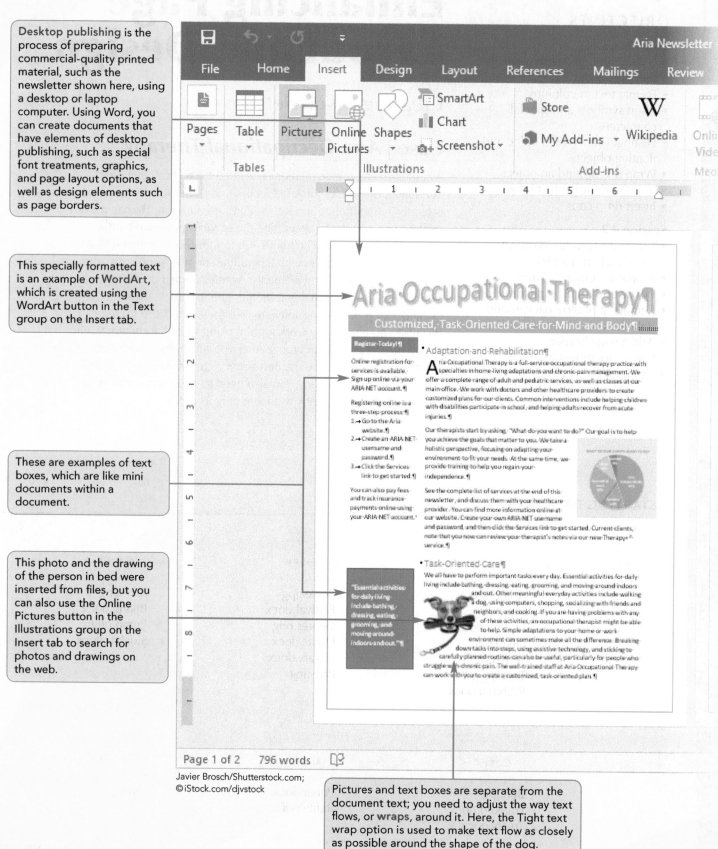

Javier Brosch/Shutterstock.com;
©iStock.com/djvstock

Pictures and text boxes are separate from the document text; you need to adjust the way text flows, or **wraps**, around it. Here, the Tight text wrap option is used to make text flow as closely as possible around the shape of the dog.

Elements of Desktop Publishing

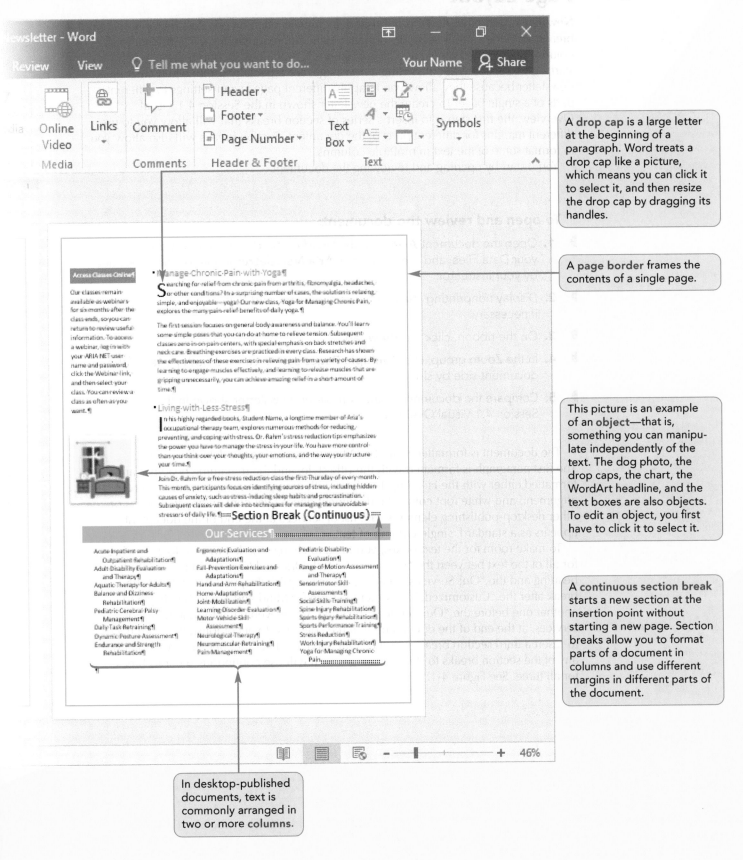

A **drop cap** is a large letter at the beginning of a paragraph. Word treats a drop cap like a picture, which means you can click it to select it, and then resize the drop cap by dragging its handles.

A **page border** frames the contents of a single page.

This picture is an example of an **object**—that is, something you can manipulate independently of the text. The dog photo, the drop caps, the chart, the WordArt headline, and the text boxes are also objects. To edit an object, you first have to click it to select it.

A **continuous section break** starts a new section at the insertion point without starting a new page. Section breaks allow you to format parts of a document in columns and use different margins in different parts of the document.

In desktop-published documents, text is commonly arranged in two or more **columns**.

Using Continuous Section Breaks to Enhance Page Layout

Newsletters and other desktop-published documents often incorporate multiple section breaks, with the various sections formatted with different margins, page orientations, column settings, and other page layout options. Continuous section breaks, which start a new section without starting a new page, are especially useful when creating a newsletter because they allow you to apply different page layout settings to different parts of a single page. To create the newsletter shown in the Session 4.1 Visual Overview, the first step is to insert a series of section breaks that will allow you to use different margins for different parts of the document. Section breaks will also allow you to format some of the text in multiple columns.

You'll start by opening and reviewing the document.

To open and review the document:

1. Open the document **Aria** from the Word4 > Module folder included with your Data Files, and then save it as **Aria Newsletter** in the location specified by your instructor.

2. Display nonprinting characters and the rulers, and switch to Print Layout view, if necessary.

3. On the ribbon, click the **View** tab.

4. In the Zoom group, click **Multiple Pages** so you can see both pages of the document side by side.

5. Compare the document to the completed newsletter shown in the Session 4.1 Visual Overview.

The document is formatted with the Office theme, using the default margins. The first paragraph is formatted with the Title style, and the remaining headings are formatted either with the Heading 1 style or with orange paragraph shading, center alignment, and white font color. The document doesn't yet contain any text boxes or other desktop-publishing elements. The list of services at the end of the document appears as a standard, single column of text.

To make room for the text boxes, you need to change the left margin to 2.5 inches for all of the text between the "Customized, Task-Oriented Care for Mind and Body" heading and the "Our Services" heading. To accomplish this, you'll insert a section break after the "Customized, Task-Oriented Care for Mind and Body" heading and another one before the "Our Services" heading. You'll eventually format the list of services, at the end of the document, in three columns. To accomplish that, you need to insert a third section break after the "Our Services" heading. Because you don't want any of the section breaks to start new pages, you will use continuous sections breaks for all three. See Figure 4-1.

| Figure 4-1 | Aria Newsletter document before adding section breaks |

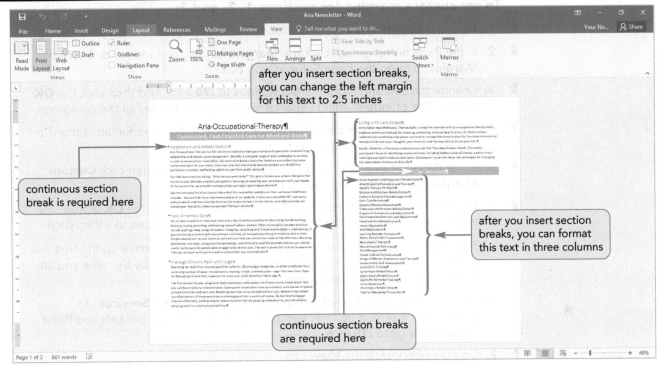

To insert continuous section breaks in the document:

1. Change the Zoom level to **120%**.

2. In the document, click at the beginning of the third paragraph, which contains the heading "Adaptation and Rehabilitation."

3. On the ribbon, click the **Layout** tab.

4. In the Page Setup group, click the **Breaks** button, and then click **Continuous**. A short dotted line, indicating a continuous section break, appears in the orange shading at the end of the preceding paragraph. If the paragraph text were shorter, you would see a longer line with the words "Section Break (Continuous)." You'll be able to see the section break text more clearly when you insert the next one.

5. Scroll down to page 2, click at the beginning of the shaded paragraph "Our Services," and then insert a continuous section break. A dotted line with the words "Section Break (Continuous)" appears at the end of the preceding paragraph.

6. Click at the beginning of the next paragraph, which contains the text "Acute Inpatient and Outpatient Rehabilitation," and then insert a continuous section break. A dotted line with the words "Section Break (Continuous)" appears in the orange shading at the end of the preceding paragraph.

Now that you have created sections within the Aria Newsletter document, you can format the individual sections as if they were separate documents. In the following steps, you'll format the first and third sections by changing their left and right margins to .75 inch. Then, you'll format the second section by changing its left margin to 2.5 inches.

To set custom margins for sections 1, 2, and 3:

1. Press the **Ctrl+Home** keys to position the insertion point in section 1.

2. In the Page Setup group, click the **Margins** button, and then click **Custom Margins** to open the Page Setup dialog box.

3. Change the Left and Right margin settings to **.75** inch, and then click the **OK** button. The orange shading expands slightly on both sides of the paragraph.

4. On page 1, click anywhere in the heading "Adaptation and Rehabilitation" to position the insertion point in section 2.

5. In the Page Setup group, click the **Margins** button, and then click **Custom Margins** to open the Page Setup dialog box.

6. Change the Left margin setting to **2.5** inches, and then click the **OK** button. The text in section 2 shifts to the right, and the document text flows to a third page.

   Throughout this module, as you add and resize various elements, the text will occasionally expand from two pages to three or four. But by the time you are finished, the newsletter will consist of only two pages.

7. Scroll down to page 2, click in the shaded heading "**Our Services**" to position the insertion point in section 3, and then change the Left and Right margin settings to **.75** inch.

8. On the ribbon, click the **View** tab.

9. In the Zoom group, click **Multiple Pages** so you can see all three pages of the document side by side. See Figure 4-2.

Figure 4-2 | Sections 1, 2, and 3 with new margins

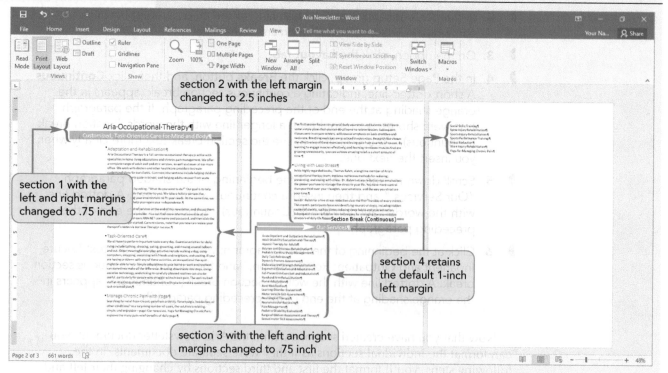

10. Save the document.

In addition to allowing you to format parts of a document with different margins, section breaks allow you to format part of a document in columns. You'll add some columns to section 4 next.

Formatting Text in Columns

Text meant for quick reading is often laid out in columns, with text flowing down one column, continuing at the top of the next column, flowing down that column, and so forth. To get started, click the Columns button in the Page Setup group on the Layout tab, and then click the number of columns you want in the Columns gallery. For more advanced column options, you can use the More Columns command to open the Columns dialog box. In this dialog box, you can adjust the column widths and the space between columns and choose to format either the entire document in columns or just the section that contains the insertion point.

As shown in the Session 4.1 Visual Overview, Avanti wants section 4 of the newsletter document, which consists of the services list, to be formatted in three columns.

To format section 4 in three columns:

▶ 1. Click anywhere in the list of services at the end of the document to position the insertion point in section 4.

▶ 2. On the ribbon, click the **Layout** tab.

▶ 3. In the Page Setup group, click the **Columns** button to display the Columns gallery. At this point, you could simply click Three to format section 4 in three columns of equal width. However, it's helpful to take a look at the columns dialog box so you can get familiar with some more advanced column options.

▶ 4. Click **More Columns** to open the Columns dialog box, and then in the Presets section, click **Three**. See Figure 4-3.

Figure 4-3 ▶ **Columns dialog box**

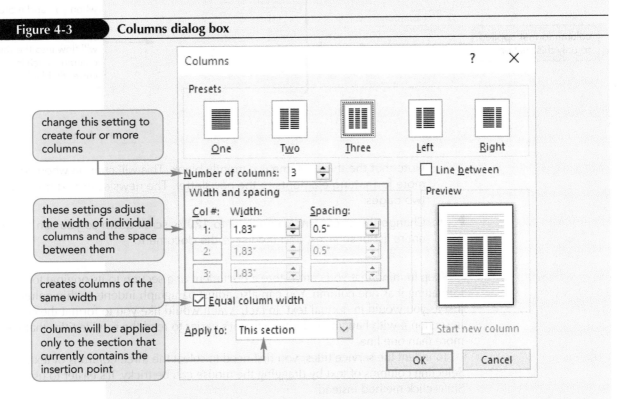

To format text in four or more columns, you can change the setting in the Number of columns box instead of selecting an option in the Presets section. By default, the Apply to box, in the lower-left corner, displays "This section," indicating that the three-column format will be applied only to the current section. To apply columns to the entire document, you could click the Apply to arrow and then click Whole document. To change the width of the individual columns or the spacing between the columns, you can use the settings in the Width and spacing section of the Columns dialog box.

▶ **5.** Click the **OK** button. Section 4 is now formatted in three columns of the default width. See Figure 4-4.

Figure 4-4   **Section 4 formatted in three columns**

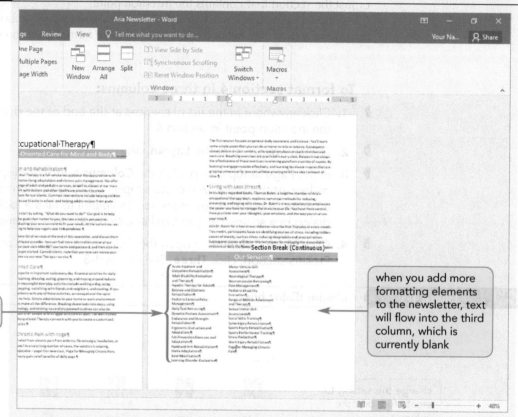

column format applied to only this section

when you add more formatting elements to the newsletter, text will flow into the third column, which is currently blank

Note that the third column is currently blank. This will change when you add more formatting elements to the newsletter. The newsletter text now fits on two pages.

▶ **6.** Change the document Zoom level to **120%**, scroll down so you can see the entire list of services, and then save the document.

Keep in mind that you can restore a document or a section to its original format by formatting it as one column. You can also adjust paragraph indents within columns, just as you would in normal text. In fact, Avanti would like you to format the columns in section 4 with hanging indents so that it's easier to read the service titles that take up more than one line.

To indent the service titles, you first need to select the three columns of text. Selecting columns of text by dragging the mouse can be tricky. It's easier to use the Shift+click method instead.

To format the columns in section 4 with hanging indents:

▶ **1.** Make sure the **Layout** tab is selected on the ribbon.

▶ **2.** Click at the beginning of the first service title ("Acute Inpatient and Outpatient Rehabilitation"), press and hold the **Shift** key, and then click at the end of the last service title ("Yoga for Managing Chronic Pain"). The entire list of services is selected.

▶ **3.** In the Paragraph group, click the **Dialog Box Launcher** to open the Paragraph dialog box with the Indents and Spacing tab displayed.

▶ **4.** In the Indentation section, click the **Special** arrow, click **Hanging**, and then change the By setting to **0.2"**.

▶ **5.** Click the **OK** button to close the Paragraph dialog box, and then click anywhere in the list to deselect it. The services list is now formatted with a hanging indent, so the second line of each paragraph is indented .2 inches. See Figure 4-5.

Figure 4-5	Text formatted in columns with hanging indent

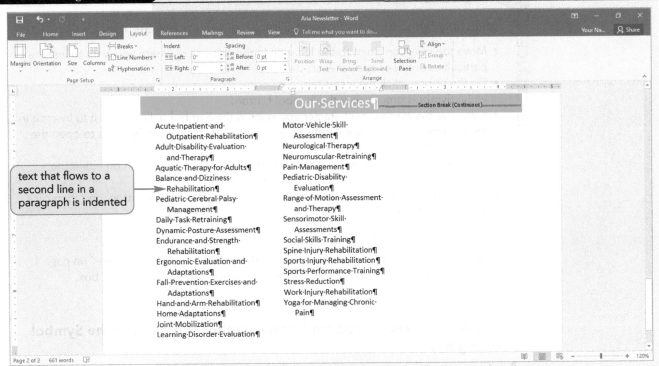

Inserting Symbols and Special Characters

When creating documents in Word, you can change some of the characters available on the standard keyboard into special characters or symbols called **typographic characters**. Word's AutoCorrect feature automatically converts some standard characters into typographic characters as you type. In some cases, you need to press the spacebar and type more characters before Word inserts the appropriate typographic character. If Word inserts a typographic character that you don't want, you can click the Undo button to revert to the characters you originally typed. See Figure 4-6.

Figure 4-6 **Common typographic characters**

To Insert This Symbol or Character	Type	Word Converts To
Em dash	word--word	word—word
Smiley face	:)	☺
Copyright symbol	(c)	©
Trademark symbol	(tm)	™
Registered trademark symbol	(r)	®
Fractions	1/2, 1/4	½, ¼
Arrows	<-- or -->	← or →

Most of the typographic characters in Figure 4-6 can also be inserted using the Symbol button on the Insert tab, which opens a gallery of commonly used symbols, and the More Symbols command, which opens the Symbol dialog box. The Symbol dialog box provides access to all the symbols and special characters you can insert into a Word document.

Inserting Symbols and Special Characters from the Symbol Dialog Box

- Move the insertion point to the location in the document where you want to insert a particular symbol or special character.
- On the ribbon, click the Insert tab.
- In the Symbols group, click the Symbol button.
- If you see the symbol or character you want in the Symbol gallery, click it to insert it in the document. For a more extensive set of choices, click More Symbols to open the Symbol dialog box.
- In the Symbol dialog box, locate the symbol or character you want on either the Symbols tab or the Special Characters tab.
- Click the symbol or special character you want, click the Insert button, and then click the Close button.

Avanti forgot to include a registered trademark symbol (®) after "Therapy+" on page 1. He asks you to add one now. After you do, you'll explore the Symbol dialog box.

To insert the registered trademark symbol and explore the Symbol dialog box:

1. Use the Navigation pane to find the term Therapy+ in the document, and then close the Navigation pane.

2. Click to the right of the plus sign to position the insertion point between the plus sign and the space that follows it.

3. Type **(r)**. AutoCorrect converts the "r" in parentheses into the superscript ® symbol.

   If you don't know which characters to type to insert a symbol or special character, you can review the AutoCorrect replacements in the AutoCorrect: English (United States) dialog box.

4. On the ribbon, click the **File** tab.

5. In the navigation bar, click **Options** to open the Word Options dialog box.

6. In the left pane, click **Proofing**, and then click the **AutoCorrect Options** button. The AutoCorrect: English (United States) dialog box opens, with the AutoCorrect tab displayed.

7. Review the table at the bottom of the AutoCorrect tab. The column on the left shows the characters you can type, and the column on the right shows what AutoCorrect inserts as a replacement. See Figure 4-7.

Figure 4-7	AutoCorrect: English (United States) dialog box

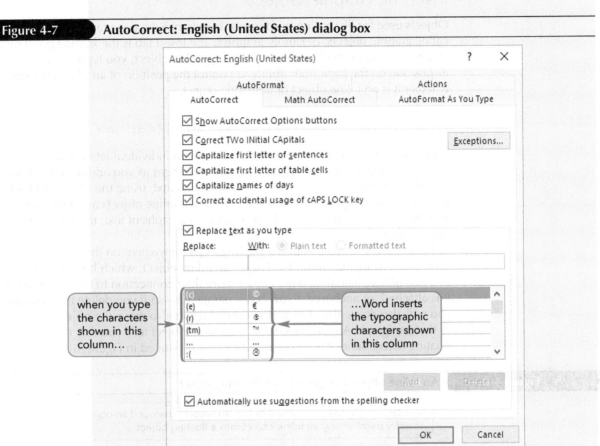

8. Scroll down to review the AutoCorrect replacements, click the **Cancel** button to close the AutoCorrect: English (United States) dialog box, and then click the **Cancel** button to close the Word Options dialog box.

Now you can explore the Symbol dialog box, which offers another way to insert symbols and special characters.

9. On the ribbon, click the **Insert** tab.

10. In the Symbols group, click the **Symbol** button, and then click **More Symbols**. The Symbol dialog box opens with the Symbols tab displayed.

11. Scroll down the gallery of symbols on the Symbols tab to review the many symbols you can insert into a document. To insert one, you would click it, and then click the Insert button.

12. Click the **Special Characters** tab. The characters available on this tab are often used in desktop publishing. Notice the shortcut keys that you can use to insert many of the special characters.

13. Click the **Cancel** button to close the Symbol dialog box.

Introduction to Working with Objects

An object is something that you can manipulate independently of the document text. In desktop publishing, you use objects to illustrate the document or to enhance the page layout. To complete the newsletter for Avanti, you'll need to add some text boxes, drop caps, and pictures. These are all examples of objects in Word.

Inserting Graphic Objects

Objects used for illustration purposes or to enhance the page layout are sometimes called **graphic objects**, or simply **graphics**. The Insert tab is the starting point for adding graphics to a document. After you insert a graphic object, you typically need to adjust its position on the page. Your ability to control the position of an object depends on whether it is an inline object or a floating object.

Distinguishing Between Inline and Floating Objects

An **inline object** behaves as if it were text. Like an individual letter, it has a specific location within a line of text, and its position changes as you add or delete text. You can align an inline object just as you would align text, using the alignment buttons in the Paragraph group on the Home tab. However, inline objects are difficult to work with because every time you add or remove paragraphs of text, the object moves to a new position.

In contrast, you can position a **floating object** anywhere on the page, with the text flowing, or wrapping, around it. Unlike an inline object, which has a specific position in a line of text, a floating object has a more fluid connection to the document text. It is attached, or **anchored**, to an entire paragraph—so if you delete that paragraph, you will also delete the object. However, you can also move the object independently of that paragraph. An anchor symbol next to an object tells you that the object is a floating object rather than an inline object, as illustrated in Figure 4-8.

| Figure 4-8 | An inline object compared to a floating object |

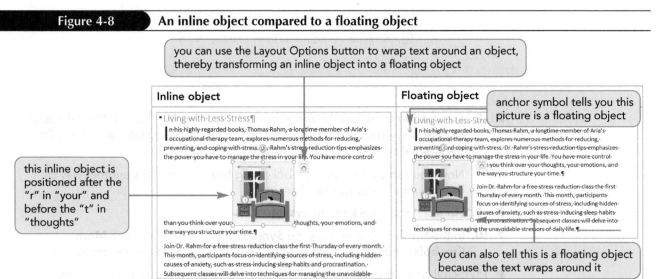

you can use the Layout Options button to wrap text around an object, thereby transforming an inline object into a floating object

Inline object

this inline object is positioned after the "r" in "your" and before the "t" in "thoughts"

Floating object

anchor symbol tells you this picture is a floating object

you can also tell this is a floating object because the text wraps around it

© iStock.com/djvstock

You'll typically want to transform all inline objects into floating objects because floating objects are far more flexible.

Wrapping Text Around an Object

To transform an inline object into a floating object, you apply a **text wrapping setting** to it. First, click the object to select it, click the Layout Options button next to the object, and then click an option in the Layout Options gallery. For example, you can select Square text wrapping to make the text follow a square outline as it flows around the object, or you can select Tight text wrapping to make the text follow the shape of the object more exactly. Figure 4-9 describes the different types of wrapping.

Figure 4-9   Text wrapping options in the Layout Options gallery

Menu Icon	Type of Wrapping	Description
	Square	Text flows in a square outline around the object, regardless of the shape of the object; by default, Square text wrapping is applied to preformatted text boxes inserted via the Text Box button on the Insert tab.
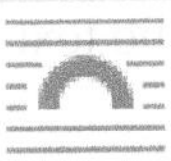	Tight	Text follows the exact outline of the object; if you want the text to flow around an object, this is usually the best option.
	Through	Text flows through the object, filling up any open areas; this type is similar to Tight text wrapping.
	Top and Bottom	Text stops above the object and then starts again below the object.
	Behind Text	The object is layered behind the text, with the text flowing over it.
	In Front of Text	The object is layered in front of the text, with the text flowing behind it; if you want to position an object in white space next to the text, this option gives you the greatest control over its exact position. By default, In Front of Text wrapping is applied to any shapes inserted via the Shapes button in the Illustrations group on the Insert tab.

Most graphic objects, including photos and SmartArt, are inline by default. All text boxes and shapes are floating by default. Objects that are inserted as floating objects by default have a specific text wrapping setting assigned to them, but you can change the default setting to any text wrapping setting you want.

INSIGHT

Displaying Gridlines

When formatting a complicated document like a newsletter, you'll often have to adjust the position of objects on the page until everything looks the way you want. To make it easier to see the relative position of objects, you can display the document's gridlines. These vertical and horizontal lines are not actually part of the document. They are simply guidelines you can use when positioning text and objects on the page. By default, when gridlines are displayed, objects align with, or **snap to**, the nearest intersection of a horizontal and vertical line. The figures in this module do not show gridlines because they would make the figures difficult to read. However, you will have a chance to experiment with gridlines in the Case Problems at the end of this module. To display gridlines, click the View tab on the ribbon, and then click the Gridlines check box to insert a check.

Inserting Text Boxes

You can choose to add a preformatted text box to a document, or you can create your own text box from scratch and adjust its appearance. To insert a preformatted text box, you use the Text Box button in the Text group on the Insert tab. Text boxes inserted this way include placeholder text that you can replace with your own text. Preformatted text boxes come with preset font and paragraph options that are designed to match the text box's overall look. However, you can change the appearance of the text in the text box by using the options on the Home tab, just as you would for ordinary text. The text box, as a whole, is designed to match the document's current theme. You could alter its appearance by using the Shape Styles options on the Drawing Tools Format tab, but there's typically no reason to do so.

Because the preformatted text boxes are so professional looking, they are usually a better choice than creating your own. However, if you want a very simple text box, you can use the Shapes button in the Illustrations group to draw a text box. After you draw the text box, you can adjust its appearance by using the Shape Styles options on the Drawing Tools Format tab. You can type any text you want inside the text box at the insertion point. When you are finished, you can format the text using the options on the Home tab.

REFERENCE

Inserting a Text Box

To insert a preformatted, rectangular text box, click in the document where you want to insert the text box.

- On the ribbon, click the Insert tab.
- In the Text group, click the Text Box button to open the Text Box gallery, and then click a text box style to select it.
- In the text box in the document, delete the placeholder text, type the text you want to include, and then format the text using the options on the Home tab.

or

- To insert and format your own rectangular text box, click the Insert tab on the ribbon.
- In the Illustrations group, click the Shapes button to open the Shapes gallery, and then click Text Box.
- In the document, position the pointer where you want to insert the text box, press and hold the mouse button, and then drag the pointer to draw the text box.
- In the text box, type the text you want to include, and then format the text using the options on the Home tab.
- Format the text box using the options in the Shape Styles group on the Drawing Tools Format tab.

Inserting a Preformatted Text Box

Avanti's newsletter requires three text boxes. You need to insert the first text box on page 1, to the left of the "Adaptation and Rehabilitation" heading. For this text box, you'll insert one that is preformatted to work as a sidebar. A **sidebar** is a text box designed to look good positioned to the side of the main document text. A sidebar is typically used to draw attention to important information.

To insert a preformatted text box in the document:

1. Scroll up to the top of page 1, and then click anywhere in the "Adaptation and Rehabilitation" heading.

2. Change the Zoom level to **Multiple Pages** so you can see both pages of the document.

3. On the ribbon, click the **Insert** tab.

4. In the Text group, click the **Text Box** button to display the Text Box gallery, and then use the scroll bar to scroll down the gallery to locate the Ion Sidebar 1 text box.

5. Click **Ion Sidebar 1**. The text box is inserted in the left margin of page 1. See Figure 4-10.

Figure 4-10   Text box inserted on page 1

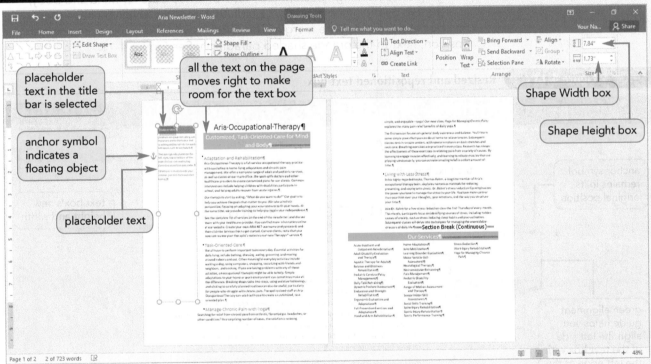

All the text on page 1 moves right to make room for the text box. Later, after you resize and move the text box, the first two paragraphs will resume their original positions, centered at the top of the page. The anchor symbol next to the text box tells you it is a floating object.

The text box consists of a blue title bar at the top that contains placeholder text, with additional placeholder text below the title bar. The dotted outline with handles indicates the borders of the text box. When you first insert a text box, the placeholder text in the title bar is selected, ready for you to type your own title. In this case, however, before you add any text, you'll resize and reposition the text box.

6. On the ribbon, click the **Drawing Tools Format** tab, if necessary.

7. In the Size group, click the **Shape Height** box, type **4.3**, click the **Shape Width** box, type **1.5**, and then press the **Enter** key. The text box is now shorter and narrower.

8. Change the Zoom level to **120%**.

Next, you need to drag the text box down below the first two paragraphs. Currently, only the placeholder text in the text box title bar is selected. Before you can move it, you need to select the entire text box.

9. Position the pointer somewhere over the text box border until the pointer changes to ⮕.

10. Click the **text box border** to select the entire text box. The text box border changes from dotted to solid, and the Layout Options button ⊡ appears to the right of the text box.

11. Position the ⮕ pointer over the text box's title bar, press and hold the **mouse button**, and then drag the text box down so that the top of the text box aligns with the first line of text below the "Adaptation and Rehabilitation" heading. The left edge of the text box should align with the left edge of the orange shaded heading "Customized, Task-Oriented Care for Mind and Body," as indicated by the green alignment guide that appears when you have the text box aligned along the margin. The anchor symbol remains in its original position, next to the orange shaded paragraph. See Figure 4-11.

Figure 4-11	**Resized and repositioned text box**

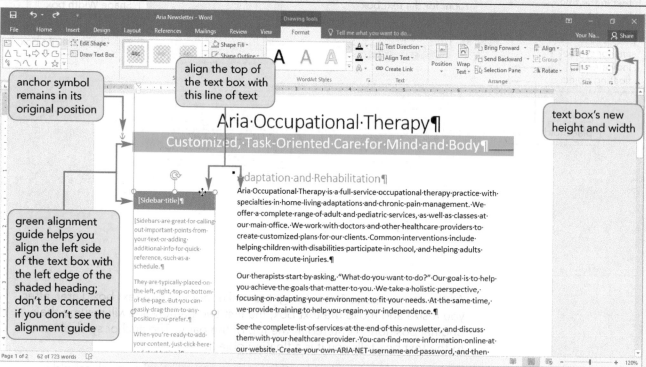

Trouble? If you don't see the green alignment guide, position the text box as described as carefully as you can.

12. When you are sure the text box is positioned as shown in Figure 4-11, release the mouse button.

After you insert a text box or other object, you usually need to adjust its relationship to the surrounding text; that is, you need to adjust its text wrapping setting.

Changing the Text Wrapping Setting for the Text Box

A preformatted text box inserted via the Text box button on the Insert tab is, by default, a floating object formatted with Square text wrapping. You will verify this when you open the Layout Options gallery in the following steps. Then you'll select the In Front of Text option instead to gain more control over the exact position of the text box on the page.

To open the Layout Options gallery and change the wrapping option:

▶ **1.** Change the Zoom level to **70%** so you can see the text box's position relative to the text on page 1.

▶ **2.** Click the **Layout Options** button . The Layout Options gallery opens with the Square option selected. See Figure 4-12.

Figure 4-12   Square text wrapping currently applied to text box

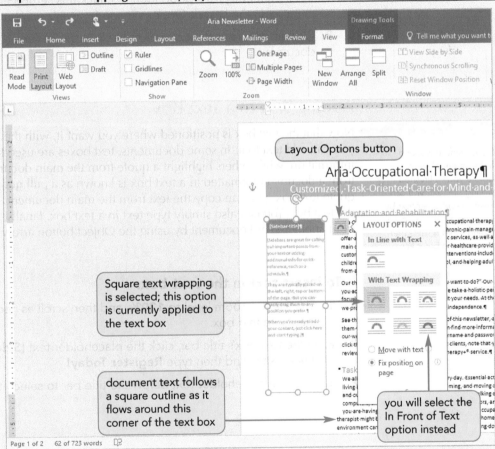

Square text wrapping is currently applied to the text box. You can see evidence of Square text wrapping where the document text flows around the lower-right corner of the text box. You'll have a chance to see some more dramatic examples of text wrapping later in this module, but it's important to be able to identify subtle examples of it.

▶ **3.** Click any of the other options in the Layout Options gallery, and observe how the document text and the text box shift position. Continue exploring the Layout Options gallery, trying out several of the options.

4. Click the **In Front of Text** option 🖻, and then click the **Close** button ⊠ in the upper-right corner of the Layout Options gallery to close the gallery. The document text shifts so that it now flows directly down the left margin, without wrapping around the text box.

Your next formatting task is to make sure the text box is assigned a fixed position on the page. You could check this setting using the Layout Options button, but you'll use the Wrap Text button in the Arrange group instead.

5. On the ribbon, click the **Drawing Tools Format** tab.

6. In the Arrange group, click the **Wrap Text** button. The Wrap Text menu gives you access to all the options in the Layout Options gallery, plus some more advanced settings.

7. Verify that **Fix Position on Page** has a checkmark next to it. To avoid having graphic objects move around unexpectedly on the page as you add or delete other elements, it's a good idea to check this setting either in the Wrap Text menu or in the Layout Options menu for every graphic object.

8. Click anywhere in the document to close the gallery, and then save the document.

Adding Text to a Text Box

Now that the text box is positioned where you want it, with the correct text wrapping, you can add text to it. In some documents, text boxes are used to present new information, while others highlight a quote from the main document. A direct quote from a document formatted in a text box is known as a **pull quote**. To create a pull quote text box, you can copy the text from the main document, and then paste it into the text box. You can also simply type text in a text box. Finally, you can insert text from another Word document by using the Object button arrow on the Insert tab.

To insert text in the text box:

1. Change the Zoom level to **120%**, and then scroll as necessary so you can see the entire text box.

2. In the text box's title bar, click the placeholder text **[Sidebar title]** to select it, if necessary, and then type **Register Today!**

3. Click the placeholder text below the title bar to select it. See Figure 4-13.

Figure 4-13   Text box with placeholder text selected

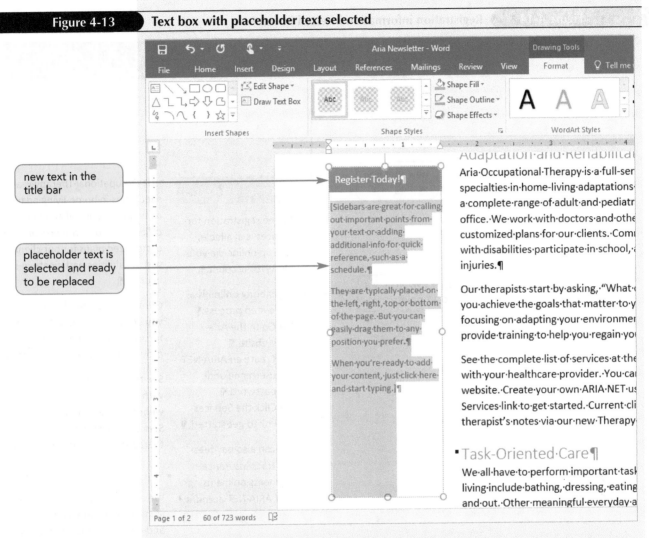

new text in the title bar

placeholder text is selected and ready to be replaced

4. Press the **Delete** key to delete the placeholder text. Now you can insert new text from another Word document.

5. On the ribbon, click the **Insert** tab.

6. In the Text group, click the **Object** button arrow to open the Object menu, and then click **Text from File**. The Insert File dialog box opens. Selecting a Word document to insert is just like selecting a document in the Open dialog box.

7. Navigate to the **Word4 > Module** folder included with your Data Files, click **Online** to select the file, and then click the **Insert** button. The registration information contained in the Online document is inserted directly into the text box. The inserted text was formatted in 9-point Calibri in the Online document, and it retains that formatting when you paste it into the Aria Newsletter document. To make the text easier to read, you'll increase the font size to 11 points.

8. With the insertion point located in the last paragraph in the text box (which is blank), press the **Backspace** key to delete the blank paragraph, and then click and drag the mouse pointer to select all the text in the text box, including the title in the shaded title box.

9. On the ribbon, click the **Home** tab.

10. In the Font group, click the **Font Size** arrow, and then click **11**. The size of the text in the text box increases to 11 points. See Figure 4-14.

Figure 4-14   **Registration information inserted in text box**

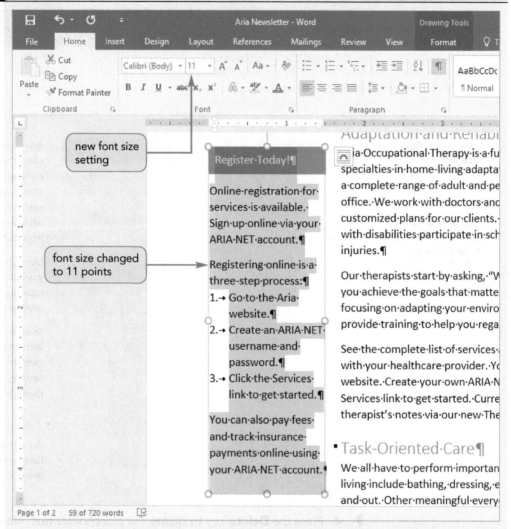

Trouble? Don't be concerned if the text in your text box wraps slightly differently from the text shown in Figure 4-14. The same fonts can vary slightly from one computer to another, causing slight differences in the way text wraps within and around text boxes.

▶ **11.** Click anywhere outside the text box to deselect it, and then save the document.

The first text box is complete. Now you need to add one more on page 1 and another on page 2. Avanti wants the second text box on page 1 to have a different look from the first one, so he asks you to use the Shapes button to draw a text box.

Drawing and Formatting a Text Box Using the Shapes Menu

A text box is considered a shape, just like the other shapes you can insert via the Shapes button on the Insert tab. This is true whether you insert a text box via the Text Box button or via the Shapes button. While text boxes are typically rectangular, you can actually turn any shape into a text box. Start by using the Shapes button to draw a shape of your choice, and then, with the shape selected, type any text you want. You won't see an insertion point inside the shape, but you can still type text inside it and then format it. You can format the shape itself by using the Shape Styles options on the Drawing Tools Format tab.

To draw and format a text box:

▶ **1.** Scroll down to display the bottom half of page 1.

▶ **2.** On the ribbon, click the **Insert** tab.

▶ **3.** In the Illustrations group, click the **Shapes** button to display the Shapes gallery. See Figure 4-15.

| Figure 4-15 | Shapes gallery |

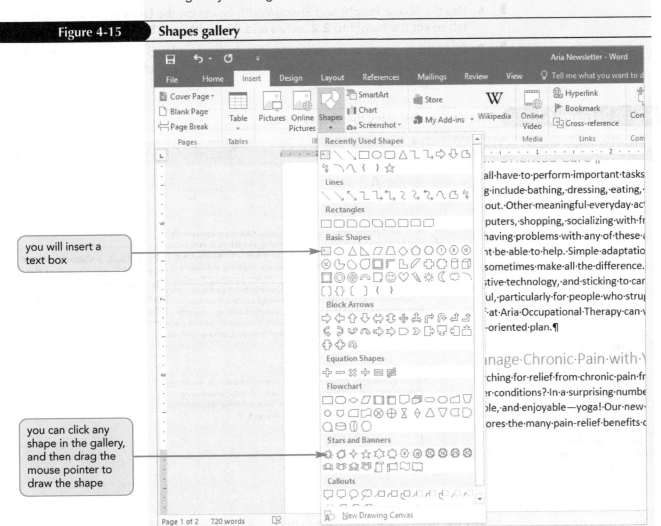

you will insert a text box

you can click any shape in the gallery, and then drag the mouse pointer to draw the shape

At this point, you could click any shape in the gallery, and then drag the pointer in the document to draw that shape. Then, after you finish drawing the shape, you could start typing in the selected shape to insert text.

▶ **4.** In the Basic Shapes section of the Shapes gallery, click the **Text Box** icon. The gallery closes, and the mouse pointer turns into a black cross +.

▶ **5.** Position the pointer in the blank area in the left margin at about the 6-inch mark (according to the vertical ruler), and then click and drag down and to the right to draw a text box approximately 1.5 inches wide and 2.5 inches tall. When you are satisfied with the text box, release the mouse button.

Don't be concerned about the text box's exact dimensions or position on the page. For now, just make sure it fits in the blank space to the left of the last two paragraphs on the page.

TIP

On computers with a touch screen, the Review tab contains the Start Inking button, which you can click to begin drawing on the screen by dragging the pointer.

The new text box is selected, with handles on its border and the insertion point blinking inside. The Layout Options button is visible, and the text box's anchor symbol is positioned to the left of the paragraph below the heading "Task-Oriented Care." By default, a shape is always anchored to the nearest paragraph that begins above the shape's top border. It doesn't matter where the insertion point is located.

▶ **6.** Use the Shape Height and Shape Width boxes on the Drawing Tools Format tab to set the height to **2.2** inches and the width to **1.5** inches.

▶ **7.** Drag the text box as necessary to align its bottom border with the last line of text on the page and its left border with the left edge of the text box above. See Figure 4-16.

Figure 4-16	Text box created using the Shapes button

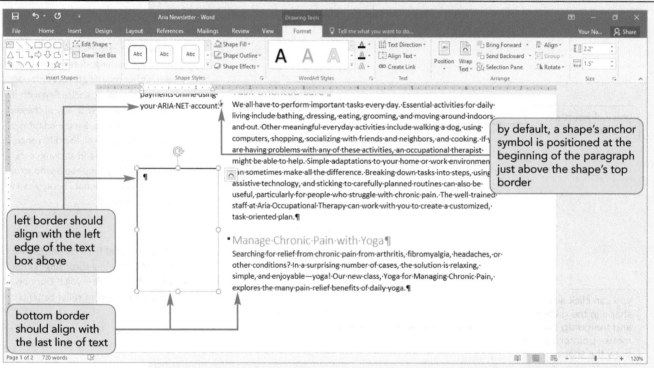

Now you need to add some text to the blank text box. Instead of inserting text from another Word document, you will copy a sentence from the newsletter and paste it into the text box to create a pull quote. After you add the text, you'll format the text box to make it match the one shown earlier in the Session 4.1 Visual Overview.

To copy text from the newsletter and paste it into the text box:

▶ **1.** Select the second sentence after the heading "Task-Oriented Care" (which begins "Essential activities for daily living. . ."), and then press the **Ctrl+C** keys to copy it to the Office Clipboard.

▶ **2.** Click in the blank text box, and then press the **Ctrl+V** keys to paste the copied sentence into the text box. The newly inserted sentence is formatted in 11-point Calibri, just as it was in the main document.

3. Add quotation marks at the beginning and end of the sentence, so it's clear the text box is a pull quote. Your next task is to center the sentence between the top and bottom borders of the text box. Then you'll add some color.

4. On the ribbon, click the **Drawing Tools Format** tab, if necessary.

5. In the Text group, click the **Align Text** button to display the Align text menu, and then click **Middle**. The text is now centered between the top and bottom borders of the text box. Next, you'll change the text's font color and add a background color.

6. In the Shape Styles group, click the **More** button to display the Shape Styles gallery. Like the text styles you have used to format text, shape styles allow you to apply a collection of formatting options, including font color and shading, with one click.

7. Move the mouse pointer over the various options in the Shape Styles gallery, and observe the Live Previews in the document. When you are finished, position the mouse pointer over the **Colored Fill - Blue, Accent 5** style, which is a dark blue box, the second from the right in the second row. See Figure 4-17.

Figure 4-17 **Shape Styles gallery**

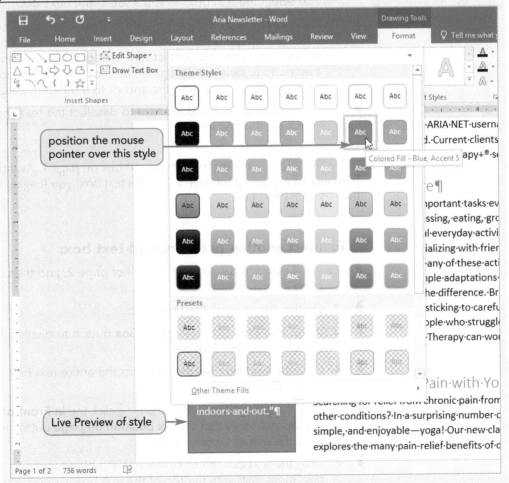

8. In the Shape Styles gallery, click the **Colored Fill - Blue, Accent 5** style. The style is applied to the text box, and the Shape Styles gallery closes.

Now, you need to make sure the text box is located in a fixed position on the page. In the following steps, you'll also experiment with making some changes involving the text box's anchor symbol. It's important to understand the role the anchor symbol plays in the document's overall layout.

To fix the text box's position on the page and experiment with the anchor symbol:

▶ **1.** Verify that the text box is still selected, with the Drawing Tools Format tab displayed on the ribbon.

▶ **2.** In the Arrange group, click the **Wrap Text** button. A checkmark appears next to Move with Text because that is the default setting for shapes.

▶ **3.** Click **Fix Position on Page** to add a checkmark and close the Wrap Text menu. This setting helps ensure that the text box will remain in its position on page 1, even if you add text above the paragraph it is anchored to. However, if you add so much text that the paragraph moves to page 2, then the text box will also move to page 2, but it will be positioned in the same location on the page that it occupied on page 1.

If you select the entire paragraph to which the text box is anchored, you will also select the text box, as you'll see in the next step.

▶ **4.** Triple-click the paragraph below the "Task-Oriented Care" heading. The entire paragraph and the text box are selected. If you pressed the Delete key at this point, you would delete the paragraph of text and the text box. If you ever need to delete a paragraph but not the graphic object that is anchored to it, you should first drag the anchor to a different paragraph.

▶ **5.** Click anywhere in the document to deselect the text and the text box, and then save the document.

You've finished creating the second text box on page 1. Avanti wants you to add a third text box at the top of page 2. For this text box, you'll again use the preformatted Ion Side Bar 1 text box.

To insert another preformatted text box:

▶ **1.** Scroll down to display the top half of page 2, and then click in the first line on page 2.

▶ **2.** On the ribbon, click the **Insert** tab.

▶ **3.** In the Text group, click the **Text Box** button to display the menu, scroll down, and then click **Ion Sidebar 1**.

▶ **4.** Click the **text box border** to select the entire text box and display the Layout Options button.

▶ **5.** Click the **Layout Options** button 🖼, click the **In Front of Text** option 🖼, if necessary, verify that the **Fix position on page** button is selected, and then close the Layout Options gallery.

▶ **6.** Drag the text box left to center it in the blank space to the left of the document text, with the top of the text box aligned with the first line of text on page 2. Note that a green alignment guide might appear if you try to position the right border of the text box too close to the document text.

▶ **7.** Change the text box's height to **3.5** inches and the width to **1.5** inches.

▶ **8.** In the title bar, replace the placeholder text with **Access Classes Online**.

▶ **9.** In the main text box, click the **placeholder text** to select it, and then press the **Delete** key.

▶ **10.** On the ribbon, click the **Insert** tab.

▶ **11.** In the Text group, click the **Object button arrow**, and then click **Text from File**.

▶ **12.** Navigate to the **Word4 > Module** folder, if necessary, and then insert the document named **Webinar**.

▶ **13.** Delete the extra paragraph at the end of the text box, increase the font size for the text to **11** points, click anywhere inside the text box to deselect the text, and then make sure your text box is positioned like the one shown in Figure 4-18.

| Figure 4-18 | Completed text box on page 2 |

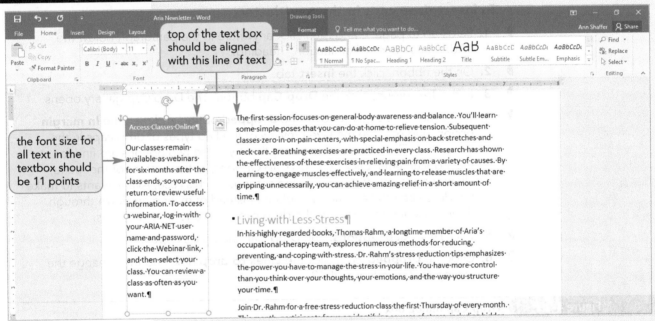

▶ **14.** Click anywhere in the document to deselect the text box, and then save the document.

INSIGHT

Linking Text Boxes

If you have a large amount of text that you want to place in different locations in a document, with the text continuing from one text box to another, you can use linked text boxes. For example, in a newsletter, you might have an article that starts in a text box on page 3 of the newsletter and continues in a text box on page 4. To flow the text automatically from one text box to a second, blank text box, click the first text box to select it (this text box should already contain some text). Next, on the ribbon, click the Drawing Tools Format tab, click the Create Link button in the Text group, and then click the empty text box. The text boxes are now linked. You can resize the first text box without worrying about how much text fits in the box. The text that no longer fits in the first text box is moved to the second text box. Note that you'll find it easier to link text boxes if you use simple text boxes without title bars.

To make the main document text look more polished, you will add some drop caps.

Inserting Drop Caps

As you saw in the Session 4.1 Visual Overview, a drop cap is a graphic that replaces the first letter of a paragraph. Drop caps are commonly used in newspapers, magazines, and newsletters to draw the reader's attention to the beginning of an article. You can place a drop cap in the margin or next to the paragraph, or you can have the text of the paragraph wrap around the drop cap. By default, a drop cap extends down three lines, but you can change that setting in the Drop Cap dialog box.

Avanti asks you to create a drop cap for some of the paragraphs that follow the headings. He wants the drop cap to extend two lines into the paragraph, with the text wrapping around it.

To insert drop caps in the newsletter:

▶ **1.** Scroll up to page 1, and then click anywhere in the paragraph below the "Adaptation and Rehabilitation" heading.

▶ **2.** On the ribbon, click the **Insert** tab.

▶ **3.** In the Text group, click the **Drop Cap** button. The Drop Cap gallery opens.

▶ **4.** Move the mouse pointer over the **Dropped** option and then the **In margin** option, and observe the Live Preview of the two types of drop caps in the document. The default settings applied by these two options are fine for most documents. Clicking Drop Cap Options, at the bottom of the menu, allows you to select more detailed settings. In this case, Avanti wants to make the drop cap smaller than the default. Instead of extending down through three lines of text, he wants the drop cap to extend only two lines.

▶ **5.** Click **Drop Cap Options**. The Drop Cap dialog box opens.

▶ **6.** Click the **Dropped** icon, click the **Lines to drop** box, and then change the setting to **2**. See Figure 4-19.

Figure 4-19   Drop Cap dialog box

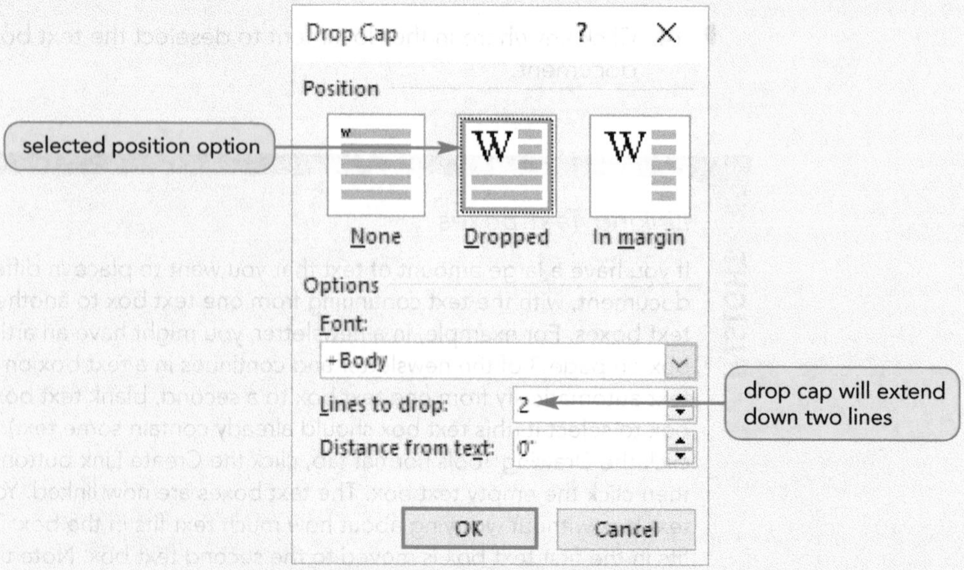

- selected position option
- drop cap will extend down two lines

TIP

To delete a drop cap, click the paragraph that contains it, open the Drop Cap dialog box, and then click None.

7. Click the **OK** button. Word formats the first character of the paragraph as a drop cap "A," as shown in the Session 4.1 Visual Overview. The dotted box with selection handles around the drop cap indicates it is selected.

8. Near the bottom of page 1, insert a similar drop cap in the paragraph following the "Manage Chronic Pain with Yoga" heading. You skipped the paragraph following the "Task-Oriented Care" heading because you'll eventually insert a graphic there. Including a drop cap there would make the paragraph look too cluttered.

9. On page 2, insert a similar drop cap in the paragraph following the "Living with Less Stress" heading.

10. Click anywhere in the text to deselect the drop cap, and then save your work.

PROSKILLS

Written Communication: Writing for a Newsletter

Pictures, WordArt, and other design elements can make a newsletter very appealing to readers. They can also be a lot of fun to create and edit. But don't let the design elements in your desktop-published documents distract you from the most important aspect of any document—clear, effective writing. Because the newsletter format feels less formal than a report or letter, some writers are tempted to use a casual, familiar tone. If you are creating a newsletter for friends or family, that's fine. But in most other settings—especially in a business or academic setting—you should strive for a professional tone, similar to what you find in a typical newspaper. Avoid jokes; you can never be certain that what amuses you will also amuse all your readers. Worse, you risk unintentionally offending your readers. Also, space is typically at a premium in any printed document, so you don't want to waste space on anything unessential. Finally, keep in mind that the best writing in the world will be wasted in a newsletter that is overburdened with too many design elements. You don't have to use every element covered in this module in a single document. Instead, use just enough to attract the reader's attention to the page, and then let the text speak for itself.

REVIEW

Session 4.1 Quick Check

1. Explain how to format a document in three columns of the default width.

2. What should you do if you don't know which characters to type to insert a symbol or special character?

3. What does the anchor symbol indicate?

4. How do you convert an inline object into a floating object?

5. What is a pull quote?

6. How many lines does a drop cap extend by default?

Session 4.2 Visual Overview:

You can use the Remove Background button for photos and some drawings. For all other pictures, you need to crop instead.

You can click the Crop button arrow to access more advanced cropping options, including cropping to a shape such as an oval or an arrow.

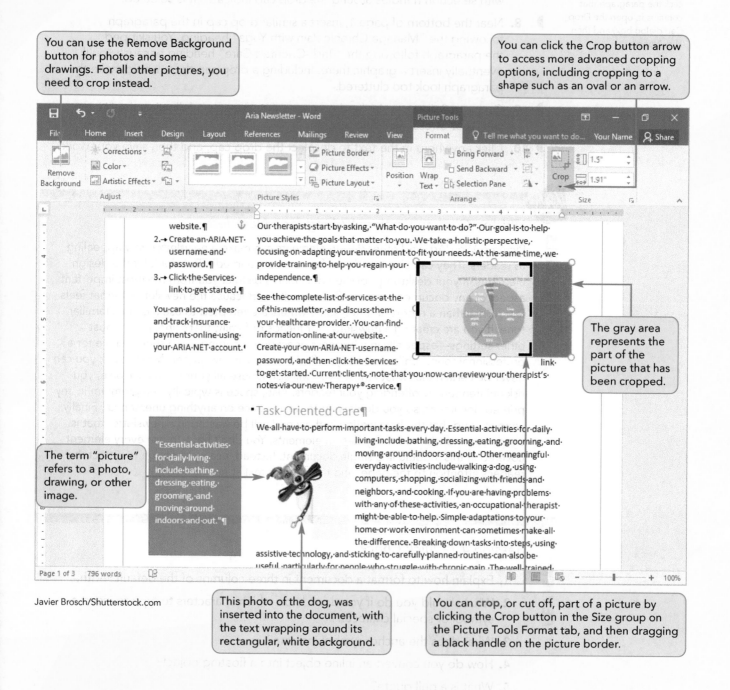

The gray area represents the part of the picture that has been cropped.

The term "picture" refers to a photo, drawing, or other image.

Javier Brosch/Shutterstock.com

This photo of the dog, was inserted into the document, with the text wrapping around its rectangular, white background.

You can **crop**, or cut off, part of a picture by clicking the Crop button in the Size group on the Picture Tools Format tab, and then dragging a black handle on the picture border.

Editing Pictures

Clicking the Remove Background button in the Adjust group on the Picture Tools Format tab displays the Background Removal tab, with tools for removing a photo's background.

The photo of the dog is displayed here with its background removed, which allows the text to wrap around the shape of the dog itself.

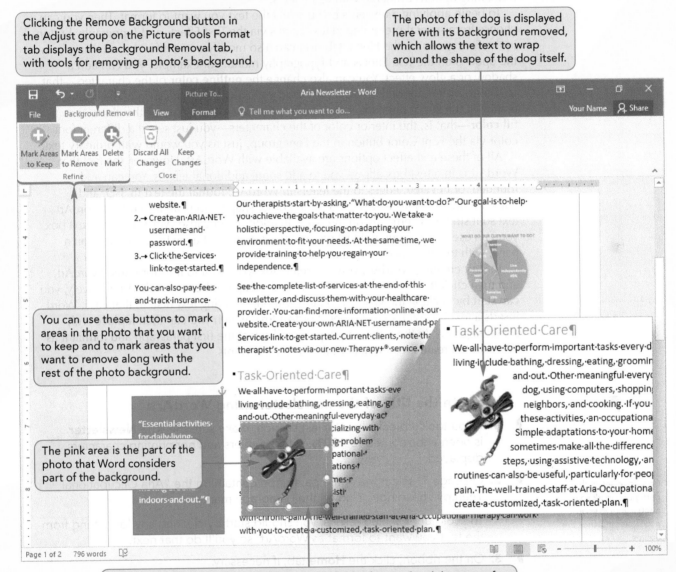

You can use these buttons to mark areas in the photo that you want to keep and to mark areas that you want to remove along with the rest of the photo background.

The pink area is the part of the photo that Word considers part of the background.

This border helps Word distinguish between the background and the parts of the image you want to keep. Any area of the image outside the border will be automatically excluded. In this case, part of the dog's head lies outside the border, so Word considers that area part of the background. To fix this problem, you can drag one of the border handles to expand the border until the dog's entire head is inside the border.

Formatting Text with WordArt

To create special text elements such as a newspaper headline, you can use decorative text known as WordArt. Essentially, WordArt is text in a text box that is formatted with a text effect. Before you move on to learning about WordArt, it's helpful to review the formatting options available with text effects.

To begin applying a text effect, you select the text you want to format. Then you can choose from several preformatted text effects via the Text Effects and Typography button in the Font group on the Home tab. You can also modify a text effect by choosing from the options on the Text Effects and Typography menu. For example, you can add a shadow or a glow effect. You can also change the **outline color** of the characters—that is, the exterior color of the characters—and you can change the style of the outline by making it thicker or breaking it into dashes, for example. To change the character's **fill color**—that is, the interior color of the characters—you just select a different font color via the Font Color button in the Font group, just as you would with ordinary text.

All of these text effect options are available with WordArt. However, the fact that WordArt is in a text box allows you to add some additional effects. You can add rounded, or **beveled**, edges to the letters in WordArt, format the text in 3-D, and transform the text into waves, circles, and other shapes. You can also rotate WordArt text so it stretches vertically on the page. In addition, because WordArt is in a text box, you can use page layout and text wrap settings to place it anywhere you want on a page, with text wrapped around it.

To start creating WordArt, you can select text you want to transform into WordArt, and then click the WordArt button in the Text group on the Insert tab. Alternatively, you can start by clicking the WordArt button without selecting text first. In that case, Word inserts a text box with placeholder WordArt text, which you can then replace with something new. In the following steps, you'll select the first paragraph and format it as WordArt to create the newsletter title that Avanti wants.

To create the title of the newsletter using WordArt:

1. If you took a break after the last session, make sure the **Aria Newsletter** is open and zoomed to **120%**, with the rulers and nonprinting characters displayed.

2. On page 1, select the entire paragraph containing the "Aria Occupational Therapy" heading, including the paragraph mark.

   To avoid unexpected results, you should start by clearing any formatting from the text you want to format as WordArt, so you'll do that next.

Be sure to select the paragraph mark so the page layout in your newsletter matches the figures.

3. On the ribbon, click the **Home** tab, if necessary.

4. In the Font group, click the **Clear All Formatting** button. The paragraph reverts to the Normal style. Now you can convert the text into WordArt.

5. On the ribbon, click the **Insert** tab.

6. In the Text group, click the **WordArt** button. The WordArt gallery opens.

7. Position the mouse pointer over the WordArt style that is second from the left in the top row. A ScreenTip describes some elements of this WordArt style—"Fill - Blue, Accent 1, Shadow." See Figure 4-20.

Figure 4-20 **WordArt gallery**

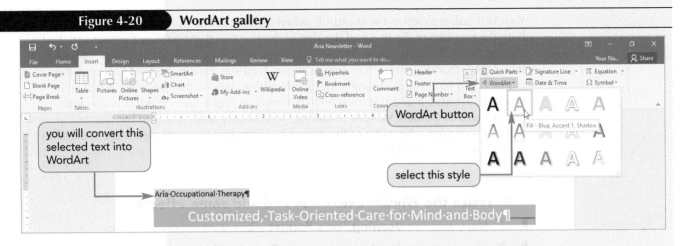

8. Click the WordArt style **Fill - Blue, Accent 1, Shadow**. The gallery closes, and a text box containing the formatted text is displayed in the document. See Figure 4-21.

Figure 4-21 **WordArt text box inserted in document**

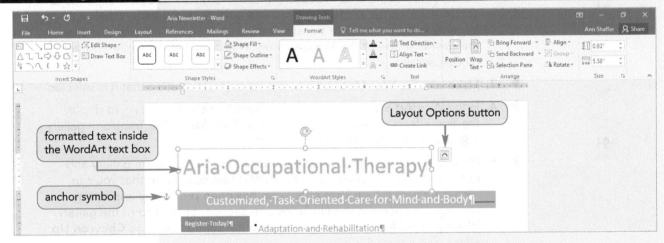

The Drawing Tools Format tab appears as the active tab on the ribbon, displaying a variety of tools that you can use to edit the WordArt. Before you change the look of the WordArt, you need to fix its position on the page and change its text wrap setting.

9. Make sure the **Drawing Tools Format** tab is selected on the ribbon.

10. In the Arrange group, click the **Wrap Text** button to open the Wrap Text menu, click **Top and Bottom**.

11. Save the document.

Next, you will modify the WordArt in several ways.

Modifying WordArt

Your first task is to resize the WordArt. When resizing WordArt, you need to consider both the font size of the text and the size of the text box that contains the WordArt. You change the font size for WordArt text just as you would for ordinary text—by selecting it and then choosing a new font size using the Font size box in the Font group on the Home tab. If you choose a large font for a headline, you might also need to resize the text box to ensure that the resized text appears on a single line. Avanti is happy with the font size of the new WordArt headline, so you only need to adjust the size of the text box so it spans the width of the page. The larger text box will then make it possible for you to add some more effects.

To resize the WordArt text box and add some effects:

▶ **1.** Make sure the **Drawing Tools Format** tab is selected on the ribbon.

▶ **2.** Change the width of the text box to **7** inches. The text box height should remain at the default .93 inches.

By default, the text is centered within the text box, which is what Avanti wants. Note, however, that you could use the alignment buttons on the Home tab to align the text any way you wanted within the text box borders. You could also increase the text's font size so that it expands to span the full width of the text box. Instead, you will take advantage of the larger text box to apply a transform effect, which will expand and change the overall shape of the WordArt text. Then you'll make some additional modifications.

▶ **3.** Make sure the **WordArt** text box is a solid line, indicating that it is selected.

▶ **4.** In the WordArt Styles group, click the **Text Effects** button Ⓐ ▾ to display the Text Effects gallery, and then point to **Transform**. The Transform gallery displays options for changing the WordArt's shape.

▶ **5.** Move the mouse pointer over the options in the Transform gallery and observe the Live Previews in the WordArt text box. Note that you can always remove a transform effect that has been previously applied by clicking the option in the No Transform section, at the top of the gallery. When you are finished, position the mouse pointer over the **Chevron Up** effect. See Figure 4-22.

Figure 4-22   Applying a Transform text effect

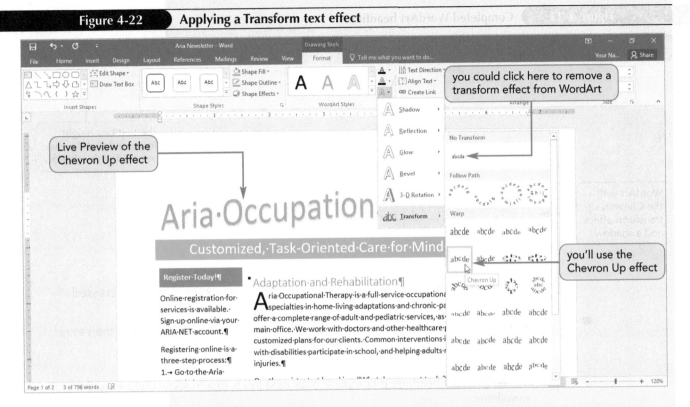

Trouble? If you don't see the Live Preview, press the Esc key twice to close the Transform and Text Effects galleries. Then, click outside the WordArt text box to deselect it, click the blue WordArt text to display the text box border, click the text box border to select it, and then begin again with Step 4.

6. Click the **Chevron Up** effect. The Transform menu closes, and the effect is applied to the WordArt. Now you will make some additional changes using the options in the WordArt Styles group. You'll start by changing the fill color.

7. In the WordArt Styles group, click the **Text Fill button arrow** A ⌄ to display the Text Fill color gallery.

8. In the Theme Colors section of the gallery, click the square that is fifth from the right in the top row to select the **Orange, Accent 2** color. The Text Fill gallery closes, and the WordArt is formatted in a shade of orange that matches the shading in the paragraph below. Next, you'll add a shadow to make the headline more dramatic.

9. In the WordArt Styles group, click the **Text Effects** button A ⌄ to display the Text Effects gallery, and then point to **Shadow** to display the Shadow gallery, which is divided into several sections.

10. In the Outer section, point to the top-left option to display a ScreenTip that reads "Offset Diagonal Bottom Right."

11. Click the **Offset Diagonal Bottom Right** shadow style. A shadow is added to the WordArt text. See Figure 4-23.

Figure 4-23   **Completed WordArt headline**

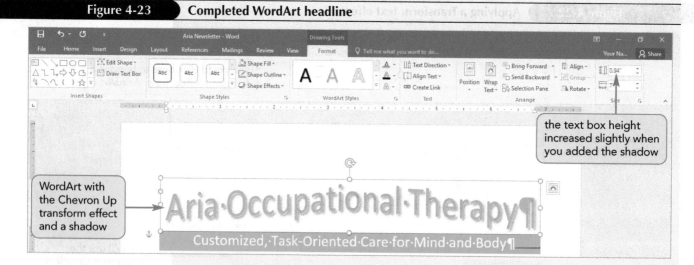

the text box height increased slightly when you added the shadow

WordArt with the Chevron Up transform effect and a shadow

Aria·Occupational·Therapy¶

Customized,·Task-Oriented·Care·for·Mind·and·Body¶

Note that the height of the text box that contains the WordArt increased slightly, to 0.94 inches.

▶ **12.** Click a blank area of the document to deselect the WordArt, and then save the document.

The WordArt headline is complete. Your next job is to add some pictures to the newsletter.

Working with Pictures

In Word, a picture is a photo, drawing, or other image. Although you can copy and paste pictures into a document from other documents, you'll typically insert pictures via either the Pictures button or the Online Pictures button, both of which are located in the Illustrations group on the Insert tab. You use the Pictures button to insert a picture from a file stored on your computer. You use the Online Pictures button to insert images that you find online using Bing Image Search or that you have stored on OneDrive. As you saw in the Session 4.1 Visual Overview, the final version of the Aria Newsletter document will contain a photograph of a dog and a drawing of someone in bed. The newsletter will also contain a picture of a chart, which Avanti's coworker created earlier and saved as a separate file.

After you insert a picture into a document, it functions as an object that you can move, resize, wrap text around, and edit in other ways using the appropriate contextual tab on the ribbon. In general, the skills you used when modifying text boxes apply to pictures as well.

PROSKILLS

Written Communication: Understanding Copyright Laws

The ownership of all forms of media, including text, drawings, photographs, and video, is governed by copyright laws. You should assume that anything you find on the web is owned by someone who has a right to control its use. It's your responsibility to make sure you understand copyright laws and to abide by them. The U.S. Copyright Office maintains a Frequently Asked Questions page that should answer any questions you might have: www.copyright.gov/help/faq.

Generally, copyright laws allow a student to reuse a photo, drawing, or other item for educational purposes, on a one-time basis, without getting permission from the owner. However, to avoid charges of plagiarism, you need to acknowledge the source of the item in your work. You don't ever want to be accused of presenting someone else's work as your own. Businesses face much more stringent copyright restrictions. To reuse any material, you must request permission from the owner, and you will often need to pay a fee.

When you use Bing Image Search in the Insert Pictures window, all of the images that initially appear as a result of your search will be licensed under a Creative Commons license. There are several types of Creative Commons licenses. One type allows you to use an image for any reason, including commercial use, and to modify the image, as long as the photographer is credited or attributed (similar to the credits under the photos in some figures in this book). Another type of license allows you to use an image with an attribution as long as it is not for commercial purposes and as long as you do not modify the image. Even if an image has a Creative Commons license, you must still review the exact license on the website on which the image is stored. When you point to an image in the search results in the Insert Pictures window, its website appears as a link at the bottom of the window.

Inserting and Cropping a Picture

You can use the Chart button in the Illustrations group on the Insert tab to enter data into a data sheet and then create a chart that illustrates the data. However, the chart Avanti wants to insert in the newsletter was created by a coworker using a different program and then saved as a PNG file named Chart.png. That means you can insert the chart as a picture using the Pictures button in the Illustrations group.

Avanti asks you to insert the chart picture on page 1.

To insert the chart picture on page 1:

▶ 1. On page 1, click at the end of the first paragraph below the "Adaptation and Rehabilitation" heading to position the insertion point between "...acute injuries." and the paragraph mark. Normally, there's no need to be so precise about where you click before inserting a picture, but doing so here will ensure that your results match the results described in these steps exactly.

▶ 2. On the ribbon, click the **Insert** tab.

▶ 3. In the Illustrations group, click the **Pictures** button to open the Insert Picture dialog box.

▶ 4. Navigate to the **Word4 > Module** folder included with your Data Files, and then insert the picture file named **Chart.png**. The chart picture is inserted in the document as an inline object. It is selected, and the Picture Tools Format tab is displayed on the ribbon.

▶ 5. Scroll down if necessary so you can see the entire chart.

The chart is wider than it needs to be and would look better as a square. So you'll need to cut off, or crop, part of it. In addition to the ability to crop part of a picture, Word offers several more advanced cropping options. One option is to crop to a shape, which means trimming the edges of a picture so it fits into a star, an oval, an arrow, or another shape. You can also crop to a specific ratio of height to width.

Whatever method you use, once you crop a picture, the part you cropped is hidden from view. However, it remains a part of the picture in case you change your mind and want to restore the cropped picture to its original form.

Before you crop off the sides of the chart, you'll try cropping it to a specific shape.

To crop the chart picture:

1. In the Size group, click the **Crop button arrow** to display the Crop menu, and then point to **Crop to Shape**. A gallery of shapes is displayed, similar to the gallery you saw in Figure 4-15.

2. In the Basic Shapes section of the gallery, click the **Lightning Bolt** shape ⚡ (third row down, sixth from the right). The chart picture takes on the shape of a lightning bolt, with everything outside the lightning bolt shape cropped off.

   Obviously, this isn't a useful option for the chart, but cropping to shapes can be very effective with photos in informal documents such as party invitations or posters, especially if you then use the Behind Text wrapping option, so that the document text flows over the photo.

3. Press the **Ctrl+Z** keys to undo the cropping.

4. In the Size group, click the **Crop** button (not the Crop button arrow). Dark black sizing handles appear around the picture borders.

5. Position the pointer directly over the middle sizing handle on the right border. The pointer changes to ⊢.

6. Press and hold down the mouse button, and drag the pointer slightly left. The pointer changes to ✛.

7. Drag the pointer toward the left until the chart border aligns with the 4-inch mark on the horizontal ruler, as shown in Figure 4-24.

Figure 4-24 **Cropping a picture**

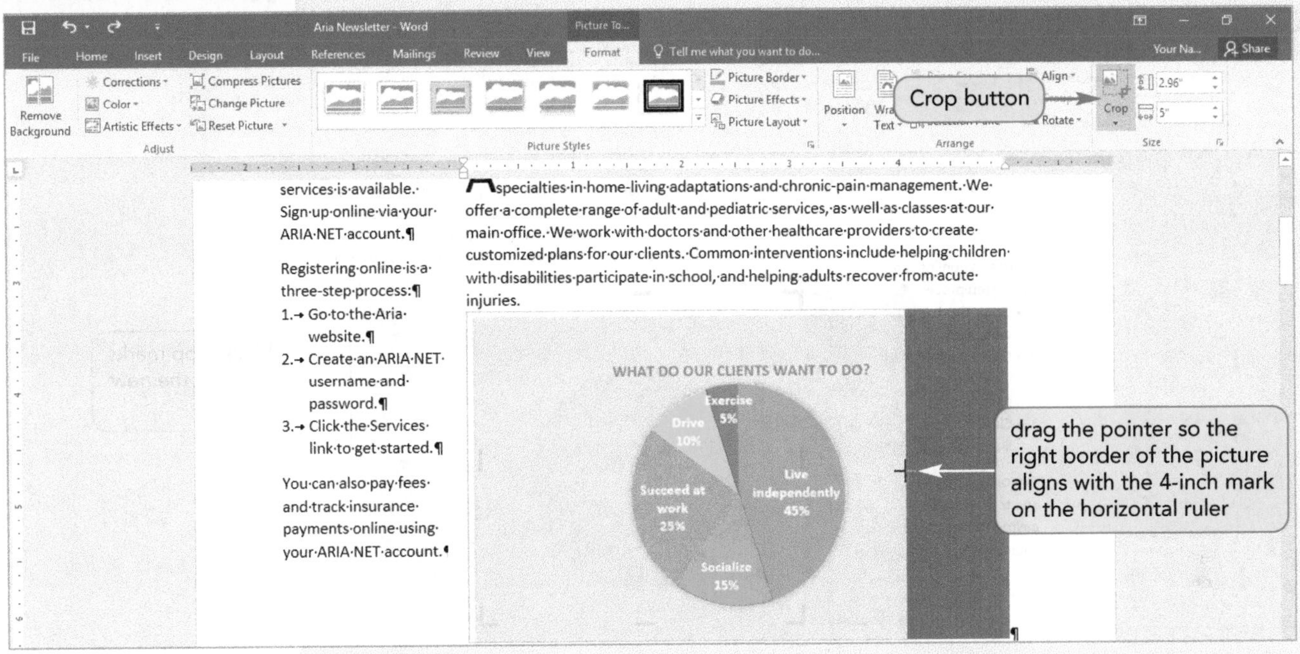

8. When the chart looks like the one shown in Figure 4-24, release the mouse button. The right portion of the chart picture is no longer visible. The chart shifts position slightly. Because the chart is an inline object, the text also shifts slightly. You can ignore the text wrapping for now. The original border remains, indicating that the cropped portion is still saved as part of the picture in case you want to undo the cropping.

9. Drag the middle handle on the left border to the right until the left border aligns with the 1.5-inch mark on the horizontal ruler.

TIP

If you aren't sure what formatting has been applied to a picture, and you want to start over, use the Reset Picture button.

The chart now takes up much less space, but it's not exactly a square. To ensure a specific ratio, you can crop the picture by changing its **aspect ratio**—that is, the ratio of width to height. You'll try that next. But first, you'll restore the picture to its original state.

10. In the Adjust group, click the **Reset Picture button arrow** to display the Reset Picture menu, and then click **Reset Picture & Size**. The chart picture returns to its original state.

11. In the Size group, click the **Crop button arrow**, and then point to **Aspect Ratio** to display the Aspect Ratio menu, which lists various ratios of width to height. A square has a 1-to-1 ratio of width to height.

12. Under "Square," click **1:1**. The chart is cropped to a square shape. See Figure 4-25.

Figure 4-25   **Chart cropped to a 1:1 aspect ratio**

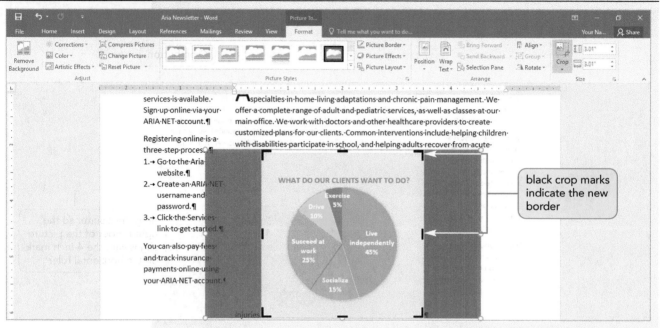

black crop marks
indicate the new
border

▶ **13.** Click anywhere outside the chart to deselect it and complete the cropping procedure.

Next, you need to change the chart from an inline object to a floating object by wrapping text around it. You also need to position it on the page. You can complete both of these tasks at the same time by using the Position button in the Arrange group.

To change the chart's position and wrapping:

▶ **1.** Change the Zoom level to **One Page**, and then click the **chart** to select it.

▶ **2.** On the ribbon, click the **Picture Tools Format** tab.

▶ **3.** In the Arrange group, click the **Position** button to display the Position gallery. You can click an icon in the "With Text Wrapping" section to move the selected picture to one of nine preset positions on the page. As with any gallery, you can see a Live Preview of the options before you actually select one.

TIP

When you select an option in the Position gallery, Fix Position on Page is also selected on the Wrap Text menu by default.

▶ **4.** Move the mouse pointer over the various icons, and observe the changing Live Preview in the document, with the chart picture moving to different locations on the page and the text wrapping around it.

▶ **5.** Point to the icon in the middle row on the far right side to display a ScreenTip that reads "Position in Middle Right with Square Text Wrapping," and then click the **Position in Middle Right with Square Text Wrapping** icon ⊞. The chart picture moves to the middle of the page along the right margin. By default, it is formatted with Tight text wrapping, so the text wraps to its left, following its square outline.

Your final step is to resize the chart picture to make it a bit smaller.

> **6.** In the Size group, click the **Shape Height** box, type **1.8**, and then press the **Enter** key. The settings in both the Shape Height and Shape Width boxes change to 1.8 inches. For most types of graphics, the aspect ratio is locked, meaning that when you change one dimension, the other changes to match. In this case, because the aspect ratio of the chart is 1:1, when you changed the height to 1.8 inches, the width also changed to 1.8 inches, ensuring that the chart retained its square shape.

> **7.** Click anywhere outside the chart picture to deselect it, and then save the document.

INSIGHT

Aligning Graphic Objects and Using the Selection Task Pane

The steps in this module provide precise directions about where to position graphic objects in the document. However, when you are creating a document on your own, you might find it helpful to use the Align button in the Arrange group on the Picture Tools Format tab to align objects relative to the margin or the edge of the page. Aligning a graphic relative to the margin, rather than the edge of the page, is usually the best choice because it ensures that you don't accidentally position a graphic outside the page margins, causing the graphic to get cut off when the page is printed.

After you choose whether to align to the page or margin, you can open the Align menu again and choose an alignment option. For example, you can align the top of an object at the top of the page or align the bottom of an object at the bottom of the page. You can also choose to have Word distribute multiple objects evenly on the page. To do this, it's helpful to open the Selection task pane first by clicking the Layout tab and then clicking Selection Pane in the Arrange group. Press and hold the Ctrl key, and then in the Selection task pane, click the objects you want to select. After the objects are selected, there's no need to switch back to the Picture Tools Format tab. Instead, you can take advantage of the Align button in the Arrange group on the Layout tab to open the Align menu, where you can then click Distribute Horizontally or Distribute Vertically.

The chart picture is finished. Next, Avanti asks you to insert the dog photo near the bottom of page 1.

Searching for and Inserting Online Pictures

The first step in using online pictures is finding the picture you want. Most image websites include a search box where you can type some descriptive keywords to help you narrow the selection down to a smaller range. To search for images from within Word, click the Online Pictures button in the Illustrations group on the Insert tab. This opens the Insert Pictures window, shown in Figure 4-26, where you can use Bing Image Search to look for images.

Figure 4-26   **Inserting an online picture**

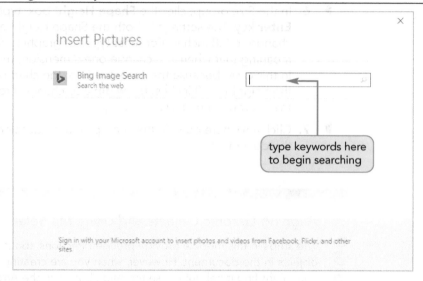

To start a search, you would type keywords, such as "walking a dog," in the Bing Image Search box and then click the Search button. Images from all over the web that have the keywords "walking a dog" and that are licensed under Creative Commons would appear below the Search box. Typically, these images are premade drawings known as **clip art**, which can be used to illustrate a wide variety of publications. To insert one of those images, you would click it, and then click the Insert button. To widen your search to all the images on the web (the vast majority of which are subject to strict copyright restrictions), you could click the Show all web results button at the bottom of the Insert Pictures window. At that point, the search results would expand to include photos in addition to clip art.

Because results from an online search are unpredictable, in the following steps you will insert an image included with your Data Files.

To insert a photo in the Aria Newsletter document:

1. Zoom in so you can read the document text at the bottom of page 1, and then click at the end of the paragraph below the "Task-Oriented Care" heading to position the insertion point between "task-oriented plan." and the paragraph mark.

2. Change the Zoom level to **Multiple Pages** so you can see the entire document.

3. On the ribbon, click the **Insert** tab.

4. In the Illustrations group, click the **Pictures** button to display the Insert Picture dialog box, and then navigate to the **Word4 > Module** folder included with your Data Files.

5. Click the image **Terrier.jpg**, and then click the **Insert** button. The dialog box closes, and the photo of a dog is inserted as an inline object at the current location of the insertion point. See Figure 4-27.

Figure 4-27	Photo inserted as inline object

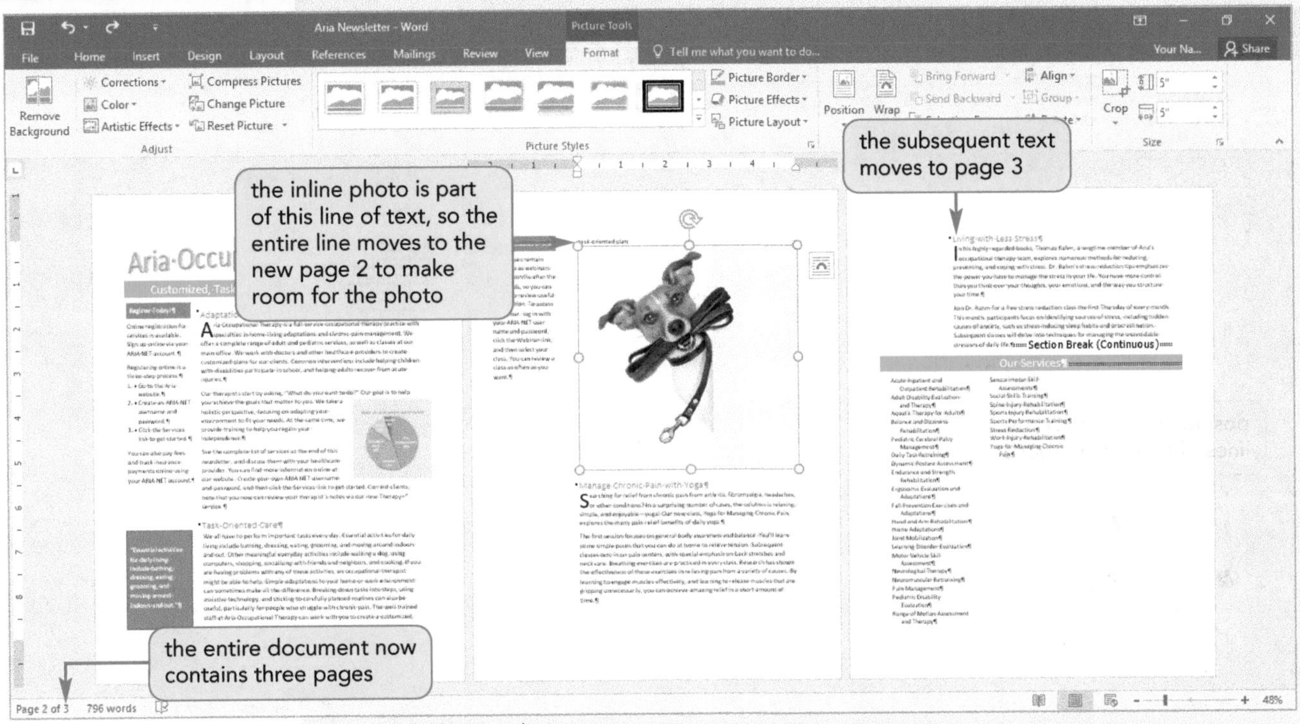

the inline photo is part of this line of text, so the entire line moves to the new page 2 to make room for the photo

the subsequent text moves to page 3

the entire document now contains three pages

Javier Brosch/Shutterstock.com

Because the photo is too large to fit on page 1, the line that contains the insertion point jumps to page 2, with the photo displayed below the text. The rest of the document text starts below the photo on page 2 and flows to page 3. The photo is selected, as indicated by its border with handles. The Picture Tools Format tab is displayed on the ribbon. Now you can reduce the photo's size, wrap text around it, and position it on the page.

6. In the Size group, click the **Shape Height** box, type **2**, and then press the **Enter** key. To maintain the photo's preset 1:1 aspect ratio, Word also changes the photo's width to 2 inches. Some of the text from page 3 moves up to fill the space below the smaller photo on page 2.

7. In the Arrange group, click the **Wrap Text** button, and then click **Tight**. The photo is now a floating object.

8. Drag the photo to page 1, and position it so the first two lines line of the paragraph under "Task-Oriented Care" wraps above it. See Figure 4-28. The anchor symbol for the photo is no longer visible because it's covered by the blue text box.

Figure 4-28   **Resized photo as a floating object**

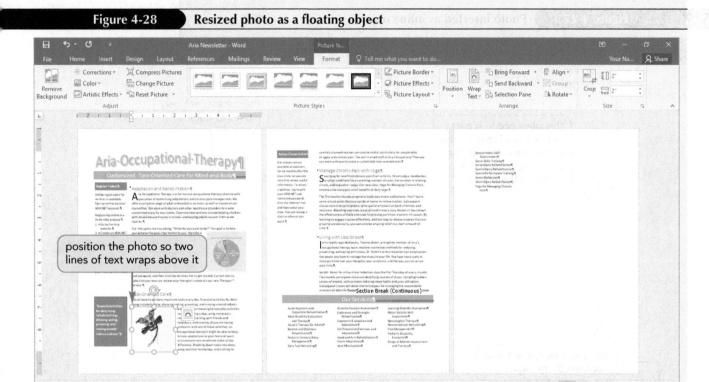

Javier Brosch/Shutterstock.com

Trouble? Don't be concerned if you can't get the text to wrap around the dog photo exactly as shown in Figure 4-28.

▶ 9. Click the **Layout Options** button 📄, click **Fix position on page**, and then close the Layout Options gallery.

Avanti likes the photo, but he asks you to make a few changes. First, he wants you to rotate the dog to the right to position it vertically on the page. Also, Avanti wants the text to wrap around the curved shape of the dog, instead of around the photo's rectangular outline. To accomplish that, you need to remove the photo's background.

Rotating a Picture

You can quickly rotate a picture by dragging the Rotation handle that appears on the photo's border when the photo is selected. To access some preset rotation options, you can click the Rotate button in the Arrange group to open the Rotate menu. To quickly rotate a picture 90 degrees, click Rotate Right 90° or Rotate Left 90° in the Rotate menu. You can also flip a picture, as if the picture were printed on both sides of a card and you wanted to turn the card over. To do this, click Flip Vertical or Flip Horizontal in the Rotate menu.

Avanti only wants to rotate the picture slightly so the dog is upright. You can do that by dragging the Rotation handle.

To rotate the photo:

1. Change the document Zoom level to **120%**, and then scroll down so you can see the bottom half of page 1.

2. Click the **dog picture**, if necessary, to select it, and then position the mouse pointer over the circular rotation handle above the middle of the photo's top border. The mouse pointer changes to ⟲.

3. Drag the mouse pointer down and to the right, until the dog rotates to a vertical position. The surrounding text wraps awkwardly around the picture's angled borders. See Figure 4-29.

Figure 4-29  **Dragging the Rotation handle**

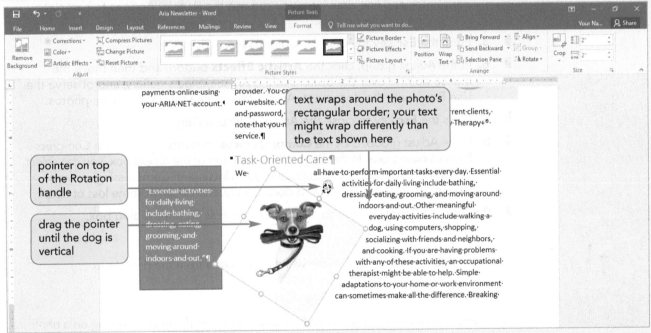

Javier Brosch/Shutterstock.com

Trouble? Don't be concerned if the text wrapping around your rotated picture looks different from the text wrapping in Figure 4-29. You'll adjust the picture's position soon.

4. Release the mouse button. The dog is displayed in the new, rotated position.

5. Save the document.

You're almost finished editing the dog photo. Your last task is to remove its background so the text wraps around the shape of the dog. But before you remove the background from the dog photo, you'll explore the options in the Adjust group.

Adjusting a Picture

The Adjust group on the Picture Tools Format tab provides several tools for adjusting a picture's overall look. Some, such as the Remove Background button, work only for photos. Others, such as the Color button, provide some options that work only for photos and some that work for both photos and line drawings. You'll explore some of these options in the following steps.

To try out some options in the Adjust group:

▶ 1. Make sure that the **dog photo** is still selected, and that the **Picture Tools Format** tab is selected on the ribbon.

▶ 2. In the Adjust group, click the **Corrections** button, and then move the mouse pointer over the various options in the Corrections gallery and observe the Live Preview in the document. You can use the Corrections gallery to sharpen or soften a photo's focus or to adjust the brightness of a photo or line drawing.

▶ 3. Press the **Esc** key to close the Corrections gallery.

▶ 4. In the Adjust group, click the **Color** button, and then move the mouse pointer over the options in the Color gallery, and observe the Live Preview in the document. For photos, you can adjust the color saturation and tone. For photos and line drawings, you can use the Recolor options to completely change the picture's colors.

▶ 5. Press the **Esc** key to close the Color gallery.

▶ 6. In the Adjust group, click the **Artistic Effects** button, and then move the mouse pointer over the options in the Artistic Effects gallery, and observe the Live Preview in the document. Artistic Effects can be used only on photos.

▶ 7. Press the **Esc** key to close the Artistic Effects gallery.

▶ 8. In the Adjust group, click the **Compress Pictures** button to open the Compress Pictures dialog box. In the Target output portion of the dialog box, you can select the option that reflects the purpose of your document. Compressing pictures reduces the file size of the Word document but can result in some loss of detail.

▶ 9. Click the **Cancel** button to close the Compress Pictures dialog box.

Now you are ready to remove the white background from the dog photo.

Removing a Photo's Background

Removing a photo's background can be tricky, especially if you are working on a photo with a background that is not clearly differentiated from the foreground image. For example, you might find it difficult to remove a white, snowy background from a photo of an equally white snowman. You start by clicking the Remove Background button in the Adjust group, and then making changes to help Word distinguish between the background that you want to exclude and the image you want to keep.

REFERENCE

Removing a Photo's Background

- Select the photo, and then on the Picture Tools Format tab, in the Adjust group, click the Remove Background button.
- Drag the handles on the border as necessary to include any parts of the photo that have been incorrectly marked for removal.
- To mark areas to keep, click the Mark Areas to Keep button in the Refine group on the Background Removal tab, and then use the drawing pointer to select areas of the photo to keep.
- To mark areas to remove, click the Mark Areas to Remove button in the Refine group on the Background Removal tab, and then use the drawing pointer to select areas of the photo to remove.
- Click the Keep Changes button in the Close group.

You'll start by zooming in so you can clearly see the photo as you edit it.

To remove the white background from the dog photo:

▶ **1.** On the Zoom slider, drag the slider button to change the Zoom level to **180%**, and then scroll as necessary to display the selected dog photo.

▶ **2.** In the Adjust group, click the **Remove Background** button. See Figure 4-30.

Figure 4-30	Removing a photo's background

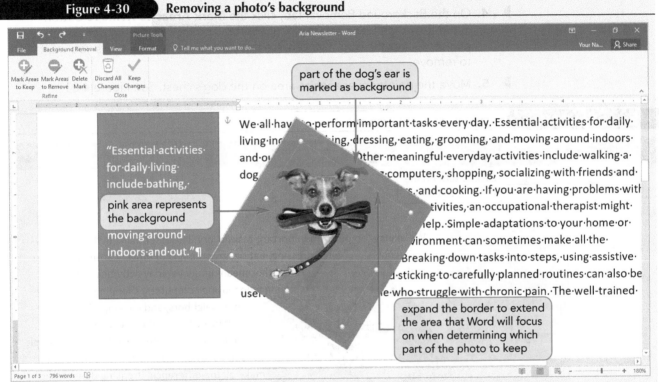

Javier Brosch/Shutterstock.com

The part of the photo that Word considers to be the background turns pink, and the Background Removal tab appears on the ribbon. A border with white handles surrounds the dog. The border helps Word narrow the area of focus as it tries to distinguish between the background and the parts of the image you want to keep. Word will automatically remove any part of the image outside the border when you click the Keep Changes button.

Trouble? If you don't see the border with the white handles, click the Mark Areas to Remove button in the Refine group on the Background Removal tab, and then click in the pink background, in the top corner of the picture. This will insert a small white circle with a negative sign inside it, which you can ignore. The border with the white handles should now be displayed.

Notice that the top of the dog's ears are pink, indicating that Word considers them to be part of the background. The same is probably true of the dog's chest, below his collar, although this can vary from one computer to another. To ensure that Word keeps the parts of the photo you want, you need to expand the border with the white handles. Then you can make additional adjustments using the tools on the Background Removal tab. In the following steps, your goal is to retain the dog's head above the collar and all of the leash.

3. If necessary, drag the handle in the top corner of the border up slightly until the border encloses the dog's entire head. The dog's ears should now be visible in their original colors, with no pink shading, indicating that Word no longer considers any part of the dog's ears to be part of the background. Depending on how far up you dragged the border handle, the border might have disappeared, or it might still be visible. At this point, most of the dog's chest is pink, which is what you want. If a few white spots are still visible, you can fix the problem by marking these white spots as areas to remove.

4. On the Background Removal tab, click the **Mark Areas to Remove** button in the Refine group to select it, if necessary, and then move the drawing pointer 🖉 over the dog. You can use this pointer to click any areas you want to remove.

5. Move the pointer over a white area on the dog's chest. See Figure 4-31.

Figure 4-31   **Marking an area to remove**

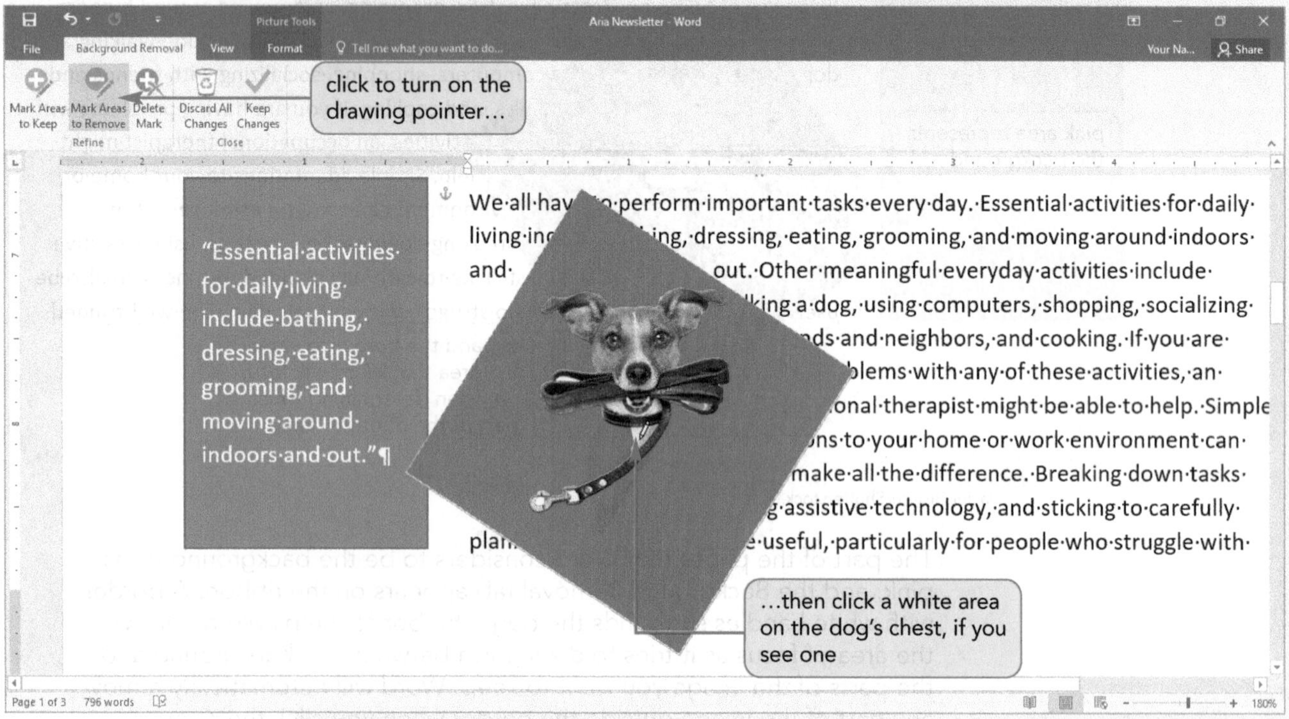

click to turn on the drawing pointer…

…then click a white area on the dog's chest, if you see one

Javier Brosch/Shutterstock.com

6. Click the mouse button. A small circle with a negative sign appears where you clicked, and the white area turns pink, indicating that Word now considers it part of the background.

7. Click any other remaining white spots on the dog's chest. You can ignore any white spots in the folds of the leash or around the dog's ears, because they will be invisible when the photo is displayed on the document's white background.

Note that you could click the Mark Areas to Keep button and then use the mouse pointer in a similar way to mark parts of the photo that you want to retain, rather than remove. You can also click and drag the Mark Areas to Remove pointer or the Mark Areas to Keep pointer to select a larger area of the photo for deletion or retention.

Now you will accept the changes you made to the photo.

8. In the Close group, click the **Keep Changes** button. The background is removed from the photo, leaving only the image of the dog with the leash. Now the text wrapping follows the curved shape of the dog, just as Avanti requested. Depending on exactly where you positioned the dog, some of the text might now wrap to the left of the leash.

9. Change the Zoom level to **100%** so that you can see the entire dog, as well as the top of page 2, and then drag the dog as necessary so the text wraps similar to the text shown in Figure 4-32.

Figure 4-32	Dog photo with background removed

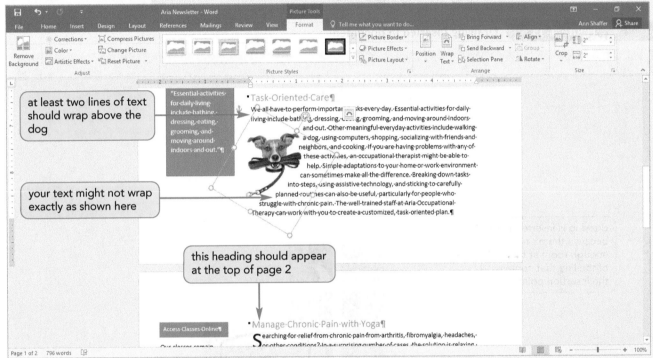

Javier Brosch/Shutterstock.com

Don't be concerned if you can't get the text wrapping to match exactly. The most important thing is that when you are finished, the "Manage Chronic Pain with Yoga" heading should be positioned at the top of page 2. Also, at least two lines of text should wrap above the dog.

10. Click outside the picture to deselect it, and then save the document.

You're finished with your work on the dog photo. Now Avanti asks you to add a drawing of someone in bed, on page 3.

Inserting and Editing a Drawing

You could search for a drawing by clicking the Online Pictures button in the Illustrations group on the Insert tab and then typing some keywords. In the following steps, however, you will insert a drawing from a file. Then, you'll add a picture style to it from the Picture Styles gallery.

To insert a drawing and add a style to it:

▶ **1.** Change the Zoom level to **120%**, and then scroll to display the middle of page 2. You'll insert the drawing in the blank space below the text box.

▶ **2.** Click at the end of the paragraph below the "Living with Less Stress" heading to position the insertion point between "…your time." and the paragraph mark.

▶ **3.** On the ribbon, click the **Insert** tab.

▶ **4.** In the Illustrations group, click the **Pictures** button, navigate to the **Word4 > Module** folder included with your Data Files, click the image **Sleep**, and then click the **Insert** button. The drawing of the person in bed is inserted as an inline object on page 3, because there is not enough room for it on page 2. See Figure 4-33.

Figure 4-33	Drawing inserted in document

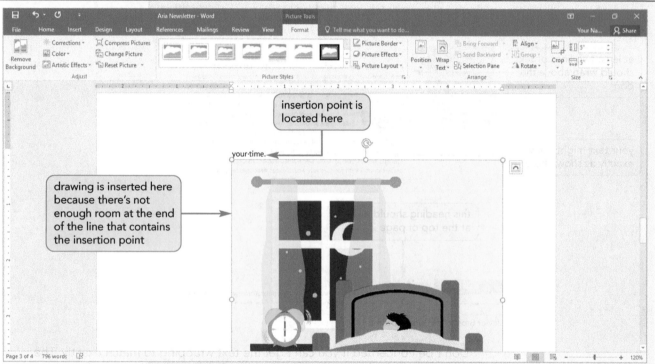

© iStock.com/djvstock

Next, you need to resize the drawing, apply a picture style, wrap text around it, and then position it on the page.

▶ **5.** In the Size group, click the **Shape Height** box, type **1.4**, and then press the **Enter** key. To maintain the picture's preset aspect ratio, the width automatically adjusts to 1.4 inches. The picture moves up to page 2 because it's now small enough to fit.

▶ **6.** Scroll up to page 2 so you can see the picture, if necessary.

▶ **7.** In the Arrange group, click the **Wrap Text** button to open the Wrap Text menu. The In Line with Text option is selected. Because the picture is still an inline picture, the Move with Text and Fix Position on Page options are grayed out, indicating that they are not available.

▶ **8.** Click **In Front of Text** to select it and close the Wrap Text menu.

9. Click the **Wrap Text** button again, and then click **Fix Position on Page**. The picture appears layered on top of the document text. Keep in mind that even though you selected Fix Position on Page, the picture is not stuck in one place. You can drag it anywhere you want. The point of the Fix Position on Page setting is that it prevents the picture from moving unexpectedly as you make changes to other parts of the document.

10. In the Picture Styles group, click the **Simple Frame, White** style, which is the first style in the visible row of the Picture Styles gallery. A frame and a shadow are applied to the drawing.

11. Drag the picture to center it in the white space below the text box in the margin, deselect it, and then save the document. See Figure 4-34.

Figure 4-34 | **Resized picture with picture style**

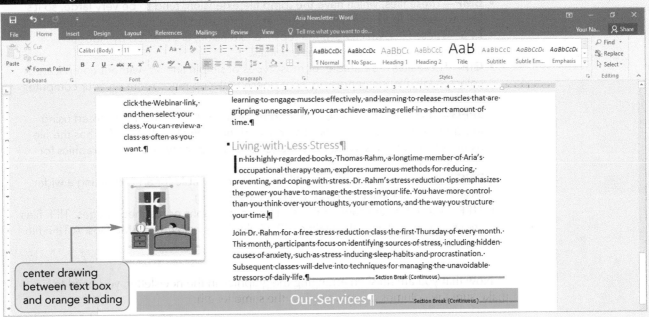

center drawing between text box and orange shading

©iStock.com/djvstock

INSIGHT

Working with Digital Picture Files

Digital picture files come in two main types—vector graphics and raster graphics. A vector graphics file stores an image as a mathematical formula, which means you can increase or decrease the size of the image as much as you want without affecting its overall quality. Vector graphics are often used for line drawings and, because they tend to be small, are widely used on the web. File types for vector graphics are often proprietary, which means they work only in specific graphics programs. In Word, you will sometimes encounter files with the .wmf file extension, which is short for Windows Metafiles. A WMF file is a type of vector graphics file created specifically for Windows. In most cases, though, you'll work with raster graphics, also known as bitmap graphics. A **bitmap** is a grid of square colored dots, called **pixels**, that form a picture. A bitmap graphic, then, is essentially a collection of pixels. The most common types of bitmap files are:

- **BMP**—These files, which have the .bmp file extension, tend to be very large, so it's best to resave them in a different format before using them in a Word document.
- **EPS**—These files, which have the .eps file extension, are created by Adobe Illustrator and can contain text as graphics.
- **GIF**—These files are suitable for most types of simple line art, without complicated colors. A GIF file is compressed, so it doesn't take up much room on your computer. A GIF file has the file extension .gif.
- **JPEG**—These files are suitable for photographs and drawings. Files stored using the JPEG format are even more compressed than GIF files. A JPEG file has the file extension .jpg. If conserving file storage space is a priority, use JPEG graphics for your document.
- **PNG**—These files are similar to GIF files but are suitable for art containing a wider array of colors. A PNG file has the file extension .png.
- **TIFF**—These files are commonly used for photographs or scanned images. TIFF files are usually much larger than GIF or JPEG files but smaller than BMP files. A TIFF file has the file extension .tif.

Now that you are finished arranging the graphics in the newsletter, you need to make sure the columns are more or less the same length.

Balancing Columns

To **balance** columns on a page—that is, to make them equal length—you insert a continuous section break at the end of the last column. Word then adjusts the flow of content between the columns so they are of equal or near-equal length. The columns remain balanced no matter how much material you remove from any of the columns later. The columns also remain balanced if you add material that causes the columns to flow to a new page; the overflow will also be formatted in balanced columns.

To balance the columns:

▶ 1. Press the **Ctrl+End** keys to move the insertion point to the end of the document, if necessary.

▶ 2. Insert a continuous section break. See Figure 4-35.

Figure 4-35 ▶ **Newsletter with balanced columns**

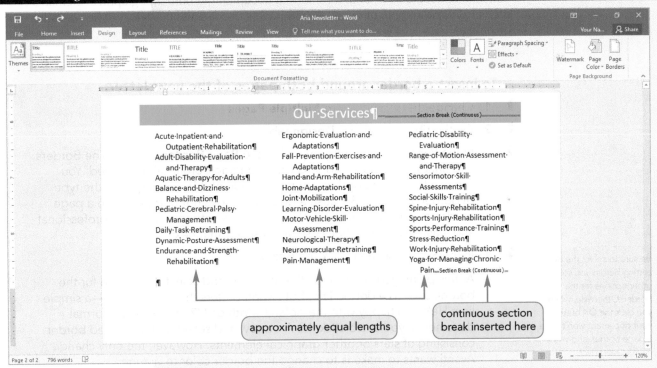

Word balances the text between the three columns, moving some text from the bottom of the left column to the middle column, and from the middle column to the right column, so the three columns are approximately the same length.

Note that you can also adjust the length of a column by inserting a column break using the Breaks button in the Page Setup group on the Layout tab. A column break moves all the text and graphics following it to the next column. Column breaks are useful when you have a multipage document formatted in three or more columns, with only enough text on the last page to fill some of the columns. In that case, balancing columns on the last page won't work. Instead, you can use a column break to distribute an equal amount of text over all the columns on the page. However, as with page breaks, you need to be careful with column breaks because it's easy to forget that you inserted them. Then, if you add or remove text from the document, or change it in some other significant way, you might end up with a page layout you didn't expect.

Inserting a Border Around a Page

The newsletter is almost finished. Your last task is to add a border around both pages. The default style for a page border is a simple black line that forms a box around each page in the document. However, you can choose more elaborate options, including a dotted line, double lines, and, for informal documents, a border of graphical elements such as stars or trees. In this case, Avanti prefers the default line style, but he wants it to be orange.

To insert a border around both pages of the newsletter:

1. Change the Zoom level to **Multiple Pages**.

2. On the ribbon, click the **Design** tab.

3. In the Page Background group, click the **Page Borders** button. The Borders and Shading dialog box opens with the Page Border tab displayed. You can use the Setting options on the left side of this tab to specify the type of border you want. Because a document does not normally have a page border, the default setting is None. The Box setting is the most professional and least distracting choice, so you'll select that next.

4. In the Setting section, click the **Box** setting.

   At this point, you could scroll the Style box and select a line style for the border, such as a dotted line, but Avanti prefers the default style—a simple line. He's also happy with the default width of 1/2 pt. For very informal documents, you could click the Art arrow and select a predesigned border consisting of stars or other graphical elements. However, the only change Avanti wants to make is to change the border color to orange.

5. Click the **Color** arrow to open the Color gallery, and then click the **Orange, Accent 2** square, which is the fifth square from the right in the top row of the Theme Colors section. The Color gallery closes and the Orange, Accent 2 color is displayed in the Color box. See Figure 4-36.

Be sure to select the Box setting before you select other options for the border. Otherwise, when you click the OK button, your document won't have a page border, and you'll have to start over.

Figure 4-36 Adding a border to the newsletter

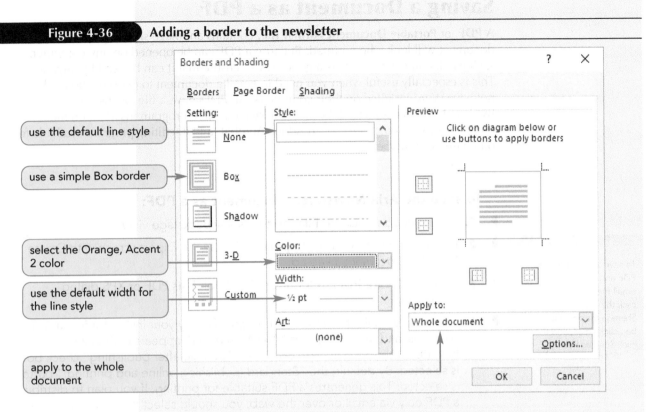

use the default line style

use a simple Box border

select the Orange, Accent 2 color

use the default width for the line style

apply to the whole document

▶ **6.** In the lower-right corner of the Borders and Shading dialog box, click the **Options** button. The Border and Shading Options dialog box opens.

By default, the border is positioned 24 points from the edges of the page. If you plan to print your document on an older printer, it is sometimes necessary to change the Measure from setting to Text, so that the border is positioned relative to the outside edge of the text rather than the edge of the page. Alternatively, you can increase the settings in the Top, Bottom, Left, and Right boxes to move the border closer to the text. For most modern printers, however, the default settings are fine.

▶ **7.** In the Border and Shading Options dialog box, click the **Cancel** button, and then click the **OK** button in the Borders and Shading dialog box. The newsletter now has a simple, orange border, as shown earlier in the Session 4.1 Visual Overview.

▶ **8.** Save the document. Finally, to get a better sense of how the document will look when printed, it's a good idea to review it with nonprinting characters turned off.

▶ **9.** On the ribbon, click the **Home** tab.

▶ **10.** In the Paragraph group, click the **Show/Hide** button to turn off nonprinting characters. Notice that the WordArt headline increases slightly in size to take up the space formerly occupied by the nonprinting paragraph mark.

▶ **11.** Change the Zoom level to **120%**, and then scroll to display page 2.

▶ **12.** On page 2, in the first line below the heading, "Living with Less Stress," replace "Thomas Rahm" with your first and last names, and then save the document.

Avanti plans to have the newsletter printed by a local printing company. Sophia, his contact at the printing company, has asked him to email her the newsletter as a PDF.

Saving a Document as a PDF

A **PDF**, or **Portable Document Format file**, contains an image showing exactly how a document will look when printed. Because a PDF can be opened on any computer, saving a document as a PDF is a good way to ensure that it can be read by anyone. This is especially useful when you need to email a document to people who might not have Word installed on their computers. All PDFs have a file extension of .pdf. By default, PDFs open in Adobe Acrobat Reader, a free program installed on most computers for reading PDFs, or in Adobe Acrobat, a PDF-editing program available for purchase from Adobe.

TIP

To save a document as a PDF and attach it to an email message in Outlook, click the File tab, click Share in the navigation bar, click Email, and then click Send as PDF.

To save the Aria Newsletter document as a PDF:

1. On the ribbon, click the **File** tab to display Backstage view.

2. In the navigation bar, click **Export** to display the Export screen with Create PDF/XPS Document selected.

3. Click the **Create PDF/XPS** button. The Publish as PDF or XPS dialog box opens.

4. If necessary, navigate to the location specified by your instructor for saving your files, and then verify that "Aria Newsletter" appears in the File name box. Below the Save as type box, the "Open file after publishing" check box is selected. By default, the "Standard (publishing online and printing)" button is selected. This generates a PDF suitable for printing. If you plan to distribute a PDF only via email or over the web, you should select the "Minimum size (publishing online)" button instead. See Figure 4-37.

Figure 4-37 **Publish as PDF or XPS dialog box**

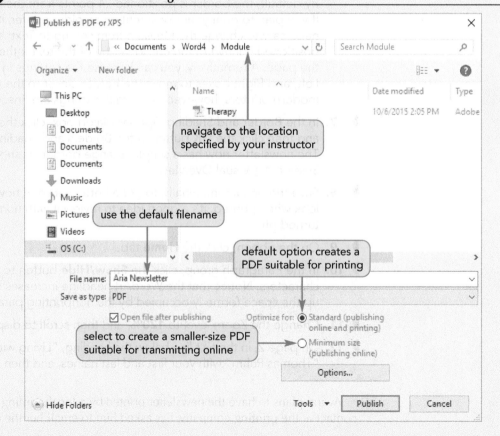

5. Click the **Publish** button. The Publish as PDF or XPS dialog box closes, and, after a pause, either Adobe Acrobat Reader or Adobe Acrobat opens with the Aria Newsletter.pdf file displayed.

Trouble? If the Aria Newsletter PDF does not open, your computer might not have Acrobat Reader or Acrobat installed. In that case, skip Step 6.

6. Scroll down and review the PDF, and then close Adobe Acrobat Reader or Adobe Acrobat.

7. In Word, close the Aria Newsletter document, saving changes if necessary, but keep Word running.

In addition to saving a Word document as a PDF, you can convert a PDF to a Word document.

Converting a PDF to a Word Document

TIP

If the PDF's creator restricted the file's security using settings available in Adobe Acrobat, you will not be able to copy text from the PDF or convert it to a Word document.

You may sometimes need to use text from a PDF in your own Word documents. Before you can do this, of course, you need to make sure you have permission to do so. Assuming you do, you can open the PDF in Acrobat or Acrobat Reader, drag the mouse pointer to select the text you want to copy, press the Ctrl+C keys, return to your Word document, and then press the Ctrl+V keys to paste the text into your document. If you need to reuse or edit the entire contents of a PDF, it's easier to convert it to a Word document. This is a very useful option with PDFs that consist mostly of text. For more complicated PDFs, such as the Aria Newsletter.pdf file you just created, the results are less predictable.

Avanti has a PDF containing some text about the Therapy+ service. He asks you to open it in Word and make some minor edits before converting it back to a PDF.

To open the PDF in Word:

1. On the ribbon, click the **File** tab to display Backstage view.

2. In the navigation bar, click **Open**, if necessary, to display the Open screen, and then navigate to the **Word4 > Module** folder included with your Data Files.

3. If necessary, click the **arrow** to the right of the File name box, and then click **All Word Documents**.

4. In the file list, click **Therapy**, click the **Open** button, and then, if you see a dialog box explaining that Word is about to convert a PDF to a Word document, click the **OK** button. The PDF opens in Word, with the name "Therapy.pdf" in the title bar. Now you can save it as a Word document.

> **5.** Click the **File** tab, click **Save As**, and then navigate to the location specified by your instructor.

> **6.** Verify that "Word Document (*.docx)" appears in the Save as type box, and then save the document as **Therapy Revised**.

> **7.** Turn on nonprinting characters, set the Zoom level to **120%**, and then review the document, which consists of a WordArt headline and a paragraph of text formatted in the Normal style. If you see some extra spaces at the end of the paragraph of text, they were added during the conversion from a PDF to a Word document. In a more complicated document, you might see graphics overlaid on top of text, or columns broken across multiple pages.

> **8.** Close the **Therapy Revised** document.

Session 4.2 Quick Check

REVIEW

1. What term refers to the interior color of the characters in WordArt?

2. Name six types of bitmap files.

3. What kind of laws govern the use of media, including text, line drawings, photographs, and video?

4. When cropping a picture, how can you maintain a specific ratio of width to height?

5. What is the most professional and least distracting style of page border?

6. What should you do if you need to ensure that your document can be read on any computer?

Review Assignments

Data Files needed for the Review Assignments: Books.jpg, Festival.docx, Genres.png, Hours.docx, Library.docx, Party.jpg

Avanti has been hired to create a newsletter for another organization, the Singleton Valley Library. This newsletter provides the latest information about the library, with articles about an upcoming celebration and a retirement. He has already written the text, and he asks you to transform it into a professional-looking newsletter. He also asks you to save the newsletter as a PDF so he can email it to the printer and to edit some text currently available only as a PDF. The finished newsletter should match the one shown in Figure 4-38.

Figure 4-38 | **Completed Library Newsletter document**

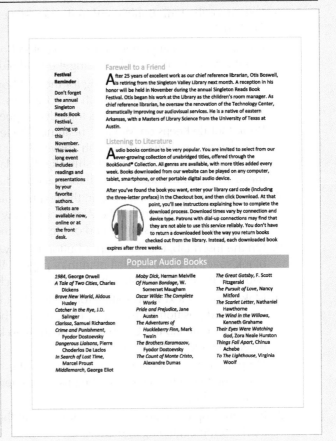

Happy_Inside/Shutterstock.com; photo.ua/Shutterstock.com

Complete the following steps:

1. Open the file **Library** from the Word4 > Review folder included with your Data Files, and then save the document as **Library Newsletter** in the location specified by your instructor.

2. Insert continuous section breaks in the following locations:

   a. On page 1, at the beginning of the "Singleton Bookmobile Keeps on Moving" heading, to the left of the "S" in "Singleton"

   b. On page 2, at the beginning of the shaded heading "Popular Audio Books," to the left of the "P" in "Popular"

   c. On page 2, at the beginning of the first book title, to the left of the "1" in "1984"

3. In sections 1 and 3, change the left and right margins to .75 inches. In section 2, change the left margin to 2.5 inches.

4. Format section 4 in three columns of equal width, and then format the entire list of book titles and authors with a 0.2-inch hanging indent.

5. Search for the term **BookSound** in the newsletter, and then add the ® symbol to the right of the final "d."

6. On page 1, click anywhere in the "Singleton Bookmobile Keeps on Moving" heading, and then insert a preformatted text box using the Grid Sidebar option.

7. Change the text wrapping setting for the text box to In Front of Text. Change the height of the text box to 4 inches and its width to 1.3 inches, and then drag it left to position it in the white space in the left margin, with its top edge aligned with the first line of text below the "Singleton Book Mobile Keeps on Moving" heading. The left border of the text box should align with the left edge of the shaded paragraph above. Verify that the text box's position is fixed on the page, but note that its placement will shift slightly relative to other elements in the newsletter as you make changes. Eventually, it will be positioned as it is in the Figure 4-38.

8. Delete all the placeholder text in the text box, and then insert the text of the Word document **Hours**, which is located in the Word4 > Review folder included with your Data Files. Delete any extra paragraph marks at the end of the text, if necessary.

9. On the Insert tab, use the Shapes button to draw a rectangular text box that roughly fills the blank space in the lower-left margin of page 1. When you are finished, adjust the height and width as necessary to make the text box 2.9 inches tall and 1.3 inches wide.

10. Make sure the text wrap setting for the text box is set to In Front of Text and that the text box has a fixed position on the page. Drag the text box's anchor up to slightly above or below the "Friends of the Library Celebration" heading to keep the text box from moving to page 2 later, when you add a graphic to page 1.

11. On page 1, in the second paragraph below the "Friends of the Library Celebration" heading, select the first sentence (which begins "The Friends of the Singleton..."), and then copy it to the Office Clipboard.

12. Paste the copied sentence into the text box at the bottom of page 1, and then add quotation marks at the beginning and end.

13. Use the Align Text button to align the text in the middle of the text box, and then apply the Subtle Effect - Blue, Accent 1 shape style (the light blue style option in the fourth row of the Shape Styles gallery).

14. On page 2, click in the heading "Listening to Literature," and then insert a preformatted text box using the Grid Sidebar option.

15. Change the text wrapping setting for the text box to In Front of Text. Change the height of the text box to 5.1 inches and its width to 1.3 inches, and then drag it left to position it in the white space in the left margin, with its top edge aligned with the first line of text. Verify that its position is fixed on the page. Don't be concerned that it overlaps the shaded paragraph below. This will change as you add more elements to the newsletter.

16. Delete all the placeholder text in the text box, and then insert the text of the Word document **Festival**, which is located in the Word4 > Review folder included with your Data Files. Delete any extra paragraph marks at the end of the text, if necessary.

17. In the first line of text after each of the four headings formatted with orange font, insert a drop cap that drops two lines.

18. On page 1, select the entire first paragraph, "Singleton Valley Library," including the paragraph mark. Clear the formatting from the paragraph, and then format the text as WordArt, using the Fill - Orange, Accent 2, Outline - Accent 2 style.

19. Use the Position button to place the WordArt in the top center of the document, with square text wrapping, and make sure the WordArt has a fixed position on the page.

20. Change the WordArt text box width to 7 inches, and retain the default height of .87 inches.

21. Apply the Chevron Up transform text effect, change the text fill to Orange, Accent 2 (the orange square in the top row of the Theme Colors section), and then add a shadow using the Offset Diagonal Bottom Right style (the first option in the top row of the Outer section).

22. Click at the end of the paragraph below the "Singleton Bookmobile Keeps on Moving" heading, and then insert the picture file named **Genres.png** from the Word4 > Review folder included with your Data Files.

23. Practice cropping the chart to a shape, and then try cropping it by dragging the cropping handles. Use the Reset Picture button as necessary to restore the picture to its original appearance. When you are finished, crop the picture using a square aspect ratio, and then change its height and width to 1.8 inches. Use the Position button to place the chart picture in the middle of the right side of page 1 with square text wrapping.

24. On page 1, click at the end of the second paragraph below the "Friends of the Library Celebration" heading, and then insert the drawing **Party.jpg** from the Word4 > Review folder included with your Data Files.

25. Apply Square text wrapping, change the picture's height to 1.7 inches, and position the picture as shown in Figure 4-38. When the picture is properly positioned, the heading "Farewell to a Friend" should be positioned at the top of page 2, as shown in Figure 4-38.

26. On page 2, click at the end of the first paragraph below the "Listening to Literature" heading, and then insert the photo **Books.jpg** from the Word4 > Review folder included with your Data Files.

27. Rotate the photo so the books are positioned vertically, with the earphones on top, change the photo's height to 1.2 inches, and retain the default width of 1.42 inches. Apply Tight text wrapping, fix its position on the page, and then remove the photo's background.

28. Drag the photo to position it as shown in Figure 4-38.

29. Balance the columns at the bottom of page 2.

30. Insert a simple box outline of the default style and width for the entire document. For the border color, use Blue, Accent 1 (the fifth square from the left in the top row of the Theme Colors). Make any additional adjustments necessary to ensure that your newsletter matches the one shown in Figure 4-38.

31. In the second line on page 2, replace "Otis Boswell" with your first and last names.

32. Save the document, and then save it again as a PDF named **Library Newsletter.pdf** in the location specified by your instructor. Wait for the PDF to open, review it, and then close the program in which it opened. Close the **Library Newsletter.docx** document, but leave Word open.

33. In Word, open the **Library Newsletter.pdf** file, save it as a Word document named **Library Newsletter from PDF.docx**, review its appearance, note the problems with the formatting that you would have to correct if you actually wanted to use this new DOCX file, and then close it.

Case Problem 1

Data Files needed for this Case Problem: Bike.png, Biking.docx, Pump.png, Sidebar.docx

Dallas Riders Bicycle Club   Philip Schuster is president of the Dallas Riders Bicycle Club, a recreational cycling organization in Dallas, Texas. He has written the text of the club's monthly newsletter. Now he needs your help to finish it. The newsletter must fit on one page so the route for this month's ride can be printed on the other side. The finished newsletter should match the one shown in Figure 4-39.

Figure 4-39   **Completed Biking Newsletter document**

Dallas Riders Bicycle Club
News From the Road

Lake View Passes

Don't forget to buy your annual pass for the Lake View Bike Path, available now on our website, or at any local bike shop. The $35 fee goes to support trail maintenance and youth programs. Daily passes are also available for out-of-town guests. Note that you can now purchase daily passes online, or at the Lake View Overlook trailhead.

See this month's ride route on the other side of this newsletter.

Dallas Riders Receive $3000 Grant

We're extremely happy to announce that the Dallas Riders Bicycle Club has been awarded a $3000 Ride the Roads grant from the Texas Department of Tourism. The money will pay for the publication of the club's "Top 100 Dallas Rides" pamphlet, which will be distributed at tourist sites throughout the Dallas-Fort Worth area.

Many thanks go to Clarice Orleans, who spent many hours completing the grant application, and to Peter Suarez and Leah Chang who compiled the information about the rides, based on a club survey. The pamphlet will be published by the end of the summer. It's packed with helpful information about biking in the Dallas-Fort Worth area.

Annual Big Southwest Ride

The Big Southwest Ride, October 15-20, is our most exciting event of the year. We encourage all participants to register before the September 15 deadline to ensure that we can accommodate everyone who wants to take part. The registration fee is $250. Online registration opens August 15.

Each rider is allowed one medium-sized backpack and one sleeping bag on the baggage truck. This year we will be staying in high school gyms along the route, so tents are not necessary. Charlie Yellow Feather, our generous volunteer chef, will once again oversee all meals. The registration fee entitles you to breakfast, lunch, and dinner. Note that this year the mid-day meal will take the form of a bagged lunch. Surveys from last year's ride suggested that most people prefer the flexibility of being able to eat lunch when and where they want.

Yellow Jersey Service Award Winners

Sasha Ann Ramirez-Beech	Carole Laydra	Seamus Brennan	Maria Morelo-Jimenez
Paul Michael Bernault	Thomas Butler	Jacqueline Fey-Esperanza	Elizabeth Juarez
Avi Cai	Lisa Erbe	Haiyan Jiang	Mario Mondre
Emma Gotlieb	Henry Douglas	Louis Jeschke	Heidi Roys
Markus Carnala	Carlos Caruccio	Jaques Lambeau	Student Name
	Cecilia Carrucio		
	Dennis McKay		

Shirstok/Shutterstock.com; Shai_Halud/Shutterstock.com

Complete the following steps:

1. Open the file **Biking** located in the Word4 > Case1 folder included with your Data Files, and then save it as **Biking Newsletter** in the location specified by your instructor.

2. Change the document margins to Narrow, and then, where indicated in the document, insert continuous section breaks. Remember to delete each instance of the highlighted text "[Insert SECTION BREAK]" before you insert a section break.

3. In section 2, change the left margin to 3 inches, and then format section 4 in four columns.

4. Format the second paragraph in the document ("News From the Road") as WordArt, using the Gradient Fill - Dark Green, Accent 1, Reflection style (second from the left in the middle row of the WordArt gallery). Change the text box height to 0.7 inches and the width to 7 inches.

5. Insert drop caps that drop two lines in the first paragraph after the "Dallas Riders Receive $3000 Grant" heading and in the first paragraph after the "Annual Big Southwest Ride" heading.

6. Click in the fourth paragraph in the document (the one with the drop cap "W"), and then insert a preformatted text box using the Ion Sidebar 1 option. Change the text wrapping setting for the text box to In Front of Text, and then change its height to 3 inches and its width to 2.3 inches.

7. Drag the text box down, and then align its top border with the "Dallas Riders Receive $3000 Grant" heading.

8. Delete the title placeholder text in the text box, and type **Lake View Passes**. In the main text box, delete the placeholder text, and insert the text of the Word document **Sidebar** from the Word4 > Case1 folder included with your Data Files. Delete any extra blank paragraphs, and change the font size for all the text in the text box, including the title, to 11 points.

9. In the blank space below the "Lake View Passes" text box, draw a rectangular text box. When you are finished, adjust the height and width to make the text box 1.3 inches tall and 2 inches wide. Apply the Moderate Effect - Blue, Accent 2 shape style (third from the left in the second row from the bottom), and then position the text box as shown in Figure 4-39, leaving room for the graphic you will add later.

10. In the text box, type **See this month's ride route on the other side of this newsletter.** Align the text in the middle of the text box, and then use the Center button to center the text between the text box's left and right borders.

11. At the end of the fifth paragraph (which begins "Many thanks go to..."), insert the drawing **Pump.png** from the Word4 > Case1 folder included with your Data Files. Crop the picture to an oval shape, apply Tight text wrapping, fix its position on the page, and then change its height to 1 inch. Drag the picture to position it so the first two lines of the fifth paragraph wrap above it, as shown in Figure 4-39.

12. At the end of the first paragraph below the "Annual Big Southwest Ride" heading, insert the drawing **Bike.png** from the Word4 > Case1 folder included with your Data Files. Change the picture's height to 1.3 inches, apply In Front of Text text wrapping, add the Center Shadow Rectangle picture style (second from right in the second row of the Picture Styles gallery), and then position the picture in the left margin, centered between the two text boxes, with a fixed position on the page, as shown in Figure 4-39.

13. Add a box page border using a line style with a thick exterior line and a thinner interior line in the default width and in the same color as the font for the "Dallas Riders Receive $3000 Grant" heading.

14. In the last paragraph, replace "Pete Del Rio" with your first and last names.

15. Make any adjustments necessary so that your newsletter matches the one shown in Figure 4-39, and then save the document.

16. Save the document as a PDF named **Biking Newsletter** in the location specified by your instructor. Review the PDF, and then close the program in which it opened.

17. In Word, open the PDF named **Biking Newsletter.pdf**, save it as **Biking Newsletter from PDF. docx**, review its contents, note the corrections you would have to make if you actually wanted to use this document, and then close it, as well as the Biking Newsletter document.

Case Problem 2

Data Files needed for this Case Problem: Ben.jpg, Franklin.docx, Treaty.docx

Benjamin Franklin Association Anne Rawson is a member of the Benjamin Franklin Association in Philadelphia, Pennsylvania, an organization of professional and amateur historians that works to promote Franklin's legacy. Anne has decided to create a series of handouts about important historical documents related to Franklin. Each handout will contain the document text, with red accent colors, along with a picture of Franklin and a text box with essential facts about Franklin and the document. Anne has asked you to help her complete her first handout, which is about the Treaty of Paris. You will create the handout shown in Figure 4-40.

Figure 4-40 **Completed Treaty of Paris handout**

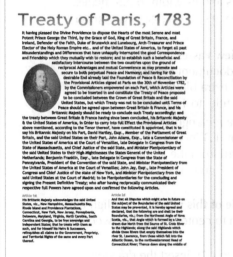

Everett Historical/Shutterstock.com

Complete the following steps:

1. Open the file **Treaty** located in the Word4 > Case2 folder included with your Data Files, and then save it as **Treaty of Paris** in the location specified by your instructor.

2. Display the document gridlines.

3. Change the theme to Facet, and format all the heading text using the Red, Accent 5 font color in the first row of the Theme Colors section of the Font Color gallery.

4. At the top of the document, add the text **Treaty of Paris, 1783** as a new paragraph, and then format it as WordArt, using the Gradient Fill - Red, Accent 1, Reflection style (the second from the left in the middle row). Add Top and Bottom text wrapping. If the position of the WordArt shifts, drag it back up to the top of the page. Change its height to .7 inches and its width to 7 inches. Apply the Square transform text effect (the first effect in the top row of the Warp section). Remove the reflection effect. Drag the WordArt as necessary to center it at the top of the page. The top edge of the text box should align with the top gridline. Don't be concerned if it extends beyond the left and right edges of the gridlines.

5. At the end of the paragraph below the WordArt, insert the picture **Ben.jpg** from the Word4 > Case2 folder included with your Data Files.

6. Apply Tight text wrapping to the photo, change the height to 2 inches, remove the portrait's gray background, leaving only the oval portrait, and then position it along the left margin, so the first six lines of regular text wrap above it, as shown in Figure 4-40.

7. Format the paragraphs containing the list of articles in two columns. (Note that the last three lines of the document are not part of the list of articles.) Use a column break to format the articles as shown in Figure 4-40, with Article 8 at the top of the second column on page 3.

8. At the end of the last paragraph on page 3, insert a preformatted text box using the Grid Sidebar style. Apply In Front of Text text wrapping, and then change the height to 3.3 inches and the width to 6.3 inches. Position the text box at the bottom of page 3, centered in the white space, with a fixed position on the page. Don't be concerned that the text box extends into the space without gridlines, at the bottom of the page.

9. Delete the placeholder text in the text box, and then insert the text of the Word document named **Franklin** from the Word4 > Case2 folder included with your Data Files. If necessary, delete any extra paragraph marks.

10. Add a box page border, using the default style in the default width and in the same color as the headings with the article numbers.

11. Make any adjustments necessary so that your newsletter matches the one shown in Figure 4-40, and then hide the gridlines.

12. At the end of the text box on page 3, insert a new, bulleted paragraph, and then insert the text **Prepared by Student Name**, with your first and last names replacing the text "Student Name." Save the document.

13. Save the document as a PDF named **Treaty of Paris.pdf** in the location specified by your instructor. Review the PDF in Acrobat or Acrobat Reader.

14. From within Acrobat or Acrobat Reader, use the appropriate keyboard shortcut to copy the text in the text box, open a new, blank Word document, and then paste the copied text into it. In a new bulleted list at the end of the document, list three differences between the formatting of the text in the current document and in the Treaty of Paris.pdf file. Format the new paragraphs in red so they are easy to spot.

15. Save the Word document as **Facts from PDF** in the location specified by your instructor, and then close it, as well as the Treaty of Paris document. Close Acrobat or Acrobat Reader.

Case Problem 3

TROUBLESHOOT

Data Files needed for this Case Problem: Porter.docx, Raffle.pdf

Porter and Mills Accounting   You are the publications manager at Porter and Mills Accounting, in Cincinnati, Ohio. Your supervisor explains that while working on the company's monthly newsletter, he left his laptop briefly unattended. His young child took advantage of the opportunity to make some unwelcome changes to his Word document. You've offered to troubleshoot the document and format the newsletter to look like the one shown in Figure 4-41. Your second task is to open a PDF containing a document announcing a charity raffle and edit the text to remove any irregularities that occurred in the conversion from a PDF to a Word document.

Figure 4-41 **Completed Porter and Mills newsletter**

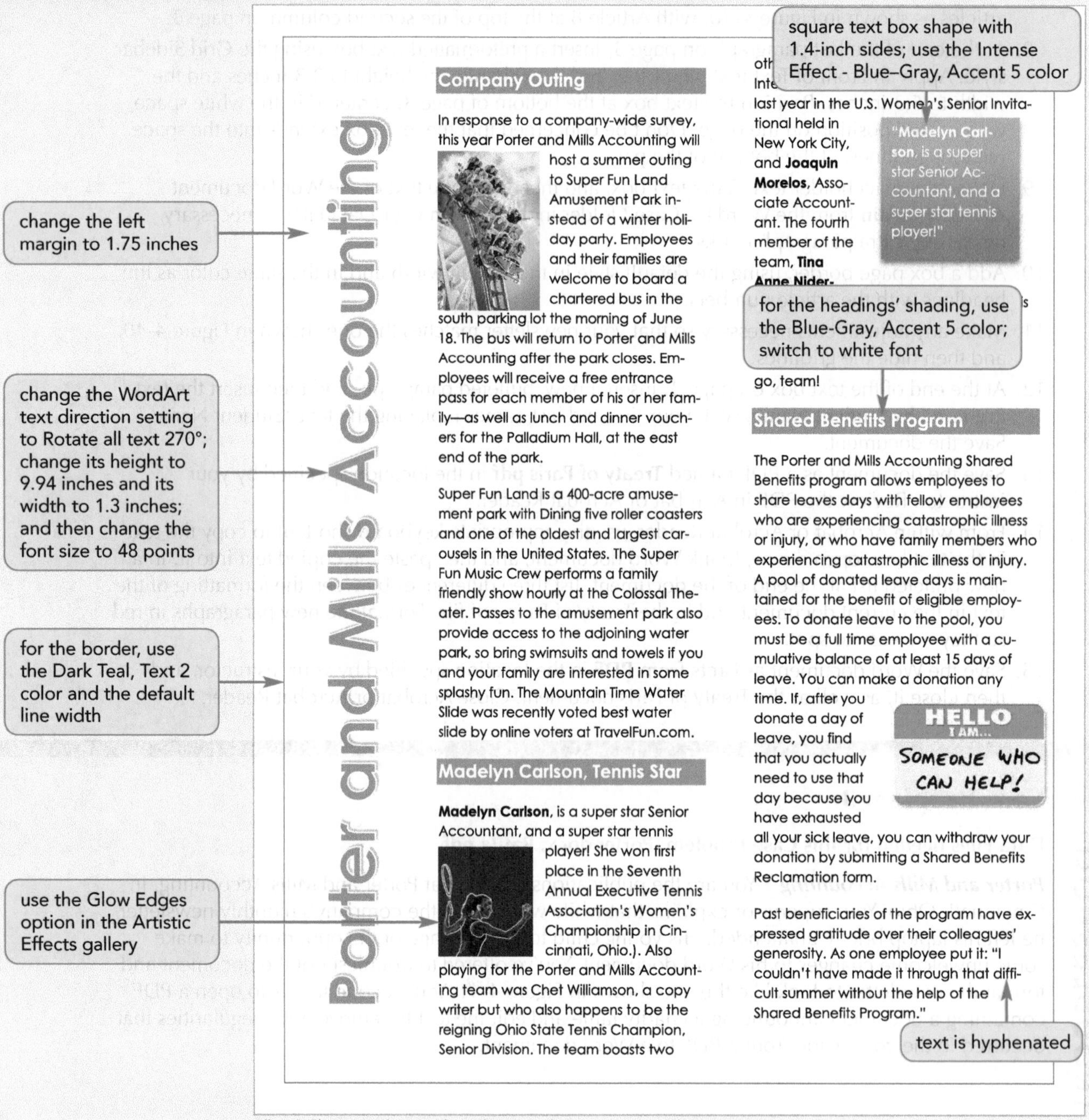

change the left margin to 1.75 inches

change the WordArt text direction setting to Rotate all text 270°; change its height to 9.94 inches and its width to 1.3 inches; and then change the font size to 48 points

for the border, use the Dark Teal, Text 2 color and the default line width

use the Glow Edges option in the Artistic Effects gallery

Porter and Mills Accounting

Company Outing

In response to a company-wide survey, this year Porter and Mills Accounting will

host a summer outing to Super Fun Land Amusement Park instead of a winter holiday party. Employees and their families are welcome to board a chartered bus in the south parking lot the morning of June 18. The bus will return to Porter and Mills Accounting after the park closes. Employees will receive a free entrance pass for each member of his or her family—as well as lunch and dinner vouchers for the Palladium Hall, at the east end of the park.

Super Fun Land is a 400-acre amusement park with Dining five roller coasters and one of the oldest and largest carousels in the United States. The Super Fun Music Crew performs a family friendly show hourly at the Colossal Theater. Passes to the amusement park also provide access to the adjoining water park, so bring swimsuits and towels if you and your family are interested in some splashy fun. The Mountain Time Water Slide was recently voted best water slide by online voters at TravelFun.com.

Madelyn Carlson, Tennis Star

Madelyn Carlson, is a super star Senior Accountant, and a super star tennis

player! She won first place in the Seventh Annual Executive Tennis Association's Women's Championship in Cincinnati, Ohio.). Also playing for the Porter and Mills Accounting team was Chet Williamson, a copy writer but who also happens to be the reigning Ohio State Tennis Champion, Senior Division. The team boasts two

oth Inte last year in the U.S. Women's Senior Invitational held in New York City, and **Joaquin Morelos**, Associate Accountant. The fourth member of the team, **Tina Anne Nider-**

square text box shape with 1.4-inch sides; use the Intense Effect - Blue–Gray, Accent 5 color

"Madelyn Carlson, is a super star Senior Accountant, and a super star tennis player!"

s

for the headings' shading, use the Blue-Gray, Accent 5 color; switch to white font

go, team!

Shared Benefits Program

The Porter and Mills Accounting Shared Benefits program allows employees to share leaves days with fellow employees who are experiencing catastrophic illness or injury, or who have family members who experiencing catastrophic illness or injury. A pool of donated leave days is maintained for the benefit of eligible employees. To donate leave to the pool, you must be a full time employee with a cumulative balance of at least 15 days of leave. You can make a donation any time. If, after you donate a day of leave, you find that you actually need to use that day because you have exhausted all your sick leave, you can withdraw your donation by submitting a Shared Benefits Reclamation form.

HELLO I AM... SOMEONE WHO CAN HELP!

Past beneficiaries of the program have expressed gratitude over their colleagues' generosity. As one employee put it: "I couldn't have made it through that difficult summer without the help of the Shared Benefits Program."

text is hyphenated

Allen.G/Shutterstock.com; Elnur/Shutterstock.com; iQoncept/Shutterstock.com

Complete the following steps:

1. Open the file **Porter** located in the Word4 > Case3 folder included with your Data Files, and then save it as **Porter and Mills** in the location specified by your instructor.

⚙ **Troubleshoot** 2. Change the border and the left margin as described in Figure 4-41.

⚙ **Troubleshoot** 3. Fix the WordArt as described in Figure 4-41, and apply column formatting as necessary.

⚙ **Troubleshoot** 4. Reset the pictures and then format, resize, and crop them to match the pictures shown in Figure 4-41. Keep in mind that you can use the Selection Task Pane to select a picture. Also, you'll need to flip one picture horizontally. You should be able to size the pictures appropriately by looking at their sizes relative to the text in Figure 4-41. You will position the pictures in the next step.

⚙ **Troubleshoot** 5. Position the pictures as shown in Figure 4-41. In the Arrange group, use the Selection Pane button and the Align Objects button to align the photo of the roller coaster and the tennis player with the left margin. Also, align the name tag image with the right margin.

6. Replace the double hyphens with an em dash.

7. In the middle of the second column, replace "Joaquin Morelos" with your first and last names.

⚙ **Troubleshoot** 8. Make any adjustments necessary so that your newsletter matches the one shown in Figure 4-41. You might need to drag the WordArt text box left slightly to keep all the text on one page. Save the document.

9. Save the document as a PDF named **Porter and Mills.pdf** in the location specified by your instructor. Review the PDF in Acrobat or Acrobat Reader, and then close Acrobat or Acrobat Reader. Close the Porter and Mills document in Word.

10. Open the PDF **Raffle.pdf** located in the Word4 > Case3 folder included with your Data Files, and then save it as a Word document named **Raffle Reminder** in the location specified by your instructor.

⚙ **Troubleshoot** 11. Edit the text to remove the WordArt and the text box, including the green textbox title. Format the remaining text as one column, and then remove any extra spaces and paragraph breaks. Keep the last two paragraphs formatted as a bulleted list. Add the default amount of paragraph spacing after each paragraph to make the text easier to read. Make any other edits necessary so that the text is formatted with consistent paragraph and line spacing throughout.

12. Save and close the document.

CREATE

Case Problem 4

There are no Data Files needed for this Case Problem.

Delicious Restaurant Design Associates   You are an intern at Delicious Restaurant Design Associates, a firm that specializes in designing restaurant interiors. As part of your training, your supervisor asks you to review examples of menu designs on the web and then re-create the first page of one of those menus in a Word document. Instead of writing the complete text of the menu, you can use placeholder text. Complete the following steps:

1. Open a new, blank document, and then save it as **Menu Design** in the location specified by your instructor.

2. Open your browser and search online for images of sample menus by searching for the keywords **restaurant menu image**. Review at least a dozen images of menus before picking a style that you want to re-create in a Word document. The style you choose should contain at least two pictures. Keep the image of the menu visible in your browser so you can return to it for reference as you work.

3. In your Word document, create the first page of the menu. To generate text that you can use to fill the page, type **=lorem()** and then press the Enter key. Change the document theme, if necessary, to a theme that provides colors and fonts that will allow you to more closely match the menu you are trying to copy. Don't worry about the menu's background color; white is fine.

4. Add at least two pictures to the menu, using pictures that you find online. Rotate or flip pictures, and remove their backgrounds as necessary to make them work in the menu layout.

5. Make any other changes necessary so that the layout and style of your document match the menu example that you found online.

6. Somewhere in the document, attach a comment that reads **I used the following webpage as a model for this menu design:**, and then include the URL for the menu image you used as a model. To copy a URL from a browser window, click the URL in the browser's Address box, and then press the Ctrl+C keys.

7. Save the document, close it, and then close your browser.

OBJECTIVES

Session 1.1
- Open and close a workbook
- Navigate through a workbook and worksheet
- Select cells and ranges
- Plan and create a workbook
- Insert, rename, and move worksheets
- Enter text, dates, and numbers
- Undo and redo actions
- Resize columns and rows

Session 1.2
- Enter formulas and the SUM and COUNT functions
- Copy and paste formulas
- Move or copy cells and ranges
- Insert and delete rows, columns, and ranges
- Create patterned text with Flash Fill
- Add cell borders and change font size
- Change worksheet views
- Prepare a workbook for printing
- Save a workbook with a new filename

Getting Started with Excel

Creating a Customer Order Report

Case | *Game Card*

Peter Lewis is part owner of Game Card, a store in Missoula, Montana, that specializes in selling vintage board games. Peter needs to track sales data, generate financial reports, create contact lists for loyal customers, and analyze market trends. He can perform all of these tasks with **Microsoft Excel 2016**, (or just **Excel**), an application used to enter, analyze, and present quantitative data. He wants to create an efficient way of tracking the company inventory and managing customer sales. Peter asks you to use Excel to create a document in which he can enter customer purchases from the store.

STARTING DATA FILES

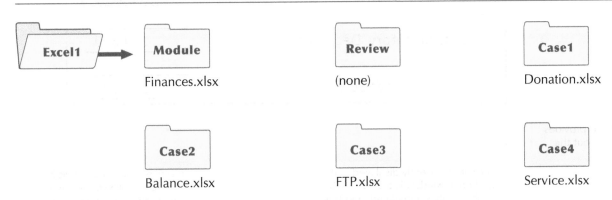

Excel1 →	**Module**	**Review**	**Case1**
	Finances.xlsx	(none)	Donation.xlsx
	Case2	**Case3**	**Case4**
	Balance.xlsx	FTP.xlsx	Service.xlsx

Session 1.1 Visual Overview:

The ribbon is organized into tabs. Each tab has commands related to particular activities or tasks.

Buttons for related commands are organized on a tab in groups.

Excel stores spreadsheets in files called workbooks. The name of the current workbook appears in the title bar.

The ribbon contains buttons that you click to execute commands to work with Excel.

The Name box displays the cell reference of the active cell. In this case, the active cell is cell H12.

The formula bar displays the value or formula entered into the active cell.

A group of cells in a rectangular block is called a cell range (or range). If the blocks are not connected, as shown here, it is a nonadjacent range.

The row headings are numbers along the left side of the workbook window that identify the different rows of the worksheet.

The status bar provides information about the workbook.

The sheet currently displayed in the workbook window is the active sheet. Its sheet tab is underlined, and the sheet name is green and bold.

Inactive sheets are not visible in the workbook window; their sheet tabs are not underlined and their sheet name is black.

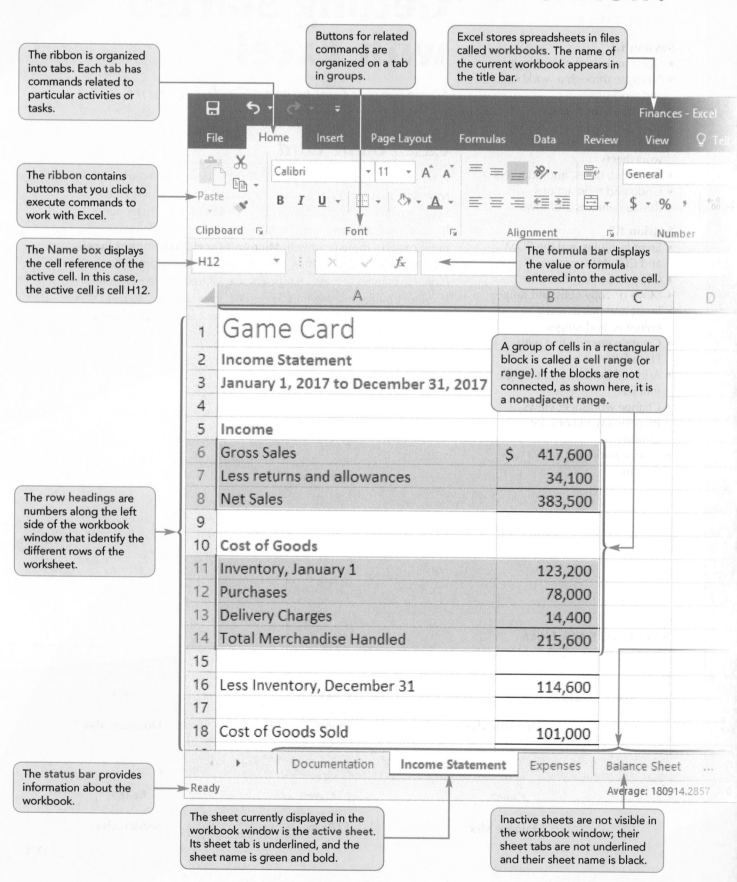

Finances - Excel

File   Home   Insert   Page Layout   Formulas   Data   Review   View

Calibri   11   A A

Paste   B I U

Clipboard   Font   Alignment   Number

H12   fx

	A	B	C	D
1	Game Card			
2	Income Statement			
3	January 1, 2017 to December 31, 2017			
4				
5	Income			
6	Gross Sales	$ 417,600		
7	Less returns and allowances	34,100		
8	Net Sales	383,500		
9				
10	Cost of Goods			
11	Inventory, January 1	123,200		
12	Purchases	78,000		
13	Delivery Charges	14,400		
14	Total Merchandise Handled	215,600		
15				
16	Less Inventory, December 31	114,600		
17				
18	Cost of Goods Sold	101,000		

Documentation   Income Statement   Expenses   Balance Sheet

Ready   Average: 180914.2857

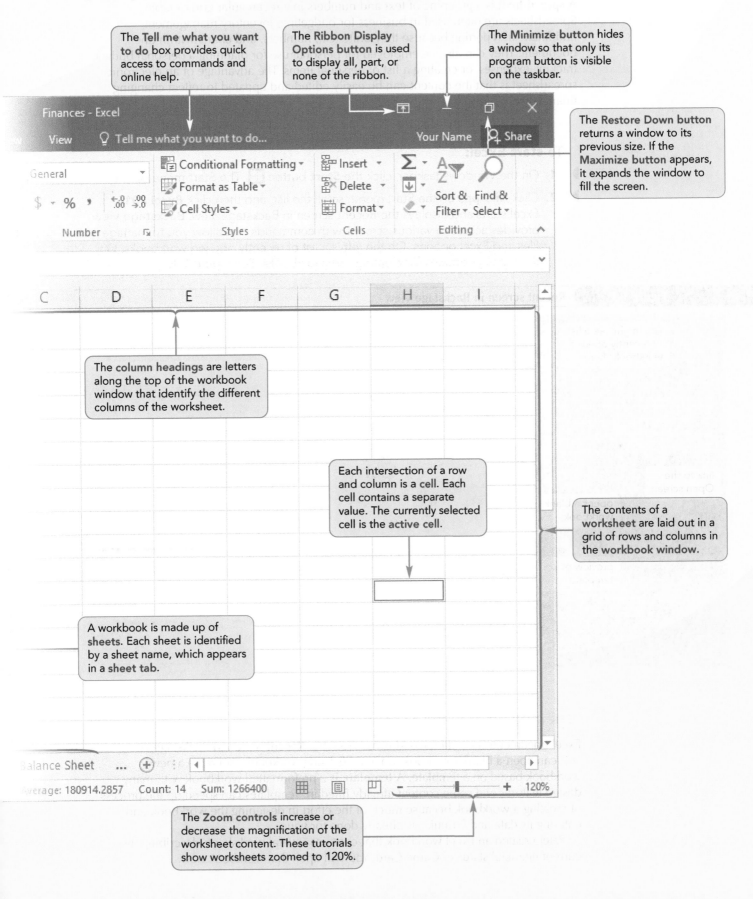

The Excel Workbook

The **Tell me what you want to do** box provides quick access to commands and online help.

The **Ribbon Display Options** button is used to display all, part, or none of the ribbon.

The **Minimize button** hides a window so that only its program button is visible on the taskbar.

The **Restore Down button** returns a window to its previous size. If the **Maximize button** appears, it expands the window to fill the screen.

The **column headings** are letters along the top of the workbook window that identify the different columns of the worksheet.

Each intersection of a row and column is a cell. Each cell contains a separate value. The currently selected cell is the **active cell**.

The contents of a **worksheet** are laid out in a grid of rows and columns in the workbook window.

A workbook is made up of **sheets**. Each sheet is identified by a sheet name, which appears in a **sheet tab**.

The **Zoom controls** increase or decrease the magnification of the worksheet content. These tutorials show worksheets zoomed to 120%.

Introducing Excel and Spreadsheets

A **spreadsheet** is a grouping of text and numbers in a rectangular grid or table. Spreadsheets are often used in business for budgeting, inventory management, and financial reporting because they unite text, numbers, and charts within one document. They can also be employed for personal use for planning a personal budget, tracking expenses, or creating a list of personal items. The advantage of an electronic spreadsheet is that the content can be easily edited and updated to reflect changing financial conditions.

To start Excel:

▶ **1.** On the Windows taskbar, click the **Start** button ⊞. The Start menu opens.

▶ **2.** Click **All Apps** on the Start menu, scroll the list, and then click **Excel 2016**. Excel starts and displays the Recent screen in Backstage view. **Backstage view** provides access to various screens with commands that allow you to manage files and Excel options. On the left is a list of recently opened workbooks. On the right are options for creating new workbooks. See Figure 1-1.

Figure 1-1	Recent screen in Backstage view

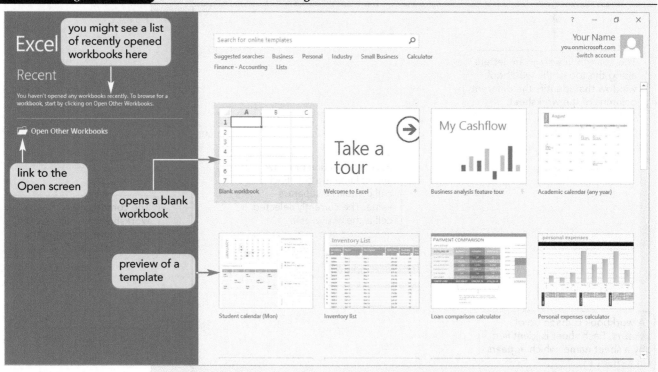

Opening an Existing Workbook

Excel documents are called workbooks. From the Recent screen in Backstage view, you can open a blank workbook, open an existing workbook, or create a new workbook based on a template. A **template** is a preformatted workbook with many design features and some content already filled in. Templates can speed up the process of creating a workbook because much of the effort in designing the workbook and entering its data and formulas is already done for you.

Peter created an Excel workbook that contains several worksheets describing the current financial status of Game Card. You will open that workbook now.

To open the Game Card financial status workbook:

▶ **1.** In the navigation bar on the Recent screen, click the **Open Other Workbooks** link. The Open screen is displayed and provides access to different locations where you might store files. The Recent Workbooks list shows the workbooks that were most recently opened on your computer.

▶ **2.** Click the **Browse** button. The Open dialog box appears.

▶ **3.** Navigate to the **Excel1 > Module** folder included with your Data Files.

   Trouble? If you don't have the starting Data Files, you need to get them before you can proceed. Your instructor will either give you the Data Files or ask you to obtain them from a specified location (such as a network drive). If you have any questions about the Data Files, see your instructor or technical support person for assistance.

▶ **4.** Click **Finances** in the file list to select it.

▶ **5.** Click the **Open** button. The workbook opens in Excel.

   Trouble? If you don't see the full ribbon as shown in the Session 1.1 Visual Overview, the ribbon may be partially or fully hidden. To pin the ribbon so that the tabs and groups are fully displayed and remain visible, click the Ribbon Display Options button, and then click Show Tabs and Commands.

▶ **6.** If the Excel window doesn't fill the screen, click the **Maximize** button in the upper-right corner of the title bar. See Figure 1-2.

| Figure 1-2 | Finances workbook |

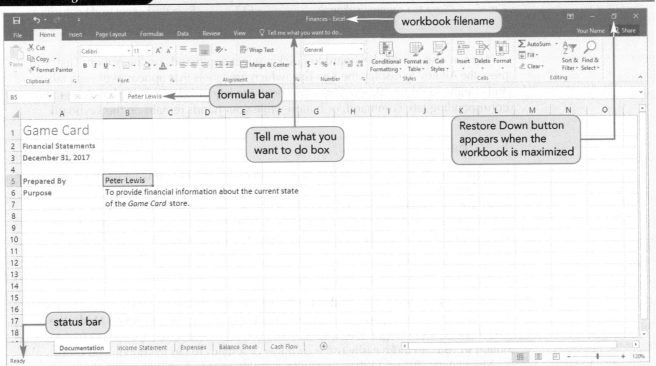

Using Keyboard Shortcuts to Work Faster

Keyboard shortcuts can help you work faster and more efficiently because you can keep your hands on the keyboard. A **keyboard shortcut** is a key or combination of keys that you press to access a feature or perform a command. Excel provides keyboard shortcuts for many commonly used commands. For example, Ctrl+S is the keyboard shortcut for the Save command, which means you hold down the Ctrl key while you press the S key to save the workbook. (Note that the plus sign is not pressed; it is used to indicate that an additional key is pressed.) When available, a keyboard shortcut is listed next to the command's name in a ScreenTip. A **ScreenTip** is a box with descriptive text about a command that appears when you point to a button on the ribbon. Figure 1-3 lists some of the keyboard shortcuts commonly used in Excel. The modules in this text show the corresponding keyboard shortcuts for accomplishing an action when available.

Figure 1-3 Excel keyboard shortcuts

Press	To	Press	To
Alt	Display the Key Tips for the commands and tools on the ribbon	Ctrl+V	Paste content that was cut or copied
Ctrl+A	Select all objects in a range	Ctrl+W	Close the current workbook
Ctrl+C	Copy the selected object(s)	Ctrl+X	Cut the selected object(s)
Ctrl+G	Go to a location in the workbook	Ctrl+Y	Repeat the last command
Ctrl+N	Open a new blank workbook	Ctrl+Z	Undo the last command
Ctrl+O	Open a saved workbook file	F1	Open the Excel Help window
Ctrl+P	Print the current workbook	F5	Go to a location in the workbook
Ctrl+S	Save the current workbook	F12	Save the current workbook with a new name or to a new location

You can also use the keyboard to quickly select commands on the ribbon. First, you press the Alt key to display the **Key Tips**, which are labels that appear over each tab and command on the ribbon. Then, you press the key or keys indicated to access the corresponding tab, command, or button while your hands remain on the keyboard.

Getting Help

If you are unsure about the function of an Excel command or you want information about how to accomplish a particular task, you can use the Help system. To access Excel Help, you either press the F1 key or enter a phrase or keyword into the Tell me what you want to do box next to the tabs on the ribbon. From this search box you can get quick access to detailed information and commands on a wide variety of Excel topics.

Using Excel 2016 in Touch Mode

You can work in Office 2016 with a keyboard and mouse or with touch. If you work with Excel on a touchscreen, you tap objects instead of clicking them. In **Touch Mode**, the ribbon increases in height, the buttons are bigger, and more space appears around each button so you can more easily use your finger or a stylus to tap the button you need.

Although the figures in these modules show the screen with Mouse Mode on, it's helpful to learn how to move between Touch Mode and Mouse Mode. You'll switch to Touch Mode and then back to Mouse Mode. If you are using a touch device, please read these steps, but do not complete them so that you remain working in Touch Mode.

To switch between Touch Mode and Mouse Mode:

▶ **1.** On the Quick Access Toolbar, click the **Customize Quick Access Toolbar** button ▾. A menu opens, listing buttons you can add to the Quick Access Toolbar as well as other options for customizing the toolbar.

   Trouble? If the Touch/Mouse Mode command on the menu has a checkmark next to it, press the Esc key to close the menu, and then skip Step 2.

▶ **2.** Click **Touch/Mouse Mode**. The Quick Access Toolbar now contains the Touch/Mouse Mode button, which you can use to switch between Mouse Mode, the default display, and Touch Mode.

▶ **3.** On the Quick Access Toolbar, click the **Touch/Mouse Mode** button. A menu opens listing Mouse and Touch, and the icon next to Mouse is shaded to indicate it is selected.

   Trouble? If the icon next to Touch is shaded, press the Esc key to close the menu and continue with Step 5.

▶ **4.** Click **Touch**. The display switches to Touch Mode with more space between the commands and buttons on the ribbon. See Figure 1-4.

| Figure 1-4 | Ribbon displayed in Touch Mode |

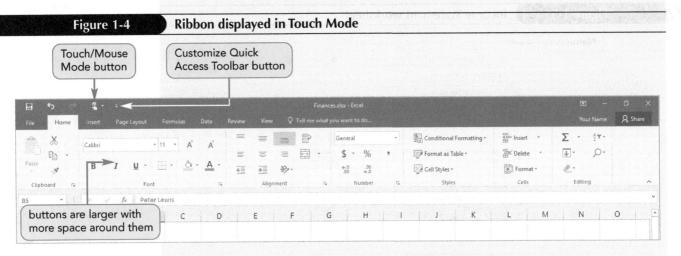

Next, you will switch back to Mouse Mode. If you are working with a touchscreen and want to use Touch Mode, skip Steps 5 and 6.

▶ **5.** On the Quick Access Toolbar, click the **Touch/Mouse Mode** button, and then click **Mouse**. The ribbon returns to Mouse Mode, as shown earlier in Figure 1-2.

▶ **6.** On the Quick Access Toolbar, click the **Customize Quick Access Toolbar** button ▾, and then click **Touch/Mouse Mode** to deselect it. The Touch/Mouse Mode button is removed from the Quick Access Toolbar.

Exploring a Workbook

Workbooks are organized into separate pages called sheets. Excel supports two types of sheets: worksheets and chart sheets. A worksheet contains a grid of rows and columns into which you can enter text, numbers, dates, and formulas and display charts. A **chart sheet** contains a chart that provides a visual representation of worksheet data. The contents of a workbook are shown in the workbook window.

Changing the Active Sheet

The sheets in a workbook are identified in the sheet tabs at the bottom of the workbook window. The Finances workbook for Game Card includes five sheets labeled Documentation, Income Statement, Expenses, Balance Sheet, and Cash Flow. The sheet currently displayed in the workbook window is the active sheet, which in this case is the Documentation sheet. To make a different sheet active and visible, you click its sheet tab. You can tell which sheet is active because its name appears in bold green.

If a workbook includes so many sheets that not all of the sheet tabs can be displayed at the same time in the workbook window, you can use the sheet tab scrolling buttons to scroll through the list of tabs. Scrolling the sheet tabs does not change the active sheet; it changes only which sheet tabs are visible.

You will view the different sheets in the Finances workbook.

To change the active sheet:

▶ **1.** Click the **Income Statement** sheet tab. The Income Statement worksheet becomes the active sheet, and its name is in bold green type. See Figure 1-5.

| Figure 1-5 | **Income Statement worksheet** |

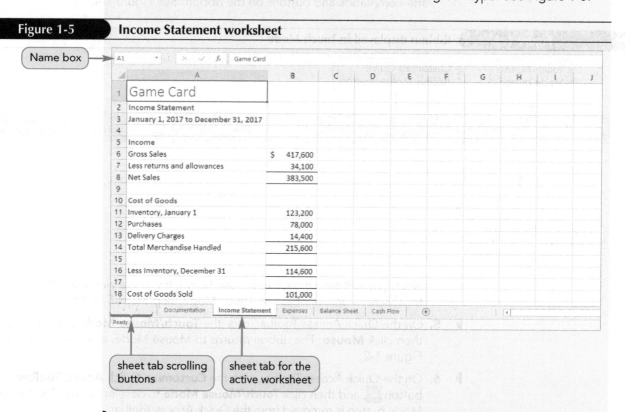

▶ **2.** Click the **Expenses** sheet tab to make it the active sheet. The Expenses sheet is an example of a chart sheet containing only an Excel chart. See Figure 1-6.

| Figure 1-6 | Expenses chart sheet |

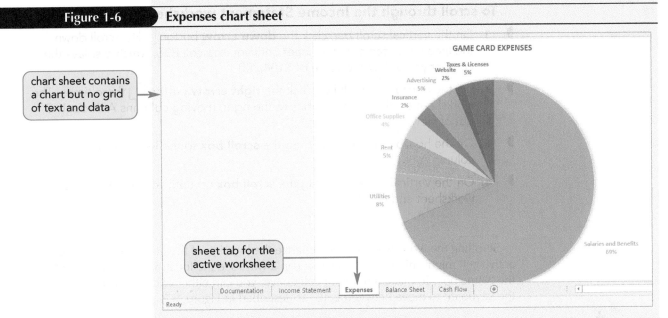

chart sheet contains a chart but no grid of text and data

GAME CARD EXPENSES

Taxes & Licenses 5%
Website 2%
Advertising 5%
Insurance 2%
Office Supplies 4%
Rent 5%
Utilities 8%
Salaries and Benefits 69%

sheet tab for the active worksheet

Documentation   Income Statement   **Expenses**   Balance Sheet   Cash Flow   ⊕

Ready

TIP

You can move to the previous or next sheet in the workbook by pressing the Ctrl+PgUp or Ctrl+PgDn keys.

▶ **3.** Click the **Balance Sheet** sheet tab to make it the active sheet. Note that this sheet contains charts embedded into the grid of data values. A worksheet can contain data values, embedded charts, pictures, and other design elements.

▶ **4.** Click the **Cash Flow** sheet tab. The worksheet with information about the company's cash flow is now active.

▶ **5.** Click the **Income Statement** sheet tab to make the Income Statement worksheet the active sheet.

Navigating Within a Worksheet

A worksheet is organized into a grid of cells. Each cell is identified by a **cell reference**, which indicates the column and row in which the cell is located. For example, in Figure 1-5, the company name, Game Card, is in cell A1, which is the intersection of column A and row 1. The column letter always appears before the row number in any cell reference. The cell that is currently selected in the worksheet is referred to as the active cell. The active cell is highlighted with a thick green border, its cell reference appears in the Name box, and the corresponding column and row headings are highlighted. The active cell in Figure 1-5 is cell A1.

Row numbers range from 1 to 1,048,576, and column labels are letters in alphabetical order. The first 26 column headings range from A to Z. After Z, the next column headings are labeled AA, AB, AC, and so forth. Excel allows a maximum of 16,384 columns in a worksheet (the last column has the heading XFD). This means that you can create large worksheets whose content extends well beyond what is visible in the workbook window.

To move different parts of the worksheet into view, you can use the horizontal and vertical scroll bars located at the bottom and right edges of the workbook window, respectively. A scroll bar has arrow buttons that you can click to shift the worksheet one column or row in the specified direction, and a scroll box that you can drag to shift the worksheet in the direction you drag.

You will scroll the active worksheet so you can review the rest of the Game Card income statement.

To scroll through the Income Statement worksheet:

▶ **1.** On the vertical scroll bar, click the **down arrow** button ▾ to scroll down the Income Statement worksheet until you see cell B36, which displays the company's net income value of $104,200.

▶ **2.** On the horizontal scroll bar, click the **right arrow** button ▶ three times. The worksheet scrolls three columns to the right, moving columns A through C out of view.

▶ **3.** On the horizontal scroll bar, drag the **scroll box** to the left until you see column A.

▶ **4.** On the vertical scroll bar, drag the **scroll box** up until you see the top of the worksheet and cell A1.

Scrolling the worksheet does not change the location of the active cell. Although the active cell might shift out of view, you can always see the location of the active cell in the Name box. To make a different cell active, you can either click a new cell or use the keyboard to move between cells, as described in Figure 1-7.

Figure 1-7	Excel navigation keys

Press	To move the active cell
↑ ↓ ← →	Up, down, left, or right one cell
Home	To column A of the current row
Ctrl+Home	To cell A1
Ctrl+End	To the last cell in the worksheet that contains data
Enter	Down one row or to the start of the next row of data
Shift+Enter	Up one row
Tab	One column to the right
Shift+Tab	One column to the left
PgUp, PgDn	Up or down one screen
Ctrl+PgUp, Ctrl+PgDn	To the previous or next sheet in the workbook

You will use both your mouse and your keyboard to change the location of the active cell in the Income Statement worksheet.

To change the active cell:

▶ **1.** Move your pointer over cell **A5**, and then click the mouse button. The active cell moves from cell A1 to cell A5. A green border appears around cell A5, the column heading for column A and the row heading for row 5 are both highlighted, and the cell reference in the Name box changes from A1 to A5.

▶ **2.** Press the → key. The active cell moves one cell to the right to cell B5.

▶ **3.** Press the **PgDn** key on your keyboard. The active cell moves down one full screen.

▶ **4.** Press the **PgUp** key. The active cell moves up one full screen, returning to cell B5.

▶ **5.** Press the **Ctrl+Home** keys. The active cell returns to the first cell in the worksheet, cell A1.

The mouse and keyboard provide quick ways to navigate the active worksheet. For larger worksheets that span several screens, you can move directly to a specific cell using the Go To command or by typing a cell reference in the Name box. You will try both of these methods.

To use the Go To dialog box and the Name box:

▶ **1.** On the Home tab, in the Editing group, click the **Find & Select** button, and then click **Go To** on the menu that opens (or press the **Ctrl+G** keys). The Go To dialog box opens.

▶ **2.** Type **B34** in the Reference box. See Figure 1-8.

Figure 1-8 ▶ **Go To dialog box**

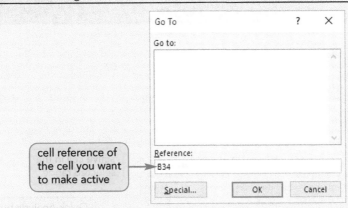

cell reference of the cell you want to make active

▶ **3.** Click the **OK** button. Cell B34 becomes the active cell, displaying 182,000, which is the total expenses for Game Card. Because cell B34 is the active cell, its cell reference appears in the Name box.

▶ **4.** Click in the Name box, type **A1**, and then press the **Enter** key. Cell A1 is again the active cell.

Selecting a Cell Range

Many tasks in Excel require you to work with a group of cells. A group of cells in a rectangular block is called a cell range (or simply a range). Each range is identified with a **range reference** that includes the cell reference of the upper-left cell of the rectangular block and the cell reference of the lower-right cell separated by a colon. For example, the range reference A1:G5 refers to all of the cells in the rectangular block from cell A1 through cell G5.

As with individual cells, you can select cell ranges using your mouse, the keyboard, or commands. You will select a range in the Income Statement worksheet.

To select a cell range:

1. Click cell **A5** to select it, and without releasing the mouse button, drag down to cell **B8**.

2. Release the mouse button. The range A5:B8 is selected. The selected cells are highlighted and surrounded by a green border. The first cell you selected in the range, cell A5, is the active cell in the worksheet. The active cell in a selected range is white. The Quick Analysis button appears, providing options for working with the range; you will use this button in another module. See Figure 1-9.

| Figure 1-9 | Range A5:B8 selected |

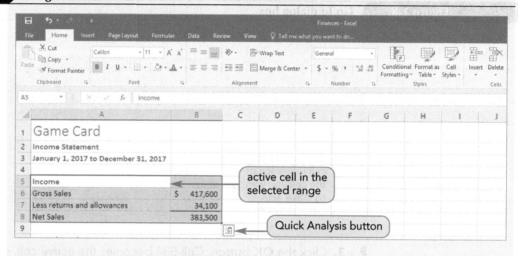

3. Click cell **A1** to deselect the range.

Another type of range is a nonadjacent range, which is a collection of separate rectangular ranges. The range reference for a nonadjacent range includes the range reference to each range separated by a comma. For example, the range reference A1:G5,A10:G15 includes two ranges—the first range is the rectangular block of cells from cell A1 to cell G5, and the second range is the rectangular block of cells from cell A10 to cell G15.

You will select a nonadjacent range in the Income Statement worksheet.

To select a nonadjacent range in the Income Statement worksheet:

1. Click cell **A5**, hold down the **Shift** key as you click cell **B8**, and then release the **Shift** key to select the range A5:B8.

2. Hold down the **Ctrl** key as you drag to select the range **A10:B14**, and then release the **Ctrl** key. The two separate blocks of cells in the nonadjacent range A5:B8,A10:B14 are selected. See Figure 1-10.

Figure 1-10   **Nonadjacent range A5:B8,A10:B14 selected**

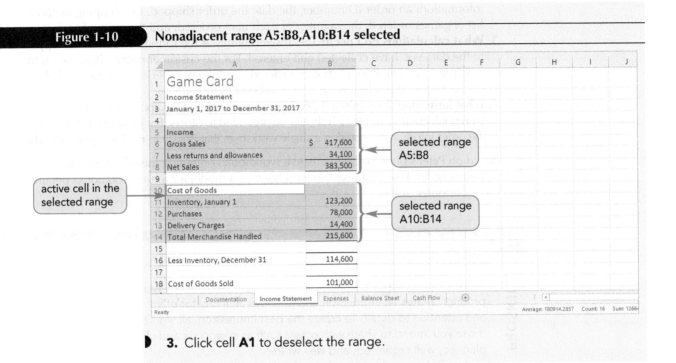

3. Click cell **A1** to deselect the range.

Closing a Workbook

Once you are finished with a workbook you can close it. When you close a workbook, a dialog box might open, asking whether you want to save any changes you may have made to the document. If you have made changes that you want to keep, you should save the workbook. Since you have finished reviewing the financial workbook for Game Card, you will close it without saving any changes you may have inadvertently made to the document contents.

To close the workbook:

1. On the ribbon, click the **File** tab to display Backstage view, and then click **Close** in the navigation bar (or press the **Ctrl+W** keys).

2. If a dialog box opens, asking whether you want to save your changes to the workbook, click the **Don't Save** button. The workbook closes without saving any changes. Excel remains opens, ready for you to create or open another workbook.

Planning a Workbook

It's good practice to plan out your workbooks before you begin creating them. You can do this by using a planning analysis sheet, which includes the following questions that help you think about the workbook's purpose and how to achieve your desired results:

1. **What problems do I want to solve?** The answer identifies the goal or purpose of the workbook. For example, Peter wants you to record customer orders and be able to analyze details from these orders.

2. **What data do I need?** The answer identifies the type of data that you need to collect and enter into the workbook. For example, Peter needs customer contact

information, an order ID number, the date the order shipped, the shipping method, a list of games ordered, the quantity of each item ordered, and the price of each item.

3. **What calculations do I need?** The answer identifies the formulas you need to apply to the data you have collected and entered. For the customer orders, Peter needs to calculate the charge for each item ordered, the total number of items ordered, the shipping cost, the sales tax, and the total cost of the order.

4. **What form should my solution take?** The answer impacts the appearance of the workbook content and how it should be presented to others. For example, Peter wants the order information stored in a single worksheet that is easy to read and prints clearly.

Based on Peter's plan, you will create a workbook containing the details of a recent customer order. Peter will use this workbook as a model for future workbooks detailing other customer orders.

PROSKILLS

Written Communication: Creating Effective Workbooks

Workbooks convey information in written form. As with any type of writing, the final product creates an impression and provides an indicator of your interest, knowledge, and attention to detail. To create the best impression, all workbooks—especially those you intend to share with others such as coworkers and clients—should be well planned, well organized, and well written.

A well-designed workbook should clearly identify its overall goal and present information in an organized format. The data it includes—both the entered values and the calculated values—should be accurate. The process of developing an effective workbook includes the following steps:

- Determine the workbook's purpose, content, and organization before you start.
- Create a list of the sheets used in the workbook, noting each sheet's purpose.
- Insert a documentation sheet that describes the workbook's purpose and organization. Include the name of the workbook author, the date the workbook was created, and any additional information that will help others to track the workbook to its source.
- Enter all of the data in the workbook. Add labels to indicate what the values represent and, if possible, where they originated so others can view the source of your data.
- Enter formulas for calculated items rather than entering the calculated values into the workbook. For more complicated calculations, provide documentation explaining them.
- Test the workbook with a variety of values; edit the data and formulas to correct errors.
- Save the workbook and create a backup copy when the project is completed. Print the workbook's contents if you need to provide a hard-copy version to others or for your files.
- Maintain a history of your workbook as it goes through different versions, so that you and others can quickly see how the workbook has changed during revisions.

By including clearly written documentation, explanatory text, a logical organization, and accurate data and formulas, you will create effective workbooks that others can use easily.

Starting a New Workbook

You create new workbooks from the New screen in Backstage view. Similar to the Recent screen that opened when you started Excel, the New screen includes templates for a variety of workbook types. You can see a preview of what the different workbooks will look like. You will create a new workbook from the Blank workbook template, in which you can add all of the content and design Peter wants for the Game Card customer order worksheet.

To start a new, blank workbook:

▶ **1.** On the ribbon, click the **File** tab to display Backstage view.

▶ **2.** Click **New** in the navigation bar to display the New screen, which includes access to templates for a variety of workbooks.

▶ **3.** Click the **Blank workbook** tile. A blank workbook opens.

In these modules, the workbook window is zoomed to 120% for better readability. If you want to zoom your workbook window to match the figures, complete Step 4. If you prefer to work in the default zoom of 100% or at another zoom level, read but do not complete Step 4; you might see more or less of the worksheet on your screen, but this will not affect your work in the modules.

▶ **4.** If you want your workbook window zoomed to 120% to match the figures, on the Zoom slider at the bottom-right of the program window, click the **Zoom In** button ➕ twice to increase the percentage to 120%. The 120% magnification increases the size of each cell but reduces the number of worksheet cells visible in the workbook window. See Figure 1-11.

TIP

You can also create a new, blank workbook by pressing the Ctrl+N keys.

Figure 1-11 **Blank workbook**

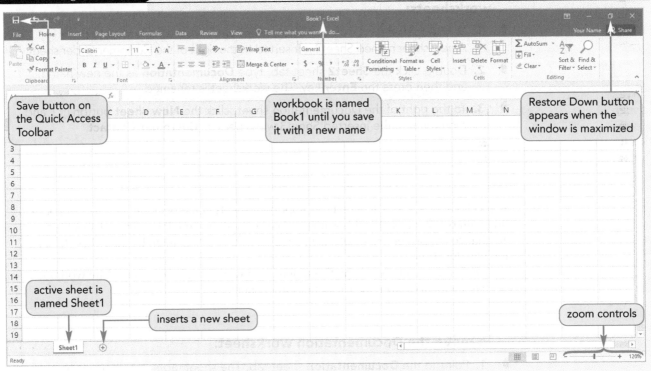

The name of the active workbook, Book1, appears in the title bar. If you open multiple blank workbooks, they are named Book1, Book2, Book3, and so forth until you save them with a more descriptive name.

Renaming and Inserting Worksheets

Blank workbooks open with a single blank worksheet named Sheet1. You can give sheets more descriptive and meaningful names. This is a good practice so that you and others can easily tell what a sheet contains. Sheet names cannot exceed 31 characters, but they can contain blank spaces and include uppercase and lowercase letters.

Because Sheet1 is not a very descriptive name, Peter wants you to rename the worksheet as Customer Order.

To rename the Sheet1 worksheet:

▶ **1.** Double-click the **Sheet1** tab. The Sheet1 label in the tab is selected.

▶ **2.** Type **Customer Order** as the new name, and then press the **Enter** key. The width of the sheet tab expands to fit the longer sheet name.

Many workbooks include multiple sheets so that data can be organized in logical groups. A common business practice is to include a worksheet named Documentation that contains a description of the workbook, the name of the person who prepared the workbook, and the date it was created.

Peter wants you to create two new worksheets. You will rename one worksheet as Documentation and the other worksheet as Customer Contact. The Customer Contact worksheet will be used to store the customer's contact information.

To insert and name the Documentation and Customer Contact worksheets:

▶ **1.** To the right of the Customer Order sheet tab, click the **New sheet** button ⊕. A new sheet named Sheet2 is inserted to the right of the Customer Order sheet.

▶ **2.** Double-click the **Sheet2** sheet tab, type **Documentation** as the new name, and then press the **Enter** key. The worksheet is renamed.

▶ **3.** To the right of the Documentation sheet, click the **New sheet** button ⊕, and then rename the inserted Sheet3 worksheet as **Customer Contact**.

Moving Worksheets

A good practice is to place the most important sheets at the beginning of the workbook (the leftmost sheet tabs) and less important sheets at the end (the rightmost sheet tabs). To change the placement of sheets in a workbook, you drag them by their sheet tabs to the new location.

Peter wants you to move the Documentation worksheet to the front of the workbook, so that it appears before the Customer Order sheet.

To move the Documentation worksheet:

▶ **1.** Point to the **Documentation** sheet tab. The sheet tab name changes to bold.

TIP

To copy a sheet, hold down the Ctrl key as you drag and drop its sheet tab.

▶ **2.** Press and hold the mouse button. The pointer changes to ▯, and a small arrow appears in the upper-left corner of the tab.

▶ **3.** Drag to the left until the small arrow appears in the upper-left corner of the Customer Order sheet tab, and then release the mouse button. The Documentation worksheet is now the first sheet in the workbook.

Deleting Worksheets

In some workbooks, you will want to delete an existing sheet. The easiest way to delete a sheet is by using a **shortcut menu**, which is a list of commands related to a selection that opens when you click the right mouse button. Peter asks you to include the customer's contact information on the Customer Order worksheet so all of the information is on one sheet.

To delete the Customer Contact worksheet from the workbook:

▶ **1.** Right-click the **Customer Contact** sheet tab. A shortcut menu opens.

▶ **2.** Click **Delete**. The Customer Contact worksheet is removed from the workbook.

Saving a Workbook

As you modify a workbook, you should save it regularly—every 10 minutes or so is a good practice. The first time you save a workbook, the Save As dialog box opens so you can name the file and choose where to save it. You can save the workbook on your computer or network or to your account on OneDrive.

To save your workbook for the first time:

▶ **1.** On the Quick Access Toolbar, click the **Save** button 🖫 (or press the **Ctrl+S** keys). The Save As screen in Backstage view opens.

▶ **2.** Click the **Browse** button. The Save As dialog box opens.

▶ **3.** Navigate to the location specified by your instructor.

▶ **4.** In the File name box, select **Book1** (the suggested name) if it is not already selected, and then type **Game Card**.

▶ **5.** Verify that **Excel Workbook** appears in the Save as type box.

▶ **6.** Click the **Save** button. The workbook is saved, the dialog box closes, and the workbook window reappears with the new filename in the title bar.

As you modify the workbook, you will need to resave the file. Because you already saved the workbook with a filename, the next time you save, the Save command saves the changes you made to the workbook without opening the Save As dialog box.

Entering Text, Dates, and Numbers

Workbook content is entered into worksheet cells. Those cells can contain text, numbers, or dates and times. **Text data** is any combination of letters, numbers, and symbols. Text data is often referred to as a **text string** because it contains a series, or string, of text characters. **Numeric data** is any number that can be used in a mathematical calculation. **Date** and **time data** are commonly recognized formats for date and time values. For example, Excel interprets the cell entry April 15, 2017 as a date and not as text. New data is placed into the active cell of the current worksheet. As you enter data, the entry appears in both the active cell and the formula bar. By default, text is left-aligned in cells, and numbers, dates, and times are right-aligned.

Entering Text

Text is often used in worksheets to label other data and to identify areas of a sheet. Peter wants you to enter some of the information from the planning analysis sheet into the Documentation sheet.

To enter text in the Documentation sheet:

1. Go to the **Documentation** sheet, and then click the **Ctrl+Home** keys to make sure cell A1 is the active cell.

2. Type **Game Card** in cell A1. As you type, the text appears in cell A1 and in the formula bar.

3. Press the **Enter** key twice. The text is entered into cell A1, and the active cell moves down two rows to cell A3.

4. Type **Author** in cell A3, and then press the **Tab** key. The text is entered and the active cell moves one column to the right to cell B3.

5. Type your name in cell B3, and then press the **Enter** key. The text is entered and the active cell moves one cell down and to the left to cell A4.

6. Type **Date** in cell A4, and then press the **Tab** key. The text is entered, and the active cell moves one column to the right to cell B4, where you would enter the date you created the worksheet. For now, you will leave the cell for the date blank.

7. Press the **Enter** key to make cell A5 the active cell, type **Purpose** in the cell, and then press the **Tab** key. The active cell moves one column to the right to cell B5.

8. Type **To record customer game orders** in cell B5, and then press the **Enter** key. Figure 1-12 shows the text entered in the Documentation sheet.

Figure 1-12   **Text entered in the Documentation sheet**

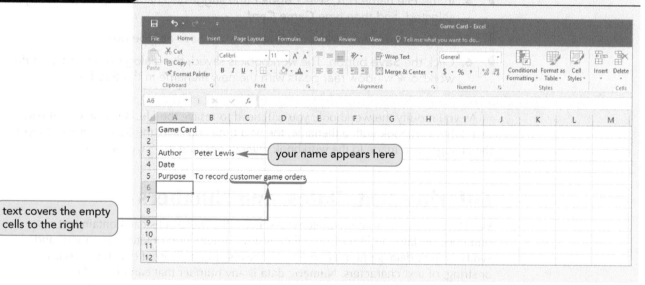

The text strings you entered in cells A1, B3, and B5 are so long that they cover the adjacent cells. Any text you enter in a cell that doesn't fit within that cell will cover the adjacent cells to the right as long as they are empty. If the adjacent cells contain data, only the text that fits into the cell is displayed. The rest of the text entry is hidden from view. The text itself is not affected. The complete text is still entered in the cell; it is just not displayed. (You will learn how to display all text in a cell in the next session.)

Undoing and Redoing an Action

As you enter data in a workbook, you might need to undo a previous action. Excel maintains a list of the actions you performed in the workbook during the current session, so you can undo most of your actions. You can use the Undo button on the Quick Access Toolbar or press the Ctrl+Z keys to reverse your most recent actions one at a time. If you want to undo more than one action, you can click the Undo button arrow and then select the earliest action you want to undo—all of the actions after the earliest action you selected are also undone.

You will undo the most recent change you made to the Documentation sheet—the text you entered into cell B5. Then you will enter more descriptive and accurate description of the worksheet's purpose.

To undo the text entry in cell B5:

▶ **1.** On the Quick Access Toolbar, click the **Undo** button ⟲ (or press the **Ctrl+Z** keys). The last action is reversed, removing the text you entered in cell B5.

▶ **2.** In cell B5, type **To record purchases of board games from Game Card**, and then press the **Enter** key.

If you want to restore actions you have undone, you can redo them. To redo one action at a time, you can click the Redo button ⟳ on the Quick Access Toolbar or press the Ctrl+Y keys. To redo multiple actions at once, you can click the Redo button arrow ⟳ ▾ and then click the earliest action you want to redo. After you undo or redo an action, Excel continues the action list starting from any new changes you make to the workbook.

Editing Cell Content

As you continue to create your workbook, you might find mistakes you need to correct or entries that you want to change. To replace all of the content in a cell, you simply select the cell and then type the new entry to overwrite the previous entry. However, if you need to replace only part of a cell's content, you can work in **Edit mode**. To switch to Edit mode, you double-click the cell. A blinking insertion point indicates where the new content you type will be inserted. In the cell or formula bar, the pointer changes to an I-beam, which you can use to select text in the cell. Anything you type replaces the selected content.

Because customers can order more than just games from Game Card, Peter wants you to edit the text in cell B5. You will do that in Edit mode.

To edit the text in cell B5:

▶ **1.** Double-click cell **B5** to select the cell and switch to Edit mode. A blinking insertion point appears within the text of cell B5. The status bar displays Edit instead of Ready to indicate that the cell is in Edit mode.

▶ **2.** Press the **arrow keys** to move the insertion point directly to the left of the word "from" in the cell text.

▶ **3.** Type **and other items** and then press the **spacebar**. The cell now reads "To record purchases of board games and other items from Game Card." See Figure 1-13.

| Figure 1-13 | Edited text in the Documentation sheet |

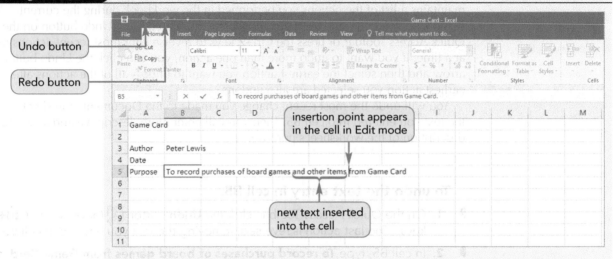

> **4.** Press the **Enter** key to exit the cell and return to Ready mode.

Understanding AutoComplete

As you type text in the active cell, Excel tries to anticipate the remaining characters by displaying text that begins with the same letters as a previous entry in the same column. This feature, known as **AutoComplete**, helps make entering repetitive text easier. To accept the suggested text, press the Tab or Enter key. To override the suggested text, continue to type the text you want to enter in the cell. AutoComplete does not work with dates or numbers or when a blank cell is between the previous entry and the text you are typing.

Next, you will enter the contact information for Leslie Ritter, a customer from Brockton, Massachusetts, who recently placed an order with Game Card. You will enter this information on the Customer Order worksheet.

To enter Leslie Ritter's contact information:

> **1.** Click the **Customer Order** sheet tab to make it the active sheet.

> **2.** In cell A1, type **Customer Order** as the worksheet title, and then press the **Enter** key twice. The worksheet title is entered in cell A1, and the active cell becomes cell A3.

> **3.** Type **Ship To** in cell A3, and then press the **Enter** key. The label is entered in the cell, and the active cell is now cell A4.

> **4.** In the range A4:A10, enter the following labels, pressing the **Enter** key after each entry and ignoring any AutoComplete suggestions: **First Name**, **Last Name**, **Address**, **City**, **State**, **Postal Code**, and **Phone**.

> **5.** Click cell **B4** to make that cell the active cell.

> **6.** In the range B4:B10, enter the following contact information, pressing the **Enter** key after each entry and ignoring any AutoComplete suggestions: **Leslie**, **Ritter**, **805 Mountain St.**, **Brockton**, **MA**, **02302**, and **(508) 555-1072**. See Figure 1-14.

| Figure 1-14 | Customer information entered in the Customer Order worksheet |

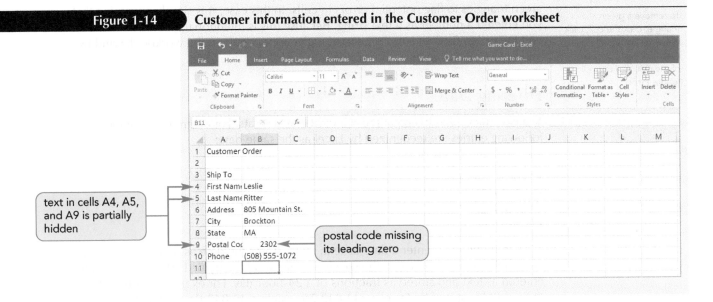

text in cells A4, A5, and A9 is partially hidden

postal code missing its leading zero

Displaying Numbers as Text

When you enter a number in a cell, Excel treats the entry as a number and ignores any leading zero. For example, in cell B9, the leading zero in the postal code 02302 is missing. Excel displays 2302 because it treats the postal code as a number, and 2302 and 02302 have the same value. To specify that a number entry should be considered text and all digits should be displayed, you include an apostrophe (') before the numbers.

To enter the postal code as text:

▶ 1. Click cell **B9** to select it. Notice that the postal code is right-aligned in the cell, unlike the other text entries, which are left-aligned—another indication that the entry is being treated as a number.

▶ 2. Type **'02302** in cell B9, and then press the **Enter** key. The text 02302 appears in cell B9 and is left-aligned in the cell, matching all of the other text entries.

▶ 3. Click cell **B9** to select it again. See Figure 1-15.

| Figure 1-15 | Number entered as text |

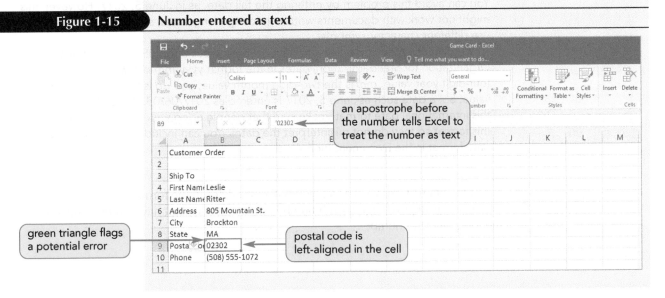

an apostrophe before the number tells Excel to treat the number as text

green triangle flags a potential error

postal code is left-aligned in the cell

TIP

To remove a green triangle, click the cell, click the yellow caution icon that appears to the left of the cell, and then click Ignore Error.

Notice that a green triangle appears in the upper-left corner of cell B9. Excel uses green triangles to flag potential errors in cells. In this case, it is simply a warning that you entered a number as a text string. Because this is intentional, you do not have to edit the cell to fix the "error." Green triangles appear only in the workbook window and not in any printouts of the worksheet.

Entering Dates

You can enter dates in any of the standard date formats. For example, all of the following entries are recognized by Excel as the same date:

- 4/6/2017
- 4/6/17
- 4-6-2017
- April 6, 2017
- 6-Apr-17

Even though you enter a date as text, Excel stores the date as a number equal to the number of days between the specified date and January 0, 1900. Times are also entered as text and stored as fractions of a 24-hour day. For example April 4, 2017 @ 6:00 PM is stored by Excel as 42,842.75 which is 42,842 days after January 0, 1900 plus 3/4 of one day. Dates and times are stored as numbers so that Excel can easily perform date and time calculations, such as determining the elapsed time between one date and another.

Based on the default date format your computer uses, Excel might alter the format of a date after you type it. For example, if you enter the date 4/6/17 into the active cell, Excel might display the date with the four-digit year value, 4/6/2017; if you enter the text April 6, 2017, Excel might change the date format to 6-Apr-17. Changing the date or time format does not affect the underlying date or time value.

International Date Formats

As business transactions become more international in scope, you may need to adopt international standards for expressing dates, times, and currency values in your workbooks. For example, a worksheet cell might contain 06/05/17. This format could be interpreted as any of the following dates: the 5th of June, 2017; the 6th of May, 2017; and the 17th of May, 2006.

The interpretation depends on which country the workbook has been designed for. You can avoid this problem by entering the full date, as in June 5, 2017. However, this might not work with documents written in foreign languages, such as Japanese, that use different character symbols.

To solve this problem, many international businesses adopt ISO (International Organization for Standardization) dates in the format *yyyy-mm-dd*, where *yyyy* is the four-digit year value, *mm* is the two-digit month value, and *dd* is the two-digit day value. So, a date such as June 5, 2017 is entered as 2017/06/05. If you choose to use this international date format, make sure that people using your workbook understand this format so they do not misinterpret the dates. You can include information about the date format in the Documentation sheet.

For the Game Card workbook, you will enter dates in the format *mm/dd/yyyy*, where *mm* is the two-digit month number, *dd* is the two-digit day number, and *yyyy* is the four-digit year number.

To enter the current date into the Documentation sheet:

▶ **1.** Click the **Documentation** sheet tab to make the Documentation sheet the active worksheet.

▶ **2.** Click cell **B4** to make it the active cell, type the current date in the *mm/dd/yyyy* format, and then press the **Enter** key. The date is entered in the cell.

   Trouble? Depending on your system configuration, Excel might change the date to the date format *dd-mmm-yy*. This difference will not affect your work.

▶ **3.** Click the **Customer Order** sheet tab to return to the Customer Order worksheet.

The next part of the Customer Order worksheet will list the items that customer Leslie Ritter purchased from Game Card. As shown in Figure 1-16, the list includes identifying information about each item, including the item's price, and the quantity of each item ordered.

Figure 1-16	Customer order from Leslie Ritter

Stock ID	Category	Manufacturer	Title	Players	Price	Qty
SG71	Strategy Game	Drebeck Brothers	Kings and Jacks: A Medieval Game of Deception	4	$39.95	2
FG14	Family Game	Misty Games	Twirple, Tweedle, and Twaddle	6	$24.55	1
PG05	Party Game	Parlor Vision	Trivia Connection	8	$29.12	1
SU38	Supplies	Parlor Vision	Box of Dice (10)		$9.95	3
SG29	Strategy Game	Drebeck Brothers	Solar Warfare	2	$35.15	1

You will enter the first four columns of the order into the worksheet.

To enter the first part of the customer order:

▶ **1.** In the Customer Order worksheet, click cell **A12** to make it the active cell, type **Stock ID** as the column label, and then press the **Tab** key to move to cell B12.

▶ **2.** In the range B12:D12, type the following labels, pressing the **Tab** key to move to the next cell: **Category**, **Manufacturer**, and **Title**.

▶ **3.** Press the **Enter** key to go to the next row of the worksheet, making cell A13 the active cell.

▶ **4.** In the range A13:D17, type the Stock ID, Category, Manufacturer, and Title text for the five items purchased by Leslie Ritter listed in Figure 1-16, pressing the **Tab** key to move from one cell to the next, and pressing the **Enter** key to move to a new row. Note that the text in some cells will be partially hidden; you will fix that problem shortly. See Figure 1-17.

Figure 1-17   Partial customer order

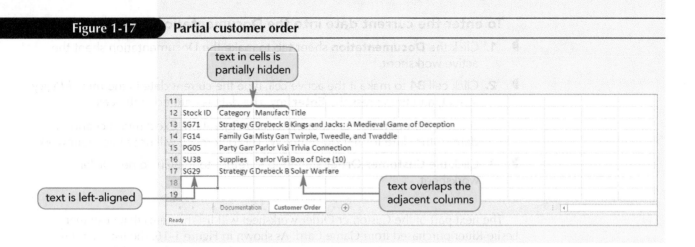

text in cells is partially hidden

text is left-aligned

text overlaps the adjacent columns

Entering Numbers

In Excel, numbers can be integers such as 378, decimals such as 1.95, or negatives such as –5.2. In the case of currency and percentages, you can include the currency symbol and percent sign when you enter the value. Excel treats a currency value such as $87.25 as the number 87.25, and a percentage such as 95% as the decimal 0.95. Much like dates, currency and percentages are formatted in a convenient way for you to read, but only the number is stored within the cell. This makes it easier to perform calculations with currency and percentage values.

You will complete Leslie Ritter's order by entering the players, price, and quantity values.

To enter the rest of the customer order:

▶ **1.** In the range E12:G12, enter **Players**, **Price**, and **Qty** as the labels.

▶ **2.** In cell E13, enter **4** as the number of players for the game Kings and Jacks.

▶ **3.** In cell F13, enter **$39.95** as the price of the game. The game price is stored as a number but displayed with the $ symbol.

▶ **4.** In cell G13, enter **2** as the quantity of the game ordered by Leslie.

▶ **5.** In the range E14:G17, enter the remaining number of players, prices, and quantities shown earlier in Figure 1-16. See Figure 1-18.

Figure 1-18   Completed customer order

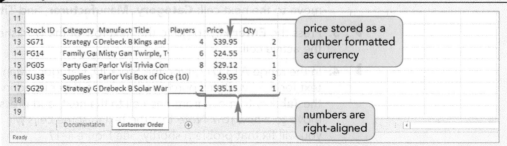

price stored as a number formatted as currency

numbers are right-aligned

▶ **6.** On the Quick Access Toolbar, click the **Save** button 🖫 (or press the **Ctrl+S** keys) to save the workbook.

Resizing Columns and Rows

Much of the information in the Customer Order worksheet is difficult to read because of the hidden text. You can display all of the cell contents by changing the size of the columns and rows in the worksheet.

Changing Column Widths

Column widths are expressed as the number of characters the column can contain. The default column width is 8.43 standard-sized characters. In general, this means that you can type eight characters in a cell; any additional text is hidden or overlaps the adjacent cell. Column widths are also expressed in terms of pixels. A **pixel** is a single point on a computer monitor or printout. A column width of 8.43 characters is equivalent to 64 pixels.

INSIGHT

Setting Column Widths

On a computer monitor, pixel size is based on screen resolution. As a result, cell contents that look fine on one screen might appear very different when viewed on a screen with a different resolution. If you work on multiple computers or share your workbooks with others, you should set column widths based on the maximum number of characters you want displayed in the cells rather than pixel size. This ensures that everyone sees the cell contents the way you intended.

You will increase the width of column A so that the contact information labels in cells A4, A5, and A9 are completely displayed.

To increase the width of column A:

▶ **1.** Point to the **right border** of the column A heading until the pointer changes to ✛.

▶ **2.** Click and drag to the right until the width of the column heading reaches **15** characters, but do not release the mouse button. The ScreenTip that appears as you resize the column shows the new column width in characters and in pixels. See Figure 1-19.

Figure 1-19   **Width of column A increased to 15 characters**

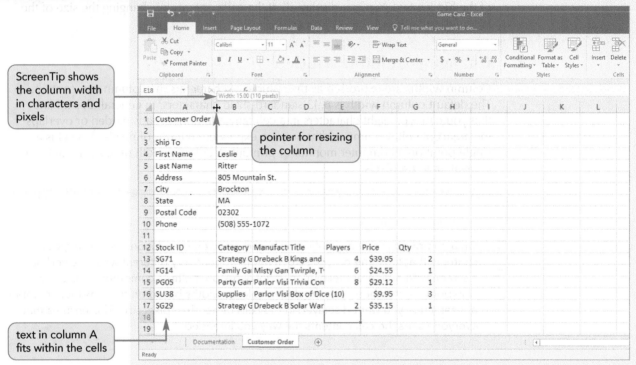

ScreenTip shows the column width in characters and pixels

pointer for resizing the column

text in column A fits within the cells

> 3. Release the mouse button. The width of column A expands to 15 characters, and all of the text within that column is visible within the cells.

You will increase the widths of columns B and C to 18 characters so that their complete entries are visible. Rather than resizing each column separately, you can select both columns and adjust their widths at the same time.

To increase the widths of columns B and C:

> 1. Click the **column B** heading. The entire column is selected.

TIP

To select adjacent columns, you can also click and drag the pointer over multiple column headings.

> 2. Hold down the **Ctrl** key, click the **column C** heading, and then release the **Ctrl** key. Both columns B and C are selected.

> 3. Point to the **right border** of the column C heading until the pointer changes to ✛.

> 4. Drag to the right until the column width changes to **18** characters, and then release the mouse button. Both column widths increase to 18 characters and display all of the entered text.

Using the mouse to resize columns can be imprecise and a challenge to some users with special needs. The Format command on the Home tab gives you precise control over column width and row height settings. You will use the Format command to set the width of column D to exactly 25 characters so that the hidden text is visible.

To set the width of column D using the Format command:

▶ **1.** Click the **column D** heading. The entire column is selected.

▶ **2.** On the Home tab, in the Cells group, click the **Format** button, and then click **Column Width.** The Column Width dialog box opens.

▶ **3.** Type **25** in the Column width box to specify the new column width.

▶ **4.** Click the **OK** button. The width of column D changes to 25 characters.

▶ **5.** Click cell **A12** to deselect column D. Figure 1-20 shows the revised column widths for the customer order columns.

Figure 1-20 ▶ Resized columns

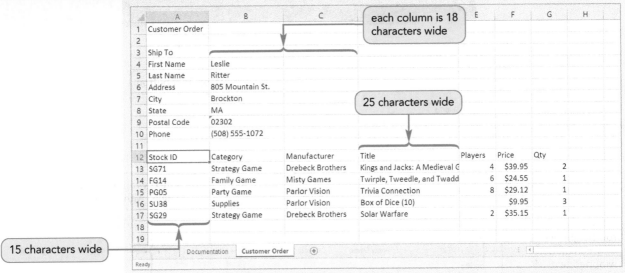

TIP

If the row or column is blank, autofitting restores its default height or width.

Notice that 25 characters is not wide enough to display all of the characters in each cell of column D. Instead of manually resizing the column width or row height to fit it to the cell contents, you can autofit the column or row. **AutoFit** changes the column width or row height to display the longest or tallest entry within the column or row. You autofit a column or a row by double-clicking the right border of the column heading or the bottom border of the row heading.

To autofit the contents of column D:

▶ **1.** Point to the **right border** of column D until the pointer changes to ✛.

▶ **2.** Double-click the **right border** of the column D heading. The width of column D increases to about 43 characters so that the longest item title is completely visible.

Wrapping Text Within a Cell

Sometimes, resizing a column width to display all of the text entered in the cells results in a cell that is too wide to read or print nicely. Another way to display long text entries is to wrap text to a new line when it would otherwise extend beyond the cell boundaries. When text wraps within a cell, the row height increases so that all of the text within the cell is displayed.

You will resize column D and then wrap the text entries in the column.

To wrap text in column D:

▶ **1.** Resize the width of column D to **25** characters.

▶ **2.** Select the range **D13:D17**. These cells include the titles that extend beyond the column width.

▶ **3.** On the Home tab, in the Alignment group, click the **Wrap Text** button. The Wrap Text button is toggled on, and text in the selected cells that exceeds the column width wraps to a new line.

▶ **4.** Click cell **A12** to make it the active cell. See Figure 1-21.

| Figure 1-21 | Text wrapped within cells |

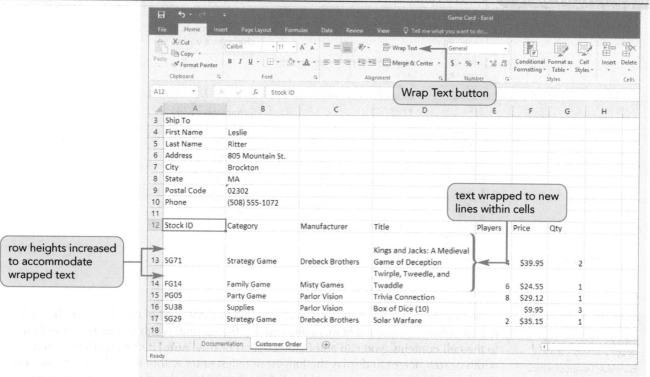

If you want to create a new line within a cell, press the Alt+Enter keys to move the insertion point to the next line within the cell. Whatever you type next will appear on the new line in the cell.

Changing Row Heights

The height of a row is measured in points or pixels. A **point** is approximately 1/72 of an inch. The default row height is 15 points, or 20 pixels. Row heights are set in the same way as column widths. You can drag the bottom border of the row heading to a new row height, specify a row height using the Format command, or autofit the row's height to match its content.

Peter notices that the height of row 13 is a little too tall for its contents. He asks you to change to it 30 points.

To change the height of row 13:

1. Point to the **bottom border** of the row 13 heading until the pointer changes to ✛.

2. Drag the **bottom border** down until the height of the row is equal to **30** points (or **40** pixels), and then release the mouse button. The height of row 13 is set to 30 points.

3. Press the **Ctrl+S** keys to save the workbook.

TIP

You can also set the row height by clicking the Format button in the Cells group on the Home tab and then using the Row Height command.

You have entered most of the data for Leslie Ritter's order at Game Card. In the next session, you will calculate the total charge for the order and print the worksheet.

REVIEW

Session 1.1 Quick Check

1. What are the two types of sheets used in a workbook?
2. What is the cell reference for the cell located in the second column and fifth row of a worksheet?
3. What is the range reference for the block of cells C2 through D10?
4. What is the reference for the nonadjacent block of cells B5 through C10 and cells B15 through D20?
5. What keyboard shortcut makes the active cell to cell A1?
6. What is text data?
7. How do you enter a number so that Excel sees it as text?
8. Cell B2 contains the entry May 3, 2017. Why doesn't Excel consider this a text entry?
9. How do you autofit a column to match the longest cell entry?

Session 1.2 Visual Overview:

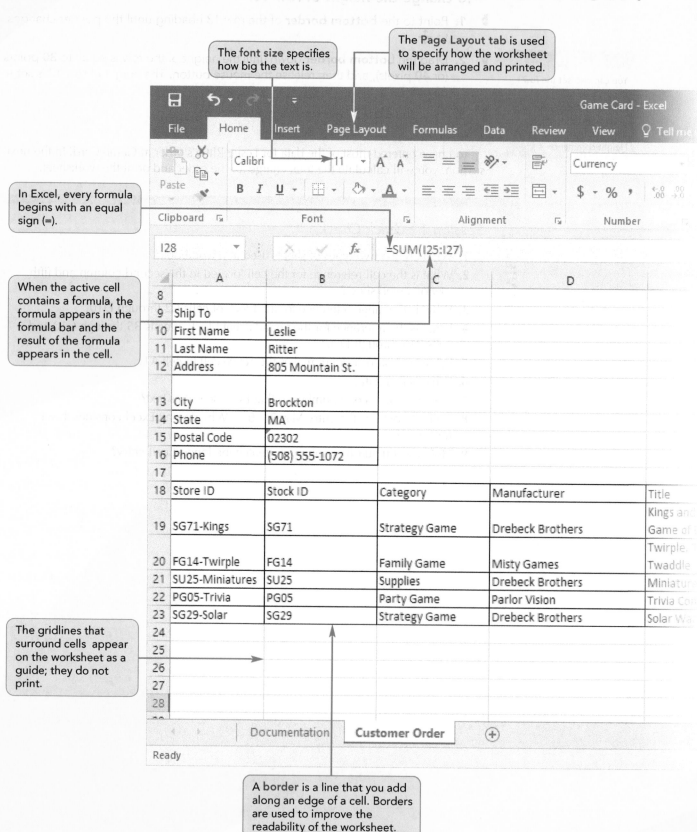

The font size specifies how big the text is.

The **Page Layout** tab is used to specify how the worksheet will be arranged and printed.

In Excel, every formula begins with an equal sign (=).

When the active cell contains a formula, the formula appears in the formula bar and the result of the formula appears in the cell.

The gridlines that surround cells appear on the worksheet as a guide; they do not print.

A **border** is a line that you add along an edge of a cell. Borders are used to improve the readability of the worksheet.

Excel Formulas and Functions

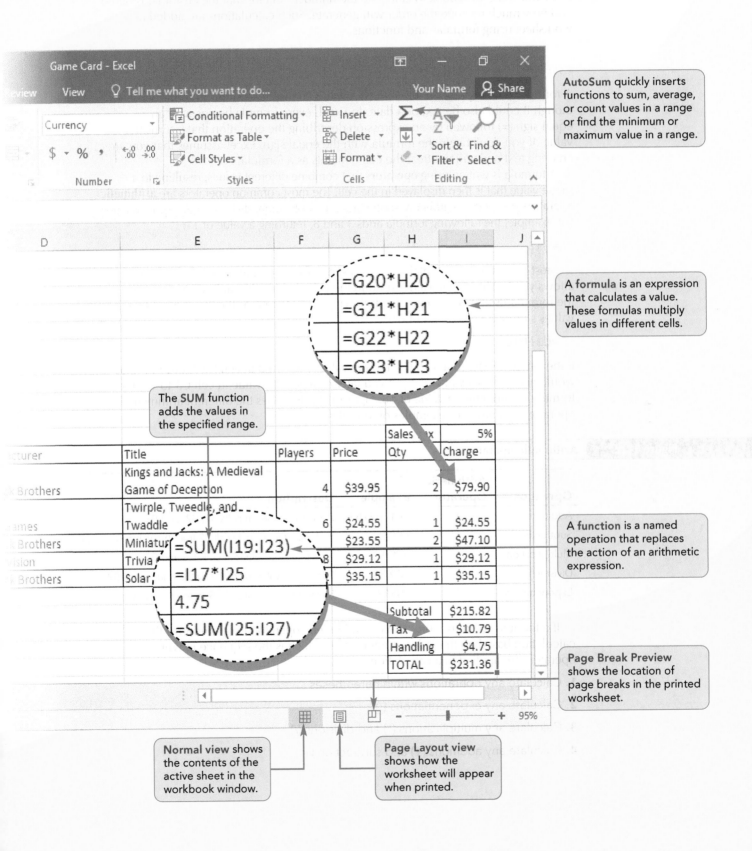

AutoSum quickly inserts functions to sum, average, or count values in a range or find the minimum or maximum value in a range.

A **formula** is an expression that calculates a value. These formulas multiply values in different cells.

=G20*H20
=G21*H21
=G22*H22
=G23*H23

The **SUM** function adds the values in the specified range.

=SUM(I19:I23)
=I17*I25
4.75
=SUM(I25:I27)

A **function** is a named operation that replaces the action of an arithmetic expression.

Game Card - Excel

View   Tell me what you want to do...   Your Name   Share

Currency

$ ▾ % ,   .0 .00

Number   Styles   Cells   Editing

Conditional Formatting ▾
Format as Table ▾
Cell Styles ▾

Insert ▾
Delete ▾
Format ▾

Sort & Filter ▾   Find & Select ▾

					Sales Tax		5%
D	E	F	G	H	I	J	
		Players	Price	Qty	Charge		
turer	Title						
Brothers	Kings and Jacks: A Medieval Game of Deception	4	$39.95	2	$79.90		
ames	Twirple, Tweedle, and Twaddle	6	$24.55	1	$24.55		
Brothers	Miniatur		$23.55	2	$47.10		
sion	Trivia	8	$29.12	1	$29.12		
Brothers	Solar		$35.15	1	$35.15		

Subtotal	$215.82
Tax	$10.79
Handling	$4.75
TOTAL	$231.36

Page Break Preview shows the location of page breaks in the printed worksheet.

95%

Normal view shows the contents of the active sheet in the workbook window.

Page Layout view shows how the worksheet will appear when printed.

Performing Calculations with Formulas

So far you have entered text, numbers, and dates in the worksheet. However, the main reason for using Excel is to perform calculations and analysis on data. For example, Peter wants the workbook to calculate the number of items that the customer ordered and how much revenue the order will generate. Such calculations are added to a worksheet using formulas and functions.

Entering a Formula

A formula is an expression that returns a value. In most cases, this is a number—though it could also be text or a date. In Excel, every formula begins with an equal sign (=) followed by an expression describing the operation that returns the value. If you don't begin the formula with the equal sign, Excel assumes that you are entering text and will not treat the cell contents as a formula.

A formula is written using **operators** that combine different values, resulting in a single value that is then displayed in the cell. The most common operators are **arithmetic operators** that perform addition, subtraction, multiplication, division, and exponentiation. For example, the following formula adds 3 and 8, returning a value of 11:

=3+8

Most Excel formulas contain references to cells rather than specific values. This allows you to change the values used in the calculation without having to modify the formula itself. For example, the following formula returns the result of adding the values stored in cells C3 and D10:

=C3+D10

If the value 3 is stored in cell C3 and the value 8 is stored in cell D10, this formula would also return a value of 11. If you later changed the value in cell C3 to 10, the formula would return a value of 18. Figure 1-22 describes the different arithmetic operators and provides examples of formulas.

Figure 1-22 Arithmetic operators

Operation	Arithmetic Operator	Example	Description
Addition	+	=B1+B2+B3	Adds the values in cells B1, B2, and B3
Subtraction	–	=C9-B2	Subtracts the value in cell B2 from the value in cell C9
Multiplication	*	=C9*B9	Multiplies the values in cells C9 and B9
Division	/	=C9/B9	Divides the value in cell C9 by the value in cell B9
Exponentiation	^	=B5^3	Raises the value of cell B5 to the third power

If a formula contains more than one arithmetic operator, Excel performs the calculation based on the **order of operations**, which is the sequence in which operators are applied in a calculation:

1. Calculate any operations within parentheses

2. Calculate any exponentiations (^)

3. Calculate any multiplications (*) and divisions (/)

4. Calculate any additions (+) and subtractions (–)

For example, the following formula returns the value 23 because multiplying 4 by 5 takes precedence over adding 3:

=3+4*5

If a formula contains two or more operators with the same level of priority, the operators are applied in order from left to right. In the following formula, Excel first multiplies 4 by 10 and then divides that result by 8 to return the value 5:

=4*10/8

When parentheses are used, the value inside them is calculated first. In the following formula, Excel calculates (3+4) first, and then multiplies that result by 5 to return the value 35:

=(3+4)*5

Figure 1-23 shows how slight changes in a formula affect the order of operations and the result of the formula.

Figure 1-23	**Order of operations applied to Excel formulas**

Formula	Order of Operations	Result
=50+10*5	10*5 calculated first and then 50 is added	100
=(50+10)*5	(50+10) calculated first and then 60 is multiplied by 5	300
=50/10–5	50/10 calculated first and then 5 is subtracted	0
=50/(10–5)	(10–5) calculated first and then 50 is divided by that value	10
=50/10*5	Two operators are at same precedence level, so the calculation is done left to right with 50/10 calculated first and that value is then multiplied by 5	25
=50/(10*5)	(10*5) is calculated first and then 50 is divided by that value	1

Peter wants the Customer Order worksheet to include the total amount charged for each item ordered. The charge is equal to the number of each item ordered multiplied by each item's price. You already entered this information in columns F and G. Now you will enter a formula to calculate the charge for each set of items ordered in column H.

To calculate the charge for the first item ordered:

1. If you took a break after the previous session, make sure the Game Card workbook is open and the Customer Order worksheet is active.

2. Click cell **H12** to make it the active cell, type **Charge** as the column label, and then press the **Enter** key. The label text is entered in cell H12, and cell H13 is now the active cell.

3. Type **=F13*G13** (the price of the Kings and Jacks game multiplied by the number of that game ordered). As you type the formula, a list of Excel function names appears in a ScreenTip, which provides a quick method for entering functions. The list will close when you complete the formula. You will learn more about Excel functions shortly. Also, after you type each cell reference, Excel color codes each cell reference and its cell. See Figure 1-24.

Figure 1-24   Formula being entered in a cell

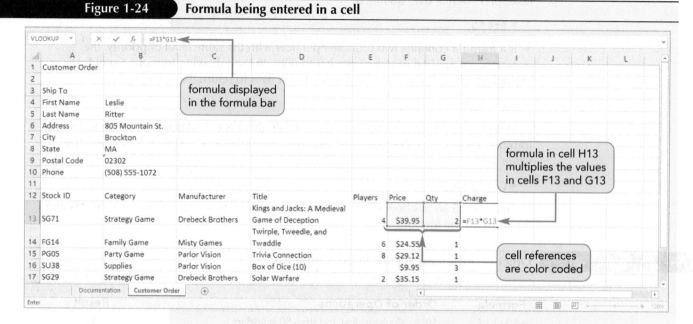

4. Press the **Enter** key. The formula is entered in cell H13 displaying the value $79.90. The result is displayed as currency because cell F13, which is referenced in the formula, contains a currency value.

5. Click cell **H13** to make it the active cell. Note that the cell displays the result of the formula, and the formula bar displays the formula you entered.

For the first item, you entered the formula by typing each cell reference in the expression. You can also insert a cell reference by clicking the cell as you type the formula. This technique reduces the possibility of error caused by typing an incorrect cell reference. You will use this method to enter the formula to calculate the charge for the second item on the order.

To enter a formula using the mouse:

1. Click cell **H14** to make it the active cell.

2. Type **=**. The equal sign indicates that you are entering a formula. Any cell you click from now on inserts the cell reference of the selected cell into the formula until you complete the formula by pressing the Enter or Tab key.

Be sure to type = first; otherwise, Excel will not recognize the entry as a formula.

3. Click cell **F14**. The cell reference is inserted into the formula in the formula bar. At this point, any cell you click changes the cell reference used in the formula. The cell reference isn't locked until you type an operator.

4. Type ***** to enter the multiplication operator. The cell reference for cell F14 is locked in the formula, and the next cell you click will be inserted after the operator.

5. Click cell **G14** to enter its cell reference in the formula. The formula is complete.

6. Press the **Enter** key. Cell H14 displays the value $24.55, which is the charge for the second item ordered.

Copying and Pasting Formulas

Sometimes you will need to repeat the same formula throughout a worksheet. Rather than retyping the formula, you can copy a formula from one cell and paste it into another cell. When you copy a formula, Excel places the formula into the **Clipboard**, which is a temporary storage location for text and graphics. When you paste, Excel takes the formula from the Clipboard and inserts it into the selected cell or range. Excel adjusts the cell references in the formula to reflect the formula's new location in the worksheet. This occurs because you usually want to copy the actions of a formula rather than the specific value the formula generates. In this case, the formula's action is to multiply the price of the item ordered by the quantity. By copying and pasting the formula, you can quickly repeat that action for every item listed in the worksheet.

You will copy the formula you entered in cell H14 to the range H15:H17 to calculate the charges on the remaining three items in Leslie Ritter's order. By copying and pasting the formula, you will save time and avoid potential mistakes from retyping the formula.

To copy and paste the formula:

▶ **1.** Click cell **H14** to select the cell that contains the formula you want to copy.

▶ **2.** On the Home tab, in the Clipboard group, click the **Copy** button (or press the **Ctrl+C** keys). Excel copies the formula to the Clipboard. A blinking green box surrounds the cell being copied.

▶ **3.** Select the range **H15:H17**. You want to paste the formula into these cells.

▶ **4.** In the Clipboard group, click the **Paste** button (or press the **Ctrl+V** keys). Excel pastes the formula into the selected cells, adjusting each formula so that the charge calculated for each ordered item is based on the corresponding values within that row. A button appears below the selected range, providing options for pasting formulas and values. See Figure 1-25.

Figure 1-25   **Copied and pasted formula**

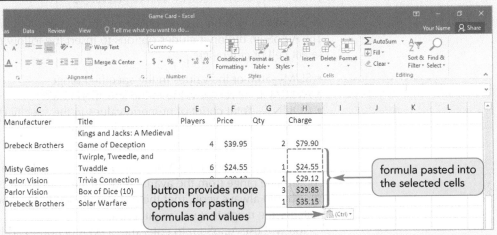

▶ **5.** Click cell **H15** and verify that the formula =F15*G15 appears in the formula bar. The formula was updated to reflect the cell references in the corresponding row.

▶ **6.** Click the other cells in column H, and verify that the corresponding formulas are entered in those cells.

Simplifying Formulas with Functions

In addition to cell references and operators, formulas can also contain functions. A function is a named operation that replaces the arithmetic expression in a formula. Functions are used to simplify long or complex formulas. For example, to add the values from cells A1 through A10, you could enter the following long formula:

```
=A1+A2+A3+A4+A5+A6+A7+A8+A9+A10
```

Or, you could use the SUM function to calculate the sum of those cell values by entering the following formula:

```
=SUM(A1:A10)
```

In both instances, Excel adds the values in cells A1 through A10, but the SUM function is faster and simpler to enter and less prone to a typing error. You should always use a function, if one is available, in place of a long, complex formula. Excel supports more than 300 different functions from the fields of finance, business, science, and engineering, including functions that work with numbers, text, and dates.

Introducing Function Syntax

Every function follows a set of rules, or **syntax**, which specifies how the function should be written. The general syntax of all Excel functions is

FUNCTION(arg1,arg2,...)

where *FUNCTION* is the function name, and *arg1*, *arg2*, and so forth are values used by that function. For example, the SUM function shown above uses a single argument, A1:A10, which is the range reference of the cells whose values will be added. Some functions do not require any arguments and are entered as *FUNCTION()*. Functions without arguments still require the opening and closing parentheses but do not include a value within the parentheses.

Entering Functions with AutoSum

A fast and convenient way to enter commonly used functions is with AutoSum. The AutoSum button includes options to insert the following functions into a select cell or cell range:

- SUM—Sum of the values in the specified range
- AVERAGE—Average value in the specified range
- COUNT—Total count of numeric values in the specified range
- MAX—Maximum value in the specified range
- MIN—Minimum value in the specified range

After you select one of the AutoSum options, Excel determines the most appropriate range from the available data and enters it as the function's argument. You should always verify that the range included in the AutoSum function matches the range that you want to use.

You will use AutoSum to enter the SUM function to add the total charges for Leslie Ritter's order.

To use AutoSum to enter the SUM function:

▶ **1.** Click cell **G18** to make it the active cell, type **Subtotal** as the label, and then press the **Tab** key to make cell H18 the active cell.

 2. On the Home tab, in the Editing group, click the **AutoSum button arrow**. The button's menu opens and displays five common functions: Sum, Average, Count Numbers, Max (for maximum), and Min (for minimum).

 3. Click **Sum** to enter the SUM function. The formula =SUM(H13:H17) is entered in cell H18. The cells being summed are selected and highlighted on the worksheet so you can quickly confirm that Excel selected the appropriate range from the available data. A ScreenTip appears below the formula describing the function's syntax. See Figure 1-26.

TIP

You can quickly insert the SUM function by pressing the Alt+= keys.

Figure 1-26   **SUM function being entered with AutoSum button**

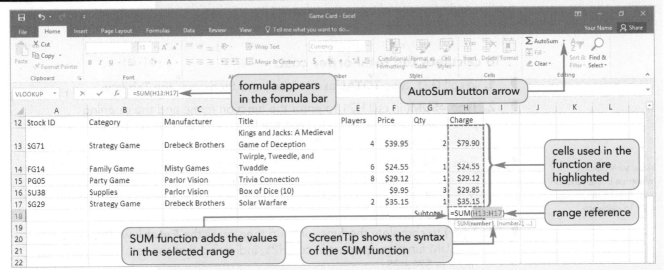

 4. Press the **Enter** key to accept the formula. The subtotal of the charges on the order returned by the SUM function is $198.57.

AutoSum makes entering a commonly used formula such as the SUM function fast and easy. However, AutoSum can determine the appropriate range reference to include only when the function is adjacent to the cells containing the values you want to summarize. If you need to use a function elsewhere in the worksheet, you will have to select the range reference to include or type the function yourself.

Each purchase made at Game Card is subject to a 5 percent sales tax and, in the case of online orders, a $4.75 handling fee. You will add these to the Customer Order worksheet so you can calculate the total charge for Leslie Ritter's order.

To add the sales tax and handling fee to the worksheet:

 1. Click cell **G11**, type **Sales Tax** as the label, and then press the **Tab** key to make cell H11 the active cell.

 2. In cell H11, type **5%** as the sales tax rate, and then press the **Enter** key. The sales tax rate is entered in the cell and can be used in other calculations. The value is displayed with the % symbol but is stored as the equivalent decimal value 0.05.

 3. Click cell **G19** to make it the active cell, type **Tax** as the label, and then press the **Tab** key to make cell H19 the active cell.

 4. Type **=H11*H18** as the formula to calculate the sales tax on the customer order, and then press the **Enter** key. The formula multiplies the sales tax

value in cell H11 by the order subtotal value in cell H18. The value $9.93 is displayed in cell H19, which is 5 percent of the subtotal value of $198.57.

▶ **5.** In cell G20, type **Handling** as the label, and then press the **Tab** key to make cell H20 the active cell. You will enter the handling fee in this cell.

▶ **6.** Type **$4.75** as the handling fee, and then press the **Enter** key.

The last part of the customer order is to calculate the total cost by adding the subtotal, the tax, and the handling fee. Rather than using AutoSum, you will type the SUM function so you can enter the correct range reference for the function. You can type the range reference or select the range in the worksheet. Remember that you must type parentheses around the range reference.

To calculate the total order cost:

▶ **1.** In cell G21, type **TOTAL** as the label, and then press the **Tab** key.

▶ **2.** Type **=SUM(** in cell H21 to enter the function name and the opening parenthesis. As you begin to type the function, a ScreenTip lists the names of all functions that start with S.

▶ **3.** Type **H18:H20** to specify the range reference of the cells you want to add. The cells referenced in the function are selected and highlighted on the worksheet so you can quickly confirm that you entered the correct range reference.

> Make sure the cell reference in the function matches the range you want to calculate.

▶ **4.** Type **)** to complete the function, and then press the **Enter** key. The value of the SUM function appears in cell H21, indicating that the total charge for the order is $213.25.

▶ **5.** Click cell **H21** to select the cell and its formula. See Figure 1-27.

Figure 1-27 | **Total charge calculated for the order**

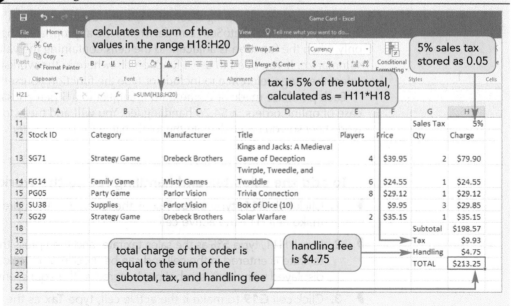

The SUM function makes it simple to quickly add the values in a group of cells.

Problem Solving: Writing Effective Formulas

You can use formulas to quickly perform calculations and solve problems. First, identify the problem you need to solve. Then, gather the data needed to solve the problem. Finally, create accurate and effective formulas that use the data to answer or resolve the problem. Follow these guidelines:

- **Keep formulas simple.** Use functions in place of long, complex formulas whenever possible. For example, use the SUM function instead of entering a formula that adds individual cells, which makes it easier to confirm that the formula is making an accurate calculation as it provides answers needed to evaluate the problem.

- **Do not hide data values within formulas.** The worksheet displays formula results, not the actual formula. For example, to calculate a 5 percent interest rate on a currency value in cell A5, you could enter the formula =0.05*A5. However, this doesn't show how the value is calculated. A better approach places the value 0.05 in a cell accompanied by a descriptive label and uses the cell reference in the formula. If you place 0.05 in cell A6, the formula =A6*A5 would calculate the interest value. Other people can then easily see the interest rate as well as the resulting interest, ensuring that the formula is solving the right problem.

- **Break up formulas to show intermediate results.** When a worksheet contains complex computations, other people can more easily comprehend how the formula results are calculated when different parts of the formula are distinguished. For example, the formula =SUM(A1:A10)/SUM(B1:B10) calculates the ratio of two sums but hides the two sum values. Instead, enter each SUM function in a separate cell, such as cells A11 and B11, and use the formula =A11/B11 to calculate the ratio. Other people can see both sums and the value of their ratio in the worksheet and better understand the final result, which makes it more likely that the best problem resolution will be selected.

- **Test formulas with simple values.** Use values you can calculate in your head to confirm that your formula works as intended. For example, using 1s or 10s as the input values lets you easily figure out the answer and verify the formula.

Finding a solution to a problem requires accurate data and analysis. With workbooks, this means using formulas that are easy to understand, clearly showing the data being used in the calculations, and demonstrating how the results are calculated. Only then can you be confident that you are choosing the best problem resolution.

Modifying a Worksheet

As you develop a worksheet, you might need to modify its content and structure to create a more logical organization. Some ways you can modify a worksheet include moving cells and ranges, inserting rows and columns, deleting rows and columns, and inserting and deleting cells.

Moving and Copying a Cell or Range

One way to move a cell or range is to select it, position the pointer over the bottom border of the selection, drag the selection to a new location, and then release the mouse button. This technique is called **drag and drop** because you are dragging the range and dropping it in a new location. If the drop location is not visible, drag the selection to the edge of the workbook window to scroll the worksheet, and then drop the selection.

You can also use the drag-and-drop technique to copy cells by pressing the Ctrl key as you drag the selected range to its new location. A copy of the original range is placed in the new location without removing the original range from the worksheet.

REFERENCE

Moving or Copying a Cell or Range

- Select the cell or range you want to move or copy.
- Move the pointer over the border of the selection until the pointer changes shape.
- To move the range, click the border and drag the selection to a new location (or to copy the range, hold down the Ctrl key and drag the selection to a new location).

or

- Select the cell or range you want to move or copy.
- On the Home tab, in the Clipboard group, click the Cut or Copy button (or right-click the selection, and then click Cut or Copy on the shortcut menu, or press the Ctrl+X or Ctrl+C keys).
- Select the cell or the upper-left cell of the range where you want to paste the content.
- In the Clipboard group, click the Paste button (or right-click the selection and then click Paste on the shortcut menu, or press the Ctrl+V keys).

Peter wants the subtotal, tax, handling, and total values in the range G18:H21 moved down one row to the range G19:H22 to set those calculations off from the list of items in the customer order. You will use the drag-and-drop method to move the range.

To drag and drop the range G18:H21:

▶ **1.** Select the range **G18:H21**. These are the cells you want to move.

▶ **2.** Point to the **bottom border** of the selected range so that the pointer changes to ⬚.

▶ **3.** Press and hold the mouse button to change the pointer to ⬚, and then drag the selection down one row. Do not release the mouse button. A ScreenTip appears, indicating that the new range of the selected cells will be G19:H22. A dark green border also appears around the new range. See Figure 1-28.

Figure 1-28   Range being moved

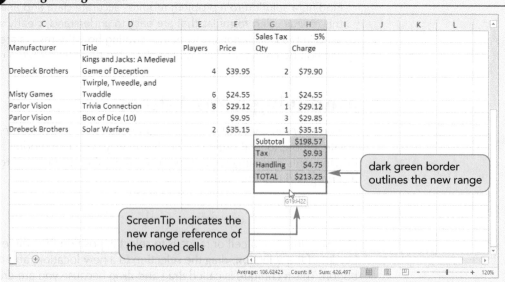

▶ **4.** Make sure the ScreenTip displays the range G19:H22, and then release the mouse button. The selected cells move to their new location.

Some people find dragging and dropping a select cell range difficult and awkward, particularly if the selected range is large or needs to move a long distance in the worksheet. In those situations, it is often more efficient to cut or copy and paste the cell contents. Cutting moves the selected content, whereas copying duplicates the selected content in the new location.

Peter wants the worksheet to include a summary of the customer order starting in row 3. You will cut the customer contact information and the item listing from range A3:A22 and paste it into range A9:H28, freeing up space for the order information.

To cut and paste the customer contact information:

▶ 1. Click cell **A3** to select it.

▶ 2. Press the **Ctrl+Shift+End** keys to extend the selection to the last cell in the lower-right corner of the worksheet (cell H22).

▶ 3. On the Home tab, in the Clipboard group, click the **Cut** button (or press the **Ctrl+X** keys). The range is surrounded by a moving border, indicating that it has been cut.

▶ 4. Click cell **A9** to select it. This is the upper-left corner of the range where you want to paste the range that you cut.

▶ 5. In the Clipboard group, click the **Paste** button (or press the **Ctrl+V** keys). The range A3:H22 is pasted into the range A9:H28. Note that the cell references in the formulas were automatically updated to reflect the new location of those cells in the worksheet.

Using the COUNT Function

Sometimes you will want to know how many unique items are included in a range, such as the number of different items in the customer order. To calculate that value, you use the COUNT function

=COUNT(*range*)

TIP

To count cells containing non-numeric values, use the COUNTA function.

where *range* is the range of cells containing numeric values to be counted. Note that any cell in the range containing a non-numeric value is not counted in the final tally.

You will include the count of the number of different items from the order in the summary information. The summary will also display the order ID (a unique number assigned by Game Card to identify the order), the shipping date, and the type of delivery (overnight, two-day, or standard) in the freed-up space at the top of the worksheet. In addition, Peter wants the total charge for the order to be displayed with the order summary so that he does not have to scroll to the bottom of the worksheet to find that value.

To add the order summary:

▶ 1. Click cell **A3**, type **Order ID** as the label, press the **Tab** key, type **C10489** in cell B3, and then press the **Enter** key. The order ID is entered, and cell A4 is the active cell.

▶ 2. Type **Shipping Date** as the label in cell A4, press the **Tab** key, type **4/3/2017** in cell B4, and then press the **Enter** key. The shipping date is entered, and cell A5 is the active cell.

▶ 3. Type **Delivery** as the label in cell A5, press the **Tab** key, type **standard** in cell B5, and then press the **Enter** key. The delivery type is entered, and cell A6 is the active cell.

4. Type **Items Ordered** as the label in cell A6, and then press the **Tab** key. Cell B6 is the active cell. Now you will enter the COUNT function to determine the number of different items ordered.

5. In cell B6, type **=COUNT(** to begin the function.

6. With the insertion point still blinking in cell B6, select the range **G19:G23**. The range reference is entered as the argument for the COUNT function.

7. Type **)** to complete the function, and then press the **Enter** key. Cell B6 displays the value 5, indicating that five items were ordered by Leslie Ritter. Cell A7 is the active cell.

8. Type **Total Charge** as the label in cell A7, and then press the **Tab** key to make cell B7 the active cell.

9. Type **=** to start the formula, and then click cell **H28** to enter its cell reference in the formula in cell B7. The formula you created, =H28, tells Excel to display the contents of cell H28 in the current cell.

10. Press the **Enter** key to complete the formula. The total charge of $213.25 appears in cell B7. See Figure 1-29.

Figure 1-29	Customer order summary

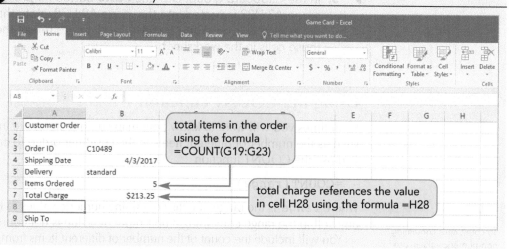

Inserting a Column or Row

You can insert a new column or row anywhere within a worksheet. When you insert a new column, the existing columns are shifted to the right, and the new column has the same width as the column directly to its left. When you insert a new row, the existing rows are shifted down, and the new row has the same height as the row above it. Because inserting a new row or column moves the location of the other cells in the worksheet, any cell references in a formula or function are updated to reflect the new layout.

REFERENCE

Inserting or Deleting a Column or Row

To insert a column or row:

- Select the column(s) or row(s) where you want to insert the new column(s) or row(s). Excel will insert the same number of columns or rows as you select to the left of the selected columns or above the selected rows.
- On the Home tab, in the Cells group, click the Insert button (or right-click a column or row heading or selected column and row headings, and then click Insert on the shortcut menu; or press the Ctrl+Shift+= keys).

To delete a column or row:

- Select the column(s) or row(s) you want to delete.
- On the Home tab, in the Cells group, click the Delete button (or right-click a column or row heading or selected column and row headings, and then click Delete on the shortcut menu; or press the Ctrl+- keys).

Peter informs you that the customer order report for Leslie Ritter is missing an item. You need to insert a new row directly above the entry for the Trivia Connection game in which you'll write the details of the missing item.

To insert a row for the missing order item:

1. Click the **row 21** heading to select the entire row.

2. On the Home tab, in the Cells group, click the **Insert** button (or press the **Ctrl+Shift+=** keys). A new row is inserted below row 20 and becomes the new row 21.

3. Enter **SU25** in cell A21, enter **Supplies** in cell B21, enter **Drebeck Brothers** in cell C21, enter **Miniatures Set (12)** in cell D21, leave cell E21 blank, enter **$23.55** in cell F21, and then enter **2** in cell G21.

4. Click cell **H20** to select the cell with the formula for calculating the item charge, and then press the **Ctrl+C** keys to copy the formula in that cell.

5. Click cell **H21** to select the cell where you want to insert the formula, and then press the **Ctrl+V** keys to paste the formula into the cell.

6. Click cell **H26**. See Figure 1-30.

> **TIP**
>
> You can insert multiple columns or rows by selecting that number of column or row headings, and then clicking the Insert button or pressing the Ctrl+Shift+= keys.

Figure 1-30   **New row inserted into the worksheet**

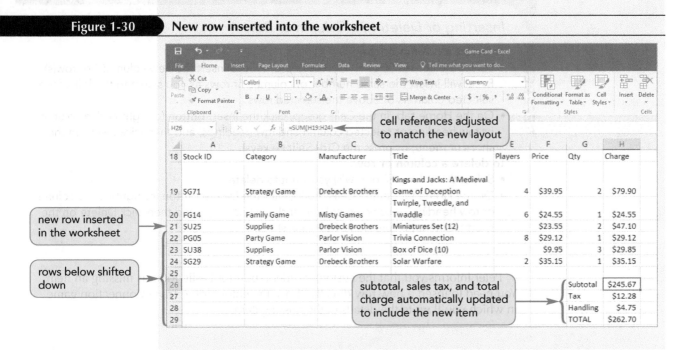

new row inserted in the worksheet

rows below shifted down

cell references adjusted to match the new layout

subtotal, sales tax, and total charge automatically updated to include the new item

Notice that the formula in cell H26 is now =SUM(H19:H24). The range reference was updated to reflect the inserted row. Also, the tax amount increased to $12.28 based on the new subtotal value of $245.67, and the total charge increased to $262.70 because of the added item. Also, the result of the COUNT function in cell B6 increased to 6 to reflect the item added to the order.

Deleting a Row or Column

You can also delete rows or columns from a worksheet. **Deleting** removes the data from the row or column as well as the row or column itself. The rows below the deleted row shift up to fill the vacated space. Likewise, the columns to the right of the deleted column shift left to fill the vacated space. Also, all cell references in the worksheet are adjusted to reflect the change. You click the Delete button in the Cells group on the Home tab to delete selected rows or columns.

Deleting a column or row is not the same as clearing a column or row. **Clearing** removes the data from the selected row or column but leaves the blank row or column in the worksheet. You press the Delete key to clear the contents of the selected row or column, which leaves the worksheet structure unchanged.

Leslie Ritter did not order the box of dice created by Parlor Vision. Peter asks you to delete the row containing this item from the report.

To delete the row containing the box of dice from the order:

1. Click the **row 23** heading to select the entire row.

2. On the Home tab, in the Cells group, click the **Delete** button (or press the **Ctrl+-** keys). Row 23 is deleted, and the rows below it shift up to fill the space.

All of the cell references in the worksheet are again updated automatically to reflect the impact of deleting row 23. The subtotal value in cell H25 is now $215.82, which is the sum of the range H19:H23. The sales tax in cell H26 decreases to $10.79. The total cost of the order decreases to $231.36. Also, the result of the COUNT function in cell B6 decreases to 5 to reflect the item deleted from the order. As you can see, one of the great advantages of using Excel is that it modifies the formulas to reflect the additions and deletions you make to the worksheet.

Inserting and Deleting a Range

You can also insert or delete cell ranges within a worksheet. When you use the Insert button to insert a range of cells, the existing cells shift down when the selected range is wider than it is long, and they shift right when the selected range is longer than it is wide, as shown in Figure 1-31. When you use the Insert Cells command, you specify whether the existing cells shift right or down, or whether to insert an entire row or column into the new range.

Figure 1-31   **Cells inserted into a worksheet**

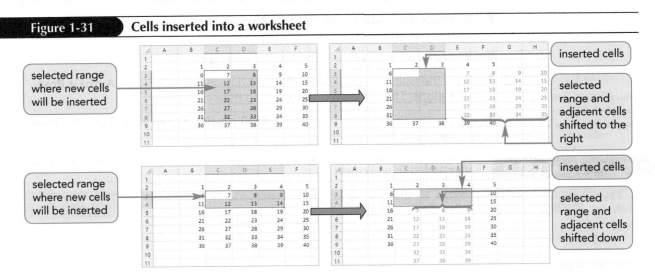

The process works in reverse when you delete a range. As with deleting a row or column, the cells adjacent to the deleted range either move up or left to fill in the space vacated by the deleted cells. The Delete Cells command lets you specify whether you want to shift the adjacent cells left or up or whether you want to delete the entire column or row.

When you insert or delete a range, cells that shift to a new location adopt the width of the columns they move into. As a result, you might need to resize columns and rows in the worksheet.

REFERENCE

Inserting or Deleting a Range

- Select a range that matches the range you want to insert or delete.
- On the Home tab, in the Cells group, click the Insert button or the Delete button.

or

- Select the range that matches the range you want to insert or delete.
- On the Home tab, in the Cells group, click the Insert button arrow and then click Insert Cells, or click the Delete button arrow and then click Delete Cells (or right-click the selected range, and then click Insert or Delete on the shortcut menu).
- Click the option button for the direction to shift the cells, columns, or rows.
- Click the OK button.

Peter wants you to insert a range into the worksheet for the ID that Game Card uses to identify the items it stocks in its store. You will insert these new cells into the range A17:A28, shifting the adjacent cells to the right.

To insert a range for the store IDs:

1. Select the range **A17:A28**.

2. On the Home tab, in the Cells group, click the **Insert button arrow**. A menu of insert options appears.

3. Click **Insert Cells**. The Insert dialog box opens.

4. Verify that the **Shift cells right** option button is selected.

5. Click the **OK** button. New cells are inserted into the selected range, and the adjacent cells move to the right. The cell contents do not fit well in the columns and rows they shifted into, so you will resize the columns and rows.

6. Resize the width of column E to **25** characters. The text is easier to read in the resized columns.

7. Select the row **19** through row **23** headings.

8. In the Cells group, click the **Format** button, and then click **AutoFit Row Height**. The selected rows autofit to their contents.

9. Resize the height of row 19 to **30 (40 pixels)**. Figure 1-32 shows the revised layout of the customer order.

> **TIP**
>
> You can also autofit by double-clicking the bottom border of row 23.

Figure 1-32   **Range added to worksheet**

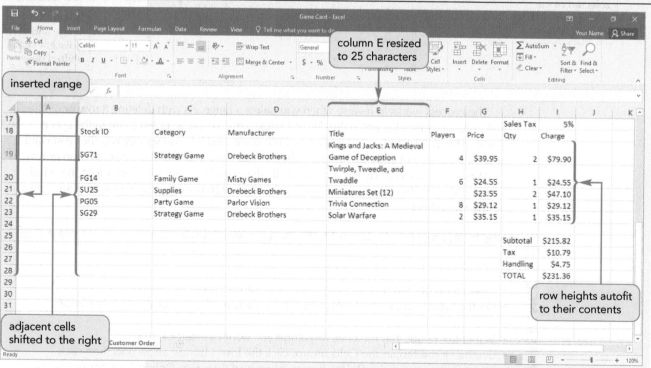

Notice that even though the customer orders will be entered only in the range A18:A23 you selected the range A17:A28 to retain the layout of the page design. Selecting the additional rows ensures that the sales tax and summary values still line up with the Qty and Charge columns. Whenever you insert a new range, be sure to consider its impact on the layout of the entire worksheet.

INSIGHT

Hiding and Unhiding Rows, Columns, and Worksheets

Workbooks can become long and complicated, filled with formulas and data that are important for performing calculations but are of little interest to readers. In those situations, you can simplify these workbooks for readers by hiding rows, columns, and even worksheets. Although the contents of hidden cells cannot be seen, the data in those cells is still available for use in formulas and functions throughout the workbook.

Hiding a row or column essentially decreases that row height or column width to 0 pixels. To a hide a row or column, select the row or column heading, click the Format button in the Cells group on the Home tab, point to Hide & Unhide on the menu that appears, and then click Hide Rows or Hide Columns. The border of the row or column heading is doubled to mark the location of hidden rows or columns.

A worksheet often is hidden when the entire worksheet contains data that is not of interest to the reader and is better summarized elsewhere in the document. To hide a worksheet, make that worksheet active, click the Format button in the Cells group on the Home tab, point to Hide & Unhide, and then click Hide Sheet.

Unhiding redisplays the hidden content in the workbook. To unhide a row or column, click in a cell below the hidden row or to the right of the hidden column, click the Format button, point to Hide & Unhide, and then click Unhide Rows or Unhide Columns. To unhide a worksheet, click the Format button, point to Hide & Unhide, and then click Unhide Sheet. The Unhide dialog box opens. Click the sheet you want to unhide, and then click the OK button. The hidden content is redisplayed in the workbook.

Although hiding data can make a worksheet and workbook easier to read, be sure never to hide information that is important to the reader.

Peter wants you to add the store ID used by Game Card to identify each item it sells. You will use Flash Fill to create these unique IDs.

Using Flash Fill

Flash Fill enters text based on patterns it finds in the data. As shown in Figure 1-33, Flash Fill generates customer names from the first and last names stored in the adjacent columns in the worksheet. To enter the rest of the names, you press the Enter key; to continue typing the names yourself, you press the Esc key.

Figure 1-33   Text being entered with Flash Fill

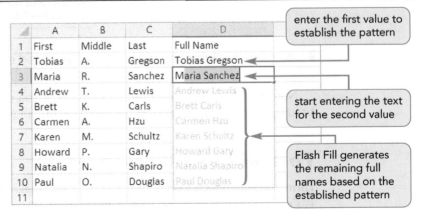

Flash Fill works best when the pattern is clearly recognized from the values in the data. Be sure to enter the data pattern in the column or row right next to the related data. The data used to generate the pattern must be in a rectangular grid and cannot have blank columns or rows.

The store IDs used by Game Card combines the Stock ID and the first name of the item. For example, the Kings and Jacks game has a Stock ID of SG71, so its Store ID is SG71-Kings. Rather than typing this for every item in the customer order, you'll use Flash Fill to complete the data entry.

To enter the Store IDs using Flash Fill:

▶ **1.** Click cell **A18**, type **Store ID** as the label, and then press the **Enter** key. The label is entered in cell A18, and cell A19 is now the active cell.

▶ **2.** Type **SG71-Kings** as the Store ID, and then press **Enter** to make cell A20 active.

▶ **3.** Type **FG** in cell A20. As soon as you complete those two characters Flash Fill generates the remaining entries in the column based on the pattern you entered. See Figure 1-34.

| Figure 1-34 | Store IDs generated by Flash Fill |

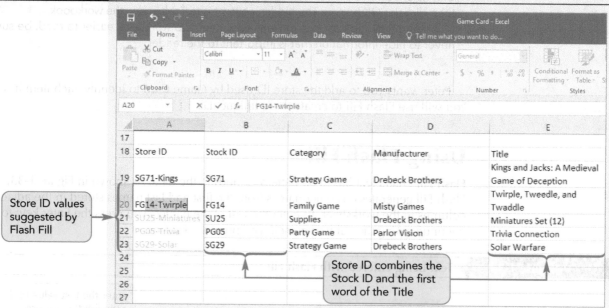

▶ **4.** Press the **Enter** key to accept the suggested entries.

Note that Flash Fill enters text, not formulas. If you edit or replace an entry originally used by Flash Fill, the content generated by Flash Fill will not be updated.

Formatting a Worksheet

Formatting changes a workbook's appearance to make the content of a worksheet easier to read. Two common formatting changes are adding cell borders and changing the font size of text.

Adding Cell Borders

Sometimes you want to include lines along the edges of cells to enhance the readability of rows and columns of data. You can do this by adding a border to the left, top, right, or bottom edge of a cell or range. You can also specify the thickness of and the number of lines in the border. This is especially helpful when a worksheet is printed because the gridlines that surround the cells are not printed by default; they appear on the worksheet only as a guide.

Peter wants to add borders around the cells that contain content in the Customer Order worksheet to make the content easier to read.

To add borders around the worksheet cells:

▶ 1. Select the range **A3:B7**. You will add borders around all of the cells in the selected range.

▶ 2. On the Home tab, in the Font group, click the **Borders button arrow** ⊞ ▾, and then click **All Borders**. Borders are added around each cell in the range. The Borders button changes to reflect the last selected border option, which in this case is All Borders. The name of the selected border option appears in the button's ScreenTip.

▶ 3. Select the nonadjacent range **A9:B16,H17:I17**. You will add borders around each cell in the selected range.

▶ 4. In the Font group, click the **All Borders** button ⊞ to add borders to all of the cells in the selected range.

▶ 5. Select the nonadjacent range **A18:I23,H25:I28**, and then click the **All Borders** button ⊞ to add borders to all of the cells in the selected range.

▶ 6. Click cell **A28** to deselect the cells. Figure 1-35 shows the borders added to the worksheet cells.

Figure 1-35   **Borders added to cells**

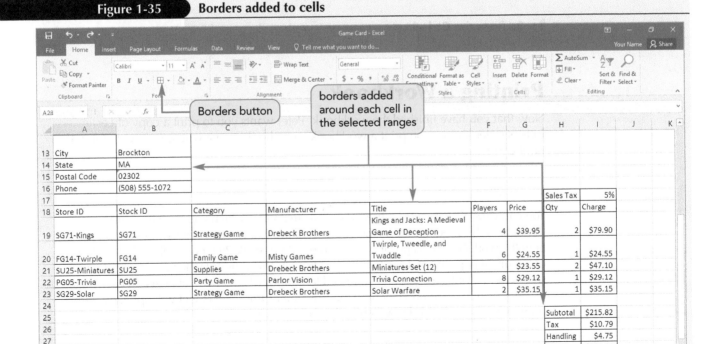

Changing the Font Size

Changing the size of text in a sheet provides a way to identify different parts of a worksheet, such as distinguishing a title or section heading from data. The size of the text is referred to as the font size and is measured in points. The default font size for worksheets is 11 points, but it can be made larger or smaller as needed. You can resize text in selected cells using the Font Size button in the Font group on the Home tab. You can also use the Increase Font Size and Decrease Font Size buttons to resize cell content to the next higher or lower standard font size.

Peter wants you to increase the size of the worksheet title to 26 points to make it more prominent.

To change the font size of the worksheet title:

▶ **1.** Click cell **A1** to select the cell containing the worksheet title.

▶ **2.** On the Home tab, in the Font group, click the **Font Size button arrow** 11 ▾ to display a list of font sizes, and then click **28**. The worksheet title changes to 28 points. See Figure 1-36.

| Figure 1-36 | Font size of the cell increased |

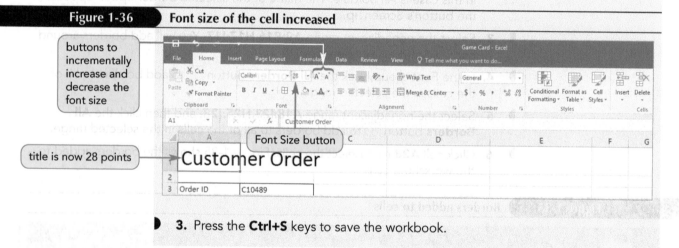

buttons to incrementally increase and decrease the font size

Font Size button

title is now 28 points

Customer Order

▶ **3.** Press the **Ctrl+S** keys to save the workbook.

Printing a Workbook

Now that you have finished the workbook, Peter wants you to print a copy of Leslie Ritter's order. Before you print a workbook, you should preview it to ensure that it will print correctly.

Changing Worksheet Views

You can view a worksheet in three ways. Normal view, which you have been using throughout this module, shows the contents of the worksheet. Page Layout view shows how the worksheet will appear when printed. Page Break Preview displays the location of the different page breaks within the worksheet. This is useful when a worksheet will span several printed pages, and you need to control what content appears on each page.

Peter wants you to preview how the Customer Order worksheet will appear when printed. You will do this by switching between views.

To switch the Customer Order worksheet to different views:

1. Click the **Page Layout** button 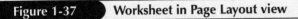 on the status bar. The page layout of the worksheet appears in the workbook window.

2. On the Zoom slider, click the **Zoom Out** button ☐ until the percentage is **50%**. The reduced magnification makes it clear that the worksheet will spread over two pages when printed. See Figure 1-37.

| Figure 1-37 | Worksheet in Page Layout view |

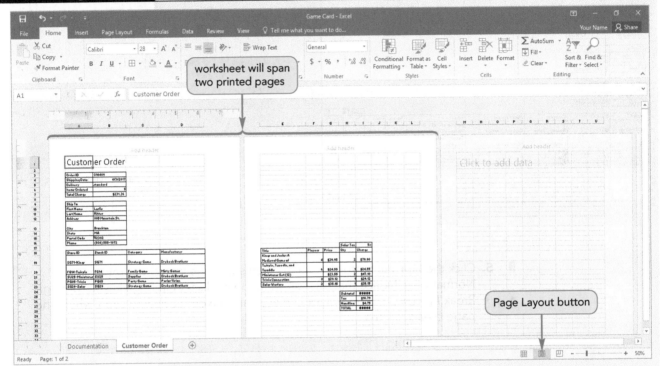

TIP

You can relocate a page break by dragging the dotted blue border in the Page Break Preview window.

3. Click the **Page Break Preview** button ☐ on the status bar. The view switches to Page Break Preview, which shows only those parts of the current worksheet that will print. A dotted blue border separates one page from another.

4. Zoom the worksheet to **70%** so that you can more easily read the contents of the worksheet. See Figure 1-38.

| Figure 1-38 | Worksheet in Page Break Preview |

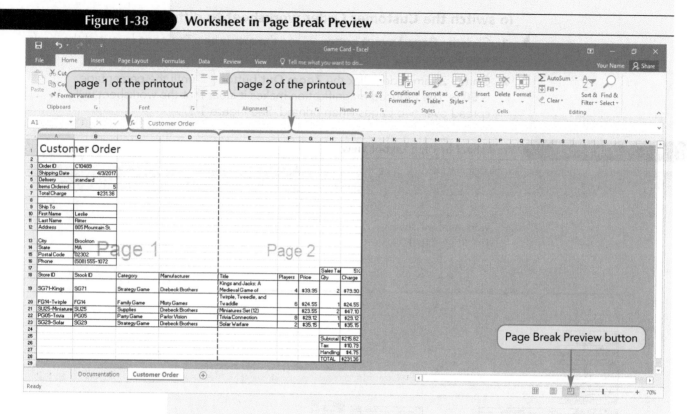

5. Click the **Normal** button ⊞ on the status bar. The worksheet returns to Normal view. Notice that after viewing the worksheet in Page Layout or Page Break Preview, a dotted black line appears in Normal view to show where the page breaks occurs.

Changing the Page Orientation

Page orientation specifies in which direction content is printed on the page. In **portrait orientation**, the page is taller than it is wide. In **landscape orientation**, the page is wider than it is tall. By default, Excel displays pages in portrait orientation. Changing the page orientation affects only the active sheet or sheets.

As you saw in Page Layout view and Page Break Preview, the Customer Order worksheet will print on two pages—columns A through D will print on the first page, and columns E through I will print on the second page, although the columns that print on each page may differ slightly depending on the printer. Peter wants the entire worksheet to print on a single page, so you'll change the page orientation from portrait to landscape.

To change the page orientation of the worksheet:

1. On the ribbon, click the **Page Layout** tab. The tab includes options for changing how the worksheet is arranged.

2. In the Page Setup group, click the **Orientation** button, and then click **Landscape**. The worksheet switches to landscape orientation.

3. Click the **Page Layout** button ▦ on the status bar to switch to Page Layout view. The worksheet will still print on two pages.

Setting the Scaling Options

You can force the printout to a single page by **scaling** the printed output. There are several options for scaling your printout. You can scale the width or the height of the printout so that all of the columns or all of the rows fit on a single page. You can also scale the printout to fit the entire worksheet (both columns and rows) on a single page. If the worksheet is too large to fit on one page, you can scale the print to fit on the number of pages you select. You can also scale the worksheet to a percentage of its size. For example, scaling a worksheet to 50% reduces the size of the sheet by half when it is sent to the printer. When scaling a printout, make sure that the worksheet is still readable after it is resized. Scaling affects only the active worksheet, so you can scale each worksheet to best fit its contents.

Peter asks you to scale the printout so that all of the Customer Order worksheet fits on one page in landscape orientation.

To scale the printout of the Customer Order worksheet:

▶ 1. On the Page Layout tab, in the Scale to Fit group, click the **Width** arrow, and then click **1 page** on the menu that appears. All of the columns in the worksheet now fit on one page.

If more rows are added to the worksheet, Peter wants to ensure that they still fit within a single sheet.

▶ 2. In the Scale to Fit group, click the **Height** arrow, and then click **1 page**. All of the rows in the worksheet now fit on one page. See Figure 1-39.

Figure 1-39   **Printout scaled to fit on one page**

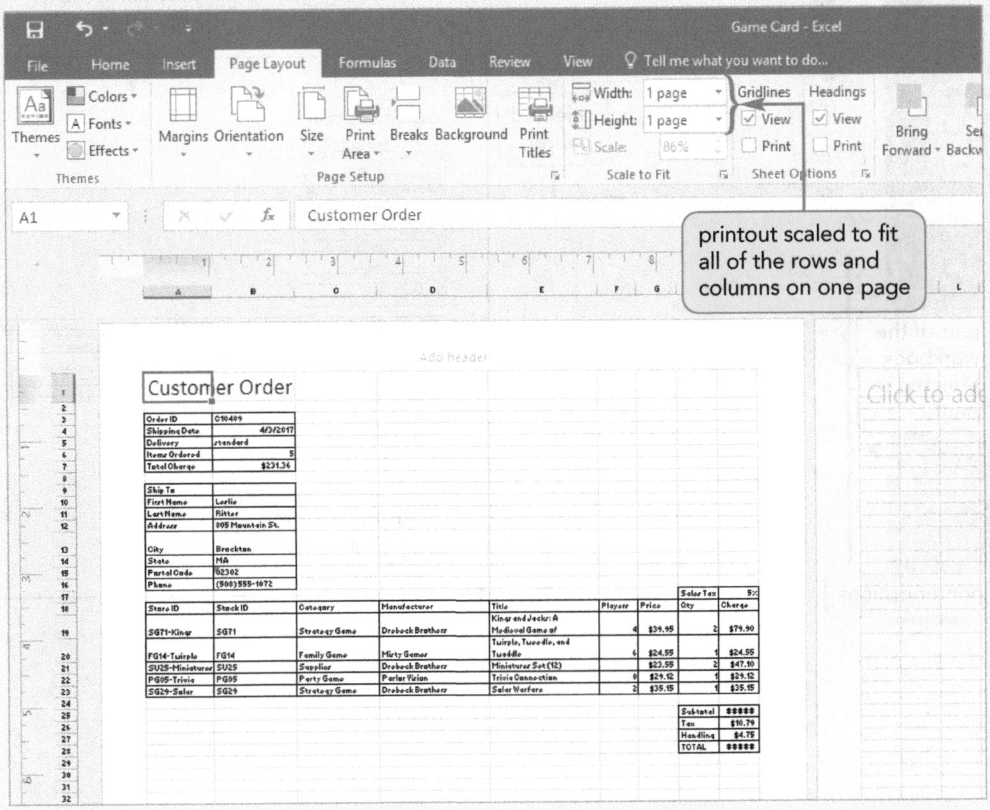

Setting the Print Options

TIP

To print the gridlines or the column and row headings, click the corresponding Print check box in the Sheet Options group on the Page Layout tab.

You can print the contents of a workbook by using the Print screen in Backstage view. The Print screen provides options for choosing where to print, what to print, and how to print. For example, you can specify the number of copies to print, which printer to use, and what to print. You can choose to print only the selected cells, only the active sheets, or all of the worksheets in the workbook that contain data. The printout will include only the data in the worksheet. The other elements in the worksheet, such as the row and column headings and the gridlines around the worksheet cells, will not print by default. The preview shows you exactly how the printed pages will look with the current settings. You should always preview before printing to ensure that the printout looks exactly as you intended and avoid unnecessary reprinting.

Peter asks you to preview and print the customer order workbook now.

Note: Check with your instructor first to make sure you should complete the steps for printing the workbook.

To preview and print the workbook:

1. On the ribbon, click the **File** tab to display Backstage view.

2. Click **Print** in the navigation bar. The Print screen appears with the print options and a preview of the Customer Order worksheet printout. See Figure 1-40.

Figure 1-40   **Print screen in Backstage view**

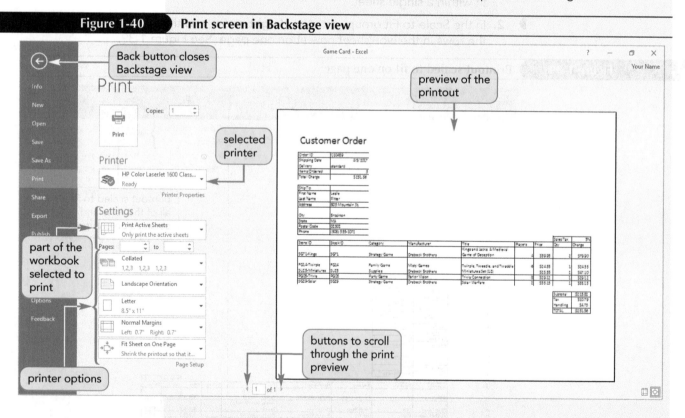

3. Click the **Printer** button, and then click the **printer** to which you want to print, if it is not already selected. By default, Excel will print only the active sheet.

4. In the Settings options, click the top button, and then click **Print Entire Workbook** to print all of the sheets in the workbook—in this case, both the Documentation and the Customer Order worksheets. The preview shows the first sheet in the workbook—the Documentation worksheet. Note that this sheet is still in the default portrait orientation.

5. Below the preview, click the **Next Page** button ▶ to view the Customer Order worksheet. As you can see, the Customer Order worksheet will print on a single page in landscape orientation.

6. If you are instructed to print, click the **Print** button to send the contents of the workbook to the specified printer. If you are not instructed to print, click the **Back** button ⬅ in the navigation bar to exit Backstage view.

Viewing Worksheet Formulas

Most of the time, you will be interested in only the final results of a worksheet, not the formulas used to calculate those results. However, in some cases, you might want to view the formulas used to develop the workbook. This is particularly useful when you encounter unexpected results and you want to examine the underlying formulas, or you want to discuss your formulas with a colleague. You can display the formulas instead of the resulting values in cells.

If you print the worksheet while the formulas are displayed, the printout shows the formulas instead of the values. To make the printout easier to read, you should print the worksheet gridlines as well as the row and column headings so that cell references in the formulas are easy to find in the printed version of the worksheet.

You will look at the Customer Order worksheet with the formulas displayed.

To display the cell formulas:

1. Make sure the Customer Order worksheet is in Page Layout view.

2. Press the **Ctrl+`** keys (the grave accent symbol ` is usually located above the Tab key). The worksheet changes to display all of the formulas instead of the resulting values. Notice that the columns widen to display all of the formula text in the cells.

3. Look at the entry in cell B4. The underlying numeric value of the shipping date (42828) is displayed instead of the formatted date value (4/3/2017). See Figure 1-41.

TIP

You can also display formulas in a worksheet by clicking the Show Formulas button in the Formula Auditing group on the Formulas tab.

| Figure 1-41 | Worksheet with formulas displayed |

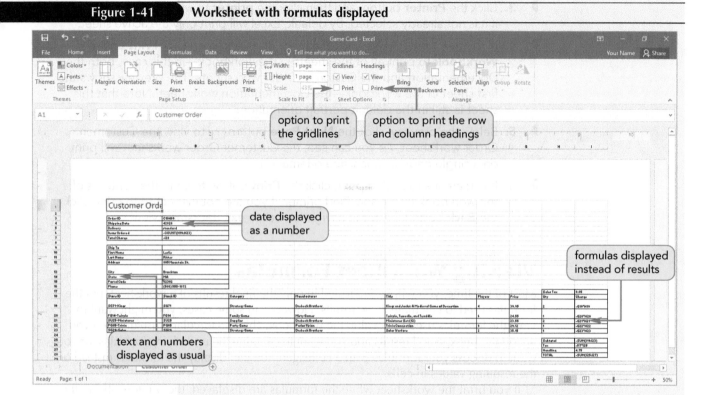

It's good practice to hide the formulas when you are done reviewing them.

▶ **4.** Press the **Ctrl+`** keys to hide the formulas and display the resulting values.

▶ **5.** Click the **Normal** button ⊞ on the status bar to return the workbook to Normal view.

Saving a Workbook with a New Filename

Whenever you click the Save button on the Quick Access Toolbar or press the Ctrl+S keys, the workbook file is updated to reflect the latest content. If you want to save a copy of the workbook with a new filename or to a different location, you need to use the Save As command. When you save a workbook with a new filename or to a different location, the previous version of the workbook remains stored as well.

You have completed the customer order workbook for Game Card. Peter wants to use the workbook as a model for other customer order reports. You will save the workbook with a new filename to avoid overwriting the Leslie Ritter order. Then you'll clear the information related to that order, leaving the formulas intact. This new, revised workbook will then be ready for the next customer order.

To save the workbook with a new filename:

▶ **1.** Press the **Ctrl+S** keys to save the workbook. This ensures that the final copy of the workbook contains the formatted version of Leslie Ritter's order.

▶ **2.** On the ribbon, click the **File** tab to display Backstage view, and then click **Save As** on the navigation bar. The Save As screen is displayed.

3. Click the **Browse** button. The Save As dialog box opens so you can save the workbook with a new filename or to a new location.

4. Navigate to the location specified by your instructor.

5. In the File name box, type **Game Card Order** as the new filename.

6. Click the **Save** button. The workbook is saved with the new filename, and you are returned to the workbook window.

7. Select the range **B3:B5**, right-click the selected range to open the shortcut menu, and then click **Clear Contents** to clear the contents of the order ID, shipping date, and delivery cells.

8. Select the nonadjacent range **B10:B16,A19:H23**, and then press the **Delete** key to clear the contact information for Leslie Ritter and the list of items she ordered.

9. Select cell **I27**, and then clear the handling fee.

10. Click cell **A3** to make that cell the active cell the next time this workbook is opened.

11. Press the **Ctrl+S** keys to save the workbook.

12. Click the **Close** button ✖ on the title bar (or press the **Ctrl+W** keys). The workbook closes, and the Excel program closes.

Peter is pleased with the workbook you created. With the calculations already in place in the new workbook, he will be able to quickly enter new customer orders and see the calculated charges without having to recreate the worksheet.

Session 1.2 Quick Check

REVIEW

1. What formula would you enter to add the values in cells C1, C2, and C3? What function would you enter to achieve the same result?
2. What formula would you enter to count how many numeric values are in the range D21:D72?
3. If you insert cells into the range C1:D10, shifting the cells to the right, what is the new location of the data that was previously in cell F4?
4. Cell E11 contains the formula =SUM(D1:D20). How does this formula change if a new row is inserted above row 5?
5. Describe four ways of viewing the content of a workbook in Excel.
6. How are page breaks indicated in Page Break Preview?
7. What orientation would you use to make the printed page wider than it is tall?
8. How do you display the formulas used in a worksheet instead of the formula results?

Review Assignments

There are no Data Files needed for the Review Assignment.

Game Card also buys and resells used games and gaming supplies. Peter wants to use Excel to record recent used purchases made by the store. The workbook should list every item the company has ordered, provide information about the item, and calculate the total order cost. Complete the following:

1. Create a new, blank workbook, and then save the workbook as **Game List** in the location specified by your instructor.
2. Rename the Sheet1 worksheet as **Documentation**, and then enter the data shown in Figure 1-42 in the specified cells.

Figure 1-42   **Documentation sheet data**

Cell	Text
A1	Game Card
A3	Author
A4	Date
A5	Purpose
B3	*your name*
B4	*current date*
B5	To record game acquisitions for Game Card

3. Set the font size of the title text in cell A1 to **28** points.
4. Add a new worksheet after the Documentation sheet, and then rename the sheet as **Game Purchases**.
5. In cell A1, enter the text **Game Purchases**. Set the font size of this text to **28** points.
6. In cell A3, enter the text **Date** as the label. In cell B3, enter the date **4/3/2017**.
7. In the range A5:F10, enter the data shown in Figure 1-43.

Figure 1-43   **Game list**

Purchase Number	Category	Manufacturer	Title	Players	Cost
83	Strategy Game	Drebeck Brothers	Secrets of Flight: Building an Airforce	6	$29.54
84	Family Game	Parlor Vision	Brain Busters and Logic Gaming	8	$14.21
85	Strategy Game	Aspect Gaming	Inspection Deduction	3	$18.91
86	Party Game	Miller Games	Bids and Buys	8	$10.81
87	Family Game	Aspect Gaming	Buzz Up	4	$21.43

8. Insert cells into the range A5:A10, shifting the other cells to the right.
9. In cell A5, enter **Stock ID** as the label. In cell A6, enter **SG83** as the first Stock ID, and then type **FG** in cell A7, allowing Flash Fill to enter the remaining Stock IDs.
10. Set the width of column A to **12** characters, columns B through D to **18** characters, and column E to **25** characters.
11. Wrap text in the range E6:E10 so that the longer game titles appear on multiple lines within the cells.

12. Autofit the heights of rows 5 through 10.

13. Move the game list in the range A5:G10 to the range A8:G13.

14. In cell F15, enter **TOTAL** as the label. In cell G15, enter a formula with the SUM function to calculate the sum of the costs in the range G9:G13.

15. In cell A4, enter **Total Items** as the label. In cell B4, enter a formula with the COUNT function to count the number of numeric values in the range G9:G13.

16. In cell A5, enter **Total Cost**. In cell B5, enter a formula to display the value from cell G15.

17. In cell A6, enter **Average Cost** as the label. In cell B6, enter a formula that divides the total cost of the purchased games (listed in cell B5) by the number of games purchased (listed in cell B4).

18. Add borders around each cell in the nonadjacent range A3:B6,A8:G13,F15:G15.

19. For the Game Purchases worksheet, change the page orientation to landscape and scale the worksheet to print on a single page for both the width and the height. If you are instructed to print, print the entire workbook.

20. Display the formulas in the Game Purchases worksheet. If you are instructed to print, print the entire worksheet.

21. Save and close the workbook.

Case Problem 1

Data File needed for this Case Problem: Donation.xlsx

Henderson Pediatric Care Center   Kari Essen is a fundraising coordinator for the Pediatric Care Center located in Henderson, West Virginia. Kari is working on a report detailing recent donations to the center and wants you to enter this data into an Excel workbook. Complete the following:

1. Open the **Donation** workbook located in the Excel1 > Case1 folder included with your Data Files. Save the workbook as **Donation List** in the location specified by your instructor.

2. In the Documentation sheet, enter your name in cell B3 and the date in cell B4.

3. Increase the font size of the text in cell A1 to 28 points.

4. Add a new sheet to the end of the workbook, and rename it as **Donor List**.

5. In cell A1 of the Donor List worksheet, enter **Donor List** as the title, and then set the font size to 28 points.

6. In the range A6:H13, enter the donor information shown in Figure 1-44. Enter the ZIP code data as text rather than as numbers.

Figure 1-44   **Donation list**

Last Name	First Name	Street	City	State	ZIP	Phone	Donation
Robert	Richards	389 Felton Avenue	Miami	FL	33127	(305) 555-5685	$150
Barbara	Hopkins	612 Landers Street	Caledonia	IL	61011	(815) 555-5865	$75
Daniel	Vaughn	45 Lyman Street	Statesboro	GA	30461	(912) 555-8564	$50
Parker	Penner	209 South Street	San Francisco	CA	94118	(415) 555-7298	$250
Kenneth	More	148 7th Street	Newberry	IN	47449	(812) 555-8001	$325
Robert	Simmons	780 10th Street	Houston	TX	77035	(713) 555-5266	$75
Donna	Futrell	834 Kimberly Lane	Ropesville	TX	79358	(806) 555-6186	$50

7. Set the width of columns A through D to 25 characters. Set the width of column G to 15 characters.

8. In cell A2, enter the text **Total Donors**. In cell A3, enter the text **Total Donations**. In cell A4, enter the text **Average Donation**.

9. In cell B2, enter a formula that counts how many numeric values are in the range H7:H13.

10. In cell B3, enter a formula that calculates the sum of the donations in the range H7:H13.

11. In cell B4, enter a formula that calculates the average donation by dividing the value in cell B3 by the value in cell B2.

12. Add borders around the nonadjacent range A2:B4,A6:H13.

13. Set the page orientation of the Donor List to landscape.

14. Scale the worksheet to print on a single page for both the width and the height. If you are instructed to print the worksheet, print the Donor List sheet.

15. Display the formulas in the Donor List worksheet. If you are instructed to print, print the worksheet.

16. Save and close the workbook.

Case Problem 2

CREATE

Data File needed for this Case Problem: Balance.xlsx

Scott Kahne Tool & Die Cheryl Hippe is a financial officer at Scott Kahne Tool & Die, a manufacturing company located in Mankato, Minnesota. Every month the company publishes a balance sheet, a report that details the company's assets and liabilities. Cheryl asked you to create the workbook with the text and formulas for this report. Complete the following:

1. Open the **Balance** workbook located in the Excel1 > Case2 folder included with your Data Files. Save the workbook as **Balance Sheet** in the location specified by your instructor.

2. In the Documentation sheet, enter your name in cell B3 and the date in cell B4.

3. Go to the Balance Sheet worksheet. Set the font size of the title in cell A1 to 28 points.

4. In cell A2, enter the text **Statement for March 2017**.

5. Set the width of columns A and E to 30 characters. Set the width of columns B, C, F, and G to 12 characters. Set the width of column D to 4 characters. (*Hint:* Hold down the Ctrl key as you click the column headings to select both adjacent and nonadjacent columns.)

6. Set the font size of the text in cells A4, C4, E4, and G4 to 18 points.

7. Set the font size of the text in cells A5, E5, A11, E11, A14, E15, A19, E20, and A24 to 14 points.

8. Enter the values shown in Figure 1-45 in the specified cells.

Figure 1-45   **Assets and liabilities**

Current Assets	Cell	Value
Cash	B6	$123,000
Accounts Receivable	B7	$75,000
Inventories	B8	$58,000
Prepaid Insurance	B9	$15,000
Long-Term Investments	**Cell**	**Value**
Available Securities	B12	$29,000
Tangible Assets	**Cell**	**Value**
Land	B15	$49,000
Building and Equipment	B16	$188,000
Less Accumulated Depreciation	B17	-$48,000
Intangible Assets	**Cell**	**Value**
Goodwill	B20	$148,000
Other Assets	B22	$14,000
Current Liabilities	**Cell**	**Value**
Accounts Payable	F6	$62,000
Salaries	F7	$14,000
Interest	F8	$12,000
Notes Payable	F9	$38,000
Long-Term Liabilities	**Cell**	**Value**
Long-Term Notes Payable	F12	$151,000
Mortgage	F13	$103,000
Stockholders' Equity	**Cell**	**Value**
Capital Stock	F16	$178,000
Retained Earnings	F17	$98,000
Comprehensive Income/Loss	F18	-$5,000

9. In cell C9, enter a formula to calculate the sum of the Current Assets in the range B6:B9.
10. In cell C12, enter a formula to display the value of B12.
11. In cell C17, enter a formula to calculate the sum of the Tangible Assets in the range B15:B17.
12. In cells C20 and C22, enter formulas to display the values of cells B20 and B22, respectively.
13. In cell C24, enter a formula to calculate the total assets in the balance sheet by adding cells C9, C12, C17, C20, and C22. Set the font size of the cell to 14 points.
14. In cell G9, enter a formula to calculate the sum of the Current Liabilities in the range F6:F9.
15. In cell G13, enter a formula to calculate the sum of the Long-Term Liabilities in the range F12:F13.
16. In cell G18, enter a formula to calculate the sum of the Stockholders' Equity in the range F16:F18.
17. In cell G20, calculate the Total Liabilities and Equity for the company by adding the values of cells G9, G13, and G18. Set the font size of the cell to 14 points.
18. Check your calculations. In a balance sheet the total assets (cell C24) should equal the total liabilities and equity (cell G20).
19. Set the page layout orientation to landscape and the Balance Sheet worksheet to print to one page for both the width and height.
20. Preview the worksheet on the Print screen in Backstage view, and then save and close the workbook.

CHALLENGE

Case Problem 3

Data File needed for this Case Problem: FTP.xslx

Succeed Gym   Allison Palmer is the owner of Succeed Gym, an athletic club in Austin, Texas, that specializes in coaching men and women aspiring to participate in triathlons, marathons, and other endurance sports. During the winter, Allison runs an indoor cycling class in which she tracks the progress of each student's fitness. One measure of fitness is FTP (Functional Threshold Power). Allison has recorded FTP levels from her students over five races and wants you to use the functions described in Figure 1-46 to analyze this data so that she can track the progress of her class and of individual students.

Figure 1-46   **Excel functions**

Function	Description
=AVERAGE(range)	Calculates the average of the values from the specified range
=MEDIAN(range)	Calculates the median or midpoint of the values from the specified range
=MIN(range)	Calculates the minimum of the values from the specified range
=MAX(range)	Calculates the maximum of the values from the specified range

Complete the following:

1. Open the **FTP** workbook located the Excel1 > Case3 folder included with your Data Files. Save the workbook as **FTP Report** in the location specified by your instructor.
2. In the Documentation sheet, enter your name in cell B3 and the date in cell B4.
3. Go to the Race Results worksheet. Change the font size of the title in cell A1 to 28 points.
4. Set the width of column A and B to 15 characters. Set the width of column I to 2 characters.
5. In the range J4:M4, enter the labels **Median**, **Average**, **Min**, and **Max**.
⊕ **Explore** 6. In cell J5, use the MEDIAN function to calculate the median (midpoint) of the FTP values of races 1 through 5 for Diana Bartlett in the range D5:H5. Copy the formula in cell J5 to the range J6:J28 to calculate the median FTP values for the other riders.
⊕ **Explore** 7. In cell K5, use the AVERAGE function to calculate the average the FTP value for races 1 through 5 for Diana Bartlett. Copy the formula to calculate the averages for the other riders.
⊕ **Explore** 8. In cell L5, use the MIN function to return the minimum FTP value for Diana Bartlett. Copy the formula to calculate the minimums for the other riders.
⊕ **Explore** 9. In cell M5, use the MAX function to return the maximum FTP value for Diana Bartlett. Copy the formula to calculate the maximums for the other riders.
10. In the range C30:C33, enter the labels **Median**, **Average**, **Min**, and **Max** to record summary information for each of the five races.
11. In cell D30, use the MEDIAN function to calculate the median FTP value from the range D5:D28. Copy the formula to the range E30:H30 to determine the median values for the other four races.
12. In the range D31:H31, use the AVERAGE function to calculate the average FTP value for each race.
13. In the range D32:H32, use the MIN function to calculate the minimum value for each race.
14. In the range D33:H33, use the MAX function to calculate the maximum FTP value for each race.
15. Move the range A4:M33 to the range A10:M39 to create space for additional summary calculations at the top of the worksheet.

16. In the range A3:A7, enter the labels **Class Size**, **Class Average**, **Class Median**, **Class Minimum**, and **Class Maximum**.

✛ **Explore** 17. In cell B3, use the COUNTA function to count the number of entries in the range A11:A34.

18. In cell B4, use the AVERAGE function to calculate the average of all FTP values in the range D11:H34.

19. In cell B5, use the MEDIAN function to calculate the median of all FTP values in the range D11:H34.

20. In cell B6, use the MIN function to calculate the minimum FTP value in the range D11:H34.

21. In cell B7, use the MAX function to calculate the maximum FTP value in the range D11:H34.

22. Set the page layout orientation for the Race Results worksheet to portrait and scale the worksheet so that its width and height fit on one page.

23. View the worksheet in Page Layout view, return to Normal view, and then save and close the workbook.

Case Problem 4

Data File needed for this Case Problem: Service.xlsx

Welch Home Appliance Repair Stefan Welch is the owner of Welch Home Appliance Repair in Trenton, New Jersey. Stefan wants to use Excel to record data from his service calls to calculate the total charge on each service call and the total charges from all service calls within a given period. Unfortunately, the workbook he has created contains several errors. He has asked you to fix the errors and complete the workbook. Complete the following:

1. Open the **Service** workbook located in the Excel1 > Case4 folder included with your Data Files. Save the workbook as **Service Calls** in the location specified by your instructor.

2. In the Documentation sheet, enter your name in cell B3 and the date in cell B4.

3. Go to the Call Sheet worksheet. Insert cells in the range A7:A27, shifting the other cells to the right.

4. In cell A7, enter **Cust ID** as the label. In cell A8, enter **Jensen-5864** (the customer's last name and last four digits on the phone number) as the customer ID for Patricia Jensen. Use Flash Fill to enter in the remaining customer IDs in the column.

5. Resize the columns of the Call Sheet worksheet so that all of the column labels and the cell contents are completely displayed.

⚙ **Troubleshoot** 6. There is a problem with the some of the customer ZIP codes. New Jersey ZIP codes begin with a 0, and these leading zeros are not showing up in the contact information. Revise the text of the ZIP code values to correct this problem.

⚙ **Troubleshoot** 7. The formula in cell L8 that calculates the total number of billable hours for the first customer is not correct. Instead of showing the number of hours, it displays the value as a percentage of a day. Fix this problem by revising the formula so that it multiplies the difference between the value in K8 and J8 by 24. (*Hint:* Use parentheses to enclose the expression that calculates the difference between starting and ending times so that the difference is calculated first.)

8. Copy the formula you entered for cell L8 to calculate the total billable hours for the rest of the entries in column L.

9. The total charge for each service call is equal to the hourly rate multiplied by the number of hours plus the charge for parts. In cell O8, enter a formula to calculate the total service charge for the first customer, and then copy that formula to calculate the rest of the service charges in column O.

10. In cell B4, enter a formula that uses the COUNT function to count the total number of service calls.

⚙ **Troubleshoot** 11. In cell B5, Stefan entered a formula to calculate the total charges from all of the service calls. Examine the formula, and correct the expression so that it adds all of the service call charges.

12. Insert two new rows above row 5.

13. In cell A5, enter the label **Total Hours**. In cell B5, enter function to calculate the total number of hours from all of the service calls.

14. In cell A6, enter the label **Average Charge**. In cell B6, enter a formula that calculates the average charge per call by dividing the total charges by the total number of calls.

15. Add borders around the cells in the nonadjacent range A4:B7,A9:O29.

16. Set the page layout of the Call Sheet worksheet so that it prints on a single page in landscape orientation.

17. View the worksheet in Page Break Preview, return to Normal view, and then save and close the workbook.

EXCEL

OBJECTIVES

Session 2.1
- Change fonts, font style, and font color
- Add fill colors and a background image
- Create formulas to calculate sales data
- Format numbers as currency and percentages
- Format dates and times
- Align, indent, and rotate cell contents
- Merge a group of cells

Session 2.2
- Use the AVERAGE function
- Apply cell styles
- Copy and paste formats with the Format Painter
- Find and replace text and formatting
- Change workbook themes
- Highlight cells with conditional formats
- Format a worksheet for printing
- Set the print area, insert page breaks, add print titles, create headers and footers, and set margins

Formatting Workbook Text and Data

Creating a Sales Report

Case | *Morning Bean*

Carol Evans is a sales manager at Morning Bean, a small but growing chain of shops specializing in coffee, tea, and other hot drinks. Carol needs to develop a workbook for the upcoming sales conference that will provide information on sales and profits for stores located in the Northwest region of the country. Carol already started the workbook by entering sales data for the previous years. She wants you to use this financial data to calculate summary statistics and then format the workbook before it's distributed to stockholders attending the conference.

STARTING DATA FILES

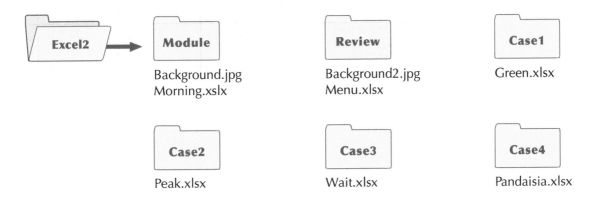

Excel2 → Module
Background.jpg
Morning.xslx

Review
Background2.jpg
Menu.xlsx

Case1
Green.xlsx

Case2
Peak.xlsx

Case3
Wait.xlsx

Case4
Pandaisia.xlsx

Session 2.1 Visual Overview:

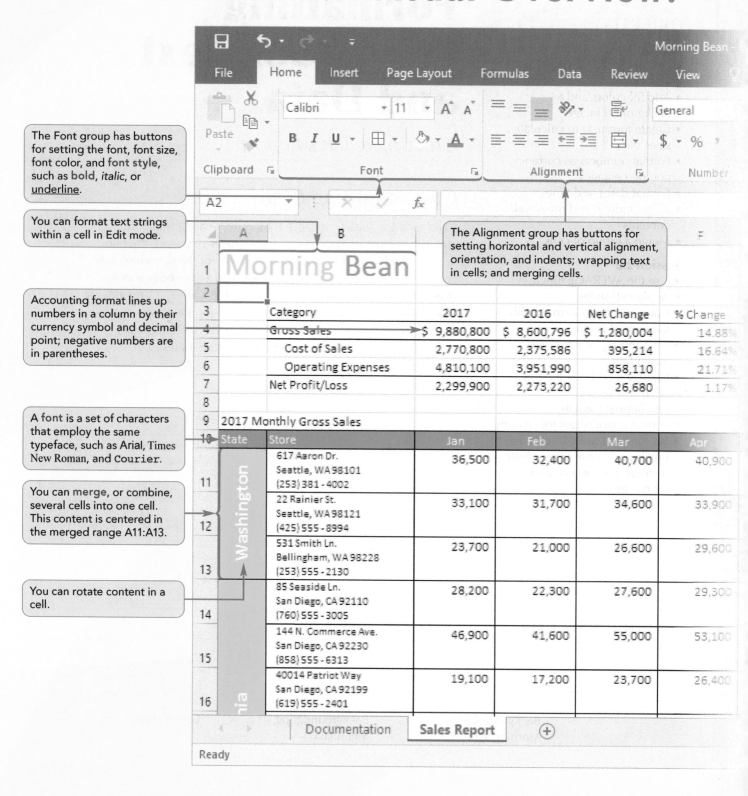

The Font group has buttons for setting the font, font size, font color, and font style, such as **bold**, *italic*, or <u>underline</u>.

You can format text strings within a cell in Edit mode.

Accounting format lines up numbers in a column by their currency symbol and decimal point; negative numbers are in parentheses.

A font is a set of characters that employ the same typeface, such as Arial, Times New Roman, and Courier.

You can merge, or combine, several cells into one cell. This content is centered in the merged range A11:A13.

You can rotate content in a cell.

The Alignment group has buttons for setting horizontal and vertical alignment, orientation, and indents; wrapping text in cells; and merging cells.

Category	2017	2016	Net Change	% Change
Gross Sales	$ 9,880,800	$ 8,600,796	$ 1,280,004	14.88%
Cost of Sales	2,770,800	2,375,586	395,214	16.64%
Operating Expenses	4,810,100	3,951,990	858,110	21.71%
Net Profit/Loss	2,299,900	2,273,220	26,680	1.17%

2017 Monthly Gross Sales

State	Store	Jan	Feb	Mar	Apr
Washington	617 Aaron Dr. Seattle, WA 98101 (253) 381 - 4002	36,500	32,400	40,700	40,900
	22 Rainier St. Seattle, WA 98121 (425) 555 - 8994	33,100	31,700	34,600	33,900
	531 Smith Ln. Bellingham, WA 98228 (253) 555 - 2130	23,700	21,000	26,600	29,600
California	85 Seaside Ln. San Diego, CA 92110 (760) 555 - 3005	28,200	22,300	27,600	29,300
	144 N. Commerce Ave. San Diego, CA 92230 (858) 555 - 6313	46,900	41,600	55,000	53,100
	40014 Patriot Way San Diego, CA 92199 (619) 555 - 2401	19,100	17,200	23,700	26,400

Documentation   **Sales Report**

Ready

Formatting a Worksheet

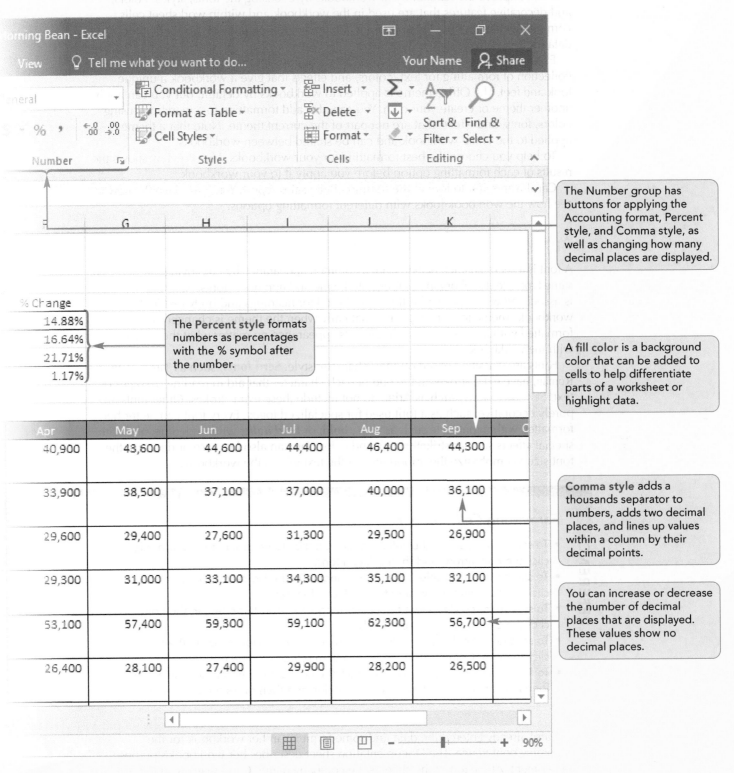

The Number group has buttons for applying the Accounting format, Percent style, and Comma style, as well as changing how many decimal places are displayed.

The **Percent style** formats numbers as percentages with the % symbol after the number.

A **fill color** is a background color that can be added to cells to help differentiate parts of a worksheet or highlight data.

Comma style adds a thousands separator to numbers, adds two decimal places, and lines up values within a column by their decimal points.

You can increase or decrease the number of decimal places that are displayed. These values show no decimal places.

% Change

14.88%	
16.64%	
21.71%	
1.17%	

Apr	May	Jun	Jul	Aug	Sep	O
40,900	43,600	44,600	44,400	46,400	44,300	
33,900	38,500	37,100	37,000	40,000	36,100	
29,600	29,400	27,600	31,300	29,500	26,900	
29,300	31,000	33,100	34,300	35,100	32,100	
53,100	57,400	59,300	59,100	62,300	56,700	
26,400	28,100	27,400	29,900	28,200	26,500	

Formatting Cell Text

You can improve the readability of workbooks by choosing the fonts, styles, colors, and decorative features that are used in the workbook and within worksheet cells. Formatting changes only the appearance of the workbook data—it does not affect the data itself.

Excel organizes complementary formatting options into themes. A **theme** is a collection of formatting for text, colors, and effects that give a workbook a unique look and feel. The Office theme is applied to workbooks by default, but you can apply another theme or create your own. You can also add formatting to a workbook using colors, fonts, and effects that are not part of the current theme. Note that a theme is applied to the entire workbook and can be shared between workbooks.

To help you choose the best formatting for your workbooks, **Live Preview** shows the results of each formatting option before you apply it to your workbook.

Carol wants you to format the Morning Bean sales report. You'll use Live Preview to see how the workbook looks with different formatting options.

Applying Fonts and Font Styles

A font is a set of characters that share a common appearance by employing the same typeface. Excel organizes fonts into theme and nontheme fonts. A **theme font** is associated with a particular theme and used for headings and body text in the workbook. Theme fonts change automatically when the theme is changed. Text formatted with a **nontheme font** retains its appearance no matter what theme is used with the workbook.

Fonts are classified based on their character style. **Serif fonts**, such as Times New Roman, have extra strokes at the end of each character that aid in reading passages of text. **Sans serif fonts**, such as Arial, do not include these extra strokes. Other fonts are purely decorative, such as a font used for specialized logos. Every font can be further formatted with a font style such as *italic*, **bold**, or ***bold italic***; with underline; and with special effects such as ~~strikethrough~~ and color. You can also increase or decrease the font size to emphasize the importance of the text within the workbook.

REFERENCE

Formatting Cell Content

- To set the font, select the cell or range. On the Home tab, in the Font group, click the Font arrow, and then select a font.
- To set the font size, select the cell or range. On the Home tab, in the Font group, click the Font Size arrow, and then select a font size.
- To set the font style, select the cell or range. On the Home tab, in the Font group, click the Bold, Italic, or Underline button.
- To set the font color, select the cell or range. On the Home tab, in the Font group, click the Font Color button arrow, and then select a theme or nontheme color.
- To format a text selection, double-click the cell to enter Edit mode, select the text to format, change the font, size, style, or color, and then press the Enter key.

Carol already entered the data and some formulas in her workbook for the upcoming conference. The Documentation sheet describes her workbook's purpose and content. At the top of the sheet is the company name. Carol wants you to format the name in large, bold letters using the default heading font from the Office theme.

To the format the company name:

1. Open the **Morning** workbook located in the **Excel2 > Module** folder included with your Data Files, and then save the workbook as **Morning Bean** in the location specified by your instructor.

2. In the Documentation sheet, enter your name in cell B4 and the date in cell B5.

3. Click cell **A1** to make it the active cell.

4. On the Home tab, in the Font group, click the **Font button arrow** to display a gallery of fonts available on your computer. Each name is displayed in its font. The first two fonts listed are the theme fonts for headings and body text—Calibri Light and Calibri.

5. Scroll down the Fonts gallery until you see Bauhaus 93 in the All Fonts list, and then point to **Bauhaus 93** (or another font). Live Preview shows the effect of the Bauhaus 93 font on the text in cell A1. See Figure 2-1.

Figure 2-1   **Font gallery**

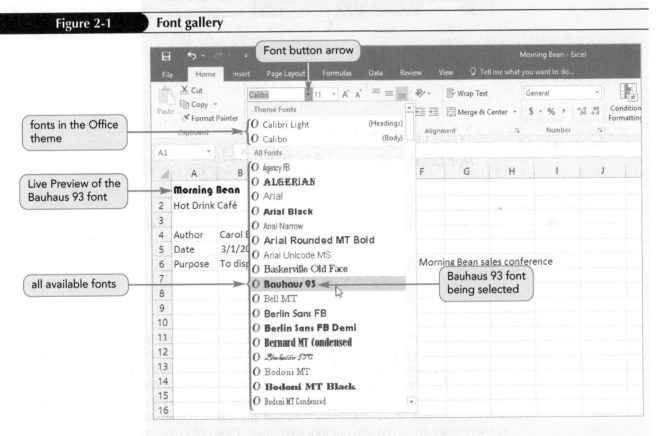

6. Point to three other fonts in the list to see the Live Preview of how the text in cell A1 would look with that font.

7. Click **Calibri Light** in the Theme Fonts list. The company name in cell A1 changes to the Calibri Light Font, the default headings font in the current theme.

8. In the Font group, click the **Font Size button arrow** to display a list of font sizes, point to **26** to preview the text in that font size, and then click **26**. The company name changes to 26 points.

9. In the Font group, click the **Bold** button **B** (or press **Ctrl+B** keys). The text changes to bold.

▶ **10.** Click cell **A2** to make it the active cell. The cell with the company description is selected.

▶ **11.** In the Font group, click the **Font Size button arrow** [11 ▾], and then click **18**. The company description changes to 18 points.

▶ **12.** In the Font group, click the **Italic** button [*I*] (or press the **Ctrl+I** keys). The company description in cell A2 is italicized.

▶ **13.** Select the range **A4:A6**, and then press the **Ctrl+B** keys. The text in the selected range changes to bold.

▶ **14.** Click cell **A7** to deselect the range. See Figure 2-2.

Figure 2-2	Formatted text in the Documentation sheet

Applying a Font Color

Color can transform a plain workbook filled with numbers and text into a powerful presentation that captures the user's attention and adds visual emphasis to the points you want to make. By default, Excel displays text in a black font color.

Like fonts, colors are organized into theme and nontheme colors. **Theme colors** are the 12 colors that belong to the workbook's theme. Four colors are designated for text and backgrounds, six colors are used for accents and highlights, and two colors are used for hyperlinks (followed and not followed links). These 12 colors are designed to work well together and to remain readable in all combinations. Each theme color has five variations, or accents, in which a different tint or shading is applied to the theme color.

Ten **standard colors**—dark red, red, orange, yellow, light green, green, light blue, blue, dark blue, and purple—are always available regardless of the workbook's theme. You can open an extended palette of 134 standard colors. You can also create a custom color by specifying a mixture of red, blue, and green color values, making available 16.7 million custom colors—more colors than the human eye can distinguish. Some dialog boxes have an automatic color option that uses your Windows default text and background colors, usually black text on a white background.

Creating Custom Colors

Custom colors let you add subtle and striking colors to a formatted workbook. To create custom colors, you use the RGB Color model in which each color is expressed with varying intensities of red, green, and blue. RGB color values are often represented as a set of numbers in the format

`(red, green, blue)`

where `red` is an intensity value assigned to red light, `green` is an intensity value assigned to green light, and `blue` is an intensity value assigned to blue light. The intensities are measured on a scale of 0 to 255—0 indicates no intensity (or the absence of the color) and 255 indicates the highest intensity. So, the RGB color value (255, 255, 0) represents a mixture of high-intensity red (255) and high-intensity green (255) with the absence of blue (0), which creates the color yellow.

To create colors in Excel using the RGB model, click the More Colors option located in a color menu or dialog box to open the Colors dialog box. In the Colors dialog box, click the Custom tab, and then enter the red, green, and blue intensity values. A preview box shows the resulting RGB color.

Carol wants the company name and description in the Documentation sheet to stand out. You will change the text in cell A1 and cell A2 to green.

To change the font color of the company name and description:

▶ **1.** Select the range **A1:A2**.

▶ **2.** On the Home tab, in the Font group, click the **Font Color button arrow** [A ▾] to display the gallery of theme and standard colors.

▶ **3.** In the Standard Colors section, point to the **Green** color (the sixth color). The color name appears in a ScreenTip, and you see a Live Preview of the text with the green font color. See Figure 2-3.

Figure 2-3   **Font Color gallery**

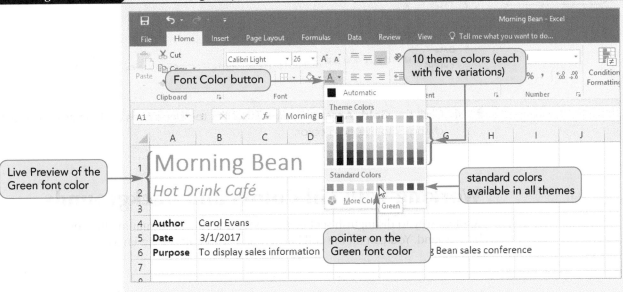

▶ **4.** Click the **Green** color. The company name and description change to green.

Formatting Text Selections Within a Cell

In Edit mode, you can select and format selections of text within a cell. You can make these changes to selected text from the ribbon or from the Mini toolbar. The **Mini toolbar** contains buttons for common formatting options used for that selection. These same buttons appear on the ribbon.

Carol asks you to format the company name in cell A1 so that the text "Morning" appears in gold.

To format part of the company name in cell A1:

1. Double-click cell **A1** to select the cell and enter Edit mode (or click cell **A1** and press the **F2** key). The status bar shows Edit to indicate that you are working with the cell in Edit mode. The pointer changes to the I-beam pointer.

2. Drag the pointer over the word **Morning** to select it. A Mini toolbar appears above the selected text with buttons to change the font, size, style, and color of the selected text in the cell. In this instance, you want to change the font color.

3. On the Mini toolbar, click the **Font Color button arrow** , and then in the Themes Colors section, point to the **Gold, Accent 4** color (the eighth color). Live Preview shows the color of the selected text as gold. See Figure 2-4.

| Figure 2-4 | Mini toolbar in Edit mode |

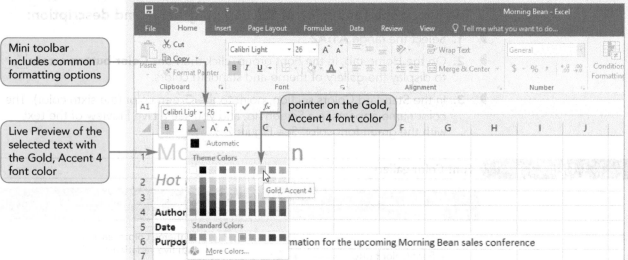

4. Click the **Gold, Accent 4** color. The Mini toolbar closes and the selected text changes to the gold color.

Working with Fill Colors and Backgrounds

Another way to distinguish sections of a worksheet is by formatting the cell background. You can fill the cell background with color or an image.

Changing a Fill Color

By default, worksheet cells do not include any background color. But background colors, also known as fill colors, can be helpful for distinguishing different parts of a worksheet or adding visual interest. The same selection of colors used to format the color of cell text can be used to format the cell background.

INSIGHT

Using Color to Enhance a Workbook

When used wisely, color can enhance any workbook. However, when used improperly, color can distract the user, making the workbook more difficult to read. As you format a workbook, keep in mind the following tips:

- Use colors from the same theme to maintain a consistent look and feel across the worksheets. If the built-in themes do not fit your needs, you can create a custom theme.
- Use colors to differentiate types of cell content and to direct users where to enter data. For example, format a worksheet so that formula results appear in cells without a fill color and users enter data in cells with a light gray fill color.
- Avoid color combinations that are difficult to read.
- Print the workbook on both color and black-and-white printers to ensure that the printed copy is readable in both versions.
- Understand your printer's limitations and features. Colors that look good on your monitor might not look as good when printed.
- Be sensitive to your audience. About 8 percent of all men and 0.5 percent of all women have some type of color blindness and might not be able to see the text when certain color combinations are used. Red-green color blindness is the most common, so avoid using red text on a green background or green text on a red background.

Carol wants you to change the background color of the range A4:A6 in the Documentation sheet to green and the font color to white.

To change the font and fill colors in the Documentation sheet:

1. Select the range **A4:A6**.

2. On the Home tab, in the Font group, click the **Fill Color button arrow**, and then click the **Green** color (the sixth color) in the Standard Colors section.

3. In the Font group, click the **Font Color button arrow**, and then click the **White, Background 1** color (the first color) in the Theme Colors section. The labels are formatted as white text on a green background.

4. Select the range **B4:B6**, and then format the cells with the **Green** font color and the **White, Background 1** fill color.

5. Increase the width of column B to **30** characters, and then wrap the text within the selected range.

6. Select the range **A4:B6**, and then add all borders around each of the selected cells.

7. Click cell **A7** to deselect the range. See Figure 2-5.

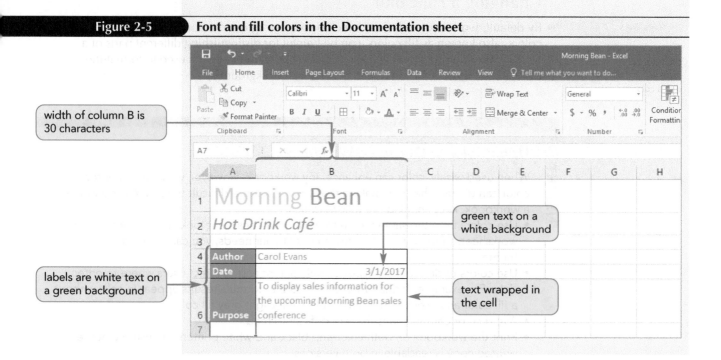

Figure 2-5 Font and fill colors in the Documentation sheet

width of column B is 30 characters

labels are white text on a green background

green text on a white background

text wrapped in the cell

Adding a Background Image

Another way to add visual interest to worksheets is with a background image. Many background images are based on textures such as granite, wood, or fibered paper. The image does not need to match the size of the worksheet; a smaller image can be repeated until it fills the entire sheet. Background images do not affect any cell's format or content. Fill colors added to cells appear on top of the image, covering that portion of the image.

Carol has provided an image that she wants you to use as the background of the Documentation sheet.

To add a background image to the Documentation sheet:

1. On the ribbon, click the **Page Layout** tab to display the page layout options.

2. In the Page Setup group, click the **Background** button. The Insert Pictures dialog box opens with options to search for an image file on your computer or local network, or use the Bing Image Search tool.

3. Click the **Browse** button next to the From a file label. The Sheet Background dialog box opens.

4. Navigate to the **Excel2 > Module** folder included with your Data Files, click the **Background** JPEG image file, and then click the **Insert** button. The image is added to the background of the Documentation sheet. The Background button changes to the Delete Background button, which you can click to remove background image. See Figure 2-6.

Figure 2-6   Background image added to the Documentation sheet

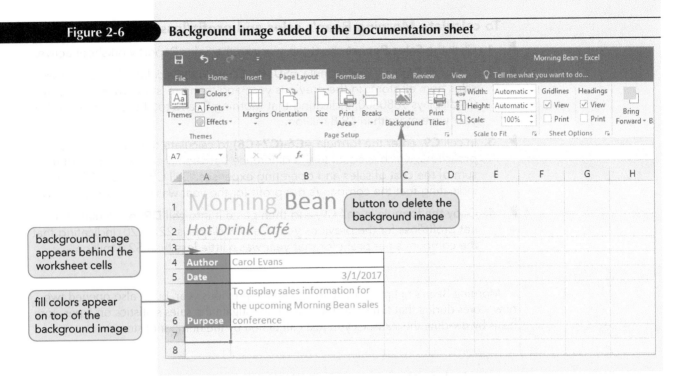

You've completed the formatting the Documentation sheet. Next, you'll work on the Sales Report worksheet.

Using Functions and Formulas to Calculate Sales Data

In the Sales Report worksheet, you will format the data on the gross sales from each of Morning Bean's 20 stores. The worksheet is divided into two areas. The table at the bottom of the worksheet displays gross sales for the past year for each month by store. The section at the top of the worksheet summarizes the sales over the past two years. Carol has compiled the following sales data:

- **Gross Sales**—the total amount of sales at all of the stores
- **Cost of Sales**—the cost of creating Morning Bean products
- **Operating Expenses**—the cost of running the individual stores including the employment and insurance costs
- **Net Profit/Loss**—the difference between the income from the gross sales and the total cost of sales and operating expenses
- **Units Sold**—the total number of menu items sold by Morning Bean during the year
- **Customers Served**—the total number of customers served by Morning Bean during the year

Carol wants you to calculate these sales statistics for the entire company and for each individual store. First, you will calculate Morning Bean's total gross sales from the past year and the company's overall net profit and loss.

To calculate Morning Bean's sales and profit/loss:

▶ 1. Click the **Sales Report** sheet tab to make the Sales Report worksheet active.

▶ 2. Click cell **C6**, type the formula **=SUM(C27:N46)** to calculate the total gross sales from all stores in the previous year, and then press the **Enter** key. Cell C6 displays 9880800, indicating that Morning Bean's total gross sales for the year were more than $9.8 million.

▶ 3. In cell **C9**, enter the formula **=C6-(C7+C8)** to calculate the current year's net profit/loss, which is equal to the difference between the gross sales and the sum of the cost of sales and operating expenses. Cell C9 displays 2299900, indicating that the company's net profit for the year was close to $2.3 million.

▶ 4. Copy the formula in cell **C9**, and then paste it into cell **D9** to calculate the net profit/loss for the previous year. Cell D9 displays 2273220, indicating that the company's net profit for that year was a little less than $2.3 million.

Morning Bean's net profit increased from the previous year, but it also opened two new stores during that time. Carol wants to investigate the sales statistics on a per-store basis by dividing the statistics you just calculated by the number of stores.

To calculate the per-store statistics:

▶ 1. In cell **C16**, enter the formula **=C6/C23** to calculate the gross sales per store for the year. The formula returns 494040, indicating each Morning Bean store had, on average, almost $500,000 in gross sales during the year.

▶ 2. In cell **C17**, enter the formula **=C7/C23** to calculate the cost of sales per store for the year. The formula returns the value 138540, indicating each Morning Bean store had a little more than $138,000 in sales cost.

▶ 3. In cell **C18**, enter the formula **=C8/C23** to calculate the operating expenses per store for the year. The formula returns the value 240505, indicating that operating expense of a typical store was a little more than $240,000.

▶ 4. In cell **C19**, enter the formula **=C9/C23** to calculate the net profit/loss per store for the year. The formula returns the value 114995, indicating that the net profit/loss of a typical store was about $115,000.

▶ 5. In cell **C21**, enter the formula **=C11/C23** to calculate the units sold per store for the year. The formula returns the value 72655, indicating that a typical store sold more than 72,000 units.

▶ 6. In cell **C22**, enter the formula **=C12/C23** to calculate the customers served per store during the year. The formula returns the value 10255, indicating that a typical store served more than 10,000 customers.

▶ 7. Copy the formulas in the range **C16:C22** and paste them into the range **D16:D22**. The cell references in the formulas change to calculate the sales data for the previous year.

▶ 8. Click cell **B24** to deselect the range. See Figure 2-7.

Figure 2-7	Overall and per-store sales statistics

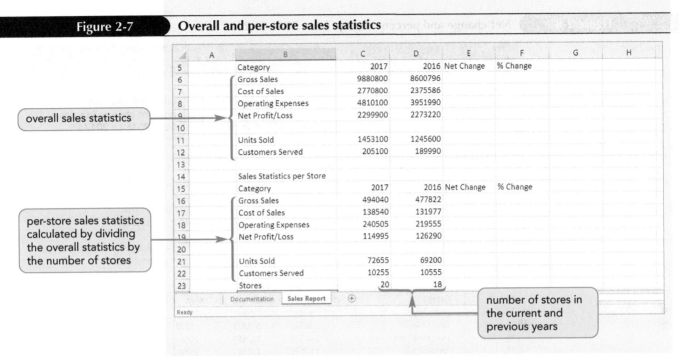

overall sales statistics

per-store sales statistics calculated by dividing the overall statistics by the number of stores

number of stores in the current and previous years

Carol also wants to report how the company's sales and expenses have changed from the previous year to the current year. To do this, you will calculate the net change in the sales statistics as well as the percent change. The percent change is calculated using the following formula:

$$\text{percent change} = \frac{\text{current year value} - \text{previous year value}}{\text{previous year value}}$$

You will calculate the net change and percentage for all of the statistics in the Sales Report worksheet.

To calculate the net and percent changes:

1. In cell **E6**, enter the formula **=C6–D6** to calculate the difference in gross sales between the previous year and the current year. The formula returns 1280004, indicating that gross sales increased by about $1.28 million.

2. In cell **F6**, enter the formula **=(C6–D6)/D6** to calculate the percent change in gross sales from the previous year to the current year. The formula returns 0.1488239, indicating an increase in gross sales of about 14.88 percent.

   Next, you'll copy and paste the formulas in cells E6 and F6 to the rest of the sales data to calculate the net change and percent change from the previous year to the current year.

3. Select the range **E6:F6**, and then copy the selected range. The two formulas are copied to the Clipboard.

4. Select the nonadjacent range **E7:F9,E11:F12,E16:F19,E21:F23**, and then paste the formulas from the Clipboard into the selected range. The net and percent changes are calculated for the remaining sales data.

5. Click cell **B24** to deselect the range, and then scroll the worksheet up to display row 5. See Figure 2-8.

Be sure to include the parentheses as shown to calculate the percent change correctly.

| Figure 2-8 | Net change and percent change from 2016 to 2017 |

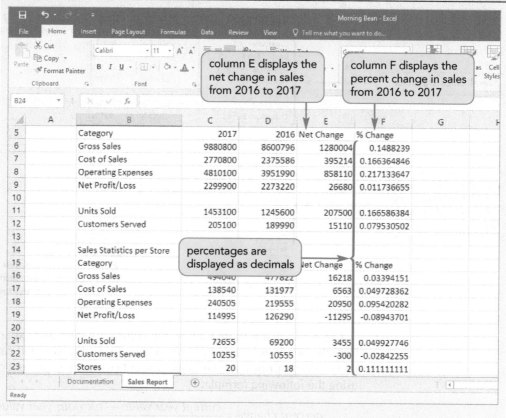

The bottom part of the worksheet contains the sales for each cafe from the current year. You will use the SUM function to calculate the total gross sales for each store during the entire year, the total monthly sales of all 20 stores, and the total gross sales of all stores and months.

To calculate different subtotals of the gross sales:

▶ 1. Click in the **Name** box to select the current cell reference, type **O26**, and then press the **Enter** key. Cell O26 is selected.

▶ 2. Type **TOTAL** as the label, and then press the **Enter** key. Cell O27 is now the active cell.

▶ 3. On the ribbon, click the **Home** tab, if necessary.

▶ 4. In the Editing group, click the **AutoSum** button, and then press the **Enter** key to accept the suggested range reference and enter the formula =SUM(C27:N27) in cell O27. The cell displays 370000, indicating gross sales in 2017 for the 85 Seaside Lane store in San Diego were $370,000.

▶ 5. Copy the formula in cell **O27**, and then paste that formula into the range **O28:O46** to calculate the total sales for each of the remaining 19 stores in the Morning Bean chain.

▶ 6. Click cell **B47**, type **TOTAL** as the label, and then press the **Tab** key. Cell C47 is now the active cell.

▶ 7. Select the range **C47:O47** so that you can calculate the total monthly sales for all of the stores.

▶ **8.** On the Home tab, in the Editing group, click the **AutoSum** button to calculate the total sales for each month as well as the total sales for all months. For example, cell C47 displays 710900, indicating that monthly sales from all stores in January were $710,900.

▶ **9.** Click cell **O48** to deselect the range. See Figure 2-9.

Figure 2-9	Gross sales by store and month

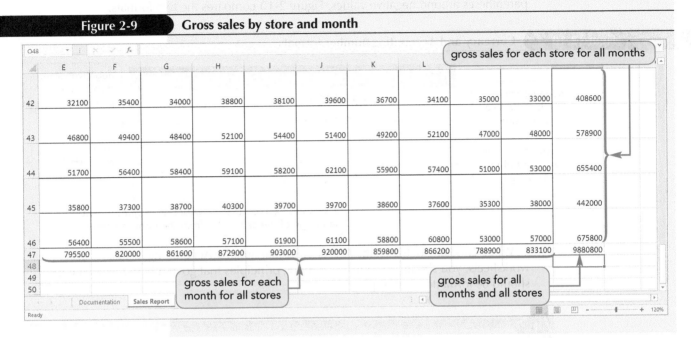

The Sales Report worksheet contains a lot of information that is difficult to read in its current form. You can improve the readability of the data by adding number formats.

Formatting Numbers

The goal in formatting any workbook is to make the content easier to interpret. For numbers, this can mean adding a comma to separate thousands, setting the number of decimal places, and using percentage and currency symbols to make numbers easier to read and understand. Changing the number format does not affect the value itself, only how that value is displayed in the worksheet.

Applying Number Formats

Cells start out formatted with the General format, which, for the most part, displays numbers exactly as they are typed. If a value is calculated from a formula or function, the General format displays as many digits after the decimal point as will fit in the cell and rounds the last digit. Calculated values that are too large to fit into the cell are displayed in scientific notation.

The General format is fine for small numbers, but some values require additional formatting to make the numbers easier to interpret. For example, you might want to:

- Change the number of digits displayed to the right of the decimal point
- Add commas to separate thousands in large numbers
- Include currency symbols to numbers to identify the monetary unit being used
- Identify percentages using the % symbol

TIP

To apply the Currency format, click the Number Format button arrow and click Currency, or press the Ctrl+Shift+$ keys.

Excel supports two monetary formats—currency and accounting. Both formats add a thousands separator to the currency values and display two digits to the right of the decimal point. However, the **Currency format** places a currency symbol directly to the left of the first digit of the currency value and displays negative numbers with a negative sign. The **Accounting format** fixes a currency symbol at the left edge of the column, and displays negative numbers within parentheses and zero values with a dash. It also slightly indents the values from the right edge of the cell to allow room for parentheses around negative values. Figure 2-10 compares the two formats.

Figure 2-10   Currency and Accounting number formats

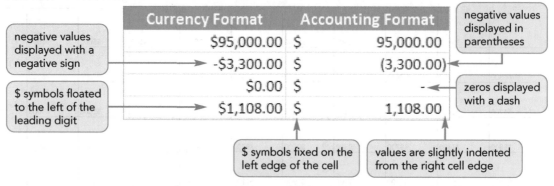

When choosing between the Currency format and the Accounting format for your worksheets, you should consider accounting principles that govern how financial data should be formatted and displayed.

PROSKILLS

Written Communication: Formatting Monetary Values

Spreadsheets commonly include monetary values. To make these values simpler to read and comprehend, keep in mind the following guidelines when formatting the currency data in a worksheet:

- **Format for your audience.** For general financial reports, round values to the nearest hundred, thousand, or million. Investors are generally more interested in the big picture than in exact values. However, for accounting reports, accuracy is important and often legally required. So, for those reports, be sure to display the exact monetary value.

- **Use thousands separators.** Large strings of numbers can be challenging to read. For monetary values, use a thousands separator to make the amounts easier to comprehend.

- **Apply the Accounting format to columns of monetary values.** The Accounting format makes columns of numbers easier to read than the Currency format. Use the Currency format for individual cells that are not part of long columns of numbers.

- **Use only two currency symbols in a column of monetary values.** Standard accounting format displays one currency symbol with the first monetary value in the column and optionally displays a second currency symbol with the last value in that column. Use the Accounting format to fix the currency symbols, lining them up within the column. Following these standard accounting principles will make your financial data easier to read both on the screen and in printouts.

Carol wants you to format the gross sales amounts in the Accounting format so that they are easier to read.

To format the gross sales in the Accounting format:

1. Select the range **C6:E6** containing the gross sales.

2. On the Home tab, in the Number group, click the **Accounting Number Format** button $. The numbers are formatted in the Accounting format. You cannot see the format because the cells display ##########.

The cells display ########## because the formatted numbers don't fit into the columns. One reason for this is that monetary values, by default, show both dollars and cents in the cell. However, you can increase or decrease the number of decimal places displayed in a cell. The displayed value might then be rounded. For example, the stored value 11.7 will appear in the cell as 12 if no decimal places are displayed to the right of the decimal point. Changing the number of decimal places displayed in a cell does not change the value stored in the cell.

Because the conference attendees are interested only in whole dollar amounts, Carol wants you to hide the cents values of the gross sales by decreasing the number of decimal places to zero.

To decrease the number of decimal places displayed in the gross sales:

1. Make sure the range **C6:E6** is still selected.

2. On the Home tab, in the Number group, click the **Decrease Decimal** button twice. The cents are hidden for gross sales.

3. Click cell **C4** to deselect the range. See Figure 2-11.

Figure 2-11   **Formatted gross sales values**

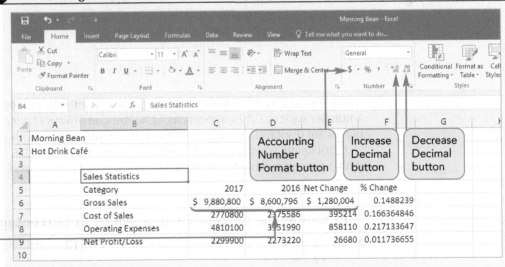

gross sales displayed in the Accounting format with no decimal places

The Comma style is identical to the Accounting format except that it does not fix a currency symbol to the left of the number. The advantage of using the Comma style and the Accounting format together is that the numbers will be aligned in the column.

Carol asks you to apply the Comma style to the remaining sales statistics.

To apply the Comma style to the sales statistics:

▶ **1.** Select the nonadjacent range **C7:E9,C11:E12** containing the sales figures for all stores in 2016 and 2017.

▶ **2.** On the Home tab, in the Number group, click the **Comma Style** button [,]. In some instances, the number is now too large to be displayed in the cell.

▶ **3.** In the Number group, click the **Decrease Decimal** button [.00→.0] twice to remove two decimal places. Digits to the right of the decimal point are hidden for all of the selected cells, and all of the numbers are now visible.

▶ **4.** Click cell **C13** to deselect the range. See Figure 2-12.

Figure 2-12	Formatted sales values

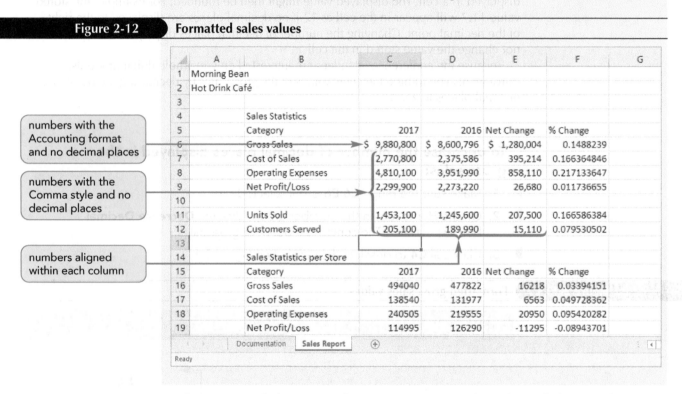

numbers with the Accounting format and no decimal places

numbers with the Comma style and no decimal places

numbers aligned within each column

The Percent style formats numbers as percentages with no decimal places so that a number such as 0.124 appears as 12%. You can always change how many decimal places are displayed in the cell if that is important to show with your data.

Carol wants you to format the percent change from the 2016 to 2017 sales statistics with a percent symbol to make the percent values easier to read.

To format the percent change values as percentages:

▶ **1.** Select the nonadjacent range **F6:F9,F11:F12** containing the percent change values.

▶ **2.** On the Home tab, in the Number group, click the **Percent Style** button [%] (or press the **Ctrl+Shift+%** keys). The values are displayed as percentages with no decimal places.

▶ **3.** In the Number group, click the **Increase Decimal** button [←.0.00] twice. The displayed number includes two decimal places.

▶ **4.** Click cell **F13** to deselect the range. See Figure 2-13.

Figure 2-13	Formatted percent change values

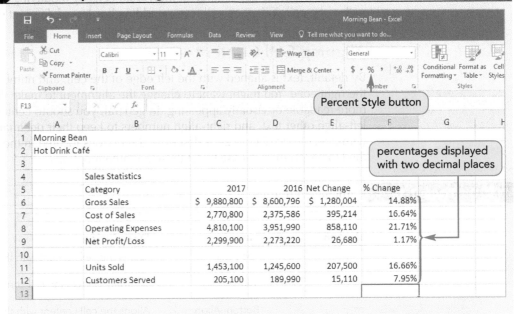

Percent Style button

percentages displayed with two decimal places

With the data reformatted, the worksheet clearly shows that Morning Bean's gross sales increased from 2016 to 2017 by almost 15 percent, but the company's net profit increased by only 1.17 percent due to increasing expenses in sales costs and operations of 16.64 percent and 21.71 percent, respectively. This type of information is very important to Morning Bean investors and to the company executives as plans are made for the upcoming year.

Formatting Dates and Times

TIP

To view the underlying date and time value, apply the General format to the cell or display the formulas instead of the formula results.

Because Excel stores dates and times as numbers and not as text, you can apply different date formats without affecting the underlying date and time value. The abbreviated format, *mm/dd/yyyy*, entered in the Documentation sheet is referred to as the Short Date format. You can also apply a Long Date format that displays the day of the week and the full month name in addition to the day of the month and the year. Other built-in formats include formats for displaying time values in 12- or 24-hour time format.

Carol asks you to change the date in the Documentation sheet to the Long Date format.

To format the date in the Long Date format:

1. Go to the **Documentation** sheet, and then select cell **B5**.

2. On the Home tab, in the Number group, click the **Number Format button arrow** to display a list of number formats, and then click **Long Date**. The date is displayed with the weekday name, month name, day, and year. Notice that the date in the formula bar did not change because you changed only the display format, not the date value.

Formatting Worksheet Cells

You can format the appearance of individual cells by modifying the alignment of text within the cell, indenting cell text, or adding borders of different styles and colors.

Aligning Cell Content

By default, text is aligned with the left edge of the cell, and numbers are aligned with the right edge. You might want to change the alignment to make the text and numbers more readable or visually appealing. In general, you should center column titles, left-align other text, and right-align numbers to keep their decimal places lined up within a column. Figure 2-14 describes the buttons located in the Alignment group on the Home tab that you use to set these alignment options.

Figure 2-14   **Alignment buttons**

Button	Name	Description
	Top Align	Aligns the cell content with the cell's top edge
	Middle Align	Vertically centers the cell content within the cell
	Bottom Align	Aligns the cell content with the cell's bottom edge
	Align Left	Aligns the cell content with the cell's left edge
	Center	Horizontally centers the cell content within the cell
	Align Right	Aligns the cell content with the cell's right edge
	Decrease Indent	Decreases the size of the indentation used in the cell
	Increase Indent	Increases the size of the indentation used in the cell
	Orientation	Rotates the cell content to any angle within the cell
	Wrap Text	Forces the cell text to wrap within the cell borders
	Merge & Center	Merges the selected cells into a single cell

The date in the Documentation sheet is right-aligned within cell B5 because Excel treats dates and times as numbers. Carol wants you to left-align the date from the Documentation sheet and center the column titles in the Sales Report worksheet.

To left-align the date and center the column titles:

1. In the Documentation sheet, make sure cell **B5** is still selected.

2. On the Home tab, in the Alignment group, click the **Align Left** button. The date shifts to the left edge of the cell.

3. Go to the **Sales Report** worksheet.

4. Select the range **C5:F5** containing the column titles.

5. In the Alignment group, click the **Center** button. The column titles are centered in the cells.

Indenting Cell Content

Sometimes you want a cell's content moved a few spaces from the cell's left edge. This is particularly useful to create subsections in a worksheet or to set off some entries from others. You can increase the indent to shift the contents of a cell away from the left edge of the cell, or you can decrease the indent to shift a cell's contents closer to the left edge of the cell.

Carol wants you to indent the Cost of Sales and Operating Expenses labels in the sales statistics table from the other labels because they represent expenses to the company.

To indent the expense categories:

▶ **1.** Select the range **B7:B8** containing the expense categories.

▶ **2.** On the Home tab, in the Alignment group, click the **Increase Indent** button ⊞ twice to indent each label two spaces in its cell.

Adding Borders to Cells

Borders are another way to make financial data easier to interpret. Common accounting practices provide guidelines on when to add borders to cells. In general, a single black border should appear above a subtotal, a single bottom border should be added below a calculated number, and a double black bottom border should appear below the total.

Carol wants you to follow common accounting practices in the Sales Report worksheet. You will add borders below the column titles and below the gross sales values. You will add a top border to the net profit/loss values. Finally, you will add a top and bottom border to the Units Sold and Customers Served rows.

To add borders to the sales statistics data:

▶ **1.** Select the range **B5:F5** containing the cell headings.

▶ **2.** On the Home tab, in the Font group, click the **Borders button arrow** ⊞ ▾, and then click **Bottom Border**. A border is added below the column titles.

▶ **3.** Select the range **B6:F6** containing the gross sales amounts.

▶ **4.** In the Font group, click the **Bottom Border** button ⊞ to add a border below the selected gross sales amounts.

▶ **5.** Select the range **B9:F9**, click the **Borders button arrow** ⊞ ▾, and then click **Top Border** to add a border above the net profit/loss amounts.

   The Units Sold and Customers Served rows do not contain monetary values as the other rows do. You will distinguish these rows by adding a top and bottom border.

▶ **6.** Select the range **B11:F12**, click the **Borders button arrow** ⊞ ▾, and then click **Top and Bottom Border** to add a border above the number of units sold and below the number of customers served.

▶ **7.** Click cell **B3** to deselect the range. See Figure 2-15.

Figure 2-15   Borders, indents, and alignment added to the sales data

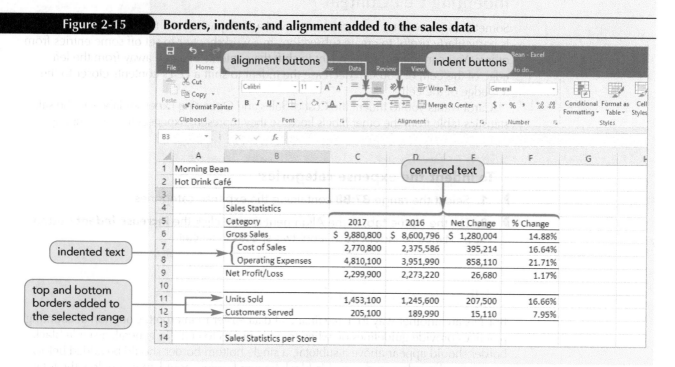

You can apply multiple formats to the same cell to create the look that best fits the data. For example, one cell might be formatted with a number format, alignments, borders, indents, fonts, font sizes, and so on. The monthly sales data needs to be formatted with number styles, alignments, indents, and borders. You'll add these formats now.

To format the monthly sales table:

1. Click in the **Name** box, type **C27:O47**, and then press the **Enter** key. The range C27:O47, containing the monthly gross sales for each store, is selected.

2. On the Home tab, in the Number group, click the **Comma Style** button to add a thousands separator to the values.

3. In the Number group, click the **Decrease Decimal** button twice to hide the cents from the sales results.

4. In the Alignment group, click the **Top Align** button to align the sales numbers with the top of each cell.

5. Select the range **C26:O26** containing the labels for the month abbreviations and the TOTAL column.

6. In the Alignment group, click the **Center** button to center the column labels.

7. Select the range **B27:B46** containing the store addresses.

8. Reduce the font size of the store addresses to **9** points.

9. In the Alignment group, click the **Increase Indent** button to indent the store addresses.

10. In the Alignment group, click the **Top Align** button to align the addresses at the top of each cell.

11. Select the range **B47:O47** containing the monthly totals.

12. In the Font group, click the **Borders button arrow**, and then click **All Borders** to add borders around each monthly totals cell.

▶ **13.** Select the range **O26:O46** containing the annual totals for each restaurant, and then click the **All Borders** button ⊞ to add borders around each restaurant total.

▶ **14.** Click cell **A24** to deselect the range. See Figure 2-16.

| Figure 2-16 | **Formatted monthly gross sales** |

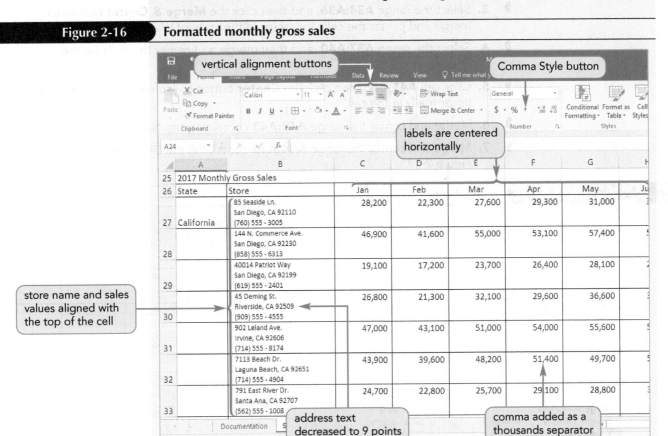

Merging Cells

You can merge, or combine, several cells into one cell. A merged cell contains two or more cells with a single cell reference. When you merge cells, only the content from the upper-left cell in the range is retained. The cell reference for the merged cell is the upper-left cell reference. So, if you merge cells A1 and A2, the merged cell reference is cell A1. After you merge cells, you can align the content within the merged cell. The Merge & Center button in the Alignment group on the Home tab includes the following options:

- **Merge & Center**—merges the range into one cell and horizontally centers the content
- **Merge Across**—merges each row in the selected range across the columns in the range
- **Merge Cells**—merges the range into a single cell but does not horizontally center the cell content
- **Unmerge Cells**—reverses a merge, returning the merged cell to a range of individual cells

The first column of the monthly sales data lists the states in which Morning Bean has stores. You will merge the cells for each state name into a single cell.

To merge the state name cells:

▶ **1.** Select the range **A27:A33** containing the cells for the California stores. You will merge these seven cells into a single cell.

▶ **2.** On the Home tab, in the Alignment group, click the **Merge & Center** button. The range A27:A33 merges into one cell with the cell reference A27, and the text is centered and bottom-aligned within the cell.

▶ **3.** Select the range **A34:A36**, and then click the **Merge & Center** button to merge and center the cells for stores in the state of Washington.

▶ **4.** Select the range **A37:A40**, and then merge and center the cells for the Oregon stores.

▶ **5.** Click cell **A41**, and then click the **Center** button ≣ to center the Idaho text horizontally in the cell.

▶ **6.** Merge and center the range **A42:A43** containing the Nevada cells.

▶ **7.** Merge and center the range **A44:A46** containing the Colorado cells. See Figure 2-17.

Figure 2-17 **Merged cells**

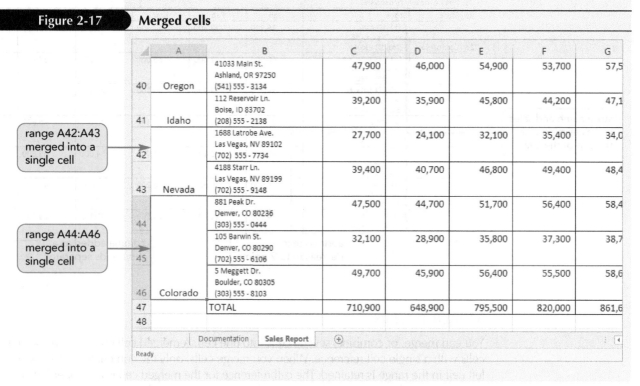

The merged cells make it easier to distinguish restaurants in each state. Next, you will rotate the cells so that the state name rotates up the merged cells.

Rotating Cell Contents

Text and numbers are displayed horizontally within cells. However, you can rotate cell text to any angle to save space or to provide visual interest to a worksheet. The state names at the bottom of the merged cells would look better and take up less room if they were rotated vertically within their cells. Carol asks you to rotate the state names.

To rotate the state names:

▶ **1.** Select the merged cell **A27**.

▶ **2.** On the Home tab, in the Alignment group, click the **Orientation** button to display a list of rotation options, and then click **Rotate Text Up**. The state name rotates 90 degrees counterclockwise.

3. In the Alignment group, click the **Middle Align** button ≡ to vertically center the rotated text in the merged cell.

4. Select the merged cell range **A34:A46**, and then repeat Steps 2 and 3 to rotate and vertically center the rest of the state names in their cells.

5. Reduce the width of column A to **7** characters because the rotated state names take up less space.

6. Select cell **A47**. See Figure 2-18.

| Figure 2-18 | Rotated cell content |

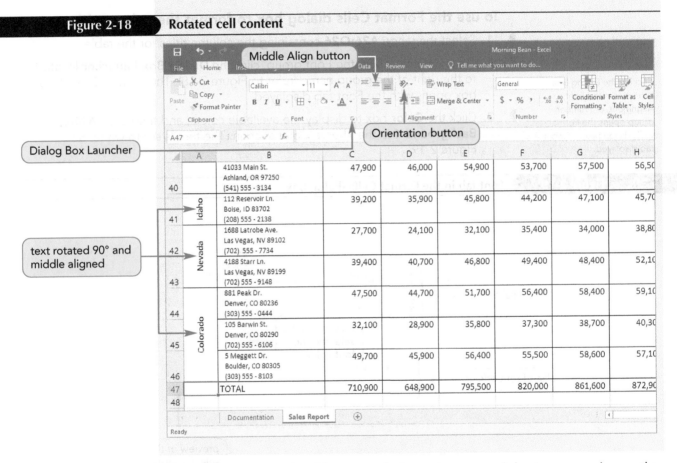

In addition to using the ribbon to apply formatting to a worksheet, you can also use the Format Cells dialog box to apply formatting.

Exploring the Format Cells Dialog Box

The buttons on the Home tab provide quick access to the most commonly used formatting choices. For more options, you can use the Format Cells dialog box. You can apply the formats in this dialog box to the selected worksheet cells. The Format Cells dialog box has six tabs, each focusing on a different set of formatting options, as described below:

- **Number**—provides options for formatting the appearance of numbers, including dates and numbers treated as text such as telephone or Social Security numbers
- **Alignment**—provides options for how data is aligned within a cell
- **Font**—provides options for selecting font types, sizes, styles, and other formatting attributes such as underlining and font colors

- **Border**—provides options for adding and removing cell borders as well as selecting a line style and color
- **Fill**—provides options for creating and applying background colors and patterns to cells
- **Protection**—provides options for locking or hiding cells to prevent other users from modifying their contents

Although you have applied many of these formats from the Home tab, the Format Cells dialog box presents them in a different way and provides more choices. You will use the Font and Fill tabs to format the column titles with a white font on a green background.

To use the Format Cells dialog box to format the column titles:

1. Select the range **A26:O26** containing the column titles for the table.

2. On the Home tab, in the Font group, click the **Dialog Box Launcher** located to the right of the group name (refer to Figure 2-18). The Format Cells dialog box opens with the Font tab displayed.

3. Click the **Color** box to display the available colors, and then click **White, Background 1** in the Theme Color section. The font is set to white. See Figure 2-19.

Figure 2-19 **Font tab in the Format Cells dialog box**

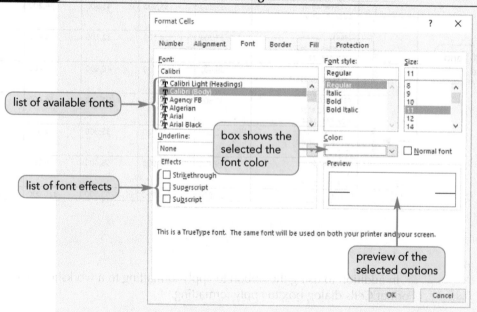

list of available fonts

box shows the selected the font color

list of font effects

preview of the selected options

4. Click the **Fill** tab to display background options.

5. In the Background Color section, click the **green** standard color (the sixth color in the last row). The background is set to green, as you can see in the Sample box.

6. Click the **OK** button. The dialog box closes, and the font and fill options you selected are applied to the column titles.

You will also use the Format Cells dialog box to change the appearance of the row titles. You'll format them to be displayed in a larger white font on a gold background.

To format the row titles:

▶ **1.** Select the range **A27:A46** containing the rotated state names.

▶ **2.** Right-click the selected range, and then click **Format Cells** on the shortcut menu. The Format Cells dialog box opens with the last tab used displayed—in this case, the Fill tab.

▶ **3.** In the Background Color section, click the **gold** theme color (the eighth color in the first row). Its preview is shown in the Sample box.

▶ **4.** Click the **Font** tab to display the font formatting options.

▶ **5.** Click the **Color** box, and then click the **White, Background 1** theme color to set the font color to white.

▶ **6.** In the Size box, click **14** to set the font size to 14 points.

▶ **7.** In the Font style box, click **Bold** to change the font to boldface.

▶ **8.** Click the **OK** button. The dialog box closes, and the font and fill formats are applied to the state names.

▶ **9.** Scroll up and click cell **A24** to deselect the A27:A46 range. See Figure 2-20.

Figure 2-20	Formatted worksheet cells

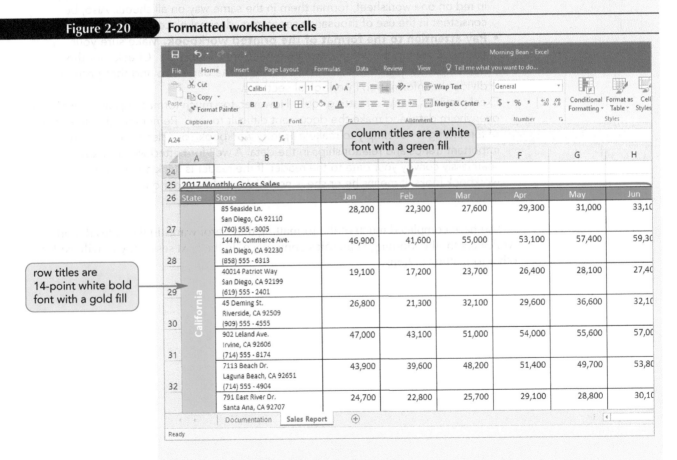

▶ **10.** Save the workbook.

With the formats you have added to the Sales Report worksheet, readers will be able to more easily read and interpret the large table of store sales.

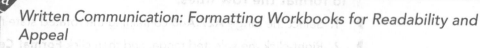

Written Communication: Formatting Workbooks for Readability and Appeal

Designing a workbook requires the same care as designing any written document or report. A well-formatted workbook is easy to read and establishes a sense of professionalism with readers. Do the following to improve the appearance of your workbooks:

- **Clearly identify each worksheet's purpose.** Include column or row titles and a descriptive sheet name.
- **Include only one or two topics on each worksheet.** Don't crowd individual worksheets with too much information. Place extra topics on separate sheets. Readers should be able to interpret each worksheet with a minimal amount of horizontal and vertical scrolling.
- **Place worksheets with the most important information first in the workbook.** Position worksheets summarizing your findings near the front of the workbook. Position worksheets with detailed and involved analysis near the end as an appendix.
- **Use consistent formatting throughout the workbook.** If negative values appear in red on one worksheet, format them in the same way on all sheets. Also, be consistent in the use of thousands separators, decimal places, and percentages.
- **Pay attention to the format of the printed workbook.** Make sure your printouts are legible with informative headers and footers. Check that the content of the printout is scaled correctly to the page size and that page breaks divide the information into logical sections.

Excel provides many formatting tools. However, too much formatting can be intrusive, overwhelm data, and make the document difficult to read. Remember that the goal of formatting is not simply to make a "pretty workbook" but also to accentuate important trends and relationships in the data. A well-formatted workbook should seamlessly convey your data to the reader. If the reader is thinking about how your workbook looks, it means he or she is not thinking about your data.

You have completed much of the formatting that Carol wants in the Sales Report worksheet for the Morning Bean sales conference. In the next session, you will explore other formatting options.

REVIEW

Session 2.1 Quick Check

1. What is the difference between a serif font and a sans serif font?

2. What is the difference between a theme color and a standard color?

3. A cell containing a number displays #######. Why does this occur, and what can you do to fix it?

4. What is the General format?

5. Describe the differences between Currency format and Accounting format.

6. The range B3:B13 is merged into a single cell. What is its cell reference?

7. How do you format text so that it is set vertically within the cell?

8. Where can you access all the formatting options for worksheet cells?

Session 2.2 Visual Overview:

The Page Layout tab has options for setting how the worksheet will print.

The Format Painter copies and pastes formatting from one cell or range to another without duplicating any data.

Print titles are rows and/or columns that are included on every page of the printout. In this case, the text in rows 1 and 2 will print on every page.

A manual page break is a page break that you set to indicate where a new page of the printout should start and is identified by a solid blue line.

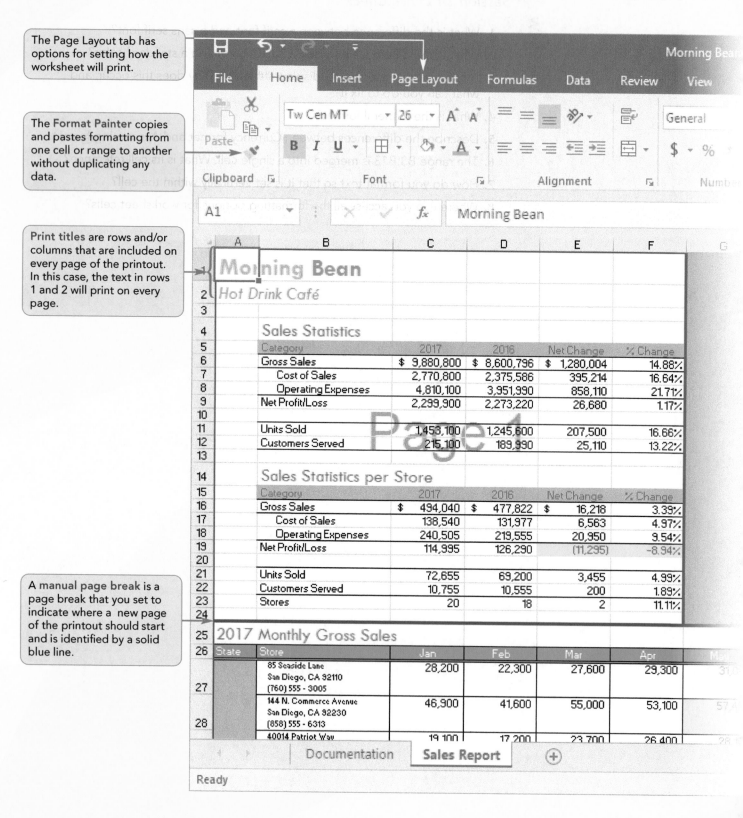

Designing a Printout

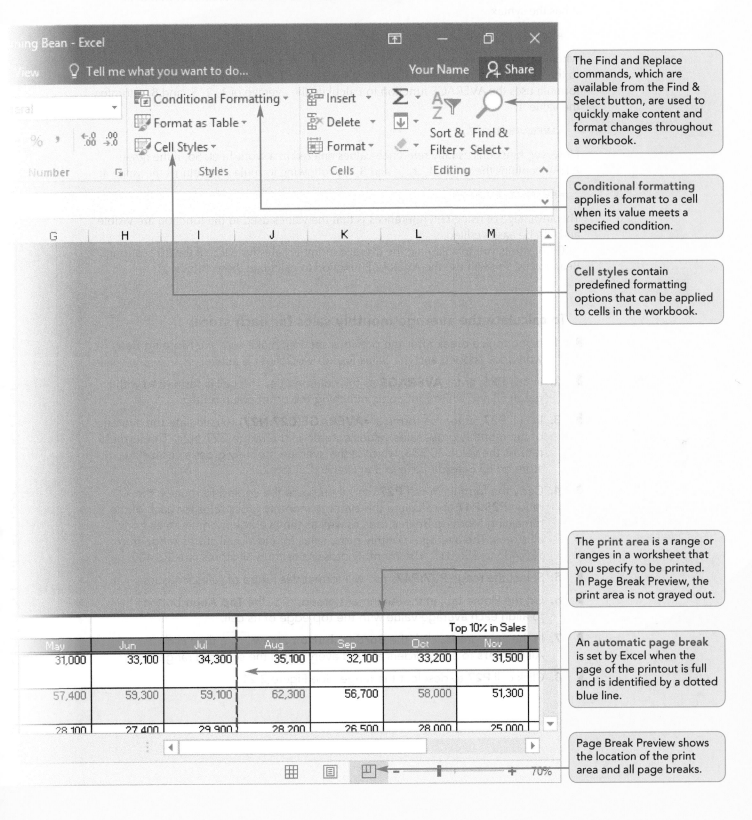

The Find and Replace commands, which are available from the Find & Select button, are used to quickly make content and format changes throughout a workbook.

Conditional formatting applies a format to a cell when its value meets a specified condition.

Cell styles contain predefined formatting options that can be applied to cells in the workbook.

The print area is a range or ranges in a worksheet that you specify to be printed. In Page Break Preview, the print area is not grayed out.

An automatic page break is set by Excel when the page of the printout is full and is identified by a dotted blue line.

Page Break Preview shows the location of the print area and all page breaks.

Calculating Averages

The **AVERAGE function** calculates the average value from a collection of numbers. It has the syntax

    AVERAGE(number1,number2,number3,…)

where *number1*, *number2*, *number3*, and so forth are either numbers or cell references to the cells or a range where the numbers are stored. For example, the following formula uses the AVERAGE function to calculate the average of 1, 2, 5, and 8, returning the value 4:

    =AVERAGE(1,2,5,8)

However, functions usually reference values entered in a worksheet. So, if the range A1:A4 contains the values 1, 2, 5, and 8, the following formula also returns the value 4:

    =AVERAGE(A1:A4)

The advantage of using cell references is that the values used in the function are visible and can be easily edited.

Carol wants you to calculate the average monthly sales for each of the 20 Morning Bean stores. You will use the AVERAGE function to calculate these values.

To calculate the average monthly sales for each store:

1. If you took a break after the previous session, make sure the Morning Bean workbook is open and the Sales Report worksheet is active.

2. In cell **P26**, enter **AVERAGE** as the column title. The cell is formatted with a green fill and white font color, matching the other column titles.

3. In cell **P27**, enter the formula **=AVERAGE(C27:N27)** to calculate the average of the monthly gross sales values entered in the range C27:N27. The formula returns the value 30,833, which is the average monthly gross sales for the store on 85 Seaside Lane in San Diego, California.

4. Copy the formula in cell **P27**, and then paste the copied formula in the range **P28:P47** to calculate the average monthly gross sales for each of the remaining Morning Bean stores as well as the average monthly sales from all stores. The average monthly gross sales for individual stores range from $25,408 to $56,317. The monthly gross sales from all stores is $823,400.

5. Select the range **P27:P47**. You will format this range of sales statistics.

6. On the Home tab, in the Alignment group, click the **Top Align** button to align each average value with the top edge of its cell.

7. In the Font group, click the **Borders button arrow**, then click **All Borders** to add borders around every cell in the selected range.

8. Click cell **P27** to deselect the range. See Figure 2-21.

Figure 2-21   Average sales results

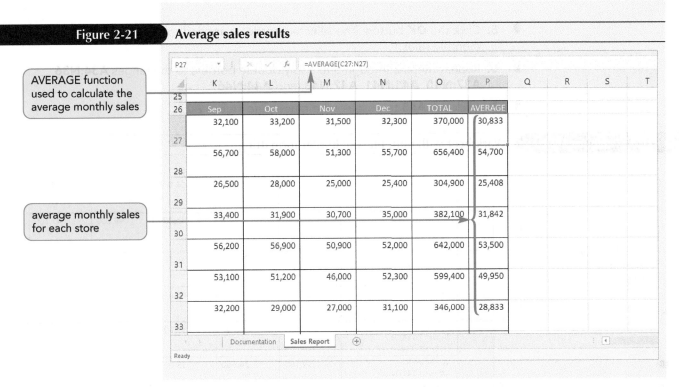

AVERAGE function used to calculate the average monthly sales

average monthly sales for each store

With so many values in the data, Carol wants you to insert double borders around the sales values for each state. The Border tab in the Format Cells dialog box provides options for changing the border style and color and placement.

To add a double border to the state results:

1. Select the range **A27:N33** containing the California monthly sales totals.

2. Open the Format Cells dialog box, and then click the **Border** tab.

3. In the Line section, click the **double line** in the lower-right corner of the Style box.

4. In the Presets section, click the **Outline** option. The double border appears around the selected cells in the Border preview. See Figure 2-22.

Figure 2-22   Border tab in the Format Cells dialog box

selected border option

selected border style

selected border color

preview of the selected border style

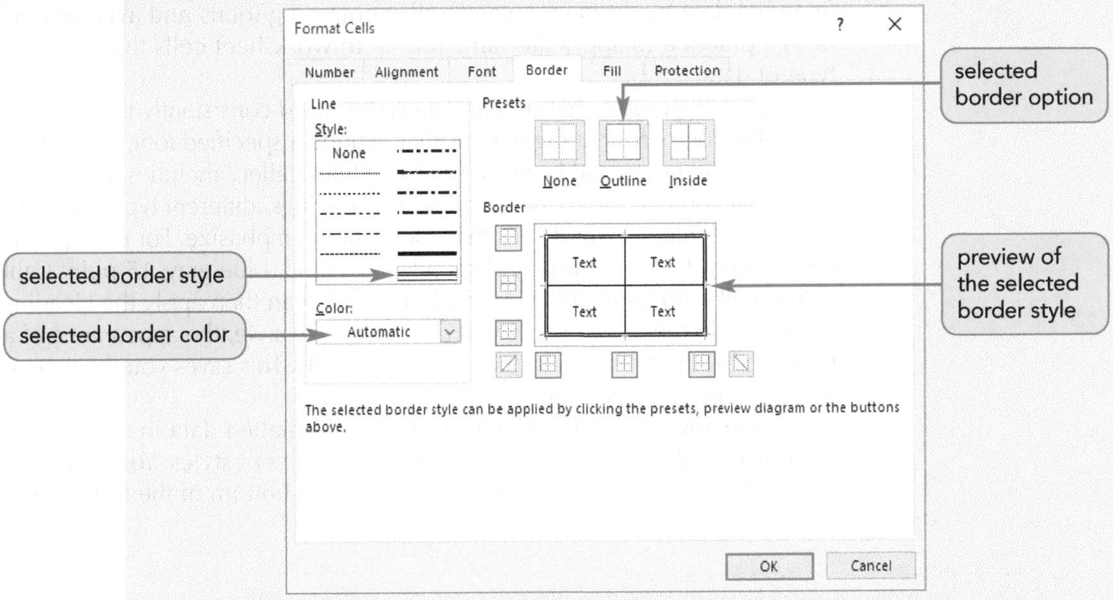

▶ **5.** Click the **OK** button. The selected border is applied to the California monthly sales.

▶ **6.** Repeat Steps 2 through 5 to apply double borders to the ranges **A34:N36**, **A37:N40**, **A41:N41**, **A42:N43**, and **A44:N46**.

▶ **7.** Click cell **A48** to deselect the range. See Figure 2-23.

Figure 2-23 | **Worksheet with font, fill, and border formatting**

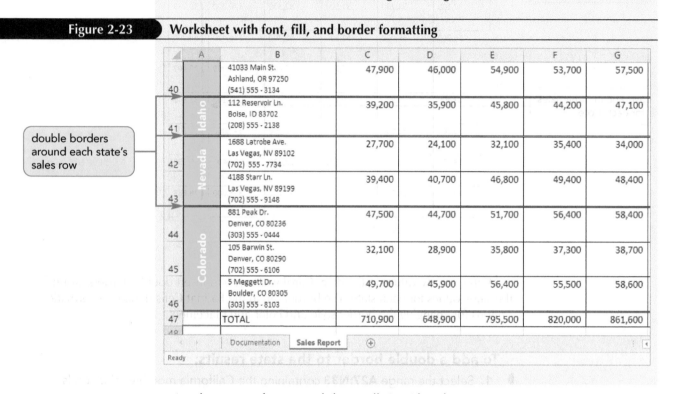

double borders around each state's sales row

Another way to format worksheet cells is with styles.

Applying Cell Styles

A workbook often contains several cells that store the same type of data. For example, each worksheet might have a cell displaying the sheet title, or a range of financial data might have several cells containing totals and averages. It is good design practice to apply the same format to worksheet cells that contain the same type of data.

One way to ensure that similar data is displayed consistently is with styles. A **style** is a collection of formatting options that include a specified font, font size, font styles, font color, fill color, and borders. The Cell Styles gallery includes a variety of built-in styles that you can use to format titles and headings, different types of data such as totals or calculations, and cells that you want to emphasize. For example, you can use the Heading 1 style to display sheet titles in a bold, blue-gray, 15-point Calibri font with no fill color and a blue bottom border. You can then apply the Heading 1 style to all titles in the workbook. If you later revise the style, the appearance of any cell formatted with that style is updated automatically. This saves you the time and effort of reformatting each cell individually.

You already used built-in styles when you formatted data in the Sales Report worksheet with the Accounting, Comma, and Percent styles. You can also create your own cell styles by clicking New Cell Style at the bottom of the Cell Styles gallery.

REFERENCE

Applying a Cell Style

- Select the cell or range to which you want to apply a style.
- On the Home tab, in the Styles group, click the Cell Styles button.
- Point to each style in the Cell Styles gallery to see a Live Preview of that style on the selected cell or range.
- Click the style you want to apply to the selected cell or range.

Carol wants you to add more color and visual interest to the Sales Report worksheet. You'll use the styles in the Cell Styles gallery to do this.

To apply cell styles to the Sales Report worksheet:

1. Click cell **B4** containing the text "Sales Statistics."

2. On the Home tab, in the Styles group, click the **Cell Styles** button. The Cell Styles gallery opens.

3. Point to the **Heading 1** style in the Titles and Headings section. Live Preview shows cell B4 in a 15-point, bold font with a solid blue bottom border. See Figure 2-24.

Figure 2-24   Cell Styles gallery

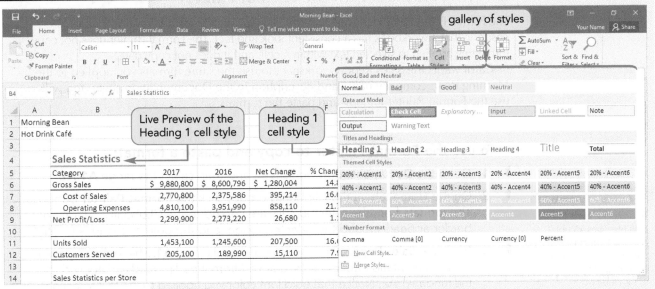

4. Move the pointer over different styles in the Cell Styles gallery to see cell B4 with a Live Preview of each style.

5. Click the **Title** style. The Title style—18-point, Blue-Gray, Text 2 Calibri Light font—is applied to cell B4.

6. Select the range **B5:F5** containing the column titles for the Sales Statistics data.

7. In the Styles group, click the **Cell Styles** button, and then click the **Accent4** style in the Themed Cell Styles section of the Cell Styles gallery.

8. Click cell **A25** containing the text "2017 Monthly Gross Sales," and then apply the **Title** cell style to the cell.

> **9.** Click cell **A3**. See Figure 2-25.

Figure 2-25 **Cell styles applied to the worksheet**

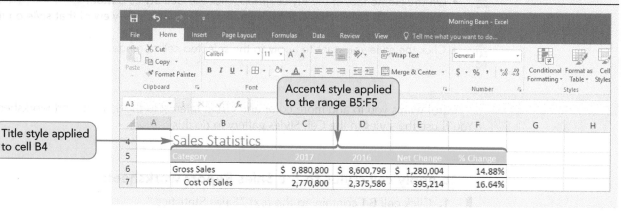

Copying and Pasting Formats

Large workbooks often use the same formatting on similar data throughout the workbook, sometimes in widely scattered cells. Rather than repeating the same steps to format these cells, you can copy the format of one cell or range and paste it to another.

Copying Formats with the Format Painter

The Format Painter provides a fast and efficient way of copying and pasting formats, ensuring that a workbook has a consistent look and feel. The Format Painter does not copy formatting applied to selected text within a cell, and it does not copy data.

Carol wants the Sales Report worksheet to use the same formats you applied to the Morning Bean company name and description in the Documentation sheet. You will use the Format Painter to copy and paste the formats.

To use the Format Painter to copy and paste a format:

> **1.** Go to the **Documentation** worksheet, and then select the range **A1:A2**.

TIP

To paste the same format multiple times, double-click the Format Painter button. Click the button again or press the Esc key to turn it off.

> **2.** On the Home tab, in the Clipboard group, click the **Format Painter** button. The formats from the selected cells are copied to the Clipboard, a flashing border appears around the selected range, and the pointer changes to ⊹🖌.

> **3.** Go to the **Sales Report** worksheet, and then click cell **A1**. The formatting from the Documentation worksheet is removed from the Clipboard and applied to the range A1:A2. Notice that gold font color you applied to the text selection "Morning" was not included in the pasted formats.

> **4.** Double-click cell **A1** to enter Edit mode, select **Morning**, and then change the font color to the **Gold, Accent 4** theme color. The format for the company title now matches what you applied earlier in the Documentation sheet.

> **5.** Press the **Enter** key to exit Edit mode and select cell A2.

You can use the Format Painter to copy all of the formats within a selected range and then apply those formats to another range that has the same size and shape by clicking the upper-left cell of the range. Carol wants you to copy all of the formats that you applied to the Sales Statistics data to the sales statistics per store data.

To copy and paste multiple formats:

▶ **1.** Select the range **B4:F12** in the Sales Report worksheet.

▶ **2.** On the Home tab, in the Clipboard group, click the **Format Painter** button.

▶ **3.** Click cell **B14**. All of the number formats, cell borders, fonts, and fill colors are pasted in the range B14:F22.

▶ **4.** Select the range **C23:E23**. You'll format this data.

▶ **5.** On the Home tab, in the Number group, click the **Comma Style** button ⟨,⟩, and then click the **Decrease Decimal** button twice to remove the decimal places to the right of the decimal point. The numbers are now vertically aligned in their columns.

▶ **6.** Click cell **F23**.

▶ **7.** In the Number group, click the **Percent Style** button ⟨%⟩ to change the number to a percentage, and then click the **Increase Decimal** button twice to display two decimal places in the percentage. The value is now formatted to match the other percentages.

▶ **8.** Click cell **B24**. See Figure 2-26.

> **TIP**
>
> If the range you paste the formats in is bigger than the range you copied, Format Painter will repeat the copied formats to fill the pasted range.

Figure 2-26 ▶ **Formatting copied and pasted between ranges**

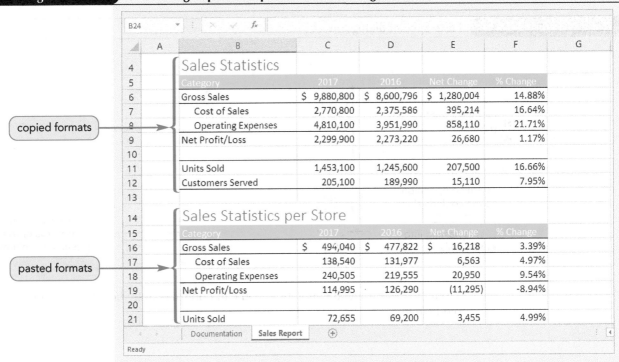

Copying Formats with the Paste Options Button

Another way to copy and paste formats is with the Paste Options button ⟨(Ctrl) ▾⟩, which provides options for pasting only values, only formats, or some combination of values and formats. Each time you paste, the Paste Options button appears in the lower-right corner of the pasted cell or range. You click the Paste Options button to open a list of pasting options, shown in Figure 2-27, such as pasting only the values or only the formatting. You can also click the Transpose button to paste the column data into a row, or to paste the row data into a column.

Figure 2-27   **Paste Options button**

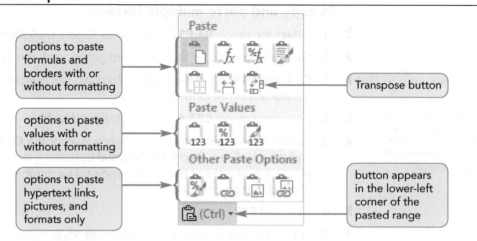

Copying Formats with Paste Special

The Paste Special command provides another way to control what you paste from the Clipboard. To use Paste Special, select and copy a range, select the range where you want to paste the Clipboard contents, click the Paste button arrow in the Clipboard group on the Home tab, and then click Paste Special to open the dialog box shown in Figure 2-28.

Figure 2-28   **Paste Special dialog box**

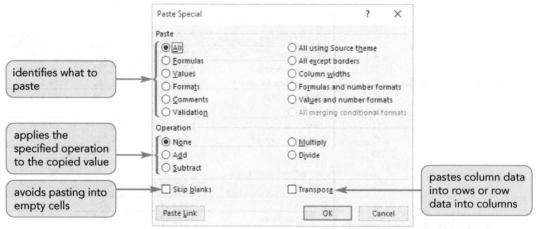

From the Paste Special dialog box, you can control exactly how to paste the copied range.

Finding and Replacing Text and Formats

The Find and Replace commands let you make content and design changes to a worksheet or the entire workbook quickly. The Find command searches through the current worksheet or workbook for the content or formatting you want to locate, and the Replace command then substitutes it with the new content or formatting you specify.

The Find and Replace commands are versatile. You can find each occurrence of the search text one at a time and decide whether to replace it. You can highlight all occurrences of the search text in the worksheet. Or, you can replace all occurrences at once without reviewing them.

Carol wants you to replace all the street title abbreviations (such as Ave.) in the Sales Report with their full names (such as Avenue). You will use Find and Replace to make these changes.

To find and replace the street title abbreviations:

▶ **1.** On the Home tab, in the Editing group, click the **Find & Select** button, and then click **Replace** (or press the **Ctrl+H** keys). The Find and Replace dialog box opens.

▶ **2.** Type **Ave.** in the Find what box.

▶ **3.** Press the **Tab** key to move the insertion point to the Replace with box, and then type **Avenue**. See Figure 2-29.

| Figure 2-29 | Find and Replace dialog box |

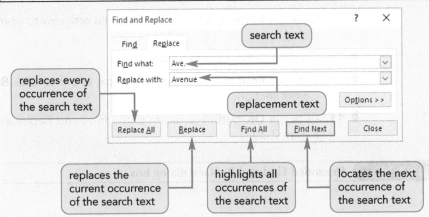

▶ **4.** Click the **Replace All** button to replace all occurrences of the search text without reviewing them. A dialog box opens, reporting that three replacements were made in the worksheet.

▶ **5.** Click the **OK** button to return to the Find and Replace dialog box.

Next, you will replace the other street title abbreviations.

▶ **6.** Repeat Steps 2 through 5 to replace all occurrences of each of the following: **St.** with **Street**, **Ln.** with **Lane**, and **Dr.** with **Drive**.

▶ **7.** Click the **Close** button to close the Find and Replace dialog box.

▶ **8.** Scroll through the Sales Report worksheet to verify that all street title abbreviations were replaced with their full names.

The Find and Replace dialog box can also be used to replace one format with another or to replace both text and a format simultaneously. Carol wants you to replace all occurrences of the white text on a gold fill in the Sales Report worksheet with blue text on a gold fill. You'll use the Find and Replace dialog box to make this formatting change.

To replace white text with blue text:

▶ **1.** On the Home tab, in the Editing group, click the **Find & Select** button, and then click **Replace** (or press the **Ctrl+H** keys). The Find and Replace dialog box opens.

▶ **2.** Delete the search text from the Find what and Replace with boxes, leaving those two boxes empty. By not specifying a text string to find and replace, the dialog box will search through all cells regardless of their content.

▶ **3.** Click the **Options** button to expand the dialog box.

▶ **4.** Click the **Format** button in the Find what row to open the Find Format dialog box, which is similar to the Format Cells dialog box you used earlier to format a range.

▶ **5.** Click the **Font** tab to make it active, click the **Color** box, and then click the **White, Background 1** theme color.

▶ **6.** Click the **Fill** tab, and then in the Background Color section, click the **gold** color (the eighth color in the first row).

▶ **7.** Click the **OK** button to close the Find Format dialog box and return to the Find and Replace dialog box.

▶ **8.** Click the **Format** button in the Replace with row to open the Replace Format dialog box.

▶ **9.** On the Fill tab, click the **gold** color.

▶ **10.** Click the **Font** tab, click the **Color** box, and then click **Blue** in the Standard Colors section.

▶ **11.** Click the **OK** button to return to the Find and Replace dialog box. See Figure 2-30.

Figure 2-30   **Expanded Find and Replace dialog box**

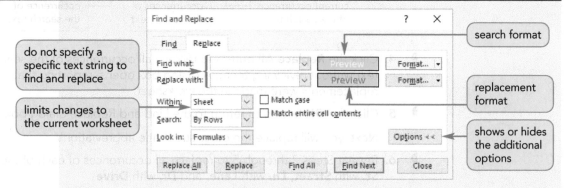

▶ **12.** Click the **Replace All** button to replace all occurrences of white text on a gold fill in the Sales Report worksheet with blue text on a gold fill. A dialog box opens, reporting that 16 replacements were made.

▶ **13.** Click the **OK** button to return to the Find and Replace dialog box.

It is a good idea to clear the find and replace formats after you are done so that they won't affect any future searches and replacements. Carol asks you to remove the formats from the Find and Replace dialog box.

To clear the options from the Find and Replace dialog box:

▶ **1.** In the Find and Replace dialog box, click the **Format button arrow** in the Find what row, and then click **Clear Find Format**. The search format is removed.

▶ **2.** Click the **Format button arrow** in the Replace with row, and then click **Clear Replace Format**. The replacement format is removed.

▶ **3.** Click the **Close** button. The Find and Replace dialog box closes.

Another way to make multiple changes to the formats used in your workbook is through themes.

Working with Themes

Recall that a theme is a coordinated selection of fonts, colors, and graphical effects that are applied throughout a workbook to create a specific look and feel. When you switch to a different theme, the theme-related fonts, colors, and effects change throughout the workbook to reflect the new theme. The appearance of nontheme fonts, colors, and effects remains unchanged no matter which theme is applied to the workbook.

Most of the formatting you have applied to the Sales Report workbook is based on the Office theme. Carol wants you to change the theme to see how it affects the workbook's appearance.

To change the workbook's theme:

▶ **1.** On the ribbon, click the **Page Layout** tab.

▶ **2.** In the Themes group, click the **Themes** button. The Themes gallery opens. Office—the current theme—is the default.

▶ **3.** Point to different themes in the Themes gallery using Live Preview to preview the impact of each theme on the fonts and colors used in the worksheet.

▶ **4.** Click the **Droplet** theme to apply that theme to the workbook. See Figure 2-31.

Figure 2-31 **Live Preview of the Droplet theme**

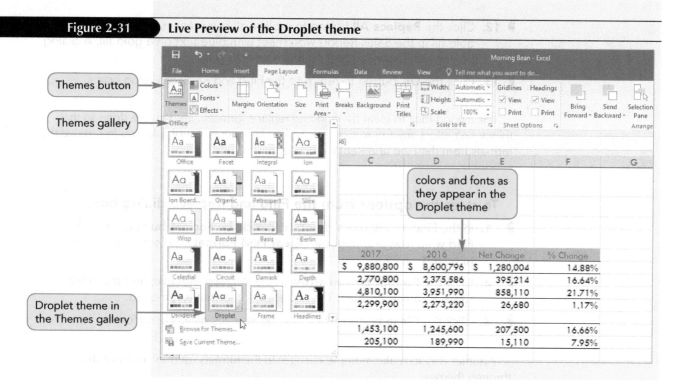

Changing the theme made a significant difference in the worksheet's appearance. The most obvious changes to the worksheet are the fill colors and the fonts. Only formatting options directly tied to a theme change when you select a different theme. Any formatting options you selected that were not theme-based remain unaffected by the change. For example, using a standard color or a nontheme font will not be affected by the choice of theme. In the Sales Report worksheet, the standard green color used for the font of the company description and the fill of the column title cells in the 2017 Monthly Gross Sales data didn't change because that green is not a theme color.

INSIGHT

Sharing Styles and Themes

Using a consistent look and feel for all the files you create in Microsoft Office is a simple way to project a professional image. This consistency is especially important when a team is collaborating on a set of documents. When all team members work from a common set of style and design themes, readers will not be distracted by inconsistent or clashing formatting.

To quickly copy the styles from one workbook to another, open the workbook with the styles you want to copy, and then open the workbook in which you want to copy those styles. On the Home tab, in the Styles group, click the Cell Styles button, and then click Merge Styles. The Merge Styles dialog box opens, listing the currently open workbooks. Select the workbook with the styles you want to copy, and then click the OK button to copy those styles into the current workbook. If you modify any styles, you must copy the styles to the other workbook; Excel does not update styles between workbooks.

Because other Office files, including those created with Word or PowerPoint, use the same file format for themes, you can create one theme to use with all your Office files. To save a theme, click the Themes button in the Themes group on the Page Layout tab, and then click Save Current Theme. The Save Current Theme dialog box opens. Select a save location, type a name in the File name box, and then click the Save button. If you saved the theme file in a default Theme folder, the theme appears in the Themes gallery and affects any Office file that uses that theme.

Highlighting Data with Conditional Formats

Conditional formatting is often used to help analyze data. Conditional formatting applies formatting to a cell when its value meets a specified condition. For example, conditional formatting can be used to format negative numbers in red and positive numbers in black. Conditional formatting is dynamic, which means that the formatting can change when the cell's value changes. Each conditional format has a set of rules that define how the formatting should be applied and under what conditions the format will be changed.

Highlighting Cells with Conditional Formatting

- Select the range in which you want to highlight cells.
- On the Home tab, in the Styles group, click the Conditional Formatting button, point to Highlight Cells Rules or Top/Bottom Rules, and then click the appropriate rule.
- Select the appropriate options in the dialog box.
- Click the OK button.

Excel has four types of conditional formatting—data bars, highlighting, color scales, and icon sets. In this module, you will use conditional formatting to highlight cells.

Highlighting Cells Based on Their Values

Cell highlighting changes the cell's font color or fill color based on the cell's value, as described in Figure 2-32. You can enter a value or a cell reference if you want to compare other cells with the value in a certain cell.

Figure 2-32   **Highlight Cells rules**

Rule	Highlights Cell Values
Greater Than	Greater than a specified number
Less Than	Less than a specified number
Between	Between two specified numbers
Equal To	Equal to a specified number
Text that Contains	That contain specified text
A Date Occurring	That contain a specified date
Duplicate Values	That contain duplicate or unique values

Carol wants to highlight important trends and sales values in the Sales Report worksheet. She asks you to highlight sales statistics that show a negative net change or negative percent change from the previous year to the current year. You will use conditional formatting to highlight the negative values in red.

To highlight negative values in red:

1. In the Sales Report worksheet, select the range **E6:F12,E16:F22** containing the net and percent changes overall and per store from the previous year to the current year.

2. On the ribbon, click the **Home** tab.

3. In the Styles group, click the **Conditional Formatting** button, and then point to **Highlight Cells Rules** to display a menu of the available rules.

4. Click **Less Than**. The Less Than dialog box opens so you can select the value and formatting to highlight negative values.

TIP

To create a format, click the right box arrow, then click Custom Format to open the Format Cells dialog box.

5. Make sure the value in the first box is selected, and then type **0** so that cells in the selected range that contain values that are less than 0 are formatted with a light red fill and dark red text. Live Preview shows the conditional formatting applied to the cells with negative numbers. See Figure 2-33.

Figure 2-33 | **Live Preview of the Less Than conditional format**

formats cells whose values are negative

with dark red text on a light red background

negative values highlighted in red

	B	C	D	E	F	G
5	Category	2017	2016	Net Change	% Change	
6	Gross Sales	$ 9,880,800	$ 8,600,796	$ 1,280,004	14.88%	
7	Cost of Sales	2,770,800	2,375,586	395,214	16.64%	
8	Operating Expenses	4,810,100	3,951,990	858,110	21.71%	
9				26,680	1.17%	
11				207,500	16.66%	
12				15,110	7.95%	
14	**Sales Statistics per Store**					
15	Category	2017	2016	Net Change	% Change	
16	Gross Sales	$ 494,040	$ 477,822	$ 16,218	3.39%	
17	Cost of Sales	138,540	131,977	6,563	4.97%	
18	Operating Expenses	240,505	219,555	20,950	9.54%	
19	Net Profit/Loss	114,995	126,290	(11,295)	-8.94%	
20						
21	Units Sold	72,655	69,200	3,455	4.99%	
22	Customers Served	10,255	10,555	(300)	-2.84%	
23	Stores	20	18	2	11.11%	

Less Than ? ×
Format cells that are LESS THAN:
0   with   Light Red Fill with Dark Red Text
OK   Cancel

Documentation   Sales Report   +

Enter   Average: $

6. Click the **OK** button to apply the highlighting rule.

The conditional formatting highlights that Morning Bean showed a decline from the previous year to the current year for two statistics: The net profit per store declined $11,295 or 8.94 percent, and the number of customers served per store declined by 300 persons or 2.84 percent. These declines occurred because the two new stores that Morning Bean opened in 2017 are still finding a market, resulting in lower profit and customer served per store for the entire franchise.

Conditional formatting is dynamic, which means that changes in the values affect the format of those cells. The total number of customers served in 2017 was incorrectly entered in cell C12 as 205,100. The correct value is 215,100. You will make this change and view its impact on the cells highlighted with conditional formatting.

To view the impact of changing values on conditional formatting:

1. Click cell **C12** to select it.

2. Type **215,100** as the new value, and then press the Enter key. The conditional formatting changes based on the new value. See Figure 2-34.

| Figure 2-34 | Cells with conditional formatting |

By changing the value in cell C12 to 215,100, the net change in customers served per store in cell E22 is now 200 and the percentage change in cell F22 is now 1.89%. Because both of these values are now positive, the cells are no longer highlighted in red.

Highlighting Cells with a Top/Bottom Rule

Another way of applying conditional formatting is with the Quick Analysis tool. The **Quick Analysis tool**, which appears whenever you select a range of cells, provides access to the most common tools for data analysis and formatting. The Formatting category includes buttons for the Greater Than and Top 10% conditional formatting rules. You can highlight cells based on their values in comparison to other cells. For example, you can highlight cells with the 10 highest or lowest values in a selected range, or you can highlight the cells with above-average values in a range.

Carol wants to know which stores and which months rank in the top 10 percent of sales. She wants to use this information to identify the most successful stores and learn which months those stores show the highest sales volume. You'll highlight those values using the Quick Analysis tool.

To use a Top/Bottom Rule to highlight stores with the highest average sales:

▶ 1. Select the range **C27:N46** containing the monthly sales values for each of the 20 Morning Bean stores.

▶ 2. Click the **Quick Analysis** button 📋, and then point to **Top 10%**. Live Preview formats the cells in the top 10 percent with red font and a red fill. See Figure 2-35.

Figure 2-35   **Quick Analysis tool applying conditional formatting**

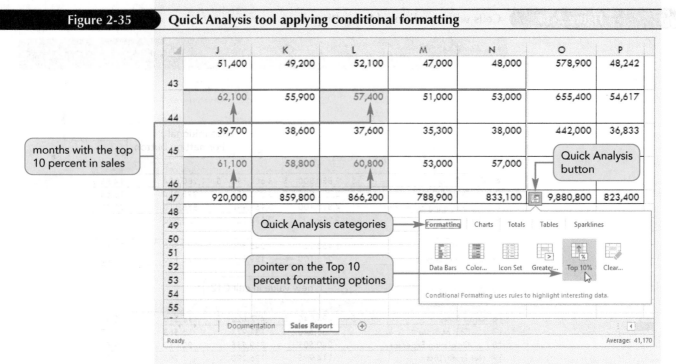

Carol doesn't like the default format used by the Quick Analysis tool because red is usually applied to negative values and results. Instead, she wants to format the top 10 percent values in green.

▶ **3.** Press the **Esc** key to close the Quick Analysis tool without applying the conditional format. The range C27:N46 remains selected.

Trouble? If the conditional formatting was applied to the worksheet, press the Ctrl+Z keys to undo the format, and then continue with Step 4.

▶ **4.** On the Home tab, in the Styles group, click the **Conditional Formatting** button, and then point to **Top/Bottom Rules** to display a list of available rules.

▶ **5.** Click **Top 10%** to open the Top 10% dialog box.

▶ **6.** Click the **with** arrow box and click **Green Fill with Dark Green Text** to apply green to cells with sales value in the top 10 percent. See Figure 2-36.

Figure 2-36   **Top 10% dialog box**

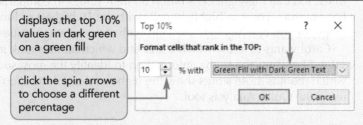

▶ **7.** Click the **OK** button, and then click cell **A24** to deselect the cells. Monthly sales that rank in the top 10 percent are formatted with green.

▶ **8.** Zoom the worksheet to **40%** so you can view all of the monthly gross sales and more easily see the sales pattern. See Figure 2-37.

| Figure 2-37 | Top 10 percent highlighted with green conditional formatting |

top 10 percent sales occur between May and October and are found in six stores

▶ **9.** Return the zoom to **120%** or whatever zoom is appropriate for your monitor.

The top 10 percent in monthly sales comes from six stores located in San Diego, Irvine, Portland, Ashland, Denver, and Boulder. The highest sales appear to be centered around the months from May to October. This information will be valuable to Carol as she compares the sales performance of different stores and projects monthly cash flows for the company.

Other Conditional Formatting Options

To create dynamic conditional formats that are based on cell values rather than a constant value, you can enter a cell reference in the conditional format dialog box. For example, you can highlight all cells whose value is greater than the value in cell B10. For this type of conditional format, enter the formula =$B$10 in the conditional formatting dialog box. Note that the $ character keeps the cell reference from changing if that formula moves to another cell.

You can remove a conditional format at any time without affecting the underlying data by selecting the range containing the conditional format, clicking the Conditional Formatting button, and then clicking the Clear Rules command. A menu opens, providing options to clear the conditional formatting rules from the selected cells or the entire worksheet. You can also click the Quick Analysis button that appears in the lower-right corner of the selected range and then click the Clear Format button in the Formatting category. Note that you might see only "Clear..." as the button name.

Creating a Conditional Formatting Legend

When you use conditional formatting to highlight cells in a worksheet, the purpose of the formatting is not always immediately apparent. To ensure that everyone knows why certain cells are highlighted, you should include a legend, which is a key that identifies each format and its meaning.

Carol wants you to add a legend to the Sales Report worksheet to document the two conditional formatting rules you created in the worksheet.

To create a conditional formatting legend:

▶ 1. In cell **M25**, enter the text **Top 10% in Sales**, and then select cell **M25** again.

▶ 2. On the Home tab, click the **Align Right** button ▤ to right-align the cell contents of the selected cell.

▶ 3. In cell **N25**, type **green** to identify the conditional formatting color you used to highlight the values in the top 10 percent, and then select cell **N25** again.

▶ 4. In the Alignment group, click the **Center** button ▤ to center the contents of the cell.

   You will use a highlighting rule to format cell N25 using dark green text on a green fill.

▶ 5. On the Home tab, in the Styles group, click the **Conditional Formatting** button, point to **Highlight Cells Rules**, and then click **Text that Contains**. The Text That Contains dialog box opens. The text string "green" is automatically entered into the left input box.

▶ 6. In the right box, click **Green Fill with Dark Green Text**.

▶ 7. Click the **OK** button to apply the conditional formatting to cell N25. See Figure 2-38.

Figure 2-38   **Conditional formatting legend**

legend explains the purpose of the conditional formatting

	Aug	Sep	Oct	Nov	Dec	TOTAL	AVERAGE
25				Top 10% In Sales	green		
26	35,100	32,100	33,200	31,500	32,300	370,000	30,833
27							
28	62,300	56,700	58,000	51,300	55,700	656,400	54,700
29	28,200	26,500	28,000	25,000	25,400	304,900	25,408
30	37,800	33,400	31,900	30,700	35,000	382,100	31,842
31	60,800	56,200	56,900	50,900	52,000	642,000	53,500
	56,100	53,100	51,200	46,000	52,300	599,400	49,950

Documentation   **Sales Report**   ⊕

Ready

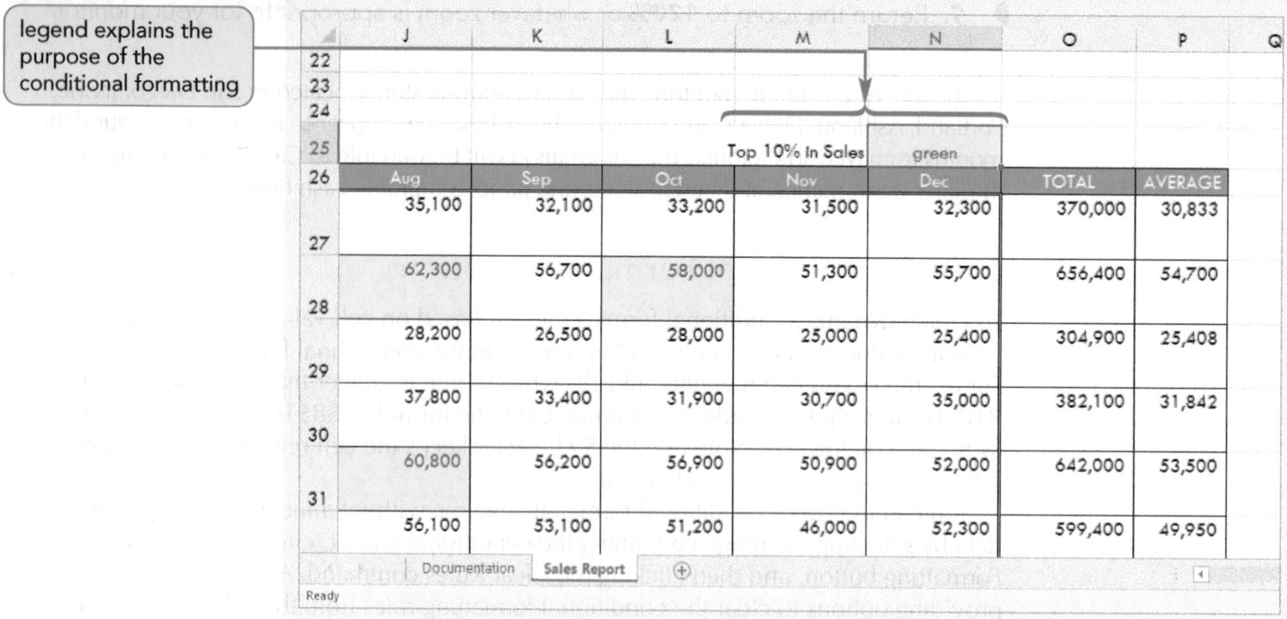

You've completed formatting the appearance of the workbook for the computer screen. Next you'll explore how to format the workbook for the printer.

Written Communication: Using Conditional Formatting Effectively

Conditional formatting is an excellent way to highlight important trends and data values to clients and colleagues. However, be sure to use it judiciously. Overusing conditional formatting might obscure the very data you want to emphasize. Keep in mind the following tips as you make decisions about what to highlight and how it should be highlighted:

- **Document the conditional formats you use.** If a bold, green font means that a sales number is in the top 10 percent of all sales, include that information in a legend in the worksheet.
- **Don't clutter data with too much highlighting.** Limit highlighting rules to one or two per data set. Highlights are designed to draw attention to points of interest. If you use too many, you will end up highlighting everything—and, therefore, nothing.
- **Use color sparingly in worksheets with highlights.** It is difficult to tell a highlight color from a regular fill color, especially when fill colors are used in every cell.
- **Consider alternatives to conditional formats.** If you want to highlight the top 10 sales regions, it might be more effective to simply sort the data with the best-selling regions at the top of the list.

Remember that the goal of highlighting is to provide a strong visual clue to important data or results. Careful use of conditional formatting helps readers to focus on the important points you want to make rather than distracting them with secondary issues and facts.

Formatting a Worksheet for Printing

You should format any worksheets you plan to print so that they are easy to read and understand. You can do this using the print settings, which enable you to set the page orientation, the print area, page breaks, print titles, and headers and footers. Print settings can be applied to an entire workbook or to individual sheets. Because other people will likely see your printed worksheets, you should format the printed output as carefully as you format the electronic version.

Carol wants you to format the Sales Report worksheet so she can distribute the printed version at the upcoming sales conference.

Using Page Break Preview

Page Break Preview shows only those parts of the active sheet that will print and how the content will be split across pages. A dotted blue border indicates a page break, which separates one page from another. As you format the worksheet for printing, you can use this view to control what content appears on each page.

Carol wants to know how the Sales Report worksheet would print in portrait orientation and how many pages would be required. You will look at the worksheet in Page Break Preview to find these answers.

To view the Sales Report worksheet in Page Break Preview:

▶ **1.** Click the **Page Break Preview** button ⊞ on the status bar. The worksheet switches to Page Break Preview.

▶ **2.** Change the zoom level of the worksheet to **30%** so you can view the entire contents of this large worksheet. See Figure 2-39.

Figure 2-39 **Sales Report worksheet in Page Break preview**

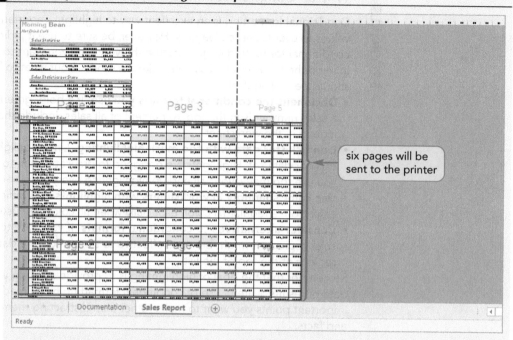

Trouble? If you see a different page layout or the worksheet is split onto a different number of pages, don't worry. Each printer is different, so the layout and pages might differ from what is shown in Figure 2-39.

Page Break Preview shows that a printout of the Sales Report worksheet requires six pages in portrait orientation, and that pages 3 and 5 would be mostly blank. Note that each printer is different, so your Page Break Preview might show a different number of pages. With this layout, each page would be difficult to interpret because the data is separated from the descriptive labels. Carol wants you to fix the layout so that the contents are easier to read and understand.

Defining the Print Area

By default, all cells in a worksheet containing text, formulas, or values are printed. If you want to print only part of a worksheet, you can set a print area, which is the region of the worksheet that is sent to the printer. Each worksheet has its own print area. Although you can set the print area in any view, Page Break Preview shades the areas of the worksheet that are not included in the print area, making it simple to confirm what will print.

Carol doesn't want the empty cells in the range G1:P24 to print, so you will set the print area to exclude those cells.

To set the print area of the Sales Report worksheet:

▶ **1.** Change the zoom level of the worksheet to **80%** to make it easier to select cells and ranges.

▶ **2.** Select the nonadjacent range **A1:F24,A25:P47** containing the cells with content.

▶ **3.** On the ribbon, click the **Page Layout** tab.

▶ **4.** In the Page Setup group, click the **Print Area** button, and then click **Set Print Area**. The print area changes to cover only the nonadjacent range A1:F24,A25:P47. The rest of the worksheet content is shaded to indicate that it will not be part of the printout.

▶ **5.** Click cell **A1** to deselect the range.

▶ **6.** Change the zoom level to **50%** so you can view more of the worksheet. See Figure 2-40.

Figure 2-40   **Print area set for the Sales Report worksheet**

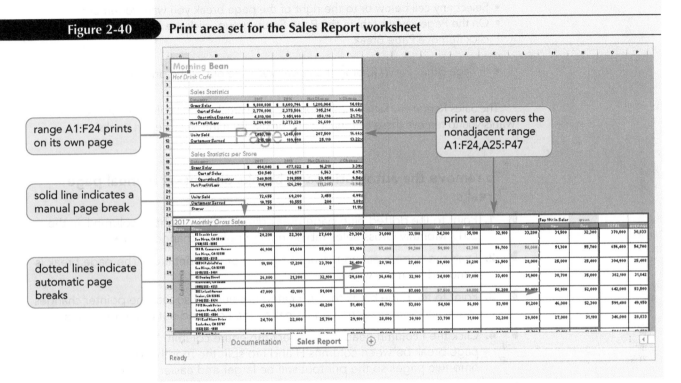

range A1:F24 prints on its own page

print area covers the nonadjacent range A1:F24,A25:P47

solid line indicates a manual page break

dotted lines indicate automatic page breaks

Inserting Page Breaks

Often, the contents of a worksheet will not fit onto a single printed page. When this happens, Excel prints as much of the content that fits on a single page without resizing, and then inserts automatic page breaks to continue printing the remaining worksheet content on successive pages. The resulting printouts might split worksheet content in awkward places, such as within a table of data.

TIP

When you remove a page break, Excel will automatically rescale the printout to fit into the allotted pages.

To split the printout into logical segments, you can insert manual page breaks. Page Break Preview identifies manual page breaks with a solid blue line and automatic page breaks with a dotted blue line. When you specify a print area for a nonadjacent range, as you did for the Sales Report worksheet, you also insert manual page breaks around the adjacent ranges. So a manual page break already appears in the print area you defined (see Figure 2-40). You can remove a page break in Page Break Preview by dragging it out of the print area.

Inserting and Removing Page Breaks

To insert a page break:
- Click the first cell below the row where you want to insert a page break, click a column heading, or click a row heading.
- On the Page Layout tab, in the Page Setup group, click the Breaks button, and then click Insert Page Break.

To remove a page break:
- Select any cell below or to the right of the page break you want to remove.
- On the Page Layout tab, in the Page Setup group, click the Breaks button, and then click Remove Page Break.

or

- In Page Break Preview, drag the page break line out of the print area.

The Sales Report worksheet has automatic page breaks along columns F and L. Carol wants you to remove these automatic page breaks from the Sales Report worksheet.

To remove the automatic page breaks and insert manual page breaks:

1. Point to the dotted blue page break directly to the right of column L in the 2017 Monthly Gross Sales table until the pointer changes to ↔.

2. Drag the page break to the right and out of the print area. The page break is removed from the worksheet.

3. Point to the page break that is located in column F so that the pointer changes to ↔, and then drag the page break to the right and out of the print area.

4. Click the **I** column heading to select the entire column. You will add a manual page break between columns H and I to split the monthly gross sales data onto two pages so the printout will be larger and easier to read.

5. On the Page Layout tab, in the Page Setup group, click the **Breaks** button, and then click **Insert Page Break**. A manual page break is added between columns H and I, forcing the monthly gross sales onto a new page after the June data.

6. Click cell **A1** to deselect the column. The printout of the Sales Report worksheet is now limited to three pages. However, the gross sales data in the range A25:P47 is split across pages. See Figure 2-41.

Figure 2-41   **Manual page break in the print area**

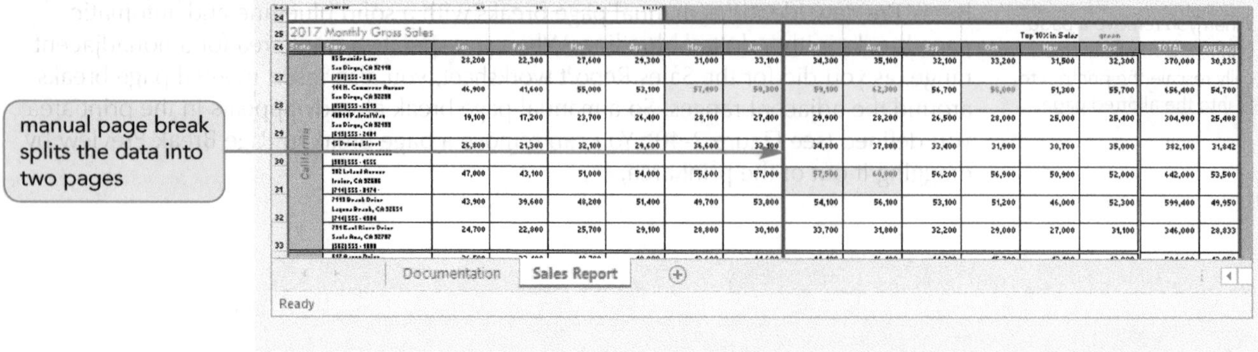

manual page break splits the data into two pages

Adding Print Titles

It is a good practice to include descriptive information such as the company name, logo, and worksheet title on each page of a printout in case a page becomes separated from the other pages. You can repeat information, such as the company name, by specifying which rows or columns in the worksheet act as print titles. If a worksheet contains a large table, you can print the table's column headings and row headings on every page of the printout by designating those columns and rows as print titles.

In the Sales Report worksheet, the company name appears on the first page of the printout but does not appear on subsequent pages. Also, the descriptive row titles for the monthly sales table in column A do not appear on the third page of the printout. You will add print titles to fix these issues.

To set the print titles:

▶ **1.** On the Page Layout tab, in the Page Setup group, click the **Print Titles** button. The Page Setup dialog box opens with the Sheet tab displayed.

▶ **2.** In the Print titles section, click the **Rows to repeat at top** box, move the pointer over the worksheet, and then select the range **A1:A2**. A flashing border appears around the first two rows of the worksheet to indicate that the contents of the first two rows will be repeated on each page of the printout. The row reference $1:$2 appears in the Rows to repeat at top box.

▶ **3.** Click the **Columns to repeat at left** box, and then select columns A and B from the worksheet. The column reference $A:$B appears in the Columns to repeat at left box. See Figure 2-42.

Figure 2-42   Sheet tab in the Page Setup dialog box

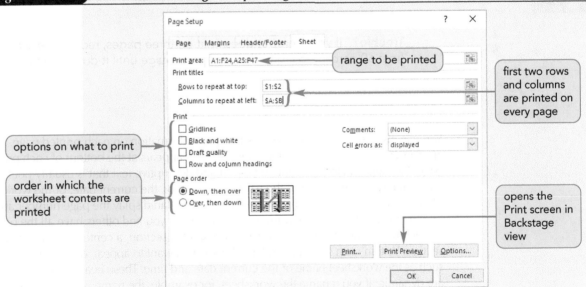

You will next rescale the worksheet so that it doesn't appear too small in the printout.

▶ **4.** In the Page Setup dialog box, click the **Page** tab.

▶ **5.** In the Scaling section, change the Adjust to amount to **60%** of normal size.

▶ **6.** Click the **Print Preview** button to preview the three pages of printed material on the Print screen in Backstage view.

7. Verify that each of the three pages has the Morning Bean title at the top of the page and that the state and store names appear in the leftmost columns of pages 2 and 3. See Figure 2-43.

Figure 2-43 | **Print titles on page 3 of the printout**

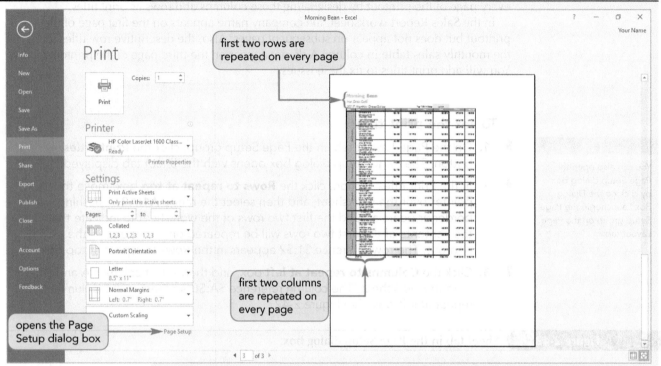

Trouble? If your printout doesn't fit on three pages, reduce the scaling factor from 60 percent to a slightly lower percentage until it does fit on three pages.

Designing Headers and Footers

You can also use headers and footers to repeat information on each printed page. A **header** appears at the top of each printed page; a **footer** appears at the bottom of each printed page. Headers and footers contain helpful and descriptive text that is usually not found within the worksheet, such as the workbook's author, the current date, or the workbook's filename. If the printout spans multiple pages, you can display the page number and the total number of pages in the printout to help ensure you and others have all the pages.

Each header and footer has three sections—a left section, a center section, and a right section. Within each section, you type the text you want to appear, or you insert elements such as the worksheet name or the current date and time. These header and footer elements are dynamic; if you rename the worksheet, for example, the name is automatically updated in the header or footer. Also, you can create one set of headers and footers for even and odd pages, and you can create another set for the first page in the printout.

Carol wants the printout to display the workbook's filename in the header's left section, and the current date in the header's right section. She wants the center footer to display the page number and the total number of pages in the printout, and the right footer to display your name as the workbook's author.

To set up the page header:

1. Near the bottom of the Print screen, click the **Page Setup** link. The Page Setup dialog box opens.

2. Click the **Header/Footer** tab to display the header and footer options.

3. Click the **Different first page** check box to select it. This lets you create one set of headers and footers for the first page, and one set for the rest of the pages.

4. Click the **Custom Header** button to open the Header dialog box. The dialog box contains two tabs—Header and First Page Header—because you selected the Different first page option.

5. On the Header tab, in the Left section box, type **Filename:**, press the **spacebar**, and then click the **Insert File Name** button 📄. The code &[File], which displays the filename of the current workbook, is added to the left section of the header.

6. Press the **Tab** key twice to move to the right section of the header, and then click the **Insert Date** button 📅. The code &[Date] is added to the right section of the header. See Figure 2-44.

TIP

You can create or edit headers and footers in Page Layout view by clicking in the header/footer section and using the tools on the Design tab.

Figure 2-44   **Header dialog box**

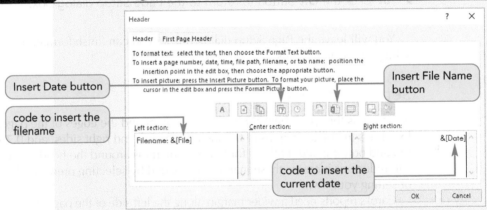

7. Click the **OK** button to return to the Header/Footer tab in the Page Setup dialog box.

You did not define a header for the first page of the printout, so no header information will be added to that page. Next, you will format the footer for all pages of the printout.

To create the page footer:

1. On the Header/Footer tab of the Page Setup dialog box, click the **Custom Footer** button. The Footer dialog box opens.

2. On the Footer tab, click the **Center section** box, type **Page**, press the **spacebar**, and then click the **Insert Page Number** button 📄. The code &[Page], which inserts the current page number, appears after the label "Page."

3. Press the **spacebar**, type **of**, press the **spacebar**, and then click the **Insert Number of Pages** button 📄. The code &[Pages], which inserts the total number of pages in the printout, is added to the Center section box. See Figure 2-45.

Figure 2-45   **Footer dialog box**

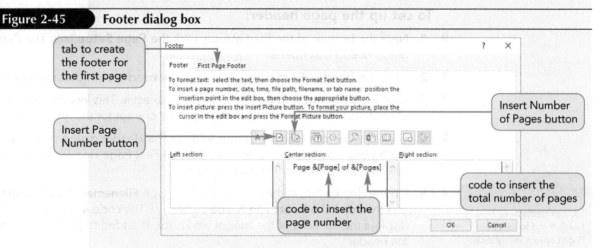

> **4.** Click the **First Page Footer** tab so you can create the footer for the first page of the printout.
>
> **5.** Click the **Right section** box, type **Prepared by:**, press the **spacebar**, and then type your name.
>
> **6.** Click the **OK** button to return to the Page Setup dialog box.

You will leave the Page Setup dialog box so you can finish formatting the printout by setting the page margins.

Setting the Page Margins

A **margin** is the space between the page content and the edges of the page. By default, Excel sets the page margins to 0.7 inch on the left and right sides, and 0.75 inch on the top and bottom; and it allows for 0.3-inch margins around the header and footer. You can reduce or increase these margins as needed by selecting predefined margin sizes or setting your own.

Carol's reports need a wider margin along the left side of the page to accommodate the binding. She asks you to increase the left margin for the printout from 0.7 inch to 1 inch.

To set the left margin:

TIP

To select preset margins, click the Margins button in the Page Setup group on the Page Layout tab.

> **1.** Click the **Margins** tab in the Page Setup dialog box to display options for changing the page margins.
>
> **2.** Double-click the **Left** box to select the setting, and then type **1** to increase the size of the left margin to 1 inch. See Figure 2-46.

| Figure 2-46 | Margins tab in the Page Setup dialog box |

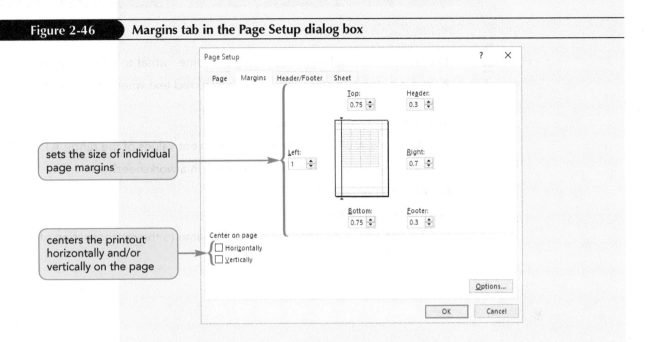

> **3.** Click the **OK** button to close the dialog box. You can see the margin change in the preview on the Print screen in Backstage view.

Now that you have formatted the printout, you can print the final version of the worksheet.

To save and print the workbook:

> **1.** With the workbook still in the Print screen in Backstage view, click the first box in the Settings section, and then click **Print Entire Workbook**.
>
> Both the Sales Report worksheet and the Documentation sheet appear in the preview. As you can see, the printout will include a header with the filename and date on every page except the first page and a footer with your name on the first page and the page number along with the total number of pages on subsequent pages.

> **2.** If you are instructed to print, print the entire workbook.

> **3.** Click the **Back** button ⊖ from the Backstage View navigation bar to return to the workbook window.

> **4.** Click the **Normal** button ▦ on the status bar to return the view of the workbook to normal.

> **5.** Save the workbook, and then close it.

Carol is pleased with the worksheet's appearance and the layout of the printout. The formatting has made the contents easier to read and understand.

REVIEW

Session 2.2 Quick Check

1. Describe two methods of applying the same format to different ranges.

2. Red is a standard color. What happens to red text when you change the workbook's theme?

3. What is a conditional format?

4. How would you highlight the top 10 percent values of the range A1:C20?

5. How do you insert a manual page break in a worksheet?

6. What is a print area?

7. What are print titles?

8. Describe how to add the workbook filename to the center section of the footer on every page of the printout.

Review Assignments

Data Files needed for the Review Assignments: Menu.xlsx, Background2.jpg

Carol created a workbook that tracks the sales of individual items from the Morning Bean menu to share at an upcoming conference. She has already entered most of the financial formulas but wants you to calculate some additional values. She also asks you to format the workbook so that it will look professional and be easy to read and understand. Complete the following:

1. Open the **Menu** workbook located in the Excel2 > Review folder included with your Data Files, and then save the workbook as **Menu Sales** in the location specified by your instructor.

2. In the Documentation sheet, enter your name in cell B4 and the date in cell B5.

3. Change the theme of the workbook to Retrospect.

4. Make the following formatting changes to the Documentation sheet:
   a. Set the background image to the **Background2** JPEG file located in the Excel2 > Review folder.
   b. Format the text in cell A1 in a 26-point bold Calibri Light.
   c. In cell A1, change the font color of the word "Morning" to the Orange, Accent 1 theme color and change the font color of the word "Bean" to the Brown, Accent 3 theme color.
   d. Format the text in cell A2 in 18-point, italic, and change the font color to the Brown, Accent 3 theme color.
   e. Format the range A4:A6 with the Accent 3 cell style.
   f. Change the font color of the range B4:B6 to the Brown, Accent 3 theme color, and change the fill color to the White, Background 1 theme color.
   g. In cell B5, format the date in the Long Date format and left-align the cell contents.

5. Use the Format Painter to copy the formatting in the range A1:A2 in the Documentation sheet and paste it to the same range in the Menu Items worksheet. Change the font colors in cell A1 of the Menu Items worksheet to match the colors used in cell A1 of the Documentation sheet.

6. Apply the Title cell style to cells B4, B12, and A20.

7. Make the following changes to the Units Sold table in the range B5:F10:
   a. Apply the Accent3 cell style to the headings in the range B5:F5. Center the headings in the range C5:F5.
   b. In cell C6, use the SUM function to calculate the total number of specialty drinks sold by the company (found in the range C22:N31 in the Units Sold per Month table). In cell C7, use the SUM function to calculate the total number of smoothies sold (in the range C32:N36). In cell C8, use the SUM function calculate the total number of sandwiches sold (in the range C37:N41). In cell C9, calculate the total number of soups sold (in the range C42:N45).
   c. In cell C10, use the SUM function to calculate the total units sold from all menu types in 2017 (based on the range C6:C9). Copy the formula to cell D10 to calculate the total units sold in 2016.
   d. In each cell of the range E6:E10, calculate the change in units sold between the 2017 and 2016 values. In each cell of the range F6:F10, calculate the percent change from 2016 to 2017. (*Hint*: The percent change is the net change divided by the 2016 value.)
   e. Format the range C6:E10 with the Comma style and no decimal places.
   f. Format the range F6:F10 with the Percent style and two decimal places.
   g. Add a top border to the range B10:F10.

8. Make the following changes to the Gross Sales table in the range B13:F18:
   a. In cells C18 and D18, use the SUM function to calculate the totals of the 2017 and 2016 sales.
   b. In the range E14:F18, enter formulas to calculate the net change and the percent change in sales.
   c. Use the Format Painter to copy the formatting from the range B5:F10 to the range B13:F18.
   d. Format the ranges C14:E14 and C18:E18 with Accounting format and no decimal places.

9. Make the following changes to the Units Sold per Month table in the range A21:O46:

   a. In the range O22:O45, use the SUM function to calculate the total units sold for each menu item. In the range C46:O46, use the SUM function to calculate the total items sold per month and overall.

   b. Format the headings in the range A21:O21 with the Accent3 cell style. Center the headings in the range C21:O21.

   c. Format the units sold values in the range C22:O46 with the Comma style and no decimal places.

   d. Change the fill color of the subtotals in the range O22:O45,C46:N46 to the White, Background 1, Darker 15% theme color (the first color in the third row).

   e. Merge each of the menu categories in the ranges A22:A31, A32:A36, A37:A41, and A42:A45 into single cells. Rotate the text of the cells up, and middle-align the cell contents.

   f. Format cell A22 with the Accent1 cell style. Format cell A32 with the Accent2 cell style. Format cell A37 with the Accent3 cell style. Format cell A42 with the Accent4 cell style. Change the font size of these four merged cells to 14 points.

   g. Add thick outside borders around each category of menu item in the ranges A22:O31, A32:O36, A37:O41, and A42:O45.

10. Use conditional formatting to highlight negative values in the range E6:F10,E14:F18 with a light red fill with dark red text to highlight which menu categories showed a decrease in units sold or gross sales from 2016 to 2017.

11. Use conditional formatting to format cells that rank in the top 10 percent of the range C22:N45 with a green fill with dark green text to highlight the menu items and months that are in the top 10 percent of units sold.

12. Create a legend for the conditional formatting you added to the worksheet. In cell O20, enter the text **Top Sellers**. Add thick outside borders around the cell, and then use conditional formatting to display this text with a green fill with dark green text.

13. Set the following print formats for the Menu Items worksheet:

   a. Set the print area to the nonadjacent range A1:F19,A20:O46.

   b. Switch to Page Break Preview, and then remove any automatic page breaks in the Units Sold per Month table. Insert a manual page break to separate the June and July sales figures. The printout of the Menu Sales worksheet should fit on three pages.

   c. Scale the printout to 70 percent.

   d. Create print titles that repeat the first three rows at the top of the sheet and the first two columns at the left of the sheet.

   e. Increase the left margin of the printout from 0.7 inch to 1 inch.

   f. Create headers and footers for the printout with a different first page.

   g. For the first page header, print **Prepared by** followed by your name in the right section. For every other page, print **Filename:** followed by the filename in the left section and the date in the right section. (*Hint*: Use the buttons in the Header dialog box to insert the filename and date.)

   h. For every footer, including the first page, print **Page** followed by the page number and then **of** followed by the total number of pages in the printout in the center section.

   i. Preview the printout to verify that the company name and description appear on every page of the Menu Items worksheet printout and that the menu category and menu item name appear on both pages with the Units Sold table. If you are instructed to print, print the entire workbook in portrait orientation.

14. Save the workbook, and then close it.

Case Problem 1

Data File needed for this Case Problem: Green.xlsx

APPLY

Green Clean Homes Sean Patel is developing a business plan for Green Clean Homes, a new professional home cleaning service in Toledo, Ohio. As part of his business plan, Sean needs to predict the company's annual income and expenses. You will help him finalize and format the Excel workbook containing the projected income statement. Complete the following:

1. Open the **Green** workbook located in the Excel2 > Case1 folder, and then save the workbook as **Green Clean** in the location specified by your instructor.

2. In the Documentation sheet, enter your name in cell B3 and the date in cell B4.

3. Display the date in cell B4 in the Long Date format and left-aligned.

4. Change the theme of the workbook to Facet.

5. Make the following formatting changes to the Documentation sheet:
   a. Merge and center cells A1 and B1.
   b. Apply the Accent2 cell style to the merged cell A1 and to the range A3:A5.
   c. In cell A1, set the font size to 22 points and bold the text. Italicize the word "Clean" in the company name.
   d. Add borders around each cell in the range A3:B5. Top-align the text in the range A3:B5.
   e. Change the font color of the text in the range B3:B5 to Dark Green, Accent 2.

6. In the Income Statement worksheet, merge and center the range A1:C1, and then apply the Accent2 cell style to the merged cell. Change the font size to 24 points and the text style to bold. Italicize the word "Clean" within the company name.

7. Make the following changes to the Income Statement worksheet:
   a. Format the range A3:C3 with the Heading 1 cell style.
   b. Format the range A4:C4,A9:C9 with the 40% - Accent1 cell style.
   c. Format cell B5 in the Accounting style with no decimal places.
   d. Format cell B6 and the range B10:B17 in the Comma style with no decimal places.

8. Add the following calculations to the workbook:
   a. In cell C7, calculate the gross profit, which is equal to the gross sales minus the cost of sales.
   b. In cell C18, calculate the company's total operating expenses, which is equal to the sum of the values in the range B10:B17. Format the value in the Accounting format with no decimal places.
   c. In cell C20, calculate the company's operating profit, which is equal to its gross profit minus its total operating expenses.
   d. In cell C21, calculate the company's incomes taxes by multiplying its total operating profit by the corporate tax rate (cell G25). Format the value in the Accounting format with no decimal places.
   e. In cell C22, calculate the company's net profit, which is equal to the total operating profit minus the income taxes.

9. Finalize the formatting of the Projected Income statement by adding the following:
   a. Add a bottom border to the ranges A6:C6, A17:C17, and A20:C20. Add a single top border and a double bottom border to the range A22:C22.
   b. Indent the expenses categories in the range A10:A17 twice.

10. Format the Financial Assumptions section as follows:
   a. Add borders around all of the cells in the range E4:G25.
   b. Format the range E3:G3 with the Heading 1 cell style.
   c. Merge the cells in the ranges E4:E7, E9:E13, E14:E15, E16:E18, and E20:E22.
   d. Top-align and left-align the range E4:E25.
   e. Change the fill color of the range E4:F25 to Green, Accent 1, Lighter 60%.

11. Use conditional formatting to highlight the net profit (cell C22) if its value is less than $50,000 with a light red fill with dark red text.

12. Change the value in cell G9 from 4 to **5**. Observe the impact that hiring another cleaner has on the projected net profit for the company in cell C22.

13. Format the printed version of the Income Statement worksheet as follows:

    a. Add a manual page break between columns D and E.

    b. For the first page, add a header that prints **Prepared by** followed by your name in the left section of the header and the current date in the right section of the header. Do not display header text on any other page.

    c. For every page, add a footer that prints the workbook filename in the left section, **Page** followed by the page number in the center section, and the worksheet name in the right section.

    d. Set the margins to 1 inch on all four sides of the printout, and center the contents of the worksheet horizontally within the printed page.

14. If you are instructed to print, print the entire contents of the workbook in portrait orientation.

15. Save and close the workbook.

Case Problem 2

APPLY

Data File needed for this Case Problem: Peak.xlsx

Peak Bytes   Peter Taylor is an engineer at Peak Bytes, an Internet service provider located in Great Falls, Montana. Part of Peter's job is to track the over-the-air connection speeds from the company's transmitters. Data from an automated program recording Internet access times has been entered into a workbook, but the data is difficult to interpret. He wants you to edit the workbook so that the data is easier to read and the fast and slow connection times are quickly visible. He also wants the workbook to provide summary statistics on the connection speeds. Complete the following:

1. Open the **Peak** workbook located in the Excel2 > Case2 folder, and then save the workbook as **Peak Bytes** in the location specified by your instructor.

2. In the Documentation sheet, enter your name in cell B3 and the date in cell B4.

3. Apply the Banded theme to the workbook.

4. Format the Documentation sheet as follows:

    a. Apply the Title cell style to cell A1. Change the font style to bold and the font size to 24 points.

    b. Add borders around the range A3:B5.

    c. Apply the Accent4 cell style to the range A3:A5.

    d. Top-align the contents in the range A3:B5.

5. In the Speed Test worksheet, move the data from the range A1:D97 to the range A12:D108.

6. Copy cell A1 from the Documentation sheet, and paste it into cell A1 of the Speed Test worksheet.

7. In cell A2, enter **Internet Speed Test Results**. Apply the Heading 1 cell style to the range A2:D2.

8. In cell A4, enter **Date** and format it using the Accent4 cell style. In cell B4, enter **4/8/2017** and format it using the Long Date format. Add a border around the cells in the range A4:B4.

9. Format the data in the Speed Test worksheet as follows:

    a. In the range A13:A108, format the numeric date and time values with the Time format. (*Hint*: The Time format is in the Number Format box in the Number group on the Home tab.)

    b. In the range C13:D108, show the numbers with three decimal places.

    c. In the range A12:D12, apply the Accent4 cell style and center the text.

    d. In the range A12:D108, add borders around all of the cells.

10. Create a table of summary statistics for the Internet Speed Test as follows:

    a. Copy the headings in the range B12:D12, and paste them into the range B6:D6.

    b. In cell A7, enter **Average**. In cell A8, enter **Minimum**. In cell A9, enter **Maximum**. Format the range A7:A9 with the Accent4 cell style.

c. In cell B7, use the AVERAGE function to calculate the average ping value of the values in the range B13:B108. In cell B8, use the MIN function to calculate the minimum ping value of the values in the range B13:B108. In cell B9, use the MAX function to calculate the maximum ping value of the values in the range B13:B108.

d. Copy the formulas from the range B7:B9 to the range C7:D9 to calculate summary statistics for the download and upload speeds from the Internet test.

e. Format the values in the range B7,C7:D9 to show two decimal places.

f. Add borders around all of the cells in the range A6:D9.

11. Use conditional formatting to highlight ping values greater than 70 in the range B13:B108 with a light red fill with dark red text to highlight times when the Internet usually appears to be slow.

12. Use conditional formatting to highlight upload values less than 3.5 in the range C13:C108 with a light red fill with dark red text.

13. Use conditional formatting to highlight download values less than 2 in the range D13:D108 with a light red fill with dark red text.

14. In cell D11, enter the text **Slow Connection**. Use conditional formatting to display this text string with a light red fill with dark red text. Center the text, and add a border around cell D11.

15. Set the print titles to repeat the first 12 rows at the top of every page of the printout.

16. For the first page of the printout, add a header that prints **Prepared by** followed by your name in the left section of the header and the current date in the right section of the header. Do not display header text on any other page.

17. For every page, add a footer that prints the workbook filename in the left section, **Page** followed by the page number followed by **of** followed by the number of pages in the center section, and then the worksheet name in the right section.

18. If you are instructed to print, print the entire contents of the workbook in portrait orientation.

19. Save and close the workbook.

Case Problem 3

Data File needed for this Case Problem: Wait.xlsx

YuriTech   Kayla Schwartz is the customer service manager at YuriTech, an electronics and computer firm located in Scottsdale, Arizona. Kayla is analyzing the calling records for technical support calls to YuriTech to determine which times are understaffed, resulting in unacceptable wait times. She has compiled several months of data and calculated the average wait times in one-hour intervals for each day of the week. You will format Kayla's workbook to make it easier to determine when YuriTech should hire more staff to assist with customer support requests. Complete the following:

1. Open the **Wait** workbook located in the Excel2 > Case3 folder, and then save the workbook as **Wait Times** in the location specified by your instructor.

2. In the Documentation sheet, enter your name in cell B3 and the date in cell B4.

3. Apply the Ion theme to the workbook.

4. Format the Documentation sheet as follows:

a. Format the title in cell A1 using a 36-point Impact font with the Purple, Accent 6 font color.

b. Format the range A3:A5 with the Accent6 cell style.

c. Add a border around the cells in the range A3:B5. Wrap the text within each cell, and top-align the cell text.

5. Copy the format you used in cell A1 of the Documentation sheet, and paste it to cell A1 of the Wait Times worksheet.

(vertical side text) CHALLENGE

6. Format the text in cell A2 with 14-point bold font and the Purple, Accent6 font color.

7. In the range A14:H39, format the average customer wait times for each hour and day of the week data as follows:

 a. Merge and center the range A14:H14, and apply the Title cell style to the merged contents.

 b. Change the number format of the data in the range B16:H39 to show one decimal place.

 c. Format the column and row labels in the range A15:H15,A16:A39 with the Accent6 cell style. Center the column headings in the range B15:H15.

8. In cell B5, enter the value **22** as an excellent wait time. In cell B6, enter **34** as a good wait time. In cell B7, enter **45** as an acceptable wait time. In cell B8, enter **60** as a poor wait time. In cell B9, enter **78** as a very poor wait time. In cell B10, enter **90** as an unacceptable wait time.

9. In the range A4:C10, apply the following formats to the wait time goals:

 a. Merge and center the range A4:C4, and apply the Accent6 cell style to the merged cells.

 b. Add borders around the cells in the range A4:C10.

10. In cell E4, enter the label **Average Wait Time (All Days)**. In cell E7, enter the label **Average Wait Time (Weekdays)**. In cell E10, enter the label **Average Wait Time (Weekends)**.

11. Merge and center the range E4:F6, wrap the text in the merged cell, center the cell content both horizontally and vertically, and then apply the Accent6 cell style to the merged cell.

12. Copy the format from the merged cell E4:F6 to cells E7 and E10.

13. In cell G4, enter a formula to calculate the average of the wait times in the range B16:H39. In cell G7, enter a formula to calculate the average weekday wait times in the range C16:G39. In cell G10, calculate the average weekend rate times in the range B16:B39,H16:H39.

14. Merge and center the ranges G4:G6, G7:G9, and G10:G12, and then center the calculated averages vertically within each merged cell.

15. Add borders around the cells in the range E4:G12.

16. Change the fill color of the range A5:C5 to a medium green, the fill color of the range A6:C6 to a light green, the fill color of the range A7:C7 to a light gold, the fill color of the range A8:C8 to a light red, and the fill color of the range A9:C9 to a medium red. Format the range A10:C10 with white text on a black background.

⊕ **Explore** 17. Use conditional formatting to highlight cells with custom formats as follows:

 a. Select the range G4:G12,B16:H39. Use conditional formatting to highlight cells with values less than 22 with a custom format that matches the fill color used in the range A5:C5.

 b. Use conditional formatting to highlight cells with values greater than 90 in the range G4:G12,B16:H39 with a custom format of a white font on a black fill.

 c. Use conditional formatting to highlight cells with values between 22 and 34 in the range G4:G12,B16:H39 with a custom format that matches the fill color used in the range A6:C6.

 d. Use conditional formatting to highlight cells with values between 34 and 60 in the range G4:G12,B16:H39 with a light gold fill color that matches the cells in the range A7:C7.

 e. Use conditional formatting to highlight cells with values between 60 and 78 in the range G4:G12,B16:H39 with light red, matching the fill color of the cells in the range A8:C8.

 f. Use conditional formatting to highlight cells with values between 78 and 90 in the range G4:G12,B16:H39 with medium red, matching the fill color of the cells in the range A9:C9.

18. In cell A41, enter the label **Notes** and then format it with the Title cell style.

19. Merge the range A42:H50. Top- and left-align the contents of the cell. Turn on text wrapping within the merged cell. Add a thick outside border to the merged cell.

20. Within the merged cell in the range A42:H50, summarize your conclusions about the wait times. Answer whether the wait times are within acceptable limits on average for the entire week, on weekdays, and on weekends. Also indicate whether there are times during the week that customers are experience very poor to unacceptable delays.

21. Format the printed version of the Wait Times worksheet as follows:

 a. Scale the sheet so that it fits on a single page in portrait orientation.

 b. Center the sheet on the page horizontally and vertically.

c. Add the header **Prepared by** followed by your name in the right section.

d. Add a footer that prints the filename in the left section, the worksheet name in the center section, and the date in the right section.

22. If you are instructed to print, print the entire contents of the workbook.

23. Save and close the workbook.

Case Problem 4

Data File needed for this Case Problem: Pandaisia.xlsx

Pandaisia Chocolates   Anne Ambrose is the owner and head chocolatier of Pandaisia Chocolates, a chocolate shop located in Essex, Vermont. Anne has asked you to create an Excel workbook in which she can enter customer orders. She wants the workbook to be easy to use and read. The final design of the order form is up to you. One possible solution is shown in Figure 2-47.

Figure 2-47   Pandaisia Chocolates order form

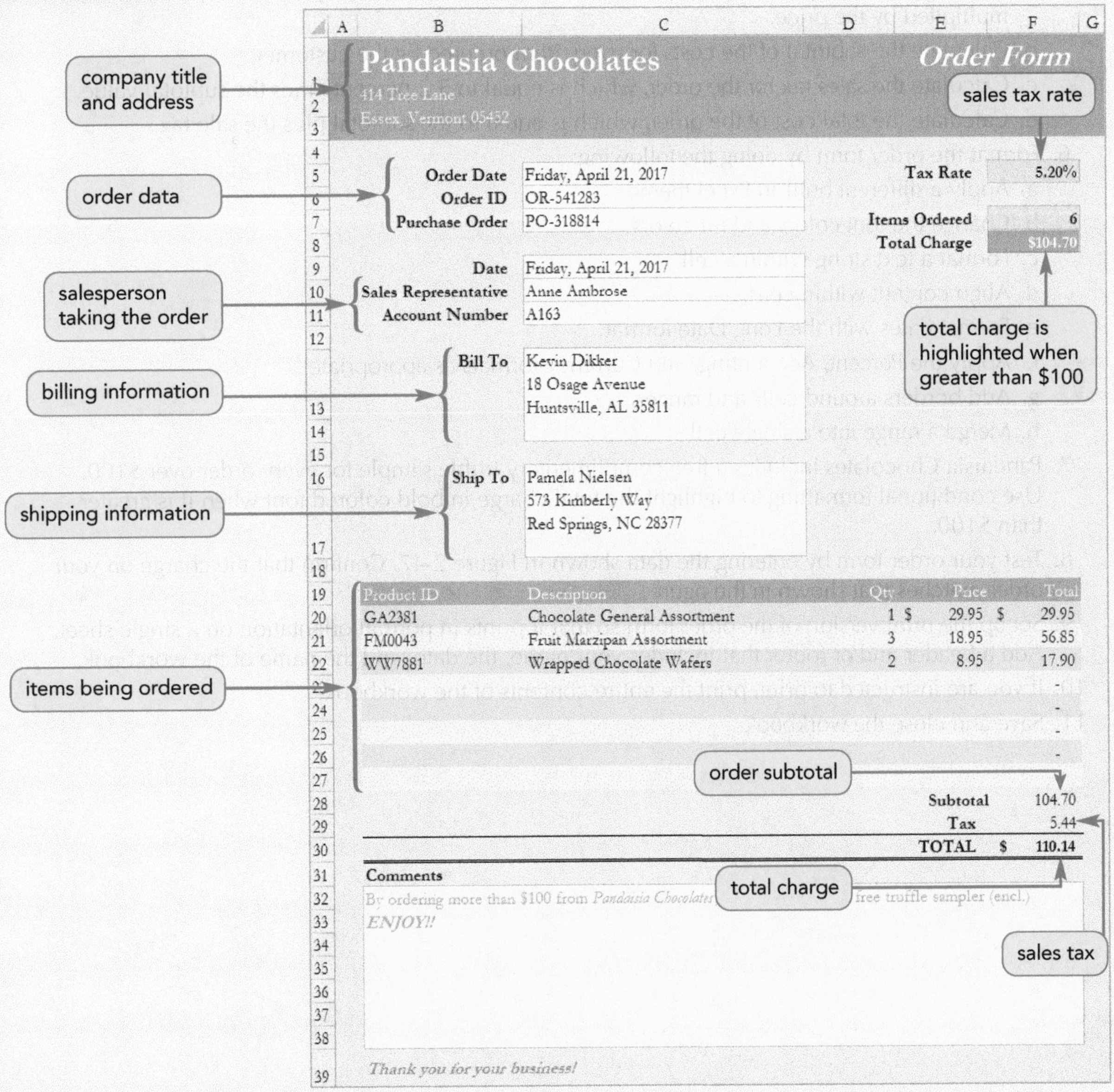

CREATE

Complete the following:

1. Open the **Pandaisia** workbook located in the Excel2 > Case3 folder, and then save the workbook as **Pandaisia Order** in the location specified by your instructor.

2. In the Documentation sheet, enter your name in cell B3 and the date in cell B4.

3. Insert a worksheet named **Order Form** after the Documentation worksheet.

4. Enter the following information in the order form:
   - The title and address of Pandaisia Chocolates
   - The order date, order ID, and purchase order ID
   - The date, sales representative, and account number for the order
   - The billing address of the order
   - The shipping address of the order
   - A table listing every item ordered including the item's product ID, description, quantity ordered, price, and total charge for the item(s)
   - A comment box where Anne can insert additional information about the order

5. Include formulas in the order form to do the following:
   a. For each item ordered, calculate the cost of the item(s), which is equal to the quantity multiplied by the price.
   b. Calculate the subtotal of the costs for every item ordered by the customer.
   c. Calculate the sales tax for the order, which is equal to 5.2 percent times the subtotal value.
   d. Calculate the total cost of the order, which is equal to the subtotal plus the sale tax.

6. Format the order form by doing the following:
   a. Apply a different built-in Excel theme.
   b. Change the font colors and fill colors.
   c. Format a text string within a cell.
   d. Align content within cells.
   e. Format dates with the Long Date format.
   f. Apply the Percent, Accounting, and Currency formats as appropriate.
   g. Add borders around cells and ranges.
   h. Merge a range into a single cell.

7. Pandaisia Chocolates includes a free complimentary truffle sample for every order over $100. Use conditional formatting to highlight the total charge in bold colored font when it is greater than $100.

8. Test your order form by entering the data shown in Figure 2-47. Confirm that the charge on your order matches that shown in the figure.

9. Set up the print version of the order form so that it prints in portrait orientation on a single sheet. Add a header and/or footer that includes your name, the date, and the name of the workbook.

10. If you are instructed to print, print the entire contents of the workbook.

11. Save and close the workbook.

OBJECTIVES

Session 3.1
- Document formulas and data values
- Explore function syntax
- Insert functions from the Formula Library
- Perform a what-if analysis

Session 3.2
- AutoFill series and formulas
- Use relative and absolute cell references
- Use the Quick Analysis tool
- Work with dates and Date functions
- Find values with Lookup functions
- Work with Logical functions

Performing Calculations with Formulas and Functions

Calculating Farm Yield and Revenue

Case | *Wingait Farm*

Jane Wingait is the owner and operator of Wingait Farm, a small farm located outside of Cascade, Iowa. Jane's cash crop is corn, and she has planted almost 140 acres of the sweet corn variety for the past 11 years. Near harvest time every year Jane samples and analyzes a portion of her crop to estimate her farm's total yield for the year. She wants you to help her design an Excel workbook that will calculate her corn yield. As Jane prepares for next year's crop, she also wants to use Excel to track her corn's growth from planting to harvesting. As you create the workbook, you will explore how Jane can use Excel formulas to help her in running her farm.

STARTING DATA FILES

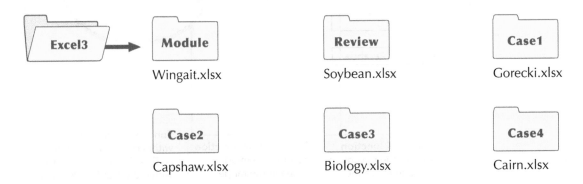

Excel3 → Module
Wingait.xlsx

Review
Soybean.xlsx

Case1
Gorecki.xlsx

Case2
Capshaw.xlsx

Case3
Biology.xlsx

Case4
Cairn.xlsx

Session 3.1 Visual Overview:

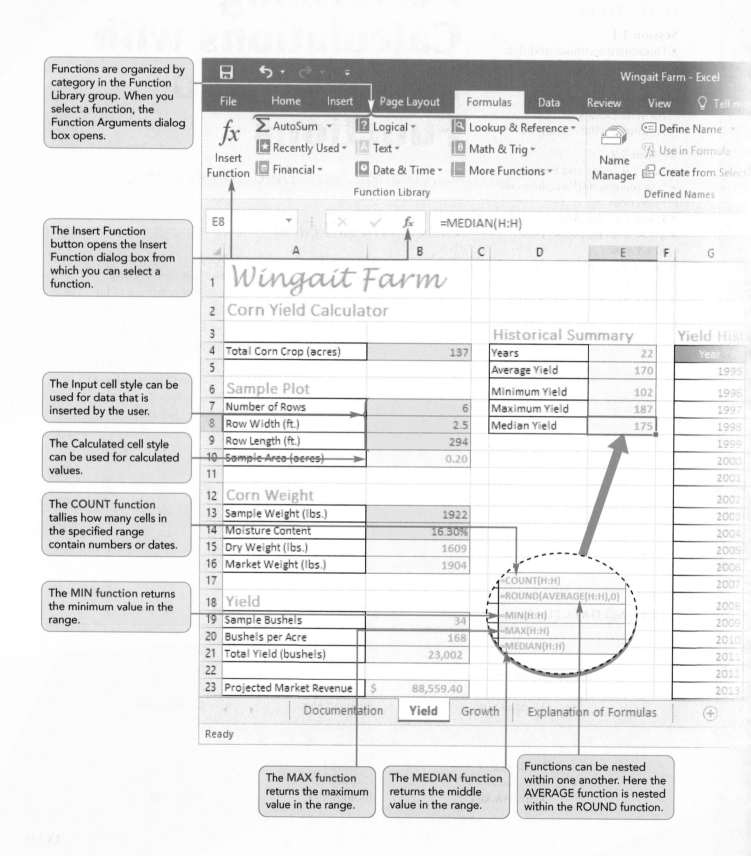

Functions are organized by category in the Function Library group. When you select a function, the Function Arguments dialog box opens.

The Insert Function button opens the Insert Function dialog box from which you can select a function.

The Input cell style can be used for data that is inserted by the user.

The Calculated cell style can be used for calculated values.

The COUNT function tallies how many cells in the specified range contain numbers or dates.

The MIN function returns the minimum value in the range.

The MAX function returns the maximum value in the range.

The MEDIAN function returns the middle value in the range.

Functions can be nested within one another. Here the AVERAGE function is nested within the ROUND function.

Wingait Farm

Corn Yield Calculator

| Total Corn Crop (acres) | 137 |

Sample Plot

Number of Rows	6
Row Width (ft.)	2.5
Row Length (ft.)	294
Sample Area (acres)	0.20

Corn Weight

Sample Weight (lbs.)	1922
Moisture Content	16.30%
Dry Weight (lbs.)	1609
Market Weight (lbs.)	1904

Yield

Sample Bushels	34
Bushels per Acre	168
Total Yield (bushels)	23,002
Projected Market Revenue	$ 88,559.40

Historical Summary

Years	22
Average Yield	170
Minimum Yield	102
Maximum Yield	187
Median Yield	175

Yield Hist...

| Year |
| 1995 |
| 1996 |
| 1997 |
| 1998 |
| 1999 |
| 2000 |
| 2001 |
| 2002 |
| 2003 |
| 2004 |
| 2005 |
| 2006 |
| 2007 |
| 2008 |
| 2009 |
| 2010 |
| 2011 |
| 2012 |
| 2013 |

=COUNT(H:H)
=ROUND(AVERAGE(H:H),0)
=MIN(H:H)
=MAX(H:H)
=MEDIAN(H:H)

E8 =MEDIAN(H:H)

Documentation | Yield | Growth | Explanation of Formulas

Formulas and Functions

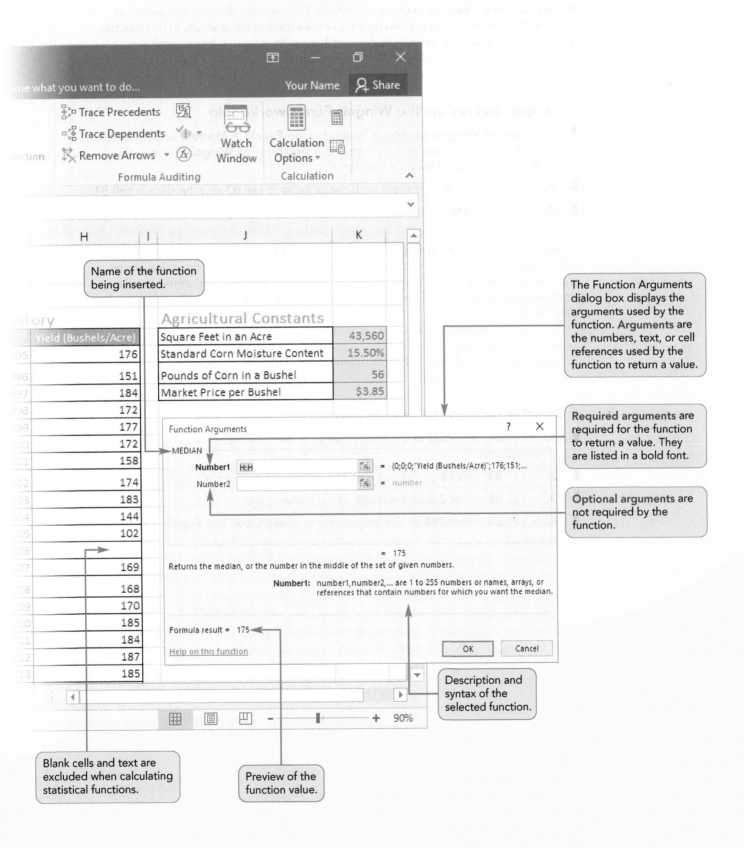

Name of the function being inserted.

The Function Arguments dialog box displays the arguments used by the function. **Arguments** are the numbers, text, or cell references used by the function to return a value.

Required arguments are required for the function to return a value. They are listed in a bold font.

Optional arguments are not required by the function.

Description and syntax of the selected function.

Blank cells and text are excluded when calculating statistical functions.

Preview of the function value.

Agricultural Constants

Square Feet in an Acre	43,560
Standard Corn Moisture Content	15.50%
Pounds of Corn in a Bushel	56
Market Price per Bushel	$3.85

Yield (Bushels/Acre)

176
151
184
172
177
172
158
174
183
144
102
169
168
170
185
184
187
185

Function Arguments

MEDIAN

Number1 H:H = {0;0;0;"Yield (Bushels/Acre)";176;151;...
Number2 = number

= 175

Returns the median, or the number in the middle of the set of given numbers.

Number1: number1,number2,... are 1 to 255 numbers or names, arrays, or references that contain numbers for which you want the median.

Formula result = 175

Help on this function

OK   Cancel

Making Workbooks User-Friendly

Excel is a powerful application for interpreting a wide variety of data used in publications from financial reports to scientific articles. To be an effective tool for data analysis, a workbook needs to be easy to use and interpret. This includes defining any technical terms in the workbook and explaining the formulas used in the analysis. In this module, you'll create a workbook to analyze the corn harvest for a farm in Iowa, employing techniques to make the workbook easily accessible to other users.

To open and review the Wingait Farms workbook:

▶ **1.** Open the **Wingait** workbook located in the **Excel3 > Module** folder included with your Data Files, and then save the workbook as **Wingait Farm** in the location specified by your instructor.

▶ **2.** In the Documentation sheet, enter your name in cell B3 and the date in cell B4.

▶ **3.** Go to the **Yield** worksheet.

Jane uses the Yield worksheet to project her farm's entire corn yield based on a small sample of harvested corn. Information about the sample and the calculations that estimate the total yield will be entered in columns A and B. Columns D and E contain important agricultural constants that Jane will use in the workbook's formulas and functions.

Jane uses a sample plot to estimate the farm's total yield. This plot, a small portion of Jane's 137-acre farm, is laid out in six rows of corn with each row 294 feet long and 2.5 feet wide. You will enter information about the size of the sample plot.

To enter data on the sample plot:

▶ **1.** In cell **B4**, enter **137** as the total acreage of the farm that Jane devotes to sweet corn.

▶ **2.** In cell **B7**, enter **6** as the number of corn rows in the sample plot.

▶ **3.** In cell **B8**, enter **2.5** as the width of each row in feet.

▶ **4.** In cell **B9**, enter **294** as the length in feet of each row. See Figure 3-1.

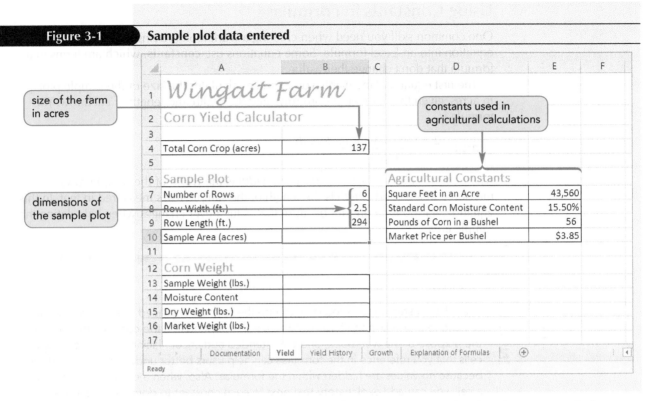

Figure 3-1 Sample plot data entered

The width and length of the sample rows are measured in feet, but Jane needs the total area expressed in acres. To calculate the area of the sample being tested, you need to refer to the agricultural equations that Jane documented for you.

Documenting Formulas

Documenting the contents of a workbook helps to avoid errors and confusion. It also makes it easier for others to interpret the analysis in the workbook. For workbooks that include many calculations, such as the Wingait Farm workbook, it is helpful to explain the formulas and terms used in the calculations. Such documentation also can serve as a check that the equations are accurate.

Jane has included explanations of equations you'll use in developing her workbook. Before proceeding, you'll review this documentation.

To review the documentation in Wingait Farm workbook:

▶ **1.** Go to the **Explanation of Formulas** worksheet.

▶ **2.** Read the worksheet contents, reviewing the descriptions of common agricultural constants and formulas. As you continue developing the Wingait Farm workbook, you'll learn about these terms and formulas in more detail.

▶ **3.** Go to the **Yield** worksheet.

Using Constants in Formulas

One common skill you need when creating a workbook is being able to translate an equation into an Excel formula. Some equations use **constants**, which are terms in a formula that don't change their value.

The first equation Jane wants you to enter calculates the size of the sample plot in acres, given the number of corn rows and the width and length of each row. The formula is

$$area = \frac{2 \times rows \times width \times length}{43560}$$

where *rows* is the number of corn rows, *width* is the width of the sample rows measured in feet, and *length* is the length of the sample rows measured in feet. In this equation, 43560 is a constant because that value never changes when calculating the sample area.

INSIGHT

Deciding Where to Place a Constant

Should a constant be entered directly into the formula or placed in a separate worksheet cell and referenced in the formula? The answer depends on the constant being used, the purpose of the workbook, and the intended audience. Placing constants in separate cells that you reference in the formulas can help users better understand the worksheet because no values are hidden within the formulas. Also, when a constant is entered in a cell, you can add explanatory text next to each constant to document how it is being used in the formula. On the other hand, you don't want a user to inadvertently change the value of a constant and throw off all the formula results. You will need to evaluate how important it is for other people to immediately see the constant and whether the constant requires any explanation for other people to understand the formula.

To convert the area equation to an Excel formula, you'll replace the *row*, *width*, and *length* values with references to the cells B7, B8, and B9, and you'll replace 43560 with a reference to cell E7. These cells provide the number of rows in the sample plot, the row width in feet, the row length in feet, and the number of square feet in one acre of land.

To calculate the area of the sample plot:

▶ 1. In cell **B10**, enter the formula **=2*B7*B8*B9/E7** to calculate the area of the sample plot. The formula returns 0.202479339.

   Trouble? If your result differs from 0.202479339, you probably entered the formula incorrectly. Edit the formula you entered in cell B10 as needed so that the numbers and cell references match those shown in the formula in Step 1.

   Jane does not need to see the acreage of the sample plot with eight decimal places.

▶ 2. Click cell **B10**, and then decrease the number of decimal places to **2**. The area of the sample plot is displayed as 0.20 acres. See Figure 3-2.

TIP

Decreasing the number decimals places rounds the displayed value; the stored value remains unchanged.

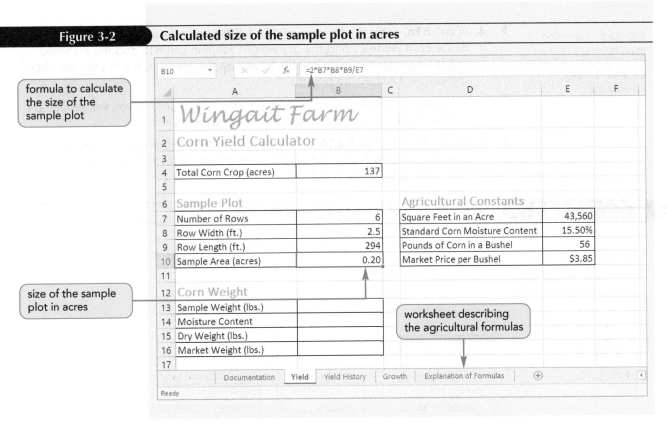

Figure 3-2   Calculated size of the sample plot in acres

formula to calculate the size of the sample plot

size of the sample plot in acres

worksheet describing the agricultural formulas

B10 f_x =2*B7*B8*B9/E7

	A	B	C	D	E	F
1	*Wingait Farm*					
2	Corn Yield Calculator					
3						
4	Total Corn Crop (acres)	137				
5						
6	Sample Plot			Agricultural Constants		
7	Number of Rows	6		Square Feet in an Acre	43,560	
8	Row Width (ft.)	2.5		Standard Corn Moisture Content	15.50%	
9	Row Length (ft.)	294		Pounds of Corn in a Bushel	56	
10	Sample Area (acres)	0.20		Market Price per Bushel	$3.85	
11						
12	Corn Weight					
13	Sample Weight (lbs.)					
14	Moisture Content					
15	Dry Weight (lbs.)					
16	Market Weight (lbs.)					
17						

Documentation   Yield   Yield History   Growth   Explanation of Formulas   ⊕

Ready

When Jane harvests the corn from the sample plot, she measures the total weight of the corn, which includes its moisture content. She then analyzes the corn to determine what percentage of its weight is due to moisture. The total weight of the corn is 1,922 pounds of which 16.3 percent is moisture. To sell the corn, Jane needs to calculate the dry weight of the corn without the moisture. She can do this with the formula

$$dry\ weight = total\ weight \times (1 - moisture)$$

where *total weight* is the weight of the corn and *moisture* is the percentage of the weight due to moisture. Market prices for corn are standardized at a moisture percentage of 15.5 percent, so to get the correct market weight of her corn, Jane uses the following formula:

$$market\ weight = \frac{dry\ weight}{1 - 0.155}$$

You will enter these two formulas in Jane's workbook to calculate the market weight of the corn she harvested from the sample plot.

To calculate the market weight of the corn:

▶ **1.** In cell **B13**, enter **1922** as the total weight of the corn sample.

▶ **2.** In cell **B14**, enter **16.3%** as the moisture content.

▶ **3.** In cell **B15**, enter the formula **=B13*(1-B14)** to calculate the dry weight of the corn kernels. Based on the formula, the dry weight of the corn harvested from the sample plot is 1608.714 pounds.

Because the expression requires dividing by two terms, you must enclose those terms within parentheses.

4. In cell **B16**, enter the formula **=B15/(1-E8)** to calculate the market weight of the corn kernels using the dry weight value in cell B15 and the standard moisture content value in cell E8. Based on the formula, the market weight of the corn is 1903.80355 pounds.

    Jane does not need to see such precise weight values, so you will reduce the number of decimal places displayed in the worksheet.

5. Select the range **B15:B16**, and then format the numbers with no decimals places to display the dry and market weights of 1609 and 1904 pounds, respectively. See Figure 3-3.

Figure 3-3 | Calculated dry and market weights of the corn

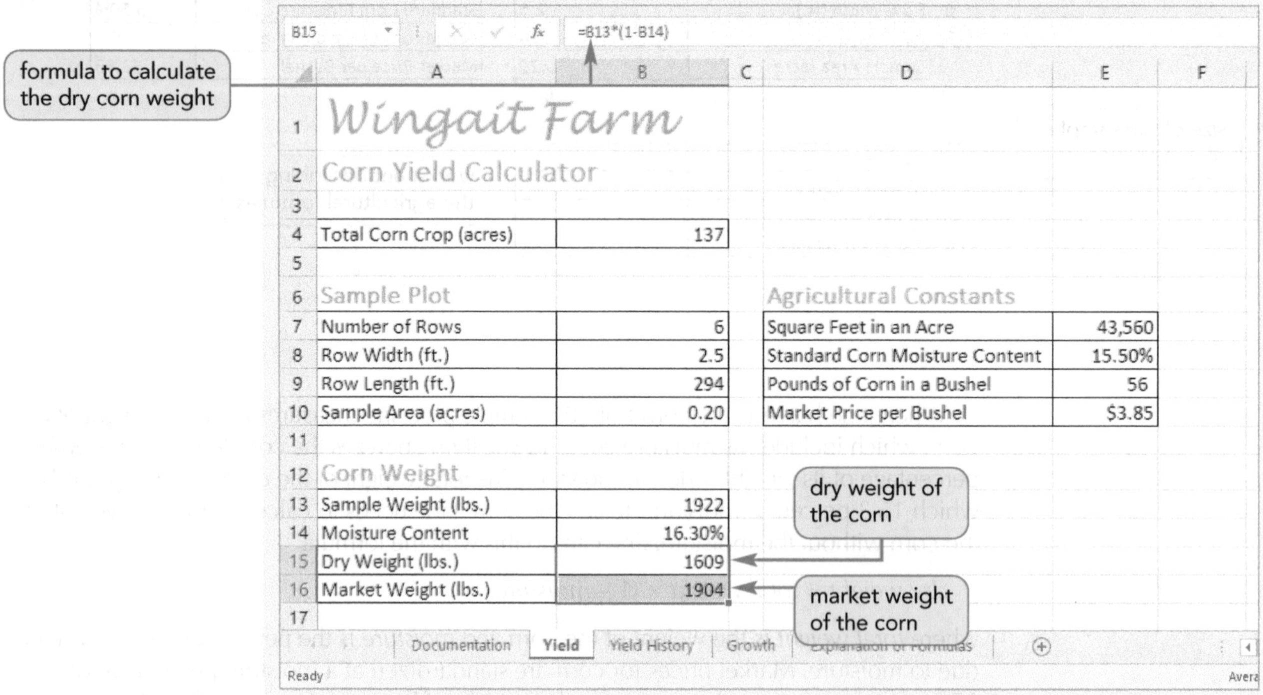

formula to calculate the dry corn weight

	A	B	C	D	E	F
	B15 ▾ ⁝ × ✓ *f*x	=B13*(1-B14)				
1	Wingait Farm					
2	Corn Yield Calculator					
3						
4	Total Corn Crop (acres)	137				
5						
6	Sample Plot		Agricultural Constants			
7	Number of Rows	6	Square Feet in an Acre		43,560	
8	Row Width (ft.)	2.5	Standard Corn Moisture Content		15.50%	
9	Row Length (ft.)	294	Pounds of Corn in a Bushel		56	
10	Sample Area (acres)	0.20	Market Price per Bushel		$3.85	
11						
12	Corn Weight					
13	Sample Weight (lbs.)	1922				
14	Moisture Content	16.30%				
15	Dry Weight (lbs.)	1609	dry weight of the corn			
16	Market Weight (lbs.)	1904	market weight of the corn			
17						

Documentation | **Yield** | Yield History | Growth | Explanation of Formulas | ⊕

Ready | Avera

Corn is not sold by the pound but rather by the bushel where 1 bushel contains 56 pounds of corn. You will calculate the number of bushels of corn in the sample plot and then use this number to estimate the farm's total yield and revenue.

To project the farm's total yield and revenue:

1. In cell **B19**, enter the formula **=B16/E9** to convert the market weight to bushels. In this case, the market weight is equal to 33.99649197 bushels.

2. In cell **B19**, format the number with no decimals places. The number is rounded to 34 bushels.

3. In cell **B20**, enter the formula **=B19/B10** to divide the number of bushels in the sample plot by the size of the plot in acres. Based on this calculation, this year's crop has yielded 167.901042 bushels per acre.

▶ **4.** In cell **B20**, format the number with no decimals places. This year's crop yielded about 168 bushels per acre.

Assuming that the rest of the farm is as productive as the sample plot, you can calculate the total bushels that the farm can produce by multiplying the bushels per acre by the total acreage of the farm.

▶ **5.** In cell **B21**, enter the formula **=B20*B4** to multiply the bushels per acre by the total acreage of the farm. Assuming that the rest of the farm is as productive as the sample plot, the total bushels that the farm can produce is 23002.44275 bushels.

▶ **6.** Format cell B21 using the Comma style with no decimal places. Cell B21 displays 23,002.

▶ **7.** In cell **B23**, enter the formula **=B21*E10** to calculate the revenue Jane can expect by selling all of the farm's corn at the market price of $3.85 per bushel.

▶ **8.** Format cell B23 with the Accounting style. The formula result is displayed as $88,559.40. See Figure 3-4.

Figure 3-4	Projected yield and revenue from the corn harvest

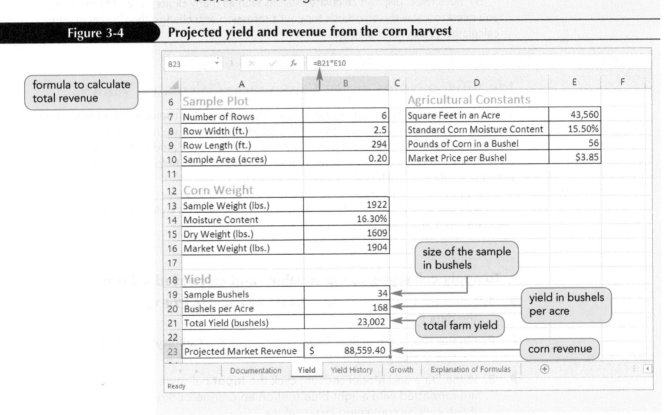

Based on your calculations, Jane projects an income of almost $90,000 from this year's corn crop.

Written Communication: Displaying Significant Digits

Excel stores numbers with up to 15 digits and displays as many digits as will fit into the cell. So even the result of a simple formula such as =10/3 will display 3.33333333333333 if the cell is wide enough.

A number with 15 digits is difficult to read, and calculations rarely need that level of accuracy. Many scientific disciplines, such as chemistry or physics, have rules for specifying exactly how many digits should be displayed with any calculation. These digits are called **significant digits** because they indicate the accuracy of the measured and calculated values. For example, an input value of 19.32 has four significant digits.

The rules are based on several factors and vary from one discipline to another. Generally, a calculated value should display no more digits than are found in any of the input values. For example, because the input value 19.32 has four significant digits, any calculated value based on that input should have no more than four significant digits. Showing more digits would be misleading because it implies a level of accuracy beyond that which was actually measured.

Because Excel displays calculated values with as many digits as can fit into a cell, you need to know the standards for your profession and change the display of your calculated values accordingly.

Identifying Notes, Input Values, and Calculated Values

When worksheets involve notes and many calculations, it is useful to distinguish input values that are used in formulas from calculated values that are returned by formulas. Formatting that clearly differentiates input values from calculated values helps others more easily understand the worksheet. Such formatting also helps prevent anyone from entering a value in a cell that contains a formula.

Jane wants to be sure that whenever she and her staff update the workbook, they can easily see where to enter data values. You will apply cell styles to distinguish between input and calculated values.

To apply cell styles to input values and calculated values:

1. Select the nonadjacent range **B4,B7:B9,B13:B14,E7:E10**. These cells contain the data that you entered for Jane.

2. On the Home tab, in the Styles group, click the **Cell Styles** button to open the Cell Styles gallery.

3. In the Data and Model section, click the **Input** cell style. The selected cells are formatted with a light blue font on an orange background, identifying those cells as containing input values.

4. Select the nonadjacent range **B10,B15:B16,B19:B21,B23**. These cells contain the formulas for calculating the weight, yield, and revenue values.

5. Format the selected cells with the **Calculation** cell style located in the Data and Model section of the Cell Styles gallery. The cells with the calculated values are formatted with a bold orange font on a light gray background.

6. Click cell **D12** to deselect the range. See Figure 3-5.

Figure 3-5	Input and calculated values formatted with cell styles

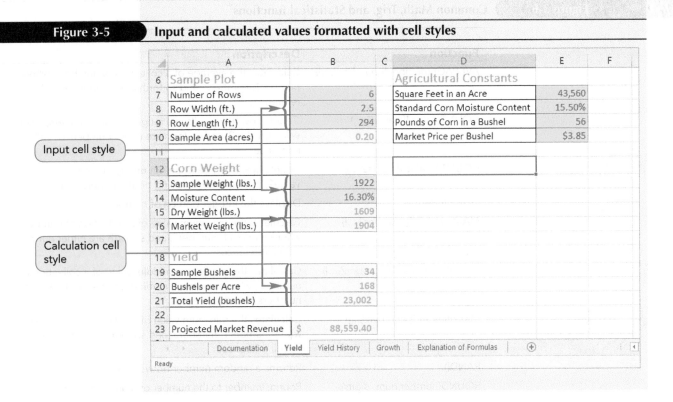

Using Excel Functions

Excel functions can be used in place of long and complicated formulas to simplify your worksheet. Jane wants to compare the estimated yield for this year's crop to historic trends. To make that comparison, you'll work with some Excel functions.

Understanding Function Syntax

Before you use functions, you should understand the function syntax. Recall that the syntax of an Excel function follows the general pattern

    FUNCTION(argument1,argument2,...)

where *FUNCTION* is the name of the function, and *argument1*, *argument2*, and so forth are arguments used by the function. An argument can be any type of value including text, numbers, cell references, or even other formulas or functions. Not all functions require arguments.

TIP

Optional arguments are always placed last in the argument list.

Some arguments are optional and can be included with the function or omitted altogether. Most optional arguments will have default values, so that if you omit an argument value, Excel will automatically apply the default. The convention is to show optional arguments within square brackets along with the argument's default value (if any), as

    FUNCTION(argument1[,argument2=value2,...])

where *argument1* is a required argument, *argument2* is optional, and *value2* is the default value for argument2. As you work with specific functions, you will learn which arguments are required and which are optional as well as any default values associated with those optional arguments.

Figure 3-6 describes some of the more commonly used Math, Trig, and Statistical functions and provides the syntax of those functions, including any optional arguments.

Figure 3-6	Common Math, Trig, and Statistical functions

Function	Description
AVERAGE(number1[,number2,...])	Calculates the average of a collection of numbers, where number1, number2, and so forth are numbers or cell references
COUNT(value1[,value2,...])	Counts how many cells in a range contain numbers, where value1, value2, and so forth are either numbers or cell references
COUNTA(value1[,value2,...])	Counts how many cells are not empty in ranges value1, value2, and so forth including both numbers and text entries
INT(number)	Displays the integer portion of number
MAX(number1[,number2,...])	Calculates the maximum value of a collection of numbers, where number1, number2, and so forth are either numbers or cell references
MEDIAN(number1[,number2,...])	Calculates the median, or middle, value of a collection of numbers, where number1, number2, and so forth are either numbers or cell references
MIN(number1[,number2,...])	Calculates the minimum value of a collection of numbers, where number1, number2, and so forth are either numbers or cell references
RAND()	Returns a random number between 0 and 1
ROUND(number,num_digits)	Rounds number to the number of digits specified by num_digits
SUM(number1[,number2,...])	Adds a collection of numbers, where number1, number2, and so forth are either numbers or cell references

Entering the COUNT function

The following COUNT function is used by Excel to count how many cells in a range contain numbers. The COUNT function syntax is

```
COUNT(value1[,value2,…])
```

where value1 is either a cell reference, range reference, or a number, and value2 and so on are optional arguments that provide additional cell references, range references, or numbers. There are no default values for the optional arguments.

The COUNT function does not include blank cells or cells that contain text in its tally. For example, the following function counts how many cells in the range A1:A10, the range C1:C5, and cell E5 contain numbers or dates:

```
COUNT(A1:A10,C1:C5,E5)
```

The COUNT function is especially helpful when data in the ranges are regularly updated.

INSIGHT

Counting Text

Excel has another important function for counting cells—the **COUNTA function**. This function counts the number of cells that contain any entries, including numbers, dates, or text. The syntax of the COUNTA function is

```
COUNTA(value1[,value2,...])
```

where *value1* is the first item or cell reference containing the entries you want to count. The remaining optional value arguments are used primarily when you want to count entries in nonadjacent ranges. The COUNTA function should be used for text data or for data in which you need to include blanks as part of the total.

You'll use the COUNT function to tally how many years of data are included in the corn yield history.

To count the number of years in the corn yield history:

▶ **1.** Go to the **Yield History** worksheet, and then click cell **B5**. You'll enter the COUNT function in this cell.

▶ **2.** Type **=COUNT(** to begin entering the COUNT function. The first argument, which is the only required argument, is the cell or range reference for the cells to be counted.

The yield values are stored in the range E5:E27. Instead of referencing this range, you will use column E as the argument for the COUNT function because Jane plans to add data to this column each year as she continues to track the farm's annual corn yield.

▶ **3.** Click the **E** column heading to select the entire column. The column reference E:E is inserted into the function as the first argument.

▶ **4.** Type **)** to end the function, and then press the **Enter** key. The formula =COUNT(E:E) is entered in cell B5 and returns 22, which is the number of years for which Jane has corn yield data.

Nesting the ROUND and AVERAGE Functions

One function can be placed inside, or **nested**, within another function. When a formula contains more than one function, Excel first evaluates the innermost function and then moves outward to evaluate the next function. The inner function acts as an argument value for the outer function. For example, the following expression nests the AVERAGE function within the ROUND function.

```
ROUND(AVERAGE(A1:A100),0)
```

Excel first uses the AVERAGE function to calculate the average of the values in the range A1:A100 and then uses the ROUND function to round that average to the nearest integer (where the number of digits to the right of the decimal point is 0.)

One challenge of nested functions is being sure to include all of the parentheses. You can check this by counting the number of opening parentheses and making sure that number matches the number of closing parentheses. Excel also displays each level of nested parentheses in different colors to make it easier for you to match the opening and closing parentheses. If the number of parentheses doesn't match, Excel will not

TIP

The ROUND function changes the value stored in the cell, not the number of decimal places displayed in the cell.

accept the formula and will provide a suggestion for how to rewrite the formula so the number of opening and closing parentheses does match.

Jane wants you to analyze the corn yield history at Wingait Farm. You'll use the COUNT function to tally the number of years in the historical sample and then use the AVERAGE function to calculate the average yield during those years. Because Jane doesn't need the exact corn yield values, you'll use the ROUND function to round that calculated average to the nearest integer.

To analyze the corn yield history:

1. Click cell **B6**. You want to enter the nested function in this cell.

2. Type **=ROUND(** to begin the formula with the ROUND function.

3. Type **AVERAGE(E:E)** to enter the AVERAGE function as the first argument of the ROUND function.

4. Type **,** (a comma) to separate the first and second arguments.

5. Type **0)** to specify the number of decimal places to include in the results. In this case, Jane doesn't want to include any decimal places.

6. Press the **Enter** key. The nested functions first calculate the average value of the numbers in column E and then round that number to the nearest integer. The formula returns 170, which is the average annual yield of Wingait Farm in bushels per acre rounded to the nearest integer. See Figure 3-7.

Figure 3-7	Nested functions calculate the average annual yield

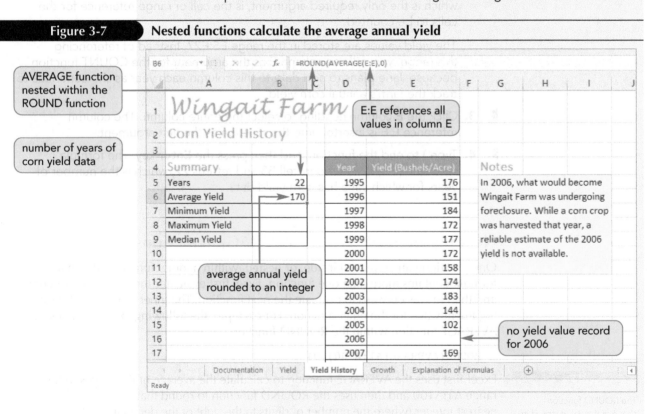

Based on values from 22 seasons of data, Jane expects her farm to yield 170 bushels of corn per acre each year.

Note that in 2006, no data on corn yield was available. Excel ignores nonnumeric data and blank cells when calculating statistical functions such as COUNT and AVERAGE. So, the count and average values in cells B5 and B6 represent only those years containing recorded corn yields. Keep in mind that a blank cell is not the same as a zero value in worksheet calculations. Figure 3-8 shows how function results differ when a zero replaces a blank in the selected range.

| Figure 3-8 | Calculations with blank cells and zero values |

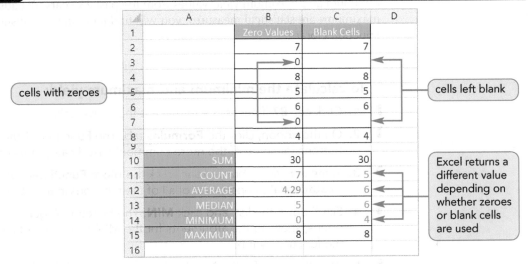

Whether you use a blank or zero depends on what you're trying to measure. For example, if Jane were to calculate average hours worked per day at the Wingait farm store, she could enter 0 for the holidays on which the store is closed, or she could enter a blank and thus calculate the average only for days in which the store is open.

Using the Function Library and the Insert Function Dialog Box

With so many Excel functions, it can difficult to locate the function you want to use for a particular application. Excel organizes its function into the 13 categories described in Figure 3-9. These function categories are available in the Function Library group on the Formulas tab and in the Insert Function dialog box.

| Figure 3-9 | Excel function categories |

Category	Description
Compatibility	Functions from Excel 2010 or earlier, still supported to provide backward compatibility
Cube	Retrieve data from multidimensional databases involving online analytical processing (OLAP)
Database	Retrieve and analyze data stored in databases
Date & Time	Analyze or create date and time values and time intervals
Engineering	Analyze engineering problems
Financial	Analyze information for business and finance
Information	Return information about the format, location, or contents of worksheet cells
Logical	Return logical (true-false) values
Lookup & Reference	Look up and return data matching a set of specified conditions from a range
Math & Trig	Perform math and trigonometry calculations
Statistical	Provide statistical analyses of data sets
Text	Return text values or evaluate text
Web	Provide information on web-based connections

Once you select a function either from the Function Library or the Insert Function dialog box, the Function Arguments dialog box opens, listing all of the arguments associated with that function. Required arguments are in bold type; optional arguments are in normal type.

Jane wants to know the range of annual corn yields, so she asks you to calculate the minimum and maximum yield values from the past 23 years. Because minimums and maximums are statistical measures, you will find them in the Statistics category in the Function Library.

To calculate the minimum and maximum yield:

▶ **1.** Click cell **B7** if necessary to make it the active cell.

▶ **2.** On the ribbon, click the **Formulas** tab. The Function Library group has buttons for some of the more commonly used categories of functions.

▶ **3.** In the Function Library group, click the **More Functions** button, and then point to **Statistical** to open a list of all of the functions in the Statistical category.

▶ **4.** Scroll down the list, and click **MIN**. The Function Arguments dialog box opens, showing the arguments for the MIN function and a brief description of the function syntax.

▶ **5.** With the entry for the Number1 argument highlighted, click the **E** column heading to select the entire column and insert the cell reference **E:E** into the Number1 input box. See Figure 3-10.

Figure 3-10	MIN function in the Function Arguments dialog box

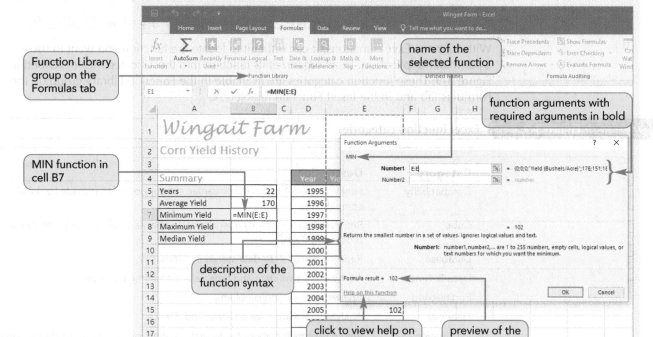

Trouble? You can click and drag the title bar in the Function Arguments dialog box to move it out of the way of the column E heading.

6. Click the **OK** button to insert the formula =MIN(E:E) into cell B7. The formula returns 102, which is the minimum value in column E.

7. Click cell **B8**, and then repeat Steps 3 through 6, selecting the **MAX** function from the Statistical category. The formula =MAX(E:E) entered in cell B8, and returns 187, which is the maximum value in column E. See Figure 3-11.

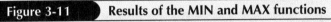

| Figure 3-11 | **Results of the MIN and MAX functions** |

formula to calculate the maximum value in column E

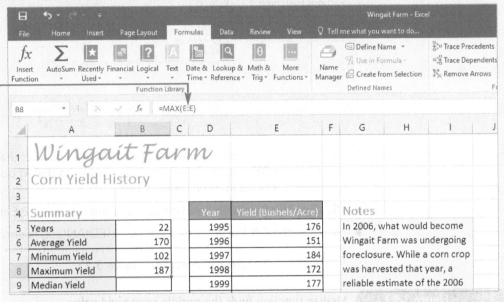

Note that like the COUNT and AVERAGE functions, the MIN and MAX functions ignore cells with text or blank cells in the selected range.

The average is one way of summarizing data from a sample. However, averages are susceptible to the effects of extremely large or extremely small values. For example, imagine calculating the average net worth of 10 people when one of them is a billionaire. An average would probably not be a good representation of the typical net worth of that group. To avoid the effect of extreme values, statisticians often use the middle, or median, value in the sample.

Jane wants you to include the median corn yield value from the farm's history. Rather than inserting the function from the Function Library, you'll search for this function in the Insert Function dialog box.

To find the median corn yield:

1. Click cell **B9** to make it the active cell.

2. Click the **Insert Function** button f_x located to the left of the formula bar. The Insert Function dialog box opens.

3. In the Search for a function box, type **middle value** as the search description, and then click the **Go** button. A list of functions matching that description appears in the Select a function box. See Figure 3-12.

Figure 3-12   **Search results in the Insert Function dialog box**

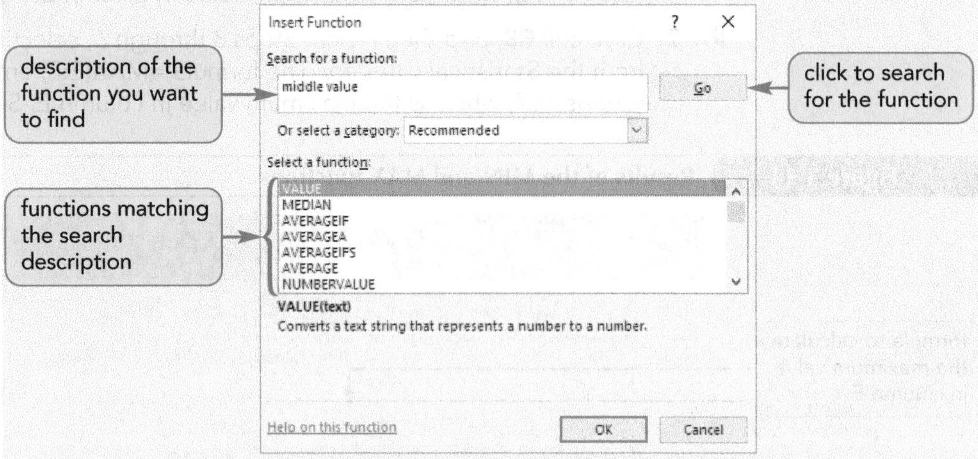

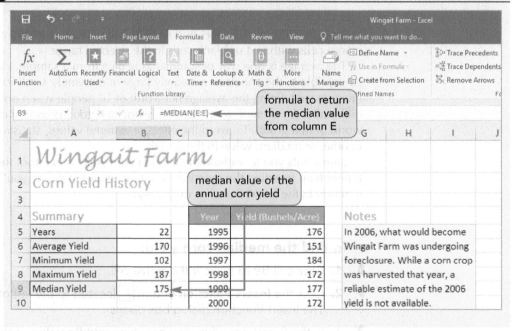

description of the function you want to find →

click to search for the function →

functions matching the search description →

4. In the Select a function box, click **MEDIAN** to select that function, and then click the **OK** button. The Function Arguments dialog box opens with the insertion point in the Number1 box.

5. Click the **E** column heading to insert the reference E:E in the Number1 box.

6. Click the **OK** button. The formula =MEDIAN(E:E) is entered in cell B9. The formula returns 175, which is the middle value from the list of annual corn yields in the farm's history. See Figure 3-13.

Figure 3-13   **Median function finds the middle corn yield value**

formula to return the median value from column E

median value of the annual corn yield

The median estimate of 175 bushels per acre is higher than the average value of 170 bushels per acre. This is due in part to the extremely low yield of 102 bushels per acre in 2005, which brought the overall average value down. Because of this, 175 bushels per acre might be a more reliable estimate of the farm's productivity.

Methods of Rounding

For cleaner and neater workbooks, you will often want to round your values. There is little need for a large corporation to show revenue to the nearest cents at the annual stockholders' convention. Excel provides several methods for rounding data values. One method is to decrease the number of decimal places displayed in the cell, leaving the underlying value unchanged but rounding the displayed value to a specified number of digits.

Another approach is to use the ROUND function, which rounds the value itself to a specified number of digits. The ROUND function also accepts negative values for the number of digits in order to round the value to the nearest multiple of 10, 100, 1000, and so forth. The formula

=ROUND(5241,-2)

returns a value of 5200, rounding the value to the nearest hundred. For rounding to the nearest of multiple of a given number, use the function

MROUND(*number*,*multiple*)

where *number* is the number to be rounded and *multiple* is the multiple that the number should be rounded to. For example, the formula

=MROUND(5241,25)

rounds 5241 to the nearest multiple of 25, returning 5250. Remember though that when you use these rounding methods, you should always have access to the original, unrounded data, in case you need to audit your calculations in the future.

Next Jane wants to explore how to increase the farm's corn revenue in future seasons. You can explore the possibilities with a what-if analysis.

Performing What-If Analyses

A **what-if analysis** explores the impact that changing input values has on calculated values. For example, Jane wants to increase the farm's total revenue from corn, which you calculated as $88,559.40 for the current year, to at least $100,000. The most obvious way to increase the farm's corn revenue is to plant and then harvest more corn. Jane asks you to perform a what-if analysis to determine how many acres of corn would be needed to generate $100,000 of income, assuming conditions remain the same as the current year in which the farm yielded 168 bushels per acre at a selling price of $3.85 per bushel.

Using Trial and Error

One way to perform a what-if analysis is with **trial and error** where you change one or more of the input values to see how they affect the calculated results. Trial and error requires some guesswork as you estimate which values to change and by how much. You will use the trial and error to study the impact of changing the cornfield acreage on the total revenue generated for the farm.

To use trial and error to find how many acres of corn will generate $100,000 revenue:

▶ **1.** Go to the **Yield** worksheet containing calculations for determining the farm's current corn revenue.

▶ **2.** In cell **B4**, change the farm acreage from 137 to **150**. Cell B23 shows that with 150 acres of corn sold at $3.85 per bushel, the farm's revenue from corn sales would increase from $88,559.40 to $96,962.85.

▶ **3.** In cell **B4**, change the farm acreage from 150 to **175**. Cell B23 shows that if the farm plants 175 acres of corn, the revenue would increase to $113,123.33.

▶ **4.** In cell **B4**, change the farm acreage back to **137**, which is the current acreage of corn on Wingait Farm.

To find the exact acreage that would result in $100,000 of revenue, you would have to continue trying different values in cell B4, gradually closing in on the correct value. This is why the method is called "trial and error." For some calculations, trial and error can be a very time-consuming way to locate the exact input value. A more direct approach to this problem is to use Goal Seek.

Using Goal Seek

TIP

Goal Seek can be used only with calculated numbers, not with text.

Goal Seek automates the trial-and-error process by allowing you to specify a value for a calculated item, which Excel uses to determine the input value needed to reach that goal. In this case, because Jane wants $100,000 of revenue, the question that Goal Seek answers is: "How many acres of corn are needed to generate $100,000?" Goal Seek starts by setting the calculated value and automatically works backward to determine the correct input value.

REFERENCE

Performing What-If Analysis and Goal Seek

To perform a what-if analysis by trial and error:
- Change the value of a worksheet cell (the input cell).
- Observe its impact on one or more calculated cells (the result cells).
- Repeat until the desired results are achieved.

To perform a what-if analysis using Goal Seek:
- On the Data tab, in the Forecast group, click the What-If Analysis button, and then click Goal Seek.
- Select the result cell in the Set cell box, and then specify its value (goal) in the To value box.
- In the By changing cell box, specify the input cell.
- Click the OK button. The value of the input cell changes to set the value of the result cell.

You will use Goal Seek to find how much acreage Wingait Farms must plant with corn to achieve $100,000 of revenue.

To use Goal Seek to find how many acres of corn will generate $100,000 revenue:

▶ **1.** On the ribbon, click the **Data** tab.

▶ **2.** In the Forecast group, click the **What-If Analysis** button, and then click **Goal Seek**. The Goal Seek dialog box opens.

▶ **3.** With Set cell box selected, click cell **B23** in the Yield worksheet. The cell reference $B$23 appears in the Set cell box. The set cell is the calculated value you want Goal Seek to change to meet your goal. (You'll learn about $ symbols in cell references in the next session.)

▶ **4.** Press the **Tab** key to move the insertion point to the To value box, and then type **100000** indicating that you want Goal Seek to set the value in cell B23 value to 100,000.

▶ **5.** Press the **Tab** key to move the insertion point to the By changing cell box.

There are often many possible input values you can change to meet a goal. In this case, you want to change the size of the farm acreage in cell B4.

▶ **6.** Click cell **B4**. The cell reference $B$4 appears in the By changing cell box. See Figure 3-14.

Figure 3-14	Goal Seek dialog box

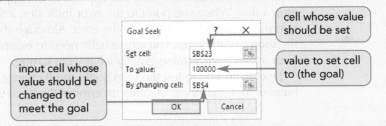

▶ **7.** Click the **OK** button. The Goal Seek dialog box closes, and the Goal Seek Status dialog box opens, indicating that Goal Seek found a solution.

▶ **8.** Click the **OK** button. The value in cell B4 changes to 154.6984204, and the value of cell B23 changes to $100,000.

If Jane increases the acreage devoted to corn production to almost 155 acres, the farm would produce a total revenue from corn of $100,000, assuming a yield of 168 bushels per acre sold at $3.85 per bushel. If the yield or market price increases, the revenue would also increase.

Interpreting Error Values

As you add formulas and values to a workbook, you might make a mistake such as mistyping a formula or entering data as the wrong type. When such errors occur, Excel displays an error value in the cell. An **error value** indicates that some part of a formula is preventing Excel from returning a value. Figure 3-15 lists the common error values you might see in place of calculated values from Excel formulas and functions. For example, the error value #VALUE! indicates that the wrong type of value is used in a function or formula.

Figure 3-15 **Excel error values**

Error Value	Description
#DIV/0!	The formula or function contains a number divided by 0.
#NAME?	Excel doesn't recognize text in the formula or function, such as when the function name is misspelled.
#N/A	A value is not available to a function or formula, which can occur when a workbook is initially set up prior to entering actual data values.
#NULL!	A formula or function requires two cell ranges to intersect, but they don't.
#NUM!	Invalid numbers are used in a formula or function, such as text entered in a function that requires a number.
#REF!	A cell reference used in a formula or function is no longer valid, which can occur when the cell used by the function was deleted from the worksheet.
#VALUE!	The wrong type of argument is used in a function or formula. This can occur when you reference a text value for an argument that should be strictly numeric.

Error values themselves are not particularly descriptive or helpful. To help you locate the error, an error indicator appears in the upper-left corner of the cell with the error value. When you point to the error indicator, a ScreenTip appears with more information about the source of the error. Although the ScreenTips provide hints as to the source of the error, you will usually need to examine the formulas in the cells with error values to determine exactly what went wrong.

Jane wants you to test the workbook. You'll change the value of cell B4 from a number to a text string, creating an error in the Yield worksheet.

To create an error value:

1. In cell **B4**, enter the text string **137 acres**. After you press the Enter key, the #VALUE! error value appears in cells whose formulas use the value in cell B4 either directly or indirectly, indicating that the wrong type of argument is used in a function or formula. In the Yield worksheet, the value in cell B4 affects the values of cells B21 and B23. See Figure 3-16.

Figure 3-16 **Error value in the worksheet**

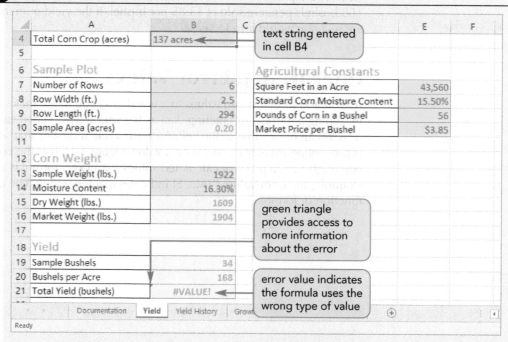

▶ **2.** Click cell **B21**, and then point to the button that appears to the left of the cell. A ScreenTip appears, providing useful information about the cause of the error value. In this case, the ScreenTip is, "A value used in the formula is of the wrong data type."

▶ **3.** Click cell **B4**, enter **137** to change the value back to the current acreage that Wingait Farm devotes to corn. After you press the Enter key, the error values disappear, the total yield in cell B21 returns to 23,002, and the projected revenue in cell B23 returns to $88,559.40.

▶ **4.** Save the workbook.

So far, you have used formulas and functions to analyze the current and past season's crop yield at Wingait Farm. In the next session, you'll use additional formulas and functions to analyze the growth of Wingait Farm's corn crop from planting to harvesting.

REVIEW

Session 3.1 Quick Check

1. Convert the following equation into an Excel formula where the *radius* value is stored in cell E31 and the value of π is stored in cell D12:

$$area = \pi \times radius^2$$

2. In Excel, the PI() function returns the decimal value of π. Rewrite your answer for the previous formula using this function.

3. Write a formula to round the value in cell A5 to the fourth decimal place.

4. Write a formula to return the middle value from the values in the range Y1:Y100.

5. The range of a set of values is defined as the maximum value minus the minimum value. Write a formula to calculate the range of values in the range Y1:Y100 and then to round that value to the nearest integer.

6. Explain the difference between the COUNT function and the COUNTA function.

7. Stephen is entering hundreds of temperature values into an Excel worksheet for a climate research project, and he wants to speed up data entry by leaving freezing point values as blanks rather than typing zeroes. Explain why this will cause complications if he later tries to calculate the average temperature from those data values.

8. What is the difference between a what-if analysis by trial and error and by Goal Seek?

9. Cell B2 contains the formula =SUME(A1:A100) with the name of the SUM function misspelled as SUME. What error value will appear in the cell?

Session 3.2 Visual Overview:

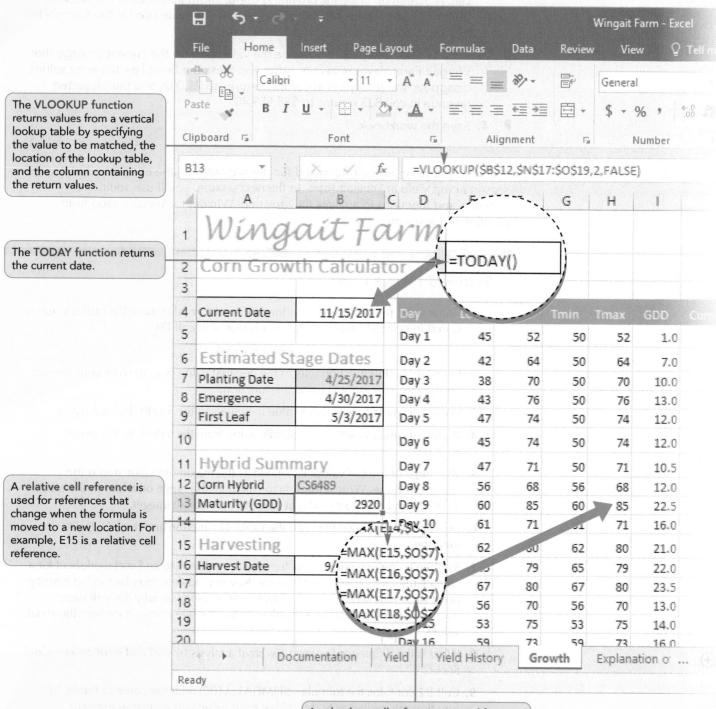

The VLOOKUP function returns values from a vertical lookup table by specifying the value to be matched, the location of the lookup table, and the column containing the return values.

The TODAY function returns the current date.

A relative cell reference is used for references that change when the formula is moved to a new location. For example, E15 is a relative cell reference.

An absolute cell reference is used for references that do not change when the formula is moved to a new location. Absolute references have "$" before the row and column components. For example, $O$7 is an absolute cell reference.

B13 =VLOOKUP($B$12,$N$17:$O$19,2,FALSE)

=TODAY()

Wingait Farm

Corn Growth Calculator

							Tmin	Tmax	GDD	
Current Date	11/15/2017		Day							
			Day 1	45	52	50	52	1.0		
Estimated Stage Dates			Day 2	42	64	50	64	7.0		
Planting Date	4/25/2017		Day 3	38	70	50	70	10.0		
Emergence	4/30/2017		Day 4	43	76	50	76	13.0		
First Leaf	5/3/2017		Day 5	47	74	50	74	12.0		
			Day 6	45	74	50	74	12.0		
Hybrid Summary			Day 7	47	71	50	71	10.5		
Corn Hybrid	CS6489		Day 8	56	68	56	68	12.0		
Maturity (GDD)	2920		Day 9	60	85	60	85	22.5		
			Day 10	61	71	61	71	16.0		
Harvesting		=MAX(E15,$O$7)		62		62	80	21.0		
Harvest Date	9/	=MAX(E16,$O$7)			79	65	79	22.0		
		=MAX(E17,$O$7)		67	80	67	80	23.5		
		MAX(E18,O		56	70	56	70	13.0		
				53	75	53	75	14.0		
			Day 16	59	73	59	73	16.0		

Documentation | Yield | Yield History | **Growth** | Explanation o ...

Ready

Cell References and Formulas

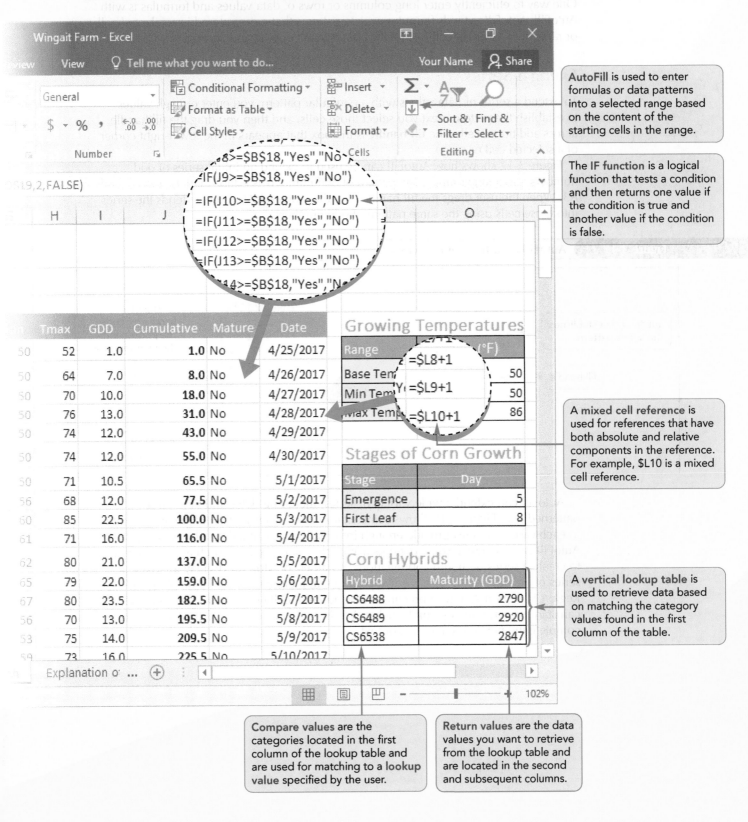

AutoFill is used to enter formulas or data patterns into a selected range based on the content of the starting cells in the range.

The IF function is a logical function that tests a condition and then returns one value if the condition is true and another value if the condition is false.

A mixed cell reference is used for references that have both absolute and relative components in the reference. For example, $L10 is a mixed cell reference.

A vertical lookup table is used to retrieve data based on matching the category values found in the first column of the table.

Compare values are the categories located in the first column of the lookup table and are used for matching to a lookup value specified by the user.

Return values are the data values you want to retrieve from the lookup table and are located in the second and subsequent columns.

Wingait Farm - Excel

View   Tell me what you want to do...   Your Name   Share

General

$ - % , .00 →.0

Number

=IF(J8>=$B$18,"Yes","No")
=IF(J9>=$B$18,"Yes","No")
=IF(J10>=$B$18,"Yes","No")
=IF(J11>=$B$18,"Yes","No")
=IF(J12>=$B$18,"Yes","No")
=IF(J13>=$B$18,"Yes","No")
=IF(J14>=$B$18,"Yes","No")

(19,2,FALSE)

Tmax	GDD	Cumulative	Mature	Date
52	1.0	1.0	No	4/25/2017
64	7.0	8.0	No	4/26/2017
70	10.0	18.0	No	4/27/2017
76	13.0	31.0	No	4/28/2017
74	12.0	43.0	No	4/29/2017
74	12.0	55.0	No	4/30/2017
71	10.5	65.5	No	5/1/2017
68	12.0	77.5	No	5/2/2017
85	22.5	100.0	No	5/3/2017
71	16.0	116.0	No	5/4/2017
80	21.0	137.0	No	5/5/2017
79	22.0	159.0	No	5/6/2017
80	23.5	182.5	No	5/7/2017
70	13.0	195.5	No	5/8/2017
75	14.0	209.5	No	5/9/2017
73	16.0	225.5	No	5/10/2017

Growing Temperatures

Range	(°F)
Base Tem... =$L8+1	50
Min Tem... =$L9+1	50
Max Tem... =$L10+1	86

Stages of Corn Growth

Stage	Day
Emergence	5
First Leaf	8

Corn Hybrids

Hybrid	Maturity (GDD)
CS6488	2790
CS6489	2920
CS6538	2847

Explanation o ... +

102%

AutoFilling Formulas and Data

One way to efficiently enter long columns or rows of data values and formulas is with AutoFill. AutoFill extends formulas or data patterns that were entered in a selected cell or range into adjacent cells. AutoFill is faster than copying and pasting.

Filling a Series

To extend a series of data values with a particular pattern, you enter enough values to establish the pattern, next you select those cells, and then you drag the fill handle across additional cells. The **fill handle** is the box that appears in the lower-right corner of a selected cell or range.

Figure 3-17 shows how AutoFill can be used to extend an initial series of odd numbers into a larger range. The pattern of odd numbers is established in cells A2 and A3. When the user drags the fill handle over the range A4:A9, Excel extends the series into those cells using the same pattern of odd numbers.

Figure 3-17 **AutoFill used to extend a series**

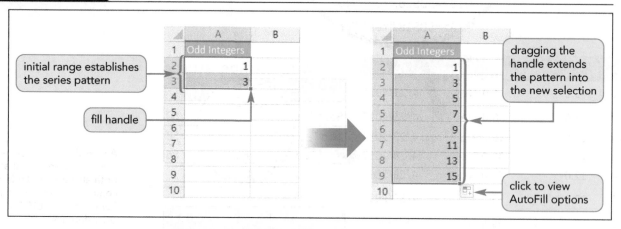

AutoFill can extend a wide variety of series, including dates and times and patterned text. Figure 3-18 shows some examples of series that AutoFill can generate. In each case, you must provide enough information for AutoFill to identify the pattern. AutoFill can recognize some patterns from only a single entry—such as Jan or January to create a series of month abbreviations or names, or Mon or Monday to create a series of the days of the week. A text pattern that includes text and a number such as Region 1, Region 2, and so on can also be automatically extended using AutoFill. You can start the series at any point, such as Weds, June, or Region 10, and AutoFill will complete the next days, months, or text.

| Figure 3-18 | Series patterns extended with AutoFill |

Type	Initial Values	Extended Values
Numbers	1, 2, 3	4, 5, 6, ..
	2, 4, 6	8, 10, 12, ...
Dates and Times	Jan	Feb, Mar, Apr, ...
	January	February, March, April, ...
	15-Jan, 15-Feb	15-Mar, 15-Apr, 15-May, ...
	12/30/2017	12/31/2017, 1/1/2018, 1/2/2018, ...
	12/31/2017, 1/31/2018	2/29/2018, 3/31/2018, 4/30/2018, ...
	Mon	Tue, Wed, Thu, ...
	Monday	Tuesday, Wednesday, Thursday, ...
	11:00AM	12:00PM, 1:00PM, 2:00PM, ...
Patterned Text	1st period	2nd period, 3rd period, 4th period, ...
	Region 1	Region 2, Region 3, Region 4, ...
	Quarter 3	Quarter 4, Quarter 1, Quarter 2, ...
	Qtr3	Qtr4, Qtr1, Qtr2, ...

With AutoFill, you can quickly fill a range with a series of numbers, dates and times, and patterned text.

REFERENCE

Creating a Series with AutoFill

- Enter the first few values of the series into a range.
- Select the range, and then drag the fill handle of the selected range over the cells you want to fill.
- To copy only the formats or only the formulas, click the Auto Fill Options button and select the appropriate option.

or

- Enter the first few values of the series into a range.
- Select the entire range into which you want to extend the series.
- On the Home tab, in the Editing group, click the Fill button, and then click Down, Right, Up, Left, Series, or Justify to set the direction in which you want to extend the series.

Jane wants you to complete the worksheet she started to explore the growth of the Wingait Farm corn crop from planting through harvesting. You need to create a column that labels each day of corn growth starting with Day 1, Day2, and so forth through the end of the season. You will create these labels using AutoFill.

To use AutoFill to extend a series of labels:

TIP

You can also fill a series down by selecting the entire range including the initial cell(s) that establish the pattern, and then pressing the Ctrl+D keys.

1. If you took a break after the previous session, make sure the Wingait Farm workbook is open.

2. Go to the **Growth** worksheet.

3. In cell **D5**, enter the text string **Day 1**. This is the initial label in the series.

4. Click cell **D5** to select the cell, and then drag the **fill handle** (located in the bottom-right corner of the cell) down over the range **D5:D163**.

▶ **5.** Release the mouse button. AutoFill enters the labels Day1 through Day 159 in the selected range. See Figure 3-19.

Figure 3-19 **Farm Day pattern extended with AutoFill**

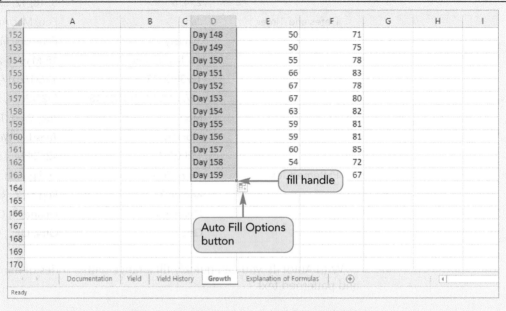

Exploring Auto Fill Options

By default, AutoFill copies both the content and the formatting of the original range to the selected range. However, sometimes you might want to copy only the content or only the formatting. The Auto Fill Options button that appears after you release the mouse button lets you specify what is copied. Figure 3-20 shows the Auto Fill Options menu for an extended series of patterned text.

Figure 3-20 **Auto Fill Options menu**

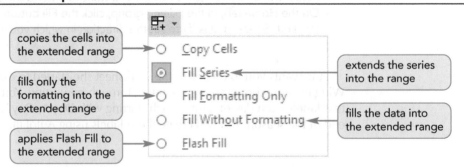

The Copy Cells option copies both the cell content and formatting but does not extend a series based on the initial values. The Fill Series option (the default) extends the initial series values into the new range. Other options allow you to fill in the values with or without the formatting used in the initial cells. Additional options (not shown in Figure 3-20) are provided when extending date values, allowing AutoFill to extend the initial dates by days, weekdays, months, or years.

The Series dialog box provides other options for how AutoFill is applied. To open the Series dialog box, click the Fill button in the Editing group on the Home tab, and then click Series. You can specify a linear or growth series for numbers; a date series for dates that increase by day, weekday, month, or year; or an AutoFill series for patterned text. With numbers, you can also specify the step value (how much each number increases over the previous entry) and a stop value (the endpoint for the entire series). See Figure 3-21.

Figure 3-21	Series dialog box

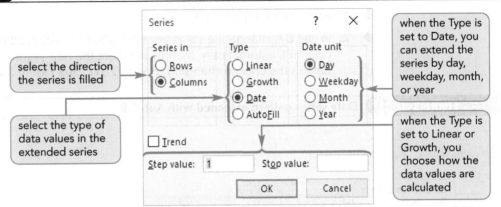

You can also use AutoFill to extend formulas into a range. AutoFill copies the formula in the initial cell or range into the extended range. Excel modifies the cell references in the formulas based on the location of the cells in the extended range.

Jane wants the Growth worksheet to include the date of each growing day starting from the planting date and extending to the last day of recorded data. Because dates are stored as numbers, you can fill in the calendar days by adding 1 to the date displayed in the previous row. Jane wants to use the date 4/15/2017 as the starting date of when the farm began planting corn.

To copy the formula with the dates for the growing season with AutoFill:

1. In cell **B7**, enter the date **4/15/2017** as the starting date of when the farm began planting corn.

2. In cell **L5**, enter the formula **=B7**. After you press the Enter key, cell L5 displays 4/15/2017, which is the first date of the growing season for corn.

3. In cell **L6**, enter the formula **=L5+1** to add one day to the date in cell L5. After you press the Enter key, the date 4/16/2017 appears in cell L6.

4. Click cell **L6** to select it, and then drag the fill handle over the range **L6:L163**. AutoFill copies the formula in cell L6 to the range L7:L163, increasing the date value by one day in each row.

AutoFill extends the formulas to display the date 4/16/2017 in cell L6 through the date 9/20/2017 in cell L163. Each date is calculated by increasing the value in the cell one row above it by one day. The formulas for these calculations are= L5+1 in cell L6, =L6+1 in cell L7, and so forth up to =L162+1 in cell L163.

Jane wants you to change the planting date to 4/25/2017, which is closer to the final date for planting corn at Wingait Farm.

To change the planting date:

▶ **1.** Scroll to the top of the workbook.

▶ **2.** In cell **B7**, change the value from 4/15/2017 to **4/25/2017**. The dates in column L automatically change to reflect the new planting date with the last date in the column changing to 9/30/2017. See Figure 3-22.

| Figure 3-22 | Date series pattern extended with AutoFill |

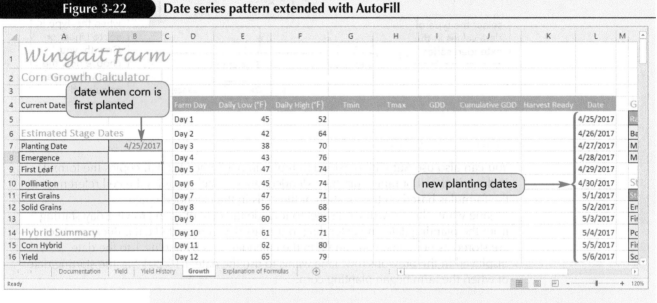

Jane wants to know when the corn crop will reach different stages of growth. In the range N11:O16 of the Growth worksheet, Jane created a table listing the number of days after planting that different growth milestones are reached. For example, the sprouts of the corn plant are often visible five days after planting (cell O12), the first small leaf appears eight days after planting (cell O13), and so forth. You will use the values in the range O12:O16 to estimate the calendar dates for when the first sprouts emerge, the first leaf appears, the corn begins to pollinate, the corn shows its first grains, and finally when the corn shows its solid grains or kernels.

To display the dates for corn growth milestones:

▶ **1.** In cell **B8**, enter the formula **=B7+O12** to add the number of days until emergence to the planting date. The date 4/30/2017, which is the estimated date when the first corn sprouts will appear, is displayed in cell B8.

▶ **2.** Click cell **B8** to select it, and then drag the fill handle over the range **B8:B12** to fill in the dates for the other growth milestones. See Figure 3-23.

Figure 3-23   **Formula extended with AutoFill**

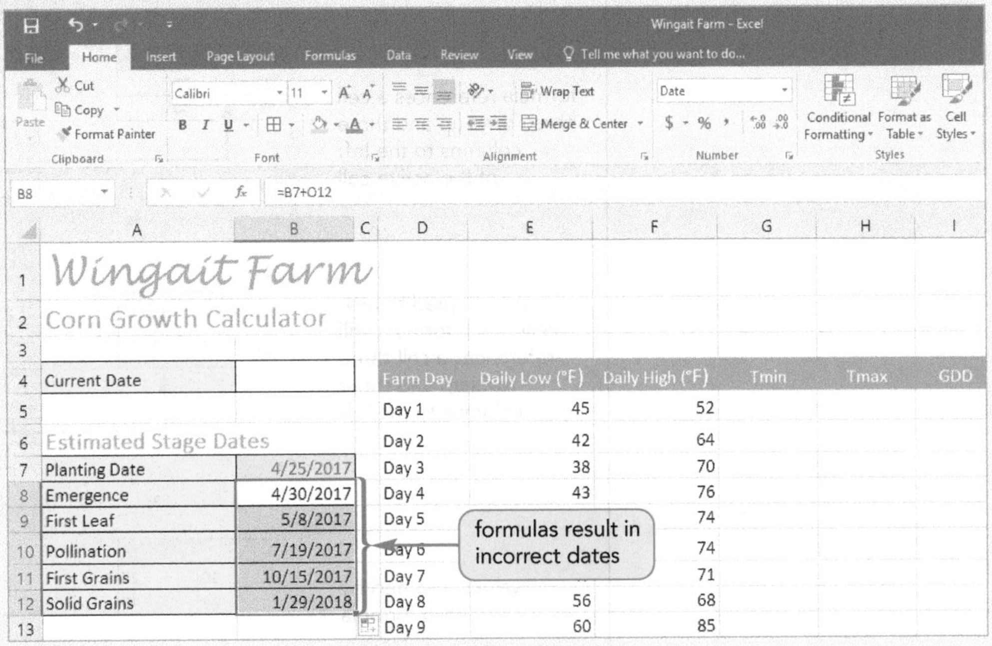

Something is wrong with the formulas that calculate the milestone dates. For example, the date for when the first corn kernels appear is January of the next year. To understand why the formulas resulted in incorrect dates, you need to look at the cell references.

Exploring Cell References

Excel has three types of cell references: relative, absolute, and mixed. Each type of cell reference in a formula is affected differently when the formula is copied and pasted to a new location.

Understanding Relative References

So far, all of the cell references you have worked with are relative cell references. When a formula includes a relative cell reference, Excel interprets the reference to each cell relative to the position of the cell containing the formula. For example, if cell A1 contains the formula =B1+B2, Excel interprets that formula as "Add the value of the cell one column to the right (B1) to the value of the cell one column to the right and one row down (B2)".

This relative interpretation of the cell reference is retained when the formula is copied to a new location. If the formula in cell A1 is copied to cell A3 (two rows down in the worksheet), the relative references also shift two rows down, resulting in the formula =B3+B4.

Figure 3-24 shows another example of how relative references change when a formula is pasted to new locations in the worksheet. In this figure, the formula =A3 entered in cell D6 displays 10, which is the number entered in cell A3. When pasted to a new location, each of the pasted formulas contains a reference to a cell that is three rows up and three rows to the left of the current cell's location.

| Figure 3-24 | Formulas using relative references |

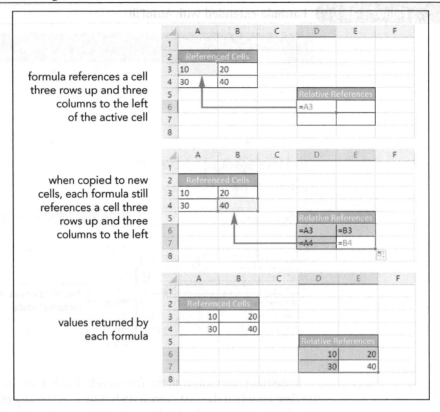

formula references a cell
three rows up and three
columns to the left
of the active cell

when copied to new
cells, each formula still
references a cell three
rows up and three
columns to the left

values returned by
each formula

This explains what happened when you used AutoFill to copy the formula =B7+O12 in cell B8 into the range B9:B12. The formula in cell B9 became =B8+O13, the formula in cell B10 became =B9+O14, the formula in cell B11 became =B10+O15, and the formula in cell B12 became =B11+O16. In each case, the stage days were added to the date in the previous row, not the original planting date entered in cell B7. As a result, date calculation for the appearance of the first solid grains was pushed out to January of the following year.

To correct this, you need a cell reference that remains fixed on cell B7 no matter where the formula is pasted. This can be accomplished with an absolute reference.

Understanding Absolute References

An absolute reference is used for a cell reference that remains fixed even when that formula is copied to a new cell. Absolute references include $ (a dollar sign) before each column and row designation. For example, B8 is a relative reference to cell B8, while $B$8 is an absolute reference to that cell.

Figure 3-25 shows an example of how copying a formula with an absolute reference results in the same cell reference being pasted in different cells regardless of their position compared to the location of the original copied cell. In this example, the formula =$A$3 will always reference cell A3 no matter where the formula is copied to.

| Figure 3-25 | Formulas using absolute references |

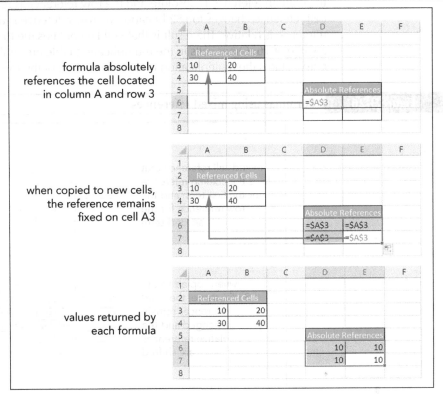

Sometimes, you'll want only one part of the cell reference to remain fixed. This requires a mixed cell reference.

Understanding Mixed References

A mixed cell reference contains both relative and absolute components. For example, a mixed reference for cell A2 can be either $A2 where the column component is absolute and the row component is relative, or it can be entered as A$2 with a relative column component and a fixed row component. A mixed reference "locks" only one part of the cell reference. When you copy and paste a cell with a mixed reference to a new location, the absolute portion of the cell reference remains fixed, and the relative portion shifts along with the new location of the pasted cell.

Figure 3-26 shows an example of using mixed references to complete a multiplication table. The first cell in the table, cell B3, contains the formula =$A3*B$2, which multiplies the first column entry (cell A3) by the first row entry (cell B2), returning 1. When this formula is copied to another cell, the absolute portions of the cell references remain unchanged, and the relative portions of the references change. For example, if the formula is copied to cell E6, the first mixed cell reference changes to $A6 because the column reference is absolute and the row reference is relative, and the second cell reference changes to E$2 because the row reference is absolute and the column reference is relative. The result is that cell E6 contains the formula =$A6*E$2 and returns a value of 16. Other cells in the multiplication table are similarly modified so that each entry returns the multiplication of the intersection of the row and column headings.

Figure 3-26   **Formulas using mixed references**

mixed cell reference that fixes the column reference for the first term and the row reference for the second term

when copied to the B3:F7 range, the fixed references remain unchanged and the relative references are shifted

values returned by each formula

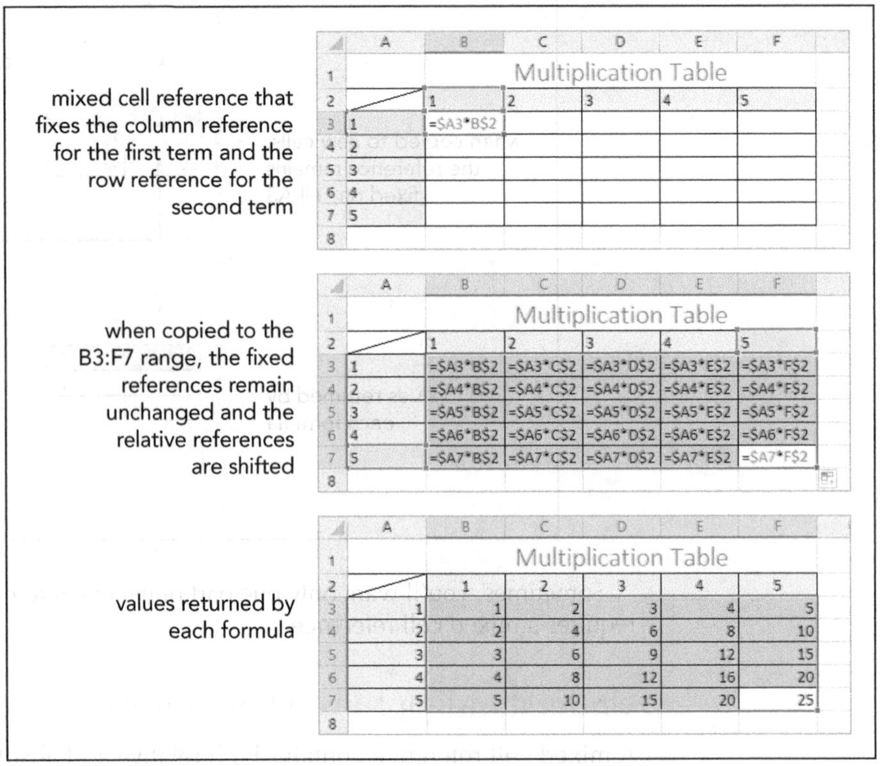

Changing Cell References in a Formula

You can quickly switch a cell reference from relative to absolute or mixed. Rather than retyping the formula, you can select the cell reference in Edit mode and then press the F4 key. As you press the F4 key, Excel cycles through the different reference types—starting with the relative reference, followed by the absolute reference, then to a mixed reference with an absolute row component followed by a mixed reference with an absolute column component.

To calculate the correct stage dates in the Growth worksheet, you will change the formula in cell B8 to use an absolute reference to cell B7 and then use AutoFill to copy that formula into range B9:B12.

To correct the stage dates formulas with absolute cell references:

▶ **1.** Double-click cell **B8** to select it and enter Edit mode.

▶ **2.** In cell B8, double-click the **B7** reference to select it, and then press the **F4** key. Excel changes the formula in cell B8 to =$B$7+O12.

▶ **3.** Press the **Enter** key to enter the formula and exit Edit mode.

▶ **4.** Click cell **B8** to select it, and then drag the fill handle over the range **B8:B12**. Figure 3-27 shows the revised dates for the different stages of corn growth.

| Figure 3-27 | Stage dates calculated with absolute cell references |

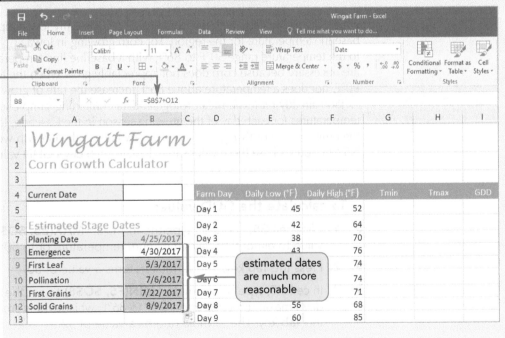

The revised dates for the different stages of the corn maturation are much more reasonable. For example, the date on which solid grains first appear is 8/9/2017, which is more in line with Jane's experience.

PROSKILLS

Problem Solving: When to Use Relative, Absolute, and Mixed References

Part of effective workbook design is knowing when to use relative, absolute, and mixed references. Use relative references when you want to apply the same formula with input cells that share a common layout or pattern. Relative references are commonly used when copying a formula that calculates summary statistics across columns or rows of data values. Use absolute references when you want your copied formulas to always refer to the same cell. This usually occurs when a cell contains a constant value, such as a tax rate, that will be referenced in formulas throughout the worksheet. Mixed references are seldom used other than when creating tables of calculated values such as a multiplication table in which the values of the formula or function can be found at the intersection of the rows and columns of the table.

Calendar days are one way of predicting crop growth, but Jane knows that five days of hot weather will result in more rapid growth than five mild days. A more accurate method to estimate growth is to calculate the crop's Growing Degree Days (GDD), which take into account the range of daily temperatures to which the crop is exposed. GDD is calculated using the formula

$$GDD = \frac{T_{max} + T_{min}}{2} - T_{base}$$

where T_{max} is the daily high temperature, T_{min} is the daily low temperature, and T_{base} is a baseline temperature for the region. For corn growing in Iowa, T_{min} and T_{max} are limited to the temperature range 50°F to 86°F with a baseline line temperature of 50°F. The limits are necessary because corn does not appreciably grow when the temperature falls below 50°F, nor does a temperature above 86°F increase the rate of growth.

Jane already retrieved meteorological data containing sample low and high temperatures for each day of the growing season in the Cascade, Iowa, region. She stored the limits of the corn's T_{min}, T_{max}, and T_{base} values in the Growth worksheet in the range N5:O8. You will use these values to calculate each day's GDD value for corn growth.

To calculate the GDD value:

1. Click cell **G5**, and then type the formula **=MAX(E5, $O$7)** to set the T_{min} value to either that day's minimum temperature or to 50°F, whichever is larger.

2. Press the **Tab** key. The formula returns a value of 50.

3. In cell H5, type the formula **=MIN(F5, $O$8)** to set the T_{max} value to that day's maximum temperature or to 86°F, whichever is smaller, and then press the **Tab** key. The formula returns a value of 52.

4. In cell I5, enter the formula **=(G5+H5)/2-$O$6** to calculate that day's GDD value using the T_{base} value of 50°F stored in cell O6. The formula returns 1.0, indicating that the GDD value for that day is 1.

   Next you'll use AutoFill to copy these formulas into the range G5:I163. Because you used absolute references in the formulas, the copied formulas will continue to reference cells O7, O8, and O6 in the extended range.

5. Select the range **G5:I5**, and then drag the fill handle down to row **163**. Figure 3-28 shows the first several rows of GDD values for the corn crop's history.

Figure 3-28	GDD values for the corn crop

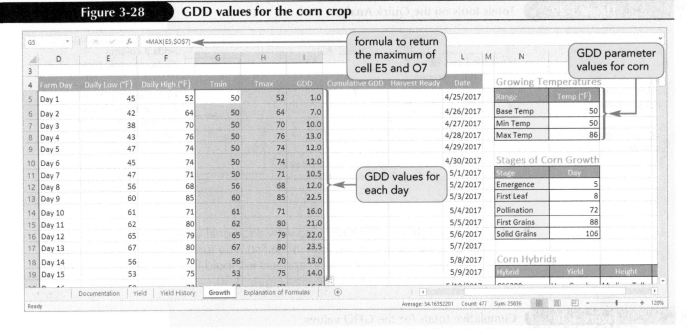

The first GDD values range between 1 and 22.5, but in July and August, GDD routinely reach the upper 20s and lower 30s, indicating that those hot days result in rapid corn growth.

Summarizing Data with the Quick Analysis Tool

The Quick Analysis tool can generate columns and rows of summary statistics and formulas that can be used for analyzing data. GDD is cumulative, which means that as the crop gains more Growing Degree Days, it continues to grow and mature. Jane needs you to calculate a running total of the GDD value for each day in the season. You will enter this calculation using the Quick Analysis tool.

To calculate a running total of GDD:

▶ **1.** Select the range **I5:I163** containing the GDD values for day of the growing season.

▶ **2.** Click the **Quick Analysis** button 📇 in the lower-right corner of the select range (or press the **Ctrl+Q** keys) to display the menu of Quick Analysis tools.

▶ **3.** Click **Totals** from the list of tools. The Quick Analysis tools that calculate summary statistics for the selected data appear. See Figure 3-29.

Figure 3-29 Totals tools on the Quick Analysis tool

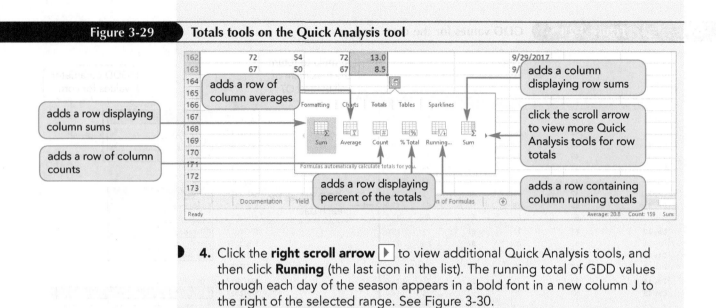

> 4. Click the **right scroll arrow** ▶ to view additional Quick Analysis tools, and then click **Running** (the last icon in the list). The running total of GDD values through each day of the season appears in a bold font in a new column J to the right of the selected range. See Figure 3-30.

Figure 3-30 Cumulative totals for the GDD values

Based on the running total in column J, Jane projects that by 9/30/2017, the corn crop will have a total of 3312 Growing Degree Days. To create the running total, the Quick Analysis tool added the following formula to cell J5 and then copied that formula over the range J5:J163:

```
=SUM($I$5:I5)
```

Note that this formula uses a combination of absolute and relative cell references. When copied to cell J6 the formula becomes

```
=SUM($I$5:I6)
```

and when copied to J7 the formula is

```
=SUM($I$5:I7)
```

In this formula, the starting cell of the range used with the SUM function is fixed at cell I5, but the ending cell is relative, causing the number of rows in the range to expand to match the cell selection. For the last date in row 163, the formula becomes:

```
=SUM($I$5:I163)
```

This approach shows how a combination of absolute and relative cell references expands the capability of Excel to create formulas for a variety of ranges.

Working with Dates and Date Functions

Excel has several functions that work with dates and times. These functions are particularly useful in workbooks that involve production schedules and calendars. Figure 3-31 describes some of the commonly used date and time functions.

Figure 3-31   Date functions

Function	Description
DATE(*year,month,day*)	Creates a date value for the date represented by the *year, month,* and *day* arguments
DAY(*date*)	Extracts the day of the month from *date*
MONTH(*date*)	Extracts the month number from *date* where 1=January, 2=February, and so forth
YEAR(*date*)	Extracts the year number from *date*
NETWORKDAYS(*start,end*[*,holidays*])	Calculates the number of whole working days between *start* and *end*; to exclude holidays, add the optional *holidays* argument containing a list of holiday dates to skip
WEEKDAY(*date*[*,return_type*])	Calculates the weekday from *date*, where 1=Sunday, 2=Monday, and so forth; to choose a different numbering scheme, set *return_type* to 1 (1=Sunday, 2=Monday, ...), 2 (1=Monday, 2=Tuesday, ...), or 3 (0=Monday, 1=Tuesday, ...)
WORKDAY(*start,days*[*,holidays*])	Returns the workday after *days* workdays have passed since the *start* date; to exclude holidays, add the optional *holidays* argument containing a list of holiday dates to skip
NOW( )	Returns the current date and time
TODAY( )	Returns the current date

Many workbooks include the current date so that any reports generated by the workbook are identified by date. To display the current date, you can use the TODAY function:

```
TODAY( )
```

Note that although the TODAY function doesn't have any arguments, you still must include the parentheses for the function to work. The date displayed by the TODAY function is updated automatically whenever you reopen the workbook or enter a new calculation.

Jane wants the Growth worksheet to show the current date each time it is used or printed. You will use the TODAY function to display the current date in cell B4.

TIP

To display the current date and time, which is updated each time the workbook is reopened, use the NOW function.

To display the current date:

▶ **1.** Scroll to the top of the worksheet, and then click cell **B4**.

▶ **2.** On the ribbon, click the **Formulas** tab.

▶ **3.** In the Function Library group, click the **Date & Time** button to display the date and time functions.

▶ **4.** Click **TODAY**. The Function Arguments dialog box opens and indicates that the TODAY function requires no arguments.

> **5.** Click the **OK** button. The formula =TODAY() is entered in cell B4, and the current date is displayed in the cell.

Note that Excel automatically formats cells containing the TODAY function to display the value in Short Date format.

INSIGHT

Date Calculations with Working Days

Businesspeople are often more interested in workdays rather than in all of the days of the week. For example, to estimate a delivery date in which packages are not shipped or delivered on weekends, it is more useful to know the date of the next weekday rather than the date of the next day.

To display the date of a weekday that is a specified number of weekdays past a start date, Excel provides the **WORKDAY function**

```
WORKDAY(start,days[,holidays])
```

where *start* is a start date, *days* is the number of workdays after that starting date, and *holidays* is an optional list of holiday dates to skip. For example, if cell A1 contains the date 12/20/2018, a Thursday, the following formula displays the date 1/2/2019, a Wednesday that is nine working days later:

```
=WORKDAY(A1,9)
```

The optional *holidays* argument references a series of dates that the WORKDAY function will skip in performing its calculations. So, if both 12/25/2018 and 1/1/2019 are entered in the range B1:B2 as holidays, the following function will return the date 1/4/2019, a Friday that is nine working days, excluding the holidays, after 12/20/2018:

```
=WORKDAY(A1,9,B1:B2)
```

To reverse the process and calculate the number of working days between two dates, use the NETWORKDAYS function

```
NETWORKDAYS(start,end[,holidays])
```

where *start* is the starting date and *end* is the ending date. So, if cell A1 contains the date 12/20/2018 and cell A2 contains the date 1/3/2019, the following function returns 9, indicating that there are nine working days between the start and ending, excluding the holidays specified in the range B1:B2:

```
=NETWORKDAYS(A1,A2,B1:B2)
```

For international applications in which the definition of working day differs between one country and another, Excel supports the WORKDAY.INTL function. See Excel Help for more information.

Corn seed is sold in a wide variety of hybrids used to create corn of different quality, size, resistance to parasites, and growth rates. Jane wants the Growth worksheet to display data about the corn hybrid she chose for Wingait Farm. You can retrieve that data using a lookup function.

Using Lookup Functions

A **lookup function** retrieves values from a table of data that match a specified condition. For example, a lookup function can be used to retrieve a tax rate from a tax table for a given annual income or to retrieve shipping rates for different delivery options.

The table that stores the data you want to retrieve is called a **lookup table**. The first row or column of the table contains compare values, which are the values that are being looked up. If the compare values are in the first row, the table is a **horizontal lookup table**; if the compare values are in the first column, the table is a vertical lookup table. The remaining rows or columns contain the return values, which are the data values being retrieved by the lookup function.

Figure 3-32 shows the range N19:Q27 in the Growth worksheet containing information about different corn hybrids. This information is a vertical lookup table because the first column of the table containing the names of the hybrids stores the compare values. The remaining columns containing type of yield, height of the corn stalk, and GDD units until the hybrid reaches maturity are the return values. To look up the Growing Degree Days required until the corn hybrid CS6478 reaches maturity, Excel scans the first column of the lookup table until it finds the entry for CS6478. Excel then moves to the right to the column containing information that needs to be returned.

Figure 3-32   **Finding an exact match from a lookup table**

Lookup tables can be constructed for exact match or approximate match lookups. In an **exact match lookup**, the lookup value must exactly match one of the compare values in the first row or column of the lookup table. Figure 3-32 is an exact match lookup because the name of the corn hybrid must match one of the compare values in the table. An **approximate match lookup** is used when the lookup value falls within a range of compare values. You will work with exact match lookups in this module.

Finding an Exact Match with the VLOOKUP Function

To retrieve the return value from a vertical lookup table, you use the VLOOKUP function

VLOOKUP(*comp_value*,*table_array*,*col_index_num*[,*range_lookup*=TRUE])

where *comp_value* is the compare value to find in the first column of the lookup table, *table_array* is the range reference to the lookup table, and *col_index_num* is the number of the column in the lookup table that contains the return value. Keep in mind that *col_index_num* refers to the number of the column within the lookup table, not the worksheet column. So, a *col_index_num* of 2 refers to the lookup table's second column. Finally, *range_lookup* is an optional argument that specifies whether the lookup should be done as an exact match or an approximate match. For an exact match, you set the *range_lookup* value to FALSE. For approximate match lookups, you set the *range_lookup* value to TRUE. The default is to assume an approximate match.

For example, the following formula performs an exact match lookup using the text "CS6478" as the compare value and the data in the range N20:Q27 (shown in Figure 3-32) as the lookup table:

```
=VLOOKUP("CS6478",N20:Q27,4,FALSE)
```

TIP

If the VLOOKUP function cannot find the lookup value in the lookup table, it returns the #N/A error value.

The function looks through the compare values in the first column of the table to locate the "CS6478" entry. When the exact entry is found, the function returns the corresponding value in the fourth column of the table, which in this case is 2795.

Jane wants you to retrieve information about the CS6478 hybrid she uses at Wingait Farm and then display that information in the range B16:B18 on the Growth worksheet. You'll use a VLOOKUP function to retrieve yield information about the hybrid.

To use the VLOOKUP function to find yield information for hybrid CS6478:

1. In cell **B15**, enter the hybrid **CS6478**.

2. Click cell **B16**, and then click the **Insert Function** button f_x to the left of the formula bar. The Insert Function dialog box opens.

3. Click the **Or select a category** box, and then click **Lookup & Reference** in the list of function categories.

4. Scroll down the Select a function box, and then double-click **VLOOKUP**. The Function Arguments dialog box for the VLOOKUP function opens.

5. In the Lookup_value box, type **$B$15** as the absolute reference to the hybrid name, and then press the **Tab** key. The insertion point moves to the Table_array box.

6. In the Growth worksheet, select the range **N20:Q27** as the Table_array value, press the **F4** key to change the range reference to the absolute reference **$N$20:$Q$27**.

7. Press the **Tab** key. The insertion point moves to the Col_index_num box. Yield information is stored in the second column of the lookup table.

8. Type **2** in the Col_index_num box to return information from the second column of the lookup table, and then press the **Tab** key. The insertion point moves to the Range_lookup box.

TIP

Exact matches are not case sensitive, so the lookup values False, false, and FALSE are considered the same.

9. Type **FALSE** in the Range_lookup box to perform an exact match lookup. See Figure 3-33.

Figure 3-33   Function Arguments dialog box for the VLOOKUP function

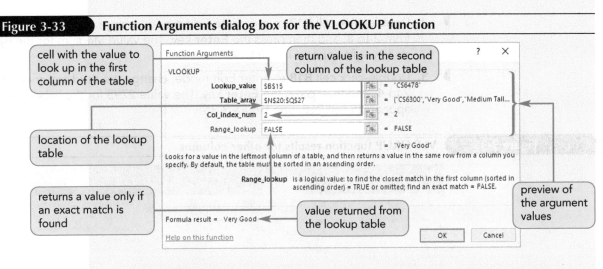

10. Click the **OK** button. The dialog box closes and the formula =VLOOKUP($B$15, $N$20:$Q$27,2,FALSE) is entered in cell B16. "Very Good," which is the yield associated with the CS6478 hybrid, is displayed in the cell. See Figure 3-34.

Figure 3-34   VLOOKUP function results

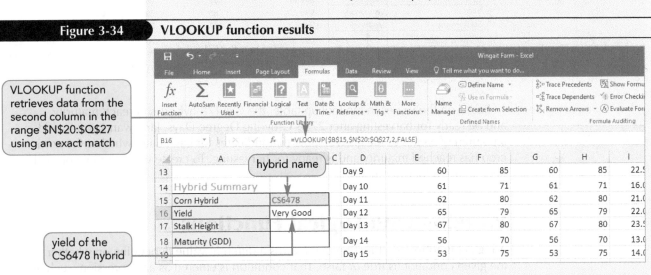

Jane wants to see the stalk height and the GDD information about the hybrid CS6478. You will use AutoFill to copy the VLOOKUP function into the other cells in the Hybrid Summary table.

To display other information about the hybrid CS6478:

1. Click cell **B16** to select it, and then drag the fill handle over the range **B16:B18** to copy the VLOOKUP formula into cells B17 and B18. The text "Very Good" appears in cells B17 and B18, because the formula is set up to retrieve text from the second column of the lookup table.

   You need to edit the formulas in cells B17 and B18 to retrieve information from the third and fourth columns of the lookup table, respectively.

2. Double-click cell **B17** to enter into Edit mode, change the third argument from 2 to **3**, and then press the **Enter** key. The value Medium for the hybrid's stalk height appears in cell B17.

3. Double-click cell **B18** to enter Edit mode, change the third argument from 2 to **4**, and then press the **Enter** key. The value 2795 for the hybrid's GDD appears in cell B18. See Figure 3-35.

Figure 3-35 **VLOOKUP function results for other columns**

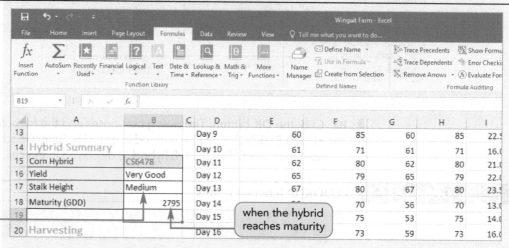

stalk height for the CS6478 hybrid

when the hybrid reaches maturity

Based on the values in the lookup table, the CS6478 hybrid will reach maturity and be ready for harvesting after 2795 Growing Degree Days. Jane wants you to add a column of values to the growth table that indicates for each date, whether the corn crop has reached maturity and is ready for harvesting. To create this column, you will need to use a logical function.

Working with Logical Functions

A **logical function** is a function that returns a different value depending on whether the given condition is true or false. That condition is entered as an expression, such as A5=3. If cell A5 is equal to 3, this expression and condition are true; if cell A5 is not equal to 3, this expression and condition are false. The most commonly used logical function is the IF function. The syntax of the IF function is

```
IF(condition,value_if_true,value_if_false)
```

where `condition` is an expression that is either true or false, `value_if_true` is the value returned by the function if the expression is true, and `value_if_false` is the value returned if the expression is false.

The value returned by the IF function can be a number, text, a date, a cell reference, or a formula. For example, the following formula tests whether the value in cell A1 is equal to the value in cell B1, returning 100 if those two cells are equal and 50 if they're not.

```
=IF(A1=B1,100,50)
```

TIP

To apply multiple logical conditions, you can nest one IF function within another.

In many cases, you will use cell references instead of values in the IF function. The following formula, for example, uses cell references, returning the value of cell C1 if A1 equals B1; otherwise, it returns the value of cell C2:

`=IF(A1=B1,C1,C2)`

The = symbol in these formulas is a **comparison operator** that indicates the relationship between two parts of the logical function's condition. Figure 3-36 describes other comparison operators that can be used within logical functions.

Figure 3-36   **Logical comparison operators**

Operator	Expression	Tests
=	A1 = B1	If the value in cell A1 is equal to the value in cell B1
>	A1 > B1	If the value in cell A1 is greater than the value in cell B1
<	A1 < B1	If the value in cell A1 is less than the value in cell B1
>=	A1 >= B1	If the value in cell A1 is greater than or equal to the value in cell B1
<=	A1 <= B1	If the value in cell A1 is less than or equal to the value in cell B1
<>	A1 <> B1	If the value in cell A1 is not equal to the value in cell B1

The IF function also works with text. For example, the following formula tests whether the value of cell A1 is equal to "yes":

`=IF(A1="yes","done","restart")`

If the condition is true (the value of cell A1 is equal to "yes"), then the formula returns the text "done"; otherwise, it returns the text "restart".

For each date in the growth record of the corn crop, Jane wants to know whether the cumulative GDD value is greater than or equal to the GDD value on which the hybrid reaches maturity and is ready for harvesting. If the crop is ready for harvesting, she wants the cell to display the text "Yes"; otherwise, it should display the text "No". You'll use the IF function to do this.

To enter the IF function to specify whether the corn is ready for harvesting:

▶ 1. Click cell **K5** to select it. You'll enter the IF function in this cell.

▶ 2. On the Formulas tab, in the Function Library group, click the **Logical** button to display the list of logical functions, and then click **IF**. The Function Arguments dialog box for the IF function opens.

▶ 3. In the Logical_test box, enter the expression **J5>=$B$18** to test whether the cumulative GDD value is greater than the maturity value in cell B18.

▶ 4. Press **Tab** key to move the insertion point to the Value_if_true box, and then type **"Yes"** as the value if the logical test is true.

▶ 5. Press **Tab** key to move the insertion point to the Value_if_false box, and then type **"No"** as the value if the logical test is false. See Figure 3-37.

Figure 3-37 **Function Arguments dialog box for the IF function**

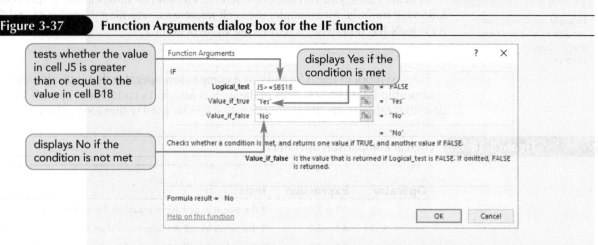

> **6.** Click the **OK** button. The formula =IF(J5>=$B$18,"Yes","No") is entered in cell K5. The cell displays the text "No," indicating that the crop is not harvest ready on this day (a logical result because this is the day when the farm starts planting the corn).

> **7.** Click cell **K5**, and then drag fill handle to select the range **K5:K163**. The formula with the IF function is applied to the remaining days of the growing season. As shown in Figure 3-38, by the end of the growing season, the crop is ready for harvesting because the cumulative GDD value for the hybrid CS6478 has exceeded 2795.

Figure 3-38 **IF function evaluates whether the crop is harvest ready**

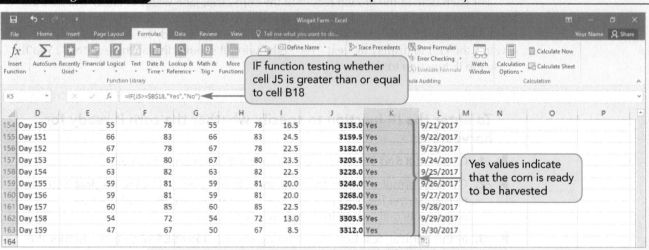

By scrolling up and down the Growth worksheet you can locate the row in which the value in the Harvest Ready column switches from No to Yes. For this data, the switch occurs in row 138 where the cumulative GDD value is equal to 2814, exceeding the minimum GDD value required for this particular hybrid to reach maturity.

Rather than scrolling through the worksheet, Jane wants the worksheet to display the calendar date on which the crop reaches maturity and is ready for harvesting. You can obtain this information by using columns K and L as a lookup table. Recall that Excel scans a lookup table from the top to the bottom and stops when it reaches the first value in the compare column that matches the lookup value. You can use this fact to find the first location in column K where the Harvest Ready value is equal to "Yes" and then apply the VLOOKUP function to return the corresponding calendar date in column L.

To display the harvest date for the corn crop:

▶ **1.** Near the top of the worksheet, click cell **B21** to select it.

▶ **2.** Click the **Insert Function** button f_x to the left of the formula bar. The Insert Function dialog box opens.

▶ **3.** Click the **Or select a category box arrow**, and then click **Most Recently Used** to display a list of the functions you have used most recently.

▶ **4.** Double-click **VLOOKUP** in the list. The Function Arguments dialog box for the VLOOKUP function opens.

▶ **5.** In the Lookup_value box, type **"Yes"** and then press the **Tab** key. The insertion point moves to the Table_array box.

▶ **6.** Select the **K** and **L** column headings to insert the reference K:L in the Table_array box, and then press the **Tab** key. The insertion point moves to the Col_index_num box.

▶ **7.** Type **2** in the Col_index_num box to retrieve the value from the second column in the lookup table, and then press the **Tab** key. The insertion point moves to the Range_lookup box.

Use FALSE to perform an exact match lookup.

▶ **8.** Type **FALSE** in the Range_lookup box to apply an exact match lookup. See Figure 3-39.

Figure 3-39 **Function Arguments for the VLOOKUP function**

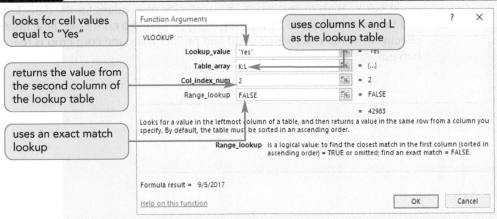

looks for cell values equal to "Yes"

returns the value from the second column of the lookup table

uses an exact match lookup

uses columns K and L as the lookup table

▶ **9.** Click the **OK** button. The formula =VLOOKUP("Yes",K:L,2,FALSE) is entered in cell B21. The cell displays 9/5/2017, which is the date when the corn crop has reached maturity and is ready for harvesting to begin.

Jane can view the impact of different hybrids on the harvest date by changing the value of cell B15.

▶ **10.** Click cell **B15**, and then change the corn hybrid from CS6478 to **CS6489**. The results from the lookup and IF functions in the worksheet change to reflect the corn hybrid CS6489. This hybrid has excellent yield and tall stalks and is ready for harvesting on 9/10/2017, five days later than the corn hybrid CS6478. See Figure 3-40.

Figure 3-40	Summary and harvesting data for the hybrid CS6489

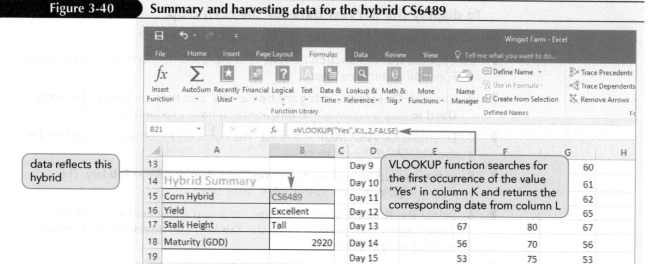

▶ **11.** Save the workbook.

You've completed your work on the Wingait Farm workbook. Jane will use this workbook to analyze next year's crop, entering new values for the daily temperatures and for the hybrid types. By tracking the growth of the corn crop, Jane hopes to more effectively increase her farm's yield and predict when the corn crop is ready for harvesting.

INSIGHT

Managing Error Values with the IF Function

An error value does not mean that you must correct the cell's formula or function. Some error values appear simply because you have not yet entered any data into the workbook. For example, if you use the VLOOKUP function without a lookup value, the #N/A error value appears because Excel cannot look up an empty value. However, as soon as you enter a lookup, the #N/A error value disappears, replaced with the result of the VLOOKUP function.

Error values of this type can make your workbook difficult to read and can confuse other users. One way to avoid error values resulting from missing input values is to nest formulas within an IF function. For example, the following formula first tests whether a value has been entered into cell B2 before attempting to use that cell as a lookup value in the VLOOKUP function:

```
=IF(B2="","",VLOOKUP(B2,$E1:$G$10,3,FALSE)
```

Note that "" is used to represent an empty text string or value. If the IF condition is true because no value has been entered into cell B2, the formula will return an empty text string instead of an error value, but if B2 has a value, the VLOOKUP function is applied using cell B2 as the lookup value. The result is a cleaner workbook that is easier for other people to read and use.

Jane appreciates all of the work you have done in developing the Wingait Farm workbook. She will continue to study the document and get back to you with future projects at the farm.

Session 3.2 Quick Check

REVIEW

1. If 4/30/2017 and 5/31/2017 are the initial values, what are the next two values AutoFill will insert?

2. You need to reference cell Q57 in a formula. What is its relative reference? What is its absolute reference? What are the two mixed references?

3. If cell R10 contains the formula =R1+R2, which is then copied to cell S20, what formula is entered in cell S20?

4. If cell R10 contains the formula =$R1+R$2, which is then copied to cell S20, what formula is entered in cell S20?

5. Explain how to use the Quick Analysis tool to calculate a running total of the values in the range D1:D10.

6. Write the formula to display the current date in the worksheet.

7. Write the formula to display a date that is four workdays after the date in cell A5. Do not assume any holidays in your calculation.

8. Write the formula to perform an exact match lookup with the lookup value from cell G5 using a vertical lookup table located in the range A1:F50. Return the value from the third column of the table.

9. If cell Q3 is greater than cell Q4, you want to display the text "OK"; otherwise, display the text "RETRY". Write the formula that accomplishes this.

Review Assignments

PRACTICE

Data File needed for the Review Assignments: Soybean.xlsx

Another cash crop grown at Wingait Farm is soybeans. Jane wants you to create a workbook for the soybean crop similar to the workbook you created for the corn crop. The workbook should estimate the total yield and revenue from a small plot sample and compare that yield to the farm's historic norms. The workbook should also track the soybean growth from planting to harvest. Complete the following:

1. Open the **Soybean** workbook located in the Excel3 > Review folder, and then save the workbook as **Soybean Crop** in the location specified by your instructor.

2. In the Documentation worksheet, enter your name in cell B3 and the date in cell B4.

3. The size of the soybean crop is **72** acres. Enter this value in cell B4 of the Yield worksheet.

4. The soybean sample comes from a plot of **4** rows each **7.5** inches wide and **21** inches long. Enter these values in the range B7:B9.

5. Within the plot, the farm has harvested **400** soybean pods with an average of **2.5** soybeans per pod. Enter these values in the B14:B15 range.

6. Apply the Input cell style to cells B4, B7:B9, and B14:B15.

7. Using the equations described in the Formulas worksheet, enter the following calculations:
   a. In cell B10, calculate the area of the plot sample in inches.
   b. In cell B11, convert the sample area to acres by dividing the value in cell B10 by the number of square inches in an acre (cell H4). Display the result to four decimal places.
   c. In cell B16, calculate the total number of seeds harvested in the sample.
   d. In cell B17, calculate the weight of the sample in pounds by dividing the number of seeds by the number of seeds in one pound (cell H5). Display the value to two decimal places.
   e. In cell B18, convert the weight to bushels by dividing the weight in pounds by the number of pounds of soybeans in one bushel (cell H6). Display the value to four decimal places.
   f. In cell B19, estimate the farm's soybean yield in bushels per acre by dividing the number of bushels in the plot sample by the area of the sample in acres. Display the value as an integer.

8. Calculate the following values for soybean yield and revenue:
   a. In cell B20, calculate the farm's average soybean yield using the values in column E. Use the ROUND function to round that average value to the nearest integer.
   b. In cell B21, calculate the farm's median soybean yield from the values in column E.
   c. In cell B24, calculate the farm's total production of soybeans in bushels by multiplying the bushels per acre value by the total number of acres that the farm devotes to soybeans. Display the value as an integer.
   d. In cell B25, calculate the total revenue from the soybean crop by multiplying the total bushels harvested by the current price per bushel (cell H7). Display the value using the Accounting format style.

9. Apply the Calculation style to the range B10:B11,B16:B21,B24:B25.

10. Use Goal Seek to determine what value in cell B4 (the number of acres devoted to soybeans) will result in a total soybean revenue of $40,000.

11. In the Growth worksheet, in cell B5, enter a formula with a function to display the current date.

12. Use AutoFill to insert the text strings Day 1 through Day 112 in the range D5:D116.

13. In cell G5, calculate the Growing Degree Days (GDD) for the first day of the season using the formula described in the Formulas worksheet and the temperature range values in the range L6:M9. (*Hint*: Use the same formula used in the tutorial for corn, but enter the T_{min}, T_{max}, and *base* values directly in the formula. Be sure to use absolute references for the temperature range values.)

14. Copy the formula in cell G5 to the range G5:G112.

15. Use the Quick Analysis tool to calculate the cumulative total of the GDD values from the range G5:G112, placing those values in the range H5:H112.

16. In cell B9, enter **5/12/2017**, which is the date the farm will start planting the soybean crop.

17. In cell J5, enter a formula to display the date from cell B9. In cell J6, enter a formula to increase the date in cell J5 by one day. Copy the formula in cell J6 to the range J6:J112 to enter the dates for the growing season.

18. In cell B8, enter **M070** as the maturity group for the current soybean hybrid.

19. In cell B10, use the VLOOKUP function to retrieve the cumulative GDD value for the M070 hybrid. (*Hint:* The range L12:M21 displays the cumulative GDD for each maturity group.)

20. In cell I5, enter an IF function that tests whether the cumulative GDD value in cell H5 is greater than the maturity value in cell B10. Use an absolute reference to cell B10. If the condition is true, return the text string "Ready"; otherwise, return the text "Not Ready". Copy the formula to the range I5:I112.

21. In cell B11, insert a VLOOKUP function using the values in the columns I and J that returns the date on which the Harvest Ready value is first equal to the text string "Ready".

22. In cell B12, calculate the number of days between planting and harvesting by subtracting the planting date (cell B9) from the harvest date (cell B11).

23. Save and close the workbook.

Case Problem 1

APPLY

Data File needed for this Case Problem: Gorecki.xlsx

Gorecki Construction   Stefan Gorecki is the owner of Gorecki Construction, a small construction firm in Chester, Pennsylvania. He wants to use Excel to track his company's monthly income and expenses and then use that information to create a monthly budget. Stefan has already entered the raw data values but has asked to you to complete the workbook by adding the formulas and functions to perform the calculations. Complete the following:

1. Open the **Gorecki** workbook located in the Excel3 > Case1 folder, and then save the workbook as **Gorecki Budget** in the location specified by your instructor.

2. In the Documentation worksheet, enter your name in cell B3 and the date in cell B4.

3. The budget values are entered based on the end-of-month values. In the Monthly Budget worksheet, enter the date **31-Jan-18** in cell E4 and **28-Feb-18** in cell F4. Use AutoFill to fill in the remaining end-of-month date in the range G4:P4.

4. Calculate the company's total monthly income by selecting the range E6:P7 and using the Quick Analysis tool to insert the SUM function automatically into the range E8:P8.

5. Calculate the company's total cost of goods sold by selecting values in range E10:P11 and using the Quick Analysis tool to insert the SUM function automatically into the range E12:P12.

6. In the range E14:P14, calculate the company's monthly gross profit, which is equal to the difference between the monthly income and the monthly cost of goods sold.

7. Select the expenses entered in the range E17:P26, and use the Quick Analysis tool to insert the sum of the monthly expenses into the range E27:P27.

8. In the range E29:P29, calculate the company's net income equal to the difference between its gross profit and its total expenses.

9. Select the values in the range E29:P29, and then use the Quick Analysis tool to insert a running total of the company's net income into the range E30:P30.

10. Calculate the year-end totals for all financial categories by selecting the range E6:P29 and using the Quick Analysis tool to insert the sum of each row into the range Q6:Q29. Delete the content of any cells that do not contain financial figures.

11. Stefan wants the monthly averages of each financial category to be displayed in range B6:B29. Select cell B6, and then enter a formula that contains a nested function that first calculates the average of the values in the range E6:P6 and then uses the ROUND function to round that average to the nearest 10 dollars. (*Hint*: Use –1 for the value of the num_digits argument.) Use AutoFill to extend formula over the range B6:B29, deleting any cells corresponding to empty values.

12. Save and close the workbook.

Case Problem 2

APPLY

Data File needed for this Case Problem: Capshaw.xlsx

Capshaw Family Dentistry Carol Lemke is a new receptionist at Capshaw Dentistry in East Point, Georgia. She wants to get a rough estimate of what her take-home pay would be after deductions for federal and local taxes. She asks you to set up an Excel worksheet to perform the wage calculations for a sample two-week period. Carol already entered the work schedule and several tables containing the federal and state tax rates but needs you to insert the formulas. (*Note:* The tax rate tables and formulas used in this example are a simplified version of the tax code and should not be used to calculate actual taxes.) Complete the following:

1. Open the **Capshaw** workbook located in the Excel3 > Case2 folder, and then save the workbook as **Capshaw Wages** in the location specified by your instructor.

2. In the Documentation worksheet, enter your name in cell B3 and the date in cell B4.

3. In the Work Schedule worksheet, enter the following information in the range B5:B9: Name **Carol Lemke**; Hourly Rate **$16.25**; Federal Marital Status **Single**; State Marital Status **Single**; and Withholding Allowances **1**.

4. In cell D6, enter the date **4/10/2017**. Use AutoFill to fill in the next day weekdays in the range D6:D15. (*Hint*: Click the AutoFill options button after dragging the fill handle, and then select the Fill Weekdays option button.)

5. In cell G6, calculate the total hours worked on the first day, which is equal to the difference between cell F6 and cell E6 multiplied by 24.

6. Carol will get overtime wages when she works more than eight hours in a day. Calculate the non-overtime hours in cell H6 by using the MIN function to return the minimum of the value in cell G6 and the value 8.

7. In cell I6, calculate the amount of overtime hours by using the IF function to test whether cell G6 is greater than 8. If it is, return the value cell G6 minus 8; otherwise, return the value 0.

8. In cell J6, calculate the salary due on the first day. The salary due is equal to the Straight Time worked multiplied by the hourly rate in cell B6 plus the Overtime multiplied by the hourly rate times 1.5 (Carol will receive time-and-a-half for each overtime hour.) Use an absolute reference to cell B6.

9. Select the range G6:J6, and then use AutoFill to copy the formulas into the range G7:J15 to calculate the salary for each of the ten days in the table.

10. In cell B11, calculate the total straight time hours worked by summing the values in column H. In cell B12, calculate the total overtime hours by summing the values in column I. In cell B13, calculate the total hours worked by summing the value in column G. In cell B14, calculate the total payments by summing the values in column J.

11. In cell B17, calculate the amount of federal tax by multiplying the Total Pay value in cell B14 by the appropriate federal tax rate for an employee with the marital status in cell B7 and withholding allowances in cell B9. (*Hint*: Use the VLOOKUP function with an exact match lookup for the lookup table in the range L6:W8. For the Col_index_num argument, use the value of cell B9 plus 2.)

12. In cell B18, calculate the Social Security tax equal to the value of cell B14 multiplied by the tax rate in cell M16.

13. In cell B19, calculate the Medicare tax equal to the value of cell B14 multiplied by the tax rate in cell M17.

14. In cell B20, calculate the amount of Georgia state tax by multiplying the value of cell B14 by the appropriate state tax rate in the range L12:W14 lookup table using the state marital status in cell B8 and the withholding allowance in cell B9. (*Hint*: Use the same type of VLOOKUP function as you did in Step 10 to retrieve the correct state tax rate.)

15. In cell B22, calculate the total deduction from pay by summing the values in the range B17:B20. In cell B23, calculate the withholding rate by dividing cell B22 by the total pay in cell B14.

16. In cell B24, calculate the take-home pay from subtracting the total withholding in cell B22 from cell B14.

17. Carol wants her take-home pay for the two weeks that she works in the sample schedule to be $1000. Use Goal Seek to find the hourly rate in cell B6 that will result in a take-home pay value of $1000.

18. Save and close the workbook.

Case Problem 3

CHALLENGE

Data File needed for this Case Problem: Biology.xlsx

Biology 221   Daivi Emani teaches biology and life sciences at Milford College in White Plains, New York. She wants to use Excel to track the test scores and calculate final averages for the students in her Biology 221 class. She has already entered the homework, quiz, and final exam scores for 66 students. The overall score is based on weighted average of the individual scores with homework accounting for 10 percent of the final grade, each of three quizzes accounting for 20 percent, and the final exam accounting for 30 percent. To calculate a weighted average you can use the SUMPRODUCT function

```
SUMPRODUCT(array1,array2)
```

where *array1* is the range containing the weights assigned to each score and *array2* is the range containing the scores themselves.

Daivi also wants you to calculate each student's rank in the class based on the student's weighted average. Ranks are calculated using the RANK function

```
RANK(number,ref[,order=0])
```

where *number* is the value to be ranked, *ref* is a reference to the range containing the values against which the ranking is done, and *order* is an optional argument that specifies whether to rank in descending order or ascending order. The default order value is 0 to rank the values in descending order.

Finally, you will create formulas that will look up information on a particular student based on that student's ID so that Daivi doesn't have to scroll through the complete class roster to find a particular student. Complete the following:

1. Open the **Biology** workbook located in the Excel3 > Case3 folder, and then save the workbook as **Biology Grades** in the location specified by your instructor.

2. In the Documentation worksheet, enter your name in cell B3 and the date in cell B4.

3. In the Biology Grades worksheet, in cell B5, calculate the number of students in the class by using the COUNTA function to count up the student IDs in the H column and subtracting 1 from that value (so as to not include cell H2 in the count).

4. In the range B8:F8, enter the weight values **10%, 20%, 20%, 20%,** and **30%.**

5. In the range B9:F9, calculate the average of the numbers in columns K, L, M, N, and O.

6. In the range B10:F10, calculate the minimum values in the corresponding student score columns.

7. In the range B11:F11, use the MEDIAN function to calculate the midpoint of each of the student scores.

8. In the range B12:F12, calculate the maximum values for each of the student scores.

⊕ **Explore** 9. In cell P3, use the SUMPRODUCT function to calculate the weighted average of the scores for the first student in the list. Use an absolute reference to the range B8:F8 for the *array1* argument, and use the relative reference to the student scores in the range K3:O3 for the *array2* argument.

⊕ **Explore** 10. In cell Q3, use the RANK function to calculate the first student's rank in class. Use cell P3 for the *number* argument and column P for the *ref* argument. You do not to specify a value for the *order* argument.

11. Calculate the weighted average and ranks for all of the students by using AutoFill to copy the formulas in the range P3:Q3 to the range P3:Q68.

12. In cell B15, enter the student ID **602-1-99** for Lawrence Fujita.

13. In cell B16, use the VLOOKUP function with the student ID from cell B15 to look up the first name of the student matching that ID. Use the range H:Q as the reference to the lookup table, and retrieve the third column from the table.

14. In the range B17:B24, use lookup functions to retrieve the other data for the student ID entered in cell B15.

15. Test the VLOOKUP function by adding other student IDs in cell B15 to confirm that you can retrieve the record for any student in class based on his or her student ID.

16. Manuel Harmon was not able to take the final exam because of a family crisis. Daivi is scheduling a makeup exam for him. A weighted average of 92.0 will give Manuel an A for the course. Use Goal Seek to determine what grade he would need on the final to get an A for the course.

17. Save and close the workbook.

CHALLENGE

Case Problem 4

Data File needed for this Case Problem: Cairn.xlsx

Cairn Camping Supplies   Diane Cho is the owner of Cairn Camping Supplies, a small camping store she runs out of her home in Fort Smith, Arkansas. To help her manage her inventory and orders, she wants to develop an Excel worksheet for recording orders. The worksheet needs to calculate the cost of each order, including the cost of shipping and sales tax. Shipping costs vary based on whether the customer wants to use standard, three-day, two-day, or overnight shipping. Diane will also offer free shipping for orders that are more than $250. The shipping form worksheet will use lookup functions so that Diane can enter each product's ID code and have the name and price of the product automatically entered into the form. To keep the worksheet clean without distracting error values when no input values have been entered, you'll use IF functions to test whether the user has entered a required value first before applying a formula using that value. Complete the following:

1. Open the **Cairn** workbook located in the Excel3 > Case4 folder, and then save the workbook as **Cairn Camping** in the location specified by your instructor.

2. In the Documentation worksheet, enter your name in cell B3 and the date in cell B4.

3. In the Order Form worksheet, enter the following sample order data: Customer **Dixie Kaufmann**; Order Number **381**; Order Date **4/5/2018**; Street **414 Topeak Lane**; City **Fort Smith**; State **AK**; ZIP **72914**; Phone **(479) 555-2081**; and Delivery Type **3 Day**.

⊕ **Explore** 4. In cell B17, calculate the number of delivery days for the order. Insert an IF function that first tests whether the value in cell B16 is equal to an empty text string (""). If it is, return an empty text string; otherwise, apply a lookup function to retrieve the lookup value from the table in the range F5:H8 using the value of cell B16 as the lookup value.

⊕ **Explore** 5. In cell B18, estimate the date of weekday delivery by inserting an IF function that tests whether cell B16 is equal to an empty text string. If it is, return an empty text string, otherwise apply the WORKDAY function using the values in cell B6 as the starting date and cell B17 as the number of days.

6. In cell D13, enter **p4981** as the initial item ordered by the customer. In cell G13, enter **2** as the number of items ordered.

7. In cell E13, enter an IF function that tests whether the value in cell D13 is equal to an empty text string. If true, return an empty text string. If false, apply the VLOOKUP function to return the name of the product ID entered into cell D13.

8. In cell F13, enter another IF function that tests whether the value in cell D13 is equal to an empty text string. If true, return an empty text string. If false, return the price of the product ID entered in cell D13.

9. In cell H13, enter another IF function to test whether the value in cell D13 is equal to an empty text string. If true, return an empty text string; otherwise, calculate the value of the price of the item multiplied by the number of items ordered.

10. Copy the formula in the range E13:F13 to the range E13:F20. Use AutoFill to copy the formula from cell H13 into the range H13:H20.

11. In cell H22, calculate the sum of the values in the range H13:H20.

12. In cell H23, calculate the sales tax equal to the total cost of the items ordered multiplied by the sales tax rate in cell G10.

13. In cell H24, calculate the shipping cost of the order by inserting an IF function that tests whether the value of cell B16 is an empty text string. If it is, return the value 0; otherwise, use a lookup function to return the shipping cost for the indicated shipping method.

14. In cell H25, insert an IF function that tests whether the value of cell H22 is greater than 250 (the minimum order needed to qualify for free shipping). If it is, return a value of cell H24; otherwise, return a value of 0.

15. In cell H27, calculate the total cost of the order by summing the values in the range H22:H24 and subtracting the value of cell H25.

16. Complete the customer order by adding the following items: Item **t7829** and Qty **1**; Item **led7331** and Qty **3**; and Item **sb8502** and Qty **5**.

17. Confirm that your worksheet correctly calculates the total cost, and then save your workbook.

18. Save the workbook as **Cairn Order Form** in the location specified by your instructor.

19. Create a blank order form sheet by deleting the input values in the ranges B4:B6, B9:B13, B16, D13:D16, G13:G16. Do *not* delete any formulas in the worksheet. Confirm that the worksheet does not show any error values when the input data is removed.

20. Save and close the workbook.

OBJECTIVES

Session 4.1
- Use the PMT function to calculate a loan payment
- Create an embedded pie chart
- Apply styles to a chart
- Add data labels to a pie chart
- Format a chart legend
- Create a clustered column chart
- Create a stacked column chart

Session 4.2
- Create a line chart
- Create a combination chart
- Format chart elements
- Modify the chart's data source
- Create a histogram and Pareto chart
- Add sparklines to a worksheet
- Format cells with data bars

Analyzing and Charting Financial Data

Preparing a Business Plan

Case | *Backspace Gear*

Haywood Mills is the owner of Backspace Gear, a new business in Kennewick, Washington, that manufactures backpacks for work, school, travel, and camping. Haywood has been working from a small shop making specialized packs for friends and acquaintances and wants to expand his business and his customer base. To do that, he needs to secure a business loan. Part of the process of securing a loan is to present a business plan that shows the current state of the market and offers projections about the company's future growth and earnings potential.

In addition to financial tables and calculations, Haywood's presentation needs to include charts and graphics that show a visual picture of the company's current financial status and where he hopes to take it. Haywood has asked for your help in creating the Excel charts and financial calculations he needs to include in his business plan.

STARTING DATA FILES

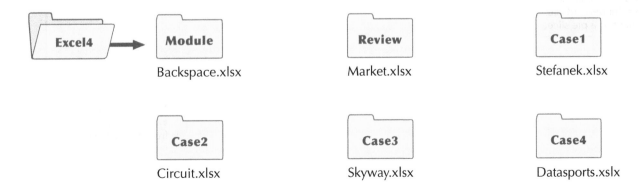

Excel4 → Module
Backspace.xlsx

Review
Market.xlsx

Case1
Stefanek.xlsx

Case2
Circuit.xlsx

Case3
Skyway.xlsx

Case4
Datasports.xslx

Session 4.1 Visual Overview:

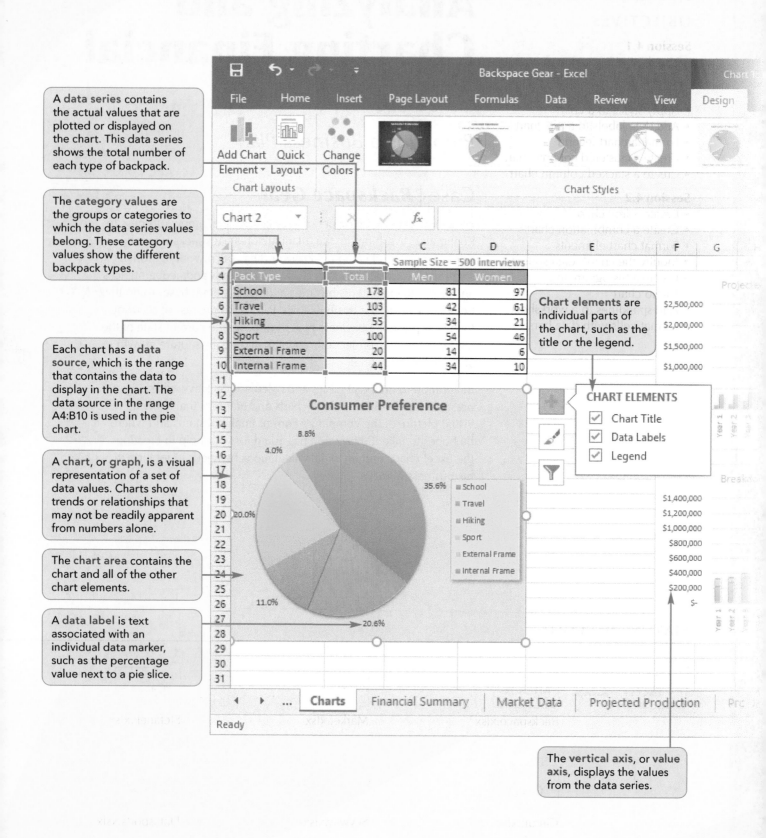

A data series contains the actual values that are plotted or displayed on the chart. This data series shows the total number of each type of backpack.

The category values are the groups or categories to which the data series values belong. These category values show the different backpack types.

Each chart has a data source, which is the range that contains the data to display in the chart. The data source in the range A4:B10 is used in the pie chart.

A chart, or graph, is a visual representation of a set of data values. Charts show trends or relationships that may not be readily apparent from numbers alone.

The chart area contains the chart and all of the other chart elements.

A data label is text associated with an individual data marker, such as the percentage value next to a pie slice.

Chart elements are individual parts of the chart, such as the title or the legend.

The vertical axis, or value axis, displays the values from the data series.

Backspace Gear - Excel

File   Home   Insert   Page Layout   Formulas   Data   Review   View   Design

Add Chart Element   Quick Layout   Change Colors

Chart Layouts   Chart Styles

Chart 2

Pack Type	Total	Men	Women
School	178	81	97
Travel	103	42	61
Hiking	55	34	21
Sport	100	54	46
External Frame	20	14	6
Internal Frame	44	34	10

Sample Size = 500 interviews

Consumer Preference

CHART ELEMENTS
- ☑ Chart Title
- ☑ Data Labels
- ☑ Legend

School, Travel, Hiking, Sport, External Frame, Internal Frame

35.6%   8.8%   4.0%   20.0%   11.0%   20.6%

$2,500,000
$2,000,000
$1,500,000
$1,000,000

$1,400,000
$1,200,000
$1,000,000
$800,000
$600,000
$400,000
$200,000
$-

Charts   Financial Summary   Market Data   Projected Production

Ready

Chart Elements

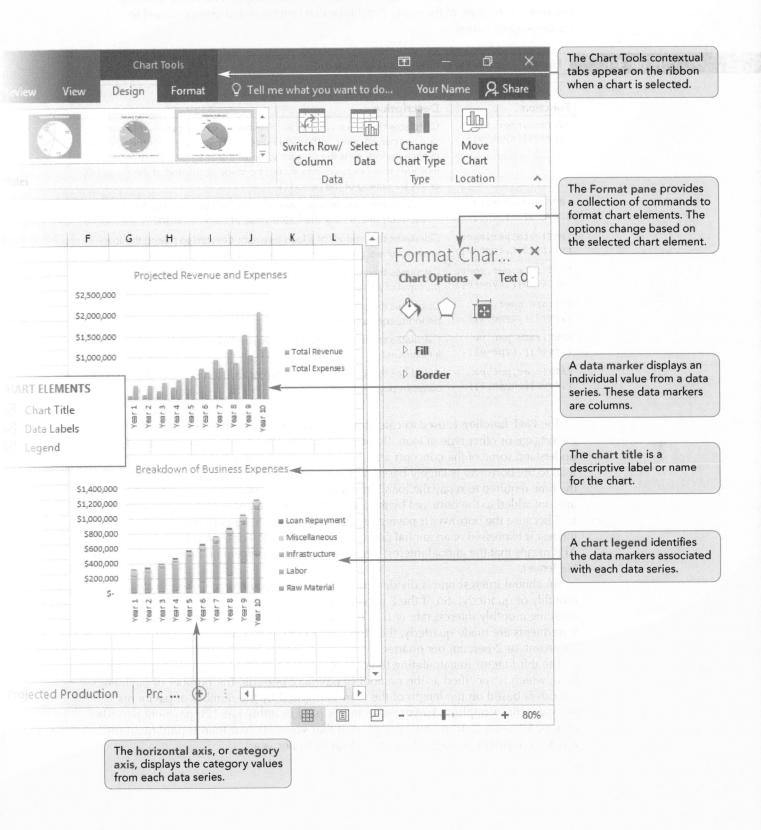

The Chart Tools contextual tabs appear on the ribbon when a chart is selected.

The Format pane provides a collection of commands to format chart elements. The options change based on the selected chart element.

A data marker displays an individual value from a data series. These data markers are columns.

The chart title is a descriptive label or name for the chart.

A chart legend identifies the data markers associated with each data series.

The **horizontal axis**, or **category axis**, displays the category values from each data series.

Introduction to Financial Functions

Financial functions are used to analyze loans, investments, and business statistics. Figure 4-1 lists some of the many Excel financial functions that are often used in business applications.

Figure 4-1 ▶ **Financial functions for loans and investments**

Function	Description
FV(*rate*,*nper*,*pmt* [,*pv*=0][,*type*=0])	Calculates the future value of an investment, where *rate* is the interest rate per period, *nper* is the total number of periods, *pmt* is the payment in each period, *pv* is the present value of the investment, and *type* indicates whether payments should be made at the end of the period (0) or the beginning of the period (1)
PMT(*rate*,*nper*,*pv* [,*fv*=0][,*type*=0])	Calculates the payments required each period on a loan or an investment, where *fv* is the future value of the investment
IPMT(*rate*,*per*,*nper*, *pv*[,*fv*=0][,*type*=0])	Calculates the amount of a loan payment devoted to paying the loan interest, where *per* is the number of the payment period
PPMT(*rate*,*per*,*nper*, *pv*[,*fv*=0][,*type*=0])	Calculates the amount of a loan payment devoted to paying off the principal of a loan
PV(*rate*,*nper*,*pmt* [,*fv*=0][,*type*=0])	Calculates the present value of a loan or an investment based on periodic, constant payments
NPER(*rate*,*pmt*,*pv* [,*fv*=0][,*type*=0])	Calculates the number of periods required to pay off a loan or an investment
RATE(*nper*,*pmt*,*pv* [,*fv*=0][,*type*=0])	Calculates the interest rate of a loan or an investment based on periodic, constant payments

The **PMT function** is used to calculate the payments required to completely repay a mortgage or other type of loan. Before you can use the PMT function, you need to understand some of the concepts and definitions associated with loans. The cost of a loan to the borrower is largely based on three factors—the principal, the interest, and the time required to repay the loan. **Principal** is the amount of the loan. **Interest** is the amount added to the principal by the lender. You can think of interest as a kind of "user fee" because the borrower is paying for the right to use the lender's money. Generally, interest is expressed at an annual percentage rate, or APR. For example, an 8 percent APR means that the annual interest rate on the loan is 8 percent of the amount owed to the lender.

An annual interest rate is divided by the number of payments per year (often monthly or quarterly). So, if the 8 percent annual interest rate is paid monthly, the resulting monthly interest rate is 1/12 of 8 percent, or about 0.67 percent per month. If payments are made quarterly, then the interest rate per quarter would be 1/4 of 8 percent, or 2 percent per quarter.

The third factor in calculating the cost of a loan is the time required to repay the loan, which is specified as the number of payment periods. The number of payment periods is based on the length of the loan multiplied by the number of payments per year. For example, a 10-year loan that is paid monthly has 120 payment periods (that is, 10 years × 12 months per year). If that same 10-year loan is paid quarterly, it has 40 payment periods (10 years × 4 quarters per year).

Using the PMT Function

To calculate the costs associated with a loan, such as the one that Haywood needs to fund the startup costs for Backspace Gear, you need the following information:

- The annual interest rate
- The number of payment periods per year
- The length of the loan in terms of the total number of payment periods
- The amount being borrowed
- When loan payments are due

The PMT function uses this information to calculate the payment required in each period to pay back the loan. The PMT function syntax is

```
PMT(rate,nper,pv[,fv=0][,type=0])
```

where $rate$ is the interest rate for each payment period, $nper$ is the total number of payment periods required to repay the loan, and pv is the present value of the loan or the amount that needs to be borrowed. The PMT function has two optional values—fv and $type$. The fv value is the future value of the loan. Because the intent with most loans is to repay them completely, the future value is equal to 0 by default. The $type$ value specifies when the interest is charged on the loan, either at the end of the payment period ($type=0$), which is the default, or at the beginning of the payment period ($type=1$).

For example, you can use the PMT function to calculate the monthly payments required to repay a car loan of $15,000 over a five-year period at an annual interest rate of 9 percent. The $rate$, or interest rate per period value, is equal to 9 percent divided by 12 monthly payments, or 0.75 percent per month. The $nper$, or total number of payments value, is equal to 12 × 5 (12 monthly payments over five years) or 60 payments. The pv, or present value of the loan, is 15,000. In this case, because the loan will be repaid completely and payments will be made at the end of the month, you can accept the defaults for the fv and $type$ values. The resulting PMT function can be written as

```
PMT(0.09/12, 5*12, 15000)
```

returning the value –311.38, or a monthly loan payment of $311.38. The PMT function returns a negative value because the monthly loan payments are treated as an expense to the borrower.

Rather than entering the argument values directly in the PMT function, you should include the loan terms in worksheet cells that are referenced in the function. This makes it clear what values are being used in the loan calculation. It also makes it easier to perform a what-if analysis exploring other loan options.

Haywood wants to borrow $150,000 to help start up his new business at a 6 percent annual interest rate. He plans to repay the loan in 10 years with monthly payments. You will calculate the amount of his monthly loan payment.

To enter the terms of the loan:

▶ 1. Open the **Backspace** workbook located in the **Excel4 > Module** folder included with your Data Files, and then save the workbook as **Backspace Gear** in the location specified by your instructor.

▶ 2. In the Documentation sheet, enter your name in cell B3 and the date in cell B4.

▶ 3. Go to the **Business Loan** worksheet. You'll use this worksheet to calculate the monthly payments that will be due on Haywood's loan.

▶ 4. In cell **B4**, enter **$150,000** as the loan amount.

▶ 5. In cell **B5**, enter **6.00%** as the annual interest rate.

▶ 6. In cell **B6**, enter **12** as the number of payments per year, indicating that the loan will be repaid monthly.

▶ 7. In cell **B7**, enter the formula **=B5/B6** to calculate the interest rate per period. In this case, the 6 percent interest rate is divided by 12 payments per year, returning a monthly interest rate of 0.50 percent.

▶ 8. In cell **B8**, enter **10** as the number of years in the loan.

▶ 9. In cell **B9**, enter **=B6*B8** to multiply the number of payments per year by the number of years in the loan, returning a value of 120 payments needed to repay the loan.

Next, you will use the PMT function to calculate the monthly payment needed to repay the loan in 10 years.

To calculate the monthly payment:

▶ 1. Select cell **B11** to make it the active cell. You will enter the PMT function in this cell.

▶ 2. On the ribbon, click the **Formulas** tab.

▶ 3. In the Function Library group, click the **Financial** button, and then scroll down and click **PMT** in the list of financial functions. The Function Arguments dialog box opens.

▶ 4. With the insertion point in the Rate box, click cell **B7** in the worksheet to enter the reference to the cell with the interest rate per month.

▶ 5. Click in the **Nper** box, and then click cell **B9** in the worksheet to enter the reference to the cell with the total number of monthly payments required to repay the loan.

▶ 6. Click in the **Pv** box, and then click cell **B4** in the worksheet to enter the reference to the cell with the present value of the loan. See Figure 4-2.

Figure 4-2   **Function Arguments dialog box for the PMT function**

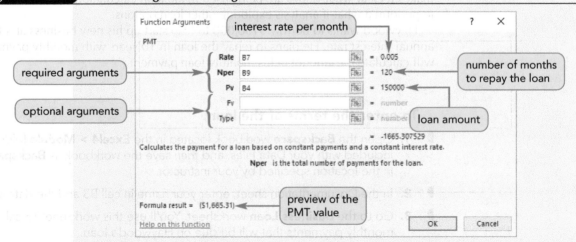

7. Click the **OK** button. The monthly payment amount ($1,665.31) appears in cell B11. The number is displayed in parentheses and in a red font to indicate a negative value because that is the payment that Backspace Gear must make rather than income it receives.

8. In cell B12, enter the formula **=B6*B11** to multiply the number of payments per year by the monthly payment amount, calculating the total payments for the entire year. The annual payments would be ($19,983.69), shown as a negative number to indicate money being paid out.

9. Select cell **B11**. The calculations for the business loan are complete. See Figure 4-3.

| Figure 4-3 | Monthly and annual costs of the business loan |

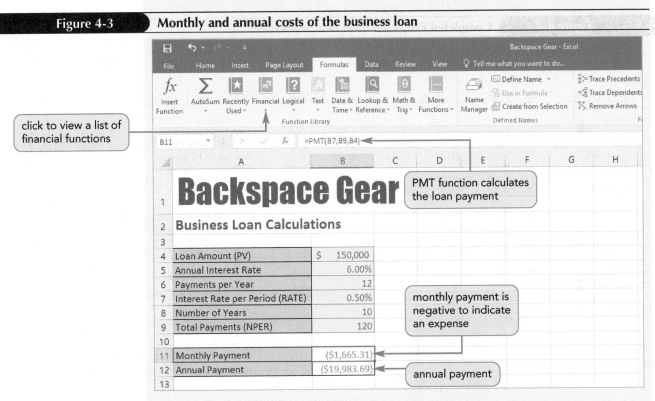

Haywood wants to see the financial impact of taking out a larger loan.

10. In cell **B4**, change the loan amount to **250,000**. With a loan of that size, the monthly payment increases to $2,775.51, and the annual total increases to $33,306.15.

Although a larger loan might help the business get off the ground, Haywood does not want the company to take such a large debt.

11. In cell **B4**, return the loan amount to **150,000**.

Based on your analysis, Backspace Gear would spend about $20,000 a year repaying the $150,000 business loan over the next 10 years. Haywood wants this information included in the Projected Cash Flow worksheet, which estimates Backspace Gear's annual revenue, expenses, and cash flow for the first 10 years of its operation. You will enter that amount as an expense for each year, completing the projected cash flow calculations.

To enter the loan repayment amount in the cash flow projection:

▶ **1.** Go to the **Projected Cash Flow** worksheet, and review the estimated annual revenue, expenses, and cash flow for the next decade.

▶ **2.** In cell **B20**, enter **20,000** as the projected yearly amount of the loan repayment. Because the projected cash flow is a rough estimate of the projected income and expenses, it is not necessary to include the exact dollar-and-cents cost of the loan.

▶ **3.** Copy the annual loan payment in cell **B20** into the range **C20:K20** to enter the projected annual loan payment in each year of the cash flow projections. See Figure 4-4.

Figure 4-4   **Completed Projected Cash Flow worksheet**

yearly loan payments

	A	B	C	D	E	F	G	H	I	J	K
13	Total Revenue	$ 100,000	$ 135,000	$ 225,000	$ 310,000	$ 535,000	$ 750,000	$ 950,000	$ 1,195,000	$ 1,550,000	$ 2,075,000
14											
15	*Expenses*										
16	Raw Material	$ 17,000	$ 20,000	$ 30,000	$ 50,000	$ 75,000	$ 150,00			400,000	$ 500,000
17	Labor	200,000	250,000	300,000	350,000	400,000	400,00			500,000	600,000
18	Infrastructure	25,000	25,000	35,000	35,000	45,000	45,00			60,000	60,000
19	Miscellaneous	75,000	35,000	25,000	25,000	35,000	50,000			75,000	75,000
20	Loan Repayment	20,000	20,000	20,000	20,000	20,000	20,000	20,000	20,000	20,000	20,000
21	Total Expenses	$ 337,000	$ 350,000	$ 410,000	$ 480,000	$ 575,000	$ 665,000	$ 770,000	$ 875,000	$ 1,055,000	$ 1,255,000
22											
23	Gross Income	$ (237,000)	$ (215,000)	$ (185,000)	$ (170,000)	$ (40,000)	$ 85,00			495,000	$ 820,000
24	Loss Carry Forward	(237,000)	(452,000)	(637,000)	(807,000)	(847,000)	(762,00			-	-
25	Income Tax @32%	-	-	-	-	-	-			(158,400)	(262,400)
26	Net Income	$ (237,000)	$ (215,000)	$ (185,000)	$ (170,000)	$ (40,000)	$ 85,000	$ 180,000	$ 320,000	$ 336,600	$ 557,600
27											
28	Capital Purchases	$ (150,000)	$ (50,000)	$ (50,000)	$ (50,000)	$ (50,000)	$ (50,000)	$ (50,000)	$ (70,000)	$ (75,000)	$ (85,000)
29	Depreciation	30,000	75,000	72,000	70,000	65,000	65,000	60,000	50,000	25,000	25,000
30	Cash Flow	$ (357,000)	$ (190,000)	$ (163,000)	$ (150,000)	$ (25,000)	$ 100,000	$ 190,000	$ 300,000	$ 286,600	$ 497,600
31											

total expenses projected over the next 10 years

net income projected over the next 10 years

Documentation | Business Loan | Market Summary | Financial Summary | Market Data | Projected Production | **Projected Cash Flow**

Ready   Average: 20,000   Count: 9   Sum: 180,000   120%

end-of-the-year cash receipts projected over the next 10 years

After including the projected annual loan payments, the Projected Cash Flow worksheet shows that Backspace Gear's projected net income at the end of the tenth year would be about $560,000, assuming all of the other projections are accurate. Based on these figures, the company should have almost $500,000 in cash at that time.

INSIGHT

Using Functions to Manage Personal Finances

Excel has many financial functions to manage personal finances. The following list can help you determine which function to use for the most common personal finance calculations:

- To determine how much an investment will be worth after a series of monthly payments at some future time, use the FV (future value) function.
- To determine how much you have to spend each month to repay a loan or mortgage within a set period of time, use the PMT (payment) function.
- To determine how much of your monthly loan payment is used to pay the interest, use the IPMT (interest payment) function.
- To determine how much of your monthly loan payment is used for repaying the principal, use the PPMT (principal payment) function.
- To determine the largest loan or mortgage you can afford given a set monthly payment, use the PV (present value) function.
- To determine how long it will take to pay off a loan with constant monthly payments, use the NPER (number of periods) function.

For most loan and investment calculations, you need to enter the annual interest rate divided by the number of times the interest is compounded during the year. If interest is compounded monthly, divide the annual interest rate by 12; if interest is compounded quarterly, divide the annual rate by four. You must also convert the length of the loan or investment into the number of payments per year. If you will make payments monthly, multiply the number of years of the loan or investment by 12.

Now that you have calculated the cost of the business loan and determined its impact on future cash flows, your next task is to summarize Haywood's business proposal for Backspace Gear. An effective tool for summarizing complex scientific and financial data is a chart.

Getting Started with Excel Charts

Charts show trends or relationships in data that are easier to see than by looking at the actual numbers. Creating a chart is a several-step process that involves choosing the chart type, selecting the data to display in the chart, and formatting the chart's appearance.

REFERENCE

Creating a Chart

- Select the range containing the data you want to chart.
- On the Insert tab, in the Charts group, click the Recommended Charts button or a button representing the general chart type, and then click the chart you want to create (or click the Quick Analysis button, click the Charts category, and then click the chart you want to create).
- On the Chart Tools Design tab, in the Location group, click the Move Chart button, select whether to embed the chart in a worksheet or place it in a chart sheet, and then click the OK button.

Excel provides 59 types of charts organized into the 10 categories described in Figure 4-5. Within each chart category are chart variations called **chart subtypes**. You can also design your own custom chart types to meet the specific needs of your reports and projects.

Figure 4-5	Excel chart types and subtypes

Chart Category	Description	Chart Subtypes
Column or Bar	Compares values from different categories. Values are indicated by the height of the columns or the length of a bar.	2-D Column, 3-D Column, 2-D Bar, 3-D Bar
Hierarchy	Displays data that is organized into a hierarchy of categories where the size of the groups is based on a number.	Treemap, Sunburst
Waterfall or Stock	Displays financial cash flow values or stock market data.	Waterfall, Stock
Line	Compares values from different categories. Values are indicated by the height of the lines. Often used to show trends and changes over time.	2-D Line, 3-D Line, 2-D Area, 3-D Area
Statistic	Displays a chart summarizing the distribution of values from a sample population.	Histogram, Pareto, Box and Whisker
Pie	Compares relative values of different categories to the whole. Values are indicated by the areas of the pie slices.	2-D Pie, 3-D Pie, Doughnut
X Y (Scatter)	Shows the patterns or relationship between two or more sets of values. Often used in scientific studies and statistical analyses.	Scatter, Bubble
Surface or Radar	Compares three sets of values in a three-dimensional chart.	Surface, Radar
Combo	Combines two or more chart types to make the data easy to visualize, especially when the data is widely varied.	Clustered Column-Line, Clustered Column-Line on Secondary Axis, Stacked Area-Clustered Column
PivotChart	Creates a chart summarizing data from a PivotTable.	*none*

Sometimes more than one chart can be used for the same data. Figure 4-6 presents the same labor cost data displayed as a line chart, a bar chart, and column charts. The column charts are shown with both a 2-D subtype that has two-dimensional, or flat, columns and a 3-D subtype that gives the illusion of three-dimensional columns. The various charts and chart subtypes are better suited for different data. You should choose the one that makes the data easiest to interpret.

Figure 4-6   Same data displayed as different chart types

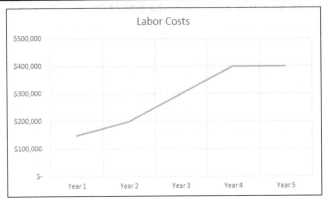

Line chart

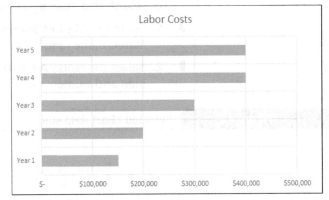

Bar chart

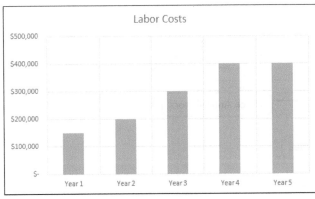

2-D Column chart

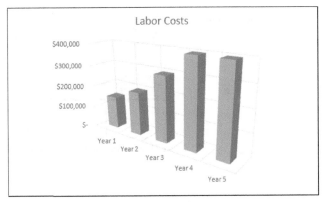

3-D Column chart

Creating a Pie Chart

The first chart you will create is a **pie chart**, which is a chart in the shape of a circle divided into slices like a pie. Each slice represents a single value from a data series. Larger data values are represented with bigger pie slices. The relative sizes of the slices let you visually compare the data values and see how much each contributes to the whole. Pie charts are most effective with six or fewer slices and when each slice is large enough to view easily.

Selecting the Data Source

The data displayed in a chart comes from the chart's data source, which includes one or more data series and a series of category values. A data series contains the actual values that are plotted on the chart, whereas the category values provide descriptive labels for each data series and are used to group those series. Category values are usually located in the first column or first row of the data source. The data series are usually placed in subsequent columns or rows. However, you can select category and data values from anywhere within a workbook.

Over the next 10 years Backspace Gear plans to produce school, travel, hiking, sport, external frame (for camping), and internal frame (for camping) packs. Haywood conducted a consumer survey of 500 adults to determine which of these will likely have the greatest demand in the Washington area. You will use the survey results, which Hayward entered in the Market Summary worksheet, as the data source for a pie chart.

To select the survey results as the pie chart's data source:

▶ **1.** Go to the **Market Summary** worksheet. A summary of the survey results is stored in the range A4:D10.

▶ **2.** Select the range **A4:B10** containing the overall results of the survey for both men and women. See Figure 4-7.

Figure 4-7 ▸ Selected chart data source

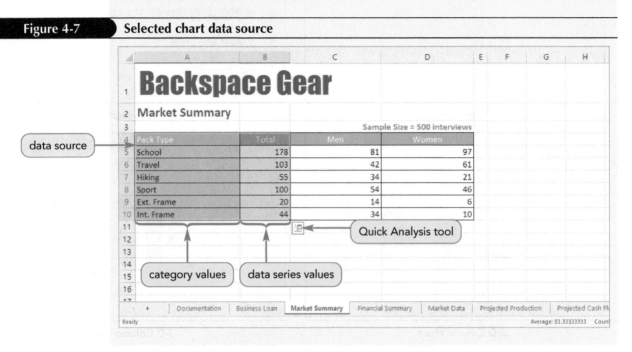

The selected data source covers two columns. The category values are located in the first column, and the data series that you will chart is located in the second column. When the selected range is taller than it is wide, Excel assumes that the category values and data series are laid out in columns. Conversely, a data source that is wider than it is tall is assumed to have the category values and data series laid out in rows. Note that the first row in this selected data source contains labels that identify the category values (Pack Type) and the data series name (Total).

Charting with the Quick Analysis Tool

After you select a data source, the Quick Analysis tool appears. The Charts category contains a list of chart types that are often appropriate for the selected data source. For the market survey results, a pie chart provides the best way to compare the preferences for the six types of packs that Backspace Gear plans to produce. You will use the Quick Analysis tool to generate the pie chart for Haywood.

To create a pie chart with the Quick Analysis tool:

TIP

You can also insert a chart by selecting a chart type in the Charts group on the Insert tab.

▶ **1.** With the range A4:B10 still selected, click the **Quick Analysis** button in the lower-right corner of the selected range (or press the **Ctrl+Q** keys) to open the Quick Analysis tool.

▶ **2.** Click the **Charts** category. The chart types you will most likely want to use with the selected data source are listed. See Figure 4-8.

Figure 4-8   **Charts category of the Quick Analysis tool**

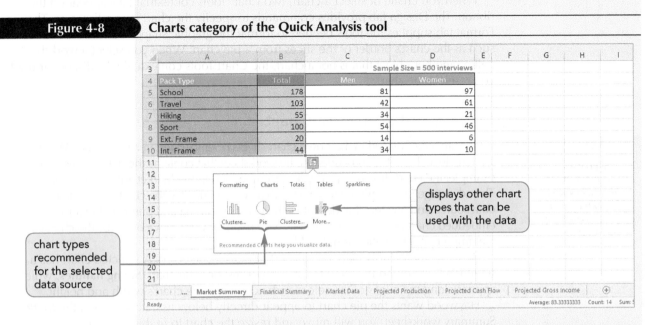

chart types recommended for the selected data source

displays other chart types that can be used with the data

3. Click **Pie**. A pie chart appears in the Market Summary worksheet. Each slice is a different size based on its value in the data series. The biggest slice represents the 178 people in the survey who selected a school pack as their most likely purchase from Backspace Gear. The smallest slice of the pie represents the 20 individuals who selected the external frame pack. See Figure 4-9.

Figure 4-9   **Pie chart in the Market Summary worksheet**

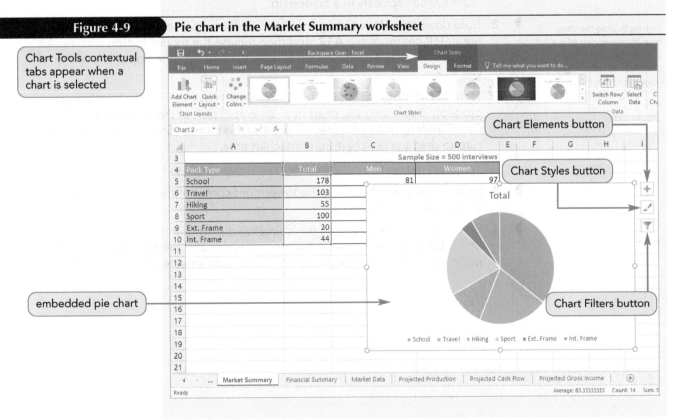

Chart Tools contextual tabs appear when a chart is selected

Chart Elements button

Chart Styles button

Chart Filters button

embedded pie chart

When you create or select a chart, two Chart Tools contextual tabs appear on the ribbon. The Design tab provides commands to specify the chart's overall design. The Format tab supplies the tools needed to format the graphic shapes found in the chart, such as the chart's border or the slices from a pie chart. When you select a worksheet cell or another object that is not a chart, the Chart Tools contextual tabs disappear until you reselect the chart.

Moving and Resizing a Chart

TIP

You can print an embedded chart with its worksheet, or you can print only the selected embedded chart without its worksheet.

Charts are either placed in their own chart sheets or embedded in a worksheet. When you create a chart, it is embedded in the worksheet that contains the data source. For example, the chart shown in Figure 4-9 is embedded in the Market Summary worksheet. The advantage of an **embedded chart** is that you can display the chart alongside its data source and any text that describes the chart's meaning and purpose. Because an embedded chart covers worksheet cells, you might have to move or resize the chart so that important information is not hidden.

Before you can move or resize a chart, it must be selected. A selected chart has a **selection box** around the chart for moving or resizing the chart. **Sizing handles**, which appear along the edges of the selection box, change the chart's width and height.

Haywood wants the pie chart to appear directly below its data source in the Market Summary worksheet. You will move and resize the chart to fit this location.

To move and resize the survey results pie chart:

1. Point to an empty area of the selected chart. The pointer changes to ⁺↖ and "Chart Area" appears in a ScreenTip.

Be sure to drag the chart from an empty part of the chart area so the entire chart moves, not just chart elements within the chart.

2. Hold down the **Alt** key, drag the chart until its upper-left corner snaps to the upper-left corner of cell **A12**, and then release the mouse button and the **Alt** key. The upper-left corner of the chart is aligned with the upper-left corner of cell A12.

    Trouble? If the pie chart resizes or does not move to the new location, you probably didn't drag the chart from an empty part of the chart area. Press the Ctrl+Z keys to undo your last action, and then repeat Steps 1 and 2, being sure to drag the pie chart from the chart area.

    The chart moves to a new location, but it still needs to be resized.

3. Point to the sizing handle in the lower-right corner of the selection box until the pointer changes to ↖.

4. Hold down the **Alt** key, drag the sizing handle up to the lower-right corner of cell **D26**, and then release the mouse button and the **Alt** key. The chart resizes to cover the range A12:D26 and remains selected. See Figure 4-10.

| Figure 4-10 | Moved and resized pie chart |

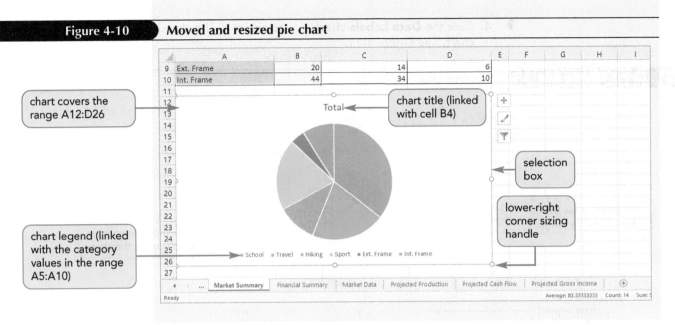

chart covers the range A12:D26

chart title (linked with cell B4)

selection box

lower-right corner sizing handle

chart legend (linked with the category values in the range A5:A10)

Note that three buttons appear to the right of the selected chart: the Chart Elements button ⊞, the Chart Styles button 🖌, and the Chart Filters button ▼. You will use these to modify the chart's appearance.

Working with Chart Elements

Every chart contains elements that can be formatted individually. For example, a pie chart has three elements—the chart title, the chart legend identifying each pie slice, and data labels that provide a data value associated with each slice. The Chart Elements button ⊞ that appears to the right of the selected chart lists the elements that can be added or removed from the chart. When you add or remove a chart element, the other elements resize to fit in the unoccupied space in the chart. Live Preview shows how changing an element will affect the chart's appearance so that you can experiment with different formats before applying them.

Haywood doesn't want the pie chart to include a title because the text in cell B4 and the data in the range A5:B10 sufficiently explain the chart's purpose. However, he does want to display the data values next to the pie slices. You will remove the chart title element and add the data labels element.

To remove the chart title and add data labels:

TIP
You can also add and remove chart elements with the Add Chart Element button in the Chart Layouts group on the Chart Tools Design tab.

1. With the pie chart still selected, click the **Chart Elements** button ⊞. A menu of chart elements that are available for the pie chart opens. As the checkmarks indicate, only the chart title and the chart legend are displayed in the pie chart.

2. Click the **Chart Title** check box to deselect it. The chart title is removed from the pie chart, and the chart elements resize to fill the space.

3. Point to the **Data Labels** check box. Live Preview shows how the chart will look when the data labels show a count of responses within each category.

4. Click the **Data Labels** check box to select it. The data labels are added to the chart. See Figure 4-11.

Figure 4-11	Displayed chart elements

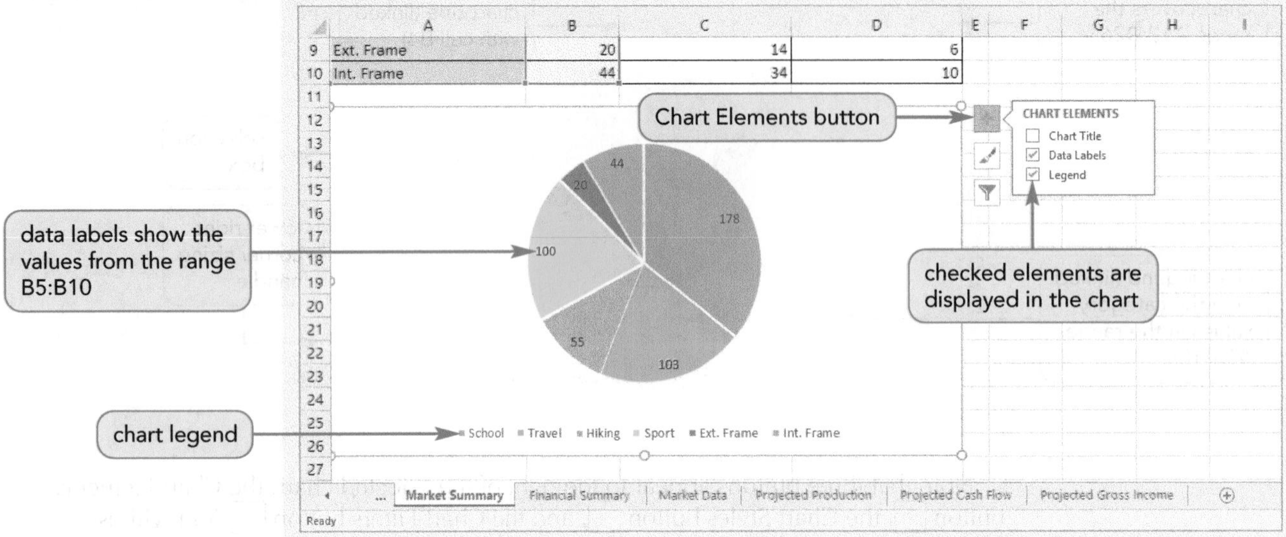

data labels show the values from the range B5:B10

chart legend

Chart Elements button

checked elements are displayed in the chart

Choosing a Chart Style

Chart elements can be formatted individually or as a group using one of the many built-in Excel chart styles. In the pie chart you just created, the format of the chart title, the location of the legend, and the colors of the pie slices are all part of the default pie chart style. You can quickly change the appearance of a chart by selecting a different style from the Chart Styles gallery. Live Preview shows how a chart style will affect the chart.

Haywood wants the pie slices to have a raised, three-dimensional look. You will explore different chart styles to find a style that best fulfills his request.

TIP

You can also select a chart style from the Chart Styles gallery in the Chart Styles group on the Chart Tools Design tab.

To choose a different chart style for the backpack production pie chart:

1. Click the **Chart Styles** button next to the selected pie chart. The Chart Styles gallery opens.

2. Point to different styles in the gallery. Live Preview shows the impact of each chart style on the pie chart's appearance.

3. Scroll to the bottom of the gallery, and then click the **Style 12** chart style. The chart style is applied to the pie chart. See Figure 4-12.

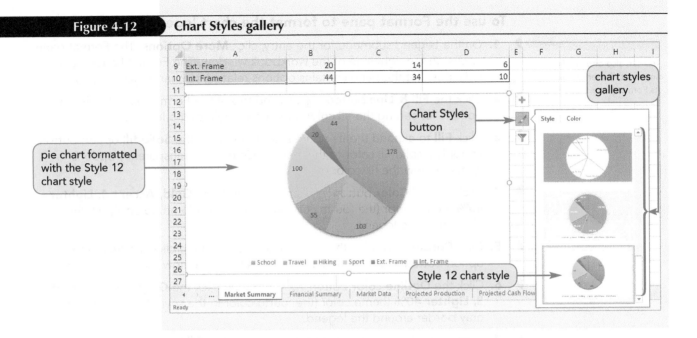

Figure 4-12   Chart Styles gallery

Formatting a Chart Legend

You can fine-tune a chart style by formatting individual chart elements. Using the Chart Elements button, you can open a submenu for each element that includes formatting options, such as the element's location within the chart. You can also open a Format pane, which has more options for formatting the selected chart element.

The default location for the pie chart legend is alongside the chart's bottom edge. Haywood thinks the chart would look better if the legend were aligned with the right edge of the chart. You'll make that change.

To format the pie chart legend:

▸ **1.** With the pie chart still selected, click the **Chart Elements** button ⊞.

▸ **2.** Point to **Legend** in the Chart Elements menu, and then click the **right arrow** icon next to the Legend entry, displaying a submenu of formatting options for that chart element.

▸ **3.** Point to **Left** to see a Live Preview of the pie chart with the legend aligned along the left side of the chart area.

▸ **4.** Click **Right** to place the legend along the right side of the chart area. The pie shifts to the left to make room for the legend.

The Chart Elements button also provides access to the Format pane, which has more design options for the selected chart element. Haywood wants you to add a drop shadow to the legend similar to the pie chart's drop shadow, change the fill color to a light gold, and add a light gray border. You'll use the Format pane to make these changes.

To use the Format pane to format the chart legend:

1. On the Legend submenu for the entry, click **More Options**. The Format pane opens on the right side of the workbook window. The Format Legend title indicates that the pane contains options relating to chart legend styles.

2. Click the **Fill & Line** button 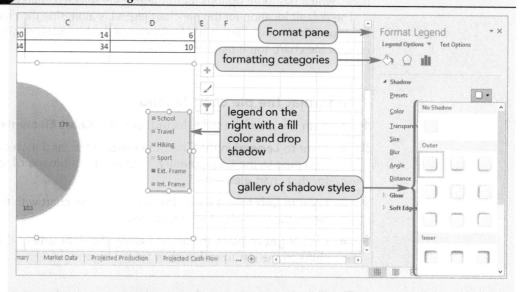 near the top of the Format pane to display options for setting the fill color and border style of the legend.

3. Click **Fill** to expand the fill options, and then click the **Solid fill** option button to apply a solid fill color to the legend. Color and Transparency options appear below the fill color options.

4. Click the **Fill Color** button, and then click the **Gold, Accent 4, Lighter 40%** theme color (the fourth color in the eighth column) to apply a light gold fill color to the legend.

5. Click **Border** to display the border options, and then click the **Solid line** option button. Additional border options appear below the border options.

6. Click the **Outline color** button, and then click the **Gray - 50%, Accent 3, Lighter 40%** theme color (the fourth color in the seventh column) to add a gray border around the legend.

7. At the top of the Format Legend pane, click the **Effects** button to display options for special visual effects.

8. Click **Shadow** to display the shadow options, and then next to the **Presets** button, click to display the Shadow gallery. See Figure 4-13.

Figure 4-13   **Formatted chart legend**

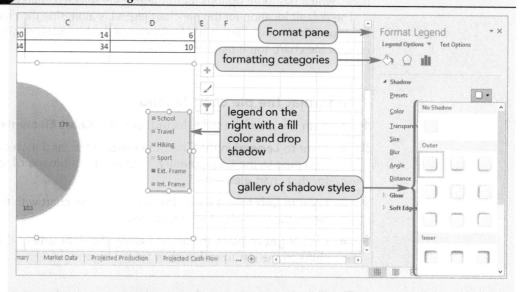

9. Click the **Offset Diagonal Bottom Right** button in the first row and first column to apply the drop shadow effect to the legend.

Formatting Pie Chart Labels

You can modify the content and appearance of data labels, selecting what the labels contain as well as where the labels are positioned. Data labels are placed where they best fit to keep the chart nicely proportioned, but you can change their location. From the Format pane, you can center the labels on the pie slices, place them outside of the slices, or set them as data callouts with each label placed in a text bubble and connected to its slice with a callout line. You can also change the text and number styles used in the data labels. You can also drag and drop individual data labels, placing them anywhere within the chart. When a data label is placed far from its pie slice, a **leader line** is added to connect the data label to its pie slice.

The pie chart data labels display the number of potential customers interested in each pack type, but this information also appears on the worksheet directly above the chart. Haywood wants to include data labels that add new information to the chart—in this case, the percentage that each pack type received in the survey. You'll change the label options.

To display percentage labels in the pie chart:

TIP

You can also format chart elements using the formatting buttons on the Home tab or on the Chart Tools Format tab.

▶ **1.** At the top of the Format pane, click the **Legend Options** arrow to display a menu of chart elements, and then click **Series "Total" Data Labels** to display the formatting options for data labels. The title of the Format pane changes to Format Data Labels and includes formatting options for data labels. Selection boxes appear around every data label in the pie chart.

▶ **2.** Near the top of the Format Data Labels pane, click the **Label Options** button ▊, and then click **Label Options**, if necessary, to display the options for the label contents and position. Data labels can contain series names, category names, values, and percentages.

▶ **3.** Click the **Percentage** check box to add the percentage associated with each pie slice to the pie chart.

▶ **4.** Click the **Value** check box to deselect it, removing the data series values from the data labels and showing only the percentages. For example, the pie chart shows that 35 percent of the survey responders indicated a willingness to buy Backspace Gear packs designed for school use.

▶ **5.** Click the **Outside End** option button to move the labels outside of the pie slices. The labels are easier to read in this location.

▶ **6.** Scroll down the Format pane, and then click **Number** to show the number formatting options for the data labels.

▶ **7.** Click the **Category** box to display the number formats, and then click **Percentage**.

▶ **8.** In the Decimal places box, select **2**, type **1**, and then press the **Enter** key. The percentages are displayed with one decimal place. See Figure 4-14.

Figure 4-14 **Formatted data labels**

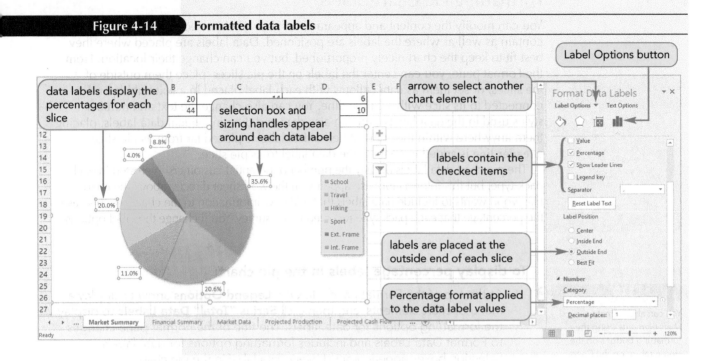

Changing the Pie Slice Colors

A pie slice is an example of a data marker representing a single data value from a data series. You can format the appearance of individual data markers to make them stand out from the others. Pie slice colors should be as distinct as possible to avoid confusion. Depending on the printer quality or the monitor resolution, it might be difficult to distinguish between similarly colored slices. If data labels are displayed within the slice, you also need enough contrast between the slice color and the data label color to make the text readable.

Haywood is concerned that the dark blue color of the Ext. Frame slice will be too dark when printed. He wants you to change it to a light shade of green.

To change the color of a pie slice:

▸ **1.** Click any pie slice to select all of the slices in the pie chart.

▸ **2.** Click the **Ext. Frame** slice, which is the darker blue slice that represents 4.0% percent of the pie. Only that slice is selected, as you can see from the sizing handles that appear at each corner of the slice.

▸ **3.** On the ribbon, click the **Home** tab.

▸ **4.** In the Font group, click the **Fill Color button arrow**, and then click the **Green, Accent 6, Lighter 40%** theme color (the fourth color in the last column) of the gallery. The pie slice changes to a light green, and the chart legend automatically updates to reflect that change.

You can also change the colors of all the pie slices by clicking the Chart Styles button ![icon] next to the selected chart, clicking the Color heading, and then selecting a color scheme.

Exploding a Pie Chart

Pie slices do not need to be fixed within the pie. An **exploded pie chart** moves one slice away from the others as if someone were taking the piece away from the pie. Exploded pie charts are useful for emphasizing one category above all of the others. For example, to emphasize the fact that Backspace Gear will be producing more school packs than any other type of pack, you could explode that single slice, moving it away from the other slices.

To explode a pie slice, first click the pie to select all of the slices, and then click the single slice you want to move. Make sure that a selection box appears around only that slice. Drag the slice away from the pie to offset it from the others. You can explode multiple slices by selecting each slice in turn and dragging them away. To explode all of the slices, select the entire pie and drag the pointer away from the pie's center. Each slice will be exploded and separated from the others. Although you can explode more than one slice, the resulting pie chart is rarely effective as a visual aid to the reader.

Formatting the Chart Area

The chart's background, which is called the chart area, can also be formatted using fill colors, border styles, and special effects such as drop shadows and blurred edges. The chart area fill color used in the pie chart is white, which blends in with the worksheet background. Haywood wants you to change the fill color to a medium green to match the worksheet's color scheme and to make the chart stand out better.

To change the chart area color:

1. Click a blank area within the chart, not containing either a pie slice or the chart legend. The chart area is selected, which you can verify because the Format pane title changes to "Format Chart Area."

2. On the Home tab, in the Font group, click the **Fill Color button arrow** ![icon], and then click the **Green, Accent 6, Lighter 60%** theme color (the last color in the third row). The chart area fill color is now medium green. See Figure 4-15.

Figure 4-15   Chart area fill color

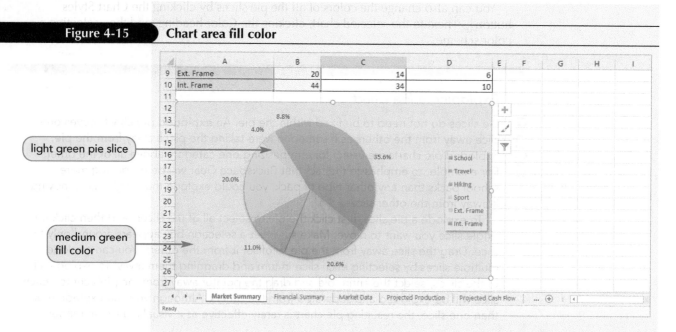

light green pie slice

medium green fill color

You are done formatting the pie chart, so you will close the Format pane to keep the window uncluttered.

3. Click the **Close** button ⊠ on the title bar of the Format pane. The pane closes, leaving more space for viewing the worksheet contents.

Performing What-If Analyses with Charts

Because a chart is linked to its data source, any changes in the data source values will be automatically reflected in the chart. For the Market Survey pie chart, the chart title is linked to the text in cell B4, the size of the pie slices is based on the production goals in the range B5:B10, and the category names are linked to the category values in the range A5:A10. Any changes to these cells affect the chart's content and appearance. This makes charts a powerful tool for data exploration and what-if analysis.

Haywood wants to see how the pie chart would change if the survey results were updated.

To apply a what-if analysis to the pie chart:

1. In cell **B7**, enter **100** to change the number of individuals who expressed an interest in Backspace hiking packs to 100. The Hiking slice automatically increases in size, changing from 11 percent to 18.3 percent. The size of the remaining slices and their percentages are reduced to compensate.

2. In cell **B7**, restore the value to **55**. The pie slices return to their initial sizes, and the percentages return to their initial values.

Haywood wants you to change the category names "Ext. Frame" and "Int. Frame" to "External Frame" and "Internal Frame."

3. Click cell **A9**, and then change the text to **External Frame**.

▶ **4.** Click cell **A10**, and then change the text to **Internal Frame**. The legend text in the pie chart automatically changes to reflect the new text.

Another type of what-if analysis is to **filter** the data source, which limits the data to fewer values. For example, the pie chart shows the survey results for all six types of packs that Backspace Gear will manufacture, but you can filter the pie chart so that it shows only the packs you select.

Haywood wants you to filter the pie chart so that it compares only the packs used for school, travel, and sport.

To filter the pie chart to show only three packs:

▶ **1.** Click the pie chart to select it.

▶ **2.** Click the **Chart Filters** button 🔽 next to the chart to open a menu listing the chart categories.

▶ **3.** Click the **Hiking**, **External Frame**, and **Internal Frame** check boxes to deselect them, leaving only the School, Travel, and Sport check boxes selected.

▶ **4.** At the bottom of the Chart Filters menu, click the **Apply** button. Excel filters the chart, showing only the three marked pack types. After filtering the data, the chart shows that 46.7 percent of the survey respondents would buy the School pack out of the choice of school, travel, and sport packs. See Figure 4-16.

| Figure 4-16 | **Filtered pie chart** |

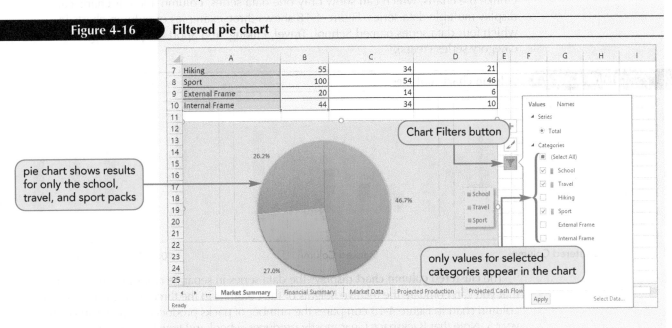

▶ **5.** In the Categories section of the Chart Filters menu, double-click the **Select All** check box to reselect all six pack types.

▶ **6.** Click the **Apply** button to update the chart's appearance.

▶ **7.** Press the **Esc** key to close the menu, leaving the chart selected.

The pie chart is complete. Next you'll create column charts to examine Haywood's proposed production schedule for the next years.

Creating a Column Chart

A **column chart** displays data values as columns with the height of each column based on the data value. A column chart turned on its side is called a **bar chart**, with the length of the bar determined by the data value. It is better to use column and bar charts than pie charts when the number of categories is large or the data values are close in value. Figure 4-17 displays the same data as a pie chart and a column chart. As you can see, it's difficult to determine which pie slice is biggest and by how much. It is much simpler to make those comparisons in a column or bar chart.

Figure 4-17	Data displayed as a pie chart and a column chart

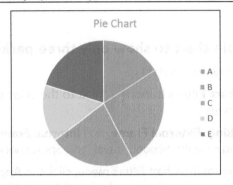 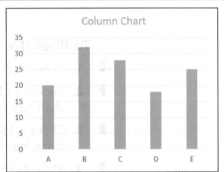

Comparing Column Chart Subtypes

Unlike pie charts, which can show only one data series, column and bar charts can display multiple data series. Figure 4-18 shows three examples of column charts in which four data series named School, Travel, Hiking, and Sport are plotted against one category series (Years).

Figure 4-18	Column chart subtypes

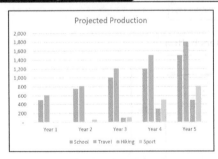 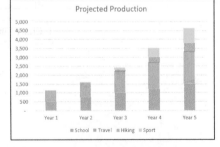 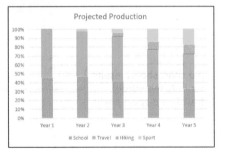

Clustered Column   Stacked Column   100% Stacked Column

The **clustered column chart** displays the data series in separate columns side by side so that you can compare the relative heights of the columns in the three series. The clustered column chart in Figure 4-18 compares the number of packs produced in year 1 through year 5. Note that Backspace Gear mostly produces school and travel packs in years 1 through 3 with hiking and sport packs production increasing in years 4 and 5.

The **stacked column chart** places the data series values within combined columns showing how much is contributed by each series. The stacked column chart in Figure 4-18 gives information on the total number of packs produced each year and how each year's production is split among the four types of packs.

Finally, the **100% stacked column chart** makes the same comparison as the stacked column chart except that the stacked sections are expressed as percentages. As you can see from the 100% stacked column chart in Figure 4-18, school and travel packs account for about 100% of the production in year 1 and steadily decline to 70% of the production in year 5 as Backspace Gear introduces hiking and sport packs.

Creating a Clustered Column Chart

The process for creating a column chart is the same as for creating a pie chart: selecting the data source and choosing a chart type and subtype. After the chart is embedded in the worksheet, you can move and resize the chart as well as change the chart's design, layout, and format.

Haywood wants his business plan to show the projected revenue and expenses for Backspace Gear's first 10 years. Because this requires comparing the data series values, you will create a clustered column chart.

To create a clustered column chart showing projected revenue and expenses:

▶ **1.** Go to the **Projected Cash Flow** worksheet.

▶ **2.** Select the nonadjacent range **A4:K4,A13:K13,A21:K21** containing the Year categories in row 4, the Total Revenue data series in row 13, and the Total Expenses data series in row 21. Because you selected a nonadjacent range, the Quick Analysis tool is not available.

TIP

You can also open the Insert Chart dialog box to see the chart types recommended for the selected data source.

▶ **3.** On the ribbon, click the **Insert** tab. The Charts group contains buttons for inserting different types of charts.

▶ **4.** In the Charts group, click the **Recommended Charts** button. The Insert Chart dialog box opens with a gallery of suggested charts for the selected data. See Figure 4-19.

| Figure 4-19 | Recommended Charts tab in the Insert Chart dialog box |

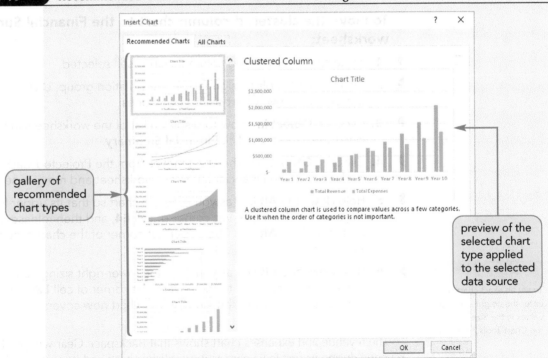

gallery of recommended chart types

preview of the selected chart type applied to the selected data source

▶ **5.** Make sure the **Clustered Column** chart is selected, and then click the **OK** button. The clustered column chart is embedded in the Projected Cash Flow worksheet.

▶ **6.** Click the **Chart Styles** button next to the selected column chart.

▶ **7.** In the Style gallery, scroll down, and click the **Style 14** chart style to format the columns with drop shadows.

▶ **8.** Click the **Chart Styles** button [icon] again to close the Style gallery.

Next, you will move the chart to a new location in the workbook.

INSIGHT

Changing a Chart Type

After creating a chart, you can easily switch the chart to a different chart type without having to recreate the chart from scratch. For example, if the data in a column chart would be more effective presented as a line chart, you can change its chart type rather than creating a new chart. Clicking the Change Chart Type button in the Type group on the Chart Tools Design tab opens a dialog box similar to the Insert Chart dialog box, from which you can select a new chart type.

Moving a Chart to a Different Worksheet

The Move Chart dialog box provides options for moving charts between worksheets and chart sheets. You can also cut and paste a chart from one location to another. Haywood wants you to move the column chart of the projected revenue and expenses to the Financial Summary worksheet.

To move the clustered column chart to the Financial Summary worksheet:

▶ **1.** Make sure the clustered column chart is still selected.

▶ **2.** On the Chart Tools Design tab, in the Location group, click the **Move Chart** button. The Move Chart dialog box opens.

▶ **3.** Click the **Object in** arrow to display a list of the worksheets in the active workbook, and then click **Financial Summary**.

▶ **4.** Click the **OK** button. The chart moves from the Projected Cash Flow worksheet to the Financial Summary worksheet and remains selected.

▶ **5.** Hold down the **Alt** key as you drag the chart so that its upper-left corner is aligned with the upper-left corner of cell **E4**, and then release the mouse button and the **Alt** key. The upper-left corner of the chart snaps to the worksheet.

TIP

To set an exact chart size, enter the height and width values in the Size group on the Chart Tools Format tab.

▶ **6.** Hold down the **Alt** key as you drag the lower-right sizing handle of the clustered column chart to the lower-right corner of cell **L20**, and then release the mouse button and the **Alt** key. The chart now covers the range E4:L20.

The revenue and expenses chart shows that Backspace Gear will produce little revenue during its first few years as it establishes itself and its customer base. It is only during year 6 that the revenue will outpace the expenses. After that, Haywood anticipates that the company's revenue will increase rapidly while expenses grow at a more moderate pace.

Editing a Chart Title

When a chart has a single data series, the name of the data series is used for the chart title. When a chart has more than one data series, *Chart Title* appears as the temporary title of the chart. You can replace the placeholder text with a more descriptive title and add a custom format.

Haywood wants you to change the chart title of the clustered column chart to "Projected Revenue and Expenses."

To change the title of the column chart:

▶ **1.** At the top of the column chart, click **Chart Title** to select the placeholder text.

▶ **2.** Type **Projected Revenue and Expenses** as the new title, and then press the **Enter** key. The new title is entered into the chart, and the chart title element remains selected.

▶ **3.** On the ribbon, click the **Home** tab, and then use the buttons in the Font group to remove the bold from the chart title, change the font to **Calibri Light**, change the font size to **16** points, and then change the font color to the **Green, Accent 6, Darker 25%** theme color. See Figure 4-20.

| Figure 4-20 | Clustered column chart |

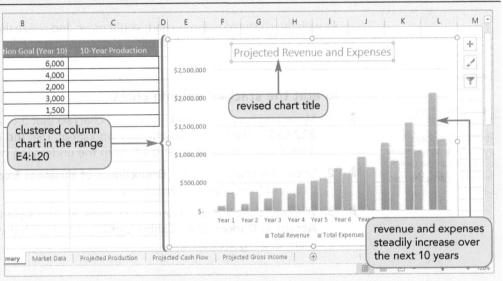

Creating a Stacked Column Chart

The next chart that Haywood wants added to the Financial Summary worksheet is a chart that projects the expenses incurred by the company over the next 10 years broken down by category. Because this chart looks at how different parts of the whole vary across time, that information would be better displayed in a stacked column chart. You will create this chart based on the data located in the Projected Cash Flow worksheet.

To create a stacked column chart:

▶ **1.** Return to the **Projected Cash Flow** worksheet, and then select the nonadjacent range **A4:K4,A16:K20** containing the year categories and five data series for different types of expenses.

▶ **2.** On the ribbon, click the **Insert** tab.

▶ **3.** In the Charts group, click the **Insert Column or Bar Chart** button ▊▊▾. A list of column and bar chart subtypes appears.

▶ **4.** Click the **Stacked Column** icon (the second chart in the 2-D Column section). The stacked column chart is embedded in the Projected Cash Flow worksheet.

▶ **5.** With the chart still selected, click the **Chart Styles** button ⬈, and then apply the **Style 11** chart style (the last style in the gallery).

You'll move this chart to the Financial Summary worksheet.

▶ **6.** On the Chart Tools Design tab, in the Location group, click the **Move Chart** button. The Move Chart dialog box opens.

▶ **7.** Click the **Object in** arrow, and then click **Financial Summary**.

▶ **8.** Click the **OK** button. The stacked column chart is moved to the Financial Summary worksheet.

As with the clustered column chart, you'll move and resize the stacked column chart in the Financial worksheet and then add a descriptive chart title.

To edit the stacked column chart:

TIP

To retain the chart's proportions as you resize it, hold down the Shift key as you drag the sizing handle.

▶ **1.** Move and resize the stacked column chart so that it covers the range **E22:L38** in the Financial Summary worksheet. Use the Alt key to help you align the chart's location and size with the underlying worksheet grid.

▶ **2.** Select the chart title, type **Breakdown of Business Expenses** as the new title, and then press the **Enter** key.

▶ **3.** With the chart title still selected, change the font style to a nonbold **Green, Accent 6, Darker 25%; Calibri Light** font to match the clustered column chart. See Figure 4-21.

Figure 4-21   Stacked column chart

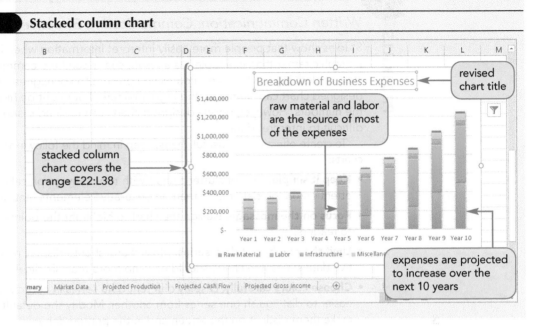

The chart clearly shows that the company's main expenses over the next 10 years will come from the raw material and labor costs. General maintenance, miscellaneous, and the business loan repayment constitute a smaller portion of the company's projected expenses. The overall yearly expense of running the company is expected to increase from about $337,000 in year 1 to $1,255,000 by year 10.

PROSKILLS

Written Communication: Communicating Effectively with Charts

Studies show that people more easily interpret information when it is presented as a graphic rather than in a table. As a result, charts can help communicate the real story underlying the facts and figures you present to colleagues and clients. A well-designed chart can illuminate the bigger picture that might be hidden by viewing only the numbers. However, poorly designed charts can mislead readers and make it more difficult to interpret data.

To create effective and useful charts, keep in mind the following tips as you design charts:

- **Keep it simple.** Do not clutter a chart with too many graphical elements. Focus attention on the data rather than on decorative elements that do not inform.

- **Focus on the message.** Design the chart to highlight the points you want to convey to readers.

- **Limit the number of data series.** Most charts should display no more than four or five data series. Pie charts should have no more than six slices.

- **Choose colors carefully.** Display different data series in contrasting colors to make it easier to distinguish one series from another. Modify the default colors as needed to make them distinct on the screen and in the printed copy.

- **Limit your chart to a few text styles.** Use a maximum of two or three different text styles in the same chart. Having too many text styles in one chart can distract attention from the data.

The goal of written communication is always to inform the reader in the simplest, most accurate, and most direct way possible. When creating worksheets and charts, everything in the workbook should be directed toward that end.

So far, you have determined monthly payments by using the PMT function and created and formatted a pie chart and two column charts. In the next session, you'll continue your work on the business plan by creating line charts, combination charts, histograms, sparklines, and data bars.

REVIEW

Session 4.1 Quick Check

1. You want to apply for a $225,000 mortgage. The annual interest on the loan is 4.8 percent with monthly payments. You plan to repay the loan in 20 years. Write the formula to calculate the monthly payment required to completely repay the loan under those conditions.

2. What function do you use to determine how many payment periods are required to repay a loan?

3. Why does the PMT function return a negative value when calculating the monthly payment due on a loan or mortgage?

4. What three chart elements are included in a pie chart?

5. A data series contains values grouped into 10 categories. Would this data be better displayed as a pie chart or a column chart? Explain why.

6. A research firm wants to create a chart that displays the total population growth of a county over a 10-year period broken down by five ethnicities. Which chart type best displays this information? Explain why.

7. If the research firm wants to display the changing ethnic profile of the county over time as a percentage of the county population, which chart type should it use? Explain why.

8. If the research firm is interested in comparing the numeric sizes of different ethnic groups over time, which chart should it use? Explain why.

9. If the research firm wants to display the ethnic profile of the county only for the current year, which chart should it use? Explain why.

Session 4.2 Visual Overview:

A combination chart combines two or more Excel chart types into a single graph. This chart combines a column chart and a line chart.

Chart gridlines extend the values of the major or minor tick marks across the plot area.

An axis title is descriptive text that appears next to an axis.

A histogram is a column chart displaying the distribution of values from a single data series.

Data values from a histogram are grouped into ascending categories called bins. The column height indicates the number of values falling within each bin.

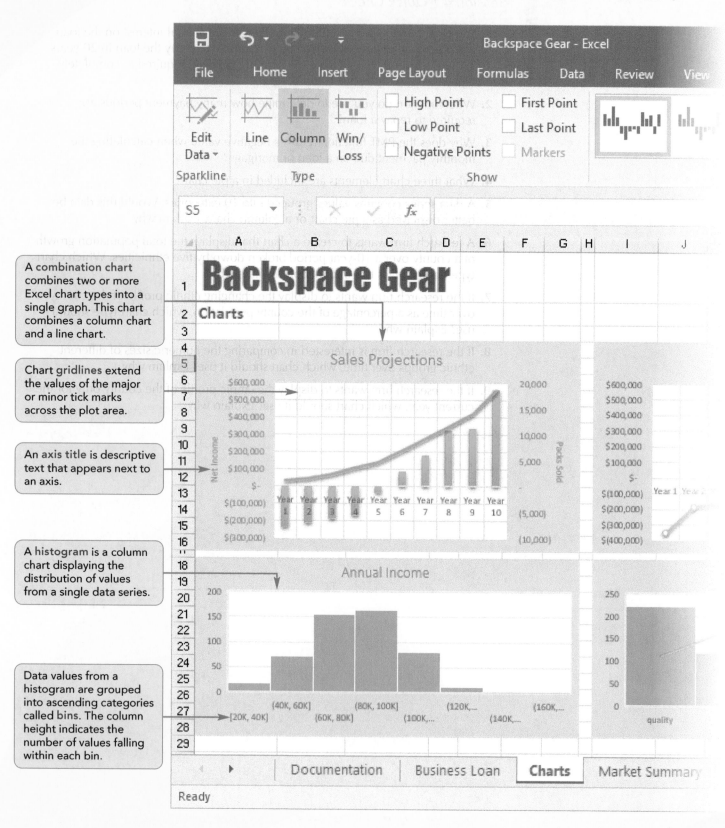

Charts, Sparklines, and Data Bars

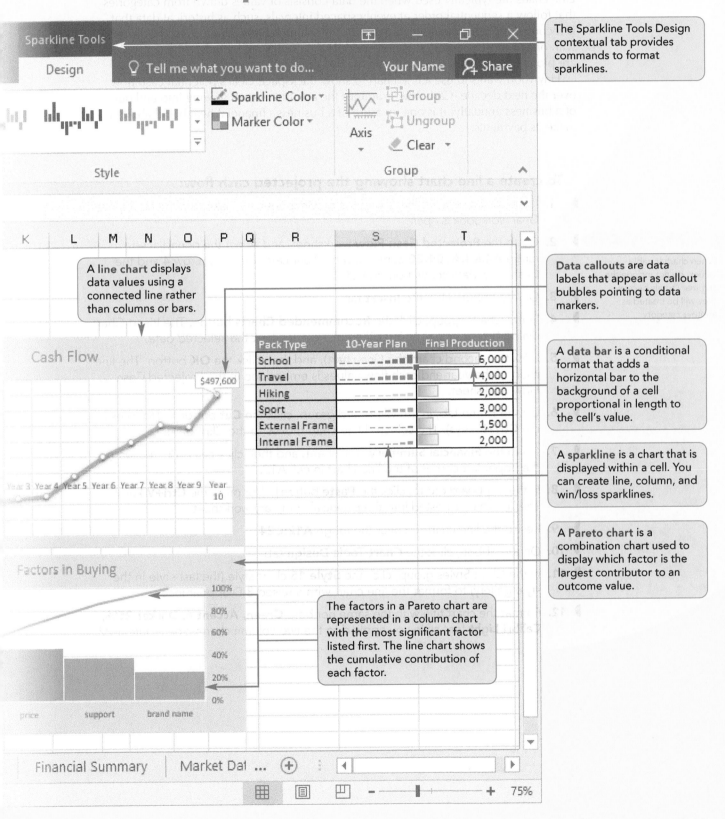

The Sparkline Tools Design contextual tab provides commands to format sparklines.

A line chart displays data values using a connected line rather than columns or bars.

Data callouts are data labels that appear as callout bubbles pointing to data markers.

A data bar is a conditional format that adds a horizontal bar to the background of a cell proportional in length to the cell's value.

A sparkline is a chart that is displayed within a cell. You can create line, column, and win/loss sparklines.

A Pareto chart is a combination chart used to display which factor is the largest contributor to an outcome value.

The factors in a Pareto chart are represented in a column chart with the most significant factor listed first. The line chart shows the cumulative contribution of each factor.

Cash Flow

$497,600

Year 3 Year 4 Year 5 Year 6 Year 7 Year 8 Year 9 Year 10

Pack Type	10-Year Plan	Final Production
School		6,000
Travel		4,000
Hiking		2,000
Sport		3,000
External Frame		1,500
Internal Frame		2,000

Factors in Buying

100%
80%
60%
40%
20%
0%

price   support   brand name

Financial Summary   Market Dat ...

75%

Creating a Line Chart

Line charts are typically used when the data consists of values drawn from categories that follow a sequential order at evenly spaced intervals, such as historical data that is recorded monthly, quarterly, or yearly. Like column charts, a line chart can be used with one or more data series. When multiple data series are included, the data values are plotted on different lines with varying line colors.

Haywood wants to use a line chart to show Backspace Gear's potential cash flow over the next decade. Cash flow examines the amount of cash flowing into and out of a business annually; it is one measure of a business's financial health and ability to make its payments.

To create a line chart showing the projected cash flow:

1. If you took a break at the end of the previous session, make sure the Backspace Gear workbook is open.

TIP

When charting table values, do not include the summary totals because they will be treated as another category.

2. Go to the **Projected Cash Flow** worksheet, and select the nonadjacent range **A4:K4,A30:K30** containing the Year categories from row 4 and the Cash Flow data series from row 30.

3. On the ribbon, click the **Insert** tab.

4. In the Charts group, click the **Recommended Charts** button. The Insert Chart dialog box opens, showing different ways to chart the selected data.

5. Click the second chart (the Line chart), and then click the **OK** button. The line chart of the year-end cash flow values is embedded in the Projected Cash Flow worksheet.

6. On the Home tab, in the Clipboard group, click the **Cut** button ✕ (or press the **Ctrl+X** keys). The selected line chart moves to the Clipboard.

7. Go to the **Financial Summary** worksheet, and then click cell **A12**. You want the upper-left corner of the line chart in cell A12.

8. In the Clipboard group, click the **Paste** button (or press the **Ctrl+V** keys). The line chart is pasted into the Financial Summary worksheet.

9. Resize the line chart to cover the range **A12:C24**.

10. On the ribbon, click the **Chart Tools Design** tab.

11. In the Chart Styles group, click the **Style 15** chart style (the last style in the style gallery) to format the line chart with a raised 3-D appearance.

12. Format the chart title with the same nonbold **Green, Accent 6, Darker 25%**; **Calibri Light** font style you applied to the two column charts. See Figure 4-22.

Figure 4-22   **Line chart showing the projected cash flow**

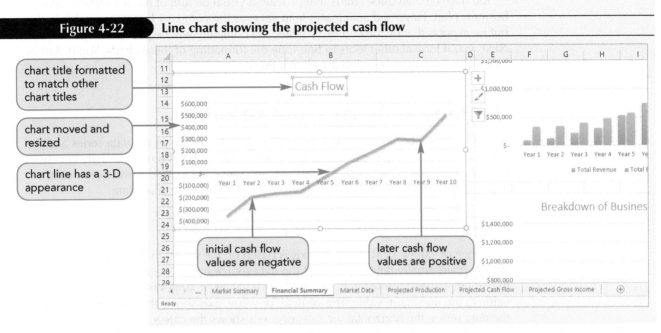

The line chart shows that Backspace Gear will have a negative cash flow in its early years and that the annual cash flow will increase throughout the decade, showing a positive cash flow starting in its sixth year.

INSIGHT

Line Charts and Scatter Charts

Line charts can sometimes be confused with XY (scatter) charts, but they are very different chart types. A line chart is more like a column chart that uses lines instead of columns. In a line chart, the data series are plotted against category values. These categories are assumed to have some sequential order. If the categories represent dates or times, they must be evenly spaced in time. For example, the Cash Flow line chart plotted the cash flow values against categories that ranged sequentially from year 1 to year 10.

A scatter chart has no category values. Instead, one series of data values is plotted against another. For example, if you were analyzing the relationship between height and weight among high school students, you would use a scatter chart because both weight and height are data values. On the other hand, if you charted weight measures against height categories (Short, Average, Tall), a line chart would be more appropriate.

Scatter charts are more often used in statistical analysis and scientific studies in which the researcher attempts to find a relationship between one variable and another. For that purpose, Excel includes several statistical tools to augment scatter charts, such as trendlines that provide the best fitting line or curve to the data. You can add a trendline by right-clicking the data series in the chart, and then clicking Add Trendline on the shortcut menu. From the Format Trendline pane that opens you can select different types of trendlines, including exponential and logarithmic lines as well as linear (straight) lines.

You have created three charts that provide a visual picture of the Backspace Gear business plan. Haywood anticipates lean years as the company becomes established, but he expects that by the end of 10 years, the company will be profitable and stable. Next, you'll look at other tools to fine-tune the formatting of these charts. You'll start by looking at the scale applied to the chart values.

Working with Axes and Gridlines

A chart's vertical and horizontal axes are based on the values in the data series and the category values. In many cases, the axes display the data in the most visually effective and informative way. Sometimes, however, you will want to modify the axes' scale, add gridlines, and make other changes to better highlight the chart data.

Editing the Scale of the Vertical Axis

The range of values, or **scale**, of an axis is based on the values in the data source. The default scale usually ranges from 0 (if the data source has no negative values) to the maximum value. If the scale includes negative values, it ranges from the minimum value to the maximum value. The vertical, or value, axis shows the range of values in the data series; the horizontal, or category, axis shows the category values.

Excel divides the scale into regular intervals, which are marked on the axis with **tick marks** and labels. For example, the scale of the vertical axis for the Projected Revenue and Expenses chart (shown in Figure 4-20) ranges from $0 up to $2,500,000 in increments of $500,000. Having more tick marks at smaller intervals could make the chart difficult to read because the tick mark labels might start to overlap. Likewise, having fewer tick marks at larger intervals could make the chart less informative. **Major tick marks** identify the main units on the chart axis while **minor tick marks** identify the smaller intervals between the major tick marks.

Some charts involve multiple data series that have vastly different values. In those instances, you can create dual axis charts. You can plot one data series against a **primary axis**, which usually appears along the left side of the chart, and the other against a **secondary axis**, which is usually placed on the right side of the chart. The two axes can be based on entirely different scales.

By default, no titles appear next to the value and category axes. This is fine when the axis labels are self-explanatory. Otherwise, you can add descriptive axis titles. In general, you should avoid cluttering a chart with extra elements such as axis titles when that information is easily understood from other parts of the chart.

Haywood thinks the value axis scale for the Projected Revenue and Expenses chart needs more tick marks and asks you to modify the axis so that it ranges from $0 to $2,500,000 in intervals of $250,000.

To change the scale of the vertical axis:

▶ 1. Click the **Projected Revenue and Expenses** chart to select it.

▶ 2. Double-click the vertical axis. The Format Axis pane opens with the Axis Options list expanded.

 Trouble? If you don't see the Axis Options section on the Format Axis pane, click the Axis Options button 📊 near the top of the pane.

 The Bounds section provides the minimum and maximum boundaries of the axis, which in this case are set from 0.0 to 2.5E6 (which stands for 2,500,000). Note that minimum and maximum values are set to Auto, which means that Excel automatically set these boundaries based on the data values.

TIP

To return a scale value
to Auto, click the Reset
button next to the value in
the Format pane.

The Units section provides the intervals between the major tick marks and
between minor tick marks. The major tick mark intervals, which are currently
500,000, are also set automatically by Excel.

3. In the Units section, click in the **Major** box, delete the current value, type
250000 as the new interval between major tick marks, and then press the
Enter key. The scale of the value axis changes. See Figure 4-23.

Figure 4-23	Formatted value axis

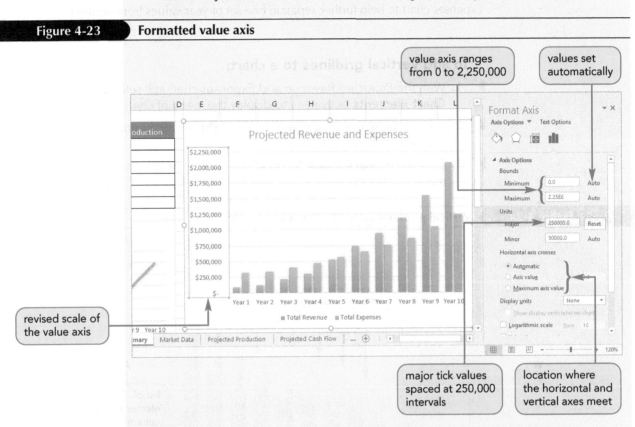

The revised axis scale makes it easier to determine the values displayed in the
column chart.

Displaying Unit Labels

INSIGHT

When a chart involves large numbers, the axis labels can take up a lot of the available
chart area and be difficult to read. You can simplify the chart's appearance by
displaying units of measure more appropriate to the data values. For example, you can
display the value 20 to represent 20,000 or 20,000,000. This is particularly useful when
space is at a premium, such as in an embedded chart confined to a small area of the
worksheet.

To display a units label, you double-click the axis to open the Format pane
displaying options to format the axis. Select the units type from the Display units box.
You can choose unit labels to represent values measured in the hundreds up to the
trillions. Excel will modify the numbers on the selected axis and add a label so that
readers will know what the axis values represent.

Adding Gridlines to a Chart

Gridlines are horizontal and vertical lines that help you compare data and category values in a chart. Depending on the chart style, gridlines may or may not appear in a chart, though you can add or remove them separately. Gridlines are placed at the major tick marks on the axes, or you can set them to appear at the minor tick marks.

The chart style used for the two column charts and the line chart includes horizontal gridlines. Haywood wants you to add vertical gridlines to the Projected Revenue and Expenses chart to help further separate one set of year values from another.

To add vertical gridlines to a chart:

▶ 1. With the Projected Revenue and Expenses chart still selected, click the **Chart Elements** button ⊞ to display the menu of chart elements.

▶ 2. Point to **Gridlines**, and then click the **right arrow** that appears to open a submenu of gridline options.

▶ 3. Click the **Primary Major Vertical** check box to add vertical gridlines at the major tick marks on the chart. See Figure 4-24.

| Figure 4-24 | Vertical gridlines added to the column chart |

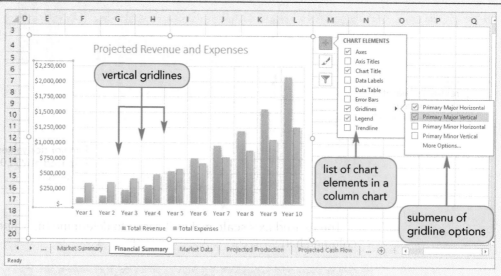

▶ 4. Click the **Chart Elements** button ⊞ to close the Chart Elements menu.

Working with Column Widths

Category values do not have the scale options used with data values. However, you can set the spacing between one column and another in your column charts. You can also define the width of the columns. As with the vertical axis, the default spacing and width are set automatically by Excel. A column chart with several categories will naturally make those columns thinner and more tightly packed.

Haywood thinks that the columns in the Projected Revenue and Expenses chart are spaced too closely, making it difficult to distinguish one year's values from another. He wants you to increase the gap between the columns.

To format the chart columns:

1. Make sure the Projected Revenue and Expenses chart is still selected and the Format pane is still open.

2. Click the **Axis Options arrow** at the top of the Format pane, and then click **Series "Total Revenue"** from the list of chart elements. The Format pane title changes to "Format Data Series," and all of the columns in the chart that show total revenue values are selected.

3. In the Format pane, click the **Series Options** button ▥ to display the list of series options.

   Series Overlap sets the amount of overlap between columns of different data series. Gap Width sets the amount of space between one group of columns and the next.

4. Drag the **Gap Width** slider until **200%** appears in the Gap Width box. The gap between groups of columns increases, and the individual column widths decrease to make room for the larger gap. See Figure 4-25.

TIP

You can use the up and down spin arrows in the Gap Width box to fine-tune the gap width in 1 percent increments.

Figure 4-25   Gap width between columns

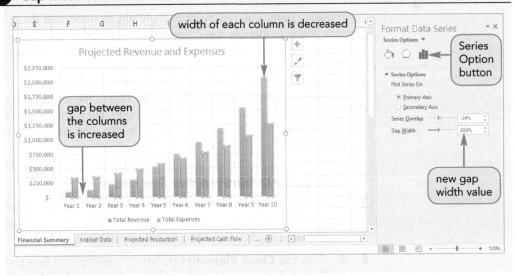

Formatting Data Markers

Each value from a data series is represented by a data marker. In pie charts, the data markers are the individual pie slices. In column charts, the columns are the data markers. In a line chart, the data markers are the points connected by the line. Depending on the line chart style, these data marker points can be displayed or hidden.

In the Cash Flow line chart, the data marker points are hidden, and only the line connecting them is visible. Haywood wants you to display these data markers and change their fill color to white so that they stand out, making the chart easier to understand.

To display and format the line chart data markers:

▶ **1.** Scroll to view the Cash Flow line chart, and then double-click the line within the chart. The Format pane changes to the Format Data Series pane.

▶ **2.** Click the **Fill & Line** button 🖾 at the top of the Format pane.

You can choose to display the format options for lines or data markers.

▶ **3.** Click **Marker**, and then click **Marker Options** to expand the list of options for the line chart data markers. Currently, the None option button is selected to hide the data markers.

▶ **4.** Click the **Automatic** option button to automatically display the markers.

The data markers are now visible in the line chart, but they have a blue fill color. You will change this fill color to white.

▶ **5.** Click **Fill** to expand the list of fill options, if necessary.

▶ **6.** Click the **Solid fill** option button, click the **Color** button, and then click the **White, Background 1** theme color. The fill color for the data markers in the line chart changes to white.

In many charts, you will want to highlight an important data point. Data labels provide a way to identify the different values in a chart. Whether you include data labels depends on the chart, the complexity of the data and presentation, and the chart's purpose. You can include data labels for every data marker or just for individual data points.

Haywood wants to highlight that at the end of the tenth year, the company should have an annual cash flow of almost $500,000. He wants you to add a data label that displays the value of the last data marker in the chart at that data point.

To add a data label to the line chart:

▶ **1.** With the line in the Cash Flow line chart still selected, click the last point on the line to select only that point. Note that selection handles appear around this data marker but not around any of the others.

▶ **2.** Click the **Chart Elements** button ⊞ next to the line chart, and then click the **Data Labels** check box to select it. The data label appears above only the selected data marker.

▶ **3.** Click the **Data Labels** arrow to display a menu of data label positions and options, and then click **Data Callout**. The data label is changed to a data callout box that includes both the category value and the data value, displaying "Year 10, $497,600." You will modify this callout to display only the data value.

▶ **4.** On the Data Labels menu, click **More Options**. The Format pane title changes to "Format Data Label."

▶ **5.** Click the **Label Options** button ▥, and then click **Label Options**, if necessary, to expand the list of those options.

▶ **6.** Click the **Category Name** check box to deselect it. The data callout now displays only $497,600. See Figure 4-26.

| Figure 4-26 | Formatted data markers and data label |

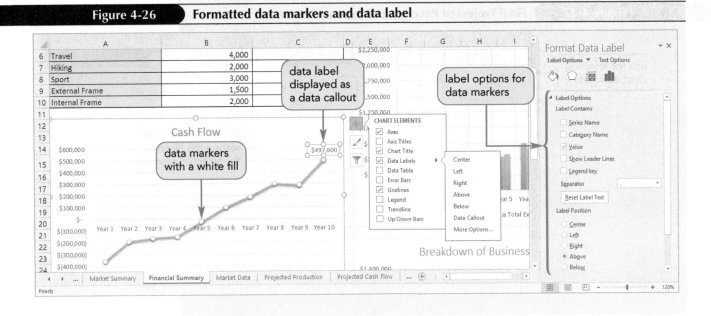

Formatting the Plot Area

The chart area covers the entire background of the chart, whereas the **plot area** includes only that portion of the chart in which the data markers, such as the columns in a column chart, have been placed or plotted. You can format the plot area by changing its fill and borders and by adding visual effects. Changes to the plot area are often made in conjunction with the chart area.

Haywood wants you to format the chart area and plot area of the Projected Revenue and Expenses chart. You will set the chart area fill color to a light green to match the pie chart background color you applied in the last session, and you will change the plot area fill color to white.

To change the fill colors of the chart and plot areas:

1. Click the **Projected Revenue and Expenses** chart to select it.

2. On the ribbon, click the **Chart Tools Format** tab.

3. In the Current Selection group, click the **Chart Elements arrow** to display a list of chart elements in the current chart, and then click **Chart Area**. The chart area is selected in the chart.

4. In the Shape Styles group, click the **Shape Fill button arrow**, and then click the **Green, Accent 6, Lighter 60%** theme color in the third row and last column. The entire background of the chart changes to light green.

5. In the Current Selection group, click the **Chart Elements arrow**, and then click **Plot Area** to select that chart element.

6. Change the fill color of the plot area to the **White, Background 1** theme color. See Figure 4-27.

Figure 4-27   **Final Projected Revenue and Expenses chart**

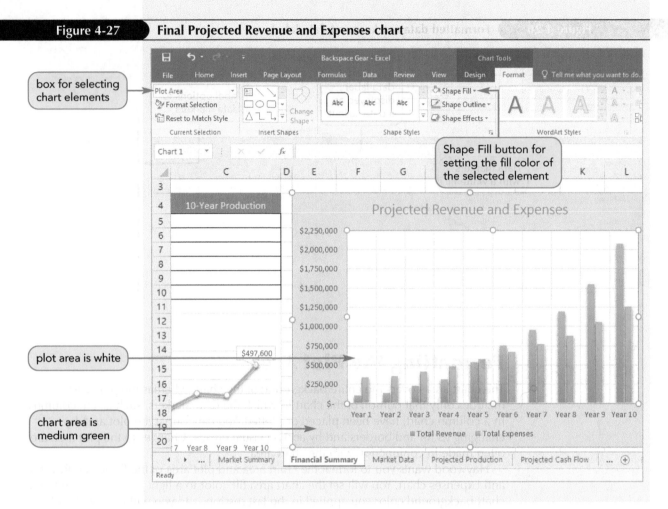

Haywood wants to apply the same general design applied to the Breakdown of Business Expenses column chart and the Cash Flow line chart. You will add vertical gridlines to each chart and then change the chart area fill color to light green and the plot area fill color to white.

To format the other charts:

1. Click the **Breakdown of Business Expenses** column chart to select it.

2. Select the **chart area**, and then set the fill color of the chart area to **Green, Accent 6, Lighter 60%** theme color.

3. Select the **plot area**, and then change the fill color to the **White, Background 1** theme color.

   Next, you'll add vertical gridlines to the chart. You can also use the Chart Tools Design tab to add chart elements such as gridlines.

4. On the ribbon, click the **Chart Tools Design** tab.

5. In the Chart Layouts group, click the **Add Chart Element** button, scroll down the chart elements, point to **Gridlines**, and then click **Primary Major Vertical** on the submenu. Vertical gridlines are added to the chart. See Figure 4-28.

| Figure 4-28 | Final Business Expenses chart |

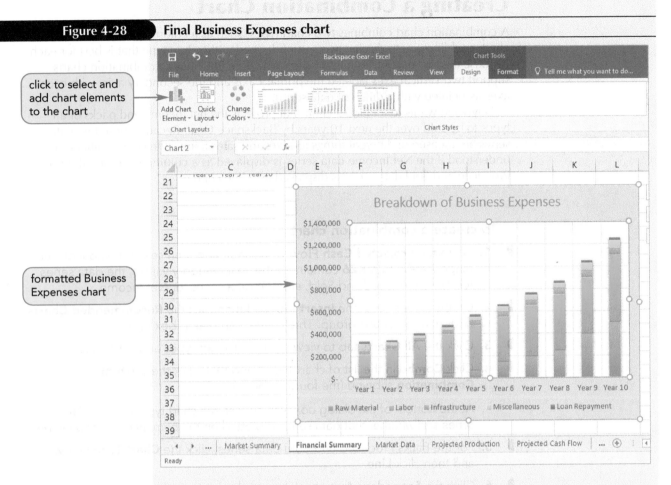

Callouts on figure:
- click to select and add chart elements to the chart
- formatted Business Expenses chart

6. Select the **Cash Flow** line chart, and then repeat Steps 2 through 5 to set the chart area fill color to light green, set the plot area fill color to white, and add major gridlines to the chart's primary axis.

The Breakdown of Business Expenses column chart and the Cash Flow line chart are now formatted with the same design.

INSIGHT

Overlaying Chart Elements

An embedded chart takes up less space than a chart sheet. However, it can be challenging to fit all of the chart elements into that smaller space. One solution is to overlay one element on top of another. The most commonly overlaid elements are the chart title and the chart legend. To overlay the chart title, click the Chart Title arrow from the list of Chart Elements and select Centered Overlay from the list of position options. Excel will place the chart title on top of the plot area, freeing up more space for other chart elements. Chart legends can also be overlaid by opening the Format pane for the legend and deselecting the Show the legend without overlapping the chart check box in the Legend Options section. Other chart elements can be overlaid by dragging them to new locations in the chart area and then resizing the plot area to recover the empty space.

Don't overuse the technique of overlaying chart elements. Too much overlaying of chart elements can make your chart difficult to read.

Creating a Combination Chart

A combination chart combines two chart types, such as a column chart and a line chart, enabling you to display two sets of data using the chart type that is best for each. Because the two data series might have vastly different values, combination charts support two vertical axes labeled the primary axis and the secondary axis, with each axes associated with a different data series.

Haywood wants to include a chart that projects the net income and packs of all types to be sold over the next 10 years by Backspace Gear. Because these two data series are measuring different things (dollars and sales items), the chart might be better understood if the Net Income data series is displayed as a column chart and the Packs Produced and Sold data series is displayed as a line chart.

To create a combination chart:

1. Go to the **Projected Cash Flow** worksheet, and then select the nonadjacent range **A4:K5,A26:K26** containing the Year category values, the data series for Packs Produced and Sold, and the data series for Net Income.

2. On the ribbon, click the **Insert** tab, and then click the **Recommended Charts** button in the Charts group. The Insert Chart dialog box opens.

3. Click the **All Charts** tab to view a list of all chart types and subtypes.

4. Click **Combo** in the list of chart types, and then click the **Custom Combination** subtype (the fourth subtype).

   At the bottom of the dialog box, you choose the chart type for each data series and whether that data series is plotted on the primary or secondary axis.

5. For the Packs Produced and Sold data series, click the **Chart Type arrow**, and then click **Line**.

6. Click the **Secondary Axis** check box to display the values for that series on a secondary axis.

7. For the Net Income data series, click the **Chart Type arrow**, and then click **Clustered Column**. See Figure 4-29.

| Figure 4-29 | Custom Combination chart in the Insert Chart dialog box |

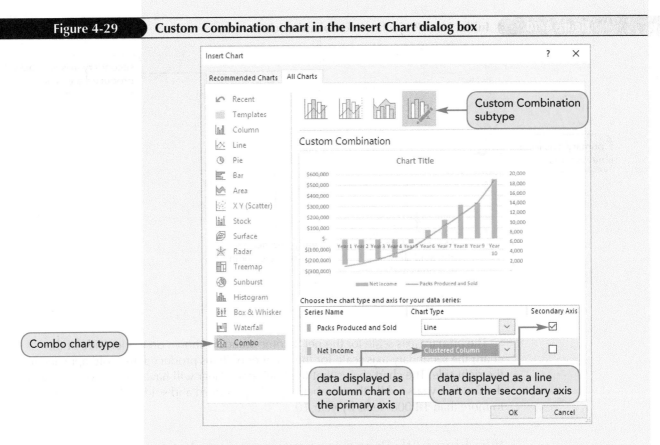

8. Click the **OK** button. The combination chart is embedded in the Projected Cash Flow worksheet.

9. Format the combination chart with the **Style 8** chart style to give both the line and the columns a raised 3-D effect.

Haywood wants the combo chart moved to the Financial Summary worksheet and formatted to match the style used for the other charts.

To move and format the combo chart:

1. Move the combination chart to the **Financial Summary** worksheet, and then resize it cover the range **A26:C38**.

2. Change the title of the combination chart to **Sales Projections**, and then format the title in the same nonbold **Green, Accent 6, Darker 25%**; **Calibri Light** font you used with the other chart titles.

3. Remove the **Legend** chart element from the combination chart.

4. Add **Primary Major Vertical** gridlines to the combination chart.

5. Change the fill color of the plot area to the **White, Background 1** theme color, and then change the fill color of the chart area to the same **Green, Accent 6, Lighter 60%** theme color as the other charts. See Figure 4-30.

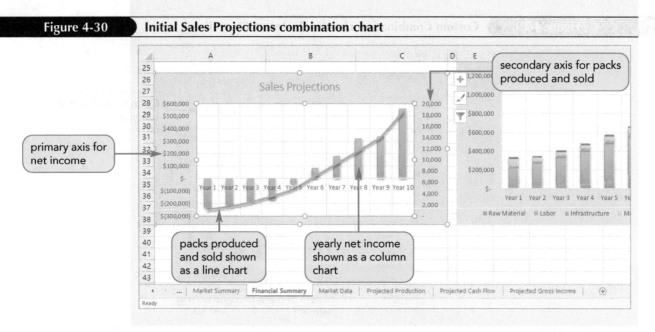

Figure 4-30 Initial Sales Projections combination chart

The primary axis scale for the net income values is shown on the left side of the chart; the secondary axis scale for the number of items produced and sold appears on the right side. The chart shows that the Backspace Gear will have a negative income for the first five years, while the number of packs produced and sold will increase steadily to more than 18,000 items by year 10.

Working with Primary and Secondary Axes

With a primary and secondary axis, combo charts can be confusing to the reader trying to determine which axis is associated with each data series. It is helpful to add an axis title to the chart with descriptive text that appears next to the axis values. As with other chart elements, you can add, remove, and format axis titles.

Haywood wants you to edit the Sales Projections chart to include labels describing what is being measured by the primary and secondary axes.

To add titles to the primary and second axes:

1. Click the **Chart Elements** button ⊞ next to the combination chart, and then click the **Axis Titles** check box to select it. Titles with the placeholders "Axis Title" are added to the primary and secondary axes.

2. Click the left axis title to select it, type **Net Income** as the descriptive title, and then press the **Enter** key.

3. With the left axis title selected, change the font color to the **Orange, Accent 2, Darker 25%** theme color to match the color of the columns in the chart.

4. Select the numbers on the left axis scale, and then change the font color to the **Orange, Accent 2, Darker 25%** theme color. The left axis title and scale are now the same color as the columns that reference that axis.

5. Select the **right axis** title, type **Packs Sold** as the descriptive title, and then press the **Enter** key.

6. With the right axis title still selected, change the font color to the **Blue, Accent 1, Darker 25%** theme color to match the color of the line in the chart.

7. On the Home tab, in the Alignment group, click the **Orientation** button , and then click **Rotate Text Down** to change the orientation of the right axis title.

8. Select the numbers on the right axis scale, and then change the font color to the **Blue, Accent 1, Darker 25%** theme color. The right axis title and scale are now the same color as the line that references that axis.

9. Click the horizontal axis title to select it, and then press the **Delete** key. The placeholder is removed from the chart, freeing up more space for other chart elements. See Figure 4-31.

| Figure 4-31 | Combination chart with axis titles |

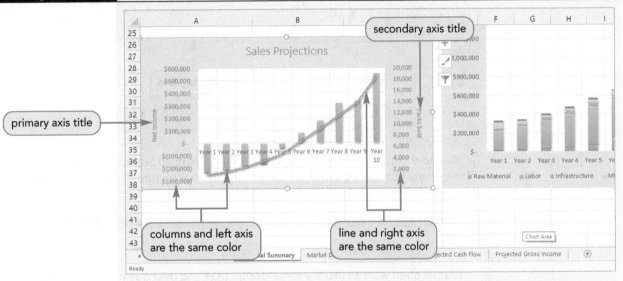

Haywood is concerned that the line chart portion of the graph makes it look as if the number of packs produced and sold was negative for the first five years. This is because the secondary axis scale, which is automatically generated by Excel, goes from a minimum of 0 to a maximum of 20,000. You will change the scale so that the 0 tick mark for Packs Sold better aligns with the $0 for Net Income.

To modify the secondary axis scale:

1. Double-click the secondary axis scale to select it and open the Format pane.

2. Click the **Axis Options** button , if necessary, to display the list of axis options.

3. In Axis Options section, click the **Minimum** box, change the value from 0.0 to **–10000**, and then press the **Enter** key. The secondary axis scale is modified. The Packs Sold scale is now better aligned with the Net Income scale, providing a clearer picture of the data.

4. Close the Format pane, and then press the **Esc** key to deselect the secondary axis. See Figure 4-32.

Figure 4-32   Final combination chart

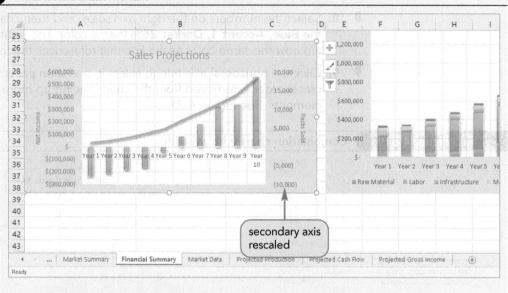

You have completed the charts portion of the Financial Summary worksheet. These charts provide a good overview of the financial picture of the first 10 years of Haywood's proposed business plan for Backspace Gear.

INSIGHT

Copying and Pasting a Chart Format

You will often want to use the same design over and over again for the charts in your worksheet. Rather than repeating the same commands, you can copy the formatting from one chart to another. To copy a chart format, first select the chart with the existing design that you want to replicate, and then click the Copy button in the Clipboard group on the Home tab (or press the Ctrl+C keys). Next, select the chart that you want to format, click the Paste button arrow in the Clipboard group, and then click Paste Special to open the Paste Special dialog box. In the Paste Special dialog box, select the Formats option button, and then click the OK button. All of the copied formats from the original chart—including fill colors, font styles, axis scales, and chart types—are then pasted into the new chart. Be aware that the pasted formats will overwrite any formats previously used in the new chart.

Editing a Chart Data Source

Excel automates most of the process of creating and formatting a chart. However, sometimes the rendered chart does not appear the way you expected. One situation where this happens is when the selected cells contain numbers you want to treat as categories but Excel treats them as a data series. When this happens, you can modify the data source to specify exactly which ranges should be treated as category values and which ranges should be treated as data values.

Modifying a Chart's Data Source

- Click the chart to select it.
- On the Chart Tools Design tab, in the Data group, click the Select Data button.
- In the Legend Entries (Series) section of the Select Data Source dialog box, click the Add button to add another data series to the chart, or click the Remove button to remove a data series from the chart.
- Click the Edit button in the Horizontal (Category) Axis Labels section to select the category values for the chart.

The Projected Gross Income worksheet contains a table that projects the company's gross income for the next 10 years. Haywood wants you to create a simple line chart of this data.

To create the line chart:

▶ 1. Go to the **Projected Gross Income** worksheet, and then select the range **A4:B14**.

▶ 2. On the ribbon, click the **Insert** tab.

▶ 3. In the Charts group, click the **Insert Line or Area Chart** button ⬚⬚.

▶ 4. In the 2-D Line charts section, click the **Line** subtype (the first subtype in the first row) to create a 2-D line chart.

▶ 5. Move the chart over the range **D2:J14**. See Figure 4-33.

| Figure 4-33 | Line chart with Year treated as a data series |

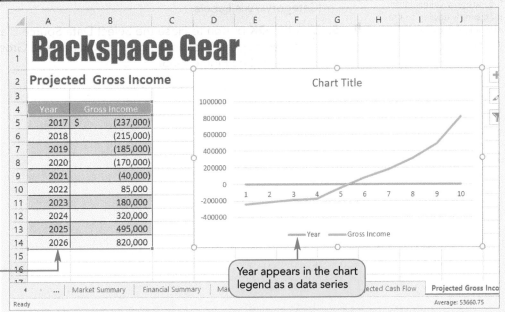

Year values should be treated as categories

Year appears in the chart legend as a data series

The line chart is incorrect because the Year values from the range A5:A14 are treated as another data series rather than category values. The line chart actually doesn't even have category values; the values are charted sequentially from the first value to the tenth. You can correct this problem from the Select Data dialog box by identifying the data series and category values to use in the chart.

To edit the chart's data source:

▶ **1.** On the Chart Tools Design tab, in the Data group, click the **Select Data** button. The Select Data Source dialog box opens. Note that Year is selected as a legend entry and the category values are simply the numbers 1 through 10. See Figure 4-34.

| Figure 4-34 | Select Data Source dialog box |

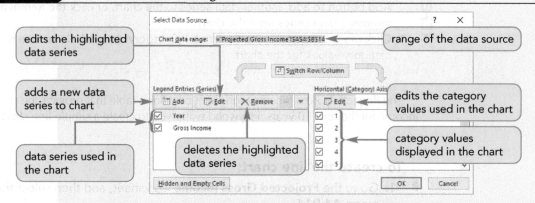

edits the highlighted data series

adds a new data series to chart

data series used in the chart

deletes the highlighted data series

range of the data source

edits the category values used in the chart

category values displayed in the chart

TIP

To organize a data series in rows, click the Switch Row/Column button.

▶ **2.** With Year selected (highlighted in gray) in the list of legend entries, click the **Remove** button. Year is removed from the line chart.

▶ **3.** Click the **Edit** button for the Horizontal (Category) Axis Labels. The Axis Labels dialog box opens. You'll specify that Year should be used as the category values.

Make sure you insert a completely new range for the category values rather than simply adding to the category values already in use.

▶ **4.** Select the range **A5:A14** containing the years as the axis label range, and then click the **OK** button. The Year values now appear in the list of Horizontal (Category) Axis Labels.

▶ **5.** Click the **OK** button to close the Select Data Source dialog box. The line chart now displays Year as the category values and Gross Income as the only data series. See Figure 4-35.

Figure 4-35	Revised Gross Income line chart

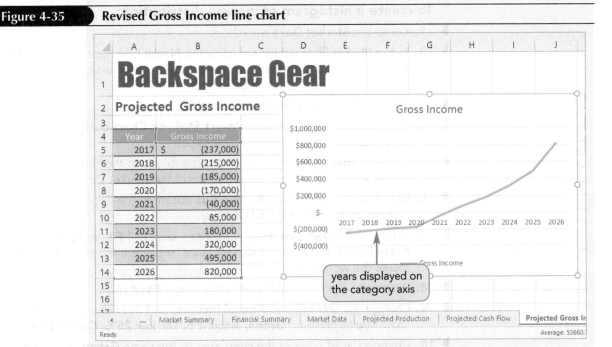

The Select Data Source dialog box is also useful when you want to add more data series to a chart. For example, if Haywood wanted to include other financial estimates in an existing chart, he could add the data series to the existing chart rather than creating a new chart. To add a data series to a chart, select the chart, click the Select Data button in the Data group on the Chart Tools Design tab to open the Select Data Source dialog box, click the Add button, and then select the range for the data series.

Exploring Other Chart Types

Excel provides many chart types tailored to specific needs in finance, statistics, science, and project management. One chart that is often used in finance and statistics is the histogram.

Creating a Histogram

A histogram is a column chart displaying the distribution of values from a single data series. For example, a professor might create a histogram to display the distribution of scores from a midterm exam. There is no category series for a histogram; instead, the data values are automatically grouped into ascending categories, or bins, with the histogram displaying the number of data points falling within the bin. So a histogram of midterm exam scores might consist of four bins corresponding to exam scores of 60 to 70, 70 to 80, 80 to 90, and 90 to 100. The number and placement of the bins is arbitrary and is chosen to best indicate the shape of the distribution.

You will use a histogram chart to summarize data from the market survey. Part of the survey included demographic information such as the respondent's gender and annual income. Haywood wants a histogram displaying the income distribution for Backspace Gear's most likely customers, which will help him better market Backspace Gear to its core customer base.

To create a histogram of income distribution:

▶ **1.** Go to the **Market Data** worksheet.

▶ **2.** In the Market Data worksheet, click the **Name** box, type the range **E6:E506**, and then press the **Enter** key to select the data values containing the annual income of the 500 survey respondents.

▶ **3.** On the ribbon, click the **Insert** tab.

▶ **4.** In the Charts group, click the **Insert Statistic Chart** button  to display a list of statistic charts supported by Excel.

▶ **5.** Click the **Histogram** subtype (the first subtype in the Histogram section). The histogram of the income data appears in the Market Data worksheet.

▶ **6.** With the chart selected, click the **Cut** button in the Clipboard group on the Home tab (or press the **Ctrl+X** keys).

▶ **7.** Go to the **Market Summary** worksheet, click cell **F4**, and then click the **Paste** button (or press the **Ctrl+V** keys) to paste the histogram chart at the top of the worksheet.

▶ **8.** Resize the chart so that it covers the range **F4:M14**.

▶ **9.** Change the chart title to **Annual Income**, and then change the color of the chart title to nonbold **Green, Accent 6, Darker 25%; Calibri Light** font.

▶ **10.** Change the fill color of the chart area to the same **Green, Accent 6, Lighter 60%** theme color used with other charts, and then change the plot area fill color to the **White, Background 1** theme color. See Figure 4-36.

Figure 4-36	Histogram of annual income

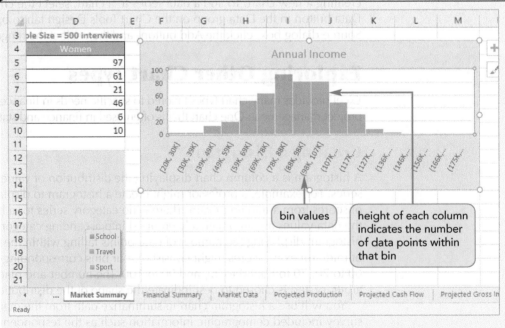

The histogram shows that most of the respondents are clustered around incomes of $59,000 to $100,000 per year. The lowest incomes are in the $20,000 to $30,000 range with some very few respondents having incomes around $175,000. Excel created the histogram with 17 bins. The number of bins is used to cover the range of values from the smallest income value up to the largest. This can result in odd-sized ranges. Haywood suggests that you change the width of each bin to 20,000. You can modify the bins by editing the values in the horizontal axis of the histogram chart.

To modify the bins used in the histogram:

▶ **1.** Double-click the horizontal axis values to select them and open the Format Axis pane.

▶ **2.** Click the **Axis Options** button ⬛ near the top of the Format pane, and then click **Axis Options** to expand the list. Excel displays a list of options to set the size and number of bins used in the histogram.

▶ **3.** Click the **Bin width** option button, change the width of the bins from the default value of 9700 to **20000**, and then press the **Tab** key. See Figure 4-37.

Figure 4-37 ▶ **Histogram with new bin widths**

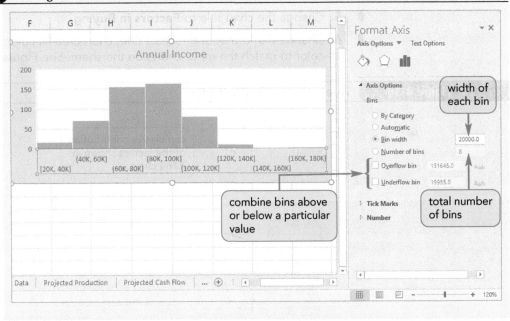

By changing the bin widths, you made the histogram easier to read and interpret. The distribution of the income values shows that there are a couple of outlying incomes in the 160,000 to 180,000 range, but almost all of the annual incomes are reported in the 60,000 to 100,000 range.

Creating a Pareto Chart

Another important statistical chart is the Pareto chart, which is used to indicate which factors are the largest contributors to an outcome value. Pareto charts are often used in quality control studies to isolate the most significant factors in the failure of a manufacturer process. They can also be used with market research to indicate which factor and combination of factors is the most crucial buying decision. Pareto charts appear as combination charts, combining a column chart and a line chart. The column chart lists the individual factors sorted from the most significant factor to the least significant. The line chart provides the cumulative percentage that each factor contributes to the whole.

Haywood's market survey asked respondents to list which one of the following factors was most important in choosing their pack: brand name, customer support, price, and quality. He wants you display this information in a Pareto chart that shows the factor that was listed most often in the survey results followed by the factor that was listed second-most often in the survey results, and so forth.

To create a Pareto chart showing buying factors:

1. Go to the **Market Data** worksheet, and then select the range **H5:I8** containing the total responses in each of the four categories: brand name, support, price, and quality.

2. On the ribbon, click the **Insert** tab.

3. In the Charts group, click the **Insert Statistic Chart** button, and then click the **Pareto** subtype (the second subtype in the Histogram section). The Pareto chart is inserted into the worksheet.

4. Move the Pareto chart to the **Market Summary** worksheet, and then resize it to cover the range **F16:M26**.

5. Change the chart title to **Factors in Buying**.

6. Change the format of the chart title, chart area fill color, and plot area fill color to match the other charts on the sheet. See Figure 4-38.

Figure 4-38 Pareto chart of buying factors

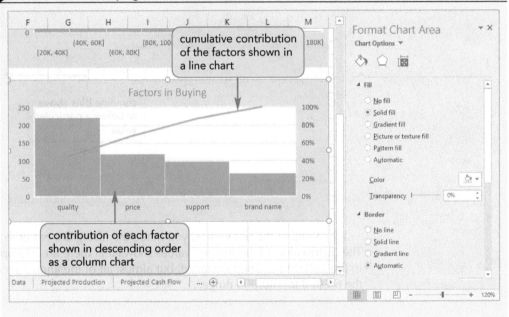

The Pareto chart quickly shows that quality is the most important factor in making a purchase for more than 200 of the respondents. The next most important factor is price, followed by support. Brand name is the least important factor. The line chart shows the cumulative effect of the four factors as a percentage of the whole. About 70 percent of the people in the survey listed quality or price as the most important factor in making a purchase, and about 90 percent listed quality, price, or customer support. Brand name, by comparison, had little impact on the respondent's buying decision, which is good for a new company entering the market.

Using a Waterfall Chart

A **waterfall chart** is used to track the effect of adding and subtracting values within a sum. Waterfall charts are often used to show the impact of revenue and expenses in profit and loss statements. The waterfall chart in Figure 4-39 is based on Backspace Gear's year 10 revenue and expenses projections.

Figure 4-39 Waterfall chart of Year 10 cash flow

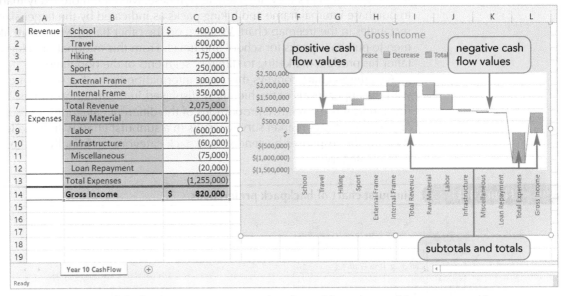

In waterfall charts, every positive value that adds to the total is represented by an increasing step, whereas negative values that subtract from the total are represented by decreasing steps. Subtotals such as the Total Revenue, Total Expenses, and Gross Income values are displayed in gray. The steps and colors in the chart show how each revenue and expense value contributes to the final gross income value.

Using a Hierarchical Chart

Hierarchy charts are like pie charts in that they show the relative contribution of groups to a whole. Unlike pie charts, a hierarchy chart also shows the organizational structure of the data with subcategories displayed within main categories. Excel supports two types of hierarchical charts: treemap charts and sunburst charts.

In a **treemap chart** each category is placed within a rectangle, and subcategories are nested as rectangles within those rectangles. The rectangles are sized to show the relative proportions of the two groups based on values from a data series. The treemap chart in Figure 4-40 measures the responses from the market survey broken down by gender and backpack type.

Figure 4-40 Treemap chart of preferences

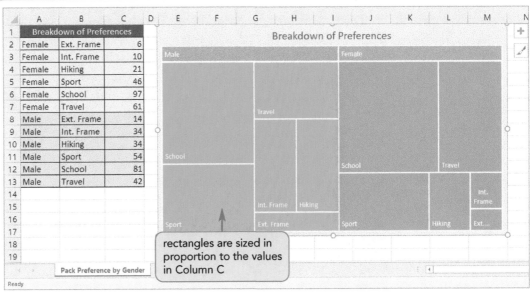

The size of the rectangles demonstrates how men and women in the survey differ in the types of packs they are likely to purchase. Men are more likely than women to purchase internal frame and hiking packs as indicated by the larger size of those rectangles in the treemap chart. Women, on the other hand, were more likely than men to purchase packs for school and travel. From this information, Haywood can tailor his product marketing to different segments of the population.

A **sunburst chart** conveys this same information through a series of concentric rings with the upper levels of the hierarchy displayed in the innermost rings. The size of the rings indicates the relative proportions of the different categories and subcategories. Figure 4-41 shows market survey results in a sunburst chart with three levels of rings showing the responses by gender, backpack category, and finally backpack type within category.

Figure 4-41   **Sunburst chart of backpack preferences**

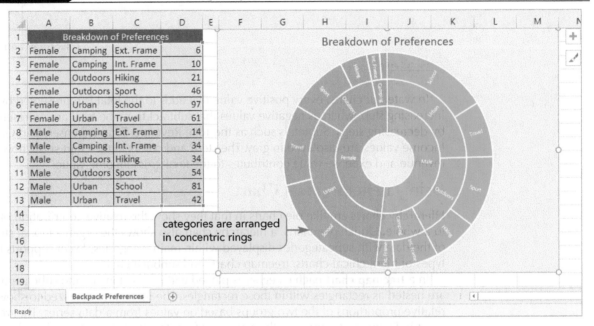

Sunburst charts are better than treemap charts at conveying information from multiple levels of nested categories and are better at displaying the relative sizes of the groups within each category level.

Decision Making: Choosing the Right Chart

Excel supports a wide variety of charts and chart styles. To decide which type of chart to use, you must evaluate your data and determine the ultimate purpose or goal of the chart. Consider how your data will appear in each type of chart before making a final decision.

- In general, pie charts should be used only when the number of categories is small and the relative sizes of the different slices can be easily distinguished. If you have several categories, use a column or bar chart.
- Line charts are best for categories that follow a sequential order. Be aware, however, that the time intervals must be a constant length if used in a line chart. Line charts will distort data that occurs at irregular time intervals, making it appear that the data values occurred at regular intervals when they did not.
- Pie, column, bar, and line charts assume that numbers are plotted against categories. In science and engineering applications, you will often want to plot two numeric values against one another. For that data, use **XY scatter charts**, which show the pattern or relationship between two or more sets of values. XY scatter charts are also useful for data recorded at irregular time intervals.

If you still can't find the right chart to meet your needs, you can create a custom chart based on the built-in chart types. Third-party vendors also sell software to allow Excel to create chart types that are not built into the software.

Creating Sparklines

Data can be displayed graphically without charts by using sparklines and data bars. A sparkline is a graphic that is displayed entirely within a worksheet cell. Because sparklines are compact in size, they don't include chart elements such as legends, titles, or gridlines. The goal of a sparkline is to convey the maximum amount of information within a very small space. As a result, sparklines are useful when you don't want charts to overwhelm the rest of your worksheet or take up valuable page space.

You can create the following types of sparklines in Excel:

- A line sparkline for highlighting trends
- A column sparkline for column charts
- A win/loss sparkline for highlighting positive and negative values

Figure 4-42 shows examples of each sparkline type. The line sparklines show the sales history from each department and across all four departments of a computer manufacturer. The sparklines provide enough information for you to examine the sales trend within and across departments. Notice that although total sales rose steadily during the year, some departments, such as Printers, showed a sales decline midway through the year.

Figure 4-42   **Types of sparklines**

line sparklines   column sparklines   win/loss sparklines

The column sparklines present a record of monthly temperature averages for four cities. Temperatures above 0 degrees Celsius are presented in blue columns; temperatures below 0 degrees Celsius are presented in red columns that extend downward. The height of each column is related to the magnitude of the value it represents.

Finally, the win/loss sparklines reveal a snapshot of the season results for four sports teams. Wins are displayed in blue; losses are in red. From the sparklines, you can quickly see that the Cutler Tigers finished their 10–2 season with six straight wins, and the Liddleton Lions finished their 3–9 season with four straight losses.

INSIGHT

Edward Tufte and Chart Design Theory

Any serious study of charts will include the works of Edward Tufte, who pioneered the field of information design. One of Tufte's most important works is *The Visual Display of Quantitative Information*, in which he laid out several principles for the design of charts and graphics.

Tufte was concerned with what he termed as "chart junk," in which a proliferation of chart elements—chosen because they look "nice"—confuse and distract the reader. One measure of chart junk is Tufte's data-ink ratio, which is the amount of "ink" used to display quantitative information compared to the total ink required by the chart. Tufte advocated limiting the use of nondata ink. Nondata ink is any part of the chart that does not convey information about the data. One way of measuring the data-ink ratio is to determine how much of the chart you can erase without affecting the user's ability to interpret the chart. Tufte would argue for high data-ink ratios with a minimum of extraneous elements and graphics.

To this end, Tufte helped develop sparklines, which convey information with a high data-ink ratio within a compact space. Tufte believed that charts that can be viewed and comprehended at a glance have a greater impact on the reader than large and cluttered graphs, no matter how attractive they might be.

To create a set of sparklines, you first select the data you want to graph, and then select the range where you want the sparklines to appear. Note that the cells in which you insert the sparklines do not need to be blank because the sparklines are part of the cell background and do not replace any content.

REFERENCE

Creating and Editing Sparklines

- On the Insert tab, in the Sparklines group, click the Line, Column, or Win/Loss button.
- In the Data Range box, enter the range for the data source of the sparkline.
- In the Location Range box, enter the range into which to place the sparkline.
- Click the OK button.
- On the Sparkline Tools Design tab, in the Show group, click the appropriate check boxes to specify which markers to display on the sparkline.
- In the Group group, click the Axis button, and then click Show Axis to add an axis to the sparkline.

Haywood's business plan for Backspace Gear involves rolling out the different types of packs gradually, starting with the school and travel packs, which have the most consumer interest, and then adding more pack types over the first five years. The company won't start producing all six types of packs until year 6. Haywood suggests that you add a column sparkline to the Financial Summary worksheet that indicates this production plan.

To create column sparklines that show projected production:

1. Go to the **Financial Summary** worksheet, and then select the range **C5:C10**. This is the location range into which you will insert the sparklines.

2. On the ribbon, click the **Insert** tab.

3. In the Sparklines group, click the **Column** button. The Create Sparklines dialog box opens. The location range is already entered because you selected it before opening the dialog box.

4. With the insertion point in the Data Range box, click the **Projected Production** sheet tab, and then select the data in the range **B5:K10**. This range contains the data you want to chart in the sparklines.

5. Click the **OK** button. The Create Sparklines dialog box closes, and the column sparklines are added to the location range in the Financial Summary worksheet. See Figure 4-43.

| Figure 4-43 | Column sparklines of projected production for pack type |

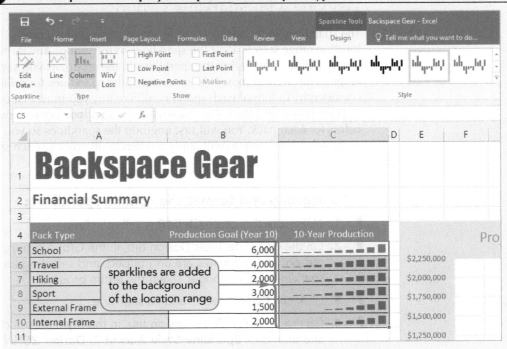

The column sparklines make it clear how the different product lines are placed into production at different times—school and travel packs first, and other models later in the production cycle. Each product, once it is introduced, is steadily produced in greater quantities as the decade progresses.

Formatting the Sparkline Axis

Because of their compact size, you have few formatting options with sparklines. One thing you can change is the scale of the vertical axis. The vertical axis will range from the minimum value to the maximum value. By default, this range is defined differently for each cell to maximize the available space. But this can be misleading. For example, the column sparklines in Figure 4-43 seem to show that Backspace Gear will be producing the same amount of each product line by the end of year 10 because the heights of the last columns are all the same. You can change the vertical axis scale to be the same for the related sparklines.

To set the scale of the column sparklines:

▶ **1.** On the Financial Summary worksheet, make sure the range **C5:C10** is still selected. Because the sparklines are selected, the Sparkline Tools contextual tab appears on the ribbon.

▶ **2.** On the Sparkline Tools Design tab, in the Group group, click the **Axis** button, and then click **Custom Value** in the Vertical Axis Maximum Value Options section. The Sparkline Vertical Axis Setting dialog box opens.

▶ **3.** Select the value in the box, and then type **6000**. You do not have to set the vertical axis minimum value because Excel assumes this to be 0 for all of the column sparklines.

▶ **4.** Click the **OK** button. The column sparklines are now based on the same vertical scale, with the height of each column indicating the number of packs produced per year.

Working with Sparkline Groups

The sparklines in the location range are part of a single group. Clicking any cell in the location range selects all of the sparklines in the group. Any formatting you apply to one sparkline affects all of the sparklines in the group, as you saw when you set the range of the vertical axis. This ensures that the sparklines for related data are formatted consistently. To format each sparkline differently, you must first ungroup them.

Haywood thinks the column sparklines would look better if they used different colors for each pack. You will first ungroup the sparklines so you can format them separately, and then you will apply a different fill color to each sparkline.

To ungroup and format the column sparklines:

▶ **1.** Make sure the range **C5:C10** is still selected.

▶ **2.** On the Sparkline Tools Design tab, in the Group group, click the **Ungroup** button. The sparklines are ungrouped, and selecting any one of the sparklines will no longer select the entire group.

▶ **3.** Click cell **C6** to select it and its sparkline.

▶ **4.** On the Sparkline Tools Design tab, in the Style group, click the **More** button, and then click **Sparkline Style Accent 2, Darker 25%** (the second style in the second row) in the Style gallery.

▶ **5.** Click cell **C7**, and then change the sparkline style to **Sparkline Style Accent 4, (no dark or light)** (the fourth style in the third row) in the Style gallery.

▶ **6.** Click cell **C8**, and then change the sparkline style to **Sparkline Style Accent 6, (no dark or light)** (the last style in the third row) in the Style gallery.

▶ **7.** Click cell **C9**, and then change the sparkline style to **Sparkline Style Dark #1** (the first style in the fifth row) in the Style gallery.

▶ **8.** Click cell **C10**, and then click **Sparkline Style Colorful #2** (the second style in the last row) in the Style gallery.

▶ **9.** Click cell **A4** to deselect the sparklines. See Figure 4-44.

Figure 4-44	Sparklines formatted with different styles

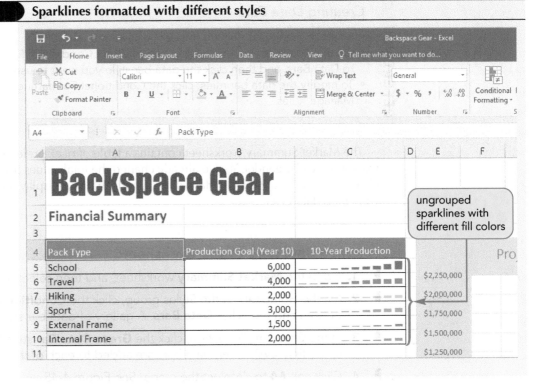

To regroup sparklines, you select all of the cells in the location range containing the sparklines and then click the Group button in the Group group on the Sparkline Tools Design tab. Be aware that regrouping sparklines causes them to share a common format, so you will lose any formatting applied to individual sparklines.

The Sparkline Color button applied a single color to the entire sparkline. You can also apply colors to individual markers within a sparkline by clicking the Marker Color button. Using this button, you can set a distinct color for negative values, maximum values, minimum values, first values, and last values. This is useful with line sparklines that track data across a time range in which you might want to identify the maximum value within that range or the minimum value.

Creating Data Bars

A data bar is a conditional format that adds a horizontal bar to the background of a cell containing a number. When applied to a range of cells, the data bars have the same appearance as a bar chart, with each cell containing one bar. The lengths of data bars are based on the value of each cell in the selected range. Cells with larger values have longer bars; cells with smaller values have shorter bars. Data bars are dynamic, changing as the cell's value changes.

Data bars differ from sparklines in that the bars are always placed in the cells containing the value they represent, and each cell represents only a single bar from the bar chart. By contrast, a column sparkline can be inserted anywhere within the workbook and can represent data from several rows or columns. However, like sparklines, data bars can be used to create compact graphs that can be easily integrated alongside the text and values stored in worksheet cells.

Creating Data Bars

- Select the range containing the data you want to chart.
- On the Home tab, in the Styles group, click the Conditional Formatting button, point to Data Bars, and then click the data bar style you want to use.
- To modify the data bar rules, click the Conditional Formatting button, and then click Manage Rules.

The Market Summary worksheet contains a table of pack preferences from the market survey by gender. You've already charted the total values from this table as a pie chart in the previous session. Haywood suggests that you display the totals for men and women as data bars.

To add data bars to the worksheet:

1. Go to the **Market Summary** worksheet, and then select the range **C5:D10**.

2. On the Home tab, in the Styles group, click the **Conditional Formatting** button, and then click **Data Bars**. A gallery of data bar styles opens.

3. In the Gradient Fill section, click the **Green Data Bar** style (the second style in the first row.) Green data bars are added to each of the selected cells.

4. Click cell **A4** to deselect the range. See Figure 4-45.

Figure 4-45   **Data bars added to the Market Summary worksheet**

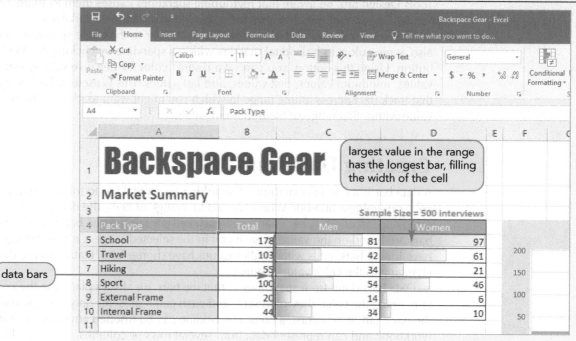

The data bars make it easy to compare the popularity of the different pack types among men and women. The bars clearly show that school packs are most popular followed by either the travel packs or the sport packs.

Modifying a Data Bar Rule

The lengths of the data bars are determined based on the values in the selected range. The cell with the largest value contains a data bar that extends across the entire width of the cell, and the lengths of the other bars in the selected range are determined relative to that bar. In some cases, this will result in the longest data bar overlapping its cell's data value, making it difficult to read. You can modify the length of the data bars by altering the rules of the conditional format.

The longest data bar is in cell D5, representing a count of 97 respondents. The length of every other data bar is proportional to this length. However, because it is the longest, it also overlaps the value of the cell. You will modify the data bar rule, setting the maximum length to 120 so that the bar no longer overlaps the cell value.

TIP

With negative values, the data bars originate from the center of the cell—negative bars extend to the left, and positive bars extend to the right.

To modify the data bar rule:

▶ **1.** Select the range **C5:D10** containing the data bars.

▶ **2.** On the Home tab, in the Styles group, click the **Conditional Formatting** button, and then click **Manage Rules**. The Conditional Formatting Rules Manager dialog box opens, displaying all the rules applied to any conditional format in the workbook.

▶ **3.** Make sure **Current Selection** appears in the Show formatting rules for box. You'll edit the rule applied to the current selection—the data bars in the Market Summary worksheet.

▶ **4.** Click the **Edit Rule** button to open the Edit Formatting Rule dialog box.

You want to modify this rule so that the maximum value for the data bar is set to 120. All data bar lengths will then be defined relative to this value.

▶ **5.** In the Type row, click the **Maximum arrow**, and then click **Number**.

▶ **6.** Press the **Tab** key to move the insertion point to the Maximum box in the Value row, and then type **120**. See Figure 4-46.

Figure 4-46   **Edit Formatting Rule dialog box**

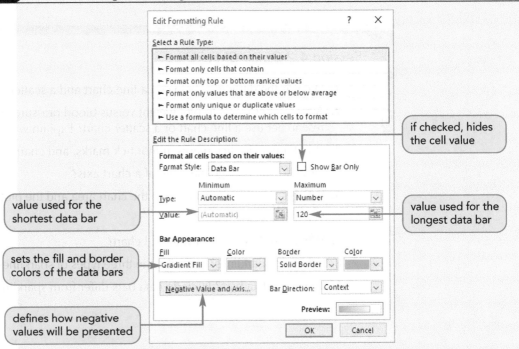

- if checked, hides the cell value
- value used for the shortest data bar
- value used for the longest data bar
- sets the fill and border colors of the data bars
- defines how negative values will be presented

▶ **7.** Click the **OK** button in each dialog box, and then select cell **A4**. The lengths of the data bars are reduced so that no cell values are obscured. See Figure 4-47.

Figure 4-47	Revised data bars

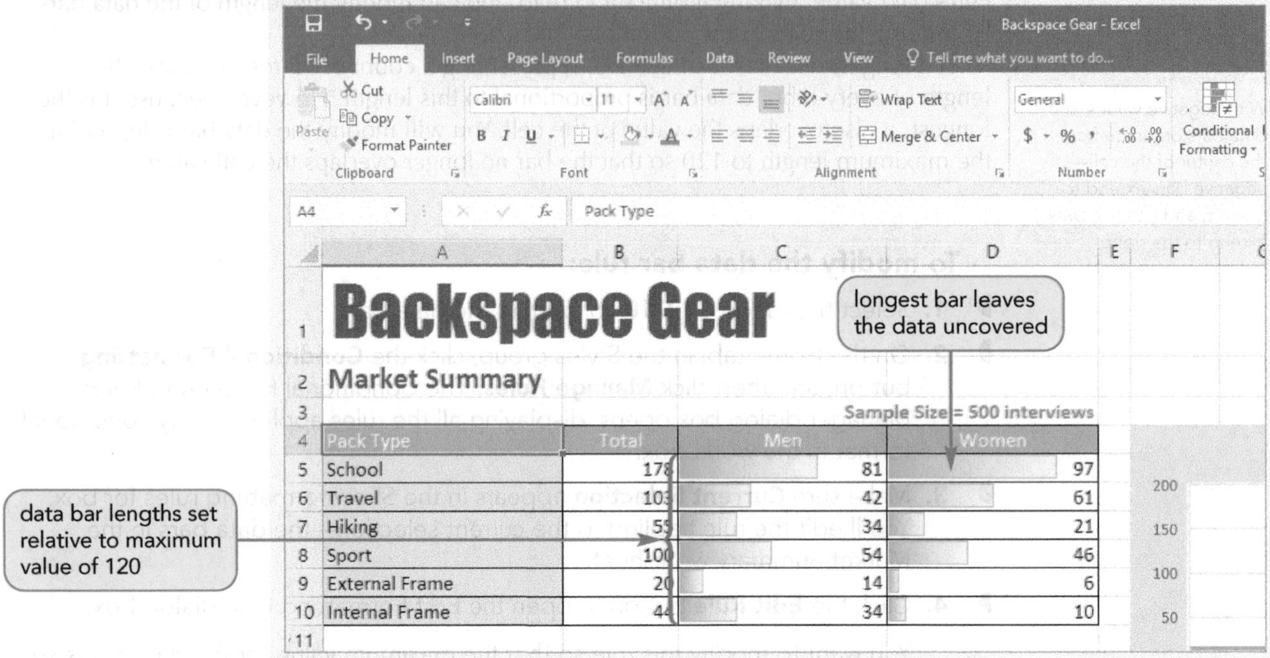

▶ **8.** Save the workbook.

You have finished your work on the Backspace Gear workbook. Haywood is pleased with the charts you created and feels that they provide useful visuals for anyone considering his business proposal.

Session 4.2 Quick Check

REVIEW

1. What is the difference between a line chart and a scatter chart?

2. A researcher wants to plot weight versus blood pressure. Should the researcher use a line chart or a scatter chart? Explain why.

3. What are major tick marks, minor tick marks, and chart gridlines?

4. How do you change the scale of a chart axis?

5. What is the difference between the chart area and the plot area?

6. What is a histogram?

7. When would you use a waterfall chart?

8. What are sparklines? Describe the three types of sparklines.

9. What are data bars? How do data bars differ from sparklines?

Review Assignments

PRACTICE

Data File needed for the Review Assignments: Market.xlsx

Haywood is creating another workbook that will have market survey data on competing manufacturers as well as more demographic data on potential Backspace Gear customers. He wants you to add charts to his workbook that show this data graphically. Complete the following:

1. Open the **Market** workbook located in the Excel4 > Review folder included with your Data Files, and then save the workbook as **Market Analysis** in the location specified by your instructor.

2. In the Documentation worksheet, enter your name in cell B3 and the date in cell B4.

3. In the Business Loan worksheet, enter the data values and formulas required to calculate the monthly payment on a business loan of **$225,000** at **6.2%** annual interest to be repaid in **15 years**. Calculate both the monthly payment and the size of the annual payment.

4. In the Market Analysis worksheet, use the data in the range A4:B9 to create a pie chart in the range A11:C24 that shows information about competitors in the Northwest region.

5. Apply the Style 11 chart style to the pie chart, and then move the legend to the left side of the chart. Place the data labels on the inside end of each pie slice.

6. In the Market Tables worksheet, create a clustered column chart of the data in the range A5:F10 to show how many units each competitor sold in the Northwest region in the past five years.

7. Move the chart to the Market Analysis worksheet, and then resize it to cover the range E4:L13. Change the chart title to **Units Sold**. Apply the Style 9 chart style to the chart. Add both primary major horizontal and vertical gridlines. Change the fill color of the chart area to the Gold Accent 4, Lighter 80% theme color and the fill color of the plot area to white. Move the legend to the right side of the chart area.

8. In the Market Tables worksheet, use the data in the range A5:F10 to create a stacked column chart. Move the chart to the Market Analysis worksheet, and then resize it to cover the range E15:L24.

9. Change the chart title to **Total Units Sold**. Format the chart with the same fill colors and gridlines you used the clustered column chart. Move the legend to the right side of the chart.

10. In the Market Tables worksheet, select the nonadjacent range A5:F5,A11:F11,A29:F29, and then create a combination chart with Total Units as a clustered column chart and Total Revenue as a line chart displayed on the secondary axis.

11. Move the chart to the Market Analysis worksheet, and then resize it to cover the range E26:L40. Change the chart title to **Units Sold and Revenue**. Format the chart with the same fill colors and gridlines you used the clustered column chart. Remove the chart legend.

12. Add axis titles to the primary and secondary vertical axes with the title **Total Units** on the primary axis and **Total Revenue** on the secondary axis. Rotate the secondary axis text down. Change the color of the scales and axis titles for the primary and secondary axes to match the color of the clustered column chart and the line chart.

13. Change the scale of the Total Revenue axis to go from $3,500,000 to $5,000,000 in intervals of $250,000.

14. In the Market Tables worksheet, select the range A23:A28,F23:F28 containing the final year revenue for each brand, and then create a Pareto chart based on this data. Move the chart to the Market Analysis worksheet, and then resize it to cover the range A26:C40.

15. Change the chart title to **Market Revenue (2017)**. Format the chart with the same fill colors and gridlines you used the clustered column chart.

16. In the Survey Data worksheet, create a histogram of the distribution of customer ages in the range E7:E506. Change the chart title to **Age Distribution**. Resize the chart to cover the range G4:P22 in the Survey Data worksheet.

17. Change the width of the histogram bins to **5** units.

18. In the Market Analysis worksheet, add gradient fill orange data bars to the values in the range B5:B9. Set the maximum value of the data bars to **0.6**.

19. In the range C5:C9, insert line sparklines based on the data in the range B15:F19 of the Market Tables worksheet to show how the competitors' share of the market has changed over the past five years.

20. Save the workbook, and then close it.

Case Problem 1

APPLY

Data File needed for this Case Problem: Stefanek.xlsx

Stefanek Budget   Edmund and Lydia Stefanek of Little Rock, Arkansas, are using Excel to track their family budget to determine whether they can afford the monthly loan payments that would come with the purchase of a new house. The couple is considering a $285,000 mortgage at a 4.30 percent interest rate to be paid back over 25 years. They want to know the impact that this mortgage will have on their budget. Complete the following:

1. Open the **Stefanek** workbook located in the Excel4 > Case1 folder included with your Data Files, and then save the workbook as **Stefanek Budget** in the location specified by your instructor.

2. In the Documentation worksheet, enter your name in cell B3 and the date in cell B4.

3. In the Budget worksheet, in the range B3:B8, enter the parameters for a **$285,000** mortgage at **4.3%** annual interest paid back over **25 years**. Calculate the interest rate per month and the total number of payments.

4. In cell B10, calculate the amount of the monthly payment needed to pay back the mortgage.

5. In the range C15:N15, calculate the total income from Edmund and Lydia's monthly salaries.

6. In the range C22:N22, use an absolute reference to insert the monthly mortgage payment you calculated in cell B10.

7. In the range C24:N24, calculate Edmund and Lydia's total expenses per month.

8. In the range C25:N25, calculate the couple's monthly net income by adding their income and their expenses. (Note that expenses are entered as negative values.)

9. In the range C28:C40, calculate the averages for the income and expenses from the 12-month budget.

10. In the range C28:C40, add data bars to the values. Note that negative data bars are displayed to the left of the center point in the cell, whereas positive data bars are displayed to the right.

11. In the range D28:D40, insert line sparklines using the values from the range C13:N25 to show how the different budget entries change throughout the year.

12. Create a pie chart of the income values in the range B28:C29 to show the breakdown of the family income between Edmund and Lydia. Resize the chart to cover the range E27:I40. Change the chart title to **Income** and apply the Style3 chart style to chart.

13. Create a pie chart of the expenses values in the range B31:C38. Resize the chart to cover the range J27:N40. Change the chart title to **Expenses** and apply the Style3 chart style to the chart. Change the position of the data labels to data callouts. If any data labels appear to overlap, select one of the overlapping data labels, and drag it to another position.

14. Save the workbook, and then close it.

Case Problem 2

Data File needed for this Case Problem: Circuit.xlsx

Circuit Realty   Alice Cho works at Circuit Realty in Tempe, Arizona. She wants to use Excel to summarize the home listings in the Tempe area. Alice has already inserted some of the new listings into an Excel workbook including descriptive statistics about the homes and their prices. She wants your help in summarizing this data using informative charts. Complete the following:

1. Open the **Circuit** workbook located in the Excel4 > Case2 folder included with your Data Files, and then save the workbook as **Circuit Realty** in the location specified by your instructor.

2. In the Documentation worksheet, enter your name in cell B3 and the date in cell B4.

3. In the Housing Tables worksheet, using the data in the range A4:B8, create a 2-D pie chart of the number of listings by region. Move the pie chart to the Summary worksheet in the range A4:E15. Change the chart title to **Listings by Region**. Add data labels showing the percentage of listings in each region, displaying the data labels outside the pie slices.

4. In the Housing Tables worksheet, using the range A10:B14, create a pie chart of the listings by the number of bedrooms. Move the pie chart to the Summary worksheet in the range A17:E28. Change the chart title to **Listings by Bedrooms**. Add data labels showing the percentage of listings in each category outside the pie slices.

5. In the Housing Tables worksheet, using the range A16:B22, create a pie chart of the listings by the number of bathrooms. Move the pie chart to the Summary worksheet in the range A30:E341. Change the chart title to **Listings by Bathrooms** and format the pie chart to match the two other pie charts.

6. In the Housing Tables worksheet, using the data in the range D4:E8, create a column chart showing the average home price in four Tempe regions. Move the chart to the Summary worksheet in the range G4:L15. Change the chart title to **Average Price by Region**.

7. In the Housing Tables worksheet, using the data in the range D10:E15, create a column chart of the average home price by age of the home. Move the chart to the Summary worksheet in the range G17:L28. Change the chart title to **Average Price by Home Age**.

8. In the Housing Tables worksheet, using the data in the range D17:E24, create a column chart of the average home price by house size. Move the chart to the Summary worksheet in the range G30:L41. Change the chart title to **Average Price by Home Size**.

9. In the Listings worksheet, create a histogram of all of the home prices in the range H4:H185. Move the histogram to the Summary worksheet in the range N4:U17. Change the chart title to **Home Prices**. Set the scale of the vertical axis to go from **0** to **50**. Set the number of bins to **6**. Set the overflow bin value to **350,000** and the underflow bin value to **150,000**.

10. Create a histogram of the distribution of home prices in each of the four regions, as follows:

    a. Use the data from the range H52:H107 in the Listings worksheet to create the North Region histogram. Place the chart in the range N18:U28 of the Summary worksheet. Change the chart title to **North Region**.

    b. Use the data from the range H5:H51 in the Listings worksheet to create the East Region histogram. Place the chart in the range N29:U39 of the Summary worksheet. Change the chart title to **East Region**.

    c. Use the data from the range H108:H143 in the Listings worksheet to create the South Region histogram. Place the chart in the range N40:U50 of the Summary worksheet. Change the chart title to **South Region**.

    d. Use the data from the range H144:H185 in the Listings worksheet to create the West Region histogram. Place the chart in the range N51:U61 of the Summary worksheet. Change the chart title to **West Region**.

11. The four regional histograms should use a common scale. For each histogram, set the scale of the vertical axis from **0** to **20**, set the number of bins to **6**, set the overflow bin value to **350,000**, and the underflow bin value to **150,000**.

12. In the Price History worksheet, use the data in the range A4:C152 to create a combination chart. Display the Average Price as a line chart on the primary axis and display the Foreclosure values as a column chart on the secondary axis. Move the chart to the Summary worksheet in the range A43:L61. Change the chart title to **Average Home Price and Foreclosure Rates**.

13. Add axis titles to the combination chart, naming the left axis **Average Home Price** and the right axis **Foreclosure (per 10,000)**. Change the horizontal axis title to **Date**. Change the minimum value on the left axis to **100,000**.

14. Change the color of the primary axis and axis title to match the color of the line in the line chart. Change the color of the secondary axis and axis title to match the color used in the column chart. Remove the chart legend.

15. Save the workbook, and then close it.

Case Problem 3

CHALLENGE

Data File needed for this Case Problem: Skyway.xlsx

Skyway Funds   Kristin Morandi is an accounts assistant at Skyway Funds, a financial consulting firm in Monroe, Louisiana. Kristin needs to summarize information on companies that are held in stock by the firm's clients. You will help her develop a workbook that will serve as a prototype for future reports. She wants the workbook to include charts of the company's financial condition, structure, and recent stock performance. Stock market charts should display the stock's daily opening; high, low, and closing values; and the number of shares traded for each day of the past few weeks. The volume of shares traded should be expressed in terms of millions of shares. Complete the following:

1. Open the **Skyway** workbook located in the Excel4 > Case3 folder included with your Data Files, and then save the workbook as **Skyway Funds** in the location specified by your instructor.

2. In the Documentation worksheet, enter your name in cell B3 and the date in cell B4.

3. In the Overview worksheet, add green data bars with a gradient fill to the employee numbers in the range B15:B19. Set the maximum value of the data bars to **20,000**.

4. Add a pie chart of the shareholder data in the range A22:B24. Resize and position the chart to cover the range A26:B37. Do not display a chart title. Add data labels to the pie chart, and then move the legend to the left edge of the chart area.

5. In the Income Statement worksheet, create a 3-D column chart of the income and expenses data from the last three years in the range A4:D4,A7:D7,A13:D13,A20:D20.

6. Move the chart to the range D6:I20 of the Overview worksheet. Change the chart title to **Income and Expenses (Thousands of Dollars)**. Remove the chart legend.

⊕ **Explore** 7. Double-click the horizontal axis values to open the Format Axis pane. Expand the Axis Options list, and click the Categories in reverse order check box in the Axis position section to display the year value in reverse order so that 2015 is listed first.

⊕ **Explore** 8. Add the data table chart element with legend keys showing the actual figures used in the column chart. (*Hint*: Use the Chart Elements button to add the data table to the chart, and use the data table submenu to show the legend keys.)

9. In the Balance Sheet worksheet, create a 3-D stacked column chart of the data in the range A4:D4,A7:D11 to show the company's assets over the past three years. Move the chart to the Overview worksheet covering the range D21:I37. Change the chart title to **Assets (Thousands of Dollars)**. Remove the chart legend.

⊕ **Explore** 10. Use the Switch Row/Column button in the Data group on the Chart Tools Design tab to switch the categories used in the chart from the asset categories to the year values. Display the values on the horizontal axis in reverse order, and add a data table chart element with legend keys to the chart.

11. Repeat Steps 9 and 10 to create a stacked column chart of the company's liabilities in the range A4:D4,A15:D18 in the Balance Sheet worksheet. Place the chart in the range J21:P37 of the Overview worksheet. Change the chart title to **Liabilities (Thousands of Dollars).**

12. Create a line chart of the company's net cash flow using the data in the range A4:D4,A26:D26 of the Cash Flow worksheet. Place the chart in the range J6:P20 of the Overview worksheet. Display the values in the horizontal axis in reverse order. Change the chart title to **Net Cash Flow (Thousands of Dollars).**

✦ **Explore** 13. In the Stock History worksheet, select the data in the range A4:F9, and then insert a Volume-Open-High-Low-Close chart that shows the stock's volume of shares traded, opening value, high value, low value, and closing value for the previous five days on the market. Move the chart to the Overview worksheet in the range A39:D54.

14. Change the chart title to **5-Day Stock Chart**. Remove the chart gridlines and the chart legend. Change the scale of the left vertical axis to go from **0** to **8**.

15. In the Stock History worksheet, create another Volume-Open-High-Low-Close chart for the 1-year stock values located in the range A4:F262. Move the chart to the Overview worksheet in the range E39:J54. Change the chart title to **1-Year Stock Chart**. Remove the chart legend and gridlines.

16. Create a stock chart for all of the stock market data in the range A4:F2242 of the Stock History worksheet. Move the chart to the range K39:P54 of the Overview worksheet. Change the chart title to **All Years Stock Chart** and remove the chart legend and gridlines.

17. Save the workbook, and then close it.

Case Problem 4

Data File needed for this Case Problem: Datasports.xlsx

Datasports   Diane Wilkes runs the Datasports website for sports fans who are interested in the statistics and data that underlie sports. She is developing a series of workbooks in which she can enter statistics and charts for recent sporting events. She wants your help designing the charts and graphics that will appear in the workbook for college basketball games. She has already created a sample workbook containing the results of a hypothetical game between the University of Maryland and the University of Minnesota. She wants you to design and create the charts. For each chart, you need to:

- Include a descriptive chart title.
- Add horizontal and vertical gridlines.
- Add and remove chart elements to effectively illustrate the data.
- Change the colors and format of chart elements to create an attractive chart.
- Insert chart data labels as needed to explain the data.
- Resize and position charts to create an attractive and effective workbook.

Complete the following:

1. Open the **Datasports** workbook located in the Excel4 > Case4 folder included with your Data Files, and then save the workbook as **Datasports Report** in the location specified by your instructor.

2. In the Documentation worksheet, enter your name in cell B3 and the date in cell B4.

3. Create two column charts, as follows, and place them in the Game Report worksheet:

   a. Use the data in the range A6:A19,I6:I19 of the Box Score worksheet to chart the points scores by the University of Maryland players.

   b. Use the data in the range A23:A32,I23:I32 of the Box Score worksheet to chart the points score by the Minnesota players.

4. Add a line chart to the Game Report worksheet tracking the changing score of the game from its beginning to its end. Use the data in the range B5:D47 of the Game Log worksheet as the chart's data source.

5. Add eight pie charts to the Game Report worksheet in comparing the Maryland and Minnesota results for points, field goal percentage, free throw percentage, 3-point field goals, assists, rebounds, turnovers, and blocked shots. Use the data in the Box Score worksheet as the data source for these pie charts.

6. In the Game Log worksheet, in the range E6:E47, calculate the value of the Minnesota score minus the value of the Maryland score.

7. Add data bars to the values in the range E6:E47 showing the score difference as the game progresses. The format of the data bars is up to you.

8. In the Season Record worksheet, in the ranges C6:C19 and G6:G19, enter –1 for every game that the team lost and 1 for every game that the team won.

9. In the Game Report worksheet, create two sparklines, as follows:

   a. In cell D6, insert a Win/Loss sparkline using the values from the range C6:C19 of the Season Record worksheet to show a graphic of Maryland's conference wins and losses.

   b. In cell D7, insert a Win/Loss sparkline using the values from the range G6:G19 of the Season Record worksheet to show a graphic of Minnesota's wins and losses.

10. Save the workbook, and then close it.

Creating a Database

Tracking Animal, Visit, and Billing Data

OBJECTIVES

Session 1.1
- Learn basic database concepts and terms
- Start and exit Access
- Explore the Microsoft Access window and Backstage view
- Create a blank database
- Create and save a table in Datasheet view
- Enter field names and records in a table datasheet
- Open a table using the Navigation Pane

Session 1.2
- Open an Access database
- Copy and paste records from another Access database
- Navigate a table datasheet
- Create and navigate a simple query
- Create and navigate a simple form
- Create, preview, navigate, and print a simple report
- Use Help in Access
- Learn how to compact, back up, and restore a database

Case | *Riverview Veterinary Care Center*

Riverview Veterinary Care Center, a veterinary care center in Cody, Wyoming, provides care for pets and livestock in the greater Cody area. In addition to caring for household pets, such as dogs and cats, the center specializes in serving the needs of livestock on ranches in the surrounding area. Kimberly Johnson, the office manager for Riverview Veterinary Care Center, oversees a small staff and is responsible for maintaining the medical records for all of the animals the care center serves.

In order to best manage the center, Kimberly and her staff rely on electronic medical records for information on the animals and their owners, billing, inventory control, purchasing, and accounts payable. Several months ago, the center upgraded to **Microsoft Access 2016** (or simply **Access**), a computer program used to enter, maintain, and retrieve related data in a format known as a database. Kimberly and her staff want to use Access to store information about the animals, their owners, billing, vendors, and products. She asks for your help in creating the necessary Access database.

STARTING DATA FILES

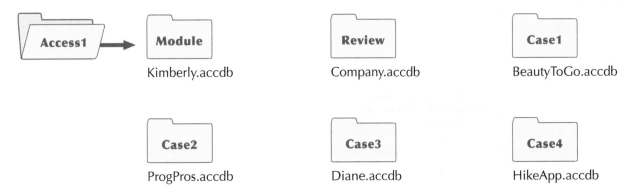

Access1 → Module	Review	Case1
Kimberly.accdb	Company.accdb	BeautyToGo.accdb

Case2	Case3	Case4
ProgPros.accdb	Diane.accdb	HikeApp.accdb

Session 1.1 Visual Overview:

The Quick Access Toolbar provides one-click access to commonly used commands, such as Save.

The Fields tab provides options for adding, removing, and formatting the fields in a table.

The Shutter Bar Open/Close Button allows you to close and open the Navigation Pane; you might want to close the pane so that you have more room on the screen to view the object's contents.

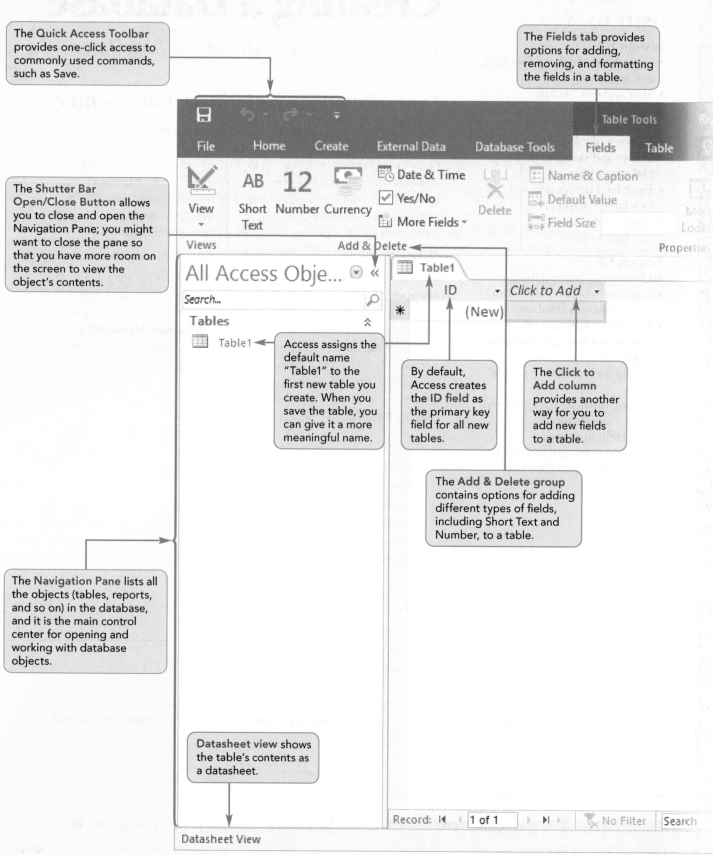

Access assigns the default name "Table1" to the first new table you create. When you save the table, you can give it a more meaningful name.

By default, Access creates the ID field as the primary key field for all new tables.

The Click to Add column provides another way for you to add new fields to a table.

The Add & Delete group contains options for adding different types of fields, including Short Text and Number, to a table.

The Navigation Pane lists all the objects (tables, reports, and so on) in the database, and it is the main control center for opening and working with database objects.

Datasheet view shows the table's contents as a datasheet.

The Access Window

The Access window is the program window that appears when you create a new database or open an existing database.

You use the window buttons to minimize, maximize, and close the Access window.

If you are signed in to your Office account, your name appears here. If you are not signed in, the Sign in link will appear here, and you can click it to sign into your Office account.

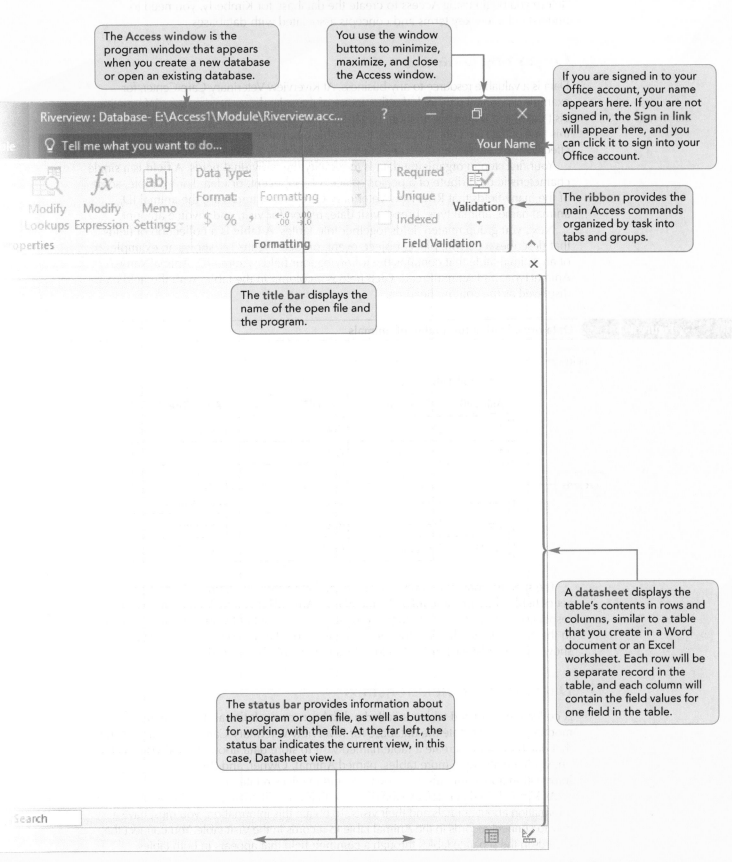

Riverview : Database- E:\Access1\Module\Riverview.acc...   ?   —   ☐   ✕

Tell me what you want to do...   Your Name

Data Type:
Modify   Modify   Memo   Format: Formatting
Lookups Expression Settings $ % ,   ←.0 .00   Validation
operties   Formatting

☐ Required
☐ Unique
☐ Indexed
Field Validation

The ribbon provides the main Access commands organized by task into tabs and groups.

The title bar displays the name of the open file and the program.

A datasheet displays the table's contents in rows and columns, similar to a table that you create in a Word document or an Excel worksheet. Each row will be a separate record in the table, and each column will contain the field values for one field in the table.

The status bar provides information about the program or open file, as well as buttons for working with the file. At the far left, the status bar indicates the current view, in this case, Datasheet view.

Search

Introduction to Database Concepts

Before you begin using Access to create the database for Kimberly, you need to understand a few key terms and concepts associated with databases.

Organizing Data

Data is a valuable resource to any business. At Riverview Veterinary Care Center, for example, important data includes the names of the animals, owners' contact information, visit dates, and billing information. Organizing, storing, maintaining, retrieving, and sorting this type of data are critical activities that enable a business to find and use information effectively. Before storing data on a computer, however, you must organize the data.

Your first step in organizing data is to identify the individual fields. A **field** is a single characteristic or attribute of a person, place, object, event, or idea. For example, some of the many fields that Riverview Veterinary Care Center tracks are the animal ID, animal name, animal type, breed, visit date, reason for visit, and invoice amount.

Next, you group related fields together into tables. A **table** is a collection of fields that describes a person, place, object, event, or idea. Figure 1-1 shows an example of an Animal table that contains the following four fields: AnimalID, AnimalName, AnimalType, and AnimalBreed. Each field is a column in the table, with the field name displayed as the column heading.

Figure 1-1	Data organization for a table of animals

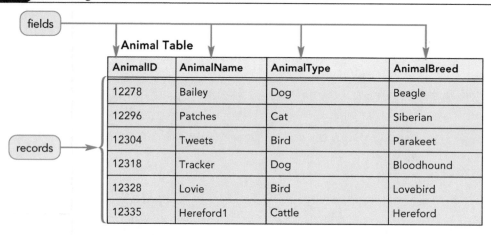

The specific content of a field is called the **field value**. In Figure 1-1, the first set of field values for AnimalID, AnimalName, AnimalType, and AnimalBreed are, respectively: 12278; Bailey; Dog; and Beagle. This set of field values is called a **record**. In the Animal table, the data for each animal is stored as a separate record. Figure 1-1 shows six records; each row of field values in the table is a record.

Databases and Relationships

A collection of related tables is called a **database**, or a **relational database**. In this module, you will create the database for Riverview Veterinary Care Center, and within that database, you'll create a table named Visit to store data about animal visits. Later on, you'll create three more tables, named Animal, Owner, and Billing, to store related information about animals, their owners, and invoices related to their care.

As Kimberly and her staff use the database that you will create, they will need to access information about animals and their visits. To obtain this information, you must have a way to connect records in the Animal table to records in the Visit table. You connect the records in the separate tables through a **common field** that appears in both tables.

In the sample database shown in Figure 1-2, each record in the Animal table has a field named AnimalID, which is also a field in the Visit table. For example, the beagle named Bailey is the first animal in the Animal table and has an AnimalID field value of 12278. This same AnimalID field value, 12278, appears in two records in the Visit table. Therefore, the beagle named Bailey is the animal that was seen at these two visits.

| Figure 1-2 | Database relationship between tables for animals and visits |

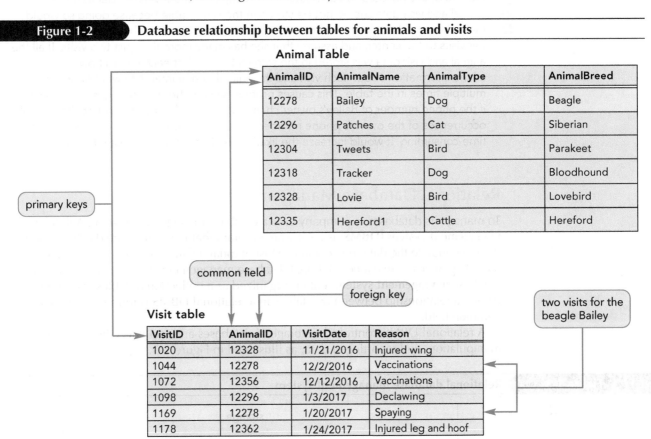

Each AnimalID value in the Animal table must be unique so that you can distinguish one animal from another. These unique AnimalID values also identify each animal's specific visits in the Visit table. The AnimalID field is referred to as the primary key of the Animal table. A **primary key** is a field, or a collection of fields, whose values uniquely identify each record in a table. No two records can contain the same value for the primary key field. In the Visit table, the VisitID field is the primary key because Riverview Veterinary Care Center assigns each visit a unique identification number.

When you include the primary key from one table as a field in a second table to form a relationship between the two tables, it is called a **foreign key** in the second table, as shown in Figure 1-2. For example, AnimalID is the primary key in the Animal table and a foreign key in the Visit table. The AnimalID field must have the same characteristics in both tables. Although the primary key AnimalID contains unique values in the Animal table, the same field as a foreign key in the Visit table does not necessarily contain unique values. The AnimalID value 12278, for example, appears two times in the Visit table because the beagle named Bailey made two visits to the center. Each foreign key value, however, must match one of the field values for the primary key in the other table. In the example shown in Figure 1-2, each AnimalID value in the Visit table must match an AnimalID value in the Animal table. The two tables are related, enabling users to connect the facts about animals with the facts about their visits to the center.

Storing Data in Separate Tables

When you create a database, you must create separate tables that contain only fields that are directly related to each other. For example, in the Riverview database, the animal and visit data should not be stored in the same table because doing so would make the data difficult to update and prone to errors. Consider the beagle Bailey and her visits to the center, and assume that she has many more than just two visits. If all the animal and visit data was stored in the same table, so that each record (row) contained all the information about each visit and the animal, the animal data would appear multiple times in the table. This causes problems when the data changes. For example, if the phone number of Bailey's owner changed, you would have to update the multiple occurrences of the owner's phone number throughout the table. Not only would this be time-consuming, it would increase the likelihood of errors or inconsistent data.

Relational Database Management Systems

To manage its databases, a company uses a database management system. A **database management system (DBMS)** is a software program that lets you create databases and then manipulate the data they contain. Most of today's database management systems, including Access, are called relational database management systems. In a **relational database management system**, data is organized as a collection of tables. As stated earlier, a relationship between two tables in a relational DBMS is formed through a common field.

A relational DBMS controls the storage of databases and facilitates the creation, manipulation, and reporting of data, as illustrated in Figure 1-3.

| Figure 1-3 | Relational database management system |

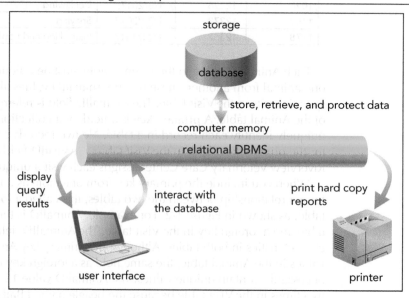

Specifically, a relational DBMS provides the following functions:

- It allows you to create database structures containing fields, tables, and table relationships.
- It lets you easily add new records, change field values in existing records, and delete records.
- It contains a built-in query language, which lets you obtain immediate answers to the questions (or queries) you ask about your data.
- It contains a built-in report generator, which lets you produce professional-looking, formatted reports from your data.
- It protects databases through security, control, and recovery facilities.

An organization such as Riverview Veterinary Care Center benefits from a relational DBMS because it allows users working in different groups to share the same data. More than one user can enter data into a database, and more than one user can retrieve and analyze data that other users have entered. For example, the database for Riverview Veterinary Care Center will contain only one copy of the Visit table, and all employees will use it to access visit information.

Finally, unlike other software programs, such as spreadsheet programs, a DBMS can handle massive amounts of data and can be used to create relationships among multiple tables. Each Access database, for example, can be up to two gigabytes in size, can contain up to 32,768 objects (tables, reports, and so on), and can have up to 255 people using the database at the same time. For instructional purposes, the databases you will create and work with throughout this text contain a relatively small number of records compared to databases you would encounter outside the classroom, which would likely contain tables with very large numbers of records.

Starting Access and Creating a Database

Now that you've learned some database terms and concepts, you're ready to start Access and create the Riverview database for Kimberly.

To start Access:

▶ **1.** On the Windows taskbar, click the **Start** button ⊞. The Start menu opens.

▶ **2.** Click **All apps** on the Start menu, and then click **Access 2016**. Access starts and displays the Recent screen in Backstage view. See Figure 1-4.

Figure 1-4 **Recent screen in Backstage view**

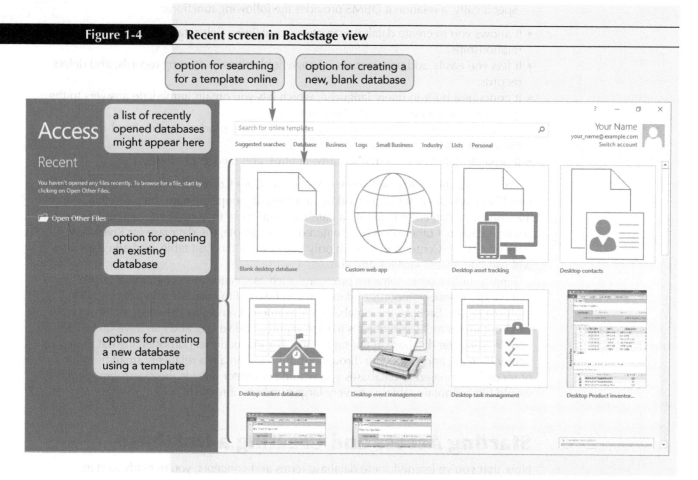

When you start Access, the first screen that appears is Backstage view, which is the starting place for your work in Access. **Backstage view** contains commands that allow you to manage Access files and options. The Recent screen in Backstage view provides options for you to create a new database or open an existing database. To create a new database that does not contain any data or objects, you use the Blank desktop database option. If the database you need to create contains objects that match those found in common databases, such as databases that store data about contacts or tasks, you can use one of the templates provided with Access. A **template** is a predesigned database that includes professionally designed tables, reports, and other database objects that can make it quick and easy for you to create a database. You can also search for a template online using the Search for online templates box.

In this case, the templates provided do not match Kimberly's needs for the center's database, so you need to create a new, blank database from scratch.

To create the new Riverview database:

1. Make sure you have the Access starting Data Files on your computer.

   Trouble? If you don't have the starting Data Files, you need to get them before you can proceed. Your instructor will either give you the Data Files or ask you to obtain them from a specified location (such as a network drive). If you have any questions about the Data Files, see your instructor or technical support person for assistance.

2. On the Recent screen, click **Blank desktop database** (see Figure 1-4). The Blank desktop database screen opens.

Be sure to type **Riverview** or you'll create a database named Database1.

3. In the File Name box, type **Riverview** to replace the selected database name provided by Access, Database1. Next you need to specify the location for the file.

4. Click the **Browse** button [icon] to the right of the File Name box. The File New Database dialog box opens.

5. Navigate to the drive and folder where you are storing your files, as specified by your instructor.

6. Make sure the Save as type box displays "Microsoft Access 2007–2016 Databases."

Trouble? If your computer is set up to show filename extensions, you will see the Access filename extension ".accdb" in the File name box.

TIP

If you don't type the filename extension, Access adds it automatically.

7. Click the **OK** button. You return to the Blank desktop database screen, and the File Name box now shows the name Riverview.accdb. The filename extension ".accdb" identifies the file as an Access 2007–2016 database.

8. Click the **Create** button. Access creates the new database, saves it to the specified location, and then opens an empty table named Table1.

Trouble? If you see only ribbon tab names and no buttons, click the Home tab to expand the ribbon, and then in the bottom-right corner of the ribbon, click the Pin the ribbon button [icon].

Refer back to the Session 1.1 Visual Overview and spend some time becoming familiar with the components of the Access window.

INSIGHT

Understanding the Database File Type

Access 2016 uses the .accdb file extension, which is the same file extension used for databases created with Microsoft Access 2007, 2010, and 2013. To ensure compatibility between these earlier versions and the Access 2016 software, new databases created using Access 2016 have the same file extension and file format as Access 2007, Access 2010, and Access 2013 databases. This is why the File New Database dialog box provides the Microsoft Access 2007–2016 Databases option in the Save as type box. In addition, the notation "(Access 2007–2016 file format)" appears in the title bar next to the name of an open database in Access 2016, confirming that database files with the .accdb extension can be used in Access 2007, Access 2010, Access 2013, and Access 2016.

Working in Touch Mode

TIP

On a touch device, you *tap* instead of *click*.

If you are working on a touch device, such as a tablet, you can switch to Touch Mode in Access to make it easier for you to tap buttons on the ribbon and perform other touch actions. Your screens will not match those shown in the book exactly, but this will not cause any problems.

Note: The following steps assume that you are using a mouse. If you are instead using a touch device, please read these steps but don't complete them, so that you remain working in Touch Mode.

To switch to Touch Mode:

1. On the Quick Access Toolbar, click the **Customize Quick Access Toolbar** button. A menu opens listing buttons you can add to the Quick Access Toolbar as well as other options for customizing the toolbar.

Trouble? If the Touch/Mouse Mode command on the menu has a checkmark next to it, press the Esc key to close the menu, and then skip to Step 3.

2. Click **Touch/Mouse Mode**. The Quick Access Toolbar now contains the Touch/Mouse Mode button, which you can use to switch between Mouse Mode, the default display, and Touch Mode.

3. On the Quick Access Toolbar, click the **Touch/Mouse Mode** button. A menu opens with two commands: Mouse, which shows the ribbon in the standard display and is optimized for use with the mouse; and Touch, which provides more space between the buttons and commands on the ribbon and is optimized for use with touch devices. The icon next to Mouse is shaded red to indicate that it is selected.

Trouble? If the icon next to Touch is shaded red, press the Esc key to close the menu and skip to Step 5.

4. Click **Touch**. The display switches to Touch Mode with more space between the commands and buttons on the ribbon. See Figure 1-5.

| Figure 1-5 | Ribbon displayed in Touch Mode |

The figures in this text show the standard Mouse Mode display, and the instructions assume you are using a mouse to click and select options, so you'll switch back to Mouse Mode.

Trouble? If you are using a touch device and want to remain in Touch Mode, skip Steps 5 and 6.

5. On the Quick Access Toolbar, click the **Touch/Mouse Mode** button, and then click **Mouse**. The ribbon returns to the standard display, as shown in the Session 1.1 Visual Overview.

6. On the Quick Access Toolbar, click the **Customize Quick Access Toolbar** button, and then click **Touch/Mouse Mode** to deselect it. The Touch/Mouse Mode button is removed from the Quick Access Toolbar.

Creating a Table in Datasheet View

Tables contain all the data in a database and are the fundamental objects for your work in Access. There are different ways to create a table in Access, including entering the fields and records for the table directly in Datasheet view.

Creating a Table in Datasheet View

- On the ribbon, click the Create tab.
- In the Tables group, click the Table button.
- Rename the default ID primary key field and change its data type, if necessary; or accept the default ID field with the AutoNumber data type.
- In the Add & Delete group on the Fields tab, click the button for the type of field you want to add to the table (for example, click the Short Text button), and then type the field name; or, in the table datasheet, click the Click to Add column heading, click the type of field you want to add from the list that opens, and then press the Tab or Enter key to move to the next column in the datasheet. Repeat this step to add all the necessary fields to the table.
- In the first row below the field names, enter the value for each field in the first record, pressing the Tab or Enter key to move from one field to the next.
- After entering the value for the last field in the first record, press the Tab or Enter key to move to the next row, and then enter the values for the next record. Continue this process until you have entered all the records for the table.
- On the Quick Access Toolbar, click the Save button, enter a name for the table, and then click the OK button.

For Riverview Veterinary Care Center, Kimberly needs to track information about each animal visit at the center. She asks you to create the Visit table according to the plan shown in Figure 1-6.

Figure 1-6   Plan for the Visit table

Field	Purpose
VisitID	Unique number assigned to each visit; will serve as the table's primary key
AnimalID	Unique number assigned to each animal; common field that will be a foreign key to connect to the Animal table
VisitDate	Date on which the animal visited the center or was seen offsite
Reason	Reason/diagnosis for the animal visit
OffSite	Whether the animal visit was offsite at a home or ranch

As shown in Kimberly's plan, she wants to store data about visits in five fields, including fields to contain the date of each visit, the reason for the visit, and if the visit was offsite. These are the most important aspects of a visit and, therefore, must be tracked. Also, notice that the VisitID field will be the primary key for the table; each visit at Riverview Veterinary Care Center has a unique number assigned to it, so this field is the logical choice for the primary key. Finally, the AnimalID field is needed in the Visit table as a foreign key to connect the information about visits to animals. The data about animals, as well as the data about their owners, and the bills for the animals' care, will be stored in separate tables, which you will create later.

Notice the name of each field in Figure 1-6. You need to name each field, table, and object in an Access database.

PROSKILLS

Decision Making: Naming Fields in Access Tables

One of the most important tasks in creating a table is deciding what names to specify for the table's fields. Keep the following guidelines in mind when you assign field names:

- A field name can consist of up to 64 characters, including letters, numbers, spaces, and special characters, except for the period (.), exclamation mark (!), grave accent ('), and square brackets ([ ]).
- A field name cannot begin with a space.
- Capitalize the first letter of each word in a field name that combines multiple words, for example VisitDate.
- Use concise field names that are easy to remember and reference and that won't take up a lot of space in the table datasheet.
- Use standard abbreviations, such as Num for Number, Amt for Amount, and Qty for Quantity, and use them consistently throughout the database. For example, if you use Num for Number in one field name, do not use the number sign (#) for Number in another.
- Give fields descriptive names so that you can easily identify them when you view or edit records.
- Although Access supports the use of spaces in field names (and in other object names), experienced database developers avoid using spaces because they can cause errors when the objects are involved in programming tasks.

By spending time obtaining and analyzing information about the fields in a table, and understanding the rules for naming fields, you can create a well-designed table that will be easy for others to use.

Renaming the Default Primary Key Field

As noted earlier, Access provides the ID field as the default primary key for a new table you create in Datasheet view. Recall that a primary key is a field, or a collection of fields, whose values uniquely identify each record in a table. However, according to Kimberly's plan, the VisitID field should be the primary key for the Visit table. You'll begin by renaming the default ID field to create the VisitID field.

TIP

A shortcut menu opens when you right-click an object and provides options for working with that object.

To rename the ID field to the VisitID field:

1. Right-click the **ID** column heading to open the shortcut menu, and then click **Rename Field**. The column heading ID is selected, so that whatever text you type next will replace it.

2. Type **VisitID** and then click the row below the heading. The column heading changes to VisitID, and the insertion point moves to the row below the heading. The **insertion point** is a flashing cursor that shows where text you type will be inserted. In this case, it is hidden within the selected field value (New). See Figure 1-7.

    Trouble? If you make a mistake while typing the field name, use the Backspace key to delete characters to the left of the insertion point or the Delete key to delete characters to the right of the insertion point. Then type the correct text. To correct a field name by replacing it entirely, press the Esc key, and then type the correct text.

| Figure 1-7 | ID field renamed to VisitID |

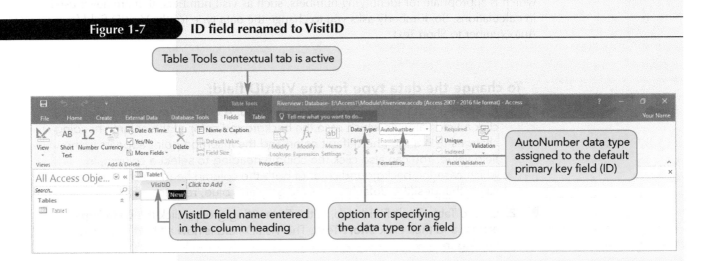

Table Tools contextual tab is active

AutoNumber data type assigned to the default primary key field (ID)

VisitID field name entered in the column heading

option for specifying the data type for a field

Notice that the Table Tools tab is active on the ribbon. This is an example of a **contextual tab**, which is a tab that appears and provides options for working with a specific object that is selected—in this case, the table you are creating. As you work with other objects in the database, other contextual tabs will appear with commands and options related to each selected object.

You have renamed the default primary key field, ID, to VisitID. However, the VisitID field still retains the characteristics of the ID field, including its data type. Your next task is to change the data type of this field.

Changing the Data Type of the Default Primary Key Field

Notice the Formatting group on the Table Tools Fields tab. One of the options available in this group is the Data Type option (see Figure 1-7). Each field in an Access table must be assigned a data type. The **data type** determines what field values you can enter for the field. In this case, the AutoNumber data type is displayed. Access assigns the AutoNumber data type to the default ID primary key field because the **AutoNumber** data type automatically inserts a unique number in this field for every record, beginning with the number 1 for the first record, the number 2 for the second record, and so on. Therefore, a field using the AutoNumber data type can serve as the primary key for any table you create.

Visit numbers at the Riverview Veterinary Care Center are specific, four-digit numbers, so the AutoNumber data type is not appropriate for the VisitID field, which is the primary key field in the table you are creating. A better choice is the **Short Text** data type, which allows field values containing letters, digits, and other characters, and which is appropriate for identifying numbers, such as visit numbers, that are never used in calculations. So, Kimberly asks you to change the data type for the VisitID field from AutoNumber to Short Text.

To change the data type for the VisitID field:

▶ **1.** Make sure that the VisitID column is selected. A column is selected when you click a field value, in which case the background color of the column heading changes to orange (the default color) and the insertion point appears in the field value. You can also click the column heading to select a column, in which case the background color of both the column heading and the field value changes (the default colors are gray and blue, respectively).

▶ **2.** On the Table Tools Fields tab, in the Formatting group, click the **Data Type arrow**, and then click **Short Text**. The VisitID field is now a Short Text field. See Figure 1-8.

| **Figure 1-8** | **Short Text data type assigned to the VisitID field** |

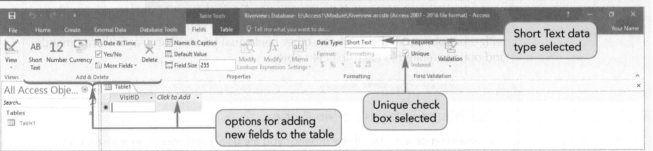

Note the Unique check box in the Field Validation group. This check box is selected because the VisitID field assumed the characteristics of the default primary key field, ID, including the fact that each value in the field must be unique. Because this check box is selected, no two records in the Visit table will be allowed to have the same value in the VisitID field.

With the VisitID field created and established as the primary key, you can now enter the rest of the fields in the Visit table.

Adding New Fields

When you create a table in Datasheet view, you can use the options in the Add & Delete group on the Table Tools Fields tab to add fields to your table. You can also use the Click to Add column in the table datasheet to add new fields. (See Figure 1-8.) You'll use both methods to add the four remaining fields to the Visit table. The next field you need to add is the AnimalID field. Similar to the VisitID field, the AnimalID field will contain numbers that will not be used in calculations, so it should be a Short Text field.

To add the rest of the fields to the Visit table:

▶ **1.** On the Table Tools Fields tab, in the Add & Delete group, click the **Short Text** button. A new field named "Field1" is added to the right of the VisitID field. See Figure 1-9.

| Figure 1-9 | New Short Text field added to the table |

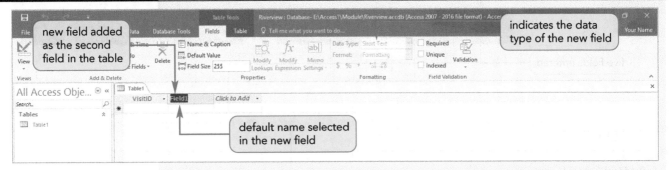

new field added as the second field in the table

indicates the data type of the new field

default name selected in the new field

The text "Field1" is selected, so you can simply type the new field name to replace it.

2. Type **AnimalID**. The second field is added to the table. Next, you'll add the VisitDate field. Because this field will contain date values, you'll add a field with the **Date/Time** data type, which allows field values in a variety of date and time formats.

3. In the Add & Delete group, click the **Date & Time** button. Access adds a third field to the table, this time with the Date/Time data type.

4. Type **VisitDate** to replace the selected name "Field1." The fourth field in the Visit table is the Reason field, which will contain brief descriptions of the reason for the visit to the center. You'll add another Short Text field—this time using the Click to Add column.

5. Click the **Click to Add** column heading. Access displays a list of available data types from which you can choose the data type for the new field you're adding.

6. Click **Short Text** in the list. Access adds a fourth field to the table.

7. Type **Reason** to replace the highlighted name "Field1," and then press the **Enter** key. The Click to Add column becomes active and displays the list of field data types.

The fifth and final field in the Visit table is the OffSite field, which will indicate whether or not the visit was at an offsite venue, such as at a home or ranch (that is, not within the center). The **Yes/No** data type is suitable for this field because it is used to define fields that store values representing one of two options—true/false, yes/no, or on/off.

TIP

You can also type the first letter of a data type to select it and close the Click to Add list.

8. Click **Yes/No** in the list, and then type **OffSite** to replace the highlighted name "Field1."

Trouble? If you pressed the Tab or Enter key after typing the OffSite field name, press the Esc key to close the Click to Add list.

9. Click in the row below the VisitID column heading. All five fields are now entered for the Visit table. See Figure 1-10.

| Figure 1-10 | Table with all fields entered |

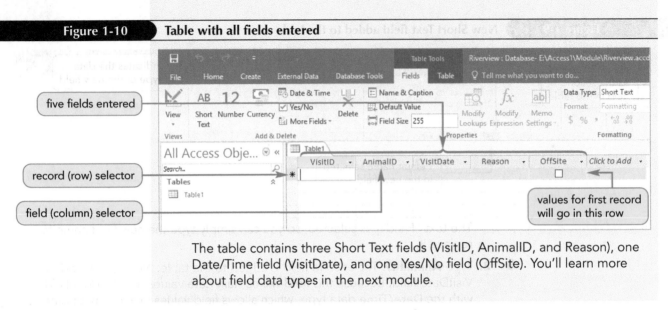

five fields entered

record (row) selector

field (column) selector

values for first record will go in this row

The table contains three Short Text fields (VisitID, AnimalID, and Reason), one Date/Time field (VisitDate), and one Yes/No field (OffSite). You'll learn more about field data types in the next module.

As noted earlier, Datasheet view shows a table's contents in rows (records) and columns (fields). Each column is headed by a field name inside a field selector, and each row has a record selector to its left (see Figure 1-10). Clicking a **field selector** or a **record selector** selects that entire column or row (respectively), which you then can manipulate. A field selector is also called a **column selector**, and a record selector is also called a **row selector**.

Entering Records

With the fields in place for the table, you can now enter the field values for each record. Kimberly requests that you enter eight records in the Visit table, as shown in Figure 1-11.

| Figure 1-11 | Visit table records |

VisitID	AnimalID	VisitDate	Reason	OffSite
1072	12356	12/12/2016	Vaccinations	Yes
1169	12278	1/20/2017	Spaying	No
1184	12443	1/25/2017	Neutering	No
1016	12345	11/18/2016	Vaccinations	Yes
1196	12455	2/1/2017	Vaccinations	No
1098	12296	1/3/2017	Declawing	No
1178	12362	1/24/2017	Injured leg and hoof	Yes
1044	12278	12/2/2016	Vaccinations	No

To enter records in a table datasheet, you type the field values below the column headings for the fields. The first record you enter will go in the first row (see Figure 1-10).

To enter the first record for the Visit table:

1. In the first row for the VisitID field, type **1072** (the VisitID field value for the first record), and then press the **Tab** key. Access adds the field value and moves the insertion point to the right, into the AnimalID column. See Figure 1-12.

Be sure to type the numbers "0" and "1" and not the letters "O" and "I" in the field value.

| Figure 1-12 | First field value entered |

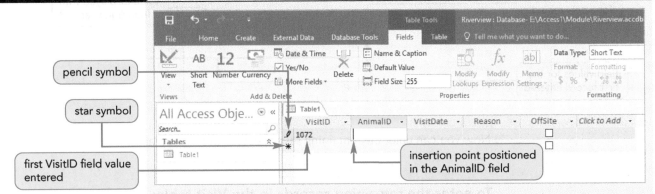

pencil symbol

star symbol

first VisitID field value entered

insertion point positioned in the AnimalID field

Trouble? If you make a mistake when typing a value, use the Backspace key to delete characters to the left of the insertion point or the Delete key to delete characters to the right of the insertion point. Then type the correct value. To correct a value by replacing it entirely, press the Esc key, and then type the correct value.

Notice the pencil symbol that appears in the row selector for the new record. The **pencil symbol** indicates that the record is being edited. Also notice the star symbol that appears in the row selector for the second row. The **star symbol** identifies the second row as the next row available for a new record.

2. Type **12356** (the AnimalID field value for the first record), and then press the **Tab** key. Access enters the field value and moves the insertion point to the VisitDate column.

3. Type **12/12/16** (the VisitDate field value for the first record), and then press the **Tab** key. Access displays the year as "2016" even though you entered only the final two digits of the year. This is because the VisitDate field has the Date/Time data type, which automatically formats dates with four-digit years.

4. Type **Vaccinations** (the Reason field value for the first record), and then press the **Tab** key to move to the OffSite column.

Recall that the OffSite field is a Yes/No field. Notice the check box displayed in the OffSite column. By default, the value for any Yes/No field is "No"; therefore, the check box is initially empty. For Yes/No fields with check boxes, you press the Tab key to leave the check box unchecked, or you press the spacebar to insert a checkmark in the check box. The record you are entering in the table is for an offsite visit, so you need to insert a checkmark in the check box to indicate "Yes."

TIP

You can also click a check box in a Yes/No field to insert or remove a checkmark.

5. Press the **spacebar** to insert a checkmark, and then press the **Tab** key. The first record is entered into the table, and the insertion point is positioned in the VisitID field for the second record. The pencil symbol is removed from the first row because the record in that row is no longer being edited. The table is now ready for you to enter the second record. See Figure 1-13.

| Figure 1-13 | Datasheet with first record entered |

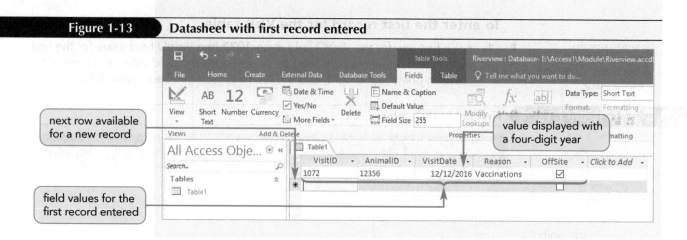

next row available for a new record

value displayed with a four-digit year

field values for the first record entered

Now you can enter the remaining seven records in the Visit table.

To enter the remaining records in the Visit table:

TIP

You can also press the Enter key instead of the Tab key to move from one field to another and to the next row.

1. Referring to Figure 1-11, enter the values for records 2 through 8, pressing the **Tab** key to move from field to field and to the next row for a new record. Keep in mind that you do not have to type all four digits of the year in the VisitDate field values; you can enter only the final two digits, and Access will display all four. Also, for any OffSite field values of "No," be sure to press the Tab key to leave the check box empty.

   Trouble? If you enter a value in the wrong field by mistake, such as entering a Reason field value in the VisitDate field, a menu might open with options for addressing the problem. If this happens, click the "Enter new value" option in the menu. You'll return to the field with the incorrect value selected, which you can then replace by typing the correct value.

   Notice that not all of the Reason field values are fully displayed. To see more of the table datasheet and the full field values, you'll close the Navigation Pane and resize the Reason column.

2. At the top of the Navigation Pane, click the **Shutter Bar Open/Close Button** [«]. The Navigation Pane closes, and only the complete table datasheet is displayed.

3. Place the pointer on the vertical line to the right of the Reason field name until the pointer changes to ✛, and then double-click the vertical line. All the Reason field values are now fully displayed. See Figure 1-14.

Figure 1-14   Datasheet with eight records entered

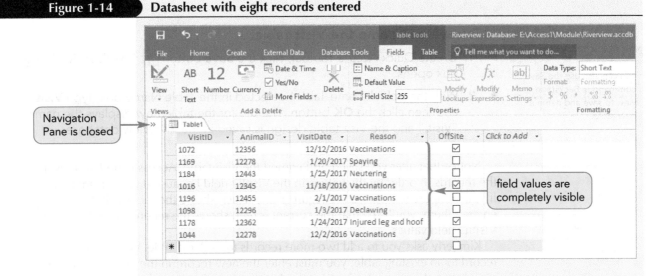

Navigation Pane is closed

field values are completely visible

When you resize a datasheet column by double-clicking the column dividing line, you are sizing the column to its **best fit**—that is, so the column is just wide enough to display the longest visible value in the column, including the field name.

Carefully compare your VisitID and AnimalID values with those in the figure, and correct any errors before continuing.

4. Compare your table to the one in Figure 1-14. If any of the field values in your table do not match those shown in the figure, you can correct a field value by clicking to position the insertion point in the value, and then using the Backspace key or Delete key to delete incorrect text. Then type the correct text and press the Enter key. To correct a value in the OffSite field, simply click the check box to add or remove the checkmark as appropriate. Also, be sure the spelling and capitalization of field names in your table match those shown in the figure exactly and that there are no spaces between words. To correct a field name, double-click it to select it, and then type the correct name; or use the Rename Field option on the shortcut menu to rename a field with the correct name.

Saving a Table

The records you enter are immediately stored in the database as soon as you enter them; however, the table's design—the field names and characteristics of the fields themselves, plus any layout changes to the datasheet—are not saved until you save the table. When you save a new table for the first time, you should give it a name that best identifies the information it contains. Like a field name, a table name can contain up to 64 characters, including spaces.

REFERENCE

Saving a Table

- Make sure the table you want to save is open.
- On the Quick Access Toolbar, click the Save button. The Save As dialog box opens.
- In the Table Name box, type the name for the table.
- Click the OK button.

According to Kimberly's plan, you need to save the table with the name "Visit."

To save and name the Visit table:

TIP

You can also use the Save command in Backstage view to save and name a new table.

1. On the Quick Access Toolbar, click the **Save** button. The Save As dialog box opens.

2. With the default name Table1 selected in the Table Name box, type **Visit**, and then click the **OK** button. The tab for the table now displays the name "Visit," and the Visit table design is saved in the Riverview database.

Notice that after you saved and named the Visit table, Access sorted and displayed the records in order by the values in the VisitID field because it is the primary key. If you compare your screen to Figure 1-11, which shows the records in the order you entered them, you'll see that the current screen shows the records in order by the VisitID field values.

Kimberly asks you to add two more records to the Visit table. When you add a record to an existing table, you must enter the new record in the next row available for a new record; you cannot insert a row between existing records for the new record. In a table with just a few records, such as the Visit table, the next available row is visible on the screen. However, in a table with hundreds of records, you would need to scroll the datasheet to see the next row available. The easiest way to add a new record to a table is to use the New button, which scrolls the datasheet to the next row available so you can enter the new record.

To enter additional records in the Visit table:

1. If necessary, click the first record's VisitID field value (**1016**) to make it the current record.

2. On the ribbon, click the **Home** tab.

3. In the Records group, click the **New** button. The insertion point is positioned in the next row available for a new record, which in this case is row 9. See Figure 1-15.

Figure 1-15	Entering a new record

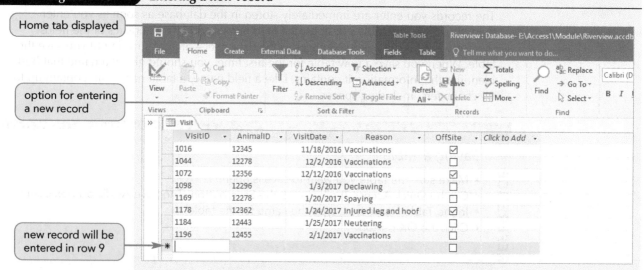

Home tab displayed

option for entering a new record

new record will be entered in row 9

4. With the insertion point in the VisitID field for the new record, type **1036** and then press the **Tab** key.

5. Complete the entry of this record by entering each value shown below, pressing the **Tab** key to move from field to field:

AnimalID = **12294**

VisitDate = **11/29/2016**

Reason = **Declawing**

OffSite = **No (unchecked)**

6. Enter the values for the next new record, as follows, and then press the **Tab** key after entering the OffSite field value:

VisitID = **1152**

AnimalID = **12318**

VisitDate = **1/13/2017**

Reason = **Not eating**

OffSite = **No (unchecked)**

Your datasheet should now look like the one shown in Figure 1-16.

| Figure 1-16 | Datasheet with additional records entered |

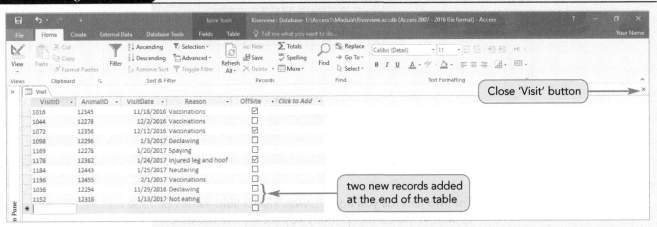

The new records you added appear at the end of the table, and are not sorted in order by the primary key field values. For example, VisitID 1036 should be the second record in the table, placed between VisitID 1016 and VisitID 1044. When you add records to a table datasheet, they appear at the end of the table. The records are not displayed in primary key order until you either close and reopen the table or switch between views.

7. Click the **Close 'Visit'** button [X] on the object tab (see Figure 1-16 for the location of this button). The Visit table closes, and the main portion of the Access window is now blank because no database object is currently open. The Riverview database file is still open, as indicated by the filename in the Access window title bar.

Opening a Table

The tables in a database are listed in the Navigation Pane. You open a table, or any Access object, by double-clicking the object name in the Navigation Pane. Next, you'll open the Visit table so you can see all the records you've entered in the correct primary key order.

To open the Visit table:

▶ **1.** On the Navigation Pane, click the **Shutter Bar Open/Close Button** 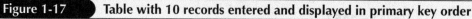 to open the pane. Note that the Visit table is listed.

▶ **2.** Double-click **Visit** to open the table in Datasheet view. See Figure 1-17.

Figure 1-17	Table with 10 records entered and displayed in primary key order

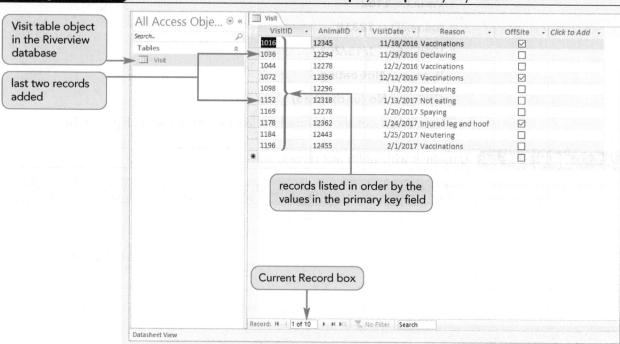

The two records you added, with VisitID field values of 1036 and 1152, now appear in the correct primary key order. The table now contains a total of 10 records, as indicated by the Current Record box at the bottom of the datasheet. The **Current Record box** displays the number of the current record as well as the total number of records in the table.

Each record contains a unique VisitID value because this field is the primary key. Other fields, however, can contain the same value in multiple records; for example, note the four values of "Vaccinations" in the Reason field.

Closing a Table and Exiting Access

When you are finished working in an Access table, it's a good idea to close the table so that you do not make unintended changes to the table data. You can close a table by clicking its Close button on the object tab, as you did earlier. Or, if you want to close the Access program as well, you can click the program's Close button. When you do, any open tables are closed, the active database is closed, and you exit the Access program.

To close the Visit table and exit Access:

TIP

To close a database without exiting Access, click the File tab to display Backstage view, and then click Close.

1. Click the **Close** button ☒ on the program window title bar. The Visit table and the Riverview database close, and then the Access program closes.

INSIGHT

Saving a Database

Unlike the Save buttons in other Office programs, the Save button on the Quick Access Toolbar in Access does not save the active document (database). Instead, you use the Save button to save the design of an Access object, such as a table (as you saw earlier), or to save datasheet format changes, such as resizing columns. Access does not have a button or option you can use to save the active database.

Access saves changes to the active database automatically when you change or add a record or close the database. If your database is stored on a removable storage device, such as a USB drive, you should never remove the device while the database file is open. If you do, Access will encounter problems when it tries to save the database, which might damage the database. Make sure you close the database first before removing the storage device.

Now that you've become familiar with database concepts and Access, and created the Riverview database and the Visit table, Kimberly wants you to add more records to the table and work with the data stored in it to create database objects including a query, form, and report. You'll complete these tasks in the next session.

REVIEW

Session 1.1 Quick Check

1. A(n) _____ is a single characteristic of a person, place, object, event, or idea.

2. You connect the records in two separate tables through a(n) _____ that appears in both tables.

3. The _____, whose values uniquely identify each record in a table, is called a(n) _____ when it is placed in a second table to form a relationship between the two tables.

4. The _____ is the area of the Access window that lists all the objects in a database, and it is the main control center for opening and working with database objects.

5. What is the name of the field that Access creates, by default, as the primary key field for a new table in Datasheet view?

6. Which group on the Fields tab contains the options you use to add new fields to a table?

7. What does a pencil symbol at the beginning of a record represent? What does a star symbol represent?

8. Explain how the saving process in Access is different from saving in other Office programs.

Session 1.2 Visual Overview:

The Create tab provides options for creating various database objects, including tables, forms, and reports. The options appear on the tab grouped by object type.

The Forms group contains options for creating a form, which is a database object you use to enter, edit, and view records in a database.

The Query Wizard button opens a dialog box with different types of wizards that guide you through the steps to create a query. One of these, the Simple Query Wizard, allows you to select records and fields quickly to display in the query results.

Riverview : Database- E:\Access1\Module\Riverview.acc

File   Home   Create   External Data   Database Tools   Tell me what you want

Application Parts ▾   Table   Table Design   SharePoint Lists ▾   Query Wizard   Query Design   Form   Form Design   Blank Form   Form Wizard   Navigation   More Forms

Templates   Tables   Queries   Forms

You use the options in the Tables group to create a table in Datasheet view or in Design view.

The Form tool quickly creates a form containing all the fields in the table (or query) on which you're basing the form.

The Form Wizard guides you through the process of creating a form.

The Queries group contains options for creating a query, which is a question you ask about the data stored in a database. In response to a query, Access displays the specific records and fields that answer your question.

Navigation Pane

Ready

The Create Tab Options

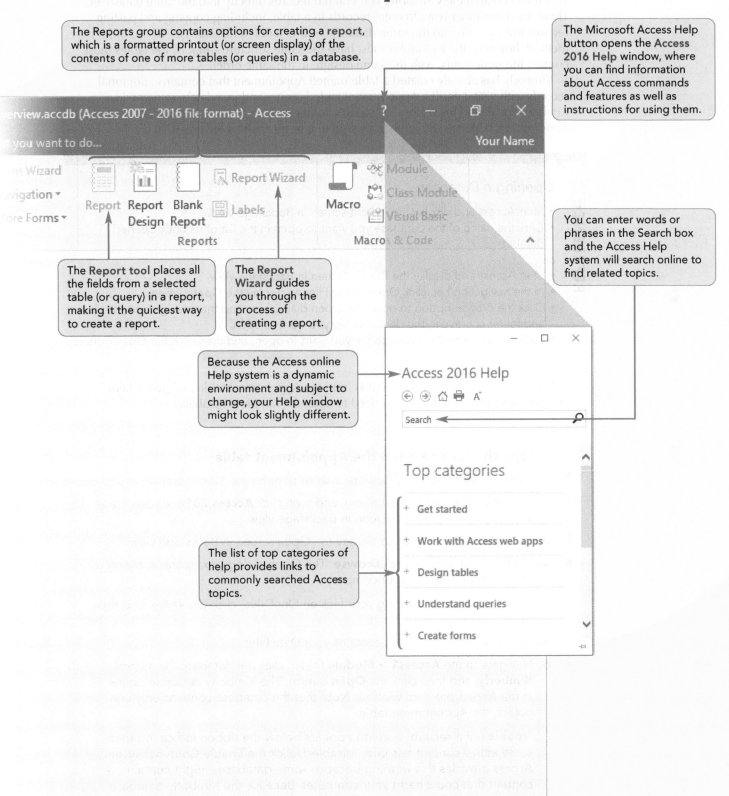

The Reports group contains options for creating a **report**, which is a formatted printout (or screen display) of the contents of one of more tables (or queries) in a database.

The Microsoft Access Help button opens the **Access 2016 Help** window, where you can find information about Access commands and features as well as instructions for using them.

The **Report tool** places all the fields from a selected table (or query) in a report, making it the quickest way to create a report.

The **Report Wizard** guides you through the process of creating a report.

You can enter words or phrases in the Search box and the Access Help system will search online to find related topics.

Because the Access online Help system is a dynamic environment and subject to change, your Help window might look slightly different.

The list of top categories of help provides links to commonly searched Access topics.

Copying Records from Another Access Database

When you created the Visit table, you entered records directly into the table datasheet. There are many other ways to enter records in a table, including copying and pasting records from a table into the same database or into a different database. To use this method, however, the two tables must have the same structure—that is, the tables must contain the same fields, with the same design, in the same order.

Kimberly has already created a table named Appointment that contains additional records with visit data. The Appointment table is contained in a database named Kimberly located in the Access1 > Module folder included with your Data Files. The Appointment table has the same table structure as the Visit table you created.

Opening a Database

- Start Access and display the Recent screen in Backstage view.
- Click the name of the database you want to open in the list of recently opened databases.

or

- Start Access and display the Recent screen in Backstage view.
- In the navigation bar, click Open Other Files to display the Open screen.
- Click the Browse button to open the Open dialog box, and then navigate to the drive and folder containing the database file you want to open.
- Click the name of the database file you want to open, and then click the Open button.

Your next task is to copy the records from the Appointment table and paste them into your Visit table. To do so, you need to open the Kimberly database.

To copy the records from the Appointment table:

1. Click the **Start** button ⊞ on the taskbar to open the Start menu.

2. Click **All apps** on the Start menu, and then click **Access 2016**. Access starts and displays the Recent screen in Backstage view.

3. Click **Open Other Files** to display the Open screen in Backstage view.

4. On the Open screen, click **Browse**. The Open dialog box opens, showing folder information for your computer.

   Trouble? If you are storing your files on OneDrive, click OneDrive, and then log in if necessary.

5. Navigate to the drive that contains your Data Files.

6. Navigate to the **Access1 > Module** folder, click the database file named **Kimberly**, and then click the **Open** button. The Kimberly database opens in the Access program window. Note that the database contains only one object, the Appointment table.

   Trouble? If a security warning appears below the ribbon indicating that some active content has been disabled, click the Enable Content button. Access provides this warning because some databases might contain content that could harm your computer. Because the Kimberly database does not contain objects that could be harmful, you can open it safely. If you are accessing the file over a network, you might also see a dialog box asking if you want to make the file a trusted document; click Yes.

7. In the Navigation Pane, double-click **Appointment** to open the Appointment table in Datasheet view. The table contains 65 records and the same five fields, with the same characteristics, as the fields in the Visit table. See Figure 1-18.

Figure 1-18   **Appointment table in the Kimberly database**

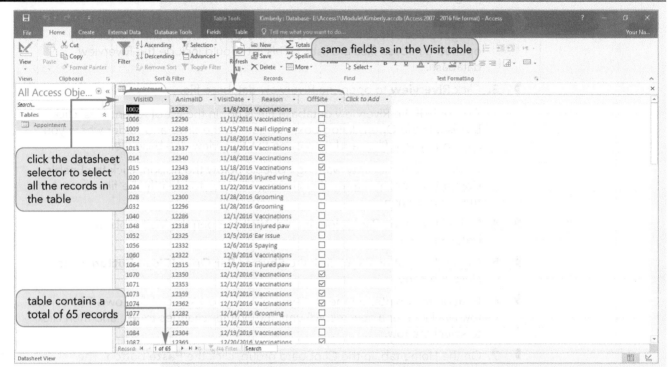

Kimberly wants you to copy all the records in the Appointment table. You can select all the records by clicking the **datasheet selector**, which is the box to the left of the first field name in the table datasheet, as shown in Figure 1-18.

8. Click the **datasheet selector** to the left of the VisitID field. All the records in the table are selected.

9. On the Home tab, in the Clipboard group, click the **Copy** button. All the records are copied to the Clipboard.

10. Click the **Close 'Appointment'** button ⊠ on the object tab. A dialog box opens asking if you want to save the data you copied to the Clipboard. This dialog box opens only when you copy a large amount of data to the Clipboard.

11. Click the **Yes** button. The dialog box closes, and then the Appointment table closes.

With the records copied to the Clipboard, you can now paste them into the Visit table. First you need to close the Kimberly database while still keeping the Access program open, and then open the Riverview database.

To close the Kimberly database and then paste the records into the Visit table:

▶ **1.** Click the **File** tab to open Backstage view, and then click **Close** in the navigation bar to close the Kimberly database. You return to a blank Access program window, and the Home tab is the active tab on the ribbon.

▶ **2.** Click the **File** tab to return to Backstage view, and then click **Open** in the navigation bar. Recent is selected on the Open screen, and the recently opened database files are listed. This list should include the Riverview database.

▶ **3.** Click **Riverview** to open the Riverview database file.

Trouble? If the Riverview database file is not in the list of recent files, click Browse. In the Open dialog box, navigate to the drive and folder where you are storing your files, and then open the Riverview database file.

Trouble? If the security warning appears below the ribbon, click the Enable Content button, and then, if necessary, click Yes to identify the file as a trusted document.

▶ **4.** In the Navigation Pane, double-click **Visit** to open the Visit table in Datasheet view.

▶ **5.** On the Navigation Pane, click the **Shutter Bar Open/Close Button** `≪` to close the pane.

▶ **6.** Position the pointer on the star symbol in the row selector for row 11 (the next row available for a new record) until the pointer changes to ➡, and then click to select the row.

▶ **7.** On the Home tab, in the Clipboard group, click the **Paste** button. The pasted records are added to the table, and a dialog box opens asking you to confirm that you want to paste all the records (65 total).

Trouble? If the Paste button isn't active, click the ➡ pointer on the row selector for row 11, making sure the entire row is selected, and then repeat Step 7.

▶ **8.** Click the **Yes** button. The dialog box closes, and the pasted records are selected. See Figure 1-19. Notice that the table now contains a total of 75 records—10 records that you entered previously and 65 records that you copied and pasted.

Figure 1-19   Visit table after copying and pasting records

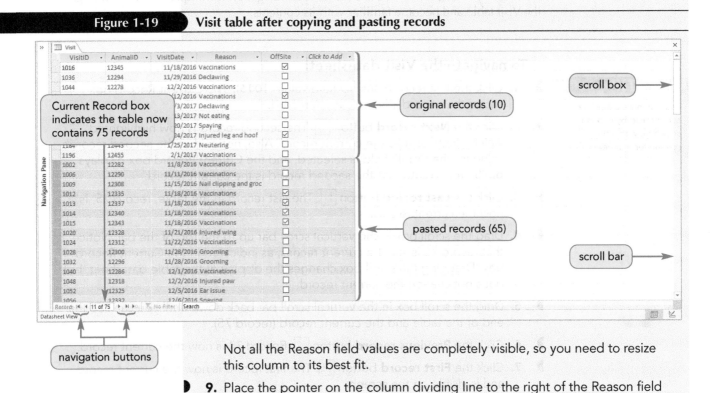

navigation buttons

Not all the Reason field values are completely visible, so you need to resize this column to its best fit.

▶ **9.** Place the pointer on the column dividing line to the right of the Reason field name until the pointer changes to ↔, and then double-click the column dividing line. The Reason field values are now fully displayed.

Navigating a Datasheet

The Visit table now contains 75 records, but only some of the records are visible on the screen. To view fields or records not currently visible on the screen, you can use the horizontal and vertical scroll bars to navigate the data. The **navigation buttons**, shown in Figure 1-19 and also described in Figure 1-20, provide another way to move vertically through the records. The Current Record box appears between the two sets of navigation buttons and displays the number of the current record as well as the total number of records in the table. Figure 1-20 shows which record becomes the current record when you click each navigation button. Note the New (blank) record button, which works in the same way as the New button on the Home tab you used earlier to enter a new record in the table.

Figure 1-20   Navigation buttons

Navigation Button	Record Selected	Navigation Button	Record Selected
◄|	First record	►|	Last record
◄	Previous record	►*	New (blank) record
►	Next record		

Kimberly suggests that you use the various navigation techniques to move through the Visit table and become familiar with its contents.

To navigate the Visit datasheet:

TIP

You can make a field the current field by clicking anywhere within the column for that field.

▶ **1.** Click the first record's VisitID field value (**1016**). The Current Record box shows that record 1 is the current record.

▶ **2.** Click the **Next record** button ▶. The second record is now highlighted, which identifies it as the current record. Also, notice that the second record's value for the VisitID field is selected, and the Current Record box displays "2 of 75" to indicate that the second record is the current record.

▶ **3.** Click the **Last record** button ▶|. The last record in the table, record 75, is now the current record.

▶ **4.** Drag the scroll box in the vertical scroll bar up to the top of the bar. Notice that record 75 is still the current record, as indicated in the Current Record box. Dragging the scroll box changes the display of the table datasheet, but does not change the current record.

▶ **5.** Drag the scroll box in the vertical scroll bar back down until you can see the end of the table and the current record (record 75).

▶ **6.** Click the **Previous record** button ◀. Record 74 is now the current record.

▶ **7.** Click the **First record** button |◀. The first record is now the current record and is visible on the screen.

Earlier you resized the Reason column to its best fit, to ensure all the field values were visible. However, when you resize a column to its best fit, the column expands to fully display only the field values that are visible on the screen at that time. If you move through the complete datasheet and notice that not all of the field values are fully displayed after conducting the resizing process on the records initially visible, you need to repeat the resizing process.

▶ **8.** Scroll down through the records and observe if the field values are fully displayed. In this case, all of the fields are fully visible, so there is no need to resize any of the field columns.

The Visit table now contains all the data about animal visits for Riverview Veterinary Care Center. To better understand how to work with this data, Kimberly asks you to create simple objects for the other main types of database objects—queries, forms, and reports.

Creating a Simple Query

As noted earlier, a query is a question you ask about the data stored in a database. When you create a query, you tell Access which fields you need and what criteria it should use to select the records that will answer your question. Then Access displays only the information you want, so you don't have to navigate through the entire database for the information. In the Visit table, for example, Kimberly might create a query to display only those records for visits that occurred in a specific month. Even though a query can display table information in a different way, the information still exists in the table as it was originally entered.

Kimberly wants to see a list of all the visit dates and reasons for visits in the Visit table. She doesn't want the list to include all the fields in the table, such as AnimalID and OffSite. To produce this list for Kimberly, you'll use the Simple Query Wizard to create a query based on the Visit table.

To start the Simple Query Wizard:

▶ **1.** On the ribbon, click the **Create** tab.

▶ **2.** In the Queries group, click the **Query Wizard** button. The New Query dialog box opens.

▶ **3.** Make sure **Simple Query Wizard** is selected, and then click the **OK** button. The first Simple Query Wizard dialog box opens. See Figure 1-21.

Figure 1-21 ▶ **First Simple Query Wizard dialog box**

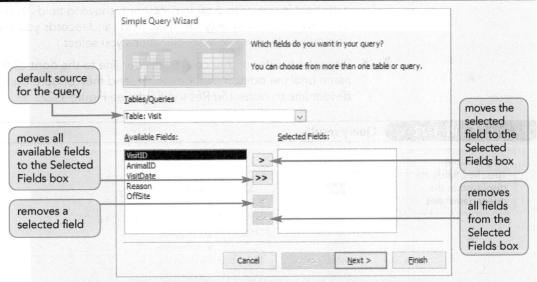

Because the Visit table is the only object in the Riverview database, it is listed in the Tables/Queries box by default. If the database contained more objects, you could click the Tables/Queries arrow and choose another table or a query as the basis for the new query you are creating. The Available Fields box lists all the fields in the Visit table.

You need to select fields from the Available Fields box to include them in the query. To select fields one at a time, click a field and then click the ⟩ button. The selected field moves from the Available Fields box on the left to the Selected Fields box on the right. To select all the fields, click the ⟩⟩ button. If you change your mind or make a mistake, you can remove a field by clicking it in the Selected Fields box and then clicking the ⟨ button. To remove all fields from the Selected Fields box, click the ⟨⟨ button.

Each Simple Query Wizard dialog box contains buttons on the bottom that allow you to move to the previous dialog box (Back button), move to the next dialog box (Next button), or cancel the creation process (Cancel button). You can also finish creating the object (Finish button) and accept the wizard's defaults for the remaining options.

Kimberly wants her query results to list to include data from only the following fields: VisitID, VisitDate, and Reason. You need to select these fields to include them in the query.

TIP

You can also double-click a field to move it from the Available Fields box to the Selected Fields box.

To create the query using the Simple Query Wizard:

▸ **1.** Click **VisitID** in the Available Fields box to select the field (if necessary), and then click the ⟩ button. The VisitID field moves to the Selected Fields box.

▸ **2.** Repeat Step 1 for the fields **VisitDate** and **Reason**, and then click the **Next** button. The second, and final, Simple Query Wizard dialog box opens and asks you to choose a name (title) for your query. The suggested name is "Visit Query" because the query you are creating is on the Visit table. You'll change the suggested name to "VisitList."

▸ **3.** Click at the end of the suggested name, use the **Backspace** key to delete the word "Query" and the space, and then type **List**. Now you can view the query results.

▸ **4.** Click the **Finish** button to complete the query. The query results are displayed in Datasheet view, on a new tab named "VisitList." A query datasheet is similar to a table datasheet, showing fields in columns and records in rows—but only for those fields and records you want to see, as determined by the query specifications you select.

▸ **5.** Place the pointer on the column divider line to the right of the Reason field name until the pointer changes to ↔, and then double-click the column divider line to resize the Reason field. See Figure 1-22.

Figure 1-22   **Query results**

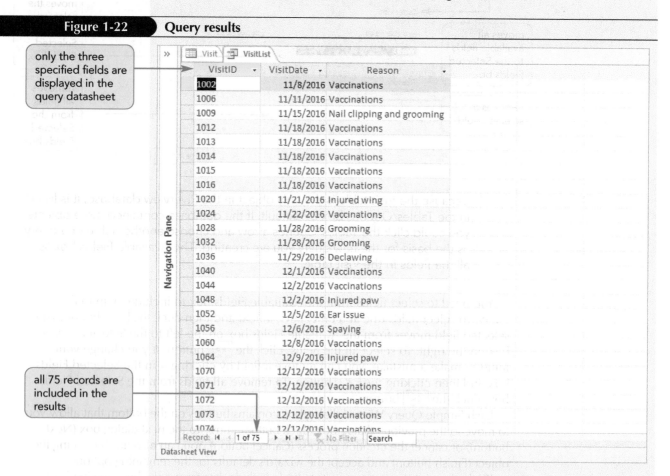

only the three specified fields are displayed in the query datasheet

all 75 records are included in the results

The VisitList query datasheet displays the three fields in the order you selected them in the Simple Query Wizard, from left to right. The records are listed in order by the primary key field, VisitID. Even though the query datasheet displays only the three fields you chose for the query, the Visit table still includes all the fields for all records.

Notice that the navigation buttons are located at the bottom of the window. You navigate a query datasheet in the same way that you navigate a table datasheet.

▶ **6.** Click the **Last record** button ⊠. The last record in the query datasheet is now the current record.

▶ **7.** Click the **Previous record** button ◀. Record 74 in the query datasheet is now the current record.

▶ **8.** Click the **First record** button ⊠. The first record is now the current record.

▶ **9.** Click the **Close 'VisitList'** button ⊠ on the object tab. A dialog box opens asking if you want to save the changes to the layout of the query. This dialog box opens because you resized the Reason column.

▶ **10.** Click the **Yes** button to save the query layout changes and close the query.

The query results are not stored in the database; however, the query design is stored as part of the database with the name you specified. You can re-create the query results at any time by opening the query again. When you open the query at a later date, the results displayed will reflect up-to-date information to include any new records entered in the Visit table.

Next, Kimberly asks you to create a form for the Visit table so that Riverview Veterinary Care Center staff can use the form to enter and work with data in the table easily.

Creating a Simple Form

As noted earlier, you use a form to enter, edit, and view records in a database. Although you can perform these same functions with tables and queries, forms can present data in many customized and useful ways.

Kimberly wants a form for the Visit table that shows all the fields for one record at a time, with fields listed one below another in a column. This type of form will make it easier for her staff to focus on all the data for a particular visit. You'll use the Form tool to create this form quickly and easily.

To create the form using the Form tool:

▶ **1.** Make sure the Visit table is still open in Datasheet view. The table or other database object you're using as the basis for the form must either be open or selected in the Navigation Pane when you use the Form tool.

Trouble? If the Visit table is not open, click the Shutter Bar Open/Close Button ⊠ to open the Navigation Pane. Then double-click Visit to open the Visit table in Datasheet view. Click the Shutter Bar Open/Close Button ⊠ to close the pane.

▶ **2.** On the ribbon, click the **Create** tab if necessary.

3. In the Forms group, click the **Form** button. The Form tool creates a simple form showing every field in the Visit table and places it on a tab named "Visit" because the form is based on the Visit table. See Figure 1-23.

Figure 1-23 ▶ **Form created by the Form tool**

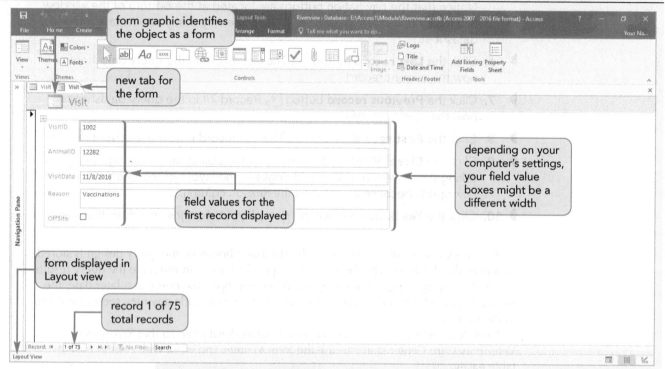

- form graphic identifies the object as a form
- new tab for the form
- field values for the first record displayed
- depending on your computer's settings, your field value boxes might be a different width
- form displayed in Layout view
- record 1 of 75 total records

Trouble? Depending on the size of your monitor and your screen resolution settings, the fields in your form might appear in multiple columns instead of a single column. This difference will not present any problems.

The form displays one record at a time in the Visit table, providing another view of the data that is stored in the table and allowing you to focus on the values for one record. Access displays the field values for the first record in the table and selects the first field value (VisitID) as indicated by the border that appears around the value. Each field name appears on a separate line and on the same line as its field value, which appears in a box to the right. Depending on your computer's settings, the field value boxes in your form might be wider or narrower than those shown in the figure. As indicated in the status bar, the form is displayed in Layout view. In **Layout view**, you can make design changes to the form while it is displaying data, so that you can see the effects of the changes you make immediately.

To view, enter, and maintain data using a form, you must know how to move from field to field and from record to record. Notice that the form contains navigation buttons, similar to those available in Datasheet view, which you can use to display different records in the form. You'll use these now to navigate the form; then you'll save and close the form.

To navigate, save, and close the form:

1. Click the **Next record** button ▶. The form now displays the values for the second record in the Visit table.

2. Click the **Last record** button ▶| to move to the last record in the table. The form displays the information for VisitID 1196.

3. Click the **Previous record** button ◀ to move to record 74.

4. Click the **First record** button |◀ to return to the first record in the Visit table.

5. Next, you'll save the form with the name "VisitData" in the Riverview database. Then the form will be available for later use.

6. On the Quick Access Toolbar, click the **Save** button 🖫. The Save As dialog box opens.

7. In the Form Name box, click at the end of the selected name "Visit," type **Data**, and then press the **Enter** key. The dialog box closes and the form is saved as VisitData in the Riverview database. The tab containing the form now displays the name VisitData.

8. Click the **Close 'VisitData'** button ☒ on the object tab to close the form.

INSIGHT

Saving Database Objects

In general, it is best to save a database object—query, form, or report—only if you anticipate using the object frequently or if it is time-consuming to create, because all objects use storage space and increase the size of the database file. For example, you most likely would not save a form you created with the Form tool because you can re-create it easily with one mouse click. (However, for the purposes of this text, you usually need to save the objects you create.)

Kimberly would like to see the information in the Visit table presented in a more readable and professional format. You'll help Kimberly by creating a report.

Creating a Simple Report

As noted earlier, a report is a formatted printout (or screen display) of the contents of one or more tables or queries. You'll use the Report tool to quickly produce a report based on the Visit table for Kimberly. The Report tool creates a report based on the selected table or query.

To create the report using the Report tool:

1. On the ribbon, click the **Create** tab.

2. In the Reports group, click the **Report** button. The Report tool creates a simple report showing every field in the Visit table and places it on a tab named "Visit" because the object you created (the report) is based on the Visit table. See Figure 1-24.

Figure 1-24 **Report created by the Report tool**

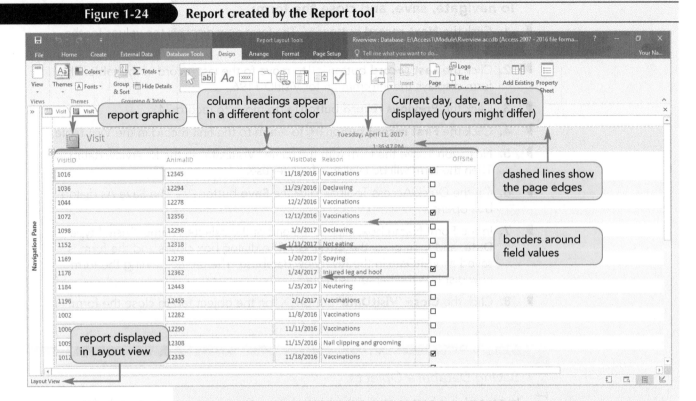

Trouble? The records in your report might appear in a different order from the records shown in Figure 1-24. This difference will not cause any problems.

The report shows each field in a column, with the field values for each record in a row, similar to a table or query datasheet. However, the report offers a more visually appealing format for the data, with the column headings in a different color, borders around each field value, a graphic of a report at the top left, and the current day, date, and time at the top right. Also notice the dashed horizontal and vertical lines on the top and right, respectively; these lines mark the edges of the page and show where text will print on the page.

The report needs some design changes to better display the data. The columns are much wider than necessary for the VisitID and AnimalID fields, and the Reason and OffSite field values and borders are not completely displayed within the page area defined by the dashed lines, which means they would not appear on the same page as the rest of the fields in the printed report. You can resize the columns easily in Layout view.

To resize the VisitID and AnimalID columns:

▶ **1.** Position the pointer on the right border of any field value in the VisitID column until the pointer changes to ↔.

▶ **2.** Click and drag the mouse to the left. Notice the dark outlines surrounding the field names and field values indicating the changing column width.

▶ **3.** Drag to the left until the column is slightly wider than the VisitID field name, and then release the mouse button. The VisitID column is now narrower, and the other four columns have shifted to the left. The Reason and OffSite fields, values, and borders are now completely within the page area. See Figure 1-25.

Figure 1-25   Report after resizing the VisitID column

field values and borders are now within the page border marked by the dashed lines

column is now narrower

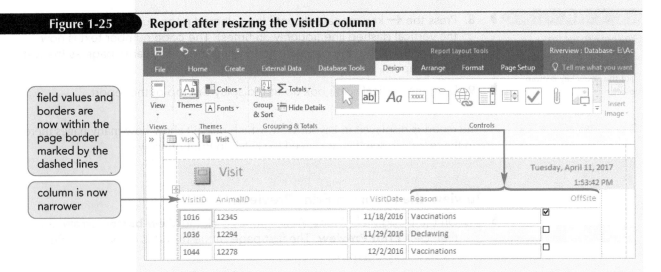

4. Click the first field value for AnimalID. AnimalID is now the current field.

5. Position the pointer on the right border of the first value in the AnimalID column until the pointer changes to ↔, click and drag to the left until the column is slightly wider than its field name, and then release the mouse button.

6. Drag the scroll box on the vertical scroll bar down to the bottom of the report to check its entire layout.

The Report tool displays the number "75" at the bottom left of the report, showing the total number of records in the report and the table on which it is based—the Visit table. The Report tool also displays the page number at the bottom right, but the text "Page 1 of 1" appears cut off through the vertical dashed line. This will cause a problem when you print the report, so you need to move this text to the left.

7. Click anywhere on the words **Page 1 of 1**. An orange outline appears around the text, indicating it is selected. See Figure 1-26.

Figure 1-26   Report page number selected

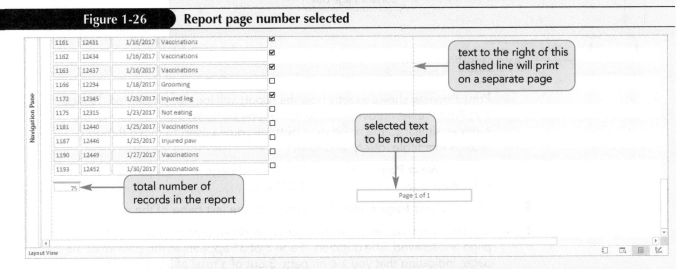

text to the right of this dashed line will print on a separate page

selected text to be moved

total number of records in the report

Page 1 of 1

With the text selected, you can use the keyboard arrow keys to move it.

TIP

You can also use the mouse to drag the selected page number, but the arrow key is more precise.

8. Press the ← key repeatedly until the selected page number is to the left of the vertical dashed line (roughly 35 times). The page number text is now completely within the page area and will print on the same page as the rest of the report.

9. Drag the vertical scroll box up to redisplay the top of the report.

The report is displayed in Layout view, which doesn't show how many pages there are in the report. To see this, you need to switch to Print Preview.

To view the report in Print Preview:

1. On the Design tab, in the Views group, click the **View button arrow**, and then click **Print Preview**. The first page of the report is displayed in Print Preview. See Figure 1-27.

Figure 1-27   **First page of the report in Print Preview**

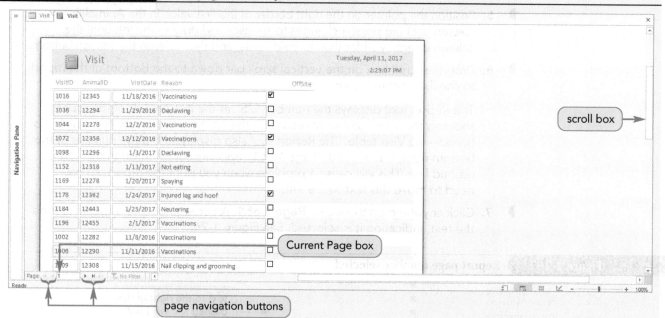

Print Preview shows exactly how the report will look when printed. Notice that Print Preview provides page navigation buttons at the bottom of the window, similar to the navigation buttons you've used to move through records in a table, query, and form.

2. Click the **Next Page** button ▶. The second page of the report is displayed in Print Preview.

3. Click the **Last Page** button ▶| to move to the last page of the report.

4. Drag the scroll box in the vertical scroll bar down until the bottom of the report page is displayed. The notation "Page 3 of 3" appears at the bottom of the page, indicating that you are on page 3 out of a total of 3 pages in the report.

Trouble? Depending on the printer you are using, your report might have more or fewer pages, and some of the pages might be blank. If so, don't worry. Different printers format reports in different ways, sometimes affecting the total number of pages and the number of records printed per page.

5. Click the **First Page** button to return to the first page of the report, and then drag the scroll box in the vertical scroll bar up to display the top of the report.

Next you'll save the report as VisitDetails, and then print it.

6. On the Quick Access Toolbar, click the **Save** button. The Save As dialog box opens.

7. In the Report Name box, click at the end of the selected word "Visit," type **Details**, and then press the **Enter** key. The dialog box closes and the report is saved as VisitDetails in the Riverview database. The tab containing the report now displays the name "VisitDetails."

Printing a Report

After creating a report, you might need to print it to distribute it to others who need to view the report's contents. You can print a report without changing any print settings, or display the Print dialog box and select options for printing.

REFERENCE

Printing a Report

- Open the report in any view, or select the report in the Navigation Pane.
- Click the File tab to display Backstage view, click Print, and then click Quick Print to print the report with the default print settings.

or

- Open the report in any view, or select the report in the Navigation Pane.
- Click the File tab, click Print, and then click Print (or, if the report is displayed in Print Preview, click the Print button in the Print group on the Print Preview tab). The Print dialog box opens, in which you can select the options you want for printing the report.

Kimberly asks you to print the entire report with the default settings, so you'll use the Quick Print option in Backstage view.

Note: To complete the following steps, your computer must be connected to a printer. Check with your instructor first to see if you should print the report.

To print the report and then close it:

1. On the ribbon, click the **File** tab to open Backstage view.

2. In the navigation bar, click **Print** to display the Print screen, and then click **Quick Print**. The report prints with the default print settings, and you return to the report in Print Preview.

Trouble? If your report did not print, make sure that your computer is connected to a printer, and that the printer is turned on and ready to print. Then repeat Steps 1 and 2.

3. Click the **Close 'VisitDetails'** button on the object tab to close the report.

4. Click the **Close 'Visit'** button on the object tab to close the Visit table.

Trouble? If you are asked to save changes to the layout of the table, click the Yes button.

You can also use the Print dialog box to print other database objects, such as table and query datasheets. Most often, these objects are used for viewing and entering data, and reports are used for printing the data in a database.

Viewing Objects in the Navigation Pane

The Riverview database now contains four objects—the Visit table, the VisitList query, the VisitData form, and the VisitDetails report. When you work with the database file—such as closing it, opening it, or distributing it to others—the file includes all the objects you created and saved in the database. You can view and work with these objects in the Navigation Pane.

To view the objects in the Riverview database:

▶ **1.** On the Navigation Pane, click the **Shutter Bar Open/Close Button** ⟫ to open the pane. See Figure 1-28.

Figure 1-28   **First page of the report in Print Preview**

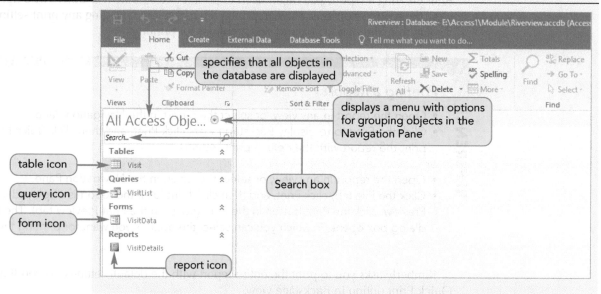

The Navigation Pane currently displays the default category, **All Access Objects**, which lists all the database objects in the pane. Each object type (Tables, Queries, Forms, and Reports) appears in its own group. Each database object (the Visit table, the VisitList query, the VisitData form, and the VisitDetails report) has a unique icon to its left to indicate the type of object. This makes it easy for you to identify the objects and choose which one you want to open and work with.

The arrow on the All Access Objects bar displays a menu with options for various ways to group and display objects in the Navigation Pane. The Search box enables you to enter text for Access to find; for example, you could search for all objects that contain the word "Visit" in their names. Note that Access searches for objects only in the categories and groups currently displayed in the Navigation Pane.

As you continue to build the Riverview database and add more objects to it in later modules, you'll use the options in the Navigation Pane to manage those objects.

Using Microsoft Access Help

Access includes a Help system you can use to search for information about specific program features. You start Help by clicking the Microsoft Access Help button in the top right of the Access window, or by pressing the F1 key.

You'll use Help now to learn more about the Navigation Pane.

To search for information about the Navigation Pane in Help:

TIP

You can also get help by typing keywords in the Tell Me box on the ribbon to access information about topics related to those words in the Access Help window.

1. Click the **Microsoft Access Help** button [?] on the title bar. The Access 2016 Help window opens, as shown earlier in the Session 1.2 Visual Overview.

2. Click in the **Search** box, type **Navigation Pane**, and then press the **Enter** key. The Access 2016 Help window displays a list of topics related to the Navigation Pane.

3. Click the topic **Manage Access database objects in the Navigation Pane**. The Access Help window displays the article you selected. See Figure 1-29.

Figure 1-29   Article displayed in the Access Help window

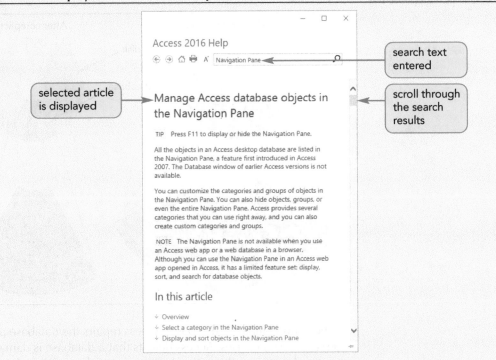

Access 2016 Help

search text entered

Navigation Pane

selected article is displayed

Manage Access database objects in the Navigation Pane

scroll through the search results

TIP   Press F11 to display or hide the Navigation Pane.

All the objects in an Access desktop database are listed in the Navigation Pane, a feature first introduced in Access 2007. The Database window of earlier Access versions is not available.

You can customize the categories and groups of objects in the Navigation Pane. You can also hide objects, groups, or even the entire Navigation Pane. Access provides several categories that you can use right away, and you can also create custom categories and groups.

NOTE   The Navigation Pane is not available when you use an Access web app or a web database in a browser. Although you can use the Navigation Pane in an Access web app opened in Access, it has a limited feature set: display, sort, and search for database objects.

In this article

↓ Overview
↓ Select a category in the Navigation Pane
↓ Display and sort objects in the Navigation Pane

Trouble? If the article on managing database objects is not listed in your Help window, choose another article related to the Navigation Pane to read.

4. Scroll through the article to read detailed information about working with the Navigation Pane.

5. When finished, click the **Close** button [X] on the Access 2016 Help window to close it.

The Access Help system is an important reference tool for you to use if you need additional information about databases in general, details about specific Access features, or support with problems you might encounter.

Managing a Database

One of the main tasks involved in working with database software is managing your databases and the data they contain. Some of the activities involved in database management include compacting and repairing a database and backing up and restoring a database. By managing your databases, you can ensure that they operate in the most efficient way, that the data they contain is secure, and that you can work with the data effectively.

Compacting and Repairing a Database

Whenever you open an Access database and work in it, the size of the database increases. Further, when you delete records or when you delete or replace database objects—such as queries, forms, and reports—the storage space that had been occupied by the deleted or replaced records or objects does not automatically become available for other records or objects. To make the space available, and also to increase the speed of data retrieval, you must compact the database. **Compacting** a database rearranges the data and objects in a database to decrease its file size, thereby making more storage space available and enhancing the performance of the database. Figure 1-30 illustrates the compacting process.

Figure 1-30   **Compacting a database**

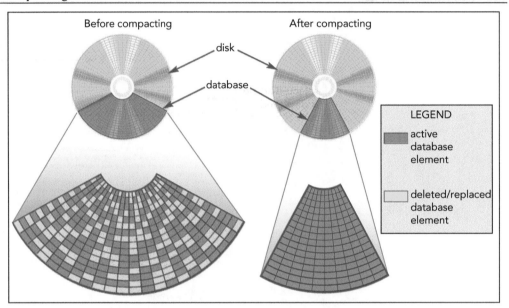

When you compact a database, Access repairs the database at the same time, if necessary. In some cases, Access detects that a database is damaged when you try to open it and gives you the option to compact and repair it at that time. For example, the data in your database might become damaged, or corrupted, if you exit the Access program suddenly by turning off your computer. If you think your database might be damaged because it is behaving unpredictably, you can use the Compact & Repair Database option to fix it.

REFERENCE

Compacting and Repairing a Database

- Make sure the database file you want to compact and repair is open.
- Click the File tab to display the Info screen in Backstage view.
- Click the Compact & Repair Database button.

Access also allows you to set an option to compact and repair a database file automatically every time you close it. The Compact on Close option is available in the Current Database section of the Access Options dialog box, which you open from

Backstage view by clicking the Options command in the navigation bar. By default, the Compact on Close option is turned off.

Next, you'll compact the Riverview database manually using the Compact & Repair Database option. This will make the database smaller and allow you to work with it more efficiently. After compacting the database, you'll close it.

To compact and repair the Riverview database:

▶ **1.** On the ribbon, click the **File** tab to open the Info screen in Backstage view.

▶ **2.** Click the **Compact & Repair Database** button. Although nothing visible happens on the screen, the Riverview database is compacted, making it smaller, and repairs it at the same time. The Home tab is again the active tab on the ribbon.

▶ **3.** Click the **File** tab to return to Backstage view, and then click **Close** in the navigation bar. The Riverview database closes.

Backing Up and Restoring a Database

Backing up a database is the process of making a copy of the database file to protect your database against loss or damage. The Back Up Database command enables you to back up your database file from within the Access program, while you are working on your database. To use this option, click the File tab to display the Info screen in Backstage view, click Save As in the navigation bar, click Back Up Database in the Advanced section of the Save Database As pane, and then click the Save As button. In the Save As dialog box that opens, a default filename is provided for the backup copy that consists of the same filename as the database you are backing up (for example, "Riverview"), and an underscore character, plus the current date. This filenaming system makes it easy for you to keep track of your database backups and when they were created. To restore a backup database file, you simply copy the backup from the location where it is stored to your hard drive, or whatever device you use to work in Access, and start working with the restored database file. (You will not actually back up the Riverview database in this module unless directed by your instructor to do so.)

INSIGHT

Planning and Performing Database Backups

Experienced database users make it a habit to back up a database before they work with it for the first time, keeping the original data intact. They also make frequent backups while continuing to work with a database; these backups are generally on flash drives, recordable CDs or DVDs, external or network hard drives, or cloud-based storage (such as OneDrive). Also, it is recommended to store the backup copy in a different location from the original. For example, if the original database is stored on a flash drive, you should not store the backup copy on the same flash drive. If you lose the drive or the drive is damaged, you would lose both the original database and its backup copy.

If the original database file and the backup copy have the same name, restoring the backup copy might replace the original. If you want to save the original file, rename it before you restore the backup copy. To ensure that the restored database has the most current data, you should update the restored database with any changes made to the original between the time you created the backup copy and the time the original database became damaged or lost.

By properly planning for and performing backups, you can avoid losing data and prevent the time-consuming effort required to rebuild a lost or damaged database.

PROSKILLS

Decision Making: When to Use Access vs. Excel

Using a spreadsheet application like Microsoft Excel to manage lists or tables of information works well when the data is simple, such as a list of contacts or tasks. As soon as the data becomes complex enough to separate into tables that need to be related, you start to see the limitations of using a spreadsheet application. The strength of a database application such as Access is in its ability to easily relate one table of information to another. Consider a table of contacts that includes home addresses, with a separate row for each person living at the same address. When an address changes, it's too easy to make a mistake and not update the home address for each person who lives there. To ensure you have the most accurate data at all times, it's important to have only one instance of each piece of data. By creating separate tables that are related and keeping only one instance of each piece of data, you'll ensure the integrity of the data. Trying to accomplish this in Excel is a complex process, whereas Access is specifically designed for this functionality.

Another limitation of using Excel instead of Access to manage data has to do with the volume of data. Although a spreadsheet can hold thousands of records, a database can hold millions. A spreadsheet containing thousands of pieces of information is cumbersome to use. Think of large-scale commercial applications such as enrollment at a college or tracking customers for a large company. It's hard to imagine managing such information in an Excel spreadsheet. Instead, you'd use a database. Finally, with an Access database, multiple users can access the information it contains at the same time. Although an Excel spreadsheet can be shared, there can be problems when users try to open and edit the same spreadsheet at the same time.

When you're trying to decide whether to use Excel or Access, ask yourself the following questions.

1. Do you need to store data in separate tables that are related to each other?
2. Do you have a very large amount of data to store?
3. Will more than one person need to access the data at the same time?

If you answer "yes" to any of these questions, an Access database is most likely the appropriate application to use.

In the following modules, you'll help Kimberly complete and maintain the Riverview database, and you'll use it to meet the specific information needs of the employees of the care center.

REVIEW

Session 1.2 Quick Check

1. To copy the records from a table in one database to another table in a different database, the two tables must have the same _____.

2. A(n) _____ is a question you ask about the data stored in a database.

3. The quickest way to create a form is to use the _____.

4. Which view enables you to see the total number of pages in a report and navigate through the report pages?

5. In the Navigation Pane, each database object has a unique _____ to its left that identifies the object's type.

6. _____ a database rearranges the data and objects in a database to decrease its file size and enhance the speed and performance of the database.

7. _____ a database is the process of making a copy of the database file to protect the database against loss or damage.

Review Assignments

PRACTICE

Data File needed for the Review Assignments: Company.accdb

For Riverview Veterinary Care Center, Kimberly asks you to create a new database to contain information about the vendors that the care center works with to obtain supplies, equipment, and resale items, and the vendors who service and maintain the equipment. Complete the following steps:

1. Create a new, blank database named **Vendor** and save it in the folder where you are storing your files, as specified by your instructor.

2. In Datasheet view for the Table1 table, rename the default ID primary key field to **SupplierID**. Change the data type of the SupplierID field to Short Text.

3. Add the following 10 fields to the new table in the order shown; all of them are Short Text fields *except* InitialContact, which is a Date/Time field: **Company**, **Category**, **Address**, **City**, **State**, **Zip**, **Phone**, **ContactFirst**, **ContactLast**, and **InitialContact**. Resize the columns as necessary so that the complete field names are displayed. Save the table as **Supplier**.

4. Enter the records shown in Figure 1-31 in the Supplier table. For the first record, be sure to enter your first name in the ContactFirst field and your last name in the ContactLast field.
   Note: When entering field values that are shown on multiple lines in the figure, do not try to enter the values on multiple lines. The values are shown on multiple lines in the figure for page spacing purposes only.

Figure 1-31   Supplier table records

SupplierID	Company	Category	Address	City	State	Zip	Phone	ContactFirst	ContactLast	InitialContact
YUM345	Yummy Dog Food	Resale	345 Riverside Dr	Charlotte	NC	28201	704-205-8725	*Student First*	*Student Last*	2/1/2017
FTS123	Flea & Tick Supplies	Resale	123 Overlook Ln	Atlanta	GA	30301	404-341-2981	Robert	Jackson	3/6/2017
PMC019	Pet Medical	Equipment	19 Waverly Ct	Blacksburg	VA	24061	540-702-0098	Julie	Baxter	2/21/2017
APL619	A+ Labs	Equipment	619 West Dr	Omaha	NE	68022	531-219-7206	Jacques	Dupont	4/10/2017
CWI444	Cat World Inc.	Supplies	444 Boxcar Way	San Diego	CA	92110	619-477-9482	Amelia	Kline	5/1/2017

5. Kimberly created a database named Company that contains a Business table with supplier data. The Supplier table you created has the same design as the Business table. Copy all the records from the **Business** table in the **Company** database (located in the Access1 > Review folder provided with your Data Files) and then paste them at the end of the Supplier table in the Vendor database.

6. Resize all datasheet columns to their best fit, and then save the Supplier table.

7. Close the Supplier table, and then use the Navigation Pane to reopen it. Note that the records are displayed in primary key order by the values in the SupplierID field.

8. Use the Simple Query Wizard to create a query that includes the Company, Category, ContactFirst, ContactLast, and Phone fields (in that order) from the Supplier table. Name the query **SupplierList**, and then close the query.

9. Use the Form tool to create a form for the Supplier table. Save the form as **SupplierInfo**, and then close it.

10. Use the Report tool to create a report based on the Supplier table. In Layout view, resize all fields except the Company field, so that each field is slightly wider than the longest entry (either the field name itself or an entry in the field). Display the report in Print Preview and verify that all the fields fit across one page in the report. Save the report as **SupplierDetails**, and then close it.

11. Close the Supplier table, and then compact and repair the Vendor database.

12. Close the Vendor database.

APPLY

Case Problem 1

Data File needed for this Case Problem: BeautyToGo.accdb

Beauty To Go Sue Miller, an owner of a nail and hair salon in Orlando, Florida, regularly checks in on her grandmother, who resides in a retirement community. On some of her visits, Sue does her grandmother's hair and nails. Her grandmother recently asked if Sue would also be willing to do the hair and nails of some of her friends in her retirement community and other surrounding communities. She said that these friends would happily pay for her services. Sue thinks this is an excellent way to expand her current business and serve the needs of the retirement community at the same time. In discussing the opportunity with some of the members of the retirement community, she found that the ladies would very much like to pay Sue in advance for her services and have them scheduled on a regular basis; however, the frequency and types of the services vary from person to person. Sue decides to come up with different options that would serve the needs of the ladies in the retirement community. Sue wants to use Access to maintain information about the customers and the types of options offered. She needs your help in creating this database. Complete the following:

1. Create a new, blank database named **Beauty** and save it in the folder where you are storing your files, as specified by your instructor.

2. In Datasheet view for the Table1 table, rename the default primary key ID field to **OptionID**. Change the data type of the OptionID field to Short Text.

3. Add the following three fields to the new table in the order shown: **OptionDescription** (a Short Text field), **OptionCost** (a Currency field), and **FeeWaived** (a Yes/No field). Save the table as **Option**.

4. Enter the records shown in Figure 1-32 in the Option table. *Hint*: When entering the OptionCost field values, you do not have to type the dollar signs, commas, or decimal places; they will be entered automatically.

Figure 1-32 **Option table records**

	OptionID	OptionDescription	OptionCost	FeeWaived
when entering currency values, you do not have to type the dollar signs, commas, or decimal places	136	Wash/cut bi-weekly for 6 months	$500.00	Yes
	101	Manicure weekly for 1 month	$125.00	No
	124	Manicure/pedicure weekly for 3 months	$700.00	Yes
	142	Wash/cut/color monthly for 6 months	$600.00	Yes
	117	Pedicure bi-weekly for 3 months	$190.00	No

5. Sue created a database named BeautyToGo that contains a MoreOptions table with plan data. The Option table you created has the same design as the MoreOptions table. Copy all the records from the **MoreOptions** table in the **BeautyToGo** database (located in the Access1 > Case1 folder provided with your Data Files), and then paste them at the end of the Option table in the Beauty database.

6. Resize all datasheet columns to their best fit, and then save the Option table.

7. Close the Option table, and then use the Navigation Pane to reopen it. Note that the records are displayed in primary key order by the values in the OptionID field.

8. Use the Simple Query Wizard to create a query that includes the OptionID, OptionDescription, and OptionCost fields from the Option table. In the second Simple Query Wizard dialog box, select the Detail option if necessary. (This option appears because the query includes a Currency field.) Save the query as **OptionData**, and then close the query.

9. Use the Form tool to create a form for the Option table. Save the form as **OptionInfo**, and then close it.

10. Use the Report tool to create a report based on the Option table. In Layout view, resize the OptionID field so it is slightly wider than the longest entry, which is the field name in this case. Resize the OptionDescription field so there are no entries with multiple lines. Also, resize the box containing the total amount that appears below the OptionCost column by clicking the box and then dragging its bottom border down so that the amount is fully displayed. (The Report Tool calculated this total automatically.) Display the report in Print Preview; then verify that all the fields are within the page area and all field values are fully displayed. Save the report as **OptionList**, print the report (only if asked by your instructor to do so), and then close it.

11. Close the Option table, and then compact and repair the Beauty database.

12. Close the Beauty database.

Case Problem 2

APPLY

Data File needed for this Case Problem: ProgPros.accdb

Programming Pros   While in college obtaining his bachelor's degree in Raleigh, North Carolina, Brent Hovis majored in computer science and learned programming. Brent found that many of his fellow classmates found it difficult to write code, and he was constantly assisting them with helpful tips and techniques. Prior to graduating, Brent began tutoring freshman and sophomore students in programming to make some extra money. As his reputation grew, high school students began contacting him for help with their programming classes. When Brent entered graduate school, he started Programming Pros, a company offering expanded tutoring service for high school and college students through group, private, and semi-private tutoring sessions. As demand for the company's services grew, Brent hired many of his fellow classmates to assist him. Brent wants to use Access to maintain information about the tutors who work for him, the students who sign up for tutoring, and the contracts they sign. He needs your help in creating this database. Complete the following steps:

1. Create a new, blank database named **Programming** and save it in the folder where you are storing your files, as specified by your instructor.

2. In Datasheet view for the Table1 table, rename the default primary key ID field to **TutorID**. Change the data type of the TutorID field to Short Text.

3. Add the following five fields to the new table in the order shown; all of them are Short Text fields *except* HireDate, which is a Date/Time field: **FirstName**, **LastName**, **Major**, **YearInSchool**, **School**, and **HireDate**. Resize the columns, if necessary, so that the complete field names are displayed. Save the table as **Tutor**.

4. Enter the records shown in Figure 1-33 in the Tutor table. For the first record, be sure to enter your first name in the FirstName field and your last name in the LastName field.

Figure 1-33   Tutor table records

TutorID	FirstName	LastName	Major	YearInSchool	School	HireDate
1060	*Student First*	*Student Last*	Computer Science	Senior	Ellings College	2/14/2017
1010	Cathy	Cowler	Computer Engineering	Graduate	Eikenville College	2/1/2017
1051	Donald	Gallager	Computer Science	Graduate	Hogan University	1/18/2017
1031	Nichole	Schneider	Computer Science	Junior	Switzer University	2/28/2017
1018	Fredrik	Karlsson	Mechatronics	Junior	Smith Technical College	2/6/2017

5. Brent created a database named ProgPros that contains a MoreTutors table with tutor data. The Tutor table you created has the same design as the MoreTutors table. Copy all the records from the **MoreTutors** table in the **ProgPros** database (located in the Access1 > Case2 folder provided with your Data Files), and then paste them at the end of the Tutor table in the Programming database.

6. Resize all datasheet columns to their best fit, and then save the Tutor table.

7. Close the Tutor table, and then use the Navigation Pane to reopen it. Note that the records are displayed in primary key order by the values in the TutorID field.

8. Use the Simple Query Wizard to create a query that includes the FirstName, LastName, and HireDate fields from the Tutor table. Save the query as **StartDate**, and then close the query.

9. Use the Form tool to create a form for the Tutor table. Save the form as **TutorInfo**, and then close it.

10. Use the Report tool to create a report based on the Tutor table. In Layout view, resize the TutorID, FirstName, LastName, Major, YearInSchool, School, and HireDate fields so they are slightly wider than the longest entry (either the field name itself or an entry in the field). All seven fields should fit within the page area after you resize the fields. At the bottom of the report, move the text "Page 1 of 1" to the left so it is within the page area. Display the report in Print Preview; then verify that the fields and page number fit within the page area and that all field values are fully displayed. Save the report as **TutorList**, print the report (only if asked by your instructor to do so), and then close it.

11. Close the Tutor table, and then compact and repair the Programming database.

12. Close the Programming database.

Case Problem 3

CHALLENGE

Data File needed for this Case Problem: Diane.accdb

Diane's Community Center   Diane Coleman is a successful businesswoman in Dallas, Georgia, but things were not always that way. Diane experienced trying times and fortunately had people in the community come into her life to assist her and her children when times were difficult. Diane now wants to give back to her community and support those in need, just as she was supported many years ago, by creating a community center in Dallas where those in need can come in for goods and services. Diane plans to open a thrift store as well to sell donated items to support the center. Diane has been contacted by many people in the community wishing to donate materials to the center as well as items to be sold at the thrift store. Diane has asked you to create an Access database to manage information about the center's patrons and donations. Complete the following steps:

1. Create a new, blank database named **Center** and save it in the folder where you are storing your files, as specified by your instructor.

2. In Datasheet view for the Table1 table, rename the default primary key ID field to **PatronID**. Change the data type of the PatronID field to Short Text.

3. Add the following five Short Text fields to the new table in the order shown: **Title**, **FirstName**, **LastName**, **Phone**, and **Email**. Save the table as **Patron**.

4. Enter the records shown in Figure 1-34 in the Patron table. For the first record, be sure to enter your title in the Title field, your first name in the FirstName field, and your last name in the LastName field.

Figure 1-34   Patron table records

PatronID	Title	FirstName	LastName	Phone	Email
3001	*Student Title*	*Student First*	*Student Last*	404-987-1234	student@example.com
3030	Mr.	David	Hampton	404-824-3381	thehamptons@example.net
3006	Dr.	Elbert	Schneider	678-492-9101	countrydoc@example.com
3041	Mr.	Frank	Miller	404-824-3431	frankmiller12@example.net
3019	Mrs.	Jane	Michaels	706-489-3310	jjmichaels@example.com

5. Diane created a database named Diane that contains a MorePatrons table with data about additional patrons. The Patron table you created has the same design as the MorePatrons table. Copy all the records from the **MorePatrons** table in the **Diane** database (located in the Access1 > Case3 folder provided with your Data Files), and then paste them at the end of the Patron table in the Center database.

6. Resize all datasheet columns to their best fit, and then save the Patron table.

7. Close the Patron table, and then use the Navigation Pane to reopen it. Note that the records are displayed in primary key order by the values in the PatronID field.

✪ **Explore** 8. Use the Simple Query Wizard to create a query that includes all the fields in the Patron table *except* the Title field. (*Hint*: Use the >> and < buttons to select the necessary fields.) Save the query using the name **PatronContactList**.

✪ **Explore** 9. The query results are displayed in order by the PatronID field values. You can specify a different order by sorting the query. Display the Home tab. Then, click the insertion point anywhere in the LastName column to make it the current field. In the Sort & Filter group on the Home tab, click the Ascending button. The records are now listed in order by the values in the LastName field. Save and close the query.

✪ **Explore** 10. Use the Form tool to create a form for the Patron table. In the new form, navigate to record 13 (the record with PatronID 3028), and then print the form *for the current record only*. (*Hint*: You must use the Print dialog box in order to print only the current record. Go to Backstage view, click Print in the navigation bar, and then click Print to open the Print dialog box. Click the Selected Record(s) option button, and then click the OK button to print the current record.) Save the form as **PatronInfo**, and then close it.

11. Use the Report tool to create a report based on the Patron table. In Layout view, resize each field so it is slightly wider than the longest entry (either the field name itself or an entry in the field). All six fields should fit within the page area after resizing. At the bottom of the report, move the text "Page 1 of 1" to the left so it is within the page area. Display the report in Print Preview, then verify that the fields and page number fit within the page area and that all field values are fully displayed. Save the report as **PatronList**. Print the report (only if asked by your instructor to do so), and then close it.

12. Close the Patron table, and then compact and repair the Center database.

13. Close the Center database.

CHALLENGE

Case Problem 4

Data File needed for this Case Problem: HikeApp.accdb

Hike Appalachia   Molly and Bailey Johnson grew up in the Blue Ridge Mountains of North Carolina. Their parents were avid outdoors people and loved to take the family on long hikes and teach the girls about the great outdoors. During middle school and high school, their friends would ask them to guide them in the surrounding area because it could be quite dangerous. One summer, the girls had an idea to expand their hiking clientele beyond their friends and help earn money for college; this was the start of their business, which they named Hike Appalachia. The girls advertised in local and regional outdoor magazines and were flooded with requests from people all around the region. They would like you to build an Access database to manage information about the hikers they guide, the tours they provide, and tour reservations. Complete the following:

1. Create a new, blank database named **Appalachia** and save it in the folder where you are storing your files, as specified by your instructor.

2. In Datasheet view for the Table1 table, rename the default primary key ID field to **HikerID**. Change the data type of the HikerID field to Short Text.

3. Add the following seven Short Text fields to the new table in the order shown: **HikerFirst**, **HikerLast**, **Address**, **City**, **State**, **Zip**, and **Phone**. Save the table as **Hiker**.

4. Enter the records shown in Figure 1-35 in the Hiker table. For the first record, be sure to enter your first name in the HikerFirst field and your last name in the HikerLast field.

Figure 1-35   **Hiker table records**

HikerID	HikerFirst	HikerLast	Address	City	State	Zip	Phone
501	*Student First*	*Student Last*	123 Jackson St	Boone	NC	28607	828-497-9128
547	Heather	Smith	412 Sentry Ln	Gastonia	NC	28052	704-998-0987
521	Zack	Hoskins	2 Hope Rd	Atlanta	GA	30301	404-998-2381
535	Elmer	Jackson	99 River Rd	Blacksburg	SC	29702	864-921-2384
509	Sarah	Peeler	32 Mountain Ln	Ridgeview	WV	25169	703-456-9381

5. Molly and Bailey created a database named HikeApp that contains a MoreHikers table with data about hikers. The Hiker table you created has the same design as the MoreHikers table. Copy all the records from the **MoreHikers** table in the **HikeApp** database (located in the Access1 > Case4 folder provided with your Data Files), and then paste them at the end of the Hiker table in the Appalachia database.

6. Resize all datasheet columns to their best fit, and then save the Hiker table.

7. Close the Hiker table, and then use the Navigation Pane to reopen it. Note that the records are displayed in primary key order.

8. Use the Simple Query Wizard to create a query that includes the following fields from the Hiker table, in the order shown: HikerID, HikerLast, HikerFirst, State, and Phone. Name the query **HikerData**.

⊕ **Explore** 9. The query results are displayed in order by the HikerID field values. You can specify a different order by sorting the query. Display the Home tab. Then, click the insertion point anywhere in the State column to make it the current field. In the Sort & Filter group on the Home tab, click the Ascending button. The records are now listed in order by the values in the State field. Save and close the query.

⊕ **Explore** 10. Use the Form tool to create a form for the Hiker table. In the new form, navigate to record 10 (the record with HikerID 527), and then print the form *for the current record only*. (*Hint:* You must use the Print dialog box in order to print only the current record. Go to Backstage view, click Print in the navigation bar, and then click Print to open the Print dialog box. Click the Selected Record(s) option button, and then click the OK button to print the current record.) Save the form as **HikerInfo**, and then close it.

11. Use the Report tool to create a report based on the Hiker table. In Layout view, resize each field so it is slightly wider than the longest entry (either the field name itself or an entry in the field). At the bottom of the report, move the text "Page 1 of 1" to the left so it is within the page area on the report's first page. All fields should fit on one page. Save the report as **HikerList**.

12. Print the report (only if asked by your instructor to do so), and then close it.

a. Close the Hiker table, and then compact and repair the Appalachia database.

b. Close the Appalachia database.

MODULE 2

Building a Database and Defining Table Relationships

Creating the Billing, Owner, and Animal Tables

OBJECTIVES

Session 2.1
- Learn the guidelines for designing databases and setting field properties
- Create a table in Design view
- Define fields, set field properties, and specify a table's primary key
- Modify the structure of a table
- Change the order of fields in Design view
- Add new fields in Design view
- Change the Format property for a field in Datasheet view
- Modify field properties in Design view

Session 2.2
- Import data from Excel
- Import an existing table structure
- Add fields to a table with the Data Type gallery
- Delete and rename fields
- Change the data type for a field in Design view
- Set the Default Value property for a field
- Import a text file
- Define a relationship between two tables

Case | *Riverview Veterinary Care Center*

The Riverview database currently contains one table, the Visit table. Kimberly Johnson also wants to track information about the clinic's animals, their owners, and the invoices sent to them for services provided by Riverview Veterinary Care Center. This information includes such items as each owner's name and address, animal information, and the amount and billing date for each invoice.

In this module, you'll create three new tables in the Riverview database—named Billing, Owner, and Animal—to contain the additional data Kimberly wants to track. You will use two different methods for creating the tables, and learn how to modify the fields. After adding records to the tables, you will define the necessary relationships between the tables in the Riverview database to relate the tables, enabling Kimberly and her staff to work with the data more efficiently.

STARTING DATA FILES

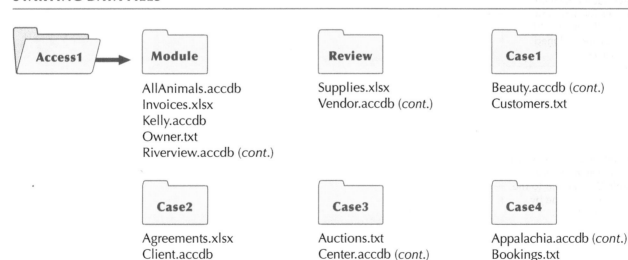

Module
AllAnimals.accdb
Invoices.xlsx
Kelly.accdb
Owner.txt
Riverview.accdb (*cont.*)

Review
Supplies.xlsx
Vendor.accdb (*cont.*)

Case1
Beauty.accdb (*cont.*)
Customers.txt

Case2
Agreements.xlsx
Client.accdb
Programming.accdb (*cont.*)
Students.txt

Case3
Auctions.txt
Center.accdb (*cont.*)
Donations.xlsx

Case4
Appalachia.accdb (*cont.*)
Bookings.txt
Travel.accdb

Session 2.1 Visual Overview:

Design view allows you to define or modify a table structure or the properties of the fields in a table.

The default name for a new table you create in Design view is Table1. This name appears on the tab for the new table.

The top portion of the Table window in Design view is called the **Table Design grid.** Here, you enter values for the Field Name, Data type, and Description field properties.

After you assign a data type to a field, the General tab displays additional field properties for that data type. Initially, most field properties are assigned default values.

When defining the fields in a table, you can move from the Table Design grid to the Field Properties pane by pressing the F6 key.

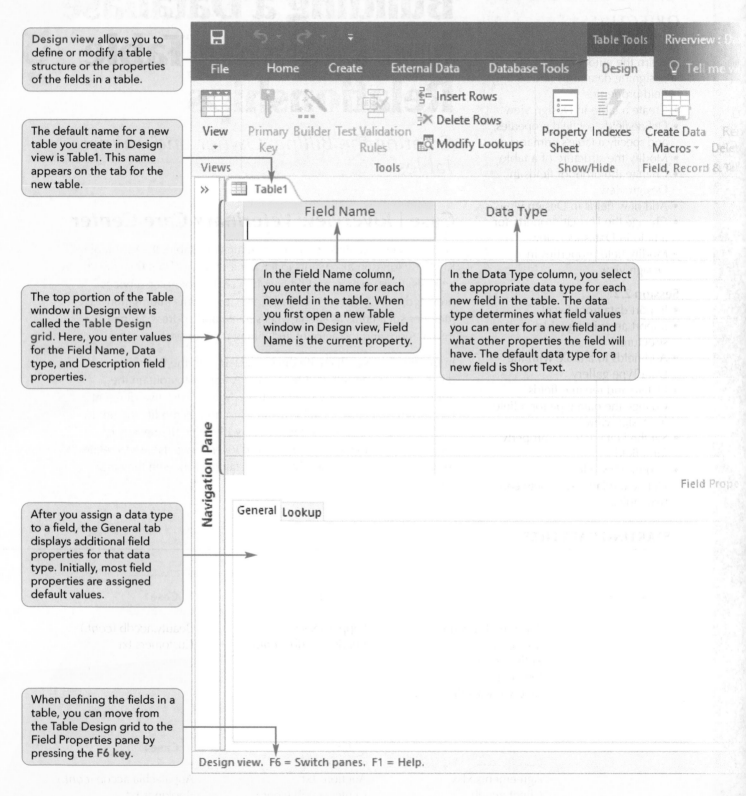

In the Field Name column, you enter the name for each new field in the table. When you first open a new Table window in Design view, Field Name is the current property.

In the Data Type column, you select the appropriate data type for each new field in the table. The data type determines what field values you can enter for a new field and what other properties the field will have. The default data type for a new field is Short Text.

Design view. F6 = Switch panes. F1 = Help.

Table Window in Design View

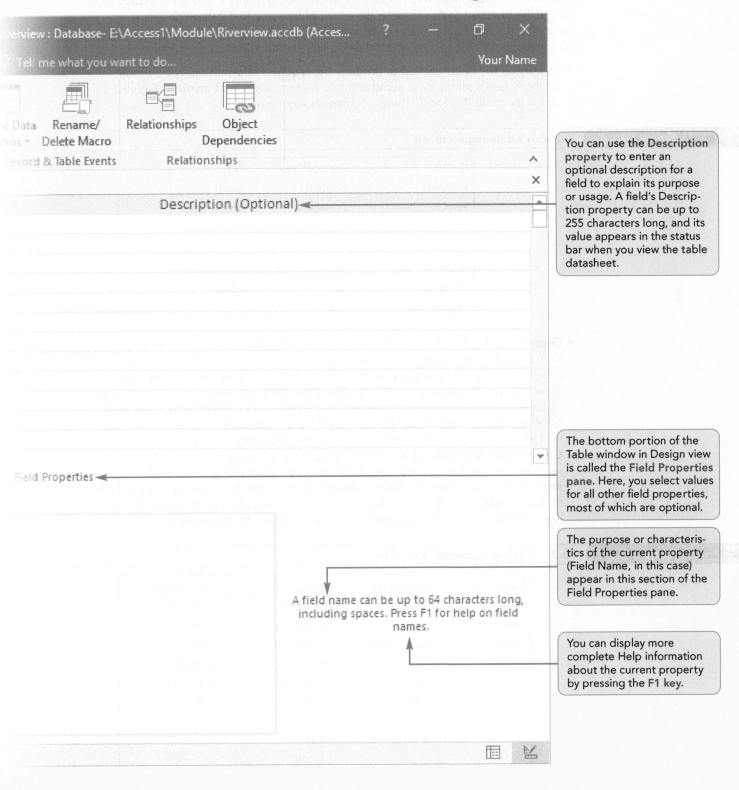

Riverview : Database- E:\Access1\Module\Riverview.accdb (Acces...   ?   —   □   ×

Tell me what you want to do...   Your Name

Data   Rename/   Relationships   Object
        Delete Macro   Dependencies
cros ▾
Record & Table Events   Relationships

Description (Optional)

You can use the **Description property** to enter an optional description for a field to explain its purpose or usage. A field's Description property can be up to 255 characters long, and its value appears in the status bar when you view the table datasheet.

Field Properties

The bottom portion of the Table window in Design view is called the **Field Properties** pane. Here, you select values for all other field properties, most of which are optional.

The purpose or characteristics of the current property (Field Name, in this case) appear in this section of the Field Properties pane.

A field name can be up to 64 characters long, including spaces. Press F1 for help on field names.

You can display more complete Help information about the current property by pressing the **F1 key**.

Guidelines for Designing Databases

A database management system can be a useful tool, but only if you first carefully design the database so that it meets the needs of its users. In database design, you determine the fields, tables, and relationships needed to satisfy the data and processing requirements. When you design a database, you should follow these guidelines:

- **Identify all the fields needed to produce the required information.** For example, Kimberly needs information about animals, owners, visits, and invoices. Figure 2-1 shows the fields that satisfy these information requirements.

Figure 2-1	Kimberly's data requirements

VisitID	AnimalBreed	Zip
VisitDate	OwnerID	Email
Reason	FirstName	InvoiceNum
OffSite	LastName	InvoiceDate
AnimalID	Phone	InvoiceAmt
AnimalName	Address	InvoiceItem
AnimalBirthDate	City	InvoicePaid
AnimalType	State	

- **Organize each piece of data into its smallest useful part.** For example, Kimberly could store each owner's complete name in one field called Name instead of using two fields called FirstName and LastName, as shown in Figure 2-1. However, doing so would make it more difficult to work with the data. If Kimberly wanted to view the records in alphabetical order by last name, she wouldn't be able to do so with field values such as "Reggie Baxter" and "Aaron Jackson" stored in a Name field. She could do so with field values such as "Baxter" and "Jackson" stored separately in a LastName field.
- **Group related fields into tables.** For example, Kimberly grouped the fields related to visits into the Visit table, which you created in the previous module. The fields related to invoices are grouped into the Billing table, the fields related to owners are grouped into the Owner table, and the fields related to animals are grouped into the Animal table. Figure 2-2 shows the fields grouped into all four tables for the Riverview database.

Figure 2-2	Kimberly's fields grouped into tables

Visit table	Billing table	Owner table	Animal table
VisitID	InvoiceNum	OwnerID	AnimalID
AnimalID	VisitID	FirstName	OwnerID
VisitDate	InvoiceDate	LastName	AnimalName
Reason	InvoiceAmt	Phone	AnimalBirthDate
OffSite	InvoiceItem	Address	AnimalType
	InvoicePaid	City	AnimalBreed
		State	
		Zip	
		Email	

- **Determine each table's primary key.** Recall that a primary key uniquely identifies each record in a table. For some tables, one of the fields, such as a credit card number, naturally serves the function of a primary key. For other tables, two or more fields might be needed to function as the primary key. In these cases, the primary key is called a **composite key.** For example, a school grade table would use a combination of student number, term, and course code to serve as the primary key. For a third category of tables, no single field or combination of fields can uniquely identify a record in a table. In these cases, you need to add a field whose sole purpose is to serve as the table's primary key. For Kimberly's tables, VisitID is the primary key for the Visit table, InvoiceNum is the primary key for the Billing table, OwnerID is the primary key for the Owner table, and AnimalID is the primary key for the Animal table.

- **Include a common field in related tables.** You use the common field to connect one table logically with another table. For example, Kimberly's Visit and Animal tables include the AnimalID field as a common field. Recall that when you include the primary key from one table as a field in a second table to form a relationship, the field in the second table is called a foreign key; therefore, the AnimalID field is a foreign key in the Visit table. With this common field, Kimberly can find all visits to the clinic made by a particular animal; she can use the AnimalID value for an animal and search the Visit table for all records with that AnimalID value. Likewise, she can determine which animal made a particular visit by searching the Animal table to find the one record with the same AnimalID value as the corresponding value in the Visit table. Similarly, the VisitID field is a common field, serving as the primary key in the Visit table and a foreign key in the Billing table. Since animals have owners responsible for their bills, there must be a relationship between the animals and owners for the clinic to contact; therefore, the OwnerID field is a foreign key in the Animal table.

- **Avoid data redundancy.** When you store the same data in more than one place, **data redundancy** occurs. With the exception of common fields to connect tables, you should avoid data redundancy because it wastes storage space and can cause inconsistencies. An inconsistency would exist, for example, if you type a field value one way in one table and a different way in the same table or in a second table. Figure 2-3, which contains portions of potential data stored in the Animal and Visit tables, shows an example of incorrect database design that has data redundancy in the Visit table. In Figure 2-3, the AnimalName field in the Visit table is redundant, and one value for this field was entered incorrectly, in three different ways.

| Figure 2-3 | Incorrect database design with data redundancy |

AnimalID	AnimalName	AnimalBirthDate	AnimalType
12286	Lady	8/12/2015	Dog
12304	Tweets	11/12/2010	Bird
12332	Smittie	5/19/2014	Cat
12345	Herford5	4/28/2015	Cattle
12359	Merino4	8/2/2014	Sheep

data redundancy

VisitID	AnimalID	AnimalName	VisitDate	OffSite
1202	12500	Bonkers	12/11/2016	No
1250	12332	Smitty	12/19/2016	No
1276	12492	Bessie	1/10/2017	Yes
1308	12332	Smity	1/23/2017	No
1325	12612	Tweets	2/6/2017	No
1342	12595	Angus	2/27/2017	Yes
1367	12332	Smittee	3/7/2017	No

Inconsistent data

- **Determine the properties of each field.** You need to identify the **properties**, or characteristics, of each field so that the DBMS knows how to store, display, and process the field values. These properties include the field's name, data type, maximum number of characters or digits, description, valid values, and other field characteristics. You will learn more about field properties later in this module.

The Billing, Owner, and Animal tables you need to create will contain the fields shown in Figure 2-2. Before creating these new tables in the Riverview database, you first need to learn some guidelines for setting field properties.

Guidelines for Setting Field Properties

As just noted, the last step of database design is to determine which values to assign to the properties, such as the name and data type, of each field. When you select or enter a value for a property, you **set** the property. Access has rules for naming fields and objects, assigning data types, and setting other field properties.

Naming Fields and Objects

You must name each field, table, and other object in an Access database. Access stores these items in the database, using the names you supply. It's best to choose a field or object name that describes the purpose or contents of the field or object so that later you can easily remember what the name represents. For example, the four tables in the Riverview database are named Visit, Billing, Owner, and Animal because these names suggest their contents. Note that a table or query name must be unique within a database. A field name must be unique within a table, but it can be used again in another table.

Assigning Field Data Types

Each field must have a data type, which is either assigned automatically by Access or specifically by the table designer. The data type determines what field values you can enter for the field and what other properties the field will have. For example, the Billing table will include an InvoiceDate field, which will store date values, so you will assign the Date/Time data type to this field. Then Access will allow you to enter and manipulate only dates or times as values in the InvoiceDate field.

Figure 2-4 lists the most commonly used data types in Access, describes the field values allowed for each data type, explains when you should use each data type, and indicates the field size of each data type. You can find more complete information about all available data types in Access Help.

Figure 2-4	Common data types

Data Type	Description	Field Size
Short Text	Allows field values containing letters, digits, spaces, and special characters. Use for names, addresses, descriptions, and fields containing digits that are *not used in calculations*.	0 to 255 characters; default is 255
Long Text	Allows field values containing letters, digits, spaces, and special characters. Use for long comments and explanations.	1 to 65,535 characters; exact size is determined by entry
Number	Allows positive and negative numbers as field values. A number can contain digits, a decimal point, commas, a plus sign, and a minus sign. Use for fields that will be used in calculations, except those involving money.	1 to 15 digits
Date/Time	Allows field values containing valid dates and times from January 1, 100 to December 31, 9999. Dates can be entered in month/day/year format, several other date formats, or a variety of time formats, such as 10:35 PM. You can perform calculations on dates and times, and you can sort them. For example, you can determine the number of days between two dates.	8 bytes
Currency	Allows field values similar to those for the Number data type, but is used for storing monetary values. Unlike calculations with Number data type decimal values, calculations performed with the Currency data type are not subject to round-off error.	Accurate to 15 digits on the left side of the decimal point and to 4 digits on the right side
AutoNumber	Consists of integer values created automatically by Access each time you create a new record. You can specify sequential numbering or random numbering, which guarantees a unique field value, so that such a field can serve as a table's primary key.	9 digits
Yes/No	Limits field values to yes and no, on and off, or true and false. Use for fields that indicate the presence or absence of a condition, such as whether an order has been filled or whether an invoice has been paid.	1 character
Hyperlink	Consists of text used as a hyperlink address, which can have up to four parts: the text that appears in a field or control; the path to a file or page; a location within the file or page; and text displayed as a ScreenTip.	Up to 65,535 characters total for the four parts of the hyperlink

Setting Field Sizes

The **Field Size property** defines a field value's maximum storage size for Short Text, Number, and AutoNumber fields only. The other data types have no Field Size property because their storage size is either a fixed, predetermined amount or is determined automatically by the field value itself, as shown in Figure 2-4. A Short Text field has a default field size of 255 characters; you can also set its field size by entering a number from 0 to 255. For example, the FirstName and LastName fields in the Owner table will be Short Text fields with sizes of 20 characters and 25 characters, respectively. These field sizes will accommodate the values that will be entered in each of these fields.

PROSKILLS

Decision Making: Specifying the Field Size Property for Number Fields

When you use the Number data type to define a field, you need to decide what the Field Size setting should be for the field. You should set the Field Size property based on the largest value that you expect to store in that field. Access processes smaller data sizes faster, using less memory, so you can optimize your database's performance and its storage space by selecting the correct field size for each field. Field Size property settings for Number fields are as follows:

- **Byte**: Stores whole numbers (numbers with no fractions) from 0 to 255 in one byte
- **Integer**: Stores whole numbers from –32,768 to 32,767 in two bytes
- **Long Integer** (default): Stores whole numbers from –2,147,483,648 to 2,147,483,647 in four bytes
- **Single**: Stores positive and negative numbers to precisely seven decimal places in four bytes
- **Double**: Stores positive and negative numbers to precisely 15 decimal places in eight bytes
- **Replication ID**: Establishes a unique identifier for replication of tables, records, and other objects in databases created using Access 2003 and earlier versions in 16 bytes
- **Decimal**: Stores positive and negative numbers to precisely 28 decimal places in 12 bytes

Choosing an appropriate field size is important to optimize efficiency. For example, it would be wasteful to use the Long Integer field size for a Number field that will store only whole numbers ranging from 0 to 255 because the Long Integer field size uses four bytes of storage space. A better choice would be the Byte field size, which uses one byte of storage space to store the same values. By first gathering and analyzing information about the number values that will be stored in a Number field, you can make the best decision for the field's Field Size property and ensure the most efficient user experience for the database.

Setting the Caption Property for Fields

The **Caption property** for a field specifies how the field name is displayed in database objects, including table and query datasheets, forms, and reports. If you don't set the Caption property, Access displays the field name as the column heading or label for a field. For example, field names such as InvoiceAmt and InvoiceDate in the Billing table can be difficult to read. Setting the Caption property for these fields to "Invoice Amt" and "Invoice Date" would make it easier for users to read the field names and work with the database.

INSIGHT

Setting the Caption Property vs. Naming Fields

Although Access allows you to include spaces in field names, this practice is not recommended because the spaces cause problems when you try to perform more complex tasks with the data in your database. Setting the Caption property allows you to follow best practices for naming fields, such as not including spaces in field names, while still providing users with more readable field names in datasheets, forms, and reports.

In the previous module, you created the Riverview database file and, within that file, you created the Visit table working in Datasheet view. According to her plan for the Riverview database, Kimberly also wants to track information about the invoices the care center sends to the owners of the animals. Next, you'll create the Billing table for Kimberly—this time, working in Design view.

Creating a Table in Design View

Creating a table in Design view involves entering the field names and defining the properties for the fields, specifying a primary key for the table, and then saving the table structure. Kimberly documented the design for the new Billing table by listing each field's name and data type; each field's size and description (if applicable); and any other properties to be set for each field. See Figure 2-5.

Figure 2-5	Design for the Billing table

Field Name	Data Type	Field Size	Description	Other
InvoiceNum	Short Text	5	Primary key	Caption = Invoice Num
VisitID	Short Text	4	Foreign key	Caption = Visit ID
InvoiceAmt	Currency			Format = Currency
				Decimal Places = 2
				Caption = Invoice Amt
InvoiceDate	Date/Time			Format = mm/dd/yyyy
				Caption = Invoice Date
InvoicePaid	Yes/No			Caption = Invoice Paid

You'll use Kimberly's design as a guide for creating the Billing table in the Riverview database.

To begin creating the Billing table:

1. Start Access and open the **Riverview** database you created in the previous module.

   Trouble? If the security warning is displayed below the ribbon, click the **Enable Content** button.

2. If the Navigation Pane is open, click the **Shutter Bar Open/Close Button** « to close it.

3. On the ribbon, click the **Create** tab.

4. In the Tables group, click the **Table Design** button. A new table named Table1 opens in Design view. Refer to the Session 2.1 Visual Overview for a complete description of the Table window in Design view.

Defining Fields

When you first create a table in Design view, the insertion point is located in the first row's Field Name box, ready for you to begin defining the first field in the table. You enter values for the Field Name, Data Type, and Description field properties, and then select values for all other field properties in the Field Properties pane. These other properties will appear when you move to the first row's Data Type box.

REFERENCE

Defining a Field in Design View

- In the Field Name box, type the name for the field, and then press the Tab key.
- Accept the default Short Text data type, or click the arrow and select a different data type for the field. Press the Tab key.
- Enter an optional description for the field, if necessary.
- Use the Field Properties pane to type or select other field properties, as appropriate.

The first field you need to define is the InvoiceNum field. This field will be the primary key for the Billing table. Each invoice at Riverview Veterinary Care Center is assigned a specific five-digit number. Although the InvoiceNum field will contain these number values, the numbers will never be used in calculations; therefore, you'll assign the Short Text data type to this field. Any time a field contains number values that will not be used in calculations—such as phone numbers, zip codes, and so on—you should use the Short Text data type instead of the Number data type.

To define the InvoiceNum field:

TIP

You can also press the Enter key to move from one property to the next in the Table Design grid.

1. Type **InvoiceNum** in the first row's Field Name box, and then press the **Tab** key to advance to the Data Type box. The default data type, Short Text, is selected in the Data Type box, which now also contains an arrow, and the field properties for a Short Text field appear in the Field Properties pane. See Figure 2-6.

Figure 2-6 Table window after entering the first field name

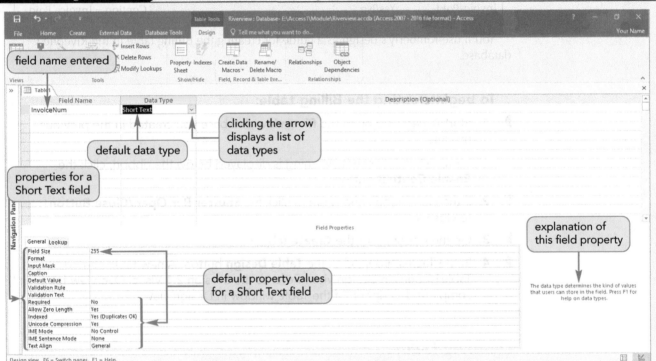

Notice that the right side of the Field Properties pane now provides an explanation for the current property, Data Type.

Trouble? If you make a typing error, you can correct it by clicking to position the insertion point, and then using either the Backspace key to delete characters to the left of the insertion point or the Delete key to delete characters to the right of the insertion point. Then type the correct text.

Because the InvoiceNum field values will not be used in calculations, you will accept the default Short Text data type for the field.

2. Press the **Tab** key to accept Short Text as the data type and to advance to the Description (Optional) box.

3. Next you'll enter the Description property value as "Primary key." The value you enter for the Description property will appear in the status bar when you view the table datasheet. Note that specifying "Primary key" for the Description property does *not* establish the current field as the primary key; you use a button on the ribbon to specify the primary key in Design view, which you will do later in this session.

4. Type **Primary key** in the Description (Optional) box.

   Notice the Field Size property for the field. The default setting of 255 for Short Text fields is displayed. You need to change this number to 5 because all invoice numbers at Riverview Veterinary Care Center contain only five digits.

5. Double-click the number **255** in the Field Size property box to select it, and then type **5**.

   Finally, you need to set the Caption property for the field so that its name appears with a space, as "Invoice Num."

6. Click the **Caption** property box, and then type **Invoice Num**. The definition of the first field is complete. See Figure 2-7.

Figure 2-7   **InvoiceNum field defined**

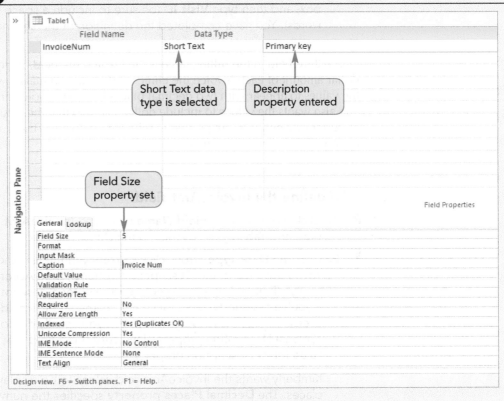

Kimberly's Billing table design (Figure 2-5) shows VisitID as the second field. Because Kimberly and other staff members need to relate information about invoices to the visit data in the Visit table, the Billing table must include the VisitID field, which is the Visit table's primary key. Recall that when you include the primary key from one table as a field in a second table to connect the two tables, the field is a foreign key in the second table. The field must be defined in the same way in both tables—that is, the field properties, including field size and data type, must match exactly.

Next, you will define VisitID as a Short Text field with a field size of 4. Later in this session, you'll change the Field Size property for the VisitID field in the Visit table to 4 so that the field definition is the same in both tables.

To define the VisitID field:

▶ **1.** In the Table Design grid, click the second row's **Field Name** box, type **VisitID**, and then press the **Tab** key to advance to the Data Type box.

▶ **2.** Press the **Tab** key to accept Short Text as the field's data type. Because the VisitID field is a foreign key to the Visit table, you'll enter "Foreign key" in the Description (Optional) box to help users of the database understand the purpose of this field.

▶ **3.** Type **Foreign key** in the Description (Optional) box. Next, you'll change the Field Size property.

▶ **4.** Press the **F6** key to move to the Field Properties pane. The current entry for the Field Size property, 255, is selected.

▶ **5.** Type **4** to set the Field Size property. Finally, you need to set the Caption property for this field.

▶ **6.** Press the **Tab** key three times to position the insertion point in the Caption box, and then type **Visit ID** (be sure to include a space between the two words). You have completed the definition of the second field.

The third field in the Billing table is the InvoiceAmt field, which will display the dollar amount of each invoice the clinic sends to the animals' owners. Kimberly wants the values to appear with two decimal places because invoice amounts include cents. She also wants the values to include dollar signs, so that the values will be formatted as currency when they are printed in bills sent to owners. The Currency data type is the appropriate choice for this field.

To define the InvoiceAmt field:

▶ **1.** Click the third row's **Field Name** box, type **InvoiceAmt** in the box, and then press the **Tab** key to advance to the Data Type box.

▶ **2.** Click the **Data Type** arrow, click **Currency** in the list, and then press the **Tab** key to advance to the Description (Optional) box. According to Kimberly's design (Figure 2-5), you do not need to enter a description for this field. If you've assigned a descriptive field name and the field does not fulfill a special function (such as primary key), you usually do not enter a value for the optional Description property. InvoiceAmt is a field that does not require a value for its Description property.

Kimberly wants the InvoiceAmt field values to be displayed with two decimal places. The **Decimal Places property** specifies the number of decimal places that are displayed to the right of the decimal point.

TIP

You can display the arrow and the list simultaneously by clicking the right side of a box.

3. In the Field Properties pane, click the **Decimal Places** box to position the insertion point there. An arrow appears on the right side of the Decimal Places box, which you can click to display a list of options.

4. Click the **Decimal Places** arrow, and then click **2** in the list to specify two decimal places for the InvoiceAmt field values.

5. Press the **Tab** key twice to position the insertion point in the Caption box, and then type **Invoice Amt**. The definition of the third field is now complete. Notice that the Format property is set to "Currency," which formats the values with dollar signs. See Figure 2-8.

| Figure 2-8 | Table window after defining the first three fields |

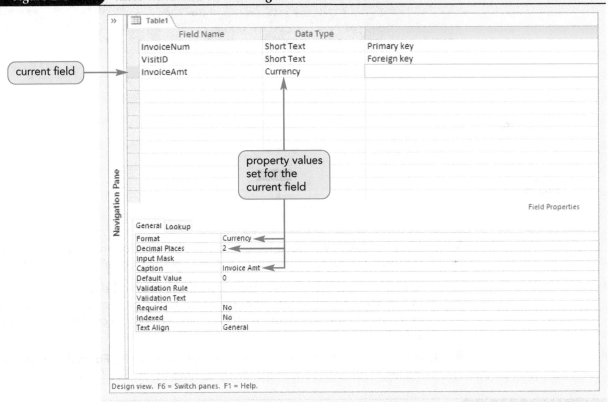

The fourth field in the Billing table is the InvoiceDate field. This field will contain the dates on which invoices are generated for the animals in the care center. You'll define the InvoiceDate field using the Date/Time data type. Also, according to Kimberly's design (Figure 2-5), the date values should be displayed in the format mm/dd/yyyy, which is a two-digit month, a two-digit day, and a four-digit year.

To define the InvoiceDate field:

1. Click the fourth row's **Field Name** box, type **InvoiceDate**, and then press the **Tab** key to advance to the Data Type box.

You can select a value from the Data Type list as you did for the InvoiceAmt field. Alternately, you can type the property value in the box or type just the first character of the property value.

2. Type **d**. Access completes the entry for the fourth row's Data Type box to "date/Time," with the letters "ate/Time" selected. See Figure 2-9.

Figure 2-9	Selecting a value for the Data Type property

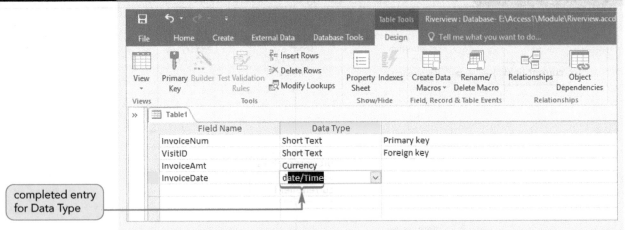

completed entry for Data Type

3. Press the **Tab** key to advance to the Description (Optional) box. Note that the value for the Data Type property changes to "Date/Time."

Kimberly wants the values in the InvoiceDate field to be displayed in a format showing the month, the day, and a four-digit year, as in the following example: 03/10/2017. You use the Format property to control the display of a field value.

4. In the Field Properties pane, click the right side of the **Format** box to display the list of predefined formats for Date/Time fields. See Figure 2-10.

Figure 2-10	Displaying available formats for Date/Time fields

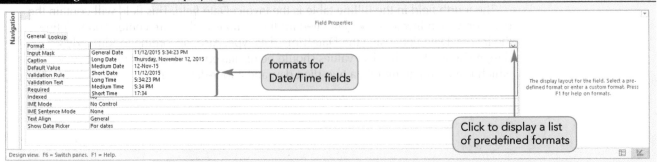

formats for Date/Time fields

Click to display a list of predefined formats

Trouble? If you see an arrow instead of a list of predefined formats, click the arrow to display the list.

As noted in the right side of the Field Properties pane, you can either choose a predefined format or enter a custom format. Even though the Short Date format seems to match the format Kimberly wants, it displays only one digit for months that contain only one digit. For example, it would display the month of March with only the digit "3"—as in 3/10/2017—instead of displaying the month with two digits, as in 03/10/2017.

Because none of the predefined formats matches the exact layout Kimberly wants for the InvoiceDate values, you need to create a custom date format. Figure 2-11 shows some of the symbols available for custom date and time formats.

Figure 2-11	Symbols for some custom date formats

Symbol	Description
/	date separator
d	day of the month in one or two numeric digits, as needed (1 to 31)
dd	day of the month in two numeric digits (01 to 31)
ddd	first three letters of the weekday (Sun to Sat)
dddd	full name of the weekday (Sunday to Saturday)
w	day of the week (1 to 7)
ww	week of the year (1 to 53)
m	month of the year in one or two numeric digits, as needed (1 to 12)
mm	month of the year in two numeric digits (01 to 12)
mmm	first three letters of the month (Jan to Dec)
mmmm	full name of the month (January to December)
yy	last two digits of the year (01 to 99)
yyyy	full year (0100 to 9999)

Kimberly wants the dates to be displayed with a two-digit month (mm), a two-digit day (dd), and a four-digit year (yyyy).

5. Click the **Format** arrow to close the list of predefined formats, and then type **mm/dd/yyyy** in the Format box.

6. Press the **Tab** key twice to position the insertion point in the Caption box, and then type **Invoice Date**. See Figure 2-12.

Figure 2-12   **Specifying the custom date format**

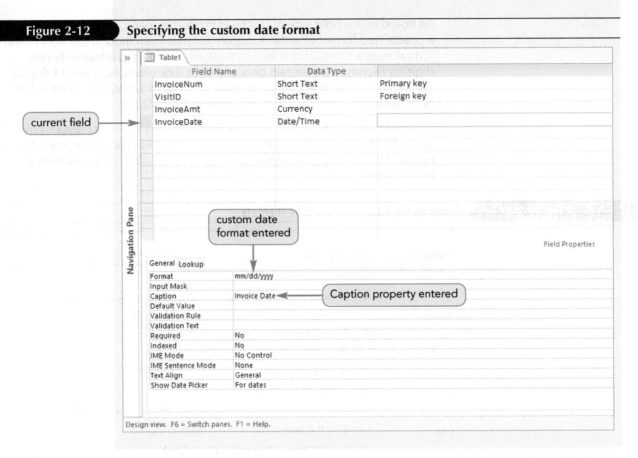

The fifth and final field to be defined in the Billing table is InvoicePaid. This field will be a Yes/No field to indicate the payment status of each invoice record stored in the Billing table. Recall that the Yes/No data type is used to define fields that store true/false, yes/no, and on/off field values. When you create a Yes/No field in a table, the default Format property is set to Yes/No.

To define the InvoicePaid field:

▶ **1.** Click the fifth row's **Field Name** box, type **InvoicePaid**, and then press the **Tab** key to advance to the Data Type box.

▶ **2.** Type **y**. Access completes the data type as "yes/No".

▶ **3.** Press the **Tab** key to select the Yes/No data type and move to the Description (Optional) box. In the Field Properties pane, note that the default format of "Yes/No" is selected, so you do not have to change this property.

▶ **4.** In the Field Properties pane, click the **Caption** box, and then type **Invoice Paid**.

You've finished defining the fields for the Billing table. Next, you need to specify the primary key for the table.

Specifying the Primary Key

As you learned earlier, the primary key for a table uniquely identifies each record in the table.

Specifying a Primary Key in Design View
- Display the table in Design view.
- Click in the row for the field you've chosen to be the primary key to make it the active field. If the primary key will consist of two or more fields, click the row selector for the first field, press and hold the Ctrl key, and then click the row selector for each additional primary key field.
- In the Tools group on the Table Tools Design tab, click the Primary Key button.

According to Kimberly's design, you need to specify InvoiceNum as the primary key for the Billing table. You can do so while the table is in Design view.

To specify InvoiceNum as the primary key:

1. Click in the row for the InvoiceNum field to make it the current field.

TIP

This button is a toggle; you can click it to remove the key symbol.

2. On the Table Tools Design tab, in the Tools group, click the **Primary Key** button. The Primary Key button in the Tools group is now selected, and a key symbol appears in the row selector for the first row, indicating that the InvoiceNum field is the table's primary key. See Figure 2-13.

Figure 2-13 **InvoiceNum field selected as the primary key**

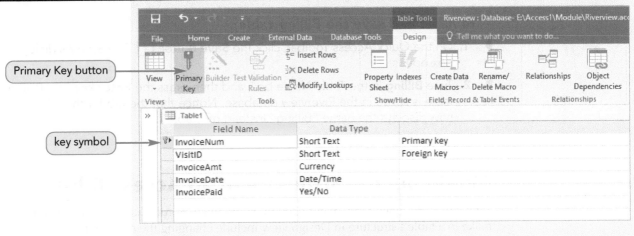

Primary Key button

key symbol

Understanding the Importance of the Primary Key

Although Access does not require a table to have a primary key, including a primary key offers several advantages:

- A primary key uniquely identifies each record in a table.
- Access does not allow duplicate values in the primary key field. For example, if a record already exists in the Visit table with a VisitID value of 1550, Access prevents you from adding another record with this same value in the VisitID field. Preventing duplicate values ensures the uniqueness of the primary key field.
- When a primary key has been specified, Access forces you to enter a value for the primary key field in every record in the table. This is known as **entity integrity**. If you do not enter a value for a field, you have actually given the field a **null value**. You cannot give a null value to the primary key field because entity integrity prevents Access from accepting and processing that record.
- You can enter records in any order, but Access displays them by default in order of the primary key's field values. If you enter records in no specific order, you are ensured that you will later be able to work with them in a more meaningful, primary key sequence.
- Access responds faster to your requests for specific records based on the primary key.

Saving the Table Structure

The last step in creating a table is to name the table and save the table's structure. When you save a table structure, the table is stored in the database file (in this case, the Riverview database file). Once the table is saved, you can enter data into it. According to Kimberly's plan, you need to save the table you've defined as "Billing."

To name and save the Billing table:

▶ 1. On the Quick Access Toolbar, click the **Save** button 🖫. The Save As dialog box opens.

▶ 2. Type **Billing** in the Table Name box, and then press the **Enter** key. The Billing table is saved in the Riverview database. Notice that the tab for the table now displays the name "Billing" instead of "Table1."

Modifying the Structure of an Access Table

Even a well-designed table might need to be modified. Some changes that you can make to a table's structure in Design view include changing the order of fields and adding new fields.

After meeting with her assistant, Kelly Flannagan, and reviewing the structure of the Billing table, Kimberly has changes she wants you to make to the table. First, she wants the InvoiceAmt field to be moved so that it appears right before the InvoicePaid field. Then, she wants you to add a new Short Text field named InvoiceItem to the table to include information about what the invoice is for, such as office visits, lab work, and so on. Kimberly would like the InvoiceItem field to be inserted between the InvoiceAmt and InvoicePaid fields.

Moving a Field in Design View

To move a field, you use the mouse to drag it to a new location in the Table Design grid. Although you can move a field in Datasheet view by dragging its column heading to a new location, doing so rearranges only the *display* of the table's fields; the table structure is not changed. To move a field permanently, you must move the field in Design view.

Next, you'll move the InvoiceAmt field so that it is before the InvoicePaid field in the Billing table.

To move the InvoiceAmt field:

▶ 1. Position the pointer on the row selector for the InvoiceAmt field until the pointer changes to ➡.

▶ 2. Click the **row selector** to select the entire InvoiceAmt row.

▶ 3. Place the pointer on the row selector for the InvoiceAmt field until the pointer changes to ⬉, press and hold the mouse button and then drag to the row selector for the InvoicePaid field. Notice that as you drag, the pointer changes to ⬉. See Figure 2-14.

| Figure 2-14 | Moving the InvoiceAmt field in the table structure |

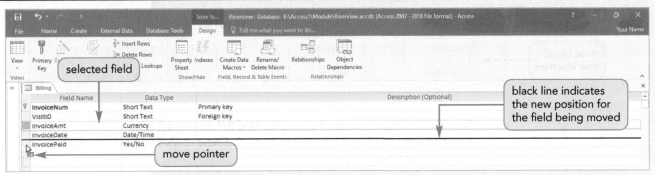

▶ 4. Release the mouse button. The InvoiceAmt field now appears between the InvoiceDate and InvoicePaid fields in the table structure.

Trouble? If the InvoiceAmt field did not move, repeat Steps 1 through 4, making sure you hold down the mouse button during the drag operation.

Adding a Field in Design View

To add a new field between existing fields, you must insert a row. You begin by selecting the row below where you want the new field to be inserted.

REFERENCE

Adding a Field Between Two Existing Fields

- In the Table window in Design view, select the row below where you want the new field to be inserted.
- In the Tools group on the Table Tools Design tab, click the Insert Rows button.
- Define the new field by entering the field name, data type, optional description, and any property specifications.

Next, you need to add the InvoiceItem field to the Billing table structure between the InvoiceAmt and InvoicePaid fields.

To add the InvoiceItem field to the Billing table:

▶ 1. Click the **InvoicePaid Field Name** box. You need to establish this field as the current field so that the row for the new record will be inserted above this field.

▶ 2. On the Table Tools Design tab, in the Tools group, click the **Insert Rows** button. A new, blank row is added between the InvoiceAmt and InvoicePaid fields. The insertion point is positioned in the Field Name box for the new row, ready for you to type the name for the new field. See Figure 2-15.

Figure 2-15	Table structure after inserting a row

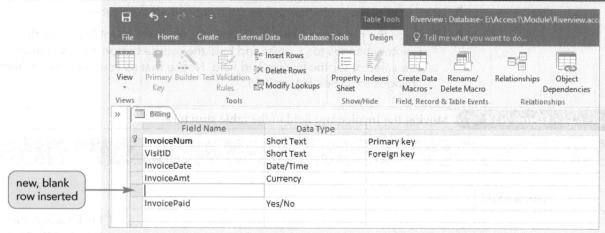

new, blank row inserted

Trouble? If you selected the InvoicePaid field's row selector and then inserted the new row, you need to click the new row's Field Name box to position the insertion point in it.

You'll define the InvoiceItem field in the new row of the Billing table. This field will be a Short Text field with a field size of 40, and you need to set the Caption property to include a space between the words in the field name.

▶ 3. Type **InvoiceItem**, press the **Tab** key to move to the Data Type property, and then press the **Tab** key again to accept the default Short Text data type.

▶ 4. Press the **F6** key to select the default field size in the Field Size box, and then type **40**.

▶ 5. Press the **Tab** key three times to position the insertion point in the Caption box, and then type **Invoice Item**. The definition of the new field is complete. See Figure 2-16.

| Figure 2-16 | InvoiceItem field added to the Billing table |

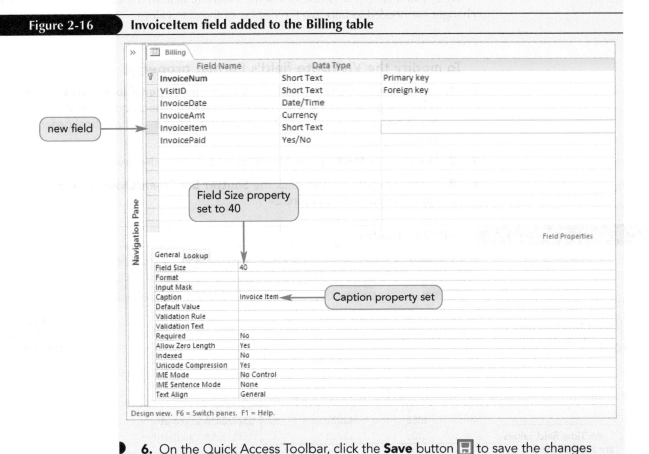

6. On the Quick Access Toolbar, click the **Save** button 💾 to save the changes to the Billing table structure.

7. Click the **Close 'Billing'** button ⊠ on the object tab to close the Billing table.

Modifying Field Properties

With the Billing table design complete, you can now go back and modify the properties of the fields in the Visit table you created in the previous module, as necessary. You can make some changes to properties in Datasheet view; for others, you'll work in Design view.

Changing the Format Property in Datasheet View

The Formatting group on the Table Tools Fields tab in Datasheet view allows you to modify some formatting for certain field types. When you format a field, you change the way data is displayed, but not the actual values stored in the table.

Next, you'll check the properties of the VisitDate field in the Visit table to see if any changes are needed to improve the display of the date values.

To modify the VisitDate field's Format property:

▶ 1. In the Navigation Pane, click the **Shutter Bar Open/Close Button** ⧠ to open the pane. Notice that the Billing table is listed above the Visit table in the Tables section. By default, objects are listed in alphabetical order in the Navigation pane.

▶ 2. Double-click **Visit** to open the Visit table in Datasheet view.

▶ 3. In the Navigation Pane, click the **Shutter Bar Open/Close Button** ⧠ to close the pane. See Figure 2-17.

Figure 2-17	Visit table datasheet

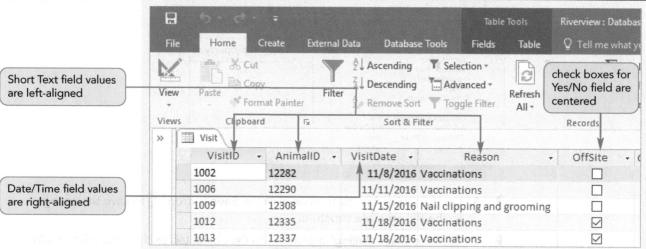

Notice that the values in the three Short Text fields—VisitID, AnimalID, and Reason—appear left-aligned within their boxes, and the values in the Date/Time field (VisitDate) appear right-aligned. In Access, values for Short Text fields are left-aligned, and values for Number, Date/Time, and Currency fields are right-aligned. The Offsite field is a Yes/No field, so its values appear in check boxes that are centered within the column.

▶ 4. On the ribbon, click the **Table Tools Fields** tab.

▶ 5. Click the **first field value** in the VisitDate column. The Data Type option shows that this field is a Date/Time field.

By default, Access assigns the General Date format to Date/Time fields. Note the Format box in the Formatting group, which you use to set the Format property (similar to how you set the Format property in the Field Properties pane in Design view.) Even though the Format box is empty, the VisitDate field has the General Date format applied to it. The General Date format includes settings for date or time values, or a combination of date and time values. However, Kimberly wants *only date values* to be displayed in the VisitDate field, so she asks you to specify the Short Date format for the field.

▶ 6. In the Formatting group, click the **Format** arrow, and then click **Short Date**. See Figure 2-18.

| Figure 2-18 | VisitDate field after modifying the format |

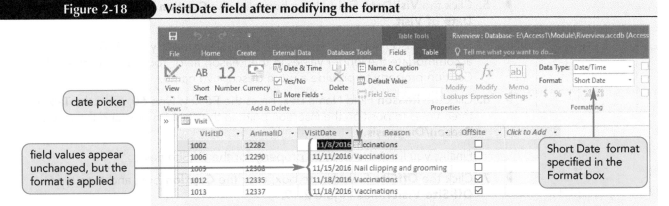

date picker

field values appear unchanged, but the format is applied

Short Date format specified in the Format box

Although no change is apparent in the datasheet—the VisitDate field values already appear with the Short Date setting (for example, 11/8/2016), as part of the default General Date format—the field now has the Short Date format applied to it. This ensures that only date field values, and not time or date/time values, are allowed in the field.

Changing Properties in Design View

Recall that each of the Short Text fields in the Visit table—VisitID, AnimalID, and Reason—still has the default field size of 255, which is too large for the data contained in these fields. Also, the VisitID and AnimalID fields need descriptions to identify them as the primary and foreign keys, respectively, in the table. Finally, each of these fields needs a caption either to include a space between the words in the field name or to make the name more descriptive. You can make all of these property changes more easily in Design view.

To modify the Field Size, Description, and Caption field properties:

1. On the Table Tools Fields tab, in the Views group, click the **View** button. The table is displayed in Design view with the VisitID field selected. You need to enter a Description property value for this field, the primary key in the table, and change its Field Size property to 4 because each visit number at Riverview Veterinary Care Center consists of four digits.

2. Press the **Tab** key twice to position the insertion point in the Description (Optional) box, and then type **Primary key**.

3. Press the **F6** key to move to and select the default setting of 255 in the Field Size box in the Fields Properties pane, and then type **4**. Next you need to set the Caption property for this field.

4. Press the **Tab** key three times to position the insertion point in the Caption box, and then type **Visit ID**.

   Next you need to enter a Description property value for the AnimalID field, a foreign key in the table, and set its Field Size property to 5 because each AnimalID number at Riverview Veterinary Care Center consists of five digits. You also need to set this field's Caption property.

5. Click the **VisitDate** Field Name box, click the **Caption** box, and then type **Date of Visit**.

For the Reason field, you will set the Field Size property to 60. This size can accommodate the longer values in the Reason field. You'll also set this field's Caption property to provide a more descriptive name.

6. Click the **Reason** Field Name box, press the **F6** key, type **60**, press the **Tab** key three times to position the insertion point in the Caption box, and then type **Reason/Diagnosis**.

Finally, you'll set the Caption property for the OffSite field.

7. Click the **OffSite** Field Name box, click the **Caption** box, and then type **Off-Site Visit?**. See Figure 2-19.

| Figure 2-19 | Visit table after modifying field properties |

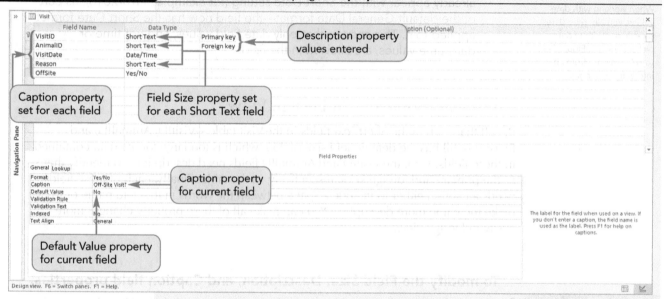

Notice that the OffSite field's Default Value property is automatically set to "No," which means the check box for this field will be empty for each new record. This is the default for this property for any Yes/No field. You can set the Default Value property for other types of fields to make data entry easier. You'll learn more about setting this property in the next session.

The changes to the Visit table's properties are now complete, so you can save the table and view the results of your changes in Datasheet view.

To save and view the modified Visit table:

1. On the Quick Access Toolbar, click the **Save** button 🖫 to save the modified table. A dialog box opens informing you that some data may be lost because you decreased the field sizes. Because all of the values in the VisitID, AnimalID, and Reason fields contain the same number of or fewer characters than the new Field Size properties you set for each field, you can ignore this message.

2. Click the **Yes** button.

3. On the Table Tools Design tab, in the Views group, click the **View** button to display the Visit table in Datasheet view. Notice that each column (field) heading now displays the text you specified in the Caption property for that field. However, now the Off-Site Visit? field caption doesn't fully display.

4. Place the pointer on the column border to the right of the Off-Site Visit? field name until the pointer changes to ↔, and then double-click the column border to fully display this field name. See Figure 2-20.

Figure 2-20 ▶ **Modified Visit table in Datasheet view**

column headings display Caption property values

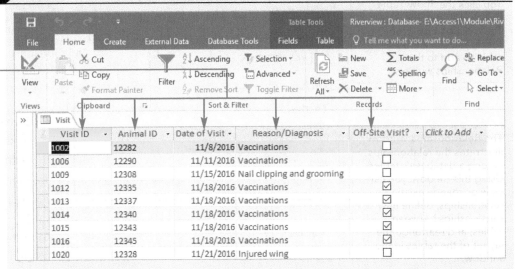

5. Click the **Close 'Visit'** button ☒ on the object tab to close the Visit table, and click **Yes** to save the changes to the Visit table.

6. If you are not continuing to Session 2.2, click the **File** tab, and then click **Close** in the navigation bar of Backstage view to close the Riverview database.

You have created the Billing table and made modifications to its design. In the next session, you'll add records to the Billing table and create the Animal and Owner tables in the Riverview database.

Session 2.1 Quick Check

1. What guidelines should you follow when designing a database?

2. What is the purpose of the Data Type property for a field?

3. The _____ property specifies how a field's name is displayed in database objects, including table and query datasheets, forms, and reports.

4. For which three types of fields can you assign a field size?

5. The default Field Size property setting for a Short Text field is _____.

6. In Design view, which key do you press to move from the Table Design grid to the Field Properties pane?

7. List three reasons why you should specify a primary key for an Access table.

Session 2.2 Visual Overview:

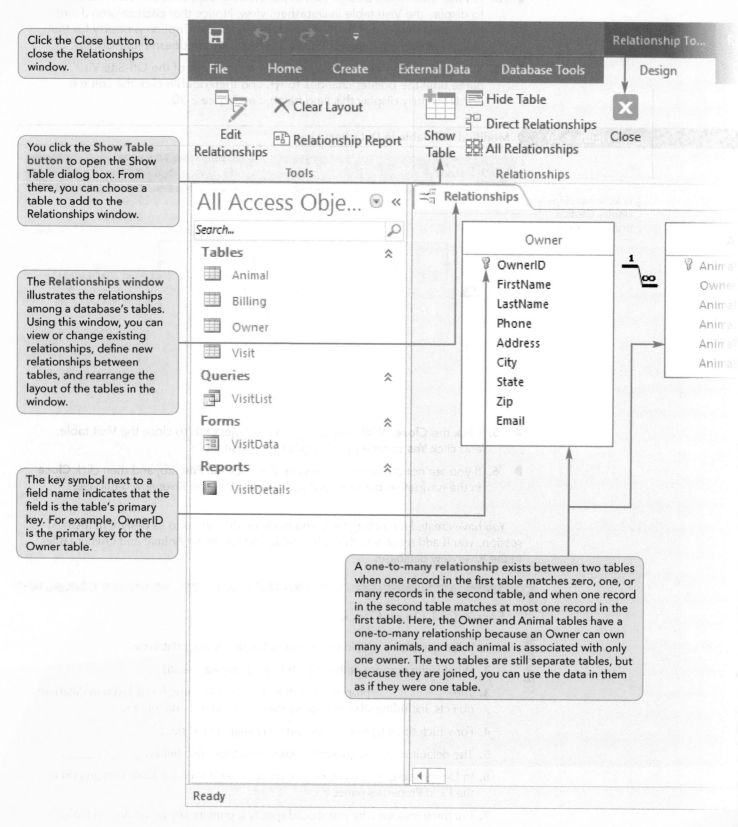

Click the Close button to close the Relationships window.

You click the **Show Table** button to open the Show Table dialog box. From there, you can choose a table to add to the Relationships window.

The Relationships window illustrates the relationships among a database's tables. Using this window, you can view or change existing relationships, define new relationships between tables, and rearrange the layout of the tables in the window.

The key symbol next to a field name indicates that the field is the table's primary key. For example, OwnerID is the primary key for the Owner table.

A **one-to-many relationship** exists between two tables when one record in the first table matches zero, one, or many records in the second table, and when one record in the second table matches at most one record in the first table. Here, the Owner and Animal tables have a one-to-many relationship because an Owner can own many animals, and each animal is associated with only one owner. The two tables are still separate tables, but because they are joined, you can use the data in them as if they were one table.

Relationship To...

File   Home   Create   External Data   Database Tools   Design

Edit Relationships   ✕ Clear Layout   Relationship Report   Show Table   Hide Table   Direct Relationships   All Relationships   Close

Tools   Relationships

All Access Obje...

Search...

Tables
- Animal
- Billing
- Owner
- Visit

Queries
- VisitList

Forms
- VisitData

Reports
- VisitDetails

Relationships

Owner
- OwnerID
- FirstName
- LastName
- Phone
- Address
- City
- State
- Zip
- Email

Ready

Modified Visit table in Datasheet view

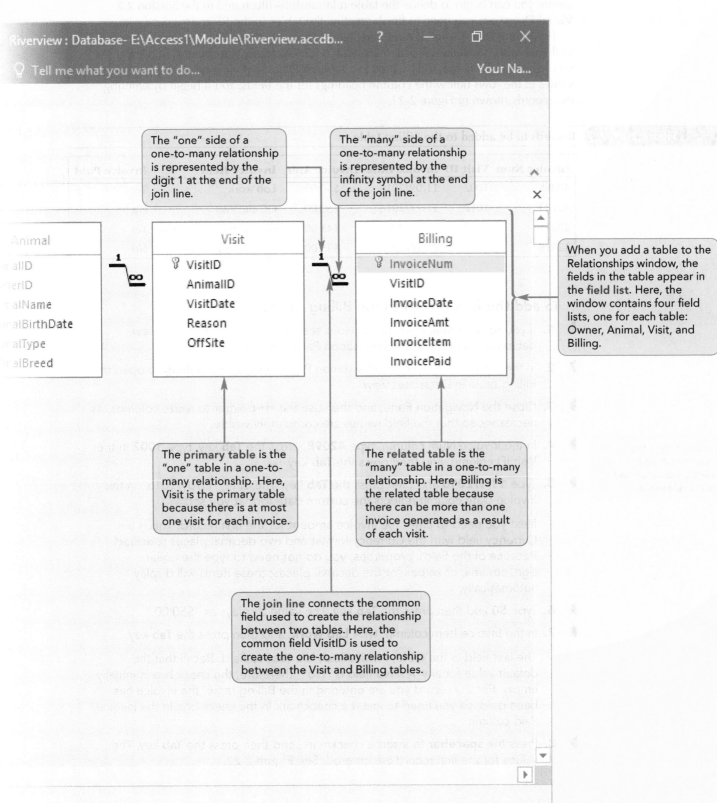

The "one" side of a one-to-many relationship is represented by the digit 1 at the end of the join line.

The "many" side of a one-to-many relationship is represented by the infinity symbol at the end of the join line.

When you add a table to the Relationships window, the fields in the table appear in the field list. Here, the window contains four field lists, one for each table: Owner, Animal, Visit, and Billing.

The primary table is the "one" table in a one-to-many relationship. Here, Visit is the primary table because there is at most one visit for each invoice.

The related table is the "many" table in a one-to-many relationship. Here, Billing is the related table because there can be more than one invoice generated as a result of each visit.

The join line connects the common field used to create the relationship between two tables. Here, the common field VisitID is used to create the one-to-many relationship between the Visit and Billing tables.

Adding Records to a New Table

Before you can begin to define the table relationships illustrated in the Session 2.2 Visual Overview, you need to finish creating the tables in the Riverview database.

The Billing table design is complete. Now, Kimberly would like you to add records to the table so it will contain the invoice data for Riverview Veterinary Care Center. As you learned earlier, you add records to a table in Datasheet view by typing the field values in the rows below the column headings for the fields. You'll begin by entering the records shown in Figure 2-21.

Figure 2-21	Records to be added to the Billing table

Invoice Num	Visit ID	Invoice Date	Invoice Amt	Invoice Item	Invoice Paid
42098	1002	11/09/2016	$50.00	Lab work	Yes
42125	1012	11/21/2016	$50.00	Off-site visit	No
42271	1077	12/15/2016	$45.00	Flea & tick medications	Yes
42518	1181	01/26/2017	$35.00	Heartworm medication	No

To add the first record to the Billing table:

▶ 1. If you took a break after the previous session, make sure the Riverview database is open and the Navigation Pane is open.

▶ 2. In the Tables section of the Navigation Pane, double-click **Billing** to open the Billing table in Datasheet view.

▶ 3. Close the Navigation Pane, and then use the ✛ pointer to resize columns, as necessary, so that the field names are completely visible.

Be sure to type the numbers "0" and "1" and *not* the letters "O" and "I" in the field values.

▶ 4. In the Invoice Num column, type **42098**, press the **Tab** key, type **1002** in the Visit ID column, and then press the **Tab** key.

▶ 5. Type **11/9/2016** and then press the **Tab** key. The date "11/09/2016" in the Invoice Date column reflects the custom date format you set.

Next you need to enter the invoice amount for the first record. This is a Currency field with the Currency format and two decimal places specified. Because of the field's properties, you do not need to type the dollar sign, comma, or zeroes for the decimal places; these items will display automatically.

▶ 6. Type **50** and then press the **Tab** key. The value displays as "$50.00."

▶ 7. In the Invoice Item column, type **Lab work**, and then press the **Tab** key.

The last field in the table, InvoicePaid, is a Yes/No field. Recall that the default value for any Yes/No field is "No"; therefore, the check box is initially empty. For the record you are entering in the Billing table, the invoice has been paid, so you need to insert a checkmark in the check box in the Invoice Paid column.

▶ 8. Press the **spacebar** to insert a checkmark, and then press the **Tab** key. The values for the first record are entered. See Figure 2-22.

| Figure 2-22 | First record entered in the Billing table |

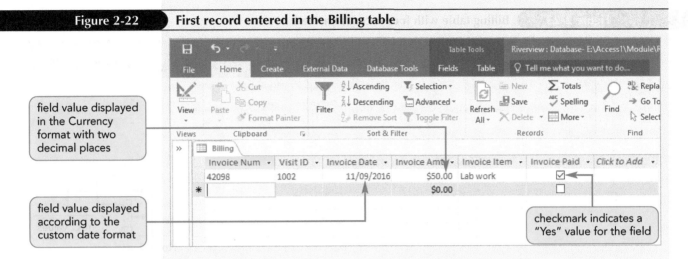

field value displayed in the Currency format with two decimal places

field value displayed according to the custom date format

checkmark indicates a "Yes" value for the field

Now you can add the remaining three records. As you do, you'll learn a keyboard shortcut for inserting the value from the same field in the previous record. A **keyboard shortcut** is a key or combination of keys you press to complete an action more efficiently.

To add the next three records to the Billing table:

1. Refer to Figure 2-21 and enter the values in the second record's Invoice Num, Visit ID, and Invoice Date columns.

   Notice that the value in the second record's Invoice Amt column is $50.00. This value is the exact same value as in the first record. You can quickly insert the value from the same column in the previous record using the Ctrl + ' (apostrophe) keyboard shortcut. To use this shortcut, you press and hold the Ctrl key, press the ' key once, and then release both keys. (The plus sign in the keyboard shortcut indicates you're pressing two keys at once; you do not press the + key.)

2. With the insertion point in the Invoice Amt column, press the **Ctrl + ' keys**. The value "$50.00" is inserted in the Invoice Amt column for the second record.

3. Press the **Tab** key to move to the Invoice Item column, and then type **Off-site visit**.

4. Press the **Tab** key to move to the Invoice Paid column, and then press the **Tab** key to leave the Invoice Paid check box unchecked to indicate the invoice has not been paid. The second record is entered in the Billing table.

5. Refer to Figure 2-21 to enter the values for the third and fourth records. Your table should look like the one in Figure 2-23.

Figure 2-23 **Billing table with four records entered**

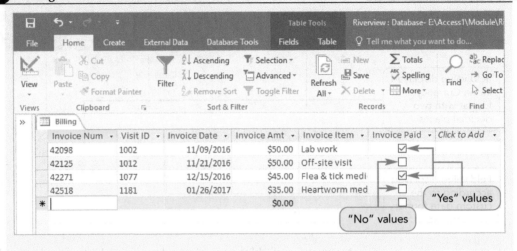

To finish entering records in the Billing table, you'll use a method that allows you to import the data.

Importing Data from an Excel Worksheet

Often, the data you want to add to an Access table exists in another file, such as a Word document or an Excel workbook. You can bring the data from other files into Access in different ways. For example, you can copy and paste the data from an open file, or you can **import** the data, which is a process that allows you to copy the data from a source without having to open the source file.

Kimberly had been using Excel to track invoice data for Riverview Veterinary Care Center and already created a worksheet, named "Invoices," containing this data. You'll import this Excel worksheet into your Billing table to complete the entry of data in the table. To use the import method, the columns in the Excel worksheet must match the names and data types of the fields in the Access table.

The Invoices worksheet contains the following columns: InvoiceNum, VisitID, InvoiceDate, InvoiceAmt, InvoiceItem, and InvoicePaid. These column headings match the field names in the Billing table exactly, so you can import the data. Before you import data into a table, you need to close the table.

> **TIP**
>
> Caption property values set for fields are not considered in the import process. Therefore make sure that the field names match the Excel worksheet column headings. If there are differences, change the column headings in the Excel worksheet to match the Access table field names.

To import the Invoices worksheet into the Billing table:

1. Click the **Close 'Billing'** button ☒ on the object tab to close the Billing table, and then click the **Yes** button in the dialog box asking if you want to save the changes to the table layout.

2. On the ribbon, click the **External Data** tab.

3. In the Import & Link group, click the **Excel** button. The Get External Data - Excel Spreadsheet dialog box opens. See Figure 2-24.

| Figure 2-24 | Get External Data – Excel Spreadsheet dialog box |

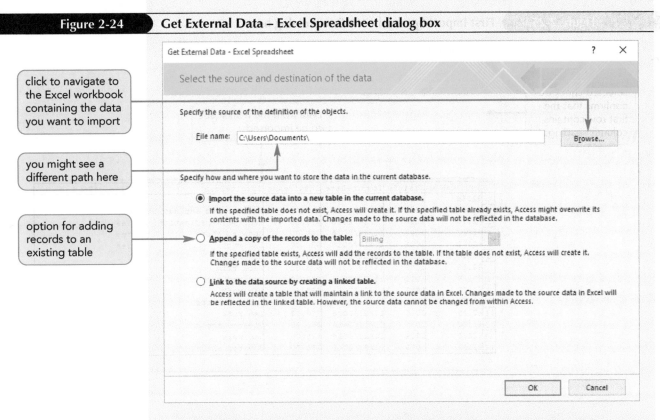

click to navigate to the Excel workbook containing the data you want to import

you might see a different path here

option for adding records to an existing table

Get External Data - Excel Spreadsheet   ?   ×

Select the source and destination of the data

Specify the source of the definition of the objects.

File name: C:\Users\Documents\   Browse...

Specify how and where you want to store the data in the current database.

◉ Import the source data into a new table in the current database.
  If the specified table does not exist, Access will create it. If the specified table already exists, Access might overwrite its contents with the imported data. Changes made to the source data will not be reflected in the database.

○ Append a copy of the records to the table: Billing
  If the specified table exists, Access will add the records to the table. If the table does not exist, Access will create it. Changes made to the source data will not be reflected in the database.

○ Link to the data source by creating a linked table.
  Access will create a table that will maintain a link to the source data in Excel. Changes made to the source data in Excel will be reflected in the linked table. However, the source data cannot be changed from within Access.

OK   Cancel

The dialog box provides options for importing the entire worksheet as a new table in the current database, adding the data from the worksheet to an existing table, or linking the data in the worksheet to the table. You need to add, or append, the worksheet data to the Billing table.

4. Click the **Browse** button. The File Open dialog box opens. The Excel workbook file is named "Invoices" and is located in the Access1 > Module folder provided with your Data Files.

5. Navigate to the **Access1 > Module** folder, where your Data Files are stored, and then double-click the **Invoices** Excel file. You return to the dialog box.

6. Click the **Append a copy of the records to the table** option button. The box to the right of this option becomes active and displays the Billing table name, because it is the first table listed in the Navigation Pane.

7. Click the **OK** button. The first Import Spreadsheet Wizard dialog box opens. The dialog box confirms that the first row of the worksheet you are importing contains column headings. The bottom section of the dialog box displays some of the data contained in the worksheet. See Figure 2-25.

Figure 2-25 | First Import Spreadsheet Wizard dialog box

selected check box
confirms that the
first row contains
column headings

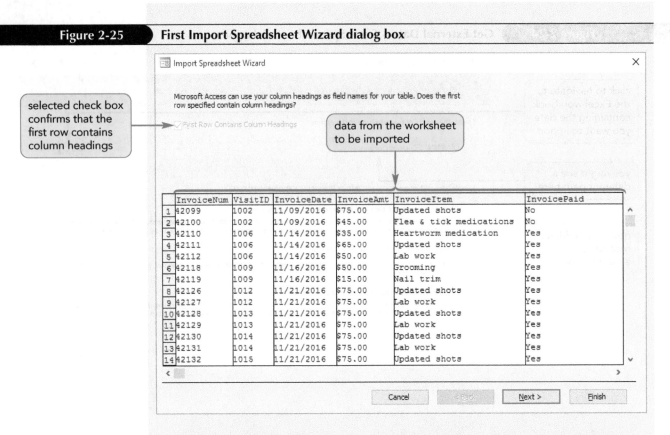

8. Click the **Next** button. The second, and final, Import Spreadsheet Wizard dialog box opens. Notice that the Import to Table box shows that the data from the spreadsheet will be imported into the Billing table.

9. Click the **Finish** button. A dialog box opens asking if you want to save the import steps. If you needed to repeat this same import procedure many times, it would be a good idea to save the steps for the procedure. However, you don't need to save these steps because you'll be importing the data only one time. Once the data is in the Billing table, Kimberly will no longer use Excel to track invoice data.

10. Click the **Close** button in the dialog box to close it without saving the steps.

The data from the Invoices worksheet has been added to the Billing table. Next, you'll open the table to view the new records.

To open the Billing table and view the imported data:

1. Open the Navigation Pane, and then double-click **Billing** in the Tables section to open the table in Datasheet view.

2. Resize the Invoice Item column to its best fit, scrolling the worksheet and resizing, as necessary.

▶ **3.** Press the **Ctrl + Home** keys to scroll to the top of the datasheet. Notice that the table now contains a total of 204 records—the four records you entered plus 200 records imported from the Invoices worksheet. The records are displayed in primary key order by the values in the Invoice Num column. See Figure 2-26.

| Figure 2-26 | Billing table after importing data from Excel |

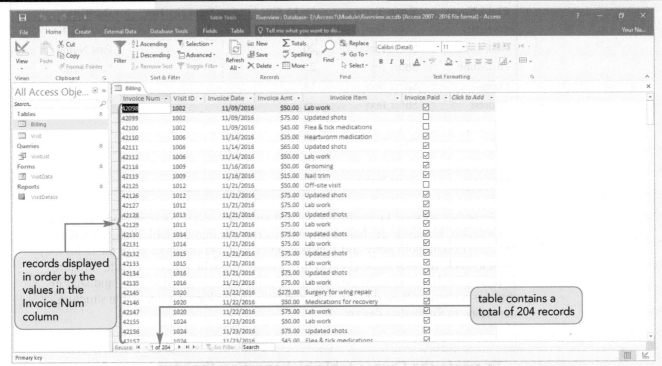

records displayed in order by the values in the Invoice Num column

table contains a total of 204 records

▶ **4.** Save and close the Billing table, and then close the Navigation Pane.

Two of the tables—Visit and Billing—are now complete. According to Kimberly's plan for the Riverview database, you still need to create the Owner and Animal tables. You'll use a different method to create these tables.

Creating a Table by Importing an Existing Table or Table Structure

If another Access database contains a table—or even just the design, or structure, of a table—that you want to include in your database, you can import the table and any records it contains or import only the table structure into your database. To create the new Owner and Animal tables per Kimberly's plan shown in Figure 2-2, you will import a table structure from a different Access database to create the Owner table and an existing table structure and records from another database to create the Animal table.

Importing an Existing Table Structure

Kimberly documented the design for the new Owner table by listing each field's name and data type, as well as any applicable field size, description, and caption property values, as shown in Figure 2-27. Note that each field in the Owner table will be a Short Text field, and the OwnerID field will be the table's primary key.

Figure 2-27	Design for the Owner table

Field Name	Data Type	Field Size	Description	Caption
OwnerID	Short Text	4	Primary key	Owner ID
FirstName	Short Text	20		First Name
LastName	Short Text	25		Last Name
Phone	Short Text	14		
Address	Short Text	35		
City	Short Text	25		
State	Short Text	2		
Zip	Short Text	10		
Email	Short Text	50		

Kimberly's assistant Kelly already created an Access database containing an Owner table design, however, she hasn't entered any records into the table. After reviewing the table design, both Kelly and Kimberly agree that it contains some of the fields they want to track, but that some changes are needed. You will import the table structure in Kelly's database to create the Owner table in the Riverview database, and later in this session, you will modify the imported table to produce the final table structure according to Kimberly's design.

To create the Owner table by importing the structure of another table:

1. Make sure the External Data tab is the active tab on the ribbon.

2. In the Import & Link group, click the **Access** button. The Get External Data - Access Database dialog box opens. This dialog box is similar to the one you used earlier when importing the Excel spreadsheet.

3. Click the **Browse** button. The File Open dialog box opens. The Access database file from which you need to import the table structure is named "Kelly" and is located in the Access1 > Module folder provided with your Data Files.

4. Navigate to the **Access1 > Module** folder, where your Data Files are stored, and then double-click the **Kelly** database file. You return to the dialog box.

5. Make sure the **Import tables, queries, forms, reports, macros, and modules into the current database** option button is selected, and then click the **OK** button. The Import Objects dialog box opens. The dialog box contains tabs for importing all the different types of Access database objects—tables, queries, forms, and so on. The Tables tab is the current tab.

6. Click the **Options** button in the dialog box to see all the options for importing tables. See Figure 2-28.

Figure 2-28 **Import Objects dialog box**

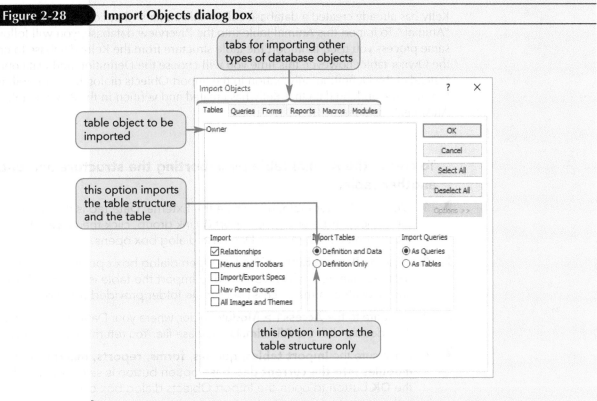

tabs for importing other types of database objects

table object to be imported

this option imports the table structure and the table

this option imports the table structure only

▶ **7.** On the Tables tab, click **Owner** to select this table.

▶ **8.** In the Import Tables section of the dialog box, click the **Definition Only** option button, and then click the **OK** button. Access creates the Owner table in the Riverview database using the structure of the Owner table in the Kelly database, and opens a dialog box asking if you want to save the import steps.

▶ **9.** Click the **Close** button to close the dialog box without saving the import steps.

▶ **10.** Open the Navigation Pane, double-click **Owner** in the Tables section to open the table, and then close the Navigation Pane. The Owner table opens in Datasheet view. The table contains no records. See Figure 2-29.

Figure 2-29 **Imported Owner table in Datasheet view**

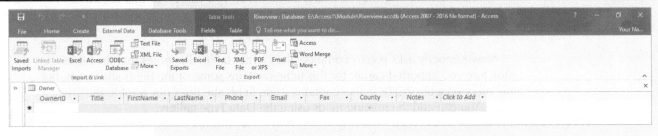

Before you add records to the Owner table and fine-tune its design, you need to first add the Animal table to the Riverview database. You will do this by importing a table and its data from another database.

Importing an Existing Table

Kelly has already created a database called "AllAnimals" that contains a table called "Animal." To import this Animal table into the Riverview database, you will follow the same process you used to import the table structure from the Kelly database to create the Owner table; however, this time you will choose the Definition and Data option, instead of the Definition only option in the Import Objects dialog box. This will import the structure and the data that Kelly has created and verified in the Animal table in the AllAnimals database.

> **To create the Animal table by importing the structure and data of another table:**
>
> ▶ **1.** Close the Owner table, make sure the External Data tab is the active tab on the ribbon, and then in the Import & Link group, click the **Access** button. The Get External Data - Access Database dialog box opens.
>
> ▶ **2.** Click the **Browse** button. The File Open dialog box opens. The Access database file from which you need to import the table is named "AllAnimals" and is located in the Access1 > Module folder provided with your Data Files.
>
> ▶ **3.** Navigate to the **Access1 > Module** folder, where your Data Files are stored, and then double-click the **AllAnimals** database file. You return to the dialog box.
>
> ▶ **4.** Make sure the **Import tables, queries, forms, reports, macros, and modules into the current database** option button is selected, and then click the **OK** button to open the Import Objects dialog box opens. The Tables tab is the current tab.
>
> ▶ **5.** Click **Animal** to select this table, click the **Options** button to display the options for importing tables, and then, in the Import Tables section, make sure the **Definition and Data** option button is selected.
>
> ▶ **6.** Click the **OK** button, and then click the **Close** button to close the dialog box without saving the import steps. Access creates the Animal table in the Riverview database using the records and structure of the Animal table in the AllAnimals database.
>
> ▶ **7.** Open the Navigation Pane, double-click **Animal** in the Tables section to open the table, and then close the Navigation Pane. The Animal table opens in Datasheet view. Kimberly reviews the new Animal table and is satisfied with its structure and the records it contains, so you can close this table.
>
> ▶ **8.** Close the Animal table.

Now Kimberly asks you to complete the Owner table. She notes that the table structure you imported earlier for this table contains some of the fields she wants, but not all (see Figure 2-27); it also contains some fields she does not want in the Owner table. You can add the missing fields using the Data Type gallery.

Adding Fields to a Table Using the Data Type Gallery

The **Data Type gallery**, available from the More Fields button located on the Add & Delete group on the Table Tools Fields tab, allows you to add a group of related fields to a table at the same time, rather than adding each field to the table individually.

The group of fields you add is called a **Quick Start selection**. For example, the **Address Quick Start selection** adds a collection of fields related to an address, such as Address, City, State, and so on, to the table at one time. When you use a Quick Start selection, the fields added already have properties set. However, you need to review and possibly modify the properties to ensure the fields match your design needs for the database.

Next, you'll use the Data Type gallery to add the missing fields to the Owner table.

To add fields to the Owner table using the Data Type gallery:

▶ **1.** Open the **Owner** table, and then on the ribbon, click the **Table Tools Fields** tab. Before inserting fields from the Data Type gallery, you need to place the insertion point in the field to the right of where you want to insert the new fields. According to Kimberly's design, the Address field should come after the Phone field, so you need to make the next field, Email, the active field.

▶ **2.** Click the **first row** in the Email field to make it the active field.

Make sure the correct field is active before adding new fields.

▶ **3.** In the Add & Delete group, click the **More Fields** button. The Data Type gallery opens and displays options for different types of fields you can add to your table.

▶ **4.** Scroll down the gallery until the Quick Start section is visible. See Figure 2-30.

| Figure 2-30 | Owner table with the Data Type gallery displayed |

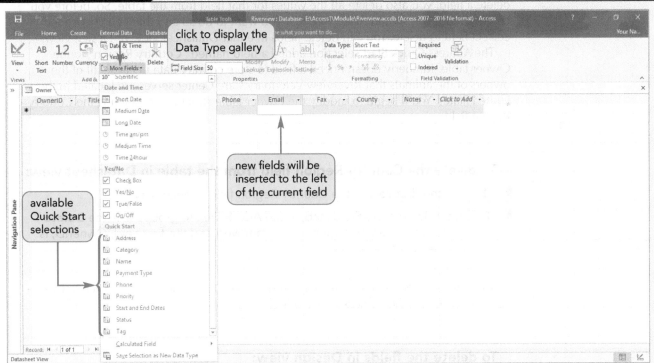

The Quick Start section provides options that will add multiple, related fields to the table at one time. The new fields will be inserted to the left of the current field.

▶ **5.** In the Quick Start section, click **Address**. Five fields are added to the table: Address, City, State Province, ZIP Postal, and Country Region. See Figure 2-31.

| Figure 2-31 | Owner table after adding fields from the Data Type gallery |

Modifying the Structure of an Imported Table

Refer back to Kimberly's design for the Owner table (Figure 2-27). To finalize the table design, you need to modify the imported table by deleting fields, renaming fields, and changing field data types. You'll begin by deleting fields.

Deleting Fields from a Table Structure

After you've created a table, you might need to delete one or more fields. When you delete a field, you also delete all the values for that field from the table. So, before you delete a field, you should make sure that you want to do so and that you choose the correct field to delete. You can delete fields in either Datasheet view or Design view.

The Address Quick Start selection added a field named "Country Region" to the Owner table. Kimberly doesn't need a field to store country data because all of the owners of the animals that Riverview Veterinary Care Center serves are located in the United States. You'll begin to modify the Owner table structure by deleting the Country Region field.

To delete the Country Region field from the table in Datasheet view:

1. Click the **first row** in the Country Region field (if necessary).

2. On the Table Tools Fields tab, in the Add & Delete group, click the **Delete** button. The Country Region field is removed and the first field, OwnerID, is now the active field.

You can also delete fields from a table structure in Design view. You'll switch to Design view to delete the other unnecessary fields.

To delete the fields in Design view:

1. On the Table Tools Fields tab, in the Views group, click the **View** button. The Owner table opens in Design view. See Figure 2-32.

Figure 2-32   Owner table in Design view

click to delete the
current field

fields to be deleted

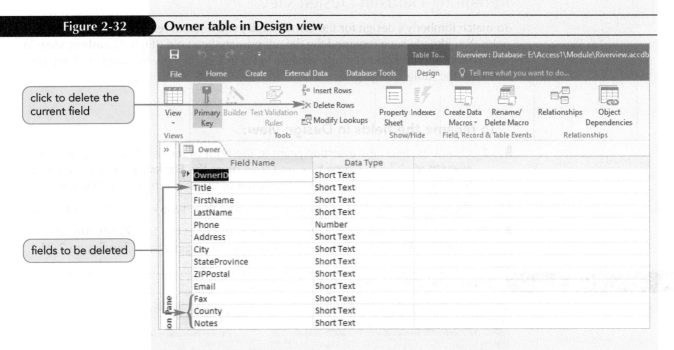

▶ **2.** Click the **Title** Field Name box to make it the current field.

▶ **3.** On the Table Tools Design tab, in the Tools group, click the **Delete Rows** button. The Title field is removed from the Owner table structure. You'll delete the Fax, County, and Notes fields next. Instead of deleting these fields individually, you'll select and delete them at the same time.

▶ **4.** On the row selector for the **Fax** field, press and hold the mouse button and then drag the mouse to select the **County** and **Notes** fields.

▶ **5.** Release the mouse button. The rows for the three fields are outlined in red, indicating all three fields are selected.

▶ **6.** In the Tools group, click the **Delete Rows** button. See Figure 2-33.

Figure 2-33   Owner table after deleting fields

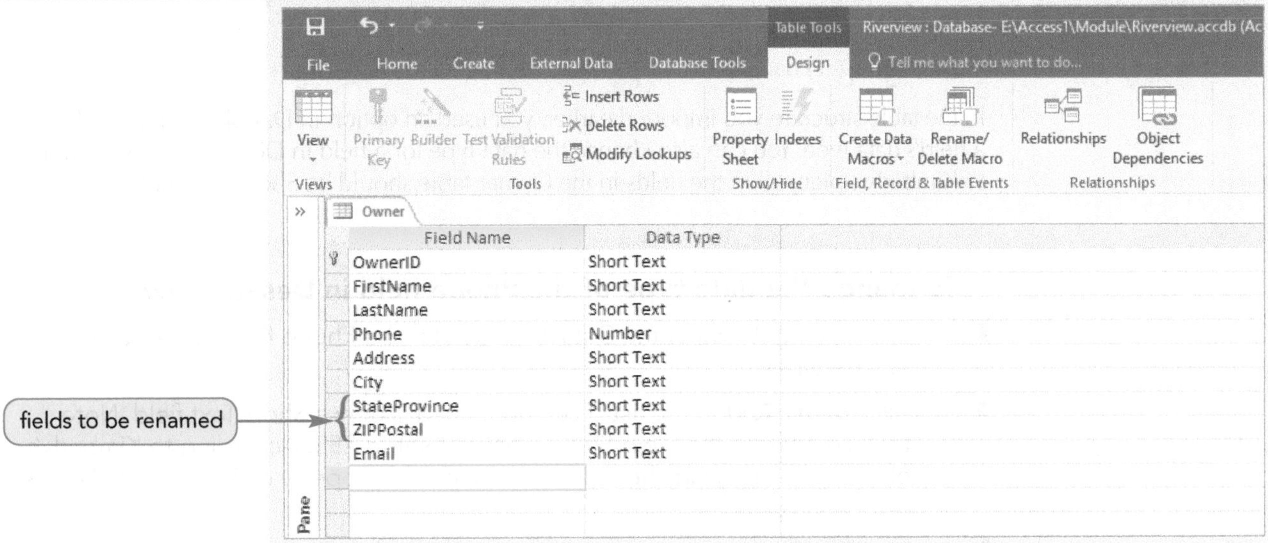

fields to be renamed

Renaming Fields in Design View

To match Kimberly's design for the Owner table, you need to rename some of the fields. You already have renamed the default primary key field (ID) in Datasheet view in the previous module. You can also rename fields in Design view by simply editing the names in the Table Design grid.

To rename the fields in Design view:

▶ **1.** Click to position the insertion point to the right of the text StateProvince in the seventh row's Field Name box, and then press the **Backspace** key eight times to delete the word "Province." The name of the seventh field is now State.

You can also select an entire field name and then type new text to replace it.

▶ **2.** In the eighth row's Field Name box, drag to select the text **ZIPPostal**, and then type **Zip**. The text you type replaces the original text. See Figure 2-34.

Figure 2-34	Owner table after renaming fields

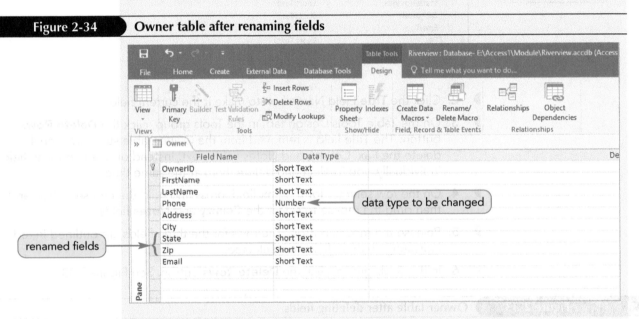

Changing the Data Type for a Field in Design View

In the table structure you imported earlier, you used an option in Datasheet view to change a field's data type. You can also change the data type for a field in Design view. According to Kimberly's plan, all of the fields in the Owner table should be Short Text fields.

To change the data type of the Phone field in Design view:

▶ **1.** Click the right side of the Data Type box for the Phone field to display the list of data types.

▶ **2.** Click **Short Text** in the list. The Phone field is now a Short Text field. Note that, by default, the Field Size property is set to 255. According to Kimberly's plan, the Phone field should have a Field Size property of 14. You'll make this change next.

▶ **3.** Press the **F6** key to move to and select the default Field Size property, and then type **14**.

Each of the remaining fields you added using the Address Quick Start selection—Address, City, State, and Zip—also has the default field size of 255. You need to change the Field Size property for these fields to match Kimberly's design. You'll also delete any Caption property values for these fields because the field names match how Kimberly wants them displayed, so captions are unnecessary.

To change the Field Size and Caption properties for the fields:

▶ **1.** Click the **Address Field Name** box to make it the current field.

▶ **2.** Press the **F6** key to move to and select the default Field Size property, and then type **35**. Note that the Caption property setting for this field is the same as the field name. This field doesn't need a caption, so you can delete this value.

▶ **3.** Press the **Tab** key three times to select Address in the Caption box, and then press the **Delete** key. The Caption property value is removed.

▶ **4.** Repeat Steps 1 through 3 for the City field to change the Field Size property to **25** and delete its Caption property value.

▶ **5.** Change the Field Size property for the State field to **2**, and then delete its Caption property value.

▶ **6.** Change the Field Size property for the Zip field to **10**, and then delete its Caption property value.

▶ **7.** On the Quick Access Toolbar, click the **Save** button 🔲 to save your changes to the Owner table.

Finally, Kimberly would like you to set the Description property for the OwnerID field and the Caption property for the OwnerID, FirstName, and LastName fields. You'll make these changes now.

To enter the Description and Caption property values:

▶ **1.** Click the **Description (Optional)** box for the OwnerID field, and then type **Primary key**.

▶ **2.** In the Field Properties pane, click the **Caption** box.

After you leave the Description (Optional) box, the Property Update Options button 📝 appears below this box for the OwnerID field. When you change a field's property in Design view, you can use this button to update the corresponding property on forms and reports that include the modified field. For example, if the Riverview database included a form that contained the OwnerID field, you could choose to propagate, or update, the modified Description property in the form by clicking the Property Update Options button, and then choosing the option to make the update everywhere the field is used. The ScreenTip on the Property Update Options button and the options it lists vary depending on the task; in this case, if you click the button, the option is "Update Status Bar Text everywhere OwnerID is used." Because the Riverview database does not include any forms or reports that are based on the Owner table, you do not need to update the properties, so you can ignore the button for now. In most cases, however, it is a good idea to perform the update.

▶ **3.** In the Caption box for the OwnerID field, type **Owner ID**.

▶ **4.** Click the **FirstName** Field Name box to make it the current field, click the **Caption** box, and then type **First Name**.

5. Click the **LastName** Field Name box to make it the current field, click the **Caption** box, and then type **Last Name**. See Figure 2-35.

Figure 2-35   **Owner table after entering descriptions and captions**

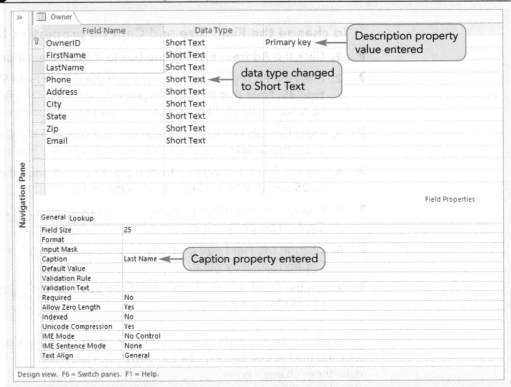

6. On the Quick Access Toolbar, click the **Save** button to save your changes to the Owner table.

7. On the Table Tools Design tab, in the Views group, click the **View** button to display the table in Datasheet view.

8. Resize each column to its best fit, and then click in the first row for the **Owner ID** column. See Figure 2-36.

Figure 2-36   **Modified Owner table in Datasheet view**

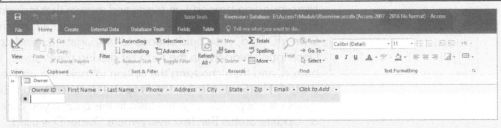

Kimberly feels that data entry would be made easier if the State field value of "WY" was automatically filled in for each new record added to the table, because all of the owners live in Wyoming. You can accomplish this by setting the Default Value property for the field.

Setting the Default Value Property for a Field

The **Default Value property** for a field specifies what value will appear, by default, for the field in each new record you add to a table.

Because all of the owners at Riverview Veterinary Care Center live in Wyoming, you'll specify a default value of "WY" for the State field in the Owner table. With this setting, each new record in the Owner table will have the correct State field value entered automatically.

To set the Default Value property for the State field:

1. On the Home tab, in the Views group, click the **View** button to display the Owner table in Design view.

2. Click the **State** Field Name box to make it the current field.

3. In the Field Properties pane, click the **Default Value** box, type **WY**, and then press the **Tab** key. See Figure 2-37.

Figure 2-37	Specifying the Default Value property for the State field

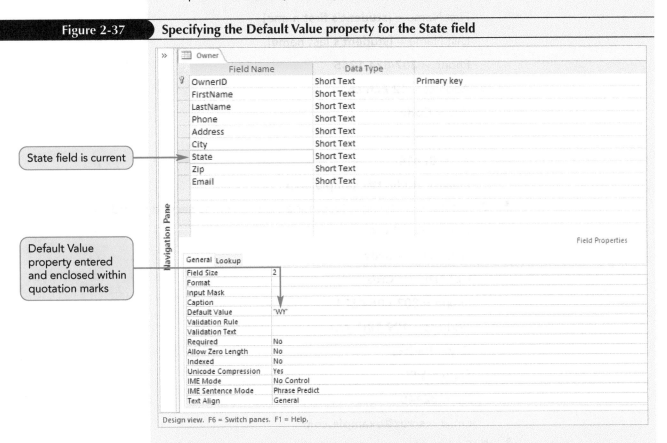

State field is current

Default Value property entered and enclosed within quotation marks

Note that a text entry in the Default Value property must be enclosed within quotation marks. If you do not type the quotation marks, Access adds them for you. However, for some entries, you would receive an error message indicating invalid syntax if you omitted the quotation marks. In such cases, you have to enter the quotation marks yourself.

4. On the Quick Access Toolbar, click the **Save** button 🖫 to save your changes to the Owner table.

5. Display the table in Datasheet view. Note that the State field for the first row now displays the default value "WY" as specified by the Default Value property. Each new record entered in the table will automatically have this State field value entered.

With the Owner table design set, you can now enter records in it. You'll begin by entering two records, and then you'll use a different method to add the remaining records.

Note: Be sure to enter your last name and first name where indicated.

To add two records to the Owner table:

1. Enter the following values in the columns in the first record; note that you can press **Tab** to move past the default State field value:

   Owner ID = **2310**

   First Name = **[student's first name]**

   Last Name = **[student's last name]**

   Phone = **307-824-1245**

   Address = **12 Elm Ln**

   City = **Cody**

   State = **WY**

   Zip = **82414**

   Email = **student@example.com**

2. Enter the following values in the columns in the second record:

   Owner ID = **2314**

   First Name = **Sally**

   Last Name = **Cruz**

   Phone = **307-406-4321**

   Address = **199 18th Ave**

   City = **Ralston**

   State = **WY**

   Zip = **82440**

   Email = **scruz@example.com**

3. Resize columns to their best fit, as necessary, and then save and close the Owner table.

Before Kimberly decided to store data using Access, Kelly managed the owner data for the care center in a different system. She exported that data into a text file and now asks you to import it into the new Owner table. You can import the data contained in this text file to add the remaining records to the Owner table.

Adding Data to a Table by Importing a Text File

There are many ways to import data into an Access database. So far, you've learned how to add data to an Access table by importing an Excel spreadsheet, and you've created a new table by importing the structure of an existing table. You can also import data contained in text files.

To complete the entry of records in the Owner table, you'll import the data contained in Kelly's text file. The file is named "Owner" and is located in the Access1 > Module folder provided with your Data Files.

To import the data contained in the Owner text file:

▶ **1.** On the ribbon, click the **External Data** tab.

▶ **2.** In the Import & Link group, click the **Text File** button. The Get External Data - Text File dialog box opens. This dialog box is similar to the one you used earlier when importing the Excel spreadsheet and the Access table structure.

▶ **3.** Click the **Browse** button. The File Open dialog box opens.

▶ **4.** Navigate to the **Access1 > Module** folder, where your Data Files are stored, and then double-click the **Owner** file. You return to the dialog box.

▶ **5.** Click the **Append a copy of the records to the table** option button. The box to the right of this option becomes active. Next, you need to select the table to which you want to add the data.

▶ **6.** Click the arrow on the box, and then click **Owner**.

▶ **7.** Click the **OK** button. The first Import Text Wizard dialog box opens. The dialog box indicates that the data to be imported is in a delimited format. A **delimited text file** is one in which fields of data are separated by a character such as a comma or a tab. In this case, the dialog box shows that data is separated by the comma character in the text file.

▶ **8.** Make sure the **Delimited** option button is selected in the dialog box, and then click the **Next** button. The second Import Text Wizard dialog box opens. See Figure 2-38.

Figure 2-38 Second Import Wizard dialog box

fields in the text file are separated by commas

preview of the data being imported

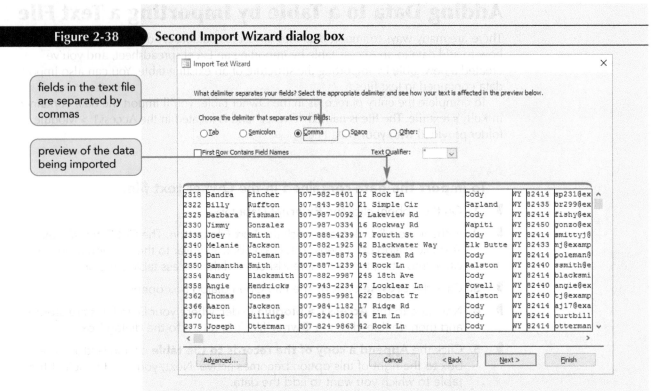

This dialog box asks you to confirm the delimiter character that separates the fields in the text file you're importing. Access detects that the comma character is used in the Owner text file and selects this option. The bottom area of the dialog box provides a preview of the data you're importing.

▶ 9. Make sure the **Comma** option button is selected, and then click the **Next** button. The third and final Import Text Wizard dialog box opens. Notice that the Import to Table box shows that the data will be imported into the Owner table.

▶ 10. Click the **Finish** button, and then click the **Close** button in the dialog box that opens to close it without saving the import steps.

Kimberly asks you to open the Owner table in Datasheet view so she can see the results of importing the text file.

To view the Owner table datasheet:

▶ 1. Open the Navigation Pane, and then double-click **Owner** to open the Owner table in Datasheet view. The Owner table contains a total of 25 records.

▶ 2. Close the Navigation Pane, and then resize columns to their best fit, scrolling the table datasheet as necessary, so that all field values are displayed. When finished, scroll back to display the first fields in the table, and then click the first row's **Owner ID** field, if necessary. See Figure 2-39.

One-to-many relationship and sample query

Figure 2-39   Owner table after importing data from the text file

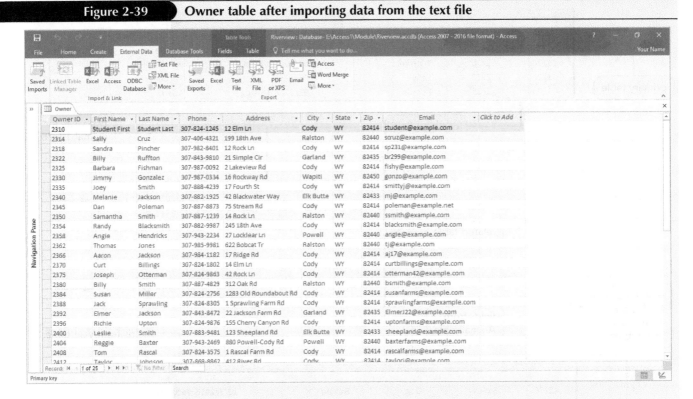

▶ **3.** Save and close the Owner table, and then open the Navigation Pane.

The Riverview database now contains four tables—Visit, Billing, Owner, and Animal—and the tables contain all the necessary records. Your final task is to complete the database design by defining the necessary relationship between its tables.

Defining Table Relationships

One of the most powerful features of a relational database management system is its ability to define relationships between tables. You use a common field to relate one table to another. The process of relating tables is often called performing a **join**. When you join tables that have a common field, you can extract data from them as if they were one larger table. For example, you can join the Animal and Visit tables by using the AnimalID field in both tables as the common field. Then you can use a query, form, or report to extract selected data from each table, even though the data is contained in two separate tables, as shown in Figure 2-40. The AnimalVisits query shown in Figure 2-40 includes the AnimalID, AnimalName, AnimalType, and AnimalBreed fields from the Animal table, and the VisitDate and Reason fields from the Visit table. The joining of records is based on the common field of AnimalID. The Animal and Visit tables have a type of relationship called a one-to-many relationship.

Figure 2-40	One-to-many relationship and sample query

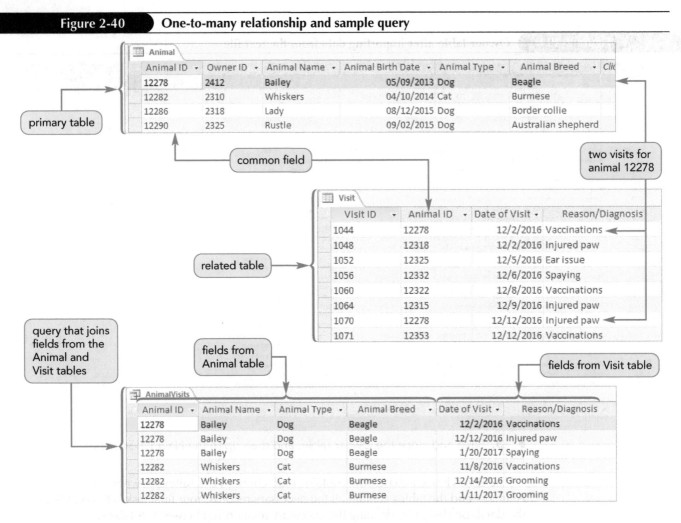

One-to-Many Relationships

As shown earlier in the Session 2.2 Visual Overview, a one-to-many relationship exists between two tables when one record in the first table matches zero, one, or many records in the second table, and when one record in the second table matches at most one record in the first table. For example, as shown in Figure 2-40, Animal 12278 has two visits in the Visit table. Other animals have one or more visits. Every visit has a single matching animal.

In Access, the two tables that form a relationship are referred to as the primary table and the related table. The primary table is the "one" table in a one-to-many relationship; in Figure 2-40, the Animal table is the primary table because there is only one animal for each visit. The related table is the "many" table; in Figure 2-40, the Visit table is the related table because an animal can have zero, one, or many visits.

Because related data is stored in two tables, inconsistencies between the tables can occur. Referring to Figure 2-40, consider the following three scenarios:

- Kimberly adds a record to the Visit table for a new animal, Fluffy (a Siberian cat), using Animal ID 12500. She did not first add the new animal's information to the animal table, so this visit does not have a matching record in the animal table. The data is inconsistent, and the visit record is considered to be an **orphaned record**.
- In another situation, Kimberly changes the AnimalID in the Animal table for Bailey the beagle from 12278 to 12510. Because there is no longer an animal with the AnimalID 12278 in the Animal table, this change creates two orphaned records in the Visit table, and the database is inconsistent.

- In a third scenario, Kimberly deletes the record for Bailey the beagle, Animal 12278, from the Animal table because this animal and its owner have moved and so the animal no longer receives care from Riverview. The database is again inconsistent; two records for Animal 12278 in the Visit table have no matching record in the Animal table.

You can avoid these types of problems and avoid having inconsistent data in your database by specifying referential integrity between tables when you define their relationships.

Referential Integrity

Referential integrity is a set of rules that Access enforces to maintain consistency between related tables when you update data in a database. Specifically, the referential integrity rules are as follows:

- When you add a record to a related table, a matching record must already exist in the primary table, thereby preventing the possibility of orphaned records.
- If you attempt to change the value of the primary key in the primary table, Access prevents this change if matching records exist in a related table. However, if you choose the **Cascade Update Related Fields option**, Access permits the change in value to the primary key and changes the appropriate foreign key values in the related table, thereby eliminating the possibility of inconsistent data.
- When you attempt to delete a record in the primary table, Access prevents the deletion if matching records exist in a related table. However, if you choose the **Cascade Delete Related Records option**, Access deletes the record in the primary table and also deletes all records in related tables that have matching foreign key values. However, you should rarely select the Cascade Delete Related Records option because doing so might cause you to inadvertently delete records you did not intend to delete. It is best to use other methods for deleting records that give you more control over the deletion process.

Defining a Relationship Between Two Tables

At the Riverview Veterinary Care Center, the owners own animals, the animals visit the clinic, and the owner receives the bill for the visits. It is important to understand these relationships in order to determine which owner to send the bill to for the visit each animal makes. Understanding these relationships also allows you to establish relationships between the tables of records in the Riverview database. When two tables have a common field, you can define a relationship between them in the Relationships window, as shown in the Session 2.2 Visual Overview.

Next, you need to define a series of relationships in the Riverview database. First, you will define a one-to-many relationship between the Owner and Animal tables, with Owner as the primary table and Animal as the related table and with OwnerID as the common field (primary key in the Owner table and a foreign key in the Animal table). Second, you will define a one-to-many relationship between the Animal and Visit tables, with Animal as the primary table and Visit as the related table and with AnimalID as the common field (the primary key in the Animal table and a foreign key in the Visit table). Finally, you will define a one-to-many relationship between the Visit and Billing tables, with Visit as the primary table and Billing as the related table and with VisitID as the common field (the primary key in the Visit table and a foreign key in the Billing table).

To define the one-to-many relationship between the Owner and Animal tables:

1. On the ribbon, click the **Database Tools** tab.

2. In the Relationships group, click the **Relationships** button to display the Relationship window and open the Show Table dialog box. See Figure 2-41.

Figure 2-41   Show Table dialog box

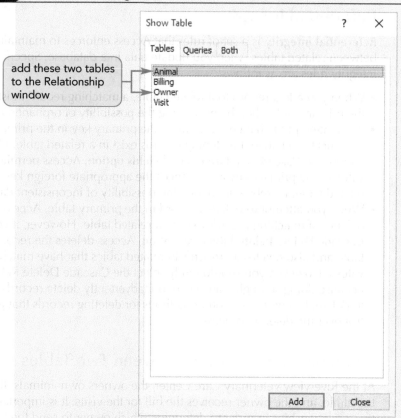

add these two tables to the Relationship window

You must add each table participating in a relationship to the Relationships window. Because the Owner table is the primary table in the relationship, you'll add it first.

TIP

You can also double-click a table in the Show Table dialog box to add it to the Relationships window.

3. Click **Owner**, and then click the **Add** button. The Owner table's field list is added to the Relationships window.

4. Click **Animal**, and then click the **Add** button. The Animal table's field list is added to the Relationships window.

5. Click the **Close** button in the Show Table dialog box to close it.

So that you can view all the fields and complete field names, you'll resize the Owner table field list.

6. Position the mouse pointer on the bottom border of the Owner table field list until it changes to ⬍, and then drag the bottom of the Owner table field list to lengthen it until the vertical scroll bar disappears and all the fields are visible.

To form the relationship between the two tables, you drag the common field of OwnerID from the primary table to the related table. Then Access opens the Edit Relationships dialog box, in which you select the relationship options for the two tables.

7. Click **OwnerID** in the Owner field list, and then drag it to **OwnerID** in the Animal field list. When you release the mouse button, the Edit Relationships dialog box opens. See Figure 2-42.

Figure 2-42   **Edit Relationships dialog box**

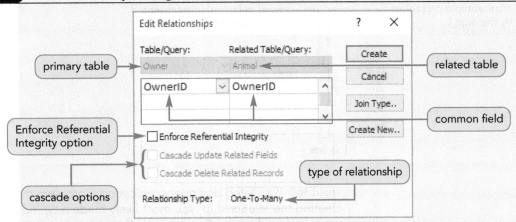

The primary table, related table, common field, and relationship type (One-To-Many) appear in the dialog box. Note that Access correctly identifies the "One" side of the relationship and places the primary table Owner in the Table/Query section of the dialog box; similarly, Access correctly identifies the "Many" side of the relationship and places the related table Animal in the Related Table/Query section of the dialog box.

8. Click the **Enforce Referential Integrity** check box. After you click the Enforce Referential Integrity check box, the two cascade options become available. If you select the Cascade Update Related Fields option, Access will update the appropriate foreign key values in the related table when you change a primary key value in the primary table. You will *not* select the Cascade Delete Related Records option because doing so could cause you to delete records that you do not want to delete; this option is rarely selected.

9. Click the **Cascade Update Related Fields** check box.

10. Click the **Create** button to define the one-to-many relationship between the two tables and to close the dialog box. The completed relationship appears in the Relationships window, with the join line connecting the common field of OwnerID in each table. See Figure 2-43.

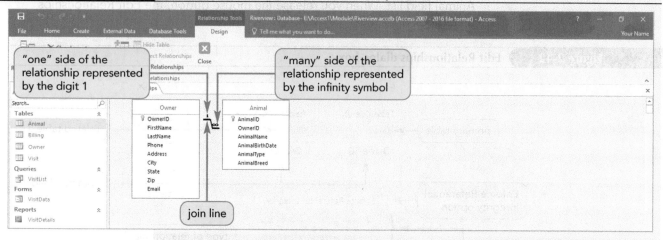

Figure 2-43 | Defined relationship in the Relationship window

Trouble? If a dialog box opens indicating a problem that prevents you from creating the relationship, you most likely made a typing error when entering the two records in the Owner table. If so, click the OK button in the dialog box and then click the Cancel button in the Edit Relationships dialog box. Refer back to the earlier steps instructing you to enter the two records in the Owner table and carefully compare your entries with those shown in the text, especially the OwnerID field values. Make any necessary corrections to the data in the Owner table, and then repeat Steps 7 through 10. If you still receive an error message, ask your instructor for assistance.

The next step is to define the one-to-many relationship between the Animal and Visit tables. In this relationship, Animal is the primary ("one") table because there is at most one animal for each visit. Visit is the related ("many") table because there are zero, one, or many visits that are generated for each animal. Similarly, you need to define the one-to-many relationship between the Visit and Billing tables. In this relationship, Visit is the primary ("one") table because there is at most one visit for each invoice. Billing is the related ("many") table because there are zero, one, or many invoices that are generated for each animal visit. For example, some visits require lab work, which is invoiced separately.

To define the relationship between the Animal and Visit tables and to define the relationship between the Visit and billing tables:

▶ **1.** On the Relationship Tools Design tab, in the Relationships group, click the **Show Table** button to open the Show Table dialog box.

▶ **2.** Click **Visit** on the Tables tab, click the **Add** button, and then click the **Close** button to close the Show Table dialog box. The Visit table's field list appears in the Relationships window to the right of the Animal table's field list.

Because the Animal table is the primary table in this relationship, you need to drag the AnimalID field from the Animal field list to the Visit field list.

▶ **3.** Drag the **AnimalID** field in the Animal field list to the **AnimalID** field in the Visit field list. When you release the mouse button, the Edit Relationships dialog box opens.

TIP

You can also use the mouse to drag a table from the Navigation Pane to add it to the Relationships window.

4. Click the **Enforce Referential Integrity** check box, click the **Cascade Update Related Fields** check box, and then click the **Create** button. The Edit Relationships dialog box closes and the completed relationship appears in the Relationships window.

Finally, you will define the relationship between the Visit and Billing tables.

5. On the Relationship Tools Design tab, in the Relationships group, click the **Show Table** button to open the Show Table dialog box.

6. Click **Billing** on the Tables tab, click the **Add** button, and then click the **Close** button to close the Show Table dialog box. The Billing table's field list appears in the Relationships window to the right of the Visit table's field list.

7. Click and drag the **VisitID** field in the Visit field list to the **VisitID** field in the Billing field list. The Edit Relationships dialog box opens.

8. In the Edit Relationships dialog box, click the **Enforce Referential Integrity** check box, click the **Cascade Update Related Fields** check box, and then click the **Create** button to define the one-to-many relationship between the two tables and to close the dialog box. The completed relationships for the Riverview database appear in the Relationships window. See Figure 2-44.

Figure 2-44	All three relationships now defined

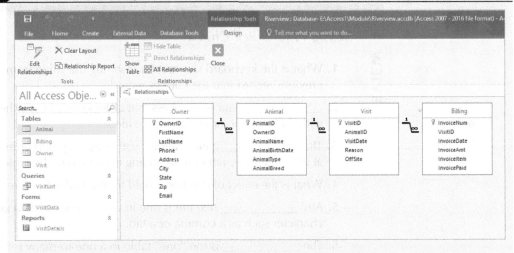

9. On the Quick Access Toolbar, click the **Save** button to save the layout in the Relationships window.

10. On the Relationship Tools Design tab, in the Relationships group, click the **Close** button to close the Relationships window.

11. Compact and repair the Riverview database, and then close the database.

PROSKILLS

Problem Solving: Creating a Larger Database

The Riverview database is a relatively small database containing only a few tables, and the data and the reports you will generate from it will be fairly simple. A larger database would most likely have many more tables and different types of relationships that can be quite complex. When creating a large database, follow this standard process:

- Consult people who will be using the data to gain an understanding of how it will be used. Gather sample reports and representative data if possible.
- Plan the tables, fields, data types, other properties, and the relationships between the tables.
- Create the tables and define the relationships between them.
- Populate the tables with sample data.
- Design some queries, forms, and reports that will be needed, and then test them.
- Modify the database structure, if necessary, based on the results of your tests.
- Enter the actual data into the database tables.

Testing is critical at every stage of creating a database. Once the database is finalized and implemented, it's not actually finished. The design of a database evolves as new functionality is required and as the data that is gathered changes.

REVIEW

Session 2.2 Quick Check

1. What is the keyboard shortcut for inserting the value from the same field in the previous record into the current record?

2. _____ data is a process that allows you to copy the data from a source without having to open the source file.

3. The _____ gallery allows you to add a group of related fields to a table at the same time, rather than adding each field to the table individually.

4. What is the effect of deleting a field from a table structure?

5. A(n) _____ text file is one in which fields of data are separated by a character such as a comma or a tab.

6. The _____ is the "one" table in a one-to-many relationship, and the _____ is the "many" table in the relationship.

7. _____ is a set of rules that Access enforces to maintain consistency between related tables when you update data in a database.

PRACTICE

Review Assignments

Data File needed for the Review Assignments: **Vendor.accdb** (*cont. from Module 1*) and **Supplies.xlsx**

In addition to tracking information about the vendors Riverview Veterinary Care Center works with, Kimberly also wants to track information about their products and services. First, Kimberly asks you to modify the necessary properties in the existing Supplier table in the Vendor database; then she wants you to create a new table in the Vendor database to contain product data. Complete the following:

1. Open the **Vendor** database you created in the previous module.
2. Open the **Supplier** table in Design view, and set the field properties as shown in Figure 2-45.

Figure 2-45	Field properties for the Supplier table

Field Name	Data Type	Description	Field Size	Other
SupplierID	Short Text	Primary key	6	Caption = Supplier ID
Company	Short Text		50	
Category	Short Text		15	
Address	Short Text		35	
City	Short Text		25	
State	Short Text		2	
Zip	Short Text		10	
Phone	Short Text		14	Caption = Contact Phone
ContactFirst	Short Text		20	Caption = Contact First Name
ContactLast	Short Text		25	Caption = Contact Last Name
InitialContact	Date/Time			Format = Short Date
				Caption = Initial Contact

3. Save the Supplier table. Click the **Yes** button when a message appears, indicating some data might be lost. Switch to Datasheet view and resize columns, as necessary, to their best fit. Then save and close the Supplier table.
4. Create a new table in Design view, using the table design shown in Figure 2-46.

Figure 2-46	Design for the Product table

Field Name	Data Type	Description	Field Size	Other
ProductID	Short Text	Primary key	5	Caption = Product ID
SupplierID	Short Text	Foreign key	6	Caption = Supplier ID
ProductName	Short Text		75	Caption = Product Name
Price	Currency			Format = Standard
				Decimal Places = 2
TempControl	Yes/No			Caption = Temp Controlled?
Sterile	Yes/No			Caption = Sterile?
Units	Number		Integer	Decimal Places = 0
				Caption = Units/Case
				Default Value = [no entry]

5. Specify ProductID as the primary key, and then save the table as **Product**.

6. Modify the table structure by adding a new field between the Price and TempControl fields. Name the new field **Weight** (data type: **Number**; field size: **Single**; Decimal Places: **2**; Caption: **Weight in Lbs**; Default Value: [no entry]). Then move the **Units** field so that it is positioned between the Price and Weight fields.

7. Enter the records shown in Figure 2-47 in the Product table. Resize all datasheet columns to their best fit. When finished, save and close the Product table.

Figure 2-47	Records for the Product table

Product ID	Supplier ID	Product Name	Price	Units/Case	Weight in Lbs	Temp Controlled?	Sterile?
PT100	KLS321	Paper tape roll	20.00	12	3	No	No
TC050	QLS002	Thermometer covers	27.00	50	1	No	Yes

8. Use the Import Spreadsheet Wizard to add data to the Product table. The data you need to import is contained in the Supplies workbook, which is an Excel file located in the Access1 > Review folder provided with your Data Files.

   a. Specify the Supplies workbook as the source of the data.

   b. Select the option for appending the data.

   c. Select Product as the table.

   d. In the Import Spreadsheet Wizard dialog boxes, make sure Access confirms that the first row contains column headings, and import to the Product table. Do not save the import steps.

9. Open the **Product** table in Datasheet view, and resize columns to their best fit, as necessary. Then save and close the Product table.

10. Define a one-to-many relationship between the primary Supplier table and the related Product table. Resize the table field lists so that all field names are visible. Select the referential integrity option and the cascade updates option for the relationship.

11. Save the changes to the Relationships window and close it, compact and repair the Vendor database, and then close the database.

Case Problem 1

Data Files needed for this Case Problem: Beauty.accdb *(cont. from Module 1)* and Customers.txt

Beauty To Go Sue Miller wants to use the Beauty database to track information about customers who subscribe to her business, which provides a variety of salon services on a subscription basis, and the plans in which customers are enrolled. She asks you to help maintain this database. Complete the following:

1. Open the **Beauty** database you created in the previous module, open the **Option** table in Design view, and then change the following field properties:

   a. OptionID: Enter **Primary key** for the description, change the field size to **3**, and enter **Option ID** for the caption.

   b. OptionDescription: Change the field size to **45** and enter **Option Description** for the caption.

   c. OptionCost: Change the format to **Standard**, specify **0** decimal places, enter **Option Cost** for the caption, no default value.

   d. FeeWaived: Enter **Fee Waived** for the caption.

2. Save and close the Option table. Click the Yes button when a message appears, indicating some data might be lost.

3. Create a new table in Design view, using the table design shown in Figure 2-48.

Figure 2-48	Design for the Member table

Field Name	Data Type	Description	Field Size	Other
MemberID	Short Text	Primary key	4	Caption = Member ID
OptionID	Short Text	Foreign key	3	Caption = Option ID
FirstName	Short Text		20	Caption = First Name
LastName	Short Text		25	Caption = Last Name
Phone	Short Text		14	
OptionEnd	Date/Time	Date Option Ends		Format = Short Date
				Caption = Option Ends

4. Specify **MemberID** as the primary key, and then save the table as **Member**.

5. Use the Address Quick Start selection in the Data Type gallery to add five fields between the LastName and Phone fields.

6. Switch to Design view, and then make the following changes to the Member table design:

   a. Address field: Change the name of this field to **Street**, change the field size to **40**, and delete the entry for the caption.

   b. City field: Change the field size to **25**, and delete the entry for the caption.

   c. StateProvince field: Change the name of this field to **State**, change the field size to **2**, delete the entry for the caption, and enter **FL** for the default value.

   d. ZIPPostal field: Change the name of this field to **Zip**, change the field size to **10**, and delete the entry for the caption.

   e. Delete the **CountryRegion** field from the Member table structure.

   f. Between the Phone and OptionEnd fields, add a new field named **OptionBegin** (data type: **Date/Time**; format: **Short Date**; Caption: **Option Begins**).

7. Enter the records shown in Figure 2-49 in the Member table. Resize all datasheet columns to their best fit. When finished, save and close the Member table. Be sure to enter your first and last name in the appropriate fields in the first record.

Figure 2-49	Records for the Member table

Member ID	Option ID	First Name	Last Name	Street	City	State	Zip	Phone	Option Begins	Option Ends
2103	123	*Student First*	*Student Last*	22 Oak St	Orlando	FL	32801	407-832-3944	2/1/17	3/1/17
2118	120	Susan	Reyes	3 Balboa St	Orlando	FL	32804	407-216-0091	11/2/16	2/2/17

8. Use the Import Text File Wizard to add data to the Member table. The data you need to import is contained in the Customers text file, which is located in the Access1 > Case1 folder provided with your Data Files.

   a. Specify the Customers text file as the source of the data.

   b. Select the option for appending the data.

   c. Select Member as the table.

   d. In the Import Text File Wizard dialog boxes, choose the options to import delimited data, to use a comma delimiter, and to import the data into the Member table. Do not save the import steps.

9. Open the **Member** table in Datasheet view and resize columns to their best fit, as necessary. Then save and close the Member table.

10. Define a one-to-many relationship between the primary Option table and the related Member table. Resize the Member table field list so that all field names are visible. Select the referential integrity option and the cascade updates option for this relationship.

11. Save the changes to the Relationships window and close it, compact and repair the Beauty database, and then close the database.

Case Problem 2

APPLY

Data Files needed for this Case Problem: Programming.accdb *(cont. from Module 1)*, Client.accdb, Students.txt, and Agreements.xlsx

Programming Pros Brent Hovis plans to use the Programming database to maintain information about the students, tutors, and contracts for his tutoring services company. Brent asks you to help him build the database by updating one table and creating two new tables in the database. Complete the following:

1. Open the **Programming** database you created in the previous module, open the **Tutor** table in Design view, and then set the field properties as shown in Figure 2-50.

Figure 2-50	Field properties for the Tutor table

Field Name	Data Type	Description	Field Size	Other
TutorID	Short Text	Primary key	4	Caption = Tutor ID
FirstName	Short Text		20	Caption = First Name
LastName	Short Text		25	Caption = Last Name
Major	Short Text		25	
YearInSchool	Short Text		12	Caption = Year In School
School	Short Text		30	
HireDate	Date/Time			Format = Short Date
				Caption = Hire Date

2. Add a new field as the last field in the Tutor table with the field name **Groups**, the **Yes/No** data type, and the caption **Groups Only**.

3. Save the Tutor table. Click the **Yes** button when a message appears, indicating some data might be lost.

4. In the table datasheet, specify that the following tutors conduct group tutoring sessions only: Carey Billings, Fredrik Karlsson, Ellen Desoto, and Donald Gallager. Close the Tutor table.

5. Brent created a table named Student in the Client database that is located in the Access1 > Case2 folder provided with your Data Files. Import the structure of the Student table in the Client database into a new table named Student in the Programming database. Do not save the import steps.

6. Open the **Student** table in Datasheet view, and then add the following two fields to the end of the table: **BirthDate** (Date/Time field) and **Gender** (Short Text field).

7. Use the Phone Quick Start selection in the Data Type gallery to add four fields related to phone numbers between the Zip and BirthDate fields. (*Hint:* Be sure to make the BirthDate field the active field before adding the new fields.)

8. Display the Student table in Design view, delete the BusinessPhone and FaxNumber fields, and then save and close the Student table.

9. Reopen the Student table and modify its design so that it matches the design in Figure 2-51, *including the revised field names and data types.*

| Figure 2-51 | Field properties for the Student table |

Field Name	Data Type	Description	Field Size	Other
StudentID	Short Text	Primary key	7	Caption = Student ID
LastName	Short Text		25	Caption = Last Name
FirstName	Short Text		20	Caption = First Name
Address	Short Text		35	
City	Short Text		25	
State	Short Text		2	Default Value = NC
Zip	Short Text		10	
HomePhone	Short Text		14	Caption = Home Phone
CellPhone	Short Text		14	Caption = Cell Phone
BirthDate	Date/Time			Format = Short Date
				Caption = Birth Date
Gender	Short Text		1	

10. Move the LastName field so it follows the FirstName field.

11. Save your changes to the table design, and then add the records shown in Figure 2-52 to the Student table.

| Figure 2-52 | Records for the Student table |

Student ID	First Name	Last Name	Address	City	State	Zip	Home Phone	Cell Phone	Date of Birth	Gender
LOP4015	Henry	Lopez	19 8th St	Raleigh	NC	27601	919-264-9981	919-665-8110	2/19/1998	M
PER4055	Rosalyn	Perez	421 Pine Ln	Cary	NC	27511	984-662-4761	919-678-0012	4/12/1996	F

12. Resize the fields to their best fit, and then save and close the Student table.

13. Use the Import Text File Wizard to add data to the Student table. The data you need to import is contained in the Students text file, which is located in the Access1 > Case2 folder provided with your Data Files.
    a. Specify the Students text file as the source of the data.
    b. Select the option for appending the data.
    c. Select Student as the table.
    d. In the Import Text File Wizard dialog boxes, choose the options to import delimited data, to use a comma delimiter, and to import the data into the Student table. Do not save the import steps.

14. Open the **Student** table in Datasheet view, resize columns in the datasheet to their best fit (as necessary), and then save and close the table.

15. Create a new table in Design view, using the table design shown in Figure 2-53.

| Figure 2-53 | Design for the Contract table |

Field Name	Data Type	Description	Field Size	Other
ContractID	Short Text	Primary key	4	Caption = Contract ID
StudentID	Short Text	Foreign key	7	Caption = Student ID
TutorID	Short Text	Foreign key	4	Caption = Tutor ID
SessionType	Short Text		15	Caption = Session Type
Length	Number		Integer	Decimal Places = 0
				Caption = Length (Hrs)
				Default Value = [no entry]
NumSessions	Number		Integer	Decimal Places = 0
				Caption = Number of Sessions
				Default Value = [no entry]
Cost	Currency			Format = Currency
				Decimal Places = 0
				Default Value = [no entry]
Assessment	Yes/No	Pre-assessment exam complete		Caption = Assessment Complete

16. Specify ContractID as the primary key, and then save the table using the name **Contract**.

17. Add a new field to the Contract table, between the TutorID and SessionType fields, with the field name **ContractDate**, the **Date/Time** data type, the description **Date contract is signed**, the **Short Date** format, and the caption **Contract Date**. Save and close the Contract table.

18. Use the Import Spreadsheet Wizard to add data to the Contract table. The data you need to import is contained in the Agreements workbook, which is an Excel file located in the Access1 > Case2 folder provided with your Data Files.

    a. Specify the Agreements workbook as the source of the data.

    b. Select the option for appending the data to the table.

    c. Select Contract as the table.

    d. In the Import Spreadsheet Wizard dialog boxes, choose the Agreements worksheet, make sure Access confirms that the first row contains column headings, and import to the Contract table. Do not save the import steps.

19. Open the **Contract** table, and add the records shown in Figure 2-54. (*Hint:* Use the New (blank) record button in the navigation buttons to add a new record.)

| Figure 2-54 | Records for the Contract table |

Contract ID	Student ID	Tutor ID	Contract Date	Session Type	Length (Hrs)	Number of Sessions	Cost	Assessment Complete
6215	PER4055	1018	7/6/2017	Group	2	5	$400	Yes
6350	LOP4015	1010	10/12/2017	Private	3	4	$720	Yes

20. Resize columns in the datasheet to their best fit (as necessary), and then save and close the Contract table.

21. Define the one-to-many relationships between the database tables as follows: between the primary Student table and the related Contract table, and between the primary Tutor table and the related Contract table. Resize the table field lists so that all field names are visible. Select the referential integrity option and the cascade updates option for each relationship.

22. Save the changes to the Relationships window and close it, compact and repair the Programming database, and then close the database.

CHALLENGE

Case Problem 3

Data Files needed for this Case Problem: Center.accdb *(cont. from Module 1)*, Donations.xlsx, and Auctions.txt

Diane's Community Center   Diane Coleman wants to use the Center database to maintain information about the patrons and donations for her not-for-profit community center. Diane asks you to help her maintain the database by updating one table and creating two new ones. Complete the following:

1. Open the **Center** database you created in the previous module, open the **Patron** table in Design view, and then change the following field properties:

   a. PatronID: Enter **Primary key** for the description, change the field size to **5**, and enter **Patron ID** for the caption.

   b. Title: Change the field size to **4**.

   c. FirstName: Change the field size to **20**, and enter **First Name** for the caption.

   d. LastName: Change the field size to **25**, and enter **Last Name** for the caption.

   e. Phone: Change the field size to **14**.

   f. Email: Change field size to **35**.

2. Save and close the Patron table. Click the Yes button when a message appears, indicating some data might be lost.

✛ **Explore** 3. Use the Import Spreadsheet Wizard to create a table in the Center database. As the source of the data, specify the Donations workbook, which is located in the Access1 > Case3 folder provided with your Data Files. Select the option to import the source data into a new table in the database.

✛ **Explore** 4. Complete the Import Spreadsheet Wizard dialog boxes as follows:

   a. Select Donation as the worksheet you want to import.

   b. Specify that the first row contains column headings.

   c. Accept the field options suggested by the wizard, and do not skip any fields.

   d. Choose DonationID as your own primary key.

   e. Import the data to a table named **Donation**, and do not save the import steps.

✛ **Explore** 5. Open the Donation table in Datasheet view. Left-justify the DonationDescription field by clicking the column heading, and then on the Home tab, clicking the Align Left button in the Text Formatting group.

6. Open the Donation table in Design view, and then modify the table so it matches the design shown in Figure 2-55, including changes to data types, field name, and field position. For the Short Text fields, delete any formats specified in the Format property boxes.

Figure 2-55 **Design for the Donation table**

Field Name	Data Type	Description	Field Size	Other
DonationID	Short Text	Primary key	4	Caption = Donation ID
PatronID	Short Text	Foreign key	5	Caption = Patron ID
DonationDate	Date/Time			Format = mm/dd/yyyy
				Caption = Donation Date
Description	Short Text		30	
DonationValue	Currency	Dollar amount or estimated value		Format = Currency
				Decimal Places = 2
				Caption = Donation Value
				Default Value = [no entry]
CashDonation	Yes/No			Caption = Cash Donation?
AuctionItem	Yes/No			Caption = Possible Auction Item?

7. Save your changes to the table design, click Yes for the message about lost data, and then switch to Datasheet view.

8. Resize the columns in the Donation datasheet to their best fit.

⊕ **Explore** 9. Diane decides that the values in the Donation Value column would look better without the two decimal places. Make this field the current field in the datasheet. Then, on the Table Tools Fields tab, in the Formatting group, use the Decrease Decimals button to remove the two decimal places and the period from these values. Switch back to Design view, and note that the Decimal Places property for the DonationValue field is now set to 0.

10. Save and close the Donation table.

11. Use Design view to create a table using the table design shown in Figure 2-56.

Figure 2-56 **Design for the Auction table**

Field Name	Data Type	Description	Field Size	Other
AuctionID	Short Text	Primary key	3	Caption = Auction ID
AuctionDate	Date/Time			Format = mm/dd/yyyy
				Caption = Date of Auction
DonationID	Short Text		4	Caption = Donation ID
MinPrice	Currency			Format = Currency
				Decimal Places = 0
				Caption = Minimum Sale Price
ItemSold	Yes/No			Caption = Item Sold at Auction?

12. Specify **AuctionID** as the primary key, save the table as **Auction**, and then close the table.

13. Use the Import Text File Wizard to add data to the Auction table. The data you need to import is contained in the Auctions text file, which is located in the Access1 > Case3 folder provided with your Data Files.

a. Specify the Auctions text file as the source of the data.

b. Select the option for appending the data.

c. Select Auction as the table.

d. In the Import Text File Wizard dialog boxes, choose the options to import delimited data, to use a comma delimiter, and to import the data into the Auction table. Do not save the import steps.

14. Open the Auction table in Datasheet view, and resize all columns to their best fit.

15. Display the Auction table in Design view. Move the DonationID field to make it the second field in the table, and enter the description **Foreign key** for the DonationID field. Save the modified Auction table design.

16. Switch to Datasheet view, and then add the records shown in Figure 2-57 to the Auction table. (*Hint:* Use the New (blank) record button in the navigation buttons to add a new record.) Close the table when finished.

Figure 2-57   **Records for the Auction table**

AuctionID	DonationID	AuctionDate	MinPrice	ItemSold
205	5132	8/12/2017	200	No
235	5217	10/14/2017	150	No

17. Define the one-to-many relationships between the database tables as follows: between the primary Patron table and the related Donation table, and between the primary Donation table and the related Auction table. Resize any field lists so that all field names are visible. Select the referential integrity option and the cascade updates option for each relationship.

18. Save the changes to the Relationships window and close it, compact and repair the Center database, and then close the database.

Case Problem 4

CHALLENGE

Data Files needed for this Case Problem: Appalachia.accdb *(cont. from Module 1)*, Travel.accdb, and Bookings.txt

Hike Appalachia   Molly and Bailey Johnson use the Appalachia database to track the data about the hikers and tours offered through their business. They ask you to help them maintain this database. Complete the following:

1. Open the **Appalachia** database you created in the previous module, open the **Hiker** table in Design view, and then change the following field properties:

   a. HikerID: Enter **Primary key** for the description, change the field size to **3**, and enter **Hiker ID** for the caption.

   b. HikerFirst: Change the field size to **20**, and enter **Hiker First Name** for the caption.

   c. HikerLast: Change the field size to **25**, and enter **Hiker Last Name** for the caption.

   d. Address: Change the field size to **35**.

   e. City: Change the field size to **25**.

   f. State: Change the field size to **2**.

   g. Zip: Change the field size to **10**.

   h. Phone: Change the field size to **14**.

2. Save the Hiker table, click the Yes button when a message appears, indicating some data might be lost, resize the Hiker First Name and Hiker Last Name columns in Datasheet view to their best fit, and then save and close the table.

   a. Import the **Trip** table structure and data from the **Travel** database into a new table in the **Appalachia** database. As the source of the data, specify the Travel database, which is located in the Access1 > Case4 folder provided with your Data Files; select the option button to import tables, queries, forms, reports, macros, and modules into the current database; and in the Import Objects dialog box, select the **Trip** table, click the **Options** button, and then make sure that the correct option is selected to import the table's data and structure (definition).

   b. Do not save your import steps.

⊕ **Explore** 3. Using a shortcut menu in the Navigation Pane, rename the Trip table as **Tour** to give this name to the new table in the Appalachia database.

4. Open the **Tour** table in Design view, and then delete the VIPDiscount field.

5. Change the following properties:

   a. TourID: Enter the description **Primary key**, change the field size to **3**, and enter **Tour ID** for the caption.

   b. TourName: Enter **Tour Name** for the caption, and change the field size to **35**.

   c. TourType: Enter **Tour Type** for the caption, and change the field size to **15**.

   d. PricePerPerson: Enter **Price Per Person** for the caption.

6. Save the modified table, click the Yes button when a message appears, indicating some data might be lost, and then display the table in Datasheet view. Resize all datasheet columns to their best fit, and then save and close the table.

7. In Design view, create a table using the table design shown in Figure 2-58.

Figure 2-58 **Design for the Reservation table**

Field Name	Data Type	Description	Field Size	Other
ReservationID	Short Text	Primary key	4	Caption = Reservation ID
HikerID	Short Text	Foreign key	3	Caption = Hiker ID
TourID	Short Text	Foreign key	3	Caption = Tour ID
TourDate	Date/Time			Caption = Tour Date
People	Number		Integer	Decimal Places = 0
				Default Value = [no entry]

8. Specify **ReservationID** as the primary key, and then save the table as **Reservation**.

⊕ **Explore** 9. Refer back to Figure 2-11 to review the custom date formats. Change the Format property of the TourDate field to a custom format that displays dates in a format similar to 02/15/17. Save and close the Reservation table.

10. Use the Import Text File Wizard to add data to the Reservation table. The data you need to import is contained in the Bookings text file, which is located in the Access1 > Case4 folder provided with your Data Files.

   a. Specify the Bookings text file as the source of the data.

   b. Select the option for appending the data.

   c. Select Reservation as the table.

   d. In the Import Text File Wizard dialog boxes, choose the options to import delimited data, to use a comma delimiter, and to import the data into the Reservation table. Do not save the import steps.

11. Open the **Reservation** table, and then resize columns in the table datasheet to their best fit (as necessary), verify that the date values in the StartDate field are displayed correctly according to the custom format, and then save and close the table.

12. Define the one-to-many relationships between the database tables as follows: between the primary Hiker table and the related Reservation table, and between the primary Tour table and the related Reservation table. (*Hint:* Place the Reservation table as the middle table in the Relationships window to make it easier to join the tables.) Resize the Hiker field list so that all field names are visible. Select the referential integrity option and the cascade updates option for each relationship.

13. Save the changes to the Relationships window and close it, compact and repair the Appalachia database, and then close the database.

OBJECTIVES

Session 3.1
- Find, modify, and delete records in a table
- Hide and unhide fields in a datasheet
- Work in the Query window in Design view
- Create, run, and save queries
- Update data using a query datasheet
- Create a query based on multiple tables
- Sort data in a query
- Filter data in a query

Session 3.2
- Specify an exact match condition in a query
- Use a comparison operator in a query to match a range of values
- Use the And and Or logical operators in queries
- Change the font size and alternate row color in a datasheet
- Create and format a calculated field in a query
- Perform calculations in a query using aggregate functions and record group calculations
- Change the display of database objects in the Navigation Pane

Maintaining and Querying a Database

Updating Tables and Retrieving Care Center Information

Case | *Riverview Veterinary Care Center*

At a recent meeting, Kimberly Johnson and her staff discussed the importance of maintaining accurate information about the animals seen by Riverview Veterinary Care Center, as well as the owners, visits, and invoices, and regularly monitoring the business activities of the care center. For example, Kelly Flannagan, Kimberly's assistant, needs to make sure she has up-to-date contact information, such as phone numbers and email addresses, for the owners of all the animals seen by the care center. The office staff also must monitor billing activity to ensure that invoices are paid on time and in full. In addition, the staff handles marketing efforts for the care center and tracks services provided to develop new strategies for promoting these services. Kimberly is also interested in analyzing other aspects of the business related to animal visits and finances. You can satisfy all these informational needs for Riverview Veterinary Care Center by updating data in the Riverview database and by creating and using queries that retrieve information from the database.

STARTING DATA FILES

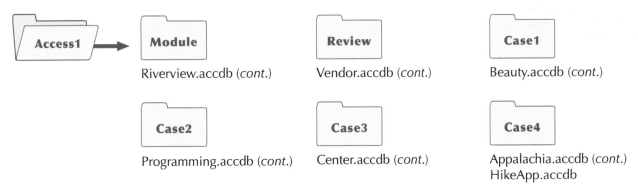

Access1 → Module
Riverview.accdb (*cont.*)

Review
Vendor.accdb (*cont.*)

Case1
Beauty.accdb (*cont.*)

Case2
Programming.accdb (*cont.*)

Case3
Center.accdb (*cont.*)

Case4
Appalachia.accdb (*cont.*)
HikeApp.accdb

Session 3.1 Visual Overview:

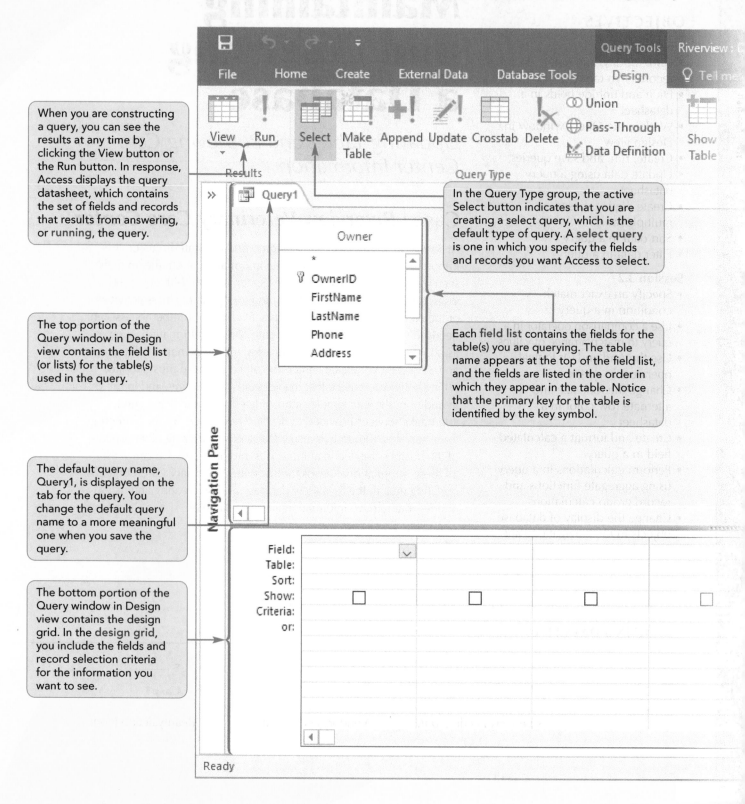

When you are constructing a query, you can see the results at any time by clicking the View button or the Run button. In response, Access displays the query datasheet, which contains the set of fields and records that results from answering, or running, the query.

In the Query Type group, the active Select button indicates that you are creating a select query, which is the default type of query. A select query is one in which you specify the fields and records you want Access to select.

The top portion of the Query window in Design view contains the field list (or lists) for the table(s) used in the query.

Each field list contains the fields for the table(s) you are querying. The table name appears at the top of the field list, and the fields are listed in the order in which they appear in the table. Notice that the primary key for the table is identified by the key symbol.

The default query name, Query1, is displayed on the tab for the query. You change the default query name to a more meaningful one when you save the query.

The bottom portion of the Query window in Design view contains the design grid. In the design grid, you include the fields and record selection criteria for the information you want to see.

Query Window in Design View

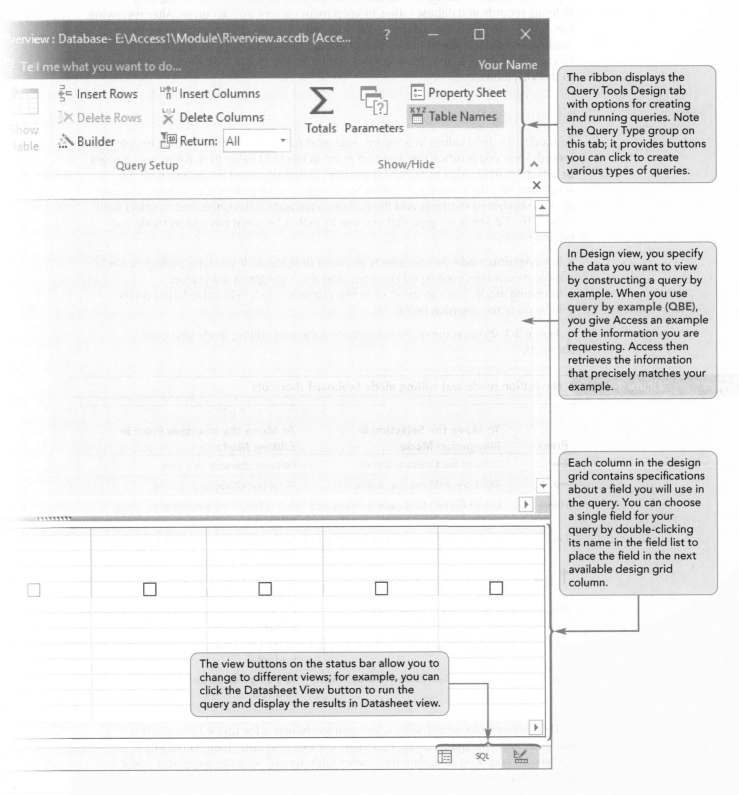

The ribbon displays the Query Tools Design tab with options for creating and running queries. Note the Query Type group on this tab; it provides buttons you can click to create various types of queries.

In Design view, you specify the data you want to view by constructing a query by example. When you use query by example (QBE), you give Access an example of the information you are requesting. Access then retrieves the information that precisely matches your example.

Each column in the design grid contains specifications about a field you will use in the query. You can choose a single field for your query by double-clicking its name in the field list to place the field in the next available design grid column.

The view buttons on the status bar allow you to change to different views; for example, you can click the Datasheet View button to run the query and display the results in Datasheet view.

Updating a Database

Updating, or **maintaining**, a database is the process of adding, modifying, and deleting records in database tables to keep them current and accurate. After reviewing the data in the Riverview database, Kelly identified some changes that need to be made to the data. She would like you to update the field values in one record in the Owner table, correct an error in one record in the Visit table, and then delete a record in the Visit table.

Modifying Records

To modify the field values in a record, you must first make the record the current record. Then you position the insertion point in the field value to make minor changes or select the field value to replace it entirely. Earlier you used the mouse with the scroll bars and the navigation buttons to navigate the records in a datasheet. You can also use keyboard shortcuts and the F2 key to navigate a datasheet and to select field values. The **F2 key** is a toggle that you use to switch between navigation mode and editing mode.

- In **navigation mode**, Access selects an entire field value. If you type while you are in navigation mode, your typed entry replaces the highlighted field value.
- In **editing mode**, you can insert or delete characters in a field value based on the location of the insertion point.

Figure 3-1 shows some of the navigation mode and editing mode keyboard shortcuts.

Figure 3-1   **Navigation mode and editing mode keyboard shortcuts**

Press	To Move the Selection in Navigation Mode	To Move the Insertion Point in Editing Mode
←	Left one field value at a time	Left one character at a time
→	Right one field value at a time	Right one character at a time
Home	Left to the first field value in the record	To the left of the first character in the field value
End	Right to the last field value in the record	To the right of the last character in the field value
↑ or ↓	Up or down one record at a time	Up or down one record at a time and switch to navigation mode
Tab or Enter	Right one field value at a time	Right one field value at a time and switch to navigation mode
Ctrl + Home	To the first field value in the first record	To the left of the first character in the field value
Ctrl + End	To the last field value in the last record	To the right of the last character in the field value

The Owner table record Kelly wants you to change is for Taylor Johnson. This owner recently moved to another location in Cody and also changed her email address, so you need to update the Owner table record with the new street address and email address.

To open the Owner table in the Riverview database:

▶ **1.** Start Access and open the **Riverview** database you created and worked with earlier.

   Trouble? If the security warning is displayed below the ribbon, click the Enable Content button.

▶ **2.** Open the **Owner** table in Datasheet view.

The Owner table contains many fields. Sometimes, when updating data in a table, it can be helpful to remove the display of some fields on the screen.

Hiding and Unhiding Fields

When you are viewing a table or query datasheet in Datasheet view, you might want to temporarily remove certain fields from the displayed datasheet, making it easier to focus on the data you're interested in viewing. The **Hide Fields** command allows you to remove the display of one or more fields, and the **Unhide Fields** command allows you to redisplay any hidden fields.

To make it easier to modify the owner record, you'll first hide a couple of fields in the Owner table.

To hide fields in the Owner table and modify the owner record:

▶ **1.** Right-click the **State** field name to display the shortcut menu, and then click **Hide Fields**. The State column is removed from the datasheet display.

▶ **2.** Right-click the **Zip** field name, and then click **Hide Fields** on the shortcut menu. The Zip column is removed from the datasheet display.

   With the fields hidden, you can now update the owner record. The record you need to modify is near the end of the table and has an OwnerID field value of 2412.

▶ **3.** Scroll the datasheet until you see the last record in the table.

▶ **4.** Click the OwnerID field value **2412**, for Taylor Johnson. The insertion point appears within the field value, indicating you are in editing mode.

▶ **5.** Press the **Tab** key to move to the First Name field value, Taylor. The field value is selected, indicating you are in navigation mode.

▶ **6.** Press the **Tab** key three times to move to the Address field and select its field value, type **458 Rose Ln**, and then press the **Tab** key twice to move to the Email field.

▶ **7.** Type **taylor.johnson@example.net**, and then press the **Tab** key to move to the insertion point to the OwnerID field in the blank record at the bottom of the table. The changes to the record are complete. See Figure 3-2.

| Figure 3-2 | Table after changing field values in a record |

field values changed

Primary key

Access saves changes to field values when you move to a new field or another record, or when you close the table. You don't have to click the Save button to save changes to field values or records.

▶ 8. Press the **Ctrl+Home** keys to move to the first field value in the first record. With the changes to the record complete, you can unhide the hidden fields.

▶ 9. Right-click any field name to display the shortcut menu, and then click **Unhide Fields**. The Unhide Columns dialog box opens. See Figure 3-3.

Figure 3-3 **Unhide Columns dialog box**

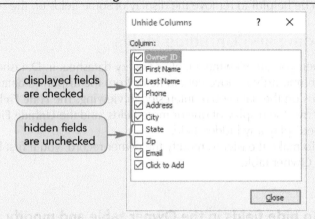

displayed fields are checked

hidden fields are unchecked

All currently displayed fields are checked in this dialog box, and all hidden fields are unchecked. To redisplay them, you simply click their check boxes to select them.

▶ 10. In the Unhide Columns dialog box, click the **State** check box to select it, click the **Zip** check box to select it, and then click the **Close** button to close the dialog box. The two hidden fields are now displayed in the datasheet.

▶ 11. Close the Owner table, and then click the **No** button in the dialog box that opens, asking if you want to save changes to the layout of the Owner table. This box appears because you hid fields and redisplayed them.

In this case, you can click either the Yes button or the No button, because no changes were actually made to the table layout or design.

Next you need to correct an error in the Visit table for a visit made by Molly, Animal ID 12312. A staff member incorrectly entered "Vaccinations" as the reason for the visit, when the animal actually came to the care center that day for a wellness exam. Ensuring the accuracy of the data in a database is an important maintenance task.

To correct the record in the Visit table:

▶ 1. Open the **Visit** table in Datasheet view. The record containing the error is for Visit ID 1024.

▶ 2. Scroll the Visit table as necessary until you locate Visit ID **1024**, and then click at the end of the **Reason/Diagnosis** field value "Vaccinations" for this record. You are in editing mode.

> **3.** Delete **Vaccinations** from the Reason/Diagnosis field, type **Wellness exam**, and then press the **Enter** key twice. The record now contains the correct value in the Reason/Diagnosis field, and this change is automatically saved in the Visit table.

The next update Kelly asks you to make is to delete a record in the Visit table. The owner of Butch, one of the animals seen by the care center, recently notified Taylor that he received an invoice for a neutering visit, but that he had canceled this scheduled appointment. Because this visit did not take place, the record for this visit needs to be deleted from the Visit table. Rather than scrolling through the table to locate the record to delete, you can use the Find command.

Finding Data in a Table

Access provides options you can use to locate specific field values in a table. Instead of scrolling the Visit table datasheet to find the visit that you need to delete—the record for Visit ID 1128—you can use the Find command to find the record. The **Find command** allows you to search a table or query datasheet, or a form, to locate a specific field value or part of a field value. This feature is particularly useful when searching a table that contains a large number of records.

To search for the record in the Visit table:

TIP

You can click any value in the column containing the field you want to search to make the field current.

> **1.** Make sure the VisitID field value **1028** is still selected, and the **Home** tab is selected on the ribbon. You need to search the VisitID field to find the record containing the value 1128, so the insertion point is already correctly positioned in the field you want to search.

> **2.** In the Find group, click the **Find** button. The Find and Replace dialog box opens. See Figure 3-4.

Figure 3-4   **Find and Replace dialog box**

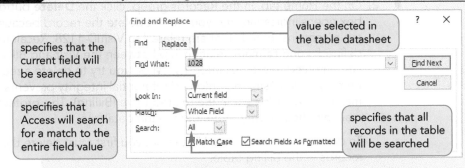

The field value 1028 appears in the Find What box because this value is selected in the table datasheet. You also can choose to search for only part of a field value, such as when you need to find all Visit IDs that start with a certain value. The Search box indicates that all the records in the table will be searched for the value you want to find. You also can choose to search up or down from the currently selected record.

Trouble? Some of the settings in your dialog box might be different from those shown in Figure 3-4 depending on the last search performed on the computer you're using. If so, change the settings so that they match those in the figure.

▶ **3.** Make sure the value 1028 is selected in the Find What box, type **1128** to replace the selected value, and then click the **Find Next** button. Record 50 appears with the field value you specified selected.

▶ **4.** Click the **Cancel** button to close the Find and Replace dialog box.

Deleting Records

To delete a record, you need to select the record in Datasheet view and then delete it using the Delete button in the Records group on the Home tab or the Delete Record option on the shortcut menu.

Deleting a Record

- With the table open in Datasheet view, click the row selector for the record you want to delete.
- In the Records group on the Home tab, click the Delete button (or right-click the row selector for the record, and then click Delete Record on the shortcut menu).
- In the dialog box asking you to confirm the deletion, click the Yes button.

Now that you have found the record with Visit ID 1128, you can delete it. To delete a record, you must first select the entire row for the record.

To delete the record:

▶ **1.** Click the row selector for the record containing the VisitID field value **1128**, which should still be highlighted. The entire row is selected.

▶ **2.** On the Home tab, in the Records group, click the **Delete** button. A dialog box opens indicating that you cannot delete the record because the Billing table contains records that are related to VisitID 1128. Recall that you defined a one-to-many relationship between the Visit and Billing tables and you enforced referential integrity. When you try to delete a record in the primary table (Visit), the enforced referential integrity prevents the deletion if matching records exist in the related table (Billing). This protection helps to maintain the integrity of the data in the database.

To delete the record in the Visit table, you first must delete the related records in the Billing table.

▶ **3.** Click the **OK** button in the dialog box to close it. Notice the plus sign that appears at the beginning of each record in the Visit table. The plus sign, also called the **expand indicator**, indicates that the Visit table is the primary table related to another table—in this case, the Billing table. Clicking the expand indicator displays related records from other tables in the database in a **subdatasheet**.

▶ **4.** Scroll down the datasheet until the selected record is near the top of the datasheet, so that you have room to view the related records for the visit record.

5. Click the **expand indicator** next to VisitID 1128. Two related records from the Billing table for this visit are displayed in the subdatasheet. See Figure 3-5.

Figure 3-5   **Related records from the Billing table in the subdatasheet**

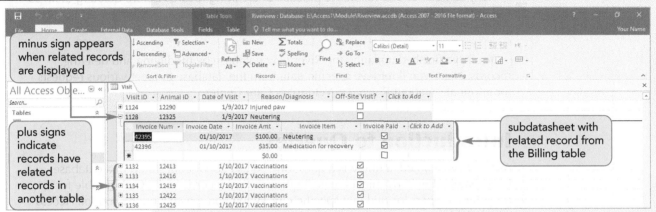

When the subdatasheet is open, you can navigate and update it, just as you can using a table datasheet. The expand indicator for an open subdatasheet is replaced by a minus sign. Clicking the minus sign, or **collapse indicator**, hides the subdatasheet.

You need to delete the records in the Billing table that are related to Visit ID 1128 before you can delete this visit record. The records are for the invoices that were mistakenly sent to the owner of Butch, who had canceled his dog's neutering visit at the care center. You could open the Billing table and find the related records. However, an easier way is to delete the records right in the subdatasheet. The records will be deleted from the Billing table automatically.

6. In the Billing table subdatasheet, click the row selector for invoice number **42395**, and then drag down one row. The rows are selected for both invoice number 42395 and invoice number 42396.

7. On the Home tab, in the Records group, click the **Delete** button. Because the deletion of records is permanent and cannot be undone, a dialog box opens asking you to confirm the deletion of two records.

8. Click the **Yes** button to confirm the deletion and close the dialog box. The records are removed from the Billing table, and the subdatasheet is now empty.

9. Click the **collapse indicator** next to VisitID 1128 to close the subdatasheet.

Now that you have deleted the related records in the Billing table, you can delete the record for Visit ID 1128. You'll use the shortcut menu to do so.

Be sure to select the correct record before deleting it.

10. Right-click the row selector for the record for Visit ID **1128** to select the record and open the shortcut menu.

11. Click **Delete Record** on the shortcut menu, and then click the **Yes** button in the dialog box to confirm the deletion. The record is deleted from the Visit table.

12. Close the Visit table.

Process for Deleting Records

When working with more complex databases that are managed by a database administrator, you typically need special permission to delete records from a table. Many companies also follow the practice of archiving records before deleting them so that the information is still available but not part of the active database.

You have finished updating the Riverview database by modifying and deleting records. Next, you'll retrieve specific data from the database to meet various requests for information about Riverview Veterinary Care Center.

Introduction to Queries

As you have learned, a query is a question you ask about data stored in a database. For example, Kimberly might create a query to find records in the Owner table for only those owners located in a specific city. When you create a query, you tell Access which fields you need and what criteria Access should use to select the records. Access provides powerful query capabilities that allow you to do the following:

- Display selected fields and records from a table
- Sort records
- Perform calculations
- Generate data for forms, reports, and other queries
- Update data in the tables in a database
- Find and display data from two or more tables

Most questions about data are generalized queries in which you specify the fields and records you want Access to select. These common requests for information, such as "Which owners are located in Ralston?" or "How many invoices have been paid?" are select queries. The answer to a select query is returned in the form of a datasheet. The result of a query is also referred to as a **recordset** because the query produces a set of records that answers your question.

Designing Queries vs. Using a Query Wizard

More specialized, technical queries, such as finding duplicate records in a table, are best formulated using a Query Wizard. A Query Wizard prompts you for information by asking a series of questions and then creates the appropriate query based on your answers. For example, earlier you used the Simple Query Wizard to display only some of the fields in the Visit table; Access provides other Query Wizards for more complex queries. For common, informational queries, designing your own query is more efficient than using a Query Wizard.

The care center staff is planning an email campaign advertising a microchipping service being offered to animals seen by Riverview Veterinary Care Center. You need to create a query to display the owner ID, last name, first name, city, and email address for each record in the Owner table. You'll open the Query window in Design view to create the query.

To open the Query window in Design view:

▶ **1.** Close the Navigation Pane, and then, on the ribbon, click the **Create** tab.

▶ **2.** In the Queries group, click the **Query Design** button to display the Query window in Design view, with the Show Table dialog box open and the Tables tab selected. See Figure 3-6.

Figure 3-6	Show Table dialog box

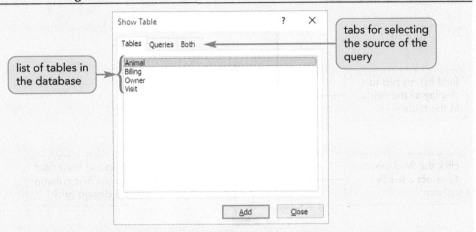

The Show Table dialog box lists all the tables in the Riverview database. You can choose to base a query on one or more tables, on other queries, or on a combination of tables and queries. The query you are creating will retrieve data from the Owner table, so you need to add this table to the Query window.

▶ **3.** In the Tables list, click **Owner**, click the **Add** button, and then click the **Close** button to close the Show Table dialog box. The Owner table's field list appears in the Query window. Refer to the Session 3.1 Visual Overview to familiarize yourself with the Query window in Design view.

Trouble? If you add the wrong table to the Query window, right-click the bar at the top of the field list containing the table name, and then click Remove Table on the shortcut menu. To add the correct table to the Query window, repeat Steps 2 and 3.

Now you'll create and run the query to display selected fields from the Owner table.

Creating and Running a Query

The default table datasheet displays all the fields in the table in the same order as they appear in the table. In contrast, a query datasheet can display selected fields from a table, and the order of the fields can be different from that of the table, enabling those viewing the query results to see only the information they need and in the order they want.

You need the OwnerID, LastName, FirstName, City, and Email fields from the Owner table to appear in the query results. You'll add each of these fields to the design grid. First you'll resize the Owner table field list to display all of the fields.

To select the fields for the query, and then run the query:

▶ **1.** Drag the bottom border of the Owner field list to resize the field list so that all the fields in the Owner table are visible.

▶ **2.** In the Owner field list, double-click **OwnerID** to place the field in the design grid's first column Field box. See Figure 3-7.

Figure 3-7   Field added to the design grid

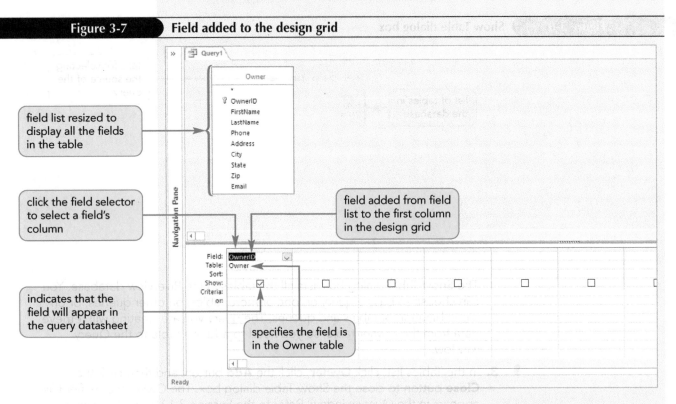

field list resized to display all the fields in the table

click the field selector to select a field's column

indicates that the field will appear in the query datasheet

field added from field list to the first column in the design grid

specifies the field is in the Owner table

In the design grid's first column, the field name OwnerID appears in the Field box, the table name Owner appears in the Table box, and the checkmark in the Show check box indicates that the field will be displayed in the datasheet when you run the query. Sometimes you might not want to display a field and its values in the query results. For example, if you are creating a query to list all owners located in Ralston, and you assign the name "RalstonOwners" to the query, you do not need to include the City field value for each record in the query results—the query design lists only owners with the City field value of "Ralston." Even if you choose not to display a field in the query results, you can still use the field as part of the query to select specific records or to specify a particular sequence for the records in the datasheet. You can also add a field to the design grid using the arrow on the Field box; this arrow appears when you click the Field box, and if you click the arrow or the right side of an empty Field box, a menu of available fields opens.

TIP

You can also use the mouse to drag a field from the field list to a column in the design grid.

3. In the design grid, click the right side of the second column's Field box to display a menu listing all the fields in the Owner table, and then click **LastName** to add this field to the second column in the design grid.

4. Add the **FirstName**, **City**, and **Email** fields to the design grid in that order.

Trouble? If you accidentally add the wrong field to the design grid, select the field's column by clicking the pointer ↓ on the field selector, which is the thin bar above the Field box, for the field you want to delete, and then press the Delete key (or in the Query Setup group on the Query Tools Design tab, click the Delete Columns button).

Now that the five fields for the query have been selected, you can run the query.

5. On the Query Tools Design tab, in the Results group, click the **Run** button. Access runs the query and displays the results in Datasheet view. See Figure 3-8.

Figure 3-8	Datasheet displayed after running the query

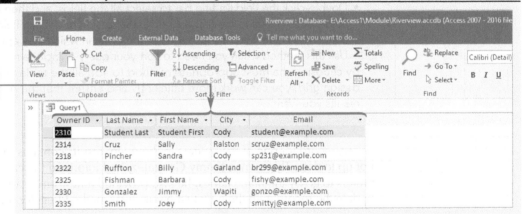

selected fields displayed

Owner ID	Last Name	First Name	City	Email
2310	Student Last	Student First	Cody	student@example.com
2314	Cruz	Sally	Ralston	scruz@example.com
2318	Pincher	Sandra	Cody	sp231@example.com
2322	Ruffton	Billy	Garland	br299@example.com
2325	Fishman	Barbara	Cody	fishy@example.com
2330	Gonzalez	Jimmy	Wapiti	gonzo@example.com
2335	Smith	Joey	Cody	smittyj@example.com

The five fields you added to the design grid appear in the datasheet in the same order as they appear in the design grid. The records are displayed in primary key sequence by OwnerID. The query selected all 25 records from the Owner table for display in the query datasheet. You will save the query as "OwnerEmail" so that you can easily retrieve the same data again.

6. On the Quick Access Toolbar, click the **Save** button 🖫. The Save As dialog box opens.

7. In the Query Name box, type **OwnerEmail** and then press the **Enter** key. The query is saved with the specified name in the Riverview database, and its name appears on the tab for the query.

PROSKILLS

Decision Making: Comparing Methods for Adding All Fields to the Design Grid

If the query you are creating includes every field from the specified table, you can use one of the following three methods to transfer all the fields from the field list to the design grid:

- Double-click (or click and drag) each field individually from the field list to the design grid. Use this method if you want the fields in your query to appear in an order that is different from the order in the field list.
- Double-click the asterisk at the top of the field list. The table name, followed by a period and an asterisk (as in "Owner.*"), appears in the Field box of the first column in the design grid, which signifies that the order of the fields is the same in the query as it is in the field list. Use this method if you don't need to sort the query or specify conditions based on the fields in the table you added in this way (for example, in a query based on more than one table). The advantage of using this method is that you do not need to change the query if you add or delete fields from the underlying table structure. Such changes are reflected automatically in the query.
- Double-click the field list title bar to select all the fields, and then click and drag one of the selected fields to the first column in the design grid. Each field appears in a separate column, and the fields are arranged in the order in which they appear in the field list. Use this method when you need to sort your query or include record selection criteria.

By choosing the most appropriate method to add all the table fields to the query design grid, you can work more efficiently and ensure that the query produces the results you want.

The record for one of the owners in the query results contains information that is not up to date. This owner, Jimmy Gonzalez, had informed the care center that he now prefers to go by the name James; he also provided a new email address. You need to update the record with the new first name and email address for this owner.

Updating Data Using a Query

A query datasheet is temporary, and its contents are based on the criteria in the query design grid; however, you can still update the data in a table using a query datasheet. In this case, you want to make changes to a record in the Owner table. Instead of making the changes in the table datasheet, you can make them in the OwnerEmail query datasheet because the query is based on the Owner table. The underlying Owner table will be updated with the changes you make.

To update data using the OwnerEmail query datasheet:

1. Locate the record with OwnerID 2330, Jimmy Gonzalez (record 6 in the query datasheet).

2. In the First Name column for this record, double-click **Jimmy** to select the name, and then type **James**.

3. Press the **Tab** key twice to move to the Email column, type **thewholething@example.com** and then press the **Tab** key.

4. Close the OwnerEmail query, and then open the Navigation Pane. Note that the OwnerEmail query is listed in the Queries section of the Navigation Pane.

Now you'll check the Owner table to verify that the changes you made in the query datasheet are reflected in the Owner table.

▶ **5.** Open the **Owner** table in Datasheet view, and then close the Navigation Pane.

▶ **6.** Locate the record for OwnerID 2330 (record 6). Notice that the changes you made in the query datasheet to the First Name and Email field values were made to the record in the Owner table.

▶ **7.** Close the Owner table.

Kelly also wants to view specific information in the Riverview database. She would like to review the visit data for animals while also viewing certain information about them. So, she needs to see data from both the Animal table and the Visit table at the same time.

Creating a Multitable Query

A multitable query is a query based on more than one table. If you want to create a query that retrieves data from multiple tables, the tables must have a common field. Earlier, you established a relationship between the Animal (primary) and Visit (related) tables based on the common AnimalID field that exists in both tables, so you can now create a query to display data from both tables at the same time. Specifically, Kelly wants to view the values in the AnimalType, AnimalBreed, and AnimalName fields from the Animal table and the VisitDate and Reason fields from the Visit table.

To create the query using the Animal and Visit tables:

▶ **1.** On the ribbon, click the **Create** tab.

▶ **2.** In the Queries group, click the **Query Design** button. The Show Table dialog box opens in the Query window. You need to add the Animal and Visit tables to the Query window.

▶ **3.** Click **Animal** in the Tables list, click the **Add** button, click **Visit**, click the **Add** button, and then click the **Close** button to close the Show Table dialog box. The Animal and Visit field lists appear in the Query window.

▶ **4.** Resize the Animal and Visit field lists if necessary so that all the fields in each list are displayed.

The one-to-many relationship between the two tables is shown in the Query window in the same way that a relationship between two tables is shown in the Relationships window. Note that the join line is thick at both ends; this signifies that you selected the option to enforce referential integrity. If you had not selected this option, the join line would be thin at both ends, and neither the "1" nor the infinity symbol would appear, even though the tables have a one-to-many relationship.

You need to place the AnimalType, AnimalBreed, and AnimalName fields (in that order) from the Animal field list into the design grid and then place the VisitDate and Reason fields from the Visit field list into the design grid. This is the order in which Taylor wants to view the fields in the query results.

▶ **5.** In the Animal field list, double-click **AnimalType** to place this field in the design grid's first column Field box.

6. Repeat Step 5 to add the **AnimalBreed** and **AnimalName** fields from the Animal table to the second and third columns of the design grid.

7. Repeat Step 5 to add the **VisitDate** and **Reason** fields (in that order) from the Visit table to the fourth and fifth columns of the design grid. The query specifications are complete, so you can now run the query.

8. In the Results group on the Query Tools Design tab, click the **Run** button. After the query runs, the results are displayed in Datasheet view. See Figure 3-9.

Figure 3-9	Datasheet for query based on the Animal and Visit tables

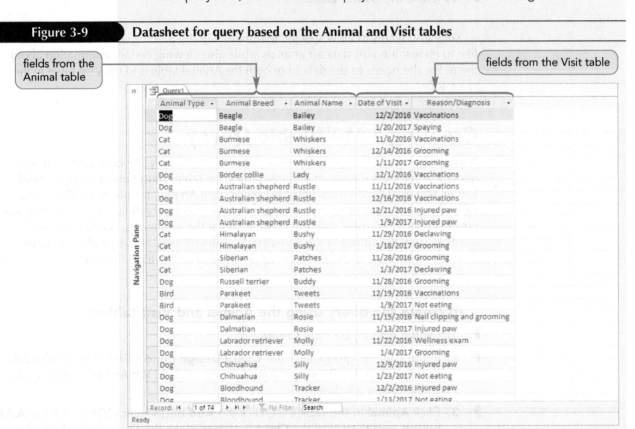

fields from the Animal table

fields from the Visit table

Only the five selected fields from the Animal and Visit tables appear in the datasheet. The records are displayed in order according to the values in the AnimalID field because it is the primary key field in the primary table, even though this field is not included in the query datasheet.

Kelly plans on frequently tracking the data retrieved by the query, so she asks you to save it as "AnimalVisits."

9. On the Quick Access Toolbar, click the **Save** button 🖫. The Save As dialog box opens.

10. In the Query Name box, type **AnimalVisits** and then press the **Enter** key. The query is saved, and its name appears on the object tab.

Kelly decides she wants the records displayed in alphabetical order by animal type. Because the query displays data in order by the field values in the AnimalID field, which is the primary key for the Animal table, you need to sort the records by the AnimalType field to display the data in the order Kelly wants.

Sorting Data in a Query

Sorting is the process of rearranging records in a specified order or sequence. Sometimes you might need to sort data before displaying or printing it to meet a specific request. For example, Kelly might want to review visit information arranged by the VisitDate field because she needs to know which months are the busiest for Riverview Veterinary Care Center in terms of animal visits. Kimberly might want to view billing information arranged by the InvoiceAmt field because she monitors the finances of the care center.

When you sort data in a query, you do not change the sequence of the records in the underlying tables. Only the records in the query datasheet are rearranged according to your specifications.

To sort records, you must select the **sort field**, which is the field used to determine the order of records in the datasheet. In this case, Kelly wants the data sorted alphabetically by animal type, so you need to specify AnimalType as the sort field. Sort fields can be Short Text, Number, Date/Time, Currency, AutoNumber, or Yes/No fields, but not Long Text, Hyperlink, or Attachment fields. You sort records in either ascending (increasing) or descending (decreasing) order. Figure 3-10 shows the results of each type of sort for these data types.

| Figure 3-10 | Sorting results for different data types |

Data Type	Ascending Sort Results	Descending Sort Results
Short Text	A to Z (alphabetical)	Z to A (reverse alphabetical)
Number	lowest to highest numeric value	highest to lowest numeric value
Date/Time	oldest to most recent date	most recent to oldest date
Currency	lowest to highest numeric value	highest to lowest numeric value
AutoNumber	lowest to highest numeric value	highest to lowest numeric value
Yes/No	yes (checkmark in check box) then no values	no then yes values

Access provides several methods for sorting data in a table or query datasheet and in a form. One of the easiest ways is to use the AutoFilter feature for a field.

Using an AutoFilter to Sort Data

TIP

You can also use the Ascending and Descending buttons in the Sort & Filter group on the Home tab to quickly sort records based on the currently selected field in a datasheet.

As you've probably noticed when working in Datasheet view for a table or query, each column heading has an arrow to the right of the field name. This arrow gives you access to the **AutoFilter** feature, which enables you to quickly sort and display field values in various ways. When you click this arrow, a menu opens with options for sorting and displaying field values. The first two options on the menu enable you to sort the values in the current field in ascending or descending order. Unless you save the datasheet or form after you've sorted the records, the rearrangement of records is temporary.

Next, you'll use an AutoFilter to sort the AnimalVisits query results by the AnimalType field.

To sort the records using an AutoFilter:

▶   **1.** Click the **arrow** on the Animal Type column heading to display the AutoFilter menu. See Figure 3-11.

| Figure 3-11 | **Using AutoFilter to sort records in the datasheet** |

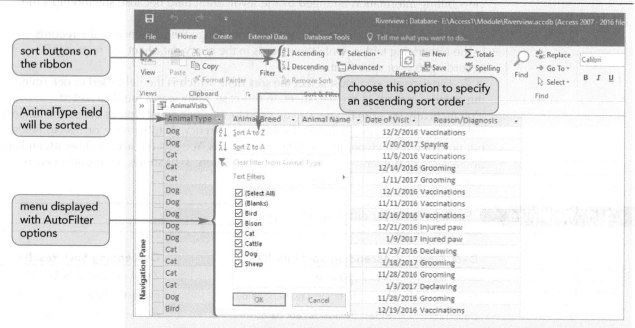

Kelly wants the data sorted in ascending (alphabetical) order by the values in the AnimalType field, so you need to select the first option in the menu.

▶   **2.** Click **Sort A to Z**. The records are rearranged in ascending alphabetical order by animal type. A small, upward-pointing arrow appears on the right side of the Animal Type column heading. This arrow indicates that the values in the field have been sorted in ascending order. If you used the same method to sort the field values in descending order, a small downward-pointing arrow would appear there instead.

After viewing the query results, Kelly decides that she would also like to see the records arranged by the values in the VisitDate field, so that the data is presented in chronological order. She still wants the records to be arranged by the AnimalType field values as well. To produce the results Kelly wants, you need to sort using two fields.

Sorting on Multiple Fields in Design View

Sort fields can be unique or nonunique. A sort field is **unique** if the value in the sort field for each record is different. The AnimalID field in the Animal table is an example of a unique sort field because each animal record has a different value in this primary key field. A sort field is **nonunique** if more than one record can have the same value for the sort field. For example, the AnimalType field in the Animal table is a nonunique sort field because more than one record can have the same AnimalType value.

TIP

The primary sort field is not the same as a table's primary key. A table has at most one primary key, which must be unique, whereas any field in a table can serve as a primary sort field.

When the sort field is nonunique, records with the same sort field value are grouped together, but they are not sorted in a specific order within the group. To arrange these grouped records in a specific order, you can specify a **secondary sort field**, which is a second field that determines the order of records that are already sorted by the **primary sort field** (the first sort field specified).

In Access, you can select up to 10 different sort fields. When you use the buttons on the ribbon to sort by more than one field, the sort fields must be in adjacent columns in the datasheet. (Note that you cannot use an AutoFilter to sort on more than one field. This method works for a single field only.) You can specify only one type of sort—either ascending or descending—for the selected columns in the datasheet. You select the adjacent columns, and Access sorts first by the first column and then by each remaining selected column in order from left to right.

Kelly wants the records sorted first by the AnimalType field values, as they currently are, and then by the VisitDate values. The two fields are in the correct left-to-right order in the query datasheet, but they are not adjacent, so you cannot use the Ascending and Descending buttons on the ribbon to sort them. You could move the AnimalType field to the left of the VisitDate field in the query datasheet, but both columns would have to be sorted with the same sort order. This is not what Kelly wants—she wants the AnimalType field values sorted in ascending order so that they are in the correct alphabetical order, for ease of reference; and she wants the VisitDate field values to be sorted in descending order, so that she can focus on the most recent animal visits first. To sort the AnimalType and VisitDate fields with different sort orders, you must specify the sort fields in Design view.

In the Query window in Design view, you must arrange the fields you want to sort from left to right in the design grid, with the primary sort field being the leftmost. In Design view, multiple sort fields do not have to be adjacent to each other, as they do in Datasheet view; however, they must be in the correct left-to-right order.

REFERENCE

Sorting a Query Datasheet

- In the query datasheet, click the arrow on the column heading for the field you want to sort.
- In the menu that opens, click Sort A to Z for an ascending sort, or click Sort Z to A for a descending sort.

or

- In the query datasheet, select the column or adjacent columns on which you want to sort.
- In the Sort & Filter group on the Home tab, click the Ascending button or the Descending button.

or

- In Design view, position the fields serving as sort fields from left to right.
- Click the right side of the Sort box for each field you want to sort, and then click Ascending or Descending for the sort order.

To achieve the results Kelly wants, you need to modify the query in Design view to specify the sort order for the two fields.

TIP

In Design view, the sort fields do not have to be adjacent, and fields that are not sorted can appear between the sort fields.

To select the two sort fields in Design view:

1. On the Home tab, in the Views group, click the **View** button to open the query in Design view. The fields are currently in the correct left-to-right order in the design grid, so you only need to specify the sort order for the two fields.

   First, you need to specify an ascending sort order for the AnimalType field. Even though the records are already sorted by the values in this field, you need to modify the query so that this sort order, and the sort order you will specify for the VisitDate field, are part of the query's design. Any time the query is run, the records will be sorted according to these specifications.

2. Click the right side of the **AnimalType Sort** box to display the arrow and the sort options, and then click **Ascending**. You've selected an ascending sort order for the AnimalType field, which will be the primary sort field. The AnimalType field is a Short Text field, and an ascending sort order will display the field values in alphabetical order.

3. Click the right side of the **VisitDate Sort** box, click **Descending**, and then click in one of the empty text boxes below the VisitDate field to deselect the setting. You've selected a descending sort order for the VisitDate field, which will be the secondary sort field because it appears to the right of the primary sort field (AnimalType) in the design grid. The VisitDate field is a Date/Time field, and a descending sort order will display the field values with the most recent dates first. See Figure 3-12.

Figure 3-12 **Selecting two sort fields in Design view**

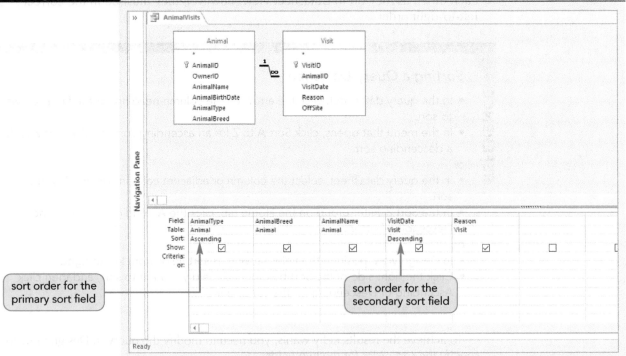

You have finished your query changes, so now you can run the query and then save the modified query with the same name.

> **4.** On the Query Tools Design tab, in the Results group, click the **Run** button. After the query runs, the records appear in the query datasheet in ascending order based on the values in the AnimalType field. Within groups of records with the same AnimalType field value, the records appear in descending order by the values of the VisitDate field. See Figure 3-13.

| Figure 3-13 | Datasheet sorted on two fields |

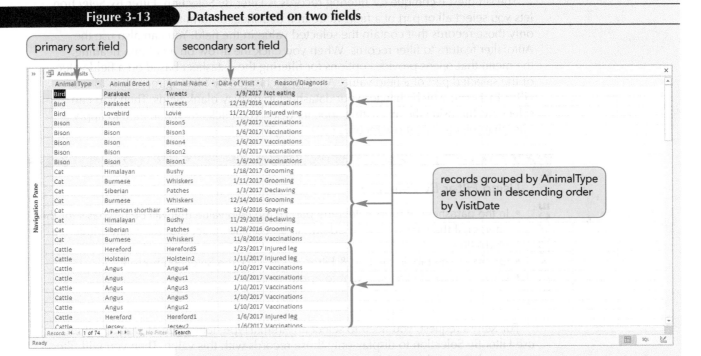

When you save the query, all of your design changes—including the selection of the sort fields—are saved with the query. The next time Kelly runs the query, the records will appear sorted by the primary and secondary sort fields.

> **5.** On the Quick Access Toolbar, click the **Save** button 🔲 to save the revised AnimalVisits query.

Kelly knows that Riverview Veterinary Care Center has seen an increase in the number of dogs receiving care. She would like to focus briefly on the information for that animal type only. Also, she is interested in knowing how many dogs have had recent vaccinations. She is concerned that, although more dogs are being brought to the care center, not enough of them are receiving regular vaccinations. Selecting only the records with an AnimalType field value of "Dog" and a Reason field value beginning with "Vaccination" is a temporary change that Kelly wants in the query datasheet, so you do not need to switch to Design view and change the query. Instead, you can apply a filter.

Filtering Data

A **filter** is a set of restrictions you place on the records in an open datasheet or form to *temporarily* isolate a subset of the records. A filter lets you view different subsets of displayed records so that you can focus on only the data you need. Unless you save a query or form with a filter applied, an applied filter is not available the next time you run the query or open the form.

The simplest technique for filtering records is Filter By Selection. **Filter By Selection** lets you select all or part of a field value in a datasheet or form and then display only those records that contain the selected value in the field. You can also use the AutoFilter feature to filter records. When you click the arrow on a column heading, the menu that opens provides options for filtering the datasheet based on a field value or the selected part of a field value. Another technique for filtering records is to use **Filter By Form**, which changes your datasheet to display blank fields. Then you can select a value using the arrow that appears when you click any blank field to apply a filter that selects only those records containing that value.

REFERENCE

Using Filter By Selection

- In the datasheet or form, select the part of the field value that will be the basis for the filter; or, if the filter will be based on the entire field value, click anywhere within the field value.
- On the Home tab, in the Sort & Filter group, click the Selection button.
- Click the type of filter you want to apply.

For Kelly's request, you need to select an AnimalType field value of Dog and then use Filter By Selection to display only those records with this value. Then you will filter the records further by selecting only those records with a Reason value that begins with "Vaccination" (for visits that include a single vaccination or multiple vaccinations).

To display the records using Filter By Selection:

▶ **1.** In the query datasheet, locate the first occurrence of an AnimalType field containing the value **Dog**, and then click anywhere within that field value.

▶ **2.** On the Home tab, in the Sort & Filter group, click the **Selection** button. A menu opens with options for the type of filter to apply. See Figure 3-14.

Figure 3-14	Using Filter By Selection

options for the type of filter to apply

current field is the basis for the filter

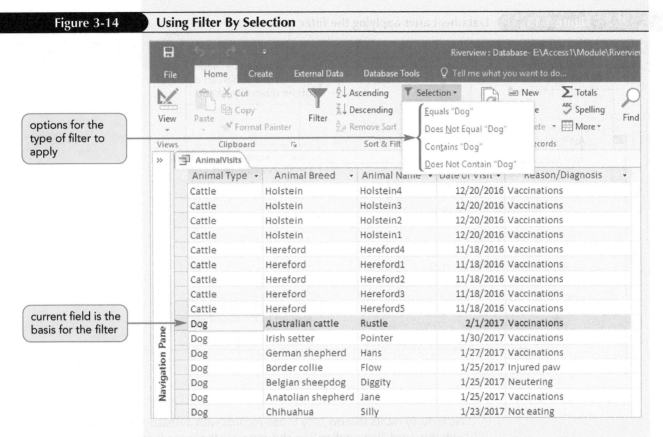

The menu provides options for displaying only those records with an AnimalType field value that equals the selected value (in this case, Dog); does not equal the value; contains the value somewhere within the field; or does not contain the value somewhere within the field. You want to display all the records whose AnimalType field value equals Dog.

3. In the Selection menu, click **Equals "Dog"**. Only the 25 records that have an AnimalType field value of Dog appear in the datasheet. See Figure 3-15.

Figure 3-15 | **Datasheet after applying the filter**

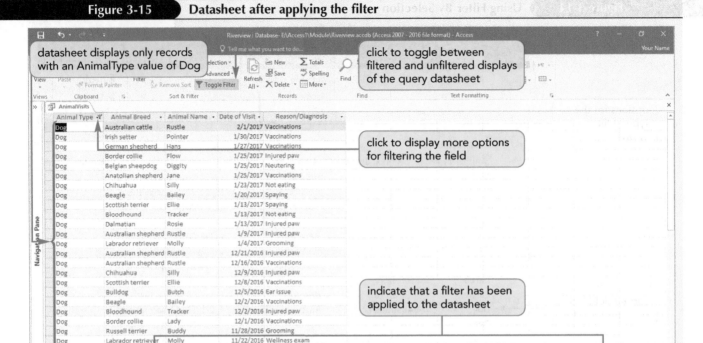

Next, Kelly wants to view only those records with a Reason field value beginning with the word "Vaccination" so she can view the records for visits that involved one or more vaccinations. You need to apply an additional filter to the datasheet.

4. In any Reason field value beginning with the word "Vaccination," select only the text **Vaccination**.

5. In the Sort & Filter group, click the **Selection** button. The same four filter types are available for this selection as when you filtered the AnimalType field.

6. On the Selection menu, click **Begins With "Vaccination"**. The first filter is applied to the query datasheet, which now shows only the nine records for dogs who have had one or more vaccinations at the care center.

   Trouble? If you do not see the Begins With "Vaccination" option, click anywhere in the datasheet to close the Selection menu, and then repeat Steps 4–6, being sure not to select the letter "s" at the end of the word "Vaccination."

   Now you can redisplay all the query records by clicking the Toggle Filter button, which you use to switch between the filtered and unfiltered displays.

TIP

The ScreenTip for this button is Remove Filter.

7. In the Sort & Filter group, click the **Toggle Filter** button. The filter is removed, and all 74 records appear in the query datasheet.

8. Close the AnimalVisits query. A dialog box opens, asking if you want to save your changes to the design of the query—in this case, the filtered display, which is still available through the Toggle Filter button. Kelly does not want the query saved with the filter because she doesn't need to view the filtered information on a regular basis.

9. Click the **No** button to close the query without saving the changes.

10. If you are not continuing to Session 3.2, click the **File** tab, and then click **Close** in the navigation bar to close the Riverview database.

Session 3.1 Quick Check

REVIEW

1. In Datasheet view, what is the difference between navigation mode and editing mode?

2. What command can you use in Datasheet view to remove the display of one or more fields from the datasheet?

3. What is a select query?

4. Describe the field list and the design grid in the Query window in Design view.

5. How are a table datasheet and a query datasheet similar? How are they different?

6. For a Date/Time field, how do the records appear when sorted in ascending order?

7. When you define multiple sort fields in Design view, describe how the sort fields must be positioned in the design grid.

8. A(n) _____ is a set of restrictions you place on the records in an open datasheet or form to isolate a subset of records temporarily.

Session 3.2 Visual Overview:

> When creating queries in Design view, you can enter criteria so that only selected records are displayed in the query results.

Field:	AnimalName	AnimalBirthDate	AnimalType	VisitDate	Reason
Table:	Animal	Animal	Animal	Visit	Visit
Sort:					
Show:	☑	☑	☑	☑	☑
Criteria:			"Bird"		
or:					

To define a condition for a field, you place the condition in the field's Criteria box in the design grid.

To indicate which records you want to select, you must specify a condition as part of the query. A **condition** is a criterion, or rule, that determines which records are selected.

Field:	InvoiceNum	InvoiceDate	InvoiceAmt	
Table:	Billing	Billing	Billing	
Sort:				
Show:	☑	☑	☑	☐
Criteria:			> 100	
or:				

A condition usually consists of an operator, often a comparison operator, and a value. A **comparison operator** compares the value in a field to the condition value and selects all the records for which the condition is true.

Field:	VisitID	AnimalID	VisitDate	Reason
Table:	Visit	Visit	Visit	Visit
Sort:				
Show:	☑	☑	☑	☑
Criteria:			Between #1/1/2017# And #1/15/2017#	
or:				

Most comparison operators (such as Between...And...) select records that match a range of values for the condition—in this case, all records with dates that fall within the range shown.

Selection Criteria in Queries

The results of a query containing selection criteria include only the records that meet the specified criteria.

BirdAnimalType

Animal Name	Animal Birth Date	Animal Type	Date of Visit
Tweets	11/12/2010	Bird	12/19/2016
Tweets	11/12/2010	Bird	1/9/2017
Lovie	02/03/2002	Bird	11/21/2016
*			

The results of this query show only birds because the condition "Bird" in the AnimalType field's Criteria box specifies that the query should select records only with AnimalType field values of bird. This type of condition is called an **exact match** because the value in the specified field must match the condition exactly in order for the record to be included in the query results.

LargeInvoiceAmts

Invoice Num	Invoice Date	Invoice Amt
42145	11/22/2016	$275.00
42182	11/30/2016	$225.00
42320	01/04/2017	$225.00
42435	01/16/2017	$125.00
42525	01/26/2017	$125.00
*		$0.00

The results of this query show only those invoices with amounts greater than $100 because the condition >100, which uses the greater than comparison operator, specifies that query should select records only with InvoiceAmt field values over $100.

EarlyJanuaryVisits

Visit ID	Animal ID	Date of Visit	Reason/Diagnosis
1098	12296	1/3/2017	Declawing
1101	12312	1/4/2017	Grooming
1120	12304	1/9/2017	Not eating
1124	12290	1/9/2017	Injured paw
1140	12282	1/11/2017	Grooming
1148	12308	1/13/2017	Injured paw
1152	12318	1/13/2017	Not eating
1156	12322	1/13/2017	Spaying
*			

The results of this query show only those visits that took place in the first half of January 2017 because the condition in the VisitDate Criteria box specifies that the query should select records only with a visit date between 1/1/2017 and 1/15/2017.

Defining Record Selection Criteria for Queries

Kimberly is considering offering a workshop on dog care at the care center, with a special emphasis on the needs of older dogs. To prepare for this, she is interested in knowing more about the level of care provided to the dogs that have visited the care center, as well as where these dogs live. For this request, you could create a query to select the correct fields and all records in the Owner, Animal, and Visit tables, select an AnimalType field value of Dog in the query datasheet, and then click the Selection button and choose the appropriate filter option to display the information for only those animals that are dogs. However, a faster way of accessing the data Kimberly needs is to create a query that displays the selected fields and only those records in the Owner, Animal, and Visit tables that satisfy a condition.

Just as you can display selected fields from a database in a query datasheet, you can display selected records. To identify which records you want to select, you must specify a condition as part of the query, as illustrated in the Session 3.2 Visual Overview. A condition usually includes one of the comparison operators shown in Figure 3-16.

Figure 3-16   **Access comparison operators**

Operator	Meaning	Example
=	equal to (optional; default operator)	="Hall"
<>	not equal to	<>"Hall"
<	less than	<#1/1/99#
<=	less than or equal to	<=100
>	greater than	>"C400"
>=	greater than or equal to	>=18.75
Between … And …	between two values (inclusive)	Between 50 And 325
In ()	in a list of values	In ("Hall", "Seeger")
Like	matches a pattern that includes wildcards	Like "706*"

Specifying an Exact Match

For Kimberly's request, you need to first create a query that will display only those records in the Animal table with the value Dog in the AnimalType field. This type of condition is an exact match because the value in the specified field must match the condition exactly in order for the record to be included in the query results. You'll create the query in Design view.

To create the query in Design view:

▶ 1. If you took a break after the previous session, make sure that the Riverview database is open and the Navigation Pane is closed, and then on the ribbon, click the **Create** tab.

▶ 2. In the Queries group, click the **Query Design** button. The Show Table dialog box opens. You need to add the Owner, Animal, and Visit tables to the Query window.

▶ 3. Click **Owner** in the Tables list, click the **Add** button, click **Animal**, click the **Add** button, click **Visit**, click the **Add** button, and then click the **Close** button. The field lists for the Owner, Animal, and Visit tables appear in the top portion of the window, and join lines indicating one-to-many relationships connect the tables.

> **4.** Resize all three field lists so that all the fields are displayed.

> **5.** Add the following fields from the Animal table to the design grid in this order: **AnimalName**, **AnimalBirthDate**, and **AnimalType**.

> Kimberly also wants information from the Visit table and the Owner table included in the query results.

> **6.** Add the following fields from the Visit table to the design grid in this order: **VisitDate** and **Reason**.

> **7.** Add the following fields from the Owner table to the design grid in this order: **FirstName**, **LastName**, **Phone**, and **Email**. All the fields needed for the query appear in the design grid. See Figure 3-17.

| Figure 3-17 | Design grid after adding fields from both tables |

enter condition here

To display the information Kimberly wants, you need to enter the condition for the AnimalType field in its Criteria box, as shown in Figure 3-17. Kimberly wants to display only those records with an AnimalType field value of Dog.

To enter the exact match condition, and then save and run the query:

> **1.** Click the **AnimalType Criteria** box, type **Dog**, and then press the **Enter** key. The condition changes to "Dog".

> Access automatically enclosed the condition you typed in quotation marks. You must enclose text values in quotation marks when using them as selection criteria. If you omit the quotation marks, however, Access will include them automatically in most cases. Some words—including "in" and "select"—are special keywords in Access that are reserved for functions and commands. If you want to enter one of these keywords as the condition, you must type the quotation marks around the text or an error message will appear indicating the condition cannot be entered.

> **2.** Save the query with the name **DogAnimalType**. The query is saved, and its name is displayed on the object tab.

> **3.** Run the query. After the query runs, the selected field values for only those records with an AnimalType field value of Dog are shown. A total of 25 records is selected and displayed in the datasheet. See Figure 3-18.

Figure 3-18 **Datasheet displaying selected fields and records**

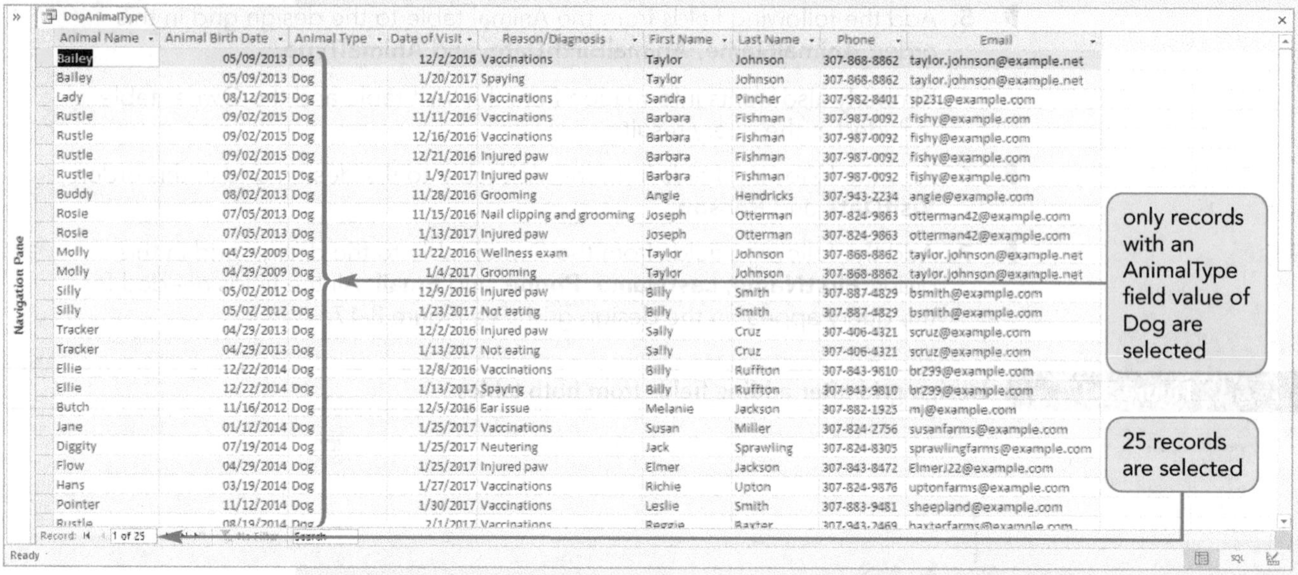

DogAnimalType

Animal Name	Animal Birth Date	Animal Type	Date of Visit	Reason/Diagnosis	First Name	Last Name	Phone	Email
Bailey	05/09/2013	Dog	12/2/2016	Vaccinations	Taylor	Johnson	307-868-8862	taylor.johnson@example.net
Bailey	05/09/2013	Dog	1/20/2017	Spaying	Taylor	Johnson	307-868-8862	taylor.johnson@example.net
Lady	08/12/2015	Dog	12/1/2016	Vaccinations	Sandra	Pincher	307-982-8401	sp231@example.com
Rustle	09/02/2015	Dog	11/11/2016	Vaccinations	Barbara	Fishman	307-987-0092	fishy@example.com
Rustle	09/02/2015	Dog	12/16/2016	Vaccinations	Barbara	Fishman	307-987-0092	fishy@example.com
Rustle	09/02/2015	Dog	12/21/2016	Injured paw	Barbara	Fishman	307-987-0092	fishy@example.com
Rustle	09/02/2015	Dog	1/9/2017	Injured paw	Barbara	Fishman	307-987-0092	fishy@example.com
Buddy	08/02/2013	Dog	11/28/2016	Grooming	Angie	Hendricks	307-943-2234	angie@example.com
Rosie	07/05/2013	Dog	11/15/2016	Nail clipping and grooming	Joseph	Otterman	307-824-9863	otterman42@example.com
Rosie	07/05/2013	Dog	1/13/2017	Injured paw	Joseph	Otterman	307-824-9863	otterman42@example.com
Molly	04/29/2009	Dog	11/22/2016	Wellness exam	Taylor	Johnson	307-868-8862	taylor.johnson@example.net
Molly	04/29/2009	Dog	1/4/2017	Grooming	Taylor	Johnson	307-868-8862	taylor.johnson@example.net
Silly	05/02/2012	Dog	12/9/2016	Injured paw	Billy	Smith	307-887-4829	bsmith@example.com
Silly	05/02/2012	Dog	1/23/2017	Not eating	Billy	Smith	307-887-4829	bsmith@example.com
Tracker	04/29/2013	Dog	12/2/2016	Injured paw	Sally	Cruz	307-406-4321	scruz@example.com
Tracker	04/29/2013	Dog	1/13/2017	Not eating	Sally	Cruz	307-406-4321	scruz@example.com
Ellie	12/22/2014	Dog	12/8/2016	Vaccinations	Billy	Ruffton	307-843-9810	br299@example.com
Ellie	12/22/2014	Dog	1/13/2017	Spaying	Billy	Ruffton	307-843-9810	br299@example.com
Butch	11/16/2012	Dog	12/5/2016	Ear issue	Melanie	Jackson	307-882-1925	mj@example.com
Jane	01/12/2014	Dog	1/25/2017	Vaccinations	Susan	Miller	307-824-2756	susanfarms@example.com
Diggity	07/19/2014	Dog	1/25/2017	Neutering	Jack	Sprawling	307-824-8305	sprawlingfarms@example.com
Flow	04/29/2014	Dog	1/25/2017	Injured paw	Elmer	Jackson	307-843-8472	ElmerJ22@example.com
Hans	03/19/2014	Dog	1/27/2017	Vaccinations	Richie	Upton	307-824-9876	uptonfarms@example.com
Pointer	11/12/2014	Dog	1/30/2017	Vaccinations	Leslie	Smith	307-883-9481	sheepland@example.com
Rustle	08/19/2014	Dog	2/1/2017	Vaccinations	Reggie	Baxter	307-943-2469	baxterfarms@example.com

Kimberly realizes that it's not necessary to include the AnimalType field values in the query results. The name of the query, DogAnimalType, indicates that the query design includes all animals with an AnimalType of Dog, so the AnimalType field values are unnecessary and repetitive in the query results. Also, she decides that she would prefer the query datasheet to show the fields from the Owner table first, followed by the Animal table fields and then the Visit table fields. You need to modify the query to produce the results Kimberly wants.

Modifying a Query

After you create a query and view the results, you might need to make changes to the query if the results are not what you expected or require. First, Kimberly asks you to modify the DogAnimalType query so that it does not display the AnimalType field values in the query results.

To remove the display of the AnimalType field values:

1. On the Home tab, in the Views group, click the **View** button. The DogAnimalType query opens in Design view.

   You need to keep the AnimalType field as part of the query design because it contains the defined condition for the query. You only need to remove the display of the field's values from the query results.

2. Click the **AnimalType Show** check box to remove the checkmark. The query will still find only those records with the value Dog in the AnimalType field, but the query results will not display these field values.

Next, you need to change the order of the fields in the query so that the owner information is listed first.

To move the Owner table fields to precede the Animal and Visit table fields:

▶ **1.** Position the pointer on the FirstName field selector until the pointer changes to ↓, and then click to select the field. See Figure 3-19.

Figure 3-19   **Selected FirstName field**

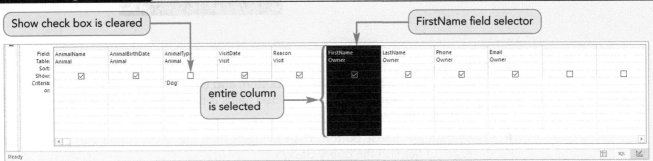

▶ **2.** Position the pointer on the FirstName field selector, and then press and hold the mouse button; notice that the pointer changes to ⬚, and a black vertical line appears to the left of the selected field. This line represents the selected field when you drag the mouse to move it.

▶ **3.** Drag the pointer to the left until the vertical line representing the selected field is positioned to the left of the AnimalName field. See Figure 3-20.

Figure 3-20   **Dragging the field in the design grid**

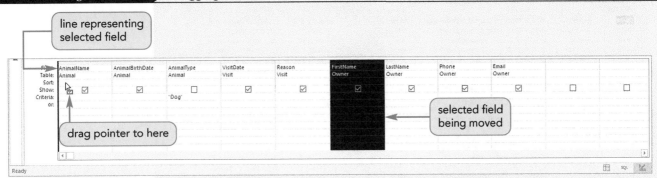

TIP

Instead of moving a field by dragging, you can also delete the field and then add it back to the design grid in the location you want.

▶ **4.** Release the mouse button. The FirstName field moves to the left of the AnimalName field.

You can also select and move multiple fields at once. You need to select and move the LastName, Phone, and Email fields so that they appear directly after the FirstName field in the query design. To select multiple fields, you click and drag the mouse over the field selectors for the fields you want.

▶ **5.** Point to the LastName field selector. When the pointer changes to ↓, press and hold the mouse button, drag to the right to select the Phone and Email fields, and then release the mouse button. All three fields are now selected. See Figure 3-21.

| Figure 3-21 | Multiple fields selected to be moved |

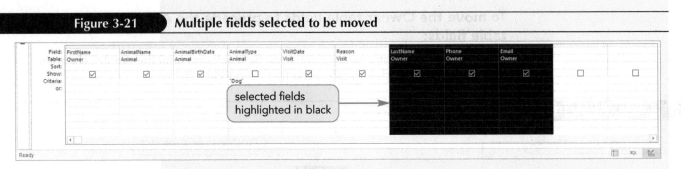

6. Position the pointer on the field selector for any of the three selected fields, press and hold the mouse button, and then drag to the left until the vertical line representing the selected fields is positioned to the left of the AnimalName field.

7. Release the mouse button. The four fields from the Owner table are now the first four fields in the query design.

You have finished making the modifications to the query Kimberly requested, so you can now run the query.

8. Run the query. The results of the modified query are displayed. See Figure 3-22.

| Figure 3-22 | Results of the modified query |

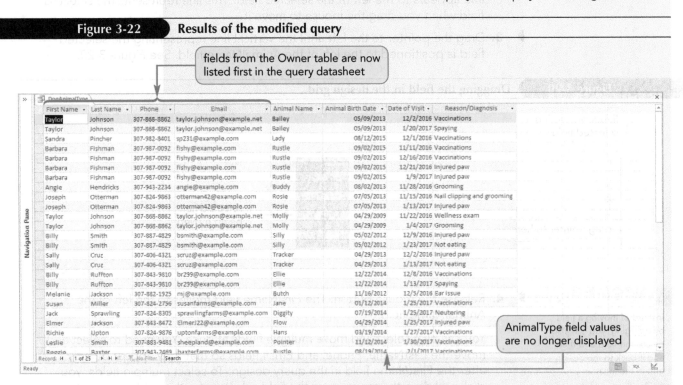

Note that the AnimalType field values are no longer displayed in the query results.

9. Save and close the DogAnimalType query.

Kimberly asks you to create a new query. She is interested to know which animals of all animal types that have not been to the care center recently, so that her staff can follow up with their owners by sending them reminder notes or emails. To create the query that will produce the results Kimberly wants, you need to use a comparison operator to match a range of values—in this case, any VisitDate value less than 1/1/2017. Because this new query will include information from several of the same fields as the DogAnimalType query, you can use that query as a starting point in designing this new query.

Using a Comparison Operator to Match a Range of Values

As you know, after you create and save a query, you can double-click the query name in the Navigation Pane to run the query again. You can then click the View button to change its design. You can also use an existing query as the basis for creating another query. Because the design of the query you need to create next is similar to the DogAnimalType query, you will copy, paste, and rename this query to create the new query. Using this approach keeps the DogAnimalType query intact.

To create the new query by copying the DogAnimalType query:

▶ **1.** Open the Navigation Pane. Note that the DogAnimalType query is listed in the Queries section.

You need to use the shortcut menu to copy the DogAnimalType query and paste it in the Navigation Pane; then you'll give the copied query a different name.

▶ **2.** In the Queries section of the Navigation Pane, right-click **DogAnimalType** to select it and display the shortcut menu.

▶ **3.** Click **Copy** on the shortcut menu.

▶ **4.** Right-click the empty area near the bottom of the Navigation Pane, and then click **Paste** on the shortcut menu. The Paste As dialog box opens with the text "Copy Of DogAnimalType" in the Query Name box. Because Kimberly wants the new query to show data for animals that have not visited the care center recently, you'll name the new query "EarlierVisits."

▶ **5.** In the Query Name box, type **EarlierVisits** and then press the **Enter** key. The new query appears in the Queries section of the Navigation Pane.

▶ **6.** Double-click the **EarlierVisits** query to open, or run, the query. The design of this query is currently the same as the original DogAnimalType query.

▶ **7.** Close the Navigation Pane.

Next, you need to open the query in Design view and modify its design to produce the results Kimberly wants—to display records for all animals and only those records with VisitDate field values that are earlier than, or less than, 1/1/2017.

To modify the design of the new query:

▶ **1.** Display the query in Design view.

▶ **2.** Click the **VisitDate Criteria** box, type **<1/1/2017** and then press the **Tab** key. Note that Access automatically encloses the date criteria with number signs. The condition specifies that a record will be selected only if its VisitDate field value is less than (earlier than) 1/1/2017. See Figure 3-23.

Figure 3-23 **Criteria entered for the VisitDate field**

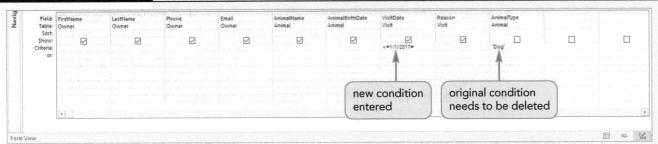

Before you run the query, you need to delete the condition for the AnimalType field. Recall that the AnimalType field is part of the query, but its values are not displayed in the query results. When you modified the query to remove the AnimalType field values from the query results, Access moved the field to the end of the design grid. You need to delete the AnimalType field's condition, specify that the AnimalType field values should be included in the query results, and then move the field back to its original position following the AnimalBirthDate field.

▶ **3.** Press the **Tab** key to select the condition for the AnimalType field, and then press the **Delete** key. The condition for the AnimalType field is removed.

▶ **4.** Click the **Show** check box for the AnimalType field to insert a checkmark so that the field values will be displayed in the query results.

▶ **5.** Use the pointer to select the AnimalType field, drag the selected field to position it to the left of the VisitDate field, and then click in an empty box to deselect the AnimalType field. See Figure 3-24.

Figure 3-24 **Design grid after moving the AnimalType field**

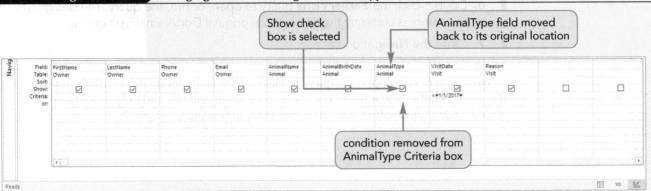

▶ **6.** Run the query. The query datasheet displays the selected fields for only those records with a VisitDate field value less than 1/1/2017, a total of 34 records. See Figure 3-25.

Figure 3-25	Running the modified query

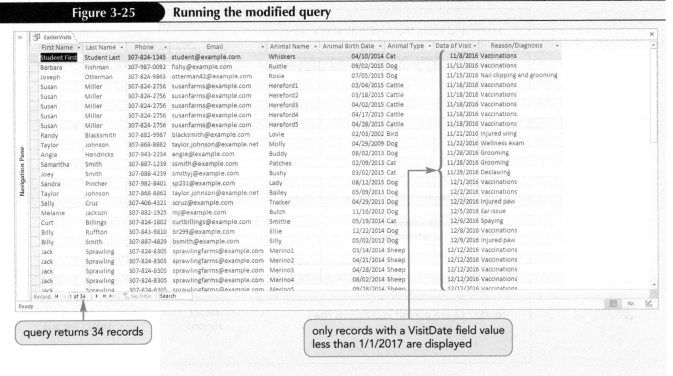

query returns 34 records

only records with a VisitDate field value less than 1/1/2017 are displayed

▶ **7.** Save and close the EarlierVisits query.

Kimberly continues to analyze animal visits to Riverview Veterinary Care Center. Although the care center offers payment plans and pet insurance options, she realizes that owners of younger animals seen off-site might not see the literature about these options that is available in the care center's waiting room. With this in mind, she would like to see a list of all animals that are less than a year old and that the care center has visited off-site. She wants to track these animals in particular so that her staff can contact their owners to review payment plans and pet insurance options. To produce this list, you need to create a query containing two conditions—one for the animal's date of birth and another for whether each visit was off-site.

Defining Multiple Selection Criteria for Queries

Multiple conditions require you to use **logical operators** to combine two or more conditions. When you want a record selected only if two or more conditions are met, you need to use the **And logical operator**. In this case, Kimberly wants to see only those records with an AnimalBirthDate field value greater than or equal to 7/1/2015 *and* an OffSite field value of "Yes" (indicating a checked box). If you place conditions in separate fields in the *same* Criteria row of the design grid, all conditions in that row must be met in order for a record to be included in the query results. However, if you place conditions in *different* Criteria rows, a record will be selected if at least one of the conditions is met. If none of the conditions are met, Access does not select the record. When you place conditions in different Criteria rows, you are using the **Or logical operator**. Figure 3-26 illustrates the difference between the And and Or logical operators.

Figure 3-26 Logical operators And and Or for multiple selection criteria

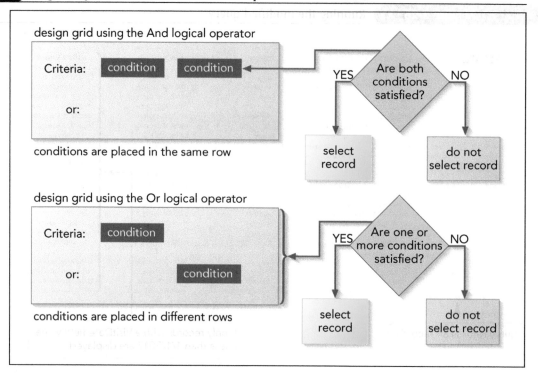

The And Logical Operator

To create the query for Kimberly, you need to use the And logical operator to show only the records for animals that were born on or after 7/1/2015 *and* who have had an off-site visit. You'll create a new query based on the Owner, Animal, and Visit tables to produce the necessary results. In the query design, both conditions you specify will appear in the same Criteria row; therefore, the query will select records only if both conditions are met.

To create a new query using the And logical operator:

▶ **1.** On the ribbon, click the **Create** tab.

▶ **2.** In the Queries group, click the **Query Design** button.

▶ **3.** Add the **Owner**, **Animal**, and **Visit** tables to the Query window in that order, and then close the Show Table dialog box. Resize all three field lists to display all the field names.

▶ **4.** Add the **AnimalName** and **AnimalBirthDate** fields from the Animal table to the design grid.

▶ **5.** Add the **FirstName**, **LastName**, and **Phone** fields from the Owner field list to the design grid.

▶ **6.** Add the **VisitDate** and **OffSite** fields from the Visit table to the design grid.

Now you need to enter the two conditions for the query.

▶ **7.** Click the **AnimalBirthDate Criteria** box, and then type **>=7/1/2015**.

▶ **8.** Press the **Tab** key five times to move to the **OffSite** box, type **Yes**, and then press the **Tab** key. Notice that for a Yes/No field such as OffSite, the criteria value is not automatically enclosed in quotes. See Figure 3-27.

Figure 3-27   **Query to find younger animals who have had off-site visits**

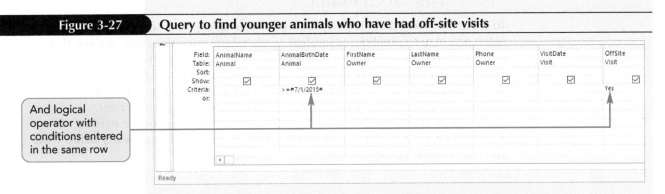

And logical operator with conditions entered in the same row

9. Run the query. The query displays only those records that meet both conditions: an AnimalBirthDate field value greater than or equal to 7/1/2015 *and* an OffSite field value of Yes. 14 records are displayed for 14 different animals. See Figure 3-28.

Figure 3-28   **Results of query using the And logical operator**

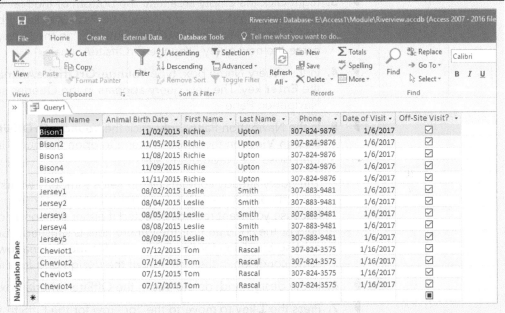

10. On the Quick Access Toolbar, click the **Save** button, and then save the query as **YoungerAndOffsiteAnimals**.

11. Close the query.

Kimberly meets with staff members to discuss the issue of owners with younger animals being informed of the care center's payment plans and insurance options. After viewing the results of the YoungerAndOffsiteAnimals query, the group agrees that the care center should reach out to the owners of all younger animals regarding these services, because first-time owners are more likely to be unaware of the care center's options. In addition, the care center should contact the owner of any animal that has received an off-site visit, because these owners are less likely to have seen the care center's waiting room literature on these payment options. To help with their planning, Kimberly asks you to produce a list of all animals that were born on or after 7/1/2015 or that received an off-site visit. To create this query, you need to use the Or logical operator.

The Or Logical Operator

To create the query that Kimberly requested, your query must select a record when either one of two conditions is satisfied or when both conditions are satisfied. That is, a record is selected if the AnimalBirthDate field value is greater than or equal to 7/1/2015 *or* if the OffSite field value is Yes *or* if both conditions are met. You will enter the condition for the AnimalBirthDate field in the Criteria row and the condition for the OffSite field in the "or" criteria row, thereby using the Or logical operator.

To display the information, you'll create a new query based on the existing YoungerAndOffsiteAnimals query, since it already contains the necessary fields. Then you'll specify the conditions using the Or logical operator.

To create a new query using the Or logical operator:

▶ 1. Open the Navigation Pane. You'll use the shortcut menu to copy and paste the YoungerAndOffsiteAnimals query to create the new query.

▶ 2. In the Queries section of the Navigation Pane, right-click **YoungerAndOffsiteAnimals**, and then click **Copy** on the shortcut menu.

▶ 3. Right-click the empty area near the bottom of the Navigation Pane, and then click **Paste** on the shortcut menu. The Paste As dialog box opens with the text "Copy Of YoungerAndOffsiteAnimals" in the Query Name box. You'll name the new query "YoungerOrOffsiteAnimals."

▶ 4. In the Query Name box, type **YoungerOrOffsiteAnimals** and then press the **Enter** key. The new query appears in the Queries section of the Navigation Pane.

▶ 5. In the Navigation Pane, right-click the **YoungerOrOffsiteAnimals** query, click **Design View** on the shortcut menu to open the query in Design view, and then close the Navigation Pane.

The query already contains all the fields Kimberly wants to view, as well as the first condition—a BirthDate field value greater than or equal to 7/1/2015. Because you want records selected if either the condition for the BirthDate field or the condition for the OffSite field is satisfied, you must delete the existing condition for the OffSite field in the Criteria row and then enter this same condition in the "or" row of the design grid for the OffSite field.

▶ 6. In the design grid, delete **Yes** in the OffSite Criteria box.

▶ 7. Press the ↓ key to move to the "or" row for the OffSite field, type **Yes**, and then press the **Tab** key. See Figure 3-29.

Figure 3-29   Query window with the Or logical operator

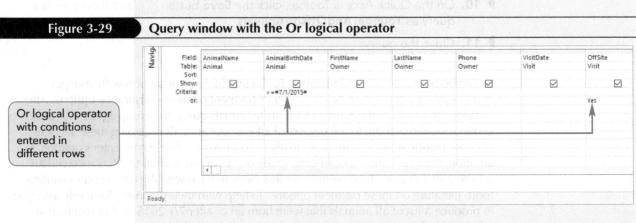

Or logical operator with conditions entered in different rows

Field:	AnimalName	AnimalBirthDate	FirstName	LastName	Phone	VisitDate	OffSite
Table:	Animal	Animal	Owner	Owner	Owner	Visit	Visit
Sort:							
Show:	☑	☑	☑	☑	☑	☑	☑
Criteria:		>=#7/1/2015#					
or:							Yes

Ready

To better analyze the data, Kimberly wants the list displayed in descending order by AnimalBirthDate.

8. Click the right side of the **AnimalBirthDate Sort** box, and then click **Descending**.

9. Run the query. The query datasheet displays only those records that meet either condition: a BirthDate field value greater than or equal to 7/1/2015 *or* an OffSite field value of Yes. The query also returns records that meet both conditions. The query displays a total of 43 records. The records in the query datasheet appear in descending order based on the values in the AnimalBirthDate field. See Figure 3-30.

Figure 3-30   Results of query using the Or logical operator

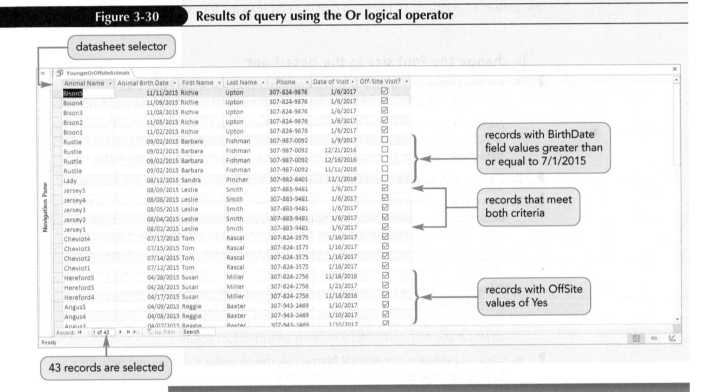

datasheet selector

43 records are selected

records with BirthDate field values greater than or equal to 7/1/2015

records that meet both criteria

records with OffSite values of Yes

Understanding the Results of Using And vs. Or

INSIGHT

When you use the And logical operator to define multiple selection criteria in a query, you *narrow* the results produced by the query because a record must meet more than one condition to be included in the results. For example, the YoungerAndOffsiteAnimals query you created resulted in only 14 records. When you use the Or logical operator, you *broaden* the results produced by the query because a record must meet only one of the conditions to be included in the results. For example, the YoungerOrOffsiteAnimals query you created resulted in 43 records. This is an important distinction to keep in mind when you include multiple selection criteria in queries, so that the queries you create will produce the results you want.

Kimberly would like to spend some time reviewing the results of the YoungerOrOffsiteAnimals query. To make this task easier, she asks you to change how the datasheet is displayed.

Changing a Datasheet's Appearance

You can make many formatting changes to a datasheet to improve its appearance or readability. Many of these modifications are familiar types of changes you can also make in Word documents or Excel spreadsheets, such as modifying the font type, size, color, and the alignment of text. You can also apply different colors to the rows and columns in a datasheet to enhance its appearance.

Modifying the Font Size

Depending on the size of the monitor you are using or the screen resolution, you might need to increase or decrease the size of the font in a datasheet to view more or fewer columns of data. Kimberly asks you to change the font size in the query datasheet from the default 11 points to 14 points so that she can read the text more easily.

To change the font size in the datasheet:

▶ **1.** On the Home tab, in the Text Formatting group, click the **Font Size** arrow, and then click **14**. The font size for the entire datasheet increases to 14 points.

 Next, you need to resize the columns to their best fit, so that all field values are displayed. Instead of resizing each column individually, you'll use the datasheet selector to select all the columns and resize them at the same time.

▶ **2.** Click the **datasheet selector**. All the columns in the datasheet are selected.

▶ **3.** Move the pointer to one of the vertical lines separating two columns in the datasheet until the pointer changes to ↔, and then double-click the vertical line. All the columns visible on the screen are resized to their best fit. Scroll down and repeat the resizing, as necessary, to make sure that all field values are fully displayed.

 Trouble? If all the columns are not visible on your screen, you need to scroll the datasheet to the right to make sure all field values for all columns are fully displayed. If you need to resize any columns, click a field value first to deselect the columns before resizing an individual column.

▶ **4.** Click any value in the Animal Name column to make it the current field and to deselect the columns in the datasheet.

Changing the Alternate Row Color in a Datasheet

Access uses themes to format the objects in a database. A **theme** is a predefined set of formats including colors, fonts, and other effects that enhance an object's appearance and usability. When you create a database, Access applies the Office theme to objects as you create them. By default, the Office theme formats every other row in a datasheet with a gray background color to distinguish one row from another, making it easier to view and read the contents of a datasheet. The gray alternate row color provides a subtle difference compared to the rows that have the default white color. You can change the alternate row color in a datasheet to something more noticeable using the Alternate Row Color button in the Text Formatting group on the Home tab. Kimberly suggests that you change the alternate row color in the datasheet to see the effect of using this feature.

To change the alternate row color in the datasheet:

1. On the Home tab, in the Text Formatting group, click the **Alternate Row Color button arrow** ⊞ ⌄ to display the gallery of color choices. See Figure 3-31.

Figure 3-31   **Gallery of color choices for alternate row color**

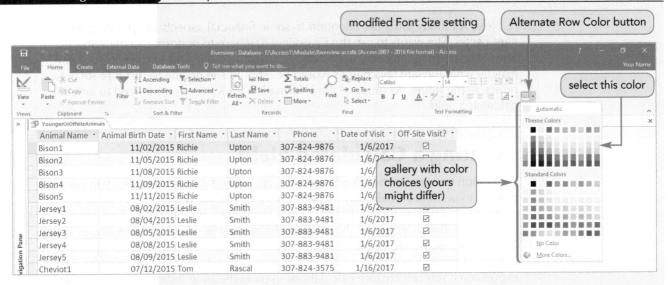

TIP

The name of the color appears in a ScreenTip when you point to a color in the gallery.

The Theme Colors section provides colors from the default Office theme, so that your datasheet's color scheme matches the one in use for the database. The Standard Colors section provides many standard color choices. You might also see a Recent Colors section, with colors that you have recently used in a datasheet. The No Color option, which appears at the bottom of the gallery, sets each row's background color to white. If you want to create a custom color, you can do so using the More Colors option. You'll use one of the theme colors.

2. In the Theme Colors section, click the **Green, Accent 6, Lighter 60%** color (third row, tenth color). The alternate row color is applied to the query datasheet. See Figure 3-32.

Figure 3-32   **Datasheet formatted with alternate row color**

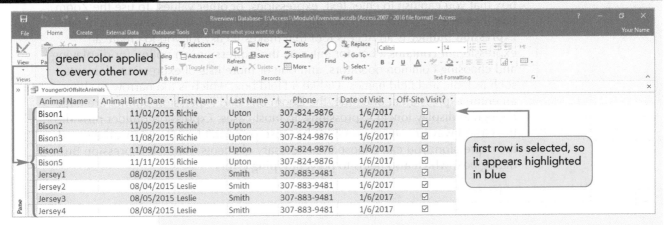

Every other row in the datasheet uses the selected theme color. Kimberly likes how the datasheet looks with this color scheme, so she asks you to save the query.

▶ **3.** Save and close the YoungerOrOffsiteAnimals query. The query is saved with both the increased font size and the green alternate row color.

Next, Kimberly turns her attention to some financial aspects of operating the care center. She wants to use the Riverview database to perform calculations. She is considering imposing a 2% late fee on unpaid invoices and wants to know exactly what the late fee charges would be, should she decide to institute such a policy in the future. To produce the information for Kimberly, you need to create a calculated field.

Creating a Calculated Field

In addition to using queries to retrieve, sort, and filter data in a database, you can use a query to perform calculations. To perform a calculation, you define an **expression** containing a combination of database fields, constants, and operators. For numeric expressions, the data types of the database fields must be Number, Currency, or Date/ Time; the constants are numbers such as .02 (for the 2% late fee); and the operators can be arithmetic operators (+ – * /) or other specialized operators. In complex expressions, you can enclose calculations in parentheses to indicate which one should be performed first; any calculation within parentheses is completed before calculations outside the parentheses. In expressions without parentheses, Access performs basic calculations using the following order of precedence: multiplication and division before addition and subtraction. When operators have equal precedence, Access calculates them in order from left to right.

To perform a calculation in a query, you add a calculated field to the query. A **calculated field** is a field that displays the results of an expression. A calculated field that you create with an expression appears in a query datasheet or in a form or report; however, it does not exist in a database. When you run a query that contains a calculated field, Access evaluates the expression defined by the calculated field and displays the resulting value in the query datasheet, form, or report.

To enter an expression for a calculated field, you can type it directly in a Field box in the design grid. Alternately, you can open the Zoom box or Expression Builder and use either one to enter the expression. The **Zoom box** is a dialog box that you can use to enter text, expressions, or other values. To use the Zoom box, however, you must know all the parts of the expression you want to create. **Expression Builder** is an Access tool that makes it easy for you to create an expression; it contains a box for entering the expression, an option for displaying and choosing common operators, and one or more lists of expression elements, such as table and field names. Unlike a Field box, which is too narrow to show an entire expression at one time, the Zoom box and Expression Builder are large enough to display longer expressions. In most cases, Expression Builder provides the easiest way to enter expressions because you don't have to know all the parts of the expression; you can choose the necessary elements from the Expression Builder dialog box, which also helps to prevent typing errors.

Creating a Calculated Field Using Expression Builder

- Create and save the query in which you want to include a calculated field.
- Open the query in Design view.
- In the design grid, click the Field box in which you want to create an expression.
- In the Query Setup group on the Query Tools Design tab, click the Builder button.
- Use the expression elements and common operators to build the expression, or type the expression directly in the expression box.
- Click the OK button.

To produce the information Kimberly wants, you need to create a new query based on the Billing and Visit tables and, in the query, create a calculated field that will multiply each InvoiceAmt field value by .02 to calculate the proposed 2% late fee.

To create the new query:

1. On the ribbon, click the **Create** tab.

2. In the Queries group, click the **Query Design** button. The Show Table dialog box opens.

   Kimberly wants to see data from both the Visit and Billing tables, so you need to add these two tables to the Query window.

3. Add the **Visit** and **Billing** tables to the Query window, and resize the field lists as necessary so that all the field names are visible. The field lists appear in the Query window, and the one-to-many relationship between the Visit (primary) and Billing (related) tables is displayed.

4. Add the following fields to the design grid in the order given: **VisitID**, **AnimalID**, and **VisitDate** from the Visit table; and **InvoiceItem**, **InvoicePaid**, and **InvoiceAmt** from the Billing table.

   Kimberly is interested in viewing data only for unpaid invoices because a late fee would apply only to them, so you need to enter the necessary condition for the InvoicePaid field. Recall that InvoicePaid is a Yes/No field. The condition you need to enter is the word "No" in the Criteria box for this field, so that Access will retrieve the records for unpaid invoices only.

5. In the **InvoicePaid Criteria box**, type **No**. As soon as you type the letter "N," a menu appears with options for entering various functions for the criteria. You don't need to enter a function, so you can close this menu.

6. Press the **Esc** key to close the menu.

7. Press the **Tab** key. The query name you'll use will indicate that the data is for unpaid invoices, so you don't need to include the InvoicePaid values in the query results.

8. Click the **InvoicePaid Show** check box to remove the checkmark.

9. Save the query with the name **UnpaidInvoiceLateFee**.

   Now you can use Expression Builder to create the calculated field for the InvoiceAmt field.

You must close the menu or you'll enter a function, which will cause an error.

To create the calculated field:

▶ **1.** Click the blank Field box to the right of the InvoiceAmt field. This field will contain the expression.

▶ **2.** On the Query Tools Design tab, in the Query Setup group, click the **Builder** button. The Expression Builder dialog box opens.

The insertion point is positioned in the large box at the top of the dialog box, ready for you to enter the expression. The Expression Categories section of the dialog box lists the fields from the query so you can include them in the expression. The Expression Elements section contains options for including other elements in the expression, including functions, constants, and operators. If the expression you're entering is a simple one, you can type it in the box; if it's more complex, you can use the options in the Expression Elements section to help you build the expression.

The expression for the calculated field will multiply the InvoiceAmt field values by the numeric constant .02 (which represents a 2% late fee).

▶ **3.** In the Expression Categories section of the dialog box, double-click **InvoiceAmt**. The field name is added to the expression box, within brackets and with a space following it. In an expression, all field names must be enclosed in brackets.

Next you need to enter the multiplication operator, which is the asterisk (*), followed by the constant.

▶ **4.** Type * (an asterisk) and then type **.02**. You have finished entering the expression. See Figure 3-33.

Figure 3-33 Completed expression for the calculated field

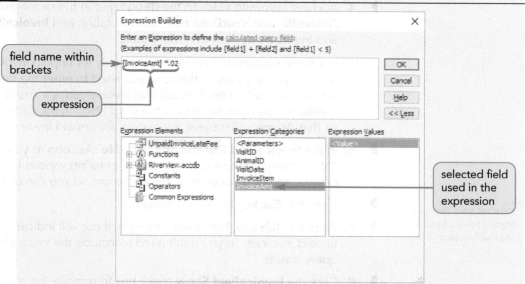

If you're not sure which operator to use, you can click Operators in the Expression Elements section to display a list of available operators in the center section of the dialog box.

▶ **5.** Click the **OK** button. The Expression Builder dialog box closes, and the expression is added to the design grid in the Field box for the calculated field.

When you create a calculated field, Access uses the default name "Expr1" for the field. You need to specify a more meaningful field name so it will appear in the query results. You'll enter the name "LateFee," which better describes the field's contents.

▶ **6.** Click to the left of the text "Expr1:" at the beginning of the expression, and then press the **Delete** key five times to delete the text **Expr1**. *Do not delete the colon*; it is needed to separate the calculated field name from the expression.

▶ **7.** Type **LateFee**. Next, you'll set this field's Caption property so that the field name will appear as "Late Fee" in the query datasheet.

▶ **8.** On the Query Tools Design tab, in the Show/Hide group, click the **Property Sheet** button. The Property Sheet for the current field, LateFee, opens on the right side of the window. See Figure 3-34.

Figure 3-34	Property Sheet for the calculated field

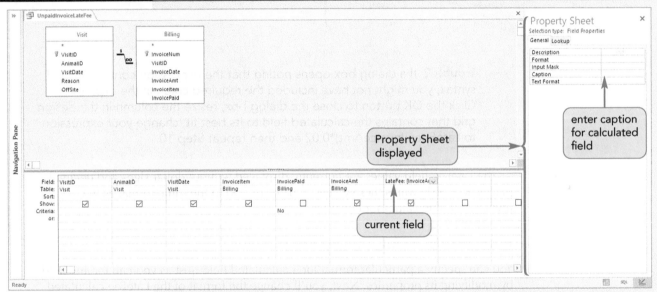

▶ **9.** In the Property sheet, click in the Caption box, type **Late Fee** and then close the Property Sheet.

▶ **10.** Run the query. The query datasheet is displayed and contains the specified fields and the calculated field with the caption "Late Fee." See Figure 3-35.

Figure 3-35	Datasheet displaying the calculated field

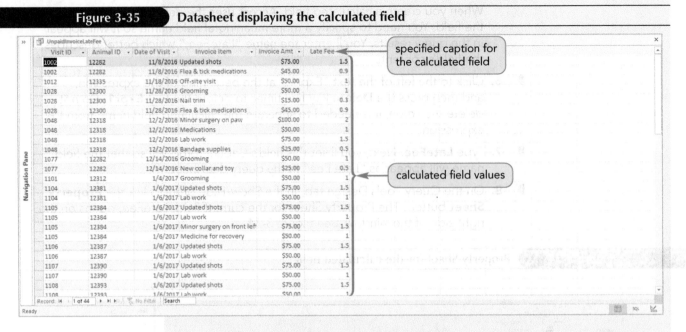

Trouble? If a dialog box opens noting that the expression contains invalid syntax, you might not have included the required colon in the expression. Click the OK button to close the dialog box, resize the column in the design grid that contains the calculated field to its best fit, change your expression to LateFee: [InvoiceAmt]*0.02 and then repeat Step 10.

The LateFee field values are currently displayed without dollar signs and decimal places. Kimberly wants these values to be displayed in the same format as the InvoiceAmt field values for consistency.

Formatting a Calculated Field

You can specify a particular format for a calculated field, just as you can for any field, by modifying its properties. Next, you'll change the format of the LateFee calculated field so that all values appear in the Currency format.

To format the calculated field:

▶ **1.** Switch to Design view.

▶ **2.** In the design grid, click in the **LateFee** calculated field to make it the current field, if necessary.

▶ **3.** On the Query Tools Design tab, in the Show/Hide group, click the **Property Sheet** button to open the Property Sheet for the calculated field.

You need to change the Format property to Currency, which displays values with a dollar sign and two decimal places.

▶ **4.** In the Property Sheet, click the right side of the **Format** box to display the list of formats, and then click **Currency**.

▶ **5.** Close the Property Sheet, and then run the query. The amounts in the LateFee calculated field are now displayed with dollar signs and two decimal places.

▶ **6.** Save and close the UnpaidInvoiceLateFee query.

PROSKILLS

Problem Solving: Creating a Calculated Field vs. Using the Calculated Field Data Type

You can also create a calculated field using the Calculated Field data type, which lets you store the result of an expression as a field in a table. However, database experts caution users against storing calculations in a table for several reasons. First, storing calculated data in a table consumes valuable space and increases the size of the database. The preferred approach is to use a calculated field in a query; with this approach, the result of the calculation is not stored in the database—it is produced only when you run the query—and it is always current. Second, the Calculated Field data type provides limited options for creating a calculation, whereas a calculated field in a query provides more functions and options for creating expressions. Third, including a field in a table using the Calculated Field data type limits your options if you need to upgrade the database at some point to a more robust DBMS, such as Oracle or SQL Server, that doesn't support this data type; you would need to redesign your database to eliminate this data type. Finally, most database experts agree that including a field in a table whose value is dependent on other fields in the table violates database design principles. To avoid such problems, it's best to create a query that includes a calculated field to perform the calculation you want, instead of creating a field in a table that uses the Calculated Field data type.

To better analyze costs at Riverview Veterinary Care Center, Kimberly wants to view more detailed information about invoices for animal care. Specifically, she would like to know the minimum, average, and maximum invoice amounts. She asks you to determine these statistics from data in the Billing table.

Using Aggregate Functions

You can calculate statistical information, such as totals and averages, on the records displayed in a table datasheet or selected by a query. To do this, you use the Access aggregate functions. **Aggregate functions** perform arithmetic operations on selected records in a database. Figure 3-36 lists the most frequently used aggregate functions.

Figure 3-36	Frequently used aggregate functions

Aggregate Function	Determines	Data Types Supported
Average	Average of the field values for the selected records	AutoNumber, Currency, Date/Time, Number
Count	Number of records selected	AutoNumber, Currency, Date/Time, Long Text, Number, OLE Object, Short Text, Yes/No
Maximum	Highest field value for the selected records	AutoNumber, Currency, Date/Time, Number, Short Text
Minimum	Lowest field value for the selected records	AutoNumber, Currency, Date/Time, Number, Short Text
Sum	Total of the field values for the selected records	AutoNumber, Currency, Date/Time, Number

Working with Aggregate Functions Using the Total Row

If you want to quickly perform a calculation using an aggregate function in a table or query datasheet, you can use the Totals button in the Records group on the Home tab. When you click this button, a row labeled "Total" appears at the bottom of the datasheet. You can then choose one of the aggregate functions for a field in the datasheet, and the results of the calculation will be displayed in the Total row for that field.

Kimberly wants to know the total amount of all invoices for the care center. You can quickly display this amount using the Sum function in the Total row in the Billing table datasheet.

To display the total amount of all invoices in the Billing table:

▶ **1.** Open the Navigation Pane, open the **Billing** table in Datasheet view, and then close the Navigation Pane.

▶ **2.** Make sure the Home tab is displayed.

▶ **3.** In the Records group, click the **Totals** button. A row with the label "Total" is added to the bottom of the datasheet.

▶ **4.** Scroll to the bottom of the datasheet to view the Total row. You want to display the sum of all the values in the Invoice Amt column.

▶ **5.** In the Total row, click the **Invoice Amt** field. An arrow appears on the left side of the field.

▶ **6.** Click the **arrow** to display the menu of aggregate functions. The functions displayed depend on the data type of the current field; in this case, the menu provides functions for a Currency field. See Figure 3-37.

Figure 3-37	**Using aggregate functions in the Total row**

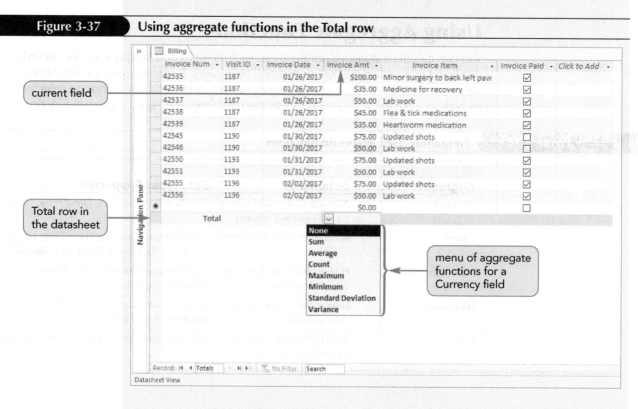

7. Click **Sum** in the menu. All the values in the Invoice Amt column are added, and the total $12,015.00 appears in the Total row for the column.

   Kimberly doesn't want to change the Billing table to always display this total. You can remove the Total row by clicking the Totals button again; this button works as a toggle to switch between the display of the Total row with the results of any calculations in the row, and the display of the datasheet without this row.

8. In the Records group, click the **Totals** button. The Total row is removed from the datasheet.

9. Close the Billing table without saving the changes.

Kimberly wants to know the minimum, average, and maximum invoice amounts for Riverview Veterinary Care Center. To produce this information for Kimberly, you need to use aggregate functions in a query.

Creating Queries with Aggregate Functions

Aggregate functions operate on the records that meet a query's selection criteria. You specify an aggregate function for a specific field, and the appropriate operation applies to that field's values for the selected records.

To display the minimum, average, and maximum of all the invoice amounts in the Billing table, you will use the Minimum, Average, and Maximum aggregate functions for the InvoiceAmt field.

To calculate the minimum of all invoice amounts:

1. Create a new query in Design view, add the **Billing** table to the Query window, and then resize the Billing field list to display all fields.

   To perform the three calculations on the InvoiceAmt field, you need to add the field to the design grid three times.

2. In the Billing field list, double-click **InvoiceAmt** three times to add three copies of the field to the design grid.

   You need to select an aggregate function for each InvoiceAmt field. When you click the Totals button in the Show/Hide group on the Design tab, a row labeled "Total" is added to the design grid. The Total row provides a list of the aggregate functions that you can select.

3. On the Query Tools Design tab, in the Show/Hide group, click the **Totals** button. A new row labeled "Total" appears between the Table and Sort rows in the design grid. The default entry for each field in the Total row is the Group By operator, which you will learn about later in this module. See Figure 3-38.

Figure 3-38   Total row inserted in the design grid

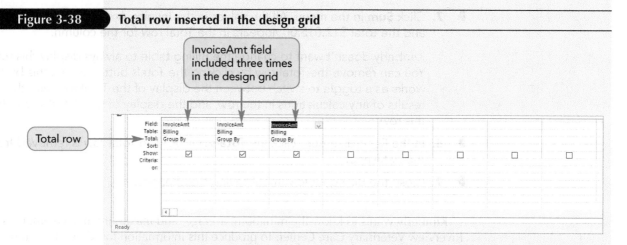

In the Total row, you specify the aggregate function you want to use for a field.

▶ **4.** Click the right side of the first column's **Total** box, and then click **Min**. This field will calculate the minimum amount of all the InvoiceAmt field values.

When you run the query, Access automatically will assign a datasheet column name of "MinOfInvoiceAmt" for this field. You can change the datasheet column name to a more descriptive or readable name by entering the name you want in the Field box. However, you must also keep the InvoiceAmt field name in the Field box because it identifies the field to use in the calculation. The Field box will contain the datasheet column name you specify followed by the field name (InvoiceAmt) with a colon separating the two names.

▶ **5.** In the first column's Field box, click to the left of InvoiceAmt, and then type **MinimumInvoiceAmt:** (including the colon).

Be sure to type the colon following the name or the query will not work correctly.

▶ **6.** Resize the column so that you can see the complete field name, MinimumInvoiceAmt:InvoiceAmt.

Next, you need to set the Caption property for this field so that the field name appears with spaces between words in the query datatsheet.

▶ **7.** On the Query Tools Design tab, in the Show/Hide group, click the **Property Sheet** button to open the Property Sheet for the current field.

▶ **8.** In the Caption box, type **Minimum Invoice Amt**, and then close the Property Sheet.

You'll follow the same process to complete the query by calculating the average and maximum invoice amounts.

To calculate the average and maximum of all invoice amounts:

▶ **1.** Click the right side of the second column's **Total** box, and then click **Avg**. This field will calculate the average of all the InvoiceAmt field values.

▶ **2.** In the second column's Field box, click to the left of InvoiceAmt, and then type **AverageInvoiceAmt:**.

▶ **3.** Resize the second column to fully display the field name, AverageInvoiceAmt:InvoiceAmt.

4. Open the Property Sheet for the current field, and then set its Caption property to **Average Invoice Amt**.

5. Click the right side of the third column's **Total** box, and then click **Max**. This field will calculate the maximum amount of all the InvoiceAmt field values.

6. In the third column's Field box, click to the left of InvoiceAmt, and then type **MaximumInvoiceAmt:**.

7. Resize the third column to fully display the field name, MaximumInvoiceAmt:InvoiceAmt.

8. In the Property Sheet, set the Caption property to **Maximum Invoice Amt**, and then close the Property Sheet. See Figure 3-39.

| Figure 3-39 | Query with aggregate functions entered |

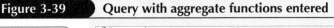

functions entered and columns resized

Trouble? Carefully compare your field names to those shown in the figure to make sure they match exactly; otherwise the query will not work correctly.

9. Run the query. One record displays containing the three aggregate function results. The single row of summary statistics represents calculations based on all the records selected for the query—in this case, all 202 records in the Billing table.

10. Resize all columns to their best fit so that the column names are fully displayed, and then click the field value in the first column to deselect the value and view the results. See Figure 3-40.

| Figure 3-40 | Result of the query using aggregate functions |

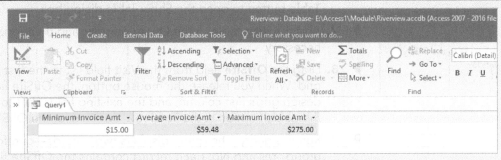

11. Save the query as **InvoiceAmtStatistics**.

Kimberly would like to view the same invoice amount statistics (minimum, average, and maximum) as they relate to both appointments at the care center and off-site visits.

Using Record Group Calculations

In addition to calculating statistical information on all or selected records in selected tables, you can calculate statistics for groups of records. The **Group By operator** divides the selected records into groups based on the values in the specified field. Those records with the same value for the field are grouped together, and the datasheet displays one record for each group. Aggregate functions, which appear in the other columns of the design grid, provide statistical information for each group.

To create a query for Kimberly's latest request, you will modify the current query by adding the OffSite field and assigning the Group By operator to it. The Group By operator will display the statistical information grouped by the values of the OffSite field for all the records in the query datasheet. To create the new query, you will save the InvoiceAmtStatistics query with a new name, keeping the original query intact, and then modify the new query.

To create a new query with the Group By operator:

▶ **1.** Display the InvoiceAmtStatistics query in Design view. Because the query is open, you can use Backstage view to save it with a new name, keeping the original query intact.

▶ **2.** Click the **File** tab to display Backstage view, and then click **Save As** in the navigation bar. The Save As screen opens.

▶ **3.** In the File Types section on the left, click **Save Object As**. The right side of the screen changes to display options for saving the current database object as a new object.

▶ **4.** Click the **Save As** button. The Save As dialog box opens, indicating that you are saving a copy of the InvoiceAmtStatistics query.

▶ **5.** Type **InvoiceAmtStatisticsByOffsite** to replace the selected name, and then press the **Enter** key. The new query is saved with the name you specified and appears in Design view.

You need to add the OffSite field to the query. This field is in the Visit table. To include another table in an existing query, you open the Show Table dialog box.

TIP

You could also open the Navigation Pane and drag the Visit table from the pane to the Query window.

▶ **6.** On the Query Tools Design tab, in the Query Setup group, click the **Show Table** button to open the Show Table dialog box.

▶ **7.** Add the **Visit** table to the Query window, and then resize the Visit field list if necessary.

▶ **8.** Drag the **OffSite** field from the Visit field list to the first column in the design grid. When you release the mouse button, the OffSite field appears in the design grid's first column, and the existing fields shift to the right. Group By, the default option in the Total row, appears for the OffSite field.

▶ **9.** Run the query. The query displays two records—one for each OffSite group, Yes and No. Each record contains the OffSite field value for the group and the three aggregate function values. The summary statistics represent calculations based on the 202 records in the Billing table. See Figure 3-41.

Figure 3-41   **Aggregate functions grouped by OffSite**

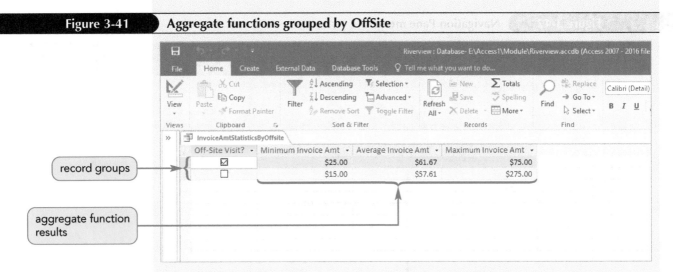

Kimberly notes that the minimum and average invoice amounts for off-site visits are slightly higher than those for visits to the care center, while the maximum amount is higher for visits to the care center.

▶ **10.** Save and close the query.

▶ **11.** Open the Navigation Pane.

You have created and saved many queries in the Riverview database. The Navigation Pane provides options for opening and managing the queries you've created, as well as the other objects in the database, such as tables, forms, and reports.

Working with the Navigation Pane

As noted earlier, the Navigation Pane is the main area for working with the objects in a database. As you continue to create objects in your database, you might want to display and work with them in different ways. The Navigation Pane provides options for grouping database objects in various ways to suit your needs. For example, you might want to view only the queries created for a certain table or all the query objects in the database.

As you know, the Navigation Pane divides database objects into categories. Each category contains groups, and each group contains one or more objects. The default category is **Object Type**, which arranges objects by type—tables, queries, forms, and reports. The default group is **All Access Objects**, which displays all objects in the database. You can also choose to display only one type of object, such as tables.

The default group name, All Access Objects, appears at the top of the Navigation Pane. Currently, each object type—Tables, Queries, Forms, and Reports—is displayed as a heading, and the objects related to each type are listed below the heading. To group objects differently, you can select another category by using the Navigation Pane menu. You'll try this next.

TIP

You can hide the display of a group's objects by clicking the button to the right of the group name; click the button again to expand the group and display its objects.

To group objects differently in the Navigation Pane:

▶ **1.** At the top of the Navigation Pane, click the **All Access Objects** button ⊙. A menu opens with options for choosing different categories and groups. See Figure 3-42.

Figure 3-42 **Navigation Pane menu**

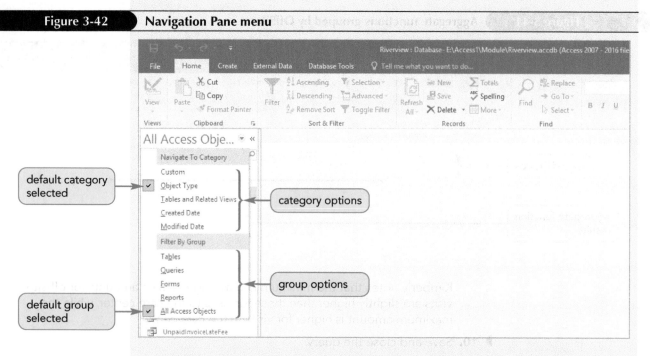

default category selected

category options

default group selected

group options

The top section of the menu provides the options for choosing a different category. The Object Type category has a checkmark next to it, signifying that it is the currently selected category. The lower section of the menu provides options for choosing a different group; these options might change depending on the selected category.

2. In the Navigate To Category section, click **Tables and Related Views**. The Navigation Pane is now grouped into categories of tables, and each table in the database—Visit, Billing, Owner, and Animal—is its own group. All database objects related to a table are listed below the table's name. Notice the UnpaidInvoiceLateFee query is based on both the Visit and Billing tables, so it is listed in the group for both tables. See Figure 3-43.

| Figure 3-43 | Database objects grouped by table in the Navigation Pane |

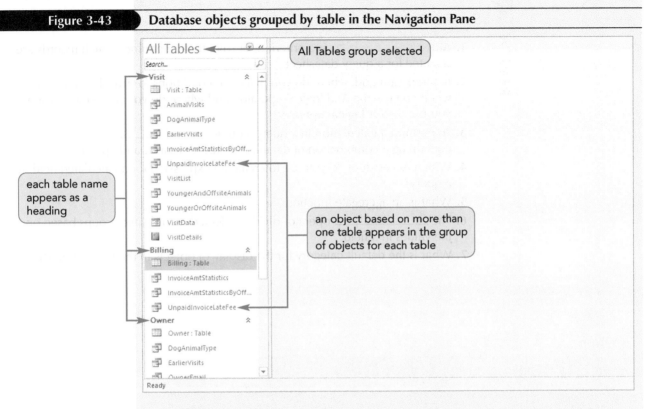

each table name appears as a heading

All Tables group selected

an object based on more than one table appears in the group of objects for each table

You can also choose to display the objects for only one table to better focus on that table.

▶ **3.** At the top of the Navigation Pane, click the **All Tables** button to display the Navigation Pane menu, and then click **Owner**. The Navigation Pane now shows only the objects related to the Owner table—the table itself plus the five queries you created that include fields from the Owner table.

▶ **4.** At the top of the Navigation Pane, click the **Owner** button, and then click **Object Type** to return to the default display of the Navigation Pane.

▶ **5.** Compact and repair the Riverview database, and then close the database.

Trouble? If a dialog box opens and warns that this action will cause Microsoft Access to empty the Clipboard, click the Yes button to continue.

The default All Access Objects category is a predefined category. You can also create custom categories to group objects in the way that best suits how you want to manage your database objects. As you continue to build a database and the list of objects grows, creating a custom category can help you to work more efficiently with the objects in the database.

The queries you've created and saved will help Kimberly and her staff to monitor and analyze the business activity of Riverview Veterinary Care Center and its patients. Now any staff member can run the queries at any time, modify them as needed, or use them as the basis for designing new queries to meet additional information requirements.

REVIEW

Session 3.2 Quick Check

1. A(n) _____ is a criterion, or rule, that determines which records are selected for a query datasheet.

2. In the design grid, where do you place the conditions for two different fields when you use the And logical operator, and where do you place them when you use the Or logical operator?

3. To perform a calculation in a query, you define a(n) _____ containing a combination of database fields, constants, and operators.

4. Which Access tool do you use to create an expression for a calculated field in a query?

5. What is an aggregate function?

6. The _____ operator divides selected records into groups based on the values in a field.

7. What is the default category for the display of objects in the Navigation Pane?

PRACTICE

Review Assignments

Data File needed for the Review Assignments: Vendor.accdb *(cont. from Module 2)*

Kimberly asks you to update some information in the Vendor database and also to retrieve specific information from the database. Complete the following:

1. Open the **Vendor** database you created and worked with in previous modules, and then click the Enable Content button next to the security warning, if necessary.

2. Open the **Supplier** table in Datasheet view, and then change the following field values for the record with the Supplier ID GGF099: Address to **738 26th St**, Contact Phone to **321-296-1958**, Contact First Name to **Carmela**, and Contact Last Name to **Montoya**. Close the table.

3. Create a query based on the Supplier table. Include the following fields in the query, in the order shown: Company, Category, ContactFirst, ContactLast, Phone, and City. Sort the query in ascending order based on the Category field values. Save the query as **ContactList**, and then run the query.

4. Use the ContactList query datasheet to update the Supplier table by changing the Phone field value for A+ Labs to **402-495-3957**.

5. Change the size of the font in the ContactList query datasheet to 12 points. Resize columns, as necessary, so that all field values and column headings are visible.

6. Change the alternate row color in the ContactList query datasheet to the Theme Color named Gold, Accent 4, Lighter 60%, and then save and close the query.

7. Create a query based on the Supplier and Product tables. Select the Company, Category, and State fields from the Supplier table, and the ProductName, Price, Units, and Weight fields from the Product table. Sort the query results in descending order based on price. Select only those records with a Category field value of Supplies, but do not display the Category field values in the query results. Save the query as **SupplyProducts**, run the query, and then close it.

8. Create a query that lists all products that cost more than $50 and are temperature controlled. Display the following fields from the Product table in the query results: ProductID, ProductName, Price, Units, and Sterile. (*Hint*: The TempControl field is a Yes/No field that should not appear in the query results.) Save the query as **HighPriceAndTempControl**, run the query, and then close it.

9. Create a query that lists information about suppliers who sell equipment or sterile products. Include the Company, Category, ContactFirst, and ContactLast fields from the Supplier table; and the ProductName, Price, TempControl, and Sterile fields from the Product table. Save the query as **EquipmentOrSterile**, run the query, and then close it.

10. Create a query that lists all resale products, along with a 10% markup amount based on the price of the product. Include the Company field from the Supplier table and the following fields from the Product table in the query: ProductID, ProductName, and Price. Save the query as **ResaleProductsWithMarkup**. Display the discount in a calculated field named **Markup** that determines a 10% markup based on the Price field values. Set the Caption property **Markup** for the calculated field. Display the query results in descending order by Price. Save and run the query.

11. Modify the format of the Markup field in the ResaleProductsWithMarkup query so that it uses the Standard format and two decimal places. Run the query, resize all columns in the datasheet to their best fit, and then save and close the query.

12. Create a query that calculates the lowest, highest, and average prices for all products using the field names **MinimumPrice**, **MaximumPrice**, and **AveragePrice**, respectively. Set the Caption property for each field to include a space between the two words in the field name. Run the query, resize all columns in the datasheet to their best fit, save the query as **PriceStatistics**, and then close it.

13. In the Navigation Pane, copy the PriceStatistics query, and then rename the copied query as **PriceStatisticsBySupplier**.

14. Modify the PriceStatisticsBySupplier query so that the records are grouped by the Company field in the Supplier table. The Company field should appear first in the query datasheet. Save and run the query, and then close it.

15. Compact and repair the Vendor database, and then close it.

Case Problem 1

APPLY

Data File needed for this Case Problem: Beauty.accdb *(cont. from Module 2)*

Beauty To Go Sue Miller needs to modify a few records in the Beauty database and analyze the data for customers that subscribe to her business. To help Sue, you'll update the Beauty database and create queries to answer her questions. Complete the following:

1. Open the **Beauty** database you created and worked with in previous modules, and then click the Enable Content button next to the security warning, if necessary.

2. In the **Member** table, find the record for MemberID 2163, and then change the Street value to **844 Sanford Ln** and the Zip to **32804**.

3. In the **Member** table, find the record for MemberID 2169, and then delete the record. Close the Member table.

4. Create a query that lists customers who did not have to pay a fee when they signed up for their current option. In the query results, display the FirstName, LastName, and OptionBegin fields from the Member table, and the OptionCost field from the Option table. Sort the records in ascending order by the option start date. Select records only for customers whose fees were waived. (*Hint*: The FeeWaived field is a Yes/No field that should not appear in the query results.) Save the query as **NoFees**, and then run the query.

5. Use the NoFees query datasheet to update the Member table by changing the Last Name value for Gilda Packson to **Washington**.

6. Use the NoFees query datasheet to display the total Option Cost for the selected members. Save and close the query.

7. Create a query that lists the MemberID, FirstName, LastName, OptionBegin, OptionDescription, and OptionCost fields for customers who signed up with Beauty To Go between January 1, 2017 and January 31, 2017. Save the query as **JanuaryOptions**, run the query, and then close it.

8. Create a query that lists all customers who live in Celebration and whose options end on or after 4/1/2017. Display the following fields from the Member table in the query results: MemberID, FirstName, LastName, Phone, and OptionEnd. (*Hint*: The City field values should not appear in the query results.) Sort the query results in ascending order by last name. Save the query as **CelebrationAndEndDate**, run the query, and then close it.

9. Copy and paste the CelebrationAndEndDate query to create a new query named **CelebrationOrEndDate**. Modify the new query so that it lists all members who live in Celebration or whose memberships expire on or after 4/1/2017. Display the City field values in the query results following the Phone field values, and sort the query results in ascending order by city (this should be the only sort in the query). Save and run the query.

10. Change the size of the font in the CelebrationOrEndDate query datasheet to 14 points. Resize columns, as necessary, so that all field values and column headings are visible.

11. Change the alternate row color in the CelebrationOrEndDate query datasheet to the Theme Color named Green, Accent 6, Lighter 80%, and then save and close the query.

12. Create a query that calculates the lowest, highest, and average cost for all options using the field names **LowestCost**, **HighestCost**, and **AverageCost**, respectively. Set the Caption property for each field to include a space between the two words in the field name. Run the query, resize all columns in the datasheet to their best fit, save the query as **CostStatistics**, and then close it.

13. Copy and paste the CostStatistics query to create a new query named **CostStatisticsByZip**.

14. Modify the CostStatisticsByZip query to display the same statistics grouped by Zip, with Zip appearing as the first field. (*Hint*: Add the Member table to the query.) Run the query, and then save and close it.

15. Compact and repair the Beauty database, and then close it.

Case Problem 2

Data File needed for this Case Problem: Programming.accdb (*cont. from Module 2*)

Programming Pros   After reviewing the Programming database, Brent Hovis wants to modify some records and then view specific information about the students, tutors, and contracts for his tutoring services company. He asks you to update and query the Programming database to perform these tasks. Complete the following:

1. Open the **Programming** database you created and worked with in previous modules, and then click the Enable Content button next to the security warning, if necessary.

2. In the **Tutor** table, change the following information for the record with TutorID 1048: Major is **Computer Science** and Year In School is **Graduate**. Close the table.

3. In the **Student** table, find the record with the StudentID RAM4025, and then delete the related record in the subdatasheet for this student. Delete the record for StudentID RAM4025, and then close the Student table.

4. Create a query based on the Student table that includes the LastName, FirstName, and CellPhone fields, in that order. Save the query as **StudentCellList**, and then run the query.

5. In the results of the StudentCellList query, change the cell phone number for Hidalgo Hickman to **919-301-2209**. Close the query.

6. Create a query based on the Tutor and Contract tables. Display the LastName field from the Tutor table, and the StudentID, ContractDate, SessionType, Length, and Cost fields, in that order, from the Contract table. Sort first in ascending order by the tutor's last name, and then in ascending order by the StudentID. Save the query as **SessionsByTutor**, run the query, and then close it.

7. Copy and paste the SessionsByTutor query to create a new query named **GroupSessions**. Modify the new query so that it displays the same information for records with a Group session type only. Do not display the SessionType field values in the query results. Save and run the query, and then close it.

8. Create and save a query that produces the results shown in Figure 3-44. Close the query when you are finished.

CREATE

Figure 3-44	RaleighPrivate query results

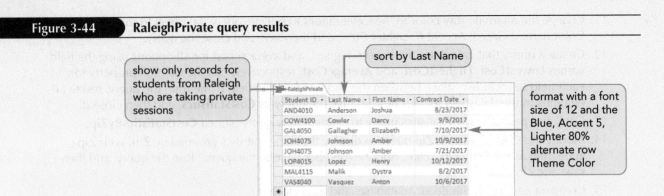

show only records for students from Raleigh who are taking private sessions

sort by Last Name

format with a font size of 12 and the Blue, Accent 5, Lighter 80% alternate row Theme Color

9. Create and save a query that produces the results shown in Figure 3-45. Close the query when you are finished.

Figure 3-45	CaryOrSemi query results

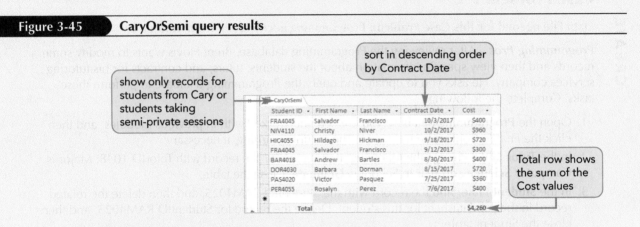

sort in descending order by Contract Date

show only records for students from Cary or students taking semi-private sessions

Total row shows the sum of the Cost values

10. Create and save a query to display statistics for the Cost field, as shown in Figure 3-46. Close the query when you are finished.

Figure 3-46	CostStatistics query results

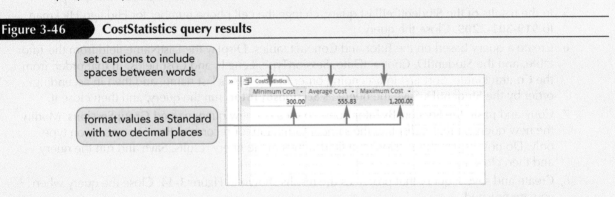

set captions to include spaces between words

format values as Standard with two decimal places

11. Copy and paste the CostStatistics query to create a new query named **CostStatisticsByCity**.

12. Modify the CostStatisticsByCity query to display the same statistics grouped by City, with City appearing as the first field. (*Hint*: Add the Student table to the query.) Run the query, and then save and close it.

13. Compact and repair the Programming database, and then close it.

Case Problem 3

CHALLENGE

Data File needed for this Case Problem: Center.accdb (*cont. from Module 2*)

Diane's Community Center   Diane Coleman needs to modify some records in the Center database, and then she wants to find specific information about the patrons, donations, and auction items for her not-for-profit community center. Diane asks you to help her update the database and create queries to find the information she needs. Complete the following:

1. Open the **Center** database you created and worked with in previous modules, and then click the Enable Content button next to the security warning, if necessary.

2. In the **Patron** table, delete the record with PatronID 3024. (*Hint*: Delete the related records in the Donation subdatasheet first.) Close the Patron table without saving changes to the table layout.

3. Create a query based on the Auction and Donation tables that includes the AuctionID, DonationID, DonationDate, and Description fields, in that order. Save the query as **AuctionItemsByDate**, and then run it.

4. Modify the AuctionItemsByDate query design so that it sorts records in ascending order first by DonationDate and then by Description. Save and run the query.

5. In the AuctionItemsByDate query datasheet, find the record for the auction item with Auction ID 250, and then change the description for this item to **New scooter**. Close the query.

6. Create a query that displays the PatronID, FirstName, and LastName fields from the Patron table, and the Description and DonationValue fields from the Donation table for all donations over $150. Sort the query in ascending order by donation value. Save the query as **LargeDonations**, run the query, and then close it.

7. Copy and paste the LargeDonations query to create a new query named **LargeCashDonations**.

⊕ **Explore** 8. Modify the LargeCashDonations query to display only those records with donations valued at more than $150 in cash. Do not include the Description field values in the query results. Use the query datasheet to calculate the average cash donation. Save and close the query.

9. Create a query that displays the PatronID, FirstName, and LastName fields from the Patron table, and the AuctionID, AuctionDate, and MinPrice fields from the Auction table. Specify that the results show records for only those items with a minimum price greater than $150. Save the query as **ExpensiveAuctionItems**, and then run the query.

10. Filter the results of the ExpensiveAuctionItems query datasheet to display records with an auction date of 10/14/2017 only.

⊕ **Explore** 11. Format the datasheet of the ExpensiveAuctionItems query so that it does not display gridlines, uses an alternate row Standard Color of Maroon 2, and displays a font size of 12. (*Hint*: Use the Gridlines button in the Text Formatting group on the Home tab to select the appropriate gridlines option.) Resize the columns to display the complete field names and values, if necessary. Save and close the query.

⊕ **Explore** 12. Create a query that displays the PatronID, FirstName, and LastName fields from the Patron table, and the Description, DonationDate, and DonationValue fields from the Donation table. Specify that the query include records for noncash donations only or for donations made in the month of September 2017. Sort the records first in ascending order by the patron's last name, and then in descending order by the donation value. Save the query as **NonCashOrSeptemberDonations**, run the query, and then close it.

13. Copy and paste the NonCashOrSeptemberDonations query to create a new query named **DonationsAfterStorageCharge**.

⊕ **Explore** 14. Modify the DonationsAfterStorageCharge query so that it displays records for noncash donations made on all dates. Create a calculated field named **NetDonation** that displays the results of subtracting $3.50 from the DonationValue field values to account for the cost of storing each noncash donated item. Set the Caption property **Net Donation** for the calculated field. Display the results in ascending order by donation value and not sorted on any other field. Run the query, and then modify it to format both the DonationValue field and the calculated field as Currency with two decimal places. Run the query again, and resize the columns in the datasheet to their best fit, as necessary. Save and close the query.

⊕ **Explore** 15. Create a query based on the **Donation** table that displays the sum, average, and count of the DonationValue field for all donations. Then complete the following:

a. Specify field names of **TotalDonations**, **AverageDonation**, and **NumberOfDonations**. Then specify captions to include spaces between words.

b. Save the query as **DonationStatistics**, and then run it. Resize the query datasheet columns to their best fit.

c. Modify the field properties so that the values in the Total Donations and Average Donation columns display two decimal places and the Standard format. Run the query again, and then save and close the query.

d. Copy and paste the DonationStatistics query to create a new query named **DonationStatisticsByDescription**.

e. Modify the DonationStatisticsByDescription query to display the sum, average, and count of the DonationValue field for all donations grouped by Description, with Description appearing as the first field. Sort the records in descending order by Total Donations. Save, run, and then close the query.

16. Compact and repair the Center database, and then close it.

Case Problem 4

Data Files needed for this Case Problem: Appalachia.accdb (cont. from Module 2) and HikeApp.accdb

Hike Appalachia   Molly and Bailey Johnson need your help to maintain and analyze data about the hikers, reservations, and tours for their hiking tour business. Additionally, you'll troubleshoot some problems in another database containing tour information. Complete the following:

1. Open the **Appalachia** database you created and worked with in previous modules, and then click the Enable Content button next to the security warning, if necessary.

2. In the **Hiker** table, change the phone number for Wilbur Sanders to **828-910-2058**, and then close the table.

3. Create a query based on the Tour table that includes the TourName, Hours, PricePerPerson, and TourType fields, in that order. Sort in ascending order based on the PricePerPerson field values. Save the query as **ToursByPrice**, and then run the query.

TROUBLESHOOT

4. Use the ToursByPrice query datasheet to display the total Price Per Person for the tours. Save and close the query.

5. Create a query that displays the HikerLast, City, and State fields from the Hiker table, and the ReservationID, TourDate, and People fields from the Reservation table. Save the query as **HikerTourDates**, and then run the query. Change the alternate row color in the query datasheet to the Theme Color Blue, Accent 1, Lighter 80%. In Datasheet view, use an AutoFilter to sort the query results from oldest to newest Tour Date. Save and close the query.

6. Create a query that displays the HikerFirst, HikerLast, City, ReservationID, TourID, and TourDate fields for all guests from North Carolina (NC). Do not include the State field in the query results. Sort the query in ascending order by the guest's last name. Save the query as **NorthCarolinaHikers** and then run it. Close the query.

7. Create a query that displays data from all three tables in the database as follows: the HikerLast, City, and State fields from the Hiker table; the TourDate field from the Reservation table; and the TourName and TourType fields from the Tour table. Specify that the query select only those records for guests from West Virginia (WV) or guests who are taking climbing tours. Sort the query in ascending order by Tour Name. Save the query as **WestVirginiaOrClimbing** and then run the query. Resize datasheet columns to their best fit, as necessary, and then save and close the query.

8. Copy and paste the **WestVirginiaOrClimbing** query to create a new query named **SouthCarolinaAndSeptember**.

9. Modify the **SouthCarolinaAndSeptember** query to select all guests from South Carolina (SC) who are taking a tour starting sometime in the month of September 2017. Do not include the State field values in the query results. Run the query. Resize datasheet columns to their best fit, as necessary, and then save and close the query.

10. Create a query that displays the ReservationID, TourDate, and People fields from the Reservation table, and the TourName and PricePerPerson fields from the Tour table for all reservations with a People field value greater than 1. Save the query as **ReservationCosts**. Add a field to the query named **TotalCost** that displays the results of multiplying the People field values by the PricePerPerson field values. Set the Caption property **Total Cost** for the calculated field. Display the results in descending order by TotalCost. Run the query. Modify the query by formatting the TotalCost field to show 0 decimal places. Run the query, resize datasheet columns to their best fit, as necessary, and then save and close the query.

11. Create a query based on the Tour table that determines the minimum, average, and maximum price per person for all tours. Then complete the following:

    a. Specify field names of **LowestPrice**, **AveragePrice**, and **HighestPrice**.

    b. Set the Caption property for each field to include a space between the two words in the field name.

    c. Save the query as **PriceStatistics**, and then run the query.

    d. In Design view, specify the Standard format and two decimal places for each column.

    e. Run the query, resize all the datasheet columns to their best fit, save your changes, and then close the query.

    f. Create a copy of the PriceStatistics query named **PriceStatisticsByTourType**.

    g. Modify the PriceStatisticsByTourType query to display the price statistics grouped by TourType, with TourType appearing as the first field. Save your changes, and then run and close the query.

    h. Compact and repair the Appalachia database, and then close it.

⚙ **Troubleshoot** 12. Open the **HikeApp** database located in the Access1 > Case4 folder provided with your Data Files, and then click the Enable Content button next to the security warning, if necessary. Run the ReservationByDateAndState query in the HikeApp database. The query is not producing the desired results. Fix the query so that the data from the Reservation table is listed first and the data is sorted only by TourDate in ascending order. Save and close the corrected query.

⚙ **Troubleshoot** 13. Run the NCGuestsFewerPeople query, which displays no records in the results. This query is supposed to show data for guests from North Carolina (NC) with fewer than four people in their booking. Find and correct the errors in the query design, run the query, and then close it.

⚙ **Troubleshoot** 14. Run the GeorgiaOrOctStart query. This query should display the records for all guests who are from Georgia (GA) or whose tour date is on or after 10/1/2017. Find and correct the errors in the query design, run the query, and then close it.

15. Compact and repair the HikeApp database, and then close it.

ACCESS

OBJECTIVES

Session 4.1
- Create a form using the Form Wizard
- Apply a theme to a form
- Add a picture to a form
- Change the color of text on a form
- Find and maintain data using a form
- Preview and print selected form records
- Create a form with a main form and a subform

Session 4.2
- Create a report using the Report Wizard
- Apply a theme to a report
- Change the alignment of field values on a report
- Move and resize fields in a report
- Insert a picture in a report
- Change the color of text on a report
- Apply conditional formatting in a report
- Preview and print a report

Creating Forms and Reports

Using Forms and Reports to Display Owner, Animal, and Visit Data

Case | *Riverview Veterinary Care Center*

Kimberly Johnson wants to continue enhancing the Riverview database to make it easier for her staff to enter, locate, and maintain data. In particular, she wants the database to include a form based on the Owner table that staff can use to enter and change data about the owners of the animals that the care center sees. She also wants the database to include a form that shows data from both the Owner and Animal tables at the same time. This form will show the basic information for each owner along with the corresponding animal data, providing a complete picture of Riverview Veterinary Care Center clients and their animals.

In addition, she would like the database to include a report of owner and visit data so that she and other staff members will have printed output when completing analyses of the owners who are clients of the care center and planning strategies for making additional veterinary services available to them. She wants the report to be formatted professionally and easy to use.

In this module, you will create the forms and reports in the Riverview database for Kimberly and her staff.

STARTING DATA FILES

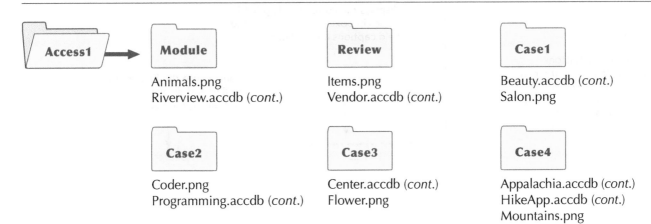

Access1 → Module
Animals.png
Riverview.accdb (*cont.*)

Review
Items.png
Vendor.accdb (*cont.*)

Case1
Beauty.accdb (*cont.*)
Salon.png

Case2
Coder.png
Programming.accdb (*cont.*)

Case3
Center.accdb (*cont.*)
Flower.png

Case4
Appalachia.accdb (*cont.*)
HikeApp.accdb (*cont.*)
Mountains.png

Session 4.1 Visual Overview:

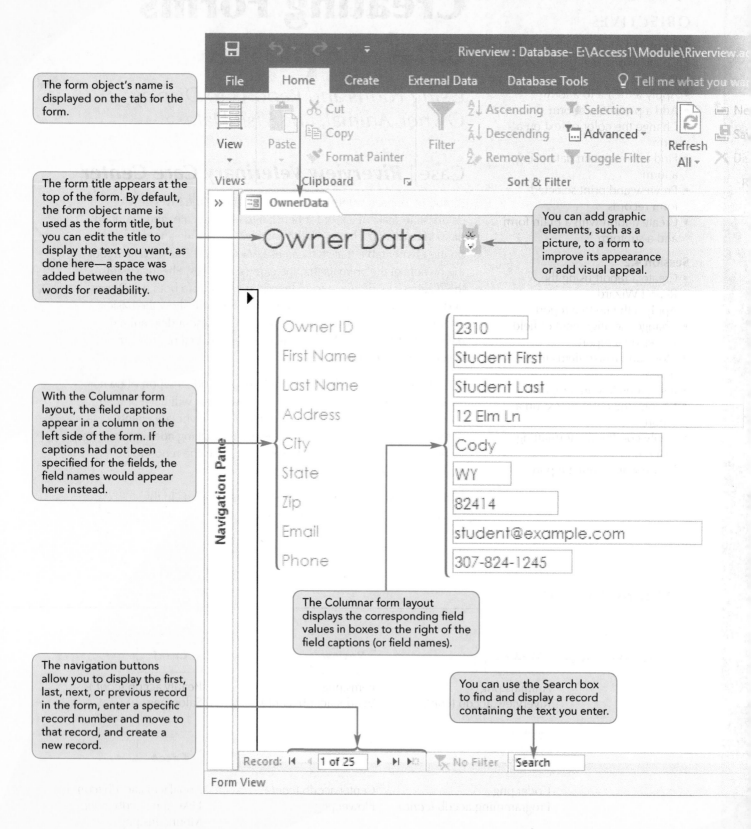

The form object's name is displayed on the tab for the form.

The form title appears at the top of the form. By default, the form object name is used as the form title, but you can edit the title to display the text you want, as done here—a space was added between the two words for readability.

You can add graphic elements, such as a picture, to a form to improve its appearance or add visual appeal.

With the Columnar form layout, the field captions appear in a column on the left side of the form. If captions had not been specified for the fields, the field names would appear here instead.

The Columnar form layout displays the corresponding field values in boxes to the right of the field captions (or field names).

The navigation buttons allow you to display the first, last, next, or previous record in the form, enter a specific record number and move to that record, and create a new record.

You can use the Search box to find and display a record containing the text you enter.

Form Displayed in Form View

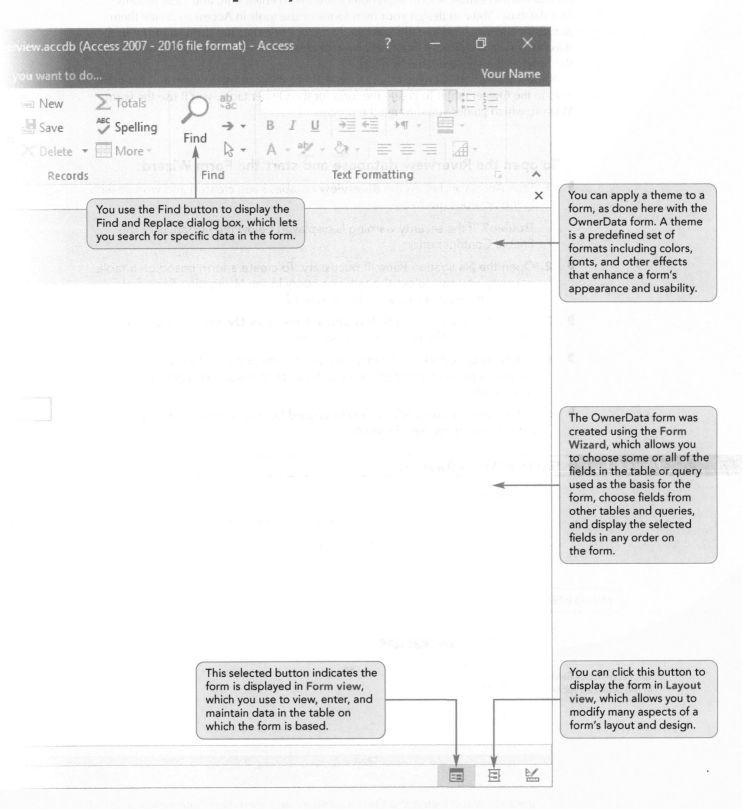

You use the Find button to display the Find and Replace dialog box, which lets you search for specific data in the form.

You can apply a theme to a form, as done here with the OwnerData form. A theme is a predefined set of formats including colors, fonts, and other effects that enhance a form's appearance and usability.

The OwnerData form was created using the Form Wizard, which allows you to choose some or all of the fields in the table or query used as the basis for the form, choose fields from other tables and queries, and display the selected fields in any order on the form.

This selected button indicates the form is displayed in Form view, which you use to view, enter, and maintain data in the table on which the form is based.

You can click this button to display the form in Layout view, which allows you to modify many aspects of a form's layout and design.

Creating a Form Using the Form Wizard

As you learned earlier, a form is an object you use to enter, edit, and view records in a database. You can design your own forms or use tools in Access to create them automatically. You have already used the Form tool to create the VisitData form in the Riverview database. Recall that the Form tool creates a form automatically, using all the fields in the selected table or query.

Kimberly asks you to create a new form that her staff can use to view and maintain data in the Owner table. To create the form for the Owner table, you'll use the Form Wizard, which guides you through the process.

To open the Riverview database and start the Form Wizard:

▶ **1.** Start Access and open the **Riverview** database you created and worked with in the previous modules.

   Trouble? If the security warning is displayed below the ribbon, click the Enable Content button.

▶ **2.** Open the Navigation Pane, if necessary. To create a form based on a table or query, you can select the table or query in the Navigation Pane first, or you can select it using the Form Wizard.

▶ **3.** In the Tables section of the Navigation Pane, click **Owner** to select the Owner table as the basis for the new form.

▶ **4.** On the ribbon, click the **Create** tab. The Forms group on the Create tab provides options for creating various types of forms and designing your own forms.

▶ **5.** In the Forms group, click the **Form Wizard** button. The first Form Wizard dialog box opens. See Figure 4-1.

| Figure 4-1 | First Form Wizard dialog box |

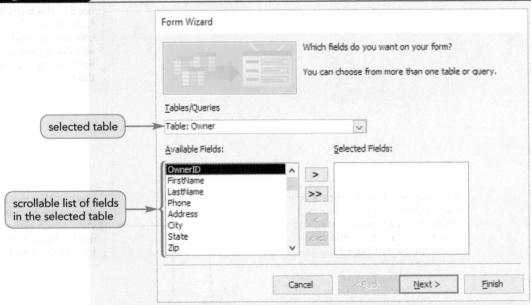

selected table

scrollable list of fields
in the selected table

Because you selected the Owner table in the Navigation Pane before starting the Form Wizard, this table is selected in the Tables/Queries box, and the fields for the Owner table are listed in the Available Fields box.

Kimberly wants the form to display all the fields in the Owner table, but in a different order. She would like the Phone field to appear at the bottom of the form so that it stands out, making it easier for someone who needs to call an animal's owner to use the form to quickly locate the phone number.

To create the form using the Form Wizard:

▶ **1.** Click the >> button to move all the fields to the Selected Fields box. Next, you need to position the Phone field so it will appear as the bottom-most field on the form. To accomplish this, you will first remove the Phone field and then add it back as the last selected field.

▶ **2.** In the Selected Fields box, click the **Phone** field, and then click the < button to move the field back to the Available Fields box.

Because a new field is always added after the selected field in the Selected Fields box, you need to first select the last field in the list and then move the Phone field back to the Selected Fields box so it will be the last field on the form.

▶ **3.** In the Selected Fields box, click the **Email** field.

▶ **4.** With the Phone field selected in the Available Fields box, click the > button to move the Phone field to the end of the list in the Selected Fields box.

▶ **5.** Click the **Next** button to display the second Form Wizard dialog box, in which you select a layout for the form. See Figure 4-2.

| Figure 4-2 | Choosing a layout for the form |

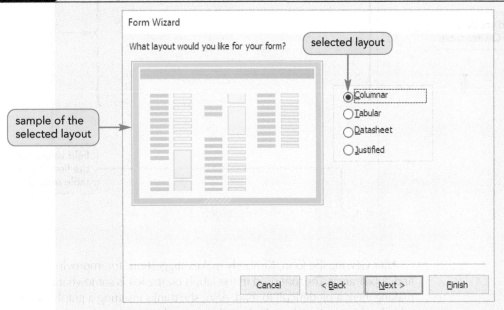

The layout choices are Columnar, Tabular, Datasheet, and Justified. A sample of the selected layout appears on the left side of the dialog box.

▶ **6.** Click each of the option buttons and review the corresponding sample layout.

The Tabular and Datasheet layouts display the fields from multiple records at one time, whereas the Columnar and Justified layouts display the fields from one record at a time. Kimberly thinks the Columnar layout is the appropriate arrangement for displaying and updating data in the table, so that anyone using the form can focus on just one owner record at a time.

7. Click the **Columnar** option button (if necessary), and then click the **Next** button.

The third and final Form Wizard dialog box shows the Owner table's name as the default form name. "Owner" is also the default title that will appear on the tab for the form.

You'll use "OwnerData" as the form name, and, because you don't need to change the form's design at this point, you'll display the form.

8. Click to position the insertion point to the right of Owner in the box, type **Data**, and then click the **Finish** button.

Close the Navigation Pane to display only the Form window. The completed form is displayed in Form view, displaying the values for the first record in the Owner table. The Columnar layout you selected places the field captions in labels on the left and the corresponding field values in boxes on the right, which vary in width depending on the size of the field. See Figure 4-3.

Figure 4-3	OwnerData form in Form view

After viewing the form, Kimberly makes suggestions for improving the form's readability and appearance. The font used in the labels on the left is somewhat light in color and small, making them a bit difficult to read. Also, she thinks inserting a graphic on the form would add visual interest, and modifying other form elements—such as the color of the title text— would improve the look of the form. You can make all of these changes working with the form in Layout view.

Modifying a Form's Design in Layout View

After you create a form, you might need to modify its design to improve its appearance or to make the form easier to use. You cannot make any design changes in Form view. However, Layout view displays the form as it appears in Form view while allowing you to modify the form's design. Because you can see the form and its data while you are modifying the form, Layout view makes it easy for you to see the results of any design changes you make.

The first modification you'll make to the OwnerData form is to change its appearance by applying a theme.

Applying a Theme to a Database Object

By default, the objects you create in a database are formatted with the Office theme. A theme provides a design scheme for the colors and fonts used in the database objects. Access, like other Microsoft Office programs, provides many built-in themes, including the Office theme, making it easy for you to create objects with a unified look. You can also create a customized theme if none of the built-in themes suit your needs.

Sometimes a theme works well for one database object but is not as suitable for other objects in that database. Therefore, when applying a theme to an object, you can choose to apply the theme just to the open object or to objects of a particular type, or you can choose to apply the theme to all the existing objects in the database and set it as the default theme for any new objects that might be created.

To change a form's appearance, you can easily apply a new theme to it.

REFERENCE

Applying a Theme to Database Objects

- Display the object in Layout view.
- In the Themes group on the Form Layout Tools Design tab or Report Layout Tools Design tab, click the Themes button.
- In the Themes gallery, click the theme you want to apply to all objects; or, right-click the theme to display the shortcut menu, and then choose to apply the theme to the current object only or to all matching objects.

Kimberly would like to see if the OwnerData form's appearance can be improved with a different theme. To apply a theme, you first need to switch to Layout view.

To apply a theme to the OwnerData form:

▶ **1.** On the ribbon, make sure the Home tab is displayed.

▶ **2.** In the Views group, click the **View** button. The form is displayed in Layout view. See Figure 4-4.

Figure 4-4   **Form displayed in Layout view**

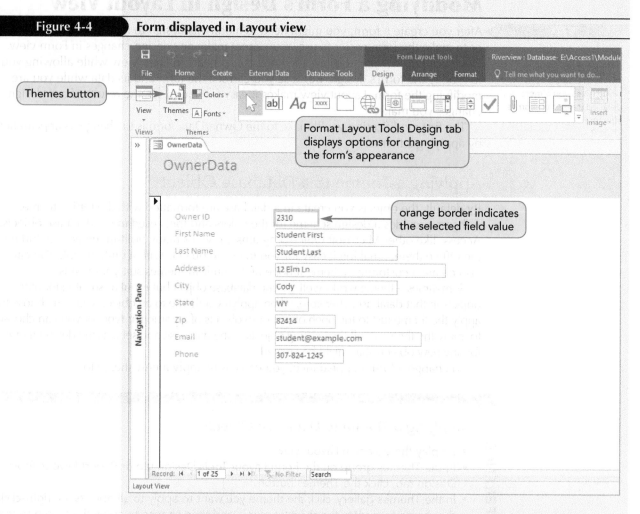

Trouble? If the Field List or Property Sheet opens on the right side of the program window, close it before continuing.

In Layout view, an orange border identifies the currently selected element on the form. In this case, the field value for the OwnerID field, 2310, is selected. You need to apply a theme to the OwnerData form.

3. On the Form Layout Tools Design tab, in the Themes group, click the **Themes** button. A gallery opens showing the available themes for the form. See Figure 4-5.

Figure 4-5   **Themes gallery**

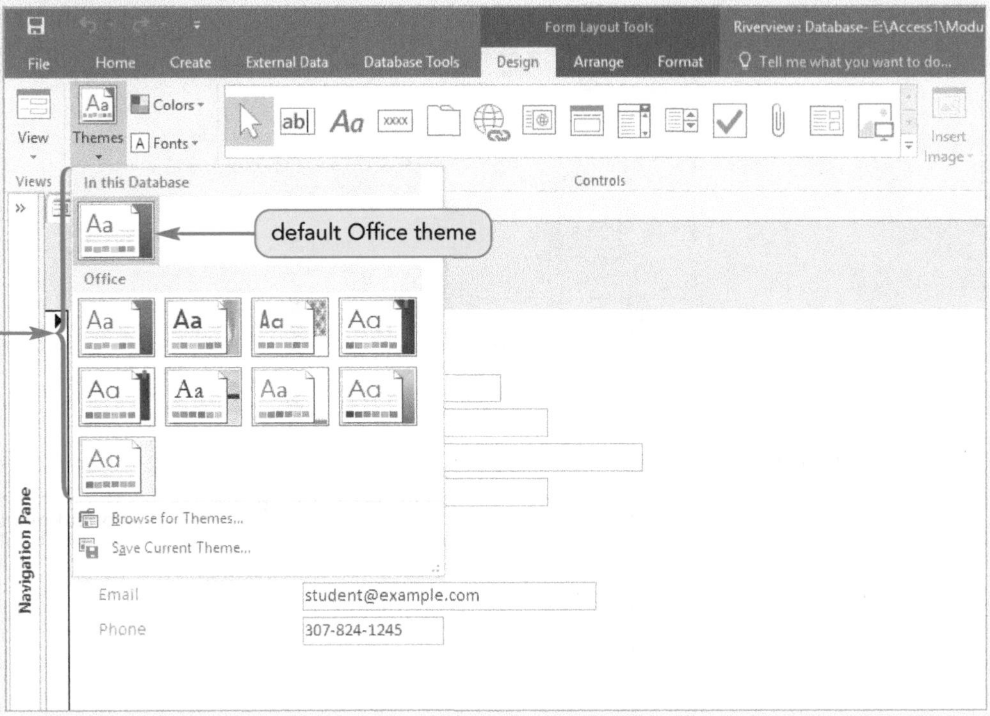

TIP

Themes other than the Office theme are listed in alphabetical order in the gallery.

The Office theme, the default theme currently applied in the database, is listed in the "In this Database" section and is also the first theme listed in the section containing other themes. You can point to each theme in the gallery to see its name in a ScreenTip. Also, when you point to a theme, the Live Preview feature shows the effect of applying the theme to the open object.

4. In the gallery, point to each of the themes to see how they would format the OwnerData form. Notice the changes in color and font type of the text, for example.

Kimberly likes the Wisp theme because of its light gray color in the title area at the top and its larger font size, which makes the text in the form easier to read.

5. Right-click the **Wisp** theme. A shortcut menu opens with options for applying the theme. See Figure 4-6.

Figure 4-6 Shortcut menu for applying the theme

Figure 4-6 | Shortcut menu for applying the theme

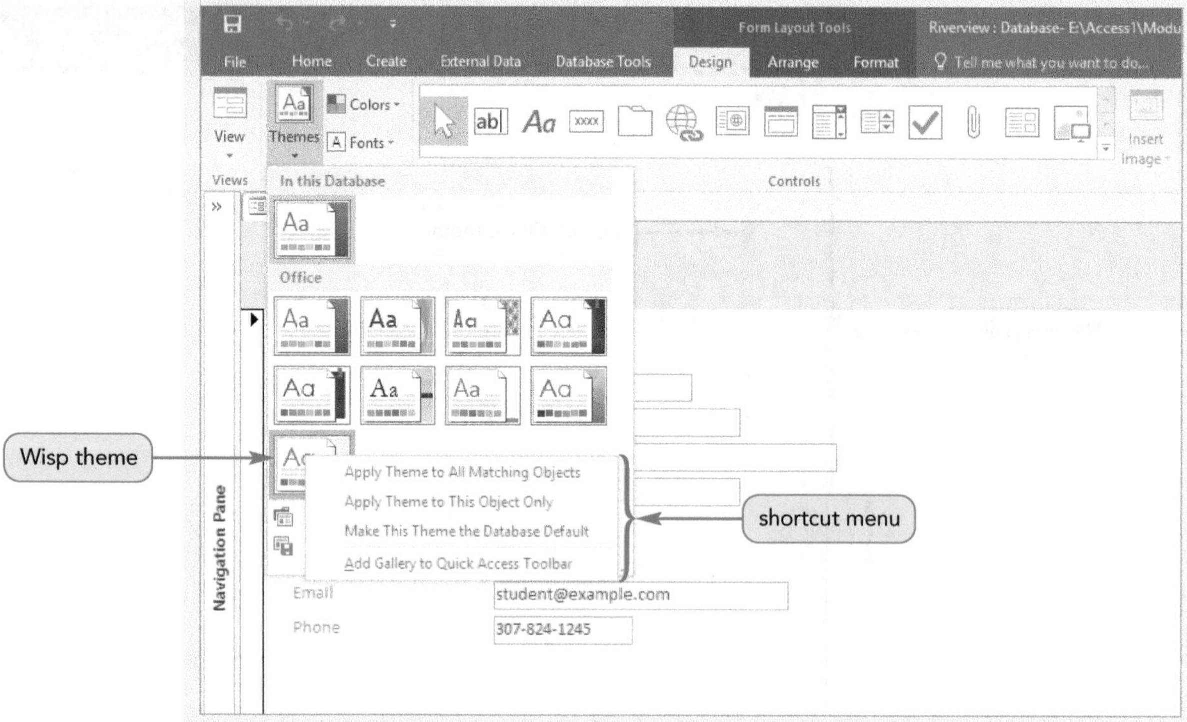

The menu provides options for applying the theme to all matching objects—for example, all the forms in the database—or to the current object only. You can also choose to make the theme the default theme in the database, which means any new objects you create will be formatted with the selected theme. Because Kimberly is not sure if all forms in the Riverview database will look better with the Wisp theme, she asks you to apply it only to the OwnerData form.

Choose this option to avoid applying the theme to other forms in the database.

6. On the shortcut menu, click **Apply Theme to This Object Only**.

The gallery closes, and the Wisp theme's colors and fonts are applied to the form.

Trouble? If you choose the wrong option by mistake, you might have applied the selected theme to other forms and/or reports in the database. Repeat Steps 3 through 6 to apply the Wisp theme to the OwnerData form. You can also follow the same process to reapply the default Office theme to the other forms and reports in the Riverview database, as directed by your instructor.

Working with Themes

INSIGHT

Themes provide a quick and easy way for you to format the objects in a database with a consistent look, which is a good design principle to follow. In general, all objects of a type in a database—for example, all forms—should have a consistent design. However, keep in mind that when you select a theme in the Themes gallery and choose the option to apply the theme to all matching objects or to make the theme the default for the database, it might be applied to all the existing forms and reports in the database as well as to new forms and reports you create. Although this approach ensures a consistent design, it can cause problems. For example, if you have already created a form or report and its design is suitable, applying a theme that includes a larger font size could cause the text in labels and field value boxes to be cut off or to extend into other objects on the form or report. The colors applied by the theme could also interfere with elements on existing forms and reports. To handle these unintended results, you would have to spend time checking the existing forms and reports and fixing any problems introduced by applying the theme. A better approach is to select the option "Apply Theme to This Object Only," available on the shortcut menu for a theme in the Themes gallery, for each existing form and report. If the newly applied theme causes problems for any individual form or report, you can then reapply the original theme to return the object to its original design.

Next, you will add a picture to the form for visual interest. The picture, which is included on various flyers and other owner correspondence for Riverview Veterinary Care Center, is a small graphic of a dog and a cat.

Adding a Picture to a Form

A picture is one of many controls you can add and modify on a form. A **control** is an item on a form, report, or other database object that you can manipulate to modify the object's appearance. The controls you can add and modify in Layout view for a form are available in the Controls group and the Header/Footer group on the Form Layout Tools Design tab. The picture you need to add is contained in a file named Animals.png, which is located in the Access1 > Module folder provided with your Data Files.

To add the picture to the form:

▶ **1.** Make sure the form is still displayed in Layout view and that the Form Layout Tools Design tab is active.

▶ **2.** In the Header/Footer group, click the **Logo** button. The Insert Picture dialog box opens.

▶ **3.** Navigate to the **Access1 > Module** folder provided with your Data Files, click the **Animals** file, and then click the **OK** button. The picture appears on top of the form's title. See Figure 4-7.

Figure 4-7   **Form with picture added**

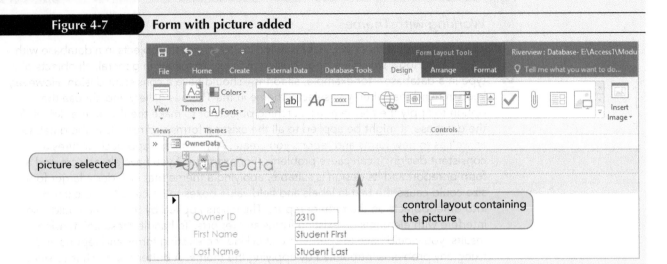

picture selected

control layout containing the picture

A solid orange border surrounds the picture, indicating it is selected. The picture is placed in a **control layout**, which is a set of controls grouped together in a form or report so that you can manipulate the set as a single control. The dotted blue outline indicates the control layout. The easiest way to move the picture off the form title is to first remove it from the control layout. Doing so allows you to move the picture independently.

▶ 4. Right-click the picture to open the shortcut menu, point to **Layout**, and then click **Remove Layout**. The dotted blue outline no longer appears, and the picture is removed from the control layout. Now you can move the picture to the right of the form title.

▶ 5. Position the pointer ⬚ on the picture, and then drag to the right of the form title. Although the image may not be visible while dragging, you can use the position of the pointer as a guide to where the image will be placed.

▶ 6. When the pointer is roughly one-half inch to the right of the form's title, release the mouse button. The picture is positioned to the right of the form title.

▶ 7. Click in a blank area to the right of the field values in the form to deselect the picture. See Figure 4-8.

Trouble? Don't be concerned if the picture is not in the exact location as the one shown in Figure 4-8. Just make sure the picture is not blocking any part of the form title and that it appears to the right of the form title and within the gray shaded area at the top of the form.

TIP

You can resize a selected image by dragging a corner of the orange selection border.

Figure 4-8   **Form with theme applied and picture repositioned**

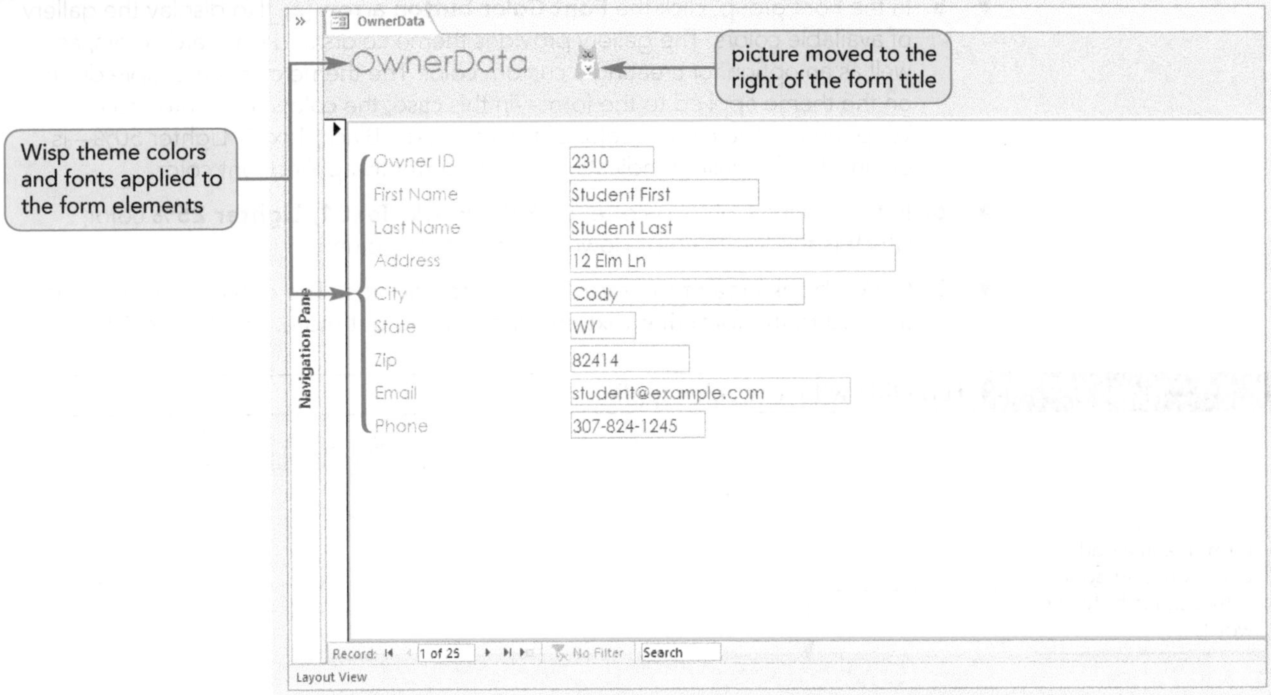

OwnerData

OwnerData ← picture moved to the right of the form title

Wisp theme colors and fonts applied to the form elements

Owner ID	2310
First Name	Student First
Last Name	Student Last
Address	12 Elm Ln
City	Cody
State	WY
Zip	82414
Email	student@example.com
Phone	307-824-1245

Navigation Pane

Record: ◄ ◄ 1 of 25 ► ►I ►☒ ☒ No Filter   Search

Layout View

Next, Kimberly asks you to change the color of the form title to a darker color so that it will stand out more on the form.

Changing the Color of Text on a Form

The Font group on the Form Layout Tools Format tab provides many options you can use to change the appearance of text on a form. For example, you can bold, italicize, and underline text; change the font, font color, and font size; and change the alignment of text. Before you change the color of the "OwnerData" title on the form, you'll change the title to two words so it is easier to read.

To change the form title's text and color:

1. Click the **OwnerData** form title. An orange border surrounds the title, indicating it is selected.

TIP

Changing the form's title does not affect the form object name; it is still OwnerData, as shown on the object tab.

2. Click between the letters "r" and "D" to position the insertion point, and then press the **spacebar**. The title on the form is now "Owner Data," but the added space caused the words to appear on two lines. You can fix this by resizing the box containing the title.

3. Position the pointer on the right edge of the box containing the form title until the pointer changes to ↔, and then drag to the right until the word "Data" appears on the same line as the word "Owner."

Trouble? You might need to repeat Step 3 until the title appears on one line. Also, you might have to move the picture further to the right to make room for the title.

Next you will change the title's font color.

4. On the ribbon, click the **Form Layout Tools Format** tab.

5. In the Font group, click the **Font Color button arrow** to display the gallery of available colors. The gallery provides theme colors and standard colors, as well as an option for creating a custom color. The theme colors available depend on the theme applied to the form—in this case, the colors are related to the Wisp theme. The current color of the title text—Black, Text 1, Lighter 50%—is outlined in the gallery, indicating it is the currently applied font color.

6. In the Theme Colors palette, click the **Black, Text 1, Lighter 25%** color, which is the fourth color down in the second column.

7. Click a blank area of the form to deselect the title. The darker black color is applied to the form title text, making it stand out more. See Figure 4-9.

Figure 4-9	Form title with new color applied

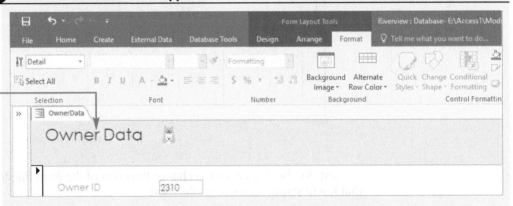

form title in a darker black font and edited with a space between words

8. On the Quick Access Toolbar, click the **Save** button to save the modified form.

9. On the status bar, click the **Form View** button to display the form in Form view.

Kimberly is pleased with the modified appearance of the form. Later, she plans to revise the existing VisitData form and make the same changes to it, so that it matches the appearance of the OwnerData form.

Written Communication: Understanding the Importance of Form Design

Similar to any document, a form must convey written information clearly and effectively. When you create a form, it's important to consider how the form will be used, so that its design will accommodate the needs of people using the form to view, enter, and maintain data. For example, if a form in a database is meant to mimic a paper form that users will enter data from, the form in the database should have the same fields in the same order as on the paper form. This will enable users to easily tab from one field to the next in the database form to enter the necessary information from the paper form. Also, it's important to include a meaningful title on the form to identify its purpose and to enhance the appearance of the form. A form that is visually appealing makes working with the database more user-friendly and can improve the readability of the form, thereby helping to prevent errors in data entry. Also, be sure to use a consistent design for the forms in your database whenever possible. Users will expect to see similar elements—titles, pictures, fonts, and so on—in each form contained in a database. A mix of form styles and elements among the forms in a database could lead to problems when working with the forms. Finally, make sure the text on your form does not contain any spelling or grammatical errors. By producing a well-designed and well-written form, you can help to ensure that users will be able to work with the form in a productive and efficient manner.

Navigating a Form

To view, navigate, and change data using a form, you need to display the form in Form view. As you learned earlier, you navigate a form in the same way that you navigate a table datasheet. Also, the same navigation mode and editing mode keyboard shortcuts you have used working with datasheets can also be used when working with a form.

Kimberly wants to view data in the Owner table. Before using the OwnerData form to display the specific information Kimberly wants to view, you will practice navigating between the fields in a record and navigating between records in the form. The OwnerData form is already displayed in Form view, so you can use it to navigate through the fields and records of the Owner table.

To navigate the OwnerData form:

▶ **1.** If necessary, click in the **Owner ID** field value box to make it current.

▶ **2.** Press the **Tab** key twice to move to the Last Name field value box, and then press the **End** key to move to the Phone field value box.

▶ **3.** Press the **Home** key to move back to the Owner ID field value box. The first record in the Owner table still appears in the form.

▶ **4.** Press the **Ctrl+End** keys to move to the Phone field value box for record 25, which is the last record in the table. The record number for the current record appears in the Current Record box between the navigation buttons at the bottom of the form.

▶ **5.** Click the **Previous record** button ◀ to move to the Phone field value box in record 24.

▶ **6.** Press the ↑ key twice to move to the Zip field value box in record 24.

▶ **7.** Click to position the insertion point within the word "Rascal" in the Address field value to switch to editing mode, press the **Home** key to move the insertion point to the beginning of the field value, and then press the **End** key to move the insertion point to the end of the field value.

▶ **8.** Click the **First record** button ◄ to move to the Address field value box in the first record. The entire field value is highlighted because you switched from editing mode to navigation mode.

▶ **9.** Click the **Next record** button ▶ to move to the Address field value box in record 2, the next record.

Kimberly wants to find the record for an owner named Thomas. The paper form containing all the original contact information for this owner was damaged. Other than the owner's first name, Kimberly knows only the street the owner lives on. You will use the OwnerData form to locate and view the complete record for this owner.

Finding Data Using a Form

As you learned earlier, the Find command lets you search for data in a datasheet so you can display only those records you want to view. You can also use the Find command to search for data in a form. You first choose a field to serve as the basis for the search by making that field the current field, and then you enter the value you want Access to match in the Find and Replace dialog box.

REFERENCE

Finding Data in a Form or Datasheet

- Open the form or datasheet, and then make the field you want to search the current field.
- On the Home tab, in the Find group, click the Find button to open the Find and Replace dialog box.
- In the Find What box, type the field value you want to find.
- Complete the remaining options, as necessary, to specify the type of search to conduct.
- Click the Find Next button to begin the search.
- Click the Find Next button to continue searching for the next match.
- Click the Cancel button to stop the search operation.

You need to find the record for the owner Kimberly wants to contact. The owner whose record she needs to find is named Thomas and he lives on Bobcat Trail. You'll search for this record using the Address field.

To find the record using the OwnerData form:

▶ **1.** Make sure the Address field value is still selected for the current record. This is the field you need to search.

You can search for a record that contains part of the address anywhere in the Address field value. Performing a partial search such as this is often easier than matching the entire field value and is useful when you don't know or can't remember the entire field value.

2. On the Home tab, in the Find group, click the **Find** button. The Find and Replace dialog box opens. The Look In box indicates that the current field (in this case, Address) will be searched. You'll search for records that contain the word "bobcat" in the address.

3. In the Find What box, type **bobcat**. Note that you do not have to enter the word as "Bobcat" with a capital letter "B" because the Match Case check box is not selected in the Find and Replace dialog box. The search will find any record containing the word "bobcat" with any combination of uppercase and lowercase letters.

4. Click the **Match** arrow to display the list of matching options, and then click **Any Part of Field**. The search will find any record that contains the word "bobcat" in any part of the Address field. See Figure 4-10.

| Figure 4-10 | Completed Find and Replace dialog box |

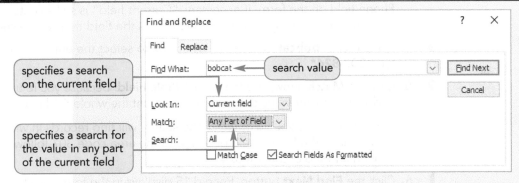

specifies a search on the current field

search value

specifies a search for the value in any part of the current field

5. Click the **Find Next** button. The Find and Replace dialog box remains open, and the OwnerData form now displays record 13, which is the record for Thomas Jones (OwnerID 2362). The word "Bobcat" is selected in the Address field value box because you searched for this word.

The search value you enter can be an exact value or it can include wildcard characters. A **wildcard character** is a placeholder you use when you know only part of a value or when you want to start or end with a specific character or match a certain pattern. Figure 4-11 shows the wildcard characters you can use when searching for data.

| Figure 4-11 | Wildcard characters |

Wildcard Character	Purpose	Example
*	Match any number of characters it can be used as the first and/or last character in the character string	th* *finds* the, that, this, therefore, *and so on*
?	Match any single alphabetic character	a?t *finds* act, aft, ant, apt, *and* art
[]	Match any single character within the brackets	a[fr]t *finds* aft *and* art *but not* act, ant, *or* apt
!	Match any character not within brackets	a[!fr]t *finds* act, ant, *and* apt *but not* aft *or* art
-	Match any one of a range of characters the range must be in ascending order (a to z, not z to a)	a[d-p]t *finds* aft, ant, *and* apt *but not* act *or* art
#	Match any single numeric character	#72 *finds* 072, 172, 272, 372, *and so on*

Next, to see how a wildcard works, you'll view the records for any owners with phone numbers that contain the exchange 824 as part of the phone number. The exchange consists of the three digits that follow the area code in the phone number. You could search for any record containing the digits 824 in any part of the Phone field, but this search would also find records with the digits 824 in any part of the phone number. To find only those records with the digits 824 as the exchange, you'll use the * wildcard character.

To find the records using the * wildcard character:

▶ **1.** Make sure the Find and Replace dialog box is still open.

▶ **2.** Click anywhere in the OwnerData form to make it active, and then press the **Tab** key until you reach the Phone field value box. This is the field you want to search.

▶ **3.** Click the title bar of the Find and Replace dialog box to make it active, and then drag the Find and Replace dialog box to the right so you can see the Phone field on the form, if necessary. "Current field" is still selected in the Look In box, meaning now the Phone field is the field that will be searched.

▶ **4.** Double-click **bobcat** in the Find What box to select the entire value, and then type **307-824***.

▶ **5.** Click the **Match** arrow, and then click **Whole Field**. Because you're using a wildcard character in the search value, you want the whole field to be searched.

With the settings you've entered, the search will find records in which any field value in the Phone field begins with the area code 307 followed by a hyphen and the exchange 824.

▶ **6.** Click the **Find Next** button. Record 15 displays in the form, which is the first record found for a customer with the exchange 824. Notice that the search process started from the point of the previously displayed record in the form, which was record 13.

▶ **7.** Click the **Find Next** button. Record 16 displays in the form, which is the next record found for a customer with the exchange 824.

▶ **8.** Click the **Find Next** button to display record 18, and then click the **Find Next** button again. Record 19 displays, the fourth record found.

▶ **9.** Click the **Find Next** button two more times to display records 21 and 24.

▶ **10.** Click the **Find Next** button again. Record 1 displays. Notice that the search process cycles back through the beginning of the records in the underlying table.

▶ **11.** Click the **Find Next** button. A dialog box opens, informing you that the search is finished.

▶ **12.** Click the **OK** button to close the dialog box, and then click the **Cancel** button to close the Find and Replace dialog box.

Kimberly has identified some owner updates she wants you to make. You'll use the OwnerData form to update the data in the Owner table.

Maintaining Table Data Using a Form

Maintaining data using a form is often easier than using a datasheet because you can focus on all the changes for a single record at one time. In Form view, you can edit the field values for a record, delete a record from the underlying table, or add a new record to the table.

Now you'll use the OwnerData form to make the changes Kimberly wants to the Owner table. First, you'll update the record for owner Sandra Pincher, who recently moved from Cody to Powell and provided a new mailing address. In addition to using the Find and Replace dialog box to locate a specific record, you can use the Search box to the right of the navigation buttons. You'll use the Search box to search for the owner's last name, Pincher, and display the owner record in the form.

To change the record using the OwnerData form:

1. To the right of the navigation buttons, click the **Search** box and then type **Pincher**. As soon as you start to type, Access begins searching through all fields in the records to match your entry. Record 3 (Sandra Pincher) is now current.

   You will first update the address in this record.

2. Select the current entry in the Address field value box, and then type **53 Verde Ln** to replace it.

3. Press the **Tab** key to select the city in the City field value box, and then type **Powell**.

4. Press the **Tab** key twice to move to and select the Zip field value, and then type **82440**. The updates to the record are complete. See Figure 4-12.

TIP

The pencil symbol appears in the upper-left corner of the form when the form is in editing mode.

Figure 4-12	Owner record after changing field values

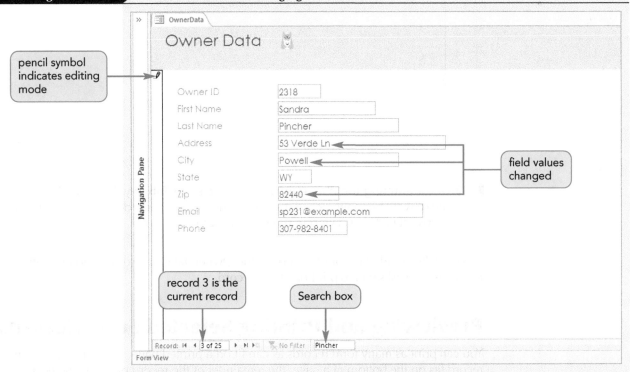

Next, Kimberly asks you to add a record for a new owner. This person indicated plans to bring a pet to the care center at a recent adoption fair in which Riverview Veterinary Care Center participated, but the owner has not yet provided information about the animal or scheduled an appointment. You'll use the OwnerData form to add the new record.

To add the new record using the OwnerData form:

▶ **1.** On the Home tab, in the Records group, click the **New** button. Record 26, the next available new record, becomes the current record. All field value boxes are empty (except the State field, which displays the default value of WY), and the insertion point is positioned in the Owner ID field value box.

▶ **2.** Refer to Figure 4-13 and enter the value shown for each field, pressing the **Tab** key to move from field to field.

| Figure 4-13 | Completed form for the new record |

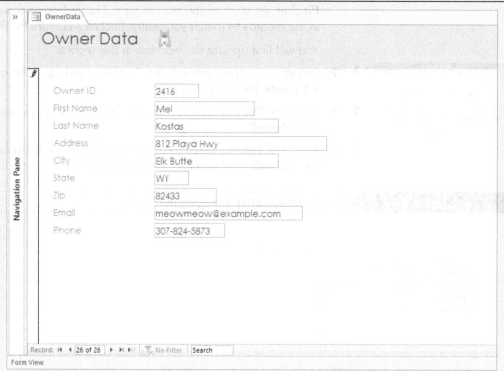

▶ **3.** After entering the Phone field value, press the **Tab** key. Record 27, the next available new record, becomes the current record, and the record for OwnerID 2416 is saved in the Owner table.

Kimberly would like a printed copy of the OwnerData form to show to her staff members. She asks you to print one form record.

Previewing and Printing Selected Form Records

You can print as many form records as can fit on a printed page. If only part of a form record fits on the bottom of a page, the remainder of the record prints on the next page. You can print all pages or a range of pages. In addition, you can print just the currently selected form record.

Kimberly asks you to use the OwnerData form to print the first record in the Owner table. Before you do, you'll preview the form record to see how it will look when printed.

To preview the form and print the data for record 1:

▶ 1. Click the **First record** button ◄ to display record 1 in the form. This is the record in which you have entered your first and last names.

▶ 2. Click the **File** tab to open Backstage view, click **Print** in the navigation bar, and then click **Print Preview**. The Print Preview window opens, showing the form records for the Owner table. Notice that each record appears in its own form and that shading is used to distinguish one record from another. See Figure 4-14.

Figure 4-14	Form records displayed in Print Preview

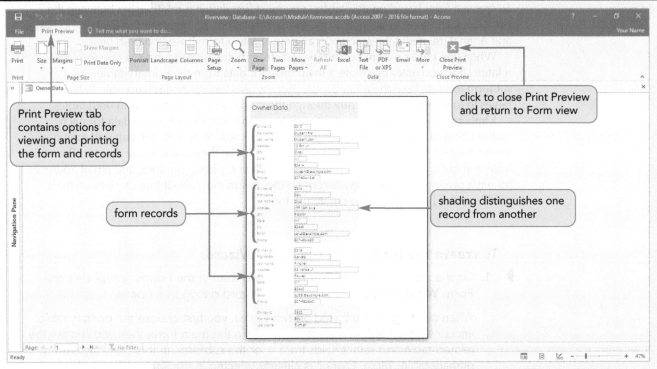

Print Preview tab contains options for viewing and printing the form and records

form records

click to close Print Preview and return to Form view

shading distinguishes one record from another

To print one selected record on a page by itself, you need to use the Print dialog box.

▶ 3. On the Print Preview tab, in the Close Preview group, click the **Close Print Preview** button. You return to Form view with the first record still displayed.

▶ 4. Click the **File** tab to open Backstage view again, click **Print** in the navigation bar, and then click **Print**. The **Print** dialog box opens.

▶ 5. Click the **Selected Record(s)** option button to print the current form record (record 1).

Trouble? Check with your instructor to be sure you should print the form, then continue to the next step. If you should not print the form, click the Cancel button, and then skip to Step 7.

▶ **6.** Click the **OK** button to close the dialog box and print the selected record.

▶ **7.** Close the OwnerData form.

After reviewing the printed OwnerData form with her staff, Kimberly realizes that it would be helpful for staff members to also have a form showing information about both owners and their animals. Because this form will need to display information from two different tables, the type of form you need to create will include a main form and a subform.

Creating a Form with a Main Form and a Subform

To create a form based on two tables, you must first define a relationship between the two tables. Earlier, you defined a one-to-many relationship between the Owner (primary) and Animal (related) tables, so you can now create a form based on both tables.

When you create a form containing data from two tables that have a one-to-many relationship, you actually create a **main form** for data from the primary table and a **subform** for data from the related table. Access uses the defined relationship between the tables to join them automatically through the common field that exists in both tables.

Kimberly would like you to create a form so that she can view the data for each owner and that owner's animals at the same time. Kimberly and her staff will then use the form when contacting the owners about care that their animals are due for. The main form will contain the owner ID, first and last names, phone number, and email address for each owner. The subform will contain the information about that owner's animals. You'll use the Form Wizard to create the form.

To create the form using the Form Wizard:

▶ **1.** On the ribbon, click the **Create** tab, and then in the Forms group, click the **Form Wizard** button. The first Form Wizard dialog box opens.

When creating a form based on two tables, you first choose the primary table and select the fields you want to include in the main form; then you choose the related table and select fields from it for the subform. In this case, the correct primary table, Table: Owner, is already selected in the Tables/Queries box.

Trouble? If Table: Owner is not currently selected in the Tables/Queries box, click the Tables/Queries arrow, and then click Table: Owner.

The form needs to include only the OwnerID, FirstName, LastName, Phone, and Email fields from the Owner table.

▶ **2.** Click **OwnerID** in the Available Fields box if necessary, and then click the
  `>` button to move the field to the Selected Fields box.

▶ **3.** Repeat Step 2 for the **FirstName**, **LastName**, **Phone**, and **Email** fields.

The subform needs to include all the fields from the Animal table, with the exception of the OwnerID field, as that field has been added already for the main form.

▶ **4.** Click the **Tables/Queries** arrow, and then click **Table: Animal**. The fields from the Animal table appear in the Available Fields box. The quickest way to add the fields you want to include is to move all the fields to the Selected Fields box, and then remove the only field you don't want to include (OwnerID).

TIP

The table name (Animal) is included in the OwnerID field name to distinguish it from the same field in the Owner table.

5. Click the >> button to move all the fields in the Animal table to the Selected Fields box.

6. Click **Animal.OwnerID** in the Selected Fields box, and then click the < button to move the field back to the Available Fields box.

7. Click the **Next** button. The next Form Wizard dialog box opens. See Figure 4-15.

| Figure 4-15 | Choosing a format for the main form and subform |

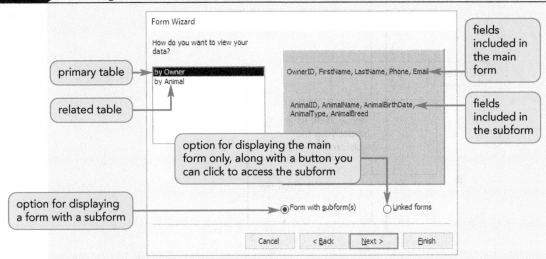

primary table

related table

option for displaying the main form only, along with a button you can click to access the subform

option for displaying a form with a subform

fields included in the main form

fields included in the subform

In this dialog box, the section on the left shows the order in which you will view the selected data: first by data from the primary Owner table, and then by data from the related Animal table. The form will be displayed as shown on the right side of the dialog box, with the fields from the Owner table at the top in the main form, and the fields from the Animal table at the bottom in the subform.

8. Click the **Next** button. The next Form Wizard dialog box opens, in which you choose the subform layout.

The Tabular layout displays subform fields as a table, whereas the Datasheet layout displays subform fields as a table datasheet. The layout choice is a matter of personal preference. You'll use the Datasheet layout.

9. Click the **Datasheet** option button to select it if necessary, and then click the **Next** button. The next Form Wizard dialog box opens, in which you specify titles for the main form and the subform. You'll use the title "OwnerAnimals" for the main form and the title "AnimalSubform" for the subform. These titles will also be the names for the form objects.

10. In the Form box, click to position the insertion point to the right of the last letter, and then type **Animals**. The main form name is now OwnerAnimals.

11. In the Subform box, delete the space between the two words so that the subform name appears as **AnimalSubform**, and then click the **Finish** button. The completed form opens in Form view. See Figure 4-16.

Figure 4-16 | **Main form with subform in Form view**

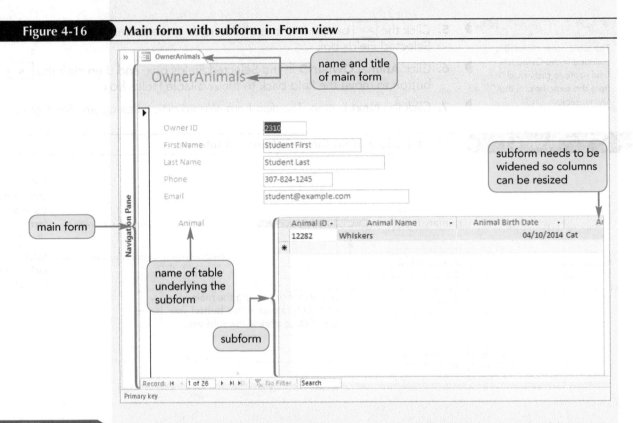

The main form displays the fields from the first record in the Owner table in a columnar format. The records in the main form appear in primary key order by OwnerID. OwnerID 2310 has one related record in the Animal table; this record, for AnimalID 12282, is shown in the subform, which uses the datasheet format. The main form name, "OwnerAnimals," appears on the object tab and as the form title. The name of the table "Animal" appears to the left of the subform indicating the underlying table for the subform. Note that only the word "Animal" and not the complete name "AnimalSubform" appears on the form. Only the table name is displayed for the subform itself, but the complete name of the object, "AnimalSubform," is displayed when you view and work with objects in the Navigation Pane. The subform designation is necessary in a list of database objects so that you can distinguish the Animal subform from other objects, such as the Animal table, but the subform designation is not needed in the OwnerAnimals form. Only the table name is required to identify the table containing the records in the subform.

TIP

The OwnerAnimals form is formatted with the default Office theme because you applied the Wisp theme only to the OwnerData form.

Next, you need to make some changes to the form. First, you'll edit the form title to add a space between the words so that it appears as "Owner Animals." Then, you'll resize the subform so that it is wide enough to allow for all the columns to be fully displayed. To make these changes, you need to switch to Layout view.

To modify the OwnerAnimals form in Layout view:

▶ **1.** Switch to Layout view.

▶ **2.** Click **OwnerAnimals** in the gray area at the top of the form. The form title is selected.

3. Click between the letters "r" and "A" to place the insertion point, and then press the **spacebar**. The title on the form is now "Owner Animals."

4. Click in a blank area of the form to the right of the field value boxes to deselect the title. Next, you'll increase the width of the subform.

5. Click the **subform**. An orange border surrounds the subform, indicating it is selected.

6. Position the pointer on the right border of the selected subform until the pointer changes to ↔, and then drag to the right approximately three inches. The wider subform makes all the columns visible. See Figure 4-17.

Figure 4-17	Modified form in Layout view

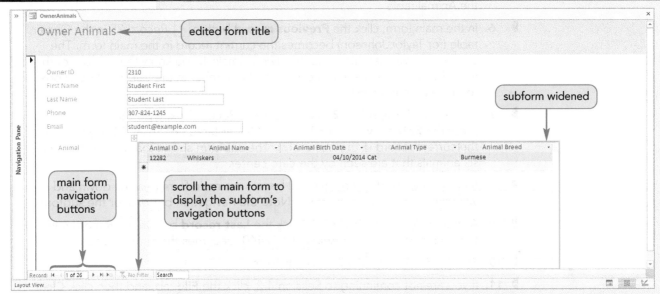

7. On the Quick Access Toolbar, click the **Save** button 🔲 to save both the main form and the subform.

8. Switch to Form view, and then if necessary, scroll up to view all the fields in the main form.

The form includes two sets of navigation buttons. You use the set of navigation buttons at the bottom of the Form window to select records from the primary table in the main form (see Figure 4-17). The second set of navigation buttons is currently not visible; you need to scroll down the main form to see these buttons, which appear at the bottom of the subform. You use the subform navigation buttons to select records from the related table in the subform.

You'll use the navigation buttons to view different records.

To navigate to different main form and subform records:

1. In the main form, click the **Next record** button ▶ six times. Record 7 of 26 total records in the Owner table (for Joey Smith) becomes the current record in the main form. The subform shows that this owner has one animal, a cat. Note that the Animal Name, Animal Birth Date, and Animal Type columns are much wider than necessary for the information displayed.

▶ **2.** Double-click the ✛ pointer on the right column divider of the Animal Name column in the subform to resize this field to its best fit.

▶ **3.** Repeat Step 2 to resize the Animal Birth Date and Animal Type columns in the subform.

▶ **4.** Use the main form navigation buttons to view each record, resizing any subform column to fully display any field values that are not completely visible.

▶ **5.** In the main form, click the **Last record** button ▶|. Record 26 in the Owner table (for Mei Kostas) becomes the current record in the main form. The subform shows that this owner currently has no animals; recall that you just entered this record using the OwnerData form. Kimberly could use the subform to enter the information on this owner's animal(s), and that information will be updated in the Animal table.

▶ **6.** In the main form, click the **Previous record** button |◀. Record 25 in the Owner table (for Taylor Johnson) becomes the current record in the main form. The subform shows that this owner has two animals. If you know the number of the record you want to view, you can enter the number in the Current Record box to move to that record.

▶ **7.** In the main form, select **25** in the Current Record box, type **18**, and then press the **Enter** key. Record 18 in the Owner table (for Susan Miller) becomes the current record in the main form. The subform shows that this owner has six animals that are seen by the care center.

▶ **8.** If necessary, use the vertical scroll bar for the main form to scroll down and view the bottom of the subform. Note the navigation buttons for the subform.

▶ **9.** At the bottom of the subform, click the **Last record** button ▶|. Record 6 in the Animal subform, for Animal ID 12440, becomes the current record.

▶ **10.** Save and close the OwnerAnimals form.

▶ **11.** If you are not continuing to Session 4.2, click the **File** tab, and then click **Close** in the navigation bar to close the Riverview database.

Both the OwnerData form and the OwnerAnimals form you created will enable Kimberly and her staff to view, enter, and maintain data easily in the Owner and Animal tables in the Riverview database.

Session 4.1 Quick Check

REVIEW

1. Describe the difference between creating a form using the Form tool and creating a form using the Form Wizard.

2. What is a theme, and how do you apply one to an existing form?

3. A(n) _____ is an item on a form, report, or other database object that you can manipulate to modify the object's appearance.

4. Which table record is displayed in a form when you press the Ctrl+End keys while you are in navigation mode?

5. Which wildcard character matches any single alphabetic character?

6. To print only the current record displayed in a form, you need to select the _____ option button in the Print dialog box.

7. In a form that contains a main form and a subform, what data is displayed in the main form and what data is displayed in the subform?

Session 4.2 Visual Overview:

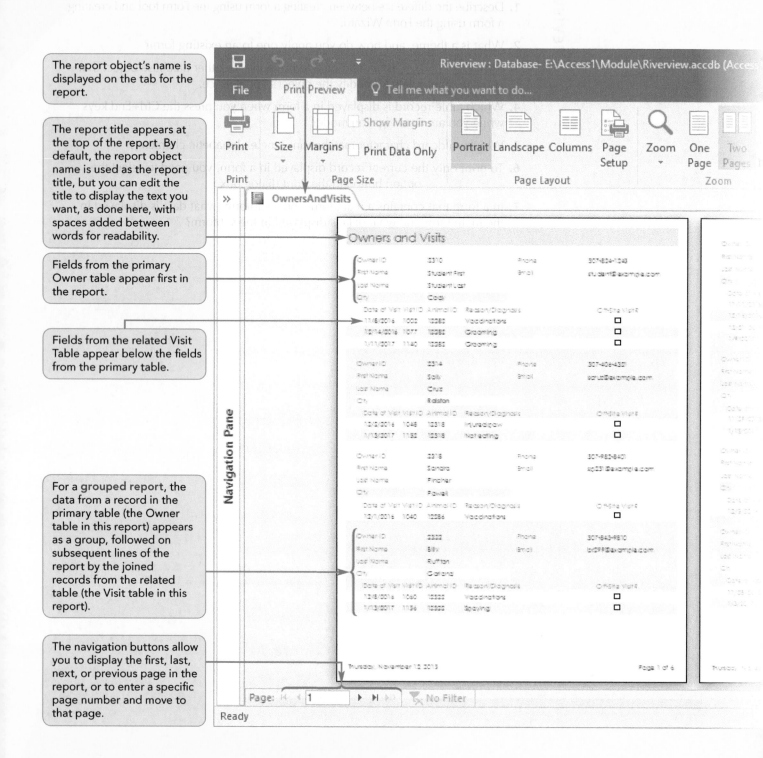

The report object's name is displayed on the tab for the report.

The report title appears at the top of the report. By default, the report object name is used as the report title, but you can edit the title to display the text you want, as done here, with spaces added between words for readability.

Fields from the primary Owner table appear first in the report.

Fields from the related Visit Table appear below the fields from the primary table.

For a grouped report, the data from a record in the primary table (the Owner table in this report) appears as a group, followed on subsequent lines of the report by the joined records from the related table (the Visit table in this report).

The navigation buttons allow you to display the first, last, next, or previous page in the report, or to enter a specific page number and move to that page.

Riverview : Database- E:\Access1\Module\Riverview.accdb (Access

File   Print Preview   ♀ Tell me what you want to do...

Print   Size   Margins   ☐ Show Margins   Portrait   Landscape   Columns   Page   Zoom   One   Two
                         ☐ Print Data Only   Setup   Page   Pages

Print   Page Size   Page Layout   Zoom

OwnersAndVisits

Navigation Pane

Page: 1   No Filter

Ready

Report Displayed in Print Preview

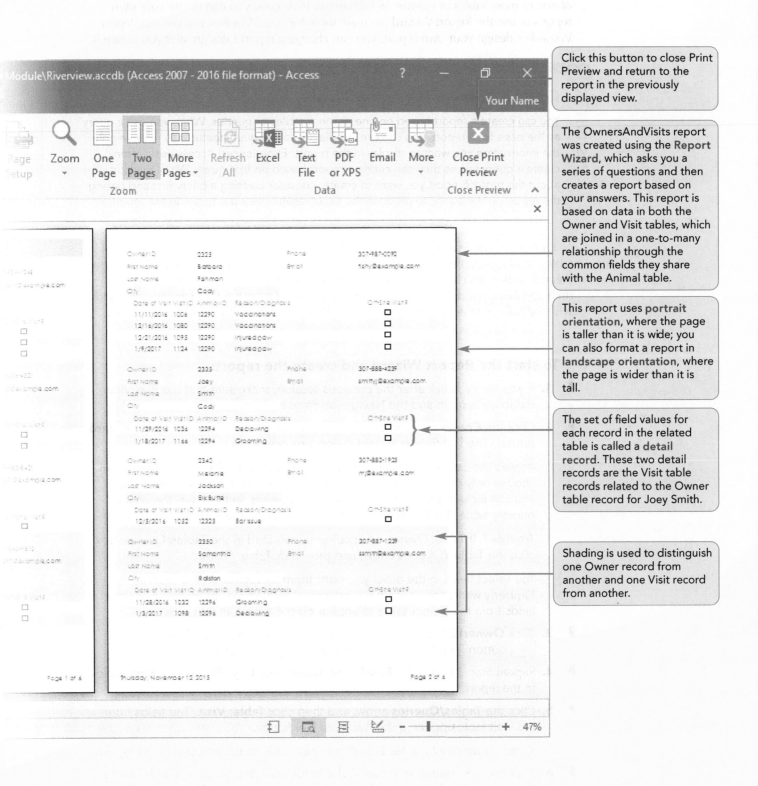

Click this button to close Print Preview and return to the report in the previously displayed view.

The OwnersAndVisits report was created using the **Report Wizard**, which asks you a series of questions and then creates a report based on your answers. This report is based on data in both the Owner and Visit tables, which are joined in a one-to-many relationship through the common fields they share with the Animal table.

This report uses **portrait orientation**, where the page is taller than it is wide; you can also format a report in **landscape orientation**, where the page is wider than it is tall.

The set of field values for each record in the related table is called a **detail record**. These two detail records are the Visit table records related to the Owner table record for Joey Smith.

Shading is used to distinguish one Owner record from another and one Visit record from another.

Creating a Report Using the Report Wizard

As you learned earlier, a report is a formatted printout or screen display of the contents of one or more tables or queries in a database. In Access, you can create your own reports or use the Report Wizard to create them for you. Whether you use the Report Wizard or design your own report, you can change a report's design after you create it.

INSIGHT

Creating a Report Based on a Query

You can create a report based on one or more tables or queries. When you use a query as the basis for a report, you can use criteria and other query features to retrieve only the information you want to display in the report. Experienced Access users often create a query just so they can create a report based on that query. When thinking about the type of report you want to create, consider creating a query first and basing the report on the query, to produce the exact results you want to see in the report.

Kimberly wants you to create a report that includes data from the Owner and Visit tables, as shown in the Session 4.2 Visual Overview. Like the OwnerAnimals form you created earlier, which includes a main form and a subform, the report will be based on both tables, which are joined in a one-to-many relationship through common fields with the Animal table. You'll use the Report Wizard to create the report for Kimberly.

To start the Report Wizard and create the report:

▶ **1.** If you took a break after the previous session, make sure that the Riverview database is open and the Navigation Pane is closed.

▶ **2.** Click the **Create** tab, and then in the Reports group, click the **Report Wizard** button. The first Report Wizard dialog box opens.

As was the case when you created the form with a subform, initially you can choose only one table or query to be the data source for the report. Then you can include data from other tables or queries. In this case, the correct primary table, Table: Owner, is already selected in the Tables/Queries box.

Trouble? If Table: Owner is not currently selected in the Tables/Queries box, click the Tables/Queries arrow, and then click Table: Owner.

You select fields in the order you want them to appear on the report. Kimberly wants the OwnerID, FirstName, LastName, City, Phone, and Email fields from the Owner table to appear on the report, in that order.

▶ **3.** Click **OwnerID** in the Available Fields box (if necessary), and then click the ⟩ button. The field moves to the Selected Fields box.

▶ **4.** Repeat Step 3 to add the **FirstName**, **LastName**, **City**, **Phone**, and **Email** fields to the report.

▶ **5.** Click the **Tables/Queries** arrow, and then click **Table: Visit**. The fields from the Visit table appear in the Available Fields box.

Kimberly wants all the fields from the Visit table to be included in the report.

▶ **6.** Click the ⟩⟩ button to move all the fields from the Available Fields box to the Selected Fields box, and then click the **Next** button. The second Report Wizard dialog box opens. See Figure 4-18.

Figure 4-18   Choosing a grouped or ungrouped report

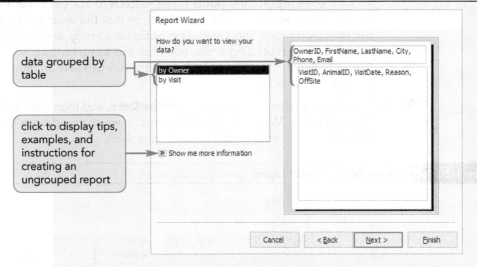

You can choose to arrange the selected data grouped by table, which is the default, or ungrouped. You're creating a grouped report; the data from each record in the Owner table will appear in a group, followed by the related records for that owner from the Visit table.

▶ **7.** Click the **Next** button. The next Report Wizard dialog box opens, in which you choose additional grouping levels.

Currently the report contains only one grouping level, which is for the owner's data. Grouping levels are useful for reports with multiple levels, such as those containing monthly, quarterly, and annual totals, or for those containing city and country groups. The report requires no further grouping levels, so you can accept the default options.

▶ **8.** Click the **Next** button. The next Report Wizard dialog box opens, in which you choose the sort order for the detail records. See Figure 4-19.

Figure 4-19   Choosing the sort order for detail records

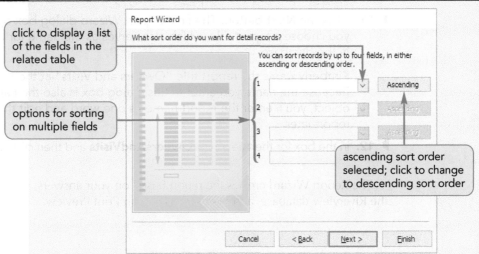

The records from the Visit table for an owner represent the detail records for Kimberly's report. She wants these records to appear in ascending order by the value in the VisitDate field, so that the visits will be shown in chronological order. The Ascending option is already selected by default. To change to descending order, you click this same button, which acts as a toggle between the two sort orders. Also, you can sort on multiple fields, as you can with queries.

▶ **9.** Click the **arrow** on the first box, click **VisitDate**, and then click the **Next** button. The next Report Wizard dialog box opens, in which you choose a layout and page orientation for the report. See Figure 4-20.

Figure 4-20   **Choosing the report layout**

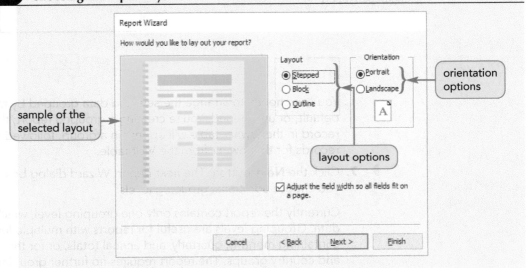

▶ **10.** Click each layout option to view each sample that appears, and then click the **Outline** option button to select that layout for the report.

Because most of the fields in both the Owner and Visit tables contain relatively short field values, the portrait page orientation should provide enough space across the page to display all the field values.

▶ **11.** Click the **Next** button. The final Report Wizard dialog box opens, in which you choose a report title, which also serves as the name for the report object in the database.

Kimberly wants the report title "Owners and Visits" at the top of the report. Because the name you enter in this dialog box is also the name of the report object, you'll enter the report name as one word and edit the title on the report later.

▶ **12.** In the box for the title, enter **OwnersAndVisits** and then click the **Finish** button.

The Report Wizard creates the report based on your answers, saves it as an object in the Riverview database, and opens the report in Print Preview.

After you create a report, you should view it in Print Preview to see if you need to make any formatting or design changes. To view the entire page, you need to change the Zoom setting.

To view the report in Print Preview:

▶ **1.** On the Print Preview tab, in the Zoom group, click the **Zoom button arrow**, and then click **Fit to Window**. The first page of the report is displayed in Print Preview.

▶ **2.** At the bottom of the window, click the **Next Page** button ▶ to display the second page of the report.

When a report is displayed in Print Preview, you can zoom in for a close-up view of a section of the report.

▶ **3.** Move the pointer to the center of the report, and then click the ⊕ pointer at the center of the report. The display changes to show a close-up view of the report. See Figure 4-21.

Figure 4-21	Close-up view of the report

shading distinguishes one Owner record from another

Visit records listed in ascending order by VisitDate

shading distinguishes one Visit record from another

Shading is used to distinguish both one Owner record from another and, within a group of each owner's Visit records, one Visit record from another.

Trouble? Depending on your computer settings, the shading and colors used in your report might look different. This difference should not cause any problems.

The detail records for the Visit table fields appear in ascending order based on the values in the VisitDate field. Because the VisitDate field is used as the basis for sorting records, it appears as the first field in this section, even though you selected the fields in the order in which they appear in the Visit table.

▶ **4.** Scroll to the bottom of the second page, checking the text in the report as you scroll. Notice the current date and page number at the bottom of the page; the Report Wizard included these elements as part of the report's design.

▶ **5.** Move the pointer onto the report, click the 🔍 pointer to zoom back out, and then click the **Next Page** navigation button ▶ to move to page 3 of the report.

▶ **6.** Continue to move through the pages of the report, and then click the **First Page** button ◀ to return to the first page.

INSIGHT

Changing a Report's Page Orientation and Margins

When you display a report in Print Preview, you can easily change the report layout using options on the Print Preview tab (refer to the Session 4.2 Visual Overview). For example, sometimes fields with longer values cause the report content to overflow onto the next page. You can fix this problem by clicking the Landscape button in the Page Layout group on the Print Preview tab to switch the report orientation to landscape, where the page is wider than it is tall. Landscape orientation allows more space for content to fit across the width of the report page. You can also use the Margins button in the Page Size group to change the margins of the report, choosing from commonly used margin formats or creating your own custom margins. Simply click the Margins button arrow to display the menu of available margin options and select the one that works best for your report.

When you created the OwnerData form, you applied the Wisp theme. Kimberly would like the OwnersAndVisits report to be formatted with the same theme. You need to switch to Layout view to make this change. You'll also make other modifications to improve the report's design.

Modifying a Report's Design in Layout View

Similar to Layout view for forms, Layout view for reports enables you to make modifications to the report's design. Many of the same options—such as those for applying a theme and changing the color of text—are provided in Layout view for reports.

Applying a Theme to a Report

The same themes available for forms are also available for reports. You can choose to apply a theme to the current report object only, or to all reports in the database. In this case, you'll apply the Wisp theme only to the OwnersAndVisits report because Kimberly isn't certain if it is the appropriate theme for other reports in the Riverview database.

To apply the Wisp theme to the report and edit the report name:

▶ **1.** On the status bar, click the **Layout View** button ▣. The report is displayed in Layout view and the Report Layout Tools Design tab is the active tab on the ribbon.

▶ **2.** In the Themes group, click the **Themes** button. The "In this Database" section at the top of the gallery shows both the default Office theme and the Wisp theme. The Wisp theme is included here because you applied it earlier to the OwnerData form.

TIP

When you point to the Wisp theme, a ScreenTip displays the names of the database objects that use the theme—in this case, the OwnerData form.

▶ **3.** At the top of the gallery, right-click the **Wisp** theme to display the shortcut menu, and then click **Apply Theme to This Object Only**. The gallery closes and the theme is applied to the report.

The larger font used by the Wisp theme has caused the report title text to be cut off on the right. You'll fix this problem and edit the title text as well.

Trouble? After you apply the theme, some VisitDate values may be displayed as a series of # symbols rather than actual date values. You'll fix this later in the session.

▶ **4.** Click the **OwnersAndVisits** title at the top of the report to select it.

▶ **5.** Position the pointer on the right border of the title's selection box until it changes to ↔, and then drag to the right until the title is fully displayed.

▶ **6.** Click between the letters "s" and "A" in the title, press the **spacebar**, change the capital letter "A" to **a**, place the insertion point between the letters "d" and "V," and then press the **spacebar**. The title is now "Owners and Visits."

▶ **7.** Click to the right of the report title in the shaded area to deselect the title.

Kimberly views the report and notices some other formatting changes she would like you to make. First, she doesn't like how the VisitDate field values are aligned compared to the other field values from the Visit table. You'll fix this next.

Changing the Alignment of Field Values

The Report Layout Tools Format tab provides options for you to easily modify the format of various report objects. For example, you can change the alignment of the text in a field value. Recall that Date/Time fields, like VisitDate, automatically right-align their field values, whereas Short Text fields, like VisitID, automatically left-align their field values. Kimberly asks you to change the alignment of the VisitDate field so its values appear left-aligned, which will improve the format of the report.

To change the alignment of the VisitDate field values:

▶ **1.** On the ribbon, click the **Report Layout Tools Format** tab. The ribbon changes to display options for formatting the report. The options for modifying the format of a report are the same as those available for forms.

▶ **2.** In the report, click the **first VisitDate** field value box, which contains the date 11/8/2016. The field value box has an orange border, indicating it is selected. Note that the other VisitDate field value boxes have a lighter orange border, indicating they are selected as well. Any changes you make will be applied to all VisitDate field values throughout the report.

▶ **3.** On the Report Layout Tools Format tab, in the Font group, click the **Align Left** button ☰. The text in the VisitDate field value boxes is now left-aligned. See Figure 4-22.

| Figure 4-22 | Report after applying a theme and changing field alignment |

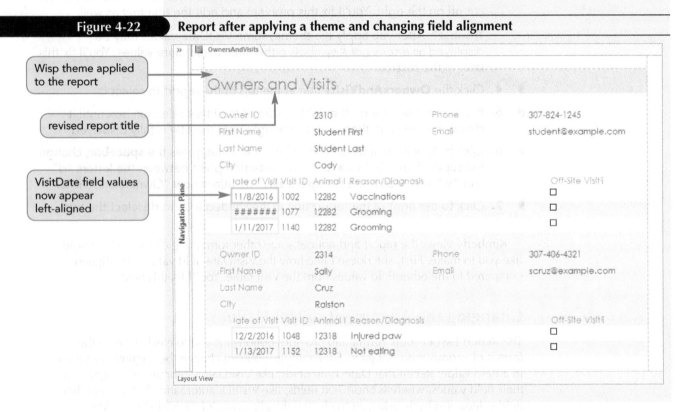

Wisp theme applied to the report

revised report title

VisitDate field values now appear left-aligned

Moving and Resizing Fields on a Report

Working in Layout view, you can resize and reposition fields and field value boxes to improve the appearance and readability of a report. You resize field value boxes by dragging their borders to the desired size. You can also move field labels and field value boxes by selecting one or more of them and then dragging them to a new location; or, for more precise control over the move, you can use the keyboard arrow keys to move selected objects.

In the OwnersAndVisits report, you need to move and resize the VisitDate, VisitID, and OffSite field labels so that the complete caption is displayed for each. Also, some of the VisitDate field values are not displayed on the report but are instead represented by a series of # symbols. This occurs when a field value box is not wide enough for its content. To fix this, you'll widen the VisitDate field value box. Before addressing these issues, you will move the OffSite field label so it appears centered over its check box.

To move and resize the OffSite field label:

1. In the report, click the first occurrence of the **Off-Site Visit?** field label. All instances of the label are selected throughout the report.

2. Press the ← key repeatedly until the label is centered (roughly) over its check box.

3. Position the pointer on the right border of the field label's selection box until the pointer changes to ↔, and then drag to the right until the label text is fully displayed.

Next, you need to move the field label and field value box for the Reason and OffSite fields to the right, to make room to widen the Animal ID field label. You also need to make adjustments to the field label and field value box for the VisitDate field.

To resize and move field labels and field value boxes in the report:

1. In the report, click the first occurrence of the **Reason/Diagnosis** field label, press and hold the **Shift** key, click the first occurrence of the **Reason** field value box, which contains the text "Vaccinations," click the first occurrence of the **Off-Site Visit?** field label, and then click the first occurrence of the **OffSite** field value box. Both field labels and their associated field value boxes are selected and can be moved. See Figure 4-23.

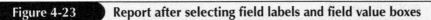

| Figure 4-23 | Report after selecting field labels and field value boxes |

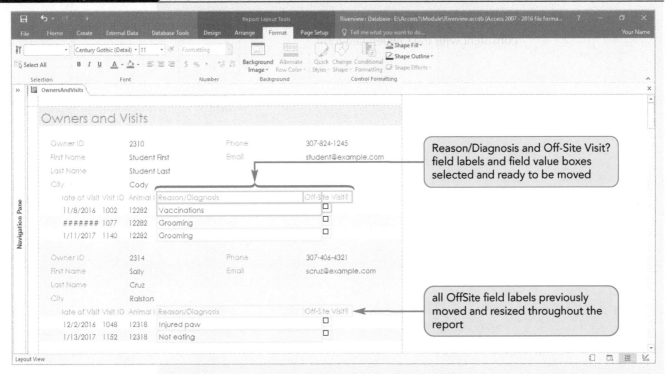

▶ **2.** Press the → key six times to move the field labels and field value boxes to the right.

Trouble? Once you press the right arrow key, the report might jump to display the end of the report. Just continue to press the right arrow key to move the labels and values. Then scroll the window back up to display the beginning of the report.

▶ **3.** Click the **Animal ID** field label to select it and deselect the moved field labels and field value boxes.

▶ **4.** Position the pointer on the right border of the Animal ID field label's selection box until it changes to ↔, and then drag to the right until the Animal ID label is fully displayed.

Now you need to modify the VisitDate field so that the # symbols that currently appear are replaced with the actual field values. You'll resize the VisitDate field value boxes to fix this problem.

▶ **5.** Scroll to the top of the report if necessary to display the first record in the report, and then click the **######** symbols that appear in the second VisitDate field value in the first record.

▶ **6.** Using the ↔ pointer, drag the left border of VisitDate field value's selection box to the left until the date value is fully displayed.

▶ **7.** Scroll through the report, resizing the VisitDate field values as necessary until all values are fully displayed, and then scroll back up to display the top of the report.

▶ **8.** Click the **Date of Visit** field label to select it, and then drag the left border of the selection box to the left until the label text is fully displayed.

▶ **9.** Click to the right of the report title in the shaded area to deselect the field label.

▶ **10.** On the Quick Access Toolbar, click the **Save** button 🖫 to save the modified report.

Next, Kimberly asks you to enhance the report's appearance to make it more consistent with the OwnerData form.

Changing the Font Color and Inserting a Picture in a Report

You can change the color of text on a report to enhance its appearance. You can also add a picture to a report for visual interest or to identify a particular section of the report.

Before you print the report for Kimberly, she asks you to change the report title color to the darker black you applied earlier to the OwnerData form and to include the Animals picture to the right of the report title.

To change the color of the report title and insert the picture:

> **1.** At the top of the report, click the **Owners and Visits** title to select it.

> **2.** Make sure the Report Layout Tools Format tab is still active on the ribbon.

Make sure the title is selected so the picture is inserted in the correct location.

> **3.** In the Font group, click the **Font Color button arrow** [A], and then in the Theme Colors section, click the **Black, Text 1, Lighter 25%** color (fourth color in the second column). The color is applied to the report title.

> Now you'll insert the picture to the right of the report title text.

> **4.** On the ribbon, click the **Report Layout Tools Design** tab. The options provided on this tab for reports are the same as those you worked with for forms.

> **5.** In the Header/Footer group, click the **Logo** button.

> **6.** Navigate to the **Access1 > Module** folder provided with your Data Files, and then double-click the **Animals** file. The picture is inserted in the top-left corner of the report, partially covering the report title.

> **7.** Position the ⁺⃗ pointer on the selected picture, and then drag it to the right of the report title.

> **8.** Click in a blank area of the shaded bar to deselect the picture. See Figure 4-24.

Figure 4-24   **Report after changing the title font color and inserting the picture**

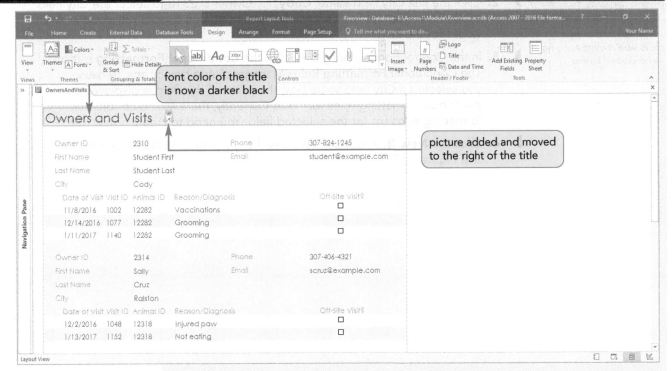

> **Trouble?** Don't be concerned if the picture in your report is not in the exact same location as the one shown in the figure. Just make sure it is to the right of the title text and within the shaded area.

Riverview Veterinary Care Center is planning a mobile clinic day in Ralston. Kimberly would like to make it easier to locate the records in the report for owners who live in Ralston by applying unique formatting to their city names. Because you don't need to apply this formatting to the city names in all the records in the report, you will use conditional formatting.

Using Conditional Formatting in a Report

Conditional formatting in a report (or form) is special formatting applied to certain field values depending on one or more conditions—similar to criteria you establish for queries. If a field value meets the condition or conditions you specify, the formatting is applied to the value.

Kimberly would like the OwnersAndVisits report to show a city name of Ralston in a bold, dark red font. This formatting will help to highlight the owner records for owners who live in this location.

To apply conditional formatting to the City field in the report:

▶ **1.** Make sure the report is still displayed in Layout view, and then click the **Report Layout Tools Format** tab on the ribbon.

To apply conditional formatting to a field, you must first make it the active field by clicking any field value in the field's column.

TIP
You must select a field value box, and not the field label, before applying a conditional format.

▶ **2.** Click the first City field value, **Cody**, for OwnerID 2310 to select the City field values in the report. The conditional formatting you specify will affect all the values for the field.

▶ **3.** In the Control Formatting group, click the **Conditional Formatting** button. The Conditional Formatting Rules Manager dialog box opens. Because you selected a City field value box, the name of this field is displayed in the "Show formatting rules for" box. Currently, there are no conditional formatting rules set for the selected field. You need to create a new rule.

▶ **4.** Click the **New Rule** button. The New Formatting Rule dialog box opens. See Figure 4-25.

| Figure 4-25 | New Formatting Rule dialog box |

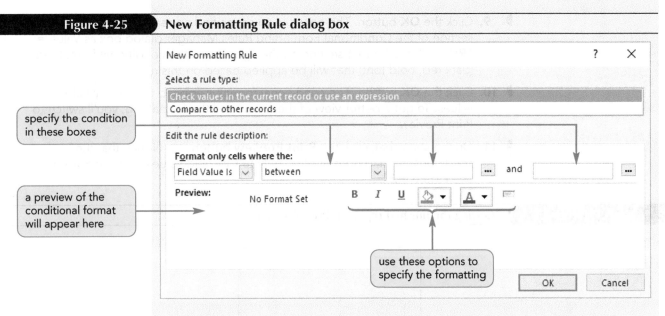

specify the condition in these boxes

a preview of the conditional format will appear here

use these options to specify the formatting

The default setting for "Select a rule type" specifies that Access will check field values and determine if they meet the condition. This is the setting you want. You need to enter the condition in the "Edit the rule description" section of the dialog box. The setting "Field Value Is" means that the conditional format you specify will be applied only when the value for the selected field, City, meets the condition.

▶ **5.** Click the **arrow** for the box containing the word "between," and then click **equal to**. You want only the city name Ralston to be formatted.

▶ **6.** Click in the next box, and then type **Ralston**.

▶ **7.** In the Preview section, click the **Font color button arrow** [A▾], and then click the **Dark Red** color (first color in the last row in the Standard Colors section).

▶ **8.** In the Preview section, click the **Bold** button [B]. The specifications for the conditional formatting are complete. See Figure 4-26.

| Figure 4-26 | Conditional formatting set for the City field |

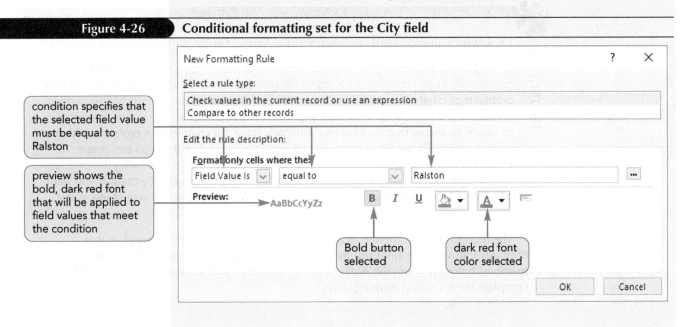

condition specifies that the selected field value must be equal to Ralston

preview shows the bold, dark red font that will be applied to field values that meet the condition

Bold button selected

dark red font color selected

9. Click the **OK** button. The new rule you specified appears in the Rule section of the Conditional Formatting Rules Manager dialog box as Value = "Ralston"; the Format section on the right shows the conditional formatting (dark red, bold font) that will be applied based on this rule.

10. Click the **OK** button. The conditional format is applied to the City field values. To get a better view of the report and the formatting, you'll switch to Print Preview.

11. On the status bar, click the **Print Preview** button. Notice that the conditional formatting is applied only to City field values equal to Ralston. See Figure 4-27.

Figure 4-27   Viewing the finished report in Print Preview

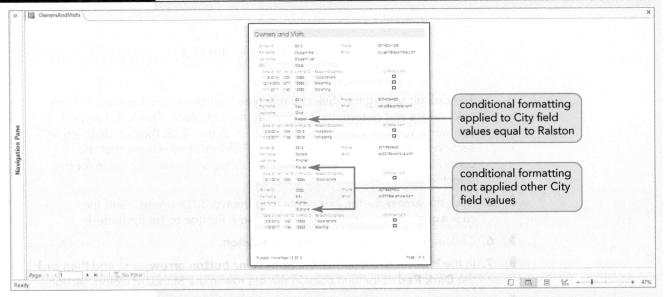

conditional formatting applied to City field values equal to Ralston

conditional formatting not applied other City field values

Problem Solving: Understanding the Importance of Previewing Reports

PROSKILLS

When you create a report, it is a good idea to display the report in Print Preview occasionally as you develop it. Doing so will give you a chance to identify any formatting problems or other issues so that you can make any necessary corrections before printing the report. It is particularly important to preview a report after you've made changes to its design to ensure that the changes you made have not created new problems with the report's format. Before printing any report, you should preview it so you can determine where the pages will break and make any necessary adjustments. Following this problem-solving approach not only will ensure that the final report looks exactly the way you want it to, but will also save you time and help to avoid wasting paper if you print the report.

The report is now complete. You'll print just the first page of the report so that Kimberly can view the final results and share the report design with other staff members before printing the entire report. (*Note*: Ask your instructor if you should complete the following printing steps.)

To print page 1 of the report:

▶ **1.** On the Print Preview tab, in the Print group, click the **Print** button. The Print dialog box opens.

▶ **2.** In the Print Range section, click the **Pages** option button. The insertion point now appears in the From box so that you can specify the range of pages to print.

▶ **3.** Type **1** in the From box, press the **Tab** key to move to the To box, and then type **1**. These settings specify that only page 1 of the report will be printed.

▶ **4.** Click the **OK** button. The Print dialog box closes, and the first page of the report is printed.

▶ **5.** Save and close the OwnersAndVisits report.

You've created many different objects in the Riverview database. Before you close it, you'll open the Navigation Pane to view all the objects in the database.

To view the Riverview database objects in the Navigation Pane:

▶ **1.** Open the **Navigation Pane** and scroll down, if necessary, to display the bottom of the pane.

The Navigation Pane now includes the OwnersAndVisits report in the Reports section of the pane. Also notice the OwnerAnimals form in the Forms section. This is the form you created containing a main form based on the Owner table and a subform based on the Animal table. The AnimalSubform object is also listed; you can open it separately from the main form. See Figure 4-28.

Figure 4-28   **Riverview database objects in the Navigation Pane**

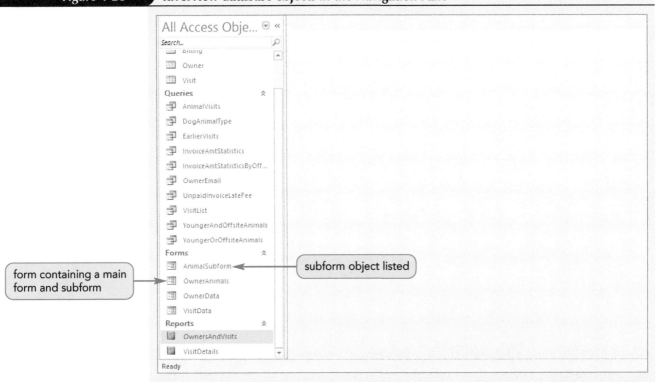

form containing a main form and subform

subform object listed

▶ **2.** Compact and repair the Riverview database, and then close the database.

Kimberly is satisfied that the forms you created—the OwnerData form and the OwnerAnimals form—will make it easier to enter, view, and update data in the Riverview database. The OwnersAndVisits report presents important information about the owners of the animals that the care center treats in an attractive and professional format, which will help Kimberly and other staff members in their work.

Session 4.2 Quick Check

REVIEW

1. In a(n) _____ report, the data from a record in the primary table appears together, followed on subsequent lines by the joined records from the related table.

2. When you create a report based on two tables that are joined in a one-to-many relationship, the field values for the records from the related table are called the _____ records.

3. Identify three types of modifications you can make to a report in Layout view.

4. Describe the process for moving a control to another location on a report in Layout view.

5. When working in Layout view for a report, which key do you press and hold down so that you can click to select multiple controls (field labels, field value boxes, and so on)?

6. _____ in a report (or form) is special formatting applied to certain field values depending on one or more conditions.

Review Assignments

PRACTICE

Data Files needed for the Review Assignments: Items.png and Vendor.accdb *(cont. from Module 3)*

Kimberly asks you to enhance the Vendor database with forms and reports. Complete the following steps:

1. Open the **Vendor** database you created and worked with in previous modules, and then click the Enable Content button next to the security warning, if necessary.

2. Use the Form Wizard to create a form based on the Product table. Select all fields for the form and the Columnar layout; specify the title **ProductData** for the form.

3. Apply the Ion theme to the ProductData form *only*.

4. Insert the **Items** picture, which is located in the Access1 > Review folder provided with your Data Files, in the ProductData form. Remove the picture from the control layout, and then move the picture to the right of the form title.

5. Edit the form title so that it appears as "Product Data" (two words), resize the title box as necessary so the title appears on a single line, and then change the font color of the form title to the Gray-25%, Background 2, Darker 75% theme color.

6. Resize the Weight in Lbs field value box so it is the same width (approximately) as the Units/Case field value box above it.

7. Change the alignment of the Price, Units/Case, and Weight in Lbs fields so that their values appear left-aligned in the field value boxes.

8. Save your changes to the form design.

9. Use the ProductData form to update the Product table as follows:

   a. Use the Find command to search for the word "premium" anywhere in the ProductName field, and then display the record for the Premium puppy food (ProductID PF200). Change the Price in this record to **44.00**.

   b. Add a new record with the following field values:

   Product ID: **CT200**
   Supplier ID: **KLS321**
   Product Name: **Cloth tape roll**
   Price: **24.00**
   Units/Case: **10**
   Weight in Lbs: **4**
   Temp Controlled?: **no**
   Sterile?: **no**

   c. Use the form to view each record with a ProductID value that starts with "CT".

   d. Save and close the form.

10. Use the Form Wizard to create a form containing a main form and a subform. Select all fields from the Supplier table for the main form, and select ProductID, ProductName, Price, TempControl, and Sterile—in that order—from the Product table for the subform. Use the Datasheet layout. Specify the title **SuppliersAndProducts** for the main form and **ProductSubform** for the subform.

11. Change the form title text to **Suppliers and Products**.

12. Resize the subform by widening it from its right side, increasing its width by approximately one inch, and then resize all columns in the subform to their best fit, working left to right. Navigate through each record in the main form to make sure all the field values in the subform are completely displayed, resizing subform columns and the subform itself, as necessary. Save and close the SuppliersAndProducts form.

13. Use the Report Wizard to create a report based on the primary Supplier table and the related Product table. Select the SupplierID, Company, City, Category, ContactFirst, ContactLast, and Phone fields—in that order—from the Supplier table, and the ProductID, ProductName, Price, and Units fields from the Product table. Do not specify any additional grouping levels, and sort the detail records in ascending order by ProductID. Choose the Outline layout and Portrait orientation. Specify the title **ProductsBySupplier** for the report.

14. Change the report title text to **Products by Supplier**.

15. Apply the Ion theme to the ProductsBySupplier report *only*.

16. Resize and reposition the following objects in the report in Layout view, and then scroll through the report to make sure all field labels and field values are fully displayed:

    a. Resize the report title so that the text of the title, Products by Supplier, is fully displayed.

    b. Move the ProductName field label and field value box to the right a bit (be sure not to move them too far so that the longest product name will still be completely visible).

    c. Resize the Product ID field label from its right side, increasing its width slightly so the label is fully displayed.

    d. Move the Price field label to the left a bit so the right side of the field label aligns with the right side of the field value below it.

    e. Move the Units/Case field label and field value box to the right a bit; then resize the label on its left side, increasing its width slightly so the label is fully displayed.

    f. Select the field value boxes *only* (not the field labels) for the following four fields: SupplierID, Company, City, and Category. Then move the four field value boxes to the left until their left edges align (roughly) with the "S" in "Supplier" in the report title.

17. Change the color of the report title text to the Gray-25%, Background 2, Darker 75% theme color.

18. Insert the **Items** picture, which is located in the Access1 > Review folder provided with your Data Files, in the report. Move the picture to the right of the report title.

19. Apply conditional formatting so that the Category field values equal to Supplies appear as dark red and bold.

20. Preview each page of the report, verifying that all the fields fit on the page. If necessary, return to Layout view and make changes so the report prints within the margins of the page and so that all field names and values are completely displayed.

21. Save the report, print its first page (only if asked by your instructor to do so), and then close the report.

22. Compact and repair the Vendor database, and then close it.

APPLY

Case Problem 1

Data Files needed for this Case Problem: Beauty.accdb *(cont. from Module 3)* **and Salon.png**

Beauty To Go   Sue Miller uses the Beauty database to track and view information about the services her business offers. She asks you to create the necessary forms and a report to help her work with this data more efficiently. Complete the following:

1. Open the **Beauty** database you created and worked with in previous modules, and then click the Enable Content button next to the security warning, if necessary.

2. Use the Form Wizard to create a form based on the Member table. Select all the fields for the form and the Columnar layout. Specify the title **MemberData** for the form.

3. Apply the Slice theme to the MemberData form *only*.

4. Edit the form title so that it appears as "Member Data" (two words); resize the title so that both words fit on the same line; and then change the font color of the form title to the Orange, Accent 5, Darker 25% theme color.

5. Use the Find command to display the record for Maita Rios, and then change the OptionEnds field value for this record to **9/3/2017**.

6. Use the MemberData form to add a new record to the Member table with the following field values:
   Member ID: **2180**
   Option ID: **135**
   First Name: **Risa**
   Last Name: **Kaplan**
   Street: **122 Bolcher Ave**
   City: **Orlando**
   State: **FL**
   Zip: **32805**
   Phone: **212-858-4007**
   Option Begins: **11/11/2017**
   Option Ends: **5/11/2018**

7. Save and close the MemberData form.

8. Use the Form Wizard to create a form containing a main form and a subform. Select all the fields from the Option table for the main form, and select the MemberID, FirstName, LastName, OptionEnd, and Phone fields from the Member table for the subform. Use the Datasheet layout. Specify the title **MembersByOption** for the main form and the title **MemberSubform** for the subform.

9. Change the form title text for the main form to **Members by Option**.

10. Resize all columns in the subform to their best fit, working from left to right; then move through all the records in the main form and check to make sure that all subform field values are fully displayed, resizing the columns as necessary.

11. Save and close the MembersByOption form.

12. Use the Report Wizard to create a report based on the primary Option table and the related Member table. Select all the fields from the Option table, and then select the MemberID, FirstName, LastName, City, Phone, OptionBegin, and OptionEnd fields from the Member table. Do not select any additional grouping levels, and sort the detail records in ascending order by MemberID. Choose the Outline layout and Landscape orientation. Specify the title **MemberOptions** for the report.

13. Apply the Slice theme to the MemberOptions report *only*.

14. Resize the report title so that the text is fully displayed; edit the report title so that it appears as "Member Options" (two words); and change the font color of the title to the Orange, Accent 5, Darker 25% theme color.

15. Change the alignment of the Option Cost field so that its values appear left-aligned in the field value boxes.

16. Resize and reposition the following objects in the report in Layout view, and then scroll through the report to make sure all field labels and field values are fully displayed:

   a. Move the FirstName label and field value box to the right a bit (be sure not to move them too far so that the longest first name will still be completely visible).

   b. Resize the MemberID field label on its right side, increasing its width until the label is fully displayed.

   c. Move the Phone label and field value box to the left; then resize the Option Begins label on its left side, increasing its width until the label is fully displayed.

   d. Scroll to the bottom of the report; note that the page number might not be completely within the page border (the dotted vertical line). If necessary, select and move the box containing the text "Page 1 of 1" until the entire text is positioned to the left of the dotted vertical line marking the right page border.

17. Insert the **Salon** picture, which is located in the Access1 > Case1 folder provided with your Data Files, in the report. Move the picture to the right of the report title.

18. Apply conditional formatting so that any OptionEnds field value less than 3/15/2017 appears as bold and with the Red color applied.

19. Preview the entire report to confirm that it is formatted correctly. If necessary, return to Layout view and make changes so that all field labels and field values are completely displayed.

20. Save the report, print its first page (only if asked by your instructor to do so), and then close the report.

21. Compact and repair the Beauty database, and then close it.

Case Problem 2

CREATE

Data Files needed for this Case Problem: Coder.png and Programming.accdb *(cont. from Module 3)*

Programming Pros Brent Hovis is using the Programming database to track and analyze the business activity of his tutoring services company. To make his work easier, you'll create a form and a report in the Programming database. Complete the following:

1. Open the **Programming** database you created and worked with in previous modules, and then click the Enable Content button next to the security warning, if necessary.
2. Create the form shown in Figure 4-29.

Figure 4-29   **Completed ContractsByTutor form**

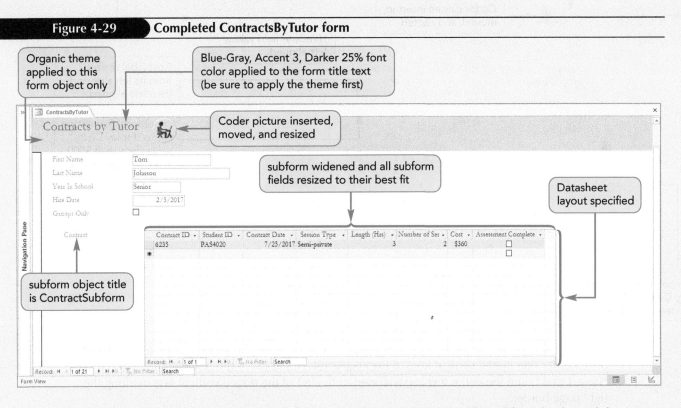

3. Using the form you just created, navigate to the second record in the subform for the eighth main record, and then change the Assessment Complete field value to **yes**.
4. Use the Find command to move to the record for Gail Fordham, and then change the value in the Year In School field to **Senior**.

5. Use the appropriate wildcard character to find all records with a Hire Date field value that begins with the month of February (2). Change the Hire Date field value for Ian Rodriguez (Tutor ID 1020) to **1/17/2017**. Save and close the form.

6. Create the report shown in Figure 4-30.

Figure 4-30 **Completed TutorsAndContracts report**

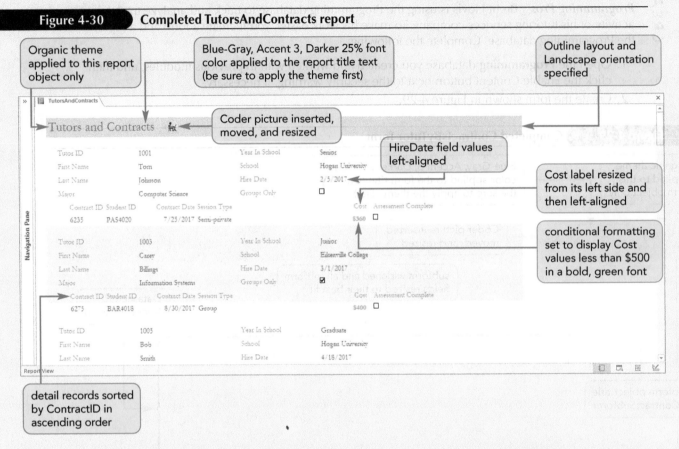

7. Scroll to the bottom of the report; note that the page number might not be completely within the page border (the dotted vertical line). If necessary, select and move the box containing the text "Page 1 of 1" until the entire text is positioned to the left of the dotted vertical line marking the right page border.

8. Preview each page of the report, verifying that all the fields fit on the page. If necessary, return to Layout view and make changes so the report prints within the margins of the page and all field names and values are completely displayed.

9. Save the report, print its first page (only if asked by your instructor to do so), and then close the report.

10. Compact and repair the Programming database, and then close it.

CHALLENGE

Case Problem 3

Data Files needed for this Case Problem: Center.accdb *(cont. from Module 3)* and Flower.png

Diane's Community Center   Diane Coleman uses the Center database to track, maintain, and analyze data about the patrons, donations, and auction items for her not-for-profit community center. You'll help Diane by creating a form and a report based on this data. Complete the following:

1. Open the **Center** database you created and worked with in previous modules, and then click the Enable Content button next to the security warning, if necessary.

2. Use the Form Wizard to create a form based on the Auction table. Select all the fields for the form and the Columnar layout. Specify the title **AuctionInfo** for the form.

3. Apply the Retrospect theme to the AuctionInfo form *only*.

4. Edit the form title so that it appears as "Auction Info" (two words), and change the font color of the form title to the Brown, Accent 3, Darker 25% theme color.

⊕ **Explore** 5. Use the appropriate button in the Font group on the Form Layout Tools Format tab to italicize the form title. Save the form.

6. Use the AuctionInfo form to update the Auction table as follows:

   a. Use the Find command to search for the record that contains the value "240" for the AuctionID field, and then change the MinimumSalesPrice field value for this record to **275**.

   b. Add a new record with the following values:

      Auction ID: **260**

      Donation ID: **5265**

      Date of Auction: **11/11/2017**

      Minimum Sales Price: **125**

      Item Sold at Auction?: [leave blank]

   ⊕ **Explore** c. Find the record with AuctionID 245, and then delete the record. (*Hint*: After displaying the record in the form, you need to select it by clicking the right-pointing triangle in the bar to the left of the field labels. Then use the appropriate button on the Home tab in the Records group to delete the record. When asked to confirm the deletion, click the Yes button.) Close the form.

7. Use the Form Wizard to create a form containing a main form and a subform. Select all the fields from the Patron table for the main form, and select all fields except PatronID from the Donation table for the subform. Use the Datasheet layout. Specify the name **PatronsAndDonations** for the main form and the title **DonationSubform** for the subform.

8. Apply the Retrospect theme to the PatronsAndDonations form *only*.

9. Edit the form title so that it appears as "Patrons and Donations." Resize the form title so that the text fits on one line. Change the font color of the title to the Brown, Accent 3, Darker 25% theme color.

10. Insert the **Flower** picture, which is located in the Access1 > Case3 folder provided with your Data Files, in the PatronsAndDonations form. Remove the picture from the control layout, and then move the picture to the right of the form title. Resize the picture so it is approximately double the original size.

⊕ **Explore** 11. Use the appropriate button in the Font group on the Form Layout Tools Format tab to apply the theme color Tan, Accent 5, Lighter 80% as a background color for all the field value boxes in the main form. Then use the appropriate button in the Control Formatting group to change the outline of all the main form field value boxes to have a line thickness of 1 pt. (*Hint*: Select all the field value boxes before making these changes.)

12. Resize the subform by extending it to the right, and then resize all columns in the subform to their best fit. Navigate through the records in the main form to make sure all the field values in the subform are completely displayed, resizing subform columns as necessary. Save and close the form.

13. Use the Report Wizard to create a report based on the primary Patron table and the related Donation table. Select all the fields from the Patron table, and select all fields except PatronID from the Donation table. Sort the detail records in *descending* order by DonationValue. Choose the Outline layout and Portrait orientation. Specify the name **PatronsAndDonations** for the report.

14. Apply the Retrospect theme to the PatronsAndDonations report *only*.

15. Resize the report title so that the text is fully displayed; edit the report title so that it appears as "Patrons and Donations"; and change the font color of the title to the Brown, Accent 3, Darker 25% theme color.

16. Move the Donation Value field label and its field value box to the left a bit. Then resize the Donation ID field label on the right to fully display the label. Move the Donation ID field label and its field value box to the left to provide space between the Donation ID and Donation Date fields, and then move the Description field label and its field value box to the right a bit, to provide more space between the Donation Date and Description fields. Widen the Cash Donation? field label so all the text is displayed, and then reposition the field label so it is centered over the CashDonation check boxes below it. Move the AuctionItem check boxes to the right so they are centered below the Possible Auction Item? field label. Finally, resize the Phone and Email field labels from their left sides to reduce the width of the label boxes, moving the words "Phone" and "Email" closer to the field value boxes. Save the report.

17. Insert the **Flower** picture, which is located in the Access1 > Case3 folder provided with your Data Files, in the PatronsAndDonations report. Move the picture to the right of the report title.

⊕ **Explore** 18. Use the appropriate button on the Report Layout Tools Format tab in the Background group to apply the theme color Tan, Accent 5, Lighter 60% as the alternate row color for the fields from the Patron table; then apply the theme color Tan, Accent 5, Lighter 80% as the alternate row color for the fields from the Donation table. (*Hint*: You must first select an entire row with no background color for the appropriate fields before applying each alternate row color.) Scroll through the report to find a patron record with multiple donations so you can verify the effect of applying the alternate row color to the Donation fields.

19. Apply conditional formatting so that any DonationValue greater than or equal to 250 is formatted as bold and with the Brown 5 font color.

⊕ **Explore** 20. Preview the report so you can see two pages at once. (*Hint*: Use a button on the Print Preview tab.) Check the report to confirm that it is formatted correctly and all field labels and field values are fully displayed. Save the report, print its first page (only if asked by your instructor to do so), and then close the report.

21. Compact and repair the Center database, and then close it.

TROUBLESHOOT

Case Problem 4

Data Files needed for this Case Problem: Appalachia.accdb *(cont. from Module 3)*, **HikeApp.accdb, and Mountains.png**

Hike Appalachia   Molly and Bailey Johnson use the Appalachia database to maintain and analyze data about the hikers, reservations, and tours for their hiking tour business. You'll help them by creating a form and a report in the Appalachia database. Additionally, you'll troubleshoot some problems in another database containing tour information. Complete the following:

1. Open the **Appalachia** database you created and worked with in previous modules, and then click the Enable Content button next to the security warning, if necessary.

2. Use the Form Wizard to create a form containing a main form and a subform. Select all the fields from the Hiker table for the main form, and select all the fields except HikerID from the Reservation table for the subform. Use the Datasheet layout. Specify the title **HikerReservations** for the main form and the title **ReservationSubform** for the subform.

3. Apply the Integral theme to the HikerReservations form *only*.

4. Edit the form title so that it appears with a space between the two words. Change the font color of the title to the Dark Teal, Text 2, Darker 25% theme color.

5. Insert the **Mountains** picture, which is located in the Access1 > Case4 folder provided with your Data Files, in the HikerReservations form. Remove the picture from the control layout, and then move the picture to the right of the form title. Resize the picture so it is approximately double the original size.

6. Resize all columns in the subform to their best fit so that the subform column titles are fully displayed. Save the form.

7. Use the Find command to search for records that contain "WV" in the State field. Display the record for Sarah Peeler (HikerID 509), and then change the Phone field value for this record to **703-599-2043**. Close the form.

8. Use the Report Wizard to create a report based on the primary Hiker table and the related Reservation table. Select all the fields from the Hiker table, and then select all the fields except HikerID from the Reservation table. Do not select any additional grouping levels, and sort the detail records in ascending order by ReservationID. Choose the Outline layout and Portrait orientation. Specify the title **HikersAndReservations** for the report.

9. Apply the Integral theme to the HikersAndReservations report *only*.

10. Edit the report title so that it appears as "Hikers and Reservations"; then change the font color of the title to the Dark Teal, Text 2, Darker 25% theme color.

11. Left-align the Tour Date field label and field value box, then move the People field label and field value box to the left, to reduce the space between the Tour Date and People columns.

12. Insert the **Mountains** picture, which is located in the Access1 > Case4 folder provided with your Data Files, in the HikersAndReservations report. Move the picture to the right of the report title.

13. Apply conditional formatting so that any People field value greater than or equal to 3 appears as bold and with the Red color applied.

14. Preview the entire report to confirm that it is formatted correctly. If necessary, return to Layout view and make changes so that all field labels and field values are completely displayed.

15. Save the report, print its first page (only if asked by your instructor to do so), and then close the report.

16. Compact and repair the Appalachia database, and then close it.

⚙️ **Troubleshoot** 17. Open the **HikeApp** database located in the Access1 > Case4 folder provided with your Data Files. Open the HikerData form in the HikeApp database. The form is not formatted correctly; it should be formatted with the Ion Boardroom theme and the theme color Plum, Accent 1, Darker 50% applied to the title. There are other problems with the form title's format as well. Additionally, some of the field labels are not properly formatted with regard to spacing between words. Identify and fix the problems with the form's format. (*Hint*: To fix the spacing between words in the necessary field labels, use the same procedure you use to fix the spacing between words in the form title text.) Save and close the corrected form.

⚙️ **Troubleshoot** 18. Open the **HikerReservations** form, which is also not formatted correctly. Modify the form so that it matches the corrected format of the HikerData form and has a consistent design, including the correctly placing the logo image and resizing it to approximately double its original size. Fix the formatting problems with the subform as well, and then save and close the corrected form with subform.

⚙️ **Troubleshoot** 19. Open the **HikersAndReservations** report. This report should have a consistent format in terms of theme, color, and so on as the two forms. Additionally, some of the field labels are not properly formatted with regard to spacing between words. (*Hint*: To fix the spacing between words in the necessary field labels, use the same procedure you use to fix the spacing between words in the report title text.) Find and fix these formatting errors. The report also has several problems with field labels and field value boxes, where the labels and values are not fully displayed. Locate and correct all of these problems, being sure to scroll through the entire report. Also, the conditional formatting applied to the People field is supposed to use a bold Red font. Edit the rule to correct the conditional formatting. Save the corrected report, and then preview it to identify and correct any remaining formatting problems.

20. Compact and repair the HikeApp database, and then close it.

POWERPOINT

OBJECTIVES

Session 1.1
- Plan and create a new presentation
- Create a title slide and slides with lists
- Edit and format text
- Move and copy text
- Convert a list to a SmartArt diagram
- Duplicate, rearrange, and delete slides
- Close a presentation

Session 1.2
- Open an existing presentation
- Change the theme and theme variant
- Insert and crop photos
- Modify photo compression options
- Resize and move objects
- Create speaker notes
- Check the spelling
- Run a slide show
- Print slides, handouts, speaker notes, and the outline

Creating a Presentation

Presenting Information About an Event Venue

Case | *Lakeside Event Center*

Lakeside Event Center is a venue in Lake Havasu City, Arizona, that opened in 1981 and is available for functions of all types, including birthdays, bar mitzvahs, corporate events, and weddings. The event center, located on the shore of Lake Havasu, has rooms that can host from 50 to 900 people. The center underwent a recent renovation including planting new gardens and updating the décor inside. Caitlin Keough-Barton was recently hired as the events manager. One of Caitlin's responsibilities is to attract new bookings. Caitlin wants to advertise the hall at upcoming wedding and event-planning conventions.

Microsoft PowerPoint 2016 (or simply **PowerPoint**) is a computer program you use to create a collection of slides that can contain text, charts, pictures, sounds, movies, multimedia, and so on. In this module, you'll use PowerPoint to create a presentation that Caitlin can use to showcase everything Lakeside Event Center has to offer when she attends the Event Planners Association annual convention. After Caitlin reviews it, you'll add graphics and speaker notes to the presentation. Finally, you'll check the spelling, run the slide show to evaluate it, and print the presentation.

STARTING DATA FILES

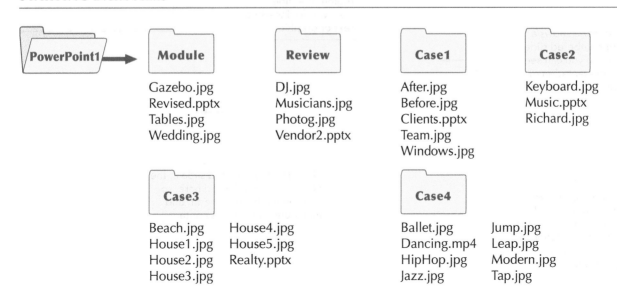

PowerPoint1 →

Module
Gazebo.jpg
Revised.pptx
Tables.jpg
Wedding.jpg

Review
DJ.jpg
Musicians.jpg
Photog.jpg
Vendor2.pptx

Case1
After.jpg
Before.jpg
Clients.pptx
Team.jpg
Windows.jpg

Case2
Keyboard.jpg
Music.pptx
Richard.jpg

Case3
Beach.jpg   House4.jpg
House1.jpg   House5.jpg
House2.jpg   Realty.pptx
House3.jpg

Case4
Ballet.jpg   Jump.jpg
Dancing.mp4   Leap.jpg
HipHop.jpg   Modern.jpg
Jazz.jpg   Tap.jpg

Session 1.1 Visual Overview:

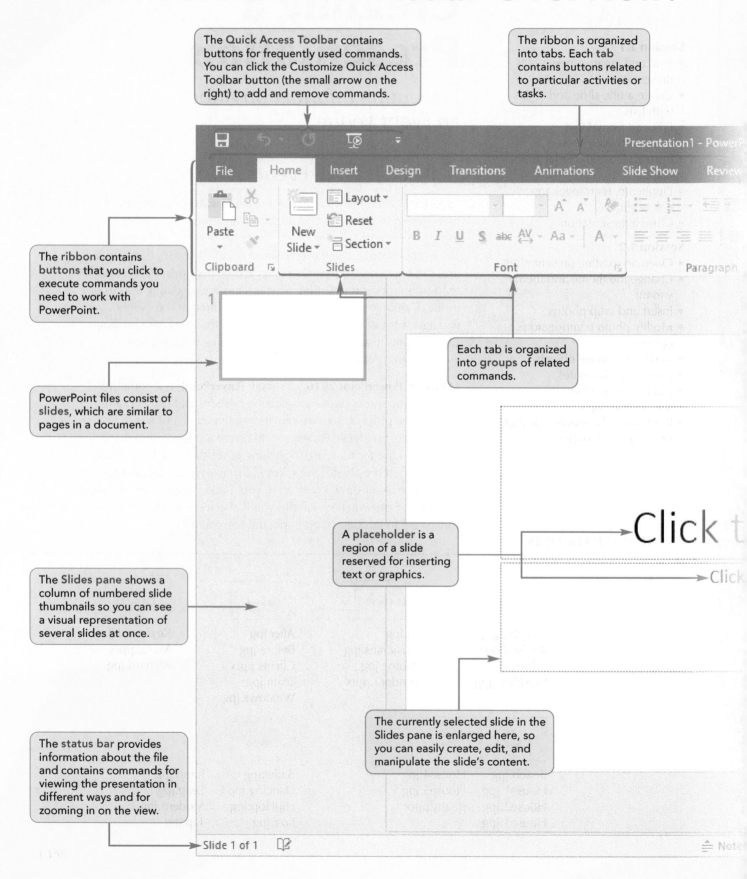

The Quick Access Toolbar contains buttons for frequently used commands. You can click the Customize Quick Access Toolbar button (the small arrow on the right) to add and remove commands.

The ribbon is organized into tabs. Each tab contains buttons related to particular activities or tasks.

The ribbon contains buttons that you click to execute commands you need to work with PowerPoint.

Each tab is organized into groups of related commands.

PowerPoint files consist of slides, which are similar to pages in a document.

A placeholder is a region of a slide reserved for inserting text or graphics.

The Slides pane shows a column of numbered slide thumbnails so you can see a visual representation of several slides at once.

The currently selected slide in the Slides pane is enlarged here, so you can easily create, edit, and manipulate the slide's content.

The status bar provides information about the file and contains commands for viewing the presentation in different ways and for zooming in on the view.

The PowerPoint Window

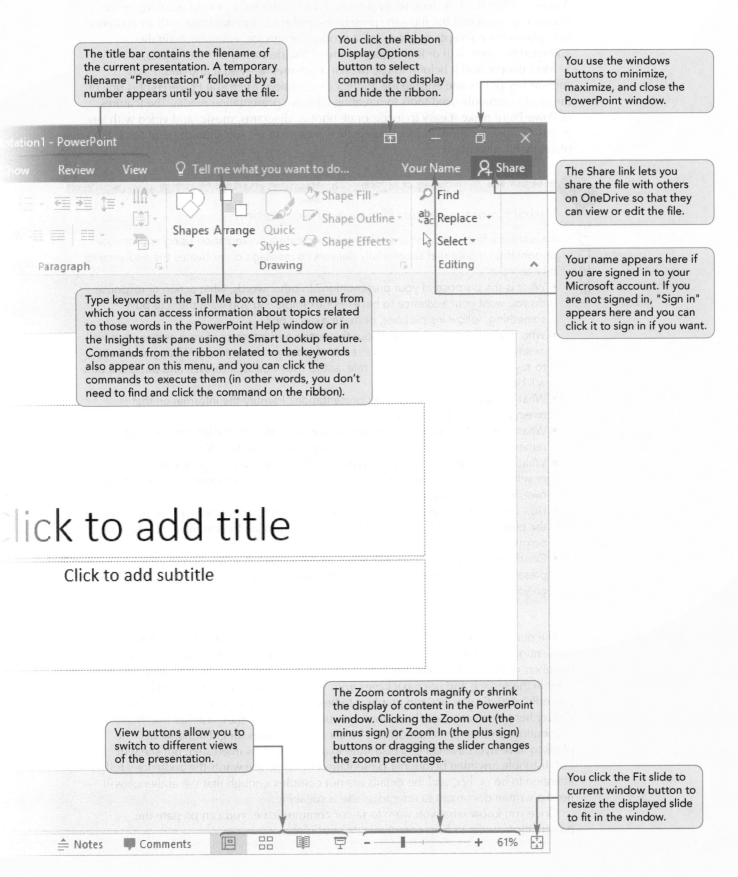

The title bar contains the filename of the current presentation. A temporary filename "Presentation" followed by a number appears until you save the file.

You click the Ribbon Display Options button to select commands to display and hide the ribbon.

You use the windows buttons to minimize, maximize, and close the PowerPoint window.

The Share link lets you share the file with others on OneDrive so that they can view or edit the file.

Type keywords in the Tell Me box to open a menu from which you can access information about topics related to those words in the PowerPoint Help window or in the Insights task pane using the Smart Lookup feature. Commands from the ribbon related to the keywords also appear on this menu, and you can click the commands to execute them (in other words, you don't need to find and click the command on the ribbon).

Your name appears here if you are signed in to your Microsoft account. If you are not signed in, "Sign in" appears here and you can click it to sign in if you want.

View buttons allow you to switch to different views of the presentation.

The Zoom controls magnify or shrink the display of content in the PowerPoint window. Clicking the Zoom Out (the minus sign) or Zoom In (the plus sign) buttons or dragging the slider changes the zoom percentage.

You click the Fit slide to current window button to resize the displayed slide to fit in the window.

Planning a Presentation

A **presentation** is a talk (lecture) or prepared file in which the person speaking or the person who prepared the file—the presenter—wants to communicate with an audience to explain new concepts or ideas, sell a product or service, entertain, train the audience in a new skill or technique, or any of a wide variety of other topics.

Most people find it helpful to use **presentation media**—visual and audio aids to support key points and engage the audience's attention. Microsoft PowerPoint is one of the most commonly used tools for creating effective presentation media. The features of PowerPoint make it easy to incorporate photos, diagrams, music, and video with key points of a presentation. Before you create a presentation, you should spend some time planning its content.

PROSKILLS

Verbal Communication: Planning a Presentation

Answering a few key questions will help you create a presentation using appropriate presentation media that successfully delivers its message or motivates the audience to take an action.

- What is the purpose of your presentation? In other words, what action or response do you want your audience to have? For example, do you want them to buy something, follow instructions, or make a decision?
- Who is your audience? Think about the needs and interests of your audience as well as any decisions they'll make as a result of what you have to say. What you choose to say to your audience must be relevant to their needs, interests, and decisions or it will be forgotten.
- What are the main points of your presentation? Identify the information that is directly relevant to your audience.
- What presentation media will help your audience absorb the information and remember it later? Do you need lists, photos, charts, or tables?
- What is the format for your presentation? Will you deliver the presentation orally or will you create a presentation file that your audience members will view on their own, without you present?
- How much time do you have for the presentation? Keep that in mind as you prepare the presentation content so that you have enough time to present all of your key points.
- Consider whether handouts will help your audience follow along with your presentation or steal your audience's attention when you want them to be focused on you, the presenter.

The purpose of Caitlin's presentation is to convince people attending wedding conventions to book their weddings at Lakeside Event Center. Her audience will be members of the local community who are planning a wedding. She also plans to explain the service and price packages from which people can choose. Caitlin will use PowerPoint to display lists and graphics to help make her message clear. She plans to deliver her presentation orally to small groups of people as they visit her booth at the convention, and her presentation will be about 10 minutes long. For handouts, she plans to have flyers available to distribute to anyone who is interested, but she will not distribute anything before her presentation because she wants the audience's full attention to be on her, and the details are not complex enough that the audience will need a written document to refer to as she is speaking.

Once you know what you want to say or communicate, you can prepare the presentation media to help communicate your ideas.

Starting PowerPoint and Creating a New Presentation

Microsoft PowerPoint 2016 is a tool you can use to create and display visual and audio aids on slides to help clarify the points you want to make in your presentation or to create a presentation that people view on their own without you being present.

When PowerPoint starts, the Recent screen in Backstage view is displayed. **Backstage view** contains commands that allow you to manage your presentation files and PowerPoint options. When you first start PowerPoint, the only actions available to you in Backstage view are to open an existing PowerPoint file or create a new file. You'll start PowerPoint now.

To start PowerPoint:

▶ 1. On the Windows taskbar, click the **Start** button ⊞. The Start menu opens.

▶ 2. Click **All apps** on the Start menu, scroll the list, and then click **PowerPoint 2016.** PowerPoint starts and displays the Recent screen in Backstage view. See Figure 1-1. In the orange bar on the left is a list of recently opened presentations, and on the right are options for creating new presentations.

Figure 1-1	Recent screen in Backstage view

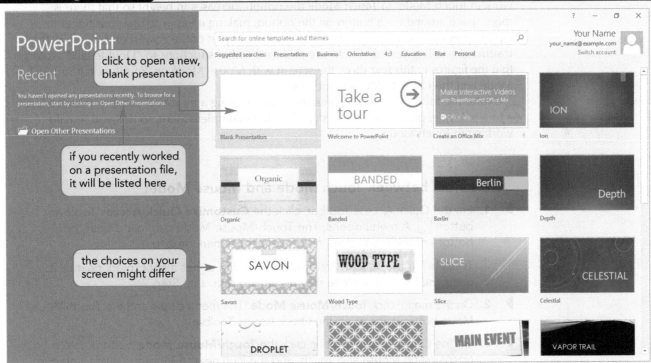

TIP

To create a new blank presentation when PowerPoint is already running, click the File tab on the ribbon, click New in the navigation bar, and then click Blank Presentation.

3. Click **Blank Presentation**. Backstage view closes and a new presentation window appears. The temporary filename "Presentation1" appears in the title bar. There is only one slide in the new presentation—Slide 1.

Trouble? If you do not see the area on the ribbon that contains buttons and you see only the ribbon tab names, click the Home tab to expand the ribbon and display the commands, and then in the bottom-right corner of the ribbon, click the Pin the ribbon button ⊞ that appears.

Trouble? If the window is not maximized, click the Maximize button ▢ in the upper-right corner.

When you create a new presentation, it is displayed in Normal view. **Normal view** displays the selected slide enlarged so you can add and manipulate objects on the slide. The Slides pane on the left side of the program window displays **thumbnails**— miniature images—of all the slides in the presentation. The Home tab on the ribbon is selected when you first open or create a presentation. The Session 1.1 Visual Overview identifies elements of the PowerPoint window.

Working in Touch Mode

In Office 2016, you can work with a mouse or, if you have a touch screen, you can work in Touch Mode. In **Touch Mode** the ribbon increases in height so that there is more space around each button on the ribbon, making it easier to use your finger to tap the specific button you need. Also, in the main part of the PowerPoint window, the instructions telling you to "Click" are replaced with instructions to "Double tap." Note that the figures in this text show the screen with Mouse Mode on. You'll switch to Touch Mode and then back to Mouse Mode now.

Note: The following steps assume that you are using a mouse. If you are instead using a touch device, please read these steps but don't complete them, so that you remain working in Touch Mode.

To switch between Touch Mode and Mouse Mode:

1. On the Quick Access Toolbar, click the **Customize Quick Access Toolbar** button ▾. A menu opens. The Touch/Mouse Mode command near the bottom of the menu does not have a checkmark next to it.

   Trouble? If the Touch/Mouse Mode command has a checkmark next to it, press the Esc key to close the menu, and then skip Step 2.

2. On the menu, click **Touch/Mouse Mode**. The menu closes and the Touch/Mouse Mode button appears on the Quick Access Toolbar.

3. On the Quick Access Toolbar, click the **Touch/Mouse Mode** button. A menu opens listing Mouse and Touch, and the icon next to Mouse is shaded orange to indicate it is selected.

   Trouble? If the icon next to Touch is shaded orange, press the Esc key to close the menu and skip Step 4.

4. On the menu, click **Touch**. The menu closes and the ribbon increases in height so that there is more space around each button on the ribbon. Notice that the instructions in the main part of the PowerPoint window changed by replacing the instruction to "Click" with the instruction to "Double tap." See Figure 1-2. Now you'll change back to Mouse Mode.

Figure 1-2   **PowerPoint window with Touch mode active**

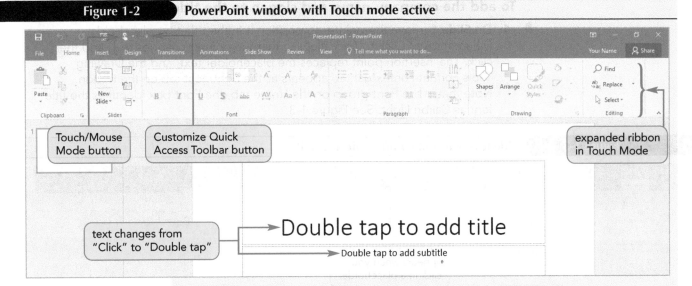

Trouble? If you are working with a touch screen and want to use Touch Mode, skip Steps 5 and 6.

5. Click the **Touch/Mouse Mode** button, and then click **Mouse**. The ribbon and the instructions change back to Mouse Mode defaults as shown in the Session 1.1 Visual Overview.

6. Click the **Customize Quick Access Toolbar** button, and then click **Touch/Mouse Mode** to deselect this option and remove the checkmark. The Touch/Mouse Mode button is removed from the Quick Access Toolbar.

Creating a Title Slide

The **title slide** is the first slide in a presentation. It generally contains the title of the presentation plus any other identifying information you want to include, such as a company's slogan, the presenter's name, or a company name. The **font**—a set of characters with the same design—used in the title and subtitle may be the same or may be different fonts that complement each other.

The title slide contains two objects called text placeholders. A **text placeholder** is a placeholder designed to contain text. Text placeholders usually display text that describes the purpose of the placeholder and instructs you to click so that you can start typing in the placeholder. The larger text placeholder on the title slide is designed to hold the presentation title, and the smaller text placeholder is designed to contain a subtitle. Once you enter text into a text placeholder, it is no longer a placeholder and becomes an object called a **text box**.

When you click in the placeholder, the **insertion point**, which indicates where text will appear when you start typing, appears as a blinking line in the center of the placeholder. In addition, a contextual tab, the Drawing Tools Format tab, appears on the ribbon. A **contextual tab** appears only in context—that is, when a particular type of object is selected or active—and contains commands for modifying that object.

You'll add a title and subtitle for Caitlin's presentation now. Caitlin wants the title slide to contain the company name and slogan.

To add the company name and slogan to the title slide:

▶ **1.** On **Slide 1**, move the pointer to position it in the title text placeholder (where it says "Click to add title") so that the pointer changes to I, and then click. The insertion point replaces the placeholder text, and the Drawing Tools Format contextual tab appears as the rightmost tab on the ribbon. Note that in the Font group on the Home tab, the Font box identifies the title font as Calibri Light. See Figure 1-3.

Figure 1-3	Title text placeholder after clicking in it

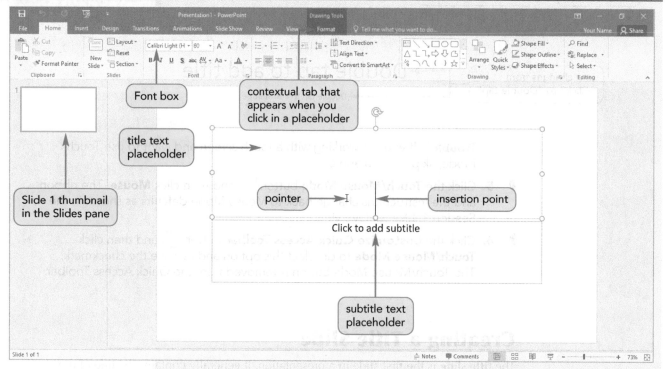

▶ **2.** Type **Lakeside Event Hall**. The placeholder is now a text box.

▶ **3.** Click a blank area of the slide. The border of the text box disappears, and the Drawing Tools Format tab no longer appears on the ribbon.

▶ **4.** Click in the **subtitle text placeholder** (where it says "Click to add subtitle"), and then type **Perfect venue for all occasions!**. Notice in the Font group that the subtitle font is Calibri, a font which works well with the Calibri Light font used in the title text.

▶ **5.** Click a blank area of the slide.

Saving and Editing a Presentation

Once you have created a presentation, you should name and save the presentation file. You can save the file on a hard drive or a network drive, on an external drive such as a USB drive, or to your account on OneDrive, Microsoft's free online storage area.

To save the presentation for the first time:

1. On the Quick Access Toolbar, point to the **Save** button 🖫. A box called a **ScreenTip** appears, identifying the button.

2. Click the **Save** button 🖫. The Save As screen in Backstage view appears. See Figure 1-4. The **navigation bar** on the left contains commands for working with the file and program options. Recently used folders on the selected drive appear in a list on the right.

Figure 1-4 Save As screen in Backstage view

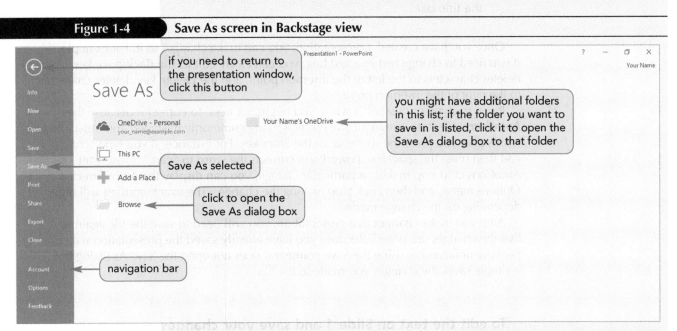

Figure 1-4 Save As screen in Backstage view

3. Click **Browse**. The Save As dialog box opens, similar to the one shown in Figure 1-5.

Figure 1-5 Save As dialog box

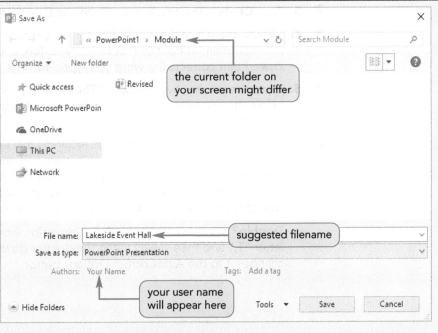

▶ **4.** Navigate to the drive and folder where you are storing your Data Files, and then click in the **File name** box. The suggested filename, Lakeside Event Hall, is selected.

▶ **5.** Type **Convention Presentation**. The text you type replaces the selected text in the File name box.

▶ **6.** Click the **Save** button. The file is saved, the dialog box and Backstage view close, and the presentation window appears again with the new filename in the title bar.

Once you have created a presentation, you can make changes to it. For example, if you need to change text in a text box, you can easily edit it. The Backspace key deletes characters to the left of the insertion point, and the Delete key deletes characters to the right of the insertion point.

If you mistype or misspell a word, you might not need to correct it because the **AutoCorrect** feature automatically corrects many commonly mistyped and misspelled words after you press the spacebar or the Enter key. For instance, if you type "cna" and then press the spacebar, PowerPoint corrects the word to "can." If you want AutoCorrect to stop making a particular change, you can display the AutoCorrect Options menu, and then click Stop making the change. (The exact wording will differ depending on the change made.)

After you make changes to a presentation, you will need to save the file again so that the changes are stored. Because you have already saved the presentation with a permanent filename, using the Save command does not open the Save As dialog box; it simply saves the changes you made to the file.

To edit the text on Slide 1 and save your changes:

▶ **1.** On Slide 1, click the **title**, and then use the ← and → keys as needed to position the insertion point to the right of the word "Hall."

▶ **2.** Press the **Backspace** key four times. The four characters to the left of the insertion point, "Hall," are deleted.

▶ **3.** Type **Center**. The title is now "Lakeside Event Center."

▶ **4.** Click to the left of the word "Perfect" in the subtitle text box to position the insertion point in front of that word, type **Teh**, and then press the **spacebar**. PowerPoint corrects the word you typed to "The."

▶ **5.** Move the pointer over the word **The**. A small, very faint rectangle appears below the first letter of the word. This indicates that an AutoCorrection has been made.

▶ **6.** Move the pointer on top of the faint rectangle that appears under the "T" so that it changes to the AutoCorrect Options button ⬚ ▾, and then click the **AutoCorrect Options** button ⬚ ▾. A menu opens, as shown in Figure 1-6. You can change the word back to what you originally typed, instruct PowerPoint to stop making this type of correction in this file, or open the AutoCorrect dialog box.

Trouble? If you can't see the AutoCorrection indicator box, point to the letter "T," and then slowly move the pointer down until it is over the box and changes it to the AutoCorrect Options button.

Figure 1-6   AutoCorrect Options button menu

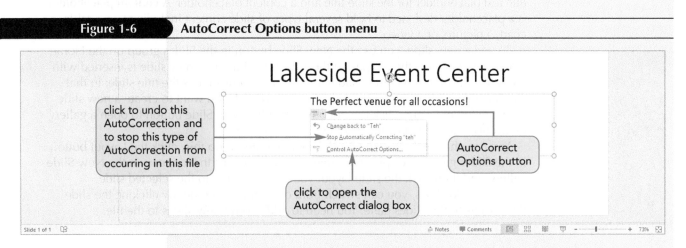

7. Click **Control AutoCorrect Options**. The AutoCorrect dialog box opens with the AutoCorrect tab selected. See Figure 1-7.

Figure 1-7   AutoCorrect tab in the AutoCorrect dialog box

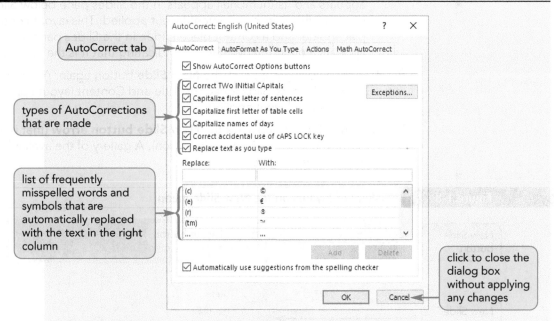

8. Examine the types of changes the AutoCorrect feature makes, and then click the **Cancel** button.

9. Click to the left of the "P" in "Perfect," if necessary, press the **Delete** key, and then type **p**. The subtitle now is "The perfect venue for all occasions!" Now that you have modified the presentation, you need to save your changes.

10. On the Quick Access Toolbar, click the **Save** button 🖫. The changes you made are saved to the Convention Presentation file.

Adding New Slides

Now that you've created the title slide, you need to add more slides. Every slide has a **layout**, which is the arrangement of placeholders on the slide. The title slide uses the Title Slide layout. A commonly used layout is the Title and Content layout, which contains a title text placeholder for the slide title and a content placeholder. A **content placeholder** is a placeholder designed to hold several types of slide content including text, a table, a chart, a picture, or a video.

To add a new slide, you use the New Slide button in the Slides group on the Home tab. When you click the top part of the New Slide button, a new slide is inserted with the same layout as the current slide, unless the current slide is the title slide; in that case the new slide has the Title and Content layout. If you want to create a new slide with a different layout, click the bottom part of the New Slide button to open a gallery of layouts, and then click the layout you want to use.

You can change the layout of a slide at any time. To do this, click the Layout button in the Slides group to display the same gallery of layouts that appears in the New Slide gallery, and then click the slide layout you want to apply to the selected slide.

As you add slides, you can switch from one slide to another by clicking the slide thumbnails in the Slides pane. You need to add several new slides to the file.

To add new slides and apply different layouts:

▶ **1.** Make sure the Home tab is displayed on the ribbon.

▶ **2.** In the Slides group, click the top part of the **New Slide** button. A new slide appears and its thumbnail appears in the Slides pane below Slide 1. The new slide has the Title and Content layout applied. This layout contains a title text placeholder and a content placeholder. In the Slides pane, an orange border appears around the new Slide 2, indicating that it is the current slide.

▶ **3.** In the Slides group, click the **New Slide** button again. A new Slide 3 is added. Because Slide 2 had the Title and Content layout applied, Slide 3 also has that layout applied.

▶ **4.** In the Slides group, click the **New Slide button arrow** (that is, click the bottom part of the New Slide button). A gallery of the available layouts appears. See Figure 1-8.

| Figure 1-8 | **Gallery of layouts on the New Slide menu** |

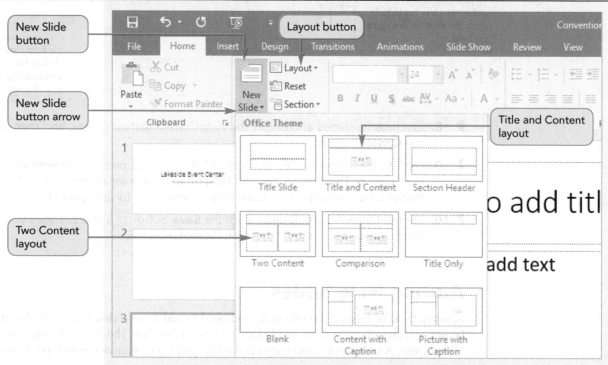

5. In the gallery, click the **Two Content** layout. The gallery closes and a new Slide 4 is inserted with the Two Content layout applied. This layout includes three objects: a title text placeholder and two content placeholders.

6. In the Slides group, click the **New Slide** button. A new Slide 5 is added to the presentation. Because Slide 4 had the Two Content layout applied, that layout is also applied to the new slide. You need to change the layout of Slide 5.

7. In the Slides group, click the **Layout** button. The same gallery of layouts that appeared when you clicked the New Slide button arrow appears. The Two Content layout is selected, as indicated by the shading behind it, showing you that this is the layout applied to the current slide, Slide 5.

8. Click the **Title and Content** layout. The layout of Slide 5 is changed to Title and Content.

9. In the Slides group, click the **New Slide** button twice to add two more slides with the Title and Content layout.

10. Add a new slide with the Two Content layout. There are now eight slides in the presentation. In the Slides pane, Slides 1 through 3 have scrolled up out of view, and vertical scroll bars are now visible in both the Slides pane and along the right side of the program window.

11. In the Slides pane, drag the **scroll box** to the top of the vertical scroll bar, and then click the **Slide 2** thumbnail. Slide 2 appears in the program window and is selected in the Slides pane. See Figure 1-9.

Figure 1-9	Slide 2 with the Title and Content layout

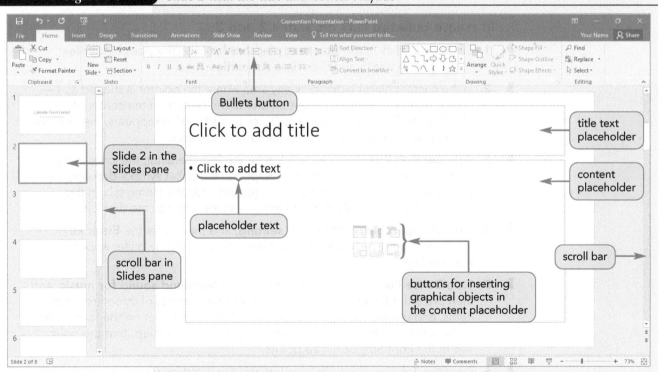

12. On the Quick Access Toolbar, click the **Save** button 🔲. The changes you made are saved in the file.

If you accidentally close a presentation without saving changes and need to recover it, you can do so by clicking the File tab, clicking Open in the navigation bar, and then clicking the Recover Unsaved Presentations button.

Creating Lists

One way to help explain the topic or concept you are describing in your presentation is to use lists. For oral presentations, the intent of lists is to enhance the oral presentation, not replace it. In self-running presentations, items in lists might need to be longer and more descriptive. However, keep in mind that PowerPoint is a presentation graphics program intended to help you present information in a visual, graphical manner, not create a written document in an alternate form.

Items in a list can appear at different levels. A **first-level item** is a main item in a list; a **second-level item**—sometimes called a **subitem**—is an item beneath and indented from a first-level item. Usually, the font size—the size of the text—in subitems is smaller than the size used for text in the level above. Text is measured in **points**, which is a unit of measurement. Text in a book is typically printed in 10- or 12-point type; text on a slide needs to be much larger so the audience can easily read it.

Creating a Bulleted List

A **bulleted list** is a list of items with some type of bullet symbol in front of each item or paragraph. When you create a subitem in the list, a different or smaller symbol is often used. You need to create a bulleted list that describes the amenities of the Lakeside Event Center and one that describes the catering packages available.

To create bulleted lists on Slides 2 and 3:

▶ **1.** On **Slide 2**, click in the **title text placeholder** (with the placeholder text "Click to add title"), and then type **Amenities**.

▶ **2.** In the content placeholder, click any area where the pointer is shaped as Ⅰ— in other words, anywhere except on one of the buttons in the center of the placeholder. The placeholder text "Click to add text" disappears, the insertion point appears, and a light gray bullet symbol appears.

▶ **3.** Type **Comfortable**. As soon as you type the first character, the icons in the center of the content placeholder disappear, the bullet symbol darkens, and the content placeholder changes to a text box. On the Home tab, in the Paragraph group, the Bullets button ⅢⅢ is shaded to indicate that it is selected.

▶ **4.** Press the **spacebar**, type **indoor seating**, and then press the **Enter** key. The insertion point moves to a new line, and a light gray bullet appears on the new line.

▶ **5.** Type **Dance floor**, press the **Enter** key, type **Surround sound for music**, and then press the **Enter** key. The bulleted list now consists of three first-level items, and the insertion point is next to a light gray bullet on the fourth line in the text box. Notice on the Home tab, in the Font group, that the point size in the Font Size box is 28 points.

▶ **6.** Press the **Tab** key. The bullet symbol and the insertion point indent one-half inch to the right, the bullet symbol changes to a smaller size, and the number in the Font Size box changes to 24. See Figure 1-10.

| Figure 1-10 | Subitem created on Slide 2 |

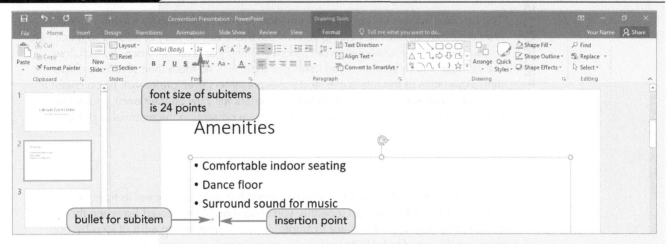

7. Type **DJs can easily plug in** and then press the **Enter** key.

8. Type **Live bands have plenty of room** and then press the **Enter** key. A third subitem is created. You will change it to a first-level item using a key combination. In this book, when you need to press two keys together, the keys will be listed separated by a plus sign.

9. Press the **Shift+Tab** keys. The bullet symbol and the insertion point shift back to the left margin of the text box, the bullet symbol changes back to the larger size, and 28 again appears in the Font Size box because this line is now a first-level bulleted item.

10. Type **Optional outdoor seating on patio**, press the **Enter** key, and then type **Additional appetizers and pasta stations available as add-ons**.

11. In the Slides pane, click the **Slide 3** thumbnail to display Slide 3, click in the **title text placeholder**, and then type **Packages**.

12. In the content placeholder, click the **placeholder text**, type **Basic--5 hours, standard catering package**, press the **Enter** key, and then type **Special-- 5 hours, deluxe catering package**. When you pressed the spacebar after typing 5, AutoCorrect changed the two dashes to an em-dash, a typographical character longer than a hyphen.

If you add more text than will fit in the text box with the default font sizes and line spacing, **AutoFit** adjusts these features to make the text fit. When AutoFit is activated, the AutoFit Options button appears below the text box. You can click this button and then select from among several options, including turning off AutoFit for this text box and splitting the text between two slides. Although AutoFit can be helpful, be aware that it also allows you to crowd text on a slide, making the slide less effective.

PROSKILLS

Written Communication: How Much Text Should I Include?

Text can help audiences retain the information you are presenting by allowing them to read the main points while hearing you discuss them. But be wary of adding so much text to your slides that your audience can ignore you and just read the slides. Try to follow the 7x7 rule—no more than seven items per slide, with no more than seven words per item. A variation of this rule is 6x6, and some presenters even prefer 4x4. If you create a self-running presentation (a presentation file others will view on their own), you will usually need to add more text than you would if you were presenting the material in person.

Creating a Numbered List

A **numbered list** is similar to a bulleted list except that numbers appear in front of each item instead of bullet symbols. Generally you should use a numbered list when the order of the items is important—for example, if you are presenting a list of step-by-step instructions that need to be followed in sequence in order to complete a task successfully. You need to create a numbered list on Slide 5 to explain how clients can reserve the event center for a function.

To create a numbered list on Slide 5:

▶ **1.** In the Slides pane, click the **Slide 5** thumbnail to display Slide 5, and then type **Reserve Lakeside Event Center for Your Function!** in the title text placeholder.

▶ **2.** In the content placeholder, click the **placeholder text**.

▶ **3.** On the Home tab, in the Paragraph group, click the **Numbering** button. The Numbering button is selected, the Bullets button is deselected, and in the content placeholder, the bullet symbol is replaced with the number 1 followed by a period.

   Trouble? If a menu containing a gallery of numbering styles appears, you clicked the Numbering button arrow on the right side of the button. Click the Numbering button arrow again to close the menu, and then click the left part of the Numbering button.

▶ **4.** Type **Specify date of function**, and then press the **Enter** key. As soon as you start typing, the number 1 darkens to black. After you press the Enter key, the insertion point moves to the next line, next to the light gray number 2.

▶ **5.** Type **Choose package**, press the **Enter** key, type **Submit deposit**, and then press the **Enter** key. The number 4 appears on the next line.

▶ **6.** In the Paragraph group, click the **Increase List Level** button. The fourth line is indented to be a subitem under the third item, and the number 4 changes to a number 1 in a smaller font size than the first-level items. Clicking the Increase List Level button is an alternative to pressing the Tab key to create a subitem.

▶ **7.** Type **Credit card**, press the **Enter** key, type **Debit from checking account**, and then press the **Enter** key.

▶ **8.** In the Paragraph group, click the **Decrease List Level** button. The sixth line is now a first-level item, and the number 4 appears next to it. Clicking the Decrease List Level button is an alternative to pressing the Shift+Tab keys to promote a subitem.

9. Type **Confirm**. The list now consists of four first-level numbered items and two subitems under number 3.

10. In the second item, click before the word "Choose," and then press the **Enter** key. A blank line is inserted above the second item.

11. Press the ↑ key. A light-gray number 2 appears in the blank line. The item on the third line in the list is still numbered 2.

12. Type **Specify number of guests**. As soon as you start typing, the new number 2 darkens in the second line, and the third item in the list is numbered 3. Compare your screen to Figure 1-11.

Figure 1-11	Numbered list on Slide 5

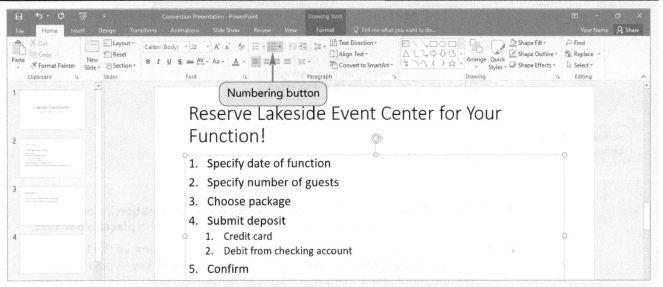

Creating an Unnumbered List

An **unnumbered list** is a list that does not have bullets or numbers preceding each item. Unnumbered lists are useful in slides when you want to present information on multiple lines without actually itemizing the information. For example, contact information for the presenter, including his or her email address, street address, city, and so on, would be clearer if it were in an unnumbered list.

As you have seen, items in a list have a little extra space between each item to visually separate bulleted items. Sometimes, you don't want the extra space between lines. If you press the Shift+Enter keys instead of just the Enter key, a new line is created, but it is still considered to be part of the item above it. Therefore, there is no extra space between the lines. Note that this also means that if you do this in a bulleted or numbered list, the new line will not have a bullet or number next to it because it is not a new item.

You need to create a slide that explains the event center's name. Also, Caitlin asks you to create a slide containing contact information.

To create unnumbered lists on Slides 4 and 7:

1. In the Slides pane, click the **Slide 4** thumbnail to display Slide 4. Slide 4 has the Two Content layout applied.

2. Type **About Us** in the title content placeholder, and then in the left content placeholder, click the **placeholder text**.

3. On the Home tab, in the Paragraph group, click the **Bullets** button. The button is no longer selected, and the bullet symbol disappears from the content placeholder.

4. Type **Lakeside**, press the **Enter** key, type **Event**, press the **Enter** key, and then type **Center**. Compare your screen to Figure 1-12.

Figure 1-12	Unnumbered list on Slide 4

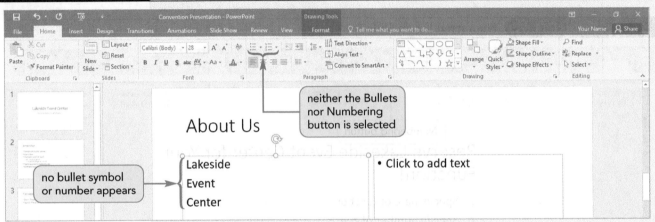

neither the Bullets nor Numbering button is selected

About Us

no bullet symbol or number appears

Lakeside
Event
Center

• Click to add text

5. Display **Slide 7** in the Slide pane, type **For More Information** in the title text placeholder, and then in the content placeholder, click the **placeholder text**.

6. In the Paragraph group, click the **Bullets** button to remove the bullets, type **Lakeside Event Center**, and then press the **Enter** key. A new line is created, but there is extra space above the insertion point. This is not how addresses usually appear.

7. Press the **Backspace** key to delete the new line and move the insertion point back to the end of the first line, and then press the **Shift+Enter** keys. The insertion point moves to the next line, and, this time, there is no extra space above it.

8. Type **15680 Shore Drive**, press the **Shift+Enter** keys, and then type **Lake Havasu City, AZ 86403**. You need to insert the phone number on the next line, the general email address for the group on the line after that, and the website address on the last line. The extra space above these lines will set this information apart from the address and make it easier to read.

9. Press the **Enter** key to create a new line with extra space above it, type **(928) 555-HALL**, press the **Enter** key, type **info@lec.example.com**, and then press the **Enter** key. The insertion point moves to a new line with extra space above it, and the email address you typed changes color to blue and is underlined.

When you type text that PowerPoint recognizes as an email or website address and then press the spacebar or Enter key, the text is automatically formatted as a link that can be clicked during a slide show. To indicate this, the color of the text is changed and the text is underlined. Links are active only during a slide show.

▶ **10.** Type **www.lec.example.com**, and then press the **spacebar**. The text is formatted as a link. Caitlin plans to click the link during her presentation to show the audience the website, so she wants it to stay formatted as a link. However, there is no need to have the email address formatted as a link because no one will click it during the presentation.

▶ **11.** Right-click **info@lec.example.com**. A shortcut menu opens.

▶ **12.** On the shortcut menu, click **Remove Hyperlink**. The email address is no longer formatted as a hyperlink. Compare your screen to Figure 1-13.

| Figure 1-13 | List on Slide 7 |

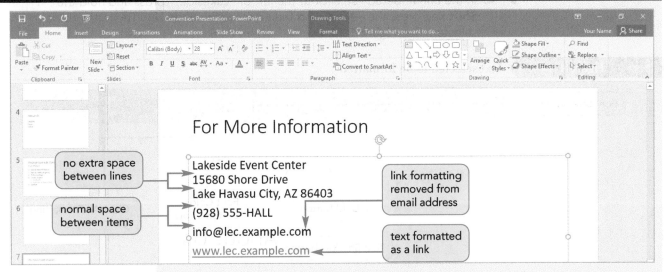

▶ **13.** On the Quick Access Toolbar, click the **Save** button 🖫 to save the changes.

Formatting Text

Slides in a presentation should have a cohesive look and feel. For example, the slide titles and the text in content placeholders should be in complementary fonts. However, there are times when you need to change the format of text. For instance, you might want to make specific words bold to make them stand out more.

To apply a format to text, either the text or the text box must be selected. If you want to apply the same formatting to all the text in a text box, you can click the border of the text box. When you do this, the dotted line border changes to a solid line to indicate that the contents of the entire text box are selected.

The commands in the Font group on the Home tab are used to apply formatting to text. Some of these commands are also available on the Mini toolbar, which appears when you select text with the mouse. The **Mini toolbar** contains commonly used buttons for formatting text. If the Mini toolbar appears, you can use the buttons on it instead of those in the Font group.

Some of the commands in the Font group use the Microsoft Office **Live Preview** feature, which previews the change on the slide so you can instantly see what the text will look like if you apply that format.

Caitlin wants the contact information on Slide 7 ("For More Information") to be larger. She also wants the first letter of each item in the unnumbered list on Slide 4 ("About Us") formatted so they are more prominent.

To format the text on Slides 4 and 7:

1. On **Slide 7** ("For More Information"), position the pointer on the border of the text box containing the contact information so that it changes to ⬚, and then click the border of the text box. The border changes to a solid line to indicate that the entire text box is selected.

2. On the Home tab, in the Font group, click the **Increase Font Size** button Ａ twice. All the text in the text box increases in size with each click, and all the text in the text box is now 36 points.

3. Display **Slide 4** ("About Us").

4. In the unnumbered list, click to the left of "Lakeside," press and hold the **Shift** key, press the → key, and then release the **Shift** key. The letter "L" is selected. See Figure 1-14.

Figure 1-14 **Text selected to be formatted**

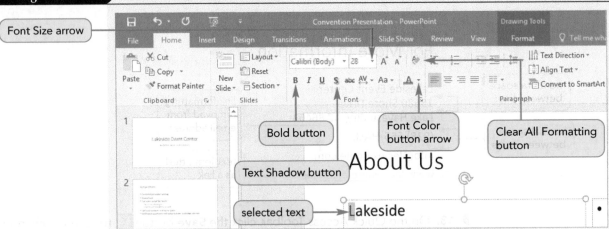

5. In the Font group, click the **Bold** button Ｂ. The Bold button becomes selected, and the selected text is formatted as bold.

6. Make sure the letter "L" is still selected, and then in the Font group, click the **Text Shadow** button Ｓ. The selected text is now bold with a slight drop shadow.

7. In the Font group, click the **Font Size arrow** to open the Font Size menu, and then click **48**. The selected text is now 48 points.

8. In the Font group, click the **Font Color button arrow** Ａ ▾. A menu containing colors opens.

9. Under Theme Colors, move the pointer over each color, noting the ScreenTips that appear and watching as Live Preview changes the color of the selected text as you point to each color. Figure 1-15 shows the pointer pointing to the Orange, Accent 2, Darker 25% color.

| Figure 1-15 | Font Color menu |

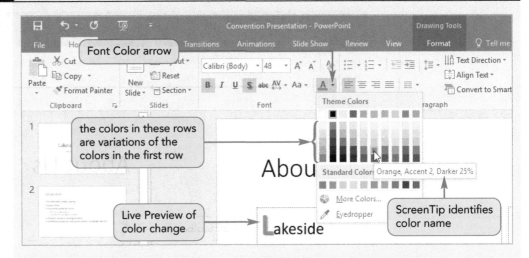

10. Using the ScreenTips, locate the **Orange, Accent 2, Darker 25%** color, and then click it. The selected text changes to the orange color you clicked.

Now you need to format the first letters in the other words in the list to match the letter "L." You can repeat the steps you did when you formatted the letter "L," or you can use the Format Painter to copy all the formatting of the letter "L" to the other letters you need to format.

Also, Caitlin wants the text in the unnumbered list to be as large as possible. Because the first letters of each word are larger than the rest of the letters, the easiest way to do this is to select all of the text, and then use the Increase Font Size button. All of the letters will increase in size by four points with each click.

To use the Format Painter to copy and apply formatting on Slide 4:

1. Make sure the letter "L" is still selected.

2. On the Home tab, in the Clipboard group, click the **Format Painter** button, and then move the pointer on top of the slide. The button is selected, and the pointer changes to ▉I.

3. Position the pointer before the letter "E" in "Event," press and hold the mouse button, drag over the letter **E**, and then release the mouse button. The formatting you applied to the letter "L" is copied to the letter "E," and the Mini toolbar appears. See Figure 1-16. The Mini toolbar appears whenever you drag over text to select it.

| Figure 1-16 | The Mini toolbar |

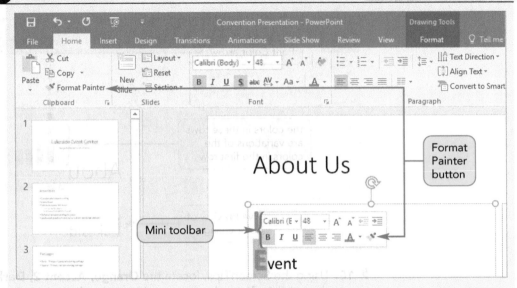

4. On the Mini toolbar, click the **Format Painter** button, and then drag across the letter **C** in "Center."

5. Click the border of the text box to select the entire text box, and then in the Font group, click the **Increase Font Size** button five times. In the Font group, the Font Size button indicates that the text is 48+ points. This means that in the selected text box, the text that is the smallest is 48 points and there is some text that is a larger point size.

6. On the Quick Access Toolbar, click the **Save** button to save the changes.

INSIGHT

Undoing and Redoing Actions

If you make a mistake or change your mind about an action as you are working, you can reverse the action by clicking the Undo button on the Quick Access Toolbar. You can undo up to the most recent 20 actions by continuing to click the Undo button or by clicking the Undo button arrow and then selecting as many actions in the list as you want. You can also Redo an action that you undid by clicking the Redo button on the Quick Access Toolbar.

When there are no actions that can be redone, the Redo button changes to the Repeat button. You can use the Repeat button to repeat an action, such as formatting text as bold. If the Repeat button is light gray, this means it is unavailable because there is no action to repeat (or to redo).

Moving and Copying Text

You can move or copy text and objects in a presentation using the Clipboard. The **Clipboard** is a temporary storage area available to all Windows programs on which text or objects are stored when you cut or copy them. To **cut** text or objects—that is, remove the selected text or objects from one location so that you can place it somewhere else—you select the text or object, and then use the Cut button in the Clipboard group on the Home tab to remove the selected text or object and place it on the Clipboard. To **copy** selected text or objects, you use the Copy button in the Clipboard group on the Home tab, which leaves the original text or object on the slide and places a copy of it on the Clipboard. You can then **paste** the text or object stored on the Clipboard anywhere in the presentation or, in fact, in any file in any Windows program.

You can paste an item on the Clipboard as many times and in as many locations as you like. However, the Clipboard can hold only the most recently cut or copied item. As soon as you cut or copy another item, it replaces the previously cut or copied item on the Clipboard.

Note that cutting text or an object is different from using the Delete or Backspace key to delete it. Deleted text and objects are not placed on the Clipboard; this means they cannot be pasted.

Caitlin wants a few changes made to Slides 5 and 3. You'll use the Clipboard as you make these edits.

To copy and paste text using the Clipboard:

▶ **1.** Display **Slide 5** ("Reserve Lakeside Event Center for Your Function!"), and then double-click the word **Reserve** in the title text. The word "Reserve" is selected.

▶ **2.** On the Home tab, in the Clipboard group, click the **Copy** button. The selected word is copied to the Clipboard.

▶ **3.** In the last item in the numbered list, click after the word "Confirm," and then press the **spacebar**.

▶ **4.** In the Clipboard group, click the **Paste** button. The text is pasted and picks up the formatting of its destination; that is, the pasted text is the 28-point Calibri font, the same font and size as the rest of the first-level items in the list, instead of 44-point Calibri Light as in the title. The Paste Options button 📋 appears below the pasted text.

▶ **5.** Click the **Paste Options** button 📋. A menu opens with four buttons on it. See Figure 1-17.

Figure 1-17   Buttons on the Paste Options menu when text is on the Clipboard

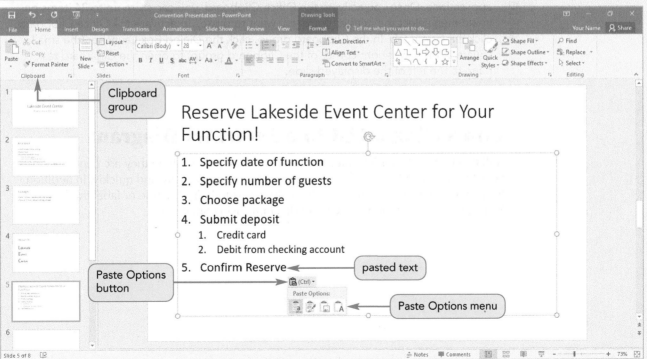

6. Point to each button on the menu, reading the ScreenTips and watching to see how the pasted text changes in appearance. The first button is the Use Destination Theme button, and this is the default choice when you paste text.

7. Click a blank area of the slide to close the menu without making a selection, press the **Backspace** key, type **ation**, click to the left of "Reservation," press the **Delete** key, and then type **r**. The word "reservation" in the numbered list is now all lowercase.

8. Display **Slide 2** ("Amenities"). The last bulleted item (starts with "Additional appetizers") belongs on Slide 3.

9. In the last bulleted item, position the pointer on top of the bullet symbol so that the pointer changes to ✛, and then click. The entire bulleted item is selected.

10. In the Clipboard group, click the **Cut** button. The last bulleted item is removed from the slide and placed on the Clipboard.

11. Display **Slide 3** ("Packages"), click after the second bulleted item, and then press the **Enter** key to create a third bulleted item.

12. In the Clipboard group, click the **Paste** button. The bulleted item you cut is pasted as the third bulleted item on Slide 3 using the default paste option of Use Destination Theme. The insertion point appears next to a fourth bulleted item.

13. Press the **Backspace** key twice to delete the extra line, and then on the Quick Access Toolbar, click the **Save** button to save the changes.

> **TIP**
> To cut text or an object, you can press the Ctrl+X keys; to copy text or an object, press the Ctrl+C keys; and to paste the item on the Clipboard, press the Ctrl+V keys.

INSIGHT

Using the Office Clipboard

The **Office Clipboard** is a special Clipboard available only to Microsoft Office applications. Once you activate the Office Clipboard, you can store up to 24 items on it and then select the item or items you want to paste. To activate the Office Clipboard, click the Home tab. In the Clipboard group, click the Dialog Box Launcher (the small square in the lower-right corner of the Clipboard group) to open the Clipboard task pane to the left of the displayed slide.

Converting a List to a SmartArt Diagram

A **diagram** visually depicts information or ideas and shows how they are connected. **SmartArt** is a feature that allows you to create diagrams easily and quickly. In addition to shapes, SmartArt diagrams usually include text to help describe or label the shapes. You can create the following types of diagrams using SmartArt:

- **List**—Shows a list of items in a graphical representation
- **Process**—Shows a sequence of steps in a process
- **Cycle**—Shows a process that is a continuous cycle
- **Hierarchy** (including organization charts)—Shows the relationship between individuals or units
- **Relationship** (including Venn diagrams, radial diagrams, and target diagrams)—Shows the relationship between two or more elements
- **Matrix**—Shows information in a grid
- **Pyramid**—Shows foundation-based relationships
- **Picture**—Provides a location for a picture or pictures that you insert

There is also an Office.com category of SmartArt, which, if you are connected to the Internet, displays additional SmartArt diagrams available in various categories on Office.com, a Microsoft website that contains tools for use with Office programs.

A quick way to create a SmartArt diagram is to convert an existing list. When you select an existing list and then click the Convert to SmartArt Graphic button in the Paragraph group on the Home tab, a gallery of SmartArt layouts appears. For SmartArt, a **layout** is the arrangement of the shapes in the diagram. Each first-level item in the list is converted to a shape in the SmartArt diagram. If the list contains subitems, you might need to experiment with different layouts to find one that best suits the information in your list.

REFERENCE

Converting a Bulleted List into a SmartArt Diagram

- Click anywhere in the bulleted list.
- In the Paragraph group on the Home tab, click the Convert to SmartArt Graphic button, and then click More SmartArt Graphics.
- In the Choose a SmartArt Graphic dialog box, select the desired SmartArt type in the list on the left.
- In the center pane, click the SmartArt diagram you want to use.
- Click the OK button.

Caitlin wants the numbered list on Slide 5 changed into a SmartArt diagram.

To convert the list on Slide 5 into a SmartArt diagram:

1. Display **Slide 5** ("Reserve Lakeside Event Center for Your Function!"), and then click anywhere in the numbered list to display the text box border.

2. On the Home tab, in the Paragraph group, click the **Convert to SmartArt** button. A gallery of SmartArt layouts appears.

3. Point to the first layout. The ScreenTip identifies this layout as the Vertical Bullet List layout, and Live Preview shows you what the numbered list will look like with that layout applied. See Figure 1-18. Notice that the subitems are not included in a shape in this diagram.

Figure 1-18   **Live Preview of the Vertical Bullet List SmartArt layout**

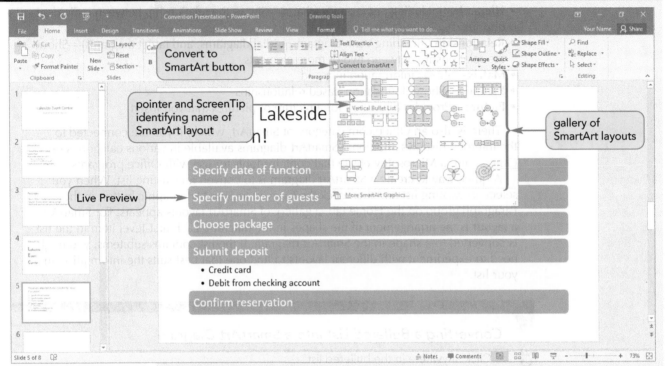

4. Point to several other layouts in the gallery, observing the Live Preview of each one. In some of the layouts, the subitems are included in a shape.

5. At the bottom of the gallery, click **More SmartArt Graphics**. The Choose a SmartArt Graphic dialog box opens. See Figure 1-19. You can click a type in the left pane to filter the middle pane to show only that type of layout.

Figure 1-19   **Choose a SmartArt Graphic dialog box**

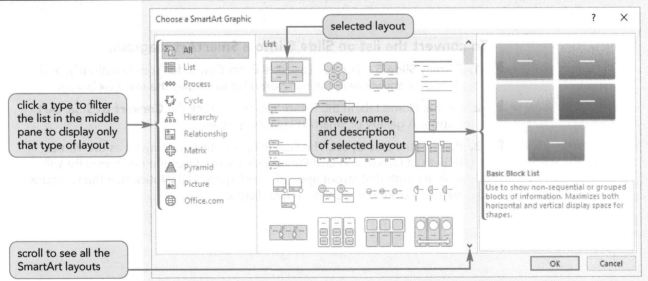

6. In the left pane, click **Process**, and then in the middle pane, click the **Step Up Process** layout, using the ScreenTips to identify it (it's the second layout in the first row). The right pane changes to show a description of that layout.

7. Click the **OK** button. The dialog box closes, and each of the first level items in the list appears in the square shapes in the diagram. The items also appear as a bulleted list in the Text pane, which is open to the left of the diagram. The SmartArt Tools contextual tabs appear on the ribbon. See Figure 1-20.

Figure 1-20   SmartArt diagram with the Step Up Process layout

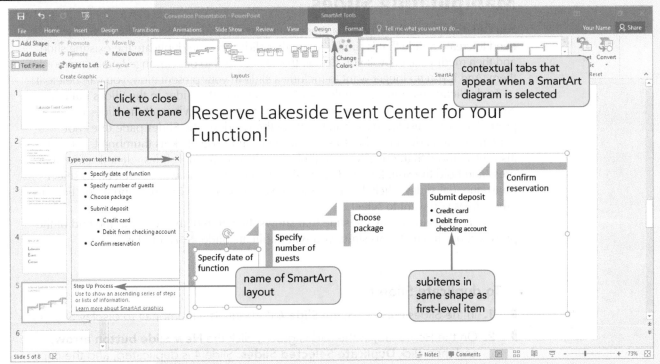

Trouble? If you do not see the Text pane, click the Text pane button on the left border of the selected SmartArt diagram.

In this layout, the subitems below "Submit deposit" are included in the fourth step shape; they are not placed in their own shapes in the diagram. Caitlin decides the information in the subitems does not need to be on the slide because people will see those options on the website when they submit their deposit.

8. In the "Submit deposit" shape, select **Debit from checking account**, and then press the **Delete** key. The text is deleted from the shape and from the Text pane.

9. In the Text pane, click to the right of the word "card," press the **Backspace** key as many times as necessary to delete all of the bullet text, and then press the **Backspace** key once more. The bullet changes to a first-level bullet and a new square shape is inserted in the diagram.

10. Press the **Backspace** key one more time. The empty bullet and the blank line are deleted in the Text pane, and the newly added shape is removed from the diagram. The "Submit deposit" shape now contains only the first-level item. Notice that AutoFit increased the size of the text in all the shapes so that the text still fills the shapes and is as large as possible. The "Submit deposit" shape is still selected. This shape should appear after the "Confirm reservation" shape.

▶ **11.** On the SmartArt Tools Design tab, in the Create Graphic group, click the **Move Down** button. The selected "Submit deposit" shape moves down one spot in the bulleted list in the text pane and one shape to the right in the SmartArt graphic on the slide.

▶ **12.** Click a blank area of the slide to deselect the diagram, and then on the Quick Access Toolbar, click the **Save** button 🖫 to save your changes.

Manipulating Slides

You can manipulate the slides in a presentation to suit your needs. For instance, if you need to create a slide that is similar to another slide, you can duplicate the existing slide and then modify the copy. If you decide that slides need to be rearranged, you can reorder them. And if you no longer want to include a slide in your presentation, you can delete it.

To duplicate, rearrange, or delete slides, you select the slides in the Slides pane in Normal view or switch to Slide Sorter view. In **Slide Sorter view** all the slides in the presentation are displayed as thumbnails in the window; the Slides pane does not appear. You already know that to select a single slide you click its thumbnail. You can also select more than one slide at a time. To select sequential slides, click the first slide, press and hold the Shift key, and then click the last slide you want to select. To select nonsequential slides, click the first slide, press and hold the Ctrl key, and then click any other slides you want to select.

Caitlin wants to display the slide that shows the name of the center at the end of the presentation. To create this slide, you will duplicate Slide 4 ("About Us").

To duplicate Slide 4:

▶ **1.** In the Slides pane, click the **Slide 4** ("About Us") thumbnail to display Slide 4.

▶ **2.** On the Home tab, in the Slides group, click the **New Slide button arrow**, and then click **Duplicate Selected Slides**. Slide 4 is duplicated, and the copy is inserted as a new Slide 5 in the Slides pane. Slide 5 is now the current slide. If more than one slide were selected, they would all be duplicated. The duplicate slide doesn't need the title; Caitlin just wants to reinforce the center's name.

▶ **3.** On Slide 5, click anywhere on the title **About Us**, click the **text box border** to select the text box, and then press the **Delete** key. The title and the title text box are deleted and the title text placeholder reappears.

You could delete the title text placeholder, but it is not necessary. When you display the presentation to an audience as a slide show, any unused placeholders will not appear.

Next you need to rearrange the slides. You need to move the duplicate of the "About Us" slide so it is the last slide in the presentation because Caitlin wants to leave it displayed after the presentation is over. She hopes this visual will reinforce the company's name for the audience. Caitlin also wants the "Packages" slide (Slide 3) moved so it appears before the "Amenities" slide (Slide 2), and she wants the original "About Us" slide (Slide 4) to be the second slide in the presentation.

To rearrange the slides in the presentation:

1. In the Slides pane, scroll up, if necessary, so that you can see Slides 2 and 3, and then drag the **Slide 3** ("Packages") thumbnail above the Slide 2 ("Amenities") thumbnail. As you drag, the Slide 3 thumbnail follows the pointer and Slide 2 moves down. The "Packages" slide is now Slide 2 and "Amenities" is now Slide 3. You'll move the other two slides in Slide Sorter view.

TIP

You can also use the buttons in the Presentation Views group on the View tab to switch views.

2. On the status bar, click the **Slide Sorter** button. The view switches to Slide Sorter view. Slide 2 appears with an orange border, indicating that it is selected.

3. On the status bar, click the **Zoom Out** button as many times as necessary until you can see all nine slides in the presentation. See Figure 1-21.

Figure 1-21   Slide Sorter view

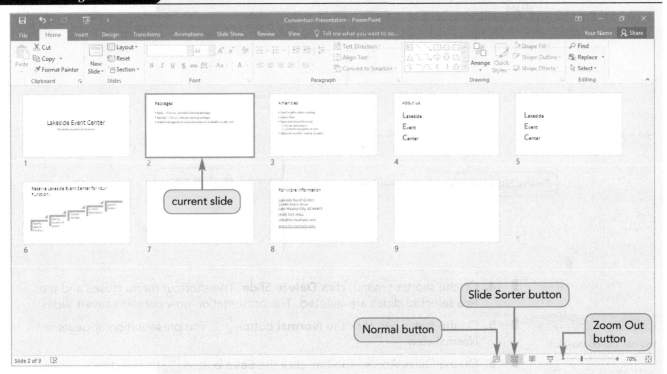

4. Drag the **Slide 4** ("About Us") thumbnail to between Slides 1 and 2. As you drag, the other slides move out of the way. The slide is repositioned, and the slides are renumbered so that the "About Us" slide is now Slide 2.

5. Drag the **Slide 5** thumbnail (the slide containing just the name of the company) so it becomes the last slide in the presentation (Slide 9).

Now you need to delete the two blank slides. To delete a slide, you can right-click its thumbnail to display a shortcut menu.

To delete the blank slides:

1. Click **Slide 6** (a blank slide), press and hold the **Shift** key, and then click **Slide 8** (the other blank slide), and then release the **Shift** key. The two slides you clicked are selected, as well as the slide between them. You want to delete only the two blank slides.

▶ **2.** Click a blank area of the window to deselect the slides, click **Slide 6**, press and hold the **Ctrl** key, click **Slide 8**, and then release the **Ctrl** key. Only the two slides you clicked are selected.

▶ **3.** Right-click either selected slide. A shortcut menu appears. See Figure 1-22.

Figure 1-22   **Shortcut menu for selected slides**

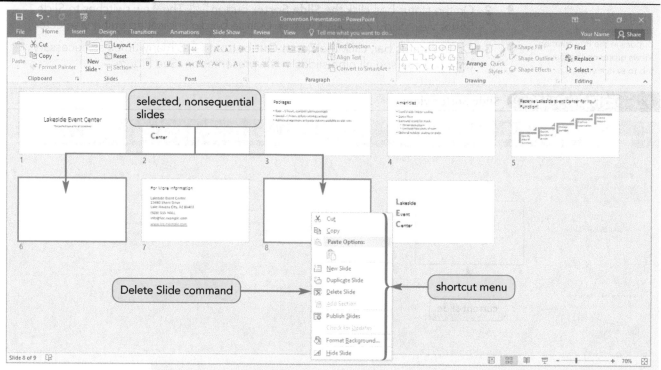

▶ **4.** On the shortcut menu, click **Delete Slide**. The shortcut menu closes and the two selected slides are deleted. The presentation now contains seven slides.

▶ **5.** On the status bar, click the **Normal** button 🔲. The presentation appears in Normal view.

▶ **6.** On the Quick Access Toolbar, click the **Save** button 🔲 to save the changes to the presentation.

Closing a Presentation

When you are finished working with a presentation, you can close it and leave PowerPoint open. To do this, you click the File tab to open Backstage view, and then click the Close command. If you click the Close button ☒ in the upper-right corner of the PowerPoint window and only one presentation is open, you will not only close the presentation, you will exit PowerPoint as well.

You're finished working with the presentation for now, so you will close it. First you will add your name to the title slide.

To add your name to Slide 1 and close the presentation:

▶ **1.** Display **Slide 1** (the title slide), click the **subtitle**, position the insertion point after "occasions!," press the **Enter** key, and then type your full name.

> **2.** Click the **File** tab. Backstage view appears with the Info screen displayed. See Figure 1-23.

| Figure 1-23 | Info screen in Backstage view |

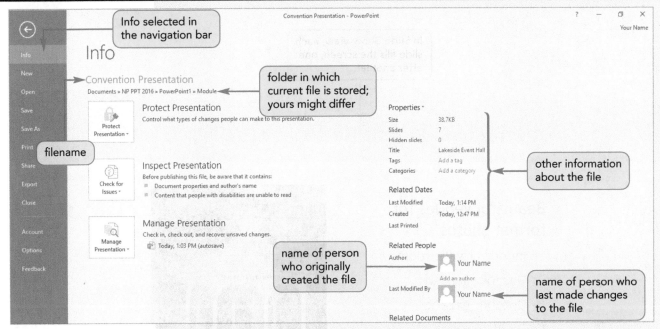

> **3.** In the navigation bar, click **Close**. Backstage view closes, and a dialog box opens, asking if you want to save your changes.

> **4.** In the dialog box, click the **Save** button. The dialog box and the presentation close, and the empty presentation window appears.

> **Trouble?** If you want to take a break, you can exit PowerPoint by clicking the Close button ☒ in the upper-right corner of the PowerPoint window.

You've created a presentation that includes slides to which you added bulleted, numbered, and unnumbered lists. You also formatted text, converted a list to SmartArt, and manipulated slides. You are ready to give the presentation draft to Caitlin to review.

Session 1.1 Quick Check

REVIEW

1. Define "presentation."
2. How do you display Backstage view?
3. What is a layout?
4. In addition to a title text placeholder, what other type of placeholder do most layouts contain?
5. What is the term for an object that contains text?
6. What is the difference between the Clipboard and the Office Clipboard?
7. How do you convert a list to a SmartArt diagram?

Session 1.2 Visual Overview:

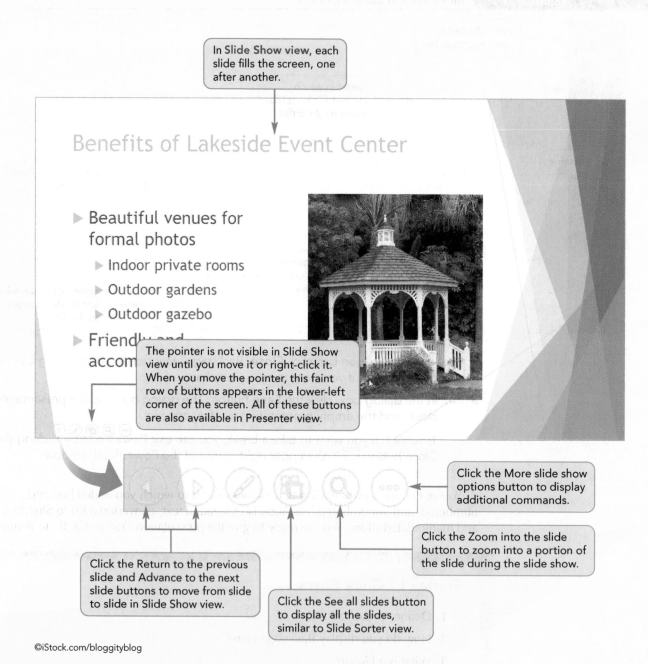

In Slide Show view, each slide fills the screen, one after another.

The pointer is not visible in Slide Show view until you move it or right-click it. When you move the pointer, this faint row of buttons appears in the lower-left corner of the screen. All of these buttons are also available in Presenter view.

Click the More slide show options button to display additional commands.

Click the Zoom into the slide button to zoom into a portion of the slide during the slide show.

Click the Return to the previous slide and Advance to the next slide buttons to move from slide to slide in Slide Show view.

Click the See all slides button to display all the slides, similar to Slide Sorter view.

©iStock.com/bloggityblog

Slide Show and Presenter Views

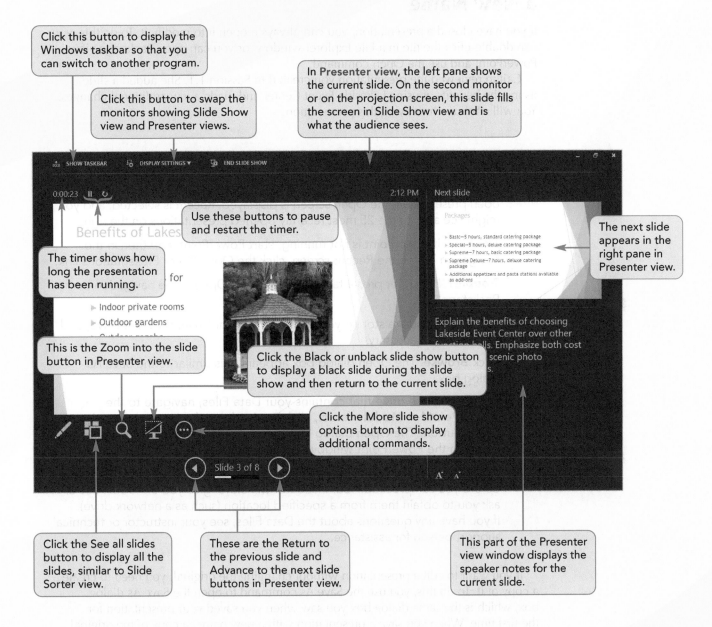

Click this button to display the Windows taskbar so that you can switch to another program.

Click this button to swap the monitors showing Slide Show view and Presenter views.

In **Presenter view**, the left pane shows the current slide. On the second monitor or on the projection screen, this slide fills the screen in Slide Show view and is what the audience sees.

Use these buttons to pause and restart the timer.

The next slide appears in the right pane in Presenter view.

The timer shows how long the presentation has been running.

This is the Zoom into the slide button in Presenter view.

Click the Black or unblack slide show button to display a black slide during the slide show and then return to the current slide.

Click the More slide show options button to display additional commands.

Click the See all slides button to display all the slides, similar to Slide Sorter view.

These are the Return to the previous slide and Advance to the next slide buttons in Presenter view.

This part of the Presenter view window displays the speaker notes for the current slide.

©iStock.com/bloggityblog

Opening a Presentation and Saving It with a New Name

If you have closed a presentation, you can always reopen it to modify it. To do this, you can double-click the file in a File Explorer window, or you can open Backstage view in PowerPoint and use the Open command.

Caitlin reviewed the presentation you created in Session 1.1. She added a slide listing the benefits of using Lakeside Event Center and made a few additional changes. You will continue modifying this presentation.

To open the revised presentation:

▶ **1.** Click the **File** tab on the ribbon to display Backstage view. Because there is no open presentation, the Open screen is displayed. Recent is selected, and you might see a list of the 25 most recently opened presentations on the right.

   Trouble? If PowerPoint is not running, start PowerPoint, and then in the navigation bar on the Recent screen, click the Open Other Presentations link.

   Trouble? If another presentation is open, click Open in the navigation bar in Backstage view.

   Trouble? If you are storing your files on your OneDrive, click OneDrive, and then log in if necessary.

▶ **2.** Click **Browse**. The Open dialog box appears. It is similar to the Save As dialog box.

▶ **3.** Navigate to the drive that contains your Data Files, navigate to the **PowerPoint1 > Module** folder, click **Revised** to select it, and then click the **Open** button. The Open dialog box closes and the Revised presentation opens in the PowerPoint window, with Slide 1 displayed.

   Trouble? If you don't have the starting Data Files, you need to get them before you can proceed. Your instructor will either give you the Data Files or ask you to obtain them from a specified location (such as a network drive). If you have any questions about the Data Files, see your instructor or technical support person for assistance.

If you want to edit a presentation without changing the original, you need to create a copy of it. To do this, you use the Save As command to open the Save As dialog box, which is the same dialog box you saw when you saved your presentation for the first time. When you save a presentation with a new name, a copy of the original presentation is created, the original presentation is closed, and the newly named copy remains open in the PowerPoint window.

To save the Revised presentation with a new name:

▶ **1.** Click the **File** tab, and then in the navigation bar, click **Save As**. The Save As screen in Backstage view appears.

▶ **2.** Click **Browse** to open the Save As dialog box.

3. If necessary, navigate to the drive and folder where you are storing your Data Files.

4. In the File name box, change the filename to **Convention Final**, and then click the **Save** button. The Save As dialog box closes, a copy of the file is saved with the new name Convention Final, and the Convention Final presentation appears in the PowerPoint window.

Changing the Theme and the Theme Variant

A **theme** is a coordinated set of colors, fonts, backgrounds, and effects. All presentations have a theme. If you don't choose one, the default Office theme is applied; that is the theme currently applied to the Convention Final presentation.

You saw the Office theme set of colors when you changed the color of the text on the "About Us" slide. You have also seen the Office theme fonts in use on the slides. In the Office theme, the font of the slide titles is Calibri Light, and the font of the text in content text boxes is Calibri. In themes, the font used for slide titles is the Headings font, and the font used for the content text boxes is the Body font.

In PowerPoint, each theme has several variants with different coordinating colors and sometimes slightly different backgrounds. A theme and its variants are called a **theme family**. PowerPoint comes with several installed themes, and many more themes are available online at Office.com. In addition, you can use a custom theme stored on your computer or network.

You can select a different installed theme when you create a new presentation by clicking one of the themes on the New or Recent screen in Backstage view instead of clicking Blank Presentation, and then clicking one of the variants. If you want to change the theme of an open presentation, you can choose an installed theme on the Design tab, or you can apply a theme applied to another presentation or a theme stored on your computer or network. When you change the theme, the colors, fonts, and slide backgrounds change to those used in the new theme.

Caitlin wants the theme of the Convention Final presentation changed to one that has more color in the background. First you'll display Slide 2 so you can see the effect a different theme has on the text formatted with a theme color.

To examine the current theme and then change the theme and theme variant:

1. Display **Slide 2** ("About Us"), and then, in the unnumbered list select the orange letter **L**.

2. On the Home tab, in the Font group, click the **Font Color button arrow** [A]. Look at the colors under Theme Colors, and note the second to last color is selected in the sixth column, which contains shades of orange. Notice also the row of Standard Colors below the theme colors.

3. In the Font group, click the **Font arrow**. A menu of fonts installed on the computer opens. At the top under Theme Fonts, Calibri (Body) is selected because the letter L that you selected is in a content text box. See Figure 1-24.

Figure 1-24 Theme fonts on the Font menu

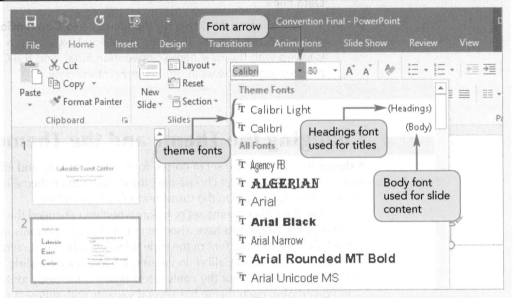

4. On the ribbon, click the **Design** tab. The Font menu closes and the installed themes appear in the Themes gallery on the Design tab. See Figure 1-25. The current theme is the first theme listed in the Themes group on the Design tab. The next theme is the Office theme, which, in this case, is also the current theme.

Figure 1-25 Themes and variants on the Design tab

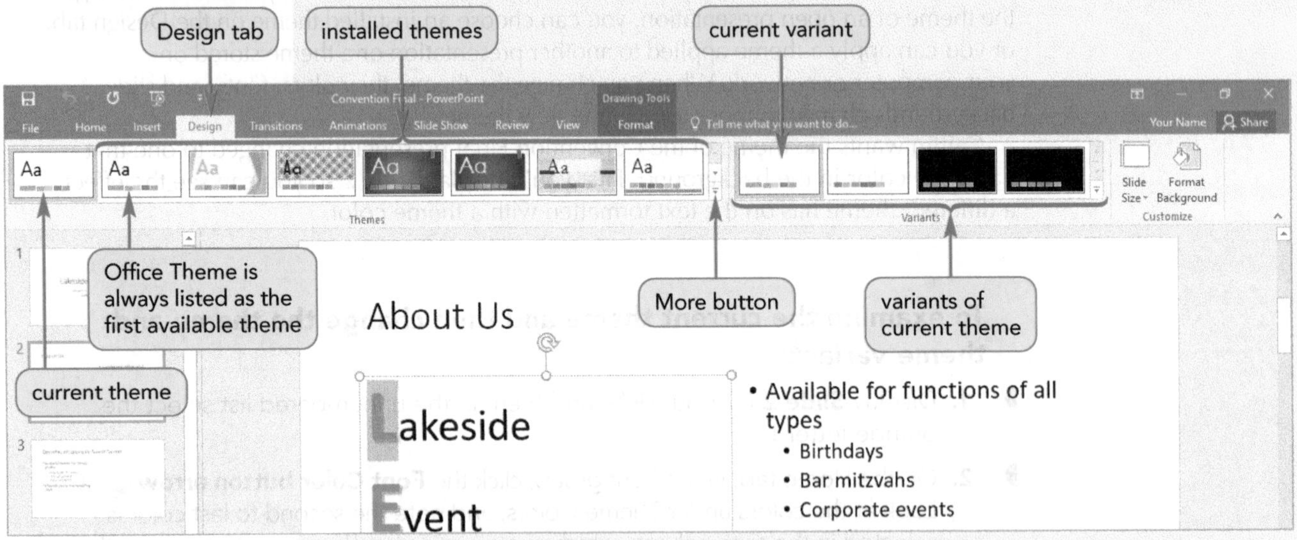

To see all of the installed themes, you need to scroll through the gallery by clicking the up and down scroll buttons on the right end of the gallery or clicking the More button to expand the gallery to see all of the themes at once. The **More button** appears on all galleries that contain additional items or commands that don't fit in the group on the ribbon.

5. In the Themes group, click the **More** button ⌄. The gallery of themes opens. See Figure 1-26. When the gallery is open, the theme applied to the current presentation appears in the first row. In the next row, the first theme is the Office theme, and then the rest of the installed themes appear. Some of these themes also appear on the Recent and New screens in Backstage view.

Figure 1-26   Themes gallery expanded

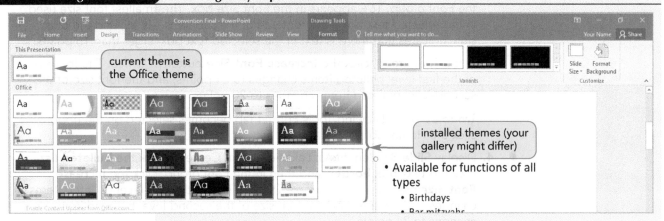

6. Point to several of the themes in the gallery to display their ScreenTips and to see a Live Preview of the theme applied to the current slide.

7. In the first row of the Office section of the gallery, click the **Facet** theme. The gallery closes, and the Facet theme is applied to all the slides with the default variant (the first variant in the Variants group). The title text on each slide changes from black to green, the letters that you had colored orange on Slide 2 are dark green, the bullet symbols change from black circles to green triangles, and in the Slides pane, you can see on the Slide 6 thumbnail that the SmartArt shapes are now green as well.

8. In the Variants group, point to the other three variants to see a Live Preview of each of them, and then click the **second variant** (the blue one).

   Trouble? If there are no variants, your installation of Office might have an extra version of the Facet theme installed. In the Themes group, click the More button, and then make sure you click the Facet theme in the first row.

9. Click the **Home** tab, and then in the Font group, click the **Font Color button arrow** [A ▾]. The selected color—the color of the selected letter "L"—is now a shade of blue in the Theme Colors of the Facet theme. Notice also that the row of Standard Colors is the same as it was when the Office theme was applied.

10. In the Font group, click the **Font arrow**. You can see that the Theme Fonts are now Trebuchet MS for both Headings (slide titles) and the Body (content text boxes).

11. Press the **Esc** key. The Font menu closes.

After you apply a new theme, you should examine your slides to make sure that they look the way you expect them to. The font sizes used for the text in lists in the Facet theme are considerably smaller than those used in the Office theme. You know that Caitlin wants the slides to be legible and clearly visible, so you will increase the font sizes on some of the slides. The title slide is fine, but you need to examine the rest of the slides.

To examine the slides with the new theme and adjust font sizes:

1. On **Slide 2** ("About Us"), in the bulleted list, click the **first bulleted item**. In the Font group, the font size is 18 points, quite a bit smaller than the font size of first-level bulleted items in the Office theme, which is 28 points. You can see that the font size of the subitems is also fairly small.

► **2.** In the bulleted list, click the **text box border** to select the entire text box. In the Font group, 16+ appears in the Font Size box. The smallest font size used in the selected text box—the font size of the subitems—is 16, and the plus sign indicates that there is text in the selected text box larger than 16 points.

► **3.** In the Font group, click the **Increase Font Size** button $\boxed{A}$ twice. The font size of the first-level bulleted items changes to 24 points, and the font size of the second-level bulleted items changes to 20 points.

    Trouble? If the Drawing Tools Format tab becomes selected on the ribbon, click the Home tab.

► **4.** Display **Slide 3** ("Benefits of Lakeside Event Center"), click the **bulleted list**, click the **text box border**, and then in the Font group, click the **Increase Font Size** button $\boxed{A}$ three times. The font size of the first-level bulleted items changes to 28 points, and the font size of the second-level bulleted items changes to 24 points.

► **5.** On **Slide 4** ("Packages") and **Slide 5** ("Amenities"), increase the size of the text in the bulleted lists so that the font size of the first-level items is 28 points and of the subitems is 24 points.

► **6.** Display **Slides 6, 7, 8,** and then **Slide 1** in the Slide pane. These remaining slides look fine.

► **7.** On the Quick Access Toolbar, click the **Save** button $\boxed{\square}$. The changes to the presentation are saved.

INSIGHT

Understanding the Difference Between Themes and Templates

As explained earlier, a theme is a coordinated set of colors, fonts, backgrounds, and effects. A **template** has a theme applied, but it also contains text, graphics, and placeholders to help direct you in creating content for a presentation. You can create and save your own custom templates or find everything from calendars to marketing templates among the thousands of templates available on Office.com. To find a template on Office.com, display the Recent or New screen in Backstage view, type keywords in the "Search for online templates and themes" box, and then click the Search button in the box to display templates related to the search terms. To create a new presentation based on the template you find, click the template and then click Create.

    If a template is stored on your computer, you can apply the theme used in the template to an existing presentation. If you want to apply the theme used in a template on Office.com to an existing presentation, you need to download the template to your computer first, and then you can apply it to an existing presentation.

Working with Photos

Most people are exposed to multimedia daily and expect to have information conveyed visually as well as verbally. In many cases, graphics are more effective than words for communicating an important point. For example, if a sales force has reached its sales goals for the year, including a photo in your presentation of a person reaching the top of a mountain can convey a sense of exhilaration to your audience.

Inserting Photos Stored on Your Computer or Network

Content placeholders contain buttons that you can use to insert things other than a list, including photos stored on your hard drive, a network drive, a USB drive, an SD card from a digital camera, or any other medium to which you have access. You can also use the Pictures button in the Images group on the Insert tab to add photos to slides.

Caitlin has photos that she wants inserted on three of the slides in the presentation. She asks you to add the photos to the presentation.

To insert photos on Slides 3, 5, and 8:

▶ 1. Display **Slide 3** ("Benefits of Lakeside Event Center"), and then in the content placeholder on the right, click the **Pictures** button 🖻. The Insert Picture dialog box opens. This dialog box is similar to the Open dialog box.

▶ 2. Navigate to the **PowerPoint1 > Module** folder included with your Data Files, click **Gazebo**, and then click the **Insert** button. The dialog box closes, and a picture of a gazebo appears in the placeholder and is selected. The contextual Picture Tools Format tab appears on the ribbon to the right of the View tab and is the active tab. See Figure 1-27.

| Figure 1-27 | Picture inserted on Slide 3 |

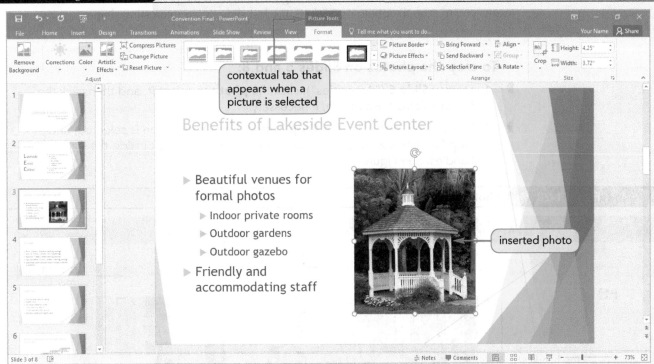

©iStock.com/bloggityblog

▶ 3. Display **Slide 5** ("Amenities"). This slide uses the Title and Content layout and does not have a second content placeholder. You can change the layout to include a second content placeholder, or you can use a command on the ribbon to insert a photo.

▶ 4. Click the **Insert** tab, and then in the Images group, click the **Pictures** button. The Insert Picture dialog box opens.

▶ **5.** In the PowerPoint1 > Module folder, click **Tables**, and then click the **Insert** button. The dialog box closes and the picture is added to the slide, covering the bulleted list. You will fix this later.

▶ **6.** Display **Slide 8** (the last slide). This slide has the Two Content layout applied, but you can still use the Pictures command on the Insert tab.

▶ **7.** Click the **Insert** tab on the ribbon.

▶ **8.** In the Images group, click the **Pictures** button, click **Wedding** in the PowerPoint1 > Module folder, and then click the **Insert** button. The picture replaces the content placeholder on the slide.

Cropping Photos

Sometimes you want to display only part of a photo. For example, if you insert a photo of a party scene that includes a bouquet of colorful balloons, you might want to show only the balloons. To do this, you can **crop** the photo—cut out the parts you don't want to include. In PowerPoint, you can crop it manually to any size you want, crop it to a preset ratio, or crop it to a shape.

Caitlin wants you to crop the photo on Slide 5 ("Amenities") to make the dimensions of the final photo smaller without making the images in the photo smaller. She also wants you to crop the photo on Slide 8 (the last slide) to an interesting shape.

To crop the photos on Slides 5 and 8:

▶ **1.** Display **Slide 5** ("Amenities"), click the **photo** to select it, and then click the **Picture Tools Format** tab, if necessary.

▶ **2.** In the Size group, click the **Crop** button. The Crop button is selected, and crop handles appear around the edges of the photo just inside the sizing handles. See Figure 1-28.

Figure 1-28	Photo with crop handles

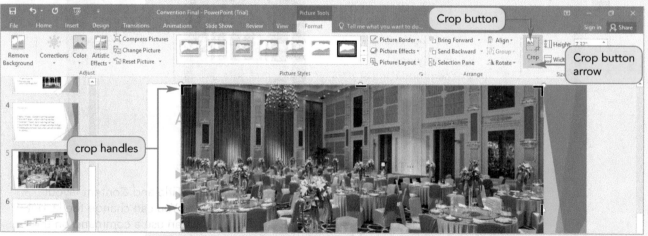

©iStock.com/kai zhang; ©iStock.com/bloggityblog

▶ **3.** Position the pointer directly on top of the right-middle crop handle so that it changes to ┝, press and hold the mouse button, and then drag the crop handle to the left approximately two inches. See Figure 1-29.

Figure 1-29   Cropped photo

Figure 1-29   Cropped photo

part of the photo that will be retained

area that will be removed from photo

©iStock.com/kai zhang; ©iStock.com/bloggityblog; Courtesy of Dina White

4. Click the **Crop** button again. The Crop feature is turned off, but the photo is still selected and the Format tab is still the active tab.

5. Display **Slide 8** (the last slide), click the **photo** to select it, and then click the **Picture Tools Format** tab, if necessary.

6. In the Size group, click the **Crop button arrow**. The Crop button menu opens. See Figure 1-30.

Figure 1-30   Crop button menu

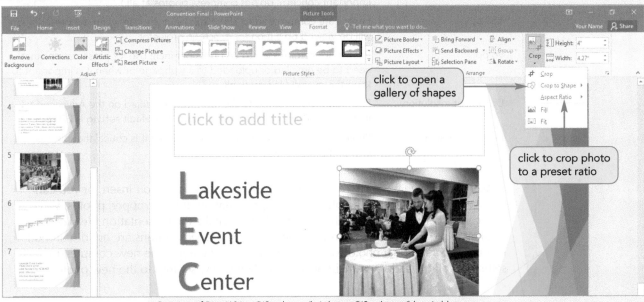

click to open a gallery of shapes

click to crop photo to a preset ratio

Click to add title

Lakeside

Event

Center

Courtesy of Dina White; ©iStock.com/kai zhang; ©iStock.com/bloggityblog

▶ **7.** Point to **Crop to Shape** to open a gallery of shapes, and then in the second row under Basic Shapes, click the **Plaque** shape. The photo is cropped to a plaque shape. Notice that the rectangular selection border of the original photo is still showing.

▶ **8.** In the Size group, click the **Crop** button. You can now see the cropped portions of the original, rectangle photo that are shaded gray.

▶ **9.** Click a blank area of the slide. The picture is no longer selected, and the Home tab is the active tab on the ribbon.

Modifying Photo Compression Options

When you save a presentation that contains photos, PowerPoint automatically compresses the photos to a resolution of 220 pixels per inch (ppi). (For comparison, photos printed in magazines are typically 300 ppi.) Compressing photos reduces the size of the presentation file, but it also reduces the quality of the photos. See Figure 1-31 for a description of the compression options available. If an option in the dialog box is gray, the photo is a lower resolution than that setting. Note that many monitors and projectors are capable of displaying resolutions only a little higher (98 ppi) than the resolution designated for email (96 ppi).

Figure 1-31 ▶ **Photo compression settings**

Compression Setting	Description
330 ppi	Photos are compressed to 330 pixels per inch; use when slides need to maintain the quality of the photograph when displayed on high-definition (HD) displays. Use when photograph quality is of the highest concern and file size is not an issue.
220 ppi	Photos are compressed to 220 pixels per inch; use when slides need to maintain the quality of the photograph when printed. This is the default setting for PowerPoint presentations. (Note that although this is minimal compression, it is still compressed, and if photograph quality is the most important concern, do not compress photos at all.)
150 ppi	Photos are compressed to 150 pixels per inch; use when the presentation will be viewed on a monitor or screen projector.
96 ppi	Photos are compressed to 96 pixels per inch; use for presentations that need to be emailed or uploaded to a webpage or when it is important to keep the overall file size small.
Document resolution	Photos are compressed to the resolution specified on the Advanced tab in the PowerPoint Options dialog box. The default setting is 220 ppi.
No compression	Photos are not compressed at all; used when it is critical that photos remain at their original resolution.

You can change the compression setting for each photo that you insert, or you can change the settings for all the photos in the presentation. If you cropped photos, you also can discard the cropped areas of the photo to make the presentation file size smaller. (Note that when you crop to a shape, the cropped portions are not discarded.) If you insert additional photos or crop a photo after you apply the new compression settings to all the slides, you will need to apply the new settings to the new photos.

Modifying Photo Compression Settings and Removing Cropped Areas

- After all photos have been added to the presentation file, click any photo in the presentation to select it.
- Click the Picture Tools Format tab. In the Adjust group, click the Compress Pictures button.
- In the Compress Pictures dialog box, click the option button next to the resolution you want to use.
- To apply the new compression settings to all the photos in the presentation, click the Apply only to this picture check box to deselect it.
- To keep cropped areas of photos, click the Delete cropped areas of pictures check box to deselect it.
- Click the OK button.

You will adjust the compression settings to make the file size of the presentation as small as possible so that Caitlin can easily send it or post it for others without worrying about file size limitations on the receiving server.

To modify photo compression settings and remove cropped areas from photos:

▶ **1.** On **Slide 8** (the last slide), click the **photo**, and then click the **Picture Tools Format** tab, if necessary.

▶ **2.** In the Adjust group, click the **Compress Pictures** button. The Compress Pictures dialog box opens. See Figure 1-32. Under Target output, the Use document resolution option button is selected. Other than that option button, only the E-mail (96 ppi) option button is selected. This is because the currently selected photo's resolution is higher than 96 ppi but lower than the next largest photo size, Web (150 ppi).

Figure 1-32   **Compress Pictures dialog box**

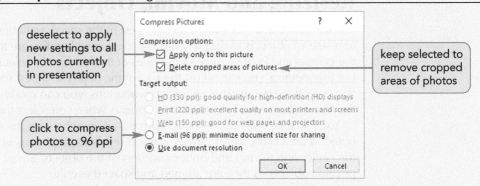

▶ **3.** Click the **E-mail (96 ppi)** option button. This setting compresses the photos to the smallest possible size. At the top of the dialog box under Compression options, the Delete cropped areas of pictures check box is already selected. This option is not applied to cropped photos until you open this dialog box and then click the OK button to apply it. Because you want the presentation file size to be as small as possible, you do want cropped portions of photos to be deleted, so you'll leave this selected. The Apply only to this picture check box is also selected; however, you want the settings applied to all the photos in the file.

Be sure you deselect the Apply only to this picture check box, and be sure you are satisfied with the way you cropped the photo on Slide 5 before you click OK to close the dialog box.

▶ **4.** Click the **Apply only to this picture** check box to deselect it.

▶ **5.** Click the **OK** button.

The dialog box closes and the compression settings are applied to all the photos in the presentation. You can confirm that the cropped areas of photos were removed by examining the photo on Slide 5. (The photo on Slide 8 was cropped to a shape, so the cropped areas on it were not removed.)

▶ **6.** Display **Slide 5** ("Amenities"), click the **photo**, and then click the **Picture Tools Format** tab, if necessary.

▶ **7.** In the Size group, click the **Crop** button. The Crop handles appear around the photo, but the portions of the photo that you cropped out no longer appear.

▶ **8.** Click the **Crop** button again to deselect it, and then save the changes to the presentation.

INSIGHT

Keeping Photos Uncompressed

Suppose you are a photographer and want to create a presentation to show your photos. In that case, you would want to display them at their original, uncompressed resolution. To do this, you need to change a setting in the PowerPoint Options dialog box before you add photos to slides. Click the File tab to open Backstage view, click Options in the navigation bar to open the PowerPoint Options dialog box, click Advanced in the navigation bar, and then locate the Image Size and Quality section. To keep images at their original resolution, click the Do not compress images in file check box to select it. Note that you can also change the default compression setting for photos in this dialog box—you can increase the compression or choose to automatically discard cropped portions of photos and other editing data. Note that these changes affect only the current presentation.

Resizing and Moving Objects

You can resize and move any object to best fit the space available on a slide. One way to resize an object is to drag a sizing handle. **Sizing handles** are the circles that appear in the corners and in the middle of the sides of the border of a selected object. When you use this method, you can adjust the size of the object so it best fits the space visually. If you need to size an object to exact dimensions, you can modify the measurements in the Size group on the Format tab that appears when you select the object.

You can also drag an object to reposition it anywhere on the slide. If more than one object is on a slide, **smart guides**, dashed red lines, appear as you drag to indicate the center and the top and bottom borders of the objects. Smart guides can help you position objects so they are aligned and spaced evenly.

In addition to using the smart guides, it can be helpful to display rulers and gridlines in the window. The rulers appear along the top and left sides of the displayed slide. Gridlines are one-inch squares made up of dots one-sixth of an inch apart. As you drag an object, it snaps to the grid, even if the grid is not visible.

Resizing and Moving Pictures

Pictures and other objects that cause the Picture Tools Format tab to appear when selected have their aspect ratios locked by default. The **aspect ratio** is the ratio of the object's height to its width. When the aspect ratio is locked, if you resize the photo by dragging a corner sizing handle or if you change one dimension in the Size group on the Picture Tools Format tab, the other dimension will change by the same percentage. However, if you drag one of the sizing handles in the middle of an object's border, you will override the locked aspect ratio setting and resize the object only in the direction you drag. Generally you do not want to do this with photos because the images will become distorted.

You need to resize and move the photos you inserted on Slides 3, 5, and 8 so the slides are more attractive. You'll display the rulers and gridlines to help you as you do this.

To move and resize the photos on Slides 3, 5, and 8:

1. Click the **View** tab, and then in the Show group, click the **Ruler** and the **Gridlines** check boxes. Rulers appear above and to the left of the displayed slide, and the gridlines appear on the slide.

2. On **Slide 5** ("Amenities"), click the **photo**, if necessary, and then position the pointer on the top-middle sizing handle so that the pointer changes to ↕.

3. Press and hold the mouse button so that the pointer changes to ┼, drag the top-middle sizing handle down approximately two inches, and then release the mouse button. The photo is two inches shorter, but the image is distorted.

4. On the Quick Access Toolbar, click the **Undo** button ⟲. You need to resize the photo by dragging a corner sizing handle to maintain the aspect ratio.

5. Click the **Picture Tools Format** tab, and then note the measurements in the Size group. The photo is 7.32 inches high and about 8.4 inches wide. (The exact width on your screen might differ depending on how much you cropped.)

6. Position the pointer on the bottom-left corner sizing handle so that it changes to ⤢, press and hold the mouse button so that the pointer changes to ┼, and then drag the bottom-left sizing handle up. Even though you are dragging in only one direction, because you are dragging a corner sizing handle, both the width and height are changing proportionately to maintain the aspect ratio.

7. When the photo is approximately 4.5 inches high and approximately 5 inches wide, release the mouse button. Note that the measurements in the Height and Width boxes changed to reflect the picture's new size.

8. Drag the photo to the right so that the right edge of the photo aligns with the 6-inch mark on the horizontal ruler above the slide, and drag it down so that smart guides appear indicating that the bottom and top of the photo is aligned with the bottom and top of the text box that contains the unnumbered list as shown in Figure 1-33.

TIP

If you don't want objects you are moving to snap to the grid, press and hold the Alt key while you are dragging.

| Figure 1-33 | Repositioning photo on Slide 5 using smart guides and gridlines |

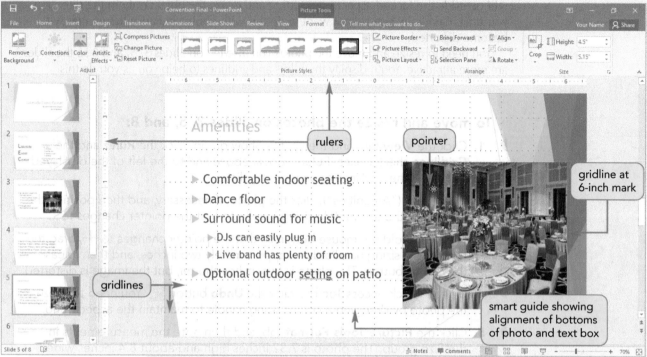

©iStock.com/kai zhang; ©iStock.com/bloggityblog

9. Release the mouse button. The photo is repositioned.

10. Display **Slide 3** ("Benefits of Lakeside Event Center"), click the **photo** to select it, and then click the **Picture Tools Format** tab if necessary.

11. In the Size group, click in the **Height** box to select the current measurement, type **4.5**, and then press the **Enter** key. The measurement in the Width box in the Size group changes proportionately to maintain the aspect ratio, and the new measurements are applied to the photo.

12. Drag the photo up and to the right until horizontal smart guides appear above and below the photo indicating that the top and bottom of the photo and the top and bottom of the text box containing the bulleted list are aligned, and so that the right edge of the photo aligns with the right edge of the title text box (at the 3.5-inch mark on the ruler), as shown in Figure 1-34.

Figure 1-34	Moving resized photo on Slide 3

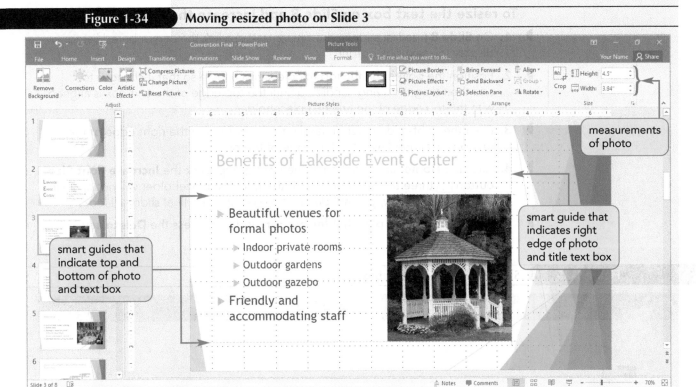

©iStock.com/bloggityblog; ©iStock.com/kai zhang

▶ **13.** When the photo is aligned as shown in Figure 1-34, release the mouse button.

▶ **14.** Display **Slide 8** (the last slide), resize the photo so it is 5.9 inches high and 6.3 inches wide, and then position it so that its bottom edge is aligned with the gridline at the 3-inch mark on the vertical ruler, and its right edge is aligned with the gridline at the 6-inch mark on the horizontal ruler.

▶ **15.** Click the **View** tab, and then click the **Ruler** and **Gridlines** check boxes to deselect them.

Resizing and Moving Text Boxes

The themes and layouts installed with PowerPoint are designed by professionals, so much of the time it's a good idea to use the layouts as provided to be assured of a cohesive look among the slides. However, occasionally there will be a compelling reason to adjust the layout of objects on a slide, by either resizing or repositioning them.

Text boxes, like other objects that cause the Drawing Tools Format tab to appear when selected, do not have their aspect ratios locked by default. This means that when you resize a text box by dragging a corner sizing handle or changing one dimension in the Size group, the other dimension is not affected.

Like any other object on a slide, you can reposition text boxes. To do this, you must position the pointer on the text box border, anywhere except on a sizing handle, to drag it to its new location.

To improve the appearance of Slide 8, you will resize the text box containing the unnumbered list so it vertically fills the slide.

To resize the text box on Slide 8 and increase the font size:

▶ **1.** On **Slide 8** (the last slide in the presentation), click the unnumbered list to display the text box border.

▶ **2.** Position the pointer on the top-middle sizing handle so that it changes to ↕, and then drag the sizing handle up until the top edge of the text box is aligned with the top edge of the title text placeholder.

▶ **3.** Drag the right-middle sizing handle to the right until the right edge of the text box is aligned with the left edge of the photo.

▶ **4.** Click the **Home** tab, and then in the Font group, click the **Increase Font Size** button A̅ three times. Even though the title text placeholder will not appear during a slide show, you will delete it to see how the final slide will look.

▶ **5.** Click the **title text placeholder border**, and then press the **Delete** key. See Figure 1-35.

Figure 1-35	Slide 8 with resized text box

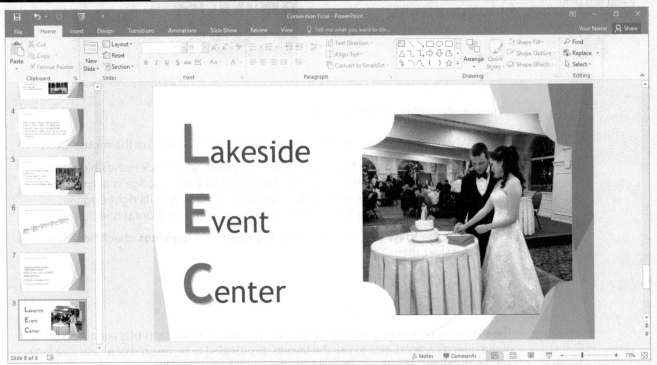

Courtesy of Dina White; ©iStock.com/bloggityblog; ©iStock.com/kai zhang

▶ **6.** Save the changes to the presentation.

Adding Speaker Notes

Speaker notes, or simply **notes**, are information you add about slide content to help you remember to bring up specific points during the presentation. Speaker notes should not contain all the information you plan to say during your presentation, but they can be a useful tool for reminding you about facts and details related to the content on specific slides. You add notes in the **Notes pane**, which you can display below the displayed slide in Normal view, or you can switch to **Notes Page view**, in which an image of the slide appears in the top half of the presentation window and the notes for that slide appear in the bottom half.

To add notes to Slides 3 and 7:

▶ **1.** Display **Slide 7** ("For More Information"), and then, on the status bar, click the **Notes** button. The Notes pane appears below Slide 7 with "Click to add notes" as placeholder text. See Figure 1-36.

Figure 1-36	Notes pane below Slide 7

Courtesy of Dina White

▶ **2.** Click in the **Notes** pane. The placeholder text disappears, and the insertion point is in the Notes pane.

▶ **3.** Type **Hand out contact information to audience. Use the link to demonstrate how to use the website**.

▶ **4.** Display **Slide 3** ("Benefits of Lakeside Event Center"), click in the **Notes** pane, and then type **Explain the benefits of choosing Lakeside Event Center over other function halls**.

▶ **5.** Click the **View** tab on the ribbon, and then in the Presentation Views group, click the **Notes Page** button. Slide 3 is displayed in Notes Page view. See Figure 1-37.

Figure 1-37	Slide 3 in Notes Page view

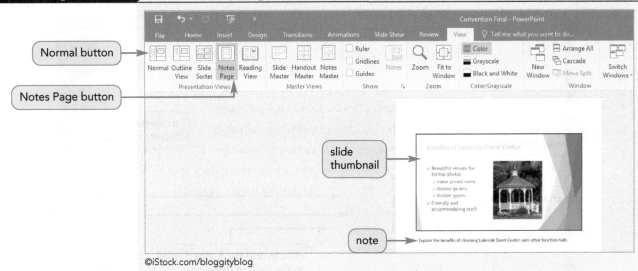

©iStock.com/bloggityblog

▶ **6.** In the note, click after the period at the end of the sentence, press the **spacebar**, and then type **Emphasize both cost benefits and scenic photo opportunities**.

▶ **7.** In the Presentation Views group, click the **Normal** button to return to Normal view. The Notes pane stays displayed until you close it again.

▶ **8.** On the status bar, click the **Notes** button to close the Notes pane, and then save the changes to the presentation.

Checking Spelling

You should always check the spelling and grammar in your presentation before you finalize it. To make this task easier, you can use PowerPoint's spelling checker. You can quickly tell if there are words on slides that are not in the built-in dictionary by looking at the Spelling button at the left end of the status bar. If there are no words flagged as possibly misspelled, the button is 🗒; if there are flagged words, the button changes to 🗒. To indicate that a word might be misspelled, a wavy red line appears under it.

To correct misspelled words, you can right-click a flagged word to see a list of suggested spellings on the shortcut menu, or you can check the spelling of all the words in the presentation. To check the spelling of all the words in the presentation, you click the Spelling button in the Proofing group on the Review tab. This opens the Spelling task pane to the right of the displayed slide and starts the spell check from the current slide. A **task pane** is a pane that opens to the right or left of the displayed slide and contains commands and options related to the task you are doing. When a possible misspelled word is found, suggestions are displayed for the correct spelling. Synonyms for the selected correct spelling are also listed.

To check the spelling of words in the presentation:

▶ **1.** Display **Slide 4** ("Packages"), and then right-click the misspelled word **Delux** in the fourth item in the list. A shortcut menu opens listing spelling options. See Figure 1-38.

Figure 1-38 **Shortcut menu for a misspelled word**

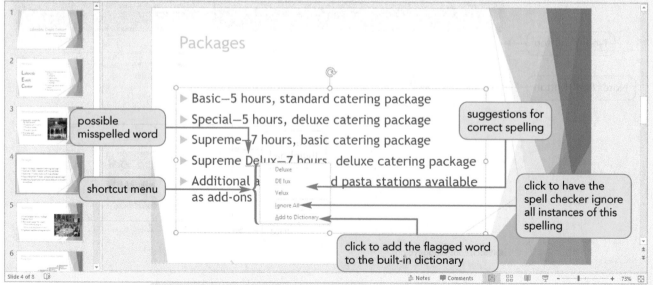

©iStock.com/bloggityblog; ©iStock.com/kai zhang

2. On the shortcut menu, click **Deluxe**. The menu closes and the spelling is corrected.

3. Click the **Review** tab, and then in the Proofing group, click the **Spelling** button. The Spelling task pane opens to the right of the displayed slide, and the next possible misspelled word on Slide 5 ("Amenities") appears with the flagged word, "seting," highlighted. See Figure 1-39. In the Spelling task pane, the first suggested correct spelling is selected. The selected correct spelling also appears at the bottom of the task pane with synonyms for the word listed below it and a speaker icon next to it.

Figure 1-39	Spelling task pane displaying a misspelled word

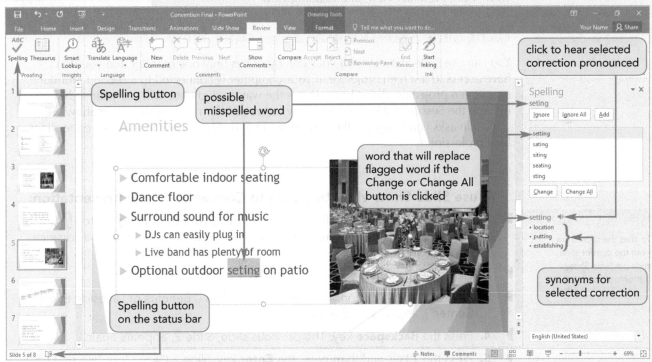

©iStock.com/kai zhang; ©iStock.com/bloggityblog

4. In the Spelling task pane, click the **speaker** icon 🔊. A male voice says the word "setting."

5. In the list of suggested corrections, click **sting**. The word at the bottom of the task pane changes to "sting," and the synonyms change also.

6. In the list of suggested corrections, click **setting**, and then click the **Change** button. The word is corrected, and the next slide containing a possible misspelled word, Slide 1, appears with the flagged word, "Keough," highlighted and listed in the Spelling task pane. This is part of Caitlin's last name so you want the spell checker to ignore this.

7. In the task pane, click the **Ignore All** button. Because that was the last flagged word in the presentation, the Spelling task pane closes, and a dialog box opens telling you that the spell check is complete.

Trouble? If the spell checker finds any other misspelled words, correct them.

▶ **8.** Click the **OK** button. The dialog box closes. The last flagged word, "Keough," is still selected on Slide 1.

▶ **9.** Click a blank area of the slide to deselect the text, and then save the changes to the presentation.

Running a Slide Show

After you have created and proofed your presentation, you should view it as a slide show to see how it will appear to your audience. There are several ways to do this—Slide Show view, Presenter view, and Reading view.

Using Slide Show View and Presenter View

You can use Slide Show view if your computer has only one monitor and you don't have access to a screen projector. If your computer is connected to a second monitor or a screen projector, Slide Show view is the way an audience will see your slides. Refer to the Session 1.2 Visual Overview for more information about Slide Show view.

Caitlin asks you to review the slide show in Slide Show view to make sure the slides look professional.

To use Slide Show view to view the Convention Final presentation:

TIP

To start the slide show from the current slide, click the Slide Show button on the status bar.

▶ **1.** On the Quick Access Toolbar, click the **Start From Beginning** button 🔲. Slide 1 appears on the screen in Slide Show view. Now you need to advance the slide show.

▶ **2.** Press the **spacebar**. Slide 2 ("About Us") appears on the screen.

▶ **3.** Click the mouse button. The next slide, Slide 3 ("Benefits of Lakeside Event Center"), appears on the screen.

▶ **4.** Press the **Backspace** key. The previous slide, Slide 2, appears again.

▶ **5.** Press the **7** key, and then press the **Enter** key. Slide 7 ("For More Information") appears on the screen.

▶ **6.** Move the mouse to display the pointer, and then position the pointer on the website address **www.lec.example.com**. The pointer changes to 🖑 to indicate that this is a link, and the ScreenTip that appears shows the full website address including "http://". If this were a real website, you could click the link to open your web browser and display the website to your audience. Because you moved the pointer, a very faint row of buttons appears in the lower-left corner. The buttons provide access to commands you need in order to run the slide show. See Figure 1-40.

Figure 1-40   **Link and row of buttons in Slide Show view**

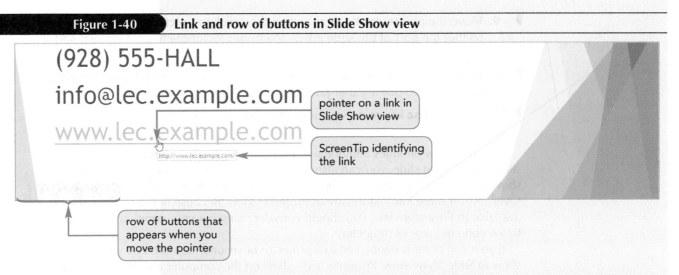

(928) 555-HALL

info@lec.example.com

www.lec.example.com

http://www.lec.example.com/

pointer on a link in Slide Show view

ScreenTip identifying the link

row of buttons that appears when you move the pointer

7. Move the pointer again, if necessary, to display the buttons that appear in the lower-left corner of the screen, and then click the **Return to the previous slide** button ◯ four times to return to Slide 3 ("Benefits of Lakeside Event Center").

Trouble? If you can't see the buttons at the bottom of the screen, move the pointer to the lower-left corner so it is on top of the first button to darken that button, and then move the pointer to the right to see the rest of the buttons.

8. Display the buttons at the bottom of the screen again, and then click the **Zoom into the slide** button ⊕. The pointer changes to ⊕, and three-quarters of the slide is darkened. See Figure 1-41.

Figure 1-41   **Zoom feature activated in Slide Show view**

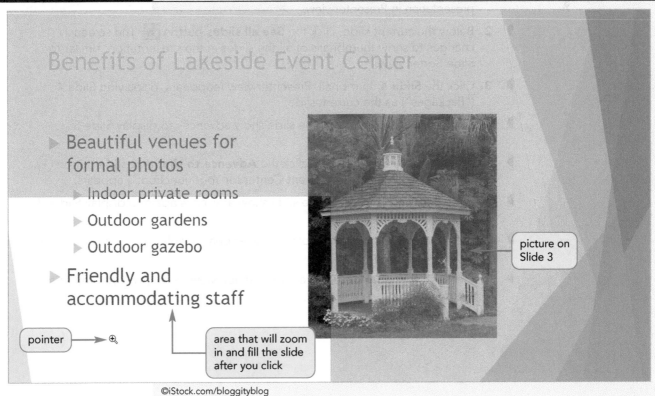

Benefits of Lakeside Event Center

Beautiful venues for formal photos

Indoor private rooms

Outdoor gardens

Outdoor gazebo

Friendly and accommodating staff

picture on Slide 3

pointer ⊕

area that will zoom in and fill the slide after you click

©iStock.com/bloggityblog

▶ **9.** Move the pointer to the picture, and then click the **picture**. The view zooms so that the part of the slide inside the bright rectangle fills the screen, and the pointer changes to ⏷.

▶ **10.** Press and hold the mouse button to change the pointer to ✋, and then drag to the right to pull another part of the zoomed in slide into view.

▶ **11.** Press the **Esc** key to zoom back out to see the whole slide.

Presenter view provides additional tools for running a slide show. In addition to seeing the current slide, you can also see the next slide, speaker notes, and a timer showing you how long the slide show has been running. Refer to the Session 1.2 Visual Overview for more information about Presenter view. Because of the additional tools available in Presenter view, you should consider using it if your computer is connected to a second monitor or projector.

If your computer is connected to a projector or second monitor, and you start a slide show in Slide Show view, Presenter view starts on the computer and Slide Show view appears on the second monitor or projection screen. If, for some reason, you don't want to use Presenter view in that circumstance, you can switch to Slide Show view. If you want to practice using Presenter view when your computer is not connected to a second monitor or projector, you can switch to Presenter view from Slide Show view.

Caitlin wants you to switch to Presenter view and familiarize yourself with the tools available there.

To use Presenter view to review the slide show:

▶ **1.** Move the pointer to display the buttons in the lower-left corner of the screen, click the **More slide show options** button ⊙ to open a menu of commands, and then click **Show Presenter View**. The screen changes to show the presentation in Presenter view.

▶ **2.** Below the current slide, click the **See all slides** button ▦. The screen changes to show thumbnails of all the slides in the presentation, similar to Slide Sorter view.

▶ **3.** Click the **Slide 4** thumbnail. Presenter view reappears, displaying Slide 4 ("Packages") as the current slide.

▶ **4.** Click anywhere on Slide 4. The slide show advances to display Slide 5 ("Amenities").

▶ **5.** At the bottom of the screen, click the **Advance to the next slide** button ⊙. Slide 6 ("Reserve Lakeside Event Center for Your Function!") appears.

▶ **6.** Press the **spacebar** twice. The slide show advances again to display Slides 7 and then 8.

▶ **7.** Press the **spacebar** again. A black slide appears displaying the text "End of slide show, click to exit."

▶ **8.** Press the **spacebar** once more. Presentation view closes, and you return to Normal view.

PROSKILLS

Decision Making: Displaying a Blank Slide During a Presentation

Sometimes during a presentation, the audience has questions about the material and you want to pause the slide show to respond. Or you might want to refocus the audience's attention on you instead of on the visuals on the screen. In these cases, you can display a blank slide (either black or white). When you do this, the audience, with nothing else to look at, will shift all of their attention to you. Some presenters plan to use blank slides and insert them at specific points during their slide shows. Planning to use a blank slide can help you keep your presentation focused and remind you that the purpose of the PowerPoint slides is to provide visual aids to enhance your presentation; the slides themselves are not the presentation.

   If you did not create blank slides in your presentation file, but during your presentation you feel you need to display a blank slide, you can easily do this in Slide Show or Presenter view by pressing the B key to display a blank black slide or the W key to display a blank white slide. You can also click the More button—⊘ in Slide Show view, ⚫ in Presenter view—or right-click the screen, point to Screen on the menu, and then click Black Screen or White Screen. To remove the black or white slide and redisplay the slide that had been on the screen before you displayed the blank slide, press any key on the keyboard or click anywhere on the screen. In Presenter view, you can also use the Black or unblack slide show button ▨ to toggle a blank slide on or off.

   An alternative to redisplaying the slide that had been displayed prior to the blank slide is to click the Advance to the next slide button ⓟ. This can be more effective than redisplaying the slide that was onscreen before the blank slide because, after you have grabbed the audience's attention and prepared them to move on, you won't lose their focus by displaying a slide they have already seen.

Using Reading View

Reading view displays the slides so that they almost fill the screen, similar to Slide Show view; however, in Reading view, a status bar appears, identifying the number of the current slide and providing buttons to advance the slide show. You can also resize the window in Reading view to allow you to work in another window on the desktop.

To use Reading view to review the presentation:

▶ 1. Display **Slide 2** ("About Us"), and then on the status bar, click the **Reading View** button ▦. The presentation changes to Reading view with Slide 2 displayed. See Figure 1-42.

Figure 1-42   **Slide 2 in Reading view**

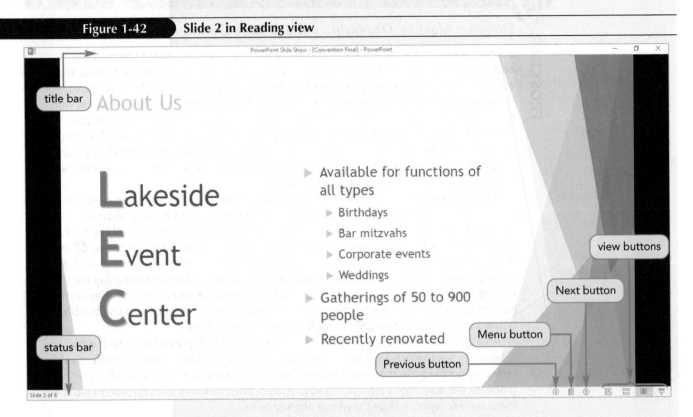

2. On the status bar, click the **Menu** button 📑. A menu appears with commands for working in Reading view, some of which are also available in Slide Show and Presenter views.

3. Click **Full Screen**. The presentation switches to Slide Show view displaying the current slide, Slide 2.

4. Press the **Esc** key. Slide Show view closes, and you return to Reading view.

5. On the status bar, click the **Next** button ▶. The next slide, Slide 3 ("Benefits of Lakeside Event Center"), appears on the screen.

6. On the status bar, click the **Normal** button 🔲 to return to Normal view with Slide 1 displayed in the Slide pane.

Printing a Presentation

Before you deliver your presentation, you might want to print it. PowerPoint provides several printing options. For example, you can print the slides in color, grayscale (white and shades of gray), or pure black and white, and you can print one, some, or all of the slides in several formats.

You use the Print screen in Backstage view to set print options such as specifying a printer and color options. First, you will add your name to the title slide.

To add your name to the title slide and choose a printer and color options:

1. Display **Slide 1**, click after Keough-Barton in the subtitle, press the **Enter** key, and then type your full name.

2. Click the **File** tab to display Backstage view, and then click **Print** in the navigation bar. Backstage view changes to display the Print screen. The Print screen contains options for printing your presentation, and a preview of the first slide as it will print with the current options. See Figure 1-43.

| Figure 1-43 | Print screen in Backstage view |

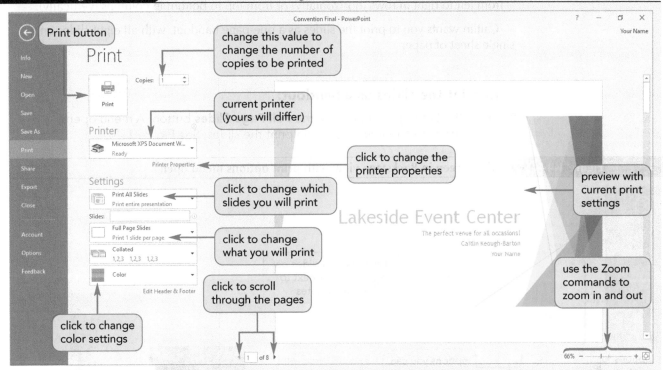

Trouble? If your screen does not match Figure 1-43, click the first button below Settings, and then click Print All Slides, and then click the second button below Settings and then click Full Page Slides.

3. If you are connected to a network or to more than one printer, make sure the printer listed in the Printer box is the one you want to use; if it is not, click the **Printer** button, and then click the correct printer in the list.

4. Click the **Printer Properties** link to open the Properties dialog box for your printer. Usually, the default options are correct, but you can change any printer settings, such as print quality or the paper source, in this dialog box.

5. Click the **Cancel** button to close the Properties dialog box. Now you can choose whether to print the presentation in color, black and white, or grayscale. If you plan to print in black and white or grayscale, you should change this setting so you can see what your slides will look like without color and to make sure they are legible.

6. Click the **Color** button, and then click **Grayscale**. The preview changes to grayscale.

7. At the bottom of the preview pane, click the **Next Page** button ▶ twice to display Slide 3 ("Benefits of Lakeside Event Center"). The slides are legible in grayscale.

8. If you will be printing in color, click the **Grayscale** button, and then click **Color**.

In the Settings section on the Print screen, you can click the Full Page Slides button to choose from among several choices for printing the presentation, as described below:

- **Full Page Slides**—Prints each slide full size on a separate piece of paper.
- **Notes Pages**—Prints each slide as a notes page.
- **Outline**—Prints the text of the presentation as an outline.
- **Handouts**—Prints the presentation with one or more slides on each piece of paper. When printing four, six, or nine slides, you can choose whether to order the slides from left to right in rows (horizontally) or from top to bottom in columns (vertically).

Caitlin wants you to print the slides as a one-page handout, with all eight slides on a single sheet of paper.

To print the slides as a handout:

▶ **1.** In the Settings section, click the **Full Page Slides** button. A menu opens listing the various ways you can print the slides. See Figure 1-44.

Figure 1-44	Print screen in Backstage view with print options menu open

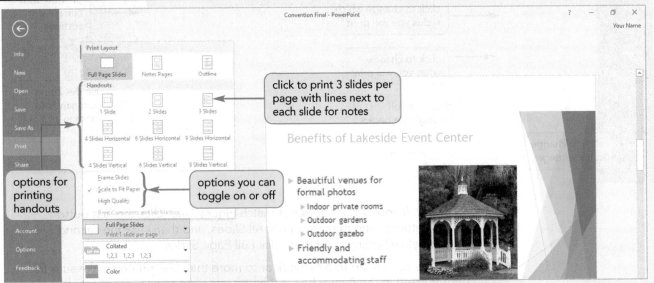

©iStock.com/bloggityblog

▶ **2.** In the Handouts section, click **9 Slides Horizontal**. The preview changes to show all eight slides in the preview pane, arranged in order horizontally, that is, in three rows from left to right. The current date appears in the top-right corner, and a page number appears in the bottom-right corner.

▶ **3.** At the top of the Print section, click the **Print** button. Backstage view closes and the handout prints.

Next, Caitlin wants you to print the title slide as a full-page slide so that she can use it as a cover page for her handouts.

To print the title slide as a full-page slide:

▶ **1.** Click the **File** tab, and then click **Print** in the navigation bar. The Print screen appears in Backstage view. The preview still shows all eight slides on one page. "9 Slides Horizontal" appears on the second button in the Settings section because that was the last printing option you chose.

2. In the Settings section, click **9 Slides Horizontal**, and then click **Full Page Slides**. Slide 1 (the title slide) appears as the preview. Below the preview of Slide 1, it indicates that you are viewing Slide 1 of eight slides to print.

3. In the Settings section, click the **Print All Slides** button. Note on the menu that opens that you can print all the slides, selected slides, the current slide, or a custom range. You want to print just the title slide as a full-page slide.

4. Click **Print Current Slide**. Slide 1 appears in the preview pane, and at the bottom, it now indicates that you will print only one slide.

5. Click the **Print** button. Backstage view closes and Slide 1 prints.

Recall that you created speaker notes on Slides 3 and 7. Caitlin would like you to print these slides as notes pages.

To print the nonsequential slides containing speaker notes:

1. Open the Print screen in Backstage view again, and then click the **Full Page Slides** button. The menu opens.

2. In the Print Layout section of the menu, click **Notes Pages**. The menu closes, and the preview displays Slide 1 as a Notes Page.

3. In the Settings section, click in the **Slides** box, type **3,7** and then click a blank area of the Print screen.

4. Scroll through the preview to confirm that Slides 3 ("Benefits of Lakeside Event Center") and 7 ("For More Information") will print, and then click the **Print** button. Backstage view closes, and Slides 3 and 7 print as notes pages.

Finally, Caitlin would like you to print the outline of the presentation. Recall that Slide 8 is designed to be a visual Caitlin can leave displayed at the end of the presentation, so you don't need to include it in the outline.

To print Slides 1 through 7 as an outline:

1. Open the Print tab in Backstage view, click the **Notes Pages** button, and then in the Print Layout section, click **Outline**. The text on Slides 3 and 7 appears as an outline in the preview pane.

2. Click in the **Slides** box, type **1-7** and then click a blank area of the Print screen. See Figure 1-45.

Figure 1-45 | **Print screen in Backstage view with Slides 1–7 previewed as an outline**

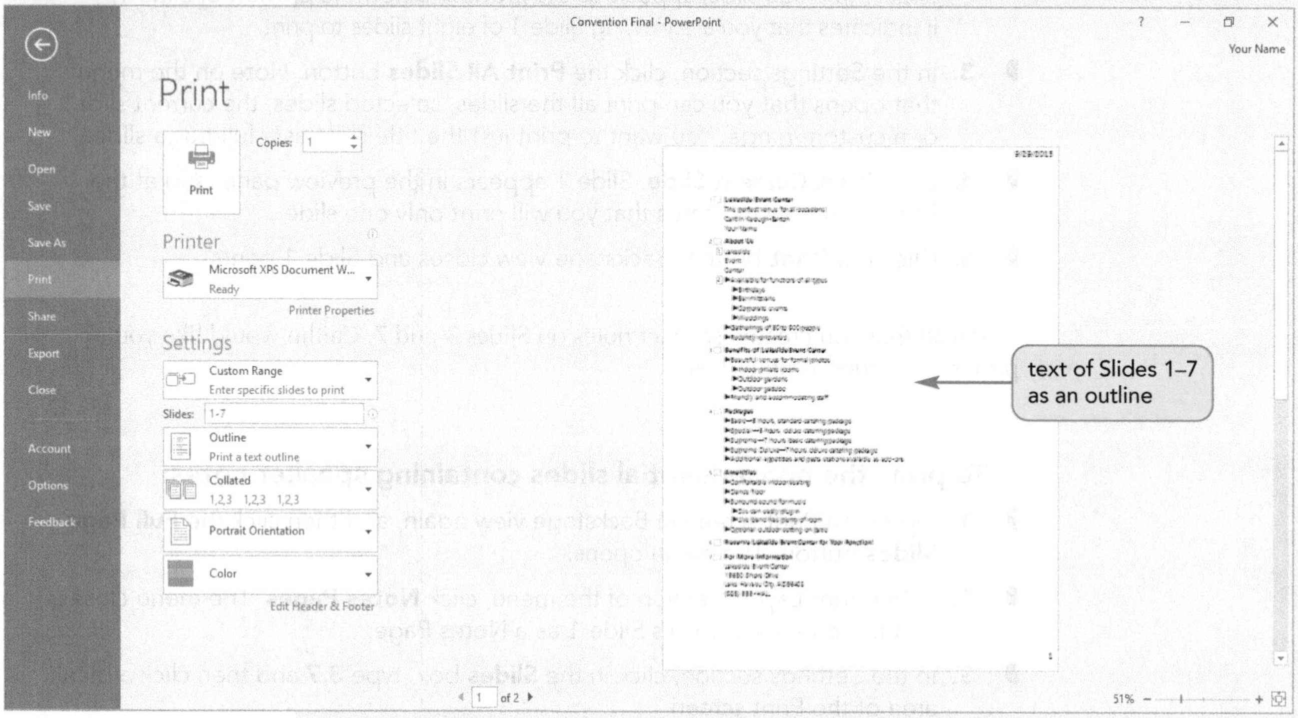

3. At the top of the Print section, click the **Print** button. Backstage view closes, and the text of Slides 1–7 prints on two sheets of paper.

Exiting PowerPoint

When you are finished working with your presentation, you can exit PowerPoint. If there is only one presentation open, you click the Close button ✕ in the upper-right corner of the program window to exit the program. If more than one presentation is open, clicking this button will only close the current presentation; to exit PowerPoint, you need to click the Close button in each of the open presentation's windows.

To exit PowerPoint:

1. In the upper-right corner of the program window, click the **Close** button ✕. A dialog box opens, asking if you want to save your changes. This is because you did not save the file after you added your name to the title slide.

2. In the dialog box, click the **Save** button. The dialog box closes, the changes are saved, and PowerPoint exits.

Trouble? If any other PowerPoint presentations are still open, click the Close button ✕ on each open presentation's program window until no more presentations are open to exit PowerPoint.

In this session, you opened an existing presentation and saved it with a new name, changed the theme, added and cropped photos and adjusted the photo compression, and resized and moved objects. You have also added speaker notes and checked the spelling. Finally, you printed the presentation in several forms and exited PowerPoint. Your work will help Caitlin give an effective presentation to potential clients of Lakeside Event Center.

Session 1.2 Quick Check

REVIEW

1. Explain what a theme is and what changes with each variant.
2. Describe what happens when you crop photos.
3. Describe sizing handles.
4. Describe smart guides.
5. Why is it important to maintain the aspect ratio of photos?
6. What is the difference between Slide Show view and Presenter view?
7. List the four formats for printing a presentation.

PRACTICE

Review Assignments

Data Files needed for the Review Assignments: DJ.jpg, Musicians.jpg, Photog.jpg, Vendor2.pptx

In addition to booking new clients, Caitlin Keough-Barton, the event manager at Lakeside Event Center, maintains a preferred vendors list for providing additional services of entertainment, music, photography, and so on that clients might want. If clients who book the hall use a preferred vendor, they receive a discount on the price of the vendor's services. Caitlin wants to create a presentation that she can use when she meets with new vendors to describe their responsibilities to both the function hall and to the clients. She asks you to begin creating the presentation.

1. Start PowerPoint and create a new, blank presentation. On the title slide, type **Information for Vendors** as the title, and then type your name as the subtitle. Save the presentation as **Vendor Info** to the drive and folder where you are storing your files.

2. Edit the slide title by adding **Lakeside Event Center** before the word "Vendors."

3. Add a new Slide 2 with the Title and Content layout, type **Types of Vendors We Partner With** as the slide title, and then in the content placeholder type the following:
   - **Photographers**
   - **Videographers**
   - **Florists**
   - **Music**
     - **DJs**
     - **Bands**

4. Create a new Slide 3 with the Title and Content layout. Add **Requirements for Vendors** as the slide title, and then type the following as a numbered list on the slide:
   1) **Supply advertisement for brochure**
   2) **Pay annual fee by January 15**
   3) **Submit availability schedule for clients**
   4) **Contact Caitlin Keough-Barton**

5. Create a new Slide 4 using the Two Content layout. Add **Questions?** as the slide title.

6. Use the Cut and Paste commands to move the last bulleted item on Slide 3 ("Contact Caitlin Keough-Barton") to the left content placeholder on Slide 4.

7. On Slide 4, remove the bullet symbol from the text you pasted, and then add the following as the next two items in the unnumbered list:
   Email: c.keoughbarton@example.com
   Cell: 602-555-8723

8. Click after "Keough-Barton" in the first item in the list, and then create a new line below it without creating a new item in the list and so that there is no extra space above the new line. On the new line, type **Events Manager**.

9. Remove the hyperlink formatting from the email address.

10. Create a new Slide 5 using the Title and Content layout. Delete the title text placeholder. In the content placeholder, type **Thank You!** as a single item in an unnumbered list. Increase the size of the text "Thank You!" to 96 points, and then change the color of this text to Blue, Accent 1.

11. On Slide 3 ("Requirements for Vendors"), change the numbered list to a SmartArt graphic. Use the Vertical Circle List layout, which is a List type of diagram.

12. Save your changes, and then close the presentation.

13. Open the file **Vendor2**, located in the PowerPoint1 > Review folder included with your Data Files, add your name as the subtitle on the title slide, and then save it as **LEC Vendor Information** to the drive and folder where you are storing your files.

14. Change the theme to Basis and choose the third variant. On Slide 2, change the size of the text in the bulleted list so that the size of the text of the first-level items is 28 points and the size of the text of the second-level items is 24 points.

15. Change the layout of Slide 4 ("Photographers") to Title and Content, and then duplicate Slide 4. In the title of Slide 5 (the duplicate slide), replace the slide title with **Music Vendors**.

16. On Slide 4, insert the photo **Photog**, located in the PowerPoint1 > Review folder. Resize the photo so it is five inches high, maintaining the aspect ratio, and reposition it so its top and right edges are aligned with the top and right edges of the slide title text box.

17. On Slide 5, change the layout to Two Content, and then in the content placeholder on the left, insert the photo **DJ**. Crop the photo from the right about one-half inch and from the top about one-quarter inch. Resize the cropped photo so it is 2.4 inches high, maintaining the aspect ratio, and then reposition the photo so its left edge is aligned with the left edge of the slide title text box and its middle is aligned with the middle of the content placeholder on the right.

18. On Slide 5, in the content placeholder on the right, insert the photo **Musicians**. Resize it so that it is 2.5 inches tall. Position it so that its right edge is aligned with the right edge of the slide title text box and its middle is aligned with the middle of the photo on the left.

19. Move Slide 5 ("Music Vendors") so it becomes Slide 7.

20. On Slide 9 ("Questions?"), crop the photo to the Oval shape. Increase the size of the text in the unnumbered list to 20 points, and then resize the text box to make it wide enough so that the line containing the email address fits on one line. Remove the hyperlink formatting from the email address.

21. Compress all the photos in the slides to 96 ppi and delete cropped areas of pictures.

22. On Slide 4 ("Photographers"), add **Must be available for the entire event. Should be able to take both formal portraits and candids.** in the Notes pane. On Slide 7 ("Music Vendors"), add **Must be available for the entire time during the event. Should be versatile and be able to play music for all audiences.** as a note on this slide.

23. Delete Slide 3 ("Vendor Requirements") and the last slide (the blank slide).

24. Check the spelling in the presentation. Correct the two spelling errors on Slide 7, ignore all instances of Caitlin's last name, and ignore the flagged instance of "candids" in the Notes pane on Slide 3 ("Photographers"). If you made any additional spelling errors, correct them as well. Save the changes to the presentation.

25. Review the slide show in Slide Show, Presenter, and Reading views.

26. View the slides in grayscale, and then print the following in color or in grayscale depending on your printer: the title slide as a full-page-sized slide; Slides 1–9 as a handout on a single piece of paper with the slides in order horizontally; Slides 3 and 6 as notes pages; and Slides 1–8 as an outline. Save and close the presentation when you are finished.

Case Problem 1

Data Files needed for this Case Problem: After.jpg, Before.jpg, Clients.pptx, Team.jpg, Windows.jpg

APPLY

Cleaning Essentials Suzanne Yang owns Cleaning Essentials, a home cleaning company in New Rochelle, New York. She markets her company at home shows in Westchester County and in New York City. She asks you to help her create PowerPoint slides that she will use at the home shows. Complete the following steps:

1. Open the presentation named **Clients**, located in the PowerPoint1 > Case1 folder included with your Data Files, and then save it as **New Clients** to the drive and folder where you are storing your files.

2. Insert a new Slide 1 that has the Title Slide layout. Add **Cleaning Essentials** as the presentation title on the title slide. In the subtitle text placeholder, type your name.

3. Create a new Slide 2 with the Title and Content layout. Add **What Is Cleaning Essentials?** as the slide title, and **An affordable door-to-door cleaning service designed to make a homeowner's life easier.** as the only item in the content placeholder. Change this to an unnumbered list.

4. Apply the Savon theme, and then apply its second variant. (If the Savon theme is not listed in the Themes gallery, choose any other theme and variant that uses a white or solid color background, places the slide titles at the top of the slides, uses bullet symbols for first-level bulleted items, and positions the content in the bulleted lists so it aligns to the top of the content text box, not the middle.)

5. On Slide 2 ("What Is Cleaning Essentials?"), increase the size of the text in the text box below the slide titles to 28 points.

6. On Slide 3 ("What Services Do We Provide?"), Slide 7 ("Extra Services Offered"), and Slide 9 ("Book Us Now!"), increase the size of the text in the bulleted list so it is 28 points.

7. On Slide 4 ("Why Choose Cleaning Essentials?"), increase the size of the text in the bulleted list so that the first-level items are 24 points.

8. On Slide 2 ("What Is Cleaning Essentials?"), insert the photo **Team**, located in the PowerPoint1 > Case1 folder. Resize the photo, maintaining the aspect ratio, so that it is 3.6 inches wide, and then use the smart guides to position it so that its center is aligned with the center of the text box above it and its bottom is aligned with the bottom border of the text box.

9. On Slide 3 ("What Services Do We Provide?"), add the speaker note **All clients are welcome to request extra services needed to completely clean their homes.**

10. On Slide 6 ("Picture Proof"), change the layout to the Comparison layout, which includes two content placeholders and a small text placeholder above each content placeholder. In the small text placeholder on the left, add **Before**, and then in the small text placeholder on the right, add **After**. Change the font size in both text boxes to 24 points.

11. In the left content placeholder, insert the photo **Before**, and in the right content placeholder, insert the photo **After**.

12. On Slide 5 ("Polish wood floors"), cut the slide title, and then paste it in on Slide 3 ("What Services Do We Provide?") as the fifth bulleted item. If a blank line is added below the pasted text, delete it.

13. On Slide 7 ("Extra Services Offered"), add **Laundry** as a third bulleted item in the list, and then add **Use in-home machines** and **Send out and pick up dry cleaning** as subitems under the "Laundry" first-level item. Change the layout to Two Content.

14. On Slide 7, in the content placeholder, insert the photo **Windows**, located in the PowerPoint1 > Case1 folder. Resize the photo so it is 5 inches high, maintaining the aspect ratio, and then reposition it so that the top of the photo and the top of the title text box are aligned and the right edge of the photo is aligned with the right edge of the title text box.

15. Compress all the photos in the presentation to 96 ppi.

16. On Slide 8 ("Cleaning Visit Options"), add **Once a week** as the second item in the list, and then add **Most popular option** and **Visit is the same day each week** as subitems below "Once a week."

17. On Slide 8, convert the bulleted list to a SmartArt diagram using the Vertical Bullet List layout, which is a List type of diagram. In the Text pane, click before "Still produces a clean and uncluttered home," and then press the Tab key to make it the second subitem under "Once a month."

18. Delete Slide 5 (a blank slide). Move Slide 4 ("Why Choose Cleaning Essentials?") so it becomes Slide 6, and then move Slide 5 ("Extra Services Offered") so it becomes Slide 4.

19. Check the spelling in the presentation and correct all misspelled words.

20. Save the changes to the presentation, view the slide show in Presenter view, and then print the title slide as a full-page slide, print Slides 2–8 as a handout using the 9 Slides Horizontal arrangement, and print Slide 3 as a notes page.

TROUBLESHOOT

Case Problem 2

Data Files needed for this Case Problem: Keyboard.jpg, Music.pptx, Richard.jpg

Dillaire Music Richard Dillaire has owned Dillaire Music in Easton, Pennsylvania, since 1991. He sells, rents, and repairs musical instruments, and he teaches students how to play instruments. He wants to expand his business and attract new students, so he asks you to help him create a presentation. He created slides containing text and a few photos that he wants to include, and he wants you to finish the presentation by inserting additional photos and formatting the presentation. Complete the following steps:

1. Open the file named **Music**, located in the PowerPoint1 > Case2 folder included with your Data Files, and then save it as **Music School** to the drive and folder where you are storing your files. Add your name as the subtitle on Slide 1.

☼ **Troubleshoot** 2. Review the presentation to identify the two slides that contain information that is repeated on another slide in the presentation, and delete those slides.

3. Display Slide 1 (the title slide), and then apply the Headlines theme to the presentation. Change the variant to the second variant.

☼ **Troubleshoot** 4. Evaluate the problem that the theme change caused on Slide 1 and fix it.

☼ **Troubleshoot** 5. Consider how changing the theme affected the readability of the lists on the slides and the size of the photos in the file. Make the appropriate changes to the slides. (*Hint:* On the slides that have pictures of a child playing an instrument on them, the first-level items should not be larger than 24 points.)

6. On Slide 8 ("Contact Info"), in the first item in the bulleted list, move "Easton, PA 18042" to a new line below the street address without creating a new bulleted item.

7. Move Slide 7 ("Lessons") so it becomes Slide 4.

8. On Slide 7 ("How to register online"), change the bulleted list to a numbered list. Add as a new item 2 **Click the green Apply button**.

9. Change the layout of Slide 8 ("Contact Info") to Two Content, and then insert the photo **Richard**, located in the PowerPoint1 > Case2 folder, in the content placeholder. Crop off about one-half inch from the top of the photo, and then increase the size of the picture, maintaining the aspect ratio, so that it is 3 inches wide. Reposition the photo so it is vertically centered below the slide title and bottom aligned with the bottom of the slide title text box.

10. On Slide 1 (the title slide), insert the photo **Keyboard** located in the PowerPoint1 > Case2 folder. Resize the photo so it is 5.25 inches square, and then position it so it is aligned with the right and bottom edges of the slide.

11. Compress all the photos in the presentation to 96 ppi and delete cropped portions of photos.

12. Check the spelling in the presentation, and then save the changes.

13. View the slide show in Presenter view, zooming in on the pictures in the presentation.

14. Print the title slide as a full-page slide in grayscale, and then print the entire presentation as an outline.

CREATE

Case Problem 3

Data Files needed for this Case Problem: Beach.jpg, House1.jpg, House2.jpg, House3.jpg, House4.jpg, House5.jpg, Realty.pptx

Shoreside Realty Karen Bridges owns Shoreside Realty, a real estate company in Scarborough, Maine, that specializes in selling and renting homes in local beach communities. As part of her marketing, she attends local events, such as the farmers' market, weekly summer concerts, and chamber of commerce events, and shows photos of houses near beaches for sale or rent. She created a presentation with slides containing the addresses and brief descriptions of newly listed properties. She asks you to finish the presentation. The completed presentation is shown in Figure 1-46. Refer to Figure 1-46 as you complete the following steps:

Figure 1-46   **Shoreside Realty presentation**

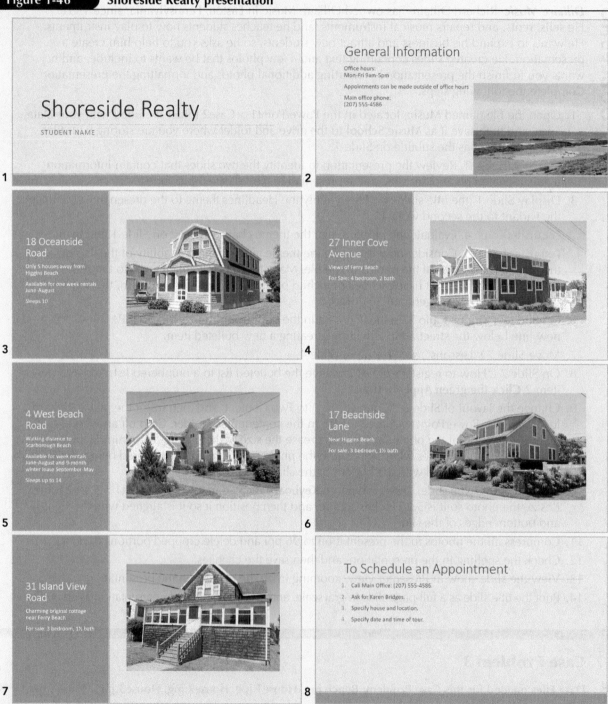

Courtesy of Helen M. Pinard

1. Open the file named **Realty**, located in the PowerPoint1 > Case3 folder included with your Data Files, and then save it as **Shoreside Realty** to the drive and folder where you are storing your files.

2. Add a new slide with the Title Slide layout, and move it so it is Slide 1. Type **Shoreside Realty** as the title and your name as the subtitle.

3. Move Slide 8 ("General Information") so it becomes Slide 2, and then delete Slide 3 ("Newest Homes on the Market").

4. Change the theme to Retrospect, and the variant of the Retrospect theme to the seventh variant. (Note that in this theme, bulleted lists do not have any bullet symbols before each item.)

5. On Slide 2 ("General Information"), in the first item in the list, move the phone number so it appears on the next line, without any additional line space above the phone number. Then move the text "Mon–Fri 9am–5pm" so it appears on the next line, without any additional line space above it.

6. On Slide 2, move the "Main office phone" list item and the phone number so these appear as the last list items on the slide.

7. On Slide 2, insert the photo **Beach**, located in the PowerPoint1 > Case3 folder. Crop two inches from the top of the photo, and then resize the photo so that it is 3.4 inches high.

8. On Slide 2, position the photo so that its right edge is flush with the right edge of the slide and so that its bottom edge is slightly on top of the lighter blue line at the bottom of the slide.

9. Change the layout of Slides 3 through 7 to Content with Caption. On all five slides, move the unnumbered list from the content placeholder on the right to the text placeholders on the left, as shown in Figure 1-46, and then change the font size of the text in the unnumbered lists you moved to 16 points. Then insert the photos named **House1** through **House5** provided in the PowerPoint1 > Case3 folder on Slides 3 through 7, using Figure 1-46 as a guide.

10. Compress all the photos in the presentation to 96 ppi.

11. On Slide 8 ("To Schedule an Appointment"), change the list to a numbered list, and then add **Specify house and location.** as a new item 3.

12. Save the changes to the presentation, and then view the presentation in Reading view.

Case Problem 4

Data Files needed for this Case Problem: Ballet.jpg, Dancing.mp4, HipHop.jpg, Jazz.jpg, Jump.jpg, Leap.jpg, Modern.jpg, and Tap.jpg

Greater Dayton Dance Academy Paul LaCroix owns Greater Dayton Dance Academy, a dance studio that teaches students ages two through adult. He has an open house every September to attract new students. He asks you to help him create a presentation that includes photos and video that he can show at the open house. Complete the following steps:

Explore 1. Create a new presentation using the Striped black border presentation template from Office.com. (*Hint:* Use "striped black border" as the search term. If you get no results, type **white** as the search term, and then choose a template with a simple theme.)

2. Replace the title text on the title slide with **Greater Dayton Dance Academy**, and replace the subtitle text with your name. Save the presentation as **New Students** to the drive and folder where you are storing your files.

3. Delete all the slides except the title slide.

4. Add a new Slide 2 with the Two Content layout. Add **About Us** as the title, and then type the following as a bulleted list in the left content placeholder:

   • **Recreational classes meet once a week**
   • **Competitive classes meet 3 to 5 times a week**
   • **Private lessons available**
   • **Annual winter and spring productions**

5. On Slide 2, in the right content placeholder, insert the photo **Leap**, located in the PowerPoint1 > Case4 folder included with your Data Files. Resize it, maintaining the aspect ratio, so it is 3.8 inches high, and then reposition it so that the top edge of the photo is aligned with the top edge of the text box and the left edge of the photo is aligned with the right edge of the text box.

6. Add a new Slide 3 with the Title and Content layout. Add **Styles Offered** as the title, and then type the following as a bulleted list in the content placeholder:

    • **Ballet**

    • **Modern**

    • **Jazz**

    • **Tap**

    • **Hip Hop**

7. On Slide 3, convert the bulleted list to a SmartArt diagram with the Bending Picture Semi-Transparent Text layout, which is a Picture type of diagram.

✪ **Explore** 8. Change the colors of the diagram to Colorful Range – Accent Colors 3 to 4 by using the Change Colors button in the SmartArt Styles group on the SmartArt Tools Design tab.

✪ **Explore** 9. Insert the following pictures, located in the PowerPoint1 > Case4 folder, in the appropriate picture placeholders in the SmartArt diagram: **Ballet**, **Modern**, **Jazz**, **Tap**, and **HipHop**.

10. Add a new Slide 4 with the Two Content layout. Add **Call Today!** as the title. In the content placeholder on the left, type the following as an unnumbered list (no bullets) without extra space between the lines:

    Greater Dayton Dance Academy

    1158 North St.

    Dayton, OH 45417

11. On Slide 4, add the phone number **(937) 555-1254** and the website address **www.daytondance.example.com** as new items in the unnumbered list. Press the spacebar after typing the website address to format it as a link.

12. On Slide 4, change the size of the text in the unnumbered list to 22 point. (*Hint:* Click in the Font Size box, type **22**, and then press the **Enter** key.)

13. On Slide 4, add the photo **Jump**, located in the PowerPoint1 > Case4 folder, to the content placeholder on the right. Resize it so it is 3.6 inches high, maintaining the aspect ratio, and then position it so the top edge aligns with the top edge of the text box on the left and there is approximately one inch of space between the right side of the photo and the right edge of the slide.

14. Compress all the photos in the presentation to 96 ppi, and then save the changes.

15. Add a new Slide 5 with the Two Content layout. Add **Classic Ballet Technique Emphasized** as the title. In the content placeholder on the right, add **Because ballet is the foundation of all dance, all students are required to take ballet technique classes.** Remove the bullet from this item.

16. Move this slide so it becomes Slide 4.

✪ **Explore** 17. On Slide 4 ("Classic Ballet Technique Emphasized"), insert the video **Dancing**, located in the PowerPoint1 > Case4 folder, in the content placeholder.

✪ **Explore** 18. Open the Info tab in Backstage view. Use the Compress Media command to compress the videos to the lowest quality possible. Use the Back button at the top of the navigation bar in Backstage view to return to Normal view.

19. Save the changes to the presentation, and then run the slide show in Slide Show view. When Slide 4 ("Classic Ballet Technique Emphasized") appears, point to the video to make a Play button appear, and then click the Play button to play the 20-second video. (*Hint:* Point to the video as it plays to display the play bar again.)

POWERPOINT

OBJECTIVES

Adding Media and Special Effects

Using Media in a Presentation for a Nonprofit River Cleaning Organization

Case | *RiverClean*

José Quiñones is a volunteer for RiverClean™, a nonprofit organization in New England that raises money and supports volunteer efforts to clean riverbanks in the area. José lives in Lowell, Massachusetts, where several intense storms have knocked down tree limbs, some of which block access to the Riverwalk trail next to the Merrimack River. In addition to the storm damage, portions of the trail are overgrown and in disrepair, and many areas along the trail have significant erosion problems. José wants to present this information to the city councilors so that he can get permission to organize a trail cleanup and obtain some funding for the project as well. José prepared the text of a PowerPoint presentation, and he wants you to add photos and other features to make the presentation more interesting and compelling.

In this module, you will modify a presentation that illustrates the poor conditions of the Riverwalk trail and estimates costs for addressing the problems. You will add formatting and special effects to photos and shapes, add transitions and animations to slides, and add and modify video.

STARTING DATA FILES

PowerPoint2 →	**Module**		**Review**	
	Barrier.jpg	Sign.jpg	Cleared.jpg	NewView.mp4
	Erosion1.jpg	Stairs.jpg	Landscape.jpg	Railings.jpg
	Erosion2.mp4	Tree.jpg	NewSign.jpg	Renewed1.pptx
	Mix.pptx	WalkTheme.pptx	NewStairs.jpg	Renewed2.pptx
	Riverwalk.pptx		NewTheme.pptx	Wall.jpg

Case1	**Case2**	**Case3**	**Case4**
Equipment.jpg	Build.jpg	Paws.pptx	Candy.png
Exercise.mp4	Finish.jpg	PawsTheme.pptx	CarePak.pptx
FitTheme.pptx	Furniture.pptx		CPTheme.pptx
HomeFit.pptx	Sand.jpg		Games.png
	Sketch.jpg		Personal.png
	Trees.jpg		Salty.png

Session 2.1 Visual Overview:

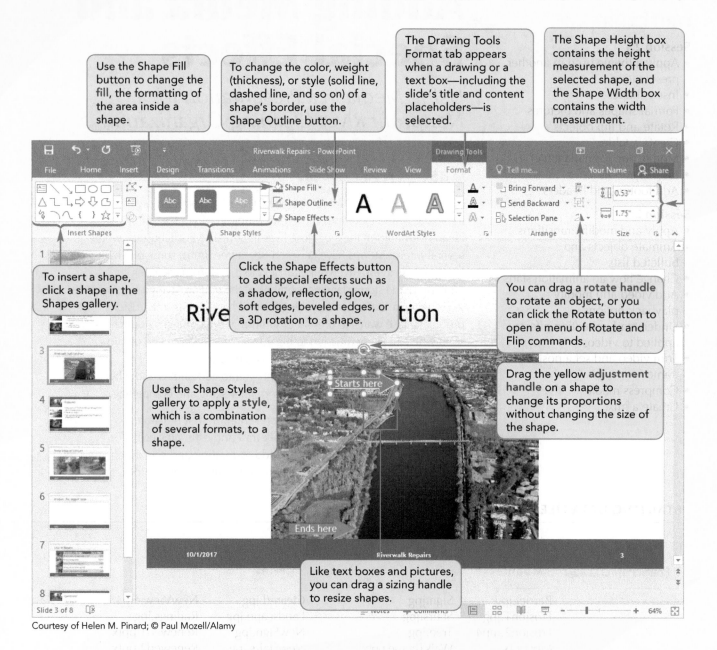

Use the Shape Fill button to change the fill, the formatting of the area inside a shape.

To change the color, weight (thickness), or style (solid line, dashed line, and so on) of a shape's border, use the Shape Outline button.

The Drawing Tools Format tab appears when a drawing or a text box—including the slide's title and content placeholders—is selected.

The Shape Height box contains the height measurement of the selected shape, and the Shape Width box contains the width measurement.

To insert a shape, click a shape in the Shapes gallery.

Click the Shape Effects button to add special effects such as a shadow, reflection, glow, soft edges, beveled edges, or a 3D rotation to a shape.

You can drag a rotate handle to rotate an object, or you can click the Rotate button to open a menu of Rotate and Flip commands.

Use the Shape Styles gallery to apply a style, which is a combination of several formats, to a shape.

Drag the yellow adjustment handle on a shape to change its proportions without changing the size of the shape.

Like text boxes and pictures, you can drag a sizing handle to resize shapes.

Courtesy of Helen M. Pinard; © Paul Mozell/Alamy

Formatting Graphics

Use the Reset Picture button to undo formatting and sizing changes you made to a picture.

To change the color, weight (thickness), or style (solid line, dashed line, and so on) of a picture's border, use the Picture Border button.

The Picture Tools Format tab appears when a picture is selected.

Like shapes, the dimensions of the picture appear in the Shape Height and Shape Width boxes.

Use the Picture Styles gallery to apply a style to a picture.

Click the Picture Effects button to add special effects to a picture, such as a shadow, reflection, glow, soft edges, beveled edges, or a 3D rotation.

Like shapes, you can rotate or flip pictures using the Rotate handle or the Rotate button.

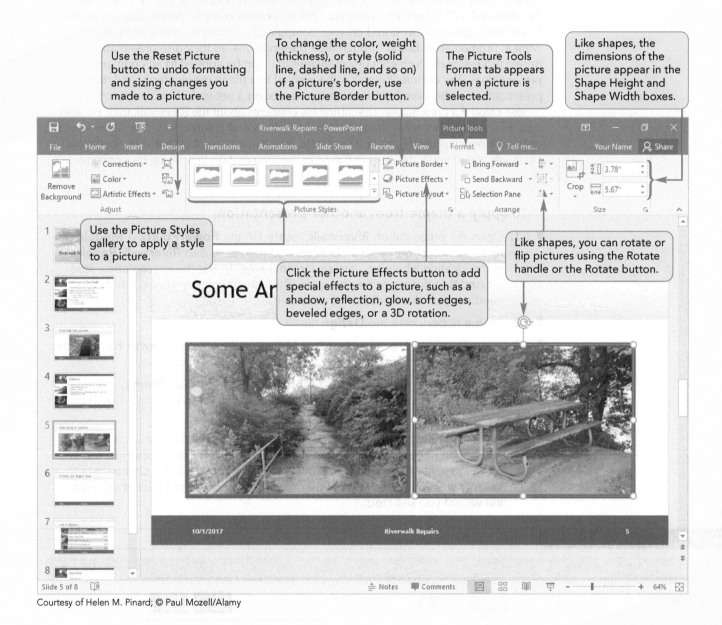

Courtesy of Helen M. Pinard; © Paul Mozell/Alamy

Applying a Theme Used in Another Presentation

As you learned earlier, an installed theme can be applied by clicking one in the Themes group on the Design tab. An installed theme is actually a special type of file that is stored with PowerPoint program files. You can also apply themes that are applied to any other presentation stored on your computer. For example, many companies want to promote their brand through their presentations, so they hire presentation design professionals to create custom themes that can be applied to all company presentations. The custom theme can be applied to a blank presentation, and this presentation can be stored on users' computers or on a network drive.

José created a presentation describing his concerns about the Riverwalk trail. He also created a custom theme by changing the theme fonts and colors, modifying layouts, and creating a new layout. He applied this theme to a blank presentation that he sent to you. He wants you to apply the custom theme to the presentation describing his concerns.

To apply a theme from another presentation:

▶ **1.** Open the presentation **Riverwalk**, located in the **PowerPoint2** > **Module** folder included with your Data Files, and then save it as **Riverwalk Repairs** in the location where you are saving your files. This is the presentation José created that describes his concerns. The Office theme is applied to it. You need to apply José's custom theme to it.

▶ **2.** On the ribbon, click the **Design** tab.

▶ **3.** In the Themes group, click the **More** button, and then click **Browse for Themes**. The Choose Theme or Themed Document dialog box opens.

▶ **4.** Navigate to the **PowerPoint2** > **Module** folder, click **WalkTheme**, and then click the **Apply** button. The custom theme is applied to the Riverwalk Repairs presentation.

▶ **5.** In the Themes group, point to the first theme in the gallery, which is the current theme. Its ScreenTip identifies it as the WalkTheme. See Figure 2-1. Although variants appear in the Variants group, these are the Office theme variants, and if you click one of them, you will reapply the Office theme with the variant you selected.

| Figure 2-1 | Custom WalkTheme applied |

ScreenTip for current theme

variants of the Office theme

Courtesy of Helen M. Pinard

▶ **6.** Click the **Home** tab, and then on Slide 1 (the title slide), click **Riverwalk Repairs**, the title text.

7. In the Font group, click the **Font arrow**. Notice that Trebuchet MS is the theme font for both the headings and the body text. This is different from the Office theme, which uses Calibri for the body text and Calibri Light for the headings.

8. In the Slides group, click the **Layout** button. The Layout gallery appears. The custom layouts that José created are listed in the gallery, as shown in Figure 2-2.

| Figure 2-2 | Custom layouts in the WalkTheme custom theme |

Courtesy of Helen M. Pinard; © Paul Mozell/Alamy

Notice the customized Title Slide layout has a photo as a slide background, the Title and Content customized layout has photos along the left edge of the slide, and the customized Photo Title and Content and the Two Content layouts include a photo under the slide title.

9. Press the **Esc** key to close the Layout gallery.

When you applied the custom theme from the WalkTheme presentation, the title slide and the slides with the Title and Content and Two Content layouts were changed to use the customized versions of these layouts. José wants you to change the layout of Slides 3, 6, and 7 to the custom layout he named Photo Title and Content.

To apply a custom layout to Slides 3, 6, and 7:

1. Display **Slide 3** ("Riverwalk Trail Location").

2. In the Slides group, click the **Layout** button. The Layout gallery appears.

▶ **3.** Click the **Photo Title and Content** layout. The custom layout is applied to Slide 3.

▶ **4.** Apply the **Photo Title and Content** layout to Slide 6 ("Erosion: The Biggest Issue") and Slide 7 ("Cost of Repairs").

▶ **5.** Save your changes.

Saving a Presentation as a Theme

If you need to use a custom theme frequently, you can save a presentation file as an Office Theme file. A theme file is a different file type than a presentation file. You can then store this file so that it appears in the Themes gallery on the Design tab. To save a custom theme, click the File tab, click Save As in the navigation bar, and then click Browse to open the Save As dialog box. To change the file type to Office Theme, click the Save as type arrow, and then click Office Theme. This changes the current folder in the Save As dialog box to the Document Themes folder, which is a folder created on the hard drive when Office is installed and where the installed themes are stored. If you save a custom theme to the Document Themes folder, that theme will be listed in its own row above the installed themes in the Themes gallery. (You need to click the More button in the Themes gallery to see this row.) You can also change the folder location and save the custom theme to any location on your computer or network or to a folder on your OneDrive. If you do this, the theme will not appear in the Themes gallery, but you can still access it using the Browse for Themes command on the Themes gallery menu.

Inserting Shapes

You can add many shapes to a slide, including lines, rectangles, stars, and more. To draw a shape, click the Shapes button in the Illustrations group on the Insert tab, click a shape in the gallery, and then click and drag to draw the shape in the size you want. Like any object, a shape can be resized after you insert it.

You've already had a little experience with one shape—a text box, which is a shape specifically designed to contain text. You can add additional text boxes to slides using the Text Box shape. You can also add text to any shape you place on a slide.

José wants you to add labels identifying the trail in the aerial photo on Slide 3. You will do this with arrow shapes. First you will add an arrow that points to the start of the trail.

To insert and position an arrow shape with text on Slide 3:

▶ **1.** Display **Slide 3** ("Riverwalk Trail Location").

▶ **2.** Click the **Insert** tab, and then in the Illustrations group, click the **Shapes** button. The Shapes gallery opens. See Figure 2-3. In addition to the Recently Used Shapes group at the top, the gallery is organized into nine categories of shapes.

Figure 2-3   Shapes gallery

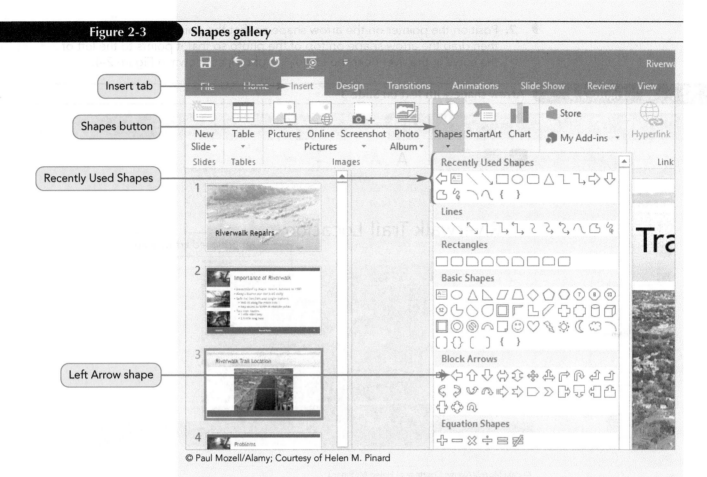

© Paul Mozell/Alamy; Courtesy of Helen M. Pinard

3. Under Block Arrows, click the **Left Arrow** shape ⬅. The gallery closes and the pointer changes to ┼.

4. On the slide, click to the right of the photo. A left-pointing arrow, approximately one inch long, appears. (Don't worry about the exact placement of the arrow; you will move it later.) Note that the Drawing Tools Format tab is the active tab on the ribbon.

5. With the shape selected, type **Starts here**. The text you type appears in the arrow, but it does not all fit.

6. Drag the middle sizing handle on the right end of the arrow to lengthen the arrow until both words fit on one line inside the arrow and the arrow is 1.75″ long as indicated in the Shape Width box in the Size group on the Drawing Tools Format tab.

   Now you need to position the arrow shape on the photo. When you drag a shape with text, it is similar to dragging a text box, which means you need to drag a border of the shape or a part of the shape that does not contain text.

▶ **7.** Position the pointer on the arrow shape so that the pointer changes to ⬚, and then drag the arrow shape on top of the photo so that it points to the left of the curve in the river near the top of the photo, as shown in Figure 2-4.

| Figure 2-4 | Arrow shape with text on Slide 3 |

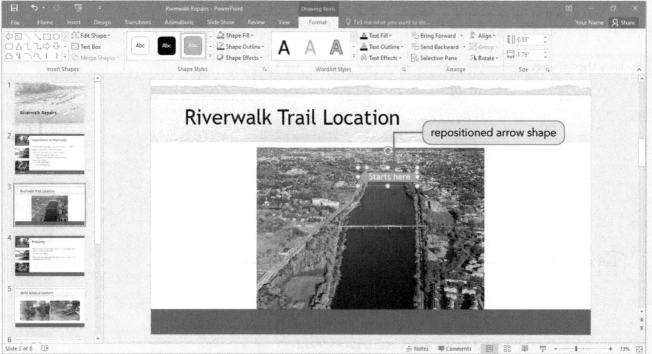

© Paul Mozell/Alamy; Courtesy of Helen M. Pinard

Next, you to need to add an arrow pointing to the end of the trail. You could draw another arrow, but instead, you'll duplicate the arrow you just drew. Duplicating is similar to copying and pasting, but nothing is placed on the Clipboard.

To duplicate the arrow on Slide 3 and edit the text in the shape:

▶ **1.** On Slide 3 ("Riverwalk Trail Location"), click the **"Starts here"** arrow to select it, if necessary.

▶ **2.** Click the **Home** tab, and then in the Clipboard group, click the **Copy button arrow**. A menu opens.

▶ **3.** On the menu, click **Duplicate**. A duplicate of the "Starts here" arrow appears on the slide.

▶ **4.** Double-click **Starts** in the duplicate arrow, and then type **Ends**.

▶ **5.** Drag the duplicate of the arrow down so that it points to the left bank of the river at the bottom of the photo as shown in Figure 2-5.

Figure 2-5   **Duplicate arrow positioned at the bottom of the photo on Slide 3**

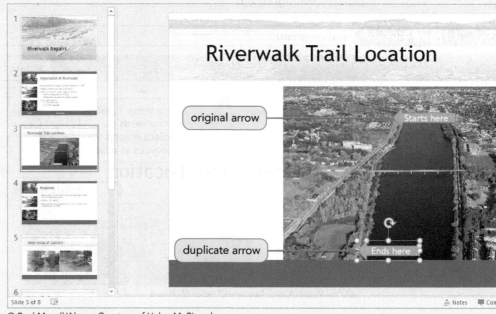

© Paul Mozell/Alamy; Courtesy of Helen M. Pinard

▶ **6.** Save your changes.

Rotating and Flipping Objects

You can rotate and flip any object on a slide. To flip an object, you click the Rotate button in the Arrange group on the Drawing Tools Format tab to access the Flip commands on the Rotate menu. To rotate an object, you can use the Rotate commands on the Rotate menu to rotate objects in 90-degree increments. You can also drag the rotate handle that appears above the top-middle sizing handle when the object is selected to rotate it to any position that you want, using the center of the object as a pivot point.

The arrows you drew on Slide 3 would look better if they were pointing from left to right. To make this change, you need to flip the arrows.

To flip the arrow shapes and reposition them on Slide 3:

▶ **1.** With Slide 3 ("Riverwalk Trail Location") displayed, click the **Starts here** arrow.

▶ **2.** Position the pointer on the Rotate handle 🔄 so that the pointer changes to ↻, and then drag the Rotate handle clockwise until the Starts here arrow is pointing to the right. The arrow is pointing in the correct direction, but the text in the arrow is now upside down.

▶ **3.** On the Quick Access Toolbar, click the **Undo** button 🔙, and then click the **Drawing Tools Format** tab, if necessary.

4. In the Arrange group, click the **Rotate** button. The Rotate menu opens. See Figure 2-6.

Figure 2-6	Rotate menu

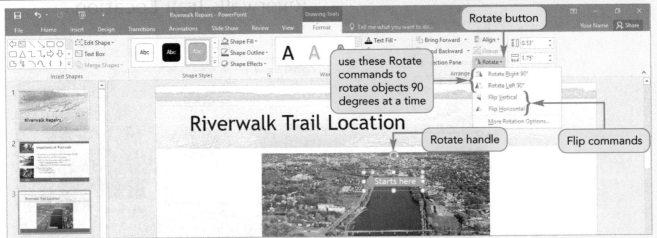

© Paul Mozell/Alamy; Courtesy of Helen M. Pinard

5. Click **Flip Horizontal**. The arrow flips horizontally and is now pointing right. Unlike when you rotated the arrow so that it pointed right, the text is still right-side up.

6. Drag the **Starts here** arrow to the left until it is pointing to the riverbank on the left side of the river at the curve at the top of the photo.

7. Click the **Ends here** arrow to select it, and then flip it horizontally. The Ends here arrow now points from the left to the right.

8. Drag the **Ends here** arrow to the left until it is pointing to the riverbank on the left side of the river at the bottom of the photo, and then click a blank area of the slide to deselect the arrow. Compare your screen to Figure 2-7, and then make any adjustments needed for your screen to match the figure.

Figure 2-7	Arrows flipped and repositioned on Slide 3

© Paul Mozell/Alamy; Courtesy of Helen M. Pinard

9. Save your changes.

Formatting Objects

Recall that both shapes and pictures, such as photos and clip art, are treated as objects in PowerPoint. The Picture Tools and Drawing Tools Format contextual tabs contain tools for formatting these objects. For both shapes and pictures, you can use these tools to apply borders or outlines, special effects such as drop shadows and reflections, and styles. You can also resize and rotate or flip these objects. Some formatting tools are available only to one or the other type of object. For example, the Remove Background tool is available only to pictures, and the Fill command is available only to shapes. Refer to the Session 2.1 Visual Overview for more information about the commands on the Format contextual tabs.

Formatting Shapes

You can modify the fill of a shape by filling it with a color, a gradient (shading in which one color blends into another or varies from one shade to another), a textured pattern, or a picture. When you add a shape to a slide, the default fill is the Accent 1 color from the set of theme colors, and the default outline is a darker shade of that color.

José wants you to change the default color of the "Starts here" arrow shape to green and the color of the "Ends here" arrow shape to red.

To change the fill and style of the arrow shapes:

▶ **1.** On Slide 3 ("Riverwalk Trail Location"), click the **Ends here** arrow, and then click the **Drawing Tools Format** tab, if necessary.

▶ **2.** In the Shape Styles group, click the **Shape Fill button arrow**. The Shape Fill menu opens. See Figure 2-8. You can fill a shape with a color, a picture, a gradient, or a texture, or you can remove the fill by clicking No Fill.

Figure 2-8	Shape Fill menu

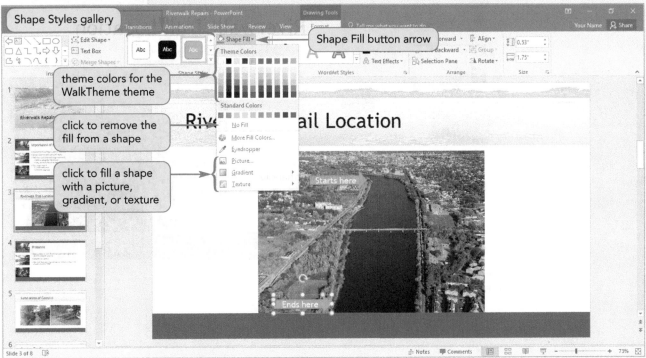

© Paul Mozell/Alamy; Courtesy of Helen M. Pinard

3. Under Standard Colors, click **Red**. The shape fill of the selected arrow changes to red. Next, you'll apply a style to the other arrow shape.

4. Click the **Starts here** arrow, and then in the Shape Styles group, click the **More** button. The Shape Styles gallery opens.

5. Click the **Light 1 Outline, Colored Fill – Dark Green, Accent 4** style. The style, which fills the shape with green and changes the shape outline to white, is applied to the shape.

On some shapes, you can drag the yellow adjustment handle to change the shape's proportions. For instance, if you dragged the adjustment handle on the arrow shape, you would change the size of the arrowhead relative to the size of the arrow.

You need to make the arrowhead larger relative to the size of the arrow shape.

To adjust the arrow shapes:

1. Click the **Starts here** shape, if necessary, to select it.

2. Drag the yellow adjustment handle at the top point on the arrowhead to the left so that the bottom point on the arrowhead aligns with the left side of the second "e" in "here."

3. Click the **Ends here** shape, and then drag the yellow adjustment handle at the top point on the arrowhead to the left so that the bottom point on the arrowhead aligns with the left side of the second "e" in "here." Compare your screen to Figure 2-9.

Figure 2-9	Formatted arrow shapes

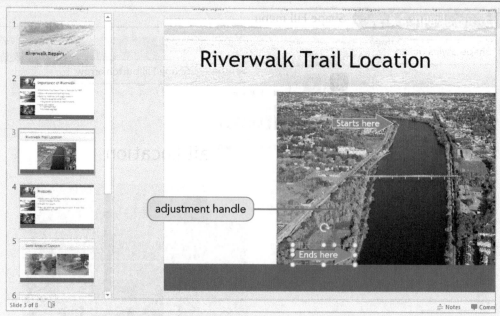

© Paul Mozell/Alamy; Courtesy of Helen M. Pinard

Formatting Pictures

You can format photos as well as shapes. To format photos, you use the tools on the Picture Tools Format tab.

José wants you to format the pictures on Slide 5 by adding a colored border. To create the border, you could apply a thick outline, or you can apply one of the styles that includes a border and then modify it.

To format the photos on Slide 5:

▶ **1.** Display **Slide 5** ("Some Areas of Concern"), click the photo on the left, and then click the **Picture Tools Format** tab.

▶ **2.** In the Picture Styles group, click the **Simple Frame, White** style. This style applies a seven-point white border to the photo.

▶ **3.** In the Picture Styles group, click the **Picture Border button arrow**, and then click the **Dark Blue, Accent 3** color. See Figure 2-10. You need to apply the same formatting to the photo on the right on Slide 5. You can repeat the same formatting steps, or you can copy the formatting.

Figure 2-10   Picture with a style and border color applied

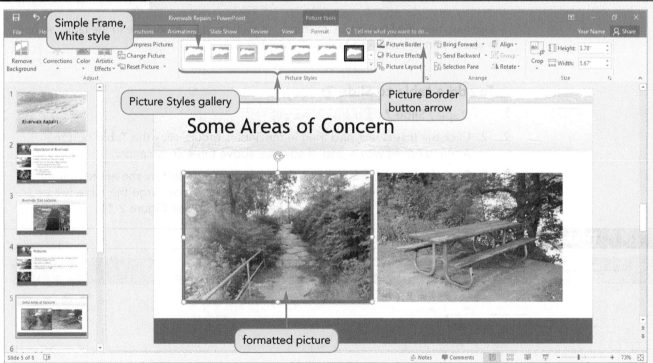

Courtesy of Helen M. Pinard; © Paul Mozell/Alamy

▶ **4.** With the left photo on Slide 5 still selected, click the **Home** tab.

▶ **5.** In the Clipboard group, click the **Format Painter** button, and then move the pointer to the slide. The pointer changes to ▷ 📌.

▶ **6.** Click the photo on the right. The style and border color of the photo on the left is copied and applied to the photo on the right.

▶ **7.** Save your changes.

Creating and Formatting Tables

A **table** is information arranged in horizontal rows and vertical columns. The area where a row and column intersect is called a **cell**. Each cell contains one piece of information. A table's structure is indicated by borders, which are lines that outline the rows and columns.

Creating a Table and Adding Data to It

José wants you to add a table to Slide 7 that itemizes the damages to the trail and associated repair costs. This table will have three columns—one to describe the damages, one to contain the expected costs for the repair, and one to list notes.

Inserting a Table

- In a content placeholder, click the Insert Table button; or, click the Insert tab on the ribbon, click the Table button in the Tables group, and then click Insert Table.
- Specify the numbers of columns and rows, and then click the OK button.

or

- On the ribbon, click the Insert tab, and then in the Tables group, click the Table button.
- Click a box in the grid to create a table of that size.

José hasn't decided how many examples of trail damages to include in the table, so he asks you to start by creating a table with four rows.

To add a table to Slide 7:

▶ **1.** Display **Slide 7** ("Cost of Repairs").

▶ **2.** Click the **Insert** tab, and then in the Tables group, click the **Table** button. A menu opens with a grid of squares above three commands.

▶ **3.** Point to the grid, and without clicking the mouse button, move the pointer over the grid. The label above the grid indicates how large the table will be, and a preview of the table appears on the slide. See Figure 2-11.

Figure 2-11	Inserting a 3x4 table on Slide 7

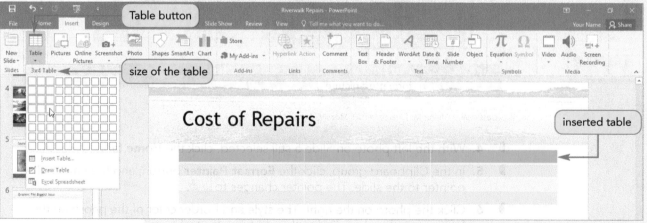

Courtesy of Helen M. Pinard

▶ **4.** When the label above the grid indicates 3x4 Table, click to insert a table with three columns and four rows. A selection border appears around the table, and the insertion point is in the first cell in the first row.

Now you're ready to fill the blank cells with the information about the trail repairs. To enter data in a table, you click in the cells in which you want to enter data and then start typing. You can also use the Tab and arrow keys to move from one cell to another.

To add data to the table:

1. In the first cell in the first row, type **Description of Damages**. The text you typed appears in the first cell.

2. Press the **Tab** key. The insertion point moves to the second cell in the first row.

3. Type **Cost of Repair**, press the **Tab** key, type **Notes**, and then press the **Tab** key. The insertion point is in the first cell in the second row.

4. In the first cell in the second row, type **Broken stairs at beginning of trail**, press the **Tab** key, and then type **$700**.

5. Click in the first cell in the third row, type **Erosion along banks**, press the **Tab** key, and then type **$2500**.

6. Click in the first cell in the last row, type **Fallen trees blocking trail**, press the **Tab** key, and then type **$350**.

Inserting and Deleting Rows and Columns

You can modify the table by adding or deleting rows and columns. You need to add more rows to the table for additional descriptions of damage to the trail.

To insert rows and a column in the table:

1. Make sure the insertion point is in the last row in the table.

2. Click the **Table Tools Layout** tab, and then in the Rows & Columns group, click the **Insert Below** button. A new row is inserted below the current row. See Figure 2-12.

| Figure 2-12 | Table with row inserted |

Courtesy of Helen M. Pinard

▶ **3.** Click in the first cell in the new last row, type **Jersey barrier blocking trail**, and then press the **Tab** key.

▶ **4.** Type **$300**, and then press the **Tab** key. The insertion point is in the last cell in the last row.

▶ **5.** Press the **Tab** key. A new row is created, and the insertion point is in the first cell in the new row.

▶ **6.** Type **Broken and vandalized signage**, press the **Tab** key, and then type **$250**. You need to insert a row above the last row.

▶ **7.** In the Rows & Columns group, click the **Insert Above** button. A new row is inserted above the current row, and all the cells in the new row are selected.

▶ **8.** Click any cell in the first column, and then in the Rows & Column group, click the **Insert Left** button.

A new first column is inserted.

Make sure you click a cell in the first column before you insert the new column. Otherwise, you will insert three new columns.

José decided he doesn't want to add notes to the table, so you'll delete the last column. He also decided that the new row you added as the second to last row in the table isn't needed, so you'll delete that row.

To delete a column and a row in the table:

▶ **1.** Click in any cell in the last column in the table. This is the column you will delete.

▶ **2.** On the Table Tools Layout tab, in the Rows & Columns group, click the **Delete** button. The Delete button menu opens.

▶ **3.** Click **Delete Columns**. The current column is deleted, and the entire table is selected.

▶ **4.** Click in any cell in the second to last row (the empty row). This is the row you want to delete.

▶ **5.** In the Rows & Columns group, click the **Delete** button, and then click **Delete Rows**. See Figure 2-13.

Figure 2-13   **Table after adding and deleting rows and columns**

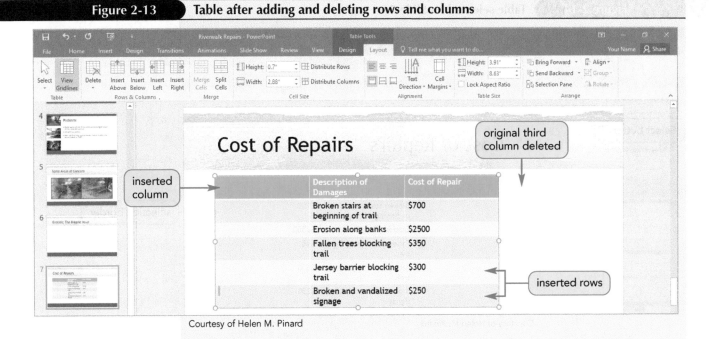

Courtesy of Helen M. Pinard

Formatting a Table

After you insert data into a table, you need to think about how the table looks and whether the table will be readable for the audience. As with any text, you can change the font, size, or color, and as with shapes and pictures, you can apply a style to a table. You can also change how the text fits in the table cells by changing the height of rows and the width of columns. You can also customize the formatting of the table by changing the border and fill of table cells.

You need to make the table text larger so that an audience will be able to read it.

To change the font size of text in the table:

▶ **1.** Click any cell in the table. You want to change the size of all the text in the table, so you will select the entire table. Notice that a selection border appears around the table. This border appears any time the table is active.

▶ **2.** Click the **Table Tools Layout** tab, if necessary, and then in the Table group, click the **Select** button. The Select menu opens with options to select the entire table, the current column, or the current row.

▶ **3.** Click **Select Table**. The entire table is selected. Because the selection border appears any time the table is active, the only visual cues you have that it is now selected are that the insertion point is no longer blinking in the cell that you clicked in Step 1 and the Select button is gray and unavailable. See Figure 2-14.

Figure 2-14   **Table selected on Slide 7**

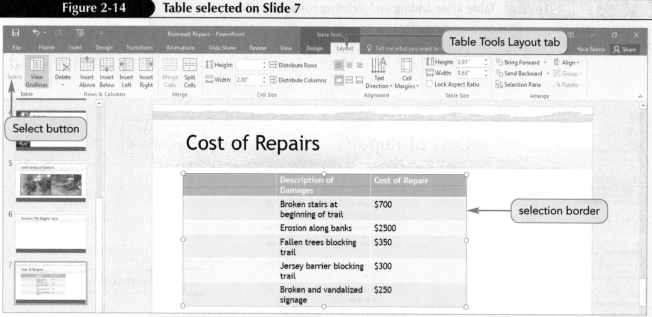

Courtesy of Helen M. Pinard

▶ **4.** On the ribbon, click the **Home** tab.

▶ **5.** In the Font group, click the **Font Size arrow**, and then click **28**. Because the entire table is selected, the size of all the text in the table changes to 28 points.

One of the rows is now off of the slide at the bottom. You will adjust the column widths so that all of the rows fit on the slide. To adjust column widths, you can drag a column border or type a number in the Width box in the Cell Size group on the Table Tools Layout tab. You can also automatically adjust a column to fit its widest entry by double-clicking its right border.

To adjust column sizes in the table:

▶ **1.** Position the pointer on the border between the first and second columns so that the pointer changes to ↔, and then drag the border to the left until it is below the "o" in the word "of" in the slide title.

▶ **2.** Click the **Table Tools Layout** tab, click any cell in the first column, and then in the Cell Size group, examine the measurement in the Width box.

▶ **3.** If the measurement in the Width box is not 1.6", click in the **Width** box, type **1.6**, and then press the **Enter** key. The width of the first column is changed to 1.6 inches.

▶ **4.** Position the pointer on the border between the second and third columns so that it changes to ↔, and then double-click. The second column widens to accommodate the widest entry in the column. See Figure 2-15.

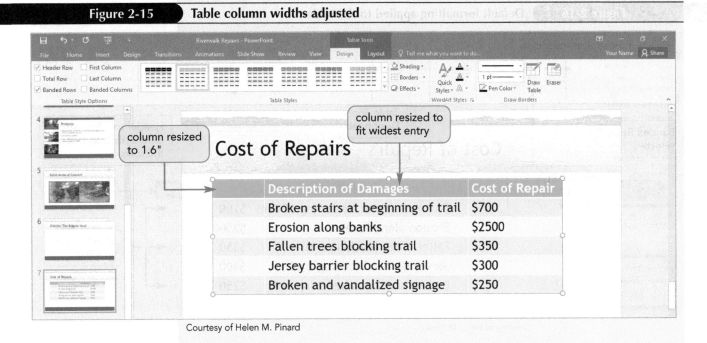

Figure 2-15   Table column widths adjusted

Courtesy of Helen M. Pinard

José wants you to change the format of the table so it looks more attractive and so that its colors complement the photo in the slide's layout. You will do this by applying a style to the table. When you apply a style to a table, you can specify whether the header and total rows and the first and last columns are formatted differently from the other rows and columns in the table. You can also specify whether to use banded rows or columns, that is, whether to fill alternating rows or columns with different shading.

To apply a style to the table:

▶ 1. Click the **Table Tools Design** tab on the ribbon, if necessary. In the Table Styles group, the second style, Medium Style 2 – Accent 1, is selected. In the Table Style Options group, the Header Row and Banded Rows check boxes are selected, which means that the header row will be formatted differently than the rest of the rows and that every other row will be filled with shading. See Figure 2-16.

Figure 2-16   **Default formatting applied to the table**

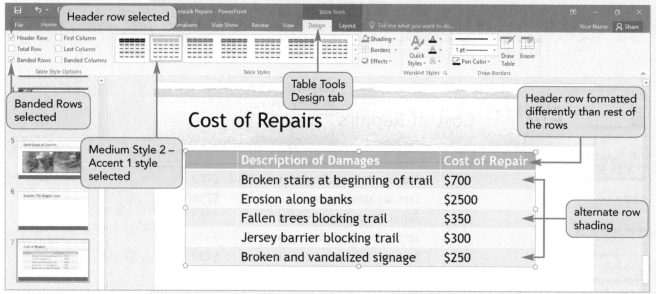

Courtesy of Helen M. Pinard

▶ **2.** In the Table Styles group, click the **More** button. The Table Styles gallery opens.

▶ **3.** Click the **Light Style 1** style, and then click a blank area of the slide to deselect the table. This style shades every other row with gray and adds a border above and below the top row and below the bottom row.

You can change the fill of table cells in the same manner that you change the fill of shapes. José wants the first row to be more prominent.

To change the fill of cells in the first row of the table:

▶ **1.** In the table, click any cell in the first row, and then click the **Table Tools Layout** tab.

▶ **2.** In the Table group, click the **Select** button, and then click **Select Row**. The first row in the table is selected.

▶ **3.** Click the **Table Tools Design** tab.

▶ **4.** In the Table Styles group, click the **Shading button arrow**. The Shading menu is similar to the Shape Fill menu you worked with earlier.

▶ **5.** Click **Dark Blue, Accent 3**. The menu closes and the cells in the first row are shaded with dark blue. The text is a little hard to read.

▶ **6.** In the WordArt Styles group, click the **Text Fill button arrow** 🅐 ▾, and then click the **White, Background 1, Darker 5%** color. The text in the selected cells changes to the white color you selected.

In addition, the table might be easier to read if the horizontal borders between the rows were visible. You can add these by using the Borders button arrow and the buttons in the Draw Borders group on the Table Tools Design tab. When you use the Borders button arrow, you can apply borders to all the selected cells at once. The borders will be the style, weight, and color specified by the Pen Style, Pen Weight, and Pen Color buttons in the Draw Borders group. Note that borders are different than gridlines. Gridlines are the lines that form the structure of a table. Borders are drawn on top of the gridlines. Gridlines are always there, but they appear only if the View Gridlines button in the Table group on the Table Tools Layout tab is selected and if the table itself is selected.

You want to see how the table looks without gridlines, then you will remove the top border on the top row in the table and make the bottom border of that row thicker.

To view and hide gridlines and modify the borders of the table:

▶ **1.** Click the **Table Tools Layout** tab, and then in the Table group, click the **View Gridlines** button to deselect it. The faint vertical lines between the table columns disappear.

   Trouble? If the View Gridlines button was already deselected, click it again to deselect it.

▶ **2.** In the Table group, click the **View Gridlines** button again to select it. The faint vertical lines between the table columns are visible again.

▶ **3.** Make sure the first row of the table is still selected. You want to remove the top border on this row.

▶ **4.** Click the **Table Tools Design** tab, and then in the Table Styles group, click the **Borders button arrow**. A menu opens listing borders that you can apply to the selected cells. Notice that the Top Border and Bottom Border commands are selected on the menu. This is because the selected cells have a top and bottom border. As indicated in the Draw Borders group, the borders are solid-line borders, one point wide, and black. See Figure 2-17. You can change any of these attributes.

Figure 2-17	Current format of borders for top row of table

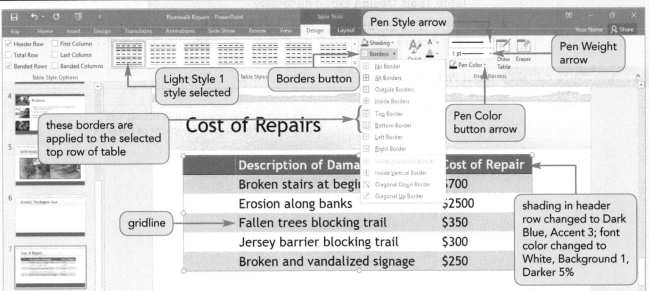

Courtesy of Helen M. Pinard

▶ **5.** Click **Top Border**. The top border on the selected row is removed.

▶ **6.** In the Table Styles group, click the **Borders button arrow**. Only the Bottom Border command is selected on the menu now.

   Trouble? If the Top Border command is still selected, click Top Border again, and then repeat Step 6.

Next you will change the first row's bottom border to a three-point line.

▶ **7.** In the Draw Borders group, click the **Pen Weight arrow**, and then click **3 pt**. The pointer changes to ⬦, and the Draw Table button in the Draw Borders group is selected. You could drag the pointer along the border you want to change, or you can use the Borders menu again.

▶ **8.** In the Table Styles group, click the **Borders button arrow**. None of the options on the Borders menu is selected because even though the selected row has a bottom border, it is a one-point border, not a three-point border.

▶ **9.** Click **Bottom Border**. The bottom border of the selected row changes to a three-point line. In the Draw Borders group, the Draw Table button is no longer selected.

Filling Cells with Pictures

Recall that one of the things you can fill a shape with is a picture. You can do the same with cells. Note that most of the table styles include shaded cells as part of the style definition, so if you want to fill table cells with pictures and apply a table style, you need to apply the table style first. Otherwise, the shading that is part of the table style definition will replace the pictures in the cells.

José wants you to add a picture to each row that shows an example of the described damage.

To fill the cells in the first column with pictures:

▶ **1.** Click in the first cell in the second row in the table, and then click the **Table Tools Design** tab, if necessary.

▶ **2.** In the Table Styles group, click the **Shading button arrow**, and then click **Picture**. The Insert Pictures window opens. See Figure 2-18.

Figure 2-18   **Insert Pictures window**

Insert Pictures

click to open the Insert Picture dialog box to locate a file on your computer or network

From a file
Browse files on your computer or local network   Browse ▸

Bing Image Search
Search the web   Search Bing

OneDrive - Personal
your_name@example.com   Browse ▸

Also insert from:

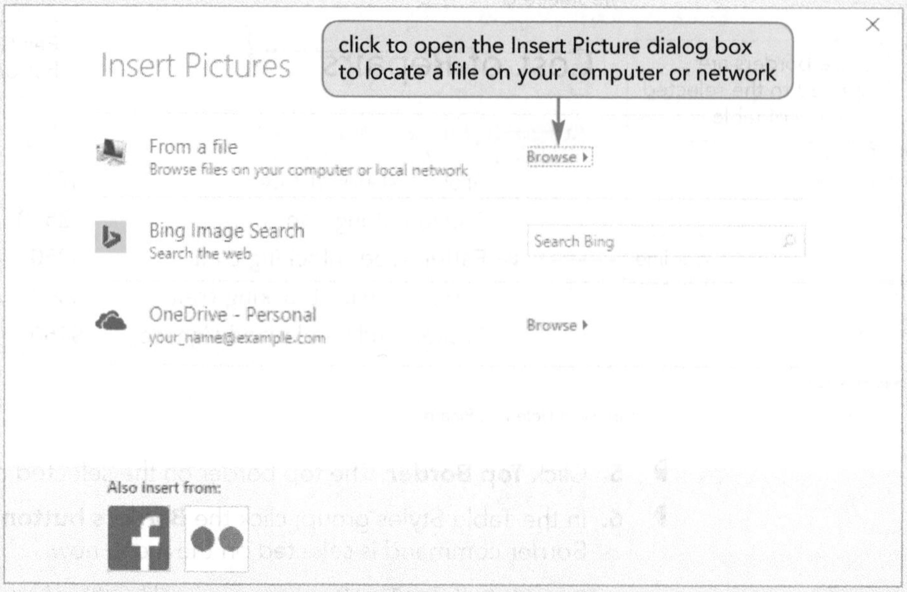

▶ **3.** Next to From a file, click **Browse**. The Insert Picture dialog box opens.

▶ **4.** Navigate to the **PowerPoint2** > **Module** folder, click **Stairs**, and then click the **Insert** button. The photo fills the cell.

▶ **5.** Insert the following photos, all located in the **PowerPoint2** > **Module** folder, in the first cells in the next four rows: **Erosion1**, **Tree**, **Barrier**, and **Sign**.

The text in the table is large enough, but the photos are too small, and some of them are distorted because they were stretched horizontally to fill the cells. To fix both of these problems, you'll increase the height of the rows containing the pictures.

To change row heights in the table:

▶ **1.** Position the pointer to the left of the second row in the table so that it changes to ➡.

▶ **2.** Press and hold the mouse button, drag down until the pointer is to the left of the bottom row in the table, and then release the mouse button. All the rows in the table except the first one are selected.

▶ **3.** Click the **Table Tools Layout** tab.

▶ **4.** In the Cell Size group, click in the **Height** box, type **.85** (make sure you type a decimal point before "85"), and then press the **Enter** key. The height of the selected rows increases to 0.85 inches.

The text in all cells in the table is horizontally left-aligned and vertically aligned at the top of the cells. The text in all the rows except the heading row would look better vertically aligned in the center of the cells. And because the data in the last column is dollar amounts, it would be better if these numbers were right-aligned. Finally, you also need to reposition the table on the slide to better fill the space. You move a table the same way you move any other object.

To adjust the alignment of text in cells and reposition the table:

▶ **1.** Make sure all the rows except the heading row are still selected.

▶ **2.** On the Table Tools Layout tab, in the Alignment group, click the **Center Vertically** button ▤. The text in the selected rows is now centered vertically in the cells.

▶ **3.** In the third column, click in the cell containing $700.

▶ **4.** Position the pointer in the last cell in the second row (the cell containing $700), press and hold the mouse button, drag down through the rest of the cells in the third column, and then release the mouse button. The cells you dragged over (all the cells in the third column except the heading cell) are selected.

▶ **5.** In the Alignment group, click the **Align Right** button ▤. The dollar amounts are now right-aligned in the cells. Now you will adjust the table's placement on the slide.

▶ **6.** In the Arrange group, click the **Align** button. A menu with commands for aligning the objects on the slide appears. Because only one object—the table—is selected, selecting a command will align the object to the borders of the slide.

7. Click **Align Center**. The table is horizontally aligned so that it is centered between the left and right borders of the slide. The bottom of the table slightly overlaps the blue bar at the bottom of the slide.

8. On the Table Tools Layout tab, in the Table group, click the **Select** button, and then click **Select Table**. The entire table is selected.

9. Press the ↑ key as many times as needed to move the table up slightly so that the bottom of the table no longer overlaps the bar at the bottom of the slide. Compare your screen to Figure 2-19.

Figure 2-19   **Final formatted table**

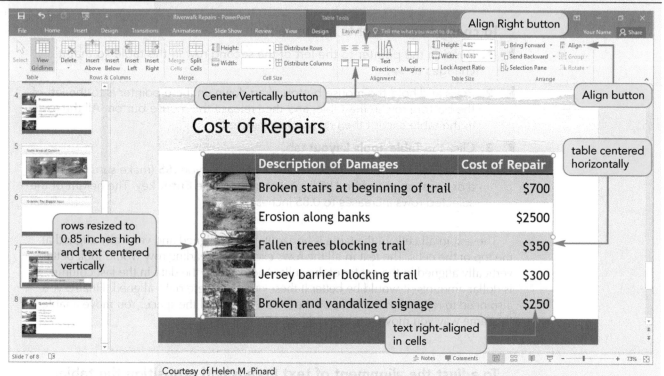

Courtesy of Helen M. Pinard

10. Click a blank area of the slide to deselect the table, and then save your changes.

Inserting Symbols

You can insert some symbols, such as the trademark symbol, the registered trademark symbol, and the copyright symbol, by typing letters between parentheses and letting AutoCorrect change the characters to a symbol. You can insert all symbols, including letters from another alphabet using a keyboard with only English letters, by using the Symbol button in the Symbols group on the Insert tab.

The nonprofit organization's name "RiverClean" is a trademarked name, so it usually appears with the trademark symbol ™ after it. You will add the trademark symbol after the organization's name on the last slide in the presentation.

To insert the trademark symbol by typing:

▶ **1.** Display **Slide 8** ("Questions?"), and then in the bulleted list, click after "RiverClean" in the second bulleted item.

▶ **2.** Type **(tm**.

▶ **3.** Type **)** (close parenthesis). The text "(tm)" changes to the trademark symbol, which is ™.

José's name contains two letters that are not in the English alphabet. You need to correct the spelling of José's first and last name. You'll do this using the Symbol dialog box.

To insert special characters:

▶ **1.** In the first bulleted item, click after "Jose," and then press the **Backspace** key. The "e" is deleted.

▶ **2.** Click the **Insert** tab, and then in the Symbols group, click the **Symbol** button. The Symbol dialog box opens.

▶ **3.** Drag the scroll box to the top of the vertical scroll bar, click the **Subset** arrow, and then click **Latin-1 Supplement**.

▶ **4.** Click the down scroll arrow three times, and then in the bottom row, click **é**. In the bottom-left corner of the Symbol dialog box, the name of the selected character is "Latin Small Letter E With Acute." See Figure 2-20.

Figure 2-20   Symbol dialog box

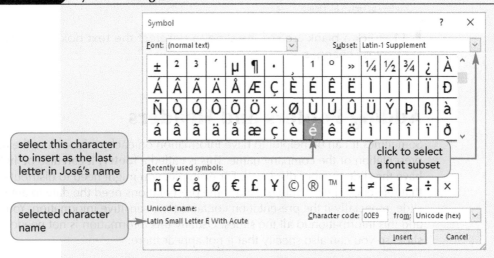

select this character to insert as the last letter in José's name

click to select a font subset

selected character name

Trouble? If the letter does not appear in the row mentioned in Step 4, someone might have resized the Symbol dialog box. Refer to Figure 2-20 for help locating the symbol.

▶ **5.** Click the **Insert** button. The letter "é" is inserted in the table, and the Cancel button in the dialog box changes to the Close button.

▶ **6.** Click the **Close** button. The first word in the first bulleted item is now "José."

▶ **7.** In the first bulleted item, click after the first "n" in "Quinones," and then press the **Backspace** key to delete the "n."

8. In the Symbols group, click the **Symbol** button to open the Symbols dialog box. The first row contains the é that you just inserted. You need to insert ñ, which appears in the row below the row containing the é.

9. In the second row in the dialog box, click **ñ**, which has the name "Latin Small Letter N With Tilde."

10. Click the **Insert** button, and then click the **Close** button. The first bulleted item is now "José Quiñones." See Figure 2-21.

| Figure 2-21 | Symbols inserted on Slide 8 |

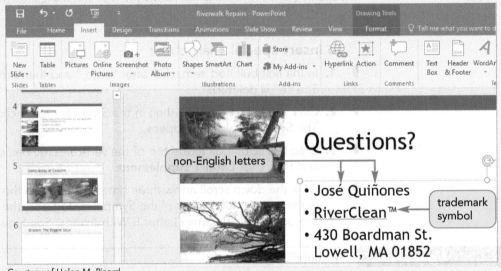

Courtesy of Helen M. Pinard

11. Click a blank area of the slide to deselect the text box, and then save your changes.

Adding Footers and Headers

Sometimes it can be helpful to have information on each slide such as the title of the presentation or the company name. This is called a **footer**. It can also be helpful to have the slide number displayed. For example, you might need to distribute handouts that reference slide numbers. And some presentations need the date to appear on each slide, especially if the presentation contains time-sensitive information. You can easily add this information to all the slides. Usually this information is not needed on the title slide, so you can also specify that it not appear there.

To add a footer, slide numbers, and the date to slides:

1. Click the **Insert** tab on the ribbon if necessary, and then in the Text group, click the **Header & Footer** button. The Header and Footer dialog box opens with the Slide tab selected.

2. Click the **Footer** check box to select it, and then click in the **Footer** box. In the Preview box on the right, the middle placeholder on the bottom is filled with black to indicate where the footer will appear on slides. See Figure 2-22. Note that the position of the footer, slide number, and date changes in different themes.

Figure 2-22   Slide tab in the Header and Footer dialog box

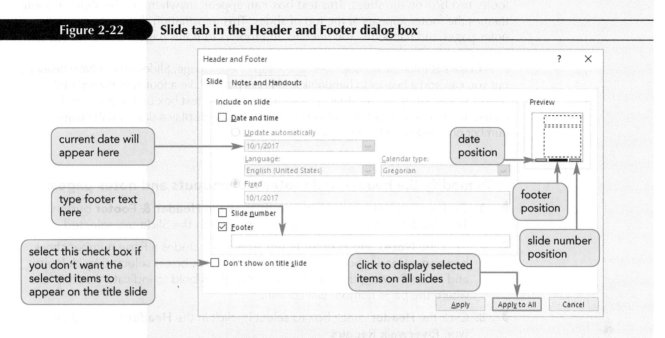

3. Type **Riverwalk Repairs**.

4. Click the **Slide number** check box to select it. In the Preview box, the box in the bottom-right is filled with black.

5. Click the **Date and time** check box to select it. The options under this check box darken to indicate that you can use them, and in the Preview box, the box in the bottom-left is filled with black.

   You don't want the date in the presentation to update automatically each time the presentation is opened. You want it to show today's date so people will know that the information is current as of that date.

6. Click the **Fixed** option button, if necessary. Now you want to prevent the footer, slide number, and date from appearing on the title slide.

7. Click the **Don't show on title slide** check box to select it, and then click the **Apply to All** button. On Slide 8, the footer, date, and slide number are displayed. See Figure 2-23.

Figure 2-23   Date, footer, and slide number on Slide 8

Courtesy of Helen M. Pinard

8. Display **Slide 1** (the title slide). Notice the footer, date, and slide number do not appear on the title slide.

In common usage, a footer is any text that appears at the bottom of every page in a document or every slide in a presentation. However, as you saw when you added the footer in the Header and Footer dialog box, in PowerPoint a footer is specifically the text that appears in the Footer box on the Slide tab in that dialog box and in the footer text box on the slides. This text box can appear anywhere on the slide; in some themes the footer appears at the top of slides. This information does not appear on notes pages and handouts. You need to add footers to notes pages and handouts separately.

A **header** is information displayed at the top of every page. Slides do not have headers, but you can add a header to handouts and notes pages. Like a footer, in PowerPoint a header refers only to the text that appears in the Header text box on handouts and notes pages. In addition to headers and footers, you can also display a date and the page number on handouts and notes pages.

To modify the header and footer on handouts and notes pages:

▶ **1.** On the Insert tab, in the Text group, click the **Header & Footer** button. The Header and Footer dialog box opens with the Slide tab selected.

▶ **2.** Click the **Notes and Handouts** tab. This tab includes a Page number check box and a Header box. The Page number check box is selected by default, and in the Preview, the lower-right rectangle is bold to indicate that this is where the page number will appear.

▶ **3.** Click the **Header** check box to select it, click in the **Header** box, and then type **Riverwalk Repairs**.

▶ **4.** Click the **Footer** check box to select it, click in the **Footer** box, and then type your name.

▶ **5.** Click the **Apply to All** button. To see the effect of modifying the handouts and notes pages, you need to look at the print preview.

▶ **6.** Click the **File** tab to open Backstage view, and then in the navigation bar, click **Print**.

▶ **7.** Under Settings, click the **Full Page Slides** button, and then click **Notes Pages**. The preview shows Slide 1 as a notes page. The header and footer you typed appear, along with the page number. See Figure 2-24.

Figure 2-24   **Header and footer on the Slide 1 notes page**

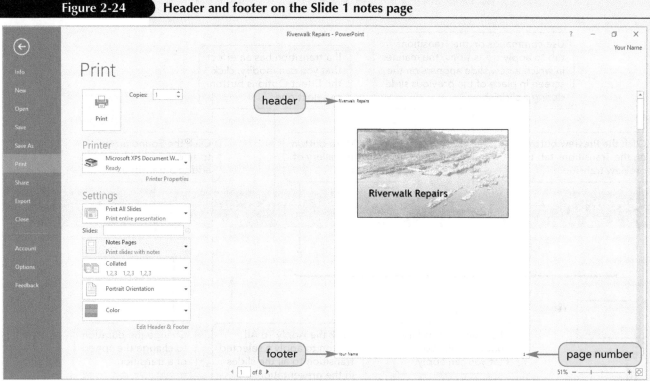

Courtesy of Helen M. Pinard

▶ **8.** At the top of the navigation bar, click the **Back** button ⊖ to return to Normal view.

▶ **9.** Save your changes.

You have modified a presentation by applying a theme used in another presentation, inserting and formatting pictures and shapes, and inserting a table and characters that are not on your keyboard. You also added footer and header information to slides and handouts. In the next session, you will continue modifying the presentation by applying and modifying transitions and animations, adding and modifying videos, and creating an Office mix.

Session 2.1 Quick Check

REVIEW

1. Which contextual tab appears on the ribbon when a shape is selected?

2. What is a style?

3. What is a shape's fill?

4. In a table, what is the intersection of a row and column called?

5. How do you know if an entire table is selected and not just active?

6. How do you insert characters that are not on your keyboard?

7. In PowerPoint, what is a footer?

Session 2.2 Visual Overview:

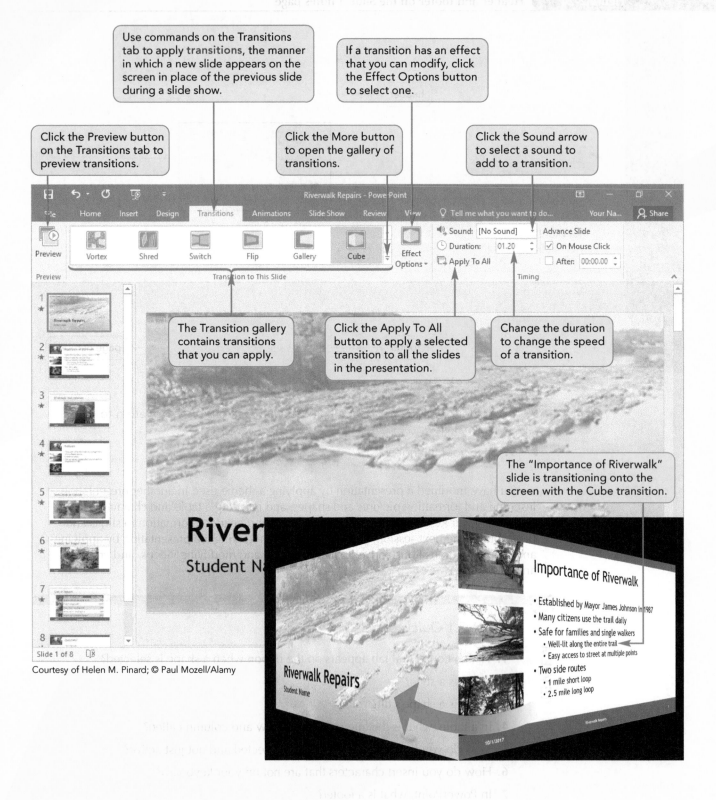

Use commands on the Transitions tab to apply transitions, the manner in which a new slide appears on the screen in place of the previous slide during a slide show.

If a transition has an effect that you can modify, click the Effect Options button to select one.

Click the Preview button on the Transitions tab to preview transitions.

Click the More button to open the gallery of transitions.

Click the Sound arrow to select a sound to add to a transition.

The Transition gallery contains transitions that you can apply.

Click the Apply To All button to apply a selected transition to all the slides in the presentation.

Change the duration to change the speed of a transition.

The "Importance of Riverwalk" slide is transitioning onto the screen with the Cube transition.

Courtesy of Helen M. Pinard; © Paul Mozell/Alamy

Using Animations and Transitions

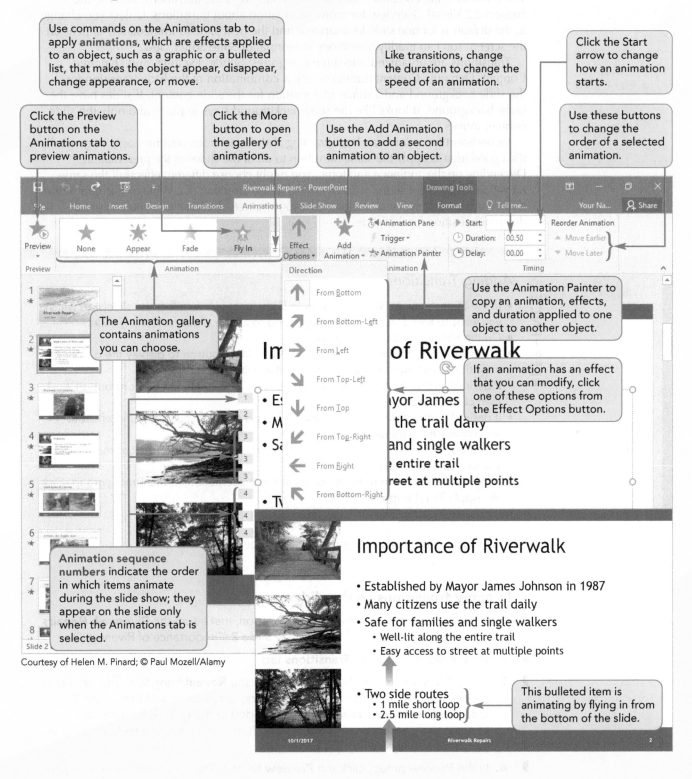

Use commands on the Animations tab to apply **animations**, which are effects applied to an object, such as a graphic or a bulleted list, that makes the object appear, disappear, change appearance, or move.

Like transitions, change the duration to change the speed of an animation.

Click the Start arrow to change how an animation starts.

Click the Preview button on the Animations tab to preview animations.

Click the More button to open the gallery of animations.

Use the Add Animation button to add a second animation to an object.

Use these buttons to change the order of a selected animation.

The Animation gallery contains animations you can choose.

Use the Animation Painter to copy an animation, effects, and duration applied to one object to another object.

If an animation has an effect that you can modify, click one of these options from the Effect Options button.

Animation sequence numbers indicate the order in which items animate during the slide show; they appear on the slide only when the Animations tab is selected.

This bulleted item is animating by flying in from the bottom of the slide.

Courtesy of Helen M. Pinard; © Paul Mozell/Alamy

Importance of Riverwalk

- Established by Mayor James Johnson in 1987
- Many citizens use the trail daily
- Safe for families and single walkers
  - Well-lit along the entire trail
  - Easy access to street at multiple points

- Two side routes
  - 1 mile short loop
  - 2.5 mile long loop

10/1/2017   Riverwalk Repairs   2

Applying Transitions

The Transitions tab contains commands for changing slide transitions. Refer to the Session 2.2 Visual Overview for more information about transitions. Unless you change it, the default is for one slide to disappear and the next slide to immediately appear on the screen. You can modify transitions in Normal or Slide Sorter view.

Transitions are organized into three categories: Subtle, Exciting, and Dynamic Content. Dynamic Content transitions are a combination of the Fade transition for the slide background and a different transition for the slide content. If slides have the same background, it looks like the slide background stays in place and only the slide content moves.

Inconsistent transitions can be distracting and detract from your message, so generally it's a good idea to apply the same transition to all of the slides in the presentation. Depending on the audience and topic, you might choose different effects of the same transition for different slides, such as changing the direction of a Wipe or Push transition. If there is one slide you want to highlight, for instance, the last slide, you can use a different transition for that slide.

REFERENCE

Adding Transitions

- In the Slides pane in Normal view or in Slide Sorter view, select the slide(s) to which you want to add a transition, or, if applying to all the slides, select any slide.
- On the ribbon, click the Transitions tab.
- In the Transition to This Slide group, click the More button to display the gallery of transitions, and then click a transition in the gallery.
- If desired, in the Transition to This Slide group, click the Effect Options button, and then click an effect.
- If desired, in the Timing group, click the Sound arrow to insert a sound effect to accompany each transition.
- If desired, in the Timing group, modify the time in the Duration box to modify the speed of the transition.
- To apply the transition to all the slides in the presentation, in the Timing group, click the Apply To All button.

José wants to add more interesting transitions between the slides.

To apply transitions to the slides:

1. If you took a break after the previous session, make sure the **Riverwalk Repairs** presentation is open, and then display **Slide 2** ("Importance of Riverwalk").

2. On the ribbon, click the **Transitions** tab.

3. In the Transition to This Slide group, click the **Reveal** transition. The transition previews as Slide 1 (the title slide) appears, fades away, and then Slide 2 fades in. The Reveal transition is now shaded in the gallery. In the Slides pane, a star appears next to the Slide 2 thumbnail. If you missed the preview, you can see it again.

4. In the Preview group, click the **Preview** button. The transition previews again.

5. In the Transition to This Slide group, click the **More** button. The gallery opens listing all the transitions. See Figure 2-25.

Figure 2-25   **Transitions gallery**

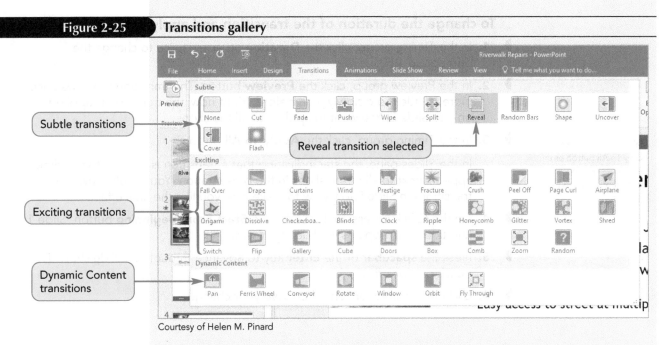

Courtesy of Helen M. Pinard

▶ **6.** Click the **Push** transition. The preview shows Slide 2 slide up from the bottom and push Slide 1 up and out of view.

Most transitions have effects that you can modify. For example, the Peel Off transition can peel from the bottom-left or the bottom-right corner, and the Wipe transition can wipe from any direction. You'll modify the transition applied to Slide 2.

To modify the transition effect for Slide 2:

▶ **1.** In the Transition to This Slide group, click the **Effect Options** button. The effects that you can modify for the Push transition are listed on the menu.

▶ **2.** Click **From Right**. The Push transition previews again, but this time Slide 2 slides from the right to push Slide 1 left. The available effects change depending on the transition selected.

▶ **3.** In the Transition to This Slide group, click the **Shape** transition. The transition previews with a brief view of Slide 1, before Slide 2 appears in the center of Slide 1 and enlarges in a circular shape to fill the slide.

▶ **4.** Click the **Effect Options** button. The effects that you can modify for the Shape transition are listed.

▶ **5.** Click **Out**. The preview of the transition with this effect displays Slide 2 in the center of Slide 1 that grows in a rectangular shape to fill the slide.

Finally, you can also change the duration of a transition. The duration is how long it takes the transition to finish, in other words, the speed of the transition. To make the transition faster, decrease the duration; to slow the transition down, increase the duration. José likes the Shape transition, but he thinks it is a little fast, so you will increase the duration. Then you can apply the modified transition to all the slides.

To change the duration of the transition and apply it to all the slides:

▶ **1.** In the Timing group, click the **Duration** up arrow twice to change the duration to 1.50.

▶ **2.** In the Preview group, click the **Preview** button. The transition previews once more, a little more slowly than before. Right now, the transition is applied only to Slide 2. You want to apply it to all the slides.

▶ **3.** In the Timing group, click the **Apply To All** button.

In the Slides pane, the star indicating that a transition is applied to the slide appears next to all of the slides in the presentation. You should view the transitions in Slide Show view to make sure you like the final effect.

▶ **4.** On the Quick Access Toolbar, click the **Start From Beginning** button. Slide 1 (the title slide) appears in Slide Show view.

▶ **5.** Press the **spacebar** or the **Enter** key to advance through the slide show. The transitions look fine.

▶ **6.** End the presentation, and then save your changes.

> Make sure you click the Apply To All button or the transition is applied only to the currently selected slide or slides.

Applying Animations

Animations add interest to a slide show and draw attention to the text or object being animated. For example, you can animate a slide title to fly in from the side or spin around like a pinwheel to draw the audience's attention to that title. Refer to the Session 2.2 Visual Overview for more information about animations.

Animation effects are grouped into four types:

- **Entrance**—Text and objects are not shown on the slide until the animation occurs; one of the most commonly used animation types.
- **Emphasis**—Text and objects on the slide change in appearance or move.
- **Exit**—Text and objects leave the screen before the slide show advances to the next slide.
- **Motion Paths**—Text and objects follow a path on a slide.

Animating Objects

You can animate any object on a slide, including pictures, shapes, and text boxes. To animate an object you click it, and then select an animation in the Animation group on the Animations tab.

REFERENCE

Applying Animations

- On the slide displayed in Normal view, select the object you want to animate.
- On the ribbon, click the Animations tab.
- In the Animation group, click the More button to display the gallery of animations, and then click an animation in the gallery.
- If desired, in the Animation group, click the Effect Options button, and then click a direction effect; if the object is a text box, click a sequence effect.
- If desired, in the Timing group, modify the time in the Duration box to modify the speed of the animation.
- If desired, in the Timing group, click the Start arrow, and then click a different start timing.

Slide 5 contains two pictures of damaged parts of the trail. José wants you to add an animation to the title text on this slide.

To animate the title on Slide 5:

▶ **1.** Display **Slide 5** ("Some Areas of Concern"), and then click the **Animations** tab on the ribbon. The animations in the Animation group are grayed out, indicating they are not available. This is because nothing is selected on the slide.

▶ **2.** Click the **Some Areas of Concern** title text. The animations in the Animation group are green to indicate that they are now available. All of the animations currently visible in the Animation group are entrance animations.

▶ **3.** In the Animation group, click the **Fly In** animation. This entrance animation previews on the slide—the title text disappears and then flies in from the bottom. In the Timing group, the Start box displays On Click, which indicates that this animation will occur when you advance the slide show by clicking the mouse or pressing the spacebar or the Enter key.

Notice the animation sequence number 1 in the box to the left of the title text box, which indicates that this is the first animation that will occur on the slide. You can preview the animation again if you missed it.

▶ **4.** In the Preview group, click the **Preview** button. The animation previews again.

▶ **5.** In the Animation group, click the **More** button. The Animation gallery opens. The animation commands are listed by category, and each category appears in a different color. At the bottom are four commands, each of which opens a dialog box listing all the effects in that category. See Figure 2-26. You will try an emphasis animation.

Figure 2-26 **Animation gallery**

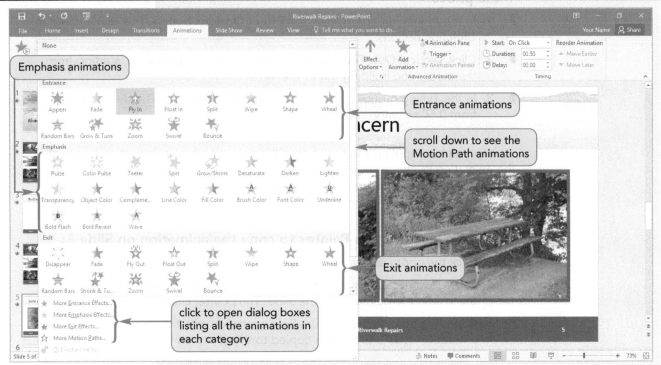

Courtesy of Helen M. Pinard

▶ **6.** Under Emphasis, click the **Underline** animation. The Underline animation replaces the Fly In animation, and the slide title is underlined in the preview.

The Underline animation you applied to the slide title is an example of an emphasis animation that is available only to text. You cannot apply that animation to objects such as pictures.

Slide 5 contains photos showing some areas of trail damage. To focus the audience's attention on one photo at time, you will apply an entrance animation to the photos so that they appear one at a time during the slide show.

To apply entrance animations to the photos on Slide 5:

▶ **1.** With Slide 5 ("Some Areas of Concern") displayed, click the picture on the right.

▶ **2.** In the Animation group, click the **More** button. Notice that in the Emphasis section, six of the animations, including the Underline animation you just applied to the slide title, are gray, which means they are not available for this object. These six animations are available only for text.

▶ **3.** In the Entrance section, click the **Split** animation. The picture appears starting from the left and right edges. In the Timing group, On Click appears in the Start box, indicating that this animation will occur when you advance the slide show. The animation sequence number to the left of the selected picture is 2, which indicates that this is the second animation that will occur on the slide when you advance the slide show.

You need to change the direction from which this animation appears, and you want to slow it down.

To change the effect and duration of the animation applied to the photo:

▶ **1.** In the Animation group, click the **Effect Options** button. This menu contains Direction options.

▶ **2.** Click **Vertical Out**. The preview shows the picture appearing, starting from the center and building out to the left and right edges.

▶ **3.** In the Timing group, click the **Duration** up arrow once. The duration changes from 0.50 seconds to 0.75 seconds.

After you have applied and customized the animation for one object, you can use the Animation Painter to copy that animation to other objects. You will copy the Split entrance animation to the other photo on Slide 5.

To use the Animation Painter to copy the animation on Slide 5:

▶ **1.** Click the photo on the right to select it.

▶ **2.** In the Advanced Animation group, click the **Animation Painter** button, and then move the pointer onto the slide. The pointer changes to ⬚ .

▶ **3.** Click the photo on the left. The Split animation with the Vertical Out effect and a duration of 0.75 seconds is copied to the photo on the left and previews.

After you apply animations, you should watch them in Slide Show, Presenter, or Reading view to see what they will look like during a slide show. Remember that On Click appeared in the Start box for each animation that you applied, which means that to see the animation during the slide show, you need to advance the slide show.

To view the animations on Slide 5 in Slide Show view:

▶ **1.** Make sure Slide 5 ("Some Areas of Concern") is displayed.

▶ **2.** On the status bar, click the **Slide Show** button ⬜. Slide 5 appears in Slide Show view. Only the photo that is part of the layout and the title appear on the slide.

▶ **3.** Press the **spacebar** to advance the slide show. The first animation, the emphasis animation that underlines the title, occurs.

▶ **4.** Press the **spacebar** again. The photo on the right appears starting at the center of the photo and building out to the left and right edges.

▶ **5.** Click anywhere on the screen. The photo on the left appears with the same animation as the photo on the right.

▶ **6.** Press the **Esc** key. Slide 5 appears in Normal view.

José doesn't like the emphasis animation on the slide title. It's distracting because the title is not the focus of this slide, the photos are. Also, it would be better if the photo on the left appeared before the photo on the right. To fix this, you can remove the animation applied to the title and change the order of the animations applied to the photos.

To remove the title animation and change the order of the photo animations:

▶ **1.** Click the **slide title**. In the Animation group, the yellow emphasis animation Underline is selected.

TIP

You can also click the animation sequence icon, and then press the Delete key to remove an animation.

▶ **2.** In the Animation group, click the **More** button, and then at the top of the gallery, click **None**. The animation that was applied to the title is removed, the animation sequence icon no longer appears next to the title text box, and the other two animation sequence icons on the slide are renumbered 1 and 2.

Now you need to select the animation applied to the photo on the left and change it so that it occurs first. You can select the object or the animation sequence icon to modify an animation.

▶ **3.** Next to the left photo, click the animation sequence icon **2**. In the Animation group, the green Split entrance animation is selected. See Figure 2-27.

| Figure 2-27 | Animation selected to change its order |

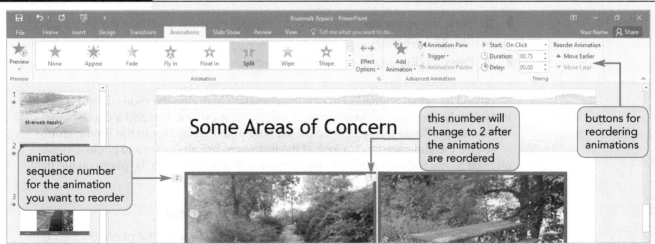

Courtesy of Helen M. Pinard; © Paul Mozell/Alamy

▶   **4.** In the Timing group, click the **Move Earlier** button. The animation sequence icon next to the photo on the left changes from 2 to 1, and the animation sequence icon next to the photo on the right changes from 1 to 2.

▶   **5.** In the Preview group, click the **Preview** button. The photo on the left appears, and then the photo on the right appears.

Changing How an Animation Starts

Remember that when you apply an animation, the default is for the object to animate On Click, which means when you advance through the slide show. You can change this so that an animation happens automatically, either at the same time as another animation or when the slide transitions, or after another animation.

José wants the photo on the right to appear automatically, without the presenter needing to advance the slide show.

To change how the animation for the photo on the right starts:

▶   **1.** With Slide 5 ("Some Areas of Concern") displayed, click the photo on the right. The entrance animation Split is selected in the Animation group, and in the Timing group, On Click appears in the Start box.

▶   **2.** In the Timing group, click the **Start** arrow. The three choices for starting an animation—On Click, With Previous, and After Previous—are listed on the menu.

▶   **3.** Click **After Previous**. Now this photo will appear automatically after the photo on the left appears. Notice that the animation sequence number next to this photo changed to 1, the same number as the animation sequence number next to the photo on the left. This is because you will not need to advance the slide show to start this animation.

When you preview an animation, it plays automatically on the slide in Normal view, even if the timing setting for the animation is On Click. To make sure the timing settings are correct, you need to watch the animation in a slide show.

To view and test the animations:

▶   **1.** On the status bar, click the **Slide Show** button 🖵. Slide 5 appears in Slide Show view.

▶   **2.** Press the **spacebar**. The photo on the left appears, and then the photo on the right appears.

▶   **3.** Press the **Esc** key to end the slide show.

When you set an animation to occur automatically during the slide show, it happens immediately after the previous action. If that is too soon, you can add a pause before the animation. To do this, you increase the time in the Delay box in the Timing group.

To give the audience time to look at the first photo before the second photo appears on Slide 5, you will add a delay to the animation that is applied to the photo on the right.

To add a delay to the After Previous animation:

▶   **1.** With Slide 5 ("Some Areas of Concern") displayed, click the photo on the right, if necessary, to select it. In the Timing group, 00.00 appears in the Delay box.

2. In the Timing group, click the **Delay** up arrow four times to change the time to one second. After the photo on the left appears (the previous animation), the photo on the right will appear after a delay of one second.

3. On the status bar, click the **Slide Show** button. Slide 5 appears in Slide Show view.

4. Press the **spacebar**. The photo on the left appears, and then after a one-second delay, the photo on the right appears.

5. Press the **Esc** key to end the slide show, and then save your changes.

Animating Lists

If you animate a list, the default is for each of the first-level items to animate On Click. This type of animation focuses your audience's attention on each item, without the distraction of items that you haven't discussed yet. José wants you to add an Entrance animation to the bulleted list on Slide 2. He wants each first-level bulleted item to appear on the slide one at a time so that the audience won't be able to read ahead while he is discussing each point.

To animate the bulleted lists:

1. Display **Slide 2** ("Importance of Riverwalk"), and then click anywhere in the bulleted list to make the text box active.

2. On the Animations tab, in the Animation group, click the **Fly In** animation. The animation previews on the slide as the bulleted items fly in from the bottom. When the "Safe for families" and "Two routes" items fly in, their subitems fly in with them. After the preview is finished, the numbers 1 through 4 appear next to the bulleted items. Notice that the subitems have the same animation sequence number as their first-level items. This means that the start timing for the subitems is set to With Previous or After Previous. See Figure 2-28.

Figure 2-28   **Fly In entrance animation applied to a bulleted list with subitems**

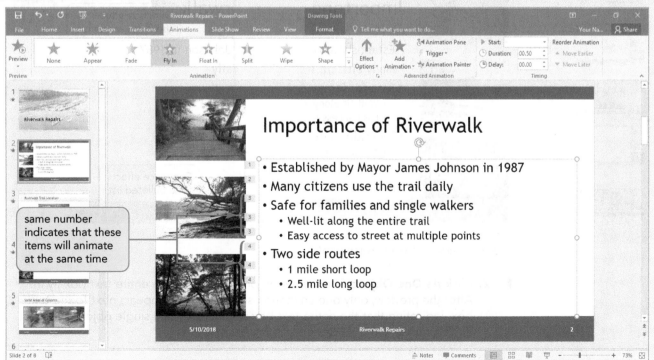

Courtesy of Helen M. Pinard; © Paul Mozell/Alamy

▶ **3.** Next to the "Safe for families and single walkers" bulleted item, click the animation sequence icon **3** to select it. In the Timing group, On Click appears in the Start box.

▶ **4.** Next to the subitem "Well-lit along the entire trail," click the animation sequence icon **3**. In the Timing group, With Previous appears in the Start box.

If you wanted to change how the items in the list animate during the slide show, you could change the start timing of each item, or you could change the sequence effect. Sequence effects appear on the Effect Options menu in addition to the Direction options when an animation is applied to a text box. The default is for the items to appear By Paragraph. This means each first-level item animates one at a time—with its subitems, if there are any—when you advance the slide show. You can change this setting so that the entire list animates at once as one object, or so that each first-level item animates at the same time but as separate objects.

To examine the Sequence options for the animated list:

▶ **1.** Click in the bulleted list, and then in the Animation group, click the **Effect Options** button. The Sequence options appear at the bottom of the menu, below the Direction options, and By Paragraph is selected. See Figure 2-29.

| Figure 2-29 | **Animation effect options for a bulleted list** |

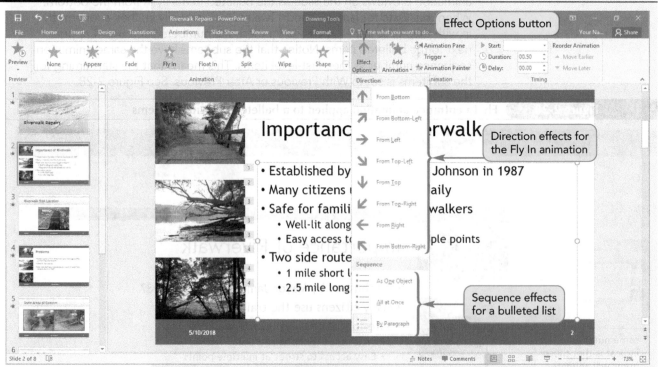

Courtesy of Helen M. Pinard; © Paul Mozell/Alamy

▶ **2.** Click **As One Object**. The animation preview shows the entire text box fly in. After the preview, only one animation sequence icon appears next to the text box, indicating that the entire text box will animate as a single object. In the Timing group, On Click appears in the Start box.

▶ **3.** In the Animation group, click the **Effect Options** button, and then under Sequence, click **All at Once**. The animation previews again, but this time each of the first-level items fly in as separate objects, although they all fly in at the same time. After the preview, animation sequence icons, all numbered 1, appear next to each bulleted item, indicating that each item will animate separately but you only need to advance the slide show once.

▶ **4.** Next to the first bulleted item, click the animation sequence icon **1**. In the Timing group, On Click appears in the Start box.

▶ **5.** Next to the second bulleted item ("Many citizens use the trail daily"), click the animation sequence icon **1**. In the Timing group, With Previous appears in the Start box.

▶ **6.** In the Animation group, click the **Effect Options** button, and then click **By Paragraph**. The sequence effect is changed back to its original setting.

▶ **7.** Save your changes.

PROSKILLS

Decision Making: Just Because You Can Doesn't Mean You Should

PowerPoint provides you with many tools that enable you to create interesting and creative slide shows. However, you need to give careful thought before deciding to use a tool to enhance the content of your presentation. Just because a tool is available doesn't mean you should use it. One example of a tool to use sparingly is sound effects with transitions. Most of the time you do not need to use sound to highlight the fact that one slide is leaving the screen while another appears.

You will also want to avoid using too many or frivolous animations. It is easy to go overboard with animations, and they can quickly become distracting and make your presentation seem less professional. Before you apply an animation, you should know what you want to emphasize and why you want to use an animation. Remember that animations should always enhance your message. When you are finished giving your presentation, you want your audience to remember your message, not your animations.

Adding and Modifying Video

You can add video to slides to play during your presentation. PowerPoint supports various file formats, but the most commonly used are the MPEG-4 format, the Windows Media Audio/Video format, and the Audio Visual Interleave format, which appears in Explorer windows as the Video Clip file type. After you insert a video, you can modify it by changing playback options, changing the length of time the video plays, and applying formats and styles to the video.

Adding Video to Slides

To insert a video stored on your computer or network, click the Insert Video button in a content placeholder, and then in the Insert Video window, in the From a file section, click Browse to open the Insert Video dialog box. You can also click the Video button in the Media group on the Insert tab, and then click Video on My PC to open the same Insert Video dialog box.

REFERENCE

Adding Videos Stored on Your Computer or Network

- In a content placeholder, click the Insert Video button to open the Insert Video window, and then in the From a file section, click Browse to open the Insert Video dialog box; or click the Insert tab on the ribbon, and then in the Media group, click the Video button, and then click Video on My PC to open the Insert Video dialog box.
- Click the video you want to use, and then click the Insert button.
- If desired, click the Video Tools Playback tab, and then in the Video Options group:
  - Click the Start arrow, and then click Automatically to change how the video starts from On Click.
  - Click the Play Full Screen check box to select it to have the video fill the screen.
  - Click the Rewind after Playing check box to select it to have the poster frame display after the video plays.
  - Click the Volume button, and then click a volume level or click Mute.

José gave you a video that he wants you to add to Slide 6. The video shows an eroded bank along the trail.

To add a video to Slide 6 and play it:

1. Display **Slide 6** ("Erosion: The Biggest Issue"), and then in the content placeholder, click the **Insert Video** button ⬚. The Insert Video window opens.

2. Next to From a file, click **Browse**. The Insert Video dialog box opens.

3. In the **PowerPoint2 > Module** folder, click **Erosion2**, and then click the **Insert** button. The video is inserted on the slide. The first frame of the video is displayed, and a play bar with controls for playing the video appears below it. See Figure 2-30.

Figure 2-30 ⟩ **Video added to Slide 6**

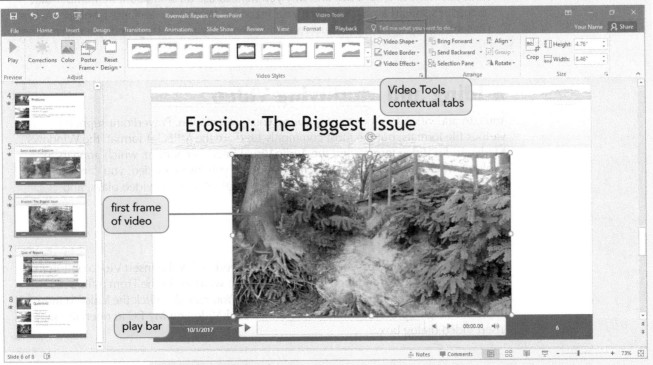

Courtesy of Helen M. Pinard

4. On the play bar, click the **Play** button ▶. The Play button changes to the Pause button ⏸ and the video plays. Watch the 13-second video (note that this video does not have any sound). Next, you'll watch the video in Slide Show view.

5. On the status bar, click the **Slide Show** button 🖵. Slide 6 appears in Slide Show view.

6. Point to the **video**. The play bar appears, and the pointer changes to 👆. You don't need to click the Play button to play the video in Slide Show view; you can click anywhere on the video to play it as long as the 👆 pointer is visible. While the video is playing, you can click it again to pause it.

7. Click anywhere on the video. The video plays.

   Trouble? If Slide 7 appeared instead of the video playing, the pointer wasn't visible or you didn't click the video object, so clicking the slide advanced the slide show. Press the Backspace key to return to Slide 6, move the mouse over the video to make the pointer visible, and then click the video.

8. Before the video finishes playing, move the pointer to make it visible, and then click the **video** again. The video pauses.

9. Move the pointer to make it visible, if necessary, click the **video** to finish playing it, and then press the **Esc** key to end the slide show.

INSIGHT

Inserting Pictures and Videos You Find Online

In addition to adding pictures and video stored on your computer or network to slides, you can also add pictures and video stored on websites. To add pictures from a website, you click the Online Pictures button in a content placeholder. When you do this, the Insert Pictures window opens, in which you can use the Bing search engine to search for images stored on the Internet. Your results will be similar to those you would get if you typed keywords in the Search box on the Bing home page in your browser. However, in the Insert Pictures window, only images that are licensed under Creative Commons appear. (When you search using Bing in a browser, you see all results, not just the images licensed under Creative Commons.)

To add a video from a website, you click the Insert Video button in a content placeholder to open the Insert Video window. There, you can type search terms in the Search YouTube box to find a video on YouTube, or, if you have the embed code from a website, you can paste the embed code in the Paste embed code here box. When you search for a video on YouTube, videos that match your search terms appear in the window. You click the video you want to add, and then click Insert. To add a video whose embed code you copied, right-click in the Paste embed code here box, click Paste on the shortcut menu, and then click the Insert button in the box.

Trimming Videos

If a video is too long, or if there are parts at the beginning or end of the video that you don't want to show during the presentation, you can trim it. To do this, click the Trim Video button in the Editing group on the Video Tools Playback tab, and then, in the Trim Video dialog box, drag the green start slider or the red stop slider to a new position to mark where the video will start and stop.

José doesn't think the audience needs to watch all 13 seconds of this video, so he wants you to trim it to 10 seconds.

To trim the video on Slide 6:

▶ **1.** With Slide 6 ("Erosion: The Biggest Issue") displayed, click the **video** to select it, if necessary, and then click the **Video Tools Playback** tab.

▶ **2.** In the Editing group, click the **Trim Video** button. The Trim Video dialog box opens. See Figure 2-31.

Figure 2-31   **Trim Video dialog box**

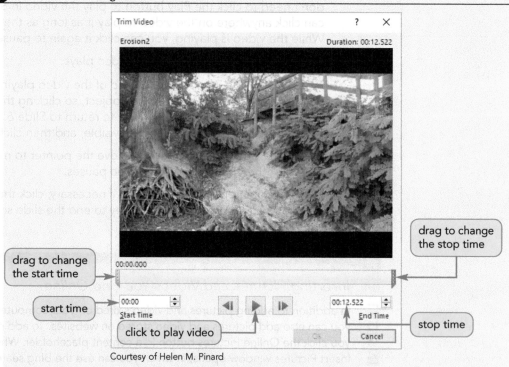

Courtesy of Helen M. Pinard

▶ **3.** Drag the red **Stop** tab to the left until the time in the End Time box is approximately 10 seconds, and then click the **OK** button.

▶ **4.** On the play bar, click the **Play** button ▶. The video plays but stops after playing for 10 seconds.

▶ **5.** Save your changes.

Setting a Poster Frame

The frame that appears on the slide when the video is not playing is called the **poster frame**. You can set the poster frame to be any frame in the video, or you can set the poster frame to any image stored in a file. The default poster frame for a video is the first frame of the video. You can change this so that any frame from the video or any image stored in a file is the poster frame. If the video is set to rewind, you can make the poster frame appear if you set the video to rewind after playing. José wants you to do this for the video on Slide 6.

To set a poster frame for the video on Slide 6:

▶ **1.** With Slide 6 ("Erosion: The Biggest Issue") displayed, click the **video** to select it, if necessary, and then click the **Video Tools Format** tab.

▶ **2.** Point to the **play bar** below the video. A ScreenTip appears identifying the time of the video at that point. See Figure 2-32.

| Figure 2-32 | Setting a poster frame |

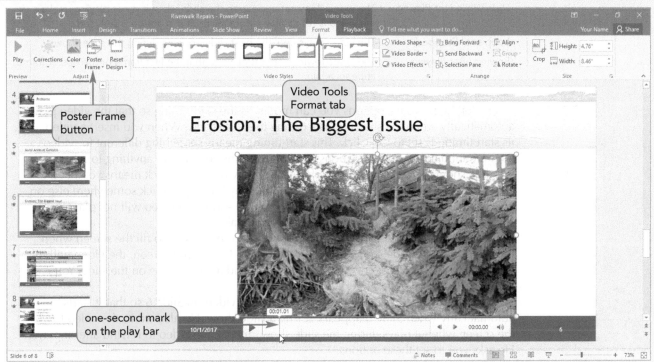

Courtesy of Helen M. Pinard

▶ **3.** On the play bar, click at approximately the one-second mark. The video advances to the one-second mark, and the frame at the one-second mark appears in the video object.

▶ **4.** In the Adjust group, click the **Poster Frame** button. The Poster Frame menu opens.

▶ **5.** Click **Current Frame**. The message "Poster Frame Set" appears in the video's play bar, and the frame currently visible in the video object is set as the poster frame.

Modifying Video Playback Options

You can change several options for how a video plays. The video playback options are listed in Figure 2-33.

Figure 2-33	Video playback options

Video Option	Function
Volume	Change the volume of the video from high to medium or low or mute it.
Start	Change how the video starts, either when the presenter clicks it or the Play button on the play bar or automatically when the slide appears during the slide show.
Play Full Screen	The video fills the screen during the slide show.
Hide While Not Playing	The video does not appear on the slide when it is not playing; make sure the video is set to play automatically if this option is selected.
Loop until Stopped	The video plays until the next slide appears during the slide show.
Rewind after Playing	The video rewinds after it plays so that the first frame or the poster frame appears again.

One of the playback options you can modify is the start timing so that the video plays automatically when the slide appears during the slide show. When you insert a video, its start timing is set to On Click. This start timing means something different for videos than for animations. For animations, On Click means you can do anything to advance the slide show to cause the animation to start. For videos, On Click means you need to click the video object or the Play button on the play bar. If you click somewhere else on the screen or do anything else to advance the slide show, the video will not play. The start timing setting is on the Video Tools Playback tab.

In addition to changing the start timing, you can set a video to fill the screen when it plays during the slide show. If you set the option to play full screen, the video will fill the screen when it plays, covering the slide title and anything else on the slide. You can also set a video to rewind after it plays.

José wants you to change the start timing of the video on Slide 6 so that it starts automatically when Slide 6 appears during a slide show. He also wants the video to fill the screen when it plays during the slide show, and for the video to rewind after it plays. He asks you to set these options.

To modify the playback options of the video:

▶ 1. With Slide 6 ("Erosion: The Biggest Issue") displayed, click the **video** to select it, if necessary.

▶ 2. On the ribbon, click the **Video Tools Playback** tab. In the Video Options group, On Click appears in the Start box. See Figure 2-34.

Figure 2-34	Options on the Video Tools Playback tab

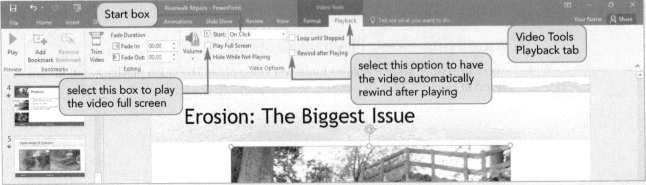

Courtesy of Helen M. Pinard

TIP

You can adjust the volume of a video while it plays, or you can set the default volume by clicking the Volume button in the Video Options group on the Playback tab and then clicking an option on the menu.

▶ **3.** In the Video Options group, click the **Start** arrow, and then click **Automatically**. Now the video will start automatically when the slide appears during the slide show.

▶ **4.** In the Video Options group, click the **Play Full Screen** check box to select it. The video will fill the screen when it plays.

▶ **5.** In the Video Options group, click the **Rewind after Playing** check box to select it. The video will reset to the beginning after it plays and display the poster frame.

▶ **6.** On the status bar, click the **Slide Show** button ▭. Slide 6 appears briefly in Slide Show view, and then the video fills the screen and plays. After the video finishes playing, Slide 6 reappears displaying the poster frame of the video.

▶ **7.** Press the **Esc** key to end the slide show, and then save the changes.

Understanding Animation Effects Applied to Videos

When you insert a video (or audio) object, an animation is automatically applied to the video so that you can click anywhere on the video to start and pause it when the slide show is run. This animation is the Pause animation in the Media animation category, and it is set to On Click. The Media animation category appears only when a media object—either video or audio—is selected on a slide. The Pause animation is what makes it possible to start or pause a video during a slide show by clicking anywhere on the video object. (When you click the video to play it, you are actually "unpausing" it.)

When you change the Start setting of a video on the Playback tab to Automatically, a second animation, the Play animation in the Media animation category, is applied to the video as well as the Pause animation, and the start timing of the Play animation is set to After Previous. If there are no other objects on the slide set to animate before the video, the Play animation has an animation sequence number of zero, which means that it will play immediately after the slide transition.

To see these animations, click the Animations tab on the ribbon, and then select a video object on a slide. The Pause and Play animations appear in the Animation gallery in the Media category.

You'll examine the video animations now.

To examine the Media animation effects for the video:

▶ **1.** With Slide 6 ("Erosion: The Biggest Issue") displayed, click the **video** to select it, if necessary.

▶ **2.** On the ribbon, click the **Animations** tab. Because you set this video to start automatically, two animation sequence icons appear next to it, one containing a zero and one containing a lightning bolt. In the Animation group, Multiple is selected because two animations are applied to this video. See Figure 2-35.

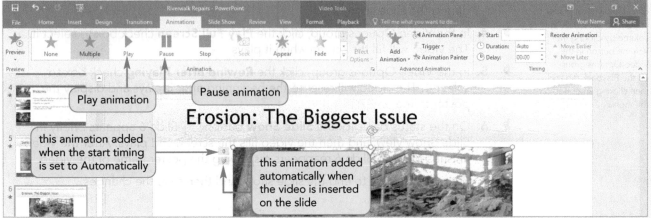

Courtesy of Helen M. Pinard

3. In the Animation group, click the **More** button. The Media category appears at the top of the Animation gallery because a media object is selected.

4. Press the **Esc** key. The gallery closes without you making a selection.

When more than one animation is applied to any object, you need to click each animation sequence icon to see which animation is associated with each icon.

5. Click the **lightning bolt** animation sequence icon. In the Animation group, the Pause animation is selected, and in the Timing group, On Click appears in the Start box. This animation is applied automatically to all videos when you add them to slides. It is because of this animation that you can click anywhere on the video object during a slide show to play or pause it.

6. Click the **0** animation sequence icon. In the Animation group, Play is selected, and in the Timing group, After Previous appears in the Start box. This Play animation was added to this video when you selected Automatically in the Start box on the Playback tab.

Compressing and Optimizing Media

As with pictures, you can compress media files. If you need to send a file via email or you need to upload it, you should compress media files to make the final PowerPoint file smaller. The more you compress files, the smaller the final presentation file will be but also the lower the quality. For videos, you can compress using the following settings:

- **Presentation Quality**—compresses the videos slightly and maintains the quality of the videos
- **Internet Quality**—compresses the videos to a quality suitable for streaming over the Internet
- **Low Quality**—compresses the videos as small as possible

With all of the settings, any parts of videos that you trimmed off will be deleted, similar to deleting the cropped portions of photos.

After you compress media, you should watch the slides containing the videos using the equipment you will be using when giving your presentation to make sure the reduced quality is acceptable. Usually, if the videos were high quality to start with, the compressed quality will be fine. However, if the original video quality was grainy, the compressed quality might be too low, even for evaluation purposes. If you decide that you don't like the compressed quality, you can undo the compression.

You will compress the media files you inserted. You need to send the presentation to José via email, so you will compress the media as much as possible.

To compress the videos in the presentation:

▶ **1.** With Slide 6 ("Erosion: The Biggest Issue") displayed, click the **File** tab. Backstage view appears displaying the Info screen. See Figure 2-36.

| Figure 2-36 | Compression options on the Info screen in Backstage view |

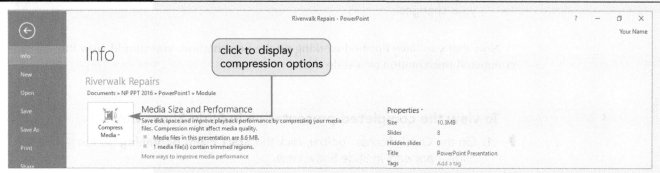

▶ **2.** Click the **Compress Media** button. A menu opens listing compression choices.

▶ **3.** Click **Low Quality**. The Compress Media dialog box opens listing the video file in the presentation with a progress bar to show you the progress of the compression. See Figure 2-37.

| Figure 2-37 | Compress Media dialog box |

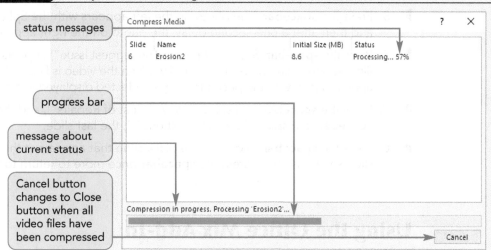

After the file is compressed, a message appears in the Status column indicating that compression for the file is complete and stating how much the video file size was reduced. A message also appears at the bottom of the dialog box stating that the compression is complete and indicating how much the file size of the presentation was reduced. Because there is only one video in this presentation, the amount the video was reduced and the amount the presentation was reduced is the same.

▶ **4.** Click the **Close** button. Next to the Compress Media button on the Info screen, the bulleted list states that the presentation's media was compressed to Low Quality and that you can undo the compression if the results are unsatisfactory. Now you need to view the compressed videos.

▶ **5.** At the top of the navigation bar, click the **Back** button ⊖ to display Slide 6.

▶ **6.** On the status bar, click the **Slide Show** button to display the slide in Slide Show view, and then watch the video. The quality is lower, but sufficient for José to get the general idea after you send the presentation to him via email.

▶ **7.** Press the **Esc** key to end the slide show.

▶ **8.** Display **Slide 1** (the title slide), add your name as the subtitle, and then save your changes.

Now that you have finished working on the presentation, you should view the completed presentation as a slide show.

To view the completed presentation in Slide Show view:

▶ **1.** On the Quick Access Toolbar, click the **Start From Beginning** button 🖳. Slide 1 appears in Slide Show view.

▶ **2.** Press the **spacebar**. Slide 2 ("Importance of Riverwalk") appears in Slide Show view displaying the photos on the slide layout, the slide title, and the footer, date, and slide number.

▶ **3.** Press the **spacebar** four times to display all the bulleted items, and then press the **spacebar** again to display Slide 3 ("Riverwalk Trail Location").

▶ **4.** Press the **spacebar** twice to display Slide 4 ("Problems") and then Slide 5 ("Some Areas of Concern").

▶ **5.** Press the **spacebar**. The photo on the left appears with the Split animation, and then after a one-second delay, the photo on the right appears.

▶ **6.** Press the **spacebar**. Slide 6 ("Erosion: The Biggest Issue") appears, the video fills the screen and plays automatically. When the video is finished, Slide 6 appears again with the poster frame you selected displayed in the video object.

▶ **7.** Press the **spacebar** to display Slide 7 ("Cost of Repairs"), and then press the **spacebar** to display Slide 8 ("Questions?"), the last slide.

▶ **8.** Press the **spacebar** to display the black slide that appears at the end of a slide show, and then press the **spacebar** once more to return to Normal view.

Using the Office Mix Add-In

The presentation with transitions, animations, and video is interesting and should enhance the presentation José will give to the city councilors. However, José wants to post the presentation to a website so that any city councilors—and any citizens—who do not attend the meeting can see the presentation.

To do this, he will use Office Mix, a PowerPoint add-in to create a mix. An **add-in** is software that you can install to add new commands and features to PowerPoint. A **mix** is an interactive video created from a PowerPoint presentation using Office Mix and posted to a website. When you use Office Mix, you can record your voice as you give your presentation and describe your slides. You can also record video of yourself as you speak; this video becomes part of the mix and appears on each slide as people view the mix. You can also record annotations (notes and drawings) that you add to slides while they are displayed. You can also add links to websites that viewers can click when they watch the mix. In addition, you can add quizzes to your mix that ask viewers questions that test their understanding of the content presented. After you create a mix, you can upload it to a Microsoft website using your Microsoft account, and anyone with the link can view it.

Installing Office Mix

In order to use Office Mix, you need to install the add-in. If the Mix tab does not appear on the ribbon to the right of the View tab, then Office Mix might not be installed.

If Office Mix is not installed as an add-in, you need to download it from Microsoft's website and then install it. You first need to close PowerPoint because you cannot install the Office Mix add-in while PowerPoint is running.

Note: The following steps were accurate at the time of publication. However, the Office Mix webpage is dynamic and might change over time, including the way it is organized and how commands are performed.

Also, if you are working in a lab or on a school-issued computer, get permission from your instructor before installing the Office Mix add-in.

To exit PowerPoint and then download and install the Office Mix add-in:

1. In the upper-right corner of the PowerPoint window, click the **Close** button ☒ to close the presentation and exit PowerPoint.

   Trouble? If there is still a PowerPoint button on the taskbar, another presentation is open. Right-click the PowerPoint button on the taskbar, and then click Close window or Close all windows.

2. Start your browser, and then go to mix.office.com.

   Trouble? If the Internet address in Step 2 is not correct, use a search engine to search for Office Mix.

3. On the Office Mix webpage, click the **Get Office Mix button**. The Welcome to Office Mix page opens, asking you to sign in.

   Trouble? If you are already signed in with your Microsoft account, the Office Mix PowerPoint Add-in page appears instead. Skip Steps 4 and 5.

4. If you have a work or school account associated with Microsoft or Office, click the **Sign in with a work or school account button**; if you do not have a work or school account associated with the computer you are using, click the **Sign in with a Microsoft account button**. The sign in page appears.

   Trouble? If you don't have a Microsoft account, click the Sign in with a Microsoft account button, on the Sign in page that appears, click the Sign up now link, fill in the requested information to create a Microsoft account, and then sign in. Skip Step 5.

5. Enter your username and password in the appropriate boxes, and then click the **Sign in** button. The Office Mix PowerPoint Add-in page appears, and the Office Mix installation file starts downloading automatically.

   Trouble? If the software does not start downloading automatically, click the "click here" link next to "If your download doesn't start automatically."

6. After the file has finished downloading, click the **Run** button in the message box that appears at the bottom of the browser window to start installing the add-in. The Office Mix license dialog box appears.

Trouble? If you are using a browser other than Microsoft Edge, you might see the name of the file—OfficeMix.Setup.exe—in a button at the bottom of the browser window. Click that button to start installing the add-in. If the downloaded file does not appear at the bottom of the window, you need to locate the folder to which the file downloaded, and then double-click the OfficeMix.Setup file. If you can't find the file, ask your technical support person for assistance.

7. Click the **I agree to the license terms and conditions** check box to accept the software license, and then click the **Install** button. The license screen closes and the User Account Control dialog box appears, asking if you want to allow this app to make changes to your PC.

Trouble? If the dialog box displays "Modify Setup" instead of the license agreement, Office Mix is already installed on your computer. Click the Close button, close your browser, skip the rest of the steps in this section, and continue with the section "Creating a Mix."

8. Click the **Yes** button. The User Account Control dialog box closes and the Office Mix Preview Setup dialog box appears. After the add-in is installed, PowerPoint starts.

9. In the Office Mix Preview Setup dialog box, click the **Close** button.

Trouble? If you don't see the Office Mix Preview Setup dialog box, click the Office Mix Preview Setup button [icon] on the taskbar, and then execute Step 9.

In the PowerPoint window, a Welcome to Office Mix slide is displayed, the Welcome task pane is open, and the Mix tab now appears on the ribbon to the right of the View tab and is the active tab. See Figure 2-38.

Figure 2-38 **Mix tab on the ribbon**

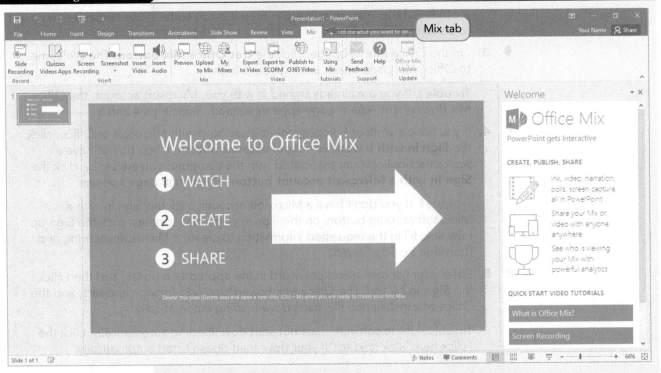

Trouble? If the Mix tab is not the active tab on the ribbon, click the Mix tab on the ribbon.

Trouble? If the Mix tab does not appear on the ribbon, click File, click Options, and then click Customize Ribbon. In the Customize the Ribbon list, click the Mix check box to select it, and then click the OK button.

▶ **10.** In the task pane title bar, click the **Close** button ☒. The Welcome task pane closes.

Trouble? If the Welcome task pane does not appear on your screen, skip Step 10.

▶ **11.** On the ribbon, click the **File** tab, and then in the navigation bar, click **Close**. The new presentation with one slide closes.

▶ **12.** On the taskbar, click your browser's program button, and then close your browser.

Now you are ready to use Office Mix to create an interactive presentation.

Creating a Mix

To create a mix, you basically record the slide show and then post it to a website. In a mix, the recording of each slide is independent of the other slides in the presentation. This means that you can reorder the slides after you have recorded them for the mix, and the timing, annotations, audio, and video that you recorded for each slide will travel with that slide. It also means that you do not need to record all of the slides in one session. You can record each slide individually if you want.

José asked you to practice recording a mix. He wants you to record yourself explaining a few of the slides, but he does not want you to include video of yourself. Because this is just practice, you will use a version of the file that contains only three slides to reduce the file size and make the upload to the Microsoft Mix server faster.

To start recording a mix:

▶ **1.** Start PowerPoint if necessary, open the file **Mix**, which is located in the **PowerPoint2 > Module** folder, and then save it as **Riverwalk Repairs Mix** to the location where you are storing your files. This file is similar to the file you created in this module, but it contains only three slides.

▶ **2.** On Slide 1 (the title slide), add your name as the subtitle.

▶ **3.** On the ribbon, click the **Mix** tab, if necessary. The Mix tab contains commands for recording and working with a mix.

Trouble? If the Mix tab is not on the ribbon, click File, click Options to open the PowerPoint Options dialog box, and then click Customize Ribbon in the navigation pane. In the Customize the Ribbon list, click the Mix check box to select it, and then click the OK button. If the Mix check box is not listed, click Add-ins in the navigation pane on the left, and then click the Go button at the bottom next to Manage COM Add-ins. In the COM Add-Ins dialog box, click the Office Mix check box to select it. (If it is already selected, do not click it.) Click the OK button. If the Mix tab still doesn't appear on the ribbon, open the Customize Ribbon screen in the PowerPoint Options dialog box again, click the Mix check box to select it, and then click the OK button.

4. In the Record group, click the **Slide Recording** button. The recording window appears with Slide 1 displayed. The ribbon in the recording window contains four groups of commands, and the Audio and Video task pane is open on the right side of the window. See Figure 2-39.

Figure 2-39 Slide recording window in Office Mix

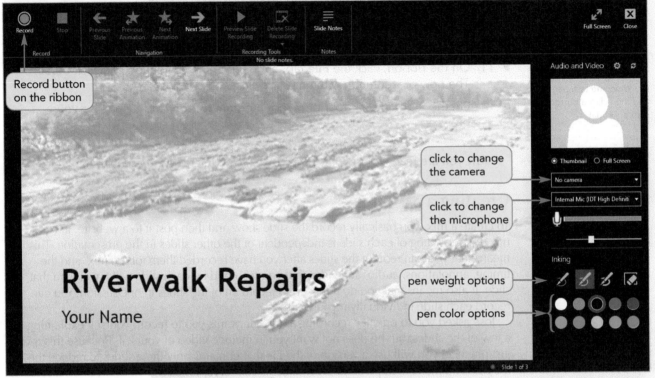

Courtesy of Helen M. Pinard

Before you start recording, you need to set the audio and video options. If you are going to record video of yourself, you need to select a camera. You also need to select a microphone if you are recording yourself speaking.

You can draw on slides while you are recording a mix. When you draw with the pointer, the lines you draw will be the color that is selected at the bottom of the Audio and Video task pane. The default color is black, and the Black color in the task pane has a faint gray border around it to indicate that it is selected. The default weight is medium, and the Medium Pen button is shaded to indicate that it is selected. You can change the pen color and weight during the recording, but it takes several seconds to do this. So in order to have a smooth recording session, you will change these options now.

To set video, audio, and pen options:

1. In the Audio and Video task pane, if the top button below the Thumbnail and Full Screen option buttons is not labeled "No camera," click it, and then click **No camera**.

2. Click the **microphone button** that appears below the No camera button. A menu of microphone options opens.

> **Trouble?** If the only menu option is No microphone, you do not have a microphone built into or connected to your computer. You need to get a microphone and connect it to your computer in order to record yourself speaking. If you do not have a microphone, you can still create the mix, but skip the rest of the steps in this set of steps.

▶ **3.** Click the microphone you want to use. The menu closes and the bar below the microphone box shows a moving white bar. The moving white bar indicates the volume level that is being detected by the microphone. You can test the microphone.

▶ **4.** Say **Testing, testing** into the microphone. (If you are using the internal microphone on a laptop, you can speak sitting in front of the laptop and the microphone will pick it up.) When you speak, the white bar increases in size.

> **Trouble?** If the white bar does not move when you speak, you either selected the wrong option on the microphone menu or the microphone you selected is not enabled in Windows. Repeat Steps 2–4, making sure you select the correct microphone. If the white bar still doesn't move, in the upper-right corner of the window, click the Close button. At the right end of the Windows taskbar, right-click the speaker icon, and then click Recording devices. In the Sound dialog box that opens, on the Recording tab, right-click the microphone you want to use, and then click Enable. (If Enable is not listed on the shortcut menu, the microphone is already enabled.) Click the OK button. In the PowerPoint window, on the Mix tab, click the Slide Recording button to return to the Slide Recording window. Repeat Steps 2–4.

▶ **5.** In the Audio and Video task pane, in the Inking section, click the **Thick Pen** button .

▶ **6.** In the Audio and Video task pane, click the **Red** color. When you draw on the slides, the lines you draw will be thick and red.

Now that the recording options are set up, you can record the mix. To do this, you click the Record button on the ribbon.

To record slides with audio for the mix:

▶ **1.** On the ribbon, in the Record group, click the **Record** button. The Record button changes to the Pause your recording button ❚❚, and a moving, dashed line appears around the slide.

▶ **2.** Move the pointer on top of the slide. The pointer changes to ✎. This indicates that you can use the pointer to draw on the slide. This also means that you cannot click to advance the slide show.

▶ **3.** Say **The Riverwalk trail is badly in need of repairs.** and then press the **spacebar**. Slide 2 ("Importance of Riverwalk") appears. On the ribbon, the Move to your next slide button ➡ is no longer available. Instead, the Go to the next animation button ⭐ is available. This is because the text on Slide 2 has animations applied, and you need to display the bulleted items before you can advance to the next slide.

> **Trouble?** If you do not have a microphone, skip the part of Step 3 in which you speak.

▶ **4.** On the ribbon click the **Go to the next animation** button ⭐, pause for a moment, click the **Go to the next animation** button ⭐ again, pause, and then press the **spacebar**. Three first-level bulleted items and associated subitems appear on the slide.

▶ **5.** In the second bullet, position the pointer below the word "Safe," press and hold the mouse button, drag below the word "Safe," and then release the mouse button. A red line appears along the path you dragged.

▶ **6.** In the Navigation group, click the **Move to your next slide** button ➡. Slide 3 ("Some Areas of Concern") appears.

▶ **7.** Press the **spacebar**. The photo on the left appears, and then after a brief delay, the photo on the right appears.

▶ **8.** On the ribbon, click the **Stop your recording** button ■.

TIP
If you want to rerecord a slide, display that slide, click the Record button, keep the slide displayed for as long as you want, click the Stop your recording button, and then click Yes in the dialog box that asks if you want to overwrite the recording on the slide.

When you record a mix, a mix media object is placed on each slide that you record. The mix media object contains the slide timing, any drawings you added while recording, and any audio or video you recorded. You can see the mix media object on each slide when the slide is displayed in Normal view.

To close the recording window and view the mix media icons:

▶ **1.** In the upper-right corner, click the **Close** button. The recording window closes, and Slide 3 ("Some Areas of Concern") appears in Normal view. In the upper-right corner of the slide, a mix media icon 🔊 appears. This is the mix media icon that appears when a microphone is selected while you record the mix.

Trouble? If you do not have a microphone, the mix media icon looks like an analog clock showing three o'clock.

▶ **2.** Display **Slide 1** (the title slide), and then point to the mix media icon 🔊. A play bar appears.

▶ **3.** On the play bar, click the **Play** button ▶. The verbal recording you made plays.

Adding Interactive Content to a Mix

Mixes can include interactive content. If you include a link to a website in a mix, people watching the mix can click the link to open their browsers and display that webpage. You can also add slides containing quiz questions that users can answer as they watch the mix. The questions can be multiple choice, true/false, or free response.

To add a quiz to a mix:

▶ **1.** Display **Slide 2** ("Importance of Riverwalk"), click the **Home** tab, and then click the **New Slide** button. A new Slide 3 with the Title and Content layout is added and is the current slide.

▶ **2.** Click in the **title text placeholder**, and then type **Quick Quiz**.

▶ **3.** Click the **Mix** tab, and then in the Insert group, click the **Quizzes Videos Apps** button. The Lab Office Add-ins window opens with the STORE tab selected. See Figure 2-40. Three types of quizzes and a poll are listed below Quizzes and Polls in the window.

Figure 2-40   **Lab Office Add-ins window**

Trouble? If Quizzes and Polls does not appear in the window on your screen, at the top of the window, click STORE.

4. In the Quizzes and Polls section, click **True False Quiz**. The window changes to describe the True False Quiz.

5. Click the **Trust It** button. The window closes, and a True False Quiz object is inserted on Slide 3. See Figure 2-41.

Figure 2-41   **True False Quiz object on Slide 3**

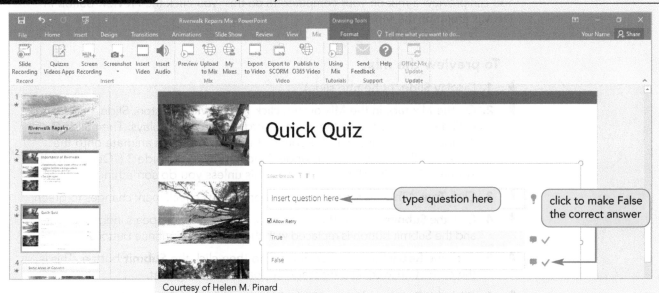

Courtesy of Helen M. Pinard

▶ 6. Click in the **Insert question here** box, and then delete all of the text in the box.

▶ 7. Type **The Riverwalk trail is poorly lit.** in the box. The answer to this is False, so you need to change the correct answer option.

▶ 8. To the right of the False box, click the **Select for correct answer** button ☑. The check mark changes to green to indicate that False is the correct answer.

▶ 9. At the bottom of the quiz object, click the **Preview** button. The borders around the question and answers disappear, and the Allow Retry check box changes to an instruction to select the correct answer. Also, the check marks that the user will click to choose True or False are both colored gray.

▶ 10. Save your changes.

Recording a Mix of a Presentation That Includes Audio and Video

In a mix, only one media element—that is, audio or video—on a slide will play. This means that if a slide contains more than one media element, only the first element will play when the mix is viewed. Therefore, if you are going to create a mix of a presentation, do not create slides with more than one media element on them.

If a slide contains a media element, you cannot record audio or video of yourself on that slide when you make the mix. This is because you would be adding a second media element to that slide. If you are recording a mix of a presentation that contains media, the recording will stop when the slide containing media appears. To continue recording the mix, you need to move to the next slide, and then restart the recording. When you upload the mix to a website, the slide with the media on it will be included in the mix, and the media (either a video or recorded audio) will play automatically when that slide appears when someone watches the mix.

Previewing and Uploading a Mix

You can preview a mix on your computer. To do this, you click the Preview button in the Mix group on the Mix tab.

To preview the mix:

▶ 1. Display **Slide 1** (the title slide).

▶ 2. On the Mix tab, in the Mix group, click the **Preview** button. Slide 1 appears in Slide Show view, and the voice recording you made plays. Then Slide 2 ("Importance of Riverwalk") appears, the bulleted items animate onto the slide, and the word "Safe" is underlined in red. Next, Slide 3 ("Quick Quiz") appears. The mix will not move past this unless you do something.

▶ 3. Click **True**. "True" is highlighted in green, and its check mark changes to green.

▶ 4. Click the **Submit** button. This is incorrect, so a message appears indicating that, and the Submit button is replaced with the Retry and Continue buttons.

▶ 5. Click the **Retry** button, click **False**, and then click the **Submit** button. This is the correct answer, so a message appears indicating that.

▶ 6. Click the **Continue** button. Slide 4 ("Some Areas of Concern") appears and the two photos appear.

▶ 7. In the bottom-left corner, click the **Close and return to presentation view** button ☒. The mix preview closes and Slide 4 appears in Normal view.

Now that the mix is complete and you have previewed it, you can upload it so that others can view it. Before you upload a mix, you should review any quizzes you added and reset them if you answered them in a preview.

To upload the mix:

1. Display **Slide 3** ("Quick Quiz"), and then at the bottom of the slide, click the **Preview** button. The quiz changes to Preview mode, and the Retry and Continue buttons appear at the bottom-right. The False option is selected. You need to reset this slide.

2. Click the **Retry** button. The quiz resets and neither answer is selected.

3. Save your changes.

4. On the Mix tab, in the Mix group, click the **Upload to Mix** button. The Upload to Mix task pane appears on the right.

5. At the bottom of the task pane, click the **Next** button. After a moment, the task pane changes to list buttons that you can click to sign in to your Microsoft account.

   Trouble? If the task pane indicates that you are signed in, skip Steps 6 and 7 and continue with Step 8.

6. If you have a work or school account associated with Microsoft or Office, click the **Sign in with a work or school account** button; if you do not have a work or school account or are using your own computer, click the **Sign in with a Microsoft account** button. The task pane changes to display boxes for your user name and password.

7. Enter your username and password in the appropriate boxes, and then click the **Sign in** button. The task pane indicates that you are signed in, and the "This is a new Mix" option button is selected.

   Trouble? If a message appears asking you if you want your browser to remember this password, click the Yes or No button depending on your preference. If the computer you are using is a school-issued or lab computer, it is safer to click the No button.

8. In the Upload to Mix task pane, click the **Next** button. The task pane changes to show the progress of the upload and the publishing processes. When the mix is published, a message appears in the task pane indicating this, and the "Show me my Mix" button changes to orange.

9. Click the **Show me my Mix** button. Your browser starts, and the webpage that contains the details for your mix appears. See Figure 2-42. You can edit the title, description, category, and tags (keywords that describe the mix content), and you can edit the permissions level (that is, change who can view the mix).

Figure 2-42 Riverwalk Repairs Mix Details webpage in the Edge browser

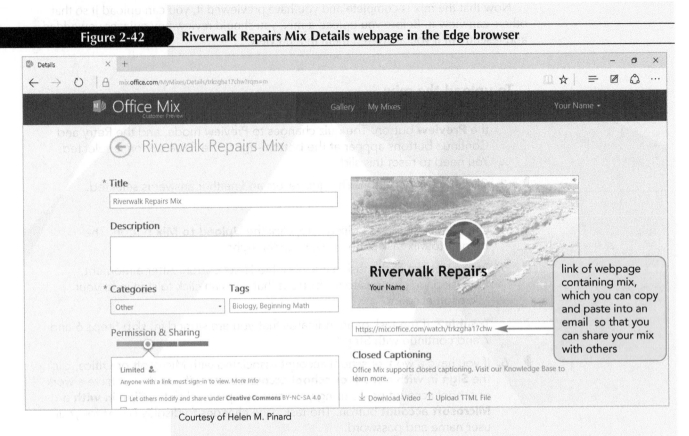

Courtesy of Helen M. Pinard

▶ **10.** Click the **video**. The webpage containing the mix appears. See Figure 2-43.

Figure 2-43 Riverwalk Repairs Mix webpage

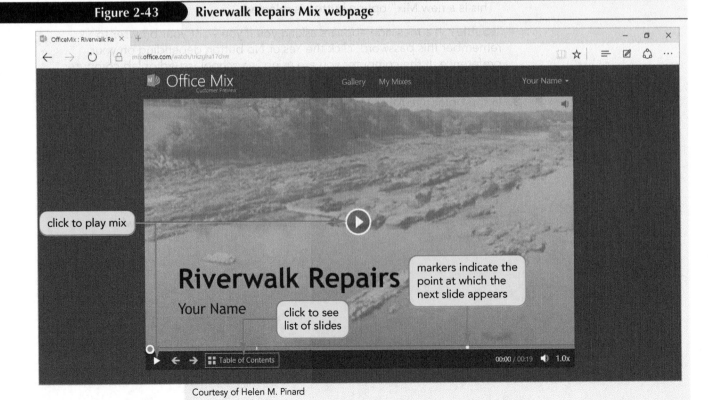

Courtesy of Helen M. Pinard

▶ **11.** Click the **Play** button ▶. The mix plays until Slide 3 ("Quick Quiz") appears. Notice that the transition between the slides is the Fade transition. The Fade transition is the only transition that is used in mixes. You can either answer the quiz or advance to the next slide without answering the quiz.

▶ **12.** In the play bar, click the **next** button ➡. Slide 4 ("Some Areas of Concern") appears, and then the photos appear.

▶ **13.** Click the browser's **Back** button to return to the page containing the details of your mix.

▶ **14.** If you want to sign out of your Microsoft account, click your username in the upper-right corner, click **Sign out**, and then close your browser.

▶ **15.** In the PowerPoint window, close the Upload to Mix task pane.

The final presentation file with transitions, animations, and video is interesting and should enhance the presentation that José will give to the city council. José also plans to record his presentation and create a new mix so that he can send the mix link to anyone who misses his presentation.

Session 2.2 Quick Check

REVIEW

1. What is a transition?

2. What are animations?

3. How do you change the speed of a transition or an animation?

4. When you apply an animation to a bulleted list with subitems, how do the first-level items animate? How do the second-level items animate?

5. What is a poster frame?

6. What does "On Click" mean for a video?

7. What animation is applied to every video that you add to a slide?

8. What is a mix created with the PowerPoint add-in Office Mix?

Review Assignments

Data Files needed for the Review Assignments: Cleared.jpg, Landscape.jpg, NewSign.jpg, NewStairs.jpg, NewTheme.pptx, NewView.mp4, Railings.jpg, Renewed1.pptx, Renewed2.pptx, Wall.jpg

José Quiñones needs to explain the improvements RiverClean™ made to the Riverwalk trail in Lowell, Massachusetts. He decides to create a presentation that will include photos and video of the improved trail. This presentation will show the city council how the money allocated was spent. José also created a new custom theme to highlight the improvements. Complete the following:

1. Open the presentation **Renewed1**, located in the PowerPoint2 > Review folder included with your Data Files, add your name as the subtitle, and then save it as **Renewed Riverwalk** to the drive and folder where you are storing your files.

2. Apply the theme from the presentation **NewTheme**, located in the PowerPoint2 > Review folder.

3. Change the layout of Slide 4 ("Projects") and Slide 6 ("New Views of the River from the Trail") to the Photo Title and Content layout, and change the layout of Slide 5 ("Views of the Trail") to the Four Content layout.

4. On Slide 5 ("Views of the Trail"), in the top, empty content placeholder, insert the photo **Landscape**, located in the PowerPoint2 > Review folder. In the bottom, empty content placeholder, insert the photo **NewStairs**, also located in the PowerPoint2 > Review folder. Apply the Drop Shadow Rectangle style to the four pictures.

5. On Slide 5, add a Right Arrow shape anywhere on the slide. Type **Improved visibility** in the arrow, and then lengthen the arrow until the text you typed just fits on one line.

6. Change the shape style of the arrow to the Subtle Effect – Orange, Accent 1 style. Then change the outline of the arrow to the Red, Accent 2 color.

7. Make three copies of the arrow. Delete the text in one of the copies, and then type **Debris and brush cleared**. Resize this arrow so that the new text just fits on one line. Delete the text in another copy, and then type **Path set back to prevent more erosion**. Resize this copy so that the new text just fits on one line. Delete the text in the last copy, and then type **New stairs**.

8. Flip the "Path set back to prevent more erosion" and the "New stairs" arrows horizontally.

9. Position the "Improved visibility" arrow so it points to the top-left picture about one-half inch from the top of the photo and so its straight end is aligned with the left edge of the slide. Position the "Debris and brush cleared" arrow so it points to the bottom-left picture about one-half inch from the bottom of that photo and so its straight end is aligned with the left edge of the slide.

10. Position the "Path set back to prevent more erosion" arrow so it points to the top-right picture with its straight end aligned with the right edge of the slide and so that it aligns with the "Improved visibility" arrow. Position the "New stairs" arrow so it points to the bottom-right picture with its straight end aligned with the right edge of the slide and so that its middle aligns with the middle of the "Debris and brush cleared" arrow.

11. On Slide 4 ("Projects"), insert a 3x4 table. Refer to Figure 2-44 to add the rest of the data to the table. Add a row if needed.

Figure 2-44 Data for table on Slide 4 in the Renewed Riverwalk presentation

Improvement	Cost	Donated?
New sign	$0	Cushing Landscaping
New stairs	$1000	No
Cleared out debris and brush	$0	Martinez and Sons
Groundcover & retaining walls	$2000	No

12. On Slide 4, add a new row above the last row in the table. Type **New railings** in the new cell in the Improvement column, type **$0** in the new cell in the Cost column, and then type **Cushing Landscaping** in the Donated? column.

13. On Slide 4, apply the Light Style 2 – Accent 4 table style.

14. On Slide 4, insert a new column to the left of the Improvement column. Fill each cell in the new column (except the first cell) with the following pictures, all located in the PowerPoint2 > Review folder, in order from the second row to the bottom row: **NewSign**, **NewStairs**, **Cleared**, **Railings**, and **Wall**.

15. On Slide 4, format the table as follows:
    - Change the font size of all of the text in the table to 20 points.
    - Change the height of rows 2 through 5 to one inch.
    - Change the width of the first column to two inches.
    - Make the second and third columns just wide enough to hold the widest entry on one line.
    - Align the text in all of the rows except the first row so it is centered vertically.
    - Right-align the data in the Cost column (do not right-align the "Cost" column head).
    - Change the borders between rows 2 through 6 to a three-point black border.

16. Reposition the table so it is centered horizontally on the slide, and then move the table up so that the top half of the top row in the table overlaps the photo behind the slide title.

17. Apply the Uncover transition to any slide. Change the Effect Options to From Bottom, and then change the duration to 0.50 seconds. Apply this transition to all of the slides.

18. On Slide 2 ("Improvements Made"), animate the bulleted list using the Wipe animation. Change the Effect Options to From Left and the duration of the animation to 0.75 seconds.

19. On Slide 5 ("Views of the Trail"), apply the Fade entrance animation to each of the photos. Apply the Wipe animation with the From Left effect to each of the two arrows on the left, and then apply the Wipe animation with the From Right effect to each of the two arrows on the right.

20. On Slide 5, reorder the animations so that the arrow associated with each photo appears immediately after the photo with the top-left photo and arrow appearing first, then the top-right objects, then the bottom-right objects, and finally the bottom-left objects.

21. On Slide 5, add a 0.25-second delay to the animations applied to the arrows.

22. On Slide 6 ("New Views of the River from the Trail"), add the video **NewView**, located in the PowerPoint2 > Review folder. Trim three seconds from the beginning of the video. Set the poster frame to the four-second mark. Finally, set the playback options so that the video starts playing automatically, fills the screen, and rewinds after playing.

23. On Slide 7 ("Thank You!"), add the trademark sign after "RiverClean" and replace the "e" in "Jose" with "é" and the first "n" in "Quinones" with "ñ".

24. Add **Renewed Riverwalk** as the footer on all the slides except the title slide, and display the slide number on all the slides except the title slide. On the notes and handouts, add **Renewed Riverwalk** as the header and your name as the footer, and show page numbers.

25. Compress all the photos in the presentation to 96 ppi, and then compress the media to Low Quality.

26. Save your changes, and then close the Renewed Riverwalk presentation.

27. Open the file **Renewed2**, located in the PowerPoint2 > Review folder, and then save it as **Riverwalk Renewed Mix**.

28. Create a mix using this presentation. Make sure the Pen color is set to red. While Slide 1 is displayed, record yourself saying, "We've made many improvements to the Riverwalk trail," and then on Slide 3 draw an exclamation point after Jose's name.

29. After you record the slides, add a new Slide 3 with the Title and Content layout. Type **Do You Know?** as the slide title. Add a True False quiz to the new Slide 3 with the question **Views of the river from the trail have been greatly improved.** and with True as the correct answer.

30. Save the changes, and then upload the mix.

APPLY

Case Problem 1

Data Files needed for this Case Problem: Equipment.jpg, Exercise.mp4, FitTheme.pptx, HomeFit.pptx

HomeFit Sam Kim is the president of HomeFit, a company in Modesto, California, that sells exercise DVDs and subscriptions to online workout videos. To help advertise his videos, he created a PowerPoint presentation that he will use when he visits local colleges. He asks you to help him finish the presentation, which will include photos, a video, and a table to provide details his audience might be interested in knowing. Complete the following steps:

1. Open the file named **HomeFit**, located in the PowerPoint2 > Case1 folder included with your Data Files, add your name as the subtitle on Slide 1, and then save it as **HomeFit Videos** to the drive and folder where you are storing your files.

2. Apply the theme from the presentation **FitTheme**, located in the PowerPoint2 > Case1 folder.

3. On Slide 2 ("Videos Include"), apply the picture style Double Frame, Black to the picture on the slide, and then change the border color to the Dark Blue, Text 2, Darker 50% color. Apply this same style to the picture on Slide 3 ("Three Phases").

4. On Slide 2, animate the bulleted list using the Float In animation with the Float Down effect, and change the duration to 0.50 seconds. Animate the bulleted list on Slide 3 using the same animation.

5. On Slide 4 ("Sample Clip from a HomeFit Video"), insert the video **Exercise**, located in the PowerPoint2 > Case1 folder. Set the movie to play automatically, fill the screen when playing, and rewind after playing. Trim about eight seconds from the end of the video so the video ends at about the 16-second mark. Set the poster frame to the frame at approximately the seven-second mark.

6. On Slide 5 ("Packages"), add a new row below the row containing "HomeFit Original" in the first column with the following data: **HomeFit Plus**, **15 hours of online video per week**, **More options for cardio and strength training**, **$45/month**.

7. Change the table style to Light Style 1 – Accent 1. In the header row, change the font to Century Gothic (Headings), change the font size to 20 points, and then align the text so it is centered horizontally. Select the text in the last column, and then center the contents of each cell horizontally.

8. On Slide 6 (the last slide), which has the Blank layout applied, insert the picture **Equipment**, located in the PowerPoint2 > Case1 folder. Crop about an inch off of the bottom of the picture, and then resize it to be the same height as the slide (it will be 7.5 inches high). Position the photo so its left edge aligns with the left edge of the slide.

9. On Slide 6, draw rectangle shape that is 3.5 inches high and 5 inches wide, and then position it so it is centered-aligned with the photo and approximately centered horizontally in the white space on the slide. Type **Subscribe or Order Your DVDs Today!**. Change the font to Century Gothic (Headings), change the font color to Black, make the text bold, and change the font size to 48 points.

10. On Slide 6, remove the fill from the rectangle containing the text, and remove the outline (that is, change the fill to No Fill and change the outline to No Outline).

11. On Slide 6, animate the rectangle containing the text using the entrance animation Grow & Turn. Set its duration to 1.25 seconds, set its start timing to After Previous, and set a delay of one-half second.

12. Compress the all the photos to 96 ppi, deleting cropped areas of pictures, and then compress the media to Low Quality.

13. Apply the Checkerboard transition to all the slides using the default From Left effect and with a duration of 1.25 seconds. Then remove the transition from Slide 1 (the title slide).

14. Save your changes, and then watch the slide show in Slide Show view. Remember, after the transition to Slide 6 (the last slide), wait for the text box to animate automatically.

15. Make sure you saved your changes, and then save a copy of the presentation to the location where you are saving your files as **HomeFit Mix**. Delete Slides 3–5, and then create a mix of the presentation. Change the Inking options to Thick Pen with the Red Color. On Slide 1, record your voice saying, "HomeFit Videos—quality instruction at a fair price." On Slide 2, circle the second subbullet under "Strength Training" after it appears.

16. Insert a new Slide 3 with the Title and Content layout. Type Quiz as the slide title, and then add a True False quiz. Type **HomeFit videos do not include warm-ups or cool-downs.** as the question, and then make False the correct answer.

17. Save your changes, and then upload the mix.

Case Problem 2

Data Files needed for this Case Problem: Build.jpg, Finish.jpg, Furniture.pptx, Sand.jpg, Sketch.jpg, Trees.jpg

Cutting Edge Furniture Carl Bertoni is the manager for Cutting Edge Furniture, in Forest Lake, Minnesota. Carl's grandfather founded the business more than 50 years ago, and they now have the resources to expand the company. To advertise this, Carl created a PowerPoint presentation that describes his custom furniture and the painstaking process used to create the pieces. He will use the presentation at home shows around the country. He asks you to help him complete the presentation. Complete the following steps:

1. Open the presentation **Furniture**, located in the PowerPoint2 > Case2 folder included with your Data Files, add your name as the subtitle, and then save the presentation as **Cutting Edge Furniture** to the drive and folder where you are storing your files.

2. On Slide 1 (the title slide), add the trademark symbol after "Furniture."

3. Refer to Figure 2-45 and insert the pictures as shown on Slides 3 through 7, and format the tables on Slide 8. The picture files are located in the PowerPoint2 > Case2 folder.

Figure 2-45 Slides 3 – 8 in the Cutting Edge Furniture presentation

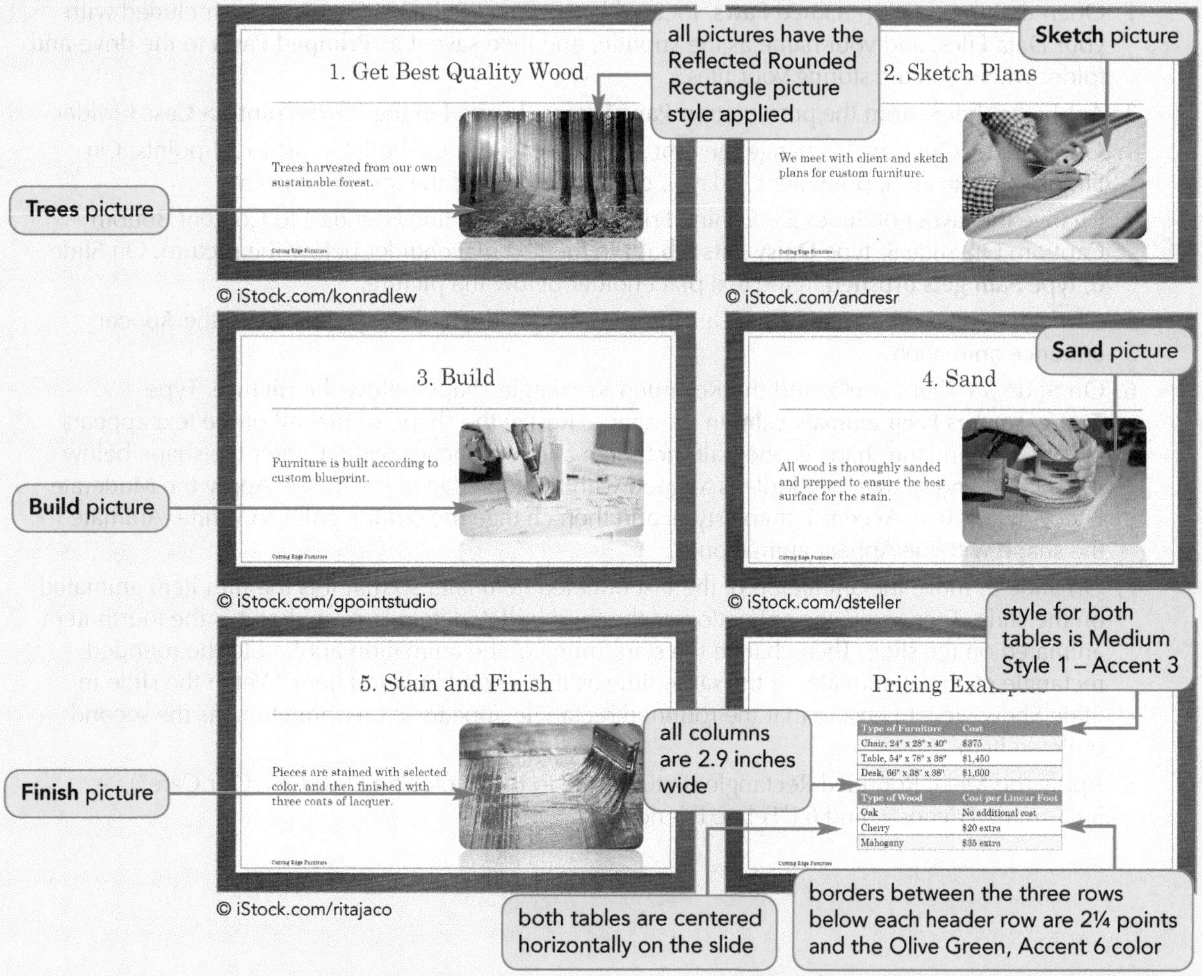

4. Compress all the photos to 96 ppi.

5. On Slide 2 ("What We Offer"), animate both bulleted lists so they appear with the Wipe animation with the From Top effect. Keep the start timing of the list on the left set to On Click, and change the start timing of the list on the right to After Previous with a delay of two seconds. Then, set the start timing of the animations applied to each of the three subitems in the list on the right to With Previous.

6. Apply the Fade transition to Slides 1, 2, 8, and 9. Apply the Conveyor transition to Slides 3 through 7.

7. Add **Cutting Edge Furniture** as a footer on all slides except the title slide. On the notes and handouts, display the current date to be updated automatically, and add your name as a header on the notes and handouts.

8. Save your changes, and then view the slide show. Remember to wait for the second bulleted list to appear on Slide 2 two seconds after the first list appears.

Case Problem 3

Data Files needed for this Case Problem: PawsTheme.pptx, Paws.pptx

Primped Paws Primped Paws is an animal-grooming service in Parkville, Maryland. Jasmine Feurman, the manager, needs to prepare a PowerPoint presentation that shows the care and attention that the groomers at Primped Paws give to animals. She will show the presentation to animal shelters and pet stores to convince them to recommend Primped Paws to new pet owners. Complete the following steps:

1. Open the presentation named **Paws**, located in the PowerPoint2 > Case3 folder included with your Data Files, add your name as the subtitle, and then save it as **Primped Paws** to the drive and folder where you are storing your files.

2. Apply the theme from the presentation **PawsTheme**, located in the PowerPoint2 > Case3 folder.

3. On Slide 3 ("Our Care"), change the font size of the text in the bulleted list to 24 points. On Slide 7 ("Make an Appointment Today"), change the size of the text to 28 points.

4. Change the layout of Slides 5 ("Canine Friends") and 6 ("Feline Friends") to Content Bottom Caption. On Slide 5, type **Daisy gets a bath** in the text placeholder below the picture. On Slide 6, type **Sam gets brushed** in the text placeholder below the picture.

5. On Slides 2 ("About Us") and 3 ("Our Care"), animate the bulleted lists on with the Appear entrance animation.

6. On Slide 3 ("Our Care"), add the Rounded Rectangle shape below the picture. Type **Two groomers keep animals calm** in the shape. Resize the shape so that all of the text appears on one line and the shape is one-half inch high and four inches wide. Center the shape below the picture and so that its middle is aligned with the top edge of the footer. Apply the Moderate Effect – Dark Teal, Accent 1 shape style, and then change the outline color to White. Animate the shape with the Appear animation.

7. On Slide 3, move the animation of the last bulleted item later so that it is the fifth item animated on the slide. Then move the animation of the third bulleted item later so that it is the fourth item animated on the slide. Then change the start timing of the animation applied to the rounded rectangle so that it animates at the same time as the second bulleted item. Watch the slide in Slide Show view to ensure that the rounded rectangle appears at the same time as the second bulleted item.

8. Apply the Metal Rounded Rectangle picture style to the photos on Slides 3 ("Our Care"), 5 ("Canine Friends"), and 6 ("Feline Friends").

9. On Slide 4 ("Pricing"), insert a 5x4 table. Enter the data shown in Figure 2-46.

| Figure 2-46 | Data for table on Slide 4 in Primped Paws presentation |

Size	Wash and Brush	Trim Fur	Trim Nails	All Three
0-15 lbs.	$15	$10	$10	$35
16-40 lbs.	$20	$15	$10	$45
41-80 lbs.	$25	$20	$10	$55

10. On Slide 4, add a new bottom row to the table. Enter the following data in the new row: **81+ lbs.**, **$30**, **$25**, **$10**, **$65**.

11. On Slide 4, increase the size of all the text in the table to 28 points.

12. On Slide 4, horizontally and vertically center the text in the first row, and then right-align all of the dollar values.

13. On Slide 4, add a three-point border (using the default White color) between all the rows and columns.

14. Add **Primped Paws** as the footer, and display the footer and slide number on all of the slides except the title slide. Add your name as a header on the notes and handouts.

15. Apply the Honeycomb transition to any slide, change the duration of the transition to 1.75 seconds, and then apply that transition to all of the slides except the first one.

16. Save your changes, and then view the slide show.

Case Problem 4

CHALLENGE

Data Files needed for this Case Problem: Candy.png, CarePak.pptx, CPTheme.pptx, Games.png, Personal.png, Salty.png

CarePak CarePak markets care packages containing snacks and games to parents of college students. They are based in Carmel, Indiana, and ship to colleges nationwide. Tim King, a sales representative for CarePak, travels to colleges to convince the colleges to partner with CarePak. In return, CarePak will give a percentage of the sales to the college. He wants to use PowerPoint to give a presentation that describes the packages. He has asked you to help him prepare the presentation. Complete the following steps:

1. Open the presentation **CarePak**, located in the PowerPoint2 > Case4 folder included with your Data Files, add your name as the subtitle, and then save the presentation as **CarePak for Students** to the drive and folder where you are storing your files.

2. Apply the theme from the presentation **CPTheme**, located in the PowerPoint2 > Case4 folder.

3. On Slide 2 ("About Us"), animate the bulleted list using the Random Bars animation with the Vertical effect.

4. On Slide 3 ("Package Options"), insert a 2x4 table. Deselect the Header Row check box on the Table Tools Design tab. In the first column, enter **Sweet Snacks Package**, **Salty Snacks Package**, **Games Package**, and **Personalized Combo Package**. In the second column, fill the cells with the pictures **Candy**, **Salty**, **Games**, **Personal**, all located in the PowerPoint2 > Case4 folder.

5. On Slide 3, change the height of all of the rows in the table to 1.2 inches, and then change the width of the second column to 1.8 inches.

6. Make all of the text in the table bold, change the color of the text to the White, Text 1 color, and then change the font size to 24 points. Center the text in the first column vertically in the cells.

7. Remove the fill from all the cells in the first column, and then remove the table borders. (*Hint:* If the View Gridlines button in the Table group on the Layout tab is selected, you will still see the table gridlines after removing the borders.)

8. On Slide 3, insert a rectangle 1.25 inches high and 7.5 inches wide, and position it on top of the first row in the table so that the text and picture of candy is covered.

9. Apply the Wipe exit animation with the From Left effect to the rectangle. (*Hint*: Make sure you use the Wipe animation in the Exit category, not the Entrance category.)

10. Duplicate the rectangle three times, and then position the three copies on top of the other three rows in the table. (The shapes will slightly overlap.)

⊕ **Explore** 11. Change the fill of each rectangle to the same color as the slide background. (*Hint*: Use the Eyedropper tool on the Shape Fill menu.) Remove the outline from the rectangles.

⊕ **Explore** 12. On Slide 4 ("Customer Reviews"), apply the Appear animation to the bulleted list, and then modify the animation so that the letters appear one by one. (*Hint*: Use the Animation group Dialog Box Launcher, and then change the setting in the Animate text box on the Effect tab.) Speed up the effect by changing the delay between letters to 0.1 seconds.

⊕ **Explore** 13. Add the Typewriter sound to the animation. (*Hint*: Use the Animate text box again.)

14. Apply the Airplane transition to all the slides except Slide 1 (the title slide).

15. Save your changes, and then run the slide show.

16. Make sure you have saved your changes, and then save a copy of the presentation as **CarePak Mix** to the location where you are saving your files, Delete Slides 2 and 4, and then create a mix. Before you record it, change the microphone setting to No microphone and change the pen color to Red. When you record it, remember to advance the slide show to make the rectangles on top of the table disappear, and then after the fourth rectangle disappears, draw a red circle around the Personalized Combo Package on Slide 2.

⊕ **Explore** 17. Add a new Slide 4 titled **Survey** with the Title and Content layout, and insert a Multiple Response Poll. Enter **Which package appeals to you?** as the question, and **Sweet Snacks**, **Salty Snacks**, **Games**, **Combo** as the four options.

18. Save your changes, and upload the mix. Ask a few people to watch the mix and take the survey.

19. Add a new Slide 5 to the CarePak Mix presentation with the Blank layout.

⊕ **Explore** 20. View the responses to your survey by opening your browser, going to www.mix.office.com, and sign in to your Microsoft account if necessary. At the top of the window, click My Mixes. Below the CarePak for Students mix, click Analytics, and then click the slide containing the survey. (It can take up to 10 minutes for the statistics to be updated.)

⊕ **Explore** 21. Switch back to Slide 5 in the CarePak Mix presentation in the PowerPoint window, and then use the Screenshot button in the Insert group on the Mix tab or in the Images group on the Insert tab to take a screenshot of your Analytics screen and paste it on Slide 5. (Note: If you are using Edge as your browser and that window does not appear as an option on the Screenshot menu, switch back to Edge, and then press the Print Screen key (usually labeled PrtScr, PrntScr, or PrtScn on your keyboard). Switch back to Slide 5 in the CarePak Mix presentation, and then on the Home tab, in the Clipboard group, click the Paste button.) With the screenshot selected, on the Picture Tools Format tab, change the height to 7.5 inches and then position the picture on the slide if necessary (the picture will be the same size as the slide).

OBJECTIVES

- Understand cloud computing
- Learn about OneDrive, Office Online, and Office 365
- Determine if you have a Microsoft account
- Learn how to access Office Online applications to create and edit files
- Learn about syncing files between your computer and OneDrive
- Explore how to upload files to and download files from OneDrive
- Learn how to share files and folders on OneDrive
- Understand co-authoring

Introduction to Cloud Computing and Office 365

Using Cloud Services and Collaborating with Others Online

The **cloud** refers to powerful computer servers that are connected to the Internet and are used to provide access to and storage for data, resources, and programs. **Cloud computing** is the process of accessing the cloud instead of using your own computer for storing and accessing information and resources. An example of a cloud storage service is Microsoft's **OneDrive**. An example of cloud computing software is **Office 365**, which is a suite of Microsoft applications and cloud services for which users pay a monthly or annual subscription fee. Another example of cloud computing is **Office Online**, a collection of free applications provided by Microsoft including limited versions of Word, Excel, and PowerPoint. To access and use any of the Microsoft cloud services, you need a Microsoft account. A **Microsoft account** is a free account that associates your email address and a password with Microsoft cloud services.

In this appendix, you will learn about cloud computing, OneDrive, Office Online, and Office 365. You will also learn how to determine if you have a Microsoft account. Then you will learn about managing files in the OneDrive cloud storage space, how to use Office Online, how to share files with others, and how to edit files at the same times as others.

> **Note:** Office Online and OneDrive are dynamic webpages and might change over time, including the way they are organized and how commands are performed. The information provided in this appendix, including the information about Office 365 subscriptions, was accurate at the time this book was published.

OFFICE

STARTING DATA FILES

There are no starting data files for this appendix.

Overview of Storage and Software in the Cloud

When you access software that is stored in the cloud and when you access and store files in the cloud, you can do so from any device that has a connection to the Internet. You can also share files that you store in the cloud with others by giving them access to the files.

Cloud computing can help businesses be more efficient and save money by shifting usage and the consumption of resources, such as servers and programs, from a local environment to the Internet. For example, consider a company that has offices in California, London, and Singapore. This company can utilize a cloud storage service such as OneDrive for storing data instead of installing and maintaining an expensive intranet of servers.

In addition, cloud computing is changing how people and companies access and pay for software applications. Instead of buying software packages sold in boxes at a store or downloaded from a website with a one-time purchase software license fee, users can buy access to software by paying a subscription fee. For example, the company with offices in California, London, and Singapore can pay a subscription for cloud computing software, such as Office 365, that all of their employees can access and use on multiple devices.

Introduction to OneDrive

If you have a free Microsoft account, you can use OneDrive, Microsoft's cloud storage service. OneDrive is like having a personal hard drive in the cloud. You store files in folders on your OneDrive, similar to the folders on your computer. You can store any type of file on your OneDrive, including Office files, photos, and videos. You can also synchronize files between your OneDrive and your computer. **Synchronize**, or **sync**, means to update files in multiple locations with the most recent information. This means that whether you access the files stored on your computer or you access the files stored on OneDrive, you will work with the most recent version of the files.

You can store files as large as 10 GB on your OneDrive until you reach the capacity of your OneDrive. Everyone with a Microsoft account has 15 GB of storage space on OneDrive, and users can pay for additional storage space if needed. Users who have an Office 365 subscription have one TB of storage space on OneDrive.

Figure A-1 shows a typical OneDrive page. Each of the tiles on the OneDrive webpage represents a file or a folder.

| **Figure A-1** | **OneDrive in Edge browser** |

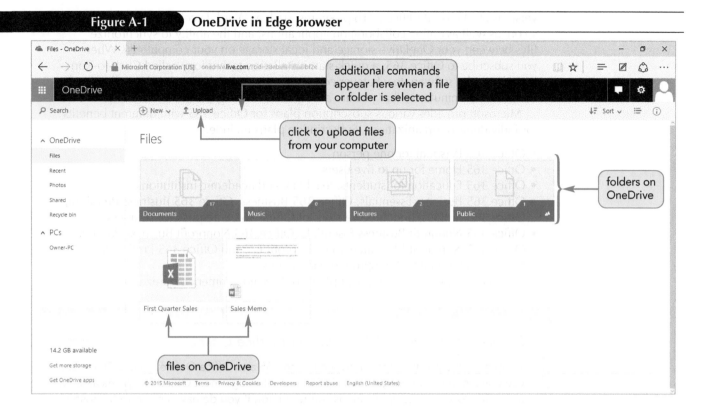

In addition to access to OneDrive, a Microsoft account gives you access to the cloud computing software Office Online.

Introduction to Office Online

Office Online is available free to anyone with a Microsoft account, a browser, and a connection to the Internet. The applications available with Office Online are stored on a Microsoft server, and you access and use them through a browser, such as Edge, Internet Explorer, or Chrome. The applications, also referred to as apps, available with Office Online are:

- **Word, Excel**, and **PowerPoint Online**—free versions of the Microsoft Word, Excel, and PowerPoint applications with limited capabilities
- **OneNote Online**—the online version of OneNote to which you can sync your OneNote notebooks
- **Sway**—a presentation application that you use to create webpages that users can scroll at their own pace
- **Outlook.com**—an email application
- **People**—a contacts application that is used by Outlook.com and the other Office Online applications when you are sharing a file
- **Calendar**—a calendar application that you use to schedule appointments
- **Docs.com**—a service that lets you publish Word, Excel, PowerPoint, PDF, Sway, and Mix files and links to webpages so that others can view them, comment on them, or download them

Overview of Office 365

Office 365 is a broad term that describes subscription plans that give subscribers access to Microsoft cloud computing software and storage. It is available in business, consumer, education, and government editions. Most of the plans include access to the complete versions of Microsoft Office 2016 programs, such as Word, Excel, PowerPoint, and so on, as well as online collaboration applications, and the ability to synchronize files between your OneDrive storage and local storage on your computer(s). When you subscribe to Office 365, a quick-start installation technology called Click-to-Run downloads the software to whatever computer you are working on and installs the basics within minutes so that you are able to start working almost immediately.

Microsoft provides various subscription plans for Office 365 with different benefits for individuals or organizations. Subscription plans include:

- Office 365 Personal for one person
- Office 365 Home for up to five users
- Office 365 Education for students, teachers, and academic institutions
- Office 365 Business Essentials, Office 365 Business, Office 365 Business Premium, Office 365 ProPlus, and three versions of Office 365 Enterprise for business
- Office 365 Nonprofit Business Essentials, Office 365 Nonprofit Business Premium, Office 365 Nonprofit E1, Office 365 Nonprofit E3, and Office 365 ProPlus for Nonprofits for qualified nonprofit organizations
- Five Office 365 U.S. Government plans for U.S. government organizations

INSIGHT

Differences Between Office 365 and Office Online

There are several differences between Office 365 and Office Online. To use Office 365, you pay a monthly or annual subscription fee. Although most Office 365 plans allow you to use Microsoft Office applications, some do not. If you do have access to Microsoft Office applications with your subscription, you have access to the full, unlimited versions of the programs included with your subscription. In addition, an Office 365 subscription includes free use of Skype, which is software that allows you to make video phone calls over the Internet. Office 365 subscriptions for business include additional features, such as access to Yammer, which is a social networking service that helps employees and team members collaborate on projects.

To use Office Online, all you need is a free Microsoft account. There is no fee for using the Office Online applications. The Word, Excel, and PowerPoint applications in Office Online are limited versions, but you can create and edit files with these applications.

Determining If You Have a Microsoft Account

If you are interested in using OneDrive or Office Online, or if you are thinking of purchasing a subscription to Office 365, you first need to determine if you already have a Microsoft account. You have a Microsoft account if you have one of the following:

- Outlook.com email account
- Hotmail email account
- live.com email account
- Xbox account
- Windows phone
- Windows 10 user account with a username that is an email address and that requires a password

If you are not sure if your Windows 10 user account is a Microsoft account, you can check on the PC settings screen. To do this, click the Start button on the Windows 10 taskbar, and then click your username at the top of the menu. Below your username, click Change account settings to display the Settings window for Accounts with Your account selected on the left. If you are signed in with a local account—that is, a Windows account that is not a Microsoft account—the words "Local Account" appear below your username as shown in Figure A-2.

Figure A-2	Windows 10 Accounts screen in the Settings window showing a user signed in with a local account

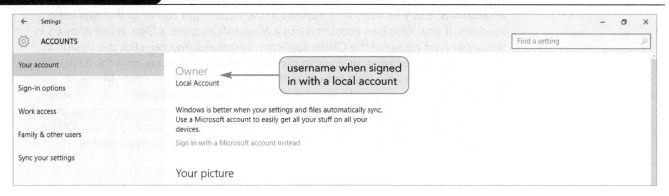

If you are signed in to Windows with a Microsoft account, the email address associated with your Microsoft account appears below your username, as shown in Figure A-3.

Figure A-3	Windows 10 Accounts screen in the Settings window showing a user signed in with a Microsoft account

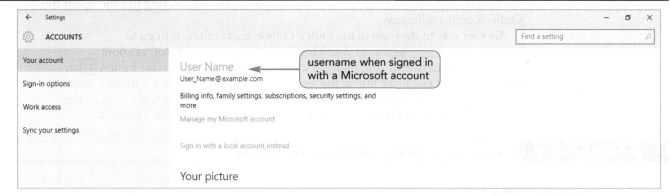

If you do not have a Microsoft account, you will need to create one in order to access Microsoft cloud services. When you attempt to access a Microsoft cloud service—for example, when you try to save to OneDrive from Backstage view in Microsoft Word, Excel, or PowerPoint, or when you try to use an app such as Mail or People—and you are not signed in to a Microsoft account, a dialog box will appear asking you to sign in or to create a new Microsoft account. Click the Sign up link, and then follow the instructions to create your account. You can also go to www. microsoft.com/account and follow the instructions there to create your Microsoft account.

How to Determine If You Are Signed In to Your Microsoft Account in an Office 2016 Application

If your Windows account is a Microsoft account, when you start Office 2016 applications, you will be automatically signed in to your Microsoft account in the applications, and your username appears in the upper-right corner of the application windows. If your Windows account is not a Microsoft account, a Sign in link appears in the upper-right corner of the Office application windows. You can click this to sign in to your Microsoft account, or you can click the File tab, click Account in the navigation pane, and then click the Sign In button. If you are not signed in to your Microsoft account and you try to save to your OneDrive, you will be prompted to sign in. After you sign in, your username will replace the Sign in link in the upper-right corner of the application windows. Note that if you sign in to your Microsoft account in one Office application, you will be signed in to your account in all the Office applications.

Using Office Online

A Microsoft account gives you access to Office Online. You can use Office Online from any computer that is connected to the Internet. To start any of the applications in Office Online, go to www.office.com. On the webpage, click the tile of the application you want to use. If you are not signed in to your Microsoft account in the browser already, you will need to sign in before you can use the application you selected. (Note that at the time of publication, Mail is listed as an application, and clicking this tile opens the Outlook.com application.)

Another way to start one of the Office Online applications is to go to www.onedrive.com, sign in to your OneDrive using your Microsoft account username and password, and then click the List of Microsoft Services button ⊞ to the left of the "OneDrive" title at the top of the webpage to display a menu listing all of the Office Online applications except for Docs.com (although you can click the Office Online tile, and then click Docs.com on that webpage). See Figure A-4.

| **Figure A-4** | **Menu of Office Online applications in OneDrive** |

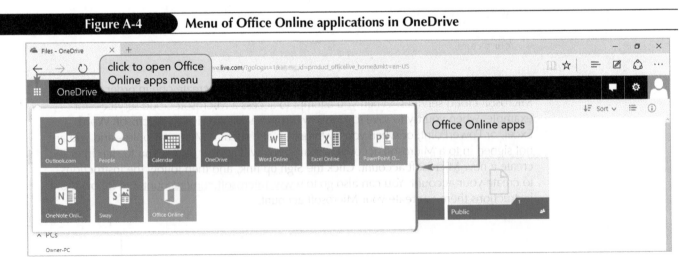

You can also create new files or open existing files in Word Online, Excel Online, PowerPoint Online, and OneNote Online from your OneDrive. To create new files while on the OneDrive webpage, click the New button at the top of your OneDrive webpage.

The menu that opens contains commands that allow you to create several types of files and a new folder. See Figure A-5. Select the Office Online program you want to use to open a new file in Edit mode in that program.

Figure A-5   New menu listing some Office Online applications

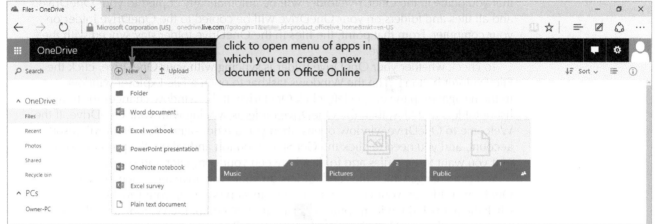

In addition, you can create Excel surveys, which are surveys whose responses are automatically collected in an Excel workbook, and plain text documents, which are text documents with no formatting.

If you store photos or videos on your OneDrive, you can click them to open them in a photo or video viewer. If you store audio files on your OneDrive, you can click them to open them in the online Groove audio player.

To open a folder, click the folder's tile. To open a Word, Excel, PowerPoint, or Plain Text file in the corresponding Office Online application, click the file's tile. If you want to open an existing Word, Excel, or PowerPoint file stored on your OneDrive in the corresponding Word 2016, Excel 2016, or PowerPoint 2016 application, point to it so that a circle appears in the upper-right corner of the file's tile, click the circle to select it, click the Open command at the top of the webpage, and then click Open in *application name*, where "application name" is the name of the full-featured application (that is, Word, Excel, or PowerPoint).

The interface for Word Online, Excel Online, and PowerPoint Online is similar to the interface of the full-featured program on your computer. Figure A-6 shows the Word Online program in edit mode.

> **TIP**
>
> When you work in an Office Online program, you do not need to save your changes. All changes are saved automatically.

Figure A-6   Word Online window

Syncing Files and Folders Between Your Computer and OneDrive

Windows 10 comes with a folder named OneDrive, and you can use this folder to sync files between your computer and OneDrive. Any files and folders on your computer that you place in the OneDrive folder will be automatically copied to your OneDrive, and all files and folders on your OneDrive will be copied to the OneDrive folder on your computer. From that point, the files in the OneDrive folder stay synced with the version on your OneDrive.

To check whether your OneDrive folder is syncing with your OneDrive, click the File Explorer button ⊞ on the Windows taskbar to open a File Explorer window. In the navigation pane on the left, click OneDrive. If the window changes to show a list of folders and files, then the OneDrive folder is syncing with your OneDrive. If the Welcome to OneDrive window opens, then you are not signed in to your Microsoft account, and you need to click the Get Started button and follow the prompts to sign in if you want to sync files and folders between your computer and your OneDrive.

You can change which files and folders on your OneDrive are synced to your OneDrive folder on your computer, or you can stop synching your OneDrive folder. Click the Show hidden icons button ⋀ at the right end of the Windows taskbar so that you can see the OneDrive icon ☁. See Figure A-7.

Figure A-7   **OneDrive icon on Show hidden icons menu**

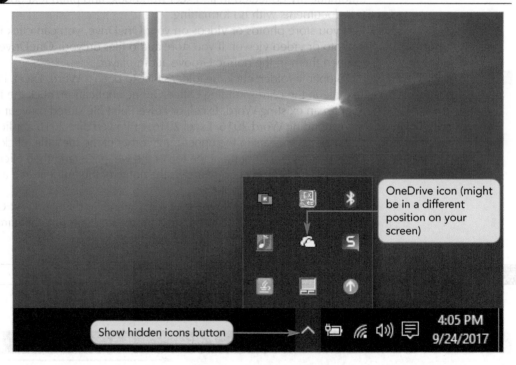

Right-click the OneDrive icon ☁, and then click Settings to open the Microsoft OneDrive dialog box. On the Settings tab, click the Unlink OneDrive button to stop synching your OneDrive folder. Click the Choose folders tab in the dialog box, and then the Choose folders button to open the Sync your OneDrive files to this PC dialog box. See Figure A-8. (This same dialog box will appear if you go through the steps to enable your OneDrive folder.) Deselect the check boxes next to any folders and files in this dialog box to stop syncing them to your OneDrive folder on your computer.

Figure A-8	Sync your OneDrive files to this PC dialog box

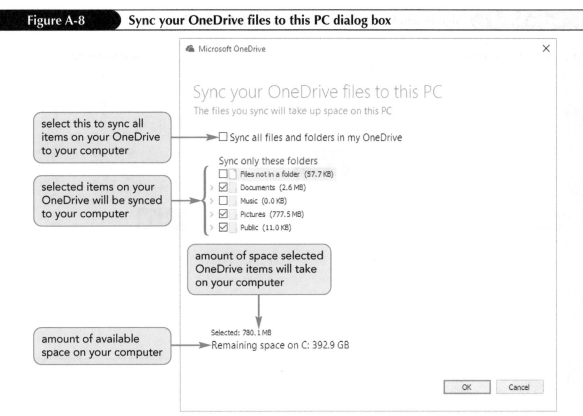

select this to sync all items on your OneDrive to your computer

selected items on your OneDrive will be synced to your computer

amount of space selected OneDrive items will take on your computer

amount of available space on your computer

Moving Files Between Your Computer and OneDrive

TIP

You cannot save to OneDrive from Backstage view in Access.

If you want to put files on your OneDrive but you don't want to sync them, you can upload files to your OneDrive from your computer from within Word 2016, Excel 2016, or PowerPoint 2016; or you can use your browser to go to www.OneDrive.com, and then use commands on the website to upload files from your computer to your OneDrive or download files from your OneDrive to your computer. To upload a file from within the Word 2016, Excel 2016, or PowerPoint 2016 applications, open the file in the application, click the File tab on the ribbon to display Backstage view, and then click Save As in the navigation bar. On the Save As screen, click OneDrive. If you are not signed in to your Microsoft account, the window changes to include a Sign In button. Click it to display the Sign in window, as shown in Figure A-9. Even if you are signed in, a similar window might appear asking you to verify your account, and you will need to enter you username (the email address associated with your Microsoft account) and password again.

Figure A-9   Sign in window on Save As screen in Backstage view

Figure A-9   Sign in window on Save As screen in Backstage view

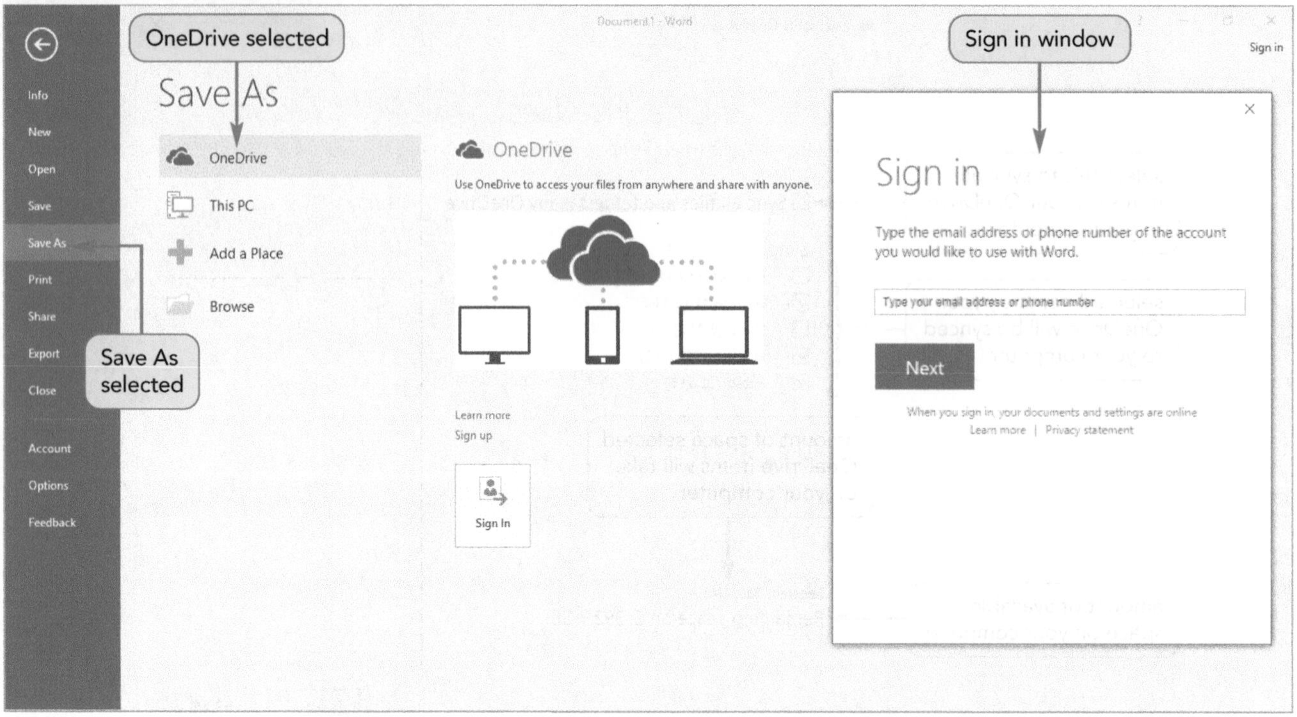

Once you are signed in, the folders on your OneDrive are listed on the Save As screen in Backstage view. See Figure A-10. You can click a folder to open the Save As dialog box; when you do so, the folder you clicked on your OneDrive will be the current location displayed in the dialog box. (You can also click Browse to open the Save As dialog box, but if you do this, you will need to click OneDrive in the navigation pane on the left in the dialog box to list the folders on your OneDrive in the dialog box. If the OneDrive folder is not enabled as described in the previous section, the folders on your OneDrive will not be listed.) Then save the file to your OneDrive in the same manner that you save files to a folder on your computer.

| Figure A-10 | Save As dialog box listing OneDrive folders on the Save As screen in Backstage view |

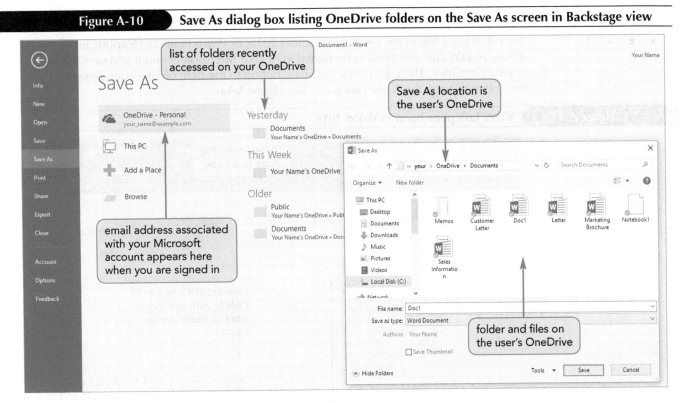

Finally, you can also move files between your OneDrive and your computer by opening a browser window, going to www.onedrive.com, and signing in to your Microsoft account on that webpage. Then you can use the Upload button at the top of the screen to open a dialog box similar to the Save As dialog box in which you can select the file you want to upload. To download a file, point to it to display a check box in the upper-right corner, and then click the check box to display additional commands at the top of the browser, including the Download command.

Sharing Files

One of the great advantages of working with OneDrive is that you can share your files and folders with others. Suppose, for example, that you want a colleague to review and edit a presentation you created in PowerPoint. You can upload the PowerPoint file to OneDrive, and then give your colleague access to the file.

Because people with whom you share a file or folder click a direct link to access the file or folder, they do not need to sign in to their Microsoft accounts in order to view or download the files you share unless you require it by selecting that option when you share the file or folder. However, if they want to use the Office Online apps to edit those files, they do need to sign in to a Microsoft account.

There are several ways to share a file stored on your OneDrive: You can share it from within Word, Excel, or PowerPoint 2016; you can share it on your OneDrive webpage from within a browser; or you can share it from within the Word Online, Excel Online, or PowerPoint Online applications. If you are working on your OneDrive webpage in a browser, you can also share entire folders on OneDrive. When you share a file, you can let others edit the file or restrict them to only viewing the file.

Sharing Files in Word, Excel, and PowerPoint 2016

You can share a file in the Word 2016, Excel 2016, or PowerPoint 2016 applications. Before you do this, you need to be signed in to your Microsoft account and save the file to your OneDrive. Then, you click the Share button to the right of your username on the ribbon to open the Share task pane. See Figure A-11.

Figure A-11 ▶ **Share task pane open in Word 2016**

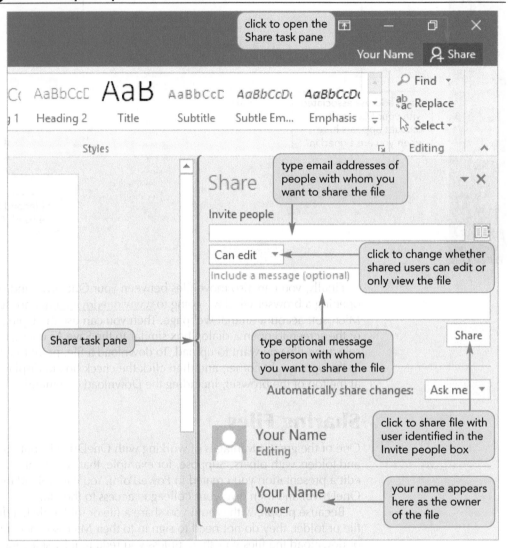

TIP

If you have not saved a file to OneDrive, when you click the Share button, a button appears in the Share task pane that you can click to save the file to your OneDrive.

In the Share task pane, you can either send an invitation to share the file via email or you can create a link that you can send to others or post on social media. To share the file via email, type the email address of the person you want to share the document with in the Invite people box. Then, if you want to change whether the person you share with can only view the file instead of edit it, you click the Can edit box and then click Can view. If you want to add a message to the recipient, click in the Include a message (optional) box, and then type your message. To send an email inviting the person to view or edit the file, click the Share button. To create a link to copy and send or post, click Get a sharing link at the bottom of the Share task pane, and then click the Create and edit link or Create a view-only link button.

Once you have shared a file, the names of the people you shared with appear below your name in the Share task pane. See Figure A-12. If you create a link, a button listing whether people with a link can edit or only view appears below the list of names of people you have shared with.

Figure A-12	Share task pane in Word 2016 after sharing a file with someone

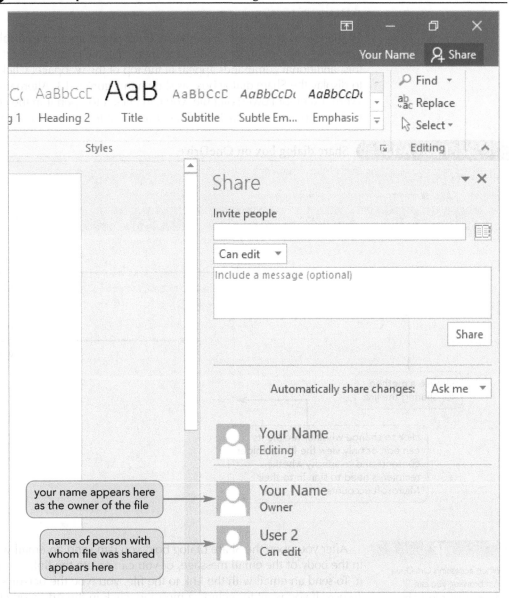

Viewing Photos and Videos on OneDrive

You can use OneDrive as a photo viewer and video player. When you click a photo or a video stored in a folder on OneDrive, the screen changes to show the photo or the video much larger on the screen. You can move the pointer to display scroll arrows on the left or right edges of the screen, and then click these to scroll through the photos and videos in the folder.

Sharing Files from Your OneDrive or Office Online Applications

To share a file from your OneDrive in a browser, point to it to display a circle in the upper-right corner of the file tile, and then click the circle to select the file. When you do this, additional commands appear at the top of the webpage. Click the Share command to display the Share dialog box, as shown in Figure A-13. Alternatively, if the file is a Word, Excel, or PowerPoint file, you can click it to open it in the corresponding Office Online app, and then click the Share button on the ribbon to open the Share dialog box.

Figure A-13   **Share dialog box on OneDrive**

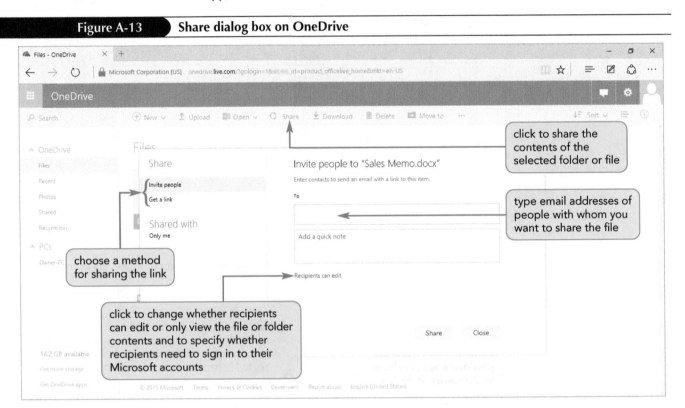

TIP

When accessing OneDrive in a browser, you can share an entire folder by selecting the folder tile or opening the folder and then clicking the Share command. When you share a folder, you are granting access to all of the files in that folder.

After you open the Share dialog box, you can send an email with the link to the file in the body of the email message, or you can create the link to the file and then copy it. To send an email with the link to the file, you type the person's email address in the To box. If you want to include a message, click in the Add a quick note box, and then type your message. If you want to restrict the person from editing the document, click the Recipients can edit link, click the Recipients can edit box, and then click Recipients can only view. To send the email, click the Share button.

You can also choose to create the link directly and then copy it to send it in an email message or post the link to your Facebook, Twitter, LinkedIn, or Webio page. To do this, click Get a link in the navigation pane on the left. In the dialog box that opens, click the Choose an option arrow, and then click Edit or View only, depending on the level of permission you want to give the person you are sharing with, and then click the Create link button.

Coauthoring Shared Word, Excel, and PowerPoint Files

If you allow others to edit a file you share on your OneDrive, you will see the changes others made the next time you access the file. Some types of files and applications allow you to coauthor. When you **coauthor** a file, you and others with whom the file is shared open the file in the appropriate application, and the changes each person makes appear on the screens of the other people editing the file.

If the file you share on OneDrive is a Word, Excel, or PowerPoint file, and you and the people you shared the file are working in the Office Online version of those programs, everyone will see the changes made by all users as the changes are being made. An icon appears on the screen next to the part of the document another person is editing. To see the name of the person editing the file, you click the icon. In addition, when someone else is editing the file, a message stating this appears on the ribbon below your username. Figure A-14 shows a file being coauthored in the Word Online application.

Figure A-14	Open file in Word Online with two people editing it

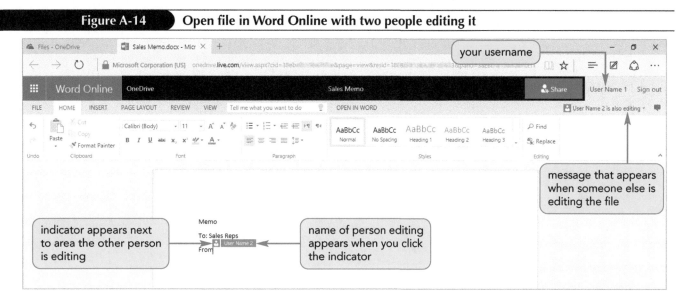

If the shared file is a Word or PowerPoint file, you can also coauthor in the Word 2016 or PowerPoint 2016 applications. (At the time this appendix was published, coauthoring was not possible in Excel 2016, but this might change.) When you coauthor a file in the Word 2016 application, you can choose to have changes made shared automatically, or you can choose to update the shared file manually. When you coauthor a file in the PowerPoint 2016 application, you must share the changes manually. To share changes automatically in Word 2016, click Yes in the dialog box that appears asking if you want to share changes automatically, or, in the Share task pane, click the Automatically share changes arrow, and then click Always. To share changes manually in either Word 2016 or PowerPoint 2016, click the Save button on the Quick Access toolbar. When you are working on a shared file in Word 2016 or PowerPoint 2016, the Save button looks like ⬚ or ⬚.

If the file you share on OneDrive is a Word, Excel, or PowerPoint file, and you and the people you shared the file are working in the Office Online version of those programs, everyone will see the changes made by all users as the changes are being made. An icon appears on the screen next to the part of the document another person is editing. To see the name of the person editing the file, you click the icon. In addition, where someone else is editing the file, a message such as this appears on the ribbon below your icon. Figure A-14 shows a file being coauthored in the Word Online application.

Figure A-14: Open file in Word Online with two people editing it

your username

message that appears when someone else is editing the file

name of person editing appears when you click the indicator

indicator appears to let you know that a certain person is editing

indicator appears to show the other person is editing

If the shared file is a Word or PowerPoint file, you can also coauthor in the Word 2016 or PowerPoint 2016 applications. (At the time this appendix was published, coauthoring was not possible in Excel 2016, but that might change.) When you coauthor a file in the Word 2016 application, you can choose to have changes made saved automatically, or you can choose to update the shared file manually. When you coauthor a file in the PowerPoint 2016 application, you must share the changes manually. To share changes automatically in Word 2016, click Yes in the dialog box that appears asking if you want to share changes automatically or tap the Share task pane, click the Automatically share changes arrow, and then click Always. To share changes manually in either Word 2016 or PowerPoint 2016, click the Save button on the Quick Access Toolbar. When you are working on a shared file in Word 2016 or PowerPoint 2016, the Save button looks like 🔁.

INDEX

Working with Excel Tables, PivotTables, and PivotCharts

Tracking Sales Data

Case | *Victoria's Veggies*

Victoria Calderon has a very large backyard farm in Watertown, Wisconsin, and a passion for local, organic, fresh vegetables. Five years ago, she started selling organic vegetables harvested from her backyard farm at a roadside stand in front of her home. Over the years, she expanded from selling fresh vegetables to individual customers to supplying restaurants, group homes, and residential care facilities. As the stand has become more popular, Victoria has hired staff to help during the busy selling times. To better accommodate both her individual customers and business clients, six months ago, she opened Victoria's Veggies as a storefront. She stocks the store with vegetables grown in her own backyard farm and supplements her supply with fresh vegetables that she purchases from the year-round farmers market in Madison.

Victoria wants to use the June data to analyze the current state of Victoria's Veggies storefront operations. Victoria has entered the June sales data into an Excel workbook and wants you to help her analyze the data. You'll work with the data as an Excel table so you can easily edit, sort, and filter the data. You'll also summarize the data using the Subtotals command, a PivotTable, and a PivotChart.

STARTING DATA FILES

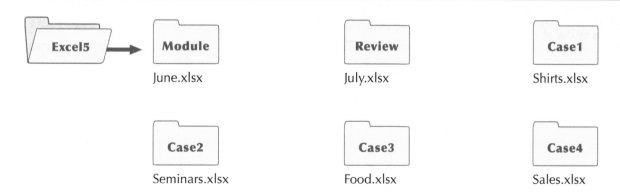

Excel5 → Module
June.xlsx

Review
July.xlsx

Case1
Shirts.xlsx

Case2
Seminars.xlsx

Case3
Food.xlsx

Case4
Sales.xlsx

Session 5.1 Visual Overview:

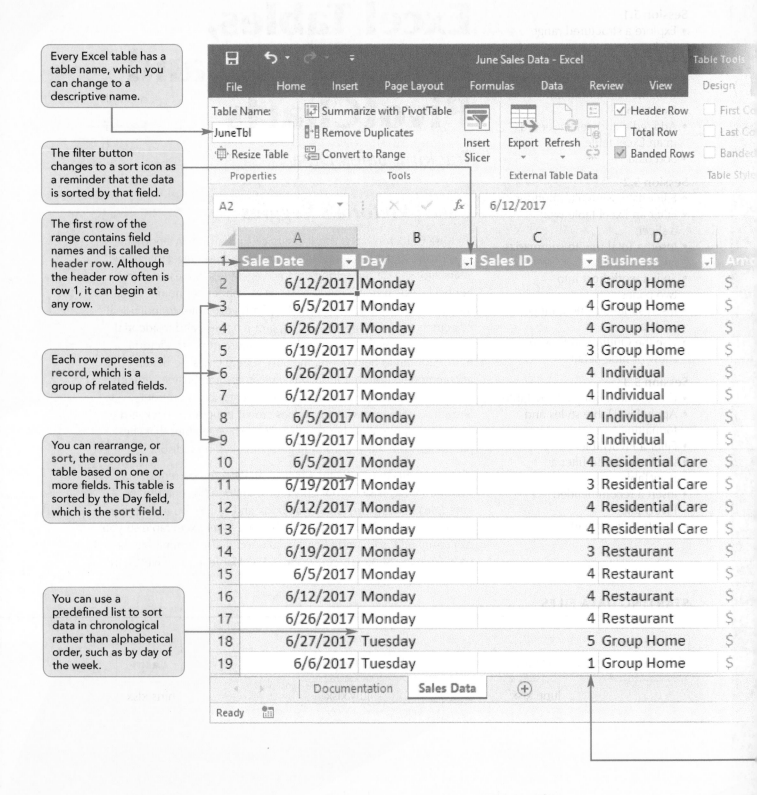

Every Excel table has a table name, which you can change to a descriptive name.

The filter button changes to a sort icon as a reminder that the data is sorted by that field.

The first row of the range contains field names and is called the header row. Although the header row often is row 1, it can begin at any row.

Each row represents a record, which is a group of related fields.

You can rearrange, or sort, the records in a table based on one or more fields. This table is sorted by the Day field, which is the sort field.

You can use a predefined list to sort data in chronological rather than alphabetical order, such as by day of the week.

Elements of an Excel Table

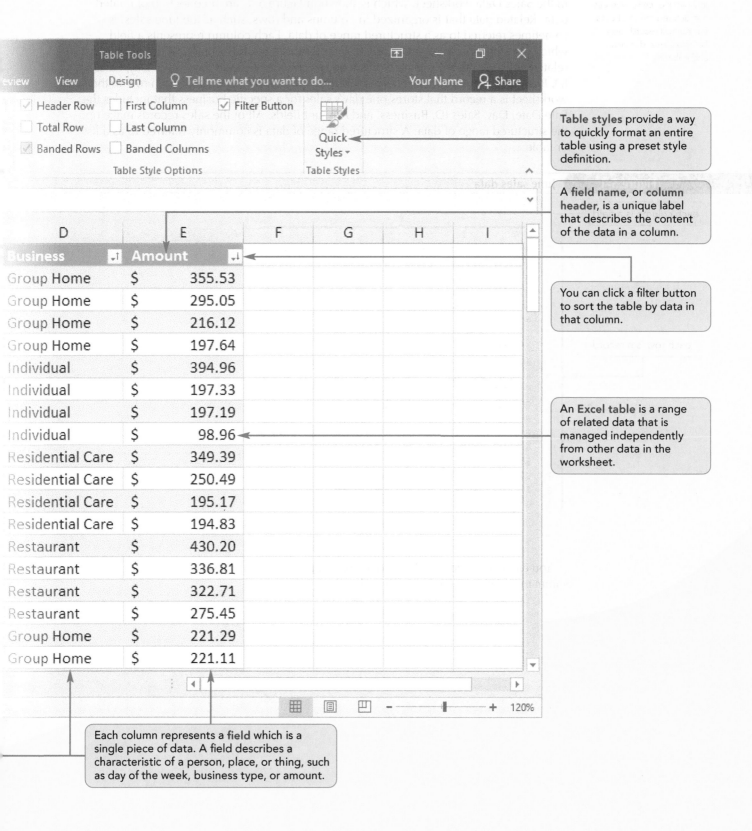

Table styles provide a way to quickly format an entire table using a preset style definition.

A field name, or column header, is a unique label that describes the content of the data in a column.

You can click a filter button to sort the table by data in that column.

An Excel table is a range of related data that is managed independently from other data in the worksheet.

Each column represents a field which is a single piece of data. A field describes a characteristic of a person, place, or thing, such as day of the week, business type, or amount.

Planning a Structured Range of Data

A worksheet is often used to manage related data, such as lists of clients, products, or transactions. For example, the June sales for Victoria's Veggies that Victoria entered in the Sales Data worksheet, which is shown in Figure 5-1, are a collection of related data. Related data that is organized in columns and rows, such as the June sales, is sometimes referred to as a structured range of data. Each column represents a field, which is a single piece of data. Each row represents a record, which is a group of related fields. In the Sales Data worksheet, the columns labeled Sale Date, Day, Sales ID, Business, and Amount are fields that store different pieces of data. Each row in the worksheet is a record that stores one day's sales for a specific business that includes the Sale Date, Day, Sales ID, Business, and Amount fields. All of the sales records make up the structured range of data. A structured range of data is commonly referred to as a list or table.

Figure 5-1   June sales data

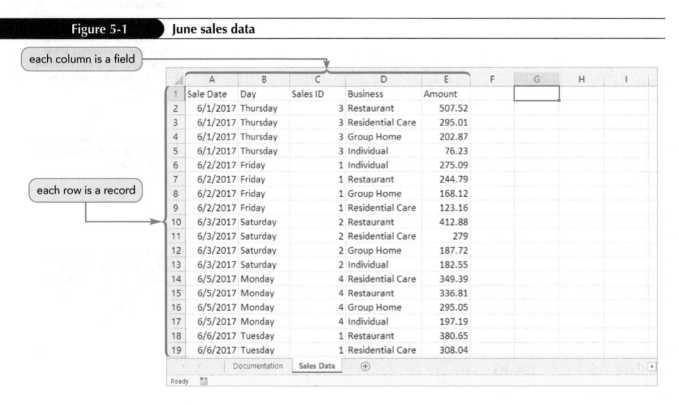

You can easily add and delete data, edit data, sort data, find subsets of data, summarize data, and create reports about related data.

PROSKILLS

Decision Making: The Importance of Planning

Before you create a structured range of data, you should create a plan. Planning involves gathering relevant information about the data and deciding your goals. The end results you want to achieve will help you determine the kind of data to include in each record and how to divide that data into fields. Specifically, you should do the following to create an effective plan:

- Spend time thinking about how you will use the data.
- Consider what reports you want to create for different audiences (supervisors, customers, directors, and so forth) and the fields needed to produce those reports.
- Think about the various questions, or queries, you want answered and the fields needed to create those results.

This information is often documented in a **data definition table**, which lists the fields to be maintained for each record, a description of the information each field will include, and the type of data (such as numbers, text, or dates) stored in each field. Careful and thorough planning will help you avoid having to redesign a structured range of data later.

Before creating the list of sales, Victoria carefully considered what information she needs and how she wants to use it. Victoria plans to use the data to track daily sales for each business type, which she has identified as group home, individual, residential care, and restaurant. She wants to be able to create reports that show specific lists of sales, such as all the sales for a specific date, day of the week, or Sales ID. Based on this information, Victoria developed the data definition table shown in Figure 5-2.

| Figure 5-2 | Data definition table for the sales data |

Data Definition Table			
Field	Description	Data Type	Notes
Sale Date	Date of the sale	Date	Use the *mm/dd/yyyy* format
Day	Day of the week	Text	Monday, Tuesday, Wednesday, …
Sales ID	Salesperson ID	Number	1=Victoria, 2=Miguel, 3=Michelle, 4=Sandy, 5=James
Business	Type of business for the sale	Text	Group Home, Individual, Residential Care, and Restaurant
Amount	Sales total for a specific transaction date and business type	Number	Use the Accounting format and show two decimal places

After you determine the fields and records you need, you can enter the data in a worksheet. You can then work with the data in many ways, including the following common operations:

- Add, edit, and delete data in the range.
- Sort the data range.
- Filter to display only rows that meet specified criteria.
- Insert formulas to calculate subtotals.
- Create summary tables based on the data in the range (usually with PivotTables).

You'll perform many of these operations on the sales data.

Creating an Effective Structured Range of Data

For a range of data to be used effectively, it must have the same structure throughout. Keep in mind the following guidelines:

- **Enter field names in the top row of the range.** This clearly identifies each field.
- **Use short, descriptive field names.** Shorter field names are easier to remember and enable more fields to appear in the workbook window at once.
- **Format field names.** Use formatting to distinguish the header row from the data. For example, apply bold, color, and a different font size.
- **Enter the same kind of data in a field.** Each field should store the smallest bit of information and be consistent from record to record. For example, enter Los Angeles, Tucson, or Chicago in a City field, but do not include states, such as CA, AZ, or IL, in the same column of data.
- **Separate the data from the rest of the worksheet.** The data, which includes the header row, should be separated from other information in the worksheet by at least one blank row and one blank column. The blank row and column enable Excel to accurately determine the range of the data.

Victoria created a workbook and entered the sales data for June based on the plan outlined in the data definition table. You'll open this workbook and review its structure.

To open and review Victoria's workbook:

1. Open the **June** workbook located in the **Excel5 > Module** folder included with your Data Files, and then save the workbook as **June Sales Data** in the location specified by your instructor.

2. In the Documentation worksheet, enter your name in cell B3 and the date in cell B4.

3. In the range A7:D13, review the data definition table. This table, which is shown in Figure 5-2, describes the different fields that are used in the Sales Data worksheet.

4. Go to the **Sales Data** worksheet. This worksheet, which is shown in Figure 5-1, contains data about the vegetable store's sales. Currently, the worksheet includes 101 sales records. Each sale record is a separate row (rows 2 through 102) and contains five fields (columns A through E). Row 1, the header row, contains labels that describe the data in each column.

5. Scroll the worksheet to row **102**, which is the last record.

When you scroll the worksheet, the first column headers in row 1 are no longer visible. Without seeing the column headers, it is difficult to know what the data entered in each column represents.

Freezing Rows and Columns

You can select rows and columns to remain visible in the workbook window as you scroll the worksheet. **Freezing** a row or column lets you keep the headers visible as you work with the data in a large worksheet. You can freeze the top row, freeze the first column, or freeze the rows and columns above and to the left of the selected cell. If you freeze the top row, row 1 remains on the screen as you scroll, leaving column headers visible and making it easier to identify the data in each record.

Victoria wants to see the column headers as she scrolls the sales records. You'll freeze row 1, which contains the column headers.

To freeze row 1 of the worksheet:

▶ **1.** Press the **Ctrl+Home** keys to return to cell A1. You want to freeze row 1.

▶ **2.** On the ribbon, click the **View** tab.

▶ **3.** In the Window group, click the **Freeze Panes** button, and then click **Freeze Top Row**. A horizontal line appears below the column labels to indicate which row is frozen.

▶ **4.** Scroll the worksheet to row **102**. This time, the column headers remain visible as you scroll. See Figure 5-3.

TIP

To freeze the columns and rows above and to the left of the selected cell, click the Freeze Panes button, and then click Freeze Panes.

Figure 5-3   **Top row of the worksheet is frozen**

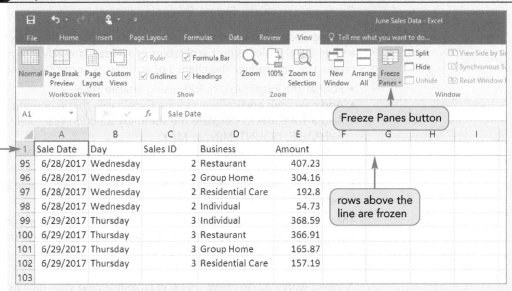

header row remains visible as you scroll the worksheet

Freeze Panes button

rows above the line are frozen

▶ **5.** Press the **Ctrl+Home** keys. Cell A2, the cell directly below the frozen row, becomes the active cell.

After you freeze panes, the first option on the Freeze Panes button menu changes to Unfreeze Panes. This option releases the frozen panes so that all the columns and rows in the worksheet shift when you scroll. Victoria wants you to use a different method to keep the column headers visible, so you will unfreeze the top row of the worksheet.

To unfreeze the top row of the worksheet:

▶ **1.** On the View tab, in the Window group, click the **Freeze Panes** button. The first Freeze Panes option is now Unfreeze Panes.

▶ **2.** Click **Unfreeze Panes**. The headers are no longer frozen, and the horizontal line below the column headers is removed. You can now scroll all the rows and columns in the worksheet.

Creating an Excel Table

You can convert a structured range of data, such as the sales data in the range A1:E102, to an Excel table. An Excel table makes it easier to identify, manage, and analyze the groups of related data. When a structured range of data is converted into an Excel table, you see the following:

- A filter button in each cell of the header row
- The range formatted with a table style
- A sizing handle (a small triangle) in the lower-right corner of the last cell of the table
- The Table Tools Design tab on the ribbon

You can create more than one Excel table in a worksheet. Although you can leave the sales data as a structured range of data and still perform all of the tasks in this section, creating an Excel table helps you to be more efficient and accurate.

INSIGHT

Saving Time with Excel Tables

Although you can perform the same operations for both a structured range of data and an Excel table, using Excel tables provides many advantages to help you be more productive and reduce the chance of error, such as the following:

- Format the Excel table quickly using a table style.
- Add new rows and columns to the Excel table that automatically expand the range.
- Add a Total row to calculate the summary function you select, such as SUM, AVERAGE, COUNT, MIN, or MAX.
- Enter a formula in one table cell that is automatically copied to all other cells in that table column.
- Create formulas that reference cells in a table by using table and column names instead of cell addresses.

These Excel table features let you focus on analyzing and understanding the data, leaving the more time-consuming tasks for the program to perform.

Victoria wants you to create an Excel table from the sales data in the Sales Data worksheet. You'll be able to work with the Excel tables to analyze Victoria's data effectively.

To create an Excel table from the sales data:

1. If necessary, select any cell in the range of sales data to make it the active cell.

2. On the ribbon, click the **Insert** tab.

3. In the Tables group, click the **Table** button. The Create Table dialog box opens. The range of data you want to use for the table is selected in the worksheet, and a formula with its range reference, =$A$1:$E$102, is entered in the dialog box.

4. Verify that the **My table has headers** check box is selected. The headers are the field names entered in row 1. If the first row did not contain field names, the My table has headers check box would be unchecked, and Excel would insert a row of headers with the names Column1, Column2, and so on.

5. Click the **OK** button. The dialog box closes, and the range of data is converted to an Excel table, which is selected. Filter buttons appear in the header row, the sizing handle appears in the lower-right corner of the last cell of the table, the table is formatted with a predefined table style, and the Table Tools Design tab appears on the ribbon. See Figure 5-4.

Figure 5-4	Excel table with the sales data

6. Select any cell in the table, and then scroll down the table. The field names in the header row replace the standard lettered column headings (A, B, C, and so on) as you scroll, so you don't need to freeze panes to keep the header row visible. See Figure 5-5.

Figure 5-5	Sales table scrolled

7. Press the **Ctrl+Home** keys to make cell A1 the active cell. The column headers return to the standard display, and the Excel table header row scrolls back into view as row 1.

Renaming an Excel Table

Each Excel table in a workbook must have a unique name. Excel assigns the name Table1 to the first Excel table created in a workbook. Any additional Excel tables you create in the workbook are named consecutively as Table2, Table3, and so forth. You can assign a more descriptive name to a table, making it easier to identify a particular table by its content. Descriptive names are especially useful when you create more than one Excel table in the same workbook because they make it easier to reference the different Excel tables.

Table names must start with a letter or an underscore but can use any combination of letters, numbers, and underscores for the rest of the name. Table names cannot include spaces, but you can use an underscore or uppercase letters instead of spaces to separate words in a table name, such as June_Records or JuneRecords. When naming objects such as tables, a best practice is to include an abbreviation that identifies that object. For example, table names often end with the letters *Tbl*, such as June_Records_Tbl or JuneTbl.

Victoria wants you to rename the Excel table you just created from the June sales data.

TIP

If you copy a worksheet that contains a table, Excel adds the next consecutive number at the end of the table name to create a unique table name.

To rename the Table1 table:

▶ 1. On the Table Tools Design tab, in the Properties group, select **Table1** in the Table Name box. See Figure 5-6.

Figure 5-6   **Table Name box**

enter a descriptive name

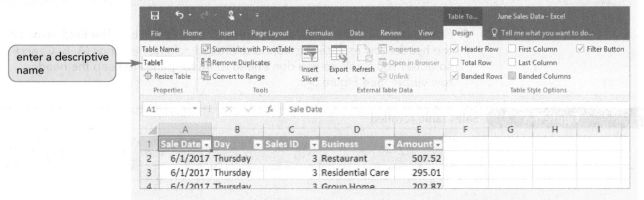

▶ 2. Type **JuneTbl** as the descriptive name, and then press the **Enter** key. The Excel table is renamed as "JuneTbl."

Modifying an Excel Table

You can modify an Excel table by adding or removing table elements or by changing the table's formatting. For every Excel table, you can display or hide the following elements:

- **Header row**—The first row of the table that includes the field names
- **Total row**—A row at the bottom of the table that applies a function to the column values
- **First column**—Formatting added to the leftmost column of the table
- **Last column**—Formatting added to the rightmost column of the table
- **Banded rows**—Formatting added to alternating rows so that even and odd rows are different colors, making it simpler to distinguish records
- **Banded columns**—Formatting added to alternating columns so they are different colors, making it simpler to distinguish fields
- **Filter buttons**—Buttons that appear in each column of the header row and open a menu with options for sorting and filtering the table data

You can also modify a table by applying a table style. As with other styles, a table style formats all of the selected table elements with a consistent, unified design. You can change the font, fill, alignment, number formats, column widths and row heights, and other formatting of selected cells in the table the same way you would for other cells in the worksheet.

Victoria wants the JuneTbl table to have a format that makes the table easier to read. You will apply a table style and make other formatting changes to the table.

To format the JuneTbl table:

1. On the Table Tools Design tab, in the Table Styles group, click the **More** button. A gallery of table styles opens.

2. In the Table Styles gallery, in the Medium section, click **Table Style Medium 7**. The table now has a green style.

TIP

To display or hide alternating column colors, click the Banded Columns check box in the Table Style Options group.

3. In the Table Style Options group, click the **Banded Rows** check box. The alternating row colors disappear. The table is more challenging to read this way, so you will reapply the banded rows formatting.

4. In the Table Style Options group, click the **Banded Rows** check box to select it. The alternating row colors reappear.

5. Change the width of columns A through E to **15** characters. The entire column headers and all of the values are now visible.

6. Select the **Amount** column, and then change the values to the **Accounting** format. See Figure 5-7.

Figure 5-7	Modified JuneTbl table

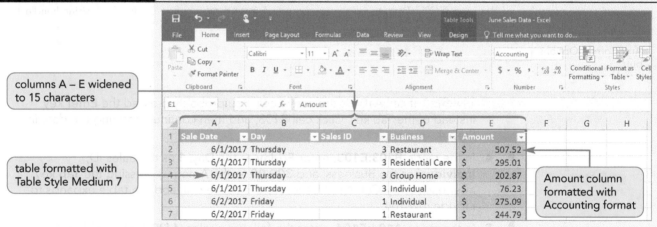

columns A – E widened to 15 characters

table formatted with Table Style Medium 7

Amount column formatted with Accounting format

7. Select cell **A1** to make it the active cell.

Maintaining Data in an Excel Table

As you develop a worksheet with an Excel table, you may need to add new records to the table, find and edit existing records in the table, and delete records from the table. Victoria wants you to make several changes to the data in the JuneTbl table.

Adding Records

As you maintain data in an Excel table, you often need to add new records. You add a record to an Excel table in a blank row. The simplest and most convenient way to add a record to an Excel table is to enter the data in the first blank row below the last record. You can then sort the data to arrange the table in the order you want. If you want the record in a specific location, you can also insert a row within the table for the new record.

The sales records for June 30 are missing from the JuneTbl table. Victoria asks you to add to the table four new records that contain the missing data.

To add four records to the JuneTbl table:

1. Press the **End** key, and then press the ↓ key to make cell A102 the active cell. This cell is in the last row of the table.

2. Press the ↓ key to move the active cell to cell A103, which is in the first blank row below the table.

TIP

You can drag the sizing handle to add columns or rows to the Excel table or delete them from it.

3. In cell A103, type **6/30/2017**, and then press the **Tab** key. Cell B103 in the Day column becomes the active cell. The table expands to include a new row with the same formatting as the rest of the table. The AutoCorrect Options button appears so you can undo the table formatting if you hadn't intended the new data to be part of the existing table. The sizing handle moves to the lower-right corner of cell E103, which is now the cell in the lower-right corner of the table. See Figure 5-8.

Figure 5-8   **New row added to the JuneTbl table**

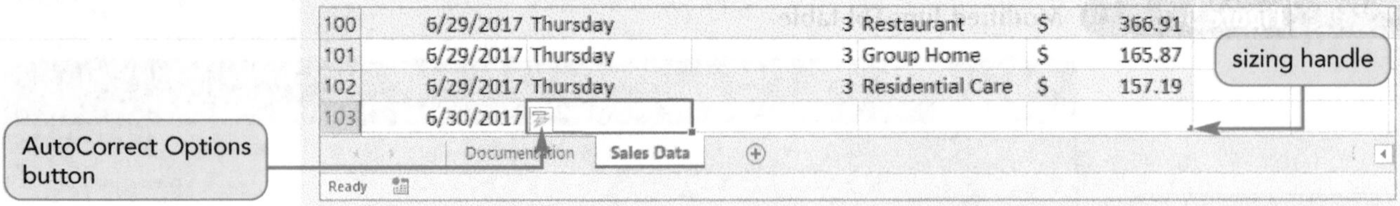

Trouble? If cell A104 is the active cell, you probably pressed the Enter key instead of the Tab key. Click cell B103, and then continue entering the data in Step 4.

4. In the range **B103:E103**, enter **Friday** as the Day, **1** as the Sales ID, **Individual** as the Business, and **309.00** as the Amount, pressing the **Tab** key after each entry. Cell A104 becomes the active cell, and the table expands to include row 104.

5. In the range **A104:E104**, enter the following sales: **6/30/2017**, **Friday**, **1**, **Restaurant**, and **464.12**.

6. In the range **A105:E105**, enter the following sales: **6/30/2017**, **Friday**, **1**, **Group Home**, and **431.12**.

7. In the range **A106:E106**, enter the following sales: **6/30/2017**, **Friday**, **1**, **Residential Care**, and **225.02**.

8. Press the **Enter** key. The records are added to the table. See Figure 5-9.

| Figure 5-9 | Records added to the JuneTbl table |

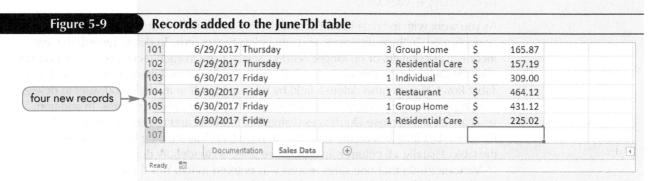

four new records →

101	6/29/2017	Thursday	3	Group Home	$	165.87
102	6/29/2017	Thursday	3	Residential Care	$	157.19
103	6/30/2017	Friday	1	Individual	$	309.00
104	6/30/2017	Friday	1	Restaurant	$	464.12
105	6/30/2017	Friday	1	Group Home	$	431.12
106	6/30/2017	Friday	1	Residential Care	$	225.02
107						

Documentation   **Sales Data**   (+)

Ready

Trouble? If a new row is added to the table, you probably pressed the Tab key instead of the Enter key after the last entry in the record. On the Quick Access Toolbar, click the Undo button ↺ to remove the extra row.

Finding and Editing Records

Although you can manually scroll through the table to find a specific record, often a quicker way to locate a record is to use the Find command. When using the Find or Replace command, it is best to start at the top of a worksheet to ensure that all cells in the table are searched. You edit the data in a table the same way as you edit data in a worksheet cell.

Victoria wants you to update the June 20 Residential Care sales amount. You'll use the Find command to locate the record, which is currently blank. Then, you'll edit the record in the table to change the amount to $309.00.

To find and edit the 6/20/2017 Residential Care record:

▸ 1. Press the **Ctrl+Home** keys to make cell A1 the active cell so that all cells in the table will be searched.

▸ 2. On the Home tab, in the Editing group, click the **Find & Select** button, and then click **Find** (or press the **Ctrl+F** keys). The Find and Replace dialog box opens.

▸ 3. In the Find what box, type **6/20/2017**, and then click the **Find Next** button. Cell A67, which contains the record for an Individual, is selected. This is not the record you want.

▸ 4. Click the **Find Next** button three times to display the record for Residential Care on 6/20/2017.

▸ 5. Click the **Close** button. The Find and Replace dialog box closes.

▸ 6. Press the **Tab** key four times to move the active cell to the Amount column, type **309**, and then press the **Enter** key. The record is updated to reflect the $309.00 amount.

▸ 7. Press the **Ctrl+Home** keys to make cell A1 the active cell.

Deleting a Record

As you work with the data in an Excel table, you might find records that are outdated or duplicated. In these instances, you can delete the records. To delete records that are incorrect, out of date, or no longer needed, select a cell in each record you want to delete, click the Delete button arrow in the Cells group on the Home tab, and then click Delete Table Rows. You can also delete a field by selecting a cell in the field you want to delete, clicking the Delete button arrow, and then clicking Delete Table Columns. In addition, you can use the Remove Duplicates dialog box to locate and remove records that have the same data in selected columns. The Remove Duplicates dialog box lists all columns in the table. Usually, all columns in a table are selected to identify duplicate records.

Victoria thinks that one sales record was entered twice. You'll use the Remove Duplicates dialog box to locate and delete the duplicate record from the table.

To find and delete the duplicate record from the JuneTbl table:

▶ **1.** Scroll to row **56**, and observe that the entries in row 56 and row 57 are exactly the same. One of these records needs to be deleted.

▶ **2.** On the ribbon, click the **Table Tools Design** tab.

▶ **3.** In the Tools group, click the **Remove Duplicates** button. The Remove Duplicates dialog box opens, and all of the columns in the table are selected. Excel looks for repeated data in the selected columns to determine whether any duplicate records exist. If duplicates are found, all but one of the records are deleted. See Figure 5-10.

| Figure 5-10 | Remove Duplicates dialog box |

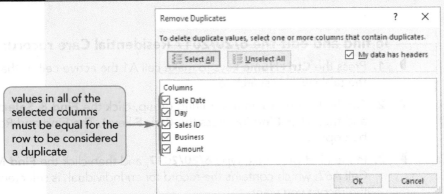

values in all of the selected columns must be equal for the row to be considered a duplicate

You want to search all of the columns in the table for duplicated data so that you don't inadvertently delete a record that has duplicate values in the selected fields but a unique value in the deselected field.

▶ **4.** Click the **OK** button. A dialog box opens, reporting "1 duplicate values found and removed; 104 unique values remain."

▶ **5.** Click the **OK** button.

Trouble? If you deleted records you did not intend to delete, you can reverse the action. On the Quick Access Toolbar, click the Undo button 🔄, and then repeat Steps 3 through 5.

▶ **6.** Press the **Ctrl+Home** keys to make cell A1 the active cell.

Sorting Data

The records in an Excel table initially appear in the order they were entered. As you work, however, you may want to view the same records in a different order. For example, Victoria might want to view the sales by business or day of the week. You can sort data in ascending or descending order. **Ascending order** arranges text alphabetically from A to Z, numbers from smallest to largest, and dates from oldest to newest. **Descending order** arranges text in reverse alphabetical order from Z to A, numbers from largest to smallest, and dates from newest to oldest. In both ascending and descending order, blank cells are placed at the end of the table.

Sorting One Column Using the Sort Buttons

You can quickly sort data with one sort field using the Sort A to Z button ⬇ or the Sort Z to A button ⬇. Victoria wants you to sort the sales in ascending order by the Business column. This will rearrange the table data so that the records appear in alphabetical order by Business.

To sort the JuneTbl table in ascending order by the Business column:

1. Select any cell in the Business column. You do not need to select the entire JuneTbl table, which consists of the range A1:E105. Excel determines the table's range when you click any cell in the table.

2. On the ribbon, click the **Data** tab.

> **TIP**
>
> You can also use the Sort & Filter button in the Editing group on the Home tab.

3. In the Sort & Filter group, click the **Sort A to Z** button ⬇. The data is sorted in ascending order by Business. The Business filter button changes to show that the data is sorted by that column. See Figure 5-11.

Figure 5-11	JuneTbl table sorted by the Business field

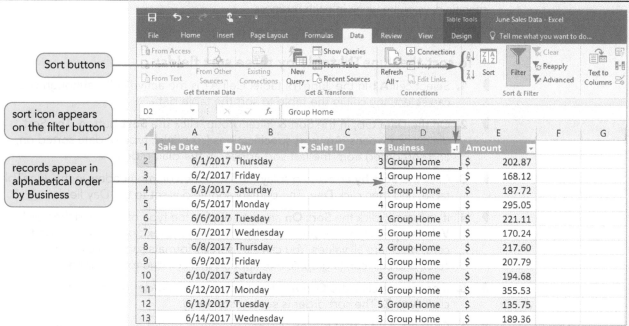

Sort buttons

sort icon appears on the filter button

records appear in alphabetical order by Business

> **Trouble?** If the data is sorted in the wrong order, you might have clicked in a different column than the Business column. Repeat Steps 1 through 3.

Sorting Multiple Columns Using the Sort Dialog Box

Sometimes one sort field is not adequate for your needs. For example, Victoria wants to arrange the JuneTbl table so that the sales are ordered first by Day (Monday, Tuesday, and so forth), then by Business for each day of the week, and then by Amount (highest to lowest). You must sort by more than one column to accomplish this. The first sort field is called the **primary sort field**, the second sort field is called the **secondary sort field**, and so forth. Although you can include up to 64 sort fields in a single sort, you typically will use one to three sort fields. In this case, the Day field is the primary sort field, the Business field is the secondary sort field, and the Amount field is the tertiary sort field. When you have more than one sort field, you should use the Sort dialog box to specify the sort criteria.

REFERENCE

Sorting Data Using Multiple Sort Fields

- Select any cell in a table or range.
- On the Data tab, in the Sort & Filter group, click the Sort button.
- If necessary, click the Add Level button to insert the Sort by row.
- Click the Sort by arrow, select the column heading for the primary sort field, click the Sort On arrow to select the type of data, and then click the Order arrow to select the sort order.
- For each additional column to sort, click the Add Level button, click the Then by arrow, select the column heading for the secondary sort field, click the Sort On arrow to select the type of data, and then click the Order arrow to select the sort order.
- Click the OK button.

Victoria wants to see the sales sorted by day, and then within day by business, and then within business by amount, with the highest amounts appearing before the smaller ones for each business. This will make it easier for Victoria to evaluate sales on specific days of the week in each business.

To sort the JuneTbl table by three sort fields:

1. Select cell **A1** in the JuneTbl table. Cell A1 is the active cell—although you can select any cell in the table to sort the table data.

2. On the Data tab, in the Sort & Filter group, click the **Sort** button. The Sort dialog box opens. Any sort specifications (sort field, type of data sorted on, and sort order) from the last sort appear in the dialog box.

3. Click the **Sort by** arrow to display the list of the column headers in the JuneTbl table, and then click **Day**. The primary sort field is set to the Day field.

4. If necessary, click the **Sort On** arrow to display the type of sort, and then click **Values**. Typically, you want to sort by the numbers, text, or dates stored in the cells, which are all values. You can also sort by formats such as cell color, font color, and cell icon (a graphic that appears in a cell due to a conditional format).

5. If necessary, click the **Order** arrow to display sort order options, and then click **A to Z**. The sort order is set to ascending.

6. Click the **Add Level** button. A Then by row is added below the primary sort field.

7. Click the **Then by** arrow and click **Business**, and then verify that **Values** appears in the Sort On box and **A to Z** appears in the Order box.

▶ **8.** Click the **Add Level** button to add a second Then by row.

▶ **9.** Click the second **Then by** arrow, click **Amount**, verify that **Values** appears in the Sort On box, click the **Order** arrow, and then click **Largest to Smallest** to specify a descending sort order for the Amount values. See Figure 5-12.

| Figure 5-12 | Sort dialog box with three sorted fields |

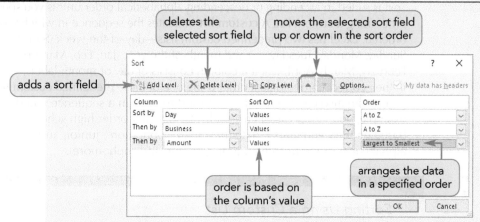

▶ **10.** Click the **OK** button. Excel sorts the table records first in ascending order by the Day field, then within each Day in ascending order by the Business field, and then within each Business in descending order by the Amount field. For example, the first 20 records are Friday sales. Of these records, the first five are Group Home, the next five are Individual, and so on. Finally, the Friday Group Home sales are arranged from highest to lowest in the Amount column. See Figure 5-13.

| Figure 5-13 | Sales sorted by Day, then by Business, and then by Amount |

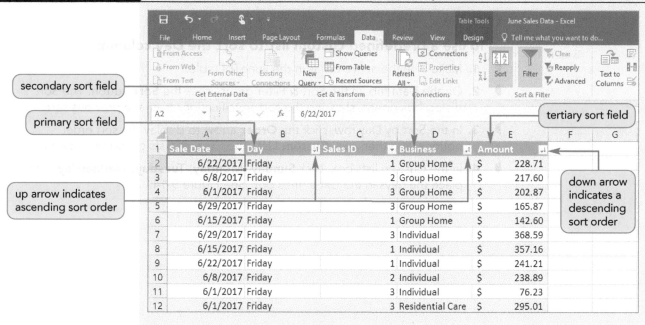

▶ **11.** Scroll the table to view the sorted table data.

The table data is sorted in alphabetical order by the day of the week—Friday, Monday, Saturday, and so forth. This default sort order for fields with text values is not appropriate for days of the week. Instead, Victoria wants you to base the sort on chronological rather than alphabetical order. You'll use a custom sort list to set up the sort order Victoria wants.

Sorting Using a Custom List

Text is sorted in ascending or descending alphabetical order unless you specify a different order using a custom list. A **custom list** indicates the sequence in which you want data ordered. Excel has two predefined custom lists—day-of-the-week (Sun, Mon, Tues, … and Sunday, Monday, Tuesday, …) and month-of-the-year (Jan, Feb, Mar, Apr, … and January, February, March, April, …). If a column consists of day or month labels, you can sort them in their correct chronological order using one of these predefined custom lists.

You can also create custom lists to sort records in a sequence you define. For example, you can create a custom list to logically order high school or college students based on their admittance date (freshman, sophomore, junior, and senior) rather than alphabetical order (freshman, junior, senior, and sophomore).

REFERENCE

Sorting Using a Custom List

- On the Data tab, in the Sort & Filter group, click the Sort button.
- Click the Order arrow, and then click Custom List.
- If necessary, in the List entries box, type each entry for the custom list (in the desired order) and press the Enter key, and then click the Add button.
- In the Custom lists box, select the predefined custom list.
- Click the OK button.

You'll use a predefined custom list to sort the records by the Day column in chronological order rather than alphabetical order.

To use a predefined custom list to sort the Day column:

▶ **1.** Make sure the active cell is in the JuneTbl table.

▶ **2.** On the Data tab, in the Sort & Filter group, click the **Sort** button. The Sort dialog box opens, showing the sort specifications from the previous sort.

▶ **3.** In the Sort by Day row, click the **Order** arrow to display the sort order options, and then click **Custom List**. The Custom Lists dialog box opens.

▶ **4.** In the Custom lists box, click **Sunday, Monday, Tuesday, Wednesday**… to place the days in the List entries box. See Figure 5-14.

Figure 5-14   **Custom Lists dialog box**

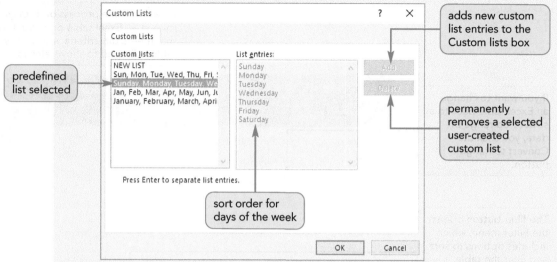

> **5.** Click the **OK** button to return to the Sort dialog box. The custom sort list—Sunday, Monday, Tuesday, Wednesday...—appears in the Order box.

> **6.** Click the **OK** button. The table is sorted based on the predefined custom list.

> **7.** Scroll the sorted table to verify that the sales are sorted by their chronological day order—Sunday, Monday, Tuesday, Wednesday, Thursday, Friday, Saturday. No sales appear for Sundays because Victoria's Veggies is closed on that day.

So far, you created an Excel table for the sales and then named and formatted the table. You updated the table by adding, editing, and deleting records. You also sorted the records and used a predefined custom list to sort the Day field by its chronological order. In the next session, you will continue to work with the JuneTbl table.

REVIEW

Session 5.1 Quick Check

1. In Excel, what is the difference between a range of data and a structured range of data?

2. Explain the difference between a field and a record.

3. What is the purpose of the Freeze Panes button in the Window group on the View tab? Why is this feature helpful?

4. What three elements indicate that a range of data is an Excel table?

5. How can you quickly find and delete duplicate records from an Excel table?

6. If you sort table data from the most recent purchase date to the oldest purchase date, in what order have you sorted the data?

7. An Excel table of college students tracks each student's first name, last name, major, and year of graduation. How can you order the table so that students graduating in the same year appear together in alphabetical order by the students' last names?

8. An Excel table of sales data includes the Month field with the values Jan, Feb, Mar, ... Dec. How can you sort the data so the sales data is sorted by Month in chronological order (Jan, Feb, Mar, ... Dec)?

Session 5.2 Visual Overview:

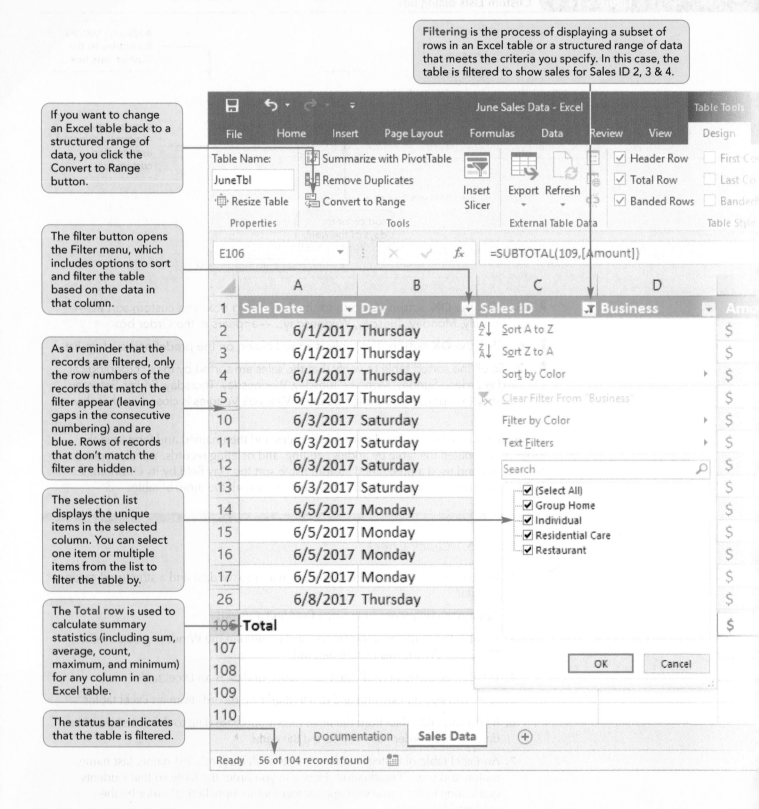

Filtering is the process of displaying a subset of rows in an Excel table or a structured range of data that meets the criteria you specify. In this case, the table is filtered to show sales for Sales ID 2, 3 & 4.

If you want to change an Excel table back to a structured range of data, you click the Convert to Range button.

The filter button opens the Filter menu, which includes options to sort and filter the table based on the data in that column.

As a reminder that the records are filtered, only the row numbers of the records that match the filter appear (leaving gaps in the consecutive numbering) and are blue. Rows of records that don't match the filter are hidden.

The selection list displays the unique items in the selected column. You can select one item or multiple items from the list to filter the table by.

The Total row is used to calculate summary statistics (including sum, average, count, maximum, and minimum) for any column in an Excel table.

The status bar indicates that the table is filtered.

Filtering Table Data

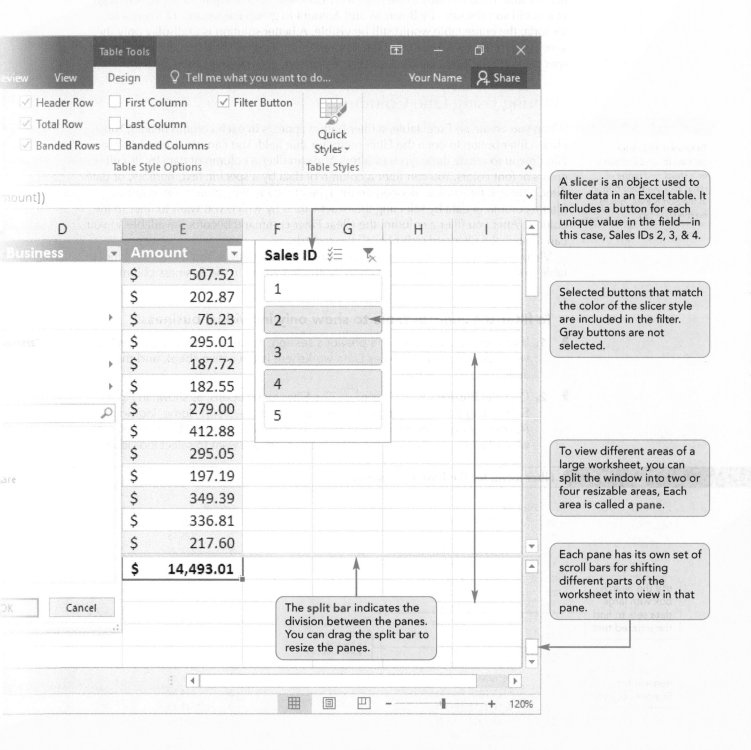

A **slicer** is an object used to filter data in an Excel table. It includes a button for each unique value in the field—in this case, Sales IDs 2, 3, & 4.

Selected buttons that match the color of the slicer style are included in the filter. Gray buttons are not selected.

To view different areas of a large worksheet, you can split the window into two or four resizable areas, Each area is called a **pane**.

Each pane has its own set of scroll bars for shifting different parts of the worksheet into view in that pane.

The **split bar** indicates the division between the panes. You can drag the split bar to resize the panes.

Filtering Data

Victoria wants to analyze the sales data to determine if she could close Victoria's Veggies to individual customers one day during the week and use that time for buying and planning. She wants to see a list of all of the individual sales and then narrow that list to see only those days with sales less than or equal to $200. Although you could sort the sales by Business and Amount to group the records of interest to Victoria, the entire table would still be visible. A better solution is to display only the specific records you want. Filtering temporarily hides any records that do not meet the specified criteria. After data is filtered, you can sort, copy, format, chart, and print it.

Filtering Using One Column

TIP

To show or hide filter buttons for an Excel table or a structured range of data, click the Filter button in the Sort & Filter group on the Data tab.

When you create an Excel table, a filter button appears in each column header. You click a filter button to open the Filter menu for that field. You can use options on the Filter menu to create three types of filters. You can filter a column of data by its cell colors or font colors. You can filter a column of data by a specific text, number, or date filter, although the choices depend on the type of data in the column. Or, you can filter a column of data by selecting the exact values by which you want to filter in the column. After you filter a column, the Clear Filter command becomes available so you can remove the filter and redisplay all the records.

Victoria wants to see the sales for only individual customers. You'll filter the JuneTbl table to show only those records with the value Individual in the Business column.

To filter the JuneTbl table to show only individual business:

▶ 1. If you took a break after the previous session, make sure the June Sales Data workbook is open, the Sales Data worksheet is the active sheet, and the JuneTbl table is active.

▶ 2. Click the **Business** filter button ⌄. The Filter menu opens, as shown in Figure 5-15, listing the unique entries in the Business field—Group Home, Individual, Residential Care, and Restaurant. All of the items are selected, but you can set which items to use to filter the data. In this case, you want to select Individual.

| Figure 5-15 | Filter menu for the Business column |

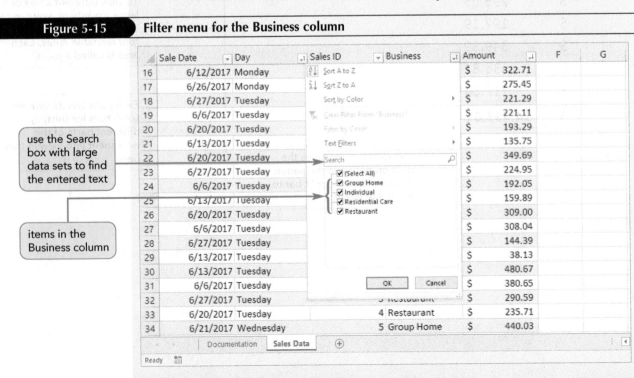

use the Search box with large data sets to find the entered text

items in the Business column

▶ 3. Click the **(Select All)** check box to remove the checkmarks from all of the Business items.

▶ 4. Click the **Individual** check box to select it. The filter will show only records that match the checked item and will hide records that contain the unchecked items.

▶ 5. Click the **OK** button. The filter is applied. The status bar lists the number of Individual rows found in the entire table—in this case, 26 of the 104 records in the table are displayed. See Figure 5-16.

| Figure 5-16 | JuneTbl table filtered to show only Individual business |

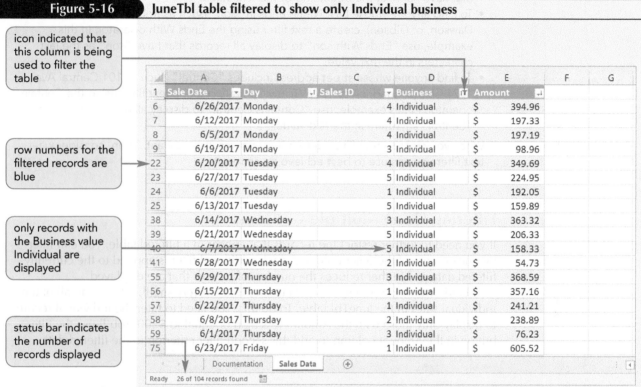

icon indicated that this column is being used to filter the table

row numbers for the filtered records are blue

only records with the Business value Individual are displayed

status bar indicates the number of records displayed

▶ 6. Review the records to verify that only records with Individual in the Business column are visible. All of the other records in this column are hidden, leaving gaps in the row numbers.

▶ 7. Point to the **Business** filter button [⊤]. A ScreenTip—Business: Equals "Individual"—describes the filter applied to the column.

The Filter menu includes options to Sort by Color and Filter by Color. These options enable you to filter and sort data using color, one of many cell attributes. Victoria could use specific cell background colors for certain sales in the JuneTbl table. For example, she might want to highlight dates when the store could have used an additional employee. So cells in the Sale Date column for busy days would be formatted with yellow as a reminder. You could click the Sort by Color option to display a list of available colors by which to sort and then click the specific color so that all the records for the days when she needed more help in the store (formatted with yellow) would appear together. Similarly, you could click the Filter by Color option to display a submenu with the available colors by which to filter, and then click a color.

INSIGHT

Exploring Text Filters

You can use different text filters to display the records you want. If you know only part of a text value or if you want to match a certain pattern, you can use the Begins With, Ends With, and Contains operators to filter a text field to match the pattern you specify. The following examples are based on a student directory table that includes First Name, Last Name, Address, City, State, and Zip fields:

- To find a student named Smith, Smithe, or Smythe, create a text filter using the Begins With operator. In this example, use "Begins With Sm" to display all records that have "Sm" at the beginning of the text value.
- To Find anyone whose Last Name ends in "son" (such as Robertson, Anderson, Dawson, or Gibson), create a text filter using the Ends With operator. In this example, use "Ends With son" to display all records that have "son" as the last characters in the text value.
- To find anyone whose street address includes "Central" (such as 101 Central Ave., 1024 Central Road, or 457 SW Willow Central), create a text filter using the Contains operator. In this example, use "Contains Central" to display all records that have "Central" anywhere in the text value.

When you create a text filter, determine what results you want. Then, consider what text filter you can use to best achieve those results.

Filtering Using Multiple Columns

If you need to further restrict the records that appear in a filtered table, you can filter by one or more of the other columns. Each additional filter is applied to the currently filtered data and further reduces the number of records that are displayed.

Victoria wants to see only individual sales that are very small, rather than all of the individual sales in the JuneTbl table. To do this, you need to filter the Individual records to display only those with the Amount less than or equal to $200. You'll use the filter button in the Amount column to add this second filter criterion to the filtered data.

To filter the Individual records to show only Amounts less than or equal to $200:

▶ **1.** Click the **Amount** filter button ⬇. The Filter menu opens.

▶ **2.** Click the **(Select All)** check box to remove the checkmarks from all of the check boxes.

▶ **3.** Click the check boxes for all of the amounts that are less than or equal to $200, starting with the **54.73** check box and ending with the **$197.33** check box. The ten check boxes are selected.

▶ **4.** Click the **OK** button. The JuneTbl table is further filtered and shows the ten records in June for Individual sales that are less than or equal to $200. See Figure 5-17.

| Figure 5-17 | JuneTbl table filtered to show Individual business with amounts less than $200 |

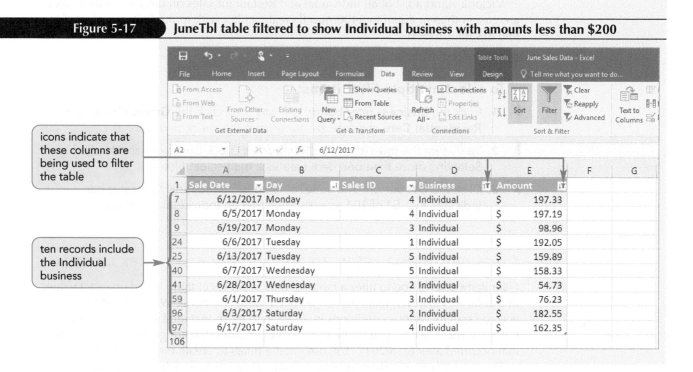

icons indicate that these columns are being used to filter the table

ten records include the Individual business

Clearing Filters

When you want to redisplay all of the data in a filtered table, you need to **clear** (or remove) the filters. When you clear a filter from a column, any other filters are still applied. For example, in the JuneTbl table, you would see all the Individual sales if you cleared the filter from the Amount field. To redisplay all of the sales in the table, you need to clear both the Amount filter and the Business filter. You will do this now to redisplay the entire table of sales.

To clear the filters to show all the records in the JuneTbl table:

▶ **1.** Click the **Amount** filter button 🔽, and then click **Clear Filter From "Amount"**. The Amount filter is removed from the table. The table shows only Individual sales because the Business filter is still in effect.

▶ **2.** Click the **Business** filter button 🔽, and then click **Clear Filter From "Business"**. The Business filter is removed, and all of the records in the JuneTbl table are displayed.

Selecting Multiple Filter Items

You can often find the information you need by selecting a single filter item from a list of filter items. Sometimes, however, you need to specify a more complex set of criteria to find the records you want. Earlier, you selected one filter item for the Business column and one filter item for the Amount column to display the records whose Business field value equals Individual *and* whose Amount field value equals less than or equal to $200. A record had to contain both values to be displayed. Now you want the Business column to display records whose Business field value equals Individual *or* Restaurant. The records must have one of these values to be displayed. You do this by selecting two filter items from the list of filter items. For example, checking the Individual and Restaurant check boxes in the Business filter items creates the filter "Business equals Individual" *or* "Business equals Restaurant."

Victoria wants a list of all Individual and Restaurant sales on days when their sales are greater than or equal to $400. You'll create a filter with multiple items selected to find this information.

To select multiple filter items:

▶ **1.** Click the **Business** filter button ⬇️, and then click the **Group Home** and **Residential Care** check boxes to remove the checkmarks.

▶ **2.** Verify that the **Individual** and **Restaurant** check boxes remain checked. Selecting more than one item creates a multiselect filter.

▶ **3.** Click the **OK** button. The JuneTbl table is filtered, and the status bar indicates that 52 of 104 records are either an Individual or a Restaurant.

Creating Criteria Filters to Specify More Complex Criteria

Filter items enable you to filter a range of data or an Excel table based on exact values in a column. However, many times you need broader criteria. With **criteria filters**, you can specify various conditions in addition to those that are based on an equals criterion. For example, you might want to find all sales that are greater than $400 or that occurred after 6/15/2017. You use criteria filters to create these conditions.

The types of criteria filters available change depending on whether the data in a column contains text, numbers, or dates. Figure 5-18 shows some of the options for text, number, and date criteria filters.

Figure 5-18	Options for text, number, and date criteria filters

Filter	Criteria	Records Displayed
Text	Equals	Exactly match the specified text
	Does Not Equal	Do not exactly match the specified text
	Begins With	Begin with the specified text
	Ends With	End with the specified text
	Contains	Have the specified text anywhere
	Does Not Contain	Do not have the specified text anywhere
Number	Equals	Exactly match the specified number
	Greater Than or Equal to	Are greater than or equal to the specified number
	Less Than	Are less than the specified number
	Between	Are greater than or equal to and less than or equal to the specified numbers
	Top 10	Are the top or bottom 10 (or the specified number)
	Above Average	Are greater than the average
Date	Today	Have the current date
	Last Week	Are in the prior week
	Next Month	Are in the month following the current month
	Last Quarter	Are in the previous quarter of the year (quarters defined as Jan, Feb, Mar; Apr, May, June; and so on)
	Year to Date	Are since January 1 of the current year to the current date
	Last Year	Are in the previous year (based on the current date)

You can use these criteria filters to find the answers to complex questions that you ask about data.

PROSKILLS

Problem Solving: Using Filters to Find Appropriate Data

Problem solving often requires finding information from a set of data to answer specific questions. When you're working with a range of data or an Excel table that contains hundreds or thousands of records, filters help you find that information without having to review each record in the table. For example, a human resources manager can use a filter to narrow the search for a specific employee out of the 2500 working at the company knowing only that the employee's first name is Elliot.

Filtering limits the data to display only the specific records that meet the criteria you set, enabling you to more effectively analyze the data. The following examples further illustrate how filtering can help people to quickly locate the data they need to answer a particular question:

- A customer service representative can use a filter to search a list of 10,000 products to find all products priced between $500 and $1000.
- A donations coordinator can use a filter to prepare a report that shows the donations received during the first quarter of the current year.
- An academic dean can use a filter to retrieve the names of all students with GPAs below 2.0 (probation) or above 3.5 (high honors).
- A professor who has 300 students in a psychology class can use a filter to develop a list of potential student assistants for next semester from the names the professor has highlighted in blue because their work was impressive. Filtering by the blue color generates a list of students to interview.
- The author of a guide to celebrity autographs can use a filter to determine whether an entry for a specific celebrity already exists in an Excel table and, if it does, determine whether the entry needs to be updated. If the entry does not exist, the author will know to add the autograph data to the table.

As these examples show, filtering is a useful tool for locating the answers to a wide variety of questions. You then can use this information to help you resolve problems.

Victoria wants you to display the records for sales to individuals or restaurants that are greater than $400. You'll modify the filtered JuneTbl table to add a criteria filter that includes records for Individual or Restaurant with Amounts greater than $400.

To add a number filter that shows sales amounts greater than $400:

1. Click the **Amount** filter button ▼, and then point to **Number Filters**. A menu opens, displaying the comparison operators available for columns of numbers.

2. Click **Greater Than**. The Custom AutoFilter dialog box opens. The upper-left box displays *is greater than*, which is the comparison operator you want to use to filter the Amount column. You enter the value you want to use for the filter criteria in the upper-right box, which, in this case, is $400.

3. Type **400** in the upper-right box. See Figure 5-19. You use the lower set of boxes if you want the filter to meet a second condition. You click the And option button to display rows that meet both criteria. You click the Or option button to display rows that meet either of the two criteria. You only want to set one criterion for this filter, so you'll leave the lower boxes empty.

Figure 5-19   **Custom AutoFilter dialog box**

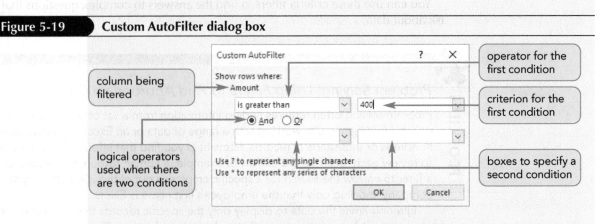

4. Click the **OK** button. The status bar indicates that 14 of 104 records were found. The 14 records that appear in the JuneTbl table are either Individual or Restaurant and have an Amount greater than $400.

Next, you'll sort the filtered data to show the largest Amount first. Although you can sort the data using Sort buttons, as you did earlier, these sort options are also available on the Filter menu. If you want to perform a more complex sort, you still need to use the Sort dialog box.

To sort the filtered table data:

1. Click the **Amount** filter button [🔽]. The Filter menu opens. The sort options are at the top of the menu.

2. Click **Sort Largest to Smallest**. The filtered records are sorted in descending order. The filtered table now displays records for individuals and restaurants with daily sales greater than $400 sorted in descending order. See Figure 5-20.

Figure 5-20   **Filtered and sorted JuneTbl table**

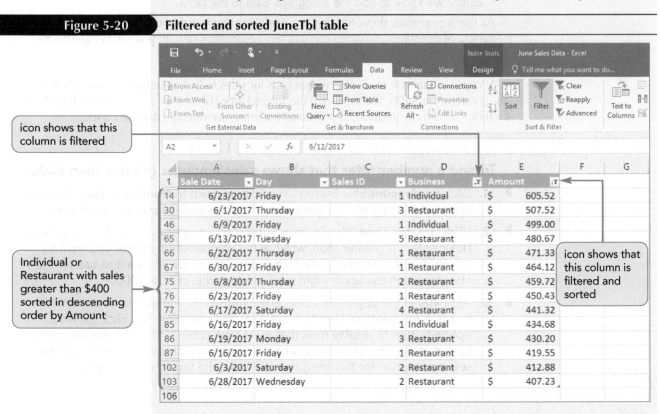

Victoria will use this data to help her decide which days she may need to hire additional workers. You need to restore the entire table of JuneTbl, which you can do by clearing all the filters at one time.

To clear all the filters from the JuneTbl table:

▶ **1.** On the ribbon, click the **Data** tab, if necessary.

▶ **2.** In the Sort & Filter group, click the **Clear** button. All of the records are redisplayed in the table.

Creating a Slicer to Filter Data in an Excel Table

Another way to filter an Excel table is with slicers. You can create a slicer for any field in the Excel table. You also can create more than one slicer for a table. Every slicer consists of an object that contains a button for each unique value in that field. For example, a slicer created for the Day field would include six buttons—one for each day of the week that Victoria's Veggies is open. One advantage of a slicer is that it clearly shows what filters are currently applied—the buttons for selected values are a different color. However, a slicer can take up a lot of space or hide data if there isn't a big enough blank area near the table. You can format the slicer and its buttons, changing its style, height, and width.

Victoria wants to be able to quickly filter the table to show sales for a specific Sales ID. You will add a slicer for the Sales ID field so she can do this.

To add the Sales ID slicer to the JuneTbl table:

▶ **1.** On the ribbon, click the **Table Tools Design** tab.

▶ **2.** In the Tools group, click the **Insert Slicer** button. The Insert Slicers dialog box opens, listing every available field in all tables in the workbook. You can select any or all of the fields.

▶ **3.** Click the **Sales ID** check box to insert a checkmark, and then click the **OK** button. The Sales ID slicer appears on the worksheet. All of the slicer buttons are selected, indicating that every Sales ID is included in the table.

▶ **4.** Drag the **Sales ID** slicer to the right of the JuneTbl table, placing its upper-left corner in cell G1.

▶ **5.** If the Slicer Tools Options tab does not appear on the ribbon, click the **Sales ID** slicer to select it. The Slicer Tools Options tab appears on the ribbon and is selected.

▶ **6.** In the Size group, enter **1.9"** in the Height box and **1.25"** in the Width box. The slicer is resized, eliminating the extra space below the buttons and to the right of the labels.

▶ **7.** In the Slicer Styles group, click the **More** button, and then click **Slicer Style Dark 6**. The slicer colors now match the formatting of the Excel table. See Figure 5-21.

Figure 5-21   **JuneTbl table with the Sales ID slicer**

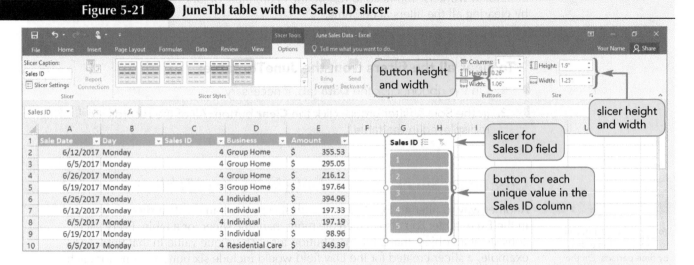

You can use the slicer to quickly filter records in an Excel table. Just click the slicer button corresponding to the data you want to display in the table. If you want to show more than one Sales ID, hold down the Ctrl key as you click the buttons that correspond to the additional data you want to show.

Victoria wants you to filter the JuneTbl table to display sales for Sales ID 1 and Sales ID 5. You will use the Sales ID slicer to do this.

To filter the JuneTbl table using the Sales ID slicer:

1. On the Sales ID slicer, click the **1** button. Only Sales ID 1 data appears in the JuneTbl table. All of the other buttons are gray, indicating that these Sales IDs are not included in the filtered data.

2. Press and hold the **Ctrl** key, click the **5** button, and then release the **Ctrl** key. Sales for Sales ID 5 are now added to the JuneTbl filtered table. See Figure 5-22.

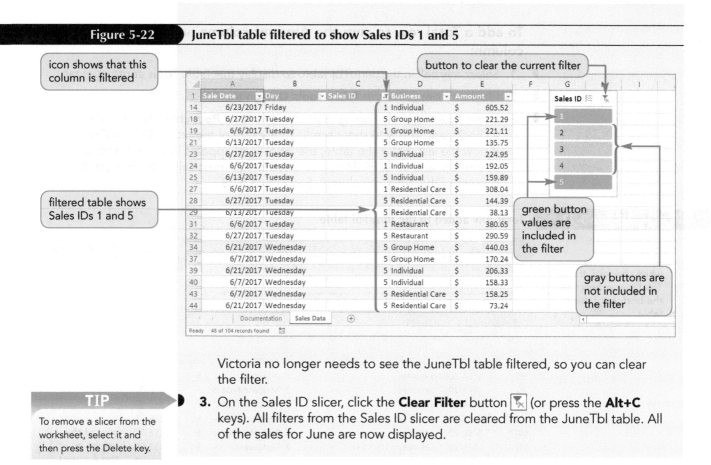

Figure 5-22   **JuneTbl table filtered to show Sales IDs 1 and 5**

icon shows that this column is filtered

button to clear the current filter

filtered table shows Sales IDs 1 and 5

green button values are included in the filter

gray buttons are not included in the filter

Ready   48 of 104 records found

Victoria no longer needs to see the JuneTbl table filtered, so you can clear the filter.

3. On the Sales ID slicer, click the **Clear Filter** button [icon] (or press the **Alt+C** keys). All filters from the Sales ID slicer are cleared from the JuneTbl table. All of the sales for June are now displayed.

Using the Total Row to Calculate Summary Statistics

The Total row is used to calculate summary statistics (including sum, average, count, maximum, and minimum) for any column in an Excel table. The Total row is inserted immediately after the last row of data in the table. A double-line border is inserted to indicate that the following row contains totals, and the label Total is added to the leftmost cell of the row. By default, the Total row adds the numbers in the last column of the Excel table or counts the number of records if the data in the last column contains text. When you click in each cell of the Total row, an arrow appears that you can click to open a list of the most commonly used functions. You can also select other functions by opening the Insert Functions dialog box.

Victoria wants to see the total amount of sales in June and the total number of records being displayed. You will add a Total row to the JuneTbl table and then use the SUM and COUNT functions to calculate these statistics for Victoria.

To add a Total row to sum the Amount column and count the Day column:

1. Select any cell in the JuneTbl table to display the Table Tools contextual tab.

2. On the ribbon, click the **Table Tools Design** tab.

3. In the Table Style Options group, click the **Total Row** check box to insert a checkmark. The worksheet scrolls to the end of the table. The Total row is now the last row in the table, the label Total appears in the leftmost cell of the row, and $27,739.26 appears in the rightmost cell of the row (at the bottom of the Amount column). See Figure 5-23.

Figure 5-23	Total row added to the JuneTbl table

when checked, the Total row appears at the bottom of the table

sum of the values in the Amount column

Total label

Next, you will use the COUNT function to add the number of records displayed.

4. Click cell **B106** (the Day cell in the Total row), and then click the **arrow** button to display a list of functions. None is the default function in all columns except the last column. See Figure 5-24.

Figure 5-24   Total row functions

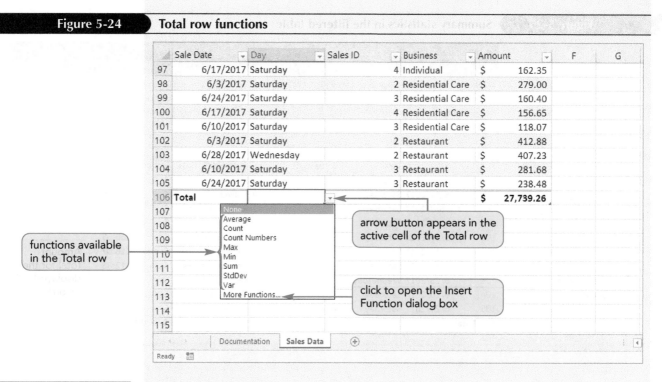

	Sale Date	Day	Sales ID	Business	Amount		F	G
97	6/17/2017	Saturday	4	Individual	$	162.35		
98	6/3/2017	Saturday	2	Residential Care	$	279.00		
99	6/24/2017	Saturday	3	Residential Care	$	160.40		
100	6/17/2017	Saturday	4	Residential Care	$	156.65		
101	6/10/2017	Saturday	3	Residential Care	$	118.07		
102	6/3/2017	Saturday	2	Restaurant	$	412.88		
103	6/28/2017	Wednesday	2	Restaurant	$	407.23		
104	6/10/2017	Saturday	3	Restaurant	$	281.68		
105	6/24/2017	Saturday	3	Restaurant	$	238.48		
106	Total				$	27,739.26		
107		None						
108		Average						
109		Count						
110		Count Numbers						
111		Max						
112		Min						
113		Sum						
114		StdDev						
115		Var						
		More Functions...						

functions available in the Total row

arrow button appears in the active cell of the Total row

click to open the Insert Function dialog box

Documentation   Sales Data   +

Ready

TIP

When you select Sum, Count, or Average, Excel uses the SUBTOTAL function to calculate the summary statistic in the Total row.

5. Click **Count**. The number 104, which is the number of records in the JuneTbl table, appears in the cell.

As you add, edit, or delete data in the table, the Total row values change. This also happens if you filter the table to show only some of the table data. Victoria wants the total sales to include sales from all seasonal employees (Sales IDs 2 through 4). You will filter the table to exclude Sales IDs 1 and 5, displaying the total Amount for Sales IDs 2 through 4 only. The COUNT function will also change to show only the number of transactions for the filtered data.

To filter sales by excluding sales from Sales ID 1 and Sales ID 5:

1. Press the **Ctrl+Home** keys to make cell A1 the active cell.

2. On the Sales ID slicer, click the **2** slicer button, press and hold the **Ctrl** key as you click the **3** and **4** slicer buttons, and then release the **Ctrl** key. The JuneTbl table is filtered to display sales for the seasonal employees in June.

3. Scroll to the end of the table. The Total row shows that the 56 records contain total sales of $14,393.01. See Figure 5-25.

Figure 5-25   Summary statistics in the filtered table

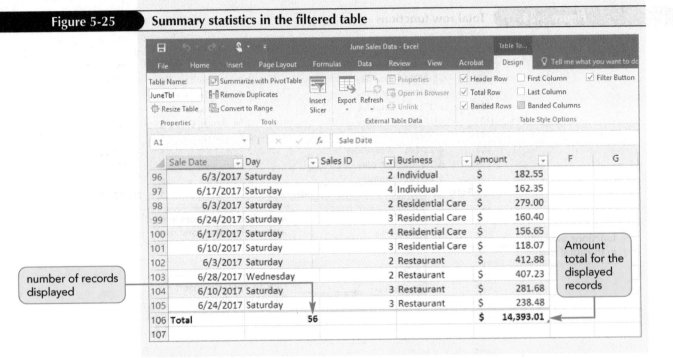

Splitting the Worksheet Window into Panes

You can split the worksheet window into two or four separate panes. This allows you to easily view data from several areas of the worksheet at the same time. Each pane has its own scroll bars so you can navigate easily within one pane or display different parts of the worksheet. You can move between panes using the mouse. To create two panes, select a cell in row 1 to split the worksheet vertically, or select a cell in column A to split the worksheet horizontally; to create four panes, select any other cell in the worksheet.

Victoria wants to view the JuneTbl summary totals at the same time she views the data on individual sales. You will divide the worksheet into two horizontal panes to view the sales records in the top pane and the totals in the bottom pane.

To split the Sales Data worksheet window into panes:

▶ **1.** Press the **Ctrl+Home** keys to make cell A1 at the top of the table the active cell.

▶ **2.** Select the cell in column A that is two rows above the last row visible on your screen.

▶ **3.** On the ribbon, click the **View** tab.

▶ **4.** In the Window group, click the **Split** button. The worksheet window splits into two panes. Each pane has its own set of scroll bars. The active cell is in the bottom pane below the split bar. See Figure 5-26.

Figure 5-26   Worksheet split into two panes

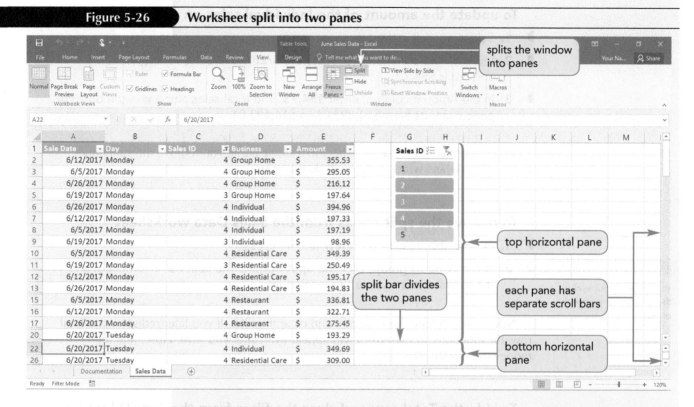

Trouble? If the window splits into four panes rather than two, click the Split button to remove all panes, and then repeat Step 1 through 4.

5. Using the lower scroll bar, scroll down until the Total row appears immediately below the split bar. See Figure 5-27.

Figure 5-27   Total row displayed in the bottom pane

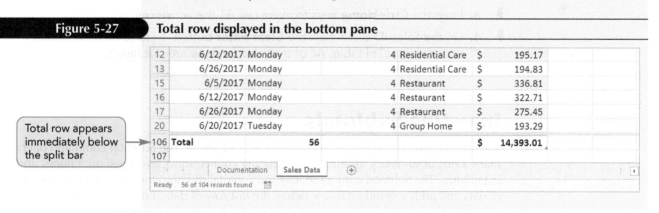

Victoria discovered a data entry error in the sales amount for Individual on 6/28/2017. It was entered as $54.73; the correct amount is $154.73. You will change the amount.

To update the amount of the Individual sales on 6/28/2017:

▶ **1.** Select any cell in the top pane.

▶ **2.** Use the Find command to locate the **6/28/2017** sales for **Individual**. The amount is $54.73.

▶ **3.** In the Amount column, enter **154.73**. The total sales amount in the bottom pane changes from $14,393.01 to $14,493.01.

When you want to see a worksheet in a single pane, you remove the split panes from the worksheet window. You will do this now.

To remove the split panes from the Sales Data worksheet

▶ **1.** On the ribbon, click the **View** tab, if necessary.

▶ **2.** In the Window group, click the **Split** button. The split bar is removed, and the worksheet is again a single window.

> **TIP**
> You can also double-click the split bar to remove the panes.

Now, you will hide the Total row and clear the filter. If you later redisplay the Total row, the functions you last used will appear even after you save, close, and then reopen the workbook.

To hide the Total row and clear the filter from the JuneTbl table:

▶ **1.** On the ribbon, click the **Table Tools Design** tab.

▶ **2.** In the Table Style Options group, click the **Total Row** check box to remove the checkmark. The Total row is no longer visible.

▶ **3.** Press the **Ctrl+Home** keys to make cell A1 the active cell.

▶ **4.** On the Sales ID slicer, click the **Clear Filter** button 🔽 to remove the filters from the JuneTbl table. All of the sales for June are displayed.

Inserting Subtotals

You can summarize data in a range by inserting subtotals. The Subtotal command offers many kinds of summary information, including counts, sums, averages, minimums, and maximums. The Subtotal command inserts a subtotal row into the range for each group of data and adds a grand total row below the last row of data. Because Excel inserts subtotals whenever the value in a specified field changes, you need to sort the data so that records with the same value in a specified field are grouped together *before* you use the Subtotal command. The Subtotal command cannot be used in an Excel table, so you must first convert the Excel table to a normal range.

REFERENCE

Calculating Subtotals for a Range of Data

- Sort the data by the column for which you want a subtotal.
- If the data is in an Excel table, on the Table Tools Design tab, in the Tools group, click the Convert to Range button, and then click the Yes button to convert the Excel table to a range.
- On the Data tab, in the Outline group, click the Subtotal button.
- Click the At each change in arrow, and then click the column that contains the group you want to subtotal.
- Click the Use function arrow, and then click the function you want to use to summarize the data.
- In the Add subtotal to box, click the check box for each column that contains the values you want to summarize.
- To calculate another category of subtotals, click the Replace current subtotals check box to remove the checkmark, and then repeat the previous three steps.
- Click the OK button.

Victoria wants to create a report that shows all the vegetable store's sales sorted by Sale Date with the total amount of the sales for each date. She also wants to see the total amount for each sale date after the last item of that date. The Subtotal command is a simple way to provide the information Victoria needs. First, you will sort the sales by Sale Date, then you will convert the Excel table to a normal range, and finally you will calculate subtotals in the Amount column for each Sale Date grouping to produce the results Victoria needs.

To sort the sales and convert the table to a range:

Be sure to sort the table and convert the table to a range before calculating subtotals.

▶ **1.** Click the **Sale Date** filter button ▼, and then click **Sort Oldest to Newest** on the Filter menu. The JuneTbl table is sorted in ascending order by the Sale Date field. This ensures one subtotal is created for each date.

▶ **2.** On the Table Tools Design tab, in the Tools group, click the **Convert to Range** button. A dialog box opens, asking if you want to convert the table to a normal range.

▶ **3.** Click the **Yes** button. The Excel table is converted to a range, and the Home tab is selected on the ribbon. You can tell the table data is now a normal range because the filter buttons, the Table Tools Design tab, and the slicer disappear.

Next, you'll calculate the subtotals.

To calculate the sales amount subtotals for each date:

▶ **1.** On the ribbon, click the **Data** tab.

▶ **2.** In the Outline group, click the **Subtotal** button. The Subtotal dialog box opens. See Figure 5-28.

Figure 5-28   Subtotal dialog box

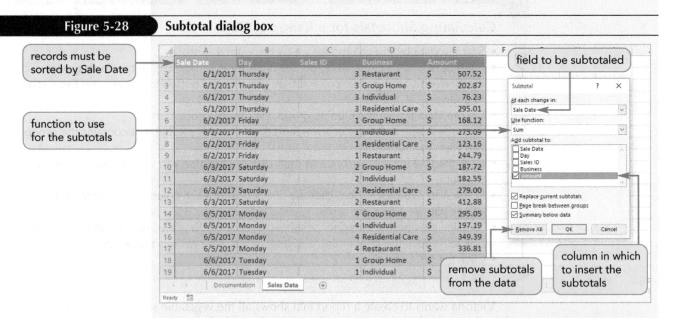

records must be sorted by Sale Date

function to use for the subtotals

field to be subtotaled

remove subtotals from the data

column in which to insert the subtotals

▶ **3.** If necessary, click the **At each change in** arrow, and then click **Sale Date**. This is the column you want Excel to use to determine where to insert the subtotals; it is the column you sorted. A subtotal will be calculated at every change in the Sale Date value.

▶ **4.** If necessary, click the **Use function** arrow, and then click **Sum**. The Use function list provides several options for subtotaling data, including counts, averages, minimums, maximums, and products.

▶ **5.** In the Add subtotal to box, make sure only the **Amount** check box is checked. This specifies the Amount field as the field to be subtotaled.

If the data already included subtotals, you would check the Replace current subtotals check box to replace the existing subtotals or uncheck the option to display the new subtotals on separate rows above the existing subtotals. Because the data has no subtotals, it makes no difference whether you select this option.

▶ **6.** Make sure the **Summary below data** check box is checked. This option places the subtotals below each group of data instead of above the first entry in each group and places the grand total at the end of the data instead of at the top of the column just below the row of column headings.

▶ **7.** Click the **OK** button. Excel inserts rows below each Sale Date group and displays the subtotals for the amount of each Sale Date in the Amount column. A series of Outline buttons appear to the left of the worksheet so you can display or hide the detail rows within each subtotal.

Trouble? If each item has a subtotal following it, or repeating subtotals appear for the same item, you probably forgot to sort the data by Sale Date. Click the Undo button ⟲ on the Quick Access Toolbar, sort the data by Sale Date, and then repeat Steps 1 through 7.

▶ **8.** Scroll through the data to see the subtotals below each category and the grand total at the end of the data. See Figure 5-29.

Figure 5-29   Subtotals and grand total added to the sales data

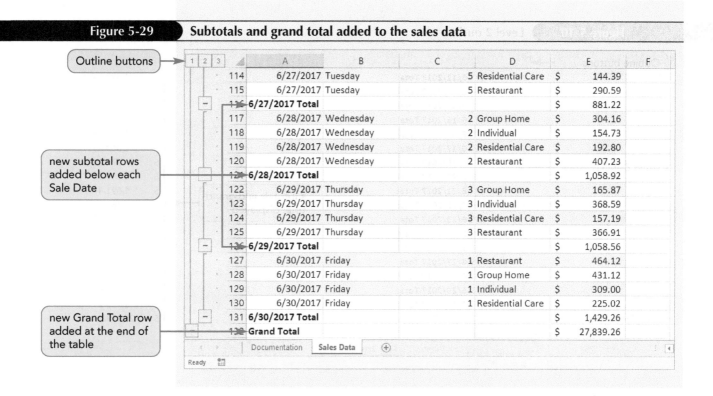

Outline buttons

new subtotal rows added below each Sale Date

new Grand Total row added at the end of the table

	A	B	C	D	E	F
114	6/27/2017	Tuesday	5	Residential Care	$ 144.39	
115	6/27/2017	Tuesday	5	Restaurant	$ 290.59	
116	6/27/2017 Total				$ 881.22	
117	6/28/2017	Wednesday	2	Group Home	$ 304.16	
118	6/28/2017	Wednesday	2	Individual	$ 154.73	
119	6/28/2017	Wednesday	2	Residential Care	$ 192.80	
120	6/28/2017	Wednesday	2	Restaurant	$ 407.23	
121	6/28/2017 Total				$ 1,058.92	
122	6/29/2017	Thursday	3	Group Home	$ 165.87	
123	6/29/2017	Thursday	3	Individual	$ 368.59	
124	6/29/2017	Thursday	3	Residential Care	$ 157.19	
125	6/29/2017	Thursday	3	Restaurant	$ 366.91	
126	6/29/2017 Total				$ 1,058.56	
127	6/30/2017	Friday	1	Restaurant	$ 464.12	
128	6/30/2017	Friday	1	Group Home	$ 431.12	
129	6/30/2017	Friday	1	Individual	$ 309.00	
130	6/30/2017	Friday	1	Residential Care	$ 225.02	
131	6/30/2017 Total				$ 1,429.26	
132	Grand Total				$ 27,839.26	

Documentation   Sales Data

Ready

Using the Subtotal Outline View

The Subtotal feature "outlines" the worksheet so you can control the level of detail that is displayed. The three Outline buttons at the top of the outline area, shown in Figure 5-29, allow you to show or hide different levels of detail in the worksheet. By default, the highest level is active; in this case, Level 3. Level 3 displays the most detail—the individual sales records, the subtotals, and the grand total. Level 2 displays the subtotals and the grand total but not the individual records. Level 1 displays only the grand total.

Victoria wants you to isolate the different subtotal sections so that she can focus on them individually. You will use the Outline buttons to prepare a report for Victoria that includes only subtotals and the grand total.

To use the Outline buttons to hide records:

▶ 1. Click the **Level 2 Outline** button 2 , and then scroll to view the daily subtotals and grand total. The individual sales records are hidden; only the subtotals for each Sale Date and the grand total are displayed. See Figure 5-30.

Figure 5-30   Level 2 outline

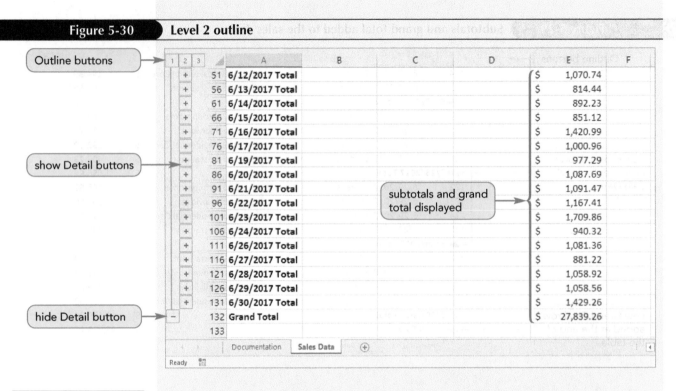

Outline buttons

show Detail buttons

subtotals and grand total displayed

hide Detail button

TIP

To collapse the outline and hide the rows with details, click the Hide Detail button.

2. Click the **Show Detail** button ⊞ to the left of 6/30/2017 to expand the outline and show the details of daily sales by unhiding rows for this date. Sales for each Business on 6/30/2017 are now displayed.

3. Click the **Level 1 Outline** button ①. The individual sales records and the subtotals for each Sale Date are hidden. Only the grand total remains visible.

4. Click the **Level 3 Outline** button ③, and then scroll up. All the records along with the subtotals and the grand total are visible.

Victoria has completed her review of the daily sales report for June. She asks you to remove the subtotals from the data.

To remove the subtotals from the Sales Data worksheet:

1. On the Data tab, in the Outline group, click the **Subtotal** button. The Subtotal dialog box opens.

2. Click the **Remove All** button. The subtotals are removed from the data, and only the records appear in the worksheet.

You'll reset the JuneTbl Excel table.

3. Make sure the active cell is a cell within the normal range of data.

4. On the ribbon, click the **Insert** tab.

5. In the Tables group, click the **Table** button. The Create Table dialog box opens.

6. Click the **OK** button to create the Excel table, and then click any cell in the table. The table structure is active.

7. On the Table Tools Design tab, in the Properties group, type **JuneTbl** in the Table Name box, and then press the **Enter** key. The Excel table is again named JuneTbl.

In this session, you filtered the table data, inserted a Total row, and determined totals and subtotals for the data. In the next session, you will work with PivotTables and PivotCharts to gather information to help Victoria with staffing and storefront opening decisions.

REVIEW

Session 5.2 Quick Check

1. Explain filtering.

2. How can you display a list of economics majors with a GPA less than 2.5 from an Excel table with records for 1000 students?

3. An Excel table includes records for 500 employees. What can you use to calculate the average salary of employees in the finance department?

4. What is a slicer, and how does it work?

5. If you have a list of employees that includes fields for gender and salary, among others, how can you determine the average salary for females using the Total row feature?

6. Explain the relationship between the Sort and Subtotal commands.

7. After you display subtotals, how can you use the Outline buttons?

Session 5.3 Visual Overview:

This PivotTable uses the data from the Business field as column labels.

A PivotTable is an interactive table used to group and summarize either a range of data or an Excel table into a concise tabular format for reporting and analysis.

This PivotTable uses the data from the Day field as row labels.

Value fields are the fields that contain summary data in a PivotTable. This PivotTable uses the total of Amount as the values field.

A PivotChart is a graphical representation of the data in the PivotTable.

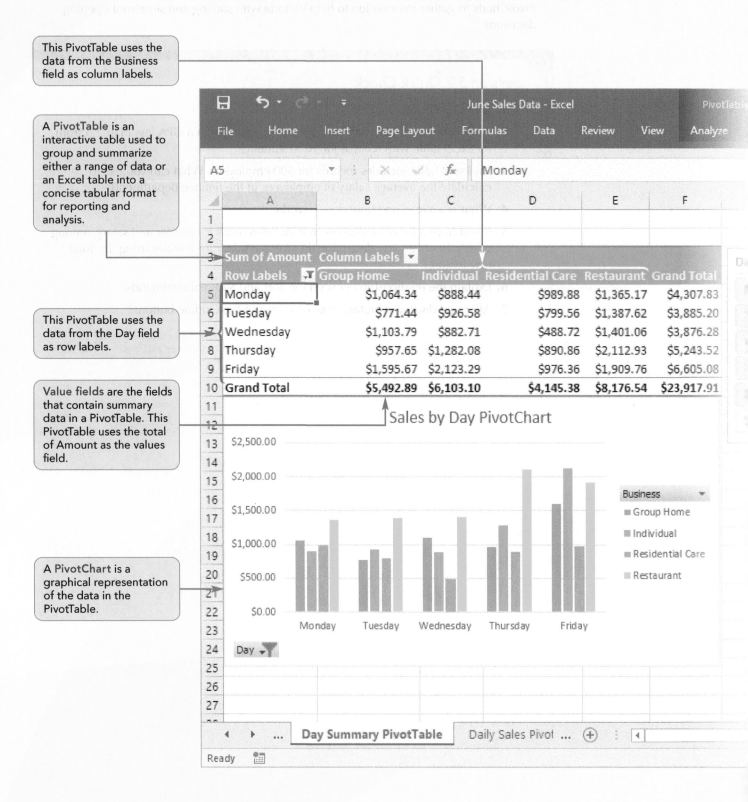

Sum of Amount	Column Labels ▼				
Row Labels ▼	Group Home	Individual	Residential Care	Restaurant	Grand Total
Monday	$1,064.34	$888.44	$989.88	$1,365.17	$4,307.83
Tuesday	$771.44	$926.58	$799.56	$1,387.62	$3,885.20
Wednesday	$1,103.79	$882.71	$488.72	$1,401.06	$3,876.28
Thursday	$957.65	$1,282.08	$890.86	$2,112.93	$5,243.52
Friday	$1,595.67	$2,123.29	$976.36	$1,909.76	$6,605.08
Grand Total	$5,492.89	$6,103.10	$4,145.38	$8,176.54	$23,917.91

Sales by Day PivotChart

PivotTable and PivotChart

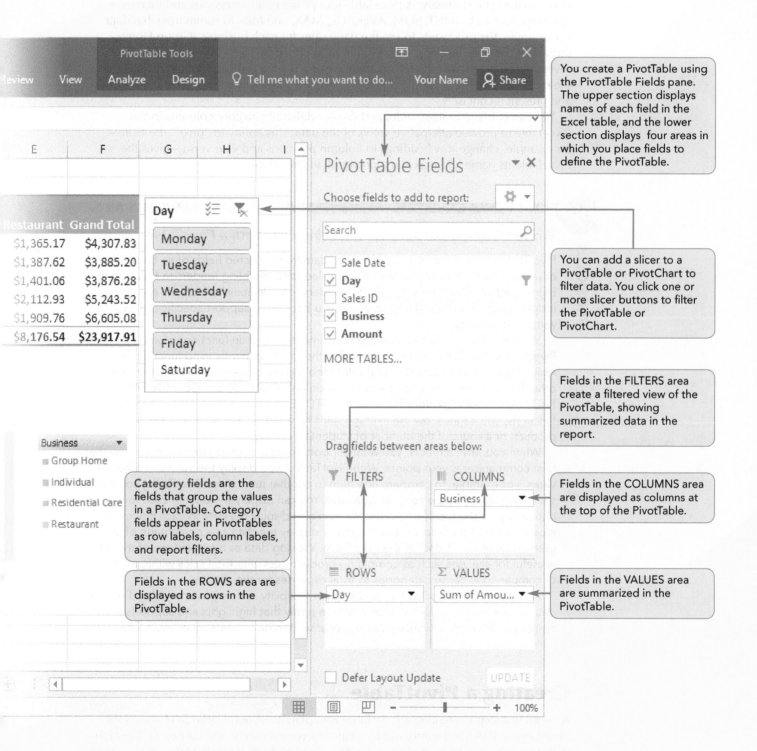

You create a PivotTable using the PivotTable Fields pane. The upper section displays names of each field in the Excel table, and the lower section displays four areas in which you place fields to define the PivotTable.

You can add a slicer to a PivotTable or PivotChart to filter data. You click one or more slicer buttons to filter the PivotTable or PivotChart.

Fields in the FILTERS area create a filtered view of the PivotTable, showing summarized data in the report.

Category fields are the fields that group the values in a PivotTable. Category fields appear in PivotTables as row labels, column labels, and report filters.

Fields in the ROWS area are displayed as rows in the PivotTable.

Fields in the COLUMNS area are displayed as columns at the top of the PivotTable.

Fields in the VALUES area are summarized in the PivotTable.

Analyzing Data with PivotTables

An Excel table can contain a wealth of information. However, when the table contains large amounts of detailed data, it often becomes more difficult to obtain a clear, overall view of that information. You can use a PivotTable to help organize the data into a meaningful summary. A PivotTable groups data into categories and then uses functions such as COUNT, SUM, AVERAGE, MAX, and MIN to summarize that data. For example, Victoria wants to see the daily sales for each business (Group Home, Individual, Residential Care, and Restaurant) grouped by week. Although there are several ways to generate the information Victoria needs, you can use a PivotTable like the one shown in the Session 5.3 Visual Overview to generate this information quickly and present it concisely.

You can easily rearrange, hide, and display different category columns in the PivotTable to provide alternative views of the data. This ability to "pivot" the table—for example, change row headings to column positions and vice versa—gives the PivotTable its name and makes it a powerful analytical tool.

PROSKILLS

Written Communication: Summarizing Data with a PivotTable

PivotTables are a great way to summarize data from selected fields of an Excel table or range. The PivotTable omits all the detailed data, enabling readers to focus on the bigger picture. This makes it easier for readers to understand the results and gain insights about the topic. It can also help you back up or support specific points in written documents.

You can show summaries in written documents based on function results in PivotTables. The SUM function is probably the most frequently used function. For example, you might show the total sales for a region. However, you can use many other functions to summarize the data, including COUNT, AVERAGE, MIN, MAX, PRODUCT, COUNT NUMBERS, STDDEV, STDDEVP, VAR, and VARP. Using these functions, you might show the average sales for a region, the minimum price of a product, or a count of the number of students by major.

When you write a report, you want supporting data to be presented in the way that best communicates your points. With PivotTables, you display the values in different views. For example, to compare one item to another item in the PivotTable, you can show the values as a percentage of a total. You can display the data in each row as a percentage of the total for the row. You can also display the data in each column as a percentage of the total for the column or display the data as a percentage of the grand total of all the data in the PivotTable. Viewing data as a percentage of the total is useful for analyses such as comparing product sales with total sales within a region or comparing expense categories to total expenses for the year.

As you can see, PivotTables provide great flexibility in how you analyze and display data. This makes it easier to present data in a way that highlights and supports the points you are communicating, making your written documents much more effective.

Creating a PivotTable

A useful first step in creating a PivotTable is to plan its layout. Figure 5-31 shows the PivotTable that Victoria wants you to create. As you can see in the figure, the PivotTable will show the total Amount of the sales organized by Sales ID, Sale Date, and Business.

Figure 5-31	PivotTable plan

Sales ID	XXXX					
Total Sales						
Sale Date		Group Home	Individual	Residential Care	Restaurant	Total
Total						

You are ready to create the PivotTable summarizing the total sales for Victoria.

Creating a PivotTable

- Click in the Excel table (or select the range of data for the PivotTable).
- On the Insert tab, in the Tables group, click the PivotTable button.
- Click the Select a table or range option button, and then verify the reference in the Table/Range box.
- Click the New Worksheet option button, or click the Existing Worksheet option button and specify a cell.
- Click the OK button.
- Click the check boxes for the fields you want to add to the PivotTable (or drag fields to the appropriate box in the layout section).
- If needed, drag fields to different boxes in the layout section.

When you create a PivotTable, you need to specify where to find the data for the PivotTable. The data can be in an Excel table or range in the current workbook or an external data source such as an Access database file. You also must specify whether to place the PivotTable in a new or an existing worksheet. If you place the PivotTable in an existing worksheet, you must also specify the cell in which you want the upper-left corner of the PivotTable to appear.

To create the PivotTable that will provide the information Victoria needs, you will use the JuneTbl table and place the PivotTable in a new worksheet.

To create a PivotTable using the JuneTbl table:

1. If you took a break after the previous session, make sure the June Sales Data workbook is open, the Sales Data worksheet is the active sheet, and the JuneTbl table is active.

2. On the ribbon, click the **Insert** tab.

3. In the Tables group, click the **PivotTable** button. The Create PivotTable dialog box opens. See Figure 5-32.

Figure 5-32   **Create PivotTable dialog box**

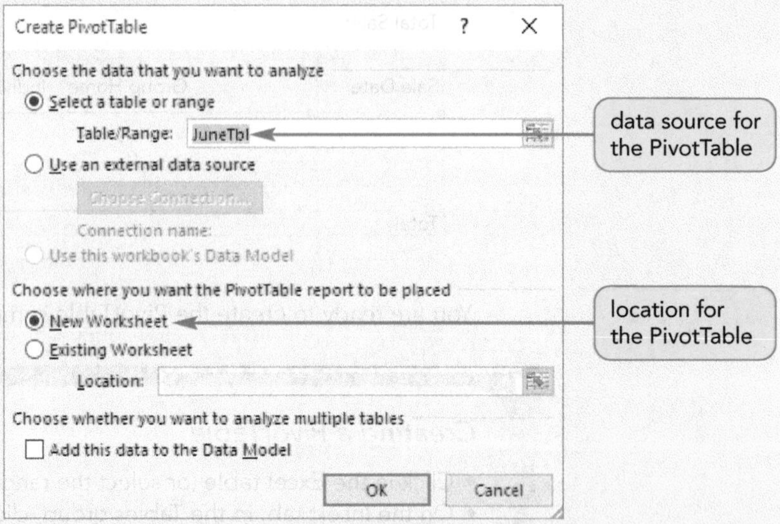

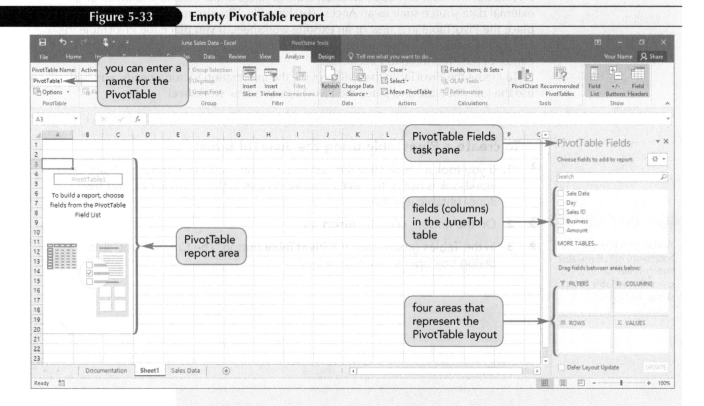

4. Make sure the **Select a table or range** option button is selected and **JuneTbl** appears in the Table/Range box.

5. Click the **New Worksheet** option button, if necessary. This sets the PivotTable report to be placed in a new worksheet.

6. Click the **OK** button. A new worksheet, Sheet1, is inserted to the left of the Sales Data worksheet. On the left is the empty PivotTable report area, where the finished PivotTable will be placed. On the right is the PivotTable Fields task pane, which you use to build the PivotTable. The PivotTable Tools tabs appear on the ribbon. See Figure 5-33.

Figure 5-33   **Empty PivotTable report**

> **Trouble?** If the PivotTable Fields task pane is not displayed, you need to display it. On the PivotTable Tools Analyze tab, in the Show group, click the Field List button.

Adding Fields to a PivotTable

To display data in a PivotTable, you add fields to the PivotTable. In PivotTable terminology, fields that contain summary data are Values fields, and fields that group the values in the PivotTable are Category fields. Category fields appear in PivotTables as row labels, column labels, and filters. You add fields to a PivotTable from the PivotTable Fields task pane, which is divided into two sections. The upper section lists the names of each field in the data source, which is the JuneTbl table, in this case. You select a field check box or drag the field into the lower section to add that field to the FILTERS, ROWS, COLUMNS, or VALUES area (described in Figure 5-34). The placement of fields in the area boxes determines the layout of the PivotTable.

Figure 5-34	Layout areas for a PivotTable

Area	Description
ROWS	Fields placed in this area appear as Row Labels on the left side of the PivotTable. Each unique item in this field is displayed in a separate row. Row fields can be nested.
COLUMNS	Fields placed in this area appear as Column Labels on the top of the PivotTable. Each unique item in this field is displayed in a separate column. Column fields can be nested.
FILTERS	Fields placed in this area appear as top-level filters above the PivotTable. These fields are used to select one or more items to display in the PivotTable.
VALUES	Fields placed in this area are numbers that are summarized in the PivotTable.

> **TIP**
>
> By default, Excel uses the COUNT function for nonnumeric fields placed in the VALUES area.

Typically, fields with text or nonnumeric data are placed in the ROWS area. Fields with numeric data are most often placed in the VALUES area and by default are summarized with the SUM function. If you want to use a different function, click the field button in the VALUES area, click Value Field Settings to open the Value Field Settings dialog box, select a different function such as AVERAGE, COUNT, MIN, MAX, and so on, and then click the OK button. You can move fields between the areas at any time to change how data is displayed in the PivotTable. You can also add the same field to the VALUES area more than once so you can calculate its sum, average, and count in one PivotTable.

Victoria wants to see the total value of sales by Sales ID. Then, within each Sales ID, she wants to see total sales for each Day. Finally, she wants each Day further divided to display sales for each Business. You'll add fields to the PivotTable so that the Sales ID, Sale Date, and Business fields are row labels, and the Amount field is the data to be summarized as the Values field.

To add fields to the PivotTable:

▶ 1. In the PivotTable Fields task pane, drag **Sales ID** from the upper section to the ROWS area in the lower section. The Sales ID field appears in the ROWS area, and the unique values in the Sales ID field—1, 2, 3, 4, and 5—appear in the PivotTable report area. See Figure 5-35.

Figure 5-35   **PivotTable with the Sales ID field values as row labels**

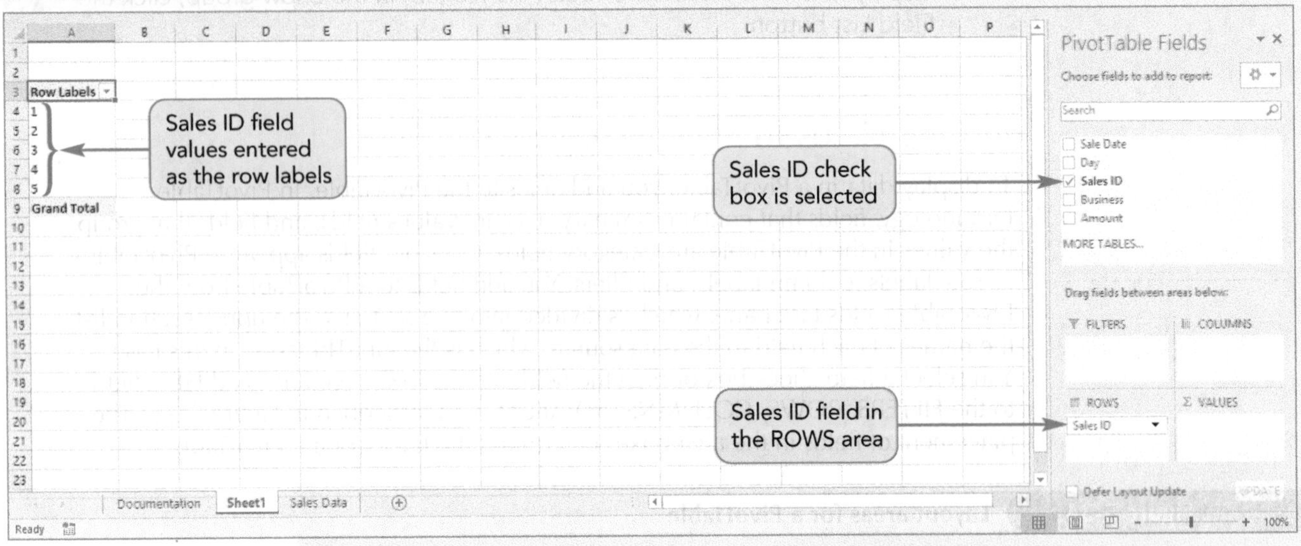

Trouble? If the Sales ID field appears in the VALUES area, you probably checked the Sales ID field, which places fields with numeric values in the VALUES area. Drag the Sales ID field from the VALUES area to the ROWS area.

▶ **2.** In the PivotTable Fields task pane, click the **Amount** check box. The Sum of Amount button is placed in the VALUES box because the field contains numeric values. The PivotTable groups the items from the JuneTbl table by Sales ID and calculates the total Amount for each week. The grand total appears at the bottom of the PivotTable. See Figure 5-36.

Figure 5-36   **PivotTable shows the sum of the Amounts field for each Sales ID**

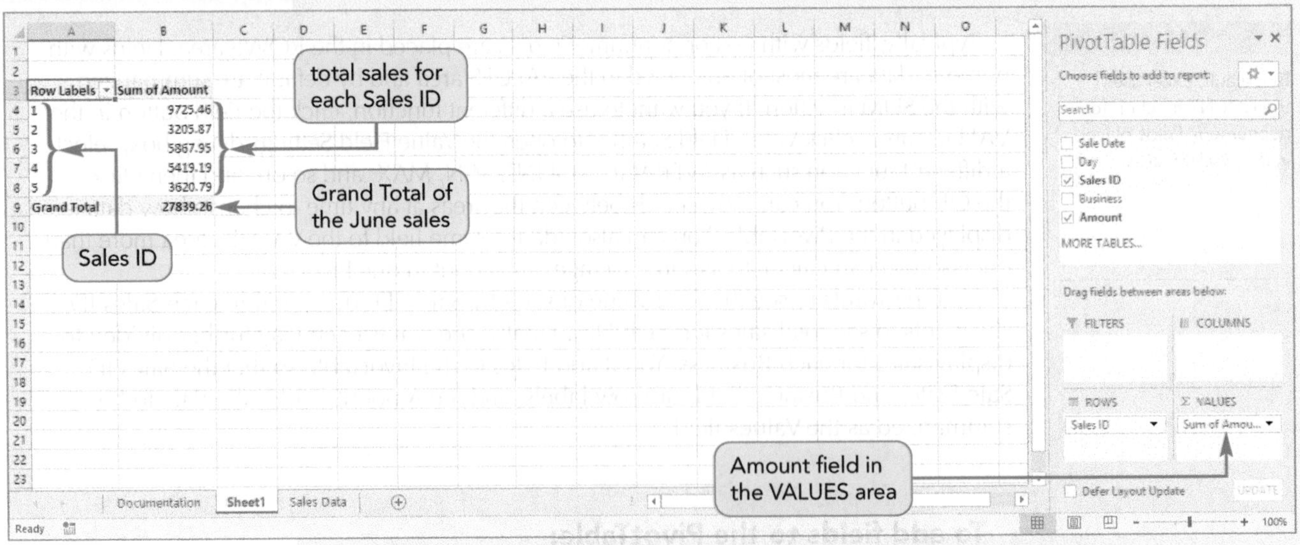

Next, you'll add the Sale Date and Business fields to the PivotTable.

▶ **3.** In the PivotTable Fields task pane, click the **Sale Date** check box. The Sale Date field appears in the ROWS area box below the Sales ID field, and the unique items in the Sale Date field are indented below each Sales ID field item in the PivotTable report.

Trouble? If the PivotTable Fields task pane is not visible, the active cell is probably not in the PivotTable. Click any cell within the PivotTable to redisplay the PivotTable Fields task pane. If the PivotTable Fields task pane is still not visible, click the PivotTable Tools Analyze tab, and then click the Field List button in the Show group.

▶ **4.** In the PivotTable Fields task pane, click the **Business** check box. The Business field appears in the ROWS area below the Sale Date field, and its unique items are indented below the Sales ID and Sale Date fields already in the PivotTable. See Figure 5-37.

| Figure 5-37 | PivotTable with Sales ID, Sale Date, and Business field items as row labels |

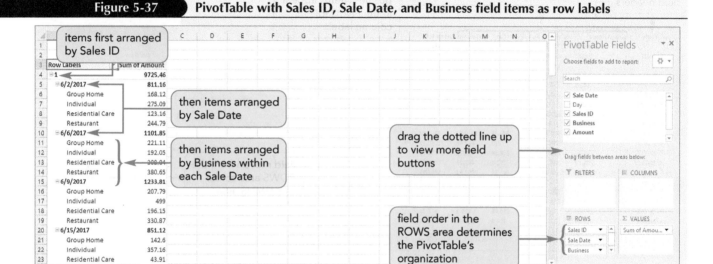

Trouble? If the Business field button is not visible in the ROWS area, drag the dotted line above the "Drag fields between areas below" label up until the Business field button is visible.

If a PivotTable becomes too detailed or confusing, you can always remove one of its fields. In the PivotTable Fields task pane, click the check box of the field you want to remove. The field is then deleted from the PivotTable and the area box.

Changing the Layout of a PivotTable

You can add, remove, and rearrange fields to change the PivotTable's layout. Recall that the benefit of a PivotTable is that it summarizes large amounts of data into a readable format. After you create a PivotTable, you can view the same data in different ways. Each time you make a change in the areas section of the PivotTable Fields task pane, the PivotTable layout is rearranged. This ability to "pivot" the table—for example, change row headings to column positions and vice versa—makes the PivotTable a powerful analytical tool.

Based on Victoria's PivotTable plan that is shown in Figure 5-31, the Business field items should be positioned as columns instead of rows in the PivotTable. You'll move the Business field now to produce the layout Victoria wants.

To move the Business field to the COLUMNS area:

▶ **1.** In the PivotTable Fields task pane, locate the **Business** field button in the ROWS area.

▶ **2.** Drag the **Business** field button from the ROWS area to the COLUMNS area. The PivotTable is rearranged so that the Business field is a column label instead of a row label. See Figure 5-38.

| Figure 5-38 | PivotTable rearranged with Business as a column label |

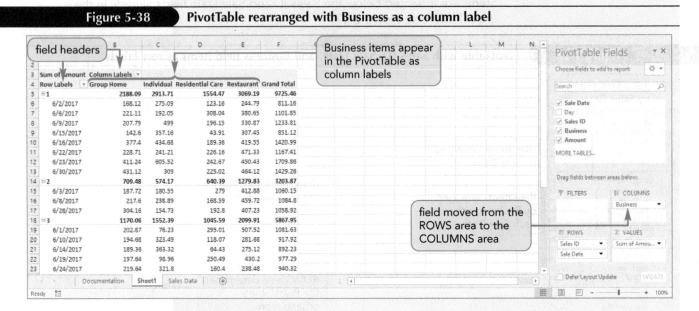

The PivotTable now has the layout that Victoria wants.

Choosing a Report Layout

There are three different report layouts available for PivotTables. The report layout shown in Figure 5-38, which is referred to as the Compact Form, is the default layout. It places all fields from the ROWS area in a single column and indents the items from each field below the outer fields. In the Outline Form layout, each field in the ROWS area takes a column in the PivotTable. The subtotal for each group appears above every group. The Tabular Form layout displays one column for each field and leaves space for column headers. A total for each group appears below each group. To select a different report layout, click the Report Layout button in the Layout group on the PivotTable Tools Design tab.

Formatting a PivotTable

Like worksheet cells and Excel tables, you can quickly format a PivotTable report using one of the built-in styles available in the PivotTable Styles gallery. As with cell and table styles, you can point to any style in the gallery to see a Live Preview of the PivotTable with that style. You also can modify the appearance of PivotTables by adding or removing banded rows, banded columns, row headers, and column headers.

Victoria wants you to apply the Pivot Style Medium 14 style, which makes each group in the PivotTable stand out and makes subtotals in the report easier to find.

To apply the Pivot Style Medium 14 style to the PivotTable:

▶ **1.** Make sure the active cell is in the PivotTable.

▶ **2.** On the ribbon, click the **PivotTable Tools Design** tab.

▶ **3.** In the PivotTable Styles group, click the **More** button to open the PivotTable Styles gallery.

▶ **4.** Move the pointer over each style to see the Live Preview of the PivotTable report with that style.

▶ **5.** Click the **Pivot Style Medium 14** style (the last style in the second row of the Medium section). The style is applied to the PivotTable.

You can format cells in a PivotTable the same way that you format cells in a worksheet. This enables you to further customize the look of the PivotTable by changing the font, color, alignment, and number formats of specific cells in the PivotTable. Victoria wants the numbers in the PivotTable to be quickly recognized as dollars. You'll change the total Amount values in the PivotTable to the Currency style.

To format the Amount field in the PivotTable as currency:

▶ **1.** In the VALUES area of the PivotTable Fields task pane, click the **Sum of Amount** button. A shortcut menu opens with options related to that field.

▶ **2.** Click the **Value Field Settings** button on the shortcut menu. The Value Field Settings dialog box opens. See Figure 5-39.

Figure 5-39	Value Field Settings dialog box

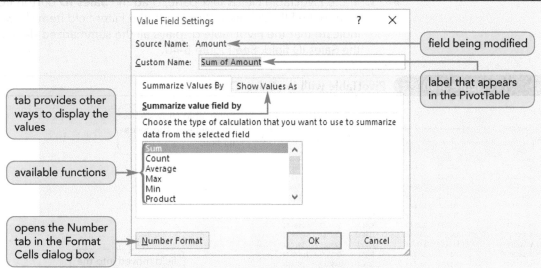

▶ **3.** In the Custom Name box, type **Total Sales** as the label for the field. You will leave Sum as the summary function for the field; however, you could select a different function.

▶ **4.** Click the **Number Format** button. The Format Cells dialog box opens. This is the same dialog box you have used before to format numbers in worksheet cells.

TIP

You can also right-click in the PivotTable data area and click Number Format or Format Cells to quickly format the PivotTable.

▶ **5.** In the Category box, click **Currency**. You will use the default number of decimal places, currency symbol, and negative number format.

▶ **6.** Click the **OK** button. The numbers in the PivotTable will be formatted as currency with two decimal places.

▶ **7.** Click the **OK** button. The Value Field Settings dialog box closes. The PivotTable changes to reflect the label you entered, and the number format for the field changes to currency.

Filtering a PivotTable

As you analyze the data in a PivotTable, you might want to show only a portion of the total data. You can do this by filtering the PivotTable. Filtering a field lets you focus on a subset of items in that field.

Adding a Field to the FILTERS Area

You can drag one or more fields to the FILTERS area of the PivotTable Fields task pane to change what values are displayed in the PivotTable. A field placed in the FILTERS area provides a way to filter the PivotTable so that it displays summarized data for one or more items or all items in that field. For example, placing the Sales ID field in the FILTERS area allows you to view or print the total sales for all Sales IDs, a specific Sales ID such as 1, or multiple Sales IDs such as 2 through 5.

Victoria wants you to move the Sales ID field from the ROWS area to the FILTERS area so that she can focus on specific subsets of the sales.

To add the Sales ID field to the FILTERS area:

▶ **1.** In the PivotTable Fields task pane, drag the **Sales ID** button from the ROWS area to the FILTERS area. By default, the Filter field item shows "(All)" to indicate that the PivotTable displays all the summarized data associated with the Sales ID field. See Figure 5-40.

Figure 5-40   **PivotTable with the Sales ID filter**

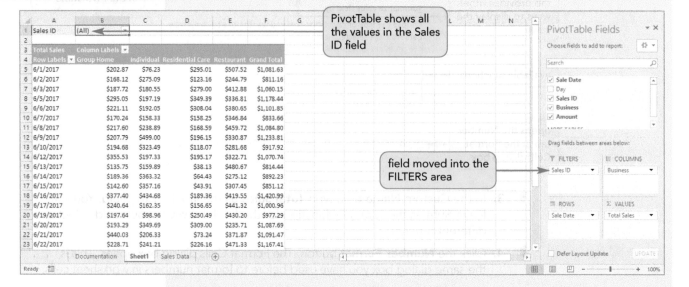

Next, you'll filter the summarized report to show only sales for Sales ID 2.

2. In cell B1, click the **filter** button [▼]. The Filter menu opens, showing the field items displayed.

3. In the Filter menu, click **2**, and then click the **OK** button. The PivotTable displays the total Amount of sales on dates associated with Sales ID 2. The filter button changes to indicate that the PivotTable is currently filtered. See Figure 5-41.

Figure 5-41 **Sales ID filter set to show sales for Sales ID 2**

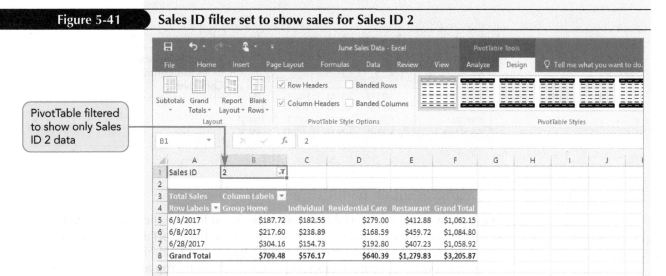

PivotTable filtered to show only Sales ID 2 data

Filtering PivotTable Fields

Another way that you can filter field items in the PivotTable is by using the Filter menu, which you open by clicking the Row Labels filter button or the Column Labels filter button. You then check or uncheck items to show or hide them, respectively, in the PivotTable.

Victoria wants to exclude Residential Care from the analysis. She asks you to remove the Residential Care sales from the PivotTable.

To filter Residential Care from the Business column labels:

1. In the PivotTable, click the **Column Labels** filter button [▼]. The Filter menu opens, listing the items in the Business field.

2. Click the **Residential Care** check box to remove the checkmark. The Select All check box is filled with black indicating that all items are not selected.

3. Click the **OK** button. The Residential Care column is removed from the PivotTable. The PivotTable includes sales from only Group Home, Individual, and Restaurant. See Figure 5-42. You can show the hidden objects by clicking the Column Labels filter button and checking the Residential Care check box.

Figure 5-42 **PivotTable report filtered by Business**

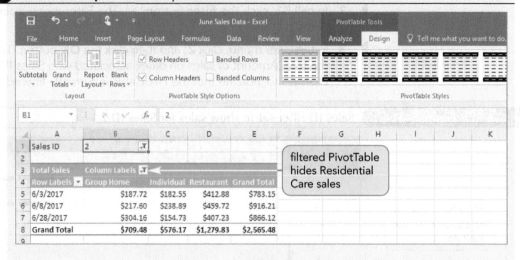

Creating a Slicer to Filter a PivotTable

Another way to filter a PivotTable is with a slicer, just like the slicer you created to filter an Excel table. You can create a slicer for any field in the PivotTable Fields task pane. The slicer contains a button for each unique value in that field. You can format the slicer and its buttons, changing its style, height, and width. You also can create more than one slicer at a time. For example, you can have a slicer for Sales ID that has a button for each unique Sales ID value and a second slicer for Business. This allows you to filter a PivotTable report so that it displays the sales amount for Sales ID 2, Group Home, Individual, and Restaurant by clicking the corresponding slicer buttons.

Victoria wants flexibility in how she views the data in the PivotTable, so she asks you to add a slicer for the Sales ID field to the current PivotTable.

To add the Sales ID slicer to the PivotTable:

▶ 1. On the ribbon, click the **PivotTable Tools Analyze** tab.

▶ 2. In the Filter group, click the **Insert Slicer** button. The Insert Slicers dialog box opens, displaying a list of available PivotTable fields. You can select any or all of the fields.

▶ 3. Click the **Sales ID** check box to insert a checkmark, and then click the **OK** button. The Sales ID slicer appears on the worksheet. Because the PivotTable is already filtered to display only the results for Sales ID 2, the 2 button is selected. The other slicer buttons are white because those weeks have been filtered and are not part of the PivotTable.

▶ 4. If the Slicer Tools Options tab does not appear on the ribbon, click the **Sales ID** slicer to select it.

▶ 5. On the Slicer Tools Options tab, in the Size group, change the height to **1.9"** and change the width to **1.25"**. The slicer object is resized, eliminating the extra space below the buttons and to the right of the labels.

▶ 6. In the Slicer Styles group, click the **More** button, and then click **Slicer Style Dark 6**. The slicer colors now match the PivotTable.

▶ 7. Drag the **Sales ID** slicer to the right of the PivotTable, placing its upper-left corner in cell G3. See Figure 5-43.

| Figure 5-43 | Sales ID slicer |

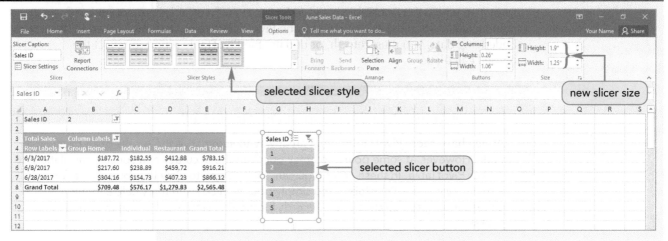

Victoria wants you to display the results of the PivotTable for all the seasonal employees in June—Sales IDs 2, 3, and 4. You can do this quickly using the Sales ID slicer.

To filter the PivotTable using the Sales ID slicer:

▸ **1.** Press and hold the **Ctrl** key, click the **3** button, and then release the **Ctrl** key. Sales ID 3 data also appears on the PivotTable.

▸ **2.** Press and hold the **Ctrl** key, click the **4** button, and then release the **Ctrl** key. Data for Sales ID 4 is added to the PivotTable.

TIP

To remove all filters from the PivotTable, click the Clear Filter button in the upper-right corner of the slicer.

▸ **3.** Click the **Sales ID 2** slicer button. Only the sales for Sales ID 2 are displayed in the PivotTable.

After you have finished creating a PivotTable, you can hide the PivotTable Fields task pane so that it won't appear when a cell is selected in the PivotTable. You can also assign more descriptive names to the PivotTable as well as the worksheet that contains the PivotTable.

To hide the PivotTable Fields task pane and rename the PivotTable and worksheet:

▸ **1.** Click in the PivotTable to display the PivotTable Tools contextual tabs on the ribbon.

▸ **2.** Click the **PivotTable Tools Analyze** tab.

▸ **3.** In the Show group, click the **Field List** button. The PivotTable Fields task pane is hidden and won't reappear when a cell in the PivotTable is selected.

▸ **4.** In the PivotTable group, select the name in the PivotTable Name box, type **SalesIDSummary** as the descriptive PivotTable name, and then press the **Enter** key.

▸ **5.** Rename the worksheet as **Sales ID Summary PivotTable**.

Refreshing a PivotTable

You cannot change data directly in a PivotTable. Instead, you must edit the data source on which the PivotTable is created. However, PivotTables are not updated automatically when the source data for the PivotTable is updated. After you edit the underlying data, you must **refresh**, or update, the PivotTable report to reflect the revised calculations.

INSIGHT

Displaying the Data Source for a PivotTable Cell

As you have seen, PivotTables are a great way to summarize the results of an Excel table. However, at some point, you may question the accuracy of a specific calculation in your PivotTable. In these cases, you can "drill down" to view the source data for a summary cell in a PivotTable. You simply double-click a summary cell, and the corresponding source data of the records for the PivotTable cell is displayed in a new worksheet.

The sales entry for Individual on 6/3/2017 should have been $180.55 (not $182.55 as currently listed). You'll edit the record in the JuneTbl table, which is the underlying data source for the PivotTable. This one change will affect the PivotTable in several locations—the Amount for Individual on 6/3/2017 (currently $182.55), the Grand Total for Individual (currently $576.17), the Grand Total for 6/3/2017 (currently $783.15), and the overall Grand Total for Sales ID 2 (currently $2,565.48).

To update the JuneTbl table and refresh the PivotTable:

▶ 1. Go to the **Sales Data** worksheet, and then find the Individual sales for 6/3/2017. The amount is $182.55.

▶ 2. Click the record's **Amount** cell, and then enter **180.55**. The sales Amount is updated in the table. You'll return to the PivotTable report to see the effect of this change.

▶ 3. Go to the **Sales ID Summary PivotTable** worksheet. The Amount for Individual on 6/3/2017 is still $182.55, the Grand Total for Individual is still $576.17, the Grand Total for 6/3/2017 is still $783.15, and the overall Grand Total is still $2,565.48.

The PivotTable was not automatically updated when the data in its source table changed, so you need to refresh the PivotTable.

▶ 4. Click any cell in the PivotTable.

▶ 5. On the ribbon, click the **PivotTable Tools Analyze** tab.

▶ 6. In the Data group, click the **Refresh** button (or press the **Alt+F5** keys). The PivotTable report is updated. The totals are now $180.55, $574.17, $781.15, and $2,563.48. See Figure 5-44.

| Figure 5-44 | **Refreshed PivotTable** |

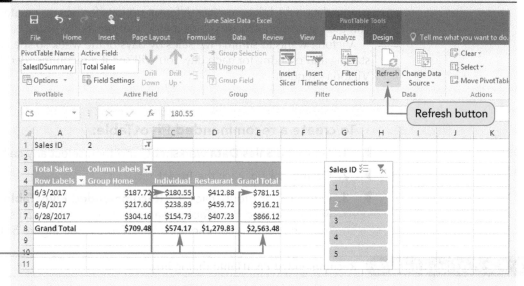

updated sales values

PivotTables provide an efficient way to display and analyze data. Like with charts, if a value displayed in the PivotTable is incorrect, you must update the data itself and then refresh the PivotTable to show that new data.

Creating Different Types of PivotTables

INSIGHT

This module only scratched the surface of the variety of PivotTables you can create. Here are a few more examples:

- Most PivotTable summaries are based on numeric data; Excel uses SUM as the default calculation. If your analysis requires a different calculation, you can select any of the 11 built-in summary calculations. For example, you could build a report that displays the minimum, maximum, and average sales for each week in June.
- You can use PivotTables to combine row label and column label items into groups. If items are numbers or dates, they can be grouped automatically using the Grouping dialog box, or they can be grouped manually using the Ctrl key to select items in a group and then clicking Group Selection from the shortcut menu. For example, you can manually combine Saturday and Sunday sales into a Weekend group, combine Monday through Friday sales into a Weekday group, and then display total sales by these groups within the PivotTable. Over time, you will also be able to group the Sale Date field to summarize daily sales by month, quarter, and year.
- You can develop PivotTables that use the percent of row, percent of column, or percent of total calculation to view each item in the PivotTable as a percent of the total in the current row, current column, or grand total. For example, you can display the total weekly sales as a percent of the total monthly sales.
- You can develop PivotTables that display how the current month/quarter/year compares to the previous month/quarter/year. For example, you can compare this month's sales for each Business to the corresponding sales for the previous month to display the difference between the two months.

Being able to enhance PivotTables by changing summary calculations, consolidating data into larger groups, and creating custom calculations based on other data in the VALUES area gives you flexibility in your analysis.

Creating a Recommended PivotTable

The Recommended PivotTables dialog box shows previews of PivotTables based on the source data, which lets you see different options for how to create the PivotTable. You can then choose the one that best meets your needs.

Victoria wants to summarize sales by days of the week so she can gain insights into staffing and ordering for each day. You will see if a recommended PivotTable meets Victoria's request.

To create a recommended PivotTable:

▶ **1.** Go to the **Sales Data** worksheet, and then select any cell in the Excel table.

▶ **2.** On the ribbon, click the **Insert** tab.

▶ **3.** In the Tables group, click the **Recommended PivotTables** button. The Recommended PivotTables dialog box opens. You can select a PivotTable from the list of recommended PivotTables. See Figure 5-45.

Figure 5-45	Recommended PivotTable dialog box

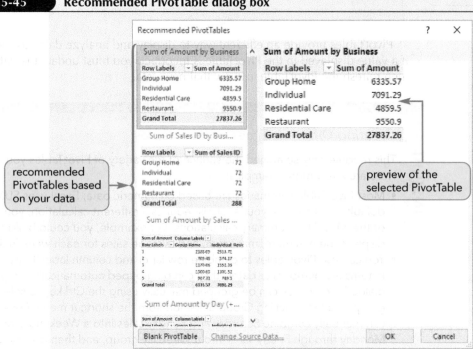

The Sum of Amount by Day PivotTable meets Victoria's request.

▶ **4.** Click **Sum of Amount by Day** (the sixth PivotTable in the left pane). An enlarged version of the selected PivotTable is displayed in the right pane of the dialog box.

▶ **5.** Click the **OK** button. A PivotTable of the sales by day appears in a new worksheet. See Figure 5-46.

Figure 5-46   **PivotTable of sales by day**

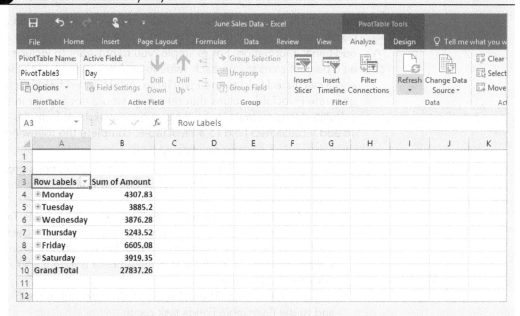

6. In the PivotTable Fields task pane, in the VALUES area, click the **Sum of Amount** button, and then click **Value Field Settings** on the shortcut menu. The Value Field Settings dialog box opens.

7. Click the **Number Format** button. The Format Cells dialog box opens.

8. In the Category box, click **Currency**, and then click the **OK** button.

9. In the Value Field Settings dialog box, click the **OK** button. The numbers in the PivotTable are formatted as currency with two decimal places.

10. On the ribbon, click the **PivotTable Tools Design** tab.

11. In the PivotTable Styles group, click the **More** button to open the PivotTable Styles gallery, and then click the **Pivot Style Medium 14** style. The style is applied to the PivotTable.

12. Rename the worksheet as **Daily Sales PivotTable**.

Victoria will use the summary of sales by days of the week in the Daily Sales PivotTable worksheet to evaluate staffing and ordering for each day.

INSIGHT

Adding a Calculated Field to a PivotTable Report

Occasionally, you might need to display more information than a PivotTable is designed to show, but it doesn't make sense to alter your data source to include this additional information. For example, you might want to include a field that shows an 8 percent sales tax on each value in an Amount field. In these instances, you can add a calculated field to the PivotTable. A **calculated field** is a formula you define to generate PivotTable values that otherwise would not appear in the PivotTable. The calculated field formula looks like a regular worksheet formula.

To add a calculated field to a PivotTable, complete the following steps:

1. Select any cell in the PivotTable report.
2. On the PivotTable Tools Analyze tab, in the Calculations group, click the Fields, Items & Sets button, and then click Calculated Field. The Insert Calculated Field dialog box opens.
3. In the Name box, type a name for the field, such as Sales Tax.
4. In the Formula box, enter the formula for the field. To use data from another field, click the field in the Fields box, and then click Insert Field. For example, to calculate an 8 percent sales tax on each value in the Amount field, enter =Amount*8%.
5. Click the Add button.
6. Click the OK button. The calculated field is added to the PivotTable's data area and to the PivotTable Fields task pane.

As you can see, you can use calculated fields to include additional information in a PivotTable.

Creating a PivotChart

A PivotChart is a graphical representation of the data in a PivotTable. You can create a PivotChart from a PivotTable. A PivotChart allows you to interactively add, remove, filter, and refresh data fields in the PivotChart similar to working with a PivotTable. PivotCharts can have all the same formatting as other charts, including layouts and styles. You can move and resize chart elements or change formatting of individual data points.

Victoria wants you to add a PivotChart next to the Sum of Amount by Day PivotTable. You will prepare a clustered column chart next to the PivotTable.

To create and format the PivotChart:

1. In the Daily Sales PivotTable worksheet, select any cell in the PivotTable.

2. On the ribbon, click the **PivotTable Tools Analyze** tab.

3. In the Tools group, click the **PivotChart** button. The Insert Chart dialog box opens.

4. If necessary, click the **Clustered Column** chart (the first chart subtype for Column charts), and then click the **OK** button. A PivotChart appears next to the PivotTable, and the task pane changes to the PivotChart Fields task pane.

   Trouble? If you selected the wrong PivotChart, delete the PivotChart you just created, and then repeat Steps 1 through 4.

5. To the right of the PivotChart, click the **Chart Elements** button ⊞, and then click the **Legend** check box to remove the checkmark. The legend is removed from the PivotChart. You do not need a legend because the PivotChart has only one data series.

TIP

You can also create a PivotChart based directly on an Excel table, which creates both a PivotTable and a PivotChart.

6. Click the PivotChart chart title, type **Sales by Day** as the new title, and then press the **Enter** key. The PivotChart displays the descriptive name.

7. To the right of the PivotChart, click the **Chart Styles** button 🖌, click **Color** at the top of the gallery, and then in the Colorful section, click **Color 4**. The columns change to green, the first color in that palette.

8. Drag the PivotChart so its upper-left corner is in cell **D3**. The PivotChart is aligned with the PivotTable. See Figure 5-47.

Figure 5-47 ▶ **PivotChart added to the PivotTable report**

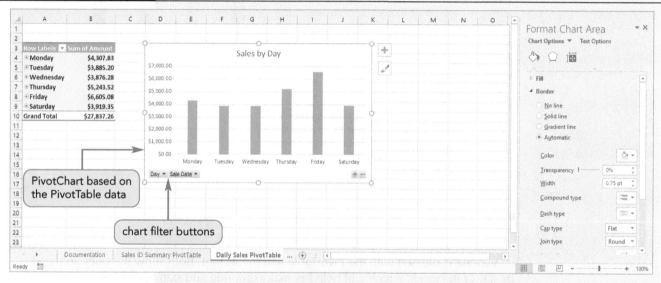

The PivotChart Tools contextual tabs enable you to work with and format the selected PivotChart the same way as an ordinary chart. A PivotChart and its associated PivotTable are linked. When you modify one, the other also changes. You can quickly display different views of the PivotChart by using the chart filter buttons on the PivotChart to filter the data.

Victoria wants you to display sales for only Monday through Friday. You will filter the PivotChart to display only those items.

To filter the PivotChart to display sales for Monday through Friday:

1. Make sure the PivotChart is selected, and then click the **Day** filter button in the lower-left corner of the PivotChart. The Filter menu opens.

2. Click the **Saturday** check box to remove its checkmark. Only the weekdays remain selected.

3. Click the **OK** button. The PivotChart updates to display only sales for weekdays. The PivotTable is automatically filtered to display the same results.

4. Select cell **A1**. See Figure 5-48.

| Figure 5-48 | Filtered PivotChart |

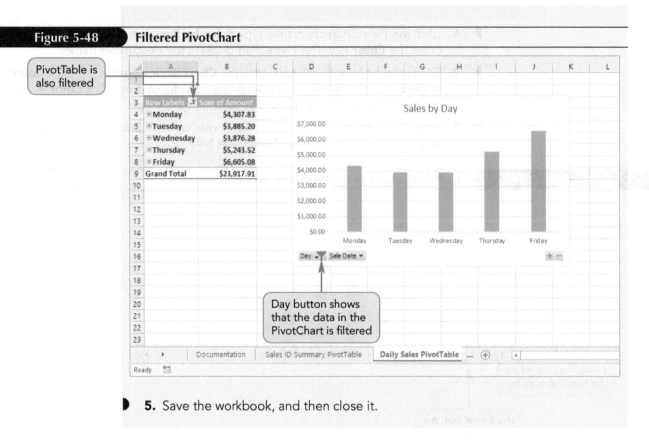

PivotTable is also filtered

Day button shows that the data in the PivotChart is filtered

5. Save the workbook, and then close it.

Victoria is pleased with the PivotTable and PivotChart. Both show the sales arranged by day of the week, which will help her make ordering and staffing decisions.

Session 5.3 Quick Check

REVIEW

1. What is a PivotTable?

2. How do you add fields to a PivotTable?

3. How are fields such as region, state, and country most likely to appear in a PivotTable?

4. How are fields such as revenue, costs, and profits most likely to appear in a PivotTable?

5. A list of college students includes a code to indicate the student's gender (male or female) and a field to identify the student's major. Would you use a filter or a PivotTable to (a) create a list of all females majoring in history and (b) count the number of males and females in each major?

6. An Excel table of professional baseball player data consists of team name, player name, position, and salary. What area of a PivotTable report would be used for the Team name field if you wanted to display the average salaries by position for all teams or an individual team?

7. After you update data in an Excel table, what must you do to a PivotTable that is based on that Excel table?

8. What is a PivotChart?

Review Assignments

Data File needed for the Review Assignments: July.xlsx

Victoria needs to analyze the sales for July. She entered this data into a new workbook and wants you to sort and filter the data, as well as create summary reports using the Subtotal command, PivotTables, and PivotCharts. Complete the following:

1. Open the **July** workbook located in the Excel5 > Review folder included with your Data Files, and then save the workbook as **July Sales Data** in the location specified by your instructor.

2. In the Documentation worksheet, enter your name and the date.

3. In the Sales Data worksheet, freeze the top row so that the headers remain on the screen as you scroll.

4. Make a copy of the Sales Data worksheet, and then rename the copied worksheet as **July Data**. (*Hint*: To make a copy of a worksheet, press and hold the Ctrl key as you drag the sheet tab to the right of the Sales Data sheet tab.)

5. In the July Data worksheet, unfreeze the top row.

6. Create an Excel table for the sales data in the July Data worksheet.

7. Format the Excel table with Table Style Medium 4, and then change the Amount field to the Accounting format with two decimal places.

8. Rename the Excel table as **JulyTbl**.

9. Make the following changes to the JulyTbl table:
   a. Add a record for 7/31/2017, Monday, 4, Group Home, 256.52.
   b. Edit the record for Individual on 7/27/2017 by changing the Amount from 462.74 to 492.05.
   c. Remove any duplicate records.

10. Make a copy of the July Data worksheet, and then rename the copied worksheet as **Sort by Sale Date**. In the Sort by Sale Date worksheet, sort the JulyTbl table by Sale Date, displaying the newest sales first, and then by Amount, displaying the largest amounts first.

11. Make a copy of the July Data worksheet, and then rename the copied worksheet as **Sort by Day**. In the Sort by Day worksheet, sort the sales data by Day (use the custom list order of Sunday, Monday,… for the chronological sort), then by Business (A to Z), and then by Amount (smallest to largest).

12. Make a copy of the July Data worksheet, and then rename the copied worksheet as **Filter to Omit Restaurant**. In the Filter to Omit Restaurant worksheet, filter the JulyTbl table to display the sales for all businesses except Restaurant.

13. In the Filter to Omit Restaurant worksheet, insert the Total row to calculate the average amount of sales for the filtered data. Change the label in the Total row to **Average**. Sort the filtered data by descending order by Amount.

14. Split the Filter to Omit Restaurant worksheet into two panes above the last row of the table. Display the sales records in the top pane, and display only the Total row in the bottom pane.

15. Make a copy of the July Data worksheet, and then rename the copied worksheet as **Filter by Sales ID**. In the Filter by Sales ID worksheet, insert a slicer for the Sales ID column. Move the slicer to row 1. Format the slicer with Slicer Style Light 3. Change the slicer's height to 1.9" and its width to 1.25". Use the slicer to display sales for Sales ID 3 and Sales ID 5.

16. Make a copy of the July Data worksheet, and then rename the copied worksheet as **July Subtotals**. In the July Subtotals worksheet, convert the JulyTbl Table to a range, and then sort the range by the Business column in ascending order.

17. In the July Subtotals worksheet, use the Subtotal command to calculate the total sales for each business in the Amount column. Display only the subtotal results. Widen columns as needed so that all of the data is visible.

18. Based on the JulyTbl table in the July Data worksheet, create a PivotTable in a new worksheet that shows the total sales Amount by Day. Format the data area with the Currency format. Rename the worksheet with the PivotTable as **PivotTableChart Sales by Day**.

19. In the PivotTableChart Sales by Day worksheet, insert a Clustered Column PivotChart based on the PivotTable you created. Move the PivotChart to row 3. Remove the legend. Change the PivotChart title to **Sales by Day of Week**.

20. Based on the JulyTbl table in the July Data worksheet, create a PivotTable in a new worksheet that shows Amount by Sale Date. Add the Business field to the FILTERS area. Format the PivotTable with Pivot Style Medium 4. Format the Amount field with the Accounting format with two decimal places. Rename that worksheet as **PivotTable by Sale Date**.

21. In the PivotTable by Sale Date worksheet, insert a slicer for the Business field of the PivotTable. Change the slicer height to 1.6" and the width to 1.5". Format the slicer with Slicer Style Dark 3. Move the slicer to row 3.

22. Use the slicer to filter the PivotTable to display only the Restaurant and Group Home sales.

23. Based on the JulyTbl table in the July Data worksheet, create the Recommended PivotTable Sum of Amount by Sales ID and Business. Rename the worksheet as **Recommended PivotTable**.

24. Save the workbook, and then close it.

Case Problem 1

APPLY

Data File needed for this Case Problem: Shirts.xlsx

Go Sports   Anton Aliyev is the store manager for Go Sports, a sports clothing store in Middletown, Ohio. In addition to its clothing inventory, the store will print logos provided by local sports teams on T-shirts, jerseys, or sweatshirts purchased at the store. Anton uses Excel for a variety of tasks, including pricing and inventory. He wants you to create an Excel table from information about current products and then analyze this data. Complete the following:

1. Open the **Shirts** workbook located in the Excel5 > Case1 folder included with your Data Files, and then save the workbook as **Shirts Inventory** in the location specified by your instructor.

2. In the Documentation worksheet, enter your name and the date.

3. In the Shirts worksheet, create an Excel table using all of the data in the worksheet. Rename the table as **ShirtsTbl**. Format the table with Table Style Medium 9. Change the Price data to the Currency format showing no decimal places. Change the In Stock data to the Number format with no decimals.

4. Make a copy of the Shirts worksheet, and then rename the copied worksheet as **Sort by Style**. (*Hint*: Press the Ctrl key as you drag and drop the Shirts sheet tab to the right of the Shirts sheet tab to make a copy of the worksheet.)

5. In the Sort by Style worksheet, sort the data in ascending order by Style, and then in descending order by In Stock.

6. Filter the ShirtsTbl table by Size to remove the youth extra small (yxsm) and ladies extra small (lxsm) sizes.

7. Insert a Total row that shows the total shirts In Stock. Change the Total row label to **Total Shirts**.

8. Split the worksheet window into two horizontal panes. Place the split bar two rows above the bottom row of the worksheet. In the top pane, display the shirt data. In the bottom pane, display only the Total row.

9. Make a copy of the Shirts worksheet, and then rename the copied worksheet as **Filter by Color**. In the Filter by Color worksheet, filter the ShirtsTbl table to display only T-shirt style.

10. Insert a slicer for Color, position the slicer so its upper-left corner is in cell G1, resize the slicer's height to 1.8" and its width to 1.2", and then format the slicer with Slicer Style Dark 1.

11. Use the Color slicer to further filter the ShirtsTbl table to display only blue T-shirts and white T-shirts.

12. Filter the ShirtsTbl table so that it displays only blue and white T-shirts with a price greater than $10. Sort the filtered data in ascending order by Price and then in descending order by In Stock.

13. Make a copy of the Shirts worksheet, and then rename the copied worksheet as **Subtotals**. Convert the table to a range because the Subtotal command cannot be used with an Excel table. Sort the table in ascending order by Style. Use the Subtotal command to display the minimum In Stock for each Style.

14. Based on the ShirtsTbl table in the Shirts worksheet, insert a PivotTable in a new worksheet that calculates the total In Stock for each Style and Color. Display both Style and Color in rows. Use the Value Field Settings dialog box to rename Sum of In Stock as **Total Inventory**. Apply the Pivot Style Medium 9 style to the PivotTable. Rename the worksheet as **PivotTable by Style and Color**.

15. In the PivotTable by Style and Color worksheet, insert a PivotChart with the Clustered Column chart subtype. Place the PivotChart to the right of the PivotTable. Remove the legend. Filter the PivotChart to exclude any white shirts. Change the chart title to **Inventory by Style and Color**.

16. Based on the ShirtsTbl table in the Shirts worksheet, insert a PivotTable in a new worksheet that displays the total In Stock and count of Item IDs by Style and Color. Place Style in the FILTERS area. Rename the worksheet as **PivotTable by Style**.

17. In the PivotTable by Style worksheet, format the PivotTable with Pivot Style Medium 2 style. In the Value Field Settings dialog box, rename the Count of Item ID as **Number of Shirts** and change the Number format to Number with no decimal places. Change the Number format of the Sum of In Stock to the Number format with no decimal places.

18. In the PivotTable, change the Style filter to show only Jersey.

19. Save the workbook, and then close it.

Case Problem 2

APPLY

Data File needed for this Case Problem: Seminars.xlsx

Collegiate Seminars   Phillip Cunningham is the new manager of Collegiate Seminars in McLean, Virginia. To help him better understand the current schedule, he created an Excel table that tracks the data he has collected about currently scheduled seminars, including topic, type, instructor, length, location, cost, and maximum enrollment. He asks you to analyze this data. Complete the following:

1. Open the **Seminars** workbook located in the Excel5 > Case2 folder included with your Data Files, and then save the workbook as **Seminar Bookings** in the location specified by your instructor.

2. In the Documentation worksheet, enter your name and the date.

3. In the Seminars worksheet, create an Excel table, and then name it **SeminarsTbl**. Format the Cost column with the Accounting format and no decimal places. Format the SeminarsTbl table with the table style of your choice.

4. Make a copy of the Seminars worksheet, and then rename the copied worksheet as **Sort by Type**. (*Hint*: Press the Ctrl key, and drag the Seminars sheet tab to the right of the Seminars sheet tab to make a copy of the worksheet.) Sort the SeminarsTbl table in ascending order by Type, then in descending order by Cost.

5. Use conditional formatting to highlight all Seminars with a cost greater than $950 with yellow fill with dark yellow text.

6. Make a copy of the Seminars worksheet, and then rename the copied worksheet as **Filter by Location**. Insert a slicer to filter by Location. Place the slicer to the right of the top of the SeminarsTbl table. Select a slicer style that matches the style you used to format the SeminarsTbl table. Resize the slicer's height and width to improve its appearance.

7. Use the slicer to filter the SeminarsTbl table to display only Seminars at the Downtown location.

8. Expand the filter to also display Beltway seminars in the SeminarsTbl table. Sort the filtered table in ascending order by cost.

9. Make a copy of the Seminars worksheet, and then rename the copied worksheet as **Filter Top 25%**. Filter the SeminarsTbl table to display Seminars whose Costs are in the top 25 percent. (*Hint*: Use the Top 10 number format.) Sort the data in descending order by Cost.

10. Use the Total row to include the average cost at the bottom of the table, and then change the Total row label to **Average**. Remove the entry in the Max column of the Total row.

11. Make a copy of the Seminars worksheet, and then rename the copied worksheet as **Subtotals**. Use the Subtotal command to display the total cost for each Topic in the Cost column. Make sure your table is sorted in the correct sequence for the required subtotals, and remember to convert the table to a range before subtotaling.

12. Based on the SeminarsTbl table in the Seminars worksheet, create a PivotTable in a new worksheet that totals cost by Type and Topic. Place the Type field in the COLUMNS area. Format the cost in the PivotTable with the Accounting format and no decimal places. Format the PivotTable with the style of your choice. Rename the worksheet as **PivotTable by Type**.

13. Insert a slicer to filter the PivotTable by Type. Resize the slicer object and buttons as needed, and then select a slicer style that matches the PivotTable. Use the slicer to filter the PivotTable to display totals for Graduate and Undergrad.

14. Based on the SeminarsTbl table in the Seminars worksheet, create a PivotTable in a new worksheet that calculates average Cost by Location and the count of Seminar IDs. Format the average cost to the Accounting format with no decimal places. Apply the same PivotTable style to this PivotTable. Rename the worksheet as **PivotTable for Average Cost**.

15. Save the workbook, and then close it.

Case Problem 3

TROUBLESHOOT

Data File needed for this Case Problem: Food.xlsx

Food for All   Samuel Hamilton started Food for All in Lake Charles, Louisiana, three years ago in response to a growing number of residents who encountered unexpected challenges with being able to feed themselves and their families. The food bank has been very successful providing healthy food for the town residents. Samuel is considering expanding the food bank's reach to include several other towns in the area and needs to analyze current donations to see whether it can support the expansion. Samuel tracks donations in Excel. He has entered donation data for the first quarter of the year in a worksheet and wants you to analyze the data. Complete the following:

1. Open the **Food** workbook located in the Excel5 > Case3 folder included with your Data Files, and then save the workbook as **Food Bank** in the location specified by your instructor.

2. In the Documentation sheet, enter your name and the date.

⚙ **Troubleshoot** 3. Samuel wants to view donations with values that are either less than $10 or greater than $100. He tried filtering the donations in the Donation Amount Filter worksheet, but it's not working as expected. Review the custom Number filter in the worksheet, and fix the problems.

4. In the Donations worksheet, create an Excel table, and then rename the table as **DonationsTbl**. Format the DonationsTbl table using the table style of your choice.

5. In the DonationsTbl table, format the Value column so that it is clear that this field contains dollars.

6. Find the record that has a year of 3018. Correct the year so that it is **2017**.

7. Make a copy of the Donations worksheet, and then rename the copied worksheet as **Sorted Donations**. (*Hint*: Press the Ctrl key and drag the sheet tab to the right of the current sheet tab to make a copy of the worksheet.) In the Sorted Donations worksheet, sort the data in ascending order by Zip and then in ascending order by Date.

8. Using conditional formatting, highlight all of the records in the sorted table that are the type Food with the format of your choice.

9. Make a copy of the Donations worksheet, and then rename the copied worksheet as **Filtered Donations**. Filter the DonationsTbl table to display records that have not been sent a receipt. Sort the data by Zip in ascending order and then by Value in descending order.

10. Insert a Total row that calculates the total of the Value column for the filtered data and the count of the Receipt column. Remove any totals that appear for other columns. Make sure that the columns are wide enough to display the values.

⚙ **Troubleshoot** 11. In the Donation Type Subtotal worksheet, Samuel is trying to include subtotals that show the total Value for each donation Type. However, the subtotal for each type appears more than once. Fix this report so it shows only one subtotal for each type.

12. Based on the DonationsTbl table in the Donations worksheet, create a PivotTable in a new worksheet that displays the Count of Value and the average Value of the donations by Type. Place the Type field in the ROWS area of the PivotTable. Apply the PivotTable style that matches the DonationsTbl table style. Format the Average values using the Accounting format. Change the labels above the average donations to **Average**, and change the label above the count of donations to **Number**.

13. Insert a slicer to filter the PivotTable by Type, and then use the slicer to filter Food from the PivotTable. Format the slicer to match the PivotTable style. Resize and position the slicer appropriately. Rename the worksheet as **PivotTable by Type**.

14. Based on the DonationsTbl table in the Donations worksheet, create a PivotTable in a new worksheet that shows the Total Value by Zip. Format the Sum of Value so that it is more readable. Apply a PivotTable style to match the style of the DonationsTbl table. Rename the worksheet as **PivotTable Value by Zip**.

15. Based on the PivotTable in the PivotTable Value by Zip worksheet, create a PivotChart using the Clustered column chart type. Move the PivotChart to row 3. Change the chart title to **Donations by Zip**. Change the fill color of the bars to a color that matches the style in the PivotTable. Remove the legend.

16. Filter the PivotChart to hide the donations in the ZIP code 70611.

17. Save the workbook, and then close it.

Case Problem 4

Data File needed for this Case Problem: Sales.xlsx

BePresent BePresent is a social networking consulting group in Yuma, Arizona, that plans, implements, and tracks social networking campaigns to help small-business owners create a strong presence on the Internet. Sales manager Alana Laidlaw regularly creates reports about the response rates for the social networking campaigns. She asks you to help her analyze data about the performance of the past year's introductory campaigns. Complete the following:

1. Open the **Sales** workbook located in the Excel5 > Case4 folder included with your Data Files, and then save the workbook as **Intro Sales** in the location specified by your instructor.

2. In the Documentation sheet, enter your name and the date.

3. In the Campaigns worksheet, create an Excel table. Rename the table as **CampaignsTbl**. Format the Responses column in the Number format with no decimal places using the comma separator. Apply a table style of your choice.

4. Make a copy of the Campaigns worksheet, and then rename the copied worksheet as **Sorted Campaigns**. (*Hint*: Press the Ctrl key, and drag the Campaigns sheet tab to the right of the Campaigns sheet tab to make a copy of the worksheet.) Sort the table in ascending order by Type of social media, then in chronological order by Month (January, February, March,…), and then in ascending order by Name.

5. Make a copy of the Campaigns worksheet, and then rename the copied worksheet as **Filter with Total Row**. Insert a slicer for the Type field. Move the slicer to row 1. Match the slicer style with the style you selected for the CampaignsTbl table. Resize the slicer height and width to eliminate any excess space.

6. Display the records for Facebook campaigns that occurred from January through June. Sort the filtered data in descending order of Responses.

7. Add a Total row to the table that calculates the average number of Responses for the filtered data. Change the label in the Total row to **Average**.

8. Make a copy of the Campaigns worksheet, and then rename the copied worksheet as **Campaign Subtotals**. Include subtotals that calculate the total Responses per Month and the total Responses per Type of Social Media. (*Hint*: Remember to sort the data, and then add two sets of subtotals. When you use the Subtotal command the second time, do not replace existing subtotals.)

9. Make a copy of the Campaigns worksheet, and then rename the copied worksheet as **Bottom 15 Campaigns**. Use the Top Number filter to display the 15 campaigns with the lowest Responses (each row represents a campaign). Sort the filtered table so that the lowest Responses appear first.

10. Based on the CampaignsTbl table in the Campaigns worksheet, create the PivotTable and the PivotChart shown in Figure 5-49 in a new worksheet to summarize the social media responses. Rename the worksheet as **PivotTableChart by Month**.

Figure 5-49	PivotTable and PivotChart of social media responses

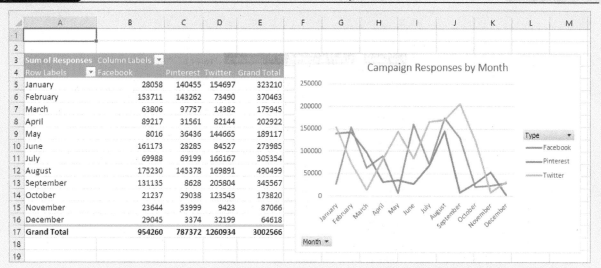

11. Based on the CampaignsTbl table in the Campaigns worksheet, create the PivotTable shown in Figure 5-50 in a new worksheet to calculate the sum of Responses categorized by Description and Type using Month as a filter. Insert slicers for Type and Month. Format the slicers to coordinate with the PivotTable, resize the slicers as needed, and then position them next to the PivotTable. Rename the worksheet as **PivotTable Response Analysis**.

Figure 5-50	PivotTable displaying sales analyzing social media responses

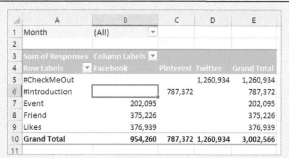

12. Based on the CampaignsTbl table in the Campaigns worksheet, create the PivotTable and slicers shown in Figure 5-51 in a new worksheet, displaying total Responses, by Name with Month as a filter. Include a second calculation that displays each of the Reponses by Name as a percentage of the total Responses. (*Hint*: In the Value Field Settings dialog box, use the Show Values As tab to show values as a percentage of the column total.) Format the PivotTable and slicers with matching styles, and adjust the height and width of the slicers as needed to improve their appearance. Rename the worksheet as **PivotTable Response by Name**.

Figure 5-51 PivotTable displaying Responses by Name

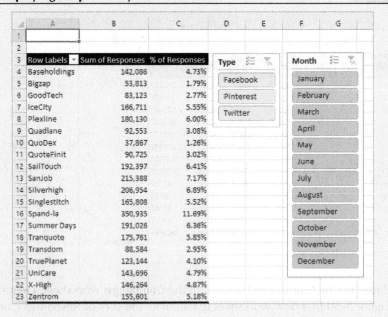

13. Save the workbook, and then close it.